CW01017655

Cambridge International
AS & A Level

Psychology

Helen J Kitching, Mandy Wood,
Kimberley Croft, Lisa Holmes,
Evie Bentley and Laura Swash

HODDER
EDUCATION
AN HACHETTE UK COMPANY

Dedication from Mandy Wood: To Zach, the cat-bombers (Luna and Jackary) and all the 'Psticklers' around the globe – you keep me smiling everyday!

Dedication from Helen Kitching: To my BFFs Nicola and Debs and my other amazing friends whose love and support got me through the past two years.

Dedication from Kimberley Croft: To my Granny, Robin, who taught me that the best life is one of adventure and to Tristan, who was my constant companion whilst writing

Dedication from Evie Bentley: With much gratitude to my support crew, thank you so much Pam, Jess, Vince, the book clubbers and the lovely Carol B.

Cambridge International copyright material in this publication is reproduced under licence and remains the intellectual property of Cambridge Assessment International Education.

Exam-style questions have been written by the authors. In examinations, the way marks are awarded may be different. References to assessment and/or assessment preparation are the publisher's interpretation of the syllabus requirements and may not fully reflect the approach of Cambridge Assessment International Education.

Cambridge International recommends that teachers consider using a range of teaching and learning resources in preparing learners for assessment, based on their own professional judgement of their students' needs.

Third-party websites and resources referred to in this publication have not been endorsed by Cambridge Assessment International Education.

Every effort has been made to trace all copyright holders, but if any have been inadvertently overlooked, the Publishers will be pleased to make the necessary arrangements at the first opportunity.

Although every effort has been made to ensure that website addresses are correct at time of going to press, Hodder Education cannot be held responsible for the content of any website mentioned in this book. It is sometimes possible to find a relocated web page by typing in the address of the home page for a website in the URL window of your browser.

Hachette UK's policy is to use papers that are natural, renewable and recyclable products and made from wood grown in well-managed forests and other controlled sources. The logging and manufacturing processes are expected to conform to the environmental regulations of the country of origin.

Orders: please contact Hachette UK Distribution, Hely Hutchinson Centre, Milton Road, Didcot, Oxfordshire, OX11 7HH. Telephone: +44 (0)1235 827827. Email education@hachette.co.uk Lines are open from 9 a.m. to 5 p.m., Monday to Friday. You can also order through our website: www.hoddereducation.com

ISBN: 978 1 3983 5300 8

© Evie Bentley, Kimberley Croft, Lisa Holmes, Helen J Kitching and Mandy Wood 2022

Laura Swash is the contributor for Sections 7.3.1–7.3.3 and Sections 7.5.2–7.5.3 in Chapter 7.

First published in 2022 by
Hodder Education
An Hachette UK Company
Carmelite House
50 Victoria Embankment
London EC4Y 0DZ

www.hoddereducation.com

Impression number   10 9 8 7 6 5 4 3

Year   2026 2025 2024

All rights reserved. Apart from any use permitted under UK copyright law, no part of this publication may be reproduced or transmitted in any form or by any means, electronic or mechanical, including photocopying and recording, or held within any information storage and retrieval system, without permission in writing from the publisher or under licence from the Copyright Licensing Agency Limited. Further details of such licences (for reprographic reproduction) may be obtained from the Copyright Licensing Agency Limited, www.cla.co.uk

Cover photo © fyb - stock.adobe.com

Illustrations by Barking Dog and Integra Software Services

Typeset by Integra Software Services Pvt. Ltd., Pondicherry, India

Printed in Spain

A catalogue record for this title is available from the British Library.

Contents

Welcome to Psychology!

We are so excited that you are here studying psychology – you now belong to one of the most vibrant, diverse and prodigious communities of students, researchers and practitioners on the planet. Millions of students study psychology around the world and take what they have learned into careers including business, sales, marketing, physical and mental health. Put simply, where there are people, there is psychology!

We hope that you enjoy your time studying and gain the confidence to question the relevance and legitimacy of psychological knowledge, before applying what you have learned to your everyday life. In a thriving, organic subject such as ours, your voice matters! For psychological knowledge to grow and evolve, the discipline requires researchers from every corner of the world – to bring together unique perspectives to challenge and demand a psychology that describes, explains, predicts and celebrates all human minds.

We learn to think critically when we can explore our ideas with others, whether that is face-to-face in a traditional classroom or virtually through online forums. We want you to enter into the dialogue, thinking, sharing, reflecting on and revising your views. This is how psychologists work and we hope it works for you too!

Safe travels and best of luck!

Helen, Mandy, Kimberley, Lisa, Evie and Laura

How to use this book

This textbook has been designed to make your study of psychology as successful and rewarding as possible.

Organisation

The book comprises nine chapters, which correspond with the topics in the Cambridge International AS & A Level Psychology syllabus. Each chapter is broken down into sections, which reflect the subtopics in the syllabus.

Features

Each chapter contains a number of features designed to help you effectively navigate the syllabus content.

Learning outcomes
At the start of each chapter, there is a blue box that provides a summary of the learning outcomes to be covered.

KEY TERMS
A list of important psychological terms.

METHODOLOGY
A list of important research methodology terms.

Chapter overview
A short introduction to the chapter and its focus.

STUDY TIP
Alerts you to common errors and difficult areas of the syllabus along with ideas to support your revision.

Main assumptions

Each of the approaches at Cambridge International AS Level has two main assumptions. These are ideas that are generally accepted by all researchers within the approach.

RESEARCH STUDIES
Highlights the aims, methodology, results and conclusions of studies and encourages the development of research-based skills.

LEARNING LINK
Numerous topics/studies in psychology are connected. This feature identifies some of these connections and encourages you to think about how the content links with other areas of the syllabus.

Each section starts with three questions; you should be able to answer them once you have finished the section.

Think!
Questions to consolidate knowledge and understanding.

Think!
Questions to apply the content to your own life or take someone else's perspective.

Think!
Questions to encourage higher order/critical thinking.

ISSUES AND DEBATES
Identifies key 'issues and debates' that apply to the content described on the page.

CHAPTER SUMMARY
At the end of each AS Level chapter, there is a list of the main points from the chapter of which you should have a good understanding.

TEST YOURSELF
Exam-style questions are placed throughout each chapter to help you to consolidate your learning and develop all the necessary skills you will need for your final assessments.

Discussion points to interact and share ideas with other learners.

A red side bar like this indicates A Level content in the AS Level section or AS Level content in the A Level section.

Glossary

Definitions of all the key terms in **blue bold** are available online at www.hoddereducation.com/cambridgeextras in a comprehensive glossary.

Notes for teachers and learners

Key concepts

Key concepts are essential ideas that help students develop a deep understanding of their subject and make links between different aspects. Key concepts may open up new ways of thinking about, understanding or interpreting the important things to be learned.

The key concepts for Cambridge International AS & A Level Psychology are:

Nature versus nurture

A key focus of contemporary psychology is to consider the relative contributions of nature versus nurture. Behaviours could be seen as resulting from innate, genetic factors (nature) or behaviours could be explained in terms of the environmental influences that begin to shape us from the moment of conception (nurture). Students should be aware of this debate while planning studies and evaluating studies as part of this course.

Ethics

Ethics must be considered when planning a psychological investigation to ensure that data is gathered without compromising the wellbeing of the participant(s). The approach to these constraints has changed over time as our understanding has developed and attitudes towards ethical and moral implications change. As a result, some of the earlier studies that were the basis of the subject no longer meet the current guidelines. We should continually evaluate the ethical and moral implications of psychological research.

Research methods

Every research method has strengths and weaknesses, and the psychologist must evaluate how the method they have chosen contributes to the validity and reliability of their specific investigation as well as to wider psychological research.

No one view in psychology is definitive

Psychological research is influenced by the approach of the researcher and the time and context they are working in. Any topic is likely to be studied from the perspective of more than one psychological approach, and each approach has its own assumptions, strengths and weaknesses.

Relevance of psychology in contemporary society

By understanding psychology, we can improve how we live our lives and society in general. Every study is undertaken with a specific purpose in mind which can then be applied in everyday life – whether it is improving how we learn, understanding how groups of people behave or treating a disorder. Students should be able to recognise how psychological studies of a specific area can be applied to other scenarios in everyday life.

The information in this section is taken from the Cambridge International AS & A Level Psychology syllabus for examination from 2024. You should always refer to the appropriate syllabus document for the year of your students' examination to confirm the details and for more information. The syllabus document is available on the Cambridge International website at **www.cambridgeinternational.org.**

The five key concepts apply to almost everything you are required to study. Research methods and ethics run through every part of the syllabus and you should always be considering nature versus nurture and the relevance of psychology in contemporary society when evaluating theories and studies in psychology, as they are part of Issues and Debates. With this in mind, we would like to add the following qualifying note: the key concepts are entwined throughout all the topics in this book and should be critically engaged with throughout. However, we have used these icons to mark areas where key concepts are particularly salient, but they should be considered against every aspect of the content.

About the authors

Evie Bentley left university with an MA and worked for the scientific civil service before moving into education. She has taught in a variety of schools; comprehensives, state and independent senior schools, sixth form and further education colleges and adult education. She describes herself as a life scientist and has been involved with World Wildlife Fund projects for teenagers, work on government committees and working parties, served a term as Chair of the Association for the Teaching of Psychology (ATP), examined for two exam boards, published textbooks, articles and more. A major interest is behaviour, and she is a current member of the Association for the Study of Animal Behaviour (ASAB). She is a happy gardener, cat owner, outdoor swimmer and granny.

Kimberley Croft studied Psychology at the University of London and gained her Masters in Education from the University of Bath. She is a passionate teacher of Psychology and has taught at a grammar school in the UK as well as been Head of Social Sciences at a British International School in Malaysia. Kimberley is also an A Level Psychology examiner for several exam boards. She has authored a book on the famous social psychologist Stanley Milgram. Kimberley currently lives in the Atacama desert with her family and enjoys hiking in the mountains, wild camping, and climbing.

Lisa Holmes studied Psychology and Sociology at Aston University. Her working life, however, began in science working in QA/QC departments in private and public health care before moving into education. She subsequently gained her PGCE from Keele University and taught at a number of schools before starting her own tutoring business nearly a decade ago, which has gone from strength to strength. Teaching psychology is her passion and she works with students at all levels, up to and including masters level. She is a current team leader and marker for a number of exam boards. Her other passion is supporting Derby County football club through all their trials and tribulations and travelling; she loves nothing more than heading to Orlando and Walt Disney World.

Helen J Kitching is an established author, having written two textbooks for Hodder Education as well as writing numerous articles for *ATP Today*, WJEC's online magazine and *Psychology Review*. She is trained as an EFL teacher and spent a number of years teaching English as a foreign language so is experienced at working with learners for whom English is an additional language. She recently edited all of the AS Level lessons for a new online version of the Cambridge International Psychology course, including ensuring the language was suitable for EAL learners. She is Chair of the Division of Academics, Researchers and Teachers and Chair of the Standing Committee for Psychology Education in Schools and Colleges of the British Psychological Society as well as Conference Organiser for the Association for the Teaching of Psychology. Helen is a Chartered Psychologist and Fellow of the BPS. She is Head of Psychology at a school in Eastbourne.

Laura Swash has been teaching psychology internationally for over twenty years. She is also an examiner, textbook author, content editor and proofreader and has her own student and teacher psychology blog where she shares studying tips and ideas. Laura lives with her husband on a small Portuguese island where she enjoys writing, reading, gardening, cycling and scuba diving.

Mandy Wood has taught A level and IB Psychology for over 20 years and is now a freelance trainer, author, editor, examiner and tutor to international students all over the world. She is an active member of the Association for the Teaching of Psychology and has recently enjoyed working with PGCE students right at the beginning of their Psychology teaching careers. Mandy's cats are regular contributors to her daily zoom calls and when she is not being upstaged by her cats, she enjoys drinking tea and binge watching *Criminal Minds*.

AS Level Issues and debates

KEY TERMS

nature

nurture

individual explanation

situational explanation

experience

assent

Think!

Can you think of one behaviour that we are born with and is therefore part of human **nature** and one behaviour that we learn from **experience** in the world, or **nurture**?

Think!

Imagine you are a researcher working with a group of children aged three to five. You need them to complete some puzzles with you as part of an experiment. Think about the children's age. Why do you think it can sometimes be difficult working with very young children? How might you need to adapt the study to get the children to focus on the puzzles?

Think!

Should all psychological research studies have applications to everyday life or is it ever acceptable to do research only for academic interest?

Psychological knowledge can be applied in so many different professions, many of which actively help to improve the lives of individuals, families and society in general.

▲ Can you think of any applications of psychology that benefit some people more than others?

When people come together to exchange their views on complex topics, such as why people are obedient or forgetful or aggressive, it often raises certain themes or issues. These issues are often fundamental questions that are linked to many topics in psychology. They are the things that seem to really matter to people. However, different things matter to different people, which is why issues often lead to debates!

Psychological differences of opinion often stem from differences between the main assumptions of the approaches. For example, biological psychologists may not always agree with social psychologists and psychologists from the learning approach may not always agree with psychologists from the cognitive approach.

In your first year, you will focus on five important issues and debates:
»» the application of psychology to everyday life
»» the use of children in psychological research
»» the use of animals in psychological research
»» **individual** and **situational explanations**
»» nature versus nurture.

Before you begin studying your first approach, it is worth taking a closer look at each of these issues and debates so that you understand how they might be used when evaluating the research that follows.

The application of psychology to everyday life

The aims of psychology are to describe, explain and predict human behaviour, but there is also one further goal. Sometimes people say the final goal is to control behaviour. Others say it is to change behaviour, but perhaps the most appealing is the idea that psychology aims to improve people's lives.

As you learn about each of the studies in this book, try to think about how the knowledge gained could be used in society. This might be within organisations such as schools, hospitals, prisons or businesses, but it could also relate to the choices made by individuals and families.

We have provided suggestions of real-life applications for each of the AS studies (in the 'evaluating' sections), but you should also try to think of your own ideas about how psychological knowledge can be applied to solving real-world issues within your local community, as well as the issues affecting us all as global citizens.

The use of children in psychological research

Some of the studies included at Cambridge International AS Level use children as their participants (e.g. Bandura *et al.*; Pozzulo *et al.*; Saavedra and Silverman). This presents some specific practical and ethical issues for the psychologists to consider when conducting their research.

In Chapter 1, you will learn about the importance of ethics in psychological research. There is a need to balance any potential costs to participants against the potential benefits to society of conducting the study. One of the most important guidelines is about the need for informed consent, so that people are not coerced into participating in studies that they do not wish to be a part of and, even more importantly, so that they actually understand that they are part of a study at all. This can be difficult with children, who may not fully understand the implications of participation. For this reason, 'The Declaration of Helsinki' (World Medical Association, 2001), a formal statement regarding the ethical treatment of participants in research, including children, details the need to obtain informed consent from parents. Wherever possible, informed consent should also be obtained from the child themselves. This may mean that psychologists need to be creative in the ways that they explain their research to make it developmentally appropriate – for example, using pictures.

The British Psychological Society (2021) also refer to the concept of **assent** (as opposed to consent). The term assent is used when participants are not yet legally adults. Assent may be gained through signing a written document with older children. Younger children may not be able to give written assent and therefore researchers must pay careful attention to their non-verbal communication (e.g. breaking eye contact) as children may not explicitly say that they do not want to participate. If the researchers detect that the child appears uncomfortable in any way, the trial, observation or interview should be terminated.

From a practical point of view, researchers must remember that children may not perform to the best of their ability unless procedures are adapted to meet their needs. Failure to do so may limit the validity of the findings. This can also include using researchers who are experienced in working with children.

As you learn about the studies where children were used as participants, think carefully about any design decisions that were made specifically to meet the developmental needs of the children. In the studies that used adults, think about how the procedures would need to be adapted if the participants were children.

The use of animals in psychological research

Your Cambridge International AS Level section of the syllabus includes two studies involving animals: Hassett *et al.*, who studied the toy preferences of rhesus monkeys, and Fagen *et al.*, who studied working elephants in Nepal. As in Fagen *et al.*'s study, psychologists sometimes investigate animal behaviour because they are simply interested in learning about animals. At other times, animals are studied in order to learn something about humans. Some psychologists believe this is possible because humans are animals too. Benvenuti (2017) defines evolutionary continuity as the idea that 'all animal capacities and behaviors exist – with variations in degree – in continuity with other species' (p. 1). People who also hold this assumption believe that conclusions about human behaviour can be drawn from studies of non-human animals.

Not everyone agrees with this and many believe that higher-order cognitive processes, including consciousness and language, mean human behaviour is much more complex. Animal research presents many practical and ethical considerations that you will be challenged to reflect on at both AS and A Level.

Individual and situational explanations

Individual explanations in psychology suggest that our behaviour stems from unique patterns of measurable traits, qualities and abilities. This suggests that, in the same situation, many different responses or reactions might occur due to differences in people's personalities and levels of intelligence, empathy or aggression. These traits are thought to remain relatively stable over time and place and can be measured using various psychometric tests (sets of questions used to measure various aspects of psychological traits). These traits are generally seen to be determined via the interaction of genetics and environmental factors which predispose us to behave in certain ways.

Situational explanations, on the other hand, suggest that despite our differing personalities, many people behave in very similar ways in certain situations. Social situations can be incredibly powerful, often eliciting behaviours from us that we may not have been able to predict. For example, immoral or criminal acts may be committed as part of a group that would not have been committed had the person been alone. Psychologists who favour situational explanations agree that our immediate circumstances often override our pre-existing personalities or preferences and can lead to unexpected outcomes.

Nature versus nurture

The nature–nurture debate in psychology relates to the extent to which different behaviours and cognitive processes are thought to result from genetic factors that are innate (inborn, sometimes referred to as hard-wired) versus experiences within our physical and social environment.

Nature

Behaviours which helped humans to survive hundreds of thousands of years ago may have been passed on through genetic inheritance. These behaviours are said to have had survival value, meaning they were adaptive as they helped the individual to survive to reproductive age. At this point, their genes would be passed to the next generation, assuming they were successful in finding a healthy mate. Behavioural traits linked to the parents' specific combination of genes would therefore also be more common in the next generation.

Nurture

Some psychologists believe that we learn how to behave through our life experiences – for example, if we pat a dog and it barks loudly at us, we learn to be more cautious about unfamiliar dogs in the future.

Typically, our experiences in the world teach us how to behave in order to be accepted by others. This process is called socialisation. Through socialisation, we learn not just about how to behave, but also about the beliefs, values and attitudes of the social group to which we belong.

Conflict and co-operation

Mass protests have been witnessed all over the world in recent years, with people campaigning for and against a diverse range of issues, from climate change to civil rights. While peaceful protests are legal and commonplace in many nations, these gatherings have sometimes descended into conflict, violence and criminality. Conversely, the pandemic years have also demonstrated the collective resilience of many communities, their ability to work together (co-operate), to support each other and to follow local 'lockdown' regulations.

Now that you are starting to understand a little more about how psychology works, try to answer the following questions:

1 How might psychologists explain conflict and co-operation in terms of:
   a nature versus nurture
   b individual explanations versus situational explanations?

Social psychologist Muzafer Sherif famously conducted a series of field experiments to investigate the situational factors that lead to conflict and co-operation. He used children as the participants in his research, which took place at an apparently normal summer camp. The experimenters divided the children into two teams and created a contest where they could win exciting prizes but only through beating the other team. What the children did not know was that their behaviour and social interactions were being covertly observed at all times (Sherif *et al.*, 1961).

2 Can you think of any practical and ethical issues that the researchers would have considered when conducting this research with children?

Elephants can be aggressive and even kill each other under certain circumstances but research suggests they are also one of the planet's most intelligent and co-operative mammals. Joshua Plotnik and colleagues demonstrated that two elephants could work together to achieve a task, even coming up with novel solutions the researchers had not previously considered (Plotnik *et al.*, 2011).

3 Can you think of any specific practical and ethical issues that the researchers would have considered when conducting this research with animals?

STUDY TIP

We have provided sections on some of the relevant issues and debates for the 12 core studies included in your AS Level syllabus in the 'evaluating' section of each study. As you learn about each study, it is important to try and apply the five issues and debates wherever possible. For example:

'Evaluate the study by Hölzel *et al.* (mindfulness and brain scans) in terms of two strengths and two weaknesses. At least one of your evaluation points must be about nature versus nurture.'

You could make a table or some other sort of diagram to show how each of the five issues and debates relate to the 12 studies.

Students Polina and Rohan are discussing a voluntary project that they saw reported on an internet news site. The project involved volunteers from many cultures who came together to collect donations and deliver aid to people affected by the COVID-19 pandemic. Rohan was surprised by how generous people were in terms of helping strangers. Polina says she feels it is understandable as people generally want to help others. The students are discussing the volunteers' behaviour in terms of nature versus nurture. Rohan believes the volunteers' behaviour is due to nurture but Polina believes that it is due to nature.

» Do you agree more with Rohan or Polina? What makes you think this?

▲ Social psychologist Philip Zimbardo favours situational explanations of human behaviour over individual explanations (Zimbardo, 2017). He believes that we are all capable of both good and evil depending on the situations we find ourselves in. Do you think our actions are shaped more by our past experiences or the present situation? What makes you think this?

1 The Biological approach

Learning outcomes

In this chapter, we will discuss:

- the main assumptions, methodology, history, issues and debates of the biological approach
- psychological concepts, theories and research relating to the three core studies:
    - Dement and Kleitman (sleep and dreams)
    - Hassett *et al.* (monkey toy preferences)
    - Hölzel *et al.* (mindfulness and brain scans)
- strengths and weaknesses of the three key studies with reference to ethical issues, **reliability, validity, objectivity** and **subjectivity, generalisations**, issues and debates, including applications to everyday life
- how to plan and evaluate your own investigations using **longitudinal studies, correlations** and **questionnaires**.

▲ Figure 1.1 Biological psychologists have studied how mindfulness affects the human brain

Where there are people, there is psychology!

Psychology is everywhere, and this woman is in Germany, the homeland of neuropsychologist Britta Hölzel. You will examine Hölzel *et al.*'s research on mindfulness on pages 29–40 of this chapter. But before finding out how this ancient practice affects the workings of the brain, you will learn about Dement and Kleitman's study of sleep and dreams and Hassett *et al.*'s study of monkey toy preferences. First, let us explore the main assumptions of the biological approach.

KEY TERMS

brain
hormones
genetic
evolutionary differences
biological factors

METHODOLOGY

experiment
longitudinal design
self-report
(questionnaire and
interview)
correlation
observation

1.0 Introducing the Biological approach

Think!

Why do you think the pituitary gland is known as the master gland?

Think!

Imagine you are working in a laboratory conducting research using female rats. Your supervisor suggests a study where you will inject the rats with testosterone. She asks you to create a way of testing the effects of this hormone on their behaviour. What would you suggest?

Think!

Many animals have evolved to sleep at night when it is dark. Using your understanding of evolution, explain why natural selection has favoured animals that sleep at night and are awake during the day.

Main assumptions

1. Behaviour, cognitions and emotions can be explained in terms of the working of the brain and the effect of **hormones**, **genetics** and **evolution**.
2. Similarities and differences between people can be understood in terms of **biological factors** and their interaction with other factors.

(Cambridge International, 2021)

Figure 1.2 shows the position of the hippocampus, a brain structure associated with memory, which underwent neuroplastic changes following Mindfulness-Based Stress Reduction in the study by Britta Hölzel and colleagues. Dr Hölzel conducted an experiment, but how would you convince her to let you conduct a case study on the role of the hippocampus?

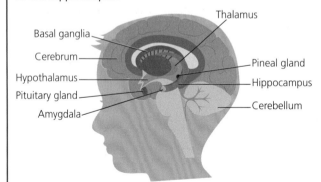

▲ Figure 1.2 The central nervous system is made up of the brain and spinal cord

The workings of the brain

Together with the spinal cord, the brain is part of the central nervous system, which controls all our bodily functions and thoughts, both conscious and unconscious. The human brain is a highly complex organ made up of billions of neurons (nerve cells), which work together in specialised neural networks. In this chapter, you will learn about localisation of function, which refers to the idea that specific structures in the brain are responsible for specific behaviours and processes. You will also learn that experience can cause changes in our neural networks, including increasing and decreasing the number of connections (synapses) between neurons. This process is called neuroplasticity and is a good example of an interaction between nature and nurture.

Throughout this course, you will learn about various brain structures, some of which are subcortical structures. This means they are buried deep within the brain, below the outside layer called the cortex (see Figure 1.2 for some of the structures you will learn about in your course). The brain is also divided into five areas, or lobes, each of which has been linked to different areas of human functioning – for example, visual (occipital lobe) and auditory processing (temporal lobe).

The effect of hormones

The endocrine system is made of glands throughout the body which produce and release various substances, including hormones. Hormones are sometimes called chemical messengers as they travel through the blood to the various bodily organs. Hormones bind to specially shaped receptors, signalling the organs to bring about important changes to help the organism to develop and respond to their environment. The most important gland in the body is called the pituitary gland and it is situated in the brain. This gland controls the release of hormones from all the other glands in the body. For example, adrenocorticotropic hormone is released by the pituitary gland and signals the adrenal glands (at the top of the kidneys) to release the stress hormone cortisol. The pituitary gland also releases oxytocin, another hormone that you will learn about in the study by Perry *et al.* (2015) in the social approach (page 143).

In this chapter, you will learn about toy preferences in monkeys (page 16). Hassett *et al.* (2008) claim that male and female monkeys prefer different types of toys due to differences in sex hormones (e.g. testosterone and oestrogen).

The effect of genetics

Genes are the basic units of heredity. They are responsible for transmitting specific characteristics from one generation to the next, e.g. from parents to their children. Genes are stretches of DNA, large chains of molecules that code for the creation of amino acids, which make up all the proteins needed to create a living organism. When psychologists talk about genetics, they are referring to the branch of biology that is concerned with the effect of genes on not only our physical development but also our behaviour and mental processing.

It is also important to understand that the way genes are expressed – that is, the way that the instructions are carried out – is affected by environmental factors, such as stress and diet. These **interactions** between nature and nurture are called epigenetic effects.

The effect of evolution

The term evolution refers to the biological process whereby the characteristics of a species gradually change over several generations. This relies on the process of natural selection: genes which code for characteristics associated with survival become more common and genes that decrease the chance of survival become less common (Darwin and Kebler, 1859).

Biological psychologists believe that behavioural differences between species depend on the amount of shared DNA. For example, humans and chimpanzees share more DNA than any other species (98.8 per cent), meaning that a small proportion of DNA (1.2 per cent) is responsible for all of the differences between these species. However, even when non-human animals and humans share the same genes, they are not always expressed in the same ways, leading to great diversity between the species.

Understanding similarities and differences between people

Similarities between people can be explained in terms of the fact that human brains typically include the same brain structures which are localised to specific behaviours and skills. Likewise, hormones typically have the same effect on their target organs for the majority of people leading to similarities in behaviour and cognition. On page 6–14 you will learn about the REM and nREM stages of sleep, which have evolved to help us to function effectively, and ultimately to survive. The majority of people exhibit similar patterns of brain activity during sleep, which is necessary for physical and psychological wellbeing.

Atypical brain development and/or brain damage may lead to differences in behaviour and cognition and may lead to loss of function. This said, cortical remapping, whereby unaffected brain structures become localised to the lost skills may mean that skills can be regained. Experiences within the environment and practice in certain skills can also lead to differences in the grey matter concentration in certain brain structures and this can account for differences in behaviour. You will learn more about this in the study by Hölzel *et al.* (mindfulness and brain scans).

As you learn more about the three core studies in the biological approach, you will begin to understand that human behaviour and cognition result from the interaction between biological factors and events within our physical and social environment. On pages 15–28 you will learn how monkey toy preferences may be shaped in part by hormonal differences between the sexes (a biological factor), however interactions with toys are also affected by the social rank of individual monkeys within the group (a social factor).

 ## Methodology in the Biological approach

Biological psychologists generally collect quantitative data, often as part of an experiment where two groups or conditions are compared. Blood, urine, saliva, cerebro-spinal fluid and faecal matter can be tested to find out about an organism's genetic make-up and/or levels of certain hormones and other substances. Other objective measures may be taken, such as heart rate or electrodermal activity, which monitors changes in sweat glands as a measure of emotional arousal.

MRI scans can be used to monitor structural changes in the brain and techniques such as voxel-based morphometry (VBM) may be used to measure the relative size of specific structures. fMRI and/or PET scans can be used to observe the activity in different brain structures while participants complete a task. This is done by monitoring neural blood flow. The more active a brain structure is, the quicker oxygen is consumed. This means blood flow to that region is increased to cope with the increased demand. On page 6, you will learn about a final imaging technique called electroencephalography (EEG), which measures changes in electrical activity (brain waves) as neurons communicate with each other.

Biological psychologists also conduct experiments on non-human animals, for the reasons discussed on page 16, and they sometimes conduct ethological studies, which means studying animals in their natural habitats.

Bonobos and chimpanzees share almost 99 per cent of their DNA with humans and, as you might expect, show many human-like behaviours, including aggression (Figure 1.3). Why do you think aggression is a common trait in these three species?

▶ Figure 1.3 Aggression is a trait shared by bonobos, chimpanzees and humans

Applications to everyday life

A better understanding of the impact of biological factors has led to the development of treatments to help people with sleep disorders and hormonal imbalances (see congenital adrenal hyperplasia, page 18) and to manage stress through practices such as mindfulness, which can trigger neuroplastic changes.

Individual and situational explanations

An understanding of the interaction between genes and environment is helpful in understanding individual differences, but an understanding of the way the brain responds to stress through the release of hormones, for example, can help explain the impact of situational factors.

Nature versus nurture

Although the biological approach is clearly allied with nature (i.e. the impact of genes on the brain and behaviour), advances in our understanding of neuroplasticity and epigenetics help to explain how nurture (experience) changes our behaviour.

The use of animals in psychological research

The biological approach often favours the use of non-human animal experiments – for example, with rodents or primates – due to biological similarities with humans.

The history of the Biological approach

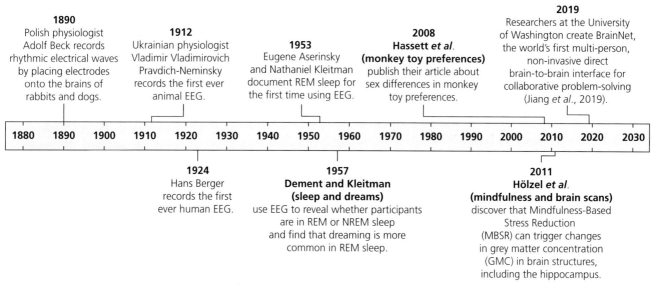

1890
Polish physiologist Adolf Beck records rhythmic electrical waves by placing electrodes onto the brains of rabbits and dogs.

1912
Ukrainian physiologist Vladimir Vladimirovich Pravdich-Neminsky records the first ever animal EEG.

1953
Eugene Aserinsky and Nathaniel Kleitman document REM sleep for the first time using EEG.

2008
Hassett *et al*. (monkey toy preferences) publish their article about sex differences in monkey toy preferences.

2019
Researchers at the University of Washington create BrainNet, the world's first multi-person, non-invasive direct brain-to-brain interface for collaborative problem-solving (Jiang *et al.*, 2019).

1880	1890	1900	1910	1920	1930	1940	1950	1960	1970	1980	1990	2000	2010	2020	2030

1924
Hans Berger records the first ever human EEG.

1957
Dement and Kleitman (sleep and dreams) use EEG to reveal whether participants are in REM or NREM sleep and find that dreaming is more common in REM sleep.

2011
Hölzel *et al*. (mindfulness and brain scans) discover that Mindfulness-Based Stress Reduction (MBSR) can trigger changes in grey matter concentration (GMC) in brain structures, including the hippocampus.

▲ Figure 1.4 Timeline of the biological approach

> **STUDY TIP**
>
> As you learn about each of the studies in the biological approach, think about how the results support the main assumptions of the approach. What has the study told us about the causes of behaviour and how they link to the workings of the brain, hormones, genetics and/or evolution? Does the study tell us anything about the interaction of these biological factors and environmental factors?

Do you remember Rohan and Polina from page xii? They were discussing an internet news story about a voluntary project where people from many cultures came together to collect and deliver aid to people affected by the COVID-19 pandemic. Rohan was surprised by how generous people were in terms of helping strangers. Polina says she feels it is understandable as people generally want to help others.

» How might biological psychologists explain the high levels of generosity and helpfulness observed during the pandemic?

» Use what you have learned in this section as a starting point, but you may also wish to conduct some research of your own.

» After you have learned about all three studies in the approach, you may like to revisit your answer and add some more ideas.

1.1 Dement and Kleitman (sleep and dreams)

1.1.1 Background

> **Think!**
>
> What are the main differences between REM and non-REM **sleep**?

> **Think!**
>
> How have your sleep patterns changed throughout your lifetime so far? Have you noticed any changes in the amount of time you sleep, or the time you wake up, as you have got older?

> **Think!**
>
> While the use of scientific equipment such as EEGs to record biological processes can make measurements more objective, what are some disadvantages of their use?

Introducing William Dement and Nathaniel Kleitman

Nathaniel Kleitman, Professor Emeritus in Physiology at the University of Chicago, is known as the founder of modern sleep research. He was also an academic supervisor of William Dement. Kleitman used many of his relatives in his sleep research and had his daughters sleep on special beds designed to track their sleep for many years. He was also interested in the effects of sleep deprivation and once spent over a month in an underground cave to record his sleep and body temperature. In 1953, another of Kleitman's graduate students, Eugene Aserinsky, discovered that periods of eye movements during sleep correspond to sudden increases in brain activity after monitoring his eight-year-old son's sleep with an EEG machine (Aserinsky and Kleitman, 1953). This was an important finding as, before this discovery, it was believed that the brain was in a restful state only during sleep.

▲ Figure 1.5 Professor Nathaniel Kleitman

How do the stages of sleep change throughout the night (Figure 1.6)? When you have slept for a longer period of time than normal, are you more likely to remember your dreams?

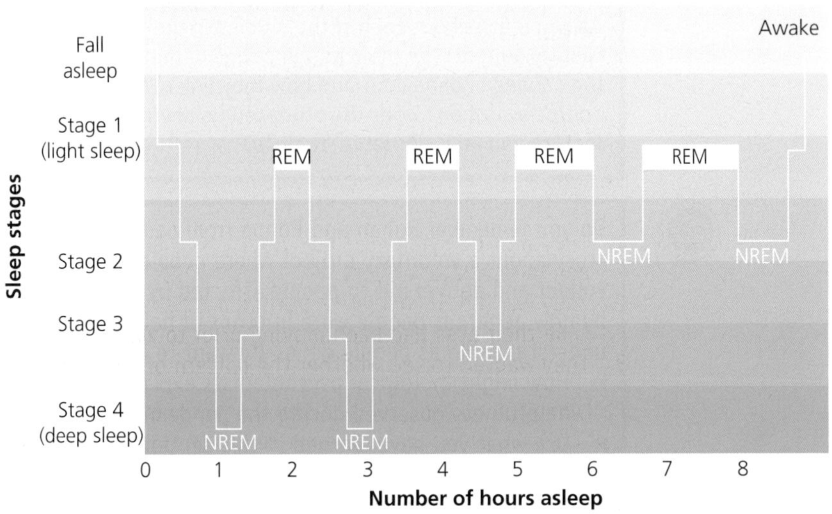

KEY TERMS

sleep

electroencephalogram (EEG)

rapid eye movement (REM)

non-rapid eye movement (non-REM)

ultradian rhythms

dreaming

▲ Figure 1.6 Sleep cycles

The psychology being investigated

Sleep

Brain wave activity during sleep can be measured via an **electroencephalogram (EEG)**, which detects activity through electrodes connected to the scalp (see page 10 for more on EEGs). Sleep researchers have identified five distinct sleep stages. Stages 1 and 2 are the lighter stages of sleep, where a person can still be woken fairly easily, and stages 3 and 4 are the deeper stages of sleep. In the deeper stages, brain waves slow down and show a pattern of high amplitude and low frequency. The final stage is **rapid eye movement (REM)** sleep. Here the brain waves are high frequency and low amplitude and are similar to those seen when we are awake. Researchers often refer to stages 1–4 as **non-rapid eye movement (non-REM)** sleep.

When we first fall asleep, we gradually enter stage (non-REM) sleep, before moving through stages 2–4 and then back into the lighter stages of sleep. Instead of re-entering stage 1, the person enters the first episode of REM sleep. During REM sleep, a person's eyes flicker and move beneath their eyelids, but other muscles in the body are paralysed. Figure 1.6 shows how we move from non-REM to REM sleep in a cyclical pattern throughout the night. As you can see, we spend a significant proportion of time in non-REM sleep in the first half of the night, and increasingly more time in REM sleep in the second half of the night.

Ultradian rhythms

Biological rhythms which repeat more frequently than once a day are called **ultradian rhythms** and the sleep stages are a good example of these as, in healthy adults, a full cycle takes roughly 90 minutes.

Dreaming

Dreams are subjective memories of what we experience while we are asleep and this study was interested in whether people are more likely to report dreams if woken in certain sleep stages compared with others.

Background

Dement and Kleitman were interested in finding a reliable way to physiologically determine when a person is **dreaming**. They believed that dreaming must have a biological basis and, therefore, there must be a way to objectively measure when it is physically taking place.

Previously, Kleitman had noticed that when people who were asleep were showing rapid eye movements and then woken up, they were often able to recall their dreams. However, when woken up during other parts of the night, they found dreams difficult to remember. Furthermore, when people were showing rapid eye movements during their sleep, this corresponded to a specific pattern of brain activity as measured by an EEG and occurred cyclically throughout the night.

Dement and Kleitman in brief

Dement and Kleitman wanted to see whether there was a relationship between eye movements and dreaming. They used the following three approaches to investigate this:
1 They wanted participants to recall their dreams without a researcher present, to avoid any investigator effects.
2 They wanted to compare a participant's estimate of their dream length to the amount of time their eyes had been moving prior to waking.
3 They wanted to see whether the pattern of eye movements was related to dream content.

Participants were invited to sleep in a sleep laboratory, where an EEG machine was used to monitor their brain waves during sleep. They were then woken up multiple times during the night and asked to report any dream content they remembered, as well as how long they estimated themselves to have been dreaming. Participants were woken up during both REM and non-REM sleep, which the researchers were able to determine by the brain wave patterns on the EEG.

Plan your own... longitudinal study

Dement and Kleitman used **experiments** and correlations to test their ideas about sleep and dreaming but there are lots of other research methods that might be used. Why not try designing a longitudinal study to investigate sleep and dreaming?

Imagine...

Merry is planning a longitudinal study to investigate whether people's total REM sleep changes over their lifespan. She wants to know if the total time spent in REM sleep changes from childhood to old age.

>> What advice would you give Merry about how to conduct this longitudinal study?

Planning a longitudinal study

A longitudinal study is an investigation that takes place over a significant period of time and can be part of an experiment. When planning a longitudinal study, it is important to consider the tests or tasks that participants will undertake, how these will be scored, how often participants will be contacted to take part in the research, how procedures will be standardised and what controls will be in place. See page 195 for more information on longitudinal studies.

▼ Table 1.1 Features of a longitudinal study

Main features of a longitudinal study	Consider...
Tests or tasks	Longitudinal studies often require participants to take part in similar tests or tasks repeatedly over a period of time. How might Merry determine the total time a person spends in REM sleep each night?
Scoring	Longitudinal studies need to compare people's data sets over time. How might Merry compare the total time spent in REM sleep per night over time?
Frequency or interval	Longitudinal studies investigate any changes that may occur over a period of time. In order to collect valid data about lifespan changes in REM sleep, how long will Merry's study last and how frequently will her participants need to be tested?
Re-contacting of participants (for repeated testing)	Participants in longitudinal studies need to be re-contacted for repeated testing. How might Merry re-contact her participants for retesting over the years?
Controls and standardisation	In order to compare data over a period of time, procedures need to be standardised and controls put in place. How can Merry ensure that her procedure is the same each time participants attend testing? What controls can she put in place?

Evaluating your plan

Merry shares your ideas with her colleagues. Some of them think it is a great idea; others are not so sure. Think about the practical strengths and weaknesses of your suggestions.

▼ Table 1.2 Evaluating your plan

	Describe	Explain
Strengths	What unique insight might be gained from Merry undertaking a longitudinal study? How would this strengthen the validity of the data?	Would it be possible for Merry to gather this data using another research method? If so, why might a longitudinal study give a more valid insight into time spent in REM sleep over the lifespan?
Weaknesses	What issues might arise with the research taking place over a very long period of time? Why might this compromise the validity of the data?	If the validity of the data is compromised by the study's length, what impact will this have on any findings about time spent in REM sleep over the lifespan?
Improvements	Consider a weakness you gave above. How might you improve Merry's procedure to overcome this issue?	How would this improvement affect the validity and/or reliability of the data Merry collects about lifespan changes in time spent in REM sleep?

Knowing that people are paralysed during REM sleep, how might these sleep trackers determine what stage of sleep a person is in?

◀ Figure 1.7 There are sleep tracking apps for both phones and watches

LEARNING LINK

Similar to Dement and Kleitman, Hölzel *et al.* (mindfulness and brain scans) also used scientific equipment to take measurements of the brain. In Hölzel *et al.*'s study, participants were awake, not asleep and an MRI scanner was used as opposed to an EEG machine. MRI scans are static (still) images of the brain, unlike an EEG machine. An MRI scanner is very restrictive as it requires a person to lie still within a very small space and can be quite claustrophobic, therefore, it is only appropriate to be used for a short amount of time. An EEG, on the other hand, is used by placing electrodes on a person's head. While this is still quite restrictive as a person is still attached to a machine via cables, it allowed Dement and Kleitman to take recordings throughout the whole night while participants slept.

STUDY TIP

A longitudinal study involves collecting and comparing data from the same group of people (or person in a longitudinal case study), on at least three occasions over an extended period. As it is a non-experimental method, there is no independent variable. However, it is also possible to have an experiment with a longitudinal design. Like any experiment, data is collected from different groups or in different conditions in order to find a cause-and-effect relationship between at least one independent and one dependent variable. The only difference is that the data collection periods may be weeks, months or years apart. Understanding that 'longitudinal' can be used to describe the method and/or its use within an experiment is important when you are planning, but also when you are evaluating, your own research or that of other people.

TEST YOURSELF

1   This study investigated rapid eye movement (REM) sleep. Outline the main features of REM sleep. [2]
2   Identify one reason for using an EEG (electroencephalogram) to record brain activity. [1]
3   Explain why the study by Dement and Kleitman is an example of the biological approach. [2]
4   Dement and Kleitman found that as dream length increased, the number of words used to describe the dream also increased. Explain which type of correlation this is. [1]
5   Dement and Kleitman relied on self-reports to investigate the content of participants' dreams. Explain one disadvantage of this. [2]
6   The study by Dement and Kleitman was conducted in a sleep laboratory. Suggest one disadvantage of conducting a study in this location. [2]

METHODOLOGY

experiment

correlation

interview

1.1.2 Describing Dement and Kleitman (sleep and dreams)

> **Think!**
>
> During which type of sleep did dream recall mostly occur in Dement and Kleitman's study?

> **Think!**
>
> How easy do you find it to recall your dreams when you wake up in the morning? Do you find it easier to remember your dreams when you sleep for longer? If so, why might this be the case?

> **Think!**
>
> Why was it important that participants did not consume alcohol or caffeine on the day of the experiment?

What does an EEG record? How might using this machine affect the participants' sleep?

◀ Figure 1.8 A modern EEG being used in a medical setting

▶ AIMS

The aims were:

1   To see if dream recall occurs during REM or non-REM sleep.
2   To see if there is a link between the estimate of dream length and length of REM period.
3   To see if the pattern of eye movements (vertical/horizontal) is related to dream content.
4   To see if there is a positive correlation between the duration of REM sleep and the number of words given in a dream narrative.

▶ RESEARCH METHODOLOGY

The study used the methods of experiment and correlation. Some qualitative data was collected using an **interview** technique. Three of the aims had independent variables, where the researchers were looking for a difference between conditions (i.e. REM vs non-REM). The fourth aim was looking for a correlation between two co-variables (time spent in REM sleep and the number of words in a dream narrative). The researchers occasionally interviewed participants after their dream recall to ask further questions.

Design and variables

The experiments used a repeated measures design, meaning participants took part in both conditions of each independent variable.

Aim 1

● Independent variable: whether woken up during REM or non-REM sleep.
● Dependent variable: whether the participant could recall the content of their dream in reasonable detail (yes or no).

Aim 2

- Independent variable: whether woken up 5 or 15 minutes after the onset of REM.
- Dependent variable: perception of whether they had been dreaming for 5 or 15 minutes (initially participants were asked to report dream length in minutes).

Aim 3

- Independent variable: eye movement pattern before waking: (a) mainly vertical eye movements, (b) mainly horizontal eye movements, (c) both vertical and horizontal eye movements, and (d) very little or no eye movements.
- Dependent variable: the description of their dream.

Aim 4

- Co-variable 1: the number of minutes spent in REM sleep.
- Co-variable 2: the number of words in the corresponding dream narrative recording.

Sample

The sample consisted of seven adult males and two adult females. Five were studied more intensively, with the data from the other four being used to confirm the results. The study took place in a sleep laboratory at the University of Chicago, in the United States of America.

▶ PROCEDURE

Each participant reported to the laboratory before their usual bedtime. They were asked to avoid consuming alcohol and caffeine on the day of the experiment, but to eat normally. Two or more electrodes were placed near their eyes to record eye movements during sleep. Two or three electrodes were then fixed to the scalp to record brain waves so the researchers knew when a person was in REM or non-REM sleep.

The participant was then taken to a quiet, dark room to sleep, where the wires were carefully tied at the top of the head to avoid becoming tangled in them during the night. An EEG was run throughout the night in the next room. Throughout the night, participants were woken at various times, in both REM and non-REM sleep, by a doorbell that

was loud enough to wake them from deep sleep. They were asked to first say whether they had been dreaming or not, and then to describe the content of their dream into a recording device near their bed. After this, they were able to go back to sleep.

Occasionally, the experimenter would enter the room to question them further about an aspect of their dream. Participants were only considered to have been dreaming if they could recall their dream content in detail.

Overall, 21 per cent of awakenings took place in the first two hours of sleep, 29 per cent in hours two to four, 28 per cent in hours four to six and 22 per cent in hours six to eight.

▶ RESULTS

All nine participants showed a regular pattern of sleep and EEG recordings, which were characterised by periods of deep sleep (high-voltage, slow pattern of EEG activity) followed by periods of REM sleep (low-voltage, fast pattern of EEG activity).

Dement and Kleitman found that REM sleep never occurred immediately after the onset of sleep but did occur at regular intervals throughout the night. The frequency of periods of REM was constant for each participant, but the length varied between them (ranging from 70 to 104 minutes, with an average of 92 minutes). The duration of REM varied from 3 to 50 minutes, with an average of 20 minutes. REM periods were also longer later in the night.

Results for aim 1

Dream recall occurred predominantly in REM sleep. Participants had a high incidence of dream recall following REM awakenings (80 per cent) and a low incidence of recall following non-REM awakenings (7 per cent).

Results for aim 2

All participants were able to determine whether they had been dreaming for 5 or 15 minutes with high accuracy

(correct 83 per cent of the time from 111 awakenings), with the exception of one participant who was only correct 65 per cent of the time and tended to underestimate the length of time he had been dreaming.

Results for aim 3

- Vertical eye movement dream reports included looking at climbers on a cliff, climbing ladders and throwing a basketball.
- The only dream report following horizontal eye movements involved watching two people throwing tomatoes at each other.
- Little or no eye movement dream reports included driving a car.
- Mixed eye movement dream reports included talking to a group of people, searching for something and fighting with someone.

Results for aim 4

There was a moderate positive correlation between duration of REM and number of words in dream narrative. The average correlation coefficient was +0.58, with individual results ranging from +0.40 to +0.71.

CONCLUSION

Dreaming occurred during periods of REM sleep in distinct episodes throughout the night. The researchers concluded that dreaming can be objectively measured by recording REM cycles during sleep.

LEARNING LINK

Dement and Kleitman included a correlation as part of their research, finding a positive correlation between length of REM period and the number of words used in a dream narrative. Similarly, Baron-Cohen *et al.* (eyes test) found a correlation between 'Eyes Test' score and Autism Spectrum Quotient. The main difference, however, is that this correlation was a negative correlation. Remember that correlations requires the collection of quantitative data, which is always plotted on a scatter graph. When plotting the data for a correlation on a scatter graph, it does not matter which co-variable goes on which axis. Are you confident in explaining the difference between a positive and negative correlation? Would you be able to sketch a scatter graph of each? For more information, check page 192 for correlations and page 220 for scatter graphs.

STUDY TIP

With four aims, there are quite a few operational definitions to learn for the independent variables, dependent variables and co-variables in this study. One way to practise your ability to operationalise variables, as well as strengthen your memory for this study, would be to write down each of the four aims and then attempt to give the operational definitions for each. Keep trying this until you can correctly define them each time with ease.

TEST YOURSELF

1 Identify the technique used in this study to measure brain activity. [1]
2 Describe the procedure for waking participants during either REM or non-REM sleep. [2]
3 Explain one methodological weakness of this study. [2]
4 Explain what is meant by a 'self-report' using the study by Dement and Kleitman as an example. [2]
5 Describe two different ways that dependent variables can be measured, using an example from this study for each. [4]
6 Describe two of the controls from the study by Dement and Kleitman. [4]

1.1.3 Evaluating Dement and Kleitman (sleep and dreams)

Think!

How might individual differences in Dement and Kleitman's study have affected the validity of the results?

Think!

Imagine that you were a participant in Dement and Kleitman's study. How do you think sleeping in the laboratory might affect your usual sleep? How might this affect the validity of this study?

> **Think!**
>
> The participants in the study were woken up on different schedules. For example, two participants were awoken randomly, using a random number generator. However, another was awoken when the experimenter decided. How might this have affected the reliability of the research?

> Research has shown that blue light from screens can disrupt sleep due to their wavelength, inhibiting melatonin release (melatonin is a hormone that is important for sleep) (Zerbini *et al.*, 2020). How might you conduct an experiment into the impact of blue light on sleep? What would your independent and dependent variables be and how would you operationalise these?

Ethical issues

Maintaining confidentiality was a strength of this research. The researchers used participants' initials when discussing their results, which kept their identity hidden. Furthermore, no other personal details about the participants were shared. This prevented any embarrassment due to the participants' personal dream content being revealed publicly.

Methodological issues

Reliability

A strength of this research was the high level of standardisation in the procedure. All participants were fitted with the same equipment, including electrodes near their eyes and scalp, with the wires tied together behind their head. They all slept in a bed in a quiet, dark room, were woken by a doorbell and were required to narrate their dream into a tape recorder. Ensuring such a consistent procedure meant that the study could be replicated to test whether the association between dreaming and REM sleep was reliable.

Validity

Avoiding investigator effects

A strength of this study is that the researchers ensured nobody else was present when the participants recalled their dreams. This was to avoid the possibility of the experimenter influencing a person's dream narrative through prompting or expectation. Although an experimenter *did* enter the room occasionally to question the participant further about their dream content, this was after the participant had given their full recording. This made the research more valid and the dream reports free from experimenter effects.

Some results discarded

In the study, one issue is that the loss of some dream recordings might have affected the validity of the data. Of the 152 dreams recalled, the recordings for six had to be discarded as they could not be understood from the tape. This may have affected the validity of the data, as these poor recordings might have been genuine dream reports during non-REM sleep, with participants simply feeling more tired after waking from deep sleep and giving a mumbled recording; there is no way to know.

Individual differences

One weakness of the operational definition of dream length (number of words used in narrative) is that there may have been significant individual differences in how verbal each participant was. For example, some participants may have a broader vocabulary and thus describe a short dream in much more detail than others. This would affect the validity of the data when correlating the number of words in a dream narrative and the length of REM sleep.

Objectivity and subjectivity

Quantitative data

A strength of this study was its use of quantitative data which can be objectively analysed. This would help to reduce the effects of subjectivity on interpretation of dream content. For example, the number of words in the dream narrative was calculated and correlated against the amount of time spent in REM sleep. This avoided researcher bias in the interpretation of data about dreaming and REM sleep, which increases the validity of the findings.

Scientific equipment

A strength is that an EEG was used in this study, which gave an objective measure of the sleep stage a participant was in. The frequency and amplitude of brain waves for both REM and non-REM can be quantified, allowing little room for subjective interpretation by the researchers. This increased the validity of the data, as the researchers could be confident of the sleep stage in which a person was being woken.

Generalisations and ecological validity

Generalising beyond the sample

One weakness of the sample is that there was a significant variation in the duration of sleep cycles even between the small number of five main participants. One participant averaged one period of eye movement every 70 minutes, while another only had a period of eye movement every 104 minutes. The researchers should, therefore, be cautious when generalising any findings to others, as the study demonstrated individual differences in sleep patterns.

Generalising to everyday life

A weakness is that the study lacks ecological validity as participants were sleeping in a laboratory attached to an EEG with electrodes on their heads. This may have affected their normal sleep patterns, as it may have been difficult to fully relax and sleep as they would normally, especially with multiple awakenings. Furthermore, participants were asked to avoid drinking caffeine and alcohol before bed, which might be a normal occurrence for them in real life. This reduces the ability of the researchers to confidently apply the findings to regular sleep conditions in a person's own home.

On the other hand, Dement and Kleitman believed that their results *were* generalisable for two reasons – firstly, because their results were similar to other studies of uninterrupted sleep and, secondly, because the physiological process of going through cycles of REM and non-REM is the same for everyone (although with individual differences in length). This would suggest that the results relating to REM sleep and dreaming could, therefore, be applied to all people.

> ## ISSUES AND DEBATES

Nature versus nurture

The research findings support the concept of nature, as all participants reported a significantly greater number of dreams during REM sleep than non-REM sleep, indicating that dreaming during REM sleep is an innate biological mechanism. Furthermore, regularly occurring periods of REM were observed in all participants on every night of sleep, indicating that this ultradian rhythm is universal for all humans and is biologically determined. The fact that people had such diverse dreams with differing content demonstrates the role of nurture in sleep and dreams, as our different life experiences will impact what we dream about.

Applications to everyday life

Treating sleep issues

An EEG can be used to determine when a person is in REM or non-REM sleep and can, therefore, be used to support the diagnosis of sleep issues, as some sleep disorders occur in certain stages of sleep only. A psychologist could also look at the output of the EEG and compare brain wave patterns with a 'typical' sleeper to see if there are any differences. This may help psychologists in determining the right course of treatment for an individual.

Monitoring external influences

Another application of the use of EEG in sleep might be to monitor how people's sleep is affected by external influences – for example, environmental changes, stress or drugs. A person's sleep patterns can be recorded before and after a change in order to determine the effects of an external factor on sleep.

Reflections

Dement and Kleitman's research demonstrating that dreaming takes place during REM sleep and that EEG can be used as a reliable measure of a person's sleep stage was pivotal in 1957 when the study was published. William Dement used the knowledge gained from this study to investigate sleep and other health disorders alongside other researchers. For example, he discovered that periods of REM occurring immediately at the onset of sleep was a biological marker for narcolepsy (a chronic sleep disorder causing sudden sleep onset) (Mitler *et al.*, 1979). Furthermore, he found that late onset of the first period of REM sleep was a biomarker for Alzheimer's disease (Bliwise *et al.*, 1989). The research findings from these studies have allowed a deeper understanding of the physiological processes involved in sleep.

► LEARNING LINK

When you study the social approach, you will discover that the study by Milgram (obedience) also suffered issues with ecological validity, having been conducted in a laboratory-type setting. The main difference in Milgram's study, however, is that participants were having their behaviour observed covertly while they were awake, rather than awake. Additionally, their external actions were being recorded. In Dement and Kleitman's study, however, internal biological processes were being monitored. Why do you think psychologists observe people's behaviour in controlled laboratory-type settings when the environment and situations presented may be very different from real life?

STUDY TIP

This study included both quantitative and qualitative data. Quantitative data included the number of participants correctly estimating whether their dream duration had been 5 or 15 minutes, for example. On the other hand, qualitative data included the content of the dream reports, which was used to see if a person's dream content matched their eye movements. Make sure that you can give examples of quantitative and qualitative data for core studies where both are collected, as well as explain the advantages and disadvantages of each.

► TEST YOURSELF

1 Explain one methodological weakness of this study. [2]
2 Suggest one real-life application from the study by Dement and Kleitman (sleep and dreams). [2]
3 Evaluate this study in terms of two strengths and two weaknesses. At least one of your evaluation points must be about qualitative data. [10]
4 Suggest one disadvantage of the way in which the dependent variable of dream context was operationalised in this study. [1]
5 Explain two advantages of using quantitative data in this study. [2]
6 Explain why measuring the length of an REM period is a valid measure of dream duration. [2]

1.2 Hassett *et al.* (monkey toy preferences)

1.2.1 Background

Think!

Do Hassett *et al.* believe that **sex differences** in **toy preferences** are due to nature or nurture? Why?

KEY TERMS

sex differences

toy preferences

play

socialisation

stereotypical

hormones

Think!

Why might increasing prenatal androgen exposure in a non-human animal experiment (e.g. Goy *et al.*, 1988) lead to different behaviour in the female monkeys compared with untreated controls? Why might female children with congenital adrenal hyperplasia (CAH) not show the same behaviour as male children and/or female monkeys exposed to high levels of prenatal androgens?

Think!

The theory that toy preferences may be biologically determined is described as controversial. Why do you think this might be? This is a good area to discuss with your peers as there are likely to be differing views and it is important to hear from both sides in order to decide how you feel about the issues.

Introducing Kim Wallen and Janice Hassett-Vick

Professor Wallen, researcher at the Yerkes National Primate Research Center, says:

> I have been working with monkeys for over 50 years, first as an undergraduate, then a graduate student, and for the last 43 years as a professor of psychology and behavioural neuroendocrinology at Emory University and the Yerkes National Primate Research Centre.

▲ Figure 1.9 Professor Kim Wallen

> Drs Melissa Hines and Gerianne Alexander had found that male vervet monkeys interacted longer with male-stereotyped toys and spent less time with female-stereotyped toys. I was interested whether monkeys would show a preference for sex-stereotyped toys if they had a choice between male and female-stereotyped toys. Janice Hassett had joined my lab for a summer internship and was somewhat surprised when I suggested we look at monkeys' preferences for human sex-typed toys. We were both quite surprised when the monkeys' behaviour almost completely paralleled what had been found in children using a human toy-preference task. This suggests that toy preferences may not be primarily the result of socialised preferences but reflect underlying sex differences in preferences for specific activities that are facilitated by toys.

> This study illustrates that sometimes investigating wild ideas results in fascinating findings. One should not hesitate to consider studies that seem doomed to failure if the question is important!

(K. Wallen, personal communication, August 2021)

Male rhesus monkeys (Figure 1.10) generally engage in more rough-and-tumble **play** than female monkeys, just like human infants, but do you think wild monkeys like these would behave any differently to monkeys raised in captivity, such as the ones in Hassett *et al.*'s study?

▲ Figure 1.10 Wild rhesus monkeys on the roof of a Buddhist temple in Cambodia

The psychology being investigated

Play

All animals play, including humans, but the concept is hard to define due to the many different types of play seen at different developmental levels. Seashore (1913) defined play as 'pleasure gained in self-expression'. This definition may apply to some forms of human play, but it does not describe non-human animal play very well as animals do not really have a sense of self to express! Bergen (2015) emphasises that play is always *voluntary*, explaining that we play because we choose to, not because we have to. We also choose what we wish to play with, how and with whom. Many psychologists agree that play allows the individual to practise the skills required in adulthood and this is true of both humans and animals. So, play may be adaptive – that is, it helps us to survive.

Sex differences and the role of nature

In mammals, biological sex is determined by our sex chromosomes, typically XX for females and XY for males, although many differences can occur. Typically, these chromosomes determine levels of **hormones** such as testosterone and oestrogen, which cause differences in the development of male and female brains. For example, the sex hormones affect neural development, including neurogenesis (cell birth) and synaptogenesis (creation of connections between neurons), and have been associated with differences in cognitive processes (Overman *et al.*, 1996).

Anyone visiting a kindergarten or nursery might see boys playing with cars and girls playing with dolls, but psychological research has demonstrated that girls are more likely to play with trucks than boys are to play with dolls. These behavioural sex differences are fairly robust and Hassett *et al.* explore the idea that these differences may be hormonal in origin. This said, their views conflict with many psychologists who believe gender roles are primarily learned through **socialisation**.

Socialisation and the role of nurture

In humans, gender refers to the individual's personal sense of their own masculinity and/or femininity. Children learn about gender and societal expectations of how males and females behave through interactions with parents and other children. For example, a little boy who bangs two trucks together may be praised for creating an exciting game, whereas a little girl may be discouraged and offered a more traditionally feminine toy, such as a doll or tea set. Daily interactions like this gradually lead boys and girls to conform to **stereotypical** gender roles and seek out specific toys. The fact that boys play less with stereotypically feminine toys than girls play with stereotypically masculine toys suggests boys may be more actively discouraged from opposite-sex behaviour, whereas opposite-sex behaviour in girls may be ignored rather than rejected. Psychologists who accept these ideas believe that sex differences in children's play result from socialisation.

Hormones and toy preferences

Hassett *et al.* reject the socialisation explanation for toy preferences. They believe male and female children prefer toys that can be used for activities that suit their specific cognitive abilities. These abilities, as stated above, depend upon the children's differing sex hormone levels. This means that toys are selected according to the different play activities they promote rather than society's attitudes regarding 'gender-appropriate' toys. This view is supported by the fact that children tend to explain their toy preferences in terms of 'what can be done with' a specific toy in contrast to its gender-appropriateness (Eisenberg *et al.*, 1982) – for example, teddies can be cuddled whereas trucks can be moved by pushing them along.

Background

Congenital adrenal hyperplasia

Hassett *et al.*'s thoughts on play, toy preference and the nature versus nurture debate were influenced by **observations** of children with congenital adrenal hyperplasia (CAH), an inherited condition where the foetus (unborn child) is exposed to higher than usual levels of prenatal androgens (male sex hormones). Research shows that girls with CAH show a preference for stereotypically male toys in comparison with their unaffected sisters (Berenbaum and Hines, 1992). Pasterski *et al.* (2005) also found that, while parents encouraged their daughters with CAH to play with stereotypically female toys more than they did their unaffected female siblings, these children still preferred stereotypically male toys. Findings like these have led researchers, including Hassett *et al.*, to favour the idea that toy preferences are shaped, initially at least, by hormones, not socialisation.

Previous research on monkeys

Studying monkeys helps to separate the effects of nature and nurture as monkeys are not socialised to play with any specific type of toys, and so any sex differences that are observed must be determined by biological not social factors.

Evolutionary continuity between monkeys and humans means findings from primates may help to determine the role of biological factors in toy preferences in human infants. Interestingly though, female vervet monkeys exposed to prenatal androgens do not always behave as expected. Although they participated in more rough-and-tumble play than untreated controls (Goy *et al.*, 1988), their interest in infants is unaffected (Herman *et al.*, 2003). Furthermore, Alexander and Hines (2002) found that male vervet monkeys played more with stereotypically male human toys than the female monkeys but, unlike humans, the males spent a similar amount of time interacting with male and female toys. In contrast, females showed a strong preference for female versus male toys.

Hassett *et al.* in brief

Building on Alexander and Hines' (2002) research, Hassett *et al.* examined toy preferences in a troop of captive rhesus monkeys. However, instead of observing the monkeys with just one toy at a time, they presented pairs of wheeled and plush (cuddly) toys, allowing observers to note the sex of any monkeys that interacted with the toys, and which toys they preferred when given a choice. They observed significant sex differences matching those seen in humans and concluded that these differences stemmed from prenatal hormone exposure.

 # Plan your own... correlation

Hassett *et al.* designed an experiment to investigate sex differences for toy preferences in monkeys. Why not try designing a correlation to investigate the relationship between age and toy preferences?

Imagine...

Aliaa is planning a correlation to investigate whether there is a relationship between the age of a boy and the typical 'masculinity' of his preferred toys.

>> What advice would you give Aliaa about how to conduct a correlation to investigate this relationship?

Planning a correlation

Correlation is a non-experimental method. There are no independent variables; instead, the researcher measures two or more co-variables to see if they are related to one another. As there are no manipulated or controlled variables, causality cannot be inferred and all that can be concluded is the strength, direction and significance of the relationship(s). See page 192 for more information on correlations.

▼ Table 1.3 Features of a correlation

Main features of a correlation	Consider...
Two co-variables	Correlations look at the relationship between two measured, quantitative variables. Think carefully about the operational definition of each. How might Aliaa operationalise how typically 'masculine' a toy is seen to be, in particular?
Measure of variable 1	How might Aliaa collect data on a child's age?
Measure of variable 2	How can Aliaa collect data on how typically 'masculine' a toy is seen to be?
Comparison and scatter graph	Correlations involve the collection of quantitative data, which is presented on a scatter graph. How will Aliaa present her data on a scatter graph?

Evaluating your plan

Aliaa shares your ideas with her peers. Some of them think it is a great idea; others are not so sure. Think about the practical strengths and weaknesses of your suggestions.

▼ Table 1.4 Evaluating your plan

	Describe	Explain
Strengths	Think about your data collection techniques. In what way did they ensure that the data collected was valid and/or reliable?	How might this strength affect any conclusions drawn about any relationship between age and perceived masculinity of 'preferred toys'?
Weaknesses	A weakness of correlations is that cause and effect cannot be established. Why is this an issue?	How might this weakness affect any conclusions drawn about any relationship between age and perceived masculinity of 'preferred toys'?
Improvements	Consider the data collection method you suggested to Aliaa for determining how 'masculine' a toy is seen to be. In what way might this be improved to collect more valid/reliable data?	What impact might this have on Aliaa's results and conclusions about any relationship between age and perceived masculinity of 'preferred toys'?

If this little girl had the option of a wheeled toy:

>> How likely do you think she would be to play with it?

>> What does the research suggest?

The idea that play allows us to practise skills needed in adulthood and therefore has survival value supports Hassett *et al.*'s view that sex differences in play may be biological (Figure 1.11). Just as playful kittens chase and pounce on things, modern humans may also have been practising the skills they needed to survive 300,000 years ago.

>> What play activities can you think of that might be linked to survival?

>> Can you think of any more modern forms of play that do not link as obviously to survival?

>> How might these types of play affect our health and wellbeing?

▲ Figure 1.11 Just like this little girl, Hassett *et al.* found that the female monkeys were drawn to the cuddly plush toys

> **LEARNING LINK**
>
> When you study the learning approach, which is about how environmental experiences affect our behaviour, you will learn about a famous study by Albert Bandura and colleagues where young children observed an adult playing aggressively with a toy (page 90). The researchers then covertly observed the children as they played with a similar style of toy. They found that the boys were more likely to imitate the physical aggression they had observed than the girls. This suggests that the observed aggression may have been seen as more socially acceptable by the male than the female children. The study by Hassett *et al.* also seems to indicate that boys are more likely to show 'sex-typed' behaviour than girls – that is, boys are more likely to show stereotypically masculine behaviours even when they do not know they are being observed, whereas girls are less consistent with regard to sex-typed feminine behaviour, both privately and in public.

STUDY TIP

Hassett *et al.* were investigating the nature versus nurture debate in terms of whether sex differences in play and toy preferences are influenced more by socialisation or hormones. Make sure you understand some of the research that inspired them including studies of congenital adrenal hyperplasia (CAH) and/or any of the previous research with monkeys (e.g. Alexander and Hines, 2002).

> **TEST YOURSELF**
>
> 1   Describe the psychology that is being investigated in the study by Hassett *et al.*   [4]
> 2   Outline what is meant by male and female stereotypical toy preferences with reference to examples from this study.   [3]
> 3   Explain one way in which hormones affect play. You must refer to research evidence in your answer.   [3]
> 4   When researching the role of hormones, psychologists sometimes use case studies. Explain one advantage of case studies as a way of investigating the effect of hormones on behaviour.   [2]
> 5   Ashley is investigating gender differences in children's play. He decides to conduct a naturalistic observation. Suggest one way Ashley could ensure that his observations are reliable.   [2]
> 6   For her dependent variable, Bethan asks a group of parents to rate the likelihood that they would give various toys as gifts to a fictional male child. The scale is numbered 0–5, where 0 is very unlikely and 5 is very likely.
>   a   State one weakness of the way Bethan has operationalised her dependent variable.   [1]
>   b   State an appropriate measure of central tendency for analysing the data.   [2]

METHODOLOGY

experiment

observation

behavioural checklist

1.2.2 Describing Hassett *et al.* (monkey toy preferences)

Think!

Hassett *et al.* used a **behavioural checklist** in their observation of the toy preferences of rhesus monkeys. Can you name three behaviours from the checklist?

Think!

In the culture where you live, are there different expectations for how female and male children should behave? Do you think people's views are becoming more or less fixed regarding what is seen as appropriate for people of different genders?

Imagine you are watching some of the video recordings made during Hassett *et al.*'s study. Can you think of any problems you might encounter when deciding how to code the monkey's behaviour using the behavioural checklist? How could you overcome these problems?

Look at Figure 1.12 which shows one of the monkeys from the study by Hassett *et al.* What sex do you think this monkey is? If your first thought was male, take another look at Hassett *et al.*'s findings; males and females were equally likely to interact with the wheeled toys, although the females did not play with them for as long as the males. This said, we have it on good authority from Professor Wallen that the monkey is actually male!

▲ Figure 1.12 One of the monkeys from the study by Hassett *et al.*, kindly contributed by Professor Kim Wallen, who supervised the study and took the original photographs

▶ AIMS

1 To test if sex differences in children's toy preferences result from biological factors – for example, from prenatal hormone exposure rather than through socialisation.
2 To investigate if male and female rhesus monkeys have similar toy preferences to human infants, despite no socialisation experience with human toys.

▶ RESEARCH METHODOLOGY

Hassett *et al.* is an experiment as the researchers were looking for a causal relationship between the monkeys' sex and their toy preferences. The monkeys were observed in their normal enclosure. This was a natural environment for them, as they had all been living together at the research centre for 25 years. However, the researchers were able to control this environment, by keeping the monkeys indoors while positioning the toys. The data was collected using observation, through analysis of video recordings of the monkeys in their outdoor enclosure.

Design and variables

The design was independent measures as two groups of monkeys were compared: males and females. Sex is a naturally occurring independent variable, determined by the appearance of the external sex organs. The dependent variable was whether the monkeys interacted more with the plush toys or the wheeled toys. Seven trials were completed, each with a different pair of toys. When the monkeys interacted with the toys, their social rank and age were recorded. Social rank had already been determined by observing grooming behaviour; the monkey doing the grooming is always subordinate (has less social status) than the monkey being groomed.

Sample

The sample was a troop of 135 monkeys at the Yerkes National Primate Research Center Field Station. The troop included both infant (juvenile) and adult monkeys. Fourteen of the monkeys had previously participated in research on prenatal hormones so they were not included in the current study. Thirty-nine babies (≤3 months) were not included as it was very hard to tell them apart, making it difficult to know which sex they were. Of the remaining monkeys (61 females and 21 males), 34 interacted with the toys on more than five occasions (23 females and 11 males) and were included in the analysis.

▶ PROCEDURE

Seven 25-minute observations were completed in the outdoor area of the monkey enclosure at the research centre. Before each observation, the observers positioned a pair of toys (one wheeled, one plush) in the outdoor area while the monkeys waited indoors. Toys were always placed ten metres apart and the positions were counterbalanced – wheeled toys were on the right and plush on the left in half of the trials and the other way around on the remaining trials. This ruled out the possibility that the monkeys preferred a certain area of the enclosure rather than genuinely preferring the properties of the toy that they found there.

The toys varied in size, shape and colour and were selected according to what you could 'do' with them rather than simply choosing traditionally 'male' or 'female' toys. There were six wheeled toys: wagon, truck, car, construction vehicle, shopping cart and dump truck, ranging from 16 to 46 cm, and seven *plush* toys: Winnie-the-Pooh™, Raggedy-Ann™, Scooby-Doo™ and four soft toy animals, including a koala, armadillo, teddy and turtle, ranging from 14 to 73 cm.

A video camera was focused on each toy so that all interactions could be recorded for later analysis. Two observers watched the videos and used a behavioural checklist to code (or categorise) every interaction between the monkeys and the toys. Using an app called Handobs, the observers recorded their data using palm pilots (digital devices similar to modern mobile phones). They recorded the start and finish times of each interaction and calculated the duration (in seconds).

The checklist included: extended touching, holding, sitting on, dragging, carrying and manipulating the toys, as well as briefly touching, sniffing, mouthing, destroying, jumping away from and throwing them (see Table 1.7 on page 28 for a description of each behaviour). Ambiguous (unclear) behaviours were discussed until the observers agreed on how to code the interaction. For each interaction, the observers also recorded the monkey's age, rank and sex.

▶ RESULTS

The observers calculated average frequencies and durations for each behaviour by adding up the totals and dividing by the number of trials each monkey participated in. Monkeys with fewer than five behaviours were discounted (3 males and 14 females). Next, the researchers calculated the total number and total duration of interactions with each toy type (plush versus wheeled) by adding up the averages for each individual behaviour.

Overall, most of the monkeys did not interact with the toys at all. Those that did often only interacted for a few

seconds, while a small number of monkeys interacted much more and for much longer periods of time.

Male monkeys preferred wheeled toys

Table 1.5 shows the male monkeys' significant preference for the wheeled toys (mean = 9.77), compared with plush toys (mean = 2.06). They also played less with plush toys compared with females. Further analysis showed that 73 per cent of the males preferred wheeled toys, 9 per cent preferred plush toys and 18 per cent showed no significant preference. These preferences did not appear to be affected by age or rank.

▼ Table 1.5 Total frequency and duration of interactions with plush and wheeled toys for male and female monkeys

		Frequency		Duration (minutes)	
		Mean	Standard deviation	Mean	Standard deviation
Plush	Male	2.06	9.21	0.53	1.41
	Female	7.97	10.48	1.49	3.81
Wheeled	Male	9.77	8.86	4.76	7.59
	Female	6.96	4.92	1.27	2.2

Female monkeys show no consistent preference

Although the females showed some preference for the plush toys (mean = 7.97) compared with the wheeled toys (mean = 6.96), the difference was not significant. There was also no significant difference between the males and females in terms of frequency of wheeled toy play.

Only 30 per cent of females preferred the plush toys, 39 per cent preferred the wheeled toys and 30 per cent showed no significant preference for either toy. Females with no preference ranked significantly lower in the social hierarchy than females who preferred plush toys but there was no significant difference in rank between females who preferred wheeled versus plush toys.

Duration of interactions

When the females played with wheeled toys, they did not play with them for as long as the males (1.27 minutes compared with 4.76 minutes) and they also played longer with the plush toys than the males did (1.49 minutes compared with 0.53 minutes). Males played significantly longer with wheeled than plush toys but the standard deviation for the duration of wheeled toy play was relatively large compared with the females (7.59 compared with 2.2). This suggests that some of the males played considerably longer with the wheeled toys than others. The females showed even greater individual differences with regard to time spent engaged in plush toy play – some individuals played longer with these toys; others interacted with them more briefly. Overall, there was no significant difference in time spent interacting with either plush (1.49 minutes) or wheeled toys (1.27 minutes) for the female monkeys.

Social rank and toy preference

When the data from both sexes was combined, there was a significant positive correlation between social rank (how dominant the monkeys were within the group) and frequency of interaction for both types of toy. Higher-ranking monkeys interacted more with the toys. Interestingly, when the data from females was examined more closely, the researchers found that the higher the rank, the more time females spent interacting with plush toys. This was not true for wheeled toys.

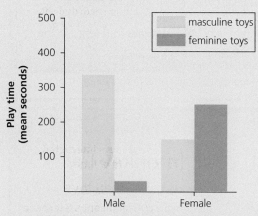

Sex difference in play with stereotypical masculine and feminine toys in a choice paradigm

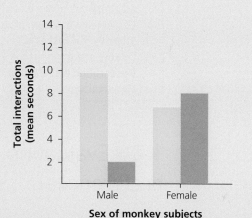

Sex difference in total frequency of interactions with plush and wheeled toys by rhesus monkeys

▲ Figure 1.13 Hassett *et al.* presented their findings using bar charts to compare their data from the rhesus monkeys (right) with data collected in a similar study with human infants (left) (Berenbaum and Hines, 1992). The human infants were presented with traditionally masculine toys (e.g. helicopter and blocks) and feminine toys (e.g. dolls and kitchen supplies)

▶ CONCLUSIONS

Based on their observations and comparisons with human infants (see Figure 1.14), Hassett *et al.* concluded that sex-typed toy preferences in humans may result from biological sex differences, as their observations suggest that rhesus monkeys show similar preferences to human infants, even without clear gender differences in socialisation. They concluded that human toy preferences, as with the monkeys, 'reflect hormonally influenced behavioural and cognitive biases' which interact with learning experiences within the social environment.

▶ LEARNING LINK

In the cognitive approach, you will learn about the study by Baron-Cohen *et al.* (eyes test). This study examines the ability to identify emotional states in others. Baron-Cohen links this skill to a concept called theory of mind, which is our ability to understand the mental states of others. This typically develops at around three years of age and research suggests that pretend play is an important forerunner of theory of mind (Leslie, 1987). This mean that children's preferred toys and differing play experiences may be important in shaping their differing skills and abilities, but do they prefer different toys due to innate sex differences or do their play experiences cause differing skills later in life?

STUDY TIP

When thinking about the findings of core studies, think about how they link with the studies' aims and what they tell us about the area of psychology being investigated. Were the findings as expected? Think about how the researchers might have felt when they got their results – do you think they were surprised, excited, confused, satisfied, frustrated? We tend to remember things that we have an emotional reaction to, so imagining how the researcher felt might just help you to remember the information better! (See page 16 for Professor Wallen's reaction to their results.)

▶ TEST YOURSELF

1 Outline the procedure from the point at which the researchers started watching the video recordings. [2]
2 Describe one result relating to the male monkeys and one relating to the female monkeys. [4]
3 Explain how one conclusion from the Hassett *et al.* study supports one of the assumptions of the biological approach. [2]
4 Explain one strength of the use of a behavioural checklist, with reference to the study by Hassett *et al.* [2]
5 Outline one way that the study by Hassett *et al.* was valid. [2]
6 Observation was used to measure the dependent variables in this experiment. Outline three features of this observation. [3]

1.2.3 Evaluating Hassett *et al.* (monkey toy preferences)

Think!

Can you think of any practical problems or issues that might have arisen with the video recordings of the monkeys' behaviour?

Think!

Once the toys had been put into position, the monkeys were allowed into the outdoor enclosure all at the same time. What problems might this have led to in terms of standardisation from one trial to the next?

Think!

How might the procedure of this study have been improved to avoid observer bias? Remember, observer bias is about how the researcher interprets what they are seeing, not the way that a participant's behaviour is affected because they are aware that they are being watched.

>> How would you know if a male monkey chooses the truck in Figure 1.14 because it has wheels or because of the colours?
>> Would green-loving females choose to play with the teddy or the truck? Think, how is the teddy in this picture similar and/or different to the one used in Hassett *et al.*?
>> How would you design a **follow-up** study to find out more about monkeys' toy preferences, in terms of colour, material and whether the toys have faces or not?

Table 1.6 shows how many of the monkeys interacted with the toys as a percentage of the group. So, for example, out of 21 males, 11 were included in the analysis as they interacted with the toys. Which groups were most likely to interact with the toys?

▲ Figure 1.14 Back in 1902, primate psychologist AJ Kinnaman suggested that the rhesus monkeys' favourite colours may be green and white

1

1.2 Hassett et al. (monkey toy preferences)

▼ Table 1.6 Male and females by social rank and age: totals and participation

	Non-natal	Ranks 1–3	Ranks 4–8	Ranks 9–13	Ranks 14–16	TOTAL
Males in group	2	1	4	6	8	21
Males participating	1 (50%)	0	3 (75%)	3 (50%)	4 (50%)	11 (52%)
Females in group	0	8	15	17	21	61
Females participating		6 (75%)	6 (40%)	4 (24%)	7 (33%)	23 (38%)
	juvenile (1–4)	subadult (5–7)	adult (8–12)	'elderly' (13+)	TOTAL	
Males in group	12	7	0	2	21	
Males participating	8 (67%)	2 (29%)		1 (50%)	11 (52%)	
Females in group	23	12	14	12	61	
Females participating	10 (43%)	5 (42%)	3 (21%)	4 (42%)	23 (38%)	

Ethical issues

A strength of Hassett *et al.* is that ethical guidelines for working with primates were upheld. The researchers followed the National Institutes of Health's *Guide for the Care and Use of Laboratory Animals*. Also, research at the Yerkes National Primate Research Center is regulated by the Emory University Institutional Animal Care and Use Committee. The monkeys were housed within their usual social groups in a 25-metre square outdoor enclosure, with a temperature-controlled indoor area. They had constant access to water, ate monkey chow twice a day and were fed fresh fruit and vegetables every day. The procedure does not present any particular ethical issues as these monkeys lived in captivity and would have been familiar with the keepers entering their enclosure, meaning they were not subjected to any more stress than usual.

Methodological issues

Reliability

Well-operationalised behavioural checklist

A strength was the use of a carefully operationalised behavioural checklist (see Table 1.7). For example, as well as the behaviour itself (e.g. 'sit on'), the checklist gives a description (e.g. 'seated on the toy or a part of the toy'). This detail means that the two independent observers should have coded behaviours in the same way, as the list is clear about whether behaviours such as sitting half on and half off should be included or not. This improves the overall reliability of toy preference observations made in this study.

An unexpected event!

A weakness was that the standardised procedure was abandoned on one of the trials. This occurred due to one of the monkeys ripping apart one of the plush toys. The trial was terminated seven minutes early as the researchers were unable to observe the monkeys' preference for one toy type over another, as the plush toy now lay in multiple pieces around the enclosure! As the data collection period was reduced to only 18 minutes for this trial, the reliability of the observations of the monkeys' toy preferences was also compromised.

Validity

The seven observational trials

One strength was that Hassett *et al.* collected data on seven separate 25-minute trials. Different pairs of plush and wheeled toys were used on each trial – for example, the wagon and Winnie the Pooh™, the truck and Raggedy-Ann™. This increased the validity of the conclusion that males were drawn to wheeled toys in general as opposed to one specific wheeled toy that might have been a colour or size that the monkeys particularly liked (see Figure 1.14).

The use of video cameras

Another strength was the use of video cameras rather than having human observers present in the monkey enclosure. The monkeys were used to the cameras, meaning their behaviour should not have been affected by them, whereas the presence of a human observer might have affected the spontaneity of their interactions/play. The monkeys may have played less if they were stressed by the humans coming into the enclosure. Alternatively, they may have played more in the hope of receiving a **reward**, suggesting that the cameras increased the validity of the data recorded.

Objectivity and subjectivity

A further strength was the use of quantitative data. For example, the researchers recorded the duration of individual behaviours (e.g. extended touch) in seconds. These measurements were taken using the palm pilots (see page 22) to record the start and finish points of each interaction. This type of data is more objective as the researchers simply have to calculate the average time spent interacting with each type of toy for the male monkeys compared with the female monkeys, avoiding any subjective interpretation of the data.

Potential observer bias

A weakness was that the researchers who analysed the videotapes were both very familiar and well acquainted with the monkeys, meaning that their knowledge of the monkey's gender could have biased their observations. For example, if they knew a monkey was male, they might have unintentionally coded his behaviour differently from how they would have coded it if they believed the monkey was female. Observer bias may have increased subjectivity, meaning that different observers who did not know the monkeys may have reached different conclusions.

Generalisations and ecological validity

Generalising beyond the sample

The lack of adult males in the sample was a weakness. The 11 male monkeys were all either juvenile, subadult or elderly. As toy play/interaction may be affected by social rank and age, generalisations should be made with caution, especially as the only high-ranking male did not interact with any of the toys. Therefore, the findings can only be generalised to lower-ranking, non-adult males.

Generalising to everyday life

A weakness of this research is that it was conducted with monkeys living in captivity. Captive monkeys may show greater interest in new objects in their territory as the lack of predators and a ready supply of food mean they may be less fearful and have more time to play. This reduces the ecological validity of the findings, meaning it is unclear whether wild monkeys would have behaved in the same way.

ISSUES AND DEBATES

1

1.2 Hassett et al. (monkey toy preferences)

Nature versus nurture

Unlike previous research, Hassett *et al.* believed that toy preference in humans may be due to nature and caused by biological not learned differences. The study seems to support this hypothesis as male monkeys showed a preference for wheeled toys over plush toys, whereas females showed no clear preference. When the females did play with a wheeled toy, the duration was shorter than when the male monkeys played with the toy.

A finding that supports the role of nurture in toy preferences is that interactions were also affected by social rank; in female monkeys, social rank was positively correlated with time spent interacting with both plush and wheeled toys. However, female dominance is also affected by testosterone levels, which may explain why the high-ranking females were equally likely to play with the trucks as the teddies, supporting the role of nature.

Applications to everyday life

Choosing toys for children

This study suggests that children may be drawn to certain toys due to innate (inborn) differences in their brains, which makes some play activities more appealing than others. If children are like monkeys, they may show preferences for certain toys over others and their skills and future talents may be shaped by these choices. Hassett *et al.*'s findings suggest that boys will be drawn to toys with moving parts. Therefore, if a parent wishes to develop skills such as empathy through imaginative play, they could choose vehicles with expressive faces. If girls are drawn more to plush toys with faces, visuospatial skills could be improved using toys with moving parts but presented as part of a more complex social situation – for example, toy ambulance or school bus with sets of dolls for acting out a scene.

Reflections

Controversially, Hassett *et al.*'s findings appear to support the gendered toy market – that is, marketing certain toys as being 'for boys' or 'for girls' based on sex differences in brain development. But, if toy choices are shaped by our hormones, as Hassett *et al.* suggest, then it is also important to recognise that there are individual differences in hormone levels; some people have higher or lower than average testosterone and/or oestrogen levels than people of the same sex, and hormone levels change over time dependent on a variety of biological and social factors. This means children may prefer to play with different types of toys at different points in time and these may or may not correspond with the sex on their birth certificate.

Hassett *et al.* demonstrated that male monkeys have a preference for wheeled toys, suggesting preferences in male children may result from hormonal differences between boys and girls.

» Does this mean that social sensitivity and verbal skills could be fostered in boys by encouraging play with wheeled characters with faces?

In this study, two observers worked together to record the data. As they watched the videos, they recorded the data onto their palm pilots, using the behavioural checklist in Table 1.7. The two observers had to agree on how each behaviour should be coded (e.g. destroy or throw). When collecting observational data in this way, it is important that each individual behaviour is carefully defined in order to improve reliability. For example, if another observer watched the videos they should end up with the same results.

» Can you think of any problems (e.g. relating to validity and/or reliability)

that might arise when recording observational data like this?

» Read the descriptions in Table 1.7 carefully. Are there any behaviours that might be hard to agree on?

» Can you think of any other behaviours that have not been included? Why do you think this might be?

▲ Figure 1.15 Could playing with vehicles with expressive faces foster social sensitivity?

▼ Table 1.7 Behavioural checklist from Hassett *et al.*

Behaviour	Description
Extended touch	Placing a hand or foot on toy
Hold	Stationary support w/one or more limbs
Sit on	Seated on the toy or a part of the toy
Carry in hand	Moving w/toy in hand and off the ground
Carry in arm	Moving w/toy in arm and off the ground
Carry in mouth	Moving w/toy in mouth and off the ground
Drag	Moving the toy along the ground behind the animal
Manipulate part	Moving, twisting or turning a part
Turn entire toy	Shifting 3D orientation of toy
Touch	Brief contact using hands or fingers
Sniff	Coming very close to the toy with the nose
Mouth	Brief oral contact – no biting or pulling
Destroy	Using mouth or hands to bite or tear toy
Jump away	Approach, then back away from toy with a jumping motion
Throw	Project into air with hands

▶ LEARNING LINK

When you get to the learning approach, you will learn about a study by Fagen *et al.* (elephant learning), in which the participants are elephants. The elephants are rewarded for washing their trunks, showing how interactions between humans and animals can alter the animals' behaviour. With this in mind, think about whether the behaviour of the rhesus monkeys in Hassett *et al.*'s study might have been affected by the fact that they live in captivity in a research centre. How do you think interactions with humans might affect the animals physically, psychologically and behaviourally?

STUDY TIP

Remember, when you are writing about an animal study such as Hassett *et al.* (or Fagen *et al.*'s study of elephants in the learning approach), it is critical that you refer to the ethical guidelines relating to the use of animals in psychological research. This may sound obvious but many students do not apply these guidelines carefully and resort to applying human ethical guidelines. Clearly, animals are unable to give or withdraw their consent and that is why we have such detailed guidelines to ensure animal welfare is a priority for all researchers.

As you revise Hassett *et al.*, you might find it helpful to draw up a table listing each of the headings from the animal ethics section in Chapter 5 (see page 209: headings include replacement, species, numbers, procedures, pain and distress, housing, reward, deprivation and aversive stimuli) and then consider how each one relates to this study. Later in your course, you will be able to add Fagen *et al.*'s study to your table.

1

1.3 Hölzel et al. (mindfulness and brain scans)

▶ **TEST YOURSELF**

1   Explain one methodological weakness of this study.   [2]
2   Suggest one real-world application of this study.   [2]
3   Evaluate the study by Hassett *et al.* in terms of two strengths and two weaknesses.
    At least one of your evaluation points must be about the use of observation.   [10]
4   Maggie decided to observe toy preferences in male and female children in a
    kindergarten.
     a   Identify two ethical issues that Maggie would need to consider when working
         with children.   [2]
     b   Explain one practical advantage of working with animals compared with
         working with children.   [2]
5   When conducting observational studies, researchers sometimes do a pilot study.
    Explain how a pilot study could improve the validity of an observational study.   [3]
6   The researchers used video cameras to record the 25-minute observations.
    Suggest one advantage and one disadvantage of the use of cameras to record
    the monkeys' behaviour.   [4]

1.3 Hölzel *et al.* (mindfulness and brain scans)

1.3.1 Background

KEY TERMS

mindfulness
MRI scan
localisation of function
brain structure

Think!

What is Mindfulness-Based Stress Reduction?

Think!

To get an accurate magnetic resonance imaging **MRI scan**, people have to lie motionless in
a noisy tunnel of about 60 cm in diameter. Often there is a carefully positioned bar (called a
bite-bar) that the person rests their teeth on to keep their head still during the scan. How do
you think you would feel in the scanner?

Think!

What are your thoughts on voxel-based morphometry (VBM)? Is this technique objective
or could the data analysis be open to bias (subjective)?

Introducing Britta Hölzel

Britta Hölzel is a psychologist, neuroscientist and Mindfulness-Based Stress Reduction
(MBSR) and yoga teacher. She discovered ancient yoga and meditation traditions
in India and meditation temples in Thailand while backpacking through Asia, after
finishing high school. Excited by the transformational power that she found in these
practices, she decided to use magnetic resonance imaging (MRI) to investigate the
structural and functional brain changes that occur following regular practice. Britta is
dedicated to developing and sharing her understanding of the potential of the human
mind for growth and virtue and runs workshops, courses and lectures on **mindfulness**,
meditation and yoga. Her articles are published in high-ranking scientific journals
and are frequently reported by international media, including the *New York Times* and
Huffington Post.

Britta shared this quote from Californian spiritual teacher Adyashanti as her inspiration:

The truth is that you already are what you are seeking.

▲ Figure 1.16 Dr Britta
Hölzel

The MRI scan shown in Figure 1.17 shows grey and white matter in a brain model created using data from a group of people who meditate regularly (Luders *et al.*, 2009). These images highlight the hippocampus, a structure where there was significantly more grey matter in meditators than non-meditators. One specific region of the hippocampus that showed increased grey matter, the subiculum, is linked to stress regulation. Eileen Luders, Associate Professor of Psychology at the University of Auckland, New Zealand, suggests increased grey matter in this region may be linked to decreased release of stress hormones. This may explain why mindfulness seems to reduce stress and improve feelings of wellbeing.

» Why is it not possible to say that meditating causes increased grey and white matter in meditators based on this study? Tip: Think about the research method and the design.

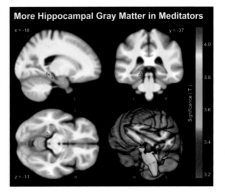

▲ Figure 1.17 MRI scan of meditators

The psychology being investigated

Mindfulness

This study focuses on the effects of mindfulness, a stress-reduction technique used to improve wellbeing. This technique develops awareness of the present moment and encourages compassionate and non-judgemental attitudes. Commonly associated with Eastern religions and philosophies, mindfulness is now practised globally by millions of people seeking calmness in their fast-paced, and sometimes stressful, lives. It has also been incorporated into treatment programmes for people with conditions including anxiety, chronic pain and substance abuse due to the increasing amount of evidence supporting its positive impact on wellbeing.

Localisation of function

The study also explores **localisation of function** – the idea that specific **brain structures** are responsible for specific behaviours/cognitive processes. For example, an area called the hippocampus is associated with memory and emotion regulation, while the insula may be at least partly responsible for awareness. One way of finding out the function of different brain structures is to monitor how they change over time following regular practice of a certain skill.

To learn about the link between mindfulness and localisation of function, Britta Hölzel and her colleagues used MRI scans to create detailed models of the human brain. These models can then be used to measure microscopic changes that occur in specific brain structures following mindfulness practice. These changes are called structural plasticity and can be quantified using voxel-based morphometry (VBM) (see page 31), a process that measures the concentration of grey matter (a type of brain tissue) in key brain structures, before and after mindfulness training. Researchers have some understanding of the function of many brain structures, and once they know which brain structures are affected by mindfulness, they can start to work out how it improves wellbeing.

Background

Mindfulness-Based Stress Reduction

Hölzel *et al.* focused on the effects of Mindfulness-Based Stress Reduction (MBSR), a technique developed in the USA by Professor Jon Kabat-Zinn, which combines Buddhist meditation with a scientific, evidence-based approach. His eight-week programme includes 2.5-hour weekly group meetings, plus one 6.5-hour training day.

Group meetings include training in three techniques, which members are encouraged to build into their everyday lives (Kabat-Zinn, 1990).

» **Body scanning:** slowly becoming aware of sensations in each area of the body, in turn, gradually developing awareness of the whole body/mind.

» **Mindful yoga:** gentle stretching, co-ordinated, slow movements and breathing with a focus on the moment-to-moment experience. Full awareness of one's presence in the here-and-now and the development of self-compassion with an awareness and acceptance of the body's potential and limitations.

» **Sitting meditation:** developing awareness of the sensation of breathing and of sensory information (e.g. sight, smell, touch, taste) and emotions, gradually developing awareness of all aspects of consciousness, including our own presence in the world.

Measuring changes in mindfulness

The Five Facets of Mindfulness Questionnaire was developed by Ruth Baer and her colleagues (Baer *et al.*, 2006) and is a way of measuring changes in five key areas of mindfulness – the ability to *observe* (1) and *describe* (2) passing thoughts and feelings in a *non-judgemental* (3) and *non-reactive* (4) way and *awareness of actions* (5).

Each facet (aspect) is positively correlated with wellbeing. Although biopsychologists are still trying to understand exactly how programmes like MBSR increase wellbeing, neuroimaging research (using brain scans) is beginning to reveal which brain structures may be involved.

Previous research on localisation of function

Studies have shown that experienced meditators have significantly more grey matter in some key brain structures compared with non-meditators. Findings are unclear, but the hippocampus and insula have each been identified in at least two studies. In one study, participants meditated while in an fMRI scanner (see page 33) and the hippocampus was especially active (Lazar *et al.*, 2000). Longitudinal studies (and experiments with longitudinal designs) have also shown that grey matter increases in key brain structures when people learn new knowledge or skills. This suggests that changes in wellbeing may be linked to increases in grey matter.

Measuring changes in grey matter concentration: voxel-based morphometry

The term voxel, from volume and pixel, is a tiny cubic measurement used to quantify the volume of three-dimensional structures. This statistical process allows researchers to compare the relative size of various brain structures between people, such as regular meditators and non-meditators (see Figure 1.17) and to monitor changes in specific brain structures over time. The process involves classifying (segmenting) the types of tissue displayed in the image, e.g. into grey matter (GM) or white matter (WM), mapping the images onto a template to control for individual differences between brains (normalising), and statistical technique called smoothing, which helps improve the overall validity of the data.

Hölzel *et al.* in brief

Hölzel *et al.* built on previous research by conducting an experiment with a longitudinal design, where they tracked changes in grey matter throughout the brain before and after MBSR training. They also measured the amount of time spent on mindfulness exercises and changes in the five facets of mindfulness to see whether there was a correlation. The team aimed to objectively measure neurological changes associated with changes in mindfulness.

Plan your own... questionnaire

Hölzel *et al.* designed an experiment with a longitudinal design to test their ideas about mindfulness and localisation of function. Why not try designing a questionnaire to investigate mindfulness meditation?

Imagine...

Abdul would like to conduct a questionnaire on people's attitudes towards the practice of mindfulness meditation.

» What advice would you give Abdul about how to conduct this questionnaire?

Planning a questionnaire

A questionnaire is a non-experimental method. When planning a questionnaire, it is important that you consider what questions will be asked to collect data on the topic being investigated, as well as how this data will be analysed. Examples of questions and the format in which the questionnaire will be delivered (i.e. on paper or online) are also essential. See page 180 for more information on questionnaires.

▼ Table 1.8 Features of a questionnaire

Main features of a questionnaire	Consider...
Question format (open and closed questions)	Questionnaires can use both open and closed questions to collect data. Would you suggest open or closed questions to collect the data required on attitudes towards mindfulness meditation? Consider how Abdul will eventually analyse this data.
Examples of questions	Can you give examples of the open and/or closed questions that Abdul might ask about attitudes towards mindfulness meditation?
Question scoring and interpretation	The data from questionnaires may be qualitative or quantitative. How would Abdul analyse this data in order to draw conclusions from the participants about their attitudes towards mindfulness meditation?
Technique (paper/pencil, online, postal)	Questionnaires can be distributed in different formats, each with their own strengths and weaknesses. How will Abdul deliver his questionnaires to participants?

Evaluating your plan

Abdul shares your ideas with his peers. Some of them think it is a great idea; others are not so sure. Think about the practical strengths and weaknesses of your suggestions.

▼ Table 1.9 Evaluating your plan

	Describe	Explain
Strengths	Which type of data will Abdul collect in his questionnaire? How would this make the data more valid and/or reliable?	How will the collection of this data benefit the study's findings on attitudes towards mindfulness meditation?
Weaknesses	What are the main weaknesses of the type of data you have chosen to collect?	Why might Abdul not gain valid and/or reliable data on participants' attitudes towards mindfulness meditation?
Improvements	Consider the weakness you gave. How might you improve Abdul's procedure to overcome this issue?	How would this improvement increase the validity and/or reliability of the data Abdul collects about attitudes towards mindfulness meditation?

What is yoga? Yoga, meaning 'union', originated in India. The word is thought to have come from the Sanskrit word for 'yoke', a harness used to keep animals like horses or cows together while working. In Hindu philosophy, yoga is a way of harnessing the human mind, allowing us to become more purposeful by linking (or yoking) the body and mind. Yoga includes both physical and mental aspects. The physical aspects have become a popular form of exercise in the West and it includes gentle stretches, building towards more challenging poses. The mental aspects include meditation, which may include breathing techniques, visualisation or chanting, as a way of achieving a state of mental calm.

» Why do you think the physical aspects of yoga have become more popular in the West than the mental aspects?

» Do you think brain scans of people who practise yoga would differ depending on whether they are from Eastern or Western cultures? Why do you think this?

▲ Figure 1.18 Yoga originated in India

1

1.3 Hölzel et al. (mindfulness and brain scans)

LEARNING LINK

Depending on which A Level options you study, you may come across studies that use fMRI. fMRIs produce *functional* scans of the brain rather than *structural* scans. They are used to identify brain structures that are particularly active while a person completes a certain task. Active brain structures require more oxygen, meaning blood flow is higher in these areas. The fMRI identifies active areas by monitoring blood flow. When reading about brain imaging studies, it is important to know whether they used MRI or fMRI scanning. As you read about Hölzel *et al.*, you will discover many links with research methodology concepts covered in Chapter 5 – turn to this chapter if you need more information on any of the research methodology terminology.

STUDY TIP

Think about how each of the 12 core studies link to the approach that they are in, e.g. Hölzel is part of the biological approach. Why not revisit the introduction to the approach (see page 2) and think about how the main assumptions match with the psychology being investigated in the study. Hölzel *et al.*, for example, were studying localisation of function – that is, which brain structures may be responsible for the changes in wellbeing that result from mindfulness. This matches up well with the assumptions of the biological approach – behaviour, cognitions and emotions can be explained in terms of the working of the brain. In this case, wellbeing may result from changes in brain structures resulting from experience. You could create a table to show how each study matches with the assumptions of the approach.

TEST YOURSELF

1 Explain what is meant by 'localisation of function' with reference to the study by Hölzel *et al.* [2]

2 Outline one psychological concept other than localisation of function that was investigated in the study by Hölzel *et al.* [2]

3 a Hölzel *et al.* used MRI scans. What does an MRI scan measure? [1]

   b Identify one reason why Hölzel *et al.* might have chosen this technique to measure brain activity. [1]

4 Hölzel *et al.* used an experiment with a longitudinal design to study localisation of function. Explain one reason why a longitudinal design was necessary in this study. [2]

5 Abigail has noticed that Buddhist monks spend a great deal of time meditating each day. She believes that the longer a person has been a monk the higher their hippocampal grey matter concentration. State the type of hypothesis Abigail might write if she wanted to investigate this relationship further and give one reason for your choice. [2]

6 A group of European travellers has signed up to spend a month volunteering at a Hindu temple in India. They will be learning to meditate as part of their experience. Abigail's friend Melis thinks this could be a good opportunity to conduct a field experiment.

Describe how Melis could conduct her field experiment on meditation and localisation of function. [10]

(See page 171 for tips on designing a field experiment, including the required features.)

(See page 171 for tips on designing a field experiment, including the required features.)

METHODOLOGY

experiment

correlation

longitudinal design

MRI scan

self-report

1.3.2 Describing Hölzel *et al.* (mindfulness and brain scans)

Think!

Was it a strength or a limitation that all the experimental participants were attending MBSR sessions at the University of Massachusetts Medical School? Why do you think this?

Think!

When was the last time you took a deep breath in and slowly let it out? Do it now! When was the last time you showed yourself some compassion? Next time you feel a little stressed, say 'May I be kind to myself in this difficult moment.' Mini-meditations can make a major difference!

Think!

Imagine you are a researcher and you want to investigate the effect of mindfulness using a case study instead of an experiment?
>> What data would you collect?
>> How would you collect this data?
>> What methodological issues might arise?
>> In what ways would your study be similar to and in what ways would it be different from Hölzel *et al.*?

Can you name the three ways in which the researchers collected quantitative data in this study? Try ranking them from the least to the most objective.

▲ Figure 1.19 Collecting data from brain scans

▶ AIMS

1 To identify if regular participation in Mindfulness-Based Stress Reduction (MBSR) leads to measurable neurological changes, which might be associated with trait changes related to mindfulness practice.
2 To identify brain structures which changed as a result of an eight-week MBSR programme.

▶ RESEARCH METHODOLOGY

Hölzel *et al.* is an experiment; the researchers were looking for a causal relationship between MBSR and grey matter concentration in various brain structures. Some measurements were taken in a controlled setting (i.e. the **MRI scans**), but other parts of the study occurred in naturalistic environments. For example, participants incorporated MBSR exercises while walking and doing housework.

Although the main method is an experiment, one part of the study was a correlation, as the researchers also wanted to know whether there was a non-causal relationship between time spent on mindfulness exercises and increases in grey matter concentration.

Design and variables

There were two independent variables:
- whether the participants received MBSR or not
- whether the data was collected at the beginning or the end of the eight-week study period.

Hölzel *et al.* measured three main dependent variables:
- grey matter concentration in specific brain structures (including the hippocampi and insulae) and throughout the brain – this was calculated using voxel-based morphometry (see page 31)
- the five facets of mindfulness measured using the Five Facets of Mindfulness Questionnaire (FFMQ) (see page 40) – this **self-report** (questionnaire) includes 39 statements which participants rate from 1 ('never or very rarely true') to 5 ('very often or always true')
- time spent on mindfulness exercises between the weekly sessions, which was recorded in a daily diary.

This was a **longitudinal design** as data was collected over an eight-week period. All participants provided two sets of data: once at the beginning and once at the end of the eight-week period.

The study also uses an independent measures design as there were two separate groups of participants: those in the experimental group, who attended weekly MBSR sessions, and those in the control group, who also had problems with stress but did not receive MBSR. This is called a waitlist control group (see 'Ethical issues' section on page 38).

Sample

An opportunity sample of 33 right-handed, healthy adults, aged 25–55 years old were recruited from four MBSR courses at the Center for Mindfulness, New England, USA. They had either self-referred or been recommended by their physician due to stress. Six males and ten females (mean age = 38, standard deviation = 4 years) were assigned to the MBSR group and eleven males and six females (mean age = 39, standard deviation = 9.2 years) to the waitlist control group. Self-reported medical information suggested they were all physically and psychologically healthy and not taking any regular medication. All agreed that they would aim to attend the full eight-week programme and complete daily 'homework'. The usual course fee was reduced for all participants to thank them for their participation. Participants all had limited meditation experience – for example, they had taken no classes in the last six months, no more than four classes in the past five years and no more than ten classes in their lifetime.

▶ PROCEDURE

Before the MBSR sessions

MRI scans of the brain were conducted two weeks before the experimental group's first MBSR session. Three-dimensional digital models were created by taking pictures of 128 sagittal slices (i.e. from the top to the bottom) of the brain and combining them using computer software. Next, the researchers analysed the models using voxel-based morphometry (VBM) to measure the concentration of grey matter in the regions of interest (bilateral hippocampi and insulae) and the brain as a whole. All participants also complete the FFMQ.

During the eight-week programme

Next, the experimental group took part in eight weekly MBSR sessions. See page 31 for information on what a typical session would include. Sessions took place at the Center for Mindfulness at the University of Massachusetts Medical School. The participants in the experimental group were given a 45-minute audio recording of guided mindfulness exercises (e.g. body scan, yoga and meditation) to help them to complete the exercises at home (e.g. while washing up, eating or taking a shower).

After the eight MBSR sessions

Further MRI scans of the brain were taken two weeks after the last MBSR session for all participants, including the control group, and everyone took the FFMQ again.

Each participant's two scans were compared using VBM computer software to measure any differences in grey matter concentration and differences in the five facets of mindfulness scores were calculated.

▶ RESULTS

Amount of mindfulness practice

The MBSR group engaged in an average of 22.6 hours of MBSR exercises. The standard deviation was relatively large at 6.3 hours, showing that some participants practised considerably more than others. Overall, participants spent around 27 minutes per day participating in mindfulness exercises. Most time was spent body scanning; participants spent more than twice as much time on this activity than yoga or meditation (see Table 1.10). There were no significant correlations between any of the individual exercises (e.g. body scanning and yoga, or yoga and meditation). This suggests that different people preferred different exercises but doing a lot of one particular exercise did not mean that you also did a lot of either of the other two.

▼ Table 1.10 Time spent engaged in MBSR activities over the course of eight weeks

	Mean	Standard deviation
Body scan	699 mins	217 mins
Yoga	327 mins	194 mins
Sitting meditation	332 mins	211 mins
Total	22.6 hours	6.3 hours

Improvements in mindfulness

The FFMQ showed that the experimental group demonstrated significant improvements in 'acting with awareness', 'observing' and 'non-judging' after MBSR training compared with the control group, but they did not show improvements in 'describing' or 'non-reactivity'.

Grey matter changes

The MBSR group experienced a significant increase in grey matter concentration in their left hippocampus, posterior cingulate cortex, temporoparietal junction and cerebellum compared with the control group. Changes in the cerebellum were observed in two locations; one of these included the brainstem. As the two groups showed no significant difference in grey matter concentration in these structures before MBSR training, it appears that the differences at eight weeks were due to the MBSR and not pre-existing individual differences.

Unlike previous research, no significant difference was found in grey matter concentration in the insulae before and after MBSR. Also, changes in grey matter concentration were not correlated with the amount of time spent engaged in mindfulness exercises or changes on the FFMQ. This suggests that time spent on mindfulness is less important than the regularity of practice.

No brain structures showed a decrease in grey matter concentration following the MBSR programme, but the control group did show a significant decrease in grey matter concentration in the posterior cingulate cortex.

▶ CONCLUSIONS

Hölzel et al. concluded that structural changes (i.e. increased grey matter concentration) in key brain regions, including the left hippocampus, posterior cingulate cortex, temporal-parietal junction and cerebellum, can occur as a result of participation in regular mindfulness practice, even after just eight weeks. They note that the brain regions identified are involved in processes such as learning, memory, emotion regulation and perspective-taking, suggesting that these areas are central to the improvements in wellbeing observed in people who make mindfulness part of their daily lives. The study did not confirm previous findings relating to the insula and the researchers conclude that changes in this region may require more than eight weeks of practice.

Which do you think would be more effective in reducing stress and/or increasing grey matter concentration: meditating alone or alongside others at a group session? Why do you think this?

▶ Figure 1.20 Hölzel *et al.* found that structural brain changes can occur as a result of regular mindfulness practice

1

1.3 Hölzel et al. (mindfulness and brain scans)

▶ LEARNING LINK

In the study by Dement and Kleitman (sleep and dreams), you learned about another way of studying the brain called an electroencephalogram (EEG). When you get to this topic, think about how an MRI scan is similar to and how it is different from an EEG. Recently, researchers have found that mindfulness increases a hormone called oxytocin as well as empathy (Bellosta-Batalla *et al.*, 2020). The social approach includes a study by Perry *et al.* (personal space), where you will learn more about the link between oxytocin, empathy and personal space (p. 139).

STUDY TIP

As you learn about the three key studies in the biological approach, think about how they relate to the issue and debates. For example, Holzel *et al.* relates to the nature versus nurture debate and individual and situational explanations. They found that participating in classes such as yoga and mindfulness can alter brain structure (e.g. increasing hippocampal grey matter) and help us to feel less stressed. This is an example of the effect of nurture overriding nature. The study also suggests that individual differences in stress, for example, may be related to structural differences in areas such as the cingulate cortex, temporoparietal junction and cerebellum and this is an example of how psychology can explain individual differences.

▶ TEST YOURSELF

1   Identify two characteristics of the sample used in Hölzel *et al.*   [2]
2   Explain how the researchers operationalised one dependent variable in this study.   [2]
3   Outline one result from Hölzel *et al.* relating to the amount of mindfulness practice engaged in by participants in the experimental group.   [2]
4   Participants in this study had two brain scans, eight weeks apart. How might order effects have affected the data in this part of the study?   [2]
5   With reference to Hölzel *et al.*:
    a   Outline what is meant by 'measure of central tendency'.   [2]
    b   Outline what is meant by 'measure of spread'.   [2]
6   The researchers wondered whether there would be a relationship between time spent on mindfulness activities over the eight weeks and increase in grey matter concentration.
    a   Explain why this part of the study was a correlation.   [2]
    b   Explain one disadvantage of using correlation to explore this.   [2]

1.3.3 Evaluating Hölzel *et al.* (mindfulness and brain scans)

> **Think!**
>
> What problems are presented by participants carrying out mindfulness activities in their own homes and recording them in a diary? Remember, problems can be ethical and/or methodological.

> **Think!**
>
> Hölzel *et al.* state that the mean average time between the two brain scans for the MBSR group was 56 days (SD = 5 days), whereas the average was 66 days (SD = 11 days) for the control group. How does this affect the validity of the findings?

> **Think!**
>
> The control group comprised more males than females (11:6) while the experimental group comprised more females than males (6:10). Could gender differences across the two groups have affected the validity of the findings in any way? Explain your answer.

> Using computer software to analyse the MRI scans made Hölzel *et al.*'s study more reliable and more objective, but why might this sort of analysis not be completely valid?

Ethical issues

Protection from harm

An important strength of this study is that the researchers took many steps to protect their participants from physical and psychological harm. They made sure that none of the participants had metallic implants (e.g. pacemakers or dental fillings) that could have been affected by the magnets in the MRI scanner. They did not allow anyone to participate who might become distressed in the scanner due to claustrophobia (fear of enclosed spaces) and two people were allowed to withdraw after their first scan due to discomfort in the scanner. Participants in the waitlist control group also received MBSR after the study was complete, so they were also able to benefit from MBSR. These examples illustrate the researchers' respect for their participants' wellbeing.

Methodological issues

Reliability

Lack of standardisation

A weakness of this study is the lack of standardisation between the weekly mindfulness sessions; participants chose which exercises they wanted to do each day, where and for how long. Some people may have completed the exercises alone in a quiet garden while others may have been surrounded by co-workers in a noisy office. This is important as it means the procedure cannot be replicated exactly, so differences in grey matter concentration post-intervention may not be reliable.

Internal consistency in the questionnaire

A strength of Hölzel *et al.*'s study was the use of the FFMQ, before and after the MBSR programme. This questionnaire is highly reliable. For example, it contains eight questions measuring 'acting with awareness'. The correlation between the answers to these eight questions is +0.87. This strong positive correlation shows that each question reliably assessed this facet of mindfulness (Baer *et al.*, 2006).

Validity

Experimental method and design

One strength of Hölzel *et al.* was the use of the independent measures design. This meant that the researchers were able to measure changes in grey matter concentration for people who have and have not taken part in MBSR. This was important as it meant that any difference in grey matter concentration in the experimental group could be put down to MBSR and not just changes that might have happened anyway, without this change to their daily routines. Therefore, the use of the control group increased the study's validity, strengthening the conclusion that MBSR *caused* an increase in grey matter concentration in certain brain structures.

Confounding variables

A weakness of Hölzel *et al.*'s design was the lack of control of confounding variables. For example, the experimental group had the added benefits of potentially making new friends at their weekly sessions and taking part in gentle exercise through yoga stretches, in addition to the mindfulness/meditation. This makes it hard to identify which factors led to their increased grey matter concentration relative to the control group (i.e. the mindfulness or the social aspects of group membership and/or exercise), which may affect the study's validity.

Self-report data

A weakness of this study was the use of self-reported quantitative data on the FFMQ. This questionnaire has 39 items, each scored on identical rating scales, where the middle value (3) is labelled 'sometimes true'. In long questionnaires like this, participants sometimes think less carefully about their answers as they go on, simply answering in a similar way to previous questions. This is called a response set and it can reduce the validity of the answers on the FFMQ, meaning the lack of correlation between self-reported mindfulness traits and grey matter concentration is also called into question.

Objectivity and subjectivity

Use of quantitative data

One strength of Hölzel *et al.* was the use of quantitative data to measure grey matter concentration. This was done using voxel-based morphometry and the analysis of this data is conducted by specialist computer software. This makes the findings more objective as it removes the need for the researcher to interpret grey matter concentration.

Generalisations and ecological validity

Generalising beyond the sample

Another weakness was the use of an opportunity sample of only 33 participants, all of whom shared certain characteristics. For example, the participants were aged 25–55 and had an average of 17.5 years of education. As structural plasticity is known to be affected by factors such as age and educational background, it would be helpful to see whether similar effects would be found with older adults or people with lower levels of formal education. This is important and would also lead to greater confidence when making generalisations about the impact of mindfulness on grey matter concentration in the wider population.

Generalising to everyday life

Another strength of Hölzel *et al.* was that the researchers encouraged the experimental participants to incorporate mindfulness into their everyday lives – for example, listening to audio-recorded guided meditations while washing up or walking. This is important as it means the findings have greater ecological validity, meaning similar changes in brain structure should be possible for other people who choose to integrate yoga, body scanning or meditation exercises into their everyday routines.

Nature versus nurture

This study supports the role of nature because it is about the workings of the brain, and the development of new synapses (synaptogenesis) is controlled by our genes. However, the study also supports the role of nurture as the findings demonstrate that experiences, such as attending a regular mindfulness class, can influence our biology/nature (e.g. increasing grey matter concentration in specific brain structures). Regular mindfulness practice appears to trigger synaptogenesis in key brain structures, leading to increased grey matter concentration. This means that, with regular mindfulness practice, even people who have a genetic predisposition to stress can experience measurable improvements in their wellbeing. The fact that grey matter concentration seems to increase in certain brain structures but not others also supports the role of nature.

Applications to everyday life

Mindfulness in schools and workplaces

With global stress levels at an all-time high, integrating regular MBSR into our daily lives may be critical. This study suggests that we do not need to spend a large amount of time on MBSR exercises, but regular, daily practice may trigger neural changes that lead to improvements in wellbeing. Just as school children have physical education lessons, it may be time for education providers to allocate time to support children's psychological wellbeing and build good habits for the future. Likewise, employers could invest in employees by providing time, space and training in MBSR, which may increase workplace productivity and decrease sick days through stress.

Reflections

Hölzel *et al.*'s findings suggest that mindfulness may increase grey matter concentration, but further research is necessary to understand why increased grey matter in key brain structures is linked to wellbeing. While the findings support the idea that structures like the hippocampus and posterior cingulate cortex may have a role to play, it is likely that different mindfulness exercises (e.g. body scanning, yoga, meditation) lead to neural changes in different structures from one another. In this study, participants were free to choose their own exercises, making it hard to unravel whether specific practices were linked to changes in specific structures.

» How do nature and nurture interact in Hölzel *et al.*'s study of mindfulness?

» Do you think everyone can benefit in the same way from mindfulness?

» Could a person's biology (nature) limit the benefits of mindfulness (nurture)?

Why not use the Five Facets of Mindfulness Questionnaire to carry out some research of your own? If you do this, you must follow all ethical guidelines. The full questionnaire is freely available online, for example, **https://novopsych.com.au/ assessments/formulation/five-facet- mindfulness-questionnaire-ffmq-15/**.

» Take a look at an online version; can you guess which facet of mindfulness is being measured by each item: observing (O), describing (D), acting with awareness (A), non-judging (n-J) and non-reactivity (n-R) to inner experience.

» Some of the questions are reverse coded. Make a list of these questions using the online version and remind yourself what this term means.

» Why not have a go at completing the questionnaire yourself; as you do so, think about what the strengths and weaknesses are of collecting quantitative data in this way.

▲ Figure 1.21 The interaction of nature and nurture

LEARNING LINK

When you get to the cognitive approach, you will learn about a study by Andrade (doodling) that looks at how doodling can improve our ability to pay attention to information in the external world, potentially by blocking our ability to daydream and/or focus too much attention on unrelated thoughts. When you get to this study, think about how this links with mindfulness, which also helps to sharpen our focus on external events and change the way we respond to thoughts which distract us from the job in-hand.

STUDY TIP

When you are evaluating studies it is important to think carefully about how you word your points. They need to be concise and clear but also give sufficient detail to show your knowledge of the study. Practise writing three-sentence paragraphs where you make a point, then elaborate it with contextual details from the study and then say why this is a strength or weakness.

TEST YOURSELF

1   Outline one ethical strength of this study.   [2]
2   Explain how one result from the study by Hölzel *et al.* supports the nature side of the nature versus nurture debate and how one result supports the nurture side.   [8]
3   Evaluate the study by Hölzel *et al.* in terms of two strengths and two weaknesses. At least one of your evaluation points must be about quantitative data.   [10]
4   Explain one aspect of the data collection in the study by Hölzel *et al.* that is objective and one that is subjective.   [2]
5   The main research method used in the study by Hölzel *et al.* was an experiment. Suggest two reasons that an experiment was chosen as the main research method for this study.   [2]
6   Hölzel *et al.* could have conducted a case study on mindfulness.
    a   Identify two ways that data could be collected in this case study.   [2]
    b   For one of your answers to question 4, explain an advantage of this way of collecting data for this case study.   [2]

CHAPTER SUMMARY

Dement and Kleitman (sleep and dreams)

Psychology investigated
The ultradian rhythm of sleep-stage cycles and whether dreaming occurs during rapid eye movement (REM) or non-rapid eye movement (non-REM) sleep, using an EEG.

Aim
To see if dream recall occurs during REM or non-REM sleep and if eye movement pattern is related to dream content.

Procedure
Participants slept in a sleep laboratory with an EEG attached to record brain waves. They were woken several times during either REM or non-REM sleep and relayed any dream content into a recording device.

Results
● Dream recall occurred predominantly in REM sleep and accuracy of dream duration estimation was high.

● Dream content matched eye gaze direction during REM sleep.
● Positive correlation between duration of REM and number of words in dream narrative.

Conclusion
Dreaming length can be objectively measured by recording REM cycles during sleep.

Strengths
● Experimenter effects were avoided as participants were woken by a doorbell and a voice recorder was used for dream narration.
● Quantitative data was collected (i.e. number of words in dream narration), increasing objectivity of data analysis.

Weaknesses
● Some data was discarded due to poor recordings, affecting validity of findings.
● Study lacks ecological validity as participants slept in a laboratory with wires attached to their head.

Links to assumptions

Dreaming occurs during REM sleep, so similarities between people can be understood in terms of biological factors.

Links to issues and debates

Participants reported a significantly greater number of dreams during REM sleep than non-REM sleep, thus dreaming during REM sleep is due to nature.

A real-life application is that an EEG can be used to determine when a person is in REM or non-REM sleep and thus used to support the diagnosis of sleep issues.

Similarities

- Both Dement and Kleitman and Hölzel *et al.* gained fully informed (valid) consent from their participants.
- Both Dement and Kleitman and Hassett *et al.* used quantitative data in their study.

Differences

- Dement and Kleitman collected qualitative data as well, while Hölzel *et al.* only collected quantitative data.
- Dement and Kleitman studied participants in a laboratory-type setting, while Hassett *et al.* used the monkeys' normal enclosure.

Hassett *et al.* (monkey toy preferences)

Psychology investigated

Whether stereotypical sex differences in toy preferences for play result from the role of hormones in prenatal exposure or due to socialisation.

Aim

To investigate if male and female rhesus monkeys have similar toy preferences to human infants, despite no socialisation experience with human toys.

Procedure

Hassett *et al.* presented pairs of wheeled and plush toys to a troop of captive rhesus monkeys in their enclosure and observers noted details of monkeys' interactions with the toys, such as sex and time spent with toy.

Results

Significant sex differences in toy preference were observed, matching those seen in humans. Male monkeys preferred wheeled toys, while female monkeys showed no consistent preference.

Conclusion

Sex differences in toy preference stem from prenatal hormone exposure.

Strengths

- Observation used a behavioural checklist to record monkey behaviour, making it reliable.
- Use of quantitative data in recording time spent with toys was objective.

Weaknesses

- Possible subjective bias as observers knew the monkeys.

- Human play may differ from monkey play, so conclusions cannot be generalised to humans.

Links to assumptions

Sex differences in toy preferences were seen in monkeys without socialisation to these toys, so this behaviour can be explained in terms of the effect of genetic and evolutionary differences between the sexes.

Links to issues and debates

Toy preference in humans may be due to nature and caused by biological not learned differences, as male monkeys showed a preference for wheeled toys over plush toys.

A real-life application may be for parents to choose vehicles with expressive faces if they wish to develop empathy skills in boys through imaginative play, as boys are more likely to be drawn to moving parts.

Similarities

- Both Hassett *et al.* and Hölzel *et al.* used an independent measures design.
- Both Hassett *et al.* and Dement and Kleitman investigated biological factors assumed to be due to nature.

Differences

- Hassett *et al.* used animal participants, while Hölzel *et al.* used humans.
- Hassett *et al.* studied behaviour while participants were awake, while Dement and Kleitman studied biological processes while participants were asleep.

Hölzel *et al.* (mindfulness and brain scans)

Psychology investigated

Using MRI scans to track changes in brain structure before and after mindfulness training (MBSR), as well as looking at localisation of function.

Aim

To see if regular participation in Mindfulness-Based Stress Reduction (MBSR) leads to changes in brain structure.

Procedure

This experiment had a longitudinal design and used MRI scans to track changes in grey matter throughout the brain before and after eight weeks of MBSR training. Time spent on mindfulness exercises (body scan, yoga and meditation) was measured, as well as changes in the five facets of mindfulness, to see if there was a correlation.

Results

The MBSR group experienced a significant increase in grey matter concentration in their left hippocampus, posterior cingulate cortex, the temporoparietal junction and cerebellum. No significant difference was found in grey matter concentration in the insulae before and after MBSR.

Conclusion

Structural changes (i.e. increased grey matter concentration) in key brain regions can occur as a result of participation in regular mindfulness practice, even after just eight weeks.

Strengths
- Use of a control group increased the validity of the conclusion that MBSR caused an increase in grey matter concentration in certain brain structures.
- Use of quantitative data from voxel-based morphometry was objective.

Weaknesses
- Lack of standardisation between the weekly mindfulness sessions – participants chose exercises and their duration daily.
- Use of self-report data from the Five Facets of Mindfulness Questionnaire (FFMQ) was subjective.

Links to assumptions
Changes in brain structure following mindfulness training show how similarities and differences between people can be understood in terms of biological factors and their interaction with other factors.

Links to issues and debates
Findings support the role of nurture as engagement in mindfulness training can lead to increases in grey matter concentration in certain areas of the brain.

A real-life application may be education providers allocating time to support regular mindfulness training for long-term improvements in wellbeing.

Similarities
- Both Hölzel *et al.* and Dement and Kleitman used brain scanning techniques.
- Both Hölzel *et al.* and Hassett *et al.* used participants in their real-life setting.

Differences
- Hölzel *et al.* used an independent measures design, while Dement and Kleitman used a repeated measures design for their experiments.
- Hölzel *et al.* investigated brain changes after mindfulness training (nurture) while Hassett *et al.* investigated whether sex differences in behaviour result from biological factors (nature).

2

The Cognitive approach

Learning outcomes

In this chapter, we will discuss:
● the main assumptions, methodology, history, issues and debates of the cognitive approach
● psychological concepts, theories and research relating to the three core studies:
  – Andrade (doodling)
  – Baron-Cohen *et al.* (eyes test)
  – Pozzulo *et al.* (line-ups)
● strengths and weaknesses of the three key studies with reference to ethical issues, **reliability**, **validity**, **objectivity** and **subjectivity**, **generalisations**, issues and debates, including applications to everyday life
● how to plan and evaluate your own investigations using **case studies**, structured **interviews** and **correlations**.

▲ Figure 2.1 What will this couple remember about their day at the lake? How similar will their memories be of this day?

Where there are people, there is psychology!

Psychology is everywhere, and these people are in Canada, the location of Joanna Pozzulo *et al.*'s line-ups study. This chapter is about **cognitive processes**, such as attention and **memory**. A great deal of cognitive research takes place in laboratories, but the reason psychologists conduct these studies is to learn about cognition in the real world. What will these people be **thinking** about as they gaze at the lake? Are they able to imagine what each other might be thinking about or how they might feel? What might have caught their attention and what will they remember about this particular point in time?

In this chapter, we will examine Jackie Andrade's study of the effect of doodling on attention and memory, Simon Baron-Cohen *et al.*'s study of how people differ in their ability to identify emotions and Joanna Pozzulo *et al.*'s study of children's behaviour when asked to identify culprits in police line-ups. In the following section, we will explore the main assumptions of the cognitive approach.

KEY TERMS

cognitive processes

input

output

language

memory

thinking

information processing approach

computer analogy

schema

2.0 Introducing the Cognitive approach

Think!

What is meant by 'incidental learning'?

Think!

Imagine you are helping a group of medical students to improve their recall of complicated terms just before their end-of-year exams. How could you design an experiment to investigate whether visual, auditory or semantic processing works best for the students?

Think!

How might cognitive processes such as attention and memory be affected by dispositional factors such as personality, cultural background and/or access to formal education?

The very first Apple home computer (Figure 2.2) was created in 1975. Cognitive psychologists say the mind is like a **computer**, but is there anything that affects the working of the human mind that could not be programmed into a computer?

▶ Figure 2.2 The original Apple Mac home computer

METHODOLOGY

laboratory experiment

correlation

interview

questionnaire

human ethics

Main assumptions

1 Information is processed through the same route in all humans: **input** – process – **output**, in a similar way to how information is processed by a computer.
2 People have individual differences in their cognitive processing, such as attention, **language**, thinking and memory. These processes can also help to explain behaviour and emotion.

(Cambridge International, 2021)

What is the information processing approach?

The cognitive approach states that behaviour is determined by mental events – for example, thoughts and memories. Cognitive psychologists often take what is called an **information processing approach**. First, information is received through the senses (sight, sound, taste, smell, touch); this information is called input. Some of this information may be filtered out at this stage, especially if it is irrelevant to what we are currently doing.

Input that gets through the initial filter may be compared with existing information stored in our memory system. This helps us to make sense of the input we have received. This process is called perception and the processing that happens at this stage can be extremely fast. Much of it happens unconsciously, meaning that we are generally unaware that it is even happening!

This additional processing determines how we respond to the information we have received. Our reactions, such as conscious thoughts, speech or bodily movements, are called output.

Cognitive theorists generally agree that humans are genetically programmed (hardwired) to process information in certain ways and this explains similarities in the ways that humans respond to certain environmental stimuli. Typically, they also agree that we have limited capacity, meaning we can only process a certain amount of information at any one time, even though we may be able to store an unlimited amount of information within our memory system.

Is the mind really like a computer?

Computers automatically process data in certain ways depending on how they have been programmed. The user supplies input through a keyboard, mouse or touch screen and the output appears on the screen. The user may then use the output to determine the nature of further input. As you can see, the computer provides a useful analogy (comparison) for the human mind. A computer comes with basic hardware and this is likened to the way that genes determine the basic architecture of the human brain, which makes cognitive processing possible. Furthermore, a computer's functionality can be developed through the addition of software, which is also true of humans who can learn new skills, such as mindfulness, juggling or how to play the ukulele.

 In recent years, many scientists have argued that the **computer analogy** is grossly oversimplified and that we can learn more about the mind and the brain by actually studying them rather than drawing analogies with other simplified, non-organic systems.

How do people differ in the way they process information?

Previously, we noted that when sensory input enters our cognitive system we make sense of it using stored information. Output or reactions may differ from person to person due to the fact that each of us perceives input differently depending on our unique past experiences and our current state (e.g. hungry, tired or scared).

Four cognitive processes

Attention

Sensory information is only retained for further processing if we pay attention to it. This involves filtering out information that we do not need, so that we can focus our limited resources on the information that is currently most important (whether that is your teacher giving instructions or a notification that has just appeared on your laptop). In this chapter, you will learn about what happens when we get bored (a state of low cognitive arousal where we find it difficult to pay attention to the outside world) and sometimes start paying greater attention to internally generated thoughts (daydreams).

Language

Humans differ from other non-human animals in terms of their complex use of spoken language. Not only do we use language to communicate, but we also use language to encode new incoming information (input) and store information in a verbal form as well as in images. Many people experience an inner voice, which allows them to verbalise their thoughts, meaning our use of language affects perception, memory and conscious thought.

Thinking

As noted above, much of our cognitive processing happens automatically and outside of conscious awareness. This processing is very fast and effortless. Kahneman (2011) refers to this sort of processing as System 1 thinking. He explains that this type of thinking can lead to errors as we do not always use all the information available to us and often rely too heavily on what we think we know (based on stored knowledge and past experience). He goes on to explain that System 2 thinking is more logical, makes use of all the available information to reach a decision and is more effortful. Unfortunately, we do not always use this sort of thinking and this can lead to the sort of miscarriages of justice that inspired Joanna Pozzulo *et al.*'s research on eyewitness testimony (see section 2.3 on page 71).

Memory

Memory involves three cognitive processes: encoding, storage and retrieval (Squire, 2009). Information may be encoded (represented in the mind) in different ways relating to how something looks (visual), sounds (acoustic) and/or what it means and how it is associated with other stored knowledge (semantic). If we are not paying attention, sensory information may only be stored for a few seconds, but when we are paying attention, short-term memories may last up to 30 seconds. Atkinson and Shiffrin's (1968) Multistore Model of Memory (see Figure 2.3) suggests that information will only be stored long-term if we consciously link that information with stored knowledge from long-term memory. This is called elaborative rehearsal. However, it is now accepted that much of our memory is incidental, meaning information can be stored long-term without conscious effort. This is seen in Andrade's doodling study (see section 2.1 on page 50), which shows that conscious attention is not always necessary for long-term recall, although these memories may be less accessible (easy to retrieve).

Individual differences in their cognitive processing

Cognitive abilities vary widely between people and the ways in which each individual experiences their world can be surprisingly different. Many people find it difficult to switch, direct and maintain attention and this can lead to difficulties in concentrating and skills such as reading, however it can also lead to exceptional ability, due to the intense ability to focus on one topic for extended periods.

On pages 60–69 you will learn about the study by Baron-Cohen *et al.* (eyes test) which examines differences in social sensitivity of people with autism spectrum disorder (ASD). The cognitive abilities of people with and without autism differ in many ways and this study focuses on differences in the way people process information about emotions. Such differences can explain differences in behaviour as our ability to decode emotions in others also affect the ways in which we respond.

Methodology in the Cognitive approach

Cognitive psychologists often use **laboratory experiments** to test their theories about memory, attention, thinking and language. Like biological psychologists, they tend to favour quantitative data. They may ask their participants to conduct some sort of standardised task to see how much information they can process at any one time (capacity) or how long they can remember something without the opportunity to rehearse (duration). For example, attention and incidental memory can be tested by asking participants to complete a dichotic listening task. Different messages may be played to each ear through headphones. The person is told to listen to one of the messages but then content played to the unattended ear may be assessed. In an experiment, the researcher would compare recall from two or more conditions – for example, words linked to the person's current state, such as food words for people who are hungry versus not hungry, or sleep words for people who are tired versus rested.

Cognitive psychologists sometimes conduct **correlational** research where there is no manipulation of an independent variable. For example, they might look at whether there is a relationship between two measured variables, such as bilingualism (proficiency in two different languages) and executive function (e.g. to switch, direct and maintain attention). Here, the psychologist might use **questionnaires** to assess the person's bilingualism and some sort of standardised task to measure executive function.

Cognitive psychologists also use case studies to investigate the impact of brain damage on cognitive processing and unusual cognition – for example, super-recognisers (people with an exceptional ability to remember faces) or prosopagnosia (people with an inability to remember faces).

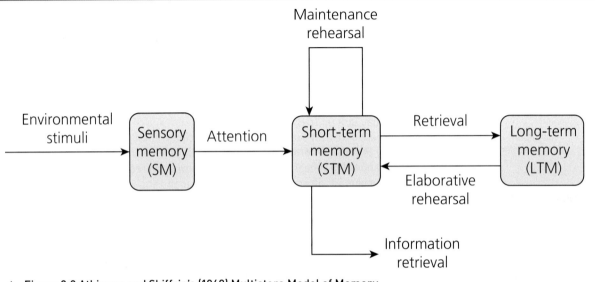

▲ Figure 2.3 Atkinson and Shiffrin's (1968) Multistore Model of Memory

Elaborative rehearsal involves making connections between information from long-term memory and the incoming information. Imagine you want to learn the following shopping list: apples, beans, noodles, eggs, flour, butter, toothpaste, ice cream, pizza, cat food. How could you remember these items by linking them to something that you already know?

ISSUES AND DEBATES

Applications to everyday life

The real-world applications of research described in this chapter are numerous – for example, recommendations for teaching and learning, improving performance in the workplace, ways of supporting neurodiverse students and employees, advising the police on the best way to **interview** witnesses.

Individual and situational explanations

Individual differences are explained as people process information in different ways according to information stored in long-term memory. Situational factors can also affect our ability to process information as we have limited cognitive capacity and we may respond differently to different people (due to anxiety or desire to please).

Nature versus nurture

Our genes shape the way our brains develop and can cause differences in the way we process information,

but social and cultural experiences can also impact the way we use our cognitive skills and, therefore, how these skills develop over time.

The use of children in psychological research

Pozzulo *et al.* (line-ups) worked with children as participants and in this chapter you will begin to think about differences in the way research is conducted with children compared with adults.

The use of animals in psychological research

Although there are no non-human animal studies in this chapter, you may like to think about how cognition in specific animals other than humans could be studied and whether or not the findings could be extrapolated (applied) to humans.

The history of the Cognitive approach

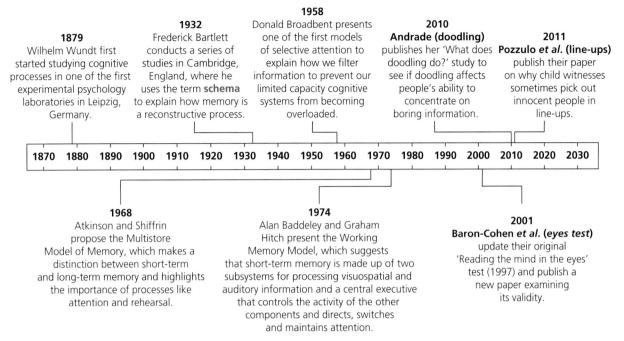

▲ Figure 2.4 Timeline of the cognitive approach

STUDY TIP

As you learn about each of the studies in the cognitive approach, think about how the results support the main assumptions of the approach. What has the study told us about the causes of behaviour and how they link to attention, memory, thinking and/or language? Does the study tell us anything about how differences in cognition may cause differences in behaviour or emotion?

Do you remember Rohan and Polina from page xii? They were discussing an internet news story about a voluntary project where people from many cultures came together to collect and deliver aid to people affected by the COVID-19 pandemic. The report included a brief interview with a doctor who had been treating COVID-19 patients throughout the pandemic. The students are discussing what they remember about the interview but each of them remember different elements of the doctor's story.

»　How might a cognitive psychologist explain Rohan and Polina's differing recall of the doctor's story?

»　Use what you have learned in this section as a starting point, but you may also wish to conduct some further research of your own.

»　After you have learned about all three studies in the approach, you may like to revisit your answer and add some more ideas.

2.1 Andrade (doodling)
2.1.1 Background

> **Think!**
>
> Do you remember Atkinson and Shiffrin's Multistore Model of Memory (see page 47)? What was the link between **attention** and **memory**? Were you paying attention?

> **Think!**
>
> Are you a daydreamer? Do you regularly find yourself thinking about things other than the task you are meant to be doing? How much of this involves thinking about real events/people and how much is purely imaginary/fantasy? What are the advantages and disadvantages of daydreaming?

> **Think!**
>
> Do you think that there are individual differences in the extent to which **doodling** would help or interfere with people's ability to pay attention? What type of person might find it helpful? Would certain types of doodles be more or less effective? How could we investigate this?

KEY TERMS

attention

memory

doodling

concentration

Introducing Jackie Andrade

Jackie Andrade is a Professor of Psychology at the University of Plymouth, UK. She uses cognitive psychology to solve real-world problems, including accidental waking up during surgery and treating post-traumatic stress disorder. Her study of doodling is a small part of her work on cravings, a kind of daydreaming or mind-wandering about consuming a favourite food or drug. Her research has shown people can achieve lifestyle goals by using mental imagery to create 'cravings' for healthy behaviours. Her best advice to psychology students of all ages is to follow your interests!

You can find out more about Professor Andrade's other research here: **www.plymouth.ac.uk/staff/jackie-andrade**

▲ Figure 2.5 Professor Jackie Andrade

Do you think doodling while listening would help the students in Figure 2.6 to concentrate or make them lose focus instead?

▶ Figure 2.6 It can be easy to lose focus in class, especially if it is rather long, late in the day or you have other things on your mind

The psychology being investigated

Jackie Andrade's paper focuses on attention and memory. She proposes that doodling, a habit often associated with loss of **concentration**, can actually *enhance* concentration when people are bored, helping them to pay attention and remember information better.

Attention

Put simply, attention refers to 'the concentration of mental effort on sensory or mental events' (Solso, 1995). Due to our limited cognitive capacity, attention is often selective, meaning we direct our attention towards certain information and filter out or ignore other input. When chatting to a friend in class, for example, you might ignore other students' conversations so you can fully focus on what your friend is saying.

Memory

Memory refers to the encoding, storage and retrieval of information, potentially leading to long-term retention. Often we try hard to remember information that we are told and make an effort to focus. We may even try a few strategies to help us remember things – for example, repeating the items to ourselves. Information that we do not focus on but we can recall is called incidental memory, meaning information that was remembered unintentionally, as is the case for so much of the input that we process every day.

Background

Concentration and doodling

A doodle is a drawing, sketch or pattern created to pass the time rather than for any particular purpose. Sometimes people think a person who is doodling has lost interest and is no longer paying attention, but Andrade's study suggests that this may not be the case at all! She explains that doodling can help us to concentrate better, but only on tasks that are not very interesting.

When we are bored, we sometimes start to daydream; we stop concentrating on events in the outside world and start focusing on our own thoughts – for example, when our next assignment is due, what we fancy for lunch or who would win in a fight between a porcupine and a puffer fish. If we want to concentrate on information that is frankly rather dull, it is important to employ strategies to stay focused.

Common sense suggests that dividing our limited cognitive capacity between two tasks (doodling and listening) would lead to decreased task performance, but because these tasks require different ways of thinking, many people find that they are able to do both things at the same time. Furthermore, doodling may actually enhance concentration, by increasing arousal levels, inhibiting daydreaming and ensuring we remain alert to external stimuli.

Andrade in brief

Forty participants listened to a very boring, pretend telephone message. Half were asked to shade printed shapes at the same time (the doodling group). All participants were asked to listen out for specific information in the message and write it down (Andrade calls this 'monitoring'). The doodlers recorded the names more accurately and remembered 29 per cent more information on a surprise memory test, which included both monitored and incidental information. Andrade concluded that doodling can enhance performance on a concurrent task through decreasing boredom, which can be an uncontrolled variable in some cognitive experiments. Her study, therefore, has important implications for both the research community and people in everyday situations, including schools and workplaces.

 # Plan your own... case study

Andrade designed a laboratory experiment to test her ideas about attention, memory and doodling, but there are many other research methods that might be used to investigate these topic areas. Why not try designing a case study?

Imagine...

Dr Viktor is planning a case study on attention, memory and doodling. He is about to meet an interesting patient called Tu, who cannot stop doodling. He doodles constantly whenever he is listening, speaking, watching television and in meetings at work, as well as when playing with his children.

▸▸ What advice would you give Dr Viktor about how to conduct a case study to investigate Patient Tu's behaviour?

Planning a case study

A case study is a non-experimental method. When planning a case study, it is important that you identify who is being studied, what data will be collected and how it will be collected and analysed. Case studies use a range of data collection methods to collect in-depth data about the participant/s they are studying (also called triangulation). See page 187 for more information on case studies.

▼ Table 2.1 Features of a case study

Main features of a case study	Consider...
Details about the participant or small group being studied	Case studies include rich and detailed information about one rare or unusual individual or small group. Who is Dr Viktor investigating as his case study? What details can you give about them?
Details about the content of the study	Case studies include qualitative and quantitative data from both primary and secondary sources. How could Dr Viktor collect quantitative and/or qualitative data about Tu? Will he use primary and/or secondary data?
Two or more techniques for data collection (triangulation)	Case studies use triangulation, meaning they collect data using two or more different techniques. Which techniques might Dr Viktor use? Can you give a detailed explanation as to how Dr Viktor will use these techniques to collect data about Tu's doodling?
Analysis and interpretation	Case studies use various techniques to analyse/interpret the data. What techniques might Dr Viktor use to analyse the data collected about Tu's doodling behaviours? Consider the type of data that he has collected.

Evaluating your plan

Dr Viktor shares your ideas with his colleagues. Some of them think it is a great idea; others are not so sure. Think about the practical strengths and weaknesses of your suggestions.

▼ Table 2.2 Evaluating your plan

	Describe	Explain
Strengths	How do case studies collect rich and in-depth data?	How might the collection of in-depth data improve the validity of Dr Viktor's research into doodling behaviour?
Weaknesses	Why might it be difficult to replicate a case study? Why might Dr Viktor be biased in his interpretation of the data?	Why is it important for Dr Viktor's research to be replicable? Why is there an issue if Dr Viktor interprets his data on Tu's doodling subjectively?
Improvements	Consider the weaknesses you gave above. How might you improve Dr Viktor's procedure to overcome one of these issues?	How would this improvement affect the validity and/or reliability of the data Dr Viktor collects in the context of doodling behaviour?

It might be a bit late for these students, but could something as simple as shading shapes help increase their end-of-term grades? Remember, Andrade only thinks doodling helps increase concentration when we are bored. What else could the teacher try to improve the students' concentration and recall?

▶ Figure 2.7 Could doodling have helped these students?

► **LEARNING LINK**

The last study in the cognitive approach, Pozzulo *et al.* (line-ups) also examines the processes of attention and memory. The participants are told to pay attention to a short film and that they will be asked some questions about it afterwards. It is a little different to Andrade's study as the input is visual (a film) not auditory (a telephone message) and they know they will be tested later. This means Pozzulo *et al.*'s participants probably tried harder to focus during the task. Unlike the Andrade study, they were not told to focus on anything specific in the film, just to watch carefully. Pozzulo *et al.* found differences between adults and children on their task. Do you think Andrade would have found differences if she had tested children as well as adults? You may like to come back to this once you have read about both studies in detail.

► **TEST YOURSELF**

1 Explain why the study by Andrade is from the cognitive approach.   [2]
2 The study by Andrade is based on the concepts of attention and memory. Explain what is meant by attention with reference to this study.   [2]
3 Outline one reason why doodling might decrease concentration and one reason why doodling might increase concentration.   [2]
4 Alexi wants to collect some qualitative data about teachers' attitudes towards students who doodle in class. Explain one research method that Alexi could use to collect qualitative data for this study.   [3]
5 Zara observes a meeting at her workplace and makes a list of everyone who was doodling during the meeting. She then tests everyone's recall of the meeting to see whether those that doodled remembered the meeting better or worse than the people who did not doodle. Describe how Zara could present her findings, with reference to an appropriate graph.   [2]
6 Irfan has read about Andrade's study. He wonders whether playing with modelling clay would also help participants to focus while completing another task. Describe how Irfan could conduct a laboratory experiment to test whether using modelling clay improves focus.   [10]
    (See page 170 for tips on designing a laboratory experiment, including the required features.)

2.1.2 Describing Andrade (doodling)

METHODOLOGY

laboratory experiment

Think!

Look at the results tables for Andrade's study. Can you spot two findings that show that doodlers found it easier to pay attention while listening to the tape than the non-doodling control group?

Think!

Are you a doodler? If so, have you ever thought about why you doodle or when you do it? What kind of doodles do you like to make?

Think!

Andrade explains in detail why she asked her participants just to shade shapes rather than create their own more elaborate doodles. If she had allowed them to create their own spontaneous images, how do you think this might have affected the validity of the results?

Andrade's participants had already participated in a study about giving directions when she asked them if they would listen to a boring message about a party. Why did she recruit them after they had already taken part in another study?

AIMS

1 To investigate whether doodling improves our ability to pay attention to (or concentrate on) auditory information (i.e. a message that is heard but not seen).
2 To investigate whether doodling affects later recall of auditory information.

RESEARCH METHODOLOGY

Andrade used a laboratory experiment to see if doodling helped people to concentrate and remember information from a mock (pretend) telephone message.

Design and variables

The study used an independent measures design as the researchers compared the performance of two separate groups of participants: an experimental/doodling group of 17 females and 3 males and a control group of 18 females and 2 males. Random allocation was used to control for participant variables – for example, differences in memory that might have affected recall of the target information. The order of recall was counterbalanced across the participants.

The independent variable was whether the participants were allowed to doodle while they listened to the phone message or not. The participants in the doodling group were asked to shade alternating rows of ten circles and ten squares (approximate size: 1 cm in diameter) printed onto standard A4 paper.

There were three main dependent variables:
1 **Monitoring accuracy**: the number of correct names (out of eight) recorded while listening to the tape; the researcher then deducted **false alarms** (i.e. wrong

answers) from the total number of correct names to give the final monitoring performance score.
2 **Memory for monitored information**: number of correct names recalled (out of eight) after false alarms were deducted.
3 **Memory for incidental information**: number of correct places recalled (out of eight).

Sample

Forty participants aged 18–55 from the MRC Applied Psychology Unit participant panel were recruited for the study. They had all just finished another experiment (about giving directions) and the researchers asked whether they would mind staying for another five minutes to complete one more study. As the participants were already part of a pre-existing and readily available group, they were an opportunity sample.

They were recruited in this way as the researcher wanted the participants to be 'ready to go home' to increase their level of boredom during the task.

The MRC Applied Psychology Unit participants were members of the general population who had volunteered to participate in research projects and all were paid a small fee for their time.

PROCEDURE

The tape (audio recording)

The researcher audio-recorded a 2.5-minute mock telephone message about a party. The message was read in a flat tone of voice at a speed of 227 words per minute. The message mentioned:
● eight people who were able to come to the party: Jane, William, Claire, Craig, Suzie, Jenny, Phil and Tony
● three people and one cat who could not come to the party: Nigel, John, Nicky and Ben the cat (Andrade refers to these names as '**lures**')
● eight places: London, Penzance, Gloucester, Colchester, Harlow, Ely, Peterborough and Edinburgh
● a lot of other irrelevant information.

Listening to the recording

Each participant completed the experiment on their own in a quiet, dull room. The standardised instructions said:
● They should pretend the speaker was a friend inviting them to a party.
● The tape is rather dull but that is okay because they do not need to remember any of it.
● Write down the names of the people who will (or probably will) come to the party (excluding themselves) and ignore the names of anyone who cannot come.
● Do not write down anything else.

The experimental group were given the A4 response sheets with the shapes to shade and a pencil. There was a 4.5 cm margin on the paper to record the target names. They were told to shade the shapes as they listened to the tape but not to worry about neatness or speed; it was 'just something to help relieve the boredom'. Those in the **control group** were given a sheet of lined paper (with no shapes to shade). The tape was played at the same 'comfortable' volume for everyone and the participants wrote down the party-goers' names as they listened.

The surprise memory test

Next, the researchers collected the response sheets and chatted to the participants for one minute. During this time, they revealed the **deception**; there would now be a surprise memory test! Half of each group were asked to recall the names first and then the places, and the other half were told to recall the places first and then the names. Finally, participants were asked whether they had guessed that there would be a memory test at the end.

Analysing the responses

The researchers included any names or places that they thought had simply been misheard as correct – for example, Greg for Craig. Incorrect names were coded as false alarms, including extra names of non-party-goers added into the message as 'lures'. Andrade included these lures to see whether people would write down all names mentioned instead of just those going to the party. Words that were neither names nor places were marked incorrect – for example, sister.

▶ RESULTS

Amount of doodling

The experimental group shaded an average of 36.3 shapes (range 3–110). One person did not shade any shapes so they were replaced with another participant. No one in the control group doodled on their lined paper.

Monitoring accuracy

▼ Table 2.3 Number of correct names recorded and number of false alarms

	Number of names correctly written down while listening to the recording		Number of people scoring full marks (8/8)	Number of people making false alarms
	Mean	Standard deviation		
Doodlers (experimental group)	7.8	0.4	15/20	1
Non-doodlers (control)	7.1	1.1	9/20	5

The researchers calculated a final monitoring performance score by subtracting the number of false alarms from the number of correct names remembered (a wrong answer theoretically cancelled out a right answer). After these deductions, the results were as follows:

▼ Table 2.4 Monitoring performance scores

	Monitoring performance score (maximum score = 8)	
	Mean	Standard deviation
Doodlers (experimental group)	7.7	0.6
Non-doodlers (control)	6.9	1.3

Monitoring performance was significantly higher in the doodling group compared with the control group.

Recall performance

▼ Table 2.5 Recall scores

	Recall score (minus false alarms)		
	Monitored information (people's names), maximum score = 8	Incidental information (place names), maximum score = 8	Total recall (monitored and incidental information), maximum score = 16
Doodlers (experimental group)	5.1 (1.7)	2.4 (1.5)	7.5
Non-doodlers (control)	4.0 (1.5)	1.8 (1.2)	5.8

The total recall score (out of 16) was 29 per cent higher in the doodling group compared with the control group. Doodlers remembered both types of information (monitored and incidental) better than the control group and remembered monitored information better than incidental. The average number of false alarms was low (0.3) and almost identical across doodlers and controls, and monitored (names) and incidental (places) information.

Andrade was concerned about the number of people who indicated that they thought there might be a surprise memory test (three in the doodling group and four in the control group). She ran the analysis again without their data. The doodling group still performed significantly better than the controls on the recall task.

▶ CONCLUSIONS

Andrade concluded that doodling can improve concentration when listening, even when the task is rather boring. She also concluded that it can help us to remember information better, even when we are not expecting to have to do so.

Andrade's participants were not told in advance that they would have to remember the names and places they heard on the tape. How do you think they felt when she revealed the 'surprise' test of recall? Were they all that surprised?

▶ LEARNING LINK

Andrade's study clearly demonstrates that, when people get bored, they get distracted and this can lead to errors in tasks that require cognitive processing. In Chapter 3, you will read a study by Fagen *et al.* (elephant learning), in which the researchers tried to teach elephants a sequence of behaviours as part of a veterinary procedure. Just like Andrade's human participants, sometimes the elephants got a little bored and distracted, especially if something more interesting was happening elsewhere! When their attention was diverted, they did not always show what they were able to do. Fagen *et al.*'s study was all about teaching a behaviour that was helpful in keeping the elephants healthy, but sometimes psychologists use animals to learn more about humans. Given that animals do not have spoken language, it is interesting to think about how boredom might affect animals in different ways to humans. Do you think elephants daydream?

STUDY TIP

The results of this study can be a little confusing. Monitoring accuracy refers to the number of correct names written down while listening to the tape. This is not the same as the monitoring performance score, which is the correct answer score *minus* false alarms. Once you have this clear in your mind, you have to remember that the researchers were not just interested in the participants' ability to pay attention (monitor and record the names while listening); they also wanted to know whether doodling improved people's ability to recall both the monitored information and the information that they heard but were not told to pay attention to (the incidental information).

▶ TEST YOURSELF

1 Outline what was meant by a false alarm in this study, with reference to one example. [2]
2 Describe the response sheets that were given to the experimental and control groups in this study. [4]
3 Identify the type of information that was most likely to be forgotten. Explain your answer with reference to the data. [2]
4 Describe two ways in which the study by Andrade is replicable. [4]
5 Explain one reason why Andrade used a control group. [2]
6 Andrade counted the number of correct names and places remembered in a surprise test of memory. What measure of spread was used to analyse this data? [1]

2.1.3 Evaluating Andrade (doodling)

Think!

The names Nigel, John, Nicky and Ben on the tape are referred to as 'lures'. What did Andrade mean by this term and how did her use of lures improve the validity of her data?

Think!

Imagine you were a participant in Andrade's doodling group. Do you think you would have shaded the shapes quickly or slowly and accurately? In the real study, one person shaded just three shapes and another shaded 110! Do you think that it was a strength or a weakness that Andrade told them it did not matter how neatly or quickly they shaded the shapes and that it was just a task to relieve the boredom?

Think!

Andrade's study is a great example of a laboratory experiment that shows how doodling can improve concentration when the information is boring. Can you think of a way of designing a field experiment to see how doodling affects concentration when the task is interesting? Remember, everyone finds different things interesting and/or boring so you will need to consider how you operationalise your independent variable. How do you think the results will differ from Andrade's study?

>> If one of Andrade's participants had included Ben the cat's name on their response sheet, how would Andrade have marked this?
>> What did she call this type of result?

▶ Figure 2.8 Ben the cat was a little disappointed not to be able to make it to the party!

Ethical issues

One weakness of Andrade's study is that the participants were deceived about the true purpose of the study. Before listening to the tape, they were told, 'The tape is rather dull but that's okay because I don't want you to remember any of it.' This was not true as after the monitoring task participants were given a surprise test of recall for not only the monitored information (the party-goers' names) but also the incidental information (the place names). Although deception was important (otherwise the participants would have concentrated more while listening to the recording), it meant that participants were unable to give their fully informed consent.

Methodological issues

Reliability

A strength of Andrade's study is the highly standardised procedure, which means the study can be easily replicated. All participants listened to the same audio-recorded message, meaning the pace and tone were identical; they all completed the study in the same quiet, dull room; and the interval between the monitoring and recall tasks was always one minute. This level of consistency in the procedure means the study can be easily replicated to see whether doodling really does improve concentration on a boring task.

Validity

Experimental method and design

A strength of the design was that the order in which the participants recalled the monitored information (names) and incidental information (places) was counterbalanced. Half the participants in each group recalled the names first then the places and the other half recalled places first and then names. This improved the validity of the findings by minimising the impact of order effects – increased memory for incidental and monitored information could be attributed to the doodling and not the order in which they had been tested.

Operational definitions

A weakness of this study was the operational definition of doodling. Andrade standardised the nature of the doodling by asking participants to shade 1 cm shapes, but in real life, doodling is generally a more creative and spontaneous activity. This is important because the conclusion that doodling aids concentration and recall may not be true for people who are allowed more freedom with regards to what, where and when they doodle.

Confounding variables

A strength of the study is that Andrade checked to see whether any of her participants had detected the deception. Eighteen per cent (three of the doodlers and four of the controls) said they had guessed there may be a memory test afterwards, although none of these participants claimed to have tried to remember the information. Andrade was concerned about the potential impact this might have had, so she re-analysed the data without their scores and found the results to be the same. This was important because it helped to improve the overall validity of her findings regarding the impact of doodling on concentration and memory.

The use of lures

A strength of Andrade's telephone message was the use of the 'lures', meaning the names of people who were not attending the party (e.g. Nigel, John and Nicky). Participants who were not really listening to the content of the message and just listening out for names might have been 'lured' into writing an incorrect answer, which would have reduced their overall monitoring performance score. This improved the validity of the findings as it ensured Andrade was really measuring participants' concentration as they had to listen carefully to what was said about each person, and not just record all the names that they heard.

Objectivity and subjectivity

A weakness of the study was the decision to mark misheard words as correct. For example, in the monitoring task, if a participant wrote Greg instead of Craig, this was recorded as correct, and then later in the recall task if they wrote Greg again, this was also marked as correct. This is a weakness as an assumption is being made that certain incorrect names are 'mishearings' and not false alarms, meaning the coding of answers is rather subjective.

Generalisations and ecological validity

Generalising beyond the sample

A weakness of this study is the overwhelming number of females in the study compared to males. Females made up 87.5 per cent of the sample, meaning it can be described as 'gynocentric'. This is important as it means that generalising the findings to males must be treated with caution, until the study has been replicated with a more balanced sample.

Generalising to everyday life

A weakness of this laboratory experiment is that the task was conducted in a highly controlled setting, which is unlikely to reflect the additional challenges of listening to a voicemail in a real-world setting. For example, the study took place in a quiet, under-stimulating room and the participants were asked to pretend that the speaker on the tape was a friend of theirs. Had the participants been in their own homes surrounded by other family members, pets, noisy neighbours and traffic sounds, doodling alone may not have been sufficient to help them concentrate on the message. This suggests doodling may be more effective in the laboratory and that the findings may lack ecological validity.

ISSUES AND DEBATES

Individual and situational explanations

A strength of this study is that it shows how attention and memory can be affected not just by participant variables (i.e. individual differences between people) but also by situational factors. Many people think of cognitive skills as fixed, measurable and relatively stable traits (e.g. 'He has a really good memory' or 'I am easily distracted'), but this study shows how other demands placed on us (e.g. not being allowed to doodle) can limit our cognitive performance. This is important and suggests that parents, teachers and employers should be aware that making small adjustments to the situation can help people to improve their performance.

Applications to everyday life

Supporting students
Leading on from the point above, a further strength of this study is that it could be used as evidence to support recommendations for teachers. Andrade's study demonstrates that a second task such as doodling can improve concentration, allowing us to remember more of what we have heard. This is an important finding as many teachers punish their students for doodling in class, but this study suggests that raising awareness of the benefits of doodling may be an important addition to teacher training.

Reflections

Andrade's findings suggest that concentration and memory can be improved by allowing people to doodle while listening to a speaker, but the small sample size means that there was little analysis of individual differences within the data. It is likely that multitasking may be beneficial to some people but not to others and it is also likely that the nature of the task in this study impacted the findings. Shading shapes is very different to creating your own spontaneous image, which is likely to require more cognitive capacity and may have the opposite effect on concentration and memory. For this reason, Andrade's findings should not be overstated as doodling can take many forms and is likely to affect people in different ways.

Andrade's sample only included adults. Do you think doodling might have a different impact on children's concentration and recall? How could you investigate this?

▶ Figure 2.9 Could doodling help children to concentrate?

In 2017, Boggs *et al.* conducted a partial replication of Andrade's doodling study aiming to extend her findings by looking at multiple different types of doodling. They argue that their findings have greater ecological validity as they included a freestyle doodling group, whose members were not constrained to shade shapes but could doodle as they pleased. The student participants (n = 93) listened to a fictional conversation about an earthquake and completed a fill-in-the-gaps quiz to test their recall of the details. In addition to a structured doodling group and control group, there were two extra groups: the free-doodlers and a note-taking group. Interestingly, the free-doodlers had less accurate recall than the structured doodlers and the notetakers.

» Think back to Andrade's explanation of why doodling should increase performance. Can you explain why free-doodling had the opposite effect?

> **LEARNING LINK**

When thinking about ethical decision-making, it is important to consider the nature of the deception and the impact it is likely to have on the participants. Andrade's participants were told they would not have to remember anything from the telephone message, yet later had to recall 16 pieces of information. Contrast this with Milgram's study of obedience, where participants were led to believe they were administering electric shocks to a complete stranger. Although both studies involved debriefing and the deception was revealed, imagine how Milgram's participants must have felt afterwards in comparison to Andrade's participants.

STUDY TIP

Andrade's study has several different dependent variables and it is important to understand how they differ from each other. For example, do you know the difference between monitoring accuracy and monitoring performance scores? What about the difference between monitoring performance and recall of monitored information? What about the difference between recall of monitored information and recall of incidental information? Conducting a replication of the study can really help with this.

> **TEST YOURSELF**

1. Suggest one real-world application of this study. [2]
2. Outline one methodological problem that could arise if children were used as participants in this study. [2]
3. Evaluate the study by Andrade in terms of two strengths and two weaknesses. At least one of your evaluation points must be about laboratory-based research. [10]
4. Explain what is meant by replicability using this study as an example. [2]
5. Andrade collected quantitative data. Give two strengths of this type of data. [4]
6. Explain one advantage and one disadvantage of using deception in psychological research. Use at least one example from Andrade's study in your answer. [5]

2.2 Baron-Cohen *et al.* (eyes test)
2.2.1 Background

Think!

Why might an individual with autism spectrum disorder find the *eyes test* challenging?

Think!

In the COVID-19 pandemic, many of us around the world were required, by law, to wear face masks. This meant that we spent more time than usual looking only at the upper half of each other's faces. Did you find it difficult to 'read' people's emotions when you could only see their eyes? How did this make you feel when interacting with others?

Think!

The *eyes test* is a 'pen and paper' test. What would be the benefits of administering the test in this way in real life?

KEY TERMS

autism

theory of mind

social sensitivity

Asperger syndrome

Introducing Simon Baron-Cohen

Simon Baron-Cohen is a cognitive-neuroscientist and Professor of Developmental Psychopathology at Cambridge University, UK. He is also Director of the university's Autism Research Centre. He is best known for his research into **autism**, including his theory that autism involves a deficit of **theory of mind** (see below) and that it is an extreme form of the male brain. You can follow Simon Baron-Cohen on Twitter @sbaroncohen

▲ Figure 2.10 Professor Simon Baron-Cohen

The psychology being investigated

Theory of mind

Theory of mind refers to the ability to determine the mental state of another person or ourselves, otherwise known as 'mentalising'. It refers to a person's ability to put oneself in the position of someone else. We use this knowledge to explain and predict the behaviour of other people. Deficits can occur in those with autism spectrum disorder. There are two stages involved in theory of mind. The first stage is determining the mental state of a person (e.g. happiness) and the second stage is determining the content of the mental state (e.g. happiness at being reunited with a sibling).

Social sensitivity

Social sensitivity refers to how effectively an individual can identify, understand and respect the feelings and views of another person during social interactions. A person with a high level of social sensitivity is aware of social cues and can respond appropriately. An example of low social sensitivity might be a person who frequently talks over others during conversations, rather than pausing to allow the other person to speak.

Background

Autism and Asperger syndrome

Autism, or autism spectrum disorder, refers to a range of conditions characterised by challenges with social interactions and communication, as well as repetitive or inflexible patterns of behaviour. The onset of the disorder occurs during childhood, usually early childhood. **Asperger syndrome** has previously been used as a diagnosis for individuals with autism who have unimpaired language skills and intellectual functioning. However, as of 1 January 2022, the term will no longer be used in the ICD-11 and all previous autism-like subgroupings will fall under the umbrella term 'autism spectrum disorder'. Genetics research has shown that there is no distinction between Asperger syndrome and high-functioning autism and the terms were not being used in a consistent way by clinicians. However, Baron-Cohen *et al.*'s study was conducted in 2001 when the diagnosis of Asperger syndrome still existed.

Measuring cognitive dysfunction

It is challenging to develop tests in psychology which are sensitive enough to detect subtle cognitive dysfunction, particularly in adults with typical intelligence who may struggle with social understanding. Most psychological tests for social cognitive functioning have been developed for children. However, adults with neurodevelopmental conditions that persist across their lifespan, such as Asperger syndrome or autism, may have developed learning strategies to compensate for their deficits, therefore requiring any tests to be sensitive to subtle differences between typical and atypical functioning.

The original 'Reading the Mind in the Eyes' test

In 1997, Baron-Cohen and colleagues devised their first test of adult social sensitivity called the 'Reading the Mind in the Eyes' test. Participants were presented with 25 photographs showing the eyes of actors and actresses and were asked to select one of two words which best fit what that person was feeling. The *eyes test* aimed to determine how sensitive a person was to another's mental state, otherwise known as 'theory of mind'. It assessed the first stage of theory of mind: determining a mental state from a fragment of a facial expression – a photograph of a person's eyes. On the original *eyes test*, males performed slightly worse than females, and adults with high-functioning autism (HFA) or Asperger syndrome (AS) scored significantly lower than sex-matched controls. The test also demonstrated that neurotypical adults could determine a person's mental state from minimal cues – a 2D image of their eyes.

This study investigated theory of mind in adults. How could you measure theory of mind in young children? Would you need to change the methodology at all?

Baron-Cohen *et al.* in brief

Baron-Cohen *et al.* wanted to test a revised version of their original *eyes test* to see whether it was a more sensitive measure of adult social intelligence for those with IQ scores within the normal range. They improved on weaknesses of the original *eyes test* in the hope of reducing the ceiling effect and ensuring that items could not be as easily guessed. Baron-Cohen *et al.* wanted to see whether adults with HFA/AS still scored lower than neurotypical adults on the *revised eyes test* and whether females scored higher than males. They also wanted to see if there was a negative correlation between the *revised eyes test* scores and Autism Spectrum Quotient (AQ), another test which measures traits of autism. All of these predicted results were found, although the difference in scores on the *revised eyes test* between males and females was not statistically significant.

Plan your own... interview

Baron-Cohen *et al.* used experiments and correlations to investigate theory of mind in adults. Why not try designing an interview to investigate social sensitivity?

Imagine...

Professor Smith is planning a structured interview to investigate social sensitivity. She is interested in people's subjective interpretation of different social situations.
» What advice would you give Professor Smith about how to conduct a structured interview to investigate social sensitivity?

Planning an interview

An interview is a non-experimental method. When planning an interview, it is important that you consider what questions will be asked to collect data on the specific topic being investigated, as well as how this data will be analysed. Examples of questions are also essential. See page 184 for more information on interviews.

▼ Table 2.6 Features of an interview

Main features of an interview	Consider...
Question format (open and closed questions)	Interviews can use both open and closed questions to collect data. Would you suggest open or closed questions to collect the data required on social sensitivity? Consider how Professor Smith will eventually analyse this data.
Examples of questions	Can you suggest examples of the open and/or closed questions that Professor Smith could ask relating to social sensitivity in the interviews?
Question scoring and interpretation	The data gathered from interviews may be qualitative or quantitative. How will Professor Smith analyse this data in order to draw conclusions from the participants about social sensitivity?

Main features of an interview	Consider...
Format (structured/semi-structured/unstructured)	Professor Smith wants to conduct a structured interview. What are the features of this and how will it be applied when interviewing participants about social sensitivity?
Technique (face-to-face, telephone)	Interviews can be conducted either face-to-face or over the telephone, for example. This may affect how much a person is willing to disclose. Which method do you feel is best for Professor Smith's research into social sensitivity?

2

2.2 Baron-Cohen et al. (eyes test)

Evaluating your plan

Professor Smith shares your ideas with her colleagues. Some of them think it is a great idea; others are not so sure. Think about the practical strengths and weaknesses of your suggestions.

▼ Table 2.7 Evaluating your plan

	Describe	Explain
Strengths	What are the strengths of conducting a structured interview over other types of interview?	Why might asking set questions be an advantage in the context of interviewing people about social sensitivity?
Weaknesses	In what way might participants' answers change due to the presence of the interviewer? Consider that the topic of the interviews is social sensitivity.	Why might the presence of the interviewer affect the validity of the data collected? Would this effect still occur with telephone interviews?
Improvements	Consider the weakness above. How might you improve Professor Smith's procedure to overcome this issue? Might the use of a different interview technique improve the validity of the data collected?	How would this improvement affect the validity of the data Professor Smith collects about social sensitivity?

> ### LEARNING LINK
> In the social approach, Perry *et al.* (personal distance) also used a questionnaire, called the Interpersonal Reactivity Index (IRI), to measure the trait of empathy in individuals. It was used by Perry *et al.* to assign people to two conditions of an independent variable: high and low empathy. What similarities and differences can you identify between Perry *et al.*'s use of a questionnaire compared to Baron-Cohen *et al.*'s *revised eyes test*? Also, in what ways did the researchers differ in how they used each questionnaire in their respective study?

STUDY TIP

It is important to be able to discuss the concept of theory of mind as part of the background to Baron-Cohen *et al.*'s study. You may wish to conduct further background reading into this, including the Sally-Anne Test.

The Sally-Anne Test is a psychological test developed by Baron-Cohen and colleagues which is used with children to see if they possess theory of mind. A scenario involving two real-life dolls called Sally and Anne is presented. Sally hides a marble in a basket within a room then leaves. While she is gone, Anne removes the marble and puts it in another box. Sally re-enters the room, at which point the child is asked the question, 'Where will Sally look for her marble?'. If a child possesses theory of mind, then they should be able to respond with Sally's false belief, as they are able to see events from Sally's perspective. Generally, children under the age of four and those with autism spectrum disorders struggle with this task and incorrectly answer 'In Anne's box'.

TEST YOURSELF

1   Describe the theory that Baron-Cohen *et al.* were investigating in their study.   [3]
2   Explain why Baron-Cohen *et al.* chose to revise their original *eyes test*.   [2]
3   Explain why this study is from the cognitive approach.   [2]
4   Baron-Cohen *et al.* used a questionnaire with fixed choices, which are closed questions. Explain one strength and one weakness of the use of closed questions in this study.   [4]
5   Baron-Cohen *et al.*'s study investigated whether there was a negative correlation between the scores of individuals with HFA/AS on the *eyes test* and the *autism spectrum quotient (AQ)*. Explain one weakness of correlations.   [2]
6   Suggest one strength and one weakness of using the *eyes test* to measure theory of mind.   [4]

2.2.2 Describing Baron-Cohen *et al.* (eyes test)

METHODOLOGY

experiment

correlation

Think!

In what ways did Baron-Cohen *et al.* revise their original *eyes test*?

Think!

Imagine that you are a researcher and want to recruit participants with HFA/AS. What might be the best way to achieve this?

Think!

Why were each of the control conditions important in this study?

AIMS

The main aims were:
1   To test adults with high-functioning autism (HFA)/Asperger syndrome (AS) on the *revised eyes test* to see if the deficits on the original test were still seen.
2   To see if there is a negative correlation between *autism spectrum quotient (AQ)* and *eyes test* scores.
3   To see if females score higher on the *eyes test* than males.

RESEARCH METHODOLOGY

Baron-Cohen *et al.* used **experiments** and **correlations**: the scores of different groups/sexes of participants were compared and the researchers also wanted to see if there was a correlation between the *AQ* and *eyes test* scores.

Design and variables

There were two main independent variables for the experiments: whether the participant had high-functioning autism/Asperger syndrome or not (divided into three groups: general population, students and IQ matched controls), and sex: male versus female. Both of these were independent measures designs. The dependent variables were the *eyes test* and *AQ* scores.

The co-variables for the correlation were the *AQ* score and *eyes test* score. The *AQ* test consisted of 50 closed questions which were answered on a four-point scale.

Sample

▼ Table 2.8 Information about Groups 1 to 4

Group	Sample	Mean age	Mean IQ	Additional information
1 HFA/AS adults	15 male adults with HFA/AS	29.7	115	Volunteer sample from adverts in UK National Autistic Society magazine or support groups. All diagnosed using established criteria. Socioeconomic status and education level matched Group 2.
2 General population controls	122 neurotypical adults	46.5	–	From adult community and education classes in Exeter or public libraries in Cambridge (both UK). Broad range of occupations and education levels.
3 Students	103 (53 male and 50 female) neurotypical undergraduate students from Cambridge University	20.8	–	Assumed to have high IQ due to very high university entry requirements.
4 IQ-matched controls	14 randomly selected people from the general population	28.0	116	Matched on IQ and age to Group 1.

▶ PROCEDURE

▼ Table 2.9 Problems with the original *eyes test*

Problems with the original test	Solutions in the new test
There were only two possible responses for each question. A person would need to score more than 17 out of 25 to ensure their score was not due to chance.	To remedy these issues, Baron-Cohen *et al.*'s new test increased the number of items on the test (from 25 to 36) and increased the number of response options for each question (from 2 to 4).
Parents of children with autism scored similarly to people with HFA or AS, even though they did not have the condition themselves.	
There were not many possible scores above chance level, leading to a ceiling effect (see page 186). This meant that the test was not very sensitive to individual differences.	
Some items were too easy as they were basic mental states such as happy, sad and angry, which can even be determined by very young children.	The new version contained only complex mental states, requiring the attribution of a belief to a person.
Some items could be guessed from eye direction, such as 'noticing'.	These were omitted on the new test.
There were more female than male faces, which may have caused bias.	An equal number of male and female faces was used.
The target word and the foil (incorrect answer) were always semantic opposites (e.g. sad versus happy), which was too easy.	In the new version, the three foils were similar to the target word to increase difficulty.
It was unclear whether some people could understand all the words.	A glossary was included on the new version.

Participants in all four groups took the *revised eyes test* in a quiet room, alone, in either Exeter or Cambridge. The test required them to select which of four words matched the expression of a set of eyes. There was one correct answer and three foils for each set of eyes. Participants with HFA/ AS (Group 1) were also asked to determine the gender of the eyes as a control task. The other groups did not need to do this as neurotypical adults' scores have a ceiling effect. Participants were also asked if they were unsure of any words in the glossary and to read the meaning of these.

Eye test development

Two authors created the target words and foils for each item. These were then presented to groups of eight judges (four female and four male), who had to pick the target word to match each pair of eyes. Five out of eight judges needed to agree on the target word for an item to pass and no more than two judges could choose the same foil.

Furthermore, the data for Groups 2 and 3 were combined. For the 225 responses, at least 50 per cent needed to select the target word and no more than 25 per cent could select the same foil. Four out of 40 items failed to meet these criteria, leaving 36 items on the revised test.

▶ RESULTS

- Group 1's *eyes test* mean was significantly lower than the mean for the other groups.
- Females scored higher than males on the *eyes test*, although this result was not found to be significant.
- Group 1 scored significantly higher than Groups 3 and 4 on the *AQ*. (Note: Group 2 did not take the *AQ* test.)
- Males scored higher on the *AQ* than females.
- There was no correlation between *eyes test* score and IQ.
- There was a negative correlation between *AQ* score and *eyes test* score (−0.53) for all three groups.
- In the student group, the *eyes test* score was negatively correlated with the social skills category (−0.27) and communication category (−0.25) of the *AQ*.
- Adults with HFA/AS scored 33 out of 36 or above on the gender recognition test.

▶ CONCLUSIONS

The *revised eyes test* was successful in being a more sensitive test for adult social intelligence than the original test. Neurotypical adults scored significantly below the ceiling, allowing the test to be a more subtle measure of individual differences. Adults with HFA/AS were impaired on the test, but they could still identify the gender of the eyes successfully on the control task. This validates the test as a useful way to detect subtle impairments in social intelligence for those with normal IQs and can be used to distinguish adults with HFA/AS from controls.

As the *AQ* and *eyes test* scores were negatively correlated, this suggests that both can be used to measure the severity of autistic traits.

▶ LEARNING LINK

Both Baron-Cohen *et al.* (eyes test) and Milgram (obedience) used volunteer samples in their research, but for very different reasons. Milgram needed participants to arrive to be tested at Yale University at a specific time, requiring a significant commitment. Therefore, he needed his participants to be highly motivated. Baron-Cohen *et al.*, on the other hand, required participants from a very specific population: those with HFA/AS. What were the specific advantages and disadvantages of using a volunteer sample in these very different studies?

STUDY TIP

An important feature of this study is the problems with the original 'Reading the Mind in the Eyes' test and how the researchers developed the *revised eyes test* as a result. It is, therefore, critical to develop your understanding of the limitations of the original test and the implications these had. You also need to ensure you can explain how the revised version was developed and how the target words and foils were selected. This study focuses on the development of a new test, which differs from other key studies.

> ## TEST YOURSELF

1 Explain how one result from this study supports the concept of theory of mind. [2]
2 a Identify two problems with the original *eyes test*. [2]
  b Explain how each of these problems was overcome on the *revised eyes test*. [2]
3 Describe the results for the *eyes test* for two groups of participants. You must use data in your answer. [3]
4 Describe one of the negative correlations found in Baron-Cohen *et al.*'s study. [2]
5 Explain why the 'ceiling effect' in the original version of the *eyes test* was a problem. [1]
6 Outline two ways in which the *eyes test* was standardised. [2]

2.2.3 Evaluating Baron-Cohen *et al.* (eyes test)

Think!

Why is it important for the *eyes test* to collect quantitative data?

Think!

The *revised eyes test* is now available in an online format so you might like to have a go yourself. Remember, if you do this activity in class, confidentiality matters. The test has 36 pairs of eyes to think about. How did you feel about your performance by the time you reached some of the later items? Did you feel that you were getting better or worse?

Think!

What real-life uses can you think of for this test? What would be the advantages and disadvantages of making the test computerised?

Ethical issues

An ethical weakness of this study is that it might have caused psychological harm to participants with HFA/AS. When completing the test, they may not have been able to understand the emotions shown by many of the sets of eyes, which might have caused them distress or embarrassment. They might have left the study with lowered self-esteem as a result.

Methodological issues

Reliability

Standardisation

A strength of Baron-Cohen *et al.*'s study is the high level of standardisation. The *revised eyes test* has a standardised procedure with each participant seeing the same 36 pairs of eyes. Additionally, the images were always the same size, in black and white, with four options, including three foils. There was only ever one correct answer and all participants were provided with a glossary of terms. This high level of standardisation means other researchers can check the reliability of the findings and re-examine non-significant findings, such as the difference between males and females.

Validity

Lack of random allocation

However, a weakness was that participants could not be randomly allocated to groups, as the independent variables were naturally occurring (i.e. diagnosis of HFA/AS or male/female).

Due to this, there may have been participant variables between the groups, particularly as some participants were recruited via volunteer sampling, with each group being recruited in different ways and from different parts of the UK. The participants within each group may have had similar features to one another, causing them to perform better or worse on the *eyes test*. This would reduce the validity of the results as any differences between the HFA/AS group and the control conditions may not have been due to the independent variable.

Theory of mind

A weakness of the study is that it may not have been measuring theory of mind, as it claimed to. At best, the study only aimed to measure the first stage of theory of mind, that is, determining the mental state of a person. Theory of mind also involves a second stage of attributing the content of a mental state to a person – that is, understanding the reason behind their emotion – which the *eyes test* cannot measure. Therefore, the test may not be a valid measure of theory of mind.

Objectivity and subjectivity

Quantitative data

A strength of this study was that the data was objective, in that there was no interpretation necessary on the part of the researchers. The participants were either right or wrong in their answers as it was a fixed-choice task with pre-determined correct answers, leading to quantitative data. This means there was no room for researcher bias when analysing participants' answers as they simply had to tick whether the participant had chosen the correct target answer or one of the incorrect foils, increasing the study's validity.

Generalisations and ecological validity

Generalising beyond the sample

A weakness is that the findings may not be generalisable to other individuals with HFA/AS. The sample in the HFA/AS group was very small, with only 15 male adults who had self-selected to take part. This means that they were particularly motivated to take part in the research or had a special interest in the study. Therefore, they may not be representative of all individuals with high-functioning autism spectrum disorder (as it is known today).

Generalising to everyday life

A weakness of the *eyes test* is that the stimuli of eyes used are static and do not reflect the processing of human emotions in a real-life setting. Usually, people will use facial movements as well as verbal and non-verbal cues to detect the emotions of another person. This reduces the mundane realism (see page 141) of the test and means that the measurements taken do not reflect a person's real-world ability to determine the mental state of another individual.

> ### ISSUES AND DEBATES
>
> ### Individual and situational explanations
>
> Adults with HFA/AS scored lower on the *eyes test* compared to neurotypical adults, supporting an individual explanation for the cognitive processing of emotions shown by the facial expressions of others. However, it could be argued that people with HFA/AS are better at recognising emotions and mental states of others in some situations compared with others. For example, they may find this harder with some emotions than others (e.g. sad versus jealous) and they may find it easier in situations where there are fewer distractions and when they are allowed sufficient processing time.

Applications to everyday life

Other clinical groups

The *eyes test* may be used with other clinical groups, such as those with brain damage, to determine whether they have suffered deficits in social intelligence. If the patients were to gain a low score on the *eyes test* then they may be given support by a therapist to help them improve on their ability to detect emotions.

Education

As the HFA/AS group scored lower than neurotypical adults on the *eyes test*, the test could be used by teachers to determine a student's level of social intelligence. A low score would indicate that the student lacks theory of mind, so extra lessons might be given by educators to help them to improve their theory of mind skills.

Reflections

Baron-Cohen *et al.*'s research was conducted in 2001 and the *eyes test* is a pencil and paper test, which they acknowledge does not represent the dynamic movements used to display emotions in real life. The researchers suggest using a computerised version of the test to record people's reaction times on the test. One step further would be to include video footage of people expressing different emotions and use these to create a more dynamic and valid test of people's social sensitivity.

▶ LEARNING LINK

This study relied on the use of questionnaires to gain quantitative data. Saavedra and Silverman (button boy) also used questionnaires to gain quantitative data about a nine-year-old boy's phobia of buttons. These two studies differed in their use of the data, however. In Baron-Cohen *et al.*'s study, they used the data to compare different groups of individuals. They were investigating a stable trait in adulthood. In the study by Saavedra and Silverman, they used their questionnaire to compare the boy's score before and after treatment to see if there was an improvement in symptoms. In both studies, there were significant advantages of using quantitative data for comparisons. What do you think these advantages are? Can you think of any disadvantages?

STUDY TIP

This research involved experiments, but these were not laboratory or field experiments as the researchers did not have any control over the independent variables (i.e. they could not assign people randomly to the HFA/AS or male/female groups as these are naturally occurring variables). In psychology, an experiment with a naturally occurring independent variable is called a 'quasi experiment', where the Latin term *quasi* means 'having some, but not all of the features'. You can simply refer to Baron-Cohen *et al.* as an experiment. However, be careful not to evaluate this study as a laboratory or field experiment, as it is neither.

▶ TEST YOURSELF

1 Suggest one disadvantage of the *eyes test* being a 'pen and paper' test. [2]
2 Suggest one real-life application of Baron-Cohen's study based on the findings. [2]
3 Evaluate the study by Baron-Cohen *et al.* in terms of two strengths and two weaknesses. At least one of your evaluation points must be about the use of self-reports. [10]
4 Explain one strength of the use of closed questions in the *eyes test*. [2]
5 Explain one strength and one weakness of using volunteer sampling to recruit the Group 1 participants with HFA/AS in this study. [2]
6 Describe two ways in which this study was not valid. [4]

2.3 Pozzulo *et al.* (line-ups)

2.3.1 Background

Think!

Are children more likely to make mistakes on **target-present** or **target-absent line-ups**? How does Pozzulo *et al.* explain this?

Think!

Imagine what it might be like to view a 'live line-up' from behind a one-way mirror (maybe you have actually had this experience and know exactly what it was like). Do you think people are more likely to make accurate **identification** when shown a live line-up or a set of photographs or video clips? Do you think it would make any difference if the images were presented simultaneously (altogether) or sequentially (one after the other)?

Think!

Previous research suggests young children perform poorly on target-absent line-ups. When the police create a line-up, they do not always know whether the true culprit is present or absent. How could the police ensure that children understand that they do not have to pick anyone out of the line-up unless they are sure that the culprit is present?

KEY TERMS

line-up (including target-present and target-absent)

identification

eyewitness testimony

confabulation

false positive responses

false memories

Introducing Joanna Pozzulo

Dr Joanna Pozzulo is Chair of the Psychology Department at Carleton University, Ontario, Canada, and Director of the Child Forensic Psychology Laboratory. Her research focuses on differences between the way children and adults perform as witnesses to a crime, specifically the cognitive and social processes involved in recalling the event and recognising the culprit. Dr Pozzulo aims to develop evidence-based, age-appropriate procedures with the ultimate goal of reducing wrongful convictions.

▲ Figure 2.11 Dr Joanna Pozzulo

Better that ten guilty persons escape, than that one innocent suffer.

William Blackstone, English jurist

You can find out more about Dr Pozzulo's work here: **https://carleton.ca/childforensicpsychology/**

To learn more about wrongful convictions based on flawed line-ups, see **https://innocenceproject.org/eyewitness-identification-reform/**

Forensic psychologist Professor Becky Milne from the University of Portsmouth, UK, describes the memory of eyewitnesses 'like snow', initially pure, it rapidly becomes dirty and contaminated. She adds, 'I would love to put police tape around everyone's head because the brain is a scene in its own right. That scene also needs protection' (Milne, 2021). Why do you think some memories become more 'contaminated' than others?

▲ Figure 2.12 Professor Becky Milne from the University of Portsmouth, UK likens eyewitness memory to snow. What are the similarities and differences between snow and memory?

The psychology being investigated

Eyewitness testimony

People who were present at the scene of an accident or crime are often questioned by the police and asked to provide a description of what they saw, heard and/or smelt. These descriptions are called **eyewitness testimonies**. They are an important part of many police investigations and often provide crucial evidence in subsequent legal proceedings. Although jurors often find eyewitness testimonies compelling, decades of research suggest they are unreliable (Hope, 2010). Memory is reconstructive, meaning it may be altered with each retelling and can become contaminated by post-event information (see Figure 2.12). Memory also degrades over time, underlining the importance of developing techniques that allow officers to elicit accurate information as quickly as possible. For this reason, eyewitness testimony has become a rich area for forensic researchers and their work has directly impacted the way witnesses are interviewed (Fisher and Schreiber, 2017).

One problem with eyewitness testimony is that memory distortion can lead people to remember things that did not happen and forget things that did. Witnesses often incorrectly remember details of real events – for example, identifying a person who is subsequently shown to have been elsewhere. Research suggests that people often 'fill in the gaps' in their memories in a process called **confabulation**. Over time, these inaccuracies can become indistinguishable from the more accurate aspects of the memory.

False positive responses

Forensic researchers often ask participants to observe a staged crime/event and then to identify the culprit (person who committed the crime) from a selection of people, called a line-up (see below). Sometimes the culprit is present (target-present line-up) and sometimes not (target-absent line-up). There are a number of possible responses in a target-present line-up: a correct identification, a **false positive response** (incorrectly choosing a foil) or a false negative (incorrectly stating that the suspect is absent). In a target-absent line-up, the participants are correct if they reject the line-up (no possibility of false negatives) but they may still make a false positive response by selecting a foil.

Background

The reliability of children as eyewitnesses is relatively understudied compared to adults, but Canadian researcher Dr Joanna Pozzulo has dedicated her research to reducing wrongful convictions through the development of evidence-based, age-appropriate techniques for working with child witnesses.

Line-ups and identification

Pozzulo *et al.*'s research focuses specifically on the use of line-ups in the identification of suspects. In real police investigations, eyewitnesses may be asked to view a line-up. They will be asked whether the culprit (the person who committed the crime) is present in a line-up made up of a suspect (someone the police believe committed the crime) and a small number of 'foils'. The foils are generally people who look physically similar to the suspect. A variety of line-up formats exist, including live line-ups (physically present suspects, who are viewed from behind a one-way mirror) and photographs and/or videos of suspects. Witnesses may view the individuals simultaneously (all at the same time) or sequentially (one after the other) (Fitzgerald *et al.*, 2018).

Children as witnesses

Joanna Pozzulo and Roderick Lindsay (1998) conducted a meta-analysis, which demonstrated that children as young as five are relatively accurate when faced with a target-present, simultaneous line-up, but children as old as 13 struggle to correctly reject target-absent line-ups. While these errors are likely due to a combination of cognitive and social factors, Pozzulo *et al.* highlight the role of social influence and the desire to please the interviewer as prominent issues affecting their accuracy with target-absent line-ups. As children are more likely to perceive the adult (researcher or police officer) as an authority figure, they are more likely to identify a foil, not realising that rejecting the line-up is also an acceptable response.

Pozzulo *et al.* in brief

To explore whether children's errors in line-ups result more from social or cognitive factors, Pozzulo *et al.* manipulated the familiarity of the target. They suggest that children who can pick out a popular cartoon character with 100 per cent accuracy, logically should be able to reject a target-absent line-up, where the character is not present. If they do not do this, social factors are implicated as a cause of false positive responses when identifying human faces. In their study, four-to-seven-year-olds and adults were shown films of easily recognisable cartoon characters and unknown human actors, before being presented with either a target-present or a target-absent line-up. As expected, the children were easily able to identify the cartoons in target-present line-ups but still made mistakes on target-absent line-ups. They made more mistakes than the adults and this was even more pronounced with unknown human faces compared with the cartoons. The influence of social factors appears to be at least partly responsible for the children's errors, suggesting that minimising these factors could allow children to give accurate testimonies.

Plan your own... correlation

Pozzulo *et al.* designed a laboratory experiment to investigate factors affecting memory for target faces in a line-up. Why not try designing a correlation to investigate the memory of eyewtinesses?

Imagine...

Kaira is planning a correlation to investigate accuracy of eyewitness testimony (EWT) and confidence levels in children who have witnessed a staged crime.
>> What advice would you give Kaira about how to conduct her correlation?

Planning a correlation

Correlation is a non-experimental method. There are no independent variables; instead the researcher measures two or more co-variables to see if they are related to one another. As there are no manipulated or controlled variables, causality cannot be inferred and all that can be concluded is the strength, direction and significance of the relationship(s). See page 192 for more information on correlations.

▼ Table 2.10 Features of a correlation

Main features of a correlation	Consider...
Two co-variables	Correlations look at the relationship between two measured, quantitative variables. Think carefully about the operational definition of each. How might Kaira operationalise 'confidence levels' and 'accuracy of eyewitness testimony (EWT)'?
Measure of variable 1	How can Kaira measure a child's confidence levels? What data will she collect on this?
Measure of variable 2	How can Kaira collect data on children's accuracy of eyewitness testimony? What data collection method might she use?
Comparison and scatter graph	Correlations involve the collection of quantitative data, which should be presented on a scatter graph. How will Kaira present her data on a scatter graph?

Evaluating your plan

▼ Table 2.11 Evaluating your plan

Kaira shares your ideas with her peers. Some of them think it is a great idea; others are not so sure. Think about the practical strengths and weaknesses of your suggestions.

	Describe	Explain
Strengths	Think about your data collection techniques. In what way did they ensure that the data collected was valid and/or reliable?	How might this strength affect any findings about any relationship between the accuracy of children's EWTs and their confidence levels?
Weaknesses	A weakness of correlations is that cause and effect cannot be established. Why is this an issue?	How might this weakness affect any findings about the relationship between the accuracy of children's EWTs and their confidence levels?
Improvements	Consider the data collection techniques you suggested to Kaira. In what way might these be improved to collect more valid/reliable data?	What impact might this have on Kaira's findings about any relationship between the accuracy of children's EWTs and their confidence levels?

In 2018, Malcolm Alexander was released from prison in Angola after serving almost 38 years for a crime he did not commit. Mistakenly identified following a photo line-up, he was finally exonerated (had his name cleared and was released) on the basis of post-conviction DNA evidence (The Innocence Project, 2021). Can you think of any ways to reduce the cases of mistaken identity such as this? You can find out more about this case here: **https://innocenceproject.org/cases/ malcolm-alexander/**

▶ LEARNING LINK

In the social approach, you will learn about social influence, which refers to the ways in which our behaviour is affected by our relationships with other people. In a now legendary experiment, Milgram (obedience) demonstrated that when we perceive a person to have legitimate authority, we will go to great lengths to obey their demands, even if they conflict with our own personal beliefs about right and wrong. Pozzulo et al.'s research highlights the relationship between the child witness and the police officer conducting the line-up. She proposes that aspects of this relationship shape the child's response. Considering Milgram's research, how do you think children's answers might differ if the police officer was in plain clothes rather than a uniform?

STUDY TIP

Some of the terms used in this study may be a bit confusing at first, such as culprit and suspect, target-absent and target-present, false positive and false negative. Why not create a video clip of a staged crime (not too dramatic – think about the ethics!) including a culprit and then create target-present and target-absent live, photo and video line-ups. This should help you to get to grips with the terminology: culprits are guilty, suspects can be guilty or innocent, and foils are chosen because they look similar to the suspect but are innocent. Create images to put in your revision notes which show your understanding of each of these important key terms.

► TEST YOURSELF

1 Describe what is meant by 'eyewitness testimony'. [2]

2 Pozzulo *et al.* studied line-ups, which are a common part of police investigations. Explain two different types of line-up used in psychological research. [2]

3 State one reason that children may be more likely to mistakenly identify a foil in target-absent line-ups compared with adults. [1]

4 Romelie is investigating whether child witnesses make more correct identifications when the culprit is a child compared with an adult. State the operationalised independent and dependent variables in her study. [4]

5 In his line-up study, Esra reminds half of his participants that the culprit may not be present, but he does not give this instruction to the other participants. He records the amount of time the participants take before giving their answer. State the graphing technique that Esra should use to present his data. [1]

6 Dasha is interested in how police officers feel about current interviewing techniques used to gather evidence from eyewitnesses. Describe how Dasha might conduct unstructured interviews to investigate how police officers feel about current interviewing techniques. [10]

(See page 184 for tips on planning a study using unstructured interviews.)

2.3.2 Describing Pozzulo *et al.* (line-ups)

Think!

Why did the line-ups include a silhouetted person?

Think!

Have you ever witnessed a crime or an incident where you have been asked to give a description of someone? How do you think it would feel to be interviewed about something like this? How might these feelings affect the information that you provide?

Think!

The researchers in this study deliberately chose to wear smart-casual clothing, but they avoided an overly formal appearance. Why do you think this was important and how might this relate to the questioning of child witnesses in the real world?

METHODOLOGY

laboratory experiment

interview

questionnaire

It looks like the police officer in Figure 2.13 is getting on well with the young witness. How might this affect the boy's response if the police officer were to ask him if he was able to pick out a culprit from a target-absent line-up?

► Figure 2.13 A child's view of an authority figure, such as a police officer, may affect their subsequent responses

AIMS

This study aimed to explore the role of social and cognitive factors in children's identification of target faces in line-ups. Specifically, they aimed to investigate whether children:

● are less able to recognise human faces than adults
● make more false positive identifications than adults when faced with:
  – target-absent line-ups versus target-present line-ups
  – human faces and cartoon characters.

RESEARCH METHODOLOGY

Participants observed video clips in a controlled setting before trying to identify the target person from the video in different types of line-up. Two of the three independent variables were manipulated by the experimenter (see below), making Pozzulo *et al.* a laboratory experiment.

Design and variables

There were three independent variables:
● age – young children or adults
● nature of target faces – familiar cartoon characters or unfamiliar human faces
● type of line-up – target-present or target-absent.

The first independent variable compares data from different people (independent measures), while the second and third independent variables compare data from different conditions, involving the same people (repeated measures).

The four videos (male cartoon – Diego, female cartoon – Dora, male actor, female actor) were randomised for each participant to avoid order effects. The order of the faces (targets and/or foils) in the line-ups was also randomised.

There were two dependent variables, correct identification rates for target-present line-ups and correct rejection rates for target-absent line-ups.

Sample

Children aged four to seven (21 female and 38 male, mean age = 4.98 years, standard deviation 0.82) were selected from three private schools in Eastern Ontario, Canada. Adults aged 17–30 (36 females and 17 males, mean age = 20.54 years, standard deviation = 3.34) were selected from the Introductory Psychology Participant Pool of an Eastern Ontario university.

PROCEDURE

Creating the video clips and photo-array line-ups

The researchers created four video clips, two starring the familiar cartoon characters Dora and Diego. Dora was speaking to the audience in one video and Diego was putting on safety gloves in the other. The other two clips separately included a male and a female main character but this time the actors were humans, matched for age and ethnicity (both were 22 years old and Caucasian). The woman was brushing her hair and the man was putting on his coat. All clips were in colour, with no sound, six seconds long and each featured a two-to-three second close-up of the person's face. There was only ever one character per clip.

Each video had an accompanying photo-array line-up of four tightly cropped, black-and-white headshots. In the target-present line-ups, one of the photographs was the target person/cartoon character (but dressed differently from the video clip) and the other three photographs were foils, meaning people who looked similar (e.g. similar facial structure, hair length and colour), but were not the target. In the target-absent condition, the target was swapped for another foil in the same position. All line-ups included a silhouette as a visual reminder that the genuine target may not be present. All images were viewed together, at the same time.

Human foils were selected from a set of 90 male and 90 female faces by a panel of three researchers. Cartoon foils were selected online due to their similarity to the target. As Dora and Diego generally wear the same brightly coloured clothes all the time, the images for the line-up were tightly cropped black-and-white photographs. This meant participants could not identify them based on their clothing rather than their faces.

Before the testing phase

The parents of the child participants completed informed consent forms and the Demographic and Cartoon Watching Form, an eight-item questionnaire. Parents were asked to estimate how long their child spent watching cartoons each week and of this how much time was spent watching *Dora the Explorer* and *Go, Diego, Go!* They were also asked their child's age, gender, primary language and ethnicity and whether they had any siblings.

Children were tested individually at their schools. The four female researchers were introduced as people from the university doing research on television shows and computer games. Before starting the experiment, the children and the researchers participated in some craft activities together to get to know each other. The adult participants completed their own paperwork and were told the study was about memory.

Watching the videos

The child participants were told they would be watching some videos and to pay attention as they would be asked some questions and shown some pictures afterwards. The first video was shown once the child seemed happy and ready. After each clip, they were asked, 'What did the cartoon character/person look like?' and 'Do you remember anything else?' If they did not answer, they were asked, 'Do you remember anything from the video?' The researcher spent two minutes on this filler task and wrote the children's answers down, although they would not be analysed. The procedure was identical for the adults, except they wrote down their own answers.

The photo-array line-ups

Participants were given the following standardised instructions: 'Please look at the photos. The person/cartoon from the video may or may not be here. If you see the person/cartoon, please point to the photo. If you do not see the person/cartoon, please point to this box.'

The line-ups were shown using presentation software on a laptop. The adults completed the same procedure, but they recorded their answers on a sheet rather than pointing to the screen.

After testing was complete

The child participants were thanked and given gifts of crayons and a colouring book. The adult participants completed the Demographic and Cartoon Watching Form after the testing phase and finally were debriefed and thanked.

▶ RESULTS

Target-present line-ups

As expected, the children were significantly better at identifying familiar cartoon characters in target-present line-ups than unfamiliar human faces. Their success rate was 0.99 compared with just 0.23 for unfamiliar human faces. The adults were also significantly better when faced with target-present cartoon line-ups (0.95) than unfamiliar faces, but their success rate was much higher than the children's (0.66). There was no significant difference in the success rate of adults and children in identifying the cartoon characters.

Target-absent line-ups

Again, as predicted, the children had a significantly higher success rate with target-absent line-ups including cartoon characters (0.74) compared with human faces (0.45). The adults also performed significantly better with the cartoon characters (0.94) compared with the human faces (0.70) and their performance was also significantly better than the children for both cartoon and human faces. Table 2.12 shows that children had a much higher rate of false positives (incorrectly choosing a foil) compared with adults. Although the rate of false negatives (incorrectly stating that the target is absent) was also higher for children, the difference was smaller than it was for false positives.

As the children were clearly able to pick out Dora and Diego in target-present line-ups, the lower rate of correct responses (0.74) in the target-absent line-ups demonstrates that their false positives are likely to be driven by social factors rather than cognitive factors – that is, the children probably knew that the character was not in the line-up but felt that the social situation required them to pick someone out, despite being told this was not the case.

▼ Table 2.12 Response rates for identifications from target-present and target-absent line-ups. False negative means the participant incorrectly rejected the line-up (stating that the target was not present when they were); false positive means a participant incorrectly identified a foil as the target

		Children	Adults
Cartoon characters	Target present	Dora: 1.0	Dora: 1.0
		Diego: 0.97 False negatives: 0.03	Diego: 0.89 False negatives: 0.11
	Target absent	Dora: 0.80 False positives: 0.20	Dora: 0.96 False positives: 0.04
		Diego: 0.67 False positives: 0.33	Diego: 0.92 False positives: 0.08
Human faces	Target present	Female 0.24 False positives: 0.38 False negatives: 0.38	Female: 0.46 False negatives: 0.54
		Male: 0.21 False positives: 0.45 False negatives: 0.34	Male: 0.85 False positives: 0.15
	Target absent	Female: 0.47 False positives: 0.53	Female: 0.72 False positives: 0.28
		Male: 0.43 False positives: 0.57	Male 0.67 False positives: 0.33

CONCLUSIONS

The researchers concluded that, since the children were able to identify the cartoon characters with almost 100 per cent accuracy in target-present line-ups, cognitive factors (e.g. faulty memory) were not responsible for the lower success rate in correctly rejecting the **foils** in the target-absent line-ups. They were clearly able to recognise the characters and, therefore, logically should have been able to recognise that none of the foils was Dora or Diego; yet some of the children still made errors. Pozzulo *et al.* conclude that these errors must be caused by social factors – that is, incorrectly believing that the researcher would prefer them to make a positive identification, regardless of whether they felt it was right or wrong, and despite the researcher saying that the target person may not be in the line-up. It was also concluded, as expected, that children are less accurate than adults when faced with unfamiliar human actors and generally more prone to giving false positive responses (incorrect identification).

Dora the Explorer is an instantly recognisable cartoon character for many kindergarten children in the USA. Figure 2.14 shows her at a Thanksgiving Day parade in Times Square, New York. Why do you think Pozzulo *et al.* used black-and-white images of both Dora and Diego and the human targets?

► Figure 2.14 Dora the Explorer

▶ LEARNING LINK

This study uses foils, meaning people placed into the line-up who are not the target person. This is done to see whether the participant is able to make an accurate identification. In the target-present line-up, there were three foils in addition to the person from the video clip. Pozzulo *et al.* were very careful when they selected their foils as they wanted the foils' physical appearance to be similar to the target person. The study by Baron-Cohen *et al.* (eyes test) also used foils. Can you think of one way in which the foils in Baron-Cohen *et al.* are similar to Pozzulo *et al.* and one way in which they are different?

STUDY TIP

Think about how the procedure and findings differed for the child versus the adult participants. Venn diagrams can be a great way to analyse studies in terms of similarities and differences. You will need two large overlapping circles, one labelled 'Adults' and one labelled 'Children'. In the intersection (where the circles overlap), write everything about the procedure that was the same for both adults and children. In the rest of the adult circle, write anything that was specific to the adults only – for example, they completed the consent forms and questionnaires themselves. Next, in the child circle, write what was unique about the procedure for them – for example, the parents completed the consent forms and questionnaire on their behalf. In a different coloured pen, you could explain why these changes were made or, in the case of the findings, why you think these differences arose, with reference to social and cognitive factors.

▶ TEST YOURSELF

1   Outline two reasons Pozzulo *et al.* asked participants to complete the Demographic and Cartoon Watching Form.   [2]
2   Pozzulo *et al.* created line-ups using photographs. Identify two things that were the same about all the photographs used in this study.   [2]
3   Explain how two results from the study by Pozzulo *et al.* support one or more of the assumptions of the cognitive approach.   [4]
4   Explain two similarities between a laboratory experiment and a field experiment, using Pozzulo *et al.* as an example.   [4]
5   Pozzulo *et al.* used standardised instructions and questions. Explain one reason standardisation may be difficult in a study comparing adults and children.   [2]
6   Describe one controlled and one uncontrolled variable from the study by Pozzulo *et al.*   [2]

2.3.3 Evaluating Pozzulo *et al.* (line-ups)

Think!

Pozzulo *et al.* randomised the order the video clips were shown in for each participant and the order of the target and foils in the line-ups. How might they have done this and how would it improve the findings of the study?

Think!

Imagine you are a research assistant on Dr Pozzulo's team. You will be testing the children at their schools. You will meet the children and do a craft activity with them before the testing. Do you think meeting the children first will affect how they perform in the study? Do you think false positive responses will be more or less likely, and why?

> **Think!**
>
> Pozzulo *et al.* compared recognition of familiar cartoon characters and unfamiliar human actors. Can you think of any other conditions that they could have used to improve their study further?

Can you think of two reasons why none of the photos in Figure 2.15 would have made it into one of Pozzulo *et al.*'s photo-arrays? The correct answer should help you to create another validity point.

▶ Figure 2.15 When creating the photo-array line-ups, three raters selected 'foils' with similar facial structure, hair length and colouring to the human actor targets

Ethical issues

One strength of Pozzulo *et al.*'s study is that, despite exploring false memory and using target-absent line-ups, there was no deception. All participants were informed before the study began that they would be asked about the videos afterwards and when shown the photo-array line-ups they were told that the person may not be present. This is important as studies of false memory often attempt to manipulate people's recall, which could make them more vulnerable to psychological harm and which means that fully informed consent is not possible.

Methodological issues

Reliability

A strength of Pozzulo *et al.*'s study is the standardised procedure and instructions, which means the study can be easily replicated. All participants were told to watch carefully as there would be questions afterwards and pictures to look at. They all completed a two-minute filler task, answering the researcher's open questions about what they remembered. Finally, they were all given the same instructions about identifying the target, including the fact that 'the person may or may not be in the line-up'. This means the study can be easily replicated to check whether the high level of false positive responses in target-absent line-ups is reliable.

A weakness regarding reliability is the fact that the researchers did not ask everyone the exact same questions as part of the two-minute filler task; some people were asked two questions and some were asked three questions. This depended on how much information they had already provided. These questions may seem inconsequential, as the data was not analysed, but participants may have gone into the line-up task with different confidence levels based on how they had answered the previous questions and this might have altered how they responded in the line-up task.

Validity

The use of the repeated measures was a strength of this study that increased the internal validity of the findings. Participants took part in both types of line-up with both types of target (human and cartoon). Performance in the target-present line-up helped to provide a baseline with which performance in the target-absent condition could be compared. If the researchers had used an independent measures design, the argument that poorer performance in the target-absent condition resulted from social not cognitive factors would not be so compelling. This is because it could have been caused by participant variables – that is, one group might have had slightly better or worse facial recognition or working memory skills.

A weakness of the design was that, although the researchers suggested that they were manipulating familiarity when they used popular cartoon characters versus unknown human actors, they were actually altering two things: familiarity and whether the character is a two-dimensional animation or a three-dimensional human. This is important as it makes it hard to interpret the findings as it is possible that we are just better at remembering two-dimensional characters due to their decreased complexity as opposed to their familiarity.

A final strength was the high degree of control that was possible due to the carefully created materials (the video clips and photo-arrays). Pozzulo *et al.* aimed to manipulate two things in the videos: whether the characters were cartoons or humans and the gender of the character (male or female). They ensured that as far as possible everything else remained the same – for example, all videos were in colour, had no sound, included a 2–3-second close-up of the target and were the same overall length (six seconds). Similar attention to detail in the construction of the photo-arrays meant that any difference in performance in the line-up task was likely to be caused by the type of target in combination with the type of line-up and not the unintentional influence of confounding variables.

Objectivity and subjectivity

A strength of the study is that Pozzulo *et al.* tried to minimise subjectivity in the choice of foils for the photo-arrays. This was done by having three raters who were shown around ten different cartoons as potential foils for each target. They rated the photographs for similarity to the target and the top four were chosen. This was important as the degree of similarity between the foils and the targets could have become a confounding variable, so it was important to establish agreement between several people as to the best faces to use in each condition.

Generalisations and ecological validity

Generalising beyond the sample

A weakness is that the findings may not be generalisable to participants from lower socioeconomic backgrounds. The children were all from private schools, suggesting that they were from relatively wealthy families, while the adults were drawn from a university participant pool, suggesting that the majority were students. They were all under 30 years of age, suggesting that the majority had limited life experience. These factors are important as children and adults from lower socioeconomic backgrounds, including those who do not speak the majority language, may be even more vulnerable to social factors when being interviewed or giving evidence. They are also more likely to be victims of crime and thus more likely to become witnesses. This suggests that researchers in the field of forensic psychology must diversify their samples to improve experiences within the justice systems for all, regardless of social background.

Generalising to everyday life

A weakness of this laboratory experiment is the artificial nature of the video clips that the participants observed. Although clips were brief, as may be the case when catching a fleeting glance of a culprit in a real-life situation, the witness would also have been exposed to other sensory information, including sound and smell, which can act as powerful memory cues. The time between encoding and retrieval was extremely short. Lastly, the mixture of cartoon character and human faces and the consecutive nature of the trials all reduce ecological validity. The difference in the number of errors made by the adults and the children may, therefore, have been less pronounced under more realistic circumstances, where adults may have made more errors and children may have made fewer.

ISSUES AND DEBATES

The use of children in psychological research

This study used young children aged four to seven, who are often particularly vulnerable to social pressure. When questioned by unfamiliar adults, they are likely to give answers that they think the adults want to hear. For this reason, the researchers told the children they 'could change their minds at any time and not get into trouble'. To help the children to feel motivated and more comfortable, the researchers participated in some crafting activities with them before introducing the experiment. They also dressed in smart but informal clothing as they knew outward signs of authority (e.g. badges/lanyards, uniforms) might make children more compliant than usual. The researchers also carefully monitored the children for signs of fatigue, anxiety and stress to protect them from harm as children may be less likely to exercise their right to withdraw.

Applications to everyday life

Police work and criminal justice

Countless miscarriages of justice have resulted from jurors' over-reliance on compelling, but questionable, eyewitness testimony. This underlines the importance of evidence-based practice, especially when working with witnesses whose testimonies may be easily influenced by the perceived expectations of others. These findings may be used to help the police to develop guidelines for interviewing child witnesses in order to reduce their tendency to make an incorrect identification instead of rejecting a target-absent line-up.

Reflections

Pozzulo *et al.*'s findings suggest that many young children may be capable of supplying invaluable evidence, if social factors that increase inaccuracy are minimised. It should be remembered that adults are not immune to these issues, meaning research that improves children's testimonies may also be helpful when working with other vulnerable witnesses, such as people with learning disabilities or mental health issues. While the findings of this study underline this problem, other research is ongoing into alternatives to the traditional line-up tasks, including the use of registered intermediaries (RIs) in the UK (Wilcock *et al.*, 2018).

How can the reliability of children's testimonies be improved according to Pozzulo *et al.*?

▶ Figure 2.16 Pozzulo and her colleagues' work has far-reaching implications. While jurors need to understand the limitations of children's testimonies, it is also critical that children's voices are not ignored in the justice system

LEARNING LINK

When evaluating research, psychologists often discuss demand characteristics, those subtle, generally unintentional cues often present in laboratory studies. These cues may lead participants to behave in ways they believe are expected of them. When participants respond to demand characteristics, it decreases the validity of the findings as behaviour is no longer spontaneous. There is a clear parallel here to the social factors that Pozzulo *et al.* say are responsible for the errors that

children (and sometimes adults) make when attempting to identify suspects (Wells and Luus, 1990). Double-blind designs can overcome such problems: the hypotheses are withheld so that the participants remain naive to the researchers' expectations and in addition the researchers responsible for collecting and analysing the data are unaware of the specific group or condition to which each participant was allocated. How could the study by Pozzulo *et al.* be adapted to reduce demand characteristics?

STUDY TIP

In the 'Test yourself' questions below, you will see an 8-mark 'issues and debates' question, which should take you around 12 minutes to answer. You may not need this long to write your answer but you do need to think carefully about what you write, so take your time. Think carefully and note down as many findings as you can think of. Next, think about the debate you have been asked about (i.e. which findings go with individual explanations and which go with situational explanations). If the researcher has manipulated a variable in order to compare behaviour under different circumstances, this will support situational explanations (i.e. that people's behaviour changes according to the situation). If the researchers find that people's behaviour differs from each other under the same circumstances, then this supports individual explanations (i.e. people experience the world and behave differently to each other due to factors such as prior experience and personality).

TEST YOURSELF

1. Studies from the cognitive approach have real-world applications. Describe how the results of the study by Pozzulo *et al.* can be applied within the criminal justice system. [4]
2. Explain one result from the study by Pozzulo *et al.* that supports individual explanations of false memory and one result that supports situational explanations of false memory. [8]
3. Evaluate the study by Pozzulo *et al.* in terms of two strengths and two weaknesses. At least one of your evaluation points must be about generalisations. [10]
4. Outline one strength of the sampling technique used to recruit the adults in the study by Pozzulo *et al.* [2]
5. Explain what is meant by 'order effects' and give one example of how they were controlled in this study. [3]
6. Give one difference between quantitative data and qualitative data. Use examples from this study in your answer. [4]

CHAPTER SUMMARY

Andrade (doodling)

Psychology investigated
Andrade proposes that doodling can enhance attention and lead to better memory.

Aim
To investigate whether doodling aids concentration on a boring task and later recall of auditory information.

Procedure
Participants were divided into two groups: doodling or control. They listened to a very boring telephone recording about a party in a quiet room alone. The doodling group shaded shapes as they listened and all participants wrote down the names of party-goers. There was a surprise memory test afterwards for names and places.

Results
- Monitoring performance was significantly higher in the doodling group.
- The total recall score (out of 16) was 29 per cent higher in the doodling group.

Conclusion
Doodling can improve concentration and memory when the task involves listening, when it is boring and when recall is unexpected.

Strengths
- The study used experimental methods, so the cause and effect of doodling on memory could be found.
- Quantitative data was collected so the results of the doodling and control groups could be compared.

Weaknesses
- A high number of females in the study means results about doodling cannot be generalised to males.
- The quiet laboratory setting does not reflect real-life memory tasks.

Links to assumptions
As recall of auditory information was significantly higher in the doodling group, this shows that memory recall can be explained in terms of the role of thinking processes like attention. People may have the same information processing pathways, which are affected by situational factors.

Links to issues and debates

Doodling was shown to aid memory recall, showing that situational factors can affect attention and memory.

A real-life application is to encourage students to doodle in the classroom to improve attention and, therefore, memory.

Similarities

● Both Andrade and Baron-Cohen *et al.* collected quantitative data.
● Both Andrade and Pozzulo *et al.* investigated memory recall.

Differences

● Andrade used both children and adults as participants, while Baron-Cohen *et al.* only used adults.
● Andrade deceived participants about a surprise test, while Pozzulo *et al.* did not use deception.

Baron-Cohen *et al.* (eyes test)

Psychology investigated

Baron-Cohen *et al.* created a test for theory of mind, which refers to the ability to determine the mental state of another person or ourselves, otherwise known as social sensitivity.

Aims

To see if the deficits on the original test were still seen for adults with HFA/AS on the Revised Eyes Test. To see if there was a negative correlation between Eyes Test score and AQ score and if females scored higher than males on the Eyes Test.

Procedure

A group of adults with HFA/AS were compared with three control groups on the Revised Eyes Test: general population, students and IQ-matched controls. Participants took the test in a quiet room and were required to select which of four words matched the expression of a set of eyes. There was one correct answer and three foils for each set of eyes.

Results

● Adults with HFA/AS performed significantly worse on the Eyes Test than the other groups.
● There was a negative correlation between AQ score and Eyes Test score (–0.53).
● Females scored higher than males on the Eyes Test, although the result was not significant.

Conclusion

The Eyes Test is a valid way to detect subtle impairments in social intelligence for those with normal IQs.

Strengths

● The Eyes Test was highly standardised: it always had the same sets of eyes and responses.
● The study used control conditions to compare to adults with HFA/AS, increasing the validity of findings.

Weaknesses

● There was a lack of random allocation to groups, which may lead to participant variables affecting Eyes Test scores.
● The Eyes Test uses static eyes, which does not reflect real-life judgements of expression.

Links to assumptions

There were differences in Eyes Test score between individuals with HFA/AS and neurotypical controls, showing that there are individual differences in people's cognitive processing of emotions shown by facial expressions.

Links to issues and debates

Adults with HFA/AS scored lower on the Eyes Test than neurotypical adults, supporting individual explanations for cognitive processing.

A real-life application is the use of the Eyes Test with other clinical groups to determine deficits in social intelligence.

Similarities

● Both Baron-Cohen *et al.* and Andrade had participants complete their tests in a quiet room.
● Both Baron-Cohen *et al.* and Pozzulo *et al.* used independent measures designs.

Differences

● Baron-Cohen *et al.* did not deceive participants, while Andrade used deception with a surprise memory test.
● Baron-Cohen *et al.* compared the performance of males and females, while Pozzulo *et al.* compared the performance of children and adults.

Pozzulo *et al.* (line-ups)

Psychology investigated

Pozzulo *et al.* investigated the accuracy of eyewitness testimonies for children, specifically factors that affect false positive responses when asked to select someone they had previously seen from a line-up.

Aim

To investigate whether children are less able to recognise human faces than adults and make more false positive identifications for target-absent line-ups.

Procedure

Four-to-seven-year-old children and adults were shown films of easily recognisable cartoon characters and unknown human actors, before being presented with either a target-present or target-absent line-up. They were asked to identify each of the characters or actors they had seen in four separate line-ups.

Results

Children were easily able to identify the cartoons in target-present line-ups but still made mistakes on target-absent line-ups. They made more mistakes than the adults and this was more pronounced with unknown human faces compared with the cartoons.

Conclusion

The influence of social factors appears to be at least partly responsible for children's errors in target-absent line-ups.

Strengths

- The standardised procedure of the instructions and line-ups means the study can be easily replicated.
- Quantitative data was collected in the form of correct or incorrect responses, reducing subjectivity in data analysis.

Weaknesses

- A lack of consistency in the number of questions asked to participants during the filler task reduced reliability.
- 2D cartoons were compared to 3D human faces, reducing the validity of the comparison.

Links to assumptions

Children were able to identify the cartoon characters in line-ups with almost 100 per cent accuracy, the same as adults, suggesting that information is processed through the same route in all humans: input – process – output.

Links to issues and debates

This study used young children, so to help them feel comfortable, the researchers participated in crafting activities with them beforehand and carefully monitored the children for signs of fatigue, anxiety and stress.

A real-life application is that the findings can be used to help police to develop guidelines for interviewing child witnesses, to reduce their tendency to make an incorrect identification instead of rejecting a target-absent line-up.

Similarities

- Both Pozzulo *et al.* and Andrade collected quantitative data.
- Both Pozzulo *et al.* and Baron-Cohen *et al.* used foils in their studies.

Differences

- Pozzulo *et al.* used a visual memory test, while Andrade used an auditory memory test.
- Pozzulo *et al.* used two groups of participants, while Baron-Cohen *et al.* used four.

3 The Learning approach

Learning outcomes

In this chapter, we will discuss:

- the main assumptions, methodology, history, issues and debates of the learning approach
- psychological concepts, theories and research relating to the three core studies:
  - Bandura *et al.* (aggression)
  - Fagen *et al.* (elephant learning)
  - Saavedra and Silverman (button phobia)
- strengths and weaknesses of the three key studies with reference to ethical issues, **reliability**, **validity**, **objectivity** and **subjectivity**, **generalisations**, issues and debates, including applications to everyday life
- how to plan and evaluate your own investigations using **naturalistic observation**, **longitudinal study** and laboratory **experiment**.

▲ Figure 3.1 Learning together in Nepal, the location of the study by Fagen *et al.*

Where there are people, there is psychology!

Psychology is everywhere, and these two young novice monks are in Nepal, the location of Fagen *et al.*'s study of elephant **learning**. The boys are learning to be Buddhist monks, but how, when, why, what and from whom do we learn? Do humans and animals all learn in the same basic ways?

In this chapter, we will examine how our behaviour changes depending upon the experiences that we have had. You will learn about three core studies: Bandura *et al.*'s (1961) study of aggression, Fagen *et al.*'s (2014) study of elephant learning and Saavedra and Silverman's (2002) study of a boy with a phobia of buttons. First, let us explore the main assumptions of the learning approach.

3.0 Introducing the Learning approach

> **Think!**
>
> What did John Locke mean when he referred to babies as **blank slates**?

> **Think!**
>
> Imagine you are one of Burrhus Skinner's students. You ask him why he keeps his pigeons at 75 per cent of their expected body weight and whether he believes that this is ethical. What do you think Skinner will say in reply? Remember, psychologists use a cost–benefit analysis when making ethical decisions; how might Skinner justify his choices?

> **Think!**
>
> Think about the stages of **classical conditioning** used by Pavlov and by Watson and Rayner. How could you use the same basic principles to help someone to overcome their fear of the dentist?

Do babies really come into the world with no skills, abilities or innate abilities at all? What do you think? Can you think of any evidence to support or dispute this view?

▲ Figure 3.2 Are babies born as 'blank slates'?

KEY TERMS

blank slate

classical conditioning

experiences

social interactions

environment

operant conditioning

social learning

stimulus–response model

learning

METHODOLOGY

laboratory experiment

case study

observation

self-report

behavioural checklist

human and animal ethics

Main assumptions

1 We all begin life as a blank slate. **Experiences** and **interactions** with the **environment** shape our behaviour and these changes are directly observable.
2 We learn through the processes of **operant conditioning**, classical conditioning and **social learning**. This can be understood using the **stimulus–response model**.

(Cambridge International, 2021)

Why are babies like blank slates?

The term blank slate (or 'tabula rasa' in Latin) refers to the small chalkboards used by schoolchildren before the days of exercise books and digital tablets. The Ancient Greeks were the first to explore the idea that humans are born as blank slates. What they meant by this is that we have no innate or inborn knowledge; everything we know we have learned through direct experience. Every interaction within the physical and social environment leaves its mark on our slate, creating an ever-changing set of rules to guide our future behaviour.

This viewpoint clearly supports the nurture side of the nature versus nurture debate and was popularised in the seventeenth century by English philosopher John Locke, who stated that 'No man's knowledge here can go beyond his experience' (see Locke, 1948).

What is learning?

Learning refers to relatively permanent changes in behaviour caused by experiences in the environment as opposed to changes that result from biological maturation (Kimble, 1961). For example, a baby may be praised for using a spoon to eat their yoghurt, meaning they are more likely to use their spoon properly in the future (this is learning). However, until they have the physical skills to co-ordinate their arms, hands and fingers to use a spoon (biological maturation) it will not matter how much praise they receive as it is just not possible yet.

The stimulus–response model

A stimulus is a change in the environment that can be detected by one of our five senses, such as a loud noise, cold breeze, nasty smell or picture of a gorgeous kitten. In behavioural psychology, something is called a stimulus if it elicits a behavioural response or reaction, like saying 'Ahhhhh!' when we see the kitten or 'Eeeuuugh!' when we smell something nasty.

Some responses are involuntary, meaning we have no control over them. These responses are called reflexes and they are often responses that are evolutionarily adaptive like flinching when we hear a sudden noise or when we see a spider scuttling across the floor!

Three theories of learning
Classical conditioning

The three studies in this chapter each focus on a different type of learning. Saavedra and Silverman studied a boy with a phobia of buttons. Phobias can be learned through classical conditioning, a process where two stimuli become associated with one another. This type of learning was discovered by Ivan Pavlov in 1927.

While studying digestion in dogs, Pavlov noticed that the dogs salivated (a reflex response) as soon as they saw a certain laboratory assistant (a stimulus). The dogs had learned to associate this person with food and were expecting their dinner! Pavlov conducted a series of famous experiments where he repeatedly paired the ticking of a metronome (a neutral stimulus) with food (an unconditioned stimulus). Eventually, the dogs began to salivate as soon as they heard the metronome, which had become a conditioned stimulus.

In 1920, John Watson and Rosalie Rayner classically conditioned an 11-month-old baby known as Little Albert to be scared of a pet rat. They paired the rat with the sound of a metal bar being struck with a hammer. After seven pairings, the boy began to cry and tried to crawl away from the rat as soon as he saw it. The researchers concluded that fear can be conditioned, leading other researchers to explore the idea that if phobias can be learned then it may be possible to unlearn them in therapy. A technique based on this theory is explored in Saavedra and Silverman's **case study** (see page 114).

Operant conditioning

Operant conditioning was discovered by Burrhus Frederic Skinner (1938), an American psychologist who mainly worked with rats and pigeons. He observed that when organisms (including humans) perform a certain behaviour, it is what happens immediately afterwards that determines whether that behaviour becomes more or less likely to occur again in the future. If the behaviour is rewarded/positively reinforced, it will become more likely, and if it is punished it will become less likely. He also discovered that negative reinforcement (the removal of an aversive or unpleasant stimulus) can also act as a reward, making behaviour more likely. The term 'primary reinforcer' is used for rewards that meet a basic human need (e.g. food), whereas a secondary reinforcer is something that does not meet a need in itself but is associated with something that does – for example, money does not meet a basic need but it can be exchanged for things that do.

You will learn about how Saavedra and Silverman used positive reinforcement to help the boy to overcome his phobia and in Fagen *et al.*'s study you will see how operant conditioning has been applied to train animals to perform behaviours that are critical for their welfare.

Social learning

Bandura *et al.* (1961) examined how children learn aggressive behaviour via the process of social learning. Albert Bandura believed that much of our behaviour is learned via **observation** and the imitation of models, or people with whom we identify or admire. They may be powerful, attractive or part of a group to which we wish to belong. We pay attention to their behaviour and store a mental representation of it. If we are able to reproduce it, and are motivated to do so, we may perform the same behaviour ourselves at some point in the future.

 # Methodology in the Learning approach

Psychologists from the learning approach argue that mental events cannot be studied empirically (i.e. directly through the senses), and this led them to abandon the study of cognitive processes and focus entirely on observable behaviour. This is why Watson, Pavlov and Skinner are also known as the behaviourists. Much of the work carried out by early behaviourists involved **laboratory experiments**, often involving animals. Animal experiments were favoured because their environments could be strictly controlled in order to observe the impact of certain stimuli on behaviour.

Behaviourists often collect quantitative data – for example, number of trials needed to learn a certain skill, number of learned behaviours observed within a certain time period. Pavlov (1927) counted the number of droplets of saliva produced in response to the metronome; his measurements were very precise as he collected the saliva in a tube (cannula) inserted through the dog's cheek.

Watson and Rayner (1920) collected qualitative data in the form of observational notes that were made about how Albert responded to various stimuli, including wooden blocks, a burning newspaper and a fur coat. In this chapter, you will learn about the case study of Saavedra and Silverman, who studied a child with a phobia of buttons. Case studies are common in clinical psychology and may be used to support the efficacy of certain therapies. The key features of a case study are the use of a variety of different data-gathering techniques (called method triangulation) and the collection of different types of data – qualitative and quantitative, primary and secondary.

> If babies are born as blank slates, what about new-born animals? Do new-born animals acquire everything they know through experience of the world too? How would you train a pet?

ISSUES AND DEBATES

Applications to everyday life

The theories and studies from the learning approach have numerous real-world applications, including treatments and therapies for clinical disorders, captive animal management (e.g. to facilitate veterinary procedures) and awareness of the role of the behavioural role models in the media and the impact they can have on children's behaviour.

Individual and situational explanations

Individual differences are explained as people experience differing sociocultural environments and, therefore, have different reinforcement histories leading to different traits. Alternatively, the approach can be linked to situational explanations as, in any given situation, exposure to a conditioned stimulus could trigger a conditioned response, while exposure to role models and the experience of reinforcement and/or punishment can affect an individual's behaviour, either at the particular time or in the future.

Nature versus nurture

This approach focuses on the role of nurture but the role of reflexive behaviours in classical conditioning also demonstrates the role of nature.

The use of children in psychological research

Bandura *et al.* and Saavedra and Silverman both worked with children and in this approach you will have an opportunity to think about the practical and ethical issues around working with children as participants.

The use of animals in psychological research

Fagen *et al.* worked with elephants in Nepal; in this study, you will have the opportunity to think about the issues presented by working with one of the planet's largest endangered species in a real-world setting, as opposed to the usual rats, cats and dogs studied in the laboratories of the learning approach's most famous contributors (i.e. Pavlov and Skinner).

The history of the Learning approach

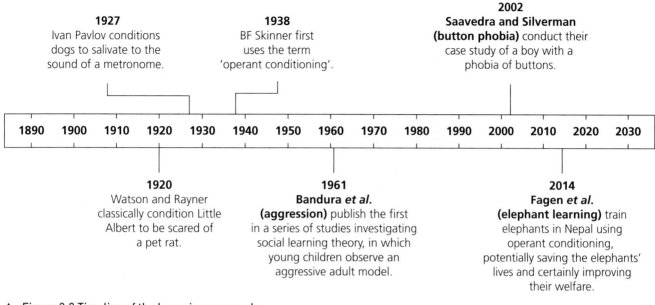

1927
Ivan Pavlov conditions dogs to salivate to the sound of a metronome.

1938
BF Skinner first uses the term 'operant conditioning'.

2002
Saavedra and Silverman (button phobia) conduct their case study of a boy with a phobia of buttons.

| 1890 | 1900 | 1910 | 1920 | 1930 | 1940 | 1950 | 1960 | 1970 | 1980 | 1990 | 2000 | 2010 | 2020 | 2030 |

1920
Watson and Rayner classically condition Little Albert to be scared of a pet rat.

1961
Bandura *et al.* (aggression) publish the first in a series of studies investigating social learning theory, in which young children observe an aggressive adult model.

2014
Fagen *et al.* (elephant learning) train elephants in Nepal using operant conditioning, potentially saving the elephants' lives and certainly improving their welfare.

▲ Figure 3.3 Timeline of the Learning approach

3.0 Introducing the Learning approach

STUDY TIP

As you learn about each of the studies in the Learning approach, think about how the results support the main assumptions of the approach. What has the study told us about the causes of behaviour and how they link to classical and operant conditioning and/or social learning theory? You should also look out for evidence that suggests the main assumptions may be incorrect or do not apply in all circumstances.

Do you remember Rohan and Polina from page xii? They were discussing an internet news story about the pandemic. The story included an interview with a doctor who sacrificed time with her own family to care for COVID-19 patients. The students are discussing what it is that makes some people go out of their way to help and care for others.

➤ How might a psychologist from the Learning approach explain the doctor's behaviour?

➤ Use what you have learned in this section as a starting point, but you may also wish to conduct some further research of your own.

➤ After you have learned about all three studies in the approach, you may like to revisit your answer and add some more ideas.

3.0 Introducing the Learning approach

3.0 Introducing the Learning approach

3.0 Introducing the Learning approach

3.0 Introducing the Learning approach

3.1 Aggression: Bandura *et al.*

3.1.1 Background

Introducing Albert Bandura

Albert Bandura was a Canadian-born American psychologist who was Chairman of the Psychology department at Stanford University. His doctorate was in Clinical Psychology. Bandura was interested in the effects of witnessing role models on others' behaviour. Following his famous experiment on the delayed imitation of aggression in 1961, he also conducted research into television violence, finding that children also imitated what they saw on video. He died on 28 July 2021 at the age of 95 years

▶ Figure 3.4 In May 2019, President Obama awarded Professor Albert Bandura the National Medal of Science for being one of the top 17 scientists, engineers and inventors.

Think!

Are children more likely to imitate a same-sex or opposite-sex role model?

Think!

Imagine you are a researcher. How might you design a study to investigate social learning theory in a real-life setting?

Think!

How do Fauls and Smith's (1956) ideas about the development of gender-appropriate behaviour differ from the explanations suggested by Hassett *et al.* (monkey toy preferences)?

The psychology being investigated

Social Learning Theory

This study investigated social learning theory, which proposes that people observe and imitate the behaviour of others, especially those with whom they identify (e.g. people who are attractive, powerful or popular). Initially, an individual will pay close attention to the behaviour of a role model, retaining this information in their memory. They need to feel motivated (and be physically able) to reproduce the behaviour, as well as be motivated to do so – for example, believing that they will be rewarded for performing the behaviour. Imitation can be immediate or delayed. Delayed imitation is when a person observes a behaviour but does not reproduce it until a later point in time.

Aggression

Aggression can be both physical (such as punching) or verbal (such as shouting). It is a behaviour where there is the intention to harm another person or object and is usually forceful or hostile. Good self-regulation can allow individuals to inhibit any aggression they feel. Bandura *et al.*'s study investigated delayed imitation of aggression in terms of both verbal and physical aggression. The study specifically looked at aggression shown towards inanimate objects.

Background

Previous research

Previous research into imitation of aggression found that children readily imitated a model's behaviour in the presence of the model. Bandura et al. wanted to see whether children would imitate behaviour when the model was no longer present and they were in a new setting. The behaviour they chose to investigate was aggression.

Imitation of aggression

In Bandura et al.'s study, children were exposed to aggressive and non-aggressive models, then moved to a new setting to see whether they imitated the behaviour they had previously observed. Bandura et al. predicted that children who had been exposed to an aggressive model would copy aggressive acts and show different behaviour to those who had seen a non-aggressive model, or no model at all. The researchers hypothesised that children learn imitative behaviours through prior reinforcement and that to some extent this tendency can also apply to adults.

Non-aggressive model

Bandura et al. also hypothesised that observing a non-aggressive model would actively inhibit any aggressive behaviour, meaning that children exposed to a non-aggressive model would show even less aggressive behaviour than those exposed to no model.

Sex of the model

Previous research by Fauls and Smith (1956) suggested that parents have a tendency to reinforce what they believe to be 'sex-appropriate' behaviour in their children. For example, a boy may not be rewarded for looking after a doll if the parents deem this to be a female-orientated activity, but a girl may be encouraged to continue. Due to the differing reinforcement histories of boys and girls, they develop a tendency to imitate same-sex models more frequently.

Therefore, Bandura et al. proposed that boys would be more likely to imitate a male model, while girls would be more likely to imitate a female model. Furthermore, they proposed that, since aggression is deemed to be a more masculine behaviour, the greatest imitation of aggression would be from boys observing an aggressive male model.

Bandura et al. in brief

In Bandura et al.'s study, children were exposed to either an aggressive model, a non-aggressive model or no model. Both male and female models were used in the experiment. The aggressive model would punch and kick a giant inflatable clown called a Bobo doll, while the non-aggressive model would play quietly. The children were then all made equally frustrated before being moved to a new setting with toys, where their subsequent behaviour was observed. As expected, the highest level of aggression seen was in boys who had been exposed to an aggressive male model. Males were more likely to imitate physical aggression while females were more likely to imitate verbal aggression. Many of these aggressive behaviours were identical to the model. Furthermore, many non-aggressive actions of the model were also imitated.

Plan your own... observation

Bandura et al. used an experiment with a controlled observation to investigate whether children would imitate the aggressive behaviour of an adult model. How might you design a naturalistic observation to investigate aggression in children?'

Imagine...

Roberto is planning a naturalistic observation into sex differences in aggression shown by children in the playground. He would like to investigate whether boys engage in more aggressive behaviour than girls.

» What advice would you give Roberto about how to conduct a naturalistic observation into sex differences in aggression on the playground?

Planning an observation

An observation is a non-experimental method, although it can also be used as a technique to collect data in an experiment. When planning an observation, it is important to consider whether participants will know they are being watched, whether the researcher will be separate from the situation they are observing, whether the observation will take place in a controlled or real-life setting and how the data will be recorded.

▼ Table 3.1 Features of an observation

Main features of an observation	Consider...
Overt vs covert	For observations, the participants may or may not know that they are being observed. Will the children in Roberto's study know that their behaviour is being observed?
Participant vs non-participant	The researcher/s may observe behaviour from afar or they may watch as part of the ongoing activity in which they are also participating. Will Roberto join in the children's activities or observe the children's behaviour from afar?
Naturalistic vs controlled	An observation can take place in a real-life setting or in a controlled laboratory environment. As this is a naturalistic observation, where will it take place? What details can you give of the location?
Structured vs unstructured	Observers may record qualitative data about a situation or use a **behavioural checklist** to record pre-determined behaviours in categories. Roberto wants to compare the behaviour of boys and girls. Would a structured or unstructured observation be more appropriate?
Behavioural categories (if appropriate)	Will Roberto use a behavioural checklist to record aggressive behaviour? If so, what behavioural categories will he include? Can you give examples of aggressive behaviours he might want to record?
Number of observers	How many observers will record data in the playground? Consider the advantages and disadvantages of having multiple observers and the effects this might have on the children's behaviour.

Evaluating your plan

Roberto shares your ideas with his colleagues. Some of them think it is a great idea; others are not so sure. Think about the practical strengths and weaknesses of your suggestions.

▼ Table 3.2 Evaluating your plan

	Describe	Explain
Strengths	Consider the features of the planned observation. Suggest ways in which you have helped Roberto ensure he gains valid/reliable data. Have you reduced the chance of demand characteristics in the design, for example?	How might the features of Roberto's observation lead to more valid/reliable data on aggressive behaviour in children? Explain why this is the case.
Weaknesses	Which features of the observation might lead to less valid/reliable data?	Why might these features reduce the validity/reliability of the data that Roberto collects on children's aggressive behaviours?
Improvements	Consider the weaknesses you gave above. How might you improve Roberto's procedure to overcome one of these issues?	How would this improvement affect the validity and/or reliability of the data Roberto collects on aggressive behaviours in children?

Bandura *et al.* investigated imitation of aggression. However, boys are generally seen to demonstrate more aggressive behaviour than girls. The findings of this study support this. Do you think this sex difference is due to nature or nurture? Can you think of a way to investigate this ethically?

▶ **LEARNING LINK**

The study by Hassett *et al.* (monkey toy preferences) also investigated sex differences. They were investigating sex differences in toy preferences; however, instead of using human children, they used rhesus monkeys. Why do you think they used monkeys instead of human children? Do you think Bandura *et al.*'s study would have been improved if they had also used monkeys to investigate sex differences in imitation of aggression? What would have been the advantages and disadvantages of having done this? (Consider the fact that they would need to have trained monkeys as 'models' and that monkeys cannot speak.) Both of these studies raise the issue of whether sex differences are due to nature or nurture.

STUDY TIP

Bandura *et al.*'s study is underpinned by Bandura's famous social learning theory, which is outlined in brief on page 91. To gain a full understanding of this theory, it is recommended that you carry out further background reading. The main stages in social learning theory are: attention, retention, reproduction and motivation. Make sure that you can briefly describe each of these steps, as well as outline the theory overall.

▶ **TEST YOURSELF**

1 Describe 'social learning theory'.   [4]
2 Explain why the study by Bandura *et al.* is from the learning approach.   [2]
3 Explain two ways in which the learning approach is different from the cognitive approach. Use the study by Bandura *et al.* as an example of the learning approach.   [4]
4 Bandura *et al.* used a controlled observation in their study. Explain what is meant by 'controlled observation'.   [2]
5 In Bandura *et al.*'s study, one variable was whether children observed a male model or a female model. State whether this was an independent variable or dependent variable. Include a reason for your answer.   [1]
6 Bandura *et al.*'s study used the experimental conditions of an aggressive model and a non-aggressive model, as well as a control condition.
   a State what the control condition was.   [1]
   b Explain one reason why a control condition is important in an experiment, using this study as an example.   [2]

3.1.2 Describing Bandura *et al.* (aggression)

METHODOLOGY

experiment

variables

observation

Think!

Why was it important to induce mild aggression arousal in the children before they were taken to the experimental room?

Think!

Consider who you view as role models in your life. Do you feel you are more likely to imitate the behaviours of same-sex or opposite-sex role models? Why do you think this is?

Think!

Why was it important for Bandura *et al.* to match participants on prior aggression levels in this study? How might participant **variables** have affected the results if they had not done this?

Do you think there are some behaviours that caregivers demonstrate that children are more likely to imitate than others? What factors do you think might increase or decrease the likelihood of a child imitating certain behaviours?

▶ AIMS

The aims were:
1 To investigate whether children imitate aggression of a model in the absence of the model.
2 To investigate whether children are more likely to imitate the behaviour of a same-sex model.

▶ RESEARCH METHODOLOGY

Bandura *et al.* used an experiment. Participants observed an aggressive model, a non-aggressive model or no model in a controlled setting. Their subsequent behaviour was then observed via a one-way mirror in a covert, structured, controlled observation.

Design and variables

There were eight experimental conditions, with six participants in each condition, as well as a control condition of 24 participants with 12 boys and 12 girls who saw no model. In the experimental conditions, half of the participants observed an aggressive model, while half observed a non-aggressive model. Within these groups, half observed a male model, while half observed a female model. Within these groups, the model was either same-sex or opposite-sex for participants.

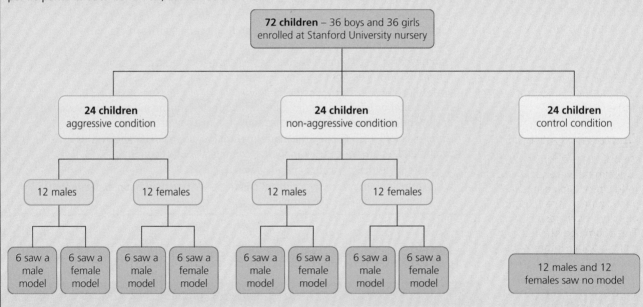

▲ Figure 3.5 Conditions in Bandura *et al.*'s study

Participants were matched on prior aggression levels. Participants were rated by their nursery teacher and the experimenter independently on their social aggression on four five-point scales measuring: physical and verbal aggression, as well as aggression towards inanimate objects and aggressive inhibition. Based on their total scores, participants were put into groups of three. Each triplet was randomly assigned to one of the three main conditions.

Sample

Seventy-two children were recruited from Stanford University nursery. There were 36 girls and 36 boys, aged from 37 to 69 months (three to six years old), with a mean age of 52 months.

▶ PROCEDURE

Experimental conditions

In the experimental conditions involving a model, the participant was brought to a room full of toys and seated at a table in the corner by the experimenter, who showed them how to make pictures with potato prints. Multi-coloured picture stickers were also provided. These two activities had been shown by previous research to have high interest value for children. The experimenter then took the model to another corner of the room which had a table and chair, tinker toy set (construction set), mallet and inflatable Bobo doll, before leaving the room.

Non-aggressive condition

In the non-aggressive condition, the model played with the tinker toys in a quiet manner and ignored the Bobo doll.

Aggressive condition

In the aggressive condition, after a minute of playing with the tinker toys, the model focused on the Bobo doll and was aggressive towards it for the remaining nine minutes. Standard actions were performed by the model each time in the same sequence. The model laid the Bobo doll on its side, sitting on it and punching its nose. They then lifted it and hit it on the head with the mallet, followed by throwing the Bobo doll up in the air aggressively and kicking it around the room. This sequence was repeated three times, along with verbally aggressive comments.

After ten minutes, the experimenter returned to the room and told the participant he or she was being taken to a game room.

Aggression arousal

Before the test for imitation, all participants in the experiment were taken to a game room to induce mild aggression arousal. This was to ensure that all participants were primed to initiate aggressive acts equally, regardless of the situation they had observed. This room had attractive toys, such as: a fire engine, a train, a fighter plane, a cable car, a colourful spinning top and a doll set. The participants were told that the toys were for them to play with, but as soon as they became engaged, the experimenter announced that these were her very best toys and they were being reserved for other children. The participant was then taken into the adjoining experimental room in a state of frustration.

Test for delayed imitation

The experimental room contained a range of toys, including those from the room with the model, such as a Bobo doll

and mallet, other novel aggressive toys, such as two dart guns, and non-aggressive toys. The non-aggressive toys included a tea set, crayons and paper, a ball, two dolls, three bears, toy vehicles and plastic farm animals. These were all presented in fixed positions for each child.

The participant spent 20 minutes in this room while their behaviour was recorded using a behavioural checklist via a one-way mirror. Behaviour was recorded every five seconds. The male model from the experiment observed all trials and for half of the trials there was a second observer.

Response measures

Three categories of imitation were observed:
● imitation of physical aggression:
  – hitting the Bobo doll with a mallet
  – sitting on the Bobo doll and punching the Bobo doll on the nose
  – kicking the Bobo doll
  – tossing the Bobo doll into the air
● imitative verbal aggression:
  – 'Sock him in the nose...'
  – 'Hit him down...'
  – 'Throw him in the air...'
  – 'Kick him...'
  – 'Pow...'
● imitative non-aggressive verbal responses:
  – 'He keeps coming back for more'
  – 'He sure is a tough fella.'

During a pre-test, it had been found that some children only partially imitated the model's behaviour, so two further categories of partially imitative behaviour were included:
● mallet aggression: striking something other than the Bobo doll with a mallet
● sits on Bobo doll: putting the Bobo doll on its side and sitting on it but non-aggressively.

Three non-imitative aggressive acts were also recorded:
● punches Bobo doll: hitting, slapping or pushing the doll aggressively
● non-imitative physical and verbal aggression: any acts or words that were aggressive but not performed by the model, such as 'Shoot the Bobo' or 'Stupid ball'
● aggressive gun play: shooting darts or firing imaginary gun shots at objects.

The number of times a participant was playing non-aggressively or sat quietly was also recorded.

▶ RESULTS

Complete imitation of models' behaviour

Participants in the aggressive model condition demonstrated more physical and verbal aggression than the non-aggressive and control groups (Table 3.3). One third of participants in the aggressive model condition also imitated the model's non-aggressive comments, while none in the other conditions did.

Partial imitation of models' behaviour

Exposure to a non-aggressive model inhibited partially imitative mallet aggression, particularly in girls. In the aggressive model and control groups, partially imitative mallet aggression was significantly higher for girls (18.0 and 13.1, respectively) than in the non-aggressive model condition (0.5). Sitting on the Bobo doll was initiated more frequently in the aggressive model condition than the other two conditions.

▼ Table 3.3 Mean aggression scores for experimental and control subjects

Response category	Sex of child	Experimental groups				Control groups
		Aggressive model		Non-aggressive model		
		Female	Male	Female	Male	
Imitative physical aggression	Female	5.5	7.2	2.5	0.0	1.2
	Male	12.4	25.8	0.2	1.5	2.0
Imitative verbal aggression	Female	13.7	2.0	0.3	0.0	0.7
	Male	4.3	12.7	1.1	0.0	1.7
Mallet aggression	Female	17.2	18.7	0.5	0.5	13.1
	Male	15.5	28.8	18.7	6.7	13.5
Punches Bobo doll	Female	6.3	16.5	5.8	4.3	11.7
	Male	18.9	11.9	15.6	14.8	15.7
Nonimitative aggression	Female	21.3	8.4	7.2	1.4	6.1
	Male	16.2	36.7	26.1	22.3	24.6
Aggressive gun play	Female	1.8	4.5	2.6	2.5	3.7
	Male	7.3	15.9	8.9	16.7	14.3

Adapted from Bandura, A., Ross, D. and Ross, S. (1961) Transmission of aggression through imitation of aggressive models. *Journal of Abnormal and Social Psychology*, 63(3), 575–582. doi.10.1037/H0045925.

Non-imitative aggression

Being in the aggressive model condition did not increase the incidence of non-imitative aggression, such as aggressive gun play or punching the Bobo doll.

Sex of participant/model

- Boys were more likely to imitate physical aggression than girls.
- Girls were slightly more likely to imitate verbal aggression than boys, but this difference was not statistically significant.
- The male model had a greater effect on participants' behaviour overall than the female model. Participants who viewed the non-aggressive male model demonstrated significantly less physical aggression, verbal aggression and mallet aggression, as well as non-imitative aggression overall, than the control group.

Same-sex models

- Children who viewed a same-sex model imitated them more than an opposite-sex model.

- Boys who witnessed an aggressive male model had the highest imitative aggression score (25.8). They showed more imitative physical and verbal aggression, as well as non-imitative aggression and aggressive gun play, compared to girls who viewed a male model.
- Girls were more verbally aggressive and showed more non-imitative aggression with a female aggressive model compared to boys.

Non-aggressive behaviour

The only sex differences in time spent playing with certain toys were:
- Girls spent more time playing with dolls, the tea set and colouring compared to boys.
- Boys spent more time playing with the gun than girls.

The non-aggressive model had some significant effects on participants' behaviour:
- Participants exposed to the non-aggressive model spent more time playing quietly with dolls than the other two conditions.
- Participants exposed to the non-aggressive model spent more than twice as much time sitting quietly than those in the aggressive model condition.

CONCLUSIONS

Bandura *et al.* made several conclusions from their data, including:
- Observing an aggressive model can lead to imitative aggression in the observer.
- Boys are more likely to imitate same-sex models than girls.
- Boys are more likely to imitate physically aggressive behaviour than girls, while girls are slightly more likely to imitate verbally aggressive behaviour than boys.
- Behaviour of male models is more likely to be imitated overall than the behaviour of female models.

This study used children as participants. If the researchers were to conduct similar research on imitation of aggressive models in adults, how might they need to adapt or change their methodology? Consider how age might affect factors such as demand characteristics and social desirability, as well as ethical considerations such as informed consent.

LEARNING LINK

This study uses a controlled observation to record data covertly through a one-way mirror. Using a controlled observation increases reliability from trial-to-trial, while being covert avoids the participants either responding to demand characteristics or acting in a socially desirable way. The study by Milgram (obedience) also used an observation to record data through a one-way mirror in a laboratory setting. In what ways was this observation similar and in what ways was it different from that used by Bandura *et al.*? Which observation do you think was more reliable and why? Which observation do you think was more valid and why? Remember that having more than one observer does not make the data collection any more reliable; it simply allows the researchers to check for inter-observer reliability.

STUDY TIP

This study investigates social learning theory so it is important that you can understand how the results both support and do not support social learning theory. For example, the results of Bandura *et al.*'s study showed that both physical and verbal aggression are imitated, which supports social learning theory. On the other hand, observing an aggressive model did not increase levels of novel aggression shown by participants compared to the non-aggressive and control groups. This evidence does not support social learning theory as a means of learning aggressive behaviour in general, as only specific acts that were observed were imitated or partially imitated.

TEST YOURSELF

1. Identify one act of physical aggression and one act of verbal aggression demonstrated by the aggressive model in the study by Bandura *et al.* [2]
2. Describe two sex differences in non-aggressive behaviour found in this study. [2]
3. Explain how two results from the study by Bandura *et al.* support one or more of the assumptions of the learning approach. [4]
4. Explain the differences between a structured and an unstructured observation, using the study by Bandura *et al.* as an example. [4]
5. A researcher proposes the following hypothesis: 'There will be a difference in the number of aggressive acts performed by children who have observed an aggressive model, compared to those who have observed a non-aggressive model.' Explain whether this is a directional or non-directional hypothesis. [1]
6. Describe how Bandura *et al.* induced mild aggression arousal in participants prior to the test for delayed imitation. [2]

3.1.3 Evaluating Bandura *et al.* (aggression)

Think!

Bandura *et al.* employed many controls in their experiment. How many of these controls can you identify? Remember that controls are things that are kept the same between levels of the independent variable.

Think!

Imagine you are a researcher. How might you conduct a similar study to Bandura *et al.* as a field experiment? What would be the advantages and disadvantages of conducting the research in this way?

Think!

Bandura *et al.* only used one observer for half of the trials and two observers for the other half of the trials. How might this have affected the results?

Why do you think the participants in this study were more likely to imitate the male model's behaviour? Do you think this finding is valid based on the study's design? What was the issue with using only two people as the male and female models?

Ethical issues

Psychological harm

One weakness of Bandura *et al.*'s study is the risk to the children of psychological harm. One third of the participants witnessed the aggressive behaviour of a model. This group of children was subsequently more likely to imitate this aggressive behaviour. Since this reproduction was after a delay, it is possible that the children continued to demonstrate delayed imitation of the aggressive behaviour even after the study had ended, or to feel in an aggressive state of mind when they returned home.

Methodological issues

Reliability

Standardisation

A strength of Bandura *et al.*'s study is the standardised procedure and instructions, which increases the reliability of the study. The layout of the toys in the experimental room was kept the same for participants in the aggressive, non-aggressive and control conditions. The length of time the children were observed for was also the same, at 20 minutes, and the same behavioural checklist was used to record behaviour every five seconds. This level of consistency makes the study's findings about children's delayed imitation of aggression more reliable.

Inter-observer reliability

A strength of this study is that high levels of inter-observer reliability were found. In one half of the trials, two observers independently recorded participants' behaviour using a behavioural checklist in five-second intervals. Their results were correlated and found to always be in the +0.90s. This ensured that there was a high level of consistency in the scoring of aggressive and non-aggressive behaviours.

Inter-rater reliability

There was strong inter-rater reliability between the researcher and the nursery teacher for the children's aggression scores. The raters' scores had a correlation at +0.89. This indicates a high level of consistency in how the children were rated across the aggression scales.

Validity

Matched aggression scores

A strength of this study was that participants were matched on prior aggression levels. They were each rated by their nursery teacher and the experimenter independently on four five-point rating scales for their: physical aggression, verbal aggression, aggression towards inanimate objects and aggressive inhibition. Using the total scores gained, participants were put into triplets, with each being randomly assigned to a different condition. This increased the validity of the findings, as individual differences in prior aggression levels should not have caused any differences between conditions.

Only two stooges

A weakness was that only one stooge was used in each male and female condition throughout the experiment. This means that the children may have imitated the model due to some individual feature that was unique to the model, rather than their sex. This confounding variable may have affected how frequently a model was imitated and thus the validity of the results.

Objectivity and subjectivity

Quantitative data

A strength was that quantitative data was collected in this study, which allows for more objective comparisons to be made between conditions of the independent variables. Data was collected on the number of aggressive acts shown by each child, using a behavioural checklist. Therefore, it was possible to compare numerical data regarding the children's levels of aggression following exposure to different types of model without bias, increasing validity.

Inside information

A weakness of this study was that the main observer for all of the trials was the male model from the experiments. This meant that he knew which children had been in the male model conditions and may have been more subjective in his interpretation of their behaviours. This would subsequently reduce the validity of the data for the male conditions, as he may have expected the children he had previously seen to act in a certain way, depending on whether they had watched him acting aggressively and interpreted their behaviour accordingly.

Single-blind

On the other hand, a strength is that the main observer did not know which condition each child had been in for any trials for which he had not been the model, which would increase his objectivity. This means that any similarities or differences between the female conditions were not due to bias on the part of the researcher, which increases the validity of the data for these conditions.

Generalisations and ecological validity

Generalising beyond the sample

A weakness is that the findings may not be generalisable to participants from lower socioeconomic backgrounds. The children were all from the nursery of a prestigious university, which was for children of staff and students. Therefore, these children may have had particularly educated parents and their home lives may not be representative of the rest of the population. Their learning experiences may have differed from other children and they may have been more or less likely to imitate adult behaviour as a result, reducing the validity of the findings.

Generalising to everyday life

A weakness of this study is that the situation presented to the children lacks mundane realism as it was an unusual set-up. It is very rare that an adult will be seen to attack a toy, with the child being provided with the opportunity to imitate this behaviour. Furthermore, the children were seen hitting an inflatable doll rather than a real person. Bobo dolls are also designed to be hit and bounce back. Therefore, it is not possible to assume that the aggressive behaviour shown towards the toys would extend to violence towards real people. Bandura *et al.*'s study did not distinguish between play fighting and violence in real life.

The use of children in psychological research

This study used young children aged 37 to 69 months, which might make them particularly vulnerable to demand characteristics. The young children may believe that the adults expect them to copy the behaviour of the stooge and so act accordingly. This would cause issues with the validity of the results. The children are also at a sensitive age in their development, which raises ethical issues for those being exposed to an aggressive model, as there may be a greater risk of psychological harm due to long-term after-effects.

Applications to everyday life

Television warnings

As Bandura *et al.*'s study demonstrated that both physical and verbal aggressive behaviour can be observed and imitated by children, it is important for television networks to either consider censoring content or provide warnings when there will be aggressive content on the screen so that parents have the option to prevent their children from viewing it. Additionally, the producers of children's television shows can ensure that characters are either non-aggressive or that aggressive content is reduced to a minimum.

Parents

Bandura *et al.* demonstrated that children were more likely to imitate a male model, so parents may wish to proactively expose their children to friendly and prosocial male role models. Additionally, children were less likely to show aggressive behaviours if they observed a non-aggressive model, so parents can direct their children to watch television programmes with models who demonstrate prosocial behaviours.

Reflections

Bandura *et al.*'s research showed that children imitated the aggressive behaviour of adults even when the model was no longer present. However, an important question is whether children only imitate real-life models or whether they are influenced by what they see on the television. Bandura *et al.* decided to research this in 1963 and found that even cartoon violence (such as the cartoon *Tom and Jerry*) might be causing children to learn aggressive behaviour. Some people believe watching aggressive behaviour on television or in sports is cathartic, meaning it allows people to release their own feelings of aggression by watching someone acting in an aggressive manner, thus reducing the desire to be violent. However, Bandura's research suggests that observing aggressive acts can make people more, not less, aggressive.

▶ LEARNING LINK

Both Bandura *et al.* (aggression) and Pozzulo *et al.* (line-ups) use children in their research, with both studies having important real-life implications in terms of policies. While Bandura *et al.*'s study raises the issue of whether violence should be shown on television and, if so, the timing and the extent, Pozzulo *et al.*'s study can be used to form guidelines around using children as witnesses for crimes. What methodological issues might arise if a researcher uses the same procedure for both children and adults in a study? Do you think it would have been possible for Bandura *et al.* to have used the same procedure on adults? How might they need to have adapted their procedure to avoid demand characteristics?

STUDY TIP

One debate that is highly relevant to Bandura *et al.*'s study is the nature versus nurture debate. It is important to know which findings support the nature side of the debate and which findings support the nurture side of the debate. Any findings from Bandura *et al.* which support social learning theory show that behaviour can be learnt from the environment (nurture), while any sex differences might be used to support the nature side of the argument, in terms of biological differences in hormones.

> **TEST YOURSELF**
> ....
>
> 1 Explain one similarity and one difference between the study by Bandura *et al.* and one other core study from the learning approach. [8]
>
> 2 Ellie believes that the findings from Bandura *et al.*'s study supports the individual side of the debate but Sri believes it supports the situational side of the debate. Outline why you think either Ellie or Sri is correct using evidence from the study. [4]
>
> 3 Evaluate the study by Bandura *et al.* in terms of two strengths and two weaknesses. At least one of your evaluation points must be about the use of children in psychological research. [10]
>
> 4 Bandura *et al.* used children as participants in their study. Explain one methodological issue that may have arisen if they had used adults instead. [2]
>
> 5 Suggest one advantage of covert observations using Bandura *et al.*'s study as an example. [2]
>
> 6 Explain two ethical guidelines that are relevant to Bandura *et al.*'s study. [4]

3.2 Fagen *et al.* (elephant learning)

3.2.1 Background

▲ Figure 3.6 Dr Ariel Fagen

Introducing Ariel Fagen

Dr Ariel Fagen is a highly qualified, board-certified veterinary behaviourist of the American College of Veterinary Behaviour, one of less than a hundred in the world. She is the Medical Director and owner of a practice in Colorado, USA, has lectured nationally and internationally, consults with shelters and private organisations and has conducted research at animal shelters, hospitals and wildlife breeding centres, including her award-winning research in Nepal. Her ground-breaking research documented the efficacy of secondary reinforcement training with captive elephants for the very first time. Ariel enjoys hiking, camping and skiing and her clients describe her as professional, compassionate and extremely knowledgeable.

KEY TERMS

shaping

behavioural chaining

reinforcement (positive, negative, primary and secondary)

operant conditioning

Think!

What is the difference between **shaping** and **behavioural chaining**?

Think!

Imagine you are working on Dr Fagen's research team. How will you find out which food the elephants like best and so would act as the most powerful **primary reinforcer**? Dr Fagen chose to use a whistle-blow as a **secondary reinforcer**. How will you test to make sure all the elephants can hear it?

Think!

Can you think of any reasons why it might be difficult to convince the mahouts (handlers) to use **positive reinforcement** to train the elephants rather than more traditional methods?

Trunk-wash training can present a few challenges as it is important that the elephants do not spill or drink any of the fluid and get as much in the bucket as possible. Can you think of any tricks to increase the amount of fluid that ends up in the bucket?

▲ Figure 3.7

The psychology being investigated

Captive elephants play an important role in Nepalese culture. Not only are they part of many religious ceremonies and customs, but they also work in the timber trade, transportation, park management and tourism. Unfortunately, elephants are vulnerable to tuberculosis (TB), a potentially fatal disease which can be transmitted between wild and captive elephants and humans. The disease affects more than 20 per cent of elephants in Nepal, meaning that finding new ways to combat this problem are crucial to both animal and human welfare.

This study investigates a way of training the elephants to actively participate in a veterinary procedure called a trunk wash, which allows them to be tested for the disease. The elephants had to learn to perform a series of behaviours in the correct order. If the behaviours were not performed accurately, the TB test result may not be accurate and an elephant could be infected without anyone knowing. This means that elephants must achieve a high standard in every behaviour that they are taught. You will learn more about the specific behaviours that were being reinforced on page 106. Here you will learn about the basic psychological principles that the researchers used.

Chopped banana (UCS) -> Happy elephant (UCR)

Whistle (NS) + Chopped banana (UCS) -> Happy elephant (UCR)

Whistle (CS) -> Happy elephant (CR)

UCS = unconditioned stimulus;
UCR = unconditioned response;
NS = neutral stimulus;
CS = conditioned stimulus;
CR = conditioned response

▲ Figure 3.8 Using classical conditioning to turn the sound of a whistle into a secondary reinforcer. Remember, this is just one small part of the training; the main training of the elephants involved operant conditioning

Operant conditioning and positive reinforcement

The researchers trained the elephants using **operant conditioning**. In this type of learning, the consequence of a behaviour determines the probability of that behaviour being performed again. Fagen *et al.* trained the elephants by rewarding them for performing specific trunk movements in the correct order. This is called positive reinforcement.

Primary and secondary reinforcement

Each time the elephant moved its trunk into the correct position, it was rewarded with chopped banana. The chopped banana is a primary reinforcer because it meets a basic need (hunger) and the elephant was likely to move its trunk in the same way again if the movement was rewarded with banana, a food that the elephants really enjoy.

Operant conditioning is most successful when the time between the behaviour (trunk movement) and the consequence is as brief as possible. For this reason, animal trainers often use secondary reinforcers, such as sounds, which the animal is taught to associate with the primary reinforcer. In this study, a short blast on a whistle was used as a secondary reinforcer. The use of the whistle allowed the researchers to reward the elephants exactly as the desired behaviour was performed, creating a strong association between the behaviour and the consequence.

The whistle is a secondary reinforcer because in itself it does not meet any of the elephants' needs, but if the researchers train the elephants to associate the whistle with banana, the whistle can become a powerful reinforcer in itself (see Figure 3.8).

Shaping and behavioural chaining

In order to perform the trunk wash, the elephants had to learn several separate behaviours. Firstly, they had to allow the trainers to inject saline solution into their trunks. Next, they had to hold their trunks upright so the fluid could travel to the base of their trunks. Then they had to spray the fluid into a bucket for testing. To begin with, the animal is rewarded for moving their trunk into any position that is similar to the desired position. Gradually, the elephant is only rewarded for movements/positions that are increasingly similar to the final desired behaviour. This is called shaping. Once the elephant has mastered the first behaviours in the trunk-wash sequence, they will move onto learning the next one.

Over time, the trainer will begin to reward the elephants only for chaining the learned behaviours together – the first behaviour must be followed by the second behaviour. Once they have learned this, they will only be rewarded for chaining three behaviours in the correct order and so on, until they are able to perform the whole trunk wash, with each behaviour performed to a satisfactory standard.

Background

In 2011, the Nepalese government introduced annual TB testing of captive elephants to reduce transmission, causing researchers to develop new training methods using positive reinforcement. They hoped that the elephants would participate voluntarily, reducing stress, improving captive animal welfare and protecting trainers from injury due to anxious and unco-operative elephants. Similar techniques had already been used with non-human primates, antelopes and giant pandas but this was the first time such techniques had been trialled with elephants.

Elephants in Nepal are generally tamed and trained by handlers called mahouts. The mahouts also use the principles of operant conditioning. Traditional training methods use aversive stimuli (see page 211), such as being prodded with sharp bamboo sticks called kocha. If a mahout wants the elephant to turn right and it turns to the left, it might be poked with the stick as a punishment. Sticks are also used for negative reinforcement – the mahout prods the elephants until they turn in the correct direction. Due to concerns over animal welfare and keeper safety, new methods such as those described above are slowly being introduced, focusing firmly on the use of positive reinforcement.

Fagen *et al.* in brief

The study explored the effectiveness of secondary positive reinforcement for training working elephants to voluntarily participate in trunk washing, a veterinary procedure used to test for TB (Fagen *et al.*, 2014). Four of the five elephants successfully mastered the necessary behaviour within 35 training sessions (average session length of 12 minutes). The training was seen to be effective in reliably producing the desired behaviour of trunk washing for juvenile (infant) elephants.

 # Plan your own... longitudinal study

Fagen *et al.* used an observation to investigate learning in captive elephants. Why not try designing a longitudinal study to investigate animal learning?

Imagine...

Dr Rogers is planning a longitudinal study to investigate whether the accuracy of the elephants' trunk wash decreases over time in the absence of positive reinforcement.

➤➤ What advice would you give Dr Rogers about how to conduct a longitudinal study to investigate this?

Planning a longitudinal study

A longitudinal study is a non-experimental method. This said, you can also have experiments with a longitudinal design (see page 195). When planning a non-experimental longitudinal study, it is important to consider the tests or tasks that participants or non-human animals will undertake, how these will be scored, how often participants or their handlers/owners will be contacted to take part in the research, how procedures will be standardised and what controls will be put in place.

▼ Table 3.4 Features of a longitudinal study

Main features of a longitudinal study	Consider...
Tests or tasks	Longitudinal studies often require participants to take part in the same tests or tasks repeatedly over a period of time. What test or tasks might Dr Rogers use to determine the elephants' accuracy at performing the trunk wash?
Scoring	Longitudinal studies need to compare people's data sets over time. What data will Dr Rogers collect about the elephants' accuracy at performing the trunk wash over time?
Frequency or interval	Longitudinal studies investigate any changes that may occur over a period of time. In order to gather valid data about how accurately the elephants perform the trunk wash, how long will Dr Roger's study last for and how frequently will the elephants need to be tested?
Recontacting of participants (for repeated testing)	Participants in longitudinal studies need to be re-approached for repeated testing. How will Dr Rogers ensure that she has access to the same elephants over the whole period of the study?
Controls and standardisation	In order to compare data over a period of time, procedures need to be standardised and controls put in place. How can Dr Rogers ensure that her procedure is the same each time elephants attend testing? What controls can she put in place?

Evaluating your plan

Dr Rogers shares your ideas with her colleagues. Some of them think it is a great idea; others are not so sure. Think about the practical strengths and weaknesses of your suggestions.

▼ Table 3.5 Evaluating your plan

	Describe	Explain
Strengths	What unique insight might be gained from Dr Rogers undertaking a longitudinal study? How would this strengthen the validity of the data?	Would it be possible for Dr Rogers to gain this data using another research method? If so, why might a longitudinal study give a more valid insight into the accuracy of the trunk-wash performance in elephants over time?
Weaknesses	What issues might arise with the research taking place over a very long period of time? Why might this compromise the validity of the data?	If the validity of the data is compromised by the study's length, what impact will this have on any findings about the elephants' ability to perform the trunk wash accurately over time?
Improvements	Consider the weakness you gave above. How might you improve Dr Rogers' procedure to overcome this issue?	How would this improvement affect the validity and/or reliability of the data Dr Rogers collects about the elephants' ability to perform the trunk wash accurately over time?

The elephants in Fagen *et al.*'s study spent many hours a day with their mahouts, grazing in the jungle and drinking from a nearby river (5.00–7.00 a.m. and 10.30–4.00 p.m.). How do you think the results might have differed if the mahouts had trained the elephants in how to perform the trunk wash rather than the researchers?

▲ Figure 3.9 The mahouts took the elephants out to graze in the jungle at 5.00–7.00 a.m. before their first training session and between 10.30 a.m. and 4.00 p.m., when the next session would start.

LEARNING LINK

On page 87, you learned about operant conditioning, a technique that can be used to modify behaviour. What type of reinforcement is being used when the elephants are given chopped banana?

STUDY TIP

The participants in this study were Asian elephants. This is important as one of the issues and debates in the Cambridge International syllabus is about the use of animals in psychological research. This study highlights the use of aversive stimuli (the sharp sticks used in the traditional methods) and rewards (used by the researchers) as ways of training animals. These terms are important with reference to the ethical guidelines relating to the use of animals. When planning hypothetical studies using animals, be sure to apply the correct ethical guidelines and think about issues such as the number and species of animals used and how they are housed. Try to avoid procedures that involve pain, distress or deprivation wherever possible.

TEST YOURSELF

1 Explain what is meant by 'operant conditioning', using this study as an example. [2]
2 Describe the psychology being investigated in the study by Fagen *et al.* [4]
3 Explain why this study is from the learning approach. [2]
4 Fagen *et al.* conducted structured observations throughout the trunk-wash training sessions. Give one strength of using structured observations in this study. [2]
5 Fagen *et al.* only used five elephants in their study. Suggest one reason why generalisations cannot be made from the sample in this study. [2]
6 Paavak has decided to interview some of the mahouts about the use of traditional methods versus secondary reinforcement training using rewards. Describe how Paavak could conduct semi-structured interviews with the mahouts about how they train their elephants. [10]
(See page 184 for tips on planning a study using semi-structured interviews, including the required features.)

3.2.2 Describing Fagen *et al.* (elephant learning)

Think!

What was the role of the mahouts in this study?

Think!

The elephants had to actively put their trunk into the trainer's hand so that saline or sterile water could be inserted. If you were the trainer, how would you use capturing, luring, shaping and primary and secondary reinforcers to encourage the elephant to be gentle and only offer the correct part of their trunk?

Think!

Why do you think the trainers did not start the performance tests until after session 10?

METHODOLOGY

observation

behavioural checklist

animal ethics

Do you think the fact that the elephants were well fed made them easier or harder to train? Which technique is being illustrated in Figure 3.10?

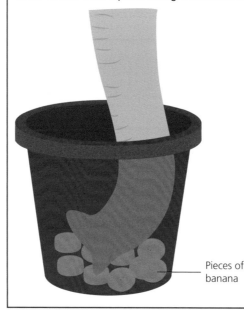

Pieces of banana

◄ Figure 3.10 Fagen *et al.* used various techniques to positively reinforce the elephants for behaviours that were part of the trunk wash.

▶ AIM

This observational study aimed to investigate whether secondary positive reinforcement could be used to train the elephants to voluntarily complete a trunk wash, a behaviour that allows the elephants to be tested for a disease called TB.

▶ RESEARCH METHODOLOGY

Fagen *et al.* conducted a controlled observation of the elephant training sessions. The observations took place while the elephants were chained in their stalls at the stable where they lived and not in the wild, for example.

It was also structured in that the observers used a behavioural checklist (see Table 3.6) to measure how successful the elephants were in completing various behaviours involved in the trunk wash.

▼ Table 3.6 Description of trained behaviours

Behaviour	Description
Trunk here	The distal end of the trunk is placed gently on top of the outstretched palm of the trainer, with the ventral aspect of the trunk in contact with the trainer's palm.
Trunk up	The distal end of the trunk is held upward either in a loose curl with the dorsal aspect of the tip of the trunk in close contact with the elephant's own forehead or is held diagonally up and outward with a completely straight trunk. The exact height or angle of the trunk is not measured.
Bucket	The distal end of the trunk is gently placed inside a bucket.
Blow	The elephant gives a strong, sharp exhale through the trunk.
Steady	The elephant holds the trunk still with the trunk held in the position previously requested (trunk here, trunk down or trunk out). The elephant can move his or her feet, ears, head, tail and body slightly as long as the trunk remains still in the previous position requested.
Syringe	The elephant holds the trunk still in the trunk-here position to have the distal end of a catheter tip syringe placed inside the nostril of the trunk and up to 60 ml of saline or water instilled into the trunk.
Blow into bucket	The elephant places the distal end of the trunk in the bucket and gives a strong, sharp exhale through the trunk.
Trunk down	The trunk is held in a relaxed position with the trunk hanging loose towards the ground.
Trunk out	The trunk is held stretched straight outward, approximately parallel to the ground.
Targeting	The elephant moves such that the centre of the forehead makes contact with the end of a targeting stick placed at the height of the forehead.

Sample

The researchers studied five female elephants – four juveniles (infants) aged 5–7 years old and one adult. The young elephants were all born in captivity. The adult elephant was at least 50 years old. The elephants were chosen as they were all relatively gentle/tame and none was pregnant, and because their mahouts (handlers) were all happy to take part. The elephants had no previous experience with secondary positive reinforcement training and had only ever been trained using traditional methods. The mahouts were present in all sessions to maintain the trainers' safety but they did not interact with the elephants.

▶ PROCEDURE

Training the elephants

Elephants were trained in the morning (7.30–10.00 a.m.) and/or afternoon (4.00–7.00 p.m.). Session times depended on the availability of the mahouts, but they were never more than two days apart.

What did the elephants have to do?

To complete a trunk wash, elephants had to:
1 Put their trunk into the trainer's hand (so saline/sterile water can be inserted).
2 Lift their trunk and hold (so the fluid can flow into the base of the trunk).
3 Lower their trunk into a bucket.
4 Blow into the bucket (to remove the fluid).
5 Hold steady (keep trunk still) – a final behaviour marking the end of the sequence, before the elephant can relax.

Initially, the syringe of saline/sterile water was not used; the elephants just had to learn the different behaviours that would be necessary. Three other steps called targeting, trunk down and trunk out were also taught but not included in this study, as they were not part of the trunk wash.

How were the elephants trained?

1 **Capturing:** The elephants were encouraged to perform natural behaviours that were already part of their usual behaviour, using rewards – for example, if an elephant spontaneously lifted her trunk up, she would be given chopped banana (a primary reinforcer); this *captured* the behaviour and made trunk lifting more common.
2 **Luring:** More unusual behaviours were encouraged by careful positioning of treats by the trainer – for example, if the trainer needed the elephant to stretch its trunk out, they would put a treat out of reach to *lure* them towards it.
3 **Shaping:** To begin with, elephants were rewarded for all behaviours that were similar to the final goal – for example, they might be rewarded for blowing fluid *near to* the bucket. However, gradually the elephants were only rewarded for accurate behaviours – for example, blowing the fluid *into* the bucket. Their behaviours were *shaped* to become more accurate over time.

4 Secondary reinforcers: The trainers taught the elephants to associate the sound of a whistle (a secondary reinforcer) with the arrival of chopped banana (a primary reinforcer). This meant the whistle could be used to reward behaviour immediately, helping the elephant to quickly learn the association between their behaviour and the reward.

Verbal cues and behavioural chaining

The trainers introduced one-syllable verbal cues to prompt the elephants once they had successfully learned all five behaviours. These cues were non-words and meant nothing specific in English or Nepali as the researchers did not want the mahouts to think the elephants could understand human language (a common myth in the area). Behavioural chaining was used to encourage the elephants to perform the five behaviours in order, following the verbal cue. Starting with just two behaviours, the elephants were only rewarded if they completed the behaviours in the correct order. Gradually, more behaviours were added until the elephant could perform all five in order.

The syringe and sample fluid

The syringe was only introduced when the elephants had learned the trunk-wash behaviours. The syringe is an aversive stimulus as the elephants might find it unpleasant. To help them to accept the syringe, the trainers gradually brought it closer to the elephant's trunk, during step 1 (trunk in hand), rewarding the elephants with banana, until they were happy to have the syringe touch their trunks. This is called desensitisation. The researchers also used counterconditioning to teach the elephants to associate the syringe with the arrival of chopped banana. Gradually, the syringe went from being an aversive stimulus to a conditioned stimulus.

Once the elephants were able to tolerate the syringe touching the outside of their trunks, the trainer gradually encouraged them to accept the syringe being placed inside the trunk, slowly moving towards injecting a droplet of fluid, building gradually from 1 to 15 ml, to the full 60 ml necessary for the test.

Measured variables

There were three main measured variables recorded by an assistant who observed each training session:
- minutes of training from the point at which the elephant was offered her first cue to her response to the last cue
- number of offers/cues made by the trainer to the elephant
- success rate for each behaviour and each sequence; starting at session 10, the elephants were tested after every fifth session. They were tested on everything they had learned up to that point. They were considered to have passed the training if they showed the correct behaviour following 8 out of 10 offers/cues (80 per cent). Behaviours were judged as successful if the trainer felt that they would function adequately in a real TB trunk-wash test.

Elephants were also graded on their ability to perform sequences of behaviours – for example, trunk in hand followed by trunk up. The success criterion was again 80 per cent and they could score between 80 and 100 per cent on any sequences they had learned. In this case, individual behaviours were not retested as the elephant had already shown them as part of the sequence. In this case, the individual behaviours were scored as 90 per cent successful. If an elephant failed a sequence, they were tested on shorter sequences and/or individual behaviours.

The only two behaviours that were regularly tested on their own were steps 3 and 5: trunk down and hold steady. Training was concluded when the elephant had a success rate of $\geq$ 80 per cent on the full five-step trunk wash.

▶ RESULTS

The four juvenile elephants all learned the full trunk wash in 25–35 sessions. The mean average session duration was 12 minutes, ranging from 10 to 13 minutes, and the overall training time for these elephants was 367 minutes, with a range of 194 minutes (257–451 minutes). Elephant 5, the older elephant, was never tested on the full trunk wash as she failed to learn the full sequence in the time available. The behaviours that she could not master were blowing into the bucket and holding her trunk steady. Elephants 2 and 4 also never fully mastered the trunk steady behaviour, except as part of the full trunk wash. Elephant 5 was also never fully desensitised to the syringe. When her training sessions were added, the mean increased to 378 minutes. Over the course of the study, the elephants' success rate for accurate individual behaviours and sequences increased from 39 per cent after 10 sessions to 89.3 per cent after 35 sessions.

▼ Table 3.7 Data on number of sessions and average session times for individual elephants

	Number of sessions to pass trunk wash	Mean average session time (minutes)	Individual behaviours failed
Elephant 2	25	10.29	Steady
Elephant 1	30	12.42	None
Elephant 3	35	13.27	None
Elephant 4	35	11.11	Steady

Individual behaviours varied significantly in terms of the amount of practice necessary to master them. For example, the most difficult behaviour was the first one (trunk here/trunk in hand), which took an average of 295 offers, compared with lower trunk into bucket (61 offers) and blow into bucket (54 offers), which required considerably less practice (see Figure 3.11).

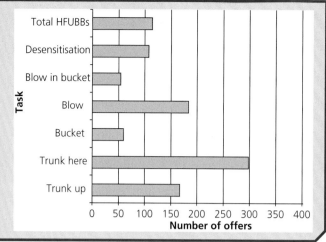

▶ Figure 3.11 Average offers made for each of the basic behavioural tasks required to pass a performance test, indicating relative difficulty in learning the task. Total HFUBBs represents the total offers made for the trunk-wash sequence (here, fluid, up, bucket, and blow)

▶ **CONCLUSIONS**

Fagen *et al.* concluded that secondary positive reinforcement is effective for training juvenile, traditionally trained elephants to voluntarily and reliably participate in a trunk wash.

▶ **LEARNING LINK**

This study uses the operant conditioning principle of reinforcement – that is, desired behaviours were rewarded meaning they become more frequent. But animals and people also learn by observation and imitation of others, as you learnt about in the study by Bandura *et al.* (page 90). In one study, Andrew *et al.* (2013) trained an elephant called Swazi to solve puzzles to receive food. Six more females observed Swazi's puzzle-solving behaviour. The young elephants showed greater focus and spent longer interacting with the puzzles they had observed Swazi solving than ones they had not seen before. This suggests elephant learning is affected by observation of other elephants.

With the Andrews *et al.* study in mind, do you think the elephants in the study by Fagen *et al.* would have learned the trunk wash faster or slower if they had been trained together in one large stable rather than separate stalls?

STUDY TIP

In this study, the exact nature of the behaviours taught and how this was done is crucial to your understanding. Why not role play a training session with a group of friends? Draw lots to see who will be the trainer, the elephant (from 1–5), the observer and the mahout. Who has the easiest job and who has the hardest? You may want to try again in a different role! Investing time in this way will help you to learn all the small study details. Reading and making notes from the original paper is also an excellent way to deepen your understanding of exactly what was done and when.

TEST YOURSELF

1 Describe three behaviours that were part of the trunk wash that were being taught to the elephants in the study by Fagen *et al.* [4]
2 Outline two results relating to Elephant 5 in this study. [2]
3 Explain one similarity and one difference between the study by Fagen *et al.* (elephant learning) and one other study from the learning approach. [8]
4 Researchers must consider ethical guidelines when using animals in psychological research. One of the guidelines is about the use of reward, deprivation and aversive stimuli. Outline what is meant by 'deprivation and aversive stimuli' using examples from this study. [4]
5 Suggest two reasons why it may not be possible to generalise the findings from this study. [4]
6 Explain two ethical guidelines relating to the use of animals in psychological research that are relevant to this study. [4]

3.2.3 Evaluating Fagen *et al.* (elephant learning)

Think!

What reasons can you think of that might explain why the oldest elephant struggled to learn the trunk wash, other than her age? Why was the youngest elephant allowed to complete fewer trials in the performance test than the older elephants?

Think!

If you could make one methodological improvement to this study, what would it be and why? Pair up with a friend to see whether you agree with their suggestion. When you have compared your answers, you may wish to change or add to your improvement.

Think!

Only five elephants participated in this study but a small sample size is sometimes considered a strength in animal studies. Can you explain why?

Elephant 1 was the youngest of the group and, like a young human, she became distracted and impatient if training sessions went on for too long. Therefore, the researchers decreased her performance tests from 8–16 offers/trials to just 5. How is this both a strength and a weakness of the study?

Ethical issues

Distress

One strength is that ethical guidelines were followed for both the animals and the trainers. Despite the elephants' leg chains, they were able to walk away from their trainers if they did not want to participate. The chains still allowed the elephants to move freely within their stalls. This is important as it helped reduce distress (psychological harm) of the animals as well as the risk of physical harm to the trainers, observers and/or mahouts, who could have been injured if an elephant became unco-operative.

Methodological issues

Reliability

Using a behavioural checklist

Another strength was the use of a behavioural checklist which detailed the exact operational descriptions of each of the taught behaviours. For example, the trunk-up behaviour was described as 'the distal end of the trunk is held upward either in a loose curl with the dorsal aspect of the tip of the trunk in close contact with the elephant's own forehead or is held diagonally up and outward with a completely straight trunk'. These detailed descriptions helped increase the reliability of the observer's decisions regarding whether the elephant passed or failed each aspect of the performance test.

If two independent observers had each rated the elephants' behaviour, they may not have found the same results. How can reliability be improved in an observational study such as Fagen *et al.*'s?

▲ Figure 3.12 Two observers may report different results

Validity

No additional cues from the mahouts

One strength was that the mahouts complied with the researchers' request not to speak to or signal to the elephants in any way. This is important as it means changes in the elephants' behaviour must have resulted from the secondary positive reinforcement training delivered by the trainer and not from additional communication from the mahout. This helps to increase the validity of the finding that secondary positive reinforcement training is helpful in training elephants to voluntarily participate in trunk washing.

Problem with the behavioural checklist

A weakness was Fagen *et al.*'s operational definition of 'steady'. To pass the steady performance test, the elephants had to stay still in various different trunk positions. They had to pass three trunk-here and trunk-down tests and four trunk-up tests (a very important part of the trunk wash). The elephants were better at trunk up and trunk here but not so good at trunk down, only reaching about 70 per cent accuracy overall. As the success criterion was 80 per cent, the elephants regularly failed the steady task. This is important as the very prescriptive operational definition meant the data did not reflect the elephants' true ability on two of the trunk positions.

Another weakness was that the total training time included training on a few behaviours that were not part of the trunk wash. For example, four elephants were trained on a behaviour called trunk out, but the trainers stopped shaping this behaviour when they realised it was not necessary. This means that the total training time does not accurately reflect the time taken to train the elephants to perform the trunk wash. The time would be reduced if the unnecessary trunk-out training sessions were subtracted from the total. This reduces the validity of the findings.

Objectivity and subjectivity

Rating success and failure

A weakness was that the measurement of the elephant's performance was subjective. Despite the detailed behavioural checklist, the trainer had to decide whether they felt the elephant would be successful if they were performing a real trunk wash, not just whether it matched the description on the checklist or not. This is a weakness because the trainers may have been biased towards viewing behaviours as successful when another observer might have interpreted the same behaviour as unsuccessful – for example, the angle of the trunk may not have been quite right or some droplets of fluid may have been spilled.

Generalisations and ecological validity

Generalising beyond the sample

Another weakness is the small sample size, specifically the lack of male and adult elephants in the sample. There was only one adult female (Elephant 5) and she failed to learn the full trunk-wash sequence. Older elephants may be able to learn using secondary positive reinforcement training as this animal suffered from physical issues that might have affected her behaviour (the mahouts said she might have impaired vision and/or trunk weakness). She also had an abscess on her foot, which made her impatient and unfocused. All of these factors mean it is not possible to generalise her lack of learning to other older elephants.

Generalising to everyday life

A strength of the study is that the data was collected in a lively, naturalistic setting. For example, large groups of tourists often gathered during training sessions, plus there were many distracting noises from animals in the surrounding jungle. This increases ecological validity, suggesting that it would be possible to achieve similar results with elephants in their normal settings, such as zoos or safari parks.

ISSUES AND DEBATES

Individual versus situational explanations

Elephant 5 was the only elephant which failed to learn the trunk-wash sequence within the time available. This could have been due to individual differences; she was much older than the other elephants, for example, and may have had some physical health problems that affected her ability to reproduce the required behaviours (e.g. blowing out the fluid).

Alternatively, her slower rate of learning may have been due to situational factors – for example, the trainers may have responded differently to her and aspects of the environment were also different, such as distractions from the young calf who often strayed into her stall.

Applications to everyday life

Improving captive animal welfare

Fagen *et al.* have developed a relatively safe and efficient way of training captive elephants to co-operate during critical veterinary procedures. The trunk wash is central to the management of TB in animal sanctuaries and zoological parks both in Nepal and overseas. This is important because not only does it help to maintain the health and wellbeing of these incredible animals, but it also reduces cases of TB in humans, who can catch the disease from infected elephants.

Furthermore, Fagen *et al.*'s technique can be easily adapted to teach other behaviours through positive reinforcement. For example, Deane (2017) explains how animals as diverse as zebras, macaws, tortoises and tropical fish have all been trained to undergo procedures including blood samples, x-rays and transportation to new environments using rewards. These important advances in veterinary practice reduce the need for manual restraint and sedative drugs, decreasing stress and improving wellbeing.

Reflections

The findings of the study by Fagen *et al.* suggest that secondary positive reinforcement is an effective way of training elephants to take an active role in the veterinary procedures needed to keep them fit and healthy, but the small sample size and the fact that the trainers were so highly experienced may mean that it is not always as easy to achieve such strong results.

> ## LEARNING LINK

This study is similar to the study by Hassett *et al.* (monkey toy preferences) in many ways. For example, both used captive animals as participants and both used behavioural checklists to collect observational data. There are a variety of differences between the studies though. Hassett *et al.* aimed to learn about humans through studying animals, whereas Fagen *et al.* aimed to improve animal welfare. Hassett *et al.* used an experimental design to compare male and female monkeys, whereas Fagen *et al.* was non-experimental as there was no independent variable. Can you think of any more similarities and differences between these two studies? Remember, when making comparisons, you can compare aspects of the methodology as well as compare their strengths and weaknesses and links to issues and debates.

STUDY TIP

One problem with this study was that the researchers only used one observer to record the duration of each session, the number of offers made by the trainer and the elephants' success rate on their performance tasks (from session 10). Remember that using just one observer means the data may be subjective as it may be affected by observer bias. If there were two observers, both of them may be affected by personal biases, but if they record similar findings, then at least the data is more reliable. If the observers do not record similar data, then the data is unreliable. Remember to rehearse the meaning of key methods terminology, such as reliability, validity, objectivity and subjectivity, regularly to keep your knowledge fresh. Also, just because there is a single observer does not mean the study lacks inter-observer reliability; you can only know this from checking with multiple observers!

> ## TEST YOURSELF

1 Explain one way in which the procedure was standardised in Fagen *et al.* [2]
2 Suggest two real-world applications of the study by Fagen *et al.*, one that applies to the elephants and one that applies to humans. [4]
3 Evaluate the study by Fagen *et al.* in terms of two strengths and two weaknesses. At least one of your evaluation points must be about the use of animals in psychological research. [10]
4 Fagen *et al.*'s study is an example of a controlled observation. Explain similarities and differences between naturalistic and controlled observations with reference to this study. [6]
5 Explain one effect of uncontrolled variables using an example from this study. [2]
6 Define qualitative and quantitative data using examples from this study. [4]

3.3 Saavedra and Silverman (button phobia)

3.3.1 Background

Introducing Wendy Silverman and Lissette Saavedra

▲ Figure 3.13 Dr Wendy Silverman

▲ Figure 3.14 Dr Lissette Saavedra

Dr Wendy Silverman is a Professor of Psychology and Child Psychiatry at the Yale School of Medicine where she is Director of the Child Study Center Anxiety and Mood Disorders Program. At the time of the case study of the boy with a button phobia, she was the graduate advisor and mentor of (now Dr) Lissette Saavedra. Lissette (therapist) and Wendy (supervisor) say they felt that 'this child's phobia would be of likely and novel interest to the field and an awesome way to show the linkage between clinical care and clinical science'.

Drs Silverman and Saavedra have continued to have satisfying and fulfilling careers advancing knowledge about anxiety and phobic disorders in children and adolescents. They shared a quote from Eleanor Roosevelt, US political figure, diplomat, activist and First Lady of the United States (1933–1945), who they both admire, saying her advice is helpful not only for anxious children, but for us all:

> You gain strength, courage, and confidence by every experience in which you really stop to look fear in the face. You must do the thing which you think you cannot do.

You can follow Lissette Saavedra on Twitter @DraSaavedra

Think!

Expectancy learning and **evaluative learning** are both linked to the development of **phobias**, but how are they different?

Think!

When was the last time you felt disgusted? Maybe you ate something that made you feel sick or smelt something really horrible. How is that different from when we feel disgusted by something that someone said or did? What other human emotions are linked to disgust? Could these feelings also lead to a phobia?

Think!

How could you create a phobia using the emotion of disgust? Do you think it is ethical to conduct research like this? Could animal experiments be used as an alternative?

KEY TERMS

evaluative learning

phobias

classical conditioning

disgust response

operant conditioning

fear response

Imagine you're eating a lovely, tasty apple; suddenly you see a maggot in your apple and you feel disgusted! Next time you see apples in the shop, you suddenly feel sick again! This is evaluative learning as you now associate apples with the nasty thought of eating a maggot. You now evaluate apples in a negative way. This is called taste aversion. Are there any foods that trigger a **disgust response** for you? Can you remember what the experience was that made you hate this particular food?

▲ Figure 3.15 Finding a maggot in your apple might put you off eating apples altogether!

The psychology being investigated

Phobias

This study explores the case of a nine-year-old boy with a phobia of buttons. A phobia is an intense fear or anxiety that occurs every time a person comes into contact with a certain object or situation. Common phobias include spiders, flying, heights, blood and injections. While these things may be scary for many people, a person with a phobia experiences a level of fear that is much higher than you might expect based on the actual level of danger. In fact, many people have phobias of things that are completely harmless. People with phobias will do whatever they can to avoid their feared object/situation and this can lead to difficulties at home, school and/or work.

Classical conditioning

One explanation of phobias is that they are learned through **classical conditioning** (see page 87). If a neutral stimulus (something that normally does not cause fear) is present at the same time as something scary, we may learn to associate the neutral stimulus with the scary stimulus. The previously neutral stimulus is now called a conditioned stimulus because it triggers the same level of fear as whatever it was that scared us in the first place. This is called expectancy learning.

Evaluative learning

Evaluative learning is a special type of classical conditioning. If a neutral stimulus is paired with something that the person finds really disgusting, then the previously neutral stimulus may now provoke the same negative reaction as the disgusting stimulus. Evaluative learning is not the same as expectancy learning; the person does not anticipate any danger or threat (they do not feel scared), they just experience an involuntary disgust response due to the strong association that has been made. They now perceive or evaluate the previously neutral stimulus in a negative way but cannot always explain why.

Operant conditioning

Saavedra and Silverman used the principles of **operant conditioning** in their treatment of the boy's button phobia. They used positive reinforcement (praise from his mother) to reward him for handling buttons during the therapy sessions. This made it more likely that he would approach buttons in a positive way in the future.

Background

Diagnosing phobias

Diagnostic manuals are used to decide whether a person's symptoms are severe enough to require a diagnosis and subsequent treatment. These contain detailed criteria that must be met, including the duration and type of symptoms. Saavedra and Silverman refer to a manual called the Diagnostic and Statistical Manual (DSM) from the USA. This classification system lists more than 300 disorders organised into 22 different categories. The boy in this study was diagnosed using a semi-structured interview schedule called the Anxiety Disorders Interview Schedule for DSM-IV–Child and Parent versions (ADIS-C/P), which was based on the DSM-IV criteria.

Disgust

Disgust is an important human emotion that helps us to survive (i.e. it is adaptive). The negative feelings that are produced, including feeling sick/nauseous, ensure that we avoid certain things that could make us ill – for example, contaminated blood or mouldy food. Saavedra and Silverman explain that through evaluative learning we can learn to associate a harmless stimulus with one which causes disgust and this leads to anxiety and avoidance of the harmless object/situation.

Previous research

Saavedra and Silverman's study was important because, at the time, few researchers had explored the role of disgust in childhood phobias. Hepburn and Page (1999) had studied 47 adults with blood-injury phobias and found that targeting disgust was helpful in reducing certain symptoms, and De Jong *et al.* (1997) had found that spider-phobic children were less disgusted by spiders as their fear reduced. However, no one had tried to reduce disgust in order to reduce fear in a phobic child.

Ants running on your arm (UCS) -> Disgust (UCR)

Flower (NS) + Ants running on your arm (UCS) -> Disgust (UCR)

Flower (CS) -> Disgust (CR)

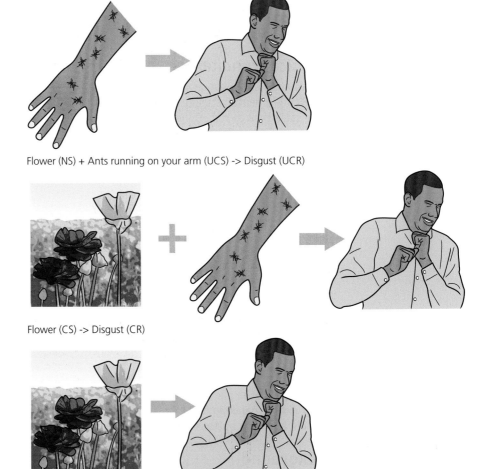

▲ Figure 3.16 Stages of evaluative learning

Saavedra and Silverman in brief

This case study describes how a young boy developed his phobias of buttons through evaluative learning, how the therapists confirmed his diagnosis of specific phobia and then how they went on to treat him using a combination of behavioural exposure and disgust imagery exposure and cognitions. Saavedra and Silverman explain that targeting disgust in this unusual phobia was central to the success of the treatment.

What are classification systems?

Classification systems help psychiatrists (medical doctors specialising in the diagnosis, prevention and treatment of mental disorders) and clinical psychologists to decide whether a person has a specific disorder or not and, if so, which disorder they have. The DSM is used in many countries around the world but was originally published in 1952. It has been revised several times since, and in 2001 (when Saavedra and Silverman completed their study) it had been updated four times. This is why it is referred to as DSM-IV – the IV stands for four in Roman numerals. In 2013, the fifth version was released and it is now referred to as DSM-5. Another commonly used system is the International Classification of Diseases and Related Health Problems (the ICD), which is published by the World Health Organization. This system has also seen many revisions and the newest version, ICD-11, will be used from 2022. Some countries also have their own systems, such as the Chinese Classification of Mental Disorders (CCMD-3).

➤➤ Can a diagnostic manual created in one culture be useful for understanding mental health and wellbeing of people in another culture?

➤➤ Do you think that it is possible to diagnose people from different cultures using the same criteria or should different cultures have different systems?

Plan your own... laboratory experiment

Saavedra and Silverman used a case study of a child with a button phobia to investigate how classical conditioning can be used to treat phobias by focusing on disgust and **fear responses**. Why not try designing a laboratory experiment to investigate treatments for phobias?

Imagine...

Professor Bins would like to conduct a laboratory experiment into a new treatment for phobias that he has developed based on classical conditioning.

➤➤ What advice would you give Professor Bins about how to conduct a laboratory experiment to investigate his new treatment?

Planning a laboratory experiment

A laboratory experiment is an experimental method that takes place in a controlled setting. The researcher manipulates the independent variable and also has a significant amount of control over extraneous variables. When planning a laboratory experiment, it is important that you identify and operationalise the independent and dependent variables, as well as identify the controls you will put in place. See page 117 for more information on laboratory experiments.

▼ Table 3.8 Features of a laboratory experiment

Main features of a laboratory experiment	Consider...
Independent variable	In laboratory experiments, researchers manipulate one or more dependent variable(s) to see how they affect other variables. What will be the operational definition of the independent variable in this study?
Dependent variable	In laboratory experiments, researchers measure dependent variable(s) to see whether they are affected by changes in the independent variable(s). What will the operational definition of the successful treatment of a phobia be in this study? How will this data be collected?
Controls	Laboratory experiments tend to have a high degree of control over anything which might affect the dependent variable(s) other than the independent variable(s). What controls would you suggest putting in place that might otherwise affect the study's findings?
Experimental design	An experiment can have an independent measures, repeated measures or matched pairs design. Which experimental design would you suggest Professor Bins uses in this study? Will the participants take part in all conditions of the independent variable, or just one?
Counterbalancing or random allocation	Depending on the experimental design being used, researchers need to consider the use of counterbalancing or random allocation to improve the validity of their data. Are you able to use either of these in your study design for Professor Bins?

Evaluating your plan

Professor Bins shares your ideas with his colleagues. Some of them think it is a great idea; others are not so sure. Think about the practical strengths and weaknesses of your suggestions.

▼ Table 3.9 Evaluating your plan

	Describe	Explain
Strengths	How might the high level of control in your study design improve the validity of the findings?	Why might this strengthen any findings about the effectiveness of the new treatment for phobias?
Weaknesses	Why might the laboratory environment be a weakness of this study?	What impact would this have on any conclusions drawn about the effectiveness of the new treatment for phobias?
Improvements	Consider the weakness you described above. How might you improve Professor Bins' procedure to overcome this issue?	How would this improvement enhance the validity and/or reliability of the data Professor Bins collects about his new treatment for phobias?

LEARNING LINK

Sometimes you will be asked to explain similarities and differences between studies, usually within the same approach. This study used a non-experimental method, the case study, whereas Bandura et al.'s study was experimental. They both used observation to collect data though. Think about how Bandura et al. did this. How was this different from Saavedra and Silverman's observation of the boy during therapy? At one point in the Bandura et al. study, the researchers collected data about the children on rating scales. Who completed these scales, and how was this similar to or different from the feelings thermometer ratings in Saavedra and Silverman's study?

STUDY TIP

The main participant in this study was a child. This is important as one of the issues and debates in the Cambridge International AS Level syllabus is about the use of children in psychological research. There are two other studies in the Cambridge International AS syllabus that use children: Bandura et al. and Pozzulo et al. You might be asked about these studies in relation to this specific issue and debate. Can you think of any special ethical considerations that apply when working with children? The children in Bandura et al.'s study were much younger than Saavedra and Silverman's participant.
● How might the age of the participants affect the way that the research is conducted?
● Which study seems least ethical of the three?

> ## ▶ TEST YOURSELF
>
> 1 Outline how a phobia can develop through evaluative learning.   [2]
> 2 One assumption of the learning approach is that people come into the world as 'a blank slate'. Explain what this means with reference to the boy in Saavedra and Silverman's study.   [4]
> 3 Hilary believes that Saavedra and Silverman support the role of nurture in the development of phobias but Chris thinks nature may also be involved. Explain why Chris might be right.   [2]
> 4 Saavedra and Silverman used a case study to explore a child's phobia of buttons. Explain one strength of this research method with reference to validity.   [2]
> 5 The therapists could have visited the boy at school and observed him in class. Explain one way that the researcher could have collected quantitative data while observing him in class.   [2]
> 6 It is difficult to generalise from case studies as only one person is studied in detail. Outline one way the researchers could have used volunteer sampling to achieve a larger sample of children with phobias.   [2]

3.3.2 Describing Saavedra and Silverman (button phobia)

> ### Think!
>
> Which button-related stimuli did the boy find least distressing (rating 2–3), moderately distressing (rating 4–6) and most distressing (rating 7–8)?

> ### Think!
>
> What do you find really disgusting? Imagine a therapist exposing you to this disgusting thing. Why do you think the boy was able to handle the buttons but felt more distressed/disgusted than he did when he first made the hierarchy?

Can you think of any ways in which the school could have supported the boy and his mother?

▲ Figure 3.17 The boy's phobias made it hard for him to concentrate at school as he worried about touching anything that had touched his shirt buttons

3

> ## AIMS

This case study aimed to:
1 Highlight the role of evaluative learning and disgust in the development and treatment of children's phobias.
2 Test the efficacy (effectiveness) of imagery exposure as part of an exposure-based cognitive-behavioural treatment for a specific phobia of buttons.

METHODOLOGY

case study

interview

rating scale

observation

> ## RESEARCH METHODOLOGY

Saavedra and Silverman is an example of a case study. The researchers present an in-depth exploration of a single case of an unusual/rare condition: button phobia. Both qualitative and quantitative data were provided using a variety of methods – structured **interview**, observation and the use of a psychometric scale to measure subjective distress. The study was longitudinal as the boy's behaviour was studied before, during and after treatment, and he also attended follow-up sessions at 6 and 12 months after treatment.

Measured variables

The boy's approach and avoidance behaviours were carefully observed and recorded during the therapy sessions. Approach behaviours included touching, holding and manipulating the buttons. A feelings thermometer was used to score the participant's subjective level of distress on a nine-point scale ranging from 0–8 (see Figure 3.18 on page 121).

Sample

The participant was a nine-year-old Hispanic-American boy from Florida, USA. He was selected for the study as his mother had brought him to the Child Anxiety and Phobia Program at Florida International University in Miami due to his phobia of buttons. His phobia had started when he was five years old and the boy had been living with his condition for four years. He did not have any other diagnosed disorders (e.g. obsessive-compulsive disorder, OCD).

> ## PROCEDURE

The initial assessment/diagnosis

The boy and his mother were interviewed using a semi-structured interview schedule called the Anxiety Disorders Interview Schedule for DSM-IV–Child and Parent versions (ADIS-C/P). This interview allowed the researchers to confirm that the boy met the criteria to be diagnosed with a specific phobia. This was due to his marked and persistent avoidance of buttons.

The researchers also asked the boy and his mother about stressful life events that may have triggered the phobia. Sometimes anxiety disorders can be triggered by traumatic events (e.g. sexual or physical abuse or accidents) and the researchers needed to rule this out before deciding on the best way to treat him.

They also checked to see whether he met the criteria for any other disorders, such as OCD. Neither the child nor his mother mentioned the key symptoms of OCD (recurrent, persistent and/or intrusive thoughts, impulses or images) and so this was ruled out.

Treatment: behavioural exposure

This phase included four 50-minute exposure-based treatment sessions, 30 minutes on his own and 20 minutes with his mother.

● Creating a disgust/fear hierarchy: The boy worked with the therapists to create a list of 11 stimuli relating to buttons. They used the feelings thermometer to help the boy identify how distressing each stimulus would be for him. They then placed the stimuli into rank order from those that caused him the least distress (large denim jean buttons = 2/8) to the type of buttons that caused him greatest distress (small coloured and small clear plastic buttons = 8/8) (see Table 3.10).

● In vivo exposures: These involved gradual exposures to buttons in vivo (in real life). If the boy was able to tolerate the buttons, his mother would reward him with praise (positive reinforcement). This is known as contingency management.

▼ Table 3.10 Disgust/fear hierarchy with child's ratings of distress

Stimuli	Distress ratings (0–8)
1 Large denim jean buttons	2
2 Small denim jean buttons	3
3 Clip-on denim jean buttons	3
4 Large plastic buttons (coloured)	4
5 Large plastic buttons (clear)	4
6 Hugging mother when she wears large plastic buttons	5
7 Medium plastic buttons (coloured)	5
8 Medium plastic buttons (clear)	6
9 Hugging mother when she wears regular medium plastic buttons	7
10 Small plastic buttons (coloured)	8
11 Small plastic buttons (clear)	8

Treatment: disgust-related imagery exposure

This phase included seven sessions where the therapists asked the boy to describe how buttons look, feel and smell and to explain how he felt while imagining them. The therapists prompted him to imagine buttons of different sizes, including small ones, which he found most distressing. They also used a technique called cognitive restructuring.

Post-treatment and the follow-up phase

The ADIS-C/P was used directly after treatment to measure the efficacy of the treatment and again 6 and 12 months later.

▶ RESULTS

When did the phobias begin?

When asked about stressful life events that might have triggered his phobia, the boy recalled a day at kindergarten (nursery school). He was working on an art project when he ran out of the buttons that he was gluing onto his poster. He went to the front of the class to take some more buttons from a large bowl on his teacher's desk. As he reached in, his hand slipped and the buttons fell onto him. He said the event was distressing. He and his mother agreed that his avoidance of buttons had increased since this event and that he had not faced any other stressful or traumatic events that might be linked to his phobia.

How was the boy's daily functioning affected?

To begin with, he did not have too many problems but gradually he became unable to touch/handle buttons. He was unable to get dressed by himself and his schoolwork suffered because he could not concentrate; he was too worried about touching his school uniform or anything that might have been touched by his shirt buttons. At home, he avoided clothes with buttons and people with buttons on their clothing.

Progress in the first four sessions: behavioural exposure

● Positive outcomes: The boy faced all 11 situations listed in his disgust hierarchy. Approach behaviours increased – for example, he could tolerate more buttons with each exposure (see Figure 3.18).

● Negative outcomes: Subjective ratings of distress (measured using the feelings thermometer) increased dramatically between sessions 2 and 3 and sessions 3 and 4 (see Figure 3.18).
  – He reported being more distressed by 'medium, coloured buttons' and 'hugging his mother when she wears large plastic buttons' than he was when he first created the hierarchy.
  – This was expected according to the theory of evaluative learning and disgust-based phobias, which differ from fear-based phobias.

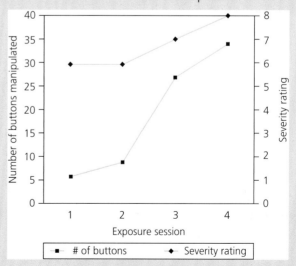

▲ Figure 3.18 Ratings of distress relative to manipulation of buttons in treatment exposure sessions

The next seven sessions: disgust-related imagery and cognitions

When asked about how buttons made him feel, the boy said the idea of buttons on his body was 'disgusting' and 'gross' but it was hard for him to put into words exactly what was disgusting about buttons, except that they smelt unpleasant.

Following the disgust-related imagery exposure, subjective ratings of distress on the feelings thermometer decreased, as seen in Table 3.11.

▼ Table 3.11 Subjective ratings of distress before, during and after disgust-related imagery exposure

	Subjective ratings of distress on the feelings thermometer (0–8)		
	Before	**During**	**After**
Asked to imagine hundreds of buttons falling all over his body	8	5	3
Hugging his mother with a 'shirt full of buttons'	7	4	3

Post-treatment: 6 and 12-month follow-up sessions

At each follow-up session, the ADIS-C/P showed that the boy no longer met the DSM-IV criteria for specific phobia. He reported no distress about button-related stimuli. He was wearing his school uniform shirt, with small clear plastic buttons, every day without any problems.

▶ CONCLUSIONS

Evaluative learning is a useful way of understanding the role of disgust in childhood-specific phobias. While exposure therapy may be helpful in treating fear-based phobias, disgust-based phobias may also require imagery exposure and cognitions, which can be more effective in targeting emotions (e.g. disgust) associated with the stimuli.

Imagery exposure was more helpful than *in vivo* (real-life) exposure where the boy actually handled buttons. Why do you think this was?

▶ LEARNING LINK

This study included an application of operant conditioning in the section on behavioural exposure and contingency management; the boy's mother provided positive reinforcement, contingent (depending) on the boy's successful handling of the buttons. In the study by Fagen *et al.*, you learned about another application of operant conditioning – training elephants in Nepal.

▶ TEST YOURSELF

1   Outline the purpose of the feelings thermometer in this study.   [2]
2   Explain two reasons that the child's mother was also present during the boy's therapy sessions.   [4]
3   Describe how the therapists used imagery exposure to target the emotion of disgust in this study.   [3]
4   Give examples of two types of data collected in this study. One example must be quantitative and the other must be qualitative.   [2]
5   Give two weaknesses of the case study as a research method. You must refer to Saavedra and Silverman in your answer.   [4]
6   Give examples of two measured variables in this study.   [2]

3.3.3 Evaluating Saavedra and Silverman (button phobia)

3

> **Think!**
>
> Can you list the seven ethical guidelines that apply to working with human participants? Which ones are relevant to this study, which includes a nine-year-old child?

> **Think!**
>
> Imagine your friend (who does not study psychology) has a phobia of the dark. She thinks she has inherited this fear from her grandfather, who also hated the dark. What might you tell your friend about whether her fear is likely to be due to nature or nurture?

> **Think!**
>
> Can you think of any ways of improving the validity of this study to make sure that the benefits of therapy are generalisable to the boy's everyday home and school life?

◀ Figure 3.19 The therapy was successful as, at the follow-up appointments at 6 and 12 months, the boy was able to wear his school uniform with a buttoned shirt without distress.

 Do you think therapy would have been as successful if it had been carried out by a different therapist?

Ethical issues

Informed consent

An important strength of this study is that the researchers gained informed consent from both the boy and his mother. Consent was provided for both the initial assessment of his condition and the treatment programme. The mother also consented to the write-up of her son's case for publication. This was a critical aspect of the study as informed consent is necessary to protect people from psychological harm. This was especially important in this study as the mother and child were particularly vulnerable due to the child's phobia.

A potential ethical weakness is that the detailed description of the bowl of buttons tipping onto the child in kindergarten, coupled with his age, ethnicity and city where he lived (Miami), may have compromised his anonymity – that is, he may have been recognisable to classmates or his kindergarten teacher. Case studies often provide very detailed information and so this can be a common problem with this method. If the child's identity was revealed, this could place him at greater risk of harm, even though his mother provided consent for publication.

Methodological issues

Reliability

Test-retest reliability of the diagnostic interviews schedule

A strength of this study was the use of the Anxiety Disorders Interview Schedule for DSM IV–Child and Parent versions (ADIS-C/P). This instrument has been shown to have excellent reliability for diagnosing specific phobias in children aged 6–11. For example, Silverman *et al.* (2001) tested children twice after 7–14 days and found a correlation of +0.84. This shows that the boy's diagnosis was reliable.

Difficulty of replication

Lack of standardisation is a weakness of the case study method as it means the procedure cannot be replicated exactly. Therapy sessions are spontaneous situations where the therapist is led by the client's individual needs. For example, if the child seemed particularly miserable one week, she might chat for longer than usual before starting the button exposures. This means the therapy sessions cannot be conducted in exactly the same way for another individual client, so it is impossible to test the findings for reliability.

Validity

The longitudinal design

A strength of this study was the follow-up sessions at 6 and 12 months. Sometimes efficacy studies do not follow up the participants and if they do it may only be for a short while after the therapy has ended. As the boy was symptom-free on both occasions, this is good evidence that imagery-exposure therapy can have long-lasting effects for children with specific disgust-related phobias. This is important as some therapies have short-term benefits but, without follow-up sessions, researchers cannot know whether they experienced a return of symptoms in the future.

Case study method

A strength of this study was the use of the case study method, which allowed the researchers to collect rich and detailed data using a variety of techniques. For example, the ADIS-C/P semi-structured interview was used to confirm his diagnosis, observations were made of how he interacted with the buttons during therapy and the feelings thermometer was used to gather self-reported data to monitor changes in disgust/distress. This is called triangulation and it improves the validity of the conclusions about the efficacy of the therapy.

Objectivity and subjectivity

One weakness was the use of self-reported data from the mother and child. The mother may have exaggerated the severity of her child's symptoms due to her anxiety about her son, whereas the child may have downplayed his worries, especially in front of his mother. He may also have wished to please his therapists, especially in the later sessions where he wanted them to feel that their work with him had been successful. This is a problem as it increases the subjectivity of the data, meaning the efficacy of the therapy may have been overestimated.

Generalisations and ecological validity

Generalising beyond the sample

A weakness of this case study is that it only focused on one child, a Hispanic-American nine-year-old boy, who was treated at a prestigious university clinic by two expert therapists. The therapy might not have been as effective for a child from a different cultural background, especially if this contrasted with the therapist's background. This means the findings may not generalise to other children and therapists, especially those who are less skilled or experienced.

The use of children in psychological research

This study focused on a nine-year-old child who attended therapy sessions with his mother. The researchers noted that they were especially interested to take this case as button phobias are unusual and also because not much had been published about evaluative learning, disgust and childhood phobias. They used a specially adapted version of the Anxiety Disorders Interview Schedule for DSM-IV that was suitable for children to make sure their diagnosis was valid and the feelings thermometer was used to measure distress in a more child-friendly way, again in the hope of improving the validity of this data.

Applications to everyday life

Training therapists to target disgust

Saavedra and Silverman's findings are important as they highlight that some phobias cannot be treated successfully with exposure therapy alone. When the aversive stimulus is harmless and unthreatening (e.g. buttons), it may be necessary to take a different approach and incorporate imagery exposure and cognitions. This may require additional training to help the therapist to know when this alternative technique might be appropriate and how to create vivid images for children in an ethical yet effective way.

Reflections

Saavedra and Silverman's findings suggest that imagery exposure can be successfully adapted to treat disgust-related phobias in children but they also note that further research must be conducted using control groups. It would also be helpful to explore whether this form of therapy is helpful for children with other types of phobia and whether other therapists can be equally successful when using it with their young clients. It would also be interesting to know whether imagery exposure without the in vivo sessions would be effective as any way of decreasing the number of sessions necessary will help make the therapy more cost-effective and accessible to a larger number of families.

Saavedra and Silverman asked the boy in their case study to show how he was feeling using a nine-point feelings thermometer to rate his level of distress (0–8). Why do you think they used a scale with nine points? Is this a strength or a weakness of the feelings thermometer? (It could be both.)

► LEARNING LINK

Look back at the design of the study by Hölzel *et al.*, which explored the effects of mindfulness on grey matter. This study had a complex design with two groups, one group that attended MBSR sessions and one that did not. Both groups were tested eight weeks apart. How could this design be adapted to further validate the use of imagery-based exposure therapy as a treatment for childhood-specific phobias?

STUDY TIP

Many students (and teachers!) wrongly use the term case study to refer to any study that they are focusing on in a specific essay or class. While this might be acceptable in some subjects, this is not the case in psychology – case study is a piece of psychological terminology with a specific meaning. Try to always label your studies using the correct method (e.g. experiment, observation, self-report, correlation or case study). If you are unsure, just say 'study' or 'investigation'.

TEST YOURSELF

1 Wilson is four years old and has a phobia of scissors. Describe three techniques that a therapist might use to help Wilson to overcome his phobia. [6]

2 This study focused on a nine-year-old child. Explain one issue that must be considered when working with children rather than adults. [3]

3 Evaluate the study by Saavedra and Silverman in terms of two strengths and two weaknesses. At least one of your evaluation points must be about the use of case studies. [10]

4 Outline two ethical guidelines relevant to this study. [2]

5 Describe what is meant by 'reliability' using one example from this study. [2]

6 Give an example of one open question and one closed question that the therapist might have asked the boy or his mother during one of the follow-up sessions. [2]

CHAPTER SUMMARY

Bandura *et al.* (aggression)

Psychology investigated
An investigation of social learning theory and whether children would imitate aggression shown by a model.

Aim
Whether children imitate aggression of a model in the absence of the model and whether they are more likely to imitate a same-sex model.

Procedure
Children observed either an aggressive or a non-aggressive model playing in a room with toys or no model. The aggressive model displayed physical and verbal aggression towards an inflatable Bobo doll. The children were then made mildly frustrated and their behaviour in a new room with toys was observed through a one-way mirror.

Results
● Participants in the aggressive model condition demonstrated more physical and verbal aggression than other groups.
● Boys are more likely to imitate physical aggression and be influenced by a same-sex model.

Conclusion
Observing an aggressive model can lead to imitative aggression, particularly if the model is the same sex.

Strengths
● There were many controls, such as a script for the model and toy placement.
● Children were matched on prior aggression levels across conditions.

Weaknesses
● Risk of psychological harm for the children who viewed the aggressive model.
● The act of watching an adult act aggressively towards an inflatable doll lacks mundane realism.

Links to assumptions
Bandura *et al.* found that children were likely to imitate the behaviour of an aggressive model, showing that we learn through the process of social learning.

Links to issues and debates
The study used young children who were at a sensitive age in their development. This increases the risk of psychological harm for those being exposed to an aggressive model.

A real-life application is to reduce the quantity of violence shown on television, or to only show it late at night when children are not watching, due to the risk of imitation.

Similarities
● Both Bandura *et al.* and Fagen *et al.* investigated how new behaviours can be learnt.
● Both Bandura *et al.* and Saavedra and Silverman used children in their studies.

Differences
● Bandura *et al.* used children as participants, while Fagen *et al.* used animals.
● Bandura *et al.* used multiple children in their study, while Saavedra and Silverman only used one.

Fagen *et al.* (elephant learning)

Psychology investigated
An investigation of how the principles of operant conditioning, including positive, negative, primary and secondary reinforcement, can be used to improve elephant welfare. Elephants are taught a procedure called the trunk wash using shaping and chaining.

Aim
To investigate whether secondary positive reinforcement could be used to train the elephants to voluntarily complete a trunk wash.

Procedure
Elephants underwent training using secondary positive reinforcement to complete each of the five steps involved in the trunk wash. Elephants were trained using capturing, luring, shaping and secondary reinforcers. Each training session was observed, with details of the session and success rate recorded.

Results
The four juvenile elephants all learned the full trunk wash in 25–35 sessions. The older elephant failed to learn the full sequence of the trunk wash in the time available.

Conclusion
Secondary positive reinforcement is effective for training juvenile, traditionally trained elephants to voluntarily participate in a trunk wash.

Strengths
- A behavioural checklist was used, which increased the reliability of observations.
- The captive elephants were observed in their normal setting.

Weaknesses
- The elephants were observed by their trainers, which was subjective.
- A very small sample of five female elephants was used.

Links to assumptions
Elephants were able to learn a new behaviour by using a stimulus–response model, showing that experiences shape behaviour and these changes are directly observable.

Links to issues and debates
One elephant was not able to successfully learn the trunk wash, which may have been due to an individual explanation for behaviour as she was older.

A real-life application of the research is improvement in captive animal welfare as it was shown that positive methods of behavioural shaping could be used to support the elephants in important health checks.

Similarities
- Both Fagen *et al.* and Bandura *et al.* used structured observations.
- Both Fagen *et al.* and Saavedra and Silverman had small sample sizes.

Differences
- Fagen *et al.* studied elephants in their normal environment, while Bandura *et al.* used a laboratory setting.
- Fagen *et al.* used female elephants as participants, while Saavedra and Silverman used a male participant.

Saavedra and Silverman (button phobia)

Psychology investigated
A boy who had developed a phobia through evaluative learning was treated using principles from operant conditioning and classical conditioning.

Aim
To test the effectiveness of imagery exposure as part of an exposure-based cognitive-behavioural treatment for a phobia of buttons.

Procedure
A boy was assessed for a phobia of buttons. He underwent four exposure-based treatment sessions, followed by seven sessions of disgust-related imagery exposure. The efficacy of the treatment was measured immediately afterwards and again 6 and 12 months later.

Results
- Following behavioural exposure, the boy could tolerate more buttons, but distress ratings increased.
- Following disgust-related imagery exposure for buttons, subjective ratings of distress on the fear thermometer decreased and the boy no longer met the diagnostic criteria for a phobia.

Conclusion
Image-exposure therapy may be a more effective treatment for disgust-based phobias than exposure-based treatments.

Strengths
- Follow-up data at 6 and 12 months showed long-lasting effects for imagery-exposure therapy.
- In-depth data was collected through triangulation of observations and self-report data.

Weaknesses
- Replication is difficult due to using a case study method.
- There was a single participant so generalisations are difficult.

Links to assumptions
The boy successfully learnt not to fear buttons through a treatment based on operant and classical conditioning. This shows that we learn through these processes.

Links to issues and debates
The child was nine years old so the researchers used a specially adapted version of the Anxiety Disorders Interview Schedule for DSM-IV suitable for children and the feelings thermometer was used to measure distress in a more child-friendly way.

A real-life application is to consider incorporating image-exposure therapy when the aversive stimulus is harmless and unthreatening.

Similarities
- Both Saavedra and Silverman and Bandura *et al.* collected quantitative data.
- Both Saavedra and Silverman and Fagen *et al.* were attempting to deliberately change/shape behaviour.

Differences
- Saavedra and Silverman collected self-report data, while Bandura *et al.* did not.
- Saavedra and Silverman used a case study as their main research method, while Fagen *et al.* used an observation

4

The Social approach

Learning outcomes

In this chapter, we will discuss:
● the main assumptions, methodology, history, issues and debates of the social approach
● psychological concepts, theories and research relating to the three core studies:
 – Milgram (obedience)
 – Perry *et al.* (personal space)
 – Piliavin *et al.* (subway Samaritans)
● strengths and weaknesses of the three core studies with reference to ethical issues, **reliability**, **validity**, **objectivity** and **subjectivity**, **generalisations**, issues and debates, including applications to everyday life
● how to plan and evaluate your own investigations using **naturalistic observation**, **longitudinal study** and laboratory **experiment**.

▲ Figure 4.1 Obedient pedestrians in New York, but would they help a collapsed passenger on the subway?

Where there are people, there is psychology!

Psychology is everywhere, and these people are in New York, in the United States of America, the location of Piliavin *et al.*'s study of passengers' reactions to an emergency on a subway (underground) train. These people are obeying the rules for behaviour in the city: crossing the street in the correct place and wearing masks to limit the spread of COVID-19, but how would they behave in a different situation, at a carnival, a mass protest or when the streets are packed with holiday shoppers?

In this chapter, we will examine how our behaviour changes in different social situations: how our perception of others, their status or how similar they appear to us affect how we behave. First, let us explore the main assumptions of the social approach.

4.0 Introducing the Social approach

KEY TERMS

social context

social environment

groups

Main assumptions

1 Behaviour, cognitions and emotions are influenced by **social contexts, social environments** and **groups**.

2 Behaviour, cognitions and emotions are influenced by the actual, implied or imagined presence of others.

(Cambridge International, 2021)

Punctuality is an important **cultural norm** – lateness is likely to lead to punishment and/or disapproval from colleagues. Is it ever socially acceptable to be late in the culture where you live? What about being early – how is this different?

▲ Figure 4.2 Being late for work is not an option in Canary Wharf, an important business district in London, in the UK

METHODOLOGY

laboratory setting

field setting

observation

interview

questionnaire

experiment

field experiment

Think!

Think of examples of two social situations – for example, watching a football match versus watching a cricket match or eating in two different types of restaurant. Can you think of some social norms that apply in one situation but not the other?

Think!

Conformity can include things like uploading specific types of content on your social media and following family traditions. Can you think of any examples of conformity from your own life, where you have changed how you behave or what you say or think to fit in with others?

Think!

Social psychologists have found some interesting ways of studying social and cultural norms. For example, Levine *et al.* (1980) observed the accuracy of public clocks, in the United States of America and Brazil, as a measure of the value placed on punctuality. In a series of **questionnaires**, they found that Americans placed more importance on being on time than Brazilians. Can you think of any cultural norms that are important where you live? How could you measure the importance of these norms in a way that is both valid and reliable?

Humans as social animals

Elliott Aronson famously described humans as 'social animals' (Aronson, 1984), emphasising the importance of relationships and **interactions** with other people as key causes of behaviour, thoughts and feelings. Social psychologists like Aronson believe that we are constantly being influenced by our social experiences, both past, present and even imagined future social events. Even when we believe we are acting independently (making our own decisions), social pressure may be affecting our actions (Tavris and Wade, 2001).

Social context versus social environment

The term 'social environment' refers to the immediate social situations where social interactions take place. For example, on page 153, you will learn about a study by Piliavin *et al.* (subway Samaritans) that was conducted in a subway (underground) train carriage involving an emergency situation. Our public behaviour in situations such as this may differ depending on whether there are other passengers on the carriage and who those people are. For example, you might behave differently if you were travelling with your parents or a teacher from your school compared with travelling alone or with a group of friends. These differences arise from our subjective interpretation of the social situation and our role within the group. This is often referred to as the social context. This means the same social environment may impact the people within it in different ways.

Social norms

Gradually, as we experience the many different types of social situations that make up everyday life, we begin to learn about the social norms or expectations that people have about how we should behave within that society. We learn which behaviours are socially acceptable and which are not, which attitudes are acceptable to express and which are not. For example, the study by Perry *et al.* (personal space) explores the concept of personal space. In some cultures, it is socially acceptable to stand very close to other people, whereas in other cultures this would make people feel very uncomfortable. The rules about personal space are just one example of differences in social norms in different social contexts.

Rules for social behaviour are generally unwritten and we must learn them through observational learning (see page 620) as well as social conditioning – we learn from experience that certain behaviours lead to approval and inclusion within **social groups**, whereas other behaviours lead to disapproval and exclusion. For example, it might be okay to stand very close to someone on a packed subway train but this would not be socially acceptable in a relatively empty elevator!

Social psychologists use the key term conformity to explain the changes in an individual's behaviour following exposure to other people and their opinions.

Why do individuals conform?

Much of the research in social psychology has shown that human beings typically have a powerful desire to belong. Many thousands of years ago, humans had to co-operate as members of social groups in order to survive. Natural selection has ensured that humans who possessed behaviours that helped them to live harmoniously within a group became more common, while humans that behaved in ways which damaged their social group became less common, as they were less likely to survive.

In the study by Perry *et al.* (personal space), you will learn about oxytocin. Previous research has shown that this hormone helps to increase social cohesion by encouraging bonding, trust and conformity. Perry *et al.* found that things are a little more complicated, as you will discover on page 144.

Groups

We have used the term groups a lot on this page and it is important to think about exactly what psychologists mean by this term. Groups comprise two or more individuals who are interdependent and share common (the same) goals. A set of individuals become a group when they are aware of each other and feel connected in some way; group norms and roles (e.g. a leader) will emerge, indicating how members should behave and what their responsibilities are within the group.

Actual, implied and imagined presence of others

As co-operative behaviour was so critical to the survival of humans living thousands of years ago, the physical presence of other humans was a powerful influence on behaviour. However, research suggests that even an image of a pair of eyes can increase prosocial behaviour (Bateson *et al.*, 2006). In this experiment, lone participants were able to take a drink and decide whether or not to donate some money in exchange for it (in some cultures, this is called an honesty box). People who saw a pair of eyes donated three times as much as a control group who did not see any eyes. This study demonstrates that cueing people just to think about the presence of others can change social behaviour.

Situational versus dispositional explanations

Social psychologists focus on the power of social situations to change people's behaviour. Social explanations of behaviour, therefore, focus on situational factors – for example, whether there is an authority figure present when deciding on behaviour. This is in contrast with psychologists who take a dispositional approach, believing that differences in behaviour are determined by characteristics that differ between individuals, such as personality, age, gender, cultural and educational background.

In the study by Milgram (obedience) (page 133), you will learn that the majority of people were willing to harm a stranger when ordered to do so. In situations like this, where there is great similarity between people's actions despite their differing personalities, it is hard to ignore the influence of situational factors. In the study by Perry *et al.* (personal space), it was found that the dispositional factor of empathy affected preferred interpersonal distance, suggesting personality still has a role to play in predicting social behaviour.

 # Methodology in the Social approach

Social psychologists use a wide variety of different research methods and often collect both quantitative and qualitative data. Laboratory experiments may be used but as social psychologists are interested, specifically, in social context, it makes sense that much of their research is conducted in real-world settings. Sometimes, researchers manipulate aspects of the setting in order to observe the effect on members of the public. In this case, we call the study a **field experiment**. A good example is the study by Piliavin *et al.* (subway Samaritans) where a confederate pretended to collapse in front of passengers on the New York subway, in the United States of America.

Before Piliavin *et al.* conducted their subway study, much of the previous work in this area had been conducted under control conditions, in university settings. While these studies may be more reliable than field experiments, it is difficult to know whether participants would have behaved in the same way in the real world. A good example of this is Milgram's study of obedience (see page 133). The study was the first in a series of experiments where he investigated aspects of a social situation that increase and/or decrease levels of obedience. As with many studies of this type, the participants were observed through a one-way mirror. Controlled **observations** of this type may use a behavioural checklist to increase reliability but qualitative observations may also be noted down and this can be extremely useful in providing a deeper understanding of why the participants behaved as they did. This can help researchers to explore individual differences between participants. Researchers may also use **interviewing** to collect further self-reported data.

Milgram (obedience) and Piliavin *et al.* (subway Samaritans) are both classic studies conducted more than 50 years ago, but today many social psychologists make use of computer technology, including virtual reality, to create realistic situations that can also be highly controlled.

ISSUES AND DEBATES

Applications to everyday life

An understanding of the influence of authority figures (e.g. see Milgram, page 133) has been incorporated into training protocols in many public and private sector jobs, such as hospitals and schools, as well as the military and the aviation industry.

Individual and situational explanations

Situational explanations focus on factors such as the individual's place within the social hierarchy. For example, are they dominant or subordinate? A leader or a follower? However, individual explanations still have a role to play as there are often individual differences between people's responses in social experiments, some of which can be understood with reference to dispositional factors.

Nature versus nurture

Social psychologists tend to believe that we are hardwired to learn how to behave in social situations – due to an innate interest in other people that encourages us to examine other people's behaviour and use it as a guide for our own. As explained above, this is linked to evolution and natural selection.

In terms of nurture, social psychologists often examine cultural differences in behaviours like conformity, obedience and bystander behaviour. Research findings suggest that, despite being hardwired for social behaviour, some cultures tolerate, and even reinforce, independent behaviour more than others. This shows that nurture can also affect social behaviour.

Solomon Asch placed his participants in the last but one seat in a group of confederates (stooges). He asked the group which line was the same length as the sample line (Asch, 1951). The confederates all gave a wrong answer and Asch was interested in observing whether the real participants would conform

▲ Figure 4.3 Replicating Asch's famous study of conformity

with the confederates' obviously incorrect answer. As a social psychologist, what do you think Asch hypothesised would happen and why?

The history of the Social approach

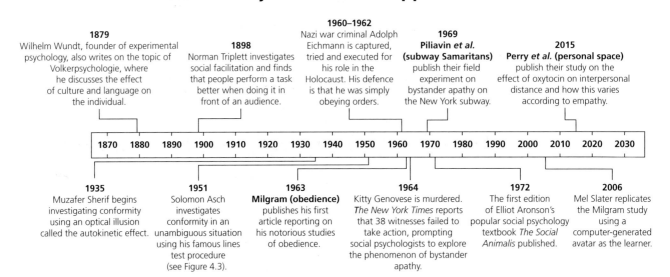

1879
Wilhelm Wundt, founder of experimental psychology, also writes on the topic of Volkerpsychologie, where he discusses the effect of culture and language on the individual.

1898
Norman Triplett investigates social facilitation and finds that people perform a task better when doing it in front of an audience.

1960–1962
Nazi war criminal Adolph Eichmann is captured, tried and executed for his role in the Holocaust. His defence is that he was simply obeying orders.

1969
Piliavin et al. (subway Samaritans) publish their field experiment on bystander apathy on the New York subway.

2015
Perry et al. (personal space) publish their study on the effect of oxytocin on interpersonal distance and how this varies according to empathy.

1870 1880 1890 1900 1910 1920 1930 1940 1950 1960 1970 1980 1990 2000 2010 2020 2030

1935
Muzafer Sherif begins investigating conformity using an optical illusion called the autokinetic effect.

1951
Solomon Asch investigates conformity in an unambiguous situation using his famous lines test procedure (see Figure 4.3).

1963
Milgram (obedience) publishes his first article reporting on his notorious studies of obedience.

1964
Kitty Genovese is murdered. *The New York Times* reports that 38 witnesses failed to take action, prompting social psychologists to explore the phenomenon of bystander apathy.

1972
The first edition of Elliot Aronson's popular social psychology textbook *The Social Animalis* published.

2006
Mel Slater replicates the Milgram study using a computer-generated avatar as the learner.

▲ Figure 4.4 Timeline of the Social approach

STUDY TIP

As you learn about each of the studies in the social approach, think about how the results support the main assumptions of the approach. What has the study told us about the causes of behaviour and how they link to aspects of the social context (e.g. whether the person has more or less authority) and the actual, implied and/or imagined presence of others? You should also look out for evidence that suggests the main assumptions may be incorrect or do not apply in all circumstances.

Do you remember Rohan and Polina from page xii? They were discussing an internet news story about a voluntary project where people from many cultures came together to collect and deliver aid to people affected by the COVID-19 pandemic. Rohan was surprised by how generous people were in terms of helping strangers. Polina says she feels it is understandable as people generally want to help others.

» How might a psychologist from the social approach explain the volunteers' behaviour?

» Use what you have learned in this section as a starting point, but you may also wish to conduct some further research of your own.

» After you have learned about all three studies in the approach, you may like to add some more ideas.

4.1 Milgram (obedience)

4.1.1 Background

▲ Figure 4.5 Stanley Milgram was an American social psychologist and professor at Yale University

Introducing Stanley Milgram

Born in 1933, Stanley Milgram was the son of Jewish immigrants from Eastern Europe who had arrived in New York during the First World War. He worked alongside several other famous social psychologists, including Solomon Asch. Milgram was a highly creative man who came up with interesting experimental techniques, which he preferred to conduct in real-world social environments. His passions included film-making and theatrics, as well as the study of urban environments. Milgram's most famous research investigated **obedience**, private prejudices, responses to queue-jumping, acquaintance chains and the mental maps people develop of cities.

KEY TERMS

obedience
social pressure
authority
situational
dispositional
personal conscience

Think!
What does the term 'legitimate authority' mean?

Think!
Imagine that someone ordered you to pick up a piece of litter that was not yours. Would your response change depending on who was asking you? Why?

Think!
Milgram initially conducted a pilot study using his own undergraduate students before the main study and was surprised to find such high levels of obedience. Why do you think he decided to conduct a pilot study first?

The psychology being investigated

Obedience and social pressure

Obedience is the result of **social pressure** whereby one person complies with the direct order of another person who they perceive to have a higher level of **authority** than themselves. Milgram proposed that a system of authority is required for any people living in a community and that people have a strong tendency to be obedient. In his paper, Milgram (1963) quotes Snow (1961), who said that:

> When you think of the long and gloomy history of man, you will find more hideous crimes have been committed in the name of obedience than have ever been committed in the name of rebellion.

However, Milgram was also quick to point out the benefits of obedience to society. Acts of charity and kindness as a result of social pressure are important for a well-functioning society.

Milgram came up with a range of explanations for why people are willing to obey others, including the perception of being asked to do so by a legitimate authority figure (someone with a higher status in the social hierarchy). He also wanted to know the extent to which **situational** factors, such as the location, or **dispositional** factors, such as **personal conscience**, were responsible for obedience.

Background

Milgram was particularly interested in the Holocaust that took place during the Second World War. At this time, obedience to orders played a significant part in the slaughter of millions of Jewish people and many other groups who were labelled as biologically inferior or socially and/or politically undesirable. Milgram believed that the Holocaust could only have been carried out on such a large scale if a significant number of people obeyed direct orders.

Milgram saw obedience as a deeply rooted social tendency to follow the orders of authority figures and that this was necessary for communal living. He proposed that the tendency to obey authority may be so strong that it may overcome our own personal conscience or feelings of sympathy for others.

It is likely that Milgram was inspired to carry out research into obedience after following the very public trial of Adolf Eichmann, one of the major organisers of the Holocaust. In 1961, Eichmann was captured by Israeli Mossad operatives in Argentina and brought to trial in Israel. An influential commentary of the trial was published in 1963 in *The New Yorker* magazine, by Hannah Arendt, an important political thinker who was born to a Jewish family in Germany (Arendt, 1963). Arendt attended the trial and described Eichmann as an ordinary family man, who was not at all antisemitic. She presented the Nazi SS officer as a regular office 'pen-pusher' who was simply following the orders of his superiors. While there is now significant evidence to completely counter this claim (Lipstadt, 2011), Arendt's article raised many questions for Stanley Milgram at the time.

Milgram in brief

Intrigued by the question of whether normal, everyday people would obey a perceived authority figure if asked to harm an innocent person, Milgram devised an infamous experimental technique into obedience. Driven by his love of theatrics, Milgram created a very professional-looking fake electric shock machine, with voltages ranging from 15 V all the way up to a lethal 450 V. He invited males from the local area through a newspaper advertisement to take part in a learning and memory experiment. He told them the study would involve administering increasingly painful electric shocks to another person, if they gave a wrong answer. This cover story was used to observe how participants responded to a series of orders by a man dressed in a grey lab coat at the prestigious setting of Yale University.

Before conducting his research, Milgram asked 14 psychology majors at Yale University to predict how 100 hypothetical Americans of various different occupations might respond in the study. All respondents estimated that only a very small minority of participants would administer the highest voltage of 450 V, with the mean estimate being 1.2 per cent. The results of the study surprised everybody: 65 per cent of participants were willing to deliver a 450 V electric shock to another innocent person.

↻ Plan your own... field experiment

Milgram used observations and an interview as techniques to investigate obedience to authority. Why not try designing a field experiment to investigate obedience?

Imagine...

Arjun is interested in whether people will be more obedient if a person is dressed in a uniform. He would like to conduct a field experiment to investigate this.

➤➤ What advice would you give Arjun about how to conduct a field experiment to investigate the effect of uniforms on obedience?

Planning a field experiment

A field experiment is an experimental method that takes place in a real-life setting. The researcher still manipulates the independent variable. When planning a field experiment, it is important that you identify and operationalise the independent and dependent variables, as well as explain the controls you will put in place. Finally, explicitly identifying the location of the study is essential. See page 134 for more information on field experiments.

▼ Table 4.1 Features of a field experiment

Main features of a field experiment	Consider...
Independent variable	In field experiments, the researcher manipulates the independent variable. What will the conditions of the independent variable be? What will the operational definition of 'uniform' be in this study?
Dependent variable	In field experiments, the researcher measures a dependent variable. What will the operational definition of 'obedience' be in this study? How will data be collected?
Controls	As field experiments take place in a real-life setting, it may be difficult to control some aspects of the environment. However, elements of the procedure can still be controlled. If Arjun uses a stooge or stooges, what might he control between the levels of his independent variable? Are there any other elements of the procedure that can be controlled?
Experimental design	Which experimental design will Arjun use in the study? Consider how he might avoid demand characteristics.
Location	As field experiments take place in a real-life setting, it is important to identify the exact location in which the study is taking place. Give as many details as you can.

Evaluating your plan

Arjun shares your ideas with his peers. Some of them think it is a great idea; others are not so sure. Think about the practical strengths and weaknesses of your suggestions.

▼ Table 4.2 Evaluating your plan

	Describe	Explain
Strengths	How might the location of the study affect the validity of Arjun's findings?	How did this allow Arjun to avoid demand characteristics and why is this important when investigating obedience?
Weaknesses	How might extraneous variables affect the validity and/or reliability of the study?	How might this affect the the findings in relation to the effect of uniforms on obedience?
Improvements	Consider a weakness you described above. How might you improve Arjun's procedure to overcome this issue?	How would this improvement affect the validity and/or reliability of the data Arjun collects in the context of uniforms and obedience?

What do you expect the outcome of Arjun's field experiment to be? Why do you think people are more likely to obey a person if they are dressed in a uniform?

▲ Figure 4.6 A uniform can change people's perceptions and behaviour towards the person wearing it

LEARNING LINK

Another study in the social approach, Piliavin *et al.* (subway Samaritans), was also a field experiment. This experiment took place on a New York subway line where confederates staged a collapse in the middle of a subway carriage in order to investigate helping behaviour. Interestingly, their findings differed from previous laboratory experiments which had investigated helping behaviour. Why do you think social psychologists often debate over whether to conduct their research in a controlled **laboratory setting** or in a real-life setting? What are the strengths and weaknesses of each type of experimental setting?

METHODOLOGY

laboratory setting

dependent variable

observation

interview

TEST YOURSELF

1   Outline the psychology being investigated in Milgram's study.   [4]
2   Describe one assumption of the social approach, using an example from this
    study.   [2]
3   Explain two ways in which the social approach is different from the learning
    approach. Use the study by Milgram as an example of the social approach.   [4]
4   Milgram gave a cover story to his participants that the study was a learning and
    memory experiment. Give one advantage and one disadvantage of using a
    cover story in this study.   [4]
5   Milgram's study took place in a laboratory setting. Suggest one strength of using
    a laboratory setting in psychological research.   [2]
6   Suggest two participant variables that may have affected the level of obedience
    in this study.   [2]

4.1.2 Describing Milgram (obedience)

Think!

The participant was asked to announce the voltage level out loud before delivering each shock. Why do you think this was included as part of the procedure?'

Think!

How do you think you would feel if you took part in this study only to later find out it had all been a set-up? Do you feel the value of the findings would outweigh any distress you might have felt while the study took place?

Think!

Participants were told that no matter what happened in the study they could keep the money, which was just for turning up. How might this have improved the study's validity?

Milgram's shock machine was carefully designed to look realistic. The shocks went from 15 V all the way up to 450 V in small 15 V increments. How might these small increments in voltage each time have affected obedience? Milgram also added labels to the machine ranging from 'SLIGHT SHOCK' beneath 15 V all the way up to 'DANGER – SEVERE SHOCK' at 375 V and 'XXX' at 435 V and 450 V. Why do you think he added these labels to the machine?

> **AIM**

To investigate the level of obedience when an authority figure orders a person to administer a physical punishment to a stranger.

> **RESEARCH METHODOLOGY**

There was only a dependent variable in this study, so it cannot be defined as an experiment. Milgram recorded data via observations through a one-way mirror and conducted interviews with participants after the study, using a laboratory setting.

Design and variables

The dependent variable was the maximum shock the participant was willing to administer before refusing to continue. This was recorded as levels from 0 to 30, with level 30 representing 450 V.

Obedience was defined by Milgram as delivering the maximum 450 V shock level and any participant who stopped before then was termed defiant.

Most sessions were recorded on video tape and some photographs were taken through a one-way mirror.

Notes were taken of unusual reactions by participants. The duration of shocks was also recorded by accurate timers.

Sample

The sample consisted of 40 males aged 20–50 from New Haven and surrounding areas in the USA, with a range of professions and educational levels.

It was a volunteer sample via a local newspaper advertisement and direct mail solicitation for a study on memory and learning at Yale University. There were a wide range of occupations, including high school teachers, postal clerks, engineers and labourers. The participants also had a range of educational levels. Participants were paid $4.50 for their participation, which they could keep no matter what.

> **PROCEDURE**

The study took place in a laboratory setting at Yale University, with a male high school teacher playing the role of the experimenter. One naive participant and a male actor playing the role of the learner took part in each trial. The actor was a 47-year-old Irish-American accountant who was mild-mannered and likeable.

The participant was told that they were taking part in a study on the effect of punishment on learning as little was known about this, or how much punishment is best for learning. The researcher explained that almost no studies in this area had been conducted on humans and they were bringing people together from a range of occupations to test this out. Participants then drew a slip of paper from a hat to determine whether they would play the role of 'teacher' or 'learner'. This was rigged so that the participant always drew the role of teacher; both slips of paper actually said 'teacher'.

Both the teacher and the learner were then taken to a room where the learner was strapped into an 'electric chair' and an electrode attached to his wrist. The experimenter explained that 'Although the shocks can be extremely painful, they cause no lasting tissue damage.' The participant was taken to a room next door and positioned in front of the electric shock generator, where they were given a real 45 V sample shock. This was applied to the wrist and came from a battery attached to the shock generator when the third switch was pressed.

Learning task

This consisted of the learner memorising word-pair associations. The participant was required to read a list of word-pairs to the learner. They would then read the first word in each word-pair along with four possible options. The learner was required to select an option by pressing a corresponding switch in front of him, which lit up one of four quadrants above the shock generator. If the answer was incorrect, the participant was required to administer an electric shock, moving one level higher with each incorrect answer. The participant was required to announce the voltage level before giving the shock.

Preliminary run

Participants undertook a preliminary run of ten trials in order to practise the procedure so it went smoothly. A pre-test had suggested that participants required this practice to master the task. Seven of these trials involved delivering shocks, going up to a maximum of 105 V. After the preliminary run, participants were given a second list of words for the regular run.

Regular run

When shock levels of 300 V and 315 V were administered, the learner was heard protesting by pounding on the wall. After 300 V, however, he stopped responding to questions completely via the switches. The participant was told to treat no response as an incorrect answer.

If a participant expressed an unwillingness to continue with the study, the experimenter used a series of standardised 'prods' in sequence:
● Prod 1: 'Please continue' or 'Please go on.'
● Prod 2: 'The experiment requires that you continue.'
● Prod 3: 'It is absolutely essential that you continue.'
● Prod 4: 'You have no other choice, you *must* go on.'

There were two special prods. If a participant expressed concern about the shocks causing permanent injury, the experimenter repeated his previous comment and instructed the participant to continue saying, 'Although the shocks may be painful, there is no permanent tissue damage, so please go on' (Milgram, 1963).

If the participant commented on the learner wishing to stop, the response was: 'Whether the learner likes it or not, you must go on until he has learned all the word pairs correctly. So please go on' (Milgram, 1963).

If a participant refused to continue after the fourth prod, the study ended. The participant then undertook an interview about their experiences and met the learner so that he knew that he had not been harmed. This was part of what Milgram called the 'dehoaxing', which he believed would mean that the participants left the study in a state of wellbeing.

▶ RESULTS

Quantitative
● 26 out of 40 of the participants were fully obedient and administered the maximum 450 V.
● 40 out of 40 of the participants went up to 300 V, which was when the victim first pounded on the wall. At this point, five participants refused to continue.

See Table 4.3 for distribution of break-off points.

Qualitative
● Extreme tension was observed, such as sweating, trembling, biting their lip, digging their nails into their flesh, groaning and stuttering.
● 14 participants showed signs of nervous laughter and smiling.
● Three participants had full-blown seizures.
● Participants who continued to 450 V seemed under extreme stress.

After the experiment, participants were asked to indicate how painful they thought the shocks were on a 14-point scale from 'Not at all painful' to 'Extremely painful'. The most common response (the mode) was 14 'Extremely painful'.

▼ Table 4.3 Distribution of break-off points in Milgram's study

Label: Description and voltage	Number of subjects for whom this was maximum shock
Slight shock	
15	0
30	0
45	0
60	0
Moderate shock	
75	0
90	0
105	0
120	0

Label: Description and voltage	Number of subjects for whom this was maximum shock
Strong shock	
135	0
150	0
165	0
180	0
Very strong shock	
195	0
210	0
225	0
240	0
Intense shock	
255	0
270	0
285	0
300	5
Extreme intensity shock	
315	4
330	2
345	1
360	1
Danger: severe shock	
375	1
390	0
405	0
420	0
XXX	
435	0
450	26

CONCLUSIONS

Milgram commented on two surprising findings in the study:

1 Firstly, the sheer strength of obedient tendencies in the study. Participants appeared willing to go against their own moral values and obey an authority figure, even when it meant harming another person.
2 He also noted that following orders to administer electric shocks to another person caused extraordinary tension and emotional strain.

Milgram provided reasons he thought obedience had occurred, which included the following:

- the prestigious location of the study: Yale University
- the experiment was seen to be a worthy contribution to science
- a sense of obligation and commitment to the experimenter
- the participants were paid to take part, increasing the sense of obligation
- the participants were explicitly told the shocks were not dangerous
- there was a conflict between the desire not to harm and the desire to obey authority.

LEARNING LINK

In another study in the social approach, Piliavin *et al.* (subway Samaritans), conducted an experiment on social behaviour in a real-life setting instead. Piliavin *et al.*'s study was a field experiment where they also covertly observed behaviour in a staged situation. Researchers are allowed to observe others' behaviour without informed consent as long as they are in a public place. What are the advantages and disadvantages of conducting an observation in a real-life setting, such as in Piliavin *et al.*'s study, versus a laboratory setting, such as in Milgram's study?

STUDY TIP

The procedure of Milgram's study contains many specific details, which were standardised, including scripts. As this is such a famous study, with many variations, it is easy to confuse the procedure. Other sources often reference a voice-feedback condition of this study where the learner is heard making distressed comments. Reading carefully through the original journal articles is important for learning small and interesting key details from each study, which are not covered by other sources.

TEST YOURSELF

1 Describe the procedure if the participant expressed concern that the learner wanted to stop. [2]
2 Describe the conditions which led to the study ending. [2]
3 Identify two examples of qualitative data from this study. [2]
4 Explain why the participants were given a sample 45 V shock at the start of the study. [2]
5 The study by Milgram used covert observation to record participants' behaviours. Explain what is meant by a 'covert observation', using this study as an example. [2]
6 Describe two of the controls from the study by Milgram. [4]

4.1.3 Evaluating Milgram (obedience)

Think!

Why did Milgram ensure that the participant met the learner at the end of the study?

Think!

Imagine how it might have felt to hear Adolf Eichmann giving his infamous defence that he was 'just following orders' in his publicly broadcast trial. Do you feel that Milgram's findings are useful in explaining the actions of Nazis, like Eichmann? Are situational factors enough to explain acts of obedience that harm others?

Think!

In 2012, Haslam and Reicher reanalysed Milgram's data and discovered that every time the fourth prod was used ('You have no other choice, you must go on!'), no participant continued. How might you explain this?

How do you think the location of Yale University affected levels of obedience in the study? How do you think levels might have changed if the experiment had been conducted at a different location?

▲ Figure 4.7 Yale University, the location of Milgram's study

Ethical issues

Debrief

One ethical strength of Milgram's research is that he was pioneering in debriefing his participants after the study was over; this was not a common procedure at the time. Following the experiment, Milgram arranged a reconciliation with the learner, who acted in a friendly manner towards the participant and reassured them that no harm was done. In this way, Milgram ensured that his participants hypothetically left the study in a state of wellbeing and any feelings of tension were reduced.

Protection from harm

One weakness of Milgram's research is the psychological harm potentially suffered by participants. Three participants had full-blown seizures in his study and most showed signs of intense distress. It is likely that some of his participants may have experienced longer term harm knowing they had been willing to deliver a 450 V shock to an innocent man, against their own morals. This means that some participants are likely to have left the study in a worse psychological state than when they entered.

Deception

One weakness is that there were several instances of deception in this study. Participants believed that they were taking part in a learning and memory experiment and that the learner (a confederate of Milgram) was actually another participant in the study, like them, when in reality their responses to orders were being covertly observed. Furthermore, they were deceived into believing they were administering real electric shocks to another person. Discovering this deception afterwards may have led to a lack of trust in psychologists and/or authority figures in the future.

Methodological issues

Reliability

Standardisation

One strength of the laboratory setting is that Milgram was able to exert tight controls over his procedure. For example, he was able to standardise the prods given by the experimenter, the responses of the learner and the environment the participant was in. This high level of standardisation meant that the study could be replicated to check that the findings relating to obedience were reliable.

Validity

Demand characteristics

A strength is that the use of a false study aim and covert observations decreased demand characteristics in Milgram's research. Participants believed that 'learning and memory' was the focus of the research and were not aware that their reactions were being observed from behind a one-way mirror. This increases the validity of the study, as participants' obedient or defiant behaviour is likely to have been genuine for the majority of participants.

A weakness is that Milgram's research lacks validity as some of the participants suspected that the shocks were not real. Many participants did not believe that Yale University would allow real harm to come to participants in a study and so they may have been responding to demand characteristics and acting in a way they believed the experimenter wanted them to. This would, therefore, reduce the validity of the conclusions drawn about obedience, as fewer participants may have administered shocks if they truly believed them to be real.

Mundane realism

A weakness is that the study lacks mundane realism. Shocking a stranger for getting an answer incorrect on a memory test is not reflective of a real-life task or situation. Therefore, this reduces the usefulness of the findings, since it does not reflect obedience situations in everyday life.

Use of qualitative data

A strength is that Milgram gathered qualitative data throughout the experiment via observation and recordings, giving a deeper insight into the high level of tension participants experienced when they obeyed. Participants' commentaries as they debated out loud whether to continue with the experiment, or in response to the experimenter, highlight the extraordinary levels of tension and internal debate they were experiencing, particularly after 300 V when the learner first pounded on the wall. This allowed for more detailed and thus valid data to be collected on participants' responses to the experimenter's prods.

Objectivity and subjectivity

Use of quantitative data

A strength is that the use of voltage as a dependent variable allowed for objective quantitative data to be collected. This meant that the data collected required no subjective interpretation on the part of the researcher. Therefore, valid results could be obtained from participants in terms of their obedience or defiance as it was free from experimenter bias.

Generalisations and ecological validity

Generalising beyond the sample

A weakness is that Milgram's study has low population validity, as the entire sample consisted of American males. We cannot be sure how obedience rates may differ in other cultures. Milgram's research was conducted in an individualist country (see page 225) where independent behaviour is more of a social norm. It may be that obedience rates would be higher in collectivist cultures where group cohesiveness is valued more highly. The findings of this study cannot, therefore, be applied to other countries, which may differ in the value they place on obedience versus independent behaviour.

Generalising to everyday life

One weakness of Milgram's research is that it was conducted in a laboratory setting, under the guise of a study into learning and memory. The participants believed that they were taking part in an academic study to further knowledge of learning and memory at the prestigious Yale University. It thus has little resemblance to real-life situations such as the Holocaust and therefore lacks ecological validity.

Individual and situational explanations

One might argue that this study supports individual explanations for obedience, as only 65 per cent of participants obeyed. This meant that 35 per cent of participants went through the uncomfortable process of resisting the experimenter's four prods in order to leave the experiment early. Personal factors, such as their sympathy for the victim, overrode their willingness to obey authority and prevented them from continuing. This highlights individual differences in behavioural responses to obedience in situations where the order goes against a person's moral code.

On the other hand, Milgram himself highlighted situational explanations for the high levels of obedience experienced. He cited the fact that participants had been paid for taking part, the 'elegant' location of the study at Yale University, the clear authority of the experimenter in a grey lab coat and the fact that participants believed they were advancing knowledge in learning and memory as situational factors that led to all 40 of the participants reaching at least 300 V.

Applications to everyday life

Training and education

Milgram's research has been very important in terms of educating people to resist obedience where it is important for the protection of others. The high levels of obedience in his study demonstrated how difficult it can be for people to resist orders from those in a higher authority position. For example, some armies have used the research in their training programmes for soldiers to highlight the importance of resisting orders on moral or ethical grounds.

Reflections

While the debate surrounding the value of Milgram's obedience research rages on, there is no doubt that it has been influential and is still highly relevant today. One reason why Milgram's experiment is so famous is due to the extremely high levels of obedience demonstrated in the study, which were surprising. Furthermore, this was not a one-off as these levels have been replicated in later research (e.g. Doliński *et al.*, 2017). This has important implications across society since positions of authority are at risk of abuse. Milgram's research has been used in training sessions for institutions – for example, by the United States Army, where it is important to encourage resistance to, or questioning of, unethical demands by superiors.

> ▶ **LEARNING LINK**
>
> Milgram's study is not the only core study that used a one-way mirror to conduct covert observations. Bandura *et al.* (aggression) also used a one-way mirror to observe children's behaviour. What do you see as the advantages and disadvantages of this methodology in terms of ethics, demand characteristics, social desirability and the validity of recorded data? Both studies gained photographic and video evidence of their participants' behaviours, which can still be viewed today.

> **STUDY TIP**
>
> It is tempting to mistake Milgram's study as a laboratory experiment; however, there was no independent variable, only a dependent variable ('voltage'). Instead, he used observations and an interview for data collection. You can still, however, evaluate this study in terms of the strengths and weaknesses of the laboratory setting it takes place in, which allowed for a high level of control over extraneous variables.

4

TEST YOURSELF

1 Explain one way in which demand characteristics may have affected the validity of Milgram's findings. [2]
2 Explain how one result from the study by Milgram supports the individual explanation of obedience and how one result supports the situational explanation of obedience. [8]
3 Evaluate the study by Milgram in terms of two strengths and two weaknesses. At least one of your evaluation points must be about quantitative data. [10]
4 Explain one way in which Milgram's study was ethical. [2]
5 The study by Milgram raised ethical issues. Explain two **ethical guidelines** that are relevant to this study. [4]
6 Suggest one real-life application of Milgram's findings. [2]

4.2 Perry *et al.* (personal space)

4.2.1 Background

▲ Figure 4.8 Dr Anat Perry

Introducing Anat Perry

Dr Anat Perry is Professor of Psychology at the Hebrew University of Jerusalem, Israel. She studies empathy and social processes from a social cognitive neuroscience perspective. Her research involves applying a range of different behavioural and biological research techniques to study both healthy and clinical populations. She hopes that a better understanding of the neural mechanisms underlying social processes could lead to an improved understanding and acceptance of others in the community and promote social change (personal communication, 2021).

You can follow Dr Anat Perry on Twitter @AnatPerry

KEY TERMS

interpersonal distance (personal space)

empathy

oxytocin

social hormones

placebo

Think!

What is the social salience hypothesis?

Think!

Imagine that you have high levels of social anxiety. How might this affect your preferred **interpersonal distance** from others?

Think!

How do you think a person's level of **empathy** might affect their preferred interpersonal distance from others?

The psychology being investigated

Interpersonal distance (personal space)

The term 'interpersonal distance' refers to the distance between two people. People's preferred distance from others may vary depending on their relationship to the other person, cultural norms or personal factors. If another person were to enter into this **personal space**, a person may feel uncomfortable or threatened. According to Hall (1966), there are four zones of interpersonal distance depending on the relationship between two people: intimate distance for close family members or intimate relationships, personal distance for everyday interactions with others, social distance for formal interactions and public distance for public figures (e.g. a lecturer).

Empathy

Empathy is a trait which plays an important role in social relationships. Empathy refers to a person's ability to understand the thoughts, feelings and experiences of another and comprises two dimensions: cognitive and affective empathy. Cognitive empathy refers to a person's ability to determine another person's emotional state, while affective empathy refers to their ability to 'feel' that same emotional state. Research points towards a person's level of empathy affecting the way they process social cues and respond emotionally.

Social hormones

Oxytocin is a **social hormone** that acts as a neurotransmitter. The hormone oxytocin plays a role in social bonding, childbirth and breastfeeding and has been seen to promote prosocial and approach behaviours. However, research has also shown that in some contexts oxytocin can actually lead to envy, risk aversion and feelings of hostility towards strangers. Scheele et al. (2012) found that administering oxytocin to males in monogamous relationships increased their preferred interpersonal distance from an attractive female when in the presence of a female researcher, compared to a control condition. This key study focuses on the role of oxytocin and how it affects people's preferences for interpersonal distance (personal space), depending on whether they are high or low in the trait of empathy.

Background

Perry et al. were interested in the effects of oxytocin on people's preferred interpersonal distances, depending on whether they were high or low in the trait of empathy.

Amygdala

The amygdala has been shown to play a role in preferred interpersonal distances. Lesions to the amygdala lead to a reduced need for interpersonal distance from others. Additionally, the more discomfort people feel with an interpersonal distance that is too close, the higher their levels of amygdala activity. Amygdala activity is known to be affected by the hormone oxytocin.

Social salience hypothesis

The leading hypothesis about the social effects of oxytocin is called the social salience hypothesis, which predicts that oxytocin increases attention to social cues, affecting how a person may process these cues and respond in different ways, depending on the social setting. While one person may feel comfortable and relaxed in a certain social setting, another person may feel stressed and intimidated. Social salience may, therefore, affect people in opposite ways.

Perry et al. wanted to test the social salience hypothesis and see whether administering oxytocin would cause people to process social situations more deeply and affect their resulting behaviour based on their evaluation of a social situation. Perry et al. believed that if a person felt comfortable in the presence of another then this feeling may be enhanced. Conversely, if a person were to feel threatened then this response might also be enhanced.

Perry et al. in brief

Perry et al. predicted that people who are highly empathetic would be more likely to prefer closer interpersonal distances following administration of oxytocin versus a **placebo** (a saline solution) while oxytocin would cause those with low empathetic traits to prefer greater interpersonal distances. They wanted to test this theory experimentally in a laboratory setting which would have high levels of control and produce quantitative data that they could statistically analyse.

Plan your own... observation

Perry *et al.* designed two experiments to test their ideas about interpersonal space, empathy and oxytocin. Why not try designing an observation to investigate factors affecting personal space?

Imagine...

Ella is planning a structured observation into personal space on public transport. She is interested in where people choose to sit or stand in relation to others.

>> What advice would you give Ella about how to conduct a structured observation into personal space on public transport?

Planning an observation

An observation is a non-experimental method. When planning an observation, it is important to consider whether participants will know they are being watched, whether the researcher will be separate from the situation they are observing, whether the observation will take place in a controlled or real-life setting and how the data will be recorded. See page 91 for more information on observations.

▼ Table 4.4 Features of an observation

Main features of an observation	Consider...
Overt vs covert	For observations, the participants may or may not know that they are being observed. As Ella's study is taking place on public transport, would an overt or covert observation be more appropriate?
Participant vs non-participant	The researcher/s may observe behaviour from afar or they may watch as part of the ongoing activity in which they are also participating. For Ella's study, will the researcher/s be part of the situation they are observing?
Naturalistic vs controlled	An observation may take place in a real-life setting or in a controlled laboratory setting. Which of these would be appropriate for Ella's study?
Structured vs unstructured	Observers may record qualitative data about a situation or use a behavioural checklist to record pre-determined behaviours in categories. As Ella would like to conduct a structured observation about personal space, how might she do this?
Behavioural categories (if appropriate)	Structured observations use behavioural checklists with pre-determined categories. What might Ella's categories be for observing personal space?
Number of observers	How many observers will record data in this study? Consider the advantages and disadvantages of having multiple observers and the effects this might have on people's behaviour.

Evaluating your plan

Ella shares your ideas with her peers. Some of them think it is a great idea; others are not so sure. Think about the practical strengths and weaknesses of your suggestions.

▼ Table 4.5 Evaluating your plan

	Describe	Explain
Strengths	Consider the features of the planned observation. Suggest ways in which you have ensured that any data collected is valid. Have you reduced the chance of demand characteristics in the design, for example?	How might the features of the observation lead to more valid/reliable data on personal space? Explain why this is the case.
Weaknesses	Which features of the observation might lead to less valid/reliable data?	Why might these features reduce the validity/reliability of the data collected on personal space?
Improvements	Consider a weakness you gave above. How might you improve the procedure to overcome this issue?	How would this improvement affect the validity and/or reliability of the data Ella collects on personal space?

In Perry *et al.*'s study, participants were administered either oxytocin or a placebo (a saline solution) on different occasions. Why do researchers use placebos in psychological research?

> ▶ **LEARNING LINK**
>
> A tool for psychological measurements is called a psychometric test (see page 186), which often takes the form of a questionnaire. Perry *et al.*'s study used the Interpersonal Reactivity Index (IRI) as a psychometric test to measure empathy levels. In an earlier study, Baron-Cohen *et al.* (eyes test), you learnt about another psychometric test, the Revised Eyes Test, which aims to measure theory of mind.
>
> The trait of empathy consists of two dimensions: cognitive and affective. Cognitive relates to the ability to interpret someone else's feelings and emotions, while affective empathy involves an involuntary emotional response to the feelings of others. Perry *et al.* used the IRI to measure both dimensions of empathy. In contrast, the psychometric test used in Baron-Cohen *et al.*'s study only aims to measure the cognitive dimension of empathy, since it focuses on detecting autism. Individuals with autism find it challenging to identify emotions based on the facial expressions of others.

> **STUDY TIP**
>
> Despite a significant focus on biological mechanisms and their impact on behaviour, this study is from the social approach. It is, therefore, important that you are able to link aspects of Perry *et al.*'s study to the assumptions of the social approach. These assumptions include the behaviours, cognitions and emotions being affected by the presence of others and the social context which a person is in. How does Perry *et al.*'s study fit in with these?

> ▶ **TEST YOURSELF**
>
> 1 Describe what is meant by the term 'empathy'. [2]
> 2 Describe the psychology being investigated in the study by Perry *et al*. [4]
> 3 Explain why this study is from the social approach. [2]
> 4 A psychologist is investigating people's preferred personal space on public transport. Suggest how you could operationalise 'personal space' in this study. [1]
> 5 Suggest one advantage of using a self-report questionnaire to measure empathy. [2]
> 6 Dennis is planning a questionnaire to investigate how individuals feel when different people invade their personal space (for example, friends or strangers). Describe how Dennis could conduct a questionnaire to investigate people's personal space preferences. [10]
> (See page 32 for tips on designing a questionnaire, including the required features).

4.2.2 Describing Perry *et al.* (personal space)

METHODOLOGICAL

experiment
questionnaire

> **Think!**
>
> What was the placebo condition in this study?

> **Think!**
>
> How do you feel if people stand too close to you? Does it make a difference to you if the person is a stranger or a close friend? Would the situation make a difference (e.g. being on a busy train versus having an intimate, face-to-face conversation)?

> **Think!**
>
> The effects of oxytocin on preferred interpersonal distance were stronger for people with high empathy. Why do you think this was?

► AIM

To investigate how oxytocin affects preferred interpersonal distance for those scoring high or low in empathy traits.

► RESEARCH METHODOLOGY

The participants took part in two experiments. Half of the participants did Experiment 1 first and the other half did Experiment 2 first. These experiments took place in a laboratory setting, where extraneous variables that might have affected preferred interpersonal distance were controlled. The researchers compared preferred interpersonal distance between different groups and conditions (see below).

Design and variables

The first independent variable was whether the participants received nasal drops containing oxytocin or a placebo (saline solution). As all participants took part in both conditions, this part of the experiment was repeated measures. To avoid order effects, the researchers randomised whether the participant received the oxytocin first or the saline. A week later, when the participants returned for the second part of the study, they received the alternative treatment (i.e. those that received saline in week one, received oxytocin in week two, and vice versa). The administration of the treatments (saline and oxytocin) was also double-blind, so neither the participant nor the experimenter knew which solution had been administered each week.

Perry *et al.* were interested in whether oxytocin affected people in different ways depending on their level of empathy (their second independent variable), so they divided the participants into two groups. As participants could only be in one group, high or low empathy, this part of the design was independent measures. High or low empathy was operationalised using a 28-item online questionnaire called the Interpersonal Reactivity Index

(IRI) (Davis, 1983). This questionnaire has four seven-item sub-sections, each assessing a different component of empathy. The people in the high empathy group (n = 20) had scores of 40 and over, while the people in the low empathy group (n = 20) had scores of 33 and under.

Experiment 1

In the first experiment, Perry *et al.* measured preferred interpersonal distance (the dependent variable) using a computer animation. Here, another independent variable was manipulated as the animation tested people on their preferred interpersonal distance from different people (a stranger, an authority figure and a friend) and an object (a ball). This part was repeated measures as all participants indicated their preferences in all conditions.

Experiment 2

The second experiment used another computer-based task called 'choosing rooms' to calculate values for two different dependent variables: the mean average preferred distance and mean average preferred angle between different items of furniture in a room. The participants were told that the task was to help plan the layout of a room where they would be having a conversation with another participant about a personal topic. This task allowed the researchers to compare preferences for the spatial arrangement of the chairs (a measure of interpersonal distance preference) and a table and plant (a control condition). This was the final independent variable in the study. As all participants gave preferences relating to both the chairs and the table and plant, this part of the design was repeated measures.

▼ Table 4.6 Summary of the differences between the independent and dependent variables in Experiments 1 and 2

Experiment	Independent variables	Dependent variable
1	1 Empathy: high or low 2 Treatment: oxytocin or placebo 3 Condition: stranger, authority, friend or ball	Preferred interpersonal distance: measured using the computerised version of the Comfortable Interpersonal Distance (CID) paradigm (a scale of 1–100, where 0 is both figures touching and 100 is the furthest distance)
2	1 Empathy: high or low 2 Treatment: oxytocin or control 3 Condition: positioning of chairs (experimental condition) versus positioning of table and plant (control condition)	The 'choosing rooms' task where participants indicate room layout preferences for a conversation on a personal topic: 1 Mean average preferred distance between the two chairs (in centimetres) 2 Mean average preferred angle of the two chairs (in degrees)

Sample

The sample consisted of 54 male undergraduates from the University of Haifa in Israel, aged 19–32 years. They received course credit or payment in exchange for their participation. Five were left-handed, none had any history of psychiatric or neurological conditions and all had normal or corrected-to-normal eyesight.

PROCEDURE

Oxytocin administration and empathy assessment

Participants visited the laboratory twice, a week apart, at the same time. On their first visit, they were randomly given either oxytocin (24 units in 250 ml of saline) or a placebo (250 ml of saline without oxytocin). Three droplets were self-administered to each nostril. The following week, they administered the alternative solution. Next, participants completed the empathy questionnaire, the IRI, as described above. Participants then had to wait for 45 minutes in a quiet room, alone, with some nature magazines. This was so that their oxytocin levels would plateau (stabilise) before taking part in the two different experiments.

Experiment 1: CID

The CID paradigm is a computer animation used to measure preferred interpersonal distance. First, the word friend, stranger, authority or ball appears on the screen for one second. Next, the participant must gaze at a fixation point which appears on the screen for 0.5 seconds. The next screen then shows a plan of a circular room with a stick person at the centre representing the participant. Next comes an animation that lasts up to three seconds: a stick person or circle (the ball) (Perry *et al.* call this the **protagonist**) enters the circle from one of eight doors around the edge, before approaching the person in the middle. The participant has to press the spacebar on the computer keyboard when they want the protagonist to stop. There were 96 trials in total with the four protagonists appearing three times from each of the eight doors. Interpersonal distance was calculated as the percentage of distance remaining between the protagonist and the central figure, from 0% to 100%, so a low score represented close proximity and a high score represented farther proximity.

Experiment 2: Choosing rooms

Participants were told they would be having a meeting with another participant to discuss personal topics and that the room would be laid out according to their preferences, as measured by a computer program. This was not true. The computer program showed the participants still colour images of pairs of rooms where the chairs, table and plant were at slightly different angles and distances from each other. Eighty-four pairs of rooms were each shown twice, giving a total of 168 pairs. During the task, participants sat 60 cm from the computer screen and were shown each pair of rooms for two seconds. They had to fixate on a point on a blank screen for 0.5 seconds between each pair.

Participants chose between the left or the right room. The experimental conditions were the distance between chairs and the angle of the chairs' positions, while the control conditions were the distance between the table and plant, as well as the angle of the positions of the table and plant. Only one of these variables differed on each trial.

RESULTS

Experiment 1: CID

- Oxytocin decreased the preferred mean distance from a protagonist in the high empathy group (placebo: 26.11 per cent vs oxytocin: 23.29 per cent) and increased it in the low empathy group (placebo: 26.98 per cent vs oxytocin: 30.20 per cent). This difference, however, was very small.
- In the high empathy group, placebo condition, there were significant differences between the preferred distances for friend and authority, as well as friend and stranger, as expected. However, not between the ball and all other conditions. When oxytocin was administered, participants were willing to be significantly closer to the ball than the stranger or authority figure.

Experiment 2: Choosing rooms

- Those in the high empathy group chose closer chair distances in the oxytocin condition compared to the placebo condition (78.07 cm versus 80.58 cm), while the opposite effect was found for the low empathy group (80.14 cm in the oxytocin condition versus 78.33 cm in the placebo condition). The effect of oxytocin on preferred chair distance was only approaching significance for the high empathy group, however.
- Oxytocin did not have an effect on preferred chair angle for either the high or the low empathy groups.

CONCLUSIONS

Oxytocin affects preferred interpersonal distance (personal space), dependent on empathy levels. Those with high empathy preferred closer interpersonal distances after oxytocin administration compared to a placebo. In contrast, oxytocin increased the preferred interpersonal distance for those with low empathy, compared to a placebo.

The researchers also suggested that oxytocin may only invoke closeness in highly empathetic people for interactions of a less threatening nature, as the effects of oxytocin were more pronounced for the ball protagonist than the stranger or authority figure.

LEARNING LINK

While Perry et al. used a computer to present their tests to participants, Baron-Cohen et al. (eyes test) used a 'pen and paper' test instead. What are the strengths and weaknesses of each technique in terms of practicality, validity and reliability? Can you think of research situations in which each technique might be preferable over the other? Do you think Baron-Cohen et al.'s procedure would be strengthened by the use of computer-generated test items? If so, in what way?

STUDY TIP

In the original journal article, there are many findings for this study, but some are not directly related to the stated aim – for example, differences in preferred interpersonal distances in general for the protagonists in Experiment 1. The most important findings relate to how oxytocin affects these distances for those scoring high and low in empathy traits, so ensure to focus your attention on these.

TEST YOURSELF

1 Outline what the participant was asked to do in Experiment 1. [2]
2 Explain how empathy was measured in this study. [2]
3 Explain how one finding from the study by Perry et al. supports one of the assumptions of the social approach. [2]
4 State how the dependent variable was operationalised in Experiment 1. [2]
5 Describe two of the independent variables used in this study. [4]
6 Identify three ways in which the procedure for Experiment 2 was standardised in this study. [3]

4.2.3 Evaluating Perry et al. (personal space)

Think!
How did the researchers operationalise 'empathy' in this study?

Think!
Imagine yourself as a researcher. How might you conduct follow-up research into the effects of empathy and oxytocin on personal space in a real-world setting?

Think!
How did the researchers avoid order effects for oxytocin versus placebo administration in Experiment 1 and why was it important in the context of this study?

This study uses computer animations. What are some of the advantages and disadvantages of using computer animations in place of real-world people and objects? Consider Perry *et al.*'s research into interpersonal distance (personal space) as well as more broadly in terms of social psychological research. Could computer animations be used as an extension of Milgram's research into obedience, for example?

Ethical issues

Deception

One key criticism of this research is that in Experiment 2 participants were deceived about choosing a room for a personal meeting. Participants were told that they would need to discuss a personal topic with another person in a room at the end of the experiment, but then only told the following week that the meeting would not take place. This may have caused some participants to feel anxious about this future meeting, since the personal topic to be discussed was not disclosed at the time, thus there was a risk of psychological harm.

Methodological issues

Reliability

Standardisation

A strength of this research is its high level of standardisation. Using a computer allowed researchers to control timings, speeds and visuals to ensure they were the same between participants. For example, in Experiment 2, each pair of rooms was presented for two seconds and all the furniture items in the room were kept the same. This means that the procedure can be replicated to see if the findings about the effects of oxytocin and empathy on interpersonal distance are reliable.

Validity

Validated paradigm

A strength of this research was its use of a widely validated paradigm to investigate preferred interpersonal distance. The CID paradigm, involving a protagonist approaching the participant in a computerised room, has been tested previously on a variety of different sex and age groups in a pen and paper format. It was found to be a valid measure of preferred interpersonal distance, which increases the validity of Perry *et al.*'s findings relating to the effects of oxytocin and empathy on interpersonal distance.

Double-blind procedure

The use of a double-blind procedure in the administration of either oxytocin or the placebo was also a strength. Neither the participant nor the experimenter knew which solution was being administered in weeks one and two. This avoided any experimenter effects or demand characteristics, whereby either the experimenter or the participant consciously or unconsciously influenced the study's findings as a result of any prior expectations about the effects of oxytocin, thus making the findings more valid.

Self-report

One weakness of the design was that participants were categorised as being high or low in empathy on the basis of their own self-report, which may be biased. Participants were required to complete the IRI themselves, which may have led some participants to demonstrate social desirability bias. Participants may have preferred to be seen as higher in empathy because it is seen as a desirable trait in society and they did not want to be evaluated negatively by the experimenter. This raises validity issues, as some people low in empathy may have ended up in the high empathy category.

Objectivity and subjectivity

A strength of this research was the use of quantitative data, which did not require subjective interpretation from the researchers. For example, Experiment 1 recorded the percentage distance remaining between the door through which a protagonist entered and the participant in the centre. This data allowed the researchers to objectively compare participants' scores in each of the different conditions in an unbiased way, which increased the validity of the results and allowed for a statistical analysis of the findings to be undertaken to determine the strength of any differences.

Generalisations and ecological validity

Generalising beyond the sample

One weakness of this study is that it only used male participants. Previous research has shown that males and females respond differently to oxytocin. For example, oxytocin may induce positive social judgements and altruism in females, while promoting the opposite effect in males. Therefore, it is not possible to apply the findings of this study relating to oxytocin's effects on personal space to females.

Generalising to everyday life

One issue with this research is the fact that it used computer-based tasks in a laboratory setting, which lacks ecological validity. Asking participants to respond to computer animations would not have recreated the intense feelings of discomfort that a person may feel in a real-life social situation of someone invading their personal space. Therefore, differences between the control and oxytocin conditions may have been minimised due to the lack of genuine feelings of discomfort, and not reflect real-life preferences.

> ## ISSUES AND DEBATES

Individual and situational explanations

Individual differences appeared to determine the effect oxytocin might have on a person's social cognition and behaviour. The researchers found that oxytocin decreased preferred interpersonal distance in those with high empathy traits, yet increased it for those low in empathy. This finding supports individual explanations for behaviour following oxytocin administration.

On the other hand, administration of oxytocin appeared to affect preferred interpersonal distance in predictable ways and this means that situations that promote oxytocin release may influence social cognition and behaviour. Research suggests that oxytocin levels increase in many situations, including socialising, especially when this involves touch and eye contact, playing with pets and even when exposing oneself to extremes of temperature (i.e. hot and cold). Therefore, preferred interpersonal distance could be affected by environmental factors that increase oxytocin, thus supporting a situational explanation for behaviour.

Applications to everyday life

Improving social behaviour

An important implication of this research is that oxytocin administration may not help individuals with social deficits who are seeking support with this – for example, autism spectrum disorders. Previous research had suggested this might be helpful (e.g. Hollander et al., 2007). Perry et al. found that when oxytocin was administered to individuals with low levels of empathy, it actually slightly increased their preferred social distance from others. Therefore, oxytocin may not be a suitable treatment for males with social disorders and may actually strengthen social biases. The study needs to be replicated with females to see whether the same effects are found.

Reflections

Perry *et al.*'s research has important implications since it highlights individual differences in how people may respond to oxytocin, which was previously believed to promote prosocial behaviour in all and has been suggested as a viable treatment option for those with social deficits. However, the main findings from this study were not statistically significant; they only demonstrated a trend. Therefore, it is essential for further research to be conducted in this area. It is likely that the lack of mundane realism of the tasks in Experiments 1 and 2 may have tempered the cognitions and emotions people felt while making their decisions, thus the effects of oxytocin on preferred interpersonal distances may actually prove to be more pronounced in real-life situations.

Perry *et al.*'s research casts doubt on earlier findings that oxytocin may promote prosocial behaviour in all people. What additional research do you think needs to be carried out before deciding whether oxytocin should be avoided as a treatment for those with social disorders?

▶ LEARNING LINK

Often participants are aware that they are taking part in psychological research, either due to the need for informed consent or because the research takes place in a laboratory setting (i.e. Milgram (obedience)). There are different methods psychologists use to avoid demand characteristics affecting the validity of their findings. How did both Perry *et al.* and Milgram (obedience) differ in the how they tried to avoid demand characteristics?

STUDY TIP

This study used a questionnaire called the Interpersonal Reactivity Index (IRI) to measure empathy. Consider the strengths and weaknesses of using a questionnaire to measure empathy and how it was operationally defined in this study. Reading through the original journal article for this key study will help you to answer these questions, as well as ensure that you understand clearly how this independent variable was operationalised.

▶ TEST YOURSELF

1 Suggest one problem with the sample used in this study. [2]
2 Explain how the results of this study support an individual explanation of personal space, referring to evidence in your answer. [4]
3 Evaluate the study by Perry *et al.* in terms of two strengths and two weaknesses. At least one of your evaluation points must be about laboratory-based studies. [10]
4 Suggest one way in which the procedure in Experiment 1 was valid and one way that it was not valid. [4]
5 Explain one advantage and one disadvantage of the use of computer-based tasks in this study. [4]
6 Explain one advantage of using a repeated measures design in this study. [2]

4.3 Piliavin *et al.* (subway Samaritans)
4.3.1 Background

Introducing Irving Piliavin

Irving Piliavin (1928–2009) was a Professor of Social Welfare and Sociology until his retirement in 1996. He was particularly interested in crime and delinquency control as well as evaluating welfare reform and foster care programmes. In addition to the present study, he was the first to conduct a longitudinal study on homelessness. Piliavin gained a doctorate in Social Work from Columbia University in 1961.

Think!

What does the term **diffusion of responsibility** mean in the context of helping behaviour?

Think!

Have you ever witnessed an emergency scenario when out in public? How did you respond? What thoughts went through your mind at the time?

Think!

How might you investigate individual differences in helping behaviour in order to determine why some people offer help immediately in an emergency situation while others hold back?

KEY TERMS

diffusion of responsibility
bystander
bystander apathy

The psychology being investigated

Bystander apathy

Bystanders are people who are physically present at the scene of an event or incident but do not take an active part in helping others in need. Interest in the psychology of bystander behaviour was triggered by the murder of an American woman called Kitty Genovese in 1964. A *New York Times* article about Genovese's death claimed that 38 witnesses ignored her cries for help. Although there is controversy over the true events of the evening (Manning *et al.*, 2007), the article inspired much interest in the field of social psychology and prompted the development of many ingenious studies to explore **bystander apathy**, the term used to describe the lack of help offered in such situations. Although some evidence suggests that bystanders may evaluate the character of a victim negatively and therefore lack compassion, a great deal of work suggests that the reason for people's inactivity often has more to do with the behaviour of people other than the victim.

Diffusion of responsibility

When an incident is observed by more than one person, there may be a diffusion of responsibility; the more people that are present the less personal responsibility each individual feels. This suggests that in situations with many people present the victim will be less likely to receive assistance as less responsibility means less guilt for people who choose not to help.

Background

Kitty Genovese's death inspired a wave of studies initiated by John Darley and Bibb Latané, all aiming to understand not only bystander apathy but also factors that encourage people to play the 'good Samaritan' and offer help to others in need. For example, people who overheard an individual supposedly having an epileptic seizure via earphones were less likely to intervene when they believed others were available to help, compared with when they believed themselves to be alone (Darley and Latané, 1968). Shortly after this, Latané and Rodin (1969) found that people in a group were less likely to help a person who had fallen over if the victim was a stranger compared with an acquaintance. Furthermore, observing the helpfulness of others (modelling) also appears to inspire Samaritanism (Bryan and Test, 1967).

Before Piliavin *et al.*'s study, the majority of social psychological research on helping behaviour in emergency situations had taken place in laboratory settings, the justification for this being the higher level of control and thus internal validity of the research. However, Piliavin *et al.* wanted to see how bystanders responded to an incident in a real-world setting, leading to findings with higher ecological validity.

Piliavin *et al.* in brief

Piliavin *et al.* were mainly interested in how the type and race of victims affected bystander behaviour in terms of the frequency of helping responses, the speed of response and the race of the helper. They decided to stage an incident in which an ill or drunk victim (a confederate of the experimenter) would collapse on a subway train. They believed that the ill victim would receive a more sympathetic response due to a lack of personal responsibility for their misfortune. They also believed that the risk of helping the drunk victim may be greater in terms of aggression or disgust. In addition, Piliavin *et al.* were interested in whether modelled help from a second confederate would inspire more help from other passengers. Finally, they wanted to determine whether group size affected the frequency and speed of help offered.

Plan your own... interview

Piliavin *et al.* designed a field experiment to test their ideas about bystander apathy and diffusion of responsibility. Why not try designing an interview to investigate helping behaviour?

Imagine...

Dr Akbar is planning a semi-structured interview investigating helping behaviour. He would like to investigate people's reasons behind choosing whether or not to help a person in need.

» What advice would you give Dr Akbar about how to conduct a semi-structured interview to investigate helping behaviour?

Planning an interview

An interview is a non-experimental method. When planning an interview, it is important that you consider what questions will be asked to collect data on the specific topic being investigated, as well as how this data will be analysed. Including example questions is also essential. See page 62 for more information on interviews.

▼ Table 4.7 Features of an interview

Main features of an interview	Consider...
Question format (open and closed questions)	Interviews can use both open and closed questions to collect data. Would you suggest open or closed questions to gather the data required on helping behaviour? Consider how the data will eventually be analysed.
Examples of questions	Can you give examples of the open and/or closed questions that you would suggest Dr Akbar asks about helping behaviour in the interviews?
Question scoring and interpretation	The data collected in interviews may be qualitative or quantitative. How will Dr Akbar analyse this data in order to draw conclusions from the participants about helping behaviour?
Format (structured/semi-structured/unstructured)	Dr Akbar wants to conduct a semi-structured interview. What are the features of this and how will it be applied when interviewing participants about helping behaviour?
Technique (face-to-face, telephone)	Interviews can be conducted either face-to-face or over the telephone, for example. This may affect how much a person is willing to disclose. Which method do you feel is best for Dr Akbar's research into helping behaviour?

Evaluating your plan

Dr Akbar shares your ideas with his colleagues. Some of them think it is a great idea; others are not so sure. Think about the practical strengths and weaknesses of your suggestions.

▼ Table 4.8 Evaluating your plan

	Describe	Explain
Strengths	What are the strengths of conducting a semi-structured interview compared with other types of interview techniques?	Why might asking set questions, with follow-up questions, be an advantage in the context of interviewing people about helping behaviour?
Weaknesses	How might the presence or absence of the interviewer affect the validity of the data gathered?	In what way might participants' answers change due to the presence or absence of an interviewer? Consider that the topic of the interviews is helping behaviour.
Improvements	Consider the weakness you gave above. How might you improve Dr Akbar's procedure to overcome this issue? Would using a different type of interview technique might improve the validity of the data collected?	How would this improvement affect the validity of the data Dr Akbar collects about helping behaviour?

The murder of Kitty Genovese took place in New York in 1964, the same city in which Piliavin *et al.* conducted their study. At that time, social psychologists were beginning to move their experiments out of the laboratory and into real-world settings. What are the strengths and weaknesses of doing this?

▶ LEARNING LINK

While it was not the main research method employed in this study, the technique used to collect data for the dependent variables was covert observation. In Milgram (obedience), covert observation was also used to collect data. In what ways were these observations similar and how were they different? What types of data were collected in each? How reliable were the observations (remember that reliability refers to the procedure being carried out consistently each time)? Were the observations participant or non-participant? How was each observation made covert?

STUDY TIP

It is important to remember the main assumptions of each approach. A useful exercise would be to write down two main assumptions for each of the four approaches, then link two findings from each study to an assumption from the relevant approach. You should end up with 24 pieces of evidence on the page. This would also help you to review all the core studies too!

▶ TEST YOURSELF

1 The study by Piliavin *et al.* (subway Samaritans) is from the social approach. Outline one assumption from the social approach, using an example from this study. [2]

2 Piliavin *et al.* wanted to investigate the theory of bystander apathy. Describe what is meant by 'bystander apathy'. [2]

3 Describe what is meant by the term 'diffusion of responsibility'. [2]

4 Describe what is meant by a field experiment, using the study by Piliavin *et al.* as an example. [2]

5 A psychologist is investigating whether anyone helps when a stooge drops a contact lens onto the floor. Suggest an operational definition for 'help'. [1]

6 Suggest one advantage of using a covert observation to investigate helping behaviour. [2]

4.3.2 Describing Piliavin *et al.* (subway Samaritans)

METHODOLOGY

field experiment

observation

Think!

How did the results for spontaneous helping differ depending on the race of the victim?

Think!

How might you use the cost–reward matrix to explain lower levels of helping for the drunk victim and higher levels of helping for the ill victim?

▶ AIMS

Piliavin *et al.* aimed to investigate factors affecting helping behaviour on a New York subway train. Specifically, they wanted to see how the following factors affected help offered to a passenger who collapsed in the carriage:

- the type of victim: drunk or ill
- the race of the victim: black or white
- modelled help provided by another passenger
- number of people in the carriage (group size).

▶ RESEARCH METHODOLOGY

The method used is a field experiment as it took place on a 7.5-minute express train between two New York stations and the researchers manipulated the independent variables.

Design and variables

The study was an independent measures design, as each scene was carried out in front of a different carriage full of passengers.

Data was also collected via covert observation:

- **Observer 1**: recorded the number of people in the car and the race, sex and location of every passenger in the critical area. She also noted how many people assisted the victim, as well as their race, sex and location.
- **Observer 2**: recorded the race, sex and location of passengers in the adjacent area, as well as the time taken to assist after the collapse.
- Both observers noted comments made by passengers and also tried to elicit them.

Variables

The independent variables were the condition of the victim (drunk or ill), the race of the victim (black or white), how close the helpful model was to the victim (critical or adjacent area), how quickly help was offered and finally group size (how many passengers were in the carriage). The dependent variables included the time taken for help to arrive (before and after modelled help), sex and race of the first helper, movement of passengers out of the critical area of the carriage (i.e. where the collapse happened) and passengers' spontaneous comments about the collapse.

Sample

The sample comprised approximately 4,450 men and women, 45 per cent of whom were black and 55 per cent white, all of whom were riding the 8th Avenue train in New York City on weekdays between 11.00 a.m. and 3.00 p.m. between 15 April and 26 June 1968. The mean number of people per car was 43; the mean number of people in the 'critical area', where the incident took place, was 8.5. Participants were an opportunity sample who did not give informed consent and were unaware they were taking part in a study.

PROCEDURE

A team of four students boarded a carriage on the New York subway train via separate doors. Two female observers took separate seats, while the two male students playing the roles of victim and model remained standing. The victim always stood centrally in the 'critical area'. Seventy seconds into the journey, the victim collapsed on the floor and laid on their back looking at the ceiling until they received help. If no help was given by the time the train reached the next station, the model helped the victim to his feet. The team would then re-board a train along the same route in the opposite direction, completing around six to eight trials per day.

Victim

There were four teams of students, each with a victim aged between 26 and 35 who were dressed identically in the same old trousers, jacket and no tie. One victim was black and three were white. There were 38 trials of the drunk condition and 65 trials of the ill condition. The ill victim carried a black cane and the drunk victim carried a liquor bottle wrapped in a brown bag and smelt of alcohol. Each student acting as the victim played both roles during the course of the study.

All of the models were white males aged between 24 and 29. There were four conditions in which the model helped the victim to a sitting position and stayed with them until the train stopped. There was also a no model condition. The order of conditions was randomised. The model conditions were:

1 Critical area-early: stood in critical area and gave help after 70 seconds.
2 Critical area-late: stood in critical area and gave help after 150 seconds.
3 Adjacent area-early: stood adjacent to the critical area and gave help after 70 seconds.
4 Adjacent area-late: stood adjacent to the critical area and gave help after 150 seconds.

RESULTS

▼ Table 4.9 The main results for each aim of the experiment

Type of victim	A person appearing ill is more likely to receive help than one appearing drunk (62/65 of trials versus 19/38 of trials). The ill victim was helped 100 per cent of the time when there was no model.
Race of victim	There was no tendency for same-race helping *unless the victim was drunk*. The drunk white victim was helped 100 per cent of the time, while the drunk black victim was only helped 73 per cent of the time and more frequently by black helpers than white. On 9 per cent of trials with a black victim, people left the critical area vs 5 per cent of trials with a white victim.
Modelled help	Early models were more likely to elicit additional help than late models (4 vs 2).
Group size	There was a weak positive correlation between group size and helping behaviour. Groups of seven or more were faster to respond than groups of three.

Table 4.10 shows a summary of quantitative results.

▼ Table 4.10 Percentage of trials on which help was given, by race and condition of victim, and total number of trials run in each condition

Trials	White victims		Black victim	
	Cane	Drunk	Cane	Drunk
No model	100%	100%	100%	73%
Number of trials run	54	11	8	11
Model trials	100%	77%	–	67%
Number of trials run	3	13	0	3
Total number of trials	57	24	8	14

Additionally, males were more likely to help the man than females. Ninety per cent of first helpers were male and 68 per cent of helpers were white. In 20 per cent of trials, people left the critical area and a total of 34 people left.

The researchers reported few interesting findings from bystander comments. Female comments included: 'It's for men to help him', 'I wish I could help him – I'm not strong enough', 'I never saw this kind of thing before – I don't know where to look', 'You feel so bad that you don't know what to do.'

CONCLUSIONS

The research did *not* support Darley and Latané's 'diffusion of responsibility' hypothesis in a real-world setting. Despite the collapses taking place on busy trains, help was offered frequently and quickly. Piliavin *et al.* proposed that witnessing an emergency situation leads to the creation of an emotional arousal state, which a person then wishes to rid themselves of. The strength and nature of this arousal depends on factors such as the level of empathy a person feels for the victim, their distance from the situation and the amount of time that passes without intervention. To reduce this arousal, a person can offer help directly, fetch help, leave the scene or decide that the victim is undeserving of help. Piliavin *et al.* suggest that people weigh up these options using a cost–reward matrix. Costs may be related to either helping (such as effort, disgust, etc.) or not helping (i.e. feelings of self-blame or the negative perceptions of others), as well as perceived rewards.

LEARNING LINK

In the study by Milgram (obedience), it was also suggested that the participants go through an internal conflict in order to decide on their behavioural response. What are the similarities and differences between the internal conflict participants went through in the Milgram (obedience) study and the Piliavin *et al.* (subway Samaritans) study?

STUDY TIP

There were several different independent variables in this study. It is important to separate each one and ensure that you can link a key finding to each of these. It may be helpful for you to create a table linking at least one key finding to each independent variable.

TEST YOURSELF

1   In Piliavin *et al.*'s study there were four conditions where a model helped the victim to a sitting position. Describe the differences between these conditions. [2]
2   Explain how race affected helping behaviour in Piliavin *et al.*'s study. Give data in your answer. [2]
3   Explain whether Darley and Latané's 'diffusion of responsibility' was supported by the findings of this study. Refer to at least one result. [3]
4   Explain what is meant by 'covert observation' using the study by Piliavin *et al.* as an example. [2]
5   Piliavin *et al.* calculated the mean number of people per subway carriage. Explain how a mean is calculated using Piliavin *et al.* as an example. [2]
6   Explain how Piliavin *et al.* avoided demand characteristics in their study. [2]

4.3.3 Evaluating Piliavin *et al.* (subway Samaritans)

Think!
Why were participants not debriefed in this study?

Think!
Piliavin *et al.* struggled to gain data for the effect of a model on helping behaviour as people tended to intervene before the model was scheduled to offer help. Imagine you are a social psychology researcher; how might you design a study to better investigate the effects of a model on helping behaviour?

Think!

Piliavin *et al.* did not believe that people were helping for altruistic/selfless reasons. Why do you think this was?

What are the advantages and disadvantages of Piliavin *et al.* conducting their research on a subway train?

▲ Figure 4.9 Piliavin *et al.* conducted their study on a New York subway train

Ethical issues

Informed consent

One key criticism of this research is the lack of informed consent. Participants were unaware that the study was taking place so this was unable to be obtained. Therefore, the participants could not give their permission to take part in the potentially distressing situation of a person collapsing in their subway carriage, which might have caused them psychological harm. Furthermore, this also meant that they were not given the opportunity to consent to their data being used in the study. Some people's comments were recorded in the published journal article, which might have caused embarrassment.

Debrief

Another weakness is that, due to the nature of the subway and the large number of participants leaving the train at their stop, no debrief could take place. This meant that the participants could not have the aims of the experiment explained to them, or have any questions answered to ensure they left the train in the same psychological state in which they had arrived. Unfortunately, the lack of debrief meant that some participants may have left the train feeling shocked at the collapse of an ill or drunk man, or potential guilt at not having offered help.

Methodological issues

Reliability

Standardisation

A strength is that the researchers controlled several aspects of the procedure. The victims always wore the same clothing and the collapse always took place when the train passed the first station on the same subway route. This ensured that the procedure could be repeated to test whether helping behaviour towards the ill and drunk victims was reliable from trial to trial.

Validity

Confounding variables

A weakness is that only one black victim was used in all of the trials. With only one person acting in this condition of the study, it is difficult to conclude that helping behaviour towards this individual was due to race as opposed to personality factors, or differences in his acting behaviour in the cane/drunk conditions (some of the students felt embarrassed to act drunk). This means that findings about helping behaviour for the independent variable of race may lack validity.

Lack of controls

Another weakness is that the location and activity of people in the carriage was not controlled. Some people may have been reading a newspaper, or were distracted in another way, not seeing the victim collapse. This would have affected the validity of the study's findings, as their reason for not helping may not have been a conscious choice.

Qualitative data

A strength was that qualitative data was also collected in this study, which allowed for further insight into bystanders' justifications for lack of helping behaviour. For example, several females made comments such as 'I wish I could help him – I'm just not strong enough'. This qualitative data allowed Piliavin *et al.* to draw more meaningful conclusions about the justifications people made when deciding not to help the victim, i.e. through their cost–reward matrix.

Objectivity and subjectivity

Quantitative data

A strength of this study was the collection of mainly quantitative data, which allowed the researchers to objectively compare helping behaviours between the drunk and cane conditions. For example, the time taken for a victim to receive help was recorded, which is a measure free from researcher bias and interpretation, allowing for valid comparisons to be made between the conditions.

Generalisations and ecological validity

Generalising beyond the sample

One strength of this research was the large sample size. It was estimated that around 4,450 men and women witnessed the victim incidents, comprising around 45 per cent black and 55 per cent white individuals. It could be argued that such a large sample may be representative of New Yorkers in general and thus the findings may be applied externally to the city's population.

However, a weakness is that the research also lacked population validity, as participants were likely to consist predominantly of commuters on a specific New York subway route. Urban residents may experience more deindividuation (loss of individuality and personal responsibility) due to their busy surroundings and individualistic culture. Therefore, this limits the extent to which the findings on helping behaviour can be applied to people living in rural areas, smaller cities or collectivist cultures.

Generalising to everyday life

A strength of this research was that it was a field experiment, taking place on a real subway route. The passengers witnessed an incident take place on their everyday commute and were unaware that they were being observed, thus demand characteristics were avoided and the participants showed genuine responses to a supposed real-life situation. This gives the research a high level of ecological validity, allowing the researchers to draw conclusions about real-life bystander behaviour in emergency situations.

Individual and situational explanations

There was evidence to support a situational explanation for helping behaviour in this study. The situation of an ill person falling appeared to trigger helping behaviour in nearby observers. On every trial without a model, someone offered help to the ill victim, thus demonstrating that the specific situation a person found themselves in was the main motivator behind their subsequent behaviour.

On the other hand, the majority of first helpers (90 per cent) of any victim was male, supporting an individual explanation for helping behaviour. Piliavin *et al.* suggested that people use a cost–reward matrix to determine whether to help; the perceived cost of helping may be lower for males and different for each person depending on their personality and personal circumstances, highlighting an individual explanation for differences in helping behaviour.

Applications to everyday life

Training and education

Educating students on the cognitive processes people go through in emergency situations may help them to change their response and be more likely to help. Understanding the cost–reward matrix would help people to recognise their own bias in interpreting heightened emotions (for example, labelling an emotion as disgust when a drunk person falls over). This understanding may then help to override negative or non-altruistic feelings in order to offer help to a victim, instead of ignoring them.

Reflections

Piliavin *et al.*'s findings contradicted those of previous researchers, as they did not find any diffusion of responsibility. However, unlike previous laboratory research in this area, the design of this study meant that observers could clearly and directly see that there was an emergency occurring. Additionally, even if many people experienced a diffusion of responsibility, the large number of people in very close proximity to the victim on the subway meant that the statistical likelihood of at least one person helping was very high. Once one individual came to their aid, there may have been a modelling effect leading others to help. Further research in both laboratory and natural settings is still required to fully understand the conditions in which diffusion of responsibility may or may not occur.

Field experiments in psychology often use confederates. What were the different roles of the confederates in Piliavin *et al.*'s study? What were the strengths and weaknesses of using confederates in this study?

> ## LEARNING LINK

Piliavin *et al.* used a confederate to model helping behaviour in the study to see if others would imitate this behaviour. This is similar to Bandura *et al.* (aggression), who used aggressive and non-aggressive models to see if children would imitate the behaviour. How did the two studies differ in the way in which the models were used? How was any subsequent imitative behaviour recorded in each study? Which study do you feel has higher validity and why?

STUDY TIP

This is the only key study which is a field experiment. When considering the strengths and weaknesses of Piliavin *et al.*'s study as a field experiment, ensure you avoid generic evaluations and include key features of the research in question when justifying your strength or weakness. For example, why were the findings in Piliavin *et al.*'s study more ecologically valid than if they had used a laboratory setting? Which specific extraneous variables were they unable to control which may have affected the study's findings related to helping behaviour?

▶ TEST YOURSELF

1 Ashay believes the study by Piliavin *et al.* supports the individual side of the debate, but Aadesh believes it supports the situational side of the debate. Outline why you think either Ashay or Aadesh is correct, using evidence from the study.   [4]

2 Explain one similarity and one difference between the study by Piliavin *et al.* and one other core study from the social approach.   [8]

3 Evaluate the study by Piliavin *et al.* in terms of two strengths and two weaknesses. At least one of your evaluation points must be about observations.   [10]

4 Explain one strength and one weakness of using confederates in this study.   [4]

5 Explain two weaknesses of field experiments using this study as an example.   [4]

6 Suggest one way in which this sample may limit the **generalisability** of the findings. [2]

▶ CHAPTER SUMMARY

Milgram (obedience)

Psychology investigated
Obedience to authority due to social pressure. The situational and dispositional factors involved in responding to the social pressure to obey an authority figure.

Aim
To investigate the level of obedience when an authority figure orders a person to administer a physical punishment to a stranger.

Procedure
A study was conducted in a laboratory setting, whereby an experimenter orders a participant to deliver increasingly higher levels of electric shocks to another person when they answer questions incorrectly in another room. Data was collected via observations and an interview and it included a dependent variable of voltage.

Results
The highest level of electric shock (450 V) was delivered by 26 out of 40 participants. All participants delivered 300 V. Participants showed physical signs of extreme tension, such as sweating and trembling. Three had full-blown seizures.

Conclusion
People are willing to go against their own moral tendencies to obey a perceived authority figure and harm another person, while showing extraordinary tension and emotional strain.

Strengths
● The measure of obedience (maximum voltage) was quantitative, which can be objectively analysed.
● The aim of the study was hidden to avoid demand characteristics, increasing validity.

Weaknesses
● The study lacks mundane realism as shocking another person as punishment is not a real-life occurrence.
● Lacks generalisability as the study used 40 males from New Haven, USA.

Links to assumptions
Behaviour can be influenced by other individuals. In Milgram's study, an experimenter in a lab coat gave participants prods to continue delivering shocks to a learner. The majority obeyed and delivered 450 V.

Links to issues and debates
All participants were willing to deliver 300 V, suggesting that situational factors, such as the prods given by an authority figure, were responsible for obedience. On the other hand, 14 out of 40 participants refused to obey the experimenter at some point, supporting an individual explanation for behaviour.

A real-life application is educating others to resist obedience as Milgram's research showed this to be challenging – for example, army training programmes to resist the orders of authority figures on moral and ethical grounds.

Similarities
● Both Milgram and Perry et al. used laboratory settings.
● Both Milgram and Piliavin et al. used stooges.

Differences
● Milgram used a laboratory setting, while Piliavin et al. used a real-life subway.
● Milgram's study had no independent variable, while Perry et al.'s study did.

Perry et al. (personal space)

Psychology investigated
How the social hormone oxytocin and the empathy levels of a person affect preferred interpersonal distance (personal space).

Aim
To investigate how oxytocin affects preferred interpersonal distance for those scoring high or low in empathy traits.

Procedure
Participants high or low in empathy traits, who received either oxytocin or a placebo, indicated their preferred interpersonal distance from different protagonists via a computer animation. They also chose between room images based on preference for distance and angle of furniture from another person.

Results
Oxytocin decreased the preferred mean distance from another person in the high empathy group and increased it in the low empathy group.

Conclusion
Oxytocin affects preferred interpersonal distance, dependent on empathy levels.

Strengths
● There was a high level of standardisation through the use of computer animations/images.
● There was high validity due to the double-blind procedure to administer oxytocin or saline solution.

Weaknesses
● Self-reports were used to categorise participants as high or low empathy, risking social desirability bias.
● Only male participants were used, so findings on the effects of oxytocin on preferred interpersonal distance cannot be generalised to females.

Links to assumptions
People have preferred interpersonal differences for different types of people, meaning that behaviour is influenced by the presence of others.

Links to issues and debates
Oxytocin decreased preferred interpersonal distance in those with high empathy traits, yet increased it for those low in empathy, supporting individual explanations for behaviour.

A real-life application is that Perry et al.'s findings counter previous research and oxytocin may not be a suitable treatment for those with social disorders.

Similarities
● Both Perry et al. and Milgram collected quantitative data.
● Both Perry et al. and Piliavin et al. used deception in their studies.

Differences
● Perry et al. used animated stooges, while Milgram used a real-life stooge.
● Perry et al. gained informed consent from participants, while Piliavin et al. did not.

Piliavin et al. (subway Samaritans)

Psychology investigated
An investigation into diffusion of responsibility and bystander apathy in emergency situations.

Aim
To see whether bystander helping behaviour, in a real-life setting, was affected by the victim's responsibility for their own situation, the race of the victim, modelling of helping behaviour and size of the group.

Procedure
A stooge, who was either white or black, acting as either an ill or drunk person, would collapse on a New York subway train. On some trials, a model standing in the critical or adjacent area would offer help either early or late. Details of bystanders who offered help, and comments from others, were recorded.

Results
● The ill person was more likely to receive help and there was no tendency for same-race helping, unless the victim was drunk. Most first helpers were male.
● There was a weak positive correlation between group size and helping behaviour.
● Early models were more likely to elicit help.

Conclusion
The findings did not support Darley and Latané's 'diffusion of responsibility' hypothesis in a real-world setting: help was offered frequently and quickly on a busy train.

Strengths
● There was high ecological validity as the setting was a real-life subway carriage.
● A **standardised procedure** was used: models only helped after a set time period, so the study can be replicated.

Weaknesses

- Ethical guidelines were broken due to no informed consent or debriefing.
- There was a lack of controls due to the real-life subway setting.

Links to assumptions

Behaviour can be influenced by groups as others may feel less responsible in an emergency situation due to others being available to help.

Links to issues and debates

On every cane trial, someone came to help, supporting a situational explanation for behaviour.

The drunk black victim was helped only 73 per cent of the time, suggesting individual differences in helping behaviour.

Similarities

- Both Piliavin *et al.* and Milgram used observations in their studies.
- Both Piliavin *et al.* and Perry *et al.* used an independent measures design.

Differences

- Piliavin *et al.* did not debrief participants, while Milgram did debrief them.
- Piliavin *et al.* used a real-life subway setting, while Perry *et al.* used a laboratory setting.

5 Research methodology

Learning outcomes

In this chapter, we will discuss:

● the six main research methods: **experiments**, **self-reports**, **observations**, **case studies**, **correlations** and **longitudinal studies**

● methodological concepts, including **aims**, **hypotheses** and variables, **experimental design**, **control** of variables and sampling

● **ethical guidelines** for working with humans and non-human animals

● ways of evaluating research: **validity**, **reliability** and **replicability**

● types of **data** and data analysis.

▲ Figure 5.1 The bustling city of Jerusalem, the location of the study by Perry *et al.*

Where there are people, there is psychology!

Psychology is everywhere, and these people are in the sacred city of Jerusalem, Israel, the nation where Anat Perry and colleagues conducted their research on oxytocin and personal space (see page 143). In this chapter, we draw on examples from Perry et al. (2015) and the other 11 AS core studies as we take an in-depth look at research methods and methodological concepts, the bedrock upon which the science of psychology is built. This chapter provides a whole new language to describe and evaluate psychological research but, before we start, we take a look at how it all began in 1783, with Ferdinand Ueberwasser, a German professor who shared something surprising in common with Dr Anat Perry and with one of the research methods discussed in this chapter.

5.0 Introducing research methodology

Think!

What is a chronoscope and how does it relate to the science of psychology?

Think!

Imagine you could join the research term of any of the psychologists named in this section, from Ferdinand Ueberwasser to Britta Hölzel, whose team would you join and why?

Think!

Do you think psychologists should spend more time studying thoughts or more time studying behaviour?

Psychologists love to observe and talk to people to try to understand what makes them think, feel and behave in the ways that they do. When they do this in a more systematic and organised way, they are conducting research and collecting data. As you can see, the circle of science is never-ending; there are always more **observations** to be made and questions to be asked.

➤➤ Have you observed anything today that made you wonder 'why'?

➤➤ You could keep a psychology diary of questions and reflections and your daily 'whys'.

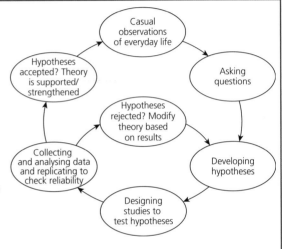

▲ Figure 5.2 The circle of science

Introducing Ferdinand Bernhard Ueberwasser: the grandfather of experimental psychology

Socrates, Plato and Aristotle were reflecting on human experience, thoughts and feelings nearly 2,500 years ago but almost 250 years ago Ferdinand Bernhard Ueberwasser appointed himself Professor of Empirical Psychology and Logic at the University of Munster, in Germany. This was the Age of Enlightenment; philosopher Immanuel Kant had coined the phrase *Sapere aude* ('Dare to know!'), people were questioning and challenging long-standing beliefs and turning to science for answers. In 1787, Ueberwasser published *Instructions*, one of psychology's first textbooks (Ueberwasser, 1787). The book explained how topics such as memory and empathy can be investigated by manipulating variables and replicating observations – as such, it shared a great deal in common with the book you are reading now.

Interestingly, Ueberwasser provided a very early account of the placebo effect, which is described in this book on page 178. We opened this chapter with a photo of Jerusalem, as a tribute to the work of Anat Perry, at the University of Haifa, in Israel. She used placebo nasal drops as a control in her scientific study of personal space and role of empathy, showing how the very earliest psychology and the psychology of today share common ground. Sadly, Ueberwasser's work ended due to the Napoleonic Wars and the closure of his university in 1849. His work has been largely forgotten and Wilhelm Wundt is heralded as the father of experimental psychology, having revived the science of psychology in 1879, in Leipzig.

Psychology through the ages

In order for psychology to break away from philosophy, as a scientific discipline, it was necessary for researchers to find ways of studying psychological processes, including sensation, perception and feelings, in ways that were objective and reliable. Wundt used an instrument called the Wheatstone-Hipp chronoscope to record reaction times, to within 1/1000 of a second. Unfortunately, his work involved attempts to observe his own private mental processes (a technique called introspection) and this approach was seen, by some, as unscientific. This is because it is impossible to verify what is going on in someone else's mind; therefore, American psychologist John Watson rejected Wundt's research into mental events in favour of studying behaviour, which can be observed and confirmed by multiple researchers. Behaviourists, like Watson, also studied animal behaviour in order to draw inferences about humans. The Cambridge International syllabus includes two animal studies: one contemporary study by Fagen *et al.*, where elephant behaviour is shaped using behaviourist principles; and the second, Hassett *et al.*, which examines the role of sex hormones in shaping monkey toy preferences, and by inference, human preferences.

> Can you think of one similarity and one difference in the way that data was collected in Fagen *et al.* versus Hassett *et al.*?

There is one important difference between Fagen *et al.* and Hassett *et al.* relating to the research methods discussed in this chapter. Hassett *et al.* were comparing groups of monkeys (males versus females) and, therefore, their study is classed as experimental, whereas Fagen *et al.* were not comparing groups or conditions; they were merely observing the elephants to see how long it would take them to learn a set of behaviours. Their study is classed as non-experimental and is a structured observation.

Focus on contemporary psychology

Despite dominating psychology for nearly 50 years, behaviourism eventually gave way to cognitive psychology in the 1950s. Interest in mental events was renewed and many psychologists agreed that cognitive processes such as memory and attention can be inferred from how people respond in experimental studies. Contemporary cognitive psychologist Joanna Pozzulo also uses laboratory experiments to explore strategies to improve eyewitness testimony, especially in children. This demonstrates one way in which science conducted in the laboratory can have far-reaching implications in the real world, in the pursuit of justice for victims and those who have been falsely convicted.

Post-behaviourist psychology not only focused on cognitive processes but also on how our behaviour is influenced by other individuals and groups. Psychology was coming out of the laboratory and into the field. For example, Piliavin *et al.* (subway Samaritans) staged a mock-emergency on the New York subway in a memorable field experiment.

> Can you think of one important difference between laboratory experiments and field experiments?

Previously, we commented that private mental processes could not be studied empirically (directly through the senses), but advances in technology in the late twentieth century onwards mean that is no longer the case. Techniques such as MRI and fMRI have provided a window into the workings of the brain. Contemporary neuroscientists like Britta Hölzel have used these techniques to study changes in brain structures over time, in experiments with longitudinal designs. One of the strengths of Hölzel *et al.*'s study was the way it combined objective, reliable, laboratory-based data collection with a real-world Mindfulness-Based Stress Reduction programme where people incorporated mindfulness into their everyday lives, practising at home while washing up or taking a walk.

Looking ahead to A Level

This research methods chapter covers everything you need to understand and to evaluate the 12 core studies at Cambridge International AS Level and to conduct your own investigations. Planning and conducting research as well as analysing data and reporting your findings are excellent ways to consolidate your growing understanding of methodological concepts (please note, ethical guidelines must be upheld at all times). The chapter also includes a few additional aspects which are relevant to the Cambridge International A Level part of the syllabus only – these are clearly identified by a red line in the margin. We have avoided using examples from the A Level options as different students/schools study different combinations. Whichever options you or your school choose (Clinical Psychology, Consumer Psychology, Health Psychology and/or Organisational Psychology), you will learn about additional research methods and methodological concepts, including randomised control trials, postal questionnaires, rating scales: forced/fixed choice, psychometric tests, writing and applying knowledge of null hypotheses and alternative directional (one-tailed) and non-directional (two-tailed) hypotheses, and temporal validity.

Before you start...

Previously, you learned about the early psychological experiments performed by Wilhelm Wundt. In tribute to his great work on reaction times, we have referred to a mock study by a fictional researcher, Dr Rox, to help you to put your new knowledge into action. Her study is introduced on page 170. You'll find that she needs your help with her study on caffeine and reaction times quite a lot! Hopefully, you'll be able to think of some more contemporary ways of measuring reaction times than the chronometer and maybe even find a way to make your measurements both valid and reliable. Good luck!

> **STUDY TIP**
>
> Although it might be tempting to claim that a certain study proved a certain theory, it is important to avoid the words 'proof', 'prove' and 'proved' in psychology. Philosopher Karl Popper noted that it is impossible to prove the claim that 'all swans are white' (Popper, 1959). You could go out searching for swans a hundred times, returning each time with a photo of a white swan, but this does not *prove* that all swans are white. Popper suggested that tracking down just one black swan would disprove (falsify) the claim – this is why psychologists test null hypotheses (see page 198). This is rather complex, but it is generally better to be cautious when writing in psychology and use phrases like 'researchers found evidence to support their theory/**hypothesis**', or 'this suggests that...', or 'this supports the idea that...'.

5.1 Research methods
5.1.1 Experiments

> **Think!**
>
> What is the difference between a **laboratory experiment** and a **field experiment**? In what way are these types of **experiment** similar?

> **Think!**
>
> Imagine you have been asked to conduct a field experiment to investigate obedience at a zoo. What would your **independent** and **dependent variables** be? Why might the data you collect be unreliable?

> **Think!**
>
> Why might the findings of laboratory experiments lack validity?

KEY TERMS

experiment (laboratory and field)

independent variable

dependent variable

controlled

standardised procedure

standardised instructions

laboratory setting

natural setting

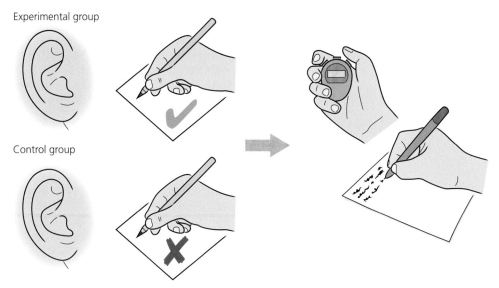

Experimental group

Control group

▲ Figure 5.3 Andrade (doodling) hypothesised that people who doodle while listening to a boring message will recall more of the message than people who do not doodle while listening to the message. She designed an experiment to test her hypothesis

What was Andrade's independent variable (what differed between the two groups)? What was one of her dependent variables (what was measured)? What type of experiment was this?

What is an experiment?

Think back to the circle of science in Figure 5.2 on page 166 and you will remember that psychologists design and conduct experiments to test hypotheses. They are interested in discovering cause-and-effect relationships between variables. To help reveal the causes of behaviour, thoughts and feelings, they compare how people behave in different situations (conditions), carefully changing one thing at a time (the independent variable) and observing how this affects another thing (the dependent variable).

To be sure that changes in the dependent variable really were caused by the independent variable, it is important to think about any other variables that might affect the dependent variable and make sure that they are **controlled** (kept the same) from one group/condition to the next. A final important feature of experiments is that there is always a carefully **standardised procedure**. The term procedure means what the experimenter must do in order to collect their data. Standardised means that each step is kept exactly the same for every participant. This includes the use of **standardised instructions**, the exact same environment (in terms of lighting, room layout, temperature, noise, etc.) and the exact same task.

The main features of experiments are as follows:
➤ Experimenters compare data collected from the experimental group or condition with data collected in the control group or control condition in order to draw conclusions about cause and effect.
➤ They have independent variables that are manipulated (changed) and dependent variables that are measured.
➤ Cause and effect can only be inferred if all other variables that could affect the dependent variable are controlled (kept the same for both groups/conditions).
➤ They have a standardised procedure and standardised instructions so that all participants have the exact same experience and so that the study can be replicated to test for reliability.

Dr Rox notices that her students always seem more alert following a cup of coffee and decides to carry out an experiment to investigate the effect of caffeine on reaction time. She gives one group of students a 300 ml cup of coffee containing 100 mg of caffeine and tests their reaction time immediately after they have drunk it. She compares their results with another group of students who are given a 300 ml glass of water (and no coffee). She predicts that the average reaction time for the caffeine group will be significantly faster than the average reaction time in the no-caffeine group.

>> The independent variable is whether the participants are given caffeine or water (this is what Dr Rox manipulated).

>> The dependent variable is participants' reaction times measured in milliseconds on the reaction time test.

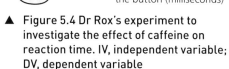

IV: the drink (coffee or water)
DV: time taken to press the button (milliseconds)

▲ Figure 5.4 Dr Rox's experiment to investigate the effect of caffeine on reaction time. IV, independent variable; DV, dependent variable

When Dr Rox analyses the results, she finds her prediction was correct, but can you think of any reasons why Dr Rox should not conclude that it was the caffeine that caused the faster reaction times?

Laboratory experiments

Location

The term **laboratory** refers to the setting (location) in which the experiment takes place. A laboratory is any setting over which the experimenter has a high level of control – for example, they can control the temperature, lighting and noise level. In Dr Rox's caffeine study, the students would be brought to a specific room at the university where they are given the coffee or water. Next, they would complete a specially designed reaction-time test on a computer – for example, touching the screen as quickly as they can every time they see the number 2 on screen. The time taken to press the button will be measured in milliseconds.

Controls

Controlled variables are kept the same between all levels (groups or conditions) of the independent variable, to ensure that only the independent variable is causing any effect on the dependent variable. Working in a laboratory setting allows researchers to control many variables. This means the researcher can be much more confident that the independent variable really did cause the changes in the dependent variable. In Dr Rox's study, if the room was rather hot on the day the coffee group took part but colder on the day the water group took part, the difference in temperature might affect reaction times. Therefore, Dr Rox should control the temperature of the room and the temperature of the water and the coffee. She would also need to control noise levels within the room, ensuring that both groups have the same quiet environment and do not become distracted.

Evaluating laboratory experiments

Validity

Another strength is that, because of the high levels of control, researchers are able to infer cause and effect because they have isolated the variable to be manipulated and the variable that is being measured. For example, in an experiment on the effects of caffeine on reaction time, if the researchers found a significant difference in the results between the caffeine and the control group, they could say that caffeine had an effect on reaction time.

A weakness of some laboratory experiments is that they can be low in ecological validity because the tasks participants are asked to perform sometimes do not reflect what they would do in real life. For example, in Pozzulo *et al.*'s (line-ups) experiment, participants were asked to watch some videos, then identify cartoon and (real) human characters from the videos in photo line-ups. This is not the same as witnessing a crime in real life, where people are unlikely to be expecting the event, may feel more intense emotions and will be viewing the situation in real life not on a screen. These factors are likely to affect their recall for faces in a different way to a calm, controlled setting. This means that the results of laboratory experiments should only be generalised to everyday life with caution as when people are in a real-life setting, they may behave very differently.

Another weakness is that validity can also be affected by demand characteristics, which are features of the environment that reveal the aim of the study. If participants are able to work out the aim of the study, they may act in a way they feel the researchers want them to, rather than behaving how they normally would.

Reliability

One strength of laboratory experiments is that the setting means the procedure can be highly standardised. This means that all participants within each group/condition have the exact same experience as each other. This is important because it means other researchers should be able to replicate the study to test the findings for reliability (i.e. consistency).

 ## Ethics

A strength is that laboratory experiments should be more ethical than field experiments (see below) because participants know they are taking part in research (even if they have not been told the exact hypothesis). They will have given their consent to take part and will be made aware of their right to withdraw. Unlike field experiments, researchers are generally able to debrief their participants following any deception. This is important as upholding ethical guidelines helps to ensure that participants are treated with respect and that they leave the research setting in the same psychological state as they were in when they arrived.

Field experiment

Location

When psychologists talk about working in 'the field', they mean conducting research in real-world settings. Away from the controlled world of the laboratory, field experiments take place in natural environments, where one might expect to see the behaviours of interest, such as the street, supermarket or workplace. One or more independent variables are still manipulated by the experiment in order to observe the effect on the dependent variable(s). However, the natural environment means that in comparison with laboratory experiments, there may be uncontrolled variables both within and between groups/conditions. These are factors that are not being measured or controlled by the researcher and can have an unwanted effect on the dependent variable. These could be things such as the temperature of the room or noise levels.

> How could Dr Rox redesign her study as a field experiment? Where would it take place and how could she measure reaction times in a more naturalistic way?

Controls

When researchers conduct field experiments, they try to maintain control over variables that could affect the dependent variable to allow cause-and-effect conclusions to be drawn, but this is much more difficult than in a laboratory environment. In natural environments, like public places (e.g. Piliavin *et al.*, subway Samaritans), it is not possible to control how many people board the train or how close people are standing to each other, for example. These uncontrolled, situational variables (see page 201) make it hard to draw firm conclusions.

Can you think of any variables that would be difficult to control if Dr Rox decided to conduct her study in a coffee shop? Imagine she has ten students in each group, would it be possible to ensure that they all have the exact same experience as each other?

Evaluating field experiments

Validity

A strength of field experiments is that they generally have higher ecological validity than a laboratory experiment, meaning that participants' behaviour is more likely to be natural as they are not in an unfamiliar laboratory setting and often unaware that they are even taking part in the research. This means their results should be generalisable to other similar situations. Another strength of field experiments is that participants are also much less likely to show demand characteristics if they do not know they are taking part in research. This means that they are unlikely to try to work out what the aim of the research is and act in the way that they think the researchers want them to.

Field experiments take place in real-world settings. The behaviours of interest are observed/measured in everyday situations. For this reason, they tend to have higher ecological validity. Also, participants are less likely to be affected by demand characteristics, especially if they do not even know they are in a study. The researcher still manipulates an aspect of the situation (e.g. Piliavin *et al.* staged an emergency on the subway, see page 154) and so the setting is not completely natural.
» Do you think it is possible for a laboratory experiment to have ecological validity?
» Do you think it is possible for a field experiment to lack ecological validity?

Reliability

A weakness is that researchers have much less control in a field experiment. For example, in the Piliavin *et al.* experiment (see page 153), researchers could not control who was sitting in the train carriage or how crowded it was when the experiment took place. Neither could they control whether the passengers had already seen the confederate collapse in a previous trial, leading them to become suspicious and potentially affecting their response. Field experiments tend to be more difficult to replicate due to the limited ability to **standardise** the procedure. This makes it difficult to test the reliability of the findings.

Ethics

A weakness of field experiments is that participants often do not know that they are taking part in research, so consent cannot be sought, which also removes the right to withdraw. When the deception is revealed, it may lead participants to doubt psychologists in the future. Deception should only be used when the research aims cannot be met without it taking place and only if the participants are unlikely to feel discomfort on finding out about the deception. The research design should protect the dignity of the participants.

Control groups and/or conditions

Experiments involve making comparisons between data obtained in two or more groups or conditions. A strength of control groups/conditions is that the data provided in this part of the experiment provides a baseline to which the data from the experimental group or condition can be compared. Control groups/conditions allow the researchers to confirm that the results of their study are due to the manipulation of the independent variable. In Dr Rox's study, the water group provides the reaction speed baseline to which the coffee group's average speed can be compared.

Can you think of a different control group that Dr Rox could have used to provide the baseline in her study?

▶ LEARNING LINK

∙∙

The study by Bandura *et al.* (aggression) used a laboratory experiment to investigate whether a child would imitate aggressive behaviour if they witnessed such behaviour in an adult. The children's behaviour was observed through a one-way mirror while they played with a standardised set of toys that were laid out in exactly the same way for each child, regardless of which group they were in (aggressive model, non-aggressive model or control). The study by Piliavin *et al.* (subway Samaritans) was a field experiment investigating helping behaviour on a subway train. The subway train was a natural environment for the passengers, who did not know that they were being observed and happened to be riding in the train carriage at the time that the study was being conducted.

- What similarities and differences are there between these two studies?
- Think about the independent and dependent variables and how the setting affects the level of control and standardisation; what impact does the setting have on the validity and reliability of the findings of each of these studies?

STUDY TIP

Sometimes it can be difficult to work out which variable is the independent variable (IV) and which is the dependent variable (DV). There are several ways to think about this. Experimenters generally want to know whether one thing causes an effect on another; they want to know whether the independent variable (I) causes (C) an effect (E) on the dependent variable (D). This spells ICED; you could ask 'Do *sales of iced coffee* (the DV) depend on *the weather, e.g. hot or cold* (the IV)?

▶ TEST YOURSELF

∙∙

1 Outline two features of a laboratory experiment. [2]
2 Explain one similarity and one difference between a laboratory experiment and a field experiment. [4]
3 Andrade used a laboratory experiment to study doodling. Outline one strength of this method with reference to this study. [2]
4 Suggest one advantage of Piliavin *et al.* (subway Samaritans) conducting their research on a New York subway. [2]
5 Sanija is conducting a study to investigate whether there is a difference in students' attention spans in school depending on whether they eat a hot or cold breakfast.
    a Suggest an appropriate research method that Sanija could use to test her theory. [1]
    b Suggest how Sanija could operationalise her dependent variables. [2]
6 Arthur is conducting an experiment into memory for instructions with a group of children with autism spectrum disorder. He thinks the children will remember the instructions better if they are presented as a written story with pictures compared with reading the instructions aloud.
    a Identify one variable that Arthur should control in his experiment. [2]
    b Outline why Arthur should use a standardised procedure in his experiment. [2]

5.1.2 Experimental designs

Think!

What is the purpose of **random allocation**?

Think!

Imagine you are investigating brain localisation and the effect of playing a certain video game. You want to see whether grey matter concentration increases in a certain brain structure following increased time spent playing the game. What research design would you use to investigate this question? How might you improve the validity of your design?

KEY TERMS

random allocation

experimental design

experimental group

control group

independent measures

baseline

repeated measures

control condition

demand characteristics

order effects (practice and fatigue)

counterbalancing

experimental condition

matched pairs

Think!

How would you rank the three **experimental designs** in terms of their practicality and validity? Put the experimental designs in order from least to most practical and least to most valid. If possible, discuss this with a classmate to see whether you agree.

In Dr Rox's caffeine experiment (see page 170), the students in the **experimental group** consumed caffeine and their average reaction time was compared with the average reaction time of the participants in the **control group**, who did not consume caffeine (the water group).
➤➤ Which experimental design was used in this study?
➤➤ What were the problems of using this design?
➤➤ How could Dr Rox have improved her experiment?

Independent measures design

In an **independent measures** design, participants are put into two or more different groups, relating to the levels of the independent variable. These groups are sometimes called the experimental group and the control group. Data from the control group provides a **baseline** to which the researcher can compare the data collected in the experimental group. For example, in the study by Andrade (doodling), participants in the experimental group were asked to shade circles and squares on an A4 piece of paper, while participants in the control group were not allowed to shade or doodle. The average number of words recalled by the two different groups of participants was then compared to see if there was a difference between them.

An independent measures design uses different participants for each condition of the experiment. In what way might using different participants for different conditions affect the validity of the results, and how might this be avoided?

Random allocation and participant variables

Another key feature of laboratory experiments is that the researchers are able to randomly allocate participants into either the experimental or the control group. This is often done by assigning each participant a number and then using a random number generator to select participants for the two or more groups.

Without random allocation, it is possible that members of one group all share some common characteristic that makes them different from the people in the other group. These characteristics are called **participant variables**, and may be things like gender, age or level of intelligence or empathy. When this happens, it is impossible to know whether differences in the dependent variable result from the manipulation of the independent variable or the participant variables. The purpose of random allocation, therefore, is to increase validity (see below).

Dr Rox realises that there might be some important participant variables affecting the students' results in her study on the effects of caffeine on reaction times (see page 170). An important participant variable in her study might be how much coffee (and other caffeinated drinks/snacks) the students usually consume. If all the heavy-caffeine users end up in the coffee group and all the light-caffeine users, by chance, end up in the water group, it would be unclear whether any difference in average reaction times results

from the drink consumed before the test or differences in the students' regular caffeine consumption. How could Dr Rox reduce the effect of participant variables in her study?

▲ Figure 5.5

Repeated measures

▲ Figure 5.6 In repeated measures designs, the same participants take part in both the experimental condition and the control condition

In a **repeated measures** design, the same group of participants provide data relating to both levels of the independent variable; they act as their own control group. This means participant variables cannot affect the validity of the data as every participant takes part in both the experimental and the **control conditions**. The control condition provides a baseline for comparison and allows the researcher to see whether the independent variable has caused the dependent variable to increase or decrease. Unfortunately, the repeated measures design has problems of its own regarding validity: **demand characteristics** and **order effects**.

Demand characteristics

Demand characteristics are cues in the set-up of the experiment, including how the researcher speaks and behaves, that provide clues about the aims and/or hypotheses of the study. Participants sometimes, consciously or unconsciously, change their behaviour in response to these cues and this reduces the spontaneity of their behaviour, meaning they may not behave as they usually would. This may be because they want to please the experimenter or behave in ways that they think are expected of them. Demand characteristics are, therefore, a threat to the validity of the study's findings and action should be taken to minimise them where possible.

Order effects, including fatigue and practice effects

When participants have to perform a task twice under different conditions, behaviour in the second condition may be different to the first, not because of the changes in the independent variable, but due to the fact they have performed the task once already. For example, they may perform better the second time due to the experience gained in the first condition (a **practice** effect) or increased motivation, or worse due to boredom, tiredness or the strain of concentrating in the first condition (a **fatigue** effect). Therefore, order effects are a threat to validity as it becomes unclear whether the independent variable is affecting the dependent variable or whether the order of the conditions has brought about any changes observed. One way researchers can reduce the impact of order effects is to leave a significant time period between first and second conditions. When this is not possible, they can be addressed using a technique like **counterbalancing**.

In Dr Rox's experiment on the effects of caffeine on reaction time (see page 170), the participants might perform better the second time they do the reaction time test because they have already done it once and had the chance to practise. Similarly, participants may perform worse in the second condition as they have already been concentrating on the screen in the first condition (fatigue effect). They might also need the toilet if they have consumed both a cup of coffee and a glass of water! How could you set up the experiment to avoid order effects?

Counterbalancing

Counterbalancing is a technique that can be used in a repeated measure design so that order effects do not compromise the validity of the findings. Participants are put into one of two groups: group one does the **experimental condition** first and then the control condition, and group two does the control condition first and then the experimental condition. This way, although practice effects will still occur, their impact on the findings is reduced.

Matched pairs design

In a **matched pairs** design, each participant in the experimental group will be matched with a participant in the control group on a number of relevant factors. This means for every participant in the experimental group, the control group will contain a person who is very similar to them on key variables that might have otherwise affected the dependent variable of the study. For example, participants could be matched on handedness (preference for using the right or left hand), gender, socioeconomic status or age. A matched pairs design overcomes the problem of participants' variables and order effects, but in practice, they can be difficult to set up as careful screening of the participants is necessary in order to match the groups. It can also be difficult to recruit people who have the necessary characteristics.

Dr Rox is still concerned that participant variables might affect the validity of her conclusions about the effect of caffeine on reaction times. She decides to use a matched pairs design where she will match the participants in each condition on age, sex, handedness and experience in playing video games, all variables which may affect the validity of her conclusions. What would she need to do to set up her matched groups of participants?

Experimental group: Soraya, female, aged 22, left-handed

Control group: Elina, female, aged 22, left-handed

▶ Figure 5.7 In matched pairs designs, participants are matched across the experimental and control conditions

▶ LEARNING LINK

The research by Hölzel *et al.* (mindfulness and brain scans) uses a combination of both independent measures design and repeated measures design (see page 29). Participants in the experimental group took part in an eight-week Mindfulness-Based Stress Reduction (MBSR) programme. MRI brain scans were conducted both before and after the intervention. Data from the scans was compared to see if the MBSR programme had changed grey matter concentration.

- Which part of Hölzel's study is independent measures and which part is repeated measures?
- Why was it important in this study to also have a control group?

STUDY TIP

Once you are confident in being able to explain the strengths and weaknesses of the different experimental designs, ensure that you are able to apply this knowledge and understanding to any new psychology experiments that you learn about in class or read about online. Working with a partner, if you can, why not design a set of experiments for each other on topics like sleep, memory, **aggression** and helpfulness? Write out the independent and dependent variables you would like to investigate. Roll a dice to see whether the design will be independent measures (odd numbers) or repeated measures (even numbers). Write a sentence on how you would set your study up and then swap with your partner and identify the problems in each study (e.g. specific participant variables, how order effects might alter the results) and re-design the studies to overcome the problems. Being able to evaluate the experimental design, using key features from the study, is an essential skill.

> **TEST YOURSELF**

1   Outline what is meant by 'counterbalancing' using any example.   [2]
2   Outline one strength and one weakness of a matched pairs design.   [4]
3   Pozzulo *et al.* used a repeated measures design so children observed both human and cartoon faces and they also participated in both target-present and target-absent line-ups. Suggest one advantage of a repeated measures design with reference to this study.   [2]
4   In Piliavin *et al.* (subway Samaritans), the researchers observed train passengers' reactions to a staged emergency. The design was independent measures. Explain one disadvantage of this design using this study as an example.   [2]
5   Javine thinks ink colour (red or black) might affect the speed at which people are able to solve anagrams. She decides to conduct a laboratory experiment with a repeated measures design to test this idea.
    a   Explain how practice effects could affect the validity of Javine's findings.   [2]
    b   Explain how Javine could use counterbalancing to improve her study.   [2]
6   Fabian shows his participants a painting. He tells one group that it took the artist six months to complete and another group was told it took six years to complete. He asks the participants to rate how much they liked it on a scale from 1–10.
    a   Identify the experimental design used in Fabian's experiment.   [1]
    b   Explain one disadvantage of using this experimental design in this study.   [2]

5.1.3 Randomised control trials

KEY TERMS

placebo effect

randomised control trial

placebo

expectancy effects

single-blind

double-blind

Think!

What is meant by a **placebo effect**? How are placebo effects controlled in a **randomised control trial** (RCT)?

Think!

Your friend says she cannot concentrate in her study periods unless she has had a can of her favourite brand of cola first. How could you design a study using a RCT to see whether your friend's favourite brand really improves her concentration or whether she just thinks that it does? Can you think of any problems with your study?

Think!

RCTs sometimes raise ethical issues as when participants are assigned to a **placebo**/control group, this may mean they have to wait for a treatment that could improve their quality of life. Can you think why such studies may be ethically justifiable?

One special type of experiment is called a randomised control trial (RCT). Randomised control trials (RCTs) are a special type of experiment. They use various techniques to increase validity and they are often referred to as the 'gold standard' in clinical and health research, such as drug testing. For example, participants might be randomly assigned to either an experimental group (who are given the new drug) or a control group. The control groups in RCTs sometimes receive no treatment or they receive a placebo.

The placebo effect

Sometimes it is hard to know whether the positive effect of a new drug is due to the drug itself or the fact that participants expect their symptoms to improve once they begin the new course of treatment. In order to isolate how much of any improvement is due to the drug and how much is due to **expectancy effects**, researchers often use placebo treatments. Here participants in the control group receive a treatment that is administered in exactly the same way as the real treatments (e.g. in the case of orally administered tablets, the tablet will look, smell and taste just like the real drug) but contains no active ingredients. Importantly, the participants do not know whether they have received the real drug or the placebo. This is called a **single-blind** design. Changes in symptoms (before and after treatment) are calculated for both groups. For example, in the study by Perry *et al.* (personal space), participants were asked to self-administer either oxytocin or a saline solution (placebo), before taking part in experiments on personal space. They were unaware whether they had received the drug or the placebo (the saline solution) to avoid this knowledge affecting their behaviour.

Often, placebo groups experience significant improvements over time (the placebo effect) but any significant difference in the amount of improvement between the experimental and control groups must be caused by the independent variable – that is, the presence of the active ingredient in the real drug.

RCTs are also used in studies investigating the efficacy of psychological treatments such as cognitive behavioural therapy (CBT) and other interventions to improve health and wellbeing. Here the placebo treatment is something that is similar to the genuine treatment/intervention in many ways (e.g. weekly appointments with a counsellor), but without the CBT element.

Double-blind design

As noted above, participants do not know whether they have received the placebo or the real drug but often the researcher who measures the severity of the participants' symptoms is also unaware whether the participants are in the placebo group or treatment group. This is called a **double-blind** design. In some studies, the person analysing the data is also unaware whether data points were contributed by people in the placebo or intervention group and this is known as a triple-blind design!

Evaluating RCTs

Validity

A strength of the double-blind design is that it reduces experimenter bias as well as reducing demand characteristics. For example, if the experimenter knew who was in the placebo group they might expect those participants to have experienced less improvement over the course of the study. The experimenter's expectations could affect the data provided by the participant, reducing the validity of the findings. A double-blind design makes sure this cannot happen, ensuring the experimenter's assessment of the participant remains objective.

Reliability

Another strength is that the double-blind design allows researchers to test interventions (e.g. treatments and therapies) in a controlled way. As none of the experimenters who come into contact with the participants are aware which groups they are in, all participants are treated in exactly the same way by the experimenters, meaning that their assessments can be replicated and tested for inter-rater reliability.

Ethics

A weakness is that valid, informed consent is not possible. Double-blind RCTs rely not only on the researchers being unaware which group (placebo or genuine treatment) the participant is in, but also the participant, meaning they are not giving fully informed consent. This is important, however, as it preserves the validity of the findings and arguably the benefits of the research outweigh the cost to participants, especially given that the participants have consented to the possibility that they will receive a placebo.

A weakness of RCTs is that it could mean that participants randomly assigned to the control group do not have access to treatments that could significantly improve their quality of life. In order to still conduct important RCTs on treatments for mental health disorders, the control groups are often offered the treatment they missed out on as soon as the study has ended. The start of treatment, however, would still be delayed, potentially causing unnecessary psychological **harm**. They are often referred to as a wait-list control group.

In Dr Rox's study about the effect of caffeine on reaction times (see page 170), the control group drank a cup of water. Now that you have a better understanding of expectancy effects, you should be able to explain why the coffee group might have experienced faster reaction times than the water group for psychological rather than biological reasons.

» How could Dr Rox have turned her study into a RCT with a placebo group and a double-blind design?

► LEARNING LINK

Lewin *et al.* (1992) used a randomised control trial to test the effectiveness of a home-based exercise programme to help improve fitness after a heart attack (see page 617). Participants were randomly assigned to receive either the self-help rehabilitation intervention or standard care plus a placebo package of information and informal counselling.

► TEST YOURSELF

1 Explain one strength and one weakness of using randomised control trials. [4]
2 Suggest one ethical issue which may arise from the use of randomised control trials, using any example. [2]
3 Dr Phil would like to test a new drug he has developed to support individuals with gambling disorders. Suggest how Dr Phil might use a randomised control trial to test whether the new drug is more effective than a placebo. [2]
4 Hajra would like to find out whether yoga has a positive impact on people's subjective wellbeing, as previous research has suggested. Suggest one reason why a randomised control trial may not be a suitable method to investigate this. [2]
5 Malcolm is investigating the effectiveness of electro-convulsive therapy (ECT) as a treatment for schizophrenia. He plans to use a randomised control trial where the control group think they have been given ECT but have not.
   a Suggest two ways that Malcolm can ensure that his data is objective. [4]
   b Outline one difference and one similarity between the experimental and control groups in Malcolm's study. [4]
6 Jolene has had pain in her shoulder for months following a car accident. She is participating in a randomised control trial to test the effectiveness of acupuncture. Explain one ethical issue relating to randomised control trials. You must refer to Jolene in your answer. [2]

5.1.4 Self-reports: questionnaires

KEY TERMS

open question

closed question

self-report

questionnaire

interview

rich (as in data)

target population

Think!

What is the difference between an **open question** and a **closed question**?

Think!

Imagine you are investigating the effect of stress on the content of people's dreams. Which type of question (open or closed) would be best to find out about people's stress levels and their dream content?

Think!

Why do you think some researchers prefer rating scales with an even number of choices, such as six-point scales from 0–5, and others prefer to use scales with an odd number, such as seven-point scales from 0–6?

Self-reports are a method of research where the participant responds to either open or closed questions. Data may be gathered about their beliefs and opinions as well how they believe they would behave in certain situations. Self-reports include both **questionnaires** and **interviews** and may collect both quantitative and qualitative data.

Questionnaires

Questionnaires can be completed in a number of ways. Printed questionnaires may be completed by hand, but nowadays most questionnaires are distributed digitally and participants complete them online. This saves printing and postage costs and data can be collated much quickly and easily. This said, online questionnaires can only be completed by participants who have access to the internet and understand the technology, meaning traditional 'pen and paper' surveys are still used and may be more convenient for many types of research.

Closed questions

Closed questions offer a fixed choice of answers. They may use some form of scale such as a Likert scale, in which the participant can circle or tick the response to show the extent to which they agree with a statement. An example of a Likert scale might be:

I do not like people invading my personal space, especially if I do not know them.

1   2   3   4   5

Please circle the response that best fits your view: 1 = Completely disagree, 2 = Disagree, 3 = Neither agree nor disagree, 4 = Agree, 5 = Completely agree.

Here is another example of a closed question is: 'Do you find mindfulness meditation relaxing? Yes/No.' This type of closed question may not provide enough options to reflect the participants' range of experiences with mindfulness meditation. For example, it is not possible to communicate that you occasionally find mindfulness meditation relaxing but often find it ineffective. In this example, a rating scale may allow participants to provide more valid responses. For example, To what extent do you agree: Mindfulness meditation helps me to relax 0 = Never found it helpful to 5 = Aways very helpful.

Although dichotomous questions (with only two answers) are often not very useful, they may be helpful if you wish to provide contingency questions. These allow the participant to ignore questions that are not relevant to them. For example:

Have you ever tried mindfulness meditation as a way of relaxing? Yes/No.

If yes, please answer questions 2–5. If no, please continue to question 6.

Rating scale: forced/fixed choice

Some of the studies in the options topics use rating scales where respondents must make a forced/fixed choice. This type of scale does not allow the participants to respond with answers like 'unsure/undecided/don't know/neutral' as it is intended to 'force' the participant to make a response and express an opinion. Forced-choice questions are often written as a statement that participants have to agree or disagree with or give a 'yes/no' answer to. Fixed-choice questionnaires produce quantitative data, which allows for objective comparisons to be made between people; however, participants' answers may lack validity as the fixed responses may not exactly match what they would like to say.

Open questions

Open questions allow the participants to express their opinion more freely and tend to start with words such as 'why' and 'how'. These words encourage participants to give detailed, qualitative answers. The data they provide is often described as **rich** because it allows the researcher to understand the complexity of the issues they are asking about. This is because participants are able to explore the reasons behind their initial thoughts and feelings in greater depth. These sorts of questions also allow the researcher to understand the diversity of an issue as the answers provided by the participants may be very different from one another.

▼ Table 5.1 Evaluating open and closed questions

	Closed questions	Open questions
Advantages	Data is quantitative (answers can be categorised and counted) and can be analysed using measures of central tendency and/or spread and displayed visually using graphs and charts. Forced/fixed-choice rating scales do not allow participants to avoid answering questions.	Data is qualitative, so it is rich and detailed, giving researchers deeper insight than would be possible with quantitative, fixed-choice answers,
Disadvantages	Limited choice reduces validity. A fixed range of answers mean participants cannot freely express their opinions; their views may not fit with the fixed-choice answers available.	Data can be harder to analyse than for closed questions. As there may be a huge amount of data, analysis can be time-consuming. It can also be subjective as researchers summarise and report on key themes in the data; other researchers might interpret the data differently, making findings less reliable than quantitative data from closed questions.

STUDY TIP

When analysing data from a questionnaire, it is useful to remember that yes/no answers can be summarised by using the mode as a measure of central tendency. If you have a Likert scale, where people indicate their agreement on a numerical scale, you can use the mode or the median. If you want to try creating an online questionnaire, there are many free programs you can use to do so.

What to avoid when creating questionnaires

1   Double-barrelled questions: these are questions where two things are asked in one question, such as:

I think that students should have more exams and coursework.

1   2   3   4   5

Please circle the response which best fits your view: 1 = Completely disagree, 2 = Disagree, 3 = Neither agree nor disagree, 4 = Agree, 5 = Completely agree.

It might be that the participant thinks that more coursework would be beneficial but does not want more exams. However, it is not possible for them to make this clear in their answer.

2 Ambiguous (unclear) questions: it is extremely important that participants can understand what the question is actually asking. If not, it will affect the validity of their responses. Pilot studies are useful to 'trial' drafts of newly developed questionnaires.

3 Technical terms: avoid using technical language unless your **target population** will understand it. For example, if you were only going to be using doctors as your target population, it would be acceptable to use medical terminology, but not if your target population had no medical training.

4 Emotive language: you should avoid using words that are likely to offend or upset your participants for ethical reasons but also emotive language may be persuasive and lead participants to give an answer that they would not have given if the question was worded differently.

> **STUDY TIP**
>
> If you are creating a questionnaire, it is best to undertake a small pilot study on a few participants before distributing it to a larger number of people. This will help you to ensure that participants understand all of the questions and are able to answer as many as possible. If the pilot study highlights any problems, these can be resolved before collecting any further data.

Evaluating questionnaires

▼ Table 5.2 Advantages and disadvantages of questionnaires

Advantages	Disadvantages
Relatively quick and easy to obtain the views of a large number of participants; large sample size means results should be more representative, although this also depends on the sampling technique (see page 199).	Participants may be less willing to elaborate fully on answers to open questions when writing, therefore limiting the depth of data collected.
Participants may be less likely to give socially desirable answers than during interviews because they are not answering face-to-face and their responses can be provided anonymously.	Participants may still give socially desirable answers. These are answers that make them look good or acceptable within their society but do not actually reflect their own viewpoint.

> **STUDY TIP**
>
> Although researcher bias and **subjectivity** can be an issue in the analysis of qualitative data, it does not mean that all researchers will show researcher bias. When evaluating methods and studies, it is best to use words such as 'could' and 'might' to show that bias is a possibility rather than a certainty.

Psychologist Hans Eysenck created a well-known personality test called the Eysenck Personality Inventory (EPI). It includes nine questions to assess whether a participant is likely to have given socially desirable answers or not (the lie scale) (Eysenck and Eysenck, 1991). Anyone scoring five or above was probably lying. This allows researchers to tell if the participant is likely to be giving truthful answers about the rest of the personality questions. For example, one question on the EPI is 'If you say you will do something do you always keep your promise, no matter how inconvenient it might be to do so?' If the participant responds 'yes' to this question, it is likely that they are lying and giving a socially desirable answer as most people at some point break a promise. Do you think it is valid to assume that participants lied on other questions based on their answers to the lie scale questions?

Postal questionnaires

Postal questionnaires refer to questionnaires that are posted out to the sample. For example, Lewin *et al.* (1992) used postal questionnaires to assess the psychological impact of a rehabilitation programme for people who had had a heart attack (see page 617). The questionnaires measured anxiety and depression, general health and use of the health services.

▼ Table 5.3 Evaluating postal questionnaires

Advantages	Disadvantages
Relatively quick and easy to obtain the views of a large number of participants; large sample size means results should be more representative, although this also depends on the sampling technique (see page 205).	The return rate for postal questionnaires is quite low due to the effort of posting them back; participants may not have the motivation to do this. Participants who do return the questionnaires may be unrepresentative of the target population – for example, they may be especially helpful, motivated or have a particular interest in the topic being studied.
Can be posted anywhere in the world; location is not an issue as it would be with a face-to-face interview.	It can be expensive to post large numbers of questionnaires, especially if return postage is included.

▶ LEARNING LINK

Questionnaires can also be used to collect data as part of an experiment. For example, Pozzulo *et al.* (line-ups) used an eight-item questionnaire called the Demographic and Cartoon Watching Form to gather information from the parents of the children in the study (see page 70). This information included age, gender, primary language and ethnicity, whether they had any siblings and how much time they spent watching cartoons. Questionnaires like this can be helpful in providing key information that is required when making **generalisations** from the sample to the target population. Also, in experiments with matched-pairs designs, questionnaires may be useful to gather data to match the participants, as part of the initial screening.

▶ TEST YOURSELF

1. Suggest one advantage of asking open questions in questionnaires. [2]
2. Suggest one disadvantage of using online questionnaires. [2]
3. Baron Cohen *et al.*'s Eyes Test is a 'pen and paper' test. Suggest one strength of using this format. [2]
4. Pozzulo *et al.* (line-ups) used a questionnaire to find out more about the children in their study. State one closed question that they could have asked about children's cartoon watching. [1]
5. Lucca works with elephant handlers (mahouts) in Nepal. He is using a questionnaire to investigate the handlers' attitudes towards training methods that focus on positive **reinforcement**.
   a. Explain how one ethical guideline would be important for Lucca's study. [2]
   b. Suggest two advantages of Lucca using a questionnaire to gather data for his study. [4]
6. Carol creates a questionnaire including a series of fixed/forced-choice questions to measure helping behaviour in a variety of different situations. Identify two questions that Carol could include in her questionnaire. [2]

KEY TERMS
structured interview
unstructured interview
semi-structured
interview
in-depth

5.1.5 Self-reports: interviews

Think!

What are the key features of a **semi-structured interview**?

Think!

Imagine you are investigating unusual phobias (e.g. buttons, flowers). You are interested to know whether people can remember any traumatic events that might have become associated with their feared object. Why might an interview be more effective than a questionnaire for collecting data about this topic?

Think!

There are many factors that can affect the validity of the data obtained in an interview, from the experience and appearance of the interviewer to the location of the interview. What advice might you give to a researcher to ensure their interview data is valid?

Interviews

Interviews differ from questionnaires in that the researcher speaks directly to individual participants, asks them questions and records their responses. Interviews are generally done on smaller numbers of participants as they are far more time-consuming to conduct.

Interviews can be conducted face-to-face or by telephone.

Just like questionnaires, interviewers can ask both open and closed questions. However, interviews are likely to have more open questions as people are often willing to speak in greater depth about a topic than they are to write about it in a questionnaire.

▼ Table 5.4 Types of interview

Interview format	Key features
Structured interviews	The researcher has a pre-determined, fixed list of questions; all participants are asked the same questions, in the same order.
Unstructured interviews	The main topics are pre-determined.
	There will be a research question that steers the direction of the interview; the interviewer does not follow a set list of questions.
	Questions are based on whatever the participant chooses to talk about.
Semi-structured interviews	The researcher has a number of key questions that guide the interview, but they can be asked in any order and the interviewer may introduce new questions based on what the participant says.
	The interviewer is also able to ask follow-up questions to clarify anything that the participant has said and to probe more deeply into interesting or unexpected areas.
	Some of the questions will be the same for each participant but not all.

Evaluating interviews

▼ Table 5.5 Advantages and disadvantages of interviews

Advantages	Disadvantages
Interviews offer researchers a much greater opportunity to gather rich, **in-depth** data from their participants.	Participants may be more likely to give socially desirable answers, due to speaking directly with the researcher and being afraid they will be judged. This would reduce the validity of the data collected.
Semi-structured or unstructured interviews allow researchers to gain a good insight into the area that they are researching as they are not constrained by set questions. They may discover thoughts and ideas that they had not previously considered.	Although semi-structured and unstructured interviews can offer a greater insight into what people think and feel about things because they are not constrained by set questions, it makes them more at risk of researcher bias.
Face-to-face interviews allow researchers to gather information about non-verbal communication (e.g. gesture, posture, facial expression); this can increase the validity of the findings as this data may provide cues about the person's emotional state and how comfortable they are with the interview.	Face-to-face interviews may be impractical for people who live in remote areas and/or have limited mobility or transport. Furthermore, people may feel uncomfortable being interviewed face-to-face about sensitive topics or in unfamiliar environments and may prefer a telephone or video call.
An advantage of telephone interviews is that they provide a quicker and more cost-effective way of gathering in-depth information than face-to-face interviews. This is because the interviewers do not have to travel to meet the participants (or the other way round), saving both time and money. This might allow them to gather a larger sample than if they were doing face-to-face interviews.	A disadvantage of telephone interviews is that some participants may not feel comfortable speaking over the phone and may be less willing to speak in-depth. Another disadvantage is that because the researcher cannot see the participants, they cannot use non-verbal signals to help them engage with the participant and get them to feel comfortable about talking to them.

STUDY TIP

While participants may be more likely to give socially desirable answers in face-to-face, or even phone, interviews due to a fear of being judged, one may also argue the opposite. The pressure of speaking to another person may prevent a participant from feeling able to lie. The topic of the interview may affect participants' potential honesty levels, and socially sensitive topics such as mental health, race or gender may be more prone to social desirability.

TEST YOURSELF

1 Describe one similarity and one difference between a semi-structured interview and an unstructured interview. [4]
2 Identify three ways that an interview differs from a questionnaire. [3]
3 Pozzulo *et al.* (line-ups) interviewed their participants after showing them videos including either human faces or cartoon characters. Outline the interview format used in this study. [2]
4 Milgram (obedience) interviewed his participants to find out more about why the majority of them obeyed. Suggest one reason why the answers that the participants gave may not have been valid. [2]
5 Tilly is planning to interview a group of parents about their attitudes towards aggression in children.
   a Suggest one open question that Tilly could use to collect data about people's attitudes towards aggressive behaviour in children. [1]
   b Suggest one strength of using open questions to collect data in Tilly's study. [2]
6 Tai and Vinh are planning to use structured interviews to ask passengers in two busy airports about their attitudes towards personal space.
   a State which type of interview Tai and Vinh should use to collect data in their study. [1]
   b Suggest one strength of using the type of interview you suggested in part a, in this study. [2]

Psychometric tests

The word psychometric literally means 'measuring the mind'. Psychometric tests are carefully designed to provide valid and reliable measures of individual differences between people relating to personality, aptitude, knowledge or skills. The tests are standardised on large random samples in order to establish norms or average scores. This means that an individual's scores can be compared to the norm to reveal whether they score higher or lower than average, and if so, how much higher or lower than other people who are comparable to them (e.g. the same age).

Floor and ceiling effects

If tested on a large enough random sample, a valid psychometric test will provide scores which range from very low to very high. Most people should score somewhere in the middle. This is called a normal distribution. Some tests do not differentiate between people very well – for example, the range of scores is low. If the majority of the scores are very high, we get a ceiling effect – people are unable to achieve any higher (they are bumping their heads on the ceiling!). Alternatively, if everyone receives a very low score, this is called a floor effect. Again, the test is not valid as it does not allow us to rank the participants from those with the highest scores to those with the lowest scores. An intelligence or IQ test, for example, must not be too hard (to avoid floor effects) or too easy (to avoid ceiling effects). In a clinical setting, researchers must also ensure that the tests cover a range of scores – for example, a test of depression must be able to show scores from not depressed at all to severely depressed.

▼ Table 5.6 Evaluating psychometric tests

Advantages	Disadvantages
Psychometric tests are objective as the tests produce numerical data, which does not require the subjective interpretation of psychologists.	Participants may respond to demand characteristics and answer in a way they think is expected of them, reducing the validity of the data collected.
Psychometric tests are a fast, cost-effective way of shortlisting job applicants before interviewing, which may allow employers to recruit more suitable candidates.	If a participant feels under stress, it may affect how they respond on a psychometric test, meaning that it is less likely to be valid or reliable (if they were tested again, when less stressed, they may respond differently).

▶ LEARNING LINK

Whichever options you are studying, you will find psychological research using psychometric tests in all the applied areas, including Clinical, Consumer, Health and Organisational Psychology. For example, a visual analogue scale (VAS) is a psychometric scale for measuring attitudes, feelings or characteristics that cannot be directly measured, like subjective perception of **pain**, along a continuum of values (see example in Figure 5.8). Can you think of any reason why a scale like this might not provide valid data? Do you think there are any groups of people in particular that might not understand this scale very well? What implications might this have?

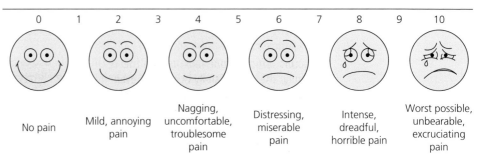

▲ Figure 5.8 An example of a visual analogue scale for measuring pain

STUDY TIP

Many of the evaluation points for questionnaires and fixed/forced-choice questions may be relevant here. It is important though to consider the purpose of psychometric tests and how they might be used to avoid general evaluations of these. Psychometric tests can be used in different contexts, so always consider what the data will be used for.

> **TEST YOURSELF**

1 Explain what is meant by a psychometric test.   [2]
2 Give two strengths of using psychometric tests to collect data.   [2]
3 Minh would like to use a visual analogue scale to measure people's overall level
   of happiness. Suggest one disadvantage of psychometric tests in this study.   [2]
4 Dr Siraj is investigating a case study of a girl who has a phobia of flowers. Explain
   how Dr Siraj might use a psychometric test to obtain data about the girl's phobia.   [2]
5 Harper is investigating whether there is a correlation between stress and illness.
   He uses a psychometric test to measure stress. Suggest one strength and one
   weakness of investigating stress using a psychometric test. You must refer to
   Harper's investigation in your answer.   [4]
6 Xanthe has designed a new psychometric test to measure leadership qualities.
   Her supervisor suggests that an observation may be a better way of assessing
   leadership qualities. Give one similarity and one difference between psychometric
   tests and observations.   [4]

5.1.6 Case studies

KEY TERMS

triangulation

case study

unit

Think!

What is meant by **triangulation**? Why is this a strength of **case studies**?

Think!

Imagine you are conducting a case study on a female child with a sex hormone imbalance. She lives with her dad and her older brother. You are interested to see whether her cognitive and social development are affected by this biological difference. You visit her every month from the age of two years old to seven years old. Can you think of any problems that might affect the objectivity and generalisability of your data?

Think!

Compared with other research methods, can you think of any reasons why it might be difficult to maintain a person's confidentiality following the publication of a case study and therefore why fully informed, valid consent is so important?

Saavedra and Silverman focused on one nine-year-old boy as the 'unit of study' but the unit can be more than one person. In Figure 5.9, we see one family, at one specific refugee camp. A case study might investigate factors affecting one individual in this family, the whole family or it could even focus on the whole camp as the unit of study, looking at factors that are specific to this particular camp. What data-collecting techniques might you like to use in a case study investigating factors affecting anxiety in refugees? Remember you need at least two different methods as triangulation is a key feature of a case study.

▲ Figure 5.9

Case studies are detailed investigations of individual people or small groups (units) of people, such as people from the same family or a single shop or health clinic. They tend to be used to study unusual or rare cases. For example, in the Saavedra and Silverman (button phobia) study, a nine-year-old Hispanic-American boy's unusual phobia was investigated.

A key feature of the case study as a research method is that data is gathered using a number of different techniques, such as interviews, observations and psychometric tests. This is known as triangulation. Data is often gathered over an extended period of time; therefore, most case studies are also longitudinal studies. The data gathered may be a combination of both qualitative and quantitative data. As well as gathering information from the participants themselves, information may also be gathered from family, friends, school records, psychiatric records, the workplace or any other relevant sources of information. When psychologists write up case studies for publication, they often begin with a case history, which provides rich and detailed background information, which often helps to put current behaviour into context.

▼ Table 5.7 Advantages and disadvantages of case studies

Evaluating case studies

Advantages	Disadvantages
Researchers can gather rich and detailed information about an individual or small group of individuals. This gives them a unique insight into their participants' lives in order to gain a good understanding of whatever aspect of behaviour they are studying.	For case studies, the researchers often work very closely with a participant, usually over an extended period of time, so they get to know the participant very well. This could result in the researcher being less objective when analysing the data because they may be influenced by how they feel about the participant, reducing the validity of the research.
As case studies use more than one method of gathering information, researchers can triangulate the data to ensure its validity.	It is very hard to replicate a case study, simply because it is a detailed analysis of one unique individual, or a small group of individuals. It might be that their specific experience leads them to act in a certain way that is not representative of others, meaning that findings may not be generalisable to others.

Case study evidence is sometimes criticised for being unreliable because it can be hard to replicate. However, some case studies include quantitative data collected using standardised procedures and/or psychometric tests. These measures can be checked for reliability. Can you think of any ways of checking the reliability of qualitative data, from interviews, for example?

▶ LEARNING LINK

Saavedra and Silverman's case study (button phobia) (see page 114) collected both qualitative and quantitative data using a variety of methods, such as structured interview, observation and the use of a psychometric scale to measure subjective distress. The study was longitudinal as the boy's behaviour was studied before, during and after treatment and he also attended follow-up sessions at 6 and 12 months after treatment. How might the researchers redesign the study to increase generalisability?

STUDY TIP

While case studies only focus on one, or a small group of, unique individual(s), making it difficult to generalise from the findings, it is important to consider the significance of the topic being investigated. Consider whether the participant/s of the case study is/are truly unique, or representative of a certain group of individuals. While the nine-year-old boy in the study by Saavedra and Silverman (button phobia) had a rare phobia of buttons, the researchers aimed to establish an effective treatment for disgust-based phobias, which could be more widely applied to others.

> # TEST YOURSELF
>
> 1 Suggest one strength and one weakness of using a case study. [4]
> 2 Outline what is meant by 'longitudinal' with reference to case studies. [2]
> 3 Saavedra and Silverman (button phobia) used a case study to investigate a nine-year-old boy's phobia of buttons. Suggest two reasons why the case study method was used in this study. [4]
> 4 Dement and Kleitman (sleep and dreams) conducted experiments and a correlation into sleep and dreams. Alternatively, they could have conducted a case study. Outline two ways that data could have been collected in this case study. [2]
> 5 Zeph has written up a case study about his work with a student called Myles. Myles has autism spectrum disorder and Zeph has been providing him with training sessions to improve his social sensitivity. Zeph's supervisor says that his case study is too subjective.
>   a Explain what is meant by 'subjectivity' using Zeph's case study of Myles as an example. [2]
>   b Outline one way that Zeph could try to reduce the subjectivity in his case study. [2]
> 6 Ruby is training to be a carer. Her client, Indie, has brain damage that is affecting his sleep. She decides to write up a case study so that other carers can learn about her work with Indie.
>   a Outline how Ruby might collect quantitative and qualitative data as part of her case study about Indie. [4]
>   b Explain one advantage of Ruby using the case study method to collect data about Indie. [2]

5.1.7 Observation

KEY TERMS
behavioural checklist
observation
participant observation
overt observation
non-participant observation
structured observation
covert observation
unstructured observation
naturalistic observation
controlled observation

> **Think!**
> **Behavioural checklists** are an important feature of which type of **observation**?

> **Think!**
> Imagine you are conducting a **participant observation** at a hairdressing salon. You are interested in the ways clients interact with each other and with their stylist. How would you record your data? Can you think of any problems with collecting data in this way?

> **Think!**
> Which type of observation do you think is better: **overt**, **non-participant** or **structured observation**?

> Hassett *et al.*'s study was an experiment as the researchers predicted that toy preference (wheeled versus plush = the dependent variable) depended on the monkeys' biological sex (male versus female = the independent variable). The data, however, was collected using observation. The researchers used a carefully operationalised behavioural checklist to code the monkeys' **interactions** with the toys. What were the four features of this observation?

▲ Figure 5.10 As predicted by Hassett *et al.* (monkey toy preferences; see page 15), this female monkey is investigating a plush toy

189

Observational research involves watching people's behaviour and recording it. Researchers may observe either human or non-human animal behaviour. There are four different features of observation, each with two alternatives.

Overt and covert

In an overt observation, participants know that they are being observed. For example, a researcher might be observing behaviour in the playground and the teacher has told the children that the researcher is there to see how they play.

In a **covert observation**, participants do not know that they are being observed. This could mean that the researcher is standing far enough away from the participants that he/she cannot be seen.

Participant and non-participant

In a participant observation, the researcher(s) join the group of participants that they want to observe in order to gain a greater understanding of the group.

There are no examples of participant observation at Cambridge International AS Level, but an interesting example was conducted by Festinger *et al.* (1956). Leon Festinger joined a cult called The Seekers, who believed that a flood would cause the world to end on 21 December 1954, but that true believers would be rescued by aliens from another planet. Festinger wanted to observe cult members first-hand so he and other researchers joined the cult, attended group meetings at the leader's house and even lived in the house for a short time. This was an interesting study that investigated the role of groups and social context, and is therefore part of the social approach. This is an example of a covert participant observation but participant observations can also be overt.

In a non-participant observation, the researcher will observe from a distance (either covertly or overtly) but will not become part of the group that they are observing and will not interact with the participants.

Structured and unstructured

With structured observations, researchers record a pre-determined, limited number of behaviours, using a behavioural checklist. Each behaviour is tightly defined (operationalised) to avoid ambiguity, and researchers keep a tally (count) of the number of times each behaviour is observed. Observers can be trained in how to observe the behavioural categories, which increases both the validity (ensuring they are scoring the correct behaviours) and reliability (ensuring that they are able to identify and score the behaviours each time they occur).

In **unstructured observations**, the researcher records all behaviour that is relevant to the aim of the research without using pre-determined behavioural categories. Often the data is qualitative as, instead of recording tallies on a checklist, the researcher writes notes or speaks into a voice recorder.

Naturalistic and controlled

In a **naturalistic observation**, the researchers observe participants (including non-human animals) in uncontrolled, real-world settings. Researchers do not interfere in any way; they simply observe behaviour within the setting. **Controlled observations** generally take place in laboratory settings where it is possible to standardise the situation for every participant.

▼ Table 5.8 Advantages and disadvantages of observations

Evaluating observations

Advantages	Disadvantages
Structured observations are more reliable than unstructured observations as the behaviours that are to be recorded are decided in advance and operationalised. This means that the behaviour that is being observed will be broken down in components that can be easily identified and recorded. This ensures that different observers are more likely to record data consistently.	Observations can also be subject to observer bias as they rely on the observer's own judgement as to what behaviour to record and are therefore subjective.

Advantages	Disadvantages
Unstructured observations can be used as part of a pilot study to give researchers a good understanding and overview of the range of behaviours that they might observe. The researchers would then choose a limited number of these to observe for their main research.	In unstructured observations, it can be difficult to record all behaviour and some of the subtler (but interesting) behaviours might be missed.
An advantage of overt observations is that it is more ethical because participants know they are being observed so it avoids having to deceive participants.	A disadvantage of overt observations is that participants may show demand characteristics because they know they are being watched and therefore may not act in a natural way
An advantage of covert observations is that it avoids any potential demand characteristics because the participants do not know they are being observed.	A disadvantage of covert observations is that they are less ethical than overt observations because participants do not know they are being observed and studied.
An advantage of participant observations is that the observer is not viewing from a distance and therefore may gain a greater understanding of the participants' behaviour.	A disadvantage of participant observations is that the observer may become too involved with the people that they are observing, and become less objective in their observations.
An advantage of non-participant observations is that the observer is likely to be more objective in their observations as they are not personally getting involved in the study.	A disadvantage of non-participant observations is that because the observer is watching from a distance some behaviours may be missed.
An advantage of naturalistic observations is that behaviour is likely to be normal as the participants are in their own natural settings and the researchers do not interfere in any way. Therefore it is likely to be high in ecological validity.	A disadvantage of naturalistic observations is that it is much harder to control for variables that might affect the participants' behaviour.
An advantage of controlled observations is that they can be more easily replicated by other researchers as they can use the same behaviour schedule and it is easier to standardise the situation for all participants. This makes controlled observations more reliable.	A disadvantage of controlled observations is that behaviour may be less natural if participants are aware that they are in a controlled setting. Researchers might also miss key behaviours if they have a very rigid behaviour schedule.

The children in Figure 5.11 have been told that the researcher will be present at lunchtimes this week, although they have not been told exactly what she is researching. She keeps her distance and does not interact with the children or the play-time supervisors.

» What are the four features of this observation?

» How could each feature be changed and what impact would this have on the validity and reliability of the data?

» How can the psychologist ensure ethical guidelines are followed in this observation?

▲ Figure 5.11 These children are being observed by a psychologist who is recording acts of physical and verbal aggression, using a behavioural checklist

▶ LEARNING LINK

In Fagen *et al.* (elephant **learning**), researchers observed whether elephants could be taught to complete a trunk wash. It was a structured observation, as the researchers were observing the elephants' training sessions using a carefully operationalised behavioural checklist. Imagine you are observing elephants in the wild and want to investigate interactions between family groups. Would your observation be naturalistic or controlled? Would you choose to use a structured or unstructured observation and why?

STUDY TIP

Observation can be used to gather data as part of a laboratory experiment (e.g. Bandura *et al.*, aggression) or a field experiment (e.g. Piliavin *et al.*, subway Samaritans). It could also be used in a case study (e.g. Saavedra and Silverman, button phobia). In all of these studies, observation was used to gather the data but was *not* the primary research method. When observation is the primary research method, researchers simply watch a group of humans or animals and record what they see, sometimes classifying or categorising individuals, but not comparing pre-existing groups. Fagen *et al.* (elephant learning) is the only study at Cambridge International AS Level where observation is the primary research method.

▶ **TEST YOURSELF**

1 Explain one similarity and one difference between naturalistic observation and controlled observation. [4]
2 Explain two weaknesses of participant observation. [4]
3 Explain what is meant by a 'structured observation' using the study by Fagen *et al.* (elephant learning) as an example. [3]
4 Bandura *et al.* (aggression) used a covert observation to study children's imitation of aggression. Suggest one strength of using a covert observation in this study. [2]
5 McKenzie is interested in the effect of culture on personal space. She decides to conduct a naturalistic observation while she is on holiday, in a city that she has not visited before.
   a Describe how McKenzie could conduct her naturalistic observation. [4]
   b Suggest one disadvantage of McKenzie using a naturalistic observation to collect her data. [2]
6 Dmitri wants to investigate people's behaviour when in their cars. He decides to conduct a structured observation of drivers at a local car park during a busy time when there are not many parking spaces.
   a Describe what is meant by a structured observation, using Dmitri's study as an example. [2]
   b Explain one ethical issue that Dmitri would have to consider. [1]

5.1.8 Correlations

Think!

What is the difference between a **correlation** and an experiment?

Think!

Imagine you are conducting a study on the correlation between empathy and preferred personal space when interacting with close friends. How will you **operationalise** your **co-variables**?

Think!

Correlational studies are often criticised as it is not possible to infer **causality** – it is unclear which variable has caused the change in the other and whether some other variable may have caused the changes in the two that have been measured. Imagine a researcher finds a **positive correlation** between the number of hours a person meditates per week and the number of items they are able to recall on a memory test. She concludes that meditation improves memory. Can you think of a third variable that might cause both time spent meditating and better memory?

KEY TERMS

correlation (positive and negative)
operational definition
co-variables
causality
correlation coefficient

Do you think time spent on video games improves reaction speed or do people with good reaction speeds play more video games?

Think back to Dr Rox's study about the effects of caffeine on reaction time (see page 170). The research method was an experiment as Dr Rox manipulated whether the participants drank coffee or water before taking the reaction time test. She now wants to conduct a correlational study on another variable that may or may not be related to reaction time. She decides to investigate the relationship between time spent playing video games each week and reaction speed.

» Do you think she will predict a positive or a **negative correlation**? How would this correlation look on a scatter graph?

» How could she measure time spent on video games in a way that is valid, reliable and ethical?

» Why is Dr Rox unable to conclude that playing video games improves reaction speed?

Correlational studies look at the relationship between two variables. These are called co-variables. For each participant, researchers will gather two sets of data which they can plot on a scatter graph to see whether there is a correlation between the two measures.

Operational definitions for co-variables

Just as it is important to operationalise your IV and DV in an experiment, it is also important to operationalise your co-variables in a correlation. This means stating exactly what they are and how they will be measured. For example, Co-variable 1: average time spent playing video games per week, measured in hours. co-variable 2: reaction speed on an app measured in minutes, seconds and milliseconds. It is always important to operationalise your hypotheses for correlations.

Correlations are often used by researchers to investigate new areas of psychology before conducting experimental research, or in cases where it is not practical or ethical to manipulate variables.

Various methods may be used to collect data for correlations, as long as the data is quantitative. In order to analyse the data, the pairs of scores are plotted against one another on a scatter graph (see Figure 5.12) to see whether there is a correlation or not.

A scatter graph is a helpful way of quickly seeing whether two variables appear to be correlated or not. It should also be possible to infer the direction and strength of the relationship.

Positive, negative and no correlation

When there is a positive correlation, the two variables being measured increase together – as one value increases so does the other. For example, in Dement and Kleitman (sleep and dreams), the longer the duration of REM sleep (in minutes) the more words participants used to describe their dream. When there is a negative correlation, as one value increases, the other decreases. In Baron-Cohen *et al.* (eyes test), the higher the Eyes Test score the lower the Autism Spectrum Quotient score. Sometimes there is no consistent relationship between the scores. In Hölzel *et al.* (mindfulness and brain scans), there was no correlation between time spent on mindfulness activities between the weekly MBSR sessions and grey matter concentration.

Figure 5.12 shows how each of these outcomes might look on a scatter graph.

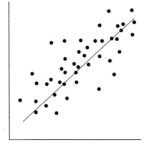
Positive correlation

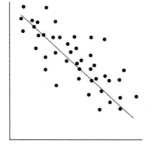
Negative correlation

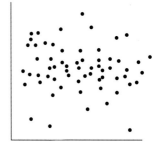
No correlation

▲ Figure 5.12 Types of correlation on scatter graphs

The strength of the relationship between the two variables can be represented by a **correlation coefficient**. In general, the closer to 1 (for a positive correlation) or –1 (for a negative correlation) that the coefficient is, the stronger the correlation is. A correlation of +0.75/–0.75 is considered to be a 'strong correlation'. This means that the two variables being studied are very strongly related.

Evaluating correlations

▼ Table 5.9 Advantages and disadvantages of correlations

Advantages	Disadvantages
Correlations allow psychologists to investigate new areas of research to see whether they are worth investigating further with experimental methods.	Correlations can only show the strength of the relationship between two variables and cause and effect cannot be inferred. They also do not tell us why that relationship has occurred.
Correlations allow researchers to investigate areas where it is not practical or ethical to manipulate variables.	The presence of a third variable cannot be ruled out in correlations. A third variable that is not being measured may have influenced the relationship.

► LEARNING LINK

Baron-Cohen *et al.* (eyes test) (see page 60) found a negative (inverse) correlation between performance on the Revised Eyes Test (where participants have to look at photographs of people's eyes and decide which word best describes the mood of the person in the photo) and the Autism Spectrum Quotient (a self-report questionnaire where a high score indicates responses consistent with traits of autism). The correlation was –0.53. What does this tell us about the relationship between the Autism Spectrum Quotient and the Eyes Test?

STUDY TIP

It is important to remember that a correlation is not an experiment. It is critical to refer to your two variables as 'co-variables' when planning a correlational study. There is no independent or dependent variable in a correlation.

► TEST YOURSELF

1 Explain what is meant by the term 'lack of causality' as a disadvantage of correlations in psychological research. [2]

2 Outline what is meant if a study says that there was 'no correlation'. [1]

3 Dement and Kleitman (sleep and dreams) found a positive correlation between length of REM and number of words in a dream report. Explain what is meant by the term 'positive correlation', using this study as an example. [2]

4 Baron-Cohen *et al.* (eyes test) used both experiments and correlations in their research. State one similarity and one difference between experiments and correlations using examples from this study. [4]

5 Trixie found a correlation between aggressive playground behaviour (scored using a structured observation, where the higher the score, the more aggressive the child) and amount of time spent playing violent video games. Explain why Trixie cannot conclude that playing violent games causes childhood aggression. [2]

6 Rebecca finds a negative correlation between empathy (measured on a self-report questionnaire, where the higher the score, the more empathetic the person) and time taken to offer help to a confederate in a staged emergency situation (in seconds).

   a Explain what the term 'negative correlation' means, using an example from Rebecca's study. [2]

   b Suggest one weakness of Rebecca using a correlation in her study. [2]

5.1.9 Longitudinal studies

KEY TERMS
longitudinal study
experiment with
longitudinal design
cohort effects
follow-up
cross-sectional
attrition

Think!

What is the difference between a **longitudinal study** and an **experiment with longitudinal design**?

Think!

Imagine you are a participant in a longitudinal study about the effects of the pandemic on loneliness. You have recently started seeing your friends much more and do not really have time to fit the sessions in any more. You decide to drop out. What type of people do you think might be left in the psychologist's sample at the end of the study? How might this affect her findings?

Think!

Longitudinal studies can take place over many years – for example, following the development of a group of people growing up after the Second World War. Can you think of any potential problems with generalisability of findings from such studies and why they might not apply to children growing up following other conflicts? A useful term here is **cohort effects**, which means that the group of people being studied may not be like similar groups growing up in other time periods.

Longitudinal research involves following the same group of individuals over an extended period of time (sometimes years) and giving them tests or tasks at various intervals during that time to see how they change and develop in their thoughts, feelings and/or behaviour. Participants of longitudinal designs need to be re-contacted over time for repeated testing. This testing needs to be standardised for valid and reliable comparisons to be made between participants' scores over time. Longitudinal studies use a variety of techniques to gather data, from psychometric testing to interviews and questionnaires. Experiments can also use a longitudinal design where the experimental group is given an intervention (such as a wellbeing programme, an educational intervention or a dietary supplement) and compared over time to a control group that is not given the intervention. **Follow-up** sessions allow psychologists to measure the long-term impact of treatments and interventions on the participants.

Evaluating longitudinal studies

▼ Table 5.10 Advantages and disadvantages of longitudinal studies

Advantages	Disadvantages
Longitudinal studies have an advantage over **cross-sectional** studies, where sub-samples from within a population are simultaneously tested and compared (such as testing cognitive differences in six-year-old, seven-year-old and eight-year-old children). Because longitudinal studies are following the same group of participants as they change and develop over time, researchers do not have the issue of participant variables where any changes found may be due to differences between participants, such as in schooling or home life.	A disadvantage of experiments with longitudinal designs is that they can have issues of **attrition** where participants drop out from the study for a number of reasons such as no longer wishing to take part.
Longitudinal studies allow some topics to be studied which might not be possible using other research methods, such as child development over time.	By the time longitudinal research is completed, it may no longer be generalisable due to changes in society (depending on the focus of the research). This means it may lack temporal validity (see page 214).
An advantage of experiments with longitudinal designs is that they avoid participant effects by following the same group of participants over an extended period of time.	

Lots of people had left Miss Steps dance class. Why do you think that might be? What does this example tell you about attrition in longitudinal studies?

▶ Figure 5.13 Posy was pleased with her progress, but was Miss Steps, the teacher, really all that good?

▶ LEARNING LINK

Hölzel *et al.* (mindfulness and brain scans) was an experiment with a longitudinal design into the effects of mindfulness on the brain, as data was collected over an eight-week period. All participants provided two sets of data, once at the beginning and once at the end of the eight-week period.

STUDY TIP

Longitudinal designs can be a research method in their own right or they can be part of an experiment with a longitudinal design, for example. An experiment with a longitudinal design will have independent and dependent variables, with the effect of the independent variable on the dependent variable being measured over time, whereas a longitudinal study will not have an independent variable and will just involve repeatedly gathering data from the participants over several weeks, months or even years.

▶ TEST YOURSELF

1 Give one strength of experiments with longitudinal designs. [2]
2 Explain one disadvantage of longitudinal studies relating to validity. [2]
3 The study by Hölzel *et al.* (mindfulness and brain scans) was an experiment with a longitudinal design. Outline what is meant by a 'longitudinal design', using this study as an example. [2]
4 Explain one reason why a psychologist might conduct a longitudinal study. Use an example from Saavedra and Silverman (button phobia) in your answer. [3]
5 Rick and his puppy, Basil, have been attending Dr Barker's puppy training classes every week for six months. Basil has done brilliantly and is now much more obedient and Rick cannot thank Dr Barker enough. At the end of the programme, many of the original puppies and owners have dropped out. Outline one reason why Rick should be cautious when making generalisations about the effectiveness of Dr Barker's classes. [2]
6 Shawna has a son who has been diagnosed with autism spectrum disorder. She and her son are part of a longitudinal study tracking children's social and emotional development. Shawna sometimes feels sad after the monthly assessments as her son is not making very good progress. She also has four other children and struggles to find the time to attend. Explain two ethical guidelines that must be considered when conducting longitudinal studies. You must refer to Shawna in your answer. [4]

5.2 Methodological concepts

5.2.1 Aims, hypotheses and variables

KEY TERMS

hypothesis (directional/one-tailed, non-directional/two-tailed, null and alternative)

operationalisation

independent variable

dependent variable

aim

operational definition

correlational

Think!

How is a **directional hypothesis** different to a **non-directional hypothesis**?

Think!

Do you have any teachers who gesture a great deal with their hands while they are teaching? Research suggests that using hand gestures can actually help students to draw logical conclusions from new information (Pilegard and Fiorella, 2021). Can you write a non-directional hypothesis that could be used to test this idea in your school?

Think!

Why do you think psychologists are so concerned about **operationalising** their variables? What is the point of doing this? What might happen if a psychologist did not operationalise their variables very well?

Pilegard and Fiorella (2021) found that understanding of complex ideas was better when lessons were delivered by a teacher who consistently used specific hand gestures than when they were delivered by a teacher who did not use hand gestures. Although the students in the experimental group (gestures) did better on the logical inferences test, they did not do any better than the control group (no gestures) on a factual recall test.

» There were three variables in this study: the teacher's hand gestures, the students' understanding and the students' recall. Which one was the **independent variable**?

» There were two **dependent variables** in this study. What were they?

» Which **hypothesis** would Pilegard and Fiorella (2021) have accepted regarding understanding of complex ideas? Which would they have accepted regarding factual recall?

Aims

The **aim** is a statement that explains why the researcher is doing the research and what they hope to achieve. For example, in Dr Rox's experiment into the effects of caffeine on reaction times (see page 170), the aim would be 'to investigate the effects of caffeine on reaction times'.

Hypotheses and operationalisation

A hypothesis is a statement where the researcher predicts what they think will happen in the research. It is important that the hypothesis is operationalised. This means that the independent and dependent variables (in an experiment) or the co-variables (in a correlation) are clearly defined. The units of measurement (e.g. milliseconds) should always be included.

When psychologists talk about **operational definitions**, they mean how something is observed or measured. For example, a phobia could be measured using a score from a self-report questionnaire, heart rate from a heart rate monitor (in beats per minute), a participant's body language from an observation (e.g. number of times they touch their face or hair, cross and uncross their legs, etc.) or a measurement of cortisol (a stress hormone) in their saliva.

Do you remember Dr Rox and her experiment about the effects of caffeine on reaction times? She's back and she needs your help. Initially, she was going to measure reaction times using a computer program, where the participant had to touch the screen every time a number 2 appeared. The computer would record the participants' average reaction time across a series of trials in milliseconds.

» Before making a decision, Dr Rox wants to know if you can think of any other ways she could measure reaction time?

» See if you can think of three alternatives. Remember, fully operationalised definitions include units.

The term experimental hypothesis is used for studies where this is an independent variable (e.g. laboratory and field experiments), whereas the term **alternative hypothesis** is used in non-experimental studies, such as **correlational** studies. Hypotheses can be directional (also known as **one-tailed**) or non-directional (or **two-tailed**).

Directional hypotheses

With a directional hypothesis, the researcher will predict whether the experimental group will perform significantly better or worse than the control group (or in a correlation, whether it will be a positive or a negative correlation). Directional hypotheses tend to be used where previous research has been done in the area, so the researcher has a good idea of what results to expect.

Dr Rox decides to use a directional hypothesis for her study on the effects of caffeine on reaction times. She quickly scribbles her hypothesis down and asks you to operationalise it for her. What does she mean and how would you do this?

Hypothesis: People who drink a cup of coffee will have quicker reaction times than people who drink a cup of water.

Tip: You need to clarify the size of the cup and the exact amount of caffeine, as well as stating exactly how reaction time will be measured and in what units.

Non-directional hypotheses

For a non-directional hypothesis, the researcher states that there will be a significant difference between the experimental and control groups but does not state in which direction that difference will be – for example, whether the experimental group will be faster or slower. Similarly, with a correlation, the researcher will state that there will be a significant correlation between two variables, but not whether it will be a positive or negative correlation.

Researchers tend to use non-directional hypotheses when there has not been previous research conducted in the area that they are researching or when the research is contradictory regarding what the possible outcome might be. Non-directional hypotheses tend to start with the words 'There will be a significant difference/correlation...'.

Dr Rox has changed her mind. She now wants you to rewrite her hypothesis but this time it should be non-directional. Look back at your fully operationalised directional hypothesis above. What do you need to change to make it non-directional? What will stay the same?

Null hypothesis

The **null hypothesis** is the statement that the independent variable will have no effect on the dependent variable, or that two variables are not correlated with each other. It is important for the null hypothesis to also be operationalised. Null hypotheses normally start with 'There will be no difference/correlation...', and they usually finish by saying that 'any difference that does arise will be due to chance'.

You are looking forward to collecting some data now and maybe even having a cup of coffee of your own, but there is one last thing to do. Dr Rox reminds you that you need to write a null hypothesis before you do anything else.

>> What will be different about the null hypothesis and what will stay the same?

Data analysis

Psychologists analyse quantitative data using descriptive statistics, as explained on page 217. These help to summarise the data and make it easier to see whether there are any obvious patterns or trends. You are not likely to encounter this in your AS studies, but sometimes it is hard to know whether these trends are significant and so psychologists use a branch of mathematics called inferential statistics, which allows them to calculate the probability (chance) that their result would have arisen if the null hypothesis was true. This is called a p value. Having completed their analysis, the researchers will decide whether to accept or reject their null hypothesis. The null hypothesis is rejected if the p value (the probability of a significant result having occurred due to chance) is less than 0.05 (1 in 20) and it is accepted if it is more than 0.05 (1 in 20). Inferential statistics are beyond the requirements of the syllabus.

▶ LEARNING LINK

In the experiment by Andrade (doodling), the independent variable was whether the participants were allowed to doodle or not while they listened to the phone message. Andrade had three dependent variables, which were operationalised as follows:
1 Monitoring accuracy: the number of correct names (out of eight) recorded while listening to the tape
2 Memory for monitored information: number of correct names recalled (out of eight)
3 Memory for incidental information: number of correct places recalled (out of eight).

What are the main advantages of the way in which Andrade operationalised these variables? Can you see any disadvantages?

STUDY TIP

Many of the core studies have more than one independent and dependent variable, which means the researchers are testing multiple different hypotheses. For example, in the study by Dement and Kleitman (sleep and dreams), there were three main experimental hypotheses, each with their own independent variables.

▶ TEST YOURSELF

1 Explain what is meant by the term 'null hypothesis', using any example. [2]
2 Explain the difference between an independent and dependent variable, using any examples. [4]
3 Describe how 'obedience' was operationalised in the study by Milgram (obedience). [2]
4 Baron-Cohen *et al.* (eyes test) hypothesised that there would be a negative correlation between score on the Eyes Test and score on the Autism Spectrum Quotient. Identify whether this is a directional (one-tailed) or non-directional (two-tailed) hypothesis, including a reason in your answer. [1]
5 Tristan would like to investigate whether people are happier in the presence of babies. Suggest how you might operationalise the dependent variable in this study. [2]
6 Nung wants to see whether meditation affects people's subjective level of wellbeing. Write an operationalised, non-directional hypothesis for Nung's study. [2]

5.2.2 Controlling of variables

KEY TERMS

standardisation
control
participant variables
situational variables
uncontrolled

> **Think!**
>
> Why is **standardisation** so important in psychological research?

> **Think!**
>
> Imagine you have to write a research proposal for an experiment on the impact of online/remote working on people's attitudes towards their colleagues. You will organise either an online or a face-to-face interview between each participant and a confederate, who they are told is a new member of staff at their workplace. You will then ask your participants to rate the confederate on a number of personality traits. How will you control **participant variables** and **situational variables**?

> **Think!**
>
> Twenty people have their memory tested individually in a quiet room. Ten complete the study in total silence and ten complete the study with quiet classical music. During the study, someone has a distracting coughing fit in the next room. What sort of variable is this? How could this affect the findings of this study?

> In order for Dr Rox to be sure about the effect of caffeine on reaction times (see page 170), she had to control a wide range of variables. How many can you think of? Try for five. If this is too easy, try for seven! Go back over your list and note down why each variable needs to be **controlled** – that is, how might it have changed the results if it was **uncontrolled**?

When conducting experiments, researchers attempt to control all variables other than the one being manipulated (the independent variable). Controlled variables are 'held constant', or standardised, between the two or more conditions. This allows the researcher to state that any changes in the dependent variable were caused by the independent variable.

Standardisation of a procedure

In order to make research replicable so that it can be checked for reliability, it is essential that the procedure is standardised for all participants. In an experiment, the only difference should be what the researcher is manipulating (the independent variable). However, all research, whether it is experimental or not, should follow standardised procedures. This includes participants all receiving the same information and instructions (unless this is something that is being manipulated as part of the independent variable).

Participant variables

Participant variables are aspects of a person's background, personality, cognitive abilities, health and wellbeing, etc., that affect how they behave or respond in a study. Individual differences between people are of course inevitable and this is why psychologists work with averages calculated from larger groups of people. However, participant variables can cause problems in experimental designs if some aspect of the participants (e.g. empathy, aggression or intelligence) varies systematically between the two or more experimental and control groups. For example, if all passengers in Piliavin *et al.*'s 'cane' condition (see page 153) were high in empathy and all the people in the drunk condition were low in empathy, it would be impossible to know whether aspects relating to the victim (drunk or cane) affected helping behaviour, or whether it was individual differences (high and low empathy) between the passengers that affected behaviour.

Random allocation of participants to the experimental and control groups can help overcome the effects of participant variables on the results. Of course this was not possible in Piliavin *et al.*'s study as it was a field experiment, but in Andrade's study (doodling) participants were randomly assigned to the experimental (doodling) and control (non-doodling) groups to ensure that people with naturally good memories did not all end up in the doodling group, for example, and obscure the true impact of doodling on recall of facts from a boring task.

Using a matched-pairs design can also help reduce the impact of participant variables, as researchers can match participants in both the experimental and the control groups on key factors that could impact on the research, such as age, handedness, cultural background or socioeconomic status. For example, in Bandura *et al.* (aggression) participants were matched on their existing aggression levels, so that each group (experimental and control groups) contained children with lower and higher levels of aggression. Again, if the most aggressive children had all ended up in one of the experimental groups, it would be unclear whether they bashed Bobo due to observing an aggressive adult or they would have done this on their own anyway.

On page 172, you were asked to list all the variables you could think of that might have reduced the validity of Dr Rox's experiment on the effects of caffeine on reaction times. Now try to label the controls with a 'P' or an 'S' depending on whether they help to control participant or situational variables. For example, the temperature of the drink is a situational variable that could have affected reaction time; a cold cup of water might have been more refreshing and made the students more alert. The researcher could have overcome this problem by serving the water and the coffee at the same temperature, or by using a cold caffeinated drink rather than a hot one.

Situational variables

Situational variables refer to any aspect of the environment that could impact participants' behaviour and affect the results. Environmental variables include factors like the temperature of the room, lighting and noise levels. It is important for researchers to control these variables as much as possible so that each participant experiences the same environment, and it is only the independent variable that is affecting the dependent variable. By controlling the environment for all participants, it also makes the research replicable.

Uncontrolled variables

These are factors that are not being measured or controlled by the researcher and can have an unwanted effect on the dependent variable. These could be things such as the temperature of the room or noise levels.

> ### ▶ LEARNING LINK
>
> In the Bandura *et al.* (aggression) study, all the children (in both the experimental and the control groups) were made to feel frustrated by being told they were not allowed to play with some attractive toys. Why was this such an important control? Can you think of any other participant and situational variables that were controlled in this experiment?

STUDY TIP

It is important to remember the difference between a standardised procedure and controls. Standardisation refers to features of the procedure being kept the same, while control variables are features of the study that are kept the same between each level of the independent variable. Standardisation is essential for replicating the study in the future, while controls are essential for ensuring that the independent variable was the only factor affecting the dependent variable.

TEST YOURSELF

1 Explain what is meant by 'situational variables', using any example.   [3]
2 Define 'control variables' and 'uncontrolled variables', using any examples.   [6]
3 Describe one control used in the study by Perry *et al.* (personal space).   [2]
4 The study by Andrade (doodling) used a standardised procedure. Explain why it
   was important to use a standardised procedure in this study.   [2]
5 Buck is investigating the effect of background music on memory for faces. The
   experimental group looks at a set of 50 faces while listening to quiet classical
   music. The control group looks at the same 50 faces in silence. Describe one
   situational variable and one participant variable that Buck must control to
   ensure the validity of his findings.   [4]
6 Georgia's teacher tells her she cannot start collecting data for her project as her
   standardised procedure is unclear. Georgia ignores this advice and goes ahead
   anyway. Explain why a standardised procedure is important for a study.   [2]

5.2.3 Types of data

KEY TERMS
quantitative data
qualitative data
subjective data
objective data

Think!

What do people mean when they say that data is subjective?

Think!

Imagine you have been asked to conduct some research on the effects of social media on teenagers' mental health. Would you rather collect **quantitative data** or **qualitative data**? What are your reasons for this answer? Your supervisor says that she would rather you collect the opposite type of data. How will you convince her to come round to your point of view?

Think!

People sometimes think that quantitative data cannot be subjective and qualitative data cannot be objective. Can you think of an example that challenges these views?

Dr Rox collected her reaction time data in milliseconds. What type of data is this?

Quantitative and qualitative data

Quantitative data refers to any data that is numerical. For example, closed questions on questionnaires produce quantitative data.

Qualitative data refers to non-numerical data, usually in words but sometimes in images (e.g. photographs). Open questions produce qualitative data as participants are able to freely express their thoughts and feelings.

▼ Table 5.11 Evaluation of quantitative and qualitative data

	Strengths	Weaknesses
Qualitative data	Qualitative data provides researchers with a more in-depth understanding of what their participants are thinking and feeling and the reasons behind their behaviour, which may give the data greater validity.	Qualitative data analysis may be more at risk of researcher bias as the interpretation of the data is more subjective. Therefore, the findings can be less reliable.
Quantitative data	Quantitative data can be more easily compared. The analysis of quantitative data is objective and so less prone to researcher bias.	Quantitative data does not always allow us to fully understand what a participant is thinking or feeling. Some scales may limit how a participant can respond and they may feel that none of the responses reflects how they feel, making the data less valid.

Subjective and objective data

Subjective data means that the data can be influenced by a person's personal thoughts, feelings or opinions. This is more likely to be an issue with qualitative data, which requires interpretation by the researcher when being analysed.

Objective data is unbiased, factual and not influenced by a person's personal thoughts or opinions. For example, research that uses ratings scales that are quantifiable is more objective as the data does not require interpretation by the researcher. In scientific research, it is important to be as objective as possible.

Researchers can improve objectivity by getting another researcher, who does not know the aim of the study, to interpret the data. This person is likely to be more objective than the primary researcher, who will have already formed hypotheses about what the data will show.

> ▶ **LEARNING LINK**
> In Piliavin *et al.* (subway Samaritans), observers collected qualitative data by recording what passengers in the carriage said about the incident. They also encouraged the passenger next to them to comment, so that they could record what they said. Can you think of any more of the core studies that collected qualitative data?

> **STUDY TIP**
> In psychology, all research methods can be adapted to collect both quantitative and qualitative data. For example, a structured observation might collect quantitative data, while an unstructured observation might collect qualitative data. When evaluating research methods, avoid implying that they can only be used to collect one type of data; for example, it might be tempting to claim that interviews only collect qualitative data and evaluate them on this basis. While it is certainly possible for an interview to only consist of open questions, it may contain both open and closed, therefore collecting both types of data.

> **TEST YOURSELF**
>
> 1 Define subjectivity using any example. [2]
> 2 Explain why data collected using an observation as a research method may be subjective. [2]
> 3 Perry *et al.* (personal space) collected quantitative data in their study.
>   a Define quantitative data using an example from this study. [2]
>   b Suggest one advantage of using quantitative data in this study. [2]
> 4 Milgram (obedience) collected data on participants' responses to orders from an authority figure. Identify one piece of quantitative data and one piece of qualitative data from this study. [2]
> 5 Jagdeep and his cousin Nishit are planning a study on mental health and therapy in India. Jagdeep thinks the findings will be more valid if they collect qualitative data, but Nishit thinks quantitative data will provide more valid findings. Explain whether you agree more with Jagdeep or Nishit. [6]
> 6 Sampson is listening to a podcast where the presenter is discussing a new piece of research on teenagers' attitudes towards climate change. The presenter says the findings were very subjective. Outline what the presenter means with reference to the study on attitudes towards climate change. [2]

5.2.4 Sampling of participants

> **Think!**
>
> When we make **generalisations** in psychology, what does this actually mean?

> **Think!**
>
> You see an advert on social media asking for participants for a memory study. The advert says that the research could have far-reaching benefits in terms of the early detection of Alzheimer's disease. Would you respond to the advert? What factors would affect your decision? How else do you think the researcher could recruit participants in order to get the largest and most diverse **sample** possible?

> **Think!**
>
> People often think the larger the sample the more **representative** it is and, therefore, the more generalisable the findings will be. Why is this not necessarily the case? Why is it still important to have a large sample?

Sample and population

Sampling refers to how researchers obtain participants for their research. Researchers will have a target **population** of people to whom they wish to generalise their findings. For example, the target population might be the global community of Cambridge International A Level psychology students. It would be practically impossible to test the entire population and instead the researcher selects a sample from the target population. Collectively, researchers refer to their participants as the sample.

Sampling techniques

Opportunity sampling

There are a number of ways that researchers can select their sample. **Opportunity sampling** is a technique in which researchers select participants who are readily available. For example,

KEY TERMS

generalisation

sample

representative

sampling techniques

population

opportunity sampling

random sampling

volunteer (self-selecting) sampling

a psychologist might know six teachers from different countries around the world who teach Cambridge International A Level. The psychologist will ask those teachers if they can use their students. Many research studies are conducted by university lecturers using their own students.

Random sampling

With **random sampling**, every person in the target population has an equal chance of being chosen to participate in the research. For example, if the target population is Cambridge International A Level students, this means that each Cambridge student across the world would have an equal chance of being selected as a member of the sample. This would involve getting the names of all of the students and putting them into a random name generator (computer program), which would pick a sample of 100 students, for example. This would involve obtaining the names of all of the students registered for this qualification and assigning each a number. A random number generator (a computer program), could then be used to select however many numbers are required for the sample. The psychologist would then contact all the students whose numbers were selected by the computer to ask whether they would like to participate in the research.

Volunteer (self-selecting) sampling

Another way for psychologists to select samples is with **volunteer (self-selecting) sampling**, where participants put themselves forward to take part in a piece of research. Researchers may advertise for participants in many ways including posters, flyers, direct mail, e-shots, newspapers, radio and online forums. For example, if the researchers were looking to study a condition such as prosopagnosia (a condition where people struggle to recognise faces), they could find a Facebook group of people with the condition and advertise their research in the group so that members can volunteer (self-select) themselves to take part.

Evaluation of sampling

▼ Table 5.12 Strengths and weaknesses of sampling techniques

Sampling technique	Strengths	Weaknesses
Opportunity sampling	Quick and easy as researchers use people who are readily available at the time of the research. May result in a larger sample and likely to mean research can be conducted without delays.	Often unrepresentative of the target population. Findings may not be generalisable.
Volunteer sampling	Participants have volunteered to take part so they are motivated and willing – drop-out rates are likely to be low. This is important in longitudinal research where attrition may significantly affect validity (see page 195).	May not be representative as only certain personality types volunteer to take part in research, such as those with more pro-social attitudes, those who are more motivated than the rest of the population and those who have a personal interest in the research topic.
Random sampling	Should be representative of the target population, making the findings more generalisable (if the sample is large enough).	Time-consuming and expensive. Potential participants may not wish to take part in the study. All potential participants must be contacted and arrangements must be made for them to visit the location where the research is being held.

Many studies use university students as their participants because the researchers work at a university and they are readily available (opportunity sampling). Some universities make it a course requirement that students take part in research studies or offer course credits for participation.
>> What are the benefits to the researchers and the students of this arrangement?
>> What are the potential practical and ethical issues of this?

►

LEARNING LINK

The study by Milgram (obedience) used a volunteer sample as he advertised for participants in the local New Haven newspaper and by directly mailing potential participants.
- Why do you think this type of sample was particularly problematic for a study on obedience?
- How might the results have been different if Milgram had used random or opportunity sampling?

STUDY TIP

Volunteer sampling can sometimes be confused with opportunity sampling. Remember that in volunteer sampling participants are self-selecting themselves to take part in the research, while in opportunity sampling they have been directly approached. Volunteer samples, therefore, tend to consist of more motivated people who may have a particular interest in the research, while an opportunity sample simply happened to be in a certain place at a certain time and did not refuse!

TEST YOURSELF

1 Define opportunity sampling using any example. [2]
2 Suggest one advantage and one disadvantage of random sampling. [4]
3 Milgram (obedience) used volunteer sampling in his research.
  a Explain how he obtained his sample. [3]
  b Suggest one disadvantage of using volunteer sampling in this study. [2]
4 Piliavin et al. (subway Samaritans) used opportunity sampling in their study investigating helping behaviour on a New York subway. Explain one reason why it may be difficult to make generalisations from this sample. [2]
5 Puangchompoo would like to interview people on their meditation habits.
  a Explain one sampling technique Puangchompoo might use to obtain her sample for this study. [2]
  b Suggest one advantage of using this sampling technique to obtain participants for this study. [2]
6 Nancibelle wants to conduct research using a questionnaire to find out what types of gifts people like. She uses opportunity sampling to obtain a sample from outside a large department store in Malaysia. Suggest one disadvantage of Nancibelle using this sampling technique in her study. [2]

5.2.5 Ethics and human participants

Think!
Why is it sometimes ethically justifiable to use deception in psychological research?

Think!
Imagine you were a participant in Milgram's study (obedience). You administered a shock of 450 V, were debriefed and met with the learner in the reconciliation phase. How do you think you would have felt when you met the learner? Do you think Milgram's actions were justified by the possible benefits of his findings?

KEY TERMS
valid consent
ethical guidelines
informed consent
right to withdraw
harm
privacy
lack of deception
debriefing
confidentiality

Think!

Why do you think it might be difficult to gain truly **valid consent** from people who are detained, such as people who are waiting for asylum requests to be processed?

Does your country have its own **ethical guidelines**? You could compare them to the British Psychological Society Code of Human Research Ethics (2021), or the guidelines of the American Psychological Association, or the Chinese Psychological Society. What do the guidelines have in common and what differences can you find?

Ethics are a critical component of all psychological research, which is why wherever in the world there is psychology, there are also ethical guidelines. Although local cultural norms and values may be reflected, many of the core principles are the same, including the need for **informed consent** and the **right to withdraw**. While ethical guidelines serve to protect the participants and ensure they do not come to any **harm**, they also help to ensure that research that benefits wider society can be pursued, as long as certain safeguards are in place.

If you carry out *any* research yourself, it is critical that you obtain ethical approval from your teacher, before collecting data from participants. All ethical guidelines must be upheld when planning and conducting your research.

Ethical guidelines in psychological research

Valid consent

This means that participants know exactly what will be happening during the research before they agree to take part. Consent must be provided before the data collection begins but is not considered valid unless it is informed; participants must know what they have signed up for and, therefore, should be given detailed, age-appropriate information before being asked for consent. Researchers must be able to provide evidence that consent was obtained; this could be by ticking a box online, signing their name on a consent form or even giving audio-recorded verbal consent.

Consent should be given by all participants, wherever possible, including children. However, in the case of some vulnerable groups, parents, family members or caregivers should also give consent. For example, consent from a close relative may be necessary when working with adults whose cognitive abilities and ability to communicate are significantly impaired, such as people with severe dementia. Parental consent must be obtained when working with children, although age restrictions may vary from country to country (e.g. under 16 versus under 18). Children should also be observed to monitor their level of assent.

Right to withdraw

Although participants give their consent, they must also be made aware that they can withdraw from the research at any time without any pressure to continue. They must also be informed that their data will be destroyed. If there is a point in the research when it is no longer possible to withdraw their data (for example, they are completing an anonymous online questionnaire and they click 'submit'), then participants must be made aware of this in advance. Researchers working with very young children or adults with significantly impaired communication ability should look out for signals (both verbal and non-verbal) that the participant is no longer happy to participate – for example, a young child that gets up and wanders round the room. If a participant shows any sign of distress, the researcher must end the trial.

Minimising harm and maximising benefit

Researchers must aim to minimise harm to participants' psychological wellbeing, personal values, **privacy** or dignity and mental health. The risk of harm should be no greater than the participant might expect to experience in their everyday lives. Researchers should aim to maximise the benefits of their research at all stages of the research process from developing the initial theories and hypotheses, to publishing their findings and applying them to help people in their everyday lives.

Lack of deception

By obtaining fully informed consent, participants will be very clear about what they will be doing and the aim and purpose of the study. **Lack of deception** means that the participants will not be deceived about anything to do with the research. In reality, it can be difficult to conduct research without any deception as simply knowing the true aim of the research could change participants' behaviour. Researchers must explore all possible ways of conducting their research before deciding to use deception. This is because it can put participants at greater risk of psychological harm (e.g. feeling upset, angry, embarrassed or ashamed). When deception is involved, full **debriefing** is essential.

Confidentiality

An individual's results should remain **confidential** before and after publication and an individual's data should not be identifiable. This is particularly important if the participants have provided qualitative data, which is more likely to be personal and thus more identifiable. It is important that any data that the researchers keep while conducting the research and analysing the data is stored confidentially. Participants' names should not be included with their data. If the participants need to return to complete another part of the research at a later point, then participants should be assigned a code number so that the data can be paired up. All data should be stored in password-protected files or in locked cupboards.

Privacy

Privacy is generally discussed in the context of observational research. Participants should only be observed in public situations where they might expect to be observed by other people, such as in a supermarket or train station. It is not acceptable to observe people in their own homes without their consent. Researchers who conduct research in public places need to gain consent from whoever owns the space – for example, the station manager, or the local government if it is an outdoor public space like a park.

Debriefing

Debriefing happens after the participant has completed the research. The purpose is to explain any deception that has taken place, to answer any questions the participant may have and to ensure they leave the research in the same state in which they entered it. For example, if the research has left the participant in a negative state of mind, it is important that the researcher ensures that they leave feeling more positive.

> ## ▶ LEARNING LINK
>
> Think about the research by Hölzel *et al.* (mindfulness and brain scans; see page 29). Participants were given brain scans, then underwent an eight-week programme of Mindfulness-Based Stress Reduction, before returning for another brain scan. It would have been important for Hölzel *et al.* to have been able to match up the participants' scores for analysis at the end. However, they also needed to ensure the data was kept confidential. Can you think of any of the other core studies that presented ethical issues?

> ## STUDY TIP
>
> It can be easy to confuse privacy and confidentiality. Maintaining confidentiality means taking steps to ensure personal information is not disclosed to anyone outside of the immediate research team (for example, using initials to refer to participants in case studies) whereas privacy refers to each participant's right not to be interrupted, observed or disturbed and this can extend to public spaces such as restaurants and shops. A good way to ensure that you fully understand each of the ethical guidelines and how they differ from each other is to form your own ethics committee with people in your class or an online study group. Whenever any practical work is undertaken, it must first be formally proposed to the committee and discussed. The committee should provide feedback and suggestions for improvements or areas that need more careful consideration. Your teacher should be head of the committee but remember, ethics is everyone's responsibility.

> ## TEST YOURSELF

1 Outline the ethical guideline of 'privacy'. [2]
2 Explain why it is sometimes necessary for researchers to use deception in psychological research. [2]
3 One ethical guideline is to obtain valid consent. Explain how this guideline might have been broken in one core study from the social approach. [2]
4 From the study by Perry *et al.* (personal space):
  a Identify two ethical guidelines followed in this study. [2]
  b For one of the ethical guidelines you identified in part a, suggest one disadvantage of following this guideline in this study. [2]
5 Boniface is assessing attention and memory in a group of elderly residents at a care home. Boniface is concerned that some of the residents do not remember him when he returns to the home a week later. He worries that the consent they have provided is not valid. Explain one way that Boniface can ensure that his study of the residents is ethical. [3]
6 Irina is conducting an experiment where half of her participants receive nasal drops containing oxytocin and the other half receive placebo nasal drops containing saline and no oxytocin. A confederate then asks if he can borrow the participant's phone to make a call. If they say yes, he asks if he can take it outside as the call is private. Irina records how many people in each group agree. Explain how Irina can ensure her study is ethical. [6]

5.2.6 Ethics and non-human animals

KEY TERMS

species

suffering

replacement

pain

housing

reward

deprivation and aversive stimuli

> ### Think!

Why do psychologists use small numbers of animals in research but try to recruit large samples of humans?

> ### Think!

You have been asked to assist on a study where cats are persistently woken up every time they enter REM sleep to see how this affects their physical and psychological wellbeing. They are woken up by dropping them into water, which they hate. Would you agree to help out on this project? Why do you feel this way?

> ### Think!

Ethical guidelines for the use of animals in psychological research are very strict, so why do researchers continue to conduct animal studies? What are the advantages from a scientific point of view?

Just as it is important to protect humans from psychological and physical harm during psychological research, it is also important that non-human animals are protected.

There are legal, as well as ethical, requirements when it comes to working with animals. These may vary from country to country, but in the United Kingdom, research involving 'protected' animal **species** is governed by the Animals (Scientific Procedures) Act 1986, amended in 2012. In this context, 'protected' does not just mean animals that are endangered, it refers to all non-human animals that have the capacity for cognition and **suffering**. Protected species include non-human vertebrates and cephalopods, such as octopuses and squid.

Ethical guidelines for non-human animals

Minimise harm and maximise benefit

As with human research, psychologists must seek to minimise harm, discomfort and suffering to the animals that they are studying and maximise the benefit of the research in applying their findings to helping either other animals of the same species or helping humans.

Replacement

The British Psychological Society guidelines recommend that, where possible, the use of animals is **replaced** with video footage from prior research or computer simulations. This is particularly important if the animals are to be used for training or teaching purposes.

Species

It is important that researchers use species of animals that are both scientifically and ethically suitable for the research. The researchers must have a good understanding of the animal's natural history and its level of sentience (its ability to feel). The researchers should know whether the animals have been bred in captivity and whether or not they have been involved in previous research. The researchers must choose the species that is likely to suffer the least while still meeting the research objectives. Researchers should discuss these choices with colleagues who are also knowledgeable about the species that they plan to use. The use of non-human primates should be avoided where possible because of their high level of sentience.

Numbers

According to the Animals (Scientific Procedures) Act 1986, researchers should use the smallest number of animals possible to meet the research aims. However, this must not mean that those animals chosen are used over an extended period of time, which could prolong any suffering. Reducing the number of animals used in an experiment can be achieved by appropriate pilot studies, reliable measures of behaviour, good experimental design and the appropriate use of statistical tests. Pilot studies should be used with a very small number of animals to ensure that the design is appropriate and testing what the researchers want to investigate, before conducting the research on larger numbers of animals. Researchers should consider using measures of behaviour that have been used in previous research and have been demonstrated to be reliable. Good experimental design ensures the minimum use of animals. It is recommended that researchers have a good understanding of statistics so that appropriate tests can be used to minimise the number of animals used.

Procedures: pain and distress

The researchers should avoid causing death, disease, psychological or physical discomfort to any animals. Where possible they should look at enriching the animals' environment rather than depriving them or using observational techniques in situations where naturally occurring instances of adverse conditions are happening. It is important that researchers carefully consider the balance between the harm or potential harm caused to the animals and the benefits that would be gained from the research. **Pain** can only be ethically justified in psychological research when there is no alternative research method available and the research would have significant scientific or educational value. Any surgical procedures should be conducted using anaesthesia to reduce any pain and prevent infection. If an animal's life needs to be terminated at the end of the research for any reason, then this should be done swiftly.

Housing

The social and natural behaviour of the species being studied should be considered when **housing** the animals. Isolating animals who would normally live in social groups could cause stress. Similarly, overcrowding could also cause stress and aggression. Using the same cage to both house and test the animals could reduce the negative impact and should be considered.

Reward, deprivation and aversive stimuli

If the researcher is considering the use of food deprivation, they must have a good understanding of the species' normal eating and drinking habits to ensure that deprivation is kept to a minimum, as feeding habits can vary greatly between species. In Skinner's classic research on **operant conditioning** in pigeons (see page 87), he deprived them of food so that they would always be motivated by the food offered as reinforcement during his experiments, but it is important that researchers consider all alternative methods to motivate the animals in their care before resorting to **deprivation and aversive stimuli**. For example, Fagen *et al.* (elephant learning) did not need to starve the elephants to get them to learn the trunk wash. Instead, she selected chopped banana, the elephants' favourite treat and, therefore, a powerful reinforcer even when they were well fed.

In order to protect creatures like the octopus, Russell and Burch (1959) suggested psychologists remember the three Rs: replace (do not use animals unless absolutely necessary), reduce (use the smallest number possible) and refine (ensure procedures minimise pain and suffering).

» Can you think of any novel ways that you could demonstrate sentience in an octopus or other aquatic animals?

» What would your hypothesis be?

◀ Figure 5.14 Octopuses are protected by the Animals (Scientific Procedures) Act in the United Kingdom due to their impressive cognitive capacity and experiments which support their sentience (ability to experience pleasure and pain) (Crook, 2021), but they are not included under a new proposed law called the Animal Welfare (Sentience) Bill

► LEARNING LINK

In Fagen *et al.* (elephant learning), elephants were chained in their stables in Nepal but able to show their desire to participate, or not, by walking away from the trainer stables. Hassett *et al.* (monkey toy preferences) worked with rhesus monkeys at the Yerkes National Primate Research Center. See if you can find the name of the ethical guidelines used here.

- What was done in each of these studies to uphold the principles listed in this section?
- Which of Russell and Burch's three Rs are considered?

STUDY TIP

It is tempting to argue that a lack of informed consent on the part of animals is an ethical issue; however, since animals cannot give valid consent, this is not included in the ethical guidelines for working with animals. Be careful not to confuse human and animal ethical guidelines when evaluating animal research, such as Hassett *et al.* (monkey toy preferences) and Fagen *et al.* (elephant learning).

▶ **TEST YOURSELF**

1 Describe the ethical guidelines of 'species' and 'replacement' in relation to animals in research, using any examples.   [6]
2 State what is meant by the ethical guideline of 'numbers' in relation to animals. [2]
3 In the study by Hassett *et al.* (monkey toy preferences), explain how two ethical guidelines relating to animals were followed.   [4]
4 In the study by Fagen *et al.* (elephant learning), explain how the ethical guideline of procedures (e.g. housing, reward, deprivation and aversive stimuli) was followed.   [3]
5 Mirabel is observing two groups of gorillas in the wild, a large group of 65 and a small group of 20. She is recording the number of close social relationships each gorilla has with other gorillas in the group. Outline why Mirabel must have a strong knowledge of the 'species' before being allowed to conduct this work. [2]
6 Yoko is conducting an experiment on mice. The mice have been genetically engineered to make them more anxious than normal. Yoko will then test a new drug on the mice to see whether she can reverse their anxiety. Describe three ethical guidelines Yoko must follow when conducting this research.   [3]

5.2.7 Validity

KEY TERMS

ecological validity

validity

subjectivity

objectivity

demand characteristics

generalisability

temporal validity

Think!

When psychologists say that a study lacks **ecological validity**, what do they actually mean?

Think!

Imagine that you are a participant in Perry *et al.*'s study (personal space). Can you remember what you had to do? If not, check page 144 for a summary. Perry has asked you to give their study a score from 1–10 for ecological validity (where 1 is very poor and 10 is amazing). If you knew your score would be confidential, would you change it? What does your answer tell you about **validity** in psychological research?

Think!

Is it possible to have a study that is high in reliability and also high in ecological validity?

Validity refers to the extent to which the researcher is measuring what they think they are measuring and the extent to which the findings are useful and meaningful.

A historical example of a psychometric test that lacked validity is the Army Alpha and Beta IQ tests. The term 'IQ' stands for 'intelligence quotient'. In 1917, a psychologist called Yerkes worked with colleagues to create IQ tests for army recruits in the United States of America, to see which section of the army would be most appropriate for them, based on their IQ levels. Many of the recruits were immigrants who had not lived in the country very long. However, the 'IQ' tests contained questions such as 'What is Crisco?' and 'Who is Christy Mathewson?'. These questions were impossible to answer unless the recruit had a good knowledge of American culture. This led to recruits from certain nations experiencing prejudice as they (understandably) received low IQ scores. This is a good example of a test that lacks validity – it was testing cultural knowledge, not IQ.

Ecological validity

Ecological validity is the extent to which behaviour that participants demonstrate during research relates to how they would behave in their real lives. Research conducted in normal, real-life settings, as in field experiments, is likely to be (but not always) higher in ecological validity. However, some laboratory experiments can also be high in ecological validity if the setting is unlikely to impact on behaviour. If research lacks ecological validity, then it cannot be generalised to real-life situations. However, where it is important for research to be conducted under controlled conditions, elements of the procedure can be made more ecologically valid. For example, if participants had to demonstrate their driving skills in a laboratory setting, it would have greater ecological validity if a participant were able to use virtual reality headsets with a steering wheel, brake and accelerator rather than using a computer keypad as controls.

Evaluating studies based on their validity

You should be able to evaluate all studies based on their validity. Here are a number of ways that you can do this.

Subjectivity/objectivity

If a researcher is required to interpret behaviour, or the data collected, in any way, there is always a risk of **subjectivity**. This is where their personal thoughts, feelings or opinions may affect the validity of the findings. An example of subjectivity in data collection might be in an observation where the researcher misinterprets a certain behaviour and records it in a way that was not meant. This would lead to the data not being valid. In terms of data analysis, qualitative data is most at risk of subjectivity as it requires a researcher to analyse the meaning behind the data and draw conclusions based on this. This process involves the researcher's own interpretation and may be influenced by their personal biases, either consciously or unconsciously, leading to low validity. For example, Milgram (obedience) needed to interpret the behaviours of the participants as they delivered what they believed to be electric shocks to another person and decide what data to record. Having previously conducted a pilot study, he may have already had certain expectations about what behaviours to expect.

If data collection or analysis is not influenced by a researcher's personal thoughts, feelings or opinions, then it is said to be **objective**. Scientific equipment – for example, brain scanning techniques such as EEGs used in Dement and Kleitman (sleep and dreams) and MRIs used in Hölzel *et al.* (mindfulness and brain scans) – is only capable of recording what biologically occurs, thus this method of collecting data is completely objective. It is worth noting, however, that the images produced by brain scans still require the subjective interpretation of researchers. Quantitative data is also more objective than qualitative as it can be statistically analysed. The less risk the data has of being influenced by another person's interpretation, the more objective and some would argue, the more valid.

> ## ▶ LEARNING LINK
>
> If you study Clinical Psychology at A Level, you will come across the case study of Little Hans, by Sigmund Freud (see page 323).
>
> Hans' father interpreted his son's dreams and fantasies and wrote letters to Freud about his child. Freud also interpreted Hans' behaviour and wrote back to the father with ideas of how to help the boy. These interpretations were subjective because they were based on the father's and Freud's own personal views of what the dreams/fantasies meant. Hans himself sometimes disagreed with his father about how he had interpreted the dreams. This meant that the findings reported by Freud were unlikely to be a valid reflection of Hans' thoughts and feelings.

> Even quantitative data can be manipulated by the researcher and presented in a way that supports their hypotheses, so it is still not free from biased analysis. For example, Burger (2009) highlighted that in the study by Milgram (obedience) only the fourth prod was a direct command: 'You have no other choice, you *must* go on' (Milgram, 1963). In his partial replication of Milgram's study, not a single person continued after this prod, highlighting the prevalence of disobedience – a quantitative finding that Milgram did not report. Why do you think it might be tempting for psychologists to only present quantitative data that supports their hypotheses?

Demand characteristics

In research studies, participants might try to guess the aim of the research and change their behaviour based on what they think the researcher is looking for. This would reduce the validity of the study. Any features of the research environment which may give away the study's aim are called **demand characteristics**. This is why some studies use deception to avoid the participants' behaviour being affected. In Milgram (obedience), participants were deceived in a variety of ways to attempt to hide the study's true purpose. However, critics have argued that participants did pick up on demand characteristics and knew that the learner could not possibly come to any harm. For example, the experimenter's total lack of concern for the learner may have cued at least some of the participants to realise that the shocks were not real (Orne and Holland, 1968).

One of the strengths of using animals as participants is that they do not actively try to work out what the study is about. Therefore, demand characteristics are reduced and validity increased. This said, animals may unconsciously pick up on subtle cues from researchers, which may affect their behaviour.

Generalisability

Findings should only be **generalised** to the target population if the sample was sufficiently representative. This will depend upon the sampling technique, for example random samples are typically more representative than opportunity or volunteer samples. The extent to which findings can be generalised beyond the sample is sometimes called 'population validity'. For example, the study by Piliavin *et al.* (subway Samaritans) looked at helping behaviour on a New York subway carriage. It may not be appropriate to generalise their findings to all cultures because helping behaviour may differ in other countries, based on cultural values. Whether the results from a study can be generalised to real-life situations or not is called ecological validity. For example, as the study by Piliavin *et al.* (subway Samaritans) took place on a normal subway journey, as part of people's real lives, it is possible to generalise the findings to similar real-life contexts.

Temporal validity

Temporal validity refers to whether the results of a study can be generalised to a different time period. For example, Bandura's study was conducted in the 1960s and the results may not be the same today as modern children have access to personal technology such as phone and tablets and gender roles have also changed significantly. This means the findings may be era-bound and said to lack temporal validity.

Other studies, such as Hassett's study of sex differences and play in monkeys, are less likely to be affected by temporal validity since they are based on a generally stable biological functions. Social psychological research may be most susceptible to issues with temporal validity, as cultural and societal norms change over time.

STUDY TIP

It is important to remember the difference between demand characteristics and socially desirable answers – demand characteristics are features of the environment that give away a study's aim, while socially desirable answers are those given by the participant to ensure they are viewed in a more positive way. Both of these, however, can affect the validity of data collected.

> **TEST YOURSELF**

1 Suggest one reason why subjectivity may cause validity issues when conducting observations. [2]
2 State what is meant by the term 'generalisability'. [2]
3 Explain one way in which demand characteristics were avoided in the study by Perry *et al.* (personal space). [2]
4 Explain why demand characteristics were not a problem in the study by Hassett *et al.* (monkey toy preferences). [2]
5 In a study looking at the effects of exercise on grey matter, the researchers cannot be sure if an increase in grey matter they observe is due to exercise or some other factor. Explain whether this is a problem with validity or reliability. [2]
6 Ichika is conducting a study on recall of items from a menu. A waiter reads out a list of nine dishes to diners in a restaurant. They are then asked which dish they would like to order. Ichika records whether they choose from the first, middle or last three menu items. She allows half of the participants to doodle on a napkin while they are listening to the waiter and the other half are not allowed to doodle. Explain one reason that Ichika's study has high validity and one reason why it has low validity. [4]

5.2.8 Reliability and replicability

KEY TERMS

replicability
reliability
test-retest reliability
inter-rater reliability
inter-observer reliability

> **Think!**
>
> What is the difference between **replicability** and **reliability**?

> **Think!**
>
> Imagine your friend has videoed ten student nurses interacting with patients on a hospital ward. With the nurses' consent, she has been asked to assess their empathy. She asks you to score five of the clips to ensure that her scoring is reliable. What is this called and how would you go about it?

> **Think!**
>
> There has been a huge replication crisis in psychology in recent years but does it really matter if some of the classic findings in psychology appear to be unreliable?

Reliability

Reliability is about consistency and can refer to the results from each participant and the overall findings, based on the whole sample. If you tested your participants again and the results were the same, we could assume the results were reliable. If we ran the whole study again, with a different set of participants (a replication), we could check the reliability of the findings. If we got the same results again, we could conclude that these findings were reliable.

Replicability

Replication means that other psychologists can repeat the study exactly to see if they get consistent results. Therefore, the ability to replicate a study is critical as it helps researchers to demonstrate the reliability of their findings – that is, to show that their findings were not due to chance. Replicability relies heavily on the extent to which the study has a standardised procedure that other researchers can follow in their replications.

Standardisation

Standardisation of the procedure and instructions provided to the participants is an important way of making a study replicable. It also means that all aspects of the research are consistent for every participant (except for the manipulation of the independent variable in experimental studies). For example, in the study by Bandura et al. (aggression), the model always displayed the same sequence of behaviours, in the same order and for the same length of time. The toys were laid out in exactly the same way in each of the rooms and the children were always given the exact same standardised instructions. The observer also scored the children's aggressive and non-aggressive behaviour in the same way according to the categories on the behavioural checklist. This high degree of standardisation means Bandura's study is easy to replicate and, therefore, his findings could be checked for reliability.

Dr Rox needs to ensure the replicability of her study on the effects of caffeine on reaction times (see page 170), so that her study can be checked for reliability.
» What can she do to make sure every participant has the exact same experience apart from whether they drink coffee or water?
» How would you ensure that everyone understands the task before they start?
» How could you ensure that everyone begins the reaction time task at exactly the right time, after finishing the drink?
» When writing up the procedure for publication, how can Dr Rox make sure that it is replicable?

▼ Table 5.13 Ways of increasing reliability

Technique	Description
Test-retest reliability	Participants repeat a test or questionnaire a few weeks or months later to see whether their scores are consistent. If they are, the researcher can say that results are reliable.
Inter-rater reliability	Inter-rater reliability refers to the extent to which two researchers agree in their scoring of a questionnaire or test. If the two raters plot their scores for each participant against each other on a scatter graph, they should see a positive correlation, suggesting that they are both applying the scoring criteria consistently (in the same way).
Inter-observer reliability	Inter-observer reliability refers to the extent to which two researchers agree in their rating or coding of behaviours in an observation.

▶ LEARNING LINK

In the learning approach, you studied the experiment by Bandura et al. (aggression). This study provides an excellent example of a highly standardised procedure, which increases replicability and the ability to check for reliability. It also included examples of both inter-rater and inter-observer reliability. Be sure to cross-reference your notes on techniques to increase reliability with this study. What level of agreement was found between the experimenter and the nursery teacher regarding the children's pre-existing aggression? What level of agreement was found between the two observers who assessed the children's behaviour in the third and final room? Tip: These are numbers between 0 and 1 – the closer to 1.0, the stronger the agreement. What do these figures tell us about the reliability of Bandura et al.'s study?

STUDY TIP
It can be easy to confuse the terms 'validity' and 'reliability' as the term 'reliability' is often used in real life to mean 'trustworthy'. In the context of science, however, it refers to how consistent something is. In the context of a study, if it was repeated again with the same participants, would the same results be obtained? The more standardised the procedure, the more reliable the study will be. Also remember that simply repeating a study many times does not make it any more reliable, in the same way that a study being conducted a single time is not unreliable. Replication of research is done to *check* for reliability.

TEST YOURSELF

1 State what is meant by 'test-retest reliability'. [2]
2 Explain what is meant by the terms 'inter-rater reliability' and 'inter-observer reliability' using any examples. [6]
3 Becky and Graham are discussing the study by Pozzulo *et al.* (line-ups). Becky thinks that the findings are reliable and Graham thinks they are not reliable. Explain why either Becky or Graham is correct. [4]
4 Explain why the study by Hölzel *et al.* (mindfulness and brain scans) may not be reliable. [2]
5 Grace asks a group of six athletes to run a marathon before coming to sleep in her laboratory. She will record the amount of REM sleep they have using an EEG. Suggest three ways Grace could improve the replicability of her procedure. [3]
6 Clara is a zookeeper. She is training Philly the leopard to open her mouth and hold it open so her teeth and gums can be checked. She wants to be sure that Philly really does understand her commands before signing the paperwork to say Philly has been fully trained. Suggest two ways Clara can check the reliability of Philly's behaviour. [2]

5.2.9 Data analysis

Think!

When should you use a **histogram** instead of a **bar chart**?

Think!

Imagine Dr Rox has asked you to collect some more **data** for her study on the effects of caffeine on reaction times (see page 170). Write out a set of scores where it would be more appropriate to use the **median** rather than the **mean** as the **measure of central tendency.**

Think!

If a histogram shows that the data in a sample is heavily skewed, what is the most appropriate measure of central tendency?

Measures of central tendency

Measures of central tendency are **descriptive statistics**. Along with **measures of spread**, they help researchers to summarise large sets of individual data points, so that trends and patterns can be identified. Measures of central tendency summarise all the data into a single

KEY TERMS
histogram
bar chart
data
median
mean
measure of central tendency
descriptive statistics
measure of spread
mode
range
standard deviation
scatter graph

score, which tells us about the midpoint or average score. In an experiment, a researcher wants to know whether there is a difference between the results of an experimental and control group. To do this, they will compare the average results of the two groups, to see whether there is a difference and how big that difference is. Altogether, there are three measures of central tendency: the **mean**, **median** and **mode**.

▼ Table 5.14 The mean, median and mode

	How to calculate	Example
The mean	Add up all of the data points (scores) and divide by the number of scores.	Andrade calculated the mean number of correct names recalled in a surprise memory test.
The median	The 'middle' value when the data points (scores) are put in rank order from smallest to greatest; all of the data must be used, even if some of the scores are the same. If there is an even number of data points, the two middle scores are added together and divided by two.	Piliavin *et al.* calculated the median number of seconds that passed before help was offered – for example, in the ill condition compared with the drunk condition.
The mode	The most frequently occurring data point (score) or category of behaviour.	Hassett *et al.* tallied whether the male and female monkeys chose to play with the wheeled toys or the plush toys; the mode could be used to demonstrate which type of toy was favoured by each sex.

Measures of spread

Measures of spread help researchers to identify how similar the data points are to one another and give an idea of the amount of variation in a data set. In an experiment, the means of both the experimental and the control groups might be very similar but this tells us nothing about how diverse the scores are. In one group, some of the scores might be very high compared with the mean and others might be low; in the other group, the scores might all be very close to the mean. There are various measures of spread and the two you need to know about are the **range** and the **standard deviation**.

▼ Table 5.15 The range and standard deviation

	Description	How to calculate	Example
The range	Tells us how widely the data is spread between the lowest and the highest data points (scores). The larger the range, the wider the data is spread. Can be used with a median or mean.	Find the highest value in the set of scores. Find the lowest value in the set of scores. Subtract the lowest value from the highest value.	Hölzel *et al.* (mindfulness and brain scans) calculated the range for the amount of time spent engaging in different mindfulness activities – for example, time spent body scanning ranged from 335 to 1002 minutes.
Standard deviation	Gives precise information about the spread around the mean. Smaller standard deviations suggest the data points are clustered more tightly around the mean; larger standard deviations suggest that the data points are more diverse.	The mean is subtracted from each data point to see how far each score deviates from the mean. The rest of the calculation allows the researcher to identify the average amount of deviation from the mean.	Baron-Cohen *et al.* (eyes test) calculated the standard deviation of the Eyes Test and IQ scores for each of his comparison groups.

Do you remember Dr Rox and her study on the effects of caffeine on reaction time (see page 170)? She has collected all her data now and wants you to look at it. She suggests that you calculate the mean average reaction time for the experimental and control groups to see whether there is any noticeable difference between them, and if there is, whether the difference is in the expected direction – that is, the caffeine group has a faster reaction time. Table 5.16 shows her results.

» Calculate the mean for each condition. Are the results as expected?
» Calculate the range for each condition. What do the ranges tell us about the effects of caffeine on reaction time?
» What will you report back to Dr Rox?

▼ Table 5.16 Raw data from Dr Rox's investigation into the effects of caffeine on reaction time

| | Reaction times (milliseconds) | |
	Experimental group (caffeine)	Control group (water)
Pp1	16	22
Pp2	23	24
Pp3	24	21
Pp4	24	23
Pp5	19	24
Pp6	32	24
Mean		

Bar charts, histograms and scatter graphs

Graphs help researchers to communicate their results visually, allowing people to quickly understand the main patterns and trends from the results.

Bar charts

Bar charts are very helpful for quickly demonstrating the relative difference between the values obtained from two or more groups or conditions in an experiment. Often bar charts compare the mean, median or modal values obtained in two or more levels of the independent variable in experimental studies but they can also be used to illustrate quantitative data from observational and self report studies.

Figure 5.15 shows some of the data from the experiment by Perry *et al.* (personal space). The bar chart illustrates how the data from two of the independent variables can be neatly compared on one graph.

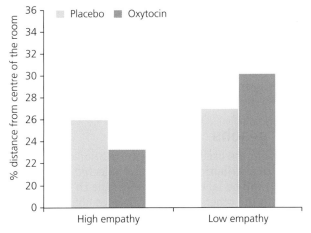

▲ Figure 5.15 A bar chart to show how oxytocin affects preferred interpersonal distance in people with high and low empathy traits, from Perry *et al.* (personal space) (see page 143)

Figure 5.16 shows the average number of offers made to the elephants in Fagen *et al.*'s study before they successfully performed each part of the trunk wash. As you can see, the bars are not touching each other as each bar represents an independent category of behaviour. In this bar chart, the behaviours are on the y axis, showing that it does not actually matter which way round you draw a bar chart, although with experimental data, you typically see the independent variable on the horizontal (x) axis and the dependent variable on the vertical (y) axis.

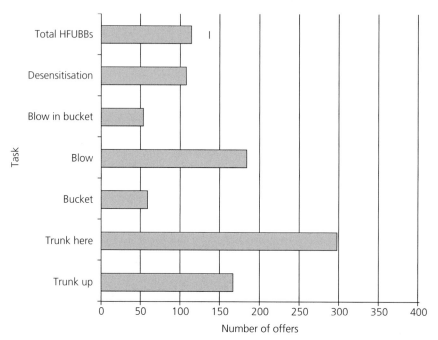

▲ Figure 5.16 A bar chart to show average number of offers necessary to teach individual behaviours from the trunk wash and the whole trunk wash sequence (HFUBB = here, fluid, up, bucket and blow), from Fagen *et al.* (elephant learning) (see page 101)

Histograms

Histograms are used when the data is continuous. Continuous data is data that can be measured on an infinite scale, where values can be infinitely large or infinitely tiny. A good example is time; units can be as large as a century or as tiny as a millionth of a nanosecond! A histogram shows the distribution of all of the collected data rather than the average. The horizontal (x) axis is divided into appropriate intervals, representing the full range of data points or scores and the vertical (y) axis is labelled frequency and shows how many people scored within each interval. As the data is continuous, the bars on a histogram should be touching and if there are no scores with a certain range, a gap should be left.

Scatter graphs

Scatter graphs are used to present correlational data. Like a histogram, they show the complete distribution of the data collected from all of the participants. The x axis (horizontal) will be labelled with one of the co-variables and the y axis (vertical) will be labelled with the other co-variable. It does not matter which co-variable goes on which axis. Next, the pairs of scores obtained from each participant are plotted using a small dot or cross. As none of the Cambridge International AS Level core studies included a scatter graph, we have included an interesting one presented in a paper by one of the researchers from the cognitive approach, Simon Baron-Cohen, and his colleagues. Baron-Cohen is known for his 'extreme male brain' theory of autism, which suggests that autism traits may be influenced by foetal testosterone exposure. Figure 5.17 shows the negative correlation between foetal testosterone exposure and scores on the Eyes-C Test, a version of the Eyes Test for children, with 28 items. The graph indicates that the lower the testosterone levels in the mother's amniotic fluid while pregnant, the higher the child's social sensitivity, as measured by the Eyes Test in childhood.

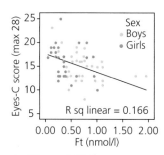

▲ Figure 5.17 A scatter graph showing the relationship between scores on the Eyes-C Test and foetal testosterone exposure for children aged 6–9 of both sexes, from Chapman *et al.* (2006)

LEARNING LINK

In Hölzel *et al.* (mindfulness and brain scans), participants in the experimental group practised yoga for between 103 and 775 minutes. Can you work out the range? Hölzel *et al.* reported that the mean amount of time spent practising yoga was 327 minutes, and the standard deviation was 194 minutes. What can you interpret from this? If you wanted to draw a graph of the amount of time spent on different mindfulness-based activities, which graph would be most suitable? Which graph would you use if you wanted to show the relationship between grey matter concentration and time spent doing mindfulness?

STUDY TIP

When drawing any type of graph/chart, remember to label both axes, including the units, and give your graph/chart a title. Titles must be informative and include the independent and the dependent variables for a bar chart, both co-variables for a scatter graph and the measured variable being shown on a histogram.

TEST YOURSELF

1   Identify the type of graph you would use if the main research method was correlation.   [2]
2   State one disadvantage of using the mode as a measure of central tendency.   [2]
3   In the study by Piliavin *et al.* (subway Samaritans), name the type of graph that would be most appropriate to compare the medians for 'time taken to help' in the cane and drunk conditions.   [1]
4   From the study by Saavedra and Silverman (button phobia), explain one conclusion from the results shown on each graph below. You must refer to the results in each conclusion.   [4]

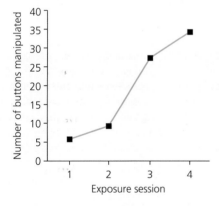
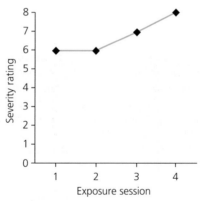

5   Petronella has plotted a scatter graph to show the relationship between testosterone levels and aggression in a group of rhesus monkeys. She tells her supervisor that she has an outlier. Describe what Petronella means by the term 'outlier', using her study as an example.   [1]
6   Christian is confused about the difference between a histogram and a bar chart. He asked his friend Angelo to help him. Explain two differences between a histogram and a bar chart.   [4]

Experiments

	Laboratory experiments	Field experiments
Description	Independent variable is manipulated by researcher. Takes place in a controlled setting.	Independent variable is manipulated by researcher. Takes place in a real-life setting.
Reliability	Highly controlled/standardised. Can be replicated and tested for reliability.	Less control, lack of standardisation. Harder to replicate and test for reliability.
Validity	Can establish cause and effect due to high level of control. Demand characteristics and artificial setting can make behaviour unnatural.	Establishing cause and effect more difficult due to lower level of control. Usually no demand characteristics; real-world setting makes behaviour more natural.
Ethics	Sometimes use deception, easier to gain consent and explain the right to withdraw. Debriefing is possible.	Sometimes use deception, often lack informed consent and right to withdraw. Debriefing not always possible.

Experimental designs

Experimental design	Strengths	Weaknesses	Solutions to problems
Independent measures: Different participants in each condition of the independent variable.	Less likely to be affected by demand characteristics than repeated measures designs. No order effects.	Participant variables can reduce validity.	Random allocation to overcome participant variables, therefore increasing validity.
Repeated measures: Same participants in all conditions of the independent variable.	No participant variables. Only needs half as many participants as they all participate twice.	More likely to be affected by demand characteristics than independent measures design. Order effects can reduce validity.	Counterbalancing to overcome order effects, therefore increasing validity.
Matched pairs: Different participants in each condition of the independent variable, matched on important key characteristics.	No order effects or participant variables. Less likely to be affected by demand characteristics than repeated measures design.	Time-consuming and difficult to set up, potentially resulting in smaller samples and decreased ability to generalise.	If possible, recruit a large sample in order to create the matched pairs, one of which will be allocated to each group.

Non-experimental research methods

Research method	Description	Strengths	Weaknesses
Self-reports: Questionnaires	Participants answer written questions on paper or online, which can include both open and closed questions.	Researchers can gather large amounts of data relatively quickly.	Participants may be less willing to elaborate on their answers when writing.
Self-reports: Interviews	Researchers question participants face-to-face or over the telephone and can ask both open and closed questions. May be structured, semi-structured or unstructured.	Rich, qualitative data can be gathered, giving a good insight into how people are thinking and feeling.	Participants may be more likely to give socially desirable answers, due to speaking directly with the researcher.
Case studies	In-depth investigations into individuals or small groups of people. Data gathered using a variety of data collection methods and triangulated.	Can give a unique insight into an individual who may have experienced unusual or difficult circumstances.	Findings cannot be generalised because one person or a small group of people is unlikely to be representative.

Research method	Description	Strengths	Weaknesses
Observations	Researchers watch people's behaviour and record it. Can be overt/covert, participant/non-participant, structured/unstructured, naturalistic/controlled.	May be high in validity if an observation is naturalistic and covert, as behaviour should be natural.	May be low in validity as interpretation of behaviour observed can be subjective.
Correlations	Researchers look for a relationship between two co-variables.	Allow researchers to investigate areas where it would be unethical or impractical to manipulate variables.	It is not possible to determine causation, only that two variables are related.
Longitudinal studies	Researchers follow the same group of individuals over a period of time. This could be from several months to many years.	Allows researchers to see how people change and develop in their thinking or behaviour over time.	If the timescale is long, participants may drop out, affecting the validity of the data.

Methodological concepts

Aims and hypotheses
Aim: the statement of why the researcher is doing the study and what they hope to achieve.

Hypotheses: the predictions that the researcher makes about what they will find.

Variables
Independent variables are the ones that the researcher manipulates to see what effect it has on the **dependent variable**, which is what the researcher is measuring. These must be **operationalised**, meaning that it is clear how they are being measured.

Controlling variables
Controls ensure that any changes to the dependent variable are due to the manipulation of the independent variable.

Uncontrolled variables are factors which may affect the study's validity.

Participant variables are individual characteristics that affect how a person behaves in a study and can affect the validity of an experiment if they vary systematically with the independent variable. **Situational variables** are features of the environment that affect how a person behaves in a study and can affect the validity of an experiment if they vary systematically with the independent variable.

Standardised procedure: the procedure is consistent/the same for every participant so the study can be replicated and tested for reliability.

Types of data
Qualitative data gathers people's thoughts and opinions. Can provide rich, in-depth data, but analysis may be **subjective** and open to researcher bias.

Quantitative data is numerical. More **objective** to analyse and easily compared.

Sampling of participants
Opportunity sampling: people nearby are asked to take part by the researcher. Quick and easy to obtain, but participants may have similar characteristics.

Volunteer (self-selecting) sampling: people respond to advertisements. Participants are often highly motivated, but sample may be biased.

Random sampling: everyone within the target population has an equal chance of taking part in the research. Can be difficult and time-consuming to obtain the sample.

Ethics
Research should follow the ethical guidelines when conducting research, including: minimising harm (maximising benefit), valid consent, including informed consent, right to withdraw, lack of deception, privacy and maintaining confidentiality.

When working with animals, researchers must follow the ethical guidelines of: minimise harm (maximise benefit of the research), replacement, species, numbers, procedures: pain, suffering and distress, housing, reward, deprivation and aversive stimuli.

Validity
Validity is the extent to which the researcher is measuring what they think they are measuring. **Ecological validity** is the extent to which the participants' behaviour reflects how they would behave in their everyday life.

Demand characteristics are features of the environment which give away the aim of the study.

Generalisability is the extent to which a study's findings can be meaningfully applied to the target population.

Temporal validity is the extent to which findings can be applied to other time periods.

Reliability
Reliability is whether the findings of a study are consistent due to standardised procedures and control variables.

Inter-rater: the extent to which two researchers agree in their scoring of a questionnaire or test.

Inter-observer: the extent to which two researchers agree in their recording of behaviours in an observation.

Test-retest: participants repeat a test or questionnaire after a time period to see if they gain similar scores.

Replicability
Replicability is whether a study can be repeated in exactly the same way again through standardised instructions and procedures.

Data analysis

Measures of central tendency
A single value that describes the whole of a data set.

Mean: calculated by adding all of the scores together and dividing by the number of scores.

Mode: the most frequently occurring score.

Median: the 'middle' value when a list of numbers (scores) is put in order from smallest to greatest.

Measures of spread
Range: the difference between the highest and lowest scores in a set.

Standard deviation: tells us how data is spread around the mean.

Graphs
Bar chart: used to show categorical data. Bars do not touch.

Histogram: used to show continuous data. Bars touch.

Scatter graph: used to show a relationship between co-variables.

Research method	Description	Strengths	Weaknesses
Randomised control trials	Participants are randomly assigned to an experimental or control (placebo) condition.	The double-blind design reduces experimenter bias as well as reducing demand characteristics.	The placebo group may be delayed in receiving an effective intervention.
Questionnaires: postal	Questionnaires that are posted out to the target population.	Location not an issue; can be posted anywhere in the world.	Return rate is quite low due to the effort of posting questionnaires back.
Questionnaires: rating scales; forced/fixed choice	'Forces' the participant to make a response from a fixed number of options, which may be on a scale.	Fixed-choice questionnaires produce quantitative data, which allows for objective comparisons to be made between people.	The fixed responses may not be valid for some participants.
Psychometric tests	These measure the individual differences between people relating to personality, aptitude, knowledge or skills.	Objective as the tests produce numerical data.	If a participant feels under stress, it may affect how they respond; data may be neither valid nor reliable.

A Level Issues and debates

KEY TERMS

cultural differences

reductionism versus holism

determinism versus free will

idiographic versus nomothetic

Think!

What does it mean if you take a holistic approach in psychology?

Think!

Think about the country where you live. Do you think it is more individualist or more collectivist? Do different parts of the country vary on this cultural dimension or is everyone quite similar in terms of their values and beliefs?

Think!

Can you think of any weaknesses of taking an idiographic approach? Think about key terms relating to methodology, including validity, reliability, objectivity and subjectivity.

On page vii, we noted that psychology is a subject that raises many competing, and often complex, points of view. Sometimes these competing views stem from basic assumptions about the best ways to approach the study of the mind, experience and behaviour, and fundamental beliefs about the human condition.

At A Level, there are four new issues and debates to consider each time you encounter a new topic:
- » cultural differences
- » reductionism versus holism
- » determinism versus free will
- » idiographic versus nomothetic.

NB: These are in addition to the five issues and debates discussed at AS Level.

Before you begin studying your first option, it is worth taking a closer look at these so that you understand how they can be used to evaluate the research that follows.

Cultural differences

At AS Level, you learned about individual explanations of behaviour as distinct from situational explanations. One of the variables that determines differences between individuals is **cultural identity**. Culture refers to shared attitudes, values, beliefs and norms for socially acceptable behaviour within groups or, as Geert Hofstede put it, 'the collective programming of the mind which distinguishes members of one group from another' (Hofstede, 1980). Many of us are exposed to multiple cultures throughout our lives and our cultural identity refers to the culture(s) or social group(s) to which we feel that we belong.

The development of our cultural identity begins with **enculturation**, the ongoing process by which we learn about the culture into which we were born. This learning starts in the home with interactions between family members but gradually the individual will learn more about their culture, both directly and indirectly, via formal education, religion and the media. Over time, most of us are exposed to a variety of cultures and our cultural identity may change as we incorporate aspects of cultural groups other than that of our immediate family.

Many people consider themselves **bi-cultural**. This may be due to having parents who identify with two or more different cultures, but it is also often the case when a person identifies with the culture of their own family as well as the majority culture of the place where they live or when people move/migrate from one culture to another.

Geert Hofstede (1980) identified six cultural dimensions which can be used to describe differences between cultures around the world. For example, the dimension of **individualism versus collectivism** refers to the degree of interdependence between group members within a culture. People from highly individualist cultures put personal goals first and value independence, competition and autonomy, whereas people from collectivist cultures value group goals, co-operation and loyalty to the group. This loyalty means the people from these cultures can expect to be supported in return.

Hofstede's five other cultural dimensions are:
>> **power distance** – the extent to which less powerful members of groups and organisations expect and accept that other people have power over them
>> **uncertainty avoidance** – how threatened people feel by ambiguous or unknown situations and create beliefs to try to avoid uncertainty
>> **long-term orientation** – the extent to which a society attempts to maintain links with its past (such as traditions) versus dealing with present and future challenges, such as through thriftiness (saving money) and investing in education
>> **indulgence versus restraint** – whether people try to control their desires and impulses or whether they allow themselves to have/take what they want
>> **masculinity versus femininity** – Hofstede defines masculine cultures as ones where people are driven by competition, achievement and success, whereas feminine cultures are those that value care for others and quality of life.

As you approach each topic in psychology, try to think how cultural differences might lead to differences in the way people think, feel and behave. Also, use this knowledge to think critically about the research you are exploring. Sometimes psychologists generalise their findings without considering the role of cultural differences, such as believing a certain therapy or intervention will be effective without realising that this may not be the case for people with cultural identities that differ from those in the original sample. This is known as **ethnocentrism**.

If you study the Clinical option, you will learn about many different therapies and ways of managing and treating symptoms of mental disorders such as schizophrenia (see page 231), depression (see page 260) and phobias (see page 307). The treatments and therapies in this chapter have been primarily developed in people from Western individualist cultures. Often they are very person-centred, meaning the individual and the therapist work collaboratively, as equal partners, with the therapist supporting the individual to find his or her own solutions.
>> In high power distance cultures (such as Malaysia and the United Arab Emirates), doctors and other clinical practitioners are highly respected members of society. How do you think this might affect the way people would interact with therapists?

>> Would this make therapy easier or more difficult?
>> If you think it might be more difficult, can you think of any ways to help make things easier?

▲ What qualities do you think make a 'good' doctor or therapist? Do you think people's views on this differ from one culture to another?

Reductionism versus holism
Reductionism

Psychology is full of interactions between multiple variables. This can make it difficult to identify which factors are the most important in determining how a person thinks, feels or behaves under certain circumstances. When psychology emerged as a social science, many people agreed that the best way to solve this problem was to take a reductionist approach, a common strategy in the natural sciences. Reductionism involves breaking down complex phenomena into their constituent parts in order to explore how they fit together and what influence they have on each other. Wilhelm Wundt, one of the world's first psychologists, took a reductionist approach to understanding conscious experience when he tried to break conscious experience down into thoughts and sensations.

As you have probably realised, when psychologists use the experimental method, they are taking a reductionist approach. Experiments involve isolating an independent variable and altering it under controlled conditions to see whether it causes a change in a dependent or measured variable. Through this process, psychologists are able to draw conclusions which allow them to identify the necessary and/or sufficient conditions under which a certain behaviour, thought or feeling will arise, for example.

Holism

Although there is a strong tradition of reductionism in experimental psychology, many psychologists favour a different approach. The holistic approach acknowledges the complexity of human experience and is guided by the principle that 'the whole is greater than the sum of its parts'. One of the most interesting things about psychology is the way behaviour can be studied in terms of many different levels of analysis, such as from the examination of genes and neurotransmitters to the impact of globalisation on our cultural identity. Psychologists that embrace explanations from each of the four approaches – biological, cognitive, learning and social – and do not overestimate the value of any one of these over the others are seen as taking a holistic approach. In practice, psychologists who take a more holistic approach tend to use a wide variety of research methods, including those that are seen as less scientific – for example, unstructured interviews and participant observation. These methods are often beneficial in understanding the broad array of individual circumstances that have led an individual to behave, think and/or feel a certain way. When we take account of all of these possible influences, we are taking a holistic approach.

As you approach each topic in psychology, try to think whether the explanations, theories, therapies, interventions and strategies that you are studying are more reductionist or more holistic. Again, use this knowledge to think critically about the research you are exploring. How has the approach the psychologist has taken affected their findings? Has this limited their research in any way? Would the applications to everyday life have had a greater impact if a different approach had been used?

If you study the Health option, you will learn about different types of pain and how the experience of pain has been explained by psychologists from different approaches (see page 567). Research in this area requires psychologists to devise ways of measuring pain through interviews, psychometric tests and rating scales, for example.

>> Which of these research methods is likely to be the most reductionist?
>> Why do you think some psychologists think it is necessary to take a holistic approach to explaining and measuring pain?
>> Why do people with the same injuries sometimes experience pain in different ways? Would you rather take a reductionist or a holistic approach to this research question?

▲ Who is in the most pain here? Is this a useful question?

Determinism versus free will

So-called **hard determinism** refers to the idea that everything that happens in the universe, including every human thought, feeling and act, has a cause – that is, it is determined by some other factor and is not a product of chance alone. As psychology is a science, it should come as no surprise that many of the theories are deterministic. For example, the biological approach suggests that our personalities, preferences and behaviour are determined by our genes, neurotransmitters and hormones (**biological determinism**), whereas the learning approach suggests our reinforcement history of past rewards and punishments is responsible for our behaviour (**environmental determinism**). As you can see, the arguments for both nature and nurture are deterministic.

One implication of determinism is that individuals have little to no ability to control their own behaviour. This said, in a survey of 40,000 people from 34 different countries, 70 per cent agreed that 'we make our own fate'. This suggests that the majority of us believe free will has a significant role to play in shaping our behaviour. Free will is not the opposite of determinism, but it is the idea that, despite being predisposed to act in certain ways, each human being possesses the ability to make conscious choices, to voluntarily control their own destiny. It is our belief in free will that means people are held morally responsible for their actions and thus provides the basis of criminal justice systems around the world.

Many psychologists believe in **soft determinism**. This is the idea that, while behaviour, thoughts and feelings are influenced by interactions between genes and environment (an individual/dispositional explanation) as well as situational factors, including the presence of other people, the fact remains that people certainly have the sense of planning their actions and behaving according to their intentions.

We might like to think that we make all of our own decisions, especially about how we spend our hard-earned cash, but if you study Consumer Psychology (see page 364), you will begin to realise that much of our consumer behaviour is determined by situational factors or retail atmospherics, including the use of colour, smell and background music, which increase the probability of us making certain purchases.

» How might a believer in biological determinism explain the behaviour of the woman in the image?
» How would a believer in soft determinism explain her behaviour?

▲ Could a psychologist really predict what this woman would purchase on her shopping trip?

Idiographic versus nomothetic

Idiographic

The word 'idiographic' comes from the Greek word *idios*, which relates to the self and our own, personal, private experiences. This is in contrast to *demos*, the Greek word for public and 'the people', referring to the wider community or group. With this in mind, the idiographic approach in psychology is about investigating the subjective experiences of individuals. Often qualitative methods are used to gather information about the individual's unique experiences, how these experiences have affected their interpretation of events and in turn the ways in which they think, feel and behave. Psychologists who take this approach often study small samples or even single participants using the case study research method. Idiographic psychologists recognise that individuals may share similar experiences, meaning their findings may be meaningful in understanding other people but, unlike psychologists who take a nomothetic approach, this is not their primary objective.

Nomothetic

The word 'nomothetic' comes from the Greek word *nomos*, meaning law. When applied to groups of people, laws are rules or standards that constrain individual behaviour, therefore making behaviour more predictable. In science, laws are statements based on repeated experiments or observations that help to describe how things happen in the natural world. The nomothetic approach in psychology is, therefore, concerned with the creation of universal laws which describe the behaviour of people, in general. It involves studying and comparing groups of people, measuring aspects of their behaviour, thoughts or feelings in a quantitative way and then, most importantly, calculating averages that describe what was typical of the group. This means that, unlike the idiographic approach, the nomothetic psychologist is describing the average person, not a real living one!

Once a data set has been reduced to a set of averages, comparisons can be made between different groups (or subsets) of people and different conditions, conclusions can be drawn and generalisations made to larger groups of people; if the larger group is similar in make-up to the smaller group, there is no reason to believe that what is typical of the sample would not also be typical of the wider population.

In summary, the idiographic approach is about studying individuals in order to learn about their subjective experiences of the world, generally in their own words, whereas the nomothetic approach involves studying smaller groups (samples) in order to create general laws that can be used to predict the behaviour of larger groups (populations).

In the Organisational Psychology chapter, you will learn a great deal about human behaviour in the world of work, including looking at topics such as job satisfaction, which is about how much people enjoy their work and how this affects people's performance and wellbeing.
>> How could you investigate job satisfaction using a nomothetic approach?
>> Imagine that, while conducting a nomothetic study, you discovered a participant with unusually high job satisfaction. How would you conduct a more idiographic investigation with this person?

>> Which types of results do you think people find more convincing – nomothetic results or idiographic results? (Tip: To answer this question, you need to think about what the results of each type of study might look like.)

▲ How would you conduct a nomothetic investigation of job satisfaction with these happy employees?

TRENDING TOPIC

The psychology of COVID-19

At A Level, you will choose two of four options topics, from Clinical, Consumer, Health and Organisational Psychology. Content from each of these topics can be discussed in the context of the COVID-19 outbreak, which the World Health Organization declared a pandemic in March 2020. You may not have started work on the options yet, but you should be able to start thinking about the A Level issues and debates in combination with the four different options topics.

1 The pandemic saw the introduction of many new behaviours into people's everyday lives, including social distancing and mask wearing. How do you think cultural differences affect people's adherence to government health advice regarding behaviours such as these?
2 Many aspects of the pandemic led to changes in people's mental health, some for the better, but sadly many for the worse. Why might it be helpful to take a nomothetic approach to research in this area?
3 Closure of shops, restaurants and leisure facilities led to dramatic increases in online consumerism. How do you think the design of online shopping websites determines the amount of time users spend on these sites?
4 Organisations including schools and businesses across the world have had to adapt to remote working, and finding adaptive and innovative solutions has been vital. Research looking into what has made some organisations more successful than others is critical, but why might it be helpful to take a more holistic approach to research in this area?

STUDY TIP

For each section in the A Level options part of this book, we have included a box alerting you to key issues and debates that you should be thinking about while reading the information in that section. Where possible, we have discussed one or more of these in the evaluation points, but you must get into the habit of thinking how each of these issues and debates (and those studied at AS Level) relate to every part of your course. One way to remember them all is to create mnemonics, such as ISCANA (Individual versus Situational explanations, Children and Animals, Nature versus nurture, Applications to everyday life) and DR CIN (Determinism versus free will, Reductionism versus holism, Cultural differences, Idiographic versus Nomothetic).

6

Clinical Psychology

Learning outcomes

In this chapter, we will discuss:

● diagnostic criteria, explanations, treatment and management of five disorders, including one key study for each (in brackets), as well as a number of supporting studies:
  – schizophrenia (Freeman *et al.*, 2003)
  – mood (affective) disorders: depressive disorder (unipolar) and bipolar disorder (Oruč *et al.*, 1997)
  – impulse control disorders (Grant *et al.*, 2008)
  – anxiety disorders and fear-related disorders (Chapman and DeLapp, 2013)
  – obsessive-compulsive disorder (OCD) (Lovell *et al.*, 2006)
● the biological approach to mental disorders, including:
  – explanations, such as genetic and biochemical
  – measures, such as blood pressure
  – treatments, such as electro-convulsive therapy
● the psychological approach to mental disorders, including:
  – explanations, such as behavioural, cognitive and psychodynamic
  – therapies, such as systematic desensitisation.

Each area will be evaluated with reference to:

● research evidence and related methodological concepts
● psychological issues and debates, including applications to the real world.

▲ Figure 6.1 The vibrant city of Rio, home of the study of by Cappi *et al.* on obsessive compulsive disorder (see page 344)

Where there are people, there is psychology!

Psychology is everywhere, and these are the colourful homes of the people of Rio de Janeiro, in Brazil, one of the world's biggest and most beautiful cities. This chapter includes various compulsory studies conducted in countries including Croatia (Oruč *et al.*, 1997), the UK (Freeman *et al.*, 2003; Lovell *et al.*, 2006) and the USA (Chapman and DeLapp, 2013; Grant *et al.*, 2008), but you will also learn about many other pieces of research to help you to evaluate the concepts, theories, treatments and therapies covered in this option. For example, on page 344, you will learn about an experiment conducted by Cappi *et al.* (2016), in Brazil. The researchers found differences in a gene called OXTR between people with obsessive-compulsive disorder and healthy controls. This gene codes for oxytocin receptors, a hormone linked to a variety of psychiatric disorders.

What is Clinical Psychology?

Clinical psychologists work with people with a wide range of mental and behavioural disorders. The job involves assessment and diagnosis using classification manuals such as the International Statistical Classification of Diseases and Related Health Problems (ICD-11), published by the World Health Organization (WHO, 2018) and the Diagnostic and Statistical Manual of Mental Disorders, Fifth Edition, published by the American Psychiatric Association (APA, 2013).

These are the main two classification manuals used around the world and they contain hundreds of different disorders, each with detailed descriptions of signs and symptoms that can be used to help make a diagnosis. Some countries have their own culturally relevant classification systems – for example, the Chinese Classification of Mental Disorders (CCMD-3), published by the Chinese Society of Psychiatry (CSP). You will discover this is an important consideration as behaviours that may seem normal in one culture may not be in another. This can make it difficult to make useful and meaningful diagnoses if behaviour, thoughts and feelings are compared with norms and standards developed in other parts of the world. This helps to explain why clinical diagnosis is so controversial as although advances are being made every day with regards to biological markers, as yet there are no objective tests for any of the disorders discussed in this chapter. Therefore, diagnosis relies upon observation and self-report, including standardised psychometric tests (see page 186) to help determine the severity of symptoms and the effect they are having on the person's daily functioning and quality of life.

Once a person has been diagnosed, this can open up options for treatment, including options based on the biological approach, such as drugs and electroconvulsive therapy (ECT), and psychological therapies based on theories from the cognitive and learning approaches. You will discover that there are many alternative explanations of each of the disorders, both biological and psychological, and each explanation has led to the development of different treatments and therapies.

Careers in Clinical Psychology

If you would like to take your studies of Psychology beyond A Level and are interested in the field of Clinical Psychology, the first step to becoming a clinical psychologist in the UK is an undergraduate degree in Psychology, accredited by the British Psychological Society, or a Master's Level conversion course. This will allow you to become a Chartered Member of the British Psychological Society, the first step to becoming a clinical psychologist. Next, you will need to gain a Doctorate Level degree in Clinical Psychology that has been approved by the Health and Care Professions Council (HCPC). Once this has been achieved, you will have the right to use the approved title 'clinical psychologist'.

In order to get onto a Doctorate Level course, you are likely to need relevant work experience as an assistant psychologist or research assistant, although other work experience in the caring occupations will also help you to gain insight and develop relevant skills and qualities to work in this area.

For further information, visit **https://careers.bps.org.uk/area/clinical**.

6.1 Schizophrenia

6.1.1 Diagnostic criteria for schizophrenia

KEY TERMS

schizophrenia

delusions

positive symptoms

negative symptoms

> **Think!**
>
> **Schizophrenia** is a heterogeneous disorder. Why do you think it is called this?

Think!

Some of you may know what it is like to live with a diagnosis of schizophrenia, as this disorder affects as many as 1 per cent of people across the world. If not, try to imagine what it might be like and how it might affect your everyday life, including your relationships with friends, family, teachers or your employer. How are people with disorders such as schizophrenia viewed in the culture where you live?

Think!

ICD-11 only requires a person to have had symptoms for one month before a diagnosis can be gained. On the one hand, this can be considered a strength, but can you think of any reasons that it might also be a weakness?

Which type of **delusion** do you think the woman in Figure 6.2 is suffering from?

▲ Figure 6.2 Even in the face of conflicting evidence, individuals who are delusional refuse to abandon their beliefs

Diagnostic criteria (ICD-11)

Schizophrenia is a **psychotic** disorder, meaning people with this diagnosis sometimes lose contact with reality. They find it difficult to tell the difference between real and imagined experiences and may not seek help as they lack insight into their condition.

According to the ICD-11, schizophrenia should be diagnosed if a person shows at least two symptoms, at least one of which (or two in less clear-cut cases) must be from the core symptoms (e.g. hallucinations, delusions, experiences of influence, passivity or control and/or disorganised thinking). The other may include a negative symptom or disorgansied movement. Other causes of the symptoms must be eliminated before a diagnosis is made – for example, substance misuse, side effects of medication or an underlying physical condition, such as a brain tumour.

The ICD-11 categorises symptoms into six dimensional descriptors (Reed *et al.*, 2019), each rated on a four-point scale (not present, mild, moderate and severe). The dimensions include **positive** and **negative symptoms**, as well as symptoms relating to mood, cognition and behaviour.

METHODOLOGY

case studies
generalisations from findings

Positive symptoms

Positive refers to the *presence* of psychological abnormality as opposed to the absence of something we might consider to be normal (negative symptoms). The core positive symptoms of schizophrenia are outlined below.

Hallucinations

These are involuntary perceptual experiences that happen in the absence of external stimuli. This means people with schizophrenia may see or hear things that others cannot, and they have no control over this. Hearing voices is a core symptom of schizophrenia, but hallucinations can also be visual, olfactory (smell) and somatosensory (touch).

Experiences of influence, passivity or control

This refers to the subjective experience that our thoughts, feelings and actions are being controlled by external forces. ICD-11 refers to these unusual feelings as experiences, noting that delusional beliefs may develop as a way of explaining them. For example, we believe aliens are implanting thoughts into our brains because we feel that our thoughts do not belong to us.
>> Thought withdrawal – the feeling that thoughts are being removed.
>> Thought insertion – the feeling that thoughts are being implanted.
>> Thought broadcasting – the feeling that thoughts are being transmitted to others.

Delusions

Delusions are fixed beliefs that conflict with reality. While some delusions relate to everyday situations, such as believing you are being monitored by the police, delusions can also be more bizarre, such as believing aliens are recruiting people to populate a new universe. There are many different types of delusion, including:
>> grandeur – the person may see themselves as exceptional in some way (e.g. having superhuman powers or abilities)
>> persecution – the person may believe that other people want to harm them and may believe they are being spied on, followed or tricked (see page 236 for 'Key study: Freeman *et al.*, 2003')
>> reference – the person may believe that situations or events have personal significance (meaning), such as they are being given a sign about how to behave or about what is going to happen in the future.

Before a person is diagnosed with schizophrenia, weaker versions of the core symptoms may be shown. These are called **prodromal** symptoms. For example, a person with persecutory ideation may hold false beliefs but they are not as strong – for example, thinking people might have been talking about you versus being convinced they were talking about you.

Other positive symptoms

Other positive symptoms include disorganised thinking: people may often lose their 'train of thought' (also known as derailment). This can lead to incoherent (muddled) speech and word salads, where ideas become jumbled. The person may also create neologisms, where new words are created by mixing words together. Behaviour may also be disorganised, meaning actions, gestures and postures may be unexpected, inappropriate or apparently purposeless.

Negative symptoms

As noted above, negative refers to an *absence* of thoughts, feelings or behaviours that would generally be considered psychologically normal. For example, people with schizophrenia sometimes experience flat affect, meaning they do not experience typical emotional highs and lows. They may experience avolition, which means they are not able to carry out goal-directed behaviours, like getting ready to go out or organising the ingredients to cook a meal. Other examples of negative symptoms include alogia (lack of spoken language), asociality (social withdrawal) and anhedonia (inability to experience pleasure).

Age of onset

The prevalence of schizophrenia is similar for males and females (about 0.3–0.7 per cent), but the age of onset is usually earlier for males (early to mid-20s) compared with females (late 20s). Late onset (i.e. from age 40) is more common in females. This disorder is rarely diagnosed in children under the age of 13 as the symptoms can overlap with various other disorders, such as autism and obsessive-compulsive disorder. This can make diagnosis difficult and unreliable.

In some cases, the diagnosis is more obvious, as with the 14-year-old boy in the study by Aneja *et al.* (2018), who shows clear symptoms and features of this disorder.

▲ Figure 6.3

Focus on: Aneja *et al.* (2018): A case study of schizophrenia

Dr Jitender Aneja is an Associate Professor of Psychiatry in AIIMS, Bathinda, India. Intrigued by human behaviour since high school, he was further inspired while working with children and their families during his undergraduate training, subsequently establishing child psychiatric units across Northern India

To bring a change in others, change is essential within oneself. Every person has a unique mind and to understand it, you need to set yourself free.

(J. Aneja, personal communication, 2021)

▶ CASE HISTORY

The boy came from a troubled home with an aggressive father. When he was ten, his parents divorced and he began living with his grandparents. His schoolwork suffered and by 12 he was not attending school at all. He was irritable, sad and often got into trouble for fighting.

▶ SYMPTOMS

- Hearing voices that teased him
- Suspicious of his mother
- Muttered, laughed and shouted at unseen others
- Spoke very little
- Poor sleep and self-care
- Preferred to be alone, away from other people
- Lack of insight into his condition

▶ TREATMENT

He was given sodium valporate, a drug often used to treat bipolar disorder (see page 260). His mood and behaviour improved for a while but soon got worse again. Eventually, he was diagnosed with very-**early-onset** schizophrenia (VEOS). His aggressive and violent outbursts increased, and he was often admitted to hospital, for his own safety. We will return to this case on page 251 when we consider the range of antipsychotic medications for the treatment of schizophrenia.

Evaluating Aneja *et al.* (2018)

One strength of this study is the detailed case history. The information about the boy's schoolwork and home life suggest that he displayed prodromal (before onset) symptoms, such as loss of interest, social withdrawal and lack of self-care. This sort of in-depth, contextual information is very helpful as it can increase the validity of a schizophrenia diagnosis, which can be difficult, especially in the case of someone of this age.

This **case study** focuses on a 14 year old child. Can you think of any practical or ethical considerations relating to the use of children in psychological research that would have been relevant to Aneja *et al.* when conducting and reporting this case study?

▲ Figure 6.4 Aneja's patient was admitted to hospital multiple times

A weakness of this study is that it only focuses on one child who may not represent the experience of children who hear voices in other cultures. The study took place in India where there is a lot of stigmatisation of people with mental health disorders (Thomas, 2018). This could mean that the family faced prejudice and lack of community support. This could have made the child's condition worse due to family stress. This is important as it means the findings may not generalise to VEOS in other cultures.

Evaluating the diagnostic criteria

A strength of the ICD-11 is that people only need to display symptoms for one month; other classification systems, such as the DSM-5, require a duration of six months before a firm diagnosis can be obtained. This is a strength as it means people should be able to access treatment more rapidly. This is important because early treatment is correlated with better outcomes (Patel *et al.*, 2014).

Another strength of ICD-11 is the removal of a set of subtypes that were previously used to classify schizophrenia (e.g. paranoid, catatonic, hebephrenic). These subtypes were based on the primary symptoms that a person displayed, but diagnoses were often unreliable as symptoms often change over time. ICD-11 replaces the subtypes with the dimensional descriptors, meaning the doctor rates each of the different categories of symptoms according to their severity. This means people are likely to receive a more reliable diagnosis that will help them to access the treatment that they require.

A weakness of the ICD-11 is that schizophrenia can be difficult to diagnose due to symptom overlap. For example, catatonia and hallucinations may be experienced by people with depression but can be caused by drug withdrawal, stress and sleep deprivation. This means different clinicians may give different diagnoses depending on whether they successfully eliminated other disorders or physical causes for the person's symptoms. This decreases the **reliability** of the diagnosis of schizophrenia.

> ## ISSUES AND DEBATES

Use of children in psychological research

One issue relating to this case study is that it focuses on the experiences of a 14-year-old child. The boy would not be able to provide his own informed consent due to his age and therefore his mother would have needed to give proxy consent for his participation in Dr Aneja's sessions and also for him to write up and publish the case study. This said, children are typically also asked for their consent and the study would not have taken place without the boy's cooperation. When working with children as participants, researchers must find ways to adapt the information they provide about their studies to make it as accessible as possible to the children and help them to understand what will be required in order to that they can make a decision about whether they would like to take part, what it means to have the right to withdraw and how their data will be stored and be used. Children with mental health difficulties are highly vulnerable and their rights and welfare are of the utmost importance.

Cultural differences

A further weakness is the subjective nature of some of the symptoms, meaning clinicians may find it difficult to diagnose people from cultural backgrounds that differ from their own. For example, in Maori culture, *matakites* are visionaries (prophets) who hear voices and these people are highly respected in the community (Lakeman, 2001). In Western cultures, the experience of hearing voices is seen as pathological (a sign of illness), and this could lead to wrongful diagnosis.

> ## LEARNING LINK

The study by Aneja *et al.* focuses on the experiences of a 14-year-old boy. Think back to your AS Level studies; can you remember another case study that focused on a child participant who was also referred for support for his mental health? What similarities and differences are there between these two **case studies**?

STUDY TIP

The case study by Aneja *et al.* is an example of the idiographic approach in Clinical Psychology. The ICD-11 encourages both idiographic and nomothetic approaches as data about symptoms is gathered through a clinical interview regarding the individual's experiences (idiographic) but the clinician also rates each of the six dimensional descriptors on a four-point scale (nomothetic). This approach could help psychologists to make generalisations about the type of symptoms that are more common in people with differing ages of onset, for example.

> **TEST YOURSELF**

1 Virat is 14 and has been diagnosed with schizophrenia. He used to love football and attended a weekly youth club. Explain how two diagnostic criteria relevant to this disorder might affect Virat's ability to participate in his usual clubs and activities. [4]

2 Explain one weakness of the diagnostic criteria for schizophrenia. [2]

3 a With reference to one research study, describe the diagnostic criteria (ICD-11) of schizophrenia. [6]

   b Evaluate the diagnostic criteria (ICD-11) of schizophrenia, including a discussion of idiographic versus nomothetic. [10]

4 Outline two features of the case study as a research method for investigating schizophrenia. [2]

5 Semi-structured interviews are often used as part of the diagnosis of schizophrenia. Explain how interviewer bias could affect the validity of the data that is obtained. [4]

6 Laila is examining the medical records of a large sample of adults with schizophrenia. She plots a graph to display the relationship between age of onset and cognitive impairment. Identify an appropriate type of graph for Laila's data. [1]

Key study: Using virtual reality to investigate persecutory ideation – Freeman *et al.* (2003)

Introducing Daniel Freeman

Daniel Freeman is Professor of Clinical Psychology at the University of Oxford and a consultant clinical psychologist. His work focuses on the development of powerful evidence-based treatments for patients diagnosed with psychosis. Driven by the brilliant work of clinical psychologists in the field of anxiety disorders, he quotes the founder of cognitive therapy, Aaron Beck, as his inspiration, commenting that his day-to-day work is underpinned by the quote 'there is more on the surface than meets the eye', which highlights how much can be learned from careful listening and questioning.

▲ Figure 6.5
Daniel Freeman

There is more on the surface than meets the eye.

(Beck, 1963)

KEY TERMS

persecutory ideation

virtual reality

Think!

Which three items from the Brief Symptoms Inventory were positively correlated with **persecutory ideation** in the virtual library?

Think!

Have you ever got the feeling that other people are talking about you? How might this affect how you interact and what you think and feel about these people?

Think!

Freeman *et al.* (2003) did not tell their participants anything about the virtual environment they were about to enter. This could be seen as both a strength and a weakness of the procedure. Why?

Virtual reality

Modern **virtual reality** (VR) experiences are delivered via headpieces which project individual digital images, separately to each eye. The images update at a rate of 60 frames per second to present a dynamic, immersive and three-dimensional virtual scene. Even the slightest movement of the head causes the scene to update. This creates the illusion of being physically present within the digital environment. The quality of this illusion relies heavily on the extent to which there is a match between body movements and the sensory information provided by the software though, so some VR experiences are more believable than others.

Have you ever experienced any sort of virtual reality? How did it feel? Did you get the sense of being present in the virtual world?

Context

According to Daniel Freeman, we are approaching a 'technological revolution in mental health care' (Freeman *et al.*, 2003) in which VR will have a major role to play in helping people to interact more effectively in everyday life. When entering a virtual situation, participants know that the setting and characters (or **avatars**) are not real, yet their reactions are very similar to real-world encounters. This has prompted psychologists to design immersive, yet highly controlled environments that can be used for both research and therapeutic purposes.

Previous studies have shown that avatars can trigger emotional reactions in people with anxiety disorders, for example (Slater *et al.*, 1999), and this led Freeman to question not just how people feel about the avatars they encounter in virtual spaces, but how they interpret their behaviour. He believes that deepening our understanding of the cognitive and emotional processes that underpin psychotic symptoms, such as delusions, is central to developing effective treatments.

▶ AIMS AND HYPOTHESES

This study examined whether neutral, non-threatening avatars could provoke persecutory thoughts in people with no previous clinical diagnoses and whether this was more common in people with higher levels of paranoia and emotional distress.

▶ METHODOLOGY

This was a **correlational study** based on quantitative data gathered via questionnaires. Qualitative data was also collected in semi-structured interviews, which were later scored to provide further quantitative data.

Sample

Twelve male and twelve female paid volunteers (mean age = 26) were recruited from University College, London, in the United Kingdom. All were mentally well. Twenty-one were students and three were administrative staff.

▶ PROCEDURE

First, participants were trained in how to use VR equipment, including lightweight headgear to track head position and orientation and a handheld joystick which allowed the participant to move around the virtual space.

Next, half the participants completed the Brief Symptom Inventory (BSI), a 53-item questionnaire to assess mood, anxiety and psychotic symptoms in the last seven days, plus two 20-item self-reports: the Spielberger State Anxiety Questionnaire and the Paranoia Scale (Fenigstein and Vanable, 1992), which measures ideas of persecution and reference.

Next, all participants completed the virtual reality task: exploring a virtual library, where five avatars sat in two small groups (a three and a pair), occasionally smiling, looking over and talking to one another. Participants were asked to 'Explore the room and try to form some impression of what you think about the people in the room and what they think about you.'

Five minutes later, all participants 'exited the room' and completed the questionnaires outlined above (half of them for the second time). They also completed the 15-item VR-Paranoia questionnaire (Table 6.1), which measured persecutory thoughts, **ideas of reference** and positive beliefs about the avatars. This was a new questionnaire, designed due to the lack of any pre-existing test of situation-specific paranoia. Finally, participants were interviewed about their experiences, including any feelings of distress. Later, a clinical psychologist watched the videotaped interviews and rated them out of six for indications of persecutory ideation – that is, their tendency to assume that other people were talking about them or out to hurt them.

▼ Table 6.1 Items in the VR-Paranoia questionnaire

1	They were hostile towards me.
2	They would have harmed me in some way if they could.
3	Someone in the room had it in for me.
4	They were trying to make me distressed.
5	They had bad intentions towards me.
6	They were talking about me behind my back.
7	They were saying negative things about me to each other.
8	They were watching me.
9	They were looking at me critically.
10	They were laughing at me.
11	They were friendly towards me.
12	They were pleasant people.
13	They were trustworthy.
14	They had kind intentions towards me.
15	I felt very safe in their company.

RESULTS

The mean paranoia score was 31.8 (minimum score 20, maximum 100) with no significant difference between male and females. This was relatively low compared with the mean of 42.7 in a previous study (Fenigstein and Vanable, 1992). Most people had positive beliefs about the avatars, but some endorsed more negative beliefs (Table 6.2).

Persecutory thoughts (items 1–5 of the VR-Paranoia questionnaire) were positively correlated with ideas of reference (items 6–10) and negatively correlated with positive beliefs. There was a positive correlation between persecutory thoughts in the questionnaire and the interviews. Finally, VR persecutory ideation was positively correlated with paranoia, **interpersonal sensitivity** and anxiety, all measured using the BSI.

Table 6.3 provides comments from the semi-structured interviews (qualitative data), illustrating the range of positive and negative beliefs that participants had about the avatars.

▼ Table 6.2 Level of agreement of participants (n = 24) with statements from the 15-item VR-Paranoia questionnaire

	Disagree	Agree a little	Moderately agree	Totally agree
Someone in the room had it in for me	15	5	3	1
They were talking about me behind my back	11	8	3	2
They were friendly towards me	4	10	9	1

▼ Table 6.3 A selection of comments made about the avatars (each comment is from a different participant)

Positive	Negative
'Friendly people just being friendly and offering a smile'	'They were very ignorant and unfriendly'
'People were nicer than real people'	'Sometimes appeared hostile, sometimes rude'
'Part of a game (flirting but being shy)'	'It was their space: you're the stranger'
'It was nice when they smiled, made me feel welcome'	'They were telling me to go away'
'They looked friendly – that was my overall impression'	'One person was very shy and another had hated me'
'I smiled and chuckled'	'The two women looked more threatening'
	'Some were intimidating'

CONCLUSIONS

Consistent with previous research, emotional processes linked to anxiety and interpersonal sensitivity contribute directly to the development of persecutory ideation, highlighting that VR holds 'great promise' not only as a tool for enhancing theoretical understanding but also as a way of helping individuals to evaluate and reduce persecutory ideation and delusions.

 ## Methodological strengths and weaknesses

One weakness was that the participants reported relatively low levels of **presence** within the virtual library. Presence refers to feelings of actually 'being there' and was measured on a six-point scale used in previous VR studies. The average presence rating was 2.3/6 (the higher the score, the more present the participants felt). This suggests that the findings may lack ecological **validity** as the participants were not fully immersed in the experience; this may be due to the short duration in the room (five minutes) and the relatively passive nature of the task.

A strength was that half the participants answered the BSI, paranoia and anxiety questionnaires before and after their time in the virtual room and the other group only completed them after the VR experience. This was done to see whether completing the questionnaires primed the participants to experience persecutory thoughts while in the room. This did not appear to be the case, suggesting that any such thoughts were triggered by the avatars and not the overall procedure.

Another weakness is **sampling bias**. The participants were all drawn from a London university, recruited via advertisements; they were all free from prior clinical diagnoses and were relatively young (mean age = 26). The participants would all have been relatively intelligent and interested in psychology and virtual reality. This means that the findings may not **generalise** to people outside this population.

> ## ISSUES AND DEBATES
>
> ### Idiographic versus nomothetic
>
> A strength of this study was that it used both **nomothetic and idiographic approaches**. Quantitative data was collected using the VR-Paranoia questionnaire (designed specifically for this study to measure situation-specific persecutory ideation – see Table 6.1). This new psychometric test collected self-reported data on 4-point scales (0–3: 'do not agree' to 'totally agree'), which can be analysed using statistics in order to draw conclusions that can be generalised to the wider target population, thus illustrated the use of the nomothetic approach. However, Freeman *et al.* also took an idiographic approach when they collected qualitative data through asking participants to explain their experiences in their own words in semi-structured interviews. Using both approaches and types of data increases the validity of Freeman *et al.*'s findings regarding the frequency of persecutory ideation in the general population.

 ## Ethics

Freeman *et al.* (2003) checked to see whether time spent in the room created any distress during the semi-structured interview and found that this was not the case. Also, anxiety scores were very similar before and after the VR task, suggesting that the experience did not leave the participants with any lasting psychological harm. Furthermore, all participants gave their consent to take part, although they were not told anything about the environment they were about to enter and were not told that the study was about persecutory thoughts. This means consent was not fully informed, but given the stress-free nature of the VR environment, this was justified due to the potential benefits to society.

Application to everyday life

A strength of this study is that it helps to deepen our understanding of the cognitive and emotional processes that underpin the development of psychotic symptoms. Exploring how people interpret mental states/intentions in others in VR settings can inform theoretical models of schizophrenia, and in turn, the development of new VR therapies where people can focus on developing new ways of interacting in the real world. This will only be possible if the VR environments have strong ecological validity, such as incorporating credible avatars that demonstrate a full range of human behaviours.

Individual and situational explanations

This study highlights the role of both **individual and situational explanations** in the development of persecutory ideation. A range of questionnaires were used to measure trait anxiety, paranoia and other clinical symptoms (e.g. The Spielberger State Anxiety Questionnaire) and these relate to individual explanations (i.e. that certain people are more vulnerable to developing psychotic symptoms due to the way they typically process information from the social and physical world). But the researchers also point to the potential for VR research to reveal environmental (situational) factors associated with persecutory thoughts, noting that experimental manipulation of aspects of the virtual environment could help to identify factors which make such thoughts more or less likely.

▶ **REFLECTION**

- Do you agree with Freeman *et al.* regarding the potential of virtual reality to revolutionise therapy for people with schizophrenia and other clinical disorders?
- If you were conducting research in this area, how might you improve this study and/or design your own study to investigate persecutory ideation using VR technology?

How could Freeman *et al.* check the reliability of their new scale?

▲ Figure 6.6 In this pioneering study, Freeman *et al.* created a brand-new questionnaire to measure situation-specific paranoia, something that had not previously been done before (see Table 6.1).

▶ **LEARNING LINKS**

Think back to the studies that you covered at AS Level, such as Hölzel *et al.* (mindfulness and brain scans), Piliavin *et al.* (subway Samaritans), Saavedra and Silverman (button phobia) and Pozzulo *et al.* (line-ups). Psychologists have used VR to research mindfulness, altruism, phobias and eyewitness testimony, showing the many and varied uses of this technology. Can you think how these studies might have been done differently if the researchers were able to incorporate VR into their procedures? Compare the original methodologies with your ideas for the new VR versions. Would the VR versions be better or worse than the originals, and why?

STUDY TIP

One thing that is a little tricky with this study is the fact that Freeman *et al.* assessed paranoia in two different ways that could be easily confused, so make sure that you understand this part of the procedure. A useful way of thinking about these two measurements is to think about *traits* versus *states*. Traits are ways of thinking and feeling that are fairly stable – they endure over time, from one situation to another. Freeman *et al.* measured 'trait paranoia' using the BSI and the paranoia scale. States refer to ways of thinking, feeling and behaving that are a reaction to a specific situation. In this study, Freeman *et al.* measured persecutory ideation and ideas of reference relating to the avatars in the virtual library using the VR-paranoia questionnaire, designed specifically for this study, in order to measure state paranoia.

▶ TEST YOURSELF

1 Explain one weakness of Freeman *et al.* (2003) relating to reliability. [2]

2 Describe how Freeman measured persecutory ideation in this study. [4]

3 a Describe the study by Freeman *et al.* (2003) on virtual reality to investigate persecutory ideation. [6]

   b Evaluate this study by Freeman *et al.* (2003), including a discussion of individual and situational explanations. [10]

4 State an appropriate fully operationalised directional hypothesis for Freeman *et al.* (2003). [2]

5 Suggest two weaknesses of self-reports (e.g. questionnaires and interviews), such as those used in Freeman *et al.* (2003). [4]

6 Explain one strength and one weakness of the sampling technique used in this study. [4]

6.1.2 Explanations of schizophrenia

Biological explanations of schizophrenia

KEY TERMS

heritability

polymorphism

allele

dopamine

upregulation

polygenic

Think!

Twin studies involve comparing concordance rates. Can you remember what this term means?

Think!

Imagine a friend of yours has just found out that their sister has schizophrenia. She asks you to explain it to her, but she does not know much about biology or psychology. How would you make it easy for her to understand?

Think!

Twin studies have historically been used to investigate the **heritability** of mental disorders, but cross-cultural studies can help to illuminate the relative contribution of nature versus nurture. If the prevalence of schizophrenia was roughly the same worldwide regardless of difference in cultural practices, what would this tell us?

What evidence can you think of that suggests that nurture can have more of an impact on our wellbeing than nature?

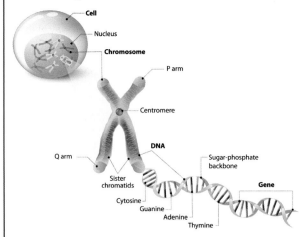

▲ Figure 6.7 The deletion of a strand of DNA during cell division could result in the loss of a whole string of genes, a biological issue which may have a lifelong impact on our psychological functioning.

Genetic explanation

Classic research

Classic family and twin studies (see page 365) suggest that, while schizophrenia is not just genetic, there is a strong argument for the heritability of this disorder. For example, the concordance rate for monozygotic (MZ) twins is 42 per cent but only 9 per cent for dizygotic (DZ) twins (Gottesman and Shields, 1966). Since the siblings in both groups (MZ and DZ) were raised in the same household, the higher concordance rate in MZ twins was thought to be due to the greater amount of shared DNA.

Contemporary research

More recently, the whole genomes of people with and without a diagnosis of schizophrenia have been compared to see whether they vary in consistent ways. These studies are called genome-wide association studies (GWAS). Some genes are **polymorphic**, meaning they come in different forms. GWAS studies have helped to identify which versions (**alleles**) are more common in people with schizophrenia.

However, the genetics of schizophrenia is extremely complex; thousands of gene variants have been linked to this complex condition (Smeland *et al.*, 2020) and, therefore, it is referred to as **polygenic**. Often the affected genes are linked to the many different proteins associated with the development (synthesis), transportation and breakdown of neurotransmitters such as **dopamine**. This means that the inheritance of certain alleles may be responsible for neurochemical imbalances associated with schizophrenia.

DiGeorge and the COMT gene

Aside from the inheritance of less than favourable alleles, sometimes problems arise during cell division and whole strands of DNA become duplicated or even deleted; this causes a 'printing error in the biological manual' and can increase a person's risk of developing schizophrenia. For example, in **DiGeorge syndrome**, a strand of DNA containing 30–40 genes is deleted from chromosome 22. One in four people with this condition develop schizophrenia, compared with less than 1 in 100 people without DiGeorge syndrome. This has been linked to the deletion of a specific gene called **COMT** (Kim *et al.*, 2020). This gene codes for an enzyme which breaks down neurotransmitters such as dopamine. This suggests that the absence of this gene could be partially responsible for the complex neurochemical imbalances that seem to underpin the symptoms of schizophrenia.

Some researchers believe the 'disrupted in schizophrenia' or the **DISC1** gene increases the risk of schizophrenia due to its association with the neurotransmitter GABA. GABA is an inhibitory neurotransmitter which helps to regulate activity in neural circuits that communicate via dopamine and glutamate. Again, an abnormality of this gene could, therefore, increase vulnerability to **excess** dopaminergic activity and subsequent symptoms of schizophrenia.

Evaluating genetic explanations

A strength of the genetic explanation of schizophrenia is that it is supported by research evidence. For example, there are two versions of the COMT gene called 'Met' and 'Val' and research suggests that the Val allele is associated with decreased dopamine activity in the prefrontal cortex, decreased cognitive performance and a slightly elevated risk of schizophrenia (Egan *et al.*, 2001). This is important evidence to support both the role of genetic factors and the dopamine deficiency hypothesis. This said, there is some evidence to suggest the effect of the Val allele on cognition may be stronger in men with schizophrenia than women (Wang *et al.*, 2020).

There is also research evidence to support the role of the DISC1 gene variant in schizophrenia. For example, in a large Scottish family with an unusually high rate of schizophrenia, 34 family members carried this gene (St Clair *et al.*, 1990). More recently, a meta-analysis of the findings of 14 animal experiments suggests that this may be linked to the impact of DISC1 on presynaptic dopamine dysregulation (Dahoun *et al.*, 2017). This is an important finding as animal experiments are tightly controlled, meaning the findings have greater internal validity. This said, the contribution of DISC1 is highly contested and has also been linked with a range of other mental health conditions, in addition to schizophrenia (Sullivan, 2013).

> ## ISSUES AND DEBATES

Nature versus nurture

Although there are a wealth of twin studies to support the role of genetics (nature) in schizophrenia, the validity of these findings is questionable. It is assumed that MZ twin pairs living in the same household will be exposed to environmental factors that are similar to pairs of DZ twins, but this is highly unlikely. As MZ twins are always the same gender, look more similar than DZ twins and are more likely to share similar temperaments, they are likely to be parented more similarly than DZ twins. This means that the degree of both genetic and environmental similarity differs between MZ and DZ twins, making it impossible to infer that the higher concordance rate for schizophrenia in MZ twins is due to them sharing 100 per cent of their DNA. This suggests that nurture may play a greater role in schizophrenia than previously thought.

Reductionism versus holism

A further weakness is this explanation is overly reductionist; taking this perspective may limit awareness of the range of treatment options. While our genome may impact the way we process information and experience the world, research suggests that it is possible to train ourselves to interpret our thoughts in more beneficial ways. On page 255, we will consider the benefits of cognitive-behavioural therapy as a way of successfully managing both positive and negative symptoms. This is important as it demonstrates that nurture can override nature when environmental experiences are carefully curated.

Biochemical

Excess dopamine as a cause of schizophrenia

In the 1960s, Arvid Carlsson and Margit Lindqvist proposed that schizophrenia was caused by an excess of the neurotransmitter dopamine, deep in the brain's **limbic system** and **mesolimbic pathways** (Carlsson and Lindqvist, 1963). Synapses that use dopamine may also be overactive due to differences in the number of receptors on the postsynaptic cell.

Over time, new evidence caused scientists to update this explanation. For example, many people who were taking dopamine **antagonists** like **chlorpromazine** (page 251) still suffered with negative symptoms and some experienced no improvement in symptoms at all.

Dopamine deficiency as a cause of schizophrenia

In the 1990s, Kenneth Davis and colleagues suggested that a lack of dopamine in the **prefrontal cortex** and **mesocortical pathways** may explain the negative and cognitive symptoms (Davis *et al.*, 1991). Symptoms such as disorganised thinking and speech could certainly result from problems with dopamine regulation as this neurotransmitter is important for shifting and directing attention.

Over the years, further contradictory evidence revealed that the updated hypothesis was still over-simplified. Overactivity in the mesolimbic pathways was thought to result from excess D2 dopamine receptors and/or low levels of the enzyme **beta-hydroxylase**, which breaks down dopamine. However, in 2006, Arvid and Maria Carlsson proposed the **dopamine deficiency hypothesis**, suggesting that the brain compensates for low levels of dopamine by increasing the number of receptors on the postsynaptic cell. This process is known as **upregulation**.

As you look at the synapse diagram in Figure 6.8, think about the stages of neurotransmission; how many different reasons can you think of as to why someone might have high (or low) levels of dopaminergic activity in their brain?

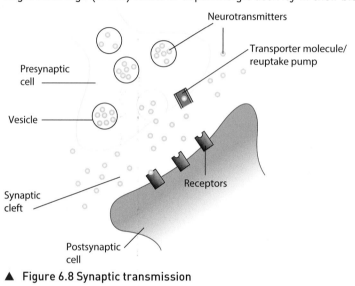

▲ Figure 6.8 Synaptic transmission

Evaluating the dopamine hypothesis

> ## ISSUES AND DEBATES

Nature versus nurture

A strength of the dopamine hypothesis and thus the role of nature is that there is wealth of research evidence to support this explanation of schizophrenia. In one study, rats were injected with **amphetamines** over a three-week period. Amphetamine is known to increase dopamine activity (Tenn *et al.*, 2003). The rats showed a range of schizophrenic-like behaviours, including strange movements and social withdrawal. Furthermore, the rats' symptoms were alleviated when they were given drugs to block their D1 dopamine receptors. This supports the role of biological factors (nature) in schizophrenia but also underlines the importance of environmental factors (nurture) such as drug taking.

Despite many studies supporting the role of a dopamine dysfunction as a potential cause of schizophrenia, Dépatie and Lal (2001) found that **apomorphine**, a dopamine **agonist**, does not worsen symptoms in people who already have a diagnosis of this disorder and neither does it trigger symptoms in those that do not. Findings such as this are hard to explain and suggest that the picture may be far more complicated, potentially, highlighting the role of nurture in predicting the impact of biological factors.

Reductionism versus holism

A limitation of all the different versions of the dopamine hypothesis is that they are highly reductionist. The idea that a single neurotransmitter is responsible for schizophrenia is no longer accepted. Drugs such as clozapine (see page 251), which block dopamine and serotonin receptors, are often more effective than drugs that only block dopamine receptors (e.g. chlorpromazine) and the efficacy of newer drugs, such as glutamate agonists, suggests that an exploration of the interactions between a wide range of neurotransmitters may prove more fruitful than studies that focus on single neurotransmitters. Taking a holistic approach and recognising how neurotransmitter levels are affected by experiences in the world and the ways in which we interpret them is also critical. Throughout this text we have focused on ways in which various lifestyle choices including mindfulness, sleep, exercise and diet can affect our neurochemistry and it is therefore important to recognise how the prognosis of conditions like schizophrenia can be affected by numerous individual and situational factors, due to their impact on our biology.

Determinism versus free will

The biological explanation of schizophrenia is deterministic in that it suggests that the workings of the brain are responsible for the symptoms of schizophrenia. Research using PET brain imaging, for example, demonstrates that people diagnosed with schizophrenia have decreased binding on their prefrontal D1 dopamine receptors in comparison with matched controls without schizophrenia (Okubo et al. 1997). Furthermore, there were significant correlations between D1 binding, severity of negative symptoms and performance on the Wisconsin Card Sorting Test (a measure of cognitive ability). This supports dopamine deficiency as an explanation of negative and cognitive symptoms and the role of biological determinism.

LEARNING LINKS

Think back to the biological approach from AS Level and you will remember the study by Dement and Kleitman (sleep and dreams). Researchers believe that REM sleep is an important time when synapses are 'cleaned out' and neurotransmitters replenished for the coming day. This suggests that improved sleep quality could help people to improve their mental health. Unfortunately, sleep is often disrupted by disorders like schizophrenia, worsening people's symptoms even more.

STUDY TIP

Comparison involves explaining how the two things are similar and how they are different. If you were asked to compare the two explanations discussed on this page, you could examine the evidence for and against each explanation, including the research methods that have been used. You could also look at the applications to the real world (e.g. treatments for schizophrenia) and you could think about how each explanation relates to the issues and debates.

TEST YOURSELF

1 Jameela has schizophrenia. She experiences hallucinations and is very socially withdrawn. Her doctor explains to her family that her symptoms may be caused by an imbalance of dopamine in her brain. Explain the dopamine hypothesis with reference to Jameela's symptoms. [4]
2 Compare the genetic and the biochemical explanations of schizophrenia. [6]
3 a Describe one or more genetic explanations of schizophrenia. [6]
  b Evaluate the genetic explanation(s) of schizophrenia, including a discussion of nature and nurture. [10]
4 Outline one advantage and one disadvantage of using animal experiments as a research method for investigating schizophrenia. [4]

5 A researcher finds a correlation between severity of schizophrenia symptoms and dopamine activity. Explain why the researcher cannot conclude that excess dopamine causes schizophrenia. [2]

6 Chase works with families where one member has schizophrenia. He has created a set of rating scales to measure people's feelings about their family member's diagnosis. Identify a suitable measure of central tendency and measure of spread for Chase's data. [2]

Psychological explanation of schizophrenia

KEY TERMS

self-monitoring error
internal monologue

Think!

What does Frith mean by **self-monitoring** and how is this related to positive symptoms of schizophrenia?

Think!

Do you hear an internal voice sometimes when you are thinking or reading? Not everyone does. Some people see their thoughts as images or actually see printed words in their heads as they think. Asking friends and family to explain how they think about certain things can be very interesting – not everyone processes information in the same way, even for people without mental disorders.

Think!

Experiments like the ones described on this page can help us to understand more about how people with schizophrenia think but the evidence they provide does not reflect the full range of people with this disorder. What sort of people do you think are more likely to take part in such studies? Why is this problematic?

'It was as if parts of my brain 'awoke' which had been dormant, and I became interested in a wide assortment of people, events, places, and ideas which normally would make no impression on me. The walk of a stranger on the street could be a 'sign' to me which I must interpret. Every face in the windows of a passing streetcar would be engraved on my mind, all of them concentrating on me and trying to pass me some sort of message.'

(MacDonald, 1960)

Which symptoms of schizophrenia do you recognise in this quote?

In Dr Longden's TED talk, she notes that the 'most violent and critical voices' related to 'the most damaged aspects of herself'. How does this fit with Frith's ideas about self-monitoring?

▲ Figure 6.9 Cognitive neuropsychologist Chris Frith cites the following quote as a guiding principle in his research into schizophrenia: 'Reality leaves a lot to the imagination' (John Lennon)

▲ Figure 6.10 In a TED talk that has reached over 5 million viewers and is translated into 37 languages, Dr Eleanor Longden speaks about her experiences of hearing voices

Cognitive explanation

Professor Chris Frith acknowledges that discussions about dopamine do not really explain the subjective experience of voice-hearing. Likewise, as fascinating as up- and down-regulation may be, neither explains the development of bizarre false beliefs, such as having one's thoughts extracted by aliens or government spies. In the 1990s, he advanced one of the first cognitive explanations of schizophrenia, assuming that both positive and negative symptoms result from faulty information processing.

Errors in self-monitoring

Many people (but not all) experience an **internal monologue** or voice – that is, we hear our thoughts as we read, write and think about what we fancy for lunch. The cognitive theory of schizophrenia suggests that people with schizophrenia have difficulty distinguishing between auditory stimuli that occur outside their own mind (e.g. in the physical and social environment) and their self-generated, inner voice. They may mistakenly perceive their sub-vocal thoughts as coming from an external source (i.e. outside of their own mind). This is known as a self-monitoring error. This helps to explain the experience of auditory hallucinations. Likewise, experiences of influence (e.g. thought insertion) can be understood with reference to the person's inability to recognise the difference between internally and externally generated stimuli. These experiences may also be a way of understanding the experience of voice-hearing – for example, 'I hear a voice, but no-one is present; the voice must have been transmitted via radio waves direct to my brain.' This shows the possible link between abnormal sensory experience (hallucinations), experiences of influence and the formation of delusions (false beliefs).

Difficulties with mentalising

In the cognitive approach, you studied the 2001 research by Baron-Cohen *et al.* (eyes test) (see page 60) about how people with autism spectrum disorder (ASD) process social information compared with people without this diagnosis. The study investigated the validity of their advanced theory of mind test ('Reading the mind in the eyes'). This test assesses the ability to attribute mental states by examining pairs of eyes. This is known as mentalising and is based on understanding that other people can have intentions and mental states/emotions that differ from our own.

Schizophrenia has some overlaps with autism (see Learning link, page 249) and Frith (1992) believes that difficulties in mentalising may result in persecutory delusions and paranoia. If people with schizophrenia have difficulties understanding mental states/intentions, neutral behaviour may be misinterpreted as hostility. Furthermore, an under-developed theory of mind may mean that people with schizophrenia believe that others have the same opinion of them as they have of themselves. Thus, if a person with schizophrenia believes they are a bad person, they may believe that others also think the same. This suggests that negative symptoms (e.g. social withdrawal) result from the difficulties that people with schizophrenia have in the social world, which may be perceived as a dangerous and threatening place.

Thinking errors and biases

As we go about our daily lives, we discover information about the world that confirms or refutes our beliefs. This leads us to modify our views in the light of new evidence. In schizophrenia, abnormal beliefs may be formed and maintained if people fail to update their understanding based on new evidence. People with schizophrenia tend to draw conclusions based on insufficient evidence and show a bias against counter-evidence – information that disconfirms their delusions. These errors of judgement and biases explain why people with schizophrenia hold bizarre beliefs, even in the face of conflicting evidence.

Evaluating the cognitive explanation

The idea that hallucinations result from the misattribution of a person's own inner speech is an example of an individual explanation of schizophrenia as it suggests that some individuals process information differently to others. This explanation is supported by experimental evidence. For example, Allen *et al.* (2007) asked participants to listen to pre-recorded words while undergoing an fMRI brain scan. The words were either spoken by the participant themselves or by someone else and were either distorted or undistorted. People with schizophrenia who hear voices were more likely to say their own words were spoken by someone else than people with and without schizophrenia who do not hear voices. Also, brain activity was the same regardless of whether the voice of the speaker belonged to them or someone else, and whether the voice was distorted or not. Control participants showed different brain activity across the four conditions, showing that they were aware of the differences between the voices. This is an important study as it shows that information is processed differently by the voice-hearers and it also indicates that this has a biological basis.

Further support for the idea that schizophrenia is caused by individual differences in terms of thinking errors and biases comes from research by Garety *et al.* (1991). Participants had to judge whether a jar contained mostly pink or mostly green beads based on the colour of beads taken one by one from the jar. The beads were in two jars, where one contained 85 pink and 15 green and the other contained 85 green and 15 pink (see Figure 6.11). People with schizophrenia requested fewer beads to be removed before making their judgement than people without schizophrenia. They were also more likely to change their mind based on a single piece of evidence – for example, following four green beads, people with schizophrenia were more likely than controls to decide the jar contained 'more pink beads' as soon as one pink bead was drawn.

A weakness of the cognitive explanation is that, although the evidence supports the contribution of underlying cognitive deficits in the development of symptoms such as delusions and hallucinations, it is unclear why some people have these cognitive deficits in the first place and this is a weakness of this overly reductionist approach. Cognitive theories suggest that symptoms develop due to faulty thinking strategies but do not explain why some people think in ways that are different to others. This means the cognitive theories only provide a partial account of schizophrenia. Taking a more holistic approach and examining interactions between biological, cognitive and social factors may provide a more comprehensive account.

Another limitation is that it does not explain why some people who have difficulties in mentalising or weak central control do not develop schizophrenia while others do. It appears that the same cognitive deficits can underpin a range of different disorders, including autism and ADHD. This suggests that other factors may determine whether schizophrenic symptoms occur, and these may be sociocultural and relate to how people interpret their differing mental experiences. For example, our beliefs, values and attitudes shape how we think about our own thinking. This means that people from certain cultural backgrounds may find 'experiences of influence', for example, more distressing than others. The stress that this generates may make their symptoms more difficult to bear. In some cultures, the experience of voice-hearing is not seen as a sign of illness. In fact, voice-hearers may be respected as healers and visionaries within the community. The attitudes of other people in society are central to our wellbeing, which is why campaigns to destigmatise mental health issues are so important.

There are many competing explanations of schizophrenia. You are only required to understand biological and cognitive explanations but there are also learning and social explanations (e.g. environmental breeder hypothesis and the social causation hypothesis [Cooper, 2005]), which examine the role of traumatic life events, poverty and stress, specifically resulting from prejudice and discrimination (Veling *et al.* 2008). Schizophrenia is best understood as the result of an interaction between genetic and environmental factors. The diathesis-stress model, for example, suggests that some people are predisposed to psychotic disorders (due to genetic inheritance or adverse childhood experiences) but only go on to develop symptoms when faced with precipitating factors or situational stressors.

Individual and situational explanations

Cognitive theory helps to explain **individual differences** in mental health by highlighting the differences in the ways people process information. What it cannot explain is the episodic nature of schizophrenia – that is, that people do not suffer from symptoms all the time, despite presumably processing information in the same way. It is possible that **situational factors**, such as high levels of stress, increase cognitive load to a point where they cannot cope, and this triggers a psychotic breakdown. This demonstrates that schizophrenia may be influenced by both **individual and situational explanations** – cognitive deficits predispose people to psychotic breaks, but precipitating factors are required for the symptoms to actually manifest themselves.

Idiographic versus nomothetic

One issue with much of the research into both biological and cognitive explanations of schizophrenia is the supporting research tends to take a nomothetic approach.

This means the studies are often experimental in nature and compare groups of people with and without schizophrenia in order to find differences between them that might explain why some people have the condition and others do not. The data is then used to draw conclusions that are generalised to larger populations. The problem with this approach is that it often fails to take account of individual differences between people with schizophrenia, which is a highly heterogeneous disorder, meaning it can manifest itself in very different ways. Taking a more idiographic approach through the use of case studies may be helpful in revealing key factors that correlate with more positive long-term outcomes. For example, the trauma-informed approach advocated by Lucy Johnstone (2018) focuses on listening to people's stories regarding events in their lives and how they have interpreted them. Not only does this approach help practitioners to understand the context of the person's symptoms (e.g. as a reaction to traumatic experiences), it also provides idiographic support for cognitive explanations of psychotic symptoms.

The participants were told that the researcher would choose one of the two jars and they had to work out which jar had been chosen by asking the researcher to randomly select one bead at a time and tell them the colour. People with schizophrenia made their decisions based on fewer beads than people without schizophrenia. Can you think of a way of making this study more ecologically valid?

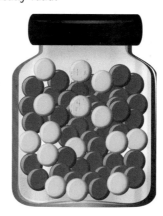

▲ Figure 6.11 The jars in the study by Garety *et al.* (1991) contained coloured beads in the ratio 85:15.

▶ LEARNING LINKS

At AS Level, you learned about the 2001 research by Baron-Cohen *et al.* (eyes test) into ASD. The terms autism and schizophrenia were first used by Swiss psychiatrist Eugen Bleuler in 1911. He included the word 'autism' as one of his 'four As of schizophrenia', to describe the way people with schizophrenia are detached from reality and other people. He believed schizophrenia only affected adults but noticed that some children also showed this symptom, believing they would develop schizophrenia as adults. The term 'childhood psychosis' was used for children who today might receive a diagnosis of autism. Although it is now understood that these are two separate conditions, research suggests that similar biological factors may contribute to both disorders.

STUDY TIP

If you are faced with a question that asks you to evaluate an explanation of a mental disorder, whether it is schizophrenia or one of the other disorders in this chapter, think about any therapies that have been developed based on the explanation. An effective therapy is a strength of the theory/explanation. You can use this to develop an evaluative paragraph by giving some detail about the therapy, but remember, the essay is asking about the explanation not the therapy, so make sure you link back by saying that, as the theory has useful applications to everyday life, it strengthens the explanation.

▶ **TEST YOURSELF**

1   Ranbir's mother died six years ago. He hears her voice criticising him and sometimes believes that people are trying to deliver secret messages from her. Outline how the cognitive explanation could explain one or more of his symptoms. [4]

2   Outline one similarity and one difference between the cognitive explanation and the genetic explanation of schizophrenia. [2]

3   a   Describe the cognitive explanation of schizophrenia. [6]

    b   Evaluate the cognitive explanation of schizophrenia, including a discussion of nature and nurture. [10]

4   Studies investigating explanations of schizophrenia often compare a group of people with schizophrenia with a control group of people who are matched with the people with schizophrenia on important variables.

    a   Outline the purpose of the control group. [4]

    b   State two variables participants might be matched on. [2]

5   Florencia asks her participants to listen to pre-recorded sentences spoken either in their own voice or in an actor's voice. She asks them to tick 'self' or 'other' for each sentence.

    a   Identify the design used in this experiment. [1]

    b   Explain one weakness of this design with reference to Florencia's study. [2]

6   Zachary asks people with and without schizophrenia to name the ink colour of 20 words as quickly as possible. He plots his data on a bar chart. State a suitable label for his *y* axis. [2]

KEY TERMS

electroconvulsive therapy

typical antipsychotic

antagonist

atypical antipsychotic

clozapine

METHODOLOGY

ethics

longitudinal studies

generalisations from findings

random control trials (RCTs)

experiments

6.1.3 Treatment and management of schizophrenia

Biological treatments

Think!

Why is clozapine unlikely to be prescribed for people who are homeless?

Think!

If you or a family member was diagnosed with schizophrenia and had to choose between antipsychotics described here, which one would you choose and why?

Think!

Biological treatments for psychological conditions are controversial; some people believe their use is unethical, describing psychoactive drugs as 'chemical straitjackets' and electroconvulsive therapy (ECT) as an assault on extremely vulnerable people. But does ECT really contravene ethical guidelines? To what extent does ECT do good (beneficence) and avoid harm (maleficence)? Can it be used with respect for personal autonomy? How does its usage ensure justice/equality of opportunity?

Double-blind, random control trials (RCTs) are the gold standard in drug testing. Participants do not know whether they have received the real drug or a placebo and neither does the clinician assessing their symptoms. Why is a double-blind RCT such a clever design in terms of finding out how effective the medications really are?

▲ Figure 6.12

Biochemical

Biochemical treatments for schizophrenia include the use of antipsychotic medications. These are generally administered orally as tablets or syrups but can also be given transdermally (through the skin) in creams, gels, patches and sprays (Abruzzo *et al.*, 2019). People who receive these medications will need regular check-ups to monitor their symptoms and any side effects. Dosages may need to be altered and it may be necessary to provide other additional medications. The boy described on page 234 (Aneja *et al.*, 2018) was prescribed five different drugs at one point and his case reveals how complex it can be to get the combination right for each individual, not least because people with schizophrenia can present such a wide range of differing symptoms.

Typical antipsychotics

In this context, the term 'typical' refers to the first-generation (early) antipsychotics that were developed in the 1950s. **Typical antipsychotic** drugs work by blocking dopamine receptors on the postsynaptic cell, but without activating them. This means dopamine cannot bind to the receptor, reducing signalling between synapses that communicate using this specific neurotransmitter. Drugs that work in this way are called dopamine **antagonists** and can be effective in reducing positive symptoms of schizophrenia. The first of these drugs was called **chlorpromazine**. Similarly, **haloperidol** also blocks dopamine receptors.

Atypical antipsychotics

From the 1980s onwards, researchers began developing **atypical antipsychotics**. These drugs block both dopamine and **serotonin** receptors. Serotonin is an inhibitory neurotransmitter which decreases the likelihood of the postsynaptic neuron firing an action potential and is involved in regulating arousal, alertness and mood. You will learn more about serotonin on page 264. Examples of these drugs include **clozapine** and **risperidone**.

The Texas Medication Algorithm Project (TMAP)

A protocol called the Texas Medication Algorithm Project (TMAP) was designed to assist doctors in the prescription of antipsychotics. Initially, the protocol suggests using an atypical drug, such as risperidone, and if this does not work moving onto a typical drug, such as haloperidol, or a different atypical, such as olanzapine. If the person still does not find any relief, clozapine may be trialled. Some patients are especially resistant to biochemical interventions and the final stages of the TMAP include combining antipsychotics with other types of medication, such as mood stabilisers like lithium. Once doctors have exhausted their options with medications, they may move onto the use of electroconvulsive therapy.

Evaluating biochemical treatments

Randomised control trials

The use of biochemical treatments is supported by experimental evidence. For example, data from over 10,000 people taking 18 different antipsychotics was examined in a meta-analysis of 56 randomised control trials (Zhao *et al.*, 2016). Seventeen drugs had lower relapse rates than the placebos. This demonstrates that drug treatments can be an effective alternative to hospitalisation, the only option for many people with schizophrenia prior to the development of drugs like chlorpromazine. This said, four of the drugs performed no better than the placebos in terms of reducing hospital admissions.

Side effects and relapse

While medications may help people to stay out of hospital, the **side effects** can be unpleasant, debilitating and even fatal. Dizziness, drowsiness and restlessness are common, as well as nausea, constipation and excessive weight gain. Typical antipsychotics often lead to **tardive dyskinesia,** characterised by uncontrollable blinking, jerking and twitching of the face and body. Atypical antipsychotics have fewer side effects but come with their own issues. Clozapine, for example, can cause **agranulocytosis**, a potentially fatal blood condition, although the risk is minimised through regular blood counts. Nonetheless, these far-reaching side effects can lead people to stop taking their medications (non-compliance) and this can be dangerous without the support of a professional.

A final weakness is that drug treatments are ineffective for 30–70 per cent of people (Howes *et al.*, 2017). **Efficacy** decreases the longer the start of treatment is delayed, and the greatest gains are made within the first five years. Furthermore, 60–80 per cent of people relapse (experience a return of symptoms) unless they continue to take a maintenance dose of their medication (Patel *et al.*, 2014).

> ## ISSUES AND DEBATES
>
> ### Idiographic versus nomothetic
>
> The advantage of large-scale studies like Zhao *et al.* (2016) is that the nomothetic approach allows generalisations to be made due to the very large sample sizes. The studies were longitudinal, lasting an average of 48 weeks (1–24 months) and studies were assessed to determine their empirical quality using the Cochrane Risk of Bias Tool. The studies differed in terms of how relapse was measured but many used numerical rating scales. The Positive and Negative Syndrome Scale (PANSS) is a common tool used for this purpose and this has high validity as it incorporates self-reported data as well as observations made by clinicians and caregivers (Opler *et al.*, 2017).
>
> These methodological features increase the overall validity of Zhao *et al.*'s (2016) findings, increasing confidence in the ability to apply the findings to others. This said, a more idiographic approach may be beneficial when evaluating the efficacy of treatment. Studies using semistructured interviewing and/or focus groups, for example, may be more likely to capture important details like the role of perceived social support from family members and the nature of the therapeutic alliance between doctor and patient. Such factors may be important in determining the effectiveness of anti-psychotic medications and may be overlooked unless researchers incorporate more idiographic methods into their research.

Electroconvulsive therapy

Electroconvulsive therapy (ECT) involves delivering electrical pulses (70–150 volts) to one or both sides of the brain via electrodes placed on the scalp. The pulses last up to one second and cause thousands of neurons to fire at the same time, inducing a brief, controlled seizure of up to one minute. The therapy includes two to three sessions per week for the first month and monthly or fortnightly 'maintenance doses' for up to one year, dependent on the individual's progress. ECT can be used to treat a range of conditions, including schizophrenia, major depressive disorder and bipolar disorder. It does not help everyone, but some people find that the symptoms start to improve after just one session. This treatment is not an alternative to medication. It is used in addition to medication, for people who are treatment-resistant. For example, the boy studied by Aneja *et al.* (2018) received eight sessions of bilateral (both sides of the brain) ECT later in his treatment.

Unlike popular media portrayals, modified ECT is now used throughout much of the world, meaning it is administered under general anaesthetic using muscle relaxants so the person cannot be injured during the seizure and has no recollection of the procedure. Despite this, the treatment is still highly controversial and is banned in some countries, such as Slovenia (Gazdag *et al.*, 2017), yet in others, such as China, more than 50 per cent of people with a diagnosis of schizophrenia receive ECT (Wang *et al.*, 2018a). It should also be noted that in many counties unmodified ECT is still the norm (Andrade *et al.*, 2012) and this presents a variety of ethical issues.

Researchers are still unsure how ECT works but it is believed the shocks trigger the release of neurotransmitters like dopamine and serotonin. Furthermore, it has also been suggested that the seizures are associated with gene expression and improved connectivity between neurons in areas such as the hippocampus (Singh and Kar, 2017).

Evaluating electroconvulsive therapy

ISSUES AND DEBATES

Applications to everyday life

A strength of ECT is that improvement can be rapid and significant in people previously classed as treatment-resistant. For example, in just eight weeks, Petrides *et al.* (2015) found that 50 per cent of their American sample showed a reduction in symptoms of 40 per cent or more when their usual dose of clozapine was combined with ECT. None of the matched control groups achieved a similar level of improvement. Despite the small sample size (n = 39), this study reveals that ECT can provide a lifeline for some of the most unwell people in society, who may be at risk of suicide.

In **single-blind studies** such as Petrides *et al.* (2015), the clinicians who assessed the participants' symptoms were unaware which treatment group they were in (i.e. clozapine or clozapine + ECT), but the participants themselves knew if they had received ECT or not. This suggests that the greater improvement in the ECT group may have been due to increased expectancy of positive outcomes. This is supported by Debora Melzer-Ribeiro and colleagues, who found no significant difference in the improvement of participants who believed they were receiving real ECT (but no seizures were induced) (n = 10) and a group who really were receiving ECT (n = 13) (Melzer-Ribeiro *et al.*, 2017). This is important as it

suggests the apparent efficacy of ECT may be nothing more than a placebo effect.

Cultural differences

Support for the use of ECT in people from non-Western cultures comes from a **meta-analysis** of 18 random control trials of ECT plus clozapine (Wang *et al.*, 2018a). Seventeen of these studies were conducted in China. ECT was found to be a highly effective and relatively safe treatment, capable of achieving rapid results in people who had failed to experience relief using even the most effective antipsychotics. This is important as, although the mechanism by which ECT works is unclear, these results suggest that ECT is an effective treatment for people in China, where the prevalence of this disorder doubled between 1990 and 2010 (Chan *et al.*, 2015).

The vast majority of the findings analysed by Wang *et al.* (2018a) were from studies conducted in China, a high power-distance culture, where people are less likely to question the wisdom of doctors. This suggests that the participants may have felt more positive about the benefits of ECT, leading to **high expectancy (placebo) effects**, for the individual and their family. This means that the results may not be generalisable to people in Western cultures, who may have had greater exposure to the negative and often brutal portrayals of unmodified ECT in popular Hollywood movies.

ECT is generally only administered with consent but sometimes this is not possible when people are very unwell. In England, independent consultant psychiatrists are asked to advise in order to protect the individual patient's rights (Care Quality Commission, 2021). Do you think it is ethical to provide ECT without consent?

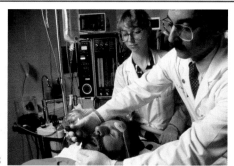

▶ Figure 6.13

LEARNING LINKS

Despite widespread, global use of ECT, the mechanism by which this controversial therapy achieves its outcomes remains unknown. Singh and Kar (2017) suggested that people who have received ECT may experience increased connectivity in the hippocampus.

If you think back to your studies of the biological approach at AS Level, you should recall that Hölzel *et al.* (mindfulness and brain scans) found that eight weeks of mindfulness-based stress reduction also resulted in increased grey matter concentration in this region as well as several others. Mindfulness has also been tried as a therapy for people with schizophrenia. Evidence suggests that it can be helpful in increasing dopamine (Esch, 2014) and a recent randomised controlled trial showed that it was effective in improving negative symptoms of schizophrenia (Lee, 2019).

STUDY TIP

Evaluation of treatments, therapies and ways of managing disorders should take a similar format to evaluations of theories in psychology. You should look at the empirical evidence for and against (e.g. research findings) and evaluate the credibility of these studies, such as how long participants were monitored (duration), how large the sample was and how participants were selected. For example, did the study use a double-blind, randomised design? Was there a control group that took a placebo? Other ways of evaluating include exploring the practical and ethical issues and making comparisons between different treatments, such as biological versus psychological, or biochemical versus electroconvulsive therapy.

TEST YOURSELF

1   Outline one similarity and one difference between typical and atypical antipsychotics. [4]
2   Compare biochemical treatments for schizophrenia with electroconvulsive therapy. [6]
3   a   Describe one or more biological treatments for schizophrenia. [6]
    b   Evaluate the biological treatment(s) for schizophrenia described in part (a), including a discussion of longitudinal studies. [10]
4   Outline one ethical strength and one ethical weakness of the use of biological treatments for schizophrenia. [4]
5   A researcher is asked whether the findings of their study can be generalised to all people with schizophrenia. Suggest two things that the researcher could mention which demonstrate that their findings can be generalised. [2]
6   Yu Yan is conducting a randomised control trial to test a new drug for schizophrenia. She is taking a nomothetic approach to her research. Han Jiao believes Yu Yan needs to take a more idiographic approach.
    a   Explain how Yu Yan might operationalise her independent and dependent variables. [4]
    b   Describe one way that Yu Yan could make her study more idiographic. [3]

Psychological treatment and management of schizophrenia

Think!

Why might a cognitive-behavioural therapist use the following techniques: **Socratic questioning, downward arrow, thought linkage**?

Think!

Imagine you are a CBT therapist. What do you think might be some of the difficulties that you would face when working with participants with schizophrenia (page 231) compared with depression (page 259) or obsessive-compulsive disorder (page 283)? If you are unsure of the symptoms of these disorders, check the pages in brackets.

KEY TERMS

Socratic questioning
downward arrow technique
thought linkage
paced activity scheduling

METHODOLOGY

ethics
longitudinal studies
generalisations from findings
experiments

Think!

As with biological treatments, it can be difficult to separate the extent to which positive gains following therapy are due to the actual therapy itself or a placebo (expectancy) effect. How did Sensky *et al.*'s study overcome this problem? Why do you think that over the longer term the befriending group showed less overall improvement than the CBT group?

Cognitive-behavioural therapists help their clients to understand how thoughts, feelings, behaviours and sensations feed into each other and how changing our beliefs can create changes in all of the other areas too. How might the physical sensations associated with experiences of passivity, influence and control be linked to beliefs, feelings and behaviour? If a therapist was able to explain why some people experience these sensations, how might this affect the person with schizophrenia?

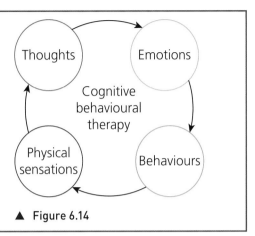

▲ Figure 6.14

Cognitive-behavioural therapy

Originally developed for mood and anxiety disorders (pages 259 and 307), cognitive-behavioural therapy (CBT) has been adapted for people with schizophrenia. The length and number of sessions will depend on the client's needs, but all CBT therapists will begin by developing a trusting and accepting relationship called a **therapeutic alliance**. This is central to the success of the therapy as CBT is a collaborative exercise, where therapists and clients work together, towards the client's goals.

Exploring events, beliefs and feelings

Therapists help their clients to develop **self-awareness** through understanding the links between daily events, physical sensations, thoughts and feelings (Figure 6.15). Focusing very much on present issues, as opposed to past life events, the therapist helps the person to explore how thoughts are interlinked and how they reflect our **core beliefs** about the world and our place within it. This in itself can be empowering as it allows people to begin to take control of their thoughts and feelings rather than being controlled by them.

Preventing relapse through stress management

The symptoms of schizophrenia can be extremely distressing and may lead to a build-up of stress, which can exacerbate symptoms and lead to further **decompensation** or loss of functioning. For this reason, CBT therapy aims to develop coping skills, including stress management. A key treatment goal is to help the person to identify early warning signs (**prodromal** symptoms) that precede decompensation, as proactive initiation of coping strategies and stress reduction can ensure that symptoms do not worsen.

Psychoeducation

Finally, CBT involves educating the person (and their family) about schizophrenia (e.g. that voice-hearing can result from misattribution of the inner voice) and how it can be affected by stress, as well as strengthening their sense of self and combating feelings of stigmatisation that can result from a diagnostic process. Providing support so that the person can reconnect with some of their former interests and hobbies and participate in a wider range of social activities can be helpful, but this must be a gradual process so that the person does not become overwhelmed, which could trigger a relapse.

You will learn more below about the specific techniques that CBT therapists use to tackle some of the positive and negative symptoms of schizophrenia (Sensky *et al.*, 2000).

Evaluating CBT for schizophrenia

One ethical strength of CBT is that the therapist and client work collaboratively, removing the imbalance of power which is a feature of biological treatments. With both ECT and drug treatments, the client's role in their recovery is minimal but with CBT they are responsible for their own progress. This is a strength as people with mental health problems often face prejudice and discrimination in society, so a therapy that also develops self-efficacy may also help to rebuild the person's self-worth.

A weakness of CBT for schizophrenia is that it relies on the quality of the therapeutic alliance and some patients may lack the necessary communication skills to connect with the therapist. Furthermore, people with low levels of literacy, organisational skills and/or motivation may be unable to complete homework exercises (e.g. keeping diaries) between sessions. This means CBT may only be effective for some clients and others may require additional support between sessions for it to be as effective for them.

Focus on: Sensky *et al.* (2000)

Tom Sensky is a psychiatrist and Emeritus Professor of Psychological Medicine at Imperial College London. He has had a longstanding clinical and research interest in understanding the psychology of people with enduring illnesses, physical and mental. The team of people who set up this study were introduced to one another by Aaron Beck, the founder of cognitive-behavioural therapy.

▲ Figure 6.15

AIM

To compare the efficacy of one-to-one CBT and a befriending intervention for people with schizophrenia.

METHODOLOGY

Ninety 16- to 60-year-old participants with schizophrenia (diagnosed using the ICD-10 and the DSM-IV) were randomly allocated to either the CBT group or the befriending group. All had been prescribed a daily dose of at least 300 mg of chlorpromazine for a minimum of six months but still experienced positive symptoms. Treatment was delivered by two experienced nurses who received regular supervision. Symptoms were assessed by 'blind' raters. They were assessed before the treatment started (to establish a **baseline**), post-treatment (up to nine months later) and nine months after treatment ended (**follow-up**).

CBT sessions

Therapists worked collaboratively with the patients to understand the development of both positive and negative symptoms and to reduce distress and disability.

Befriending

The befriending (control) group received the same amount of contact time with a therapist, at similarly spaced intervals. Therapists were empathic and non-directive. They talked about hobbies, sport and current affairs.

▼ Table 6.4 CBT techniques used to treat different symptoms in Sensky *et al.* (2000)

Hearing voices	Patients kept diaries to document their experiences. The therapist encouraged a critical analysis of their client's beliefs about the origin and nature of the voice(s) and helped them to devise coping strategies.
Delusions	Guided discovery using Socratic questioning was used to verbally challenge and reflect on the client's irrational beliefs; clients were asked probing questions and encouraged to present evidence for their claims; the therapist helped the client to rigorously examine any evidence they presented, gradually helping them recognise that their delusional beliefs were unfounded. The downward arrow technique was used to explore the subjective meaning of the client's thoughts to reveal underlying beliefs, and alternative interpretations of events were discussed.
Disorganised thinking	Therapists used the technique of thought linkage, repeatedly asking patients to explain the connections between their seemingly unrelated thoughts.
Negative symptoms	Strategies including **paced activity scheduling** were suggested to minimise fatigue and stress and clients were encouraged to keep a diary of times when they felt pleasure and/or a sense of accomplishment.

RESULTS

Participants attended an average of 19 sessions in nine months. There was no significant difference in the number of sessions attended by the CBT group compared with the befriending group. Both groups showed a reduction in post-treatment symptoms but only the CBT group showed continued improvement at the nine-month follow-up assessment. There was no difference in medication use between these groups.

CONCLUSIONS

CBT was more effective than befriending; patients continued to improve post-treatment to follow-up, unlike befriending, where initial improvements were no longer evident at follow-up.

Evaluating Sensky *et al.* (2000)

One strength was that all treatment sessions were audiotaped and a blind rater randomly selected a sample of the tapes to assess the quality of the treatment. This improved internal validity as the rater was able to check that the befriending sessions did not contain elements of CBT and that the CBT sessions covered all of the expected elements.

Another strength was that the sample was selected from five clinical services in London, Newcastle, Cleveland and Durham, UK. This means generalisations can be made with greater confidence as the sample included people living in a variety of urban and more rural locations.

A weakness is that it is unclear whether CBT would be as effective on its own as, in this study, it was combined with drug treatment. Although initially the participants were not responding to their medications, they were still taking them. Therefore, it is possible that it was the combination of drugs and CBT that was effective as opposed to just CBT on its own.

A final weakness relates to the longitudinal design, which meant that some of the participants were excluded due to not completing a sufficient number of therapy sessions (six failed to engage at all and nine dropped out before they had received sufficient therapy). Participant drop-out can reduce the representativeness of the sample, thus limiting generalisations that can be drawn. For example, CBT may only lead to enduring benefits for a certain subset of people with schizophrenia, such as those that have coherent speech.

People in the befriending group in Sensky *et al.* (2000) also showed improvement in their symptoms following regular contact with an empathic, non-directive therapist. Can you think why this might have helped relieve their symptoms but also why the benefits diminished when the sessions concluded?

You have now studied both biological treatments (i.e. biochemical treatment and electro-convulsive therapy) and an example of the use of psychological therapy (i.e. cognitive-behavioural therapy). You should be able to see now that there is no definitive approach to treatment; unlike many medical conditions, psychological disorders are often extremely heterogeneous. Different people present differing combinations of symptoms and respond in different ways to treatment, doubtless due to their unique combinations of genes and life experiences. The best approaches to treatment are often eclectic, meaning practitioners will combine biological and psychological treatments to get the best fit for each individual patient.

▶ LEARNING LINKS

You will come across different versions of cognitive-behavioural therapy throughout this chapter, specifically when we examine Aaron Beck and Albert Ellis's therapies for unipolar and bipolar depression (page 280), as well as a version of CBT adapted for use with people with obsessive-compulsive disorder (page 302). Although each version is slightly different, you should be able to think of some practical and ethical evaluation points that you could use in any question about CBT. For example, compared with drug treatments, CBT does not have any unpleasant side effects, although sessions may be challenging and distressing for some. Can you think of any weaknesses of CBT compared with drug treatments?

STUDY TIP

You do not have to choose Sensky *et al.* (2000) to study cognitive-behavioural therapy for schizophrenia, but if you choose another study, make sure that it is a longitudinal study so that you really understand why this method is important – that is, to compare symptoms before, during and after therapy. Make sure you understand the difference between relapse (the return of symptoms that had previously improved) and remission (a reduction in symptoms to the point where the person no longer meets the threshold for diagnosis); these terms are often used when discussing the efficacy of therapies, such as CBT.

▶ TEST YOURSELF

1   Outline the procedure of one study of cognitive-behavioural therapy as a
    psychological treatment for schizophrenia.   [4]
2   Compare one biological and one psychological treatment for schizophrenia.   [6]
3   a   Describe cognitive-behavioural therapy for schizophrenia.   [6]
    b   Evaluate cognitive-behavioural therapy for schizophrenia, including a
        discussion of idiographic versus nomothetic. You must include research
        evidence in your answer.   [10]
4   Explain one methodological weakness of one study investigating a psychological
    therapy for schizophrenia.   [2]
5   Explain two ethical issues that researchers would need to consider when
    investigating psychological therapies for schizophrenia.   [4]
6   Paul is a clinical psychologist. He is reading an article about CBT for schizophrenia.
    He wants to know whether the findings from the study are generalisable to clinics
    like his. Identify two pieces of information that might lead Paul to think that the
    results may not be generalisable.   [2]

KEY TERMS

mood (affective) disorder
depressive disorder (unipolar)
unipolar disorder
bipolar disorder
manic episode
depressive episode
Beck depression inventory

METHODOLOGY

validity
psychometrics
quantitative and qualitative data

6.2 Mood (affective) disorders

6.2.1 Diagnostic criteria (ICD-11) for mood (affective) disorders

Think!

How long does a person need to have been experiencing symptoms to receive a diagnosis of **unipolar** versus **bipolar disorder**? Why do you think the time frame is shorter for bipolar disorder?

Think!

Can you think of any reasons why it might be difficult to make a valid and reliable diagnosis of unipolar and/or bipolar disorder? If you need to refresh your memory, check the glossary to revisit the difference between reliability and validity in the context of diagnosis.

Think!

If you or someone you know is showing signs or experiencing symptoms of a **mood disorder**, talk to a teacher, parent or friend for support. There are suggestions at the end of this chapter for agencies who can support you. Reaching out and talking to each other about difficult thoughts and feelings sometimes saves lives.

Systems like the ICD-11 include information to help clinicians to make better decisions when working with people from different cultural backgrounds from themselves. Why do you think this additional information is necessary?

▶ Figure 6.16 Diagnosis relies on open and effective communication between the person with symptoms and the clinician

Mood (affective) disorders

In psychology, **affect** (a noun) is another word for **emotion**, so **affective** disorders are conditions that affect (a verb!) our emotions. Usually, our emotions are relatively temporary and change according to the situation. Moods, on the other hand, are more stable, meaning they last longer and do not change as quickly as emotions. People with mood disorders often experience extended periods of time where either negative and/or positive emotions dominate and affect their thoughts and feelings in ways that can lead to **dysfunction**, distress and even danger.

The ICD-11 categorises mood disorders according to the types of mood generated and how the person's mood changes over time. The key term **episode** is used to refer to a time period in which a certain mood dominates. Episodes may be **depressive**, **manic** or **hypomanic**, or mixed (see below). The term 'polar' refers to the idea that our moods are on a continuum (or scale). The ends of the scale are the two 'poles' (like North and South!), with very high mood at one end and very low mood at the other. We all experience changes in mood each day, but generally these average out within the normal range. Therefore, mood disorders are characterised by the duration and intensity of the moods experienced.

Depressive disorder (unipolar)

People who experience unipolar depressive episodes typically experience moods within the normal range but sometimes their mood drops to the very low end of the scale. This is known as a depressive episode. The ICD-11 defines a depressive episode as follows:

> a period of depressed mood or diminished interest in activities occurring most of the day, nearly every day during a period lasting at least two weeks accompanied by other symptoms such as difficulty concentrating, feelings of worthlessness or excessive or inappropriate guilt, hopelessness, recurrent thoughts of death or suicide, changes in appetite or sleep, psychomotor agitation or retardation, and reduced energy or fatigue.

(World Health Organization, 2018)

This definition demonstrates the diversity of **cognitive**, **affective**, **behavioural** and **somatic (bodily)** symptoms related to depression. A person who has experienced at least two depressive episodes will be diagnosed with **recurrent** depressive disorder. A doctor may add a **specifier** of mild, moderate or severe to describe the intensity of the episode. This is determined by the range of symptoms experienced and their impact on the person's daily functioning (e.g. how they behave at home, work and/or school, and in social situations). The doctor will also note whether the depressive episode occurred with or without psychotic symptoms, which can also be part of mood disorders.

Bipolar disorders (manic and depressive episodes)

People with a diagnosis of bipolar disorder (type 1) also experience very low moods as well as the other symptoms of unipolar depression, but in addition, they also experience periods of very high mood. These periods are called manic episodes, which the ICD-11 defines as 'an extreme mood state lasting at least one week unless shortened by a treatment intervention' (World Health Organization, 2018).

Symptoms include **euphoria**, irritability and expansiveness, meaning they may have an inflated sense of self-importance (grandiosity) and behave in an overly enthusiastic, friendly, flamboyant or exuberant manner. They may be highly active or have a subjective sense of increased energy. Rapid speech may reflect rapidly changing thoughts and ideas. There may be decreased need for sleep and the person may be easily distracted, impulsive and reckless. In bipolar disorder, the person may alternate between depressive and manic episodes that last a week or more or they may experience mixed episodes where aspects of both mania and depression may be apparent within the same day or week. Bipolar disorder is characterised by lability of mood, which refers to the changeability and intensity with which moods may be experienced and expressed.

People with a diagnosis of bipolar (type 2) experience the same intensity of depressive episodes as people with bipolar disorder (type 1) but they tend to experience hypomanic rather than manic episodes. The prefix 'hypo-' means under or below and in this context means that the person does not experience full-blown manic episodes as described above but some of the symptoms may be present in an attenuated (less intense) form. Type 2 is also diagnosed when the person's daily functioning is less impaired and they are still coping relatively well in different areas of their life.

Other mood disorders

Further to the disorders mentioned in this chapter, it may be helpful to know of other disorders beyond the ones required by the syllabus. **Dysthymia** may be diagnosed when a person experiences depressive symptoms for much of the time but never quite reaches the threshold for a diagnosis of a depressive episode. Similarly, **cyclothymia** may be diagnosed if a person experiences numerous **hypomanic** episodes and depressive symptoms within a two-year period. Unlike the disorders above, people with these conditions have little respite between episodes and experience symptoms more of the time than not. Although the symptoms may be less intense, they are relentless and as such have a significant impact on daily functioning.

Measure of depression: Beck Depression Inventory

Typically, diagnoses are made following detailed **clinical interviews**, using interview schedules that are based on the guidelines stated in the ICD (and/or DSM). Interviews gather qualitative data, but doctors may also use **psychometric tests** (see page 186) to gauge the range, intensity and duration of a person's symptoms. These tests gather quantitative data and are a good example of the **nomothetic approach** in clinical psychology.

One such test is the **Beck Depression Inventory (BDI)**, named after its creator, Aaron Beck (see page 272). This test can only be used with people over the age of 13 and, when answering, people should think about the last two weeks, including the day the test is taken. It comprises 21 items (e.g. self-dislike, pessimism and indecisiveness) and takes around 5–10 minutes to complete (see extract in Table 6.5). The test helps to determine the severity of a person's symptoms. For example, a score of 14–19 is common in people with mild depression, 20–28 moderate depression and 29–63 severe depression (Gebrie, 2018). This test was designed to be used by qualified health professionals; if you complete the test online and feel like you need some support, see the advice at the end of this chapter.

▼ Table 6.5 Extract from the Beck Depression Inventory

1.	Sadness
	0. I do not feel sad.
	1. I feel sad much of the time.
	2. I am sad all the time.
	3. I am so sad or unhappy that I can't stand it.
2.	Pessimism
	0. I am not discouraged about my future.
	1. I feel more discouraged about my future than I used to.
	2. I do not expect things to work out for me.
	3. I feel my future is hopeless and will only get worse.
3.	Past failure
	0. I do not feel like a failure.
	1. I have failed more than I should have.
	2. As I look back, I see a lot of failures.
	3. I feel I am a total failure as a person.

The questions in Table 6.5 are from the Beck Depression Inventory (Beck *et al.*, 1996). Can you think of any reasons why the data gathered from a test like this might be invalid?

Evaluating the Beck Depression Inventory

One strength of the BDI, as a psychometric measure of depressive symptoms, is that evidence suggests that it is both reliable and valid. It has excellent test–retest reliability for people tested twice, one week apart. In one study, scores on the BDI were positively correlated with scores on another well-respected test of depression, the Hamilton Psychiatric Rating Scale for Depression (Arbisi, 2001; Farmer, 2001). This is important as it suggests that the BDI provides useful, meaningful and accurate information about depressive symptoms.

Another strength is that the BDI is quick to administer, yet it provides precise and accurate data. For these reasons, it is widely used by both researchers and clinicians to assess the efficacy of treatments such as antidepressants and cognitive-behavioural therapy (CBT). The speed at which it can be completed makes it particularly popular as time is often extremely limited in real-world settings (Piotrowski and Keller, 1989).

A weakness of the BDI is that it relies on self-reported data which may be provided during a semi-structured interview with a doctor. The doctor may then complete the BDI based on the participants' answers. This means that the data may be affected by social desirability bias – that is, information may be withheld or the person may exaggerate their symptoms if they believe this will lead to better services or support. These factors reduce the validity of the test, limiting its usefulness as a measure of depression.

ISSUES AND DEBATES

Individual versus situational explanations

A weakness of psychometric tests such as the BDI is that they collect purely quantitative data with the objective of deciding upon the extent to which a person's symptoms match agreed definitions of depression. This approach assumes that depression resides with the person, reflecting an individual approach to diagnosis rather than collecting qualitative data about the context in which the person is experiencing their symptoms. Modern approaches to diagnosis, e.g. Lucy Johnstone's trauma-informed approach focus on psychological formulation, a technique that involves gathering detailed information, about the person *and* the situation in order to develop individualised treatment plans based on each person's specific personal, social and cultural needs. Psychological formulations are derived from listening carefully to the patient, allowing them to tell their story 'in their own words'. This means the information they provide is less likely to be distorted due to the use of questions that are based on someone else's experiences and/or assumptions.

Evaluating the diagnostic criteria

One strength is that clinicians are able to arrive at reliable diagnoses of mood disorders using the ICD-11. In a study involving nearly 2000 participants and more than 300 clinicians from 13 countries, high levels of agreement between independent raters were found for diagnoses of bipolar disorder (type 1) (84 per cent) and recurrent depressive disorder (74 per cent). Reliable diagnosis is an essential step in accessing the best treatment and support; so far it appears that ICD-11 is superior to ICD-10 in this respect (Reed *et al.*, 2018).

Despite impressive results for some mood disorders, others returned less favourable results; this is a weakness of ICD-11. For example, clinicians were less likely to agree when diagnosing bipolar (type 2) (62 per cent) than bipolar (type 1) (74 per cent) and dysthymic disorder returned a relatively low rate of agreement of just 45 per cent (Reed *et al.*, 2018). This suggests that some mood disorders are harder to diagnose than others, questioning the utility of these labels from a practical point of view.

► LEARNING LINKS

Like the BDI, several of the studies that you examined at AS Level also collected self-reported quantitative data. Can you think of any? If you can, then some of the evaluation points you made may also be relevant here, and vice versa. For example, questionnaires that include many items formatted in a similar way (rating scales), such as the Five Facets of Mindfulness Questionnaire and the Autism Spectrum Quotient, sometimes lead to a response set where people give the same answer to a whole set of questions, without really considering their answers. This means the data lacks validity. This criticism has also been levelled at the Beck Depression Inventory.

ISSUES AND DEBATES

Cultural differences

A strength of the ICD-11 is that cultural differences in depressive symptoms are acknowledged. Although the focus is on affective and cognitive symptoms of depression, clinicians are informed that in many low-to-middle-income countries (LMICs) people may be more likely to report somatic (bodily) symptoms such as aches and pains (Sharan and Hans, 2021). The inclusion of this information means clinicians are more informed and so can diagnose more rapidly and with greater sensitivity.

STUDY TIP

Negative thoughts and feelings can be a real nuisance when you are studying. The body's physiological stress response can interfere with your ability to concentrate. This can make further study counterproductive as you become increasingly worried about your inability to take information in. Building in regular breaks for fresh air, water and a laugh with your family or a friend could make all the difference. If you find yourself becoming overwhelmed, step away from the books or the screen and take some time to relax and unwind. Investing an hour or so in self-care (whether it is watching a film or kicking a ball around) may actually pay back on results day!

TEST YOURSELF

1 Describe two symptoms of bipolar disorder and explain how they might affect a person's functioning in everyday life. [4]
2 Outline one similarity and one difference between depressive disorder (unipolar) and bipolar disorder. [2]
3 a Describe the diagnostic criteria (ICD-11) of mood disorders. [6]
  b Evaluate the diagnostic criteria (ICD-11) of mood disorders, including a discussion of psychometrics. [10]
4 Explain one strength and one weakness of the use of quantitative data to measure depressive symptoms, such as using the Beck Depression Inventory. [4]
5 Explain one way that a diagnosis of depression could be checked for reliability. [2]
6 With reference to the BDI, outline what is meant by psychometrics. [2]

6.2.2 Explanations of mood (affective) disorders: depressive disorder (unipolar)

Biological explanations

KEY TERMS

serotonin
transporter molecules
noradrenaline
monoamine hypothesis
monoamine oxidase
association analysis

METHODOLOGY

reliability
experiments

Think!

Which gene has been linked to **serotonin** reuptake (i.e. the development of **transporter molecules** on the presynaptic cell)? And which gene is linked to the development of serotonin receptor sites on the postsynaptic cell?

Think!

Imagine you are a molecule of serotonin. You live in the brain of someone who is always happy and has never experienced a depressive episode. What is life like for you? Can you describe a day in the life of a serotonin molecule? Now, imagine how life might be different for your cousin, a serotonin molecule who lives in the brain of someone with either (a) bipolar disorder or (b) recurrent depressive episodes.

Think!

Considering what you have learned on these pages, what ideas do you have about ways of treating depression? Try to think of some possible ways you could increase the availability of serotonin using drugs but also some lifestyle changes that could decrease depressive symptoms.

Can you redraw Figure 6.17 and show how it might look for someone with:

a low tryptophan levels

b low stress levels?

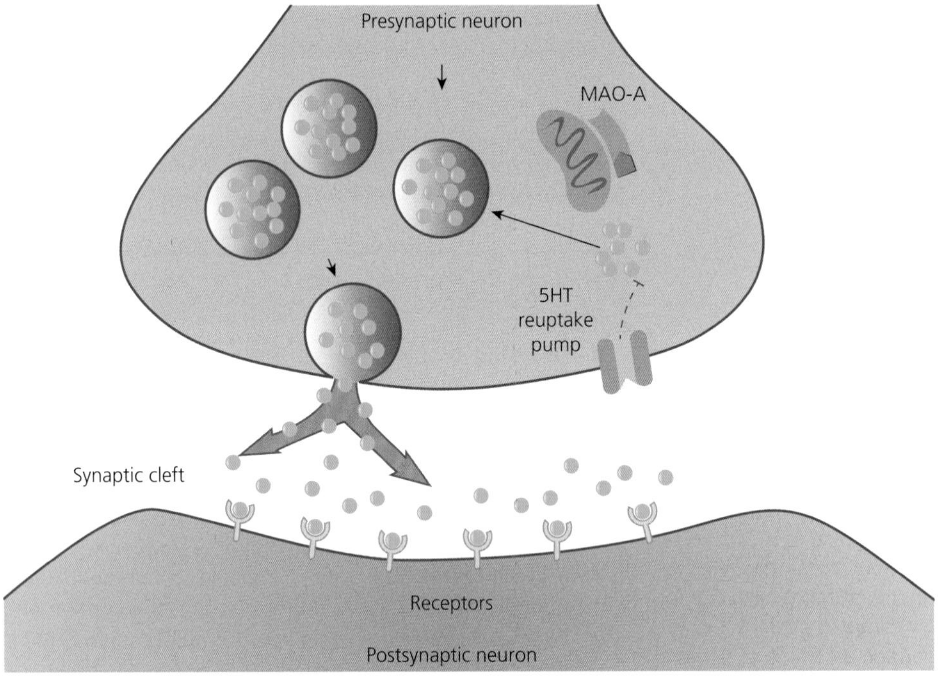

Presynaptic neuron

MAO-A

5HT reuptake pump

Synaptic cleft

Receptors

Postsynaptic neuron

▲ Figure 6.17 This diagram shows molecules of serotonin contained in vesicles on the presynaptic cells before they have been released. You can also see a 5HT reuptake pump (transporter molecule) in the presynaptic membrane.

Biochemical

Monoamine hypothesis

Early biochemical explanations of mood disorders focused on **noradrenaline**, a neurotransmitter which is central to the communication of neurons in the brain's emotion centres, such as the amygdala, hypothalamus and hippocampus (Schildkraut, 1965). Researchers had observed that **reserpine** (a drug used to treat high blood pressure) causes depression as a side effect. As this drug reduces noradrenaline levels, noradrenaline **deficiency** was proposed as a potential cause of depression. Next, researchers turned their attention to another neurotransmitter, serotonin (e.g. Prange *et al.*, 1974). This neurotransmitter had been found to control noradrenaline levels. Thus, an imbalance of serotonin could allow noradrenaline levels to drop, leading to a depressive episode. Alternatively, if serotonin allowed noradrenaline levels to become too high it could lead to manic episodes. Noradrenaline and serotonin are called 'monoamines', so together these ideas are referred to as the **monoamine hypothesis**.

Serotonin imbalances

Serotonin levels can rise and fall for numerous reasons. For example, changes in diet could affect mood as serotonin is created from an amino acid called **tryptophan**, which is found in certain foods. Production can also be inhibited by cortisol, a hormone associated with chronic stress (Dinan, 1994).

Problems with the receptor sites on the postsynaptic cell could also interfere with the communication between neighbouring neurons. For example, receptors may become over-sensitive, particularly when serotonin levels are low. As mentioned on page 244, the postsynaptic cell may also attempt to compensate for low levels of serotonin by creating more receptors (upregulation), but this can create more problems than it solves!

Following transmission, serotonin is absorbed back into the presynaptic cell via transporter molecules in the presynaptic cell membrane. Problems with these molecules can mean serotonin is either not cleared out of the synapse effectively or, if it is taken back into the presynaptic cell too readily, it can reduce the availability of serotonin molecules for binding on the postsynaptic cell. Serotonin levels may also fall if we have too much **monoamine oxidase**, an enzyme that breaks down serotonin.

Evaluating the biochemical explanation

One strength of the biochemical explanation is that it is supported by research evidence. For example, Moreno *et al.* (1999) reduced participants' tryptophan levels using a chocolate-flavoured drink in an attempt to experimentally reduce serotonin production. They found a significant increase in depressive symptoms measured using the Hamilton Depression Scale (HAM-D) in the 24 hours following the drink in people with a history of depression and an age- and gender-matched control group. Experimental research such as this supports the idea that depression may be related to a deficiency of serotonin. The use of a control group increases internal validity and helps to establish a cause and effect relationship between the reduction in tryptophan and the subsequent increase in depressive symptoms.

> ## ISSUES AND DEBATES

Nature versus nurture

A weakness of the biochemical explanation is that its focus on nature means that the role of nurture is undervalued. For example, Raleigh *et al.* (1984) found that a change in social status from dominant to subordinate caused a reduction in serotonin of approximately 40 per cent in adult vervet monkeys. The new leader experienced an increase in serotonin of around 60 per cent. An awareness of the interaction between biochemical and environmental factors can lead to a more holistic understanding of depression, and this is critical when thinking about treatment options.

Determinism versus free will

A weakness is that the monoamine hypothesis is overly deterministic, suggesting that everyone responds in the same way to alterations to neurochemicals like serotonin and noradrenaline. Yet, this is not the case. Contrary to previous research, Strickland *et al.* (2002) found that depressed women had higher serotonin levels than non-depressed women. This suggests individual differences resulting from complex interactions between dozens of genes cannot be ignored and our personal vulnerability to depression cannot always be predicted from current biochemical levels.

Genetic

Biopsychologists believe our thoughts, feelings and behaviours are determined by signals passed between clusters of neurons in our nervous systems. Genes provide the instructions that dictate how these networks develop, meaning depressive or manic episodes may be determined via genetic inheritance and/or mutations occurring during cell division.

Twin studies

In an enormous twin study (n=>42,000), Kendler *et al.* (2006) found a concordance rate of 44 per cent for female monozygotic (MZ) twins compared with only 16 per cent for female dizygotic (DZ) twins, and rates of 31 per cent for male MZ twins and 11 per cent for male DZ twins. This suggests that depression has a genetic component but that the condition is more heritable in females. Bipolar disorder appears to be more heritable than unipolar depression, returning rates of 62 per cent concordance in MZ twins compared with just 8 per cent for DZ twins (Bertelsen *et al.*, 1977).

Candidate genes

Given the huge amount of evidence highlighting the role of serotonin in the development of mood disorders, genetic research has focused on genes that code for postsynaptic serotonin receptors (e.g. **5-HT2c**) and presynaptic transporter molecules (e.g. **5-HTT**; see Key study: Oruč *et al.*, 1997, page 267). The 5-HTT gene, for example, has a polymorphism that results in two different alleles, identified by their length, short and long. Individuals who inherit two short alleles have an increased risk of depression following a stressful life event than those who inherit either two long alleles or a combination of both. Caspi *et al.* (2003) found that people carrying two copies of the short allele were more likely to become depressed following a stressful life event than people carrying one short allele, or two long alleles. The more negative life events the person had faced, the stronger the effect. Despite strong evidence of a genetic component, large **genome wide association studies (GWAS)** have failed to identify consistent patterns of genes associated with depression (Hek *et al.*, 2013).

 Nature and nurture

The genetics of depression, as with other disorders, is highly complex and may involve countless genes, each of which increase our vulnerability by a tiny degree. Moreover, gene expression is shaped by environmental factors and genes may be switched 'on' and 'off' according to our changing life circumstances; it is this level of complexity that makes it difficult to predict phenotype from a knowledge of genotype alone.

Evaluating genetic explanations

ISSUES AND DEBATES

Nature versus nurture

One weakness of the genetic explanation of mood disorders is that twin studies such as Kendler *et al.* (2006) and Bertelsen *et al.* (1977) assume that differences in concordance rates are due to differences in the quantity of shared DNA, but these differences may, in fact, result from differences in how MZ and DZ twin pairs are treated by others. As MZ twins look similar and are always the same sex, they are likely to be treated more similarly to each other than DZ twins. This makes it difficult to establish whether shared genes (nature) or aspects of the shared environment (nurture) are responsible for the higher concordance rates seen in MZ twin pairs.

A further weakness of the genetic argument is that adoption studies support the role of nurture in the development of mood disorders. For example, Kendler *et al.* (2018) found an increased risk for depression in adoptive children where the adoptive parent had depression. This is important as the child and parent do not share DNA yet share the same diagnosis. This suggests that the transmission of depression is not always due to genetic inheritance but may also result from differences in upbringing and exposure of family members to similar stressors.

This said, adoption studies also support the genetic explanation of bipolar disorder. For example, 31 per cent of biological parents of adopted children with bipolar disorder had also been diagnosed with a mood disorder, compared with only 12 per cent of adoptive parents (Mendlewicz and Rainer, 1977). This suggests that, although environmental factors have a role to play, genetic inheritance does increase vulnerability to mood disorders.

Cultural differences

A final strength is that progress has been made with regards to identifying specific genes linked to some of the subtypes of depression, such as recurrent and early onset. For example, a study involving more than 10,000 Chinese women revealed significant associations between recurrent depression and two genes called SIRT1 and LHPP (CONVERGE Consortium, 2015). Interestingly, though, this finding did not replicate in women of European heritage, illustrating another layer of complexity in the genetics of depression (Hyde *et al.*, 2016).

LEARNING LINKS

Think back to the biological approach from AS Level and you will remember the study by Hölzel *et al.* (mindfulness and brain scans). The participants in this study underwent Mindfulness-Based Stress Reduction (MBSR). Stress increases cortisol production, which inhibits serotonin production in regions such as the hippocampus, meaning interventions that reduce stress should increase serotonin production by reducing cortisol. Research has shown that mindfulness training can lead to epigenetic effects specific to the 5-HTT gene and this research helps to explain how this intervention improves psychological wellbeing (Stoffel *et al.*, 2019).

STUDY TIP

If you find it difficult to remember the names of the different genes or neurotransmitters and what they do, just spend some time coming up with your own way to remember them by creating a silly image, rhyme or link between the name and the function. For example, the gene that causes problems with reuptake is called 5-HTT, you could think of it as the 'troublesome transport' gene. As long as you know that transporter molecules take serotonin out of the synapse and back into the presynaptic cells then all is well! You could think of these molecules like a taxi (T for transport, T for taxi and T for 5-HTT), taking serotonin home after a day out in the synapse!

► TEST YOURSELF

1   a   Outline what is meant by determinism versus free will.   [2]

    b   Explain one strength of one biological explanation for depressive disorders from the determinism side of the debate.   [2]

2   Gray is a school teacher. He has been diagnosed with unipolar depression. Explain how two symptoms of this disorder might affect Gray's daily life.   [4]

3   a   Describe the neurochemical explanation of depressive disorder.   [6]

    b   Evaluate the neurochemical explanation of depressive disorder, including a discussion of reductionism versus holism.   [10]

4   Some people believe that depressive disorders are determined by aspects of our biology.

    Plan a laboratory experiment to investigate one biological explanation of mood disorders. Your plan must include details about sampling technique and a directional or non-directional hypothesis.   [10]

5   For one piece of psychological knowledge that has informed your plan:

    a   Describe this psychological knowledge.   [4]

    b   Explain how two features of this psychological knowledge informed your plan.   [4]

Key study: Association analysis of the 5-HT2C receptor and 5HT transporter genes in bipolar disorder – Oruč *et al.* (1997)

Introducing Lilijana Oruč

Lilijana Oruč is Professor of Neuropsychiatry and Clinical Psychiatry at the Sarajevo School of Science and Technology Medical School, in Bosnia and Herzegovina, in south-eastern Europe. She has more than 35 years of experience and has published approximately 170 papers and authored and co-authored numerous books about biological and clinical psychiatry. She guest lectures at many universities and regularly participates in conferences, workshops and seminars. In addition, she supervises masters and doctorate students and serves on the editorial board of many professional journals.

KEY TERMS

polymorphism

heterozygotic

genetic heterogeneity

METHODOLOGY

reliability

experiments

Think!

Which allele was more common in females with bipolar than females without bipolar? Why was this result unusual compared with the other results?

Think!

Imagine a friend has just found out that her identical twin sister has bipolar disorder. Thinking about what you have learned from Oruč *et al.*'s study, should she be concerned for her own mental health?

Think!

The study by Oruč *et al.* (1997) is not an experiment as there is no manipulation of an **independent variable** (i.e. genotype was a naturally occurring variable) and there is no control of factors that might have affected the development of bipolar disorder, yet the study is still highly scientific. What features of the study make it scientific?

Oruč *et al.* (1997) extracted DNA from blood tests to determine their participants' genotype. They wanted to know whether certain alleles were more common in people with bipolar disorder. What do their findings tell us about the debate about nature versus nurture?

▲ Figure 6.18

Context

Selecting candidate genes

Biochemical research had already underlined the importance of serotonin in mood disorders and suicidal behaviour, so genetic research began to focus on candidate genes known to code for proteins involved in serotonergic transmission in the central nervous system.

The serotonin antagonist clozapine has great **affinity** for 5-HT2c receptors on the postsynaptic cell and Oruč *et al.* note that these receptors are also linked with appetite control. As appetite is frequently disrupted in major depressive episodes, Oruč *et al.* suggest that bipolar disorder may also be linked to irregularities of these receptors. Research into antidepressant drugs had also revealed that problems with the serotonin transporter protein 5-HTT may increase vulnerability to mood disorders (see page 343).

▶ AIM

This study aimed to determine whether specific polymorphisms of two genes associated with serotonin transmission (5-HT2c and the 5-HTT gene) were more common in people with bipolar disorder.

▶ METHODOLOGY

This study investigated whether there is a difference in the alleles for two specific candidate genes in people with and without bipolar disorder. The researchers examined the frequency of these alleles using blood samples from people with and without a diagnosis of bipolar disorder (type 1), assessed via diagnostic interview and hospital case notes.

Sample

All participants were Croatian and recruited via opportunity sampling. The researchers recruited 25 females and 17 males, aged 31–70, with bipolar disorder (type 1), from psychiatric hospitals in Zagreb, Croatia. The average age of onset was 32. Medical records showed that 16 of the participants had at least one first-degree relative (i.e. a parent or sibling) with a mood disorder.

An age- and sex-matched control group of 25 females and 15 males were also recruited via opportunity sampling of hospital staff, friends and family. None had first-degree relatives with a psychiatric diagnosis.

PROCEDURE

Blood samples were analysed to see which alleles participants were carrying for two specific genes: the **serotonin receptor 2c gene (5-HTR2c)**, which codes for a specific type of serotonin receptor, and the **serotonin transporter gene (5-HTT)**, which codes for the serotonin transporters. Each gene had two possible alleles; the alleles of the 5-HTR2c gene are called Cys (C) and Ser (S), while the 5-HTT alleles are referred to as 1 and 2.

RESULTS

The researchers found that there was no significant difference in the specific polymorphisms of interest on either of the genes; however, they did find some sex differences in allele frequency. Firstly, there was a difference in the distribution of the S allele of the 5-HTR2c gene; this was somewhat more common in females with bipolar disorder than the female controls. Also, it is interesting to note that this was only the case with **heterozygotic** females (CS). Furthermore, the females with bipolar were slightly more likely to carry allele 1 of the 5-HTT gene than the female controls.

CONCLUSIONS

This study focused on two specific polymorphisms of genes associated with serotonergic function but neither appear to play a major role in increasing vulnerability to bipolar disorder. This said, the study suggests that females may be more vulnerable to genetic alterations to serotonergic transmission.

How does the idea of a genotype relate to the debate around free will and determinism? Does free will have a role to play in conditions like bipolar disorder? This study is all about our genes, specifically it is about the pairs of alleles we inherit from our parents, our genotype.

Life is like a game of cards. The hand that is dealt you represents determinism; the way you play it is free will

▲ Figure 6.19

Methodological strengths and weaknesses

One strength was that all participants were carefully assessed to check that they reached the criteria for a diagnosis of bipolar disorder (type 1). Two experienced psychiatrists assessed each patient using a Croatian language version of the Schedule for Affective Disorders and Schizophrenia-Lifetime Version (SADS-L). This was important as this disorder is difficult to diagnose due to the overlaps between bipolar disorder, schizoaffective disorder and other mood disorders.

Another strength is that the findings strengthen the reliability of other studies. For example, Oruč *et al.* replicated the findings of a study by Gutiérrez *et al.* (1996), who also found no significant difference between people with bipolar disorder and healthy controls with regard to allele or genotype frequency for the 5-HTR2c receptor gene. Likewise, Oruč *et al.* replicated the non-significant findings of Kelsoe *et al.* (1996) with regard to the 5-HTT gene. This is important as replication is an important hallmark of scientific research.

A weakness is the small sample size, which meant there was not a good spread of people with different versions of the alleles of interest. For example, there were only three people (all male) with the SS genotype of the 5-HTR2c gene. This is important as it means the importance of these genes may have been overlooked and this is why replication is so crucial, even in studies where the null hypothesis was accepted.

Ethics

Studies like Oruč *et al.* (1997) present a range of ethical issues, including the importance of informed consent and confidentiality. In order to protect the participants from psychological harm, it would have been important that participants fully understood what the researchers were testing for and the implications of discovering that they were carrying a certain combination of alleles – for example, that bipolar disorder is polygenic and the results cannot tell them whether they are at increased risk of the disorder due to the complex interaction with other genes and environmental factors.

Application to everyday life

A strength of this study is that increased understanding of the genetic underpinning of disorders like bipolar may gradually help to improve drug treatments. Due to the complex **genetic heterogeneity** of the disorder, it is likely that personalised drug treatments matching the person's genome will provide the most effective therapy. This emerging field is known as pharmacogenomics and could revolutionise care for people with bipolar disorder, although this is still a long way off at present (Pisanu *et al.*, 2018).

> **ISSUES AND DEBATES**
>
> **Reductionism versus holism**
>
> Studies such as Oruč *et al.* (1997) could be accused of biological **reductionism** as they examine single genes, and in this case specific polymorphisms which may affect synaptic transmission. This study does not examine epigenetic factors, which can affect whether a gene is expressed or silenced, and a more **holistic** examination of the interaction between specific genotypes and environmental risk factors could provide richer insight into the contribution of these genes to bipolar disorder.

> **REFLECTION**
>
> - Having considered the findings of Oruč *et al.*, how do you think researchers should move forward; should they continue to study these two genes or move onto something new?
> - If you could ask Oruč one question about her research study, what would it be and why?

> **LEARNING LINKS**
>
> You will look at a variety of genetic explanations and studies throughout this chapter, including in your studies of anxiety and fear-related disorders (page 307) and obsessive-compulsive disorder (page 346). For this reason, it is worth investing the extra time now to ensure that you feel completely comfortable with this section.

> **STUDY TIP**
>
> The vocabulary of genetics can be difficult to remember; why not create a collage or illustration to help you remember the difference between some of the important terminology, The online glossary is there to help you. You could also play a game with coloured sweets and a dice to help you think about the ways in which different alleles are passed from parents to children and how the alleles come together to create a new genotype, which may mean that the person is more or less vulnerable to bipolar disorder. Remember though, Oruč *et al.* (1997) suggest that the S allele of the 5-HTR2c gene and 1 allele of the 5-HTT gene only increased vulnerability for this disorder in females.

TEST YOURSELF

1 Describe the aim of the study by Oruč *et al.* (1997) investigating the genetics of bipolar disorder. [2]
2 Describe two findings of Oruč *et al.* (1997). [4]
3 a Describe the study by Oruč *et al.* (1997) on the genetics of bipolar disorder. [6]
  b Evaluate the study by Oruč *et al.* (1997), including a discussion of determinism versus free will. [10]
4 Outline one strength and one weakness of the sampling technique used in Oruč *et al.* (1997). [4]
5 Outline one feature of the study by Oruč *et al.* (1997) that improved the reliability of the findings. [2]
6 Describe what is meant by reductionism. You must refer to the study by Oruč *et al.* (1997) in your answer. [3]

Psychological explanations of mood (affective) disorders

KEY TERMS

catastrophising
arbitrary inference
pessimism/optimism
negative cognitive triad
dichotomous
personalising

METHODOLOGY

reliability
experiments

Think!

What do you understand by the terms **catastrophising** and **arbitrary inference**?

Think!

Do you ever think in the **pessimistic** way that Seligman describes? Many people do. If this is something you do a great deal, imagine that these thoughts belong to someone you really care about. How would you help them to think differently? When you catch yourself thinking pessimistically again, be kind to yourself, and offer yourself an alternative way of thinking if you can.

Think!

Seligman *et al.* (1988) compared data from two groups of people with depressive symptoms who received therapy and one control group with no depressive symptoms. Can you think of another control that could have been used that would have improved the design even further?

Can you think of any ways of disrupting or interfering with negative automatic thinking, to break the chain? Negative thoughts can trigger sadness and feelings of worthlessness. People become pessimistic and passive, believing nothing will change ('giving up').

▲ Figure 6.20 Dr Aaron Beck

Beck's cognitive theory of depression

Dr Aaron Beck states that depressive symptoms are caused by negative thoughts, linked to dysfunctional (unhelpful) core beliefs (Beck, 1962). The more negative thoughts a person has, the worse their symptoms. Depressed people hold negative beliefs about the self, the world and the future, such as 'I am worthless', 'Everything is doomed to failure', 'The future is hopeless/Nothing will ever change'. Together these three areas are called the **negative cognitive triad** (Figure 6.21).

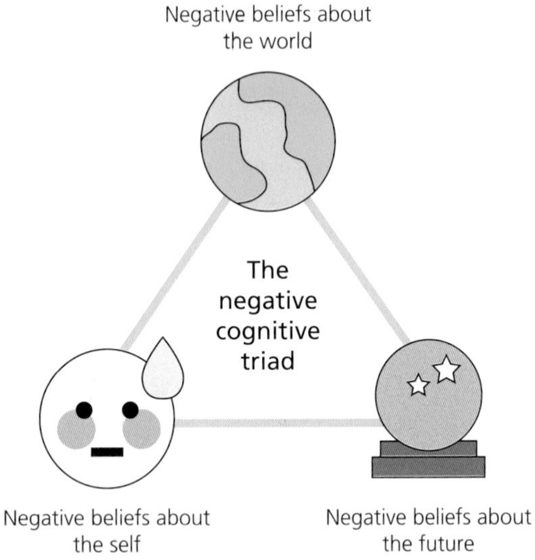

Negative beliefs about the world

The negative cognitive triad

Negative beliefs about the self

Negative beliefs about the future

▲ Figure 6.21

These beliefs develop in childhood as a result of experiences of criticism and/or rejection from important people in their lives, including parents, peers and/or teachers. Neglect, abuse, bullying, bereavement and other experiences of loss, even overprotective parenting, all contribute to the development of negative core beliefs. Later in life, these beliefs affect how people select information from the world for further processing. Evidence that does not match their beliefs is filtered out and evidence that confirms their negative views is focused upon and stored. The importance of negative information is exaggerated (magnified) and the importance of contradictory evidence is minimised – for example, 'I only got a good grade because my teacher felt sorry for me.'

Beck also discusses a number of cognitive biases or faulty thinking patterns that can increase the risk of depression. These biases may occasionally affect everyone, but people who are vulnerable to depression tend to use them consistently and automatically in comparison with those who are less vulnerable. See 'Faulty thinking strategies' for examples of these biases.

Faulty thinking strategies
Do you do any of these? Rate each one from 1 to 10 (1: 'I never do this', to 10: 'I do this every day').
» **Dichotomous thinking** ('all or nothing'): classifying events into two categories with no middle ground, such as success and failure. Sometimes called 'black or white' thinking.
» **Arbitrary inferences:** drawing negative conclusions in the absence of sufficient supporting evidence. This can lead people to make assumptions about what other people think about them ('mind reading') and how things will turn out in the future ('fortune telling'). Also linked to over-generalising – for example, not being offered a job leads the person to think they are unemployable.
» **Catastrophising:** something relatively insignificant triggers a flood of negative thoughts, resulting in overwhelming anxiety about worst-case scenarios. For example, you find a freckle you have not noticed before and end up terrified you have skin cancer, sick with worry about death and leaving behind family members with no-one to look after them.
» **Personalisation:** taking the blame for negative outcomes and failing to acknowledge situational factors, such as 'I was made redundant because I am useless', not due to the company's financial difficulties.

Learned helplessness/attributional style

Animal research

Following an initial experiment with dogs, Seligman proposed that depression in humans may be a learned response to a negative experience. The experimental dogs were classically conditioned (see page 87) to associate a neutral stimuli (e.g. a light) with an unavoidable electric shock. Next, they were tested to see how they would react to the light when placed in a new enclosure with a low barrier. If the dogs jumped the barrier, they could easily escape the electric shock, which was delivered through the enclosure floor. In comparison with a control group (dogs who could turn off the original shocks by pressing a panel with their noses), the experimental dogs made no attempt to escape (Maier and Seligman, 1976). The dogs had developed a negative expectation that anything they did to control the shocks would be hopeless and, therefore, passively accepted the situation. This overgeneralisation from the negative experience in the first enclosure is an example of learned helplessness.

▼ Table 6.6 Following the breakdown of a relationship, Person A is at greater risk of developing depression due to their pessimistic attributional style

Depression in humans

Seligman developed his theory of human depression based on these early experiments, believing that the way we **attribute** (reason about) our circumstances can be a cause of depressive symptoms. He explains that the attributional style of people who are vulnerable to depression differs from others in three ways. Depressed people make attributions that are internal, global and stable, whereas people who are unlikely to become depressed make attributions that are external, specific and unstable (see Table 6.6).

	Person A: Pessimistic	**Person B: Optimistic**
Personalisation	Internal: 'I wasn't good enough for them.'	External: 'We weren't spending enough time together.'
Global/specific	Global: 'My friends think it's my fault, I'm rubbish at my job, I'm going to fail my exams.'	Specific: 'At least I've got my friends, my job and I'm doing okay in school.'
Pervasiveness	Stable: 'I'm going to be single forever.'	Unstable: 'I'll meet someone new when I'm ready.'

Focus on: Seligman *et al.* (1988)

▶ AIM

Seligman *et al.* (1988) aimed to replicate previous research that showed a positive correlation between depressive attributional style and severity of depressive symptoms.

▶ METHODOLOGY

Fifty-one patients with mood disorder (39 unipolar and 12 bipolar) completed the Beck Depression Inventory (BDI) (see page 261) and the Attributional Style Questionnaire (ASQ), in which respondents make attributions about 12 hypothetical positive and negative events, plus various additional measures of mental health symptoms. Next, they completed six months of weekly cognitive therapy (average: 22.5 sessions). All were carefully diagnosed, and the data collection began with an interview using the Schedule for Affective Disorders and Schizophrenia (SADS). Thirty-two were reassessed within a month of their last therapy session. Twenty-six were followed up 12 months later. Findings were compared with those of a matched control group of non-depressed participants.

▶ RESULTS

There was a positive correlation between depressive attributions for negative events and severity of depressive symptoms before and after therapy, as well as at the follow-up assessment. This was true for both unipolar and bipolar disorder and scores were lower for pessimism in the non-depressed control group than the depressed group.

The greater the decrease in pessimism in therapy, the greater the improvement in depressive symptoms. Improvements in symptoms were impressive and stable over time. There was no significant difference in pessimism for people with unipolar versus bipolar disorder; however, pessimism was significantly higher in people with bipolar disorder who were high in trait-anxiety compared with those who were low in trait-anxiety.

There was also a link between pessimism scores at the end of therapy and risk of relapse at 12 months, even in those who had benefited a great deal from therapy. Finally, the study found that explanatory/attributional style was fairly stable over time in the control group, suggesting pessimism is a trait, not an effect of low mood or circumstances.

▶ CONCLUSIONS

People with both unipolar and bipolar disorder share a cognitive attributional style which favours internal, global and stable attributions of negative events in comparison with people without depression, but this tendency can be altered in therapy, and this is associated with greater probability of remission at 12 months.

Evaluating Seligman *et al.* (1988)

One strength was the use of a matched control group. This allowed the researchers to monitor the extent to which pessimism changes over time. This is important as it helps to provide evidence that pessimism is a stable trait as opposed to a reaction to one's current circumstances (state-pessimism). Evidence to support pessimism as a relatively fixed trait helps to support the cognitive explanation of depression – that depressed mood is a result of pessimism as opposed to a cause.

Another strength is the use of method triangulation. For example, depressive symptoms were rated on the BDI by the participants, but they were also rated by the clinicians who had observed the patients during the SADS interview. This is important as it means the measurement of depressive symptoms is more valid as it was assessed using more than one technique.

A weakness is the gender imbalance in the sample. There were 31 females but only 20 males. This means the findings should be generalised with caution as the relationship between pessimism and unipolar depression may differ in males in comparison with females.

Another weakness is that the dropout rate also reduces generalisability. Only 26 people from the original 39 completed the assessments at follow-up. This is important as they may not have been representative of the original sample or indeed of the target population. People who dropped out may have had more severe symptoms and the relationship between pessimism, depression, treatment efficacy and relapse may have been different had these people still been part of the final sample.

Evaluating the psychological explanations

One strength of attributional style as an explanation of depression is that it is supported by research evidence. For example, Seligman *et al.* (1988) found that severity of depressive symptoms decreased following a course of cognitive therapy which targeted pessimistic attributional style. This suggests that pessimism may have been a cause of the symptoms as when this thinking style was replaced with a more optimistic outlook, mood and other symptoms improved.

One weakness of depressive attributional style is that it may not be a cause of depression, it may be an effect. Although Seligman *et al.*'s study shows that changing from pessimism to optimism is followed by a reduction in depressive symptoms, the findings are correlational, and it is therefore impossible to say that therapy *caused* symptoms to decrease in severity.

How do the views of cognitive psychologists about depression fit with the debate around free will and determinism?

▶ Figure 6.22 According to cognitive psychologists, people with depression 'carry around' a great deal of negativity. These negative views of themselves, the world and the future are thought to result from early experiences

As you can see, there are multiple explanations of mood disorders and no one view is definitive. Viewing biological and psychological explanations separately makes little sense as we now understand that somatic (bodily), cognitive, affective and behavioural symptoms result from an interaction between biological and environmental factors, which affect how we interpret events in the world around us. Cognitive psychologists do not necessarily believe that biological factors are unimportant, however they may take a view that psychological therapies may be more effective than a purely medical approach. Likewise, biopsychologists may also value cognitive models recognising that drug treatments, for example, are often more effective when combined with cognitive therapy. These ideas will be explored further in the next section.

ISSUES AND DEBATES

Determinsim versus free will

Cognitive explanations of depression seems to suggest that depressive symptoms are inevitable in people with negative thinking biases, however this may not necessarily be the case. Those who believe in free will would argue that despite life experiences that may have predisposed us towards hopelessness, we always have the power to override this way of thinking; the success of cognitive behavioural therapy is evidence of this. This said, it must be remembered that many people face challenges in life, including discrimination and poverty that make it difficult, if not impossible, for them to access support and acceptance within their communities.

▶ LEARNING LINKS

At AS Level, you learned that cognitive psychologists take an information processing approach. They are interested in the input that we receive from the environment, which input we selectively attend to or filter out, how we organise the input in terms of what we already have stored in our long-term memory and finally how the input affects our subsequent output, or behaviour. Beck explains how information stored in long-term memory about ourselves, the world and the future can act as a lens through which we see the world. Depressed people may selectively attend to negative information about themselves, the world and the future. This then leads to selective memory as well, whereby depressed people tend to remember negative events better than positive ones, all strengthening their view of themselves and their lives as inferior and hopeless. On page 291, you will learn more about how cognitive therapy can adjust this negative bias.

STUDY TIP

If you are asked to evaluate any explanation in psychology, think: Evidence, Applications, Alternatives! You can evaluate the cognitive explanation of depression using evidence from Seligman *et al.*'s study – if you can show how this is *strong* evidence, then even better (a study is strong if it has good validity, reliability and generalisability) as strong evidence is a strength of the theory. Another way to evaluate a theory in Clinical Psychology is to show how the theory inspired an effective therapy. A final way is to compare the theory with an alternative, such as the biological explanation, and identify points that make one theory stronger than the other.

▶ TEST YOURSELF

1. Explain what is meant by attributional style. You should refer to one example. [4]
2. Faraji has unipolar depression. He has had an argument with his father. With reference to Beck's cognitive explanation of depression, outline two thoughts Faraji might have about the argument. [2]
3. a Describe one study that investigates the cognitive explanation of unipolar depression. [6]
   b Evaluate one study that investigates the cognitive explanation of unipolar depression, including a discussion of reliability. [10]
4. Studies of depression sometimes have a longitudinal design. Explain one weakness of longitudinal designs, with reference to one example from Clinical Psychology. [2]
5. The Beck Depression Inventory is a questionnaire that uses rating scales to collect quantitative data about severity of symptoms. Outline one strength of this type of questionnaire with reference to reliability. [2]
6. Angelika is planning to investigate the correlation between severity of depressive symptoms and the number of negative thoughts per day. Write a suitable directional hypothesis for Angelika's study. [2]

6.2.3 Treatment and management of mood (affective) disorders

Biological treatments

KEY TERMS

selective serotonin reuptake inhibitors (SSRIs)

monoamine oxidase inhibitors (MAOIs)

tricyclics

METHODOLOGY

generalisations from findings

Think!

Can you think of one similarity and one difference between **specific serotonin reuptake inhibitors (SSRIs)** and **monoamine oxidase inhibitors (MAOIs)**?

Think!

Imagine you are a doctor. A patient who you have known for a long time has developed moderate depression. You give them a prescription for an SSRI drug. How will you explain what you have prescribed to your patient? Don't just think about what you would say but also how you would say it, including your body language. Now think, how might your communication increase expectancy and potential placebo effects in your patient?

Think!

Biological treatments for depression are sometimes described as reductionist. Why do you think this is? How might this relate to relapse rates in comparison with other therapies, such as cognitive-behavioural therapy?

The antidepressant drugs outlined below are believed to affect the availability of monoamine neurotransmitters, such as serotonin, noradrenaline and dopamine.

Tricyclics

Tricyclics improve depressive symptoms by blocking serotonin transporter molecules (SERT) and noradrenaline transporter molecules (NET) in the presynaptic cell membrane. This means molecules of these neurotransmitters cannot be reabsorbed and remain in the synapse ready to bind to postsynaptic receptors. Some tricyclic drugs are more effective at binding SERT and some are better at binding to NET. This may be why certain tricyclics work better than others for some people. Tricyclics also bind to a range of different types of receptors, but this is not thought to increase their antidepressant effect and is in fact the reason that they have certain side effects.

MAOIs

MAOI stands for monoamine oxidase inhibitor. Serotonin, noradrenaline and dopamine are called monoamines and monoamine oxidase is an enzyme which breaks down these neurotransmitters following reabsorption by the transporter molecules in the presynaptic cell membrane. One way of increasing serotonin and noradrenaline levels is to stop monoamine oxidase from breaking down these molecules. This increases the amount of serotonin available for release into the synapse. There are two subtypes of MAO (enzyme), subtype A and subtype B. MAO-A is better at breaking down serotonin and noradrenaline whereas, MAO-B is better at breaking down dopamine. Drugs that inhibit MAO-A seem to have more of an antidepressant effect than those that block MAO-B.

Although MAOIs are effective in improving depressive symptoms, they are only used if other drugs have not worked. This is because they can have harmful interactions with other drugs and certain foods. MAOs in the gut break down monoamines from food. When they are inhibited, this can lead to a build-up of a substance called tyramine. This can increase the risk of a stroke, a dangerous medical condition where the blood supply to the brain is cut off. For this reason, it is very important that people taking MAOIs avoid certain foods that contain a lot of tyramine.

SSRIs

SSRI stands for selective serotonin reuptake inhibitor. These drugs work by increasing the amount of serotonin that is available to bind with 5HT receptors on the postsynaptic cell. The drug binds to serotonin transporter molecules (SERT) in the presynaptic cell membrane. This means that serotonin that has been released into the synapse cannot be reabsorbed for recycling and remains in the synapse. The reuptake process has therefore been inhibited. They are known as specific serotonin reuptake inhibitors as they only inhibit serotonin transporters, whereas some other similar drugs inhibit only noradrenaline transporters (SNRIs). A well-known example of an SSRI is fluoxetine, commonly known as Prozac. Later in this chapter, we look at the use of SSRIs as a treatment for other disorders, including generalised anxiety disorder and obsessive-compulsive disorder.

Evaluating the use of antidepressants

Research evidence

One strength of antidepressants is that research evidence suggests they are effective for many people. For example, Cipriani *et al.* (2018) found that all 21 of the drugs they investigated in a meta-analysis of 522 double-blind trials were more effective than placebos. This is important as this study included a very large sample of 116,477 participants, suggesting that drug treatments are effective in reducing depressive symptoms. This said, it should be noted that the people who take part in drug trials may not be representative of the wider population meaning that the findings may not be **generalisable**. For example, these people may have mild to moderate as opposed to severe symptoms otherwise it would not be safe for them to be taken off their existing medicines in order to enter the trial.

A weakness, however, is that the improvement in people's symptoms is relatively small. There are wide individual differences between drugs and some of the most effective drugs have the worst compliance rates. Furthermore, critics of antidepressants have questioned the very low level of improvement that is sometimes counted as clinically significant (i.e. just two points on the Hamilton Depression Rating Scale, HDRS; Hamilton, 1960), suggesting such small differences are likely to make little difference to patients in their day-to-day lives.

Supporters of antidepressants argue that scales such as the HDRS sometimes mask the true impact of antidepressants as they measure so many different symptoms. For example, Hieronymous *et al.* (2016) found that when the one core symptom of depressed mood was evaluated on its own, 90 per cent (29/32) of studies showed drug treatments outperformed placebos compared with just 44 per cent when all symptoms were considered. This suggests that antidepressants may be helpful in targeting some symptoms more than others.

> ## ISSUES AND DEBATES

Individual versus situational explanations

Critics of biological treatments for depression argue that the focus on the individual undermines the role of situational factors in creating stress and anxiety that can lead to depressive symptoms. Supporting a person to remove themselves from unjust and toxic situations may be sufficient to allow them to thrive and rebuild themselves without the need for medication. This suggests that support for people with depression needs to be more holistic and that practitioners need to take the time to find out what is happening in people's lives before suggesting a medical route.

Applications to everyday life

One weakness of SSRIs is that they can have some unpleasant side effects. For example, increased anxiety, insomnia, nausea and dizziness are common. Further problems include fatigue, headaches and weight gain. These issues mean that non-adherence in the early weeks, before the person starts to experience any improvement, can be a problem as they may decide to stop taking their medication, believing that the benefits will not outweigh the costs.

A further weakness of antidepressants is that relapse is common – that is, symptoms return for many people when they stop taking their medication. Factors affecting relapse have been difficult to identify but initial symptom severity is a risk factor. This is important as it means people may need to take a maintenance dose of their medication for at least six months to reduce the risk of a further depressive episode (Kato *et al.*, 2021).

Ethical issues

The controversy over the efficacy of antidepressants presents a variety of ethical issues, not least the need to protect people from physical and psychological harm. The global antidepressant industry is currently valued at around US$16 billion, and this is argued to lead to sponsorship bias and publication bias (Wang *et al.*, 2018b), whereby only studies that highlight the benefits of antidepressants are published. For example, Turner *et al.* (2008) showed that only 8 per cent of antidepressants trials that found negative results were published, compared with 97 per cent with positive results. Thirty per cent of studies with negative results were published with misleading results which made them appear positive. These findings suggest false hope may be given to patients and their families regarding the potential efficacy of drug treatments for depression.

This said, it should be noted that Driessen *et al.* (2015) highlight that publication bias has also led to an overestimation of the efficacy of psychological treatments, suggesting that the bias is towards publishing positive outcomes as opposed to promoting biological treatments versus psychological treatments.

Placebos and nocebos

A further fascinating finding about **placebos** is that people who have taken antidepressants in the past sometimes experience **nocebo** effects. This refers to negative outcomes that a person may experience if they expect certain side effects – for example, a person who thinks they have taken an antidepressant but has actually taken a placebo may experience headaches, fatigue and nausea. Professor Kirsch believes that the positive effects of antidepressants are primarily due to placebo effects and that studies that support their efficacy are often scientifically flawed (Kirsch, 2019). He advocates the use of exercise and psychotherapy to treat depression, saying they are safer and can lead to equally beneficial outcomes.

A placebo effect is a self-reported improvement in a person's symptoms that arises when the person believes they have taken an active drug (e.g. a pill containing an antidepressant). As they expect to get better, they start to actually feel better. Dr Irving Kirsch of Harvard Medical School explains that sometimes people even improve when they know they are taking a placebo drug! Impressive improvement on the HDRS can be achieved by either a placebo or the real antidepressant but the difference between the two is very small. Why do you think placebos are so effective at decreasing depressive symptoms?

▲ Figure 6.23

▶ LEARNING LINKS

At AS Level, you learned about classical conditioning, whereby a neutral stimulus can trigger a response over which we have no control. One possible explanation for the nocebo effect is that the appearance of the tablet, the packaging, the glass of water and so on have become powerful conditioned stimuli for patients who have taken antidepressants in the past. The act of taking a pill may have become associated with the unpleasant side effects of the real drugs and this means that, even if the person knows they are taking a placebo, they still experience the same involuntary bodily responses. Not everyone who has experienced a placebo effect has had previous experience with antidepressants though; how might cognitive and/or social psychologists explain the efficacy of antidepressants and/or placebos?

STUDY TIP

One way to evaluate biological treatments for depression is to make a comparison with psychological treatments, such as cognitive-behavioural therapy (CBT). The theme of your comparison could be about practical issues, ethical issues and/or the evidence supporting the efficacy of the treatment.

For example, you could say that: 'A weakness of antidepressants is that they can make you feel worse before you feel better and they take at least two weeks to work, whereas face-to-face support from an expert cognitive-behavioural therapist may be effective from the very first meeting.'

Remember, it is important to state why your point is important. For example, 'This is important because people often wait until they are at crisis point before seeking help from a doctor, meaning daily support in the early weeks may be critical.'

▶ **TEST YOURSELF**

1 Describe one practical issue relating to the use of monoamine oxidase inhibitors. [2]
2 Compare two biological treatments for mood (affective) disorders. [4]
3 a Describe one or more biological treatments for mood (affective) disorders. [6]
  b Evaluate one or more biological treatments for mood (affective) disorders, including a discussion of applications to everyday life. You must include research evidence in your answer. [10]
4 Studies investigating the efficacy of antidepressant drugs often use samples of people who are not representative of the wider population of people who seek help for depression. Explain one disadvantage of this. [2]
5 The Hamilton Depression Rating Scale (HDRS) is often used to evaluate the efficacy of drug treatments. The scale is to be completed following a structured interview and is made up of many rating scales.
  a Describe one strength of the HDRS as a measure of depressive symptoms. [2]
  b Describe one weakness of the HDRS as a measure of depressive symptoms. [2]
6 Randomised control trials (RCTs) are often used to investigate the efficacy of antidepressants. Explain two ways in which this design improves the validity of the findings. [4]

Psychological treatments and management of mood (affective) disorders

KEY TERMS

disputing
cognitive restructuring
rational emotive behaviour therapy (REBT)
psychoeducation
musturbation
cognitive flexibility

METHODOLOGY

generalisations from findings

Think!

What is meant by **disputing**?

Think!

Your friend, who has suffered from depression in the past, went for a job interview but they did not get the job. They are very upset and angry as they feel they had all the right experience and performed well in the interview. Imagine they are seeing a cognitive therapist; how might the conversation go? How might the conversation differ if the therapist used **cognitive restructuring** compared with **rational emotive behaviour therapy (REBT)**?

Think!

Can you think of any characteristics of the therapist that might affect the success of the therapy they deliver? Now think about why the efficacy of cognitive restructuring and REBT might be overexaggerated in research studies compared with people's experiences in real life.

▲ Figure 6.24 Socrates was an ancient Greek philosopher who wandered the streets asking people challenging questions to encourage them to reflect on their lives. Today, cognitive therapists use a technique called Socratic questioning to help their clients to reflect on their negative thoughts and reach fairer, more balanced conclusions

Beck's cognitive restructuring

Aaron Beck believed that depression is caused by irrational beliefs about the self, the world and the future. These beliefs affect how we interpret events in the world, and it is our interpretation of events that can lead to depressive symptoms. Beck used the term 'cognitive restructuring' to refer to the process of identifying and challenging negative thoughts. Cognitive therapists collaborate (work together) with their clients using many different techniques to support the restructuring process. For example:

» **psychoeducation** – the therapist teaches their client about the links between thoughts, feelings and behaviour and the problems that can result from cognitive distortions and faulty thinking patterns (see page 272)
» homework – the client must complete homework exercises between sessions, such as keeping a thought/mood diary to record their thoughts and feelings for discussion in their next session; the diary should help to increase awareness of situations that trigger negative thinking
» Socratic questioning – the therapist ask questions to help the client to analyse and reflect on their thoughts; together they will seek alternative explanations for negative attributions.

The overall goal is to help people to rely less on their dysfunctional beliefs and more on the available evidence when making attributions. Clients will be challenged to think about the evidence for and against their thoughts. The target is not to replace negativity with positivity, or pessimism with optimism, but to come to more objective, balanced views of the self, the world and the future. Throughout the restructuring process, the therapist will draw attention to the person's mood, such as how they feel when they are thinking differently.

Between five and twenty weekly sessions may be necessary to train the person to embed these new thinking strategies into their everyday life. Gradually, they should begin to reframe/restructure their thoughts without support from the therapist.

Rational emotive behaviour therapy

ABC model

Albert Ellis's cognitive explanation of depression is based on his ABC model: where A stands for activating events, B for beliefs and C for consequences. He believed that therapy should focus on our interpretation of events/situations, as opposed to focusing on the events themselves. The model helps explain the interactions between how we think, feel and act.

Musturbation

Based on his theory, Ellis developed rational emotive behaviour therapy (REBT) in 1955. He believed it was important to focus on the present not the past and to actively challenge self-defeating thoughts (ideas that stop us from reaching our potential). Like cognitive restructuring, REBT therapists work collaboratively with their clients to help them to reduce negative emotions (e.g. guilt, anger) and behaviours (e.g. aggression, overeating) through targeting unhelpful beliefs. REBT therapists help their clients to identify whether any of the three basic musts (see above) are affecting their happiness and day-to-day functioning. Ellis used the term **musturbation** to describe the way that some people allow 'the three musts' to control their thoughts, feelings, behaviour and ultimately their ability to enjoy life and contribute to society.

The three basic musts (Ellis, 1997)
People who place the following sorts of demands upon themselves and others often find themselves disappointed. Seeing them as goals rather than essential can help to ease some of the negative feelings and behaviours that are associated with these unhelpful beliefs:

1 People must approve of everything I do.
2 Other people must treat me well.
3 I must get what I want and not what I do not want.

On a scale of 1 to 10 (where 1 is 'not like me at all' and 10 is 'this is exactly like me'), how would you rate yourself on each of the three musts. How do you think these beliefs affect your wellbeing?

Disputing

REBT therapists use a technique called disputing (the D of the ABC model!) to reduce musturbation. The therapist will dispute the person's thoughts, asking them to provide evidence for why everything must be as their beliefs demand, such as 'Why must you win everyone's approval? What will happen if you don't?' The therapist will explore the person's answers until the person realises that their beliefs are irrational and the therapist's questions do not lead to logical answers. Gradually, the person will develop new alternative ways of thinking about their lives that do not lead to feelings of sadness. The end point of REBT is for clients to accept themselves, other people and their life, including all the good and bad points.

Evaluating cognitive restructuring

One strength of cognitive restructuring is that the risk of relapse following drug treatment is lower when the person has also received cognitive therapy than when antidepressants are used without additional cognitive therapy. For example, Fava *et al.* (1998) found that 75 per cent of people who had received cognitive restructuring in addition to antidepressants were symptom-free 24 months after treatment ended, compared with only 25 per cent of a matched group who received antidepressants but no cognitive therapy. This suggests that cognitive therapy can help to break the association between negative thinking and depressive symptoms as it provides people with the skills they need to combat negative thinking if and when it resurfaces.

ISSUES AND DEBATES

Individual and situational explanations

One weakness of cognitive restructuring is that it may be less effective for older adults. For example, Johnco *et al.* (2015) found that depressed adults aged 60–86 showed poorer **cognitive flexibility** (see page 282) than an age-matched control group. Cognitive flexibility was correlated with ability to restructure negative thoughts and those with weaker skills in these areas had greater subjective distress post-treatment. This suggests that a different approach to treatment may be required for older adults with poor cognitive flexibility. This said, cognitive restructuring may be effective for some older adults, as decreases in cognitive flexibility will depends not just on age but on situational factors such as availability of social support and engagement with intellectually stimulating hobbies, for example. Practitioners should be mindful of stereotyping clients due to gender, age or ethnicity and design treatment programmes that are personalised

not just to the individual but also to the social situation in which that person resides, otherwise the plan may be ineffective.

Applications to everyday life

One weakness of cognitive restructuring is that the success of the therapy may depend on the client's motivation to complete activities between sessions. For example, Neimeye *et al.* (2008) found that reduction in depressive symptoms was dependent upon interactions between willingness to complete homework, actual completion of homework (compliance) and skill acquisition (successfully being able to restructure negative thoughts). This is important as it means time should be invested in finding ways to make homework engaging for undermotivated clients, such as gamifying the activities so that people are rewarded for their progress.

Evaluating REBT

One strength of REBT is that it can be as effective as antidepressants for young people with depression. For example, Iftene *et al.* (2015) compared three groups of Romanian teenagers aged 11–17 (n=88): REBT, an SSRI (sertraline) and REBT plus sertraline. All groups showed increased serotonin and noradrenaline measured via blood tests and reduced negative automatic thoughts and depressive symptoms. This is important as the study demonstrates that REBT may be an effective alternative to drug treatments, which can cause unpleasant side effects leading to non-compliance.

One weakness of REBT is that the supporting studies have been shown to be flawed. For example, Lyons and Woods (1991) conducted a meta-analysis of 70 longitudinal studies of REBT. They found it to be as effective as other forms of therapy; however, they also comment that attrition may have affected the extent to which the findings can be generalised to other people with depression. Attrition refers to participant dropout, which can mean that the final sample is made up of people who attended the full number of therapy sessions. This means that REBT may be less effective for people who attend fewer sessions.

Ethical issues

One ethical issue with REBT is that Ellis's 'musts' suggest that people should accept the 'fact' that the world is not fair and that people do not always behave towards you in a fair manner. While this may be true, this does not empower people to challenge injustice, but rather to accept their place in an unjust society. This is important as, although adjusting our interpretation of negative events that have happened to us can be helpful, achieving justice can also be critical to the psychological recovery of people who have been victims of crime (e.g. Calton and Cattaneo, 2014).

REBT involves disputing or challenging people's core beliefs about themselves and the world; the therapeutic alliance, or relationship between therapist and client, is central to the way in which the client responds. How do you think factors such as the gender, age and ethnicity of both client and therapist affect the efficacy of REBT?

ISSUES AND DEBATES

Determinism versus free will

Cognitive therapists recognise the power of free will in helping people to overcome negative thinking biases that cause depression. They believe we have the power to take action and that through regular practice we can train our minds to overwrite long-standing thinking processes and challenge core beliefs that have previously fueled depressive symptoms. This challenges the deterministic view that depression is predestined by our genes and childhood experiences, granting people the opportunity to regain control and make potentially lasting changes in their lives.

Reductionism versus holism

As with each of the disorders discussed in this chapter, evidence suggests that taking a holistic (or eclectic) approach to treating depression may lead to the greatest reduction in symptoms and also help to reduce the risk of relapse. Combining the use of antidepressants with either REBT or cognitive restructuring may mean people are able to learn new skills and ways of thinking that will combat relapse while the antidepressants help to improve mood, sleep, motivation and concentration to a point where the person can benefit from therapy. This approach recognises the complex multi-factorial nature of depression that may be overlooked if a more reductionist approach is taken.

▶ LEARNING LINKS

Think back to the learning approach and the case study of the boy with the button phobia by Saavedra and Silverman (button phobia). When he started handling the buttons more, his distress increased and the researchers began using some techniques in addition to systematic desensitisation. Cognitive restructuring was used to target his irrational beliefs about buttons. Can you think of any reasons why cognitive restructuring in this situation might have been easier (or more difficult) than using it to treat depression?

Cognitive flexibility is a person's ability to change between cognitive tasks, such as applying a new or different rule when doing a task and/or retaining multiple items of information and switching attention between them. How could you measure cognitive flexibility in a way that was both reliable and ecologically valid?

▲ Figure 6.25

STUDY TIP

Throughout this chapter, you will learn about many types of psychological therapy. Some of these are very similar and could be easy to mix up.

Why not have a go at role-playing conversations between clients and therapists where you focus on key techniques, such as psychoeducation, discussing a **thought record**, musturbation or disputing?

If you film your work, you could create a webpage/blog or channel where you collect your examples together. Why not wear different coloured clothing for each of the different therapies, such as red for REBT and carrot-orange for cognitive restructuring?

If you are studying independently, you could write a script and create an animation.

▶ **TEST YOURSELF**

1   Explain what is meant by cognitive restructuring.   [4]
2   Compare two psychological treatments for mood (affective) disorders.   [4]
3   a   Describe one or more psychological treatments for mood (affective) disorders.   [6]
    b   Evaluate one or more psychological treatments for mood (affective) disorders, including a discussion of determinism versus free will. You must include research evidence in your answer.   [10]
4   a   Plan a longitudinal experiment to investigate the effectiveness of cognitive restructuring and/or REBT to treat mood (affective) disorders. Your plan must include:
        i   details of your sampling technique and how you will measure changes in symptoms
        ii   a directional or non-directional hypothesis.   [10]
    b   For one piece of psychological knowledge that has informed your plan:
        i   Describe this psychological knowledge.   [4]
        ii   Explain how two features of this psychological knowledge informed your plan.   [4]

6.3 Impulse control disorders

6.3.1 Diagnostic criteria (ICD-11)

KEY TERMS

kleptomania
pyromania
gambling disorder
impulse control disorders
K-SAS

METHODOLOGY

questionnaires
case studies
quantitative and qualitative data
objective and subjective data

Think!

What score would you need to achieve of the K-SAS to be diagnosed with severe kleptomania?

Think!

Some of you may know what it is like to live with a diagnosis of an impulse control disorder as these disorders affect approximately 5 per cent of people across the world (Dell'Osso *et al.*, 2006). If not, try to imagine what it might be like – how might it affect your everyday life, including your relationships with friends, family, teachers or your employer? Do you think disorders like **kleptomania**, **pyromania** or intermittent explosive disorder are more or less prevalent than 5 per cent in the culture where you live?

Think!

You are reading about a psychologist who says she takes an idiographic approach to studying pyromania. What methods would you expect her to use and how might her data differ from someone who takes a more nomothetic approach?

The woman in the case study by Glover (1985) stole items that she did not need, like baby shoes. How would the woman's feelings have changed before, during and after stealing?

▲ Figure 6.26

Impulse control disorders all involve build up in tension that is relieved when the person engages in a specific behaviour, which they feel an irresistible urge to carry out. These behaviours are often referred to as compulsions, which you will learn more about in the final part of this chapter ('Obsessive-compulsive disorder', page 337). In impulse control disorders, the behaviour leads to a euphoric rush of pleasure, which immediately relieves the tension. This pleasurable 'high' is short-lived, however, and the longer-term impact of these behaviours often leads to significant distress and dysfunction, including financial and personal losses. In this section, you will learn about three specific disorders: kleptomania, pyromania and **gambling disorder**.

Kleptomania

Kleptomania is a rare condition affecting up to 0.6 per cent of the population and can develop at any age. It is more common in females than males and the main characteristic is a recurrent, irresistible urge to steal. Unlike shoplifting, people with this disorder rarely want or need the items they steal and may throw them away or give them to other people. In one study, only 4 per cent of a sample of shoplifters met the criteria for kleptomania (Bradford and Balmaceda, 1983). In this disorder, thefts are often unplanned and carried out in response to a building sense of tension that is released when item(s) are stolen. As with all impulse control disorders, the behaviour is reinforced by the resulting short-term pleasure and relief, but the majority of people with this disorder also suffer with crippling depression and/or anxiety due to the shame and guilt associated with their criminality. To be diagnosed with kleptomania, doctors must rule out all other possible causes of stealing, such as checking whether the person is hearing voices that tell them to steal. On page 299 you will learn about a **case study** of a woman with kleptomania (Glover, 1985) who stole items for which she had no use (see Figure 6.26). Turn to page 300 now to find out more her symptoms.

Pyromania

People with pyromania have a fascination with fire. They repeatedly and intentionally light fires, but they do not always intend to cause damage. As with kleptomania, they may feel an urge to start a fire. Tension builds until a fire is lit and is released once a fire has been started. The person experiences relief and pleasure as the fire grows. People with pyromania are often also fascinated by equipment for starting, accelerating and extinguishing fires, including firefighters, fire engines and fire alarms.

This is a very rare condition, although between 3 and 6 per cent of psychiatric **inpatients** are thought to meet the criteria for diagnosis (Burton *et al.*, 2012). The age of onset is usually relatively young (i.e. teenage years), with the severity of the condition increasing over time. Risk factors include boredom, stress, feelings of inadequacy and conflict at home and/or school. Disorders such as mood substance disorders are common, with 90 per cent of people with pyromania saying they feel intensely guilty for the damage they cause and putting others' lives at risk. More than 30 per cent are suicidal.

Gambling disorder

Gambling disorder destroys lives and is sadly becoming increasingly prevalent due to the legalisation of online gambling in many countries across the world. In the USA, the lifetime prevalence is 4 per cent (Black and Shaw, 2019), underlining the critical nature of understanding this condition. As with kleptomania and pyromania, gambling disorder also involves a build-up of tension, relieved in this case not through stealing or fire-starting but by placing a bet, whether that is in a traditional betting shop (e.g. betting on horses or football), in a casino or arcade or an instant-win lottery on your phone.

When the new version of the ICD was published in 2018, gambling disorder was reclassified from an impulse control disorder to a disorder due to addictive behaviours, alongside gaming disorder (WHO, 2018). This is because research has demonstrated that, like substance addictions (e.g. cocaine or alcohol), people who engage in excessive gambling and gaming often show a similar profile of physical and behavioural signs and symptoms. For example, Griffiths (1993) found signs of tolerance in regular gamblers whose heart rates returned to normal significantly faster than non-regular gamblers, following placing a bet. This suggests that regular gamblers would need to gamble longer or with more money to experience the same level of arousal as the non-regular gamblers. Also in one study, 65 per cent of gamblers experienced withdrawal symptoms when abstaining from gambling, such as insomnia, headaches and upset stomach, and in fact these symptoms were worse for gamblers than people with substance addictions (Rosenthal and Lesieur, 1992).

To be diagnosed with this disorder, people must demonstrate impaired control over their gambling, such as where and when this happens, how often and how much they bet. Gambling will take priority over other activities necessary for typical daily functioning, such as work or family life, and the person will find it difficult to stop despite significant negative consequences. Often a pattern of persistent or recurrent gambling will have been exhibited for at least 12 months before a diagnosis is made, although this can be less in severe and obvious cases. When making a diagnosis, it is important to eliminate mania as the cause of excessive gambling, which can be common in people with bipolar disorder. You will learn more about gambling disorder throughout this chapter. Turn to page 299 now to find out more about the case study of John (Miller, 2010).

Measuring impulse control disorders

The Kleptomania Symptom Assessment Scale

Kleptomania is a relatively under-researched disorder and, as such, there is only one scale which measures the severity of symptoms: the Kleptomania Symptom Assessment Scale, **K-SAS**. This 11-item self-report scale requires the respondent to consider their thoughts, feelings and actions over the past week. Each item is scored from 0–4 (see Figure 6.27 for sample items). The maximum score is 44; a person with a score of over 31 is said to have severe symptoms, whereas a score of over 21 is classified as moderate. Most people with this disorder score between 22 and 37. As well as diagnosis, the K-SAS is used to assess changes in severity of symptoms over time – for example, following treatment (Grant *et al.*, 2003).

1 If you had urges to steal during the past WEEK, on average, how strong were your urges?
   Please circle the most appropriate number:

   None (0)   Mild (1)   Moderate (2)   Severe (3)   Extreme (4)

2 During the past WEEK, how many times did you experience urges to steal?
   Please circle the most appropriate number:

   None (0)   Once (1)   Two or three times (2)   Several to many times (3)   Constant or near constant (4)

3 During the past WEEK, how many hours (add up hours) were you preoccupied with your urges to steal? Please circle the most appropriate number:

   None (0)   1 hour or less (1)   1 to 4 hours (2)   4 to 10 hours (3)   Over 10 hours (4)

▲ Figure 6.27 Sample items from the Kleptomania Symptom Assessment Scale (K-SAS)

Evaluating the K-SAS

A strength of the K-SAS is that it only takes around ten minutes to complete and the person making a diagnosis does not need any special training to administer or score this **questionnaire**. It also covers all aspects of kleptomania, including thoughts, urges, behaviour and distress (Hollander and Berlin, 2007). This is important as a diagnosis can be made quickly, meaning the person can be referred for treatment without delay.

A further strength is the use of **quantitative data**, which does not require any interpretation, whereas qualitative data from an interview, for example, could lead to a **subjective** analysis, where factors such as age, gender and socioeconomic background may influence the diagnosing doctor's conclusions. Use of a standardised procedure for assessing symptoms should reduce the bias, leading to a more **objective** diagnosis.

A weakness is that the K-SAS is a self-report questionnaire, so people may not tell the truth about their symptoms. People with kleptomania are often deeply ashamed of their urges and actions, meaning they are likely to under-report the true extent of their disorder. This is important because it means the K-SAS scores may not be valid.

> ## ISSUES AND DEBATES

Idiographic versus nomothetic

A strength of the K-SAS is the nomothetic approach that it takes, i.e. large amounts of data have been collected over the years in order that people's scores can be compared with normative data and judgments made about whether symptoms are mild, moderate or severe, thus allowing people to be prioritised for treatment using relatively objective quantitative data. However, this approach means that symptoms may be seen 'out of context', i.e there is no explanations of why a person has been stealing. Case studies use more than one approach to gathering data (triangulation) meaning that it is possible to gain information using idiographic methods such as interviewing to ask open questions, which help practitioners to understand the 'why' as well as the 'what'. For example, in Glover's case study (Glover, 1985) the information about the woman's husband's conviction for embezzlement (see page 299) may have helped the doctor to decide on a suitable form of therapy for her. Quantitative data alone may not be as helpful in this respect, suggesting that the K-SAS should only be one part of the information obtained about a client.

People with impulse control disorders experience a build-up of tension before they act on their urge, which is then released and followed by feelings of pleasure and relief. Think back to the learning approach:

» Which type of conditioning ensures that the person keeps on repeating the behaviours that are reinforced?
» What type of reinforcement is happening in pyromania? Can you think of any ways of helping the person to modify their behaviour?

▲ Figure 6.28

> ## LEARNING LINKS

At AS Level, you learned that biological psychologists believe that different areas of the brain are responsible for different skills and behaviours. This is called localisation of function. Experimental research with rats suggests that damage to the nucleus accumbens may be linked to impulse control disorders (Cardinal *et al.*, 2001). This brain region is linked to reward, cravings and addiction and so it is possible that it is also linked to disorders like kleptomania and pyromania.

STUDY TIP

This clinical chapter includes a number of case studies, including Aneja *et al.* (2018) (page 234), Glover (1985) (page 299), Little Hans (Freud, 1909; page 323) and the case of Charles by Rapoport (1989). The details of these studies could easily get mixed up.

One way to really get to know these characters would be to write a play where they all meet up with each other. How do you think they would get along?

You could create a description of each character with instructions for the actor who is to play them. Be sure to provide plenty of information about the person and their disorder to help the actor to get into character.

> **TEST YOURSELF**

1 Ricky's mother is in prison and he lives with his grandmother. Ricky has been arrested three times for starting fires. His care worker, Morgan, thinks that he may have pyromania. Explain two reasons why Morgan might think Ricky has pyromania. [4]

2 Outline two symptoms of kleptomania with reference to evidence from one case study. [4]

3 a Describe the Kleptomania Symptom Assessment Scale (K-SAS). [6]
   b Evaluate the Kleptomania Symptom Assessment Scale (K-SAS), including a discussion of objective versus subjective data. [10]

4 Identify two strengths of the type of data collected by the Kleptomania Symptom Assessment Scale (K-SAS). [2]

5 Morgan is interviewing 16-year-old Ricky about his fascination with fire to try to decide whether he has pyromania. Give one open question and one closed question that Morgan could ask Ricky. [2]

6 Questionnaires sometimes ask forced/fixed-choice questions. Give an example of a forced/fixed-choice question that could be used to investigate kleptomania. [2]

6.3.2 Explanations of impulse control disorders

Biological explanation: dopamine

KEY TERMS

septal region
nucleus accumbens
euphoria
striatum
D2 receptors
Parkinson's disease
agonist

Think!

Which brain structures were stimulated in the study by Olds and Milner (1954)?

Think!

Imagine you are a dopamine molecule in the brain of someone carrying the **A1** allele of the D2 dopamine receptor gene. What is your biggest problem in life? What about if you are a dopamine molecule in the brain of an A2 allele carrier?

Think!

Why do you think many researchers conduct their experiments on rats rather than people when disorders like kleptomania, pyromania and gambling disorder all involve behaviours that only apply to humans?

Look carefully at parts (a) and (b) in Figure 6.29.

» What is the main difference between them?

» How might this affect the individual's thoughts, feelings and behaviour?

a) A1 allele

b) A2 allele

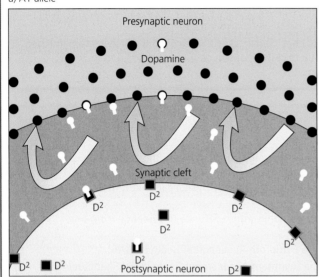
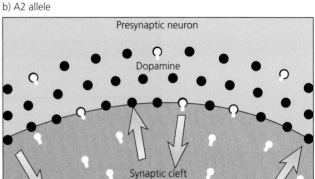

▲ Figure 6.29 These diagrams represent the difference between dopamine synapses in people carrying: (a) the A1 allele or (b) the A2 allele

On page 242, you learned that an imbalance of dopamine is associated with schizophrenia, but this neurotransmitter is also associated with impulse control disorders. Dopamine is often called the 'pleasure molecule' or the 'happy chemical' because dopamine receptors exist in very high numbers in the neural circuits (pathways) related to reward/reinforcement.

Early dopamine research

Olds and Milner (1954) placed rats into a Skinner box (see page 87) where they had access to a lever. If the rat pressed the lever, the researcher would electrically stimulate different brain regions to see how this affected the rat's behaviour. The **septal region** and the **nucleus accumbens** each have a high concentration of dopamine receptors and when these regions were stimulated the rats pressed the lever up to 2000 times an hour. The researchers concluded that these regions are important reward centres as stimulation clearly caused the rats to experience a rush of pleasure ('high') that was irresistible. This is an example of operant conditioning, where the consequences of a behaviour determine whether it is repeated. Further studies showed that the rats even tolerated painful shocks in order to get to the lever (Olds, 1956).

Anticipation

More recently, researchers have noted that animals seem to experience a high level of dopamine activity *before* they perform behaviours that have previously been rewarded. At this stage, the rat is showing signs of classical conditioning; just seeing the lever (conditioned stimulus) is enough to get the rat to experience a 'high' (conditioned response). This is due to the association that has formed between the sight of the lever and the electrical stimulation of the septal region and nucleus accumbens (the unconditioned stimulus). Biologically, this subjective feeling of **euphoria** (intense pleasure) is caused by the release of high levels of dopamine.

Reward deficiency syndrome

Comings and Blum (2000) explain that impulse control disorders may result from low levels of dopamine in brain regions like the **striatum** (which contains the nucleus accumbens). This deficiency is thought to result from an interaction between specific genes and environmental factors (Williams and Potenza, 2008). It can result in people finding little pleasure in everyday life, meaning they seek out opportunities that lead to a dopamine rush.

Researchers have identified that people with impulse control disorders are more likely to be carriers of the A1 allele of a gene which codes for **D2 receptors** (Blum *et al.*, 1996). This allele is carried by about 25 per cent of the population and can result in carriers developing 30 per cent fewer D2 receptors (Noble *et al.*, 1991). With fewer receptor sites for dopamine to bind with, communication in certain neural networks is reduced, causing the individual to seek dopamine highs in other ways, such as through compulsive fire-starting, stealing, overeating or shopping.

Evaluating the biochemical explanation: dopamine

One strength of reward deficiency syndrome as an explanation of impulse control disorders is that it is supported by research evidence. In one study, the A1 allele was carried by 51 per cent of people with gambling disorder (Comings *et al.*, 1996), yet it is only observed in 25 per cent of the population in general (Blum *et al.*, 1996). The probability of carrying this allele was even higher in those with the most severe symptoms. This is important support for the role of dopamine in gambling disorder, although it is unclear whether this explanation applies to those with kleptomania and/or pyromania.

ISSUES AND DEBATES

Application to everyday life

A strength of the dopamine explanation is that it has important applications to everyday life. For example, it helps to explain why many people with **Parkinson's disease** develop impulse control disorders, especially following treatment. This disease is associated with low levels of dopamine and is often treated using drugs that elevate dopamine (dopamine **agonists**) (Weintraub *et al.*, 2006). This is a strength as this knowledge can be used to help people to make informed decisions about their medication and ensure people who are prescribed these drugs are monitored regularly to avoid the development of an impulse control disorder.

Nature versus nurture

A weakness of this explanation is that the focus on the A1 allele as a biological cause of impulse control disorders (nature) means the role of the environment (nurture) may be underestimated. A famous series of experiments called 'Rat Park' demonstrated that rats that lived in an under stimulating/poor environment were more likely to become addicted to morphine when given the opportunity than rats who lived in an enriched environment (Alexander *et al.*, 1981). This suggests that behavioural addictions in humans could be prevented through community-based projects that target inequality and improve quality of life. Studies such as these demonstrate that even if some people are genetically predisposed towards addiction, nurture and environments play a central role in eliciting such behaviours. Understanding the complex interactions between nature and nurture may help people to recognise

the power they have to create small lifestyle changes which over time can help them to begin their recovery journey.

Determinism versus free will

Biological explanations tend to overlook the role of free will. Although people with impulse control disorders report an uncontrollable urges to engage in their specific compulsions, with the right support, people with impulse control disorders can, and do, take control of their lives, actively choosing and creating environmental experiences that support their recovery. Explanations that focus too exclusively on genes and neural pathways minimise the role of personal agency presenting a rather pessimistic viewpoint, which could be damaging to sufferers and their families.

Reductionism versus holism

A weakness of the biological explanations is that they tend to present an overly reductionist view, which may mean people underestimate the role of cognitive and social factors in driving impulsive behaviour. A person may inherit certain genes that predispose them towards a dopamine deficiency, however the expression of these genes is dictated by environmental experiences. For example Archer *et al.* (2012) identify numerous environmental factors, including prenatal tobacco exposure, maternal depression and childhood bullying all of which could affect the way the developing brain responds to stress therefore indirectly increasing the probability of impulse control disorders in later life.

The word 'compulsion' strongly suggests that people have no power to stop their behaviour, that they are programmed by brain structures and chemical imbalances over which they have no voluntary control. This underlines the role of free will – when we believe we can change, we can change! What are the implications of believing in free will (versus determinism) when it comes to people with impulse control disorders?

▲ Figure 6.30

► LEARNING LINKS

In the section on mood disorders (page 259), you learned about the short allele of the 5-HTT gene, which has been associated with depression, but research suggests that carrying two copies of short allele is more common in some parts of the world, yet rates of depression are lower not higher (Chiao and Blizinsky, 2010). This indicates that we must be careful about making over-simplified conclusions about the role of the A1 allele; this allele may not affect behaviour in the same way in everyone around the world. Given that most of the research in this area has been conducted either on animals or on people from largely individualist nations, caution should certainly be exercised (see page 225).

STUDY TIP

With a variety of different genetic and biochemical theories for different disorders, it can be easy to confuse them. You could draw up a table with a row for each of the five disorders when you have completed the whole chapter and fill in the details of which genes, alleles and neurotransmitters are involved. You could also use a Venn diagram to compare either two or three disorders at a time, such as impulse control disorders and obsessive-compulsive disorder.

► TEST YOURSELF

1 Isaac often feels tense and irritable at work. He has started going into a local arcade on the way home. Sitting at the machine and placing his money in the slot, he barely notices the result before reaching for another coin. Describe the dopamine explanation of impulse control disorders using Isaac's behaviour as an example. [4]

2 Explain one weakness of the dopamine explanation of impulse control disorders. [2]

3 a Describe one biological explanation of impulse control disorders. [6]

  b Evaluate one biological explanation of impulse control disorders, including a discussion of free will versus determinism. [10]

4 Research into impulse control disorders often uses rats. Explain one practical and one ethical issue that must be considered when using animals in research into biological explanations of impulse control disorders. [4]

5 Samuel increases dopamine levels in ten participants using a new drug called 'Do-plus'. He gives another ten participants a placebo. Next, he records the number of tokens each participant spends while playing an online gambling game for one hour.

  a Write a null hypothesis for Samuel's study. [2]

  b Identify the type of graph that Samuel should use to display his results. [1]

6 Erika wants to conduct a semi-structured interview with a group of people attending a support group for gambling disorders. Suggest one open and one closed question that Erika could ask as part of her interview. [2]

Psychological explanations

KEY TERMS

continuous reinforcement

partial reinforcement schedules

variable ratio

state-dependent memory

addictive memory (AM)

feeling-state

context-dependent memory

Think!

According to Skinner's research on reinforcement schedules, why do you think people spend so much time and money playing on 'slot machines', like the one in Figure 6.31?

Think!

O'Guinn and Faber (1989) collected both quantitative and qualitative data, which increased the validity of their findings, but what problems might a researcher face when collecting data using interviews to investigate impulse control disorders. Can you think of any other ways of collecting data that might avoid some of the issues that you have outlined?

Think!

Imagine you are talking to a teenager who has been diagnosed with pyromania. What questions would you like to ask to help you to decide whether the behavioural or the cognitive explanations are more useful in understanding impulse control disorders? Can you foresee any problems talking to the teenager about this topic? If you could choose one other person to talk to about this, who would it be and why?

Skinner stated that, 'If the gambling establishment cannot persuade a patron to turn over money with no return, it may achieve the same effect by returning part of the patron's money on a variable-ratio schedule' (Skinner, 1953, page 397) It is easy to understand why someone becomes addicted to slot machines, but why is it harder to explain a disorder like kleptomania?

Behavioural explanation: positive reinforcement

Skinner's theory of operant conditioning states that behaviours that are rewarded will be repeated. In Olds and Milner (1954) (see page 288), the behaviour of the rats was rewarded using electrical stimulation of reward pathways in the brain, resulting in compulsive lever pressing. In humans, the act of placing a bet, slotting a coin into a machine or scraping the surface from an immediate-win scratch card may occasionally be reinforced by the thrill of a win, or even a near-miss (Chase and Clark, 2010)!

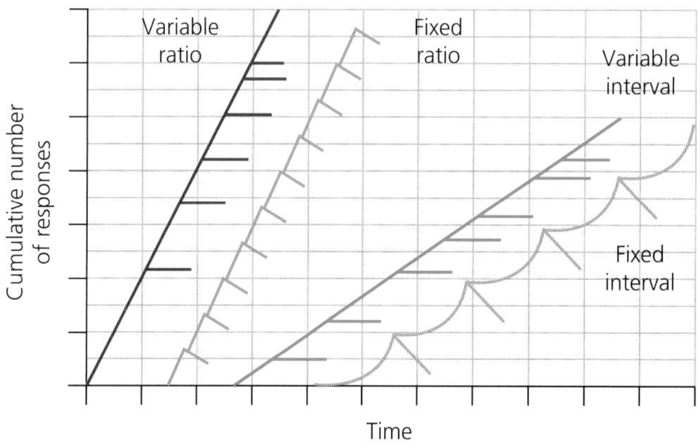

What is more difficult to explain is why the losses, which far outweigh the wins when gambling, do not inhibit (stop) the behaviour. However, this can also be explained by Skinner's research with rats. Initially, he undertook experiments where the rats were rewarded every time they pressed the lever. This is known as **continuous reinforcement**. Next, he experimented with **partial reinforcement schedules**. Here, the rats were only rewarded for some of their lever presses. The schedule that led to the highest response rate was a **variable ratio** schedule, whereby rewards were unpredictable – for example, the rat might be reinforced every fifth time it pressed the lever, but sometimes only three presses were required, whereas other times it might be eight or nine.

Figure 6.31 illustrates the rate of responding for variable ratio reinforcement versus three other reinforcement schedules.

Skinner believed that behaviours such as excessive gambling could be explained in the same way. Furthermore, the anticipation of a win learned through previous

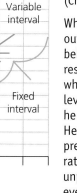

▲ Figure 6.31 The effect of four partial reinforcement schedules on response rates: variable ratio, where the ratio of rewards to responses is unpredictable, gives the steadiest and highest rate of responding compared with fixed ratio (rewarded every *n*th response), variable interval (unpredictable amount of time must pass between rewards) and fixed interval (rewarded after a predictable time period)

experience can also become rewarding in itself. Skinner showed that this variable ratio reinforcement schedule is highly resistant to extinction, meaning even in the absence of any reinforcement, the learned behaviour persists.

Evaluating the behavioural explanation

A weakness of the positive reinforcement explanation is that it fails to acknowledge the role of negative reinforcement. Impulse control disorders are characterised by building a sense of tension and anxiety before the act, which is immediately relieved when the compulsion has been enacted. The alleviation of a negative feeling is negatively reinforcing and the person is, therefore, more likely to exhibit this behaviour in future. This view is supported by Blaszczynski *et al.* (1986), who state that gambling is driven by the desire to avoid 'noxious physiological states and/or dysphoria mood'. This is important as understanding the function of the behaviour for the individual is key to helping the person to break the habit.

A strength of the behavioural explanation is that the focus on nurture explains findings that cannot easily be explained by biological explanations alone. On page 269, it was noted that carrying allele 1, which codes for D2 dopamine receptors, is associated with impulse control disorders, but not everyone who carries one or even two copies of this allele develops an impulse control disorder as such variants only minimally increase the risk. This suggests that environmental/learning experiences may also be necessary for a person with a genetic vulnerability to actually develop an impulse control disorder.

Cognitive explanation: Miller's feeling-state theory

State-dependent memory refers to the idea that, when we are in a certain emotional state, we begin to retrieve memories from the last time we were in the same state. So when we are happy this can lead us to retrieve memories of happy times and when we are sad this can trigger the retrieval of memories of sad times. Miller (2010) uses the term **addictive memory (AM)** to describe memories for past experiences relating to the problem behaviour in people with impulse control disorders, such as fire-starting, stealing or gambling. For example, when a person with pyromania feels tense and anxious, they may remember that the last time they felt tense and anxious, they started a fire. The recall of the fire triggers recall of the sense of euphoria associated with fire-starting. Miller refers to this as a **feeling-state**.

Feeling-states may include sensations and thoughts as well as feelings, such as feelings of empowerment and control. If these feelings are typically missing in a person's life due to their personal or family circumstances, they may be more vulnerable to developing an impulse control disorder as the feelings are so powerful and motivating. Memories can also be **context-dependent**, meaning specific people, objects and events may trigger a feeling-state which triggers the compulsive behaviour – for example, the sight of items associated with fire-starting may trigger a feeling-state, which generates the irresistible urge. When the person does start a fire, the same sense of relief is triggered and the memory is strengthened and becomes a more powerful motivator for future behaviour. A sense of shame and anxiety may quickly develop following the behaviour but unfortunately this then triggers the feeling-state again, creating a vicious cycle.

Miller believes that strong associations formed between both positive and negative feeling-states and specific behaviours explain how these behaviours become habitual.

Evaluating the cognitive explanation

A weakness of Miller's theory is that much of the evidence to support it comes from **case studies**, such as that of John, a man with gambling disorder. John's positive feeling-state was tied to a memory of winning $16,000 and he reported positive feelings around belonging with the other people at the casino, but he also revealed to Miller that his father used to call him a 'loser' and he felt that no-one liked him. Reduction of these negative feeling-states had also become strongly associated with gambling. Although this evidence seems to support Miller's theory, case study evidence tends to be unreliable as it is often based on unstructured interviews and cannot be generalised as John's experiences are unique to his personal circumstances and only relate to gambling disorder.

That said, O'Guinn and Faber (1989) have also provided detailed qualitative data from compulsive shoppers that clearly supports the role of positive feeling-states. For example, '...the attention I got in there was incredible. She waited on me very nicely' and 'I know the

UPS drivers in my neighbourhood really well. They all wave and say hello by first name.' The participants also refer to physiological arousal and sensations (e.g. sweating, heart racing) as they describe the process of shopping in contrast to the pleasure of the actual purchases. The social elements, such as feeling in control and 'belonging', can make people with low self-esteem especially vulnerable to compulsive shopping. In O'Guinn and Faber (1989), self-esteem was significantly lower in the compulsive shoppers than in a matched control group.

ISSUES AND DEBATES

Individual and situational explanations

A strength of the cognitive explanation is that it acknowledges the role of both individual and situational factors in triggering impulsive acts. For example, the case study of John points to events in his life (e.g. his father calling him a loser) that created negative feeling-states, which were reduced through gambling, but it also takes into account situational factors acting on people at the time the urges arise, e.g. the actions of others as described by O'Guinn and Faber (1989) (see above). Here, compulsive shoppers spoke of the behaviour of shop assistants and delivery drivers who unwittingly helped to create a positive-feeling state that strengthened their impulsive behaviour. Explanations that emphasise interactions between multiple factors provide a more holistic perspective and this is often helpful in identifying a variety of possibilities for treatment.

LEARNING LINKS

In Chapter 3, we discussed how children can acquire new behaviours via observation and imitation of adults (i.e. social learning). In Bandura et al. (aggression), the problem behaviour was aggression towards the Bobo doll. In a variation of this experiment, the adult was rewarded for being aggressive to the Bobo doll and this had the effect of increasing the children's later aggression towards the Bobo doll. Bandura called this vicarious reinforcement – that is, watching someone else being reinforced for an action makes it more likely that the observer will also repeat the behaviour. The same could also be true of behaviours such as gambling, meaning a child will be more likely to gamble as an adult if they have observed first-degree relatives being rewarded for this behaviour. Which of the theories that you have learned about on pages 287–293 best explain why some people's gambling gets out of control?

STUDY TIP

Drawing diagrams or models to show the links between different aspects of a theory can be very helpful for fixing the ideas in your mind. This could be especially helpful for the feeling-state theory to help provide an overview of the interactions between feelings, memories and behaviours, past and future. Illustrating your model with images helps make it even more memorable and the process of simply selecting the best images to represent each concept should deepen your memory of the theory. You could also make up characters, with kleptomania, pyromania and gambling disorder (perhaps give them names to help them come to life, e.g. Khloe, Poroto and Grzegorz) and think about how the theories apply to their specific stories you have created for your characters.

TEST YOURSELF

1   Outline what is meant by positive reinforcement using an example relating to pyromania.   [2]
2   Give one similarity and one difference between the dopamine explanation of impulse control disorders and the behavioural explanation of impulse control disorders.   [4]
3   a   Describe Miller's feeling-state theory of impulse control disorders.   [6]
    b   Evaluate Miller's feeling-state theory of impulse control disorders, including a discussion of nature versus nurture.   [10]

4   Professor Ronaldo places rats (Arnie and Bert) in two cages, each with a lever. Arnie is rewarded with one food pellet every fifth time he presses the lever. Bert is sometimes rewarded with three food pellets if he presses the lever but often he receives nothing at all.

Using your knowledge of positive reinforcement, explain which rat will press the lever the most.   [4]

5   Dr Kira believes that shopping habits are affected by self-esteem. She decides to collect some quantitative data using self-reports about positive feelings while shopping and self-esteem. Her main research method will be correlation. Write a suitable fully operationalised, directional hypothesis for Dr Kira.   [2]

6   Draw a sketch of a scatter graph to show the expected relationship between Dr Kira's two variables. Label the x and y axes appropriately.   [2]

7   Baz measures the heart rate of a group of people with pyromania before and after starting a fire.
    a   State the design of Baz's experiment.   [1]
    b   State a suitable measure of spread for Baz's results.   [1]

6.3.3 Treatment and management of impulse control disorders

Biological treatments

KEY TERMS

opiates
opioid receptors
endogenous
endorphins

METHODOLOGY

interviews
generalisations from findings

Think!

How do **opiate** antagonists help people to reduce gambling urges and behaviour? Try to use as many key terms in your answer as you can.

Think!

Imagine you are one of the researchers on Grant's team. He has asked you to write a set of standardised instructions that can be used to tell participants about the study. What are the top three things you think you should include?

Think!

Based on your understanding of how opiate antagonists work, can you think of any possible negative side effects of drugs like nalmefene and naltrexone that could reduce patient compliance?

Biological treatments for impulse control disorders such as kleptomania, pyromania and gambling disorder involve the use of medications such as selective serotonin reuptake inhibitors (SSRIs), also used to treat mood and anxiety disorders (see page 277) and mood stabilisers such as lithium, used to treat bipolar disorder. Other drugs including the anticonvulsant drug topiramate, commonly used to treat epilepsy, has also been found to be effective in treating kleptomania (Talih, 2011; Dannon, 2003). However, these ICDs are also commonly treated with a class of drugs called opioid antagonists, which will be the focus of this section.

Key study: Treating gambling disorder with drugs and placebo – Grant *et al.* (2008)

Introducing Dr Jon Grant

Dr Jon Grant is Professor of Psychiatry and Behavioral Neuroscience at the University of Chicago, in the USA. He is the director of a Center of Excellence in Gambling Research, but his research also includes biological explanations and treatments for impulse control disorders, including stealing and shopping, as well as obsessive-compulsive disorder and drug addictions. He is editor-in-chief of the *Journal of Gambling Studies*, is part of the editorial board of nine other scientific journals and has written numerous books and articles.

Some people would argue that treating gambling disorder with medication is reductionist, meaning that chemically blocking the 'high' that reinforces the behaviour may mean the behaviour becomes extinct, but the person may be left with residual symptoms of depression and anxiety which they are unable to reduce. Do you think drug treatments like nalmefene can ever cure a person with gambling disorder?

Context

Opiates are a class of drugs produced from **opium**, a naturally occurring substance found in poppies. Opiates, including **morphine**, are used as painkillers. The molecules bind to **opioid receptors**, which exist throughout the nervous system. You may wonder why the body has receptors for a substance found in poppies. This is because the body creates its own **endogenous** morphine, better known as **endorphins**. Endorphins are released in response to exercise, sex and eating, but also as a reaction to pain and stress. They have two main effects: to increase pleasure and to decrease pain.

When opioid receptors are activated, they inhibit the release of a neurotransmitter called **GABA**. One of GABA's jobs is to regulate **dopamine**. This means that, while opioid receptors are occupied, dopamine activity increases and this is why opiates are associated with euphoria (extreme pleasure). Antagonists reduce the effects of neurochemicals by occupying receptors without activating them. Opiate antagonists block opiate receptors and, therefore, reduce the ability to experience euphoria. For this reason, these drugs are used to treat substance addictions, behavioural addictions (e.g. gambling disorder) and impulse control disorders, including kleptomania and pyromania.

▶ AIMS AND HYPOTHESES

To investigate factors that predict the effectiveness of opiate antagonists in the treatment of gambling disorder (or pathological gambling as it was called at the time of this study).

Grant *et al.* hypothesised that opiate antagonists would be more effective for people with a family history of alcoholism, stronger urges to gamble and euphoria in response to alcohol compared with people with no family history of alcoholism, weaker gambling urges and a less pronounced response to alcohol. They also predicted that people with less severe gambling urges may experience a placebo effect – that is, they would respond positively to the drugs but there would be no difference in the level of improvement between the real drug and the placebo.

▶ METHODOLOGY

The study combined the results of two randomised control trials and, therefore, can be described as a meta-analysis. Both RCTs were double-blind, placebo-controlled experiments with **independent measures**. Data-gathering techniques included structured and semi-structured interviews, questionnaires and psychometric tests.

Sample

All 284 American participants were diagnosed with pathological gambling using the DSM-IV and scored five or more on the South Oaks Gambling Screen (SOGS). Forty-eight per cent were female, none were pregnant or breastfeeding and all used regular contraception. There were 207 **outpatients** from 15 psychiatric centres who participated in a 16-week trial of nalmefene. The remaining 77 participated in an 18-week trial of naltrexone. All had gambled in the past two weeks and gambled more than once a week. None had used either of the trial drugs before.

▶ PROCEDURE

Participants were randomly assigned to either the placebo group or the low, medium or higher dose in the drug group. Daily doses of nalmefene doses were either 25 mg, 50 mg or 100 mg, while naltrexone doses were 50 mg, 100 mg or 150 mg. Comorbid diagnoses were identified using a structured interview and gambling behaviour was investigated using a questionnaire. Severity of gambling disorder symptoms (e.g. urges and gambling behaviour) was assessed before and after treatment using a modified version of the Yale-Brown Obsessive-Compulsive Scale (see page 340). A decrease of more than 35 per cent was classified as a positive response to treatment. Daily functioning, anxiety and depression were assessed using questionnaires and a semi-structured interview was used to collect information about family history of psychiatric diagnoses, including alcoholism in first-degree relatives.

▶ RESULTS

Demographics

- Average age of onset was 29, but there was an average of 11 years (range 1–40) between starting to gamble and being diagnosed.
- Thirty per cent had attended Gamblers Anonymous and only 19 per cent had previously sought professional help for their gambling.
- Forty-eight per cent played non-strategic games, such as slots and bingo, 16 per cent played only strategic games, such as blackjack and poker, and 36 per cent played both non-strategic and strategic games.
- Twenty-four per cent met criteria for mood disorders, 7 per cent for anxiety disorders, 3 per cent for eating disorders and 42 per cent were regular tobacco users.

Response to opiate antagonists and placebos

Initially, the data from the two drugs were analysed separately but as the findings were so similar, the researchers decided to analyse the data from each trial together to increase the sample size. Of all the data collected, only family history of alcoholism was robustly associated with a positive response to treatment outcome. Stronger baseline 'urge to gamble' scores were mildly associated with positive treatment response to the higher doses of both drugs.

Younger participants were more likely to respond positively to the placebo, which was 30 per cent less effective for every ten years in participant age.

▶ CONCLUSIONS

Family history of alcoholism and, to a lesser extent, strength of urges to gamble are associated with a positive response to opiate antagonists as a treatment for gambling disorder

 ## Methodological strengths and weaknesses

A strength of this study was the double-blind, placebo-controlled design, which increases validity. For example, the Y-BOCS test used to assess symptom severity was administered by a researcher who was unaware of the condition to which the participant had been allocated (e.g. active versus placebo) and the outcomes of the screening measures (e.g. family history of alcoholism). This is important; had the researcher been aware of this information, differences in the way they interacted with each participant could have unintentionally conveyed their expectations about the efficacy of the treatment. This could have affected participants' expectations about the efficacy of their treatment, thus increasing the placebo effects.

A further strength is that the nalmefene participants were recruited from 15 treatment centres, making the result more representative of the target population. Participants were aged 19–72, and a range of people of different ethnicities, marital status and employment status were included. This increases the **generalisability** of the results regarding family history of alcoholism and efficacy of opiate antagonists. That said, these findings may not always apply with naltrexone, as there were fewer participants in this group, 90 per cent of whom were Caucasian, and they were only from one geographical area (Minnesota, USA).

A weakness is that family history of alcoholism was self-reported in semi-structured interviews and so may not be valid. As this information is personal/sensitive, participants may not have accurate knowledge regarding all of their first-degree relatives, especially if those relatives are deceased or if they were adopted. The reliance on self-reported data without checking secondary data, such as medical records, means the importance of family history of alcoholism may be over- or underestimated as a predictor of positive response to opiate antagonists. Furthermore the use of semistructured interviews makes this part of the study difficult to replicate as the interviewers will have asked different questions depending on the interviewees responses.

A further weakness was that Grant *et al.* (2008) did not conduct a follow-up assessment after the 16- and 18-week trial periods had finished. Family history of alcoholism may, therefore, only have been predictive of short-term positive effects of opiate antagonists. Also, one or more of the other variables may have been indicative of relapse/remission over the longer term. This sort of data is crucial as relapse is a common feature of gambling disorder. Opiate antagonists stop the person experiencing euphoria and help people to 'break the habit' as the behaviour no longer has positive consequences. However, if the person is not motivated to take the medication each day, they may relapse and thus may have been more likely once the trial was over and there was less support available.

 ## Ethics

These drug trials were approved by the institutional review board of the University of Minnesota. Written informed consent was provided by all participants after potential risks had been explained and they had been given information about alternative treatments. Unlike some studies, the number of participants who received a placebo only was much lower than the active treatment groups (1:3), meaning as many people as possible were treated without compromising the design of the study. All participants were carefully screened to ensure that no-one would be at additional risk of physical or psychological harm. For example, people with unstable medical conditions, people taking medications that could interact negatively with the opiate antagonists and people with various psychiatric conditions and/or suicidality were all excluded.

> ## ISSUES AND DEBATES

Application to everyday life

These findings should help health professionals to ask questions that will help them to make more informed decisions about the best drugs to offer to people with gambling disorders. Asking simple questions about family history is a quick and cheap way to gain valuable information that will help inform the patient of the probability of a positive response to the medication. Opiate antagonists may still work for people without any family history of alcoholism, but it may be helpful to use a different drug in the first instance, such as an antidepressant or an antipsychotic.

Idiographic versus nomothetic

This study takes a nomothetic approach; the objective was to draw conclusions about factors that predict the efficacy of opiate antagonists that can be applied universally to people with gambling disorder. Information about many possible factors was gathered, including age of onset, type of gambling and tobacco use. All data was quantitative, meaning statistical techniques could be used to determine which, if any, of the factors were most important in predicting treatment response. Although the nomothetic approach may be helpful in determining probable outcomes, these probabilities are based on averages drawn from groups of people rather than focusing on the unique treatment journeys of individuals. Taking an idiographic approach could help to provide a more detailed understanding of the experience of taking medication and the impact that it has on individuals and their family members.

Reductionism versus holism

One problem with opiate antagonists as a treatment for impulse control disorders is that the focus on biological factors is reductionist. Without additional support to develop coping mechanisms, people may quickly relapse if they stop taking their medication. Although the behaviour may no longer feel rewarding, underpinning beliefs remain the same. This suggests that pairing opiate antagonists with psychological therapies that focus on stress management and coping skills may provide a more comprehensive treatment package.

REFLECTION

- What do you think the major strengths and weaknesses are of this study?
- If you were conducting research in this area, how might you improve this study and/or design your own study to investigate gambling disorder and the use of opiate antagonists?

LEARNING LINKS

We talked about placebos for the first time in the study by Perry et al. (personal space) (see page 143), which investigated how oxytocin affects preferred interpersonal distance differently depending on whether a person has high or low empathy. Some of the participants took nasal drops that only contained saline and no oxytocin to see whether just thinking you had taken the drug affected the participants' preferences. In this study, the placebos also contained no active ingredients but looked, tasted and smelt exactly like the real opiate antagonists.

The researchers ensured that none of the participants had ever taken naltrexone or nalmefene before, but why was this important? If they had taken these drugs before, how might this have affected the blinding process? For example, could it have helped the participants to know whether they were in the placebo or active treatment group?

STUDY TIP

The mode of action for opiate antagonists (how they change thoughts, feelings and behaviour) is rather complicated. Drawing a cartoon strip of the relationships between opiates, GABA, dopamine and opiate antagonists will help to fix this in your long-term memory.

You could also draw a diagram to show the overall design of this study, which is also rather complex as it combines results from two RCTs, one on each drug, each with four groups. If you prefer, why not make up a rhyme or rap to remember the details. The rhyming words should cue you to remember the details – for example, 'Trying to quit gambling but think you can't? Try out nalmefene and help from Jon Grant.'

TEST YOURSELF

1 Explain one reason why Grant et al. (2008) used placebos in their study on treating gambling disorder. [2]
2 Describe two features of the sample used by Grant et al. (2008). [4]
3 a Describe the study by Grant et al. (2008) on treating gambling disorder with drugs and placebo. [6]
  b Evaluate the study by Grant et al. (2008), including a discussion about applications to everyday life. [10]
4 Grant et al. (2008) used both structured and semi-structured interviews. Explain one difference between these two interview formats using the study by Grant et al. as an example. [2]
5 Bhaavik and Ishir are talking about the study by Grant et al. (2008). Bhaavik thinks that it is possible to generalise from findings, but Ishir disagrees. Explain whether you agree more with Bhaavik or Ishir. [4]
6 Mr Nguyen tells his class that the study by Grant et al. (2008) is reductionist, but his student Khánh thinks it could be seen as holistic. Explain one reason why Mr Nguyen is correct and one reason why Khánh is correct. [4]

KEY TERMS

covert sensitisation

aphantasia

Psychological (cognitive-behavioural) therapies

Covert sensitisation

> **Think!**
>
> How many relapses did the woman have during and following treatment? What did she take?

> **Think!**
>
> Imagine a character on your favourite television programme is having **covert sensitisation** therapy for kleptomania. When they walk out of the therapist's office, they are smiling and laughing. Do you think this is very believable? How do you think it might feel to have this type of therapy? Do you think the feelings differ depending on how many sessions you have had?

> **Think!**
>
> What sort of skills do you think a therapist needs if they are going to successfully deliver covert sensitisation to clients? Can you think of any problems that might arise during therapy sessions? How might the therapist solve these problems?

In covert sensitisation, therapists may encourage people with kleptomania to imagine being arrested and prosecuted for their crimes as a way of increasing negative emotions associated with stealing. The woman in Glover's study said this had not worked for her in the past. Can you think of any reasons why the covert sensitisation approach outlined in Figure 6.32 might not work? In the learning approach (page 85), we noted that something is only a reinforcer or a punisher if it actually changes the behaviour. Could some people possibly find the thought of being arrested exciting or motivating?

▲ Figure 6.32

The learning approach assumes that all behaviours, except the most basic reflexes, are learned; this means that they can also be unlearned, via the same principles. Covert sensitisation uses classical conditioning to create unpleasant associations with the behaviour the person wishes to stop, such as stealing, gambling or fire-starting.

On page 114, you learned how disgust-based phobias are acquired via evaluative learning and the same principles are used here. The therapist will help the client to visualise disturbing images (unconditioned stimulus) that create unpleasant feelings, such as disgust or shame (unconditioned response). These images are then paired with thoughts of the target behaviour. If a strong enough association can be formed between the two, thoughts of the target behaviour will now trigger negative feelings that override the urge to enact the behaviour.

Focus on: Glover (1985)

> **CASE HISTORY**
>
> The client was a 56-year-old married woman. She had been stealing every day for 14 years. A year before her stealing began, her husband was found guilty of embezzlement (stealing from his workplace). He received a big fine and took a new, low-paid job. The woman said her previous friendships had 'melted away'. She had taken on extra work to support them. She mainly stole from supermarkets on her lunch break. She resented her husband's behaviour and was unable to forgive him. She had been prescribed antidepressants over the years.

▶ SYMPTOMS

- Waking every morning with compulsive thoughts about stealing
- Attempts to resist the thought, which she found repugnant (awful)
- Giving in to the urge to steal and taking items for which she had no need, such as baby shoes
- Described her urges as 'overwhelming' and wished she was 'chained to a wall' to stop her from stealing

▶ METHODOLOGY

The woman attended four covert sensitisation sessions, once every two weeks. As she had previously tried to cure herself by imagining she was being arrested and prosecuted, with her therapist, she decided to use imagery relating to vomiting. The therapist encouraged her to imagine approaching items in a shop, as though she were about to steal them, but then to imagine herself vomiting. He asked her to imagine other shoppers staring at her. She was encouraged to imagine the vomiting stopping as she replaced the items that she was about to steal. She was asked to continue the visualisations several times a day as homework.

In the first two sessions, muscle-relaxing medication was used to help her to fully immerse herself in the imagery. In the last two sessions, she used self-hypnosis, which she felt increased the vividness of her visualisations.

The therapist encouraged her never to shop without a strict 'shopping list' and she was also advised to leave the bag she had previously used for stealing at home.

After the initial two months of treatment, she had a follow-up once every three months to reassess her progress.

▶ RESULTS

▼ Table 6.7 Progress reported in Glover (1985)

Months since therapy began	Progress
After four sessions over two months	Preoccupation with stealing and urges to steal were reduced; she stole on two occasions, taking five low-value items from four shops; in comparison with her previous daily stealing this was a vast improvement.
Three-month follow-up	She continued the homework exercises several times a day, visualising the unpleasant imagery; she was becoming more confident to shop alone.
Nine-month follow-up	She stole a bar of soap from a chemist's supermarket; she said this did not relieve tension as it once would have done.
Nineteen-month follow-up	No further relapses; more cheerful, confident and outgoing, no longer shunning social contact due to shame, shopping alone, rarely thought about stealing; if she did think of stealing, it was no longer overwhelming; it made her feel unwell but this was relieved by walking away from tempting items.

▶ CONCLUSIONS

Glover says it is impossible to know exactly which aspects of the therapy were most effective in helping the woman to overcome her kleptomania but states that, in the woman's opinion, her urge to steal was reduced by her ability to clearly imagine the unpleasant scenes.

Evaluating Glover (1985)

One weakness of this study is that it only examined a case of kleptomania in one middle-aged woman, who may not be representative of the wider population of people with this condition. This woman's issues developed following her husband's own stealing and the sense of shame she experienced regarding his crime was echoed in her feelings about her own stealing. This woman noted herself that the therapy was effective due to her ability to create vivid imagery. This is important as it means the therapy may be less effective for someone who is unable to fully immerse themselves in the imagery exposure. That said, there is evidence to suggest that this therapy is effective with other types of client. For example, Kohn and Antonuccio (2002) used this form of therapy to successfully treat a 39-year-old man who had been stealing from the age of six. This demonstrates that covert sensitisation may be effective regardless of age of onset and gender.

> ## ISSUES AND DEBATES

Idiographic versus nomothetic

A strength of Glover's case study was the idiographic approach characterised by the collection of solely qualitative data. The detailed case history means readers can determine the extent to which the client's experiences may be transferable to other clients and therapists. For example, the woman was highly motivated and had made active choices about the therapeutic approach, such as using imagery of vomiting rather than police involvement and using self-hypnosis rather than muscle relaxants. The idiographic approach is helpful as Glover's goal was not to create generalisable conclusions about the efficacy of covert sensitisation, as characterised by the nomothetic approach, but to explore how it can be personalised to a single client's needs.

Evaluating covert sensitisation

A strength of covert sensitisation is that it is supported by research evidence, including the case studies by Glover (1985) and Kohn and Antonuccio (2002). These studies show that a disorder that may have dominated a person's life for several decades can be treated in as little as two months. Although the therapy may be intense and unpleasant for a brief period, this may be seen as favourable to taking medication such as opiate antagonists, which can have unpleasant side effects, including nausea, vomiting, stomach pain, hypertension, fever, dizziness, joint and muscle pain and dysphoria. This is important as these negative side effects could make a person stop taking their medication leading to a relapse, whereas the study by Glover showed that the woman was still doing well more than a year and a half after her therapy ended.

A weakness of covert sensitisation is that it relies on the person being able to imagine scenes in detail to prompt unpleasant emotional and physical sensations. Some neurodiverse people may find this very difficult, not least those with **aphantasia**, an unusual condition which means that people are unable to wilfully bring images to mind. Wicken *et al.* (2021) demonstrated that people with aphantasia have flattened physiological responses when listening to frightening stories, suggesting that this therapy would be ineffective for people with impulse control disorders who also have aphantasia.

> ## LEARNING LINKS
>
> This is an interesting therapy from a practical and ethical point of view. If you think back to the learning approach, we looked at how some phobias are acquired via evaluative learning (see page 114). A person may learn to associate a neutral stimulus with something negative; they learn to avoid it and may even find it disgusting. In Saavedra and Silverman (button phobia), the boy seemed to associate buttons with the negative event of spilling the bowl of buttons in front of his classmates. In covert sensitisation, therapists intentionally create phobic-like reactions towards situations/objects that the person wants to avoid, such as lighters or matches in the case of someone with pyromania.
>
> Why do you think some people are critical of the ethics of this therapy? How might the therapy be altered for people who find it hard to imagine a suitable disgusting scene or painful event? Would this be ethical?

> ### STUDY TIP
>
> Many of the therapies that you learn about throughout this chapter are very similar and it is crucial to understand the differences fully. To this end, it might be sensible to create a table or a series of Venn diagrams once you reach the end of the chapter. For example, the goal of systematic desensitisation is to reduce avoidance of the feared stimuli, whereas the goal of covert sensitisation is to increase avoidance of stimuli associated with undesirable behaviour, such as gambling, fire-starting and stealing. Often exposures are in vivo (in real life) with systematic desensitisation but they are imagined (or in vitro) in covert sensitisation.

> ## TEST YOURSELF

1 Describe the results of one study of covert sensitisation. [4]
2 Compare one biological and one psychological treatment for impulse control disorders. [4]
3 a Describe one cognitive-behavioural therapy for impulse control disorders. [6]
   b Evaluate the cognitive-behavioural therapy you described above, including a discussion of applications to everyday life. [10]
4 Impulse control disorders can be treated using cognitive-behavioural therapy, such as covert sensitisation, but this may be more effective for some people than others.
   a Plan a correlational study to investigate factor(s) which might be related to the effectiveness of this treatment. Your plan must include:
      • how the variables will be measured
      • the types of data and how it will be analysed. [10]
   b i State one reason for your decision about how to measure your variables. [2]
      ii Explain one strength of the type of data in your planned study. [2]
      iii Explain one reason why the findings of the planned study will lack causality. [2]

Imaginal desensitisation

Think!

What is meant by 'having second thoughts' in the context of **imaginal desensitisation**?

Think!

Imagine you are the director of a centre of excellence for the treatment of impulse control disorders. Imaginal desensitisation is a popular choice for many clients and you need a new therapist. You are writing a job advert. What will you write for the personal specification – what skills and qualities would you want the therapist to have?

Think!

On page 299, you learned about a woman with kleptomania (Glover, 1985). Can you think of any reasons why imaginal desensitisation might have been a better option for this woman? If you were her friend, would you rather she participated in covert sensitisation or imaginal desensitisation?

KEY TERMS

imaginal desensitisation

progressive muscle relaxation

guided imagery

scripts

handouts

stressors

comorbid

The most important part of an imaginal desensitisation therapist's job is to construct a script that is highly personalised to the individual's situation and capable of evoking the appropriate reactions; getting a good understanding of the client's personal circumstances beforehand is therefore critical. What sort of skills and qualities do you think an imaginal desensitisation therapist would need in order to do their job effectively?

▲ Figure 6.33

For people with impulse control disorders, specific environmental cues often trigger irresistible urges to engage in behaviours, including gambling, stealing and fire-starting. Imaginal desensitisation uses relaxation-based imagery to reduce the strength of these urges, by reducing excitement and physiological arousal relating to the triggering stimulus.

The therapy empowers the client through developing coping skills and building a sense of self efficacy. It is based on McConaghy's (1980) Behaviour Completion Mechanism, an idea which suggests that compulsive behaviours are repeated because the person never completes a full behavioural sequence, which leads to tension and the urge to carry out the behaviour again. Imaginal desensitisation works by helping the person to imagine a full behavioural sequence and all the feelings that go with it in order to reduce urges, behaviour and the tension that reinforces the habit.

Progressive muscle relaxation

Sessions typically take place in a quiet room and begin with four to five minutes of **progressive muscle relaxation** (PMR), a technique that involves tensing different muscle groups while breathing in and relaxing the muscles while breathing out. This technique can bring about a state of relaxation that means anxiety cannot interfere with the person's concentration during the **guided imagery** session. Once learned, it can also be applied in situations which trigger arousal and urges. For example, a shopping bag that has been previously used for stealing may become a cue (conditioned stimulus). Seeing the bag increases arousal and triggers the urge, but PMR may help the person to quickly regain a sense of calm, neutralising the urge to steal.

Guided imagery

Guided imagery is also used to reverse physiological arousal to the point where the stimulus no longer leads to the same bodily response, making way for alternative, more adaptive responses. Guided imagery sessions can be highly personalised and **scripts** are typically written for each client based on their own personal circumstances (see Table 6.8). They are designed to evoke a range of feelings and thoughts, ultimately emphasising the negative consequences of the behaviour. In a guided imagery session, the person will listen to the script, either read by the therapist in person or via an audio-recording. Scripts usually comprise six scenes or stages (see Table 6.8) separated by a few minutes of PMR. The regular PMR helps to maintain a state of deep relaxation throughout the script.

Therapists typically prepare two or three different scripts each focusing on a different sequence of events linked to the target behaviour. These may focus on different triggers, venues, etc. If clients have similar behaviours to previous clients, therapists may sometimes use a generic script – that is, one that is not specific to any particular client, but may be useful in many situations.

Designing a script

During the initial session, the therapist will use open questions to identify typical behavioural sequences linked to the onset of urges. Some environmental cues may be easy to identify, such as radio adverts for the lottery, but personal cues, such as 'feeling lonely', can be more difficult. Clients may be asked to monitor urges before the initial discussion using **handouts** to identify cues.

The therapist will then break the sequence of events into four to six scenes that lead up to the target behaviour, such as awareness of urge, collecting required items for the behaviour, travelling to the venue where the behaviour will take place and starting the behaviour.

Next, the therapist will write a personalised guided imagery script of approximately 20 minutes, including the six stages. This script will then be used in face-to-face sessions with the client and made into an audio-recording for use between sessions.

Homework

As with all types of cognitive-behavioural therapy, clients are asked to participate in guided imagery two to three times a day for five to seven days, recording their progress on specially prepared handouts provided by the therapist. Blaszczynski and Nower (2003) advise a minimum of 15 sessions within seven days, with each 20-minute session being completed at the same time each day, such as first thing in the morning, late afternoon and before bed. The handouts are designed to track the guided imagery sessions, as well as monitoring strength of urges and any incidents of the target behaviour.

Clients may only have two or three face-to-face sessions with the therapist, one to inform the design of the script, another to practise the relaxation strategies and run through the script, plus details of how to practise at home to greatest effect, and finally one further session to check on the client's progress and to see whether the script needs modifying.

Focus on: Blaszczynski and Nower (2003)

▶ CASE HISTORY

Mary Doe was a 52-year-old, divorced, American mother of two grown-up children. She worked as a bookkeeper and lived alone. Her fascination with gambling began while watching her grandmother play cards as a child. She started playing for money while still at school. Shy and overweight, she did not socialise much but became pregnant with twins while still in high school. She did not have a boyfriend and her mother helped her raise the children.

Mary's gambling

When gambling was legalised in her state (Missouri, USA), she began daily visits to a local casino after work. Her losses amounted to $25,000 and caused her to imagine stealing to get money to continue gambling.

▶ TREATMENT

The therapist spoke to Mary about **stressors** in her life that were triggering the behaviour and explained that they would create a script to use in the guided imagery sessions. They spoke together about patterns of behaviour associated with her gambling and the therapist created one full behavioural sequence relating to her gambling but ending positively (see Table 6.8).

▼ Table 6.8 A full behavioural sequence, with examples of the script used to treat Mary Doe

Scene	Purpose of each stage	Application to Mary's script
1	Initiating the urge, such as describing time of day, location, who is present and what had just happened	Time of day: 17.00; seeing people begin to leave work, feelings of loneliness as she thought about going home to her empty flat; urge to go to the casino; sadness strengthens the urge; anticipation and excitement about gambling reduce sadness
		Example: 'You are at work and notice that it is getting close to 5 o'clock. As you see others starting to leave, you become aware of an urge to gamble. You have been working all day and need to unwind. You are tired but the last thing you want is to spend another night alone in your apartment. You begin to feel anxious as more and more workers leave for the day.'
2	Planning to act on the urge, such as collecting required items, travelling to venue	Drives to the casino, feeling exhilarated
		Example: 'You start to think of what you will do after work. Everything seems too lonely. Where could you go to be with people and have fun? You decide to drive by the casino on the way home. You know you're low on money, but just seeing the lights would make you feel so much better. You pack your things and leave work, feeling excited.'
3	Arriving at the venue, such as looking round the location	Looking at the lights and hearing the music, noise of the machines
		Example: 'As you drive up to the casino and approach the entrance, your excitement builds. You can hardly wait to get inside. You see others entering the casino, you see the doors opening and hear the music. As you enter, you look around. You see the lights, the colours, you smell the popcorn and vanilla scent in the air.'
4	Generating arousal and excitement, such as aspects of the venue that create positive feelings about the behaviour	Finds her favourite table and dealer to play poker
		Example: 'You see your favourite dealer. He smiles at you. You have $1 in your purse and an ATM card in case you need it. As you approach his table, you feel confident you will win. You will be lucky tonight. You plan your bet and the dealer deals you the first hand.'

Scene	Purpose of each stage	Application to Mary's script
5	Having 'second thoughts', such as identifying negative aspects of the venue, other people there and the behaviour, focus on boredom, reducing the sense of arousal	As the game unfolds, her thoughts turn to prior losses and thoughts about her unpaid bills; feels sense of shame/guilt *Example: 'As the dealer deals you a card, you start to get second thoughts. You look around and see the other people at the tables. They look discouraged. You start to think of past times when you lost, remember the despair of losing. You are not so confident any more. You start thinking of all your debts and other things you could do with your money.'*
6	Decreasing attractiveness of behaviour, such as getting clients to think about negative outcomes that have happened in the past and potential alternative	Leaves the casino (feeling relieved and accomplished); goes to a movie theatre (cinema) instead *Example: 'You are remembering more and more times in the past when you lost, and you know that losing is a likely outcome. As you think of your bills, your inability to pay your mortgage, gambling no longer seems attractive. You leave the table and walk out of the club. You are happy with your decision and think of other things you could do with your time and money.'*

Evaluating Blaszczynski and Nower (2003)

One strength of the case study of Mary is that the case history provides detailed qualitative data of Mary's family and gambling history. For example, Blaszczynski and Nower (2003) provide details of her losses, preferred type of gambling and age of onset, all of which may be relevant in terms of positive response to treatment. This level detail is important as it will enable other therapists to make decisions about the extent to which the findings might be transferable to their own clients.

A weakness of this case study is that the researchers do not provide any information about the success of the therapy. Mary's story is used more as an illustrative example to other therapists regarding how to write a suitable script based on details from the case history. This is important as without the findings other therapists may know how to conduct the therapy but may not be completely convinced of its long-term efficacy and so would need to seek further evidence before using it with their own clients.

Evaluating imaginal desensitisation

A strength of imaginal desensitisation is that it is supported by research evidence. For example, 80 per cent of people with gambling disorder found long-term relief following six sessions of this therapy (Grant *et al.*, 2011). After six months, gambling urges and behaviour were much improved compared with pre-treatment. This shows that, despite the reduction in hours with a therapist (due to the use of audio-recordings), the therapy can still have long-term success. This said, there was a small increase in symptoms at the six-month follow-up compared with immediate post-treatment, suggesting relapse is possible without maintenance sessions or regular practice.

From a practical perspective, the therapy has a high level of client satisfaction, not least because it is quicker and so cheaper than other types of cognitive-behavioural therapy. As sessions can be recorded, the therapist's time is primarily spent interviewing clients in order to write personalised scripts rather than delivering one-to-one therapy sessions. This is a strength as it makes the therapy more cost-effective for both the client and the service provider, thus increasing access to therapy for people who may not otherwise be able to afford it.

A weakness is that the therapy may not work for clients who are under-motivated or poorly organised as they may forget their daily guided imagery sessions. Specifically, the Blaszczynski and Nower (2003) study suggests that imaginal desensitisation may be less effective for people with attention deficit disorder or **comorbid** disorders, including depression. That said, Grant *et al.* (2012) successfully treated a 17-year-old Korean-American client with autism spectrum disorder, obsessive-compulsive disorder and kleptomania. This is important as it demonstrates that therapists should make decisions based on individual clients, building on their personal strengths, as sometimes a therapy may be successful even for clients with complex needs, depending on the support that they have available to them.

A final weakness of the therapy is that it relies on the client being able to reach a state of deep relaxation in order to fully immerse themselves in the imagery. Some clients might find this very difficult and may require medication to help them to relax sufficiently. Furthermore, the therapy takes a good deal of effort in terms of carrying out the guided imagery sessions three times a day, if only for one week. For these reasons some clients may prefer to either augment imaginal desensitisation with anti-anxiety medication to help them to relax while conducting the guided imagery sessions or they may simply prefer to use opiate antagonists or another drug treatment as with drug treatments there is very minimal effort required, other than remembering to take the medication.

> ## ▶ LEARNING LINKS
>
> One of the assumptions of the social approach (see page 129) is that our behaviour is shaped by the social and cultural groups to which we see ourselves as belonging. Cultural differences (see page 225) can also affect how people respond in therapy. Gambling disorder is twice as common in people with Asian cultural identity than the white Caucasian population. Tse *et al.* (2004) and Scalia (2003) found that 19 per cent of Chinese restaurant workers in Montreal were pathological gamblers. As psychological therapies for gambling disorder were developed and tested on people from individualist backgrounds, it is critical that research is conducted with people with Asian, and especially Chinese, cultural identity. Raylu *et al.* (2013) report a number of ways that therapists can work more effectively with clients with strong collectivist cultural values. For example, in these cultures, clinicians are seen as highly respected experts, meaning some Asian clients may not fully understand their collaborative role in helping the therapists to write personalised scripts. Also, when asked questions like 'Do you understand what you need to do?', some Asian clients may agree, whether they understand or not, as it would be seen as disrespectful to say 'No'. This suggests that therapists may sometimes need to ask more open questions and find other ways of checking that clients fully understand homework exercises, for example.

> ## STUDY TIP
>
> You will need to invest significant time into learning the differences between each of the therapies in this chapter. You could create a character with pyromania; write a case history for this person and then write a script for their first therapy session where they are being interviewed by the therapist to obtain information to create the six-stage, personalised guided imagery session.
>
> Swap with someone else at this point (if you can) and write a guided imagery session for your partner's client. You could even record it as a podcast to remind you that this is exactly how the therapy is delivered in real life.

> ## ▶ TEST YOURSELF
>
> 1 Ulrike has pyromania. Her mother, Freya, has booked a session with an imaginal desensitisation therapist, but Ulrike is nervous and does not want to go. Based on your knowledge of imaginal desensitisation, explain two ways Freya could reassure her daughter. [4]
>
> 2 Compare one biological treatment and one psychological therapy for impulse control disorders. [4]
>
> 3 a Describe imaginal desensitisation as a psychological therapy for impulse control disorders. [6]
>
>   b Evaluate imaginal desensitisation as a psychological therapy for impulse control disorders, including a discussion of reductionism versus holism. [10]
>
> 4 Ling wants to conduct a semi-structured interview with a man who had received imaginal desensitisation therapy for gambling disorder, but her friend Aaron thinks she should use a structured interview. Explain whether you agree more with Ling or Aaron. [4]

5   Case studies are often used in clinical psychology. Explain one reason why it may not be possible to generalise the findings of case studies investigating impulse control disorders.   [2]

6   a   State one research method that could be used to investigate impulse control disorders, other than case studies.   [1]

    b   Explain two strengths of using the research method you have suggested in part a to investigate impulse control disorders.   [4]

6.4 Anxiety and fear-related disorders

6.4.1 Diagnostic criteria (ICD-11)

Think!

Two people watch a presentation in class including images of medical needles and flowers. What important differences might there be in the reactions of a person with trypanophobia (phobia of needles) compared with a person with a specific phobia of flowers?

Think!

Some of you may know what it is like to live with an **anxiety** disorder like **generalised anxiety disorder (GAD)**, as this disorder affects as many as 3 per cent of people at some point in their lives. If not, try to imagine what it might be like. How might it affect your everyday life, including your relationships with friends, family, teachers or your employer? Do people talk about anxiety in your culture(s) or do people tend to hide their worries from other people?

Think!

Can you think of any reasons why **blood, injection and injury phobias** are more common than other types of specific phobia? Can you think of reasons that relate to nature as well as nurture?

KEY TERMS

anxiety

generalised anxiety disorder (GAD)

blood-injection-injury phobia

sympathetic branch of the autonomic nervous system

insomnia

GAD-7

agoraphobia

Blood Injection Phobia Inventory (BIPI)

METHODOLOGY

questionnaires

validity

subjective and objective data

reliability

psychometric tests

Blood and needle phobias are one of the more common specific phobias, but they can have a serious impact on people's lives.

» Can you think of any situations that people with a blood phobia might avoid in order to limit the probability of coming into contact with their own blood or that of another person or animal?

» How might their attempts to avoid blood impact their health and wellbeing and that of their family?

The autonomic nervous system and the stress response

In the study by Hölzel *et al.* (mindfulness and brain scans), you learned about localisation of function in the brain and how mindfulness can help to reduce stress. The brain is part of the central nervous system (CNS), but the nervous system is in fact broken into several divisions. The second main division is called the peripheral nervous system (PNS), which connects the CNS to the organs, limbs and skin. This is divided into the somatic nervous system (which controls voluntary actions) and the autonomic nervous system (ANS), which controls involuntary processes in the body. The ANS transmits signals to and from our vital organs. It controls breathing, heart rate, digestion and how we respond to threats (the stress response). The **sympathetic branch of the ANS** increases arousal and makes us alert and ready for fight or flight (i.e. to defend ourselves or run away), while the parasympathetic branch returns the body to its normal resting state.

» Can you remember the last time your cheeks blushed, your heart raced or you broke out in a sweat due to an immediate stress response?

» How long does this usually take to go away after an immediate shock?

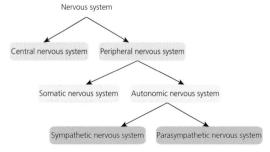

▲ **Figure 6.34 Divisions of the nervous system**

Generalised anxiety disorder (GAD) is characterised by intense, persistent and unreasonable anxiety about everyday things. This disorder is only diagnosed if a person experiences symptoms almost every day, for several months. Symptoms include a general sense of **apprehension** called free floating anxiety and excessive worries about family, health, finance, school or work. Symptoms can be:

» physical, such as muscle aches and pains, insomnia, digestive problems like constipation and diarrhoea
» behavioural, such as restlessness, irritability
» affective, such as feeling nervous
» cognitive, such as being unable to concentrate.

Diagnoses are only made if the person is experiencing high levels of distress and disruption to their daily functioning at work, home or school. Before making a diagnosis, other conditions must be ruled out (eliminated), such as social phobia or panic disorder. The doctor must be sure that symptoms are not caused by prescribed medication or recreational drug use.

Unlike schizophrenia, people with GAD often have good insight into their condition; they often are aware that their anxieties are irrational but they cannot control their thoughts and feelings and find this distressing. Like the other disorders discussed in this chapter, GAD may be mild, moderate or severe, meaning some people are able to function relatively well, whereas for other people anxiety can have a major impact on the person's ability to perform everyday tasks, such as shopping or socialising with friends and family.

The prevalence of GAD is estimated to be around 2–5 per cent and Spitzer *et al.* (2006) found that in a large sample from Missouri, USA, the prevalence was 9 per cent in women and 4 per cent in men.

The Generalised Anxiety Disorder Assessment (GAD-7)

The **GAD-7** (Spitzer *et al.*, 2006) is a seven-item **questionnaire** that can also be used as a structured interview schedule. Respondents are asked how often they have experienced anxiety-related symptoms in the last two weeks. Items are rated on a four-point scale, from 0–3 (see Figure 6.35 for sample items and the labelling of the four points on the scale).

1 Feeling nervous, anxious or on edge?

| Not at all (0) | Several days (1) | More than half the days (2) | Nearly every day (4) |

2 Trouble relaxing?

| Not at all (0) | Several days (1) | More than half the days (2) | Nearly every day (4) |

3 Being so restless that it is hard to sit still?

| Not at all (0) | Several days (1) | More than half the days (2) | Nearly every day (4) |

▲ Figure 6.35 Sample items from the Generalised Anxiety Disorder Assessment (GAD-7)

A score of 5 out of 21 indicates mild GAD, whereas a score of 10 out of 21 indicates moderate GAD and should trigger a referral to a psychiatrist for a more detailed assessment and/or a therapist for support. Scores of more than 15 are indicative of severe GAD, suggesting that these people should be prioritised, due to the significant negative impact their condition is likely to be having on their lives.

Initially, the GAD-7 had 13 items, but following research with 2739 people from Missouri, the final seven items were selected. This study revealed the people diagnosed with GAD (n=73) had an average GAD-7 score of 14.4 and those without GAD averaged 4.9 (Spitzer *et al.*, 2006).

Evaluating the GAD-7

One strength of the GAD-7 is that research evidence suggests that this psychometric test has strong test-retest reliability. For example, Spitzer *et al.* (2006) tested participants twice, one week apart, and found a strong positive correlation between the pairs of scores (+0.83).

This is important as tests need to be reliable in order to provide useful and meaningful data that can be used to prioritise cases appropriately.

Another strength is that the GAD-7 is quick and easy to use. In comparison with the BIPI, which is a very long and detailed **questionnaire**, the GAD-7 has just seven items, yet it still has excellent validity (as shown through its strong positive correlation with scores obtained on other respected measures of anxiety; Spitzer *et al.*, 2006). This is important as, in practice, doctors often have very limited time to assess patients before having to make critical decisions about whether to refer the patient to another professional. Unnecessary referrals lead to longer waiting lists for patients who may need urgent help, meaning that doctors need tests like the GAD-7 that are quick to administer but differentiate effectively between mild, moderate and severe cases.

A weakness of the GAD-7 is that it is unclear whether it provides an accurate reflection of the severity of symptoms over time. For example, Spitzer *et al.* (2006) conducted two assessments just one week apart rather than conducting a lengthier longitudinal study. This is important because, for a diagnosis to be made, a person must have experienced symptoms over several months and it is difficult to know from the GAD-7 alone whether a person's symptoms are likely to get better or worse over time as it merely provides a snapshot of their current mental state and this may not be **reliable**.

Agoraphobia

The prefix *agora* comes from the Ancient Greek word for an open, public space, such as a marketplace, and *phobia* refers to excessive fear or anxiety shown in response to a specific object or situation. To receive a diagnosis of **agoraphobia** a person's fear response will be triggered by multiple situations from which 'escape might be difficult or help might not be available, such as using public transportation, being in crowds, being outside the home alone (e.g. in shops, theatres, standing in line)' (World Health Organization, 2018).

People with agoraphobia often avoid such situations due to fear of having a panic attack or suffering from other symptoms in public. If they do put themselves into their feared situations, it will generally only be with a well-trusted friend or relative and they may endure high levels of anxiety while doing so. As with GAD, a diagnosis will not be made unless the person has experienced symptoms for several months and their fear/anxiety is causing them significant distress and affecting their personal, social and occupational functioning (i.e. their ability to cope with the demands of everyday life at home, work and/or school).

Specific phobia (blood-injection-injury)

People with specific phobias show irrational and/or excessive fear of certain situations (e.g. flying, heights) or in the presence of certain objects or animals. In the learning approach, you learned about Saavedra and Silverman's (button phobia) case study of a nine-year-old boy with a specific phobia of buttons (page 114); button phobia is an example of a relatively unusual specific phobia. An example of a more common specific phobia is the fear of blood (haemophobia), injections/medical needles (trypanophobia) and injury. Although many phobias cause an increase in heart rate and blood pressure, people with blood and needle phobias often experience a sudden decrease in blood pressure causing them to faint (lose consciousness).

Mas *et al.* (2010) (see page 310) report that most people with blood, injection and injury phobias self-report that they have had this phobia since childhood (72 per cent) and, in nearly half of all cases, there is a first-degree relative with the same disorder (46 per cent). The majority say that the disorder causes significant impairment to their daily functioning (86 per cent) and half reported that fainting was a common part of their response.

The Blood Injection Phobia Inventory

An **inventory** is a detailed list of items. In the **Blood Injection Phobia Inventory (BIPI)**, the items are 18 situations relating to blood and injections/medical needles, involving themselves and/or others. Some of the items relate to **situational anxiety** – that is, how a person would feel, think and behave when actually confronting the situation, whereas others assess **anticipatory anxiety** – how they would feel, think and behave in the time leading up to the event. Participants have to rate how often they experience 27 different cognitive, biological and behavioural reactions. The rating scale ranges from 0 (never) to 3 (always).

Here are some sample items from the BIPI:
1   When I see an injured person after an accident, bleeding in the road or on the television.
2   When I think about a pool of blood on the floor.
3   When I think I have to accompany a relative to have a blood test or to treat an open wound.

▼ Table 6.9 Sample responses from the BIPI

Cognitive	'I think that people will notice how distressed I feel.'	'I think I'm going to faint.'
Biological	'My palms and armpits sweat.'	'I feel my face is hot.'
Behavioural	'My legs and/or hands shake.'	'My words don't come out fluidly or my voice is uneven.'

Evaluating the BIPI

One strength of the BIPI is that it provides **valid** evidence regarding phobic symptoms in people from Spanish-speaking cultures. For example, Mas *et al.* (2010) found a strong positive correlation between scores on the BIPI and the blood subscale of the Fear Questionnaire (FQ), a psychometric scale developed to measure phobic symptoms in English-language users. This is important as if the BIPI is to be used in research with Spanish-language users, outcomes must be comparable with research conducted in other languages.

A weakness of the BIPI is that the self-reported data relies on the person's interpretation of their symptoms and is, therefore, **subjective**. For example, people are asked about how they think they would respond in certain situations rather than actually observing their behaviour in real life. This is important as there may be a mismatch between how people think they would respond and how they would actually respond.

Another strength of the BIPI is that it is thorough in terms of the breadth of situations and symptoms that it measures. It covers 27 different cognitive, biological and behavioural symptoms and 18 situations, giving a total of 486 data points per person. This detailed approach means the BIPI should be extremely helpful to therapists in designing individualised treatment programmes focused on each patient's specific symptoms, such as whether they are more fearful of their own blood or that of other people or animals, for example.

Focus on: Mas *et al.* (2010)

▶ AIM

To develop a valid and reliable measure of blood anxiety and blood phobia symptoms for people who speak Spanish as their first language. At the time, there was no questionnaire specifically designed for this population.

METHODOLOGY

Thirty-nine people with a diagnosis of blood phobia and 135 matched controls completed a questionnaire containing 50 situations relating to agoraphobia, social phobia (fear of social situations) and blood-injection phobia. They rated how often they experienced cognitive, biological and behavioural phobic responses on a four-point Likert-style scale.

To create the final list of items that would make up the BIPI, the researchers removed ten items that resulted in no significant difference between the average scores obtained by the phobic group versus the control group.

After further analysis, the 18 items that were best at identifying people with blood phobia from those without the disorder were selected.

All participants were from Andalusia in Spain and the average age was 24. The two groups were matched for age, marital status and educational level.

The phobic group were also interviewed to gather additional information about their phobia and completed the Fear Questionnaire (FQ) (Marks and Mathews, 1979) to assess symptoms of agoraphobia, social phobia and blood-injection phobia.

RESULTS

There was a strong positive correlation between BIPI score and scores on the blood sub-section of the FQ. People with blood phobias obtained significantly higher scores on the BIPI than people without a previous diagnosis of blood phobia.

CONCLUSIONS

The scale was found to be a reliable and valid measure of blood phobia in Spanish speakers and, therefore, useful in diagnosing this disorder.

Evaluating Mas *et al.* (2010)

One weakness of Mas *et al.* (2010) is that the sample included significantly more females than males in the blood phobic group. There were three times as many females as males (female n=30, male n=9). This matters because it may mean that the BIPI is better at detecting blood-injection phobia in females as males were not well represented in the original sample.

A strength of Mas *et al.* (2010) is the rigorous statistical analysis that was used to select the final 18 situations from the original list of 50. A technique called factor analysis was used to ensure that items that were least helpful in diagnosing blood phobia were removed, leaving only the most useful items. This is important as all the data obtained by psychometric tests like the BIPI should be useful in identifying vulnerable people who need support.

People with anxiety disorders generally know that their worries are irrational and/or excessive; often people become even more anxious about their inability to control their anxiety. We all have worries that arrive in our minds without warning but it's often what we do with these worries that determines whether they develop into anxiety. What strategies do you find helpful to shift your focus away from your worries?

▲ Figure 6.36

> **LEARNING LINKS**
....

You have now learned about several questionnaires designed to diagnose mental disorders such as depressive disorder (the Beck Depression Inventory) and blood-injection phobia (the BIPI). At AS Level, you learned about the FFMQ used by Hölzel *et al.* (mindfulness and brain scans) to measure the five facets of mindfulness and the ASQ used by Baron-Cohen *et al.* (eyes test) to measure autism spectrum traits. One problem with lengthy questionnaires is that participants sometimes begin to answer all the questions in a very similar way, without considering the differences between each of the items. When this happens, we call it a response set and generally the data is less valid as it is not an accurate reflection of the participants' thoughts, feelings and experiences.

Which do you think is likely to obtain the most valid data – a longer questionnaire like the BIPI or a really short questionnaire like the GAD-7?

STUDY TIP

Remember, a measurement is valid if it is useful, meaningful and accurate. There are many different ways of deciding whether a psychometric test is valid. Firstly, you could see whether the test is able to differentiate (tell the difference) between people who are known to have a certain disorder and people who do not have the disorder. The people with the disorder should achieve a higher average score than those who do not have the disorder. Another way to assess the validity of a test is to see whether there is a correlation between scores on the test and scores on another test of the same disorder. A test would not be valid if the same person received a high score on one test and a low score on the other if both tests were measuring the same thing.

> **TEST YOURSELF**
....

1   Kaamil works in a busy office but recently he has been unable to concentrate, he is restless, is unable to relax and feels nervous all the time. His doctor thinks he may have generalised anxiety disorder. Suggest two questions Kaamil's doctor might ask to help her to decide whether Kaamil has generalised anxiety disorder. [2]

2   Outline one similarity and one difference between agoraphobia and generalised anxiety disorder. [2]

3   a   Describe the Blood Injection Phobia Inventory (BIPI). [6]

   b   Evaluate the Blood Injection Phobia Inventory (BIPI), with reference to one research study, including a discussion of psychometric tests. [10]

4   Outline two features of the questionnaire as a research method for investigating anxiety and fear-related disorders. [2]

5   The data collected using the BIPI is subjective. Give one objective way that a researcher could collect data about blood, injection and/or injury phobias. [2]

6   Jaycee is developing a questionnaire to measure agoraphobia. She has listed 20 situations that she thinks might trigger anxiety-related symptoms in people with this disorder. She will ask her participants to rate their thoughts and feelings in each situation on a five-point scale, such as 'I think that something bad is going to happen' and 'I feel like I might be sick'.

   a   Identify one way that Jaycee could check that her scale is reliable. [2]

   b   Identify one way that Jaycee could check that her scale is valid. [2]

KEY TERMS

NTRK3 gene

de novo

DUP25

transgenic mice

METHODOLOGY

case studies

longitudinal studies

validity

6.4.2 Explanations of anxiety and fear-related disorders

Think!

How is the **NTRK3 gene** linked to anxiety?

Think!

Imagine you are one of the participants in Öst's study. You have completed the interview and questionnaires and had your heart rate and blood pressure recorded. You have just found out about the behavioural tests (watching the surgery video or the finger-prick blood test). How would you feel? Would you withdraw at this point? What are your thoughts on the ethics of this study?

Think!

Imagine a person with a blood phobia sees their child fall over and cut their knees. Can you think of reasons why they might show more and/or less fear than the participants in Öst's study who watched a video of thoracic surgery?

Do you or any of your family or friends get nervous or feel sick when watching hospital dramas, violent crime programmes or horror films? Using the information on these pages, can you explain why some people find hospital dramas, violent crime programmes or horror films more difficult to watch than other people?

▲ Figure 6.37

Biological explanation

Genetic inheritance

Before the Human Genome Project was completed in 2003, biological psychologists relied on family, twin and adoption studies to investigate the role of nature and nurture in the development of anxiety disorders and fear-related disorders. Below you will learn about Lars-Göran Öst's study of blood-injection phobias (Öst, 1992). This study suggests that blood phobia may be more heritable than other specific phobias as more of the blood phobics said that they had either a parent or a sibling with the same disorder than the injection phobics.

De novo mutations

Vulnerability to anxiety disorders and fear-related disorders may be genetic but differences between people with and without these disorders may not necessarily be due to genetic inheritance. Instead, vulnerability may arise due to new or *de novo* genetic mutations that can affect the child's mental health but are not present in all or even any of the biological parents' cells.

A *de novo* mutation thought to be linked with agoraphobia and specific phobias disorder was discovered by Gratacòs *et al.* (2001) in a sample of Spanish participants. Ninety per cent of people with fear-related disorders in this study had a duplication of a stretch of DNA on chromosome 15 (called **DUP25**) compared with only 7 per cent of his control group of people without fear-related disorders. The link between DUP25 and anxiety/fear is believed to be associated with the duplication of the NTRK3 gene. Previous research has linked this gene to emotional and behavioural arousal in response to external stimuli. Over-expression could, therefore, increase vulnerability to anxiety and fear-related disorders.

How is NTRK3 gene linked to anxiety and fear-related disorders?

Neurotrophins are proteins that are essential for the healthy function and development of our neurons. NTRK3 provides the instructions for the development of a type of neurotrophin receptor called NT-3. There are many of these receptors in a brain structure called the locus coeruleus in the brain stem and this brain structure has been linked to arousal, vigilance and attention. Over-expression of the NTRK gene in this brain structure may be linked to high levels of noradrenaline, a neurotransmitter linked with stress and anxiety (Armengol et al., 2002).

Focus on: Öst (1992)

▶ AIM

To compare people with blood-injection phobias in terms of cognitive, biological and behavioural variables in order to determine whether these phobias should be separated into blood phobia and injection phobia or whether they are so similar they should be treated as one phobia (i.e. blood-injection phobia).

▶ METHODOLOGY

Self-report data

Interviews and questionnaires were conducted with 81 people with blood phobia and 59 people with injection phobia to gather data about the origin of their phobias, age of onset, family history (i.e. whether any other relatives had the same disorder), age when treatment started and history of fainting in the feared situation. Data from another study of people with claustrophobia, animal and dental phobias was used for comparison (Öst, 1987). Participants had to picture themselves in anxiety-arousing situations and rate the severity of 11 biological and 10 cognitive reactions on a scale of 0 (no reaction) to 4 (very strong reaction).

Behavioural tests

Blood phobics watched a colour-video of thoracic surgery and injection phobics had a finger-prick blood test. Participants could withdraw at any point. Time taken before withdrawal was noted and fainting was rated on a scale of 0–4. Participants self-reported their anxiety on a scale of 0–10 and indicated which of five positive and negative thoughts they had experienced. Heart rate and blood pressure were recorded before and after the tests.

▶ RESULTS

▼ Table 6.10 Findings from Öst (1992)

	Blood phobics	Injection phobics
Met criteria for diagnosis of both phobias	69%	31%
Phobia is shared with at least one parent and/or sibling	61%	29%
Feared fainting when exposed to source of their phobia	77%	48%

Questionnaires and interviews

People with blood phobia were more likely to meet criteria for injection phobia than people with injection phobia were to meet criteria for blood phobia. Blood phobics were more likely to have a first-degree relative with the same phobia as them than injection phobics. Blood phobics were also more fearful of fainting than infection phobics. Injection phobics only had higher average scores than the blood phobics for two of the eleven biological reactions.

Behavioural tests

Injection phobics had higher heart rates and blood pressure than blood phobics at the point of withdrawal. The blood phobics experienced small decreases in heart rate and blood pressure at this point. Both groups withdrew approximately one third of the way through the tests and experienced similar levels of anxiety. Fainting was much more common in the blood-phobic group.

6

CONCLUSIONS

There are more similarities than differences between people with blood and injection phobias and, therefore, these phobias should not be separated into two different diagnoses. Blood phobia appears to have a stronger genetic component than injection phobia and biological reactions are more severe. When compared with non-blood-injection-injury (BII) phobias (e.g. claustrophobia, animal and dental), injection phobia was more commonly shared by first-degree relatives and more likely to lead to fainting.

Evaluating Öst (1992)

One strength of Öst is that the initial diagnosis of blood-injection phobias was checked before further testing was conducted. Following an interview using the Anxiety Disorders Interview Schedule, seven people were deselected as they did not meet the DSM-III criteria for specific phobia. This is a strength as relying on secondary data can mean results may not be **valid**.

A further strength of this study was the use of behavioural tests which provided **objective data**. For example, the observers recorded how long participants were able to endure their feared stimuli rather than relying on participants' recall of encounters with blood or injections. This is important as memory, especially of emotional situations, can be highly unreliable.

A weakness of the behavioural tests is that the findings may lack ecological **validity**. For example, the participants with blood phobia watched a video of an operation and this is not the same as being confronted with one's own blood or the blood of a close friend or family member. This is important as the number of people who fainted and the amount of time they endured their feared stimuli may have differed in real life.

A final weakness was that the data about first-degree relatives with the same disorder may not have been **valid**. The participants were asked whether either of their parents or any of their siblings had the same phobia as them. These relatives were not tracked down and assessed properly, meaning the data may not have been accurate.

Evaluating the genetic explanation

One strength of the genetic explanation of blood-injection-injury phobia is that it is supported by evidence from twin studies. For example, Distel *et al.* (2008) found a concordance rate of 39 per cent for monozygotic (MZ) twins but only 9 per cent for dizygotic (DZ) twins, where one twin was diagnosed with the disorder. As both twins in each pair shared similar environmental circumstances, the difference in the concordance rates can only be explained by the difference in the amount of shared DNA between MZ and DZ twin pairs (i.e. 100 per cent compared with 50 per cent).

Further support for the genetic explanation comes from research with **transgenic mice**. For example, Dierssen *et al.* (2006) found that mice that over-expressed the NTRK3 gene showed increased anxiety-like behaviour and panic responses when encountering threatening stimuli and situations in a test called the Mouse Defense Test Battery. These mice also had a higher density of neurons that communicate via noradrenaline in the locus coeruleus. This suggests that DUP25 may increase vulnerability to anxiety disorders and fear-related disorders in humans.

ISSUES AND DEBATES

Determinism versus free will debate

A weakness is that the genetic explanation is overly deterministic. For example, it suggests that over- or under-expression of certain genes determines how we think, feel and behave. This ignores the role of free will. Some people may be more vulnerable to anxiety due to their genes, but they deliberately choose to use techniques such as mindfulness and yoga (see page 29) to control their anxiety. Research demonstrates that such behaviours can be effective in altering our brain chemistry, suggesting that free will also has an important role to play in shaping our wellbeing (see page 227).

Nature versus nurture

A further weakness of the genetic explanation is that it ignores the role of nurture. Although epigenetic research suggests that environmental factors can affect gene expression and cause *de novo* mutations, the genetic explanation alone cannot explain why 60 per cent of people with DUP25 do not develop anxiety disorders. This is important as it demonstrates that the genetic explanation alone is over-simplified and reductionist and that important environmental factors may protect genetically predisposed individuals from developing symptoms.

Transgenic mice had their genome altered in order to study the function of specific genes. Dierssen *et al.* (2006) studied the link between the NTRK gene and anxiety and panic in mice. Why do you think scientists use mice for genetic research such as Dierssen *et al.* (2006)?

▲ Figure 6.38

▶ LEARNING LINKS

At AS Level, you looked at two animal studies, Hassett *et al.* (monkey toy preferences) and Fagen *et al.* (elephant learning). You will also have studied the ethical guidelines for use of animals in psychological research. If you decide to use the Dierssen *et al.* (2006) study as an example in your writing, you may wish to think about how the species, number and procedures would all have been carefully considered before the researchers were allowed to begin the study. This study presents particularly sensitive ethical issues as the mouse genome was deliberately altered to increase the amount of distress experienced by the mice when exposed to aversive stimuli. How could you argue that studies like this are ethical?

STUDY TIP

It is important to understand not only the details of studies (e.g. aims, procedures, results and conclusions) but also *why* you are learning about them. Öst (1992) is included as it investigates the genetic explanation of anxiety and fear-related disorders by asking participants whether they have first-degree relatives with the same phobia. This section also discusses two other studies that investigate the genetics of anxiety and fear-related disorders – the twin study by Distel *et al.* (2008) and the animal experiment by Dierssen *et al.* (2006). When you are thinking about the validity of these studies, you need to question whether the data is objective and also if it is not reliable, it will not be valid either.

▶ TEST YOURSELF

1   Tanzy's grandmother and her mother, Shania, both have a phobia of blood. Tanzy remembers her mother fainting once when she had a nosebleed. Tanzy worries that she will develop a fear of blood too. Using your knowledge of the genetic explanation of anxiety disorders and fear-related disorders, explain whether Tanzy's worries are justified. [4]

2   a   Outline what is meant by nature versus nurture. [2]

    b   Explain one weakness of explanations for anxiety disorders and fear-related disorders from the nature side of the debate. [2]

3 a Describe the genetic explanation of anxiety disorders and fear-related disorders. [6]

b Evaluate the genetic explanation of anxiety disorders and fear-related disorders, including a discussion of validity. [10]

4 Explain how a researcher might use a longitudinal study to test the genetic explanation of anxiety disorders and fear-related disorders. [4]

5 Questionnaires are sometimes used to investigate phobias. Give an example of a rating scale and a forced/fixed-choice question that could be used to investigate the biological explanations of phobias. [2]

6 Compare two research methods used to investigate phobias. [4]

Psychological explanations

KEY TERMS

unconditioned stimulus

conditioned stimulus

unconditioned response

conditioned response

extinction

neutral stimulus

negative reinforcement

positive reinforcement

transfer/generalise

Think!

What was the purpose of showing Albert the building blocks after he cried when he saw the rat?

Think!

Do you have any fears or phobias? If so, do you remember a specific occasion when you learned your fear? If not, why not make up your own example. How might someone become afraid of the dentist or elevators or balloons? Try to use the terms **unconditioned stimulus, conditioned stimulus, unconditioned response** and **conditioned response** to explain your example.

Think!

Extinction is the process by which a previously learned/conditioned response is no longer triggered by the presence of a conditioned stimulus. With phobias, the conditioned fear response does not become extinct. With this in mind, can you think of a way of extinguishing conditioned fear?

Little Albert was shown different animals in the Watson and Rayner study.

» Which of these animals were not shown to Little Albert as part of Watson and Rayner's study of fear conditioning?

» Can you rate the remaining animals from the least feared to the most feared following the classical conditioning trials?

» Why did Albert fear some of the animals more than others?

▲ Figure 6.39

Behavioural

Classical conditioning

On page 87, you learned about Ivan Pavlov's research on salivation, an involuntary or unconditioned response which occurs in the presence of food (unconditioned stimulus) (Pavlov, 1927). When Pavlov presented a **neutral stimulus** (e.g. a bell or ticking metronome) at the same time or immediately before food, the two stimuli became associated. The dogs now salivated (conditioned response) in the presence of the neutral stimulus. The bell or metronome was now a conditioned stimulus. You also learned briefly about a classic study in the history of psychology, where the founder of behaviourism, John Watson, and Rosalie Rayner demonstrated that fear responses can also be conditioned (Watson and Rayner, 1920; see below).

Maintenance of fear reactions

Once a fear has been acquired through classical conditioning, Mowrer (1947) believes that fears are maintained through operant conditioning. Classically conditioned behaviours usually become extinct as the person learns that the conditioned stimulus is not always followed by the unconditioned stimulus. For example, Albert's fear of rats should become less intense as he learns that the rat is not always followed by a loud noise.

Operant conditioning

If you are interested in evaluating this further beyond the syllabus requirements, you can look at fear-related disorders through the lens of operant conditioning. People with intense fears usually avoid their feared objects/situations. Avoidance helps them to escape the unpleasant feelings of fear. Avoidant behaviour is, therefore, **negatively reinforced** and becomes more frequent. Unfortunately, this also means that the person rarely comes into close contact with their feared object/situation, meaning that there is no opportunity to unlearn the association between the conditioned and unconditioned stimulus.

Fear reactions may also be **positively reinforced** (rewarded) as others often provide comfort and reassurance. These behaviours, though well-intentioned, tend to reinforce or strengthen the fear.

Focus on: Watson and Rayner (1920)

▶ AIM

1   To determine whether a fear response to a rat could be classically conditioned by pairing the rat with a loud noise
2   To determine whether conditioned fear would **transfer (generalise)** to animals/objects similar to the conditioned stimulus
3   To determine the effect of time on learned fears
4   To investigate how learned fears can be removed

▶ METHODOLOGY AND RESULTS

The participant in this three-month longitudinal case study was Albert B (known as Little Albert), a healthy and typically calm nine-month-old infant. He lived in a children's hospital where his mother worked as a nurse.

At approximately nine months: Albert's reactions to various stimuli were observed under controlled conditions, his behaviour was filmed and qualitative data was recorded in a diary. No emotional reaction was shown towards a rabbit, rat, dog, monkey, masks with and without hair, cotton wool or burning newspaper – these were, therefore, referred to as neutral stimuli. When a loud noise (the unconditioned stimulus) was made, by hitting a steel bar with a hammer, Albert was startled, his lip trembled and he cried (unconditioned response).

At 11 months, 3 days: Albert was shown the rat and as he reached towards it the steel bar was hit with the hammer. He flinched, hid his face and gave a distressed whimper.

At 11 months, 10 days: Albert was cautious of, but not scared by, the rat; he played happily with the blocks; the researchers repeated the pairing of the rat and the loud noise five times. After the third pairing, Albert whimpered at the sight of the rat. After two more pairings, he rapidly crawled away, when he saw the rat. Albert was given the building blocks after each trial to quieten him down.

At 11 months, 15 days: Albert was shown the rat, a rabbit, a dog, a fur coat, cotton wool and white hair on a Santa Claus mask. Fear was shown towards all three animals; the dog triggered less fear than the rabbit. Again, he played happily with the blocks but was distressed by the white fluffy items, including Watson's own white hair (not the other two observers' hair).

At 11 months, 20 days: Albert seemed less scared when shown the rat, but his fear quickly returned following one more pairing of the rat and the loud noise. When tested in a different room, he still showed fear towards the rat, but the response was less intense.

At 12 months, 21 days: Albert was still fearful of white fluffy stimuli and animals. His mother withdrew consent and the researchers did not attempt to reverse his fears.

▶ CONCLUSIONS

Watson and Rayner (1920) concluded that it is possible to learn to fear previously neutral stimuli. They suggest that many phobias are conditioned emotional reactions learned in childhood, either through direct association of a neutral and unconditioned stimulus or through transfer of fear to similar stimuli.

Evaluating Watson and Rayner (1920)

One strength is that this study was **longitudinal**; Albert was observed on multiple occasions within a three-month period (between nine and twelve months of age). Collecting data at multiple time points meant that the researchers were able to observe the way his fear increased and decreased over time. This is important as, had they only observed this twice, before and after conditioning, they may have missed important findings about learned fear.

A further strength of this study was the collection of qualitative data. The researchers made detailed observations of his behaviour, describing exactly what he did, how and when with notes about bodily movement and facial expressions as well as attempts to self-soothe (i.e. thumb sucking). This is important as individual children may display fear and efforts to self-soothe in different ways.

A weakness of this study was the use of the laboratory setting where Albert was observed. Although the environment would have become familiar to him over the three-month study, his reaction may have differed if he was observed in his own home. This is important as a child's fear reactions are likely to be greater in unfamiliar environments with people they do not know, compared to how they would respond in a familiar environment with their parents or grandparents. This suggests that the findings may lack ecological validity.

Another weakness is that this study was only conducted on one individual child. Although Watson and Rayner (1920) say that 'at no time did this infant ever show fear in any situation' (p. 1) and that he was a generally unemotional child, it is possible that he developed fears more readily than another child might have done. For example, Alexander and Wilcox (2012) provide a detailed review of sex differences in the first year, suggesting that a female infant may have behaved differently in this study. This is important as it means that the findings should only be generalised with care to people of different ages and genders.

Evaluating the behavioural explanation

A strength of classical conditioning as an explanation of phobias is that it is supported by research evidence. For example, Watson and Rayner (1920) conditioned an 11-month-old baby to be frightened of a pet rat through repeatedly pairing it with a loud bang. This study highlights the role of learning experiences (nurture) in the development of phobias.

A further strength of Watson's explanation is the idea that phobias can be learned, which suggests that phobias can also be unlearned and/or replaced with new behaviours. This realisation inspired the development of therapies such as systematic desensitisation (SD) (see page 328), where the fear response is substituted for a relaxation response in the presence of the feared object. This is important as the real-world applications of this explanation strengthen its validity.

▶ ISSUES AND DEBATES

Nature versus nurture

A weakness is that this explanation ignores the role of biological factors (nature) in the acquisition of phobias. Watson's explanation does not explain why some fears can be conditioned with much greater ease than others. For example, Ohman *et al.* (1975) showed that a fear of snakes can be conditioned with just one pairing of a picture of a snake and an electric shock, whereas at least five pairings are necessary to condition a fear of a picture of a house. This is important as it suggests we may be genetically prepared to acquire some phobias more quickly than others due to the significance of snakes in our evolutionary past.

Determinism versus free will

A further weakness is that the explanation is too deterministic; research findings simply do not match up with its predictions. For example, Di Nardo *et al.* (1988) noted that 50 per cent of a sample of people who were scared of dogs had never had a traumatic experience that might have triggered their phobia and many participants in their non-phobic control group recalled that they in fact had experienced a traumatic event with a dog but had not become phobic. This is important as it suggests that the explanation is over-simplified and that how we interpret events may be more important that than the events themselves.

Watson and Rayner (1920) have been criticised for deliberately setting out to create a fear of animals in an 11-month old baby.
» Which ethical guidelines are violated in this study and which are upheld?
» Can you think of any reason to argue that the benefits to society outweigh the cost to the participant and his mother in this study?

▲ Figure 6.40

▶ LEARNING LINKS

You learned about treatments for phobias when you studied Saavedra and Silverman's (button phobia) case study of the boy with a button phobia. The researchers explained that the phobia developed due to evaluative learning as opposed to expectancy learning. In the case of Little Albert, when he saw the rat, he *expected* a loud bang and reacted to the potential threat before it had actually happened. With the boy with the button phobia, he had not learned to expect any danger or threat, but instead he *evaluated* buttons in a negative way; he found them disgusting. It was not fully explained in the study why this was, but it was potentially linked to feeling embarrassed or ashamed of spilling the bowl of buttons in front of his peers.

STUDY TIP

Whenever you want to apply classical conditioning to a scenario/extract, it is always a good idea to first write out the three stages of classical conditioning, before, during and after (see Table 6.11). Then you can start trying to work out how the aspects of the extract match up with the terms from the theory. Think carefully – in the questions below, you are asked about Duane's fear of flames and fire. The behaviourist explanation states that the thing a phobic person is scared of is a conditioned stimulus and this leads to a conditioned response. You need to think about something that might have frightened Duane that was present at the same time as the flames or that happened just after he saw a flame/fire. This will be the unconditioned stimulus.

▼ Table 6.11 Three stages of classical conditioning

Before conditioning	UCS → UCR
During conditioning	NS + UCS → UCR
After conditioning	CS → CR

TEST YOURSELF

1　Duane has a phobia of flames and fire. On an evening out with his girlfriend, he walked out of a restaurant and sat outside shaking as there were lit candles on the table. Explain Duane's reaction with reference to classical conditioning.　[4]

2　Compare one biological and one psychological explanation of fear-related disorders.　[4]

3　a　Describe one study investigating the behavioural explanation of fear-related disorders.　[6]

　　b　Evaluate one study investigating the behavioural explanation of fear-related disorders, including a discussion of nature versus nurture.　[10]

4　Researchers investigating fear-related disorder collect qualitative data and quantitative data.

　　a　Suggest one way that quantitative data could be used in a study of fear-related disorders.　[2]

　　b　Give one weakness of the suggestion that you made in part a.　[2]

5　Explain one strength and one weakness of using laboratory settings to study fear-related disorders.　[4]

6　a　Outline what is meant by demand characteristics.　[2]

　　b　Explain one reason that demand characteristics are unlikely to affect the validity of studies investigating classical conditioning and fear-related disorders.　[2]

Psychodynamic

KEY TERMS

displacement
unconscious
id
ego
superego
conscience
defence mechanisms
dreamwork
manifest content
latent content
psychosexual stages
fixation
Oedipus complex
castration anxiety
identification
repression

Think!

What is **displacement** and how is it linked to phobias?

Think!

Imagine you are a psychoanalytic therapist. A child with a phobia of scissors comes to your clinic. How might you interpret this phobia?

Think!

Hans once saw a horse collapse in the street and became very distressed, as he thought that the horse had died. How might John Watson have explained Hans' phobia using the principles of classical conditioning?

Five-year-old Hans had a phobia of white horses. On page 324, you will see that Harold Blum (2007) presents an alternative explanation for Hans' phobias, based on mistreatment by his mother, Olga Graf.

» Does this alternative explanation mean that all of Freud's psychodynamic concepts are incorrect or just his interpretation of this child's phobia?
» Could displacement still be used to explain Hans' phobia?

▲ Figure 6.41

Freud believed that, without therapy, people with phobias will never know why they have these irrational fears. This is because the reasons for these symptoms are stored below the level of conscious awareness, in the **unconscious**. For Freud, symptoms of mental disorder, including phobias, are caused by unresolved conflicts from early infancy and childhood.

The id, the ego and the superego

Freud believed that personality has three parts that develop between birth and age five. At birth, the personality has one part, the **id**, which is contained within the unconscious. For babies, life is all about meeting their needs, the sooner the better.

Age two, infants develop their **ego**, the part of the personality that allows them to make rational plans about how to get what they need. Between the ages of three and five, the **superego** develops. This is the child's sense of morality. Part of the superego is the **conscience**, which makes us feel guilty about thoughts and wishes that conflict with society's norms for socially acceptable behaviour.

The id and superego are often in conflict. For example, the id may desire the mother's love and want to keep her all to themselves, but the superego demands that the child must share the mother's love with the rest of the family and become more independent.

Defence mechanisms

Conflicts between the id and the superego are generally resolved by the ego using **defence mechanisms**. These are short-term coping strategies that protect us from becoming aware of anything that could overwhelm the conscious mind with negative emotions (e.g. shame, anger or fear). Defence mechanisms often allow the id's socially unacceptable impulses to be expressed but in a socially acceptable way. The id's strongest impulses in Freud's mind were for sexual pleasure and aggression.

In Freud's case study of Little Hans (below), Hans' phobia of horses was interpreted as a result of fear of the father (Freud, 1909), who Hans believed was angry with him due to his desire to keep his mother to himself. Freud suggested that Hans was using a defence mechanism called displacement, which involved redirecting his fear of his father onto something else – in this case, horses. In other phobias, other types of socially unacceptable urges might be redirected, such as a person may have an aggressive urge to kill their father who is a rival for the mother's attention. An injury-blood phobia may develop as a way of expressing the anxiety associated with the desire to injure the father.

Dreamwork and wish fulfilment

Freud believed that the ego uses a process called **dreamwork** to turn unconscious desires into symbols, which are then linked together into a dream. In Freud's opinion, dreams help people to express the id's desires and, therefore, he refers to the purpose of dreams as wish fulfilment. He believed that the **manifest content** of our dreams (what we remember) can be interpreted in order to reveal the **latent content** (the true unconscious meaning of the dream). For example, a dream about vigorously beating eggs in a bowl may symbolise the unconscious desire to attack a rival.

The psychosexual stages of development

Freud divided the first five years of life into three stages (see Table 6.12), each focusing on a different area of the body (called an erogenous zone) from which the child derives interest and pleasure. Each **psychosexual stage** is also associated with a specific conflict (challenge) that the individual must overcome and Freud believed that if the conflict was not fully resolved it could lead to the development of certain personality traits through a process called **fixation**.

▼ Table 6.12 Summary of Freud's psychosexual stages (first three stages only)

Name	Age	Erogenous zone	Pleasure and interest focused on	Conflict
Oral	Birth to 18 months	Mouth	Sucking and biting	Weaning (moving from milk to solid food)
Anal	18 months to three years	Anus, rectum	Withholding and expelling faeces	Potty training (moving from nappies to using the toilet/lavatory)
Phallic	Three to five/six years	Genitals	Touching genitals and receiving attention from opposite-sex parent	The **Oedipus complex** (moving from negative to positive emotions towards the same sex)

Freud believed that at age three to six, male infants wish to spend all of their time with their mothers and become angry and jealous of their fathers. Next, the child becomes fearful of castration (the removal of the penis and/or testes) as a punishment. Freud calls this fear **castration anxiety**. Gradually, these negative emotions are resolved using a defence mechanism called **identification**. The child develops positive feelings, wishing to be like their father rather than competing with him. If the conflict is unresolved, negative emotions are moved into the unconscious via a final defence mechanism called **repression**. Freud called this conflict the Oedipus complex. Once this conflict has been resolved, the next part of personality to develop is the superego, which is concerned with societal expectations and morality. A poorly resolved Oedipus complex may, therefore, weaken the superego and increase the likelihood of immoral and impulsive behaviour.

Focus on: Freud (1909)

AIM

To describe the development of a phobia of white horses in a five-year-old boy (Little Hans) and his subsequent recovery.

CASE HISTORY

This longitudinal case study tracks Hans' development between the ages of three and five years. Hans' father was a great supporter of Freud's work and wrote him many letters, including information from conversations and observations of his son. Freud spoke directly to Hans only once but offered the father advice about how to talk to his son about his fears.

Interest in widdlers

Hans talked a great deal about 'widdlers', his word for penis, asking his parents whether they had widdlers and pointing out the widdlers of large animals, such as horses, lions and cows. Aged three and a half, his mother told him off for touching his penis, saying the doctor would cut it off. This was interpreted as the start of his castration anxiety.

Interpreting Hans' giraffe fantasy

Hans told his mother of a fantasy he'd had about giraffes. A large giraffe and a smaller 'crumpled' giraffe were in his room. Hans took the crumpled one away and the big one called out. When the big one stopped calling out, Hans sat on the crumpled one. This was thought to symbolise Hans' desire for his mother. His mother often let him get into bed with her, but his father had said that he should stop doing this, suggesting the large giraffe represents the father and the smaller one, the mother.

Fear of white horses

Hans developed a fear of white horses, specifically being bitten. He became very distressed when in the street with his mother, eventually not wanting to leave the house. His father thought this fear was linked to his son's desire to be at home with his mother but might also be linked to horses' large 'widdlers'. Freud believed Hans had used the defence mechanism of displacement to transfer his fear of castration by his father to a fear of being bitten by a horse. When Freud met Hans, he told him his father was not angry with him about his love for his mother and his father loved him too.

Identification with his father

Aged five, Hans told his father about a dream where a plumber removed his penis with pliers and replaced it with a bigger one. He also played a game where he became the father, and his father became the grandfather. Both the dream and the game were interpreted as Hans finding resolutions for the Oedipus complex as both indicated that Hans wanted to become more like his father.

► CONCLUSION

Hans' fear of horses signified castration anxiety, an important feature of the Oedipus complex. Identification with his father helped him to resolve the complex and his phobia.

Evaluating Freud (1909)

A strength of this study is that Freud collected a wealth of qualitative data from the letters from Hans' father. For example, the letters included extracts of conversations that happened within the privacy of the family home. Furthermore, the father made notes about interesting conversations as they happened rather than relying on his memory when writing to Freud about the boy's fears. This is important as it is rare that a therapist gains access to this level of insight into the nature of relationships between a child and his or her parents.

The father and Freud corresponded for several years and this is also a strength. For example, Freud gained information about events around the time that Hans' fears first developed and as well as how they intensified and were gradually resolved. This is important as taking a longitudinal approach meant that multiple observations were of the same child over time, allowing comparisons to be made between Hans' behaviour at the beginning and the end of the phallic stage.

A weakness is that the study only focuses on the experiences of one child. Hans was the first child of a two-parent family from a very wealthy district of Vienna, Austria. He spent a great deal of time with his mother, who like many wealthy women at this time did not go to work outside the home. This is important as modern children may not experience the Oedipus complex in the same way, making it a less valid explanation for childhood phobias.

A final weakness is the selective nature of the information. In recent years, it has been reported that Olga Graf (the mother) lost her father and brother to suicide, suggesting a possible genetic predisposition towards anxiety and depression that ran in her family. Furthermore, Olga is said to have physically abused Hans' little sister, Hanna, and frequently abandoned and rejected the children. Blum (2007) highlights the role of trauma and child abuse as causes of Hans' phobia, suggesting that Freud's interpretation was based on limited information about the private life of the family.

► ISSUES AND DEBATES

Use of children in psychological research

At AS Level, you learned about the study by Pozzulo *et al.* (line-ups) that children's behaviour is often affected by social factors when they act as research participants, i.e. the difference in power between adults and the children mean they are more likely to show demand characteristics answers than adults. In the Freud case study, Hans' father asked him 'Did you think of Daddy'? when Hans talked about the horse collapsing in the street. It is possible that Hans said 'Maybe, yes' simply to agree with his father and not because he really thought this.

Evaluating psychodynamic theory of fear-related disorders

A strength is that this explanation is supported by the Little Hans **case study**. Hans' dislike of white horses with black blinkers and harnesses is seen as symbolic of his fear of his father's glasses and black moustache. Hans had once admired his father's white skin as he washed and likened his moustache to a horse's whiskers. This supports the theory, as Freud suggests we cannot be consciously aware of the cause of our fears and, therefore, Hans does not show fear towards his father but displaces it onto something else, which he then discusses with his father.

A further strength is that the theory led to the development of psychoanalytic therapy. Freud developed techniques, including free association and dream interpretation, which he used in therapy with his adult patients, helping them to explore troubling memories and resolve past conflicts. This is important as, although Freudian therapy is controversial due to lack of scientific evidence, it inspired the development of newer talking therapies which provide effective alternatives to biological treatment and confinement in long-stay hospitals.

A weakness is Freud's over-reliance on case study data, meaning the evidence is highly subjective. The information obtained about Little Hans, for example, was entirely from the father's point of view, a man with a great interest in Freud's theories. When Hans saw a horse collapse in the street, his father asked, 'Did you think of Daddy'? This leading question prompted Hans to say, 'Maybe, yes', but this is clearly not valid evidence to support the link between the horse and his father. Issues such as this weaken the evidence for the theory in comparison with other theories such as Watson's behavioural explanation (see page 317).

Another weakness is that the theory is unscientific. Contrary to Freud's claims, many people say they know the cause of their phobias. The trauma of seeing a horse collapse may have led Hans to develop a conditioned fear. Freud would say that this is just an explanation created by the ego to protect the person from the real reasons, which are contained within the unconscious and inaccessible without therapy. However, there is no way of testing whether this interpretation is accurate as the contents of the unconscious can only be inferred and not observed directly.

Freud argues that male infants go through the Oedipus complex between the ages of three and six and at this time may have unconscious feelings of aggression towards their fathers, who they perceive as rivals for their mothers' love and attention. Freud's theory may be said to have limited temporal validity, meaning it does not explain the development of children in the twenty-first century. How has family life changed over time and why might Freud's theories be irrelevant for many modern families?

▲ Figure 6.42

> ### LEARNING LINKS

Freud's psychodynamic explanation of development suggests that aggression is a universal feature of the human psyche as all human behaviour is driven by the id's unconscious desires. The ego finds ways to express the id's desires so they are acceptable in order to satisfy the superego. You learned about two studies at AS Level that suggested that children and adults alike will demonstrate aggression if put into situations in which it appears to be acceptable. In the study by Bandura *et al.* (aggression), children quickly showed aggressive behaviour towards the Bobo doll when the adult gave the impression that this was acceptable, although this was more common in males. Furthermore, the male participants in Milgram's (obedience) study readily administered electric shocks to the learner when instructed to do so.

With reference to Freudian theory, can you think why anxiety disorders may be more common in females than males in many parts of the world?

STUDY TIP

Remember, when you are evaluating an explanation or theory, always use research evidence where possible. For example, if asked to evaluate Freud's explanation of fear-related disorders, you should include the findings of the Little Hans case study as evidence for his claims. Having done this, you may wish to comment on weaknesses of the evidence. If a study is scientifically weak, then it does not provide strong evidence for the theory. It is important that you always point this out in your written work. You should also ensure all evaluation points are linked back to the question. If you give too much evaluation of the Little Hans case study, then your essay will start to become unfocused, so keep it brief and move onto another strength or weakness of the theory itself, such as an application to real life or one of the issues and debates.

TEST YOURSELF

1   Pedro has a phobia of snakes and refuses to walk in the countryside or take his children to the zoo in case he sees one. Outline how a psychodynamic therapist might explain Pedro's phobia.   [4]
2   a   Outline what is meant by free will versus determinism.   [2]
    b   Explain one weakness of psychodynamic explanations of fear-related disorders.   [2]
3   a   Describe the psychodynamic explanation of fear-related disorders.   [6]
    b   Evaluate the psychodynamic explanation of fear-related disorders, including a discussion of nature versus nurture.   [10]
4   Case studies are often longitudinal. With reference to the study of fear-related disorders, outline one strength and one weakness of studying one person over a long period of time.   [4]
5   Shawn and Buffy are discussing the best way to carry out an investigation into the causes of fear-related disorders. Shawn thinks they should collect quantitative data, but Buffy disagrees, saying she thinks they should collect qualitative data. Explain whether you agree more with Shawn or Buffy.   [4]
6   Guido is comparing people who grew up in single-parent households with people who grew up in two-parent households to see whether there is a difference in the number of people who have phobias.
    a   Describe one way that Guido could recruit participants for his study.   [2]
    b   Explain one weakness of the sampling technique that you have described in part a.   [2]

6.4.3 Treatment and management of anxiety and fear-related disorders

Behavioural therapy

KEY TERMS

reciprocal inhibition
fear hierarchy
behavioural therapy
counter-conditioning
systematic desensitisation
flooding
implosive therapy

METHODOLOGY

self-reports
longitudinal studies

Think!

What is meant by **reciprocal inhibition**?

Think!

Imagine you are a behavioural therapist working with a client, Audrey, who has agoraphobia (see page 309). In your first session, you work together to create a **fear hierarchy**, including six situations involving being alone in public places. Audrey ranks the situations from least to most distressing. What might these situations be and what order might she put them in?

Think!

Lipsedge *et al.* (1973) collected data from both the patient/clients with agoraphobia and a clinician who was unaware of the treatment each participant had received. Which way of collecting data do you think provided the most valid assessment of the participants' levels of anxiety and avoidance? Can you think of another valid way of collecting data in this study?

Jones (1924) allowed other children to join in her sessions with Peter. Like these children, one child loved animals and enjoyed holding and petting the rabbit. Peter watched the other child with the rabbit and Jones believed that this played an important role in helping him to overcome his phobia. Like Watson, Jones used classical conditioning to help Peter. Which other theory from the learning approach explains why the presence of the other child was so helpful?

▲ Figure 6.43

Mary Cover Jones and the case of Little Peter

Four years after Watson and Rayner (1920) demonstrated that fears could be learned through classical conditioning, a New York-based developmental psychologist reported the case of Little Peter, a child with a phobia of small animals. Inspired by Watson's research, Mary Cover Jones conducted her own research into **behavioural therapy** for children with phobias (Jones, 1924). Initially, Jones encouraged three-year-old Peter to play with other children in the presence of a rabbit. He tolerated the animal well but, following some time in hospital, his fears returned.

Jones decided to try something new, which has become known as **counter-conditioning**. She sat Peter in a highchair and allowed him to eat some candy, his favourite treat. Next, she placed a caged rabbit near his highchair while he ate. Over the course of several visits to her laboratory, she moved the rabbit closer as he ate, until eventually he ate the candy with the uncaged rabbit sitting next to him.

Ethical standards were very different in the 1920s, as the study of Little Albert (see page 319) clearly demonstrates. Imagine you are replicating Mary Cover Jones' study of Little Peter, can you think of any specific practical and ethical issues that you would need to consider given that your participant will be just three years old?

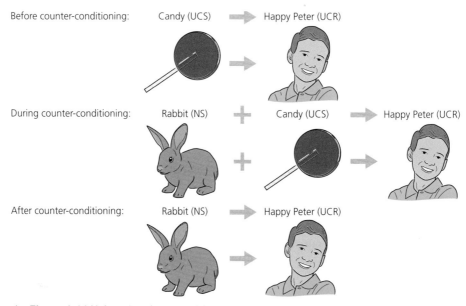

▲ Figure 6.44 Using classical conditioning to treat learned fear

Systematic desensitisation

In the 1950s, South African psychiatrist Joseph Wolpe developed Mary Jones' original work and created the behavioural therapy we now know as **systematic desensitisation** (SD). This therapy combines two important features: the use of a fear hierarchy and a technique called 'reciprocal inhibition'. The treatment has been successful in helping people with a wide range of specific phobias, from snakes to feathers, but has also been used to successfully treat agoraphobia (Wolpe, 1958).

Reciprocal inhibition

Reciprocal inhibition refers to the way in which relaxation and fear responses cancel each other out. Little Peter, for example, could not feel scared of the rabbit while also feeling relaxed and happy because of the candy. Wolpe (1968) taught his phobic patients to relax using deep muscle relaxation (see page 328) before the first exposure to their feared object/situation, but sometimes anti-anxiety drugs may also be used to achieve a state of relaxation (see Lipsedge *et al.*, 1973).

Fear hierarchy

At AS Level, you studied Saavedra and Silverman's (button phobia) case study of a boy with a button phobia (see page 114). In the first session, the therapists asked the boy to describe various situations involving buttons and then rank them from the least to the most distressing, to form a hierarchy. Likewise, Jones avoided the feelings of fear towards the rabbit being transferred to the candy by gradually exposing the boy to closer and closer contact with the rabbit. Initially, the caged rabbit was placed 12 feet away from Peter but over time the rabbit was moved nearer until Peter allowed it to nibble his fingers.

Over about six sessions, the therapist helps the patient to enter a deeply relaxed state before exposing them to each stage of the fear hierarchy, starting with the least distressing contact with the feared object/situation to the most feared contact. Contact can be in real life (*in vivo*) or the therapist may help the person to imagine the situation. The therapist will only move up the hierarchy when they are confident that the person is able to tolerate the current situation without distress.

Evaluating systematic desensitisation

One strength of SD is that it is supported by animal experiments. For example, Wolpe (1976) conditioned cats to fear (CR) a specific cage (CS) using electric shocks (UCS). He then counter-conditioned them by giving them food pellets (UCS) in a series of cages that were increasingly similar to the original feared cage. At first, the cats showed some fear towards the similar cages due to generalisation but gradually they began to eat the food. Over time, the previous fear response became extinct. The cats now entered the original cage without fear due to its new association with food in contrast to the earlier electric shocks. This is an important study as animal experiments can be more tightly controlled than human experiments, increasing the validity of the findings.

In addition to animal experiments, there have been many experiments with **longitudinal** designs using humans to demonstrate the efficacy of this therapy. For example, Lipsedge *et al.* (1973) compared the efficacy of SD with and without the use of barbiturate drugs to create deep relaxation during the exposure sessions. The participants were 60 outpatients with severe agoraphobia (see page 309). Self-reported and clinician-rated measures of anxiety and avoidance were collected before and after eight weeks of treatment. The greatest improvements were seen in people who received the barbiturate drug before exposures, although the standard SD treatment was also more effective in reducing anxiety and avoidance than no treatment. These findings suggest that SD can be an effective treatment for agoraphobia as well as specific object/situation phobias (e.g. spiders, flying).

A weakness of SD is that the fear hierarchy may be unnecessary, meaning it takes longer than other forms of therapy and may therefore not be as cost-effective. For example, **flooding (implosive therapy)** therapy involves confronting the person with the most distressing situation with no gradual build-up and can be highly effective in just one session. This said, SD is arguably more ethical as it does not cause the client as much distress.

ISSUES AND DEBATES

Reductionism versus holism

A further weakness of SD for agoraphobia is that it is reductionist. Some might argue that this therapy ignores the role of conscious and unconscious beliefs about the world and one's place within it. For example, Cynthia Shilkret believes that avoidant behaviour is maintained due to irrational beliefs, such as 'the world is a dangerous place' and 'I don't deserve a better life' (Shilkret, 2002). She explains that, although behavioural therapies involving exposure (as in SD and flooding) are important, many people are left with residual symptoms and only 50 per cent show substantial improvement. To this end, she advocates the use of cognitive-behavioural and psychodynamic therapies over the longer term to reduce the residual symptoms. This is an important alternative perspective that demonstrates that a more holistic approach to therapy may lead to longer-lasting outcomes.

The original research that supported systematic desensitisation therapy was carried out using cats. Although this animal research has many benefits, can you think of any reasons why this research may not be helpful in understanding whether this type of therapy could help a person with agoraphobia?

▲ Figure 6.45

LEARNING LINKS

At AS Level, you learned about the study by Saavedra and Silverman (button phobia) where a nine-year-old boy received therapy for his phobia, which was explained with reference to evaluative learning and the negative emotion of disgust. The therapy was similar to SD because Saavedra and Silverman used a hierarchy to organise the exposure sessions.

Which feature of SD was missing from Saavedra and Silverman's treatment plan? What additional features did they include that made their treatment plan more holistic?

STUDY TIP

When you are evaluating therapies, try to think about how either the therapy itself or the supporting evidence relate to each of the issues and debates. Question 3b in 'Test yourself' below asks you to consider the debate about idiographic versus nomothetic approaches to research.

The nomothetic approach to research usually involves quantitative data and the aim is to generalise to wider groups of people in society. Lipsedge *et al.* (1973) takes a nomothetic approach as they asked their participants to rate their anxiety before and after treatment on a five-point scale (where 0 equalled 'Absence of discomfort when going out alone' and 4 equalled 'Feeling terrified to the point of panic when going out alone').

The idiographic approach often involves qualitative data and the aim is to obtain detailed information but not necessarily to make generalisations. Shilkret (2002) provides qualitative accounts of her therapy sessions with two patients with agoraphobia. Her comprehensive approach to understanding her patients' core beliefs appears to have been helpful in reducing their symptoms of agoraphobia in the long term.

▶ TEST YOURSELF
....

1   Urzila has been diagnosed with agoraphobia. She is unable to walk beyond the end of her street, has not used public transport for ten years and the thought of going on holiday makes her feel sick. Outline how a behavioural therapist might treat Urzila's phobia.   [4]

2   Explain one ethical strength of using systematic desensitisation as a treatment for agoraphobia.   [2]

3   a   Describe one behavioural therapy for fear-related disorders.   [6]

    b   Evaluate the behavioural therapy you described in part a, including a discussion of idiographic versus nomothetic.   [10]

4   Agoraphobia can be treated using behavioural therapy, such as systematic desensitisation.

    a   Plan an experiment to investigate the effectiveness of systematic desensitisation to treat agoraphobia. Your plan must include details about the design, the type of data and how it will be analysed.   [10]

    b   For one piece of psychological knowledge that has informed your plan:

        i   Describe this psychological knowledge.   [4]

        ii   Explain how two features of this psychological knowledge informed your plan.   [4]

Psychological therapy

Cognitive-behavioural therapy (CBT)

Psychological therapy for anxiety disorders such as generalised anxiety disorder, agoraphobia and specific phobias includes the many variations of cognitive-behavioural therapy (CBT). You learned about the basic principles of CBT as they are applied to the treatment of schizophrenia (pages 231–258), mood disorders (pages 259–282) and impulse control disorders (pages 283–306) and the approach to the treatment of anxiety and fear has many similarities in that CBT practitioners believe that the fear and/or anxiety result from dysfunctional thinking patterns. Through systematically challenging these unhelpful beliefs, CBT practitioners aim to change not only the way people think, but also how they feel and behave. A course of CBT is usually time-limited to a maximum of around 20 sessions. In contrast with other types of psychological therapy, CBT practitioners do not spend time looking into the past for reasons for the person's behaviour, instead they help to find solutions to problems the person is facing in their present (current) daily life.

The term cognitive fear structures is used to describe networks of stored information (similar to Bartlett's concept of schema) about threatening stimuli (Kaczkurkin and Foa, 2015). For example, a person with a phobias of dogs will have a cognitive fear structure for dogs that contains concepts such as big teeth, fierce, aggressive, dangerous. It may also include memory of bodily sensations associated with dogs, e.g. rapid heart rate which may then trigger further associations with heart attacks, hospital and even death.

In a person with a phobias of dogs their cognitive fear structures may be activated even by small, calm dogs leading them to avoid dogs completely. Avoidance means they are never able to assimilate new information about the positive qualities of many dogs, e.g. that they can be affectionate and completely harmless. The CBT practitioner will attempt to disconfirm the person's inaccurate beliefs about their feared stimuli through exposure with the aim of replacing the fear structure with new positive memories.

Exposure theory is typically combined with cognitive therapy. As with Beck's cognitive restructuring (see page 261), CBT practitioners will use psychoeducation to teach people with fear and anxiety disorders about the links between thoughts, emotions and behaviour, encourage them to provide evidence for their automatic negative thoughts, gradually encouraging the development of a more objective view of themselves, the future and the world. Homework is an important part of the CBT for anxiety and people will be encouraged to practise skills and strategies between sessions and report back on their experiences.

KEY TERMS

applied tension (also applied muscle tension)

fainting

diphasic biological response

vasovagal syncope

animal reminder disgust

core disgust

in vivo graduated exposure

modelling

selfmonitoring

Subjective Units of Discomfort Scale (SUDS)

▲ Figure 6.46 Dr Kevin Chapman

Applied tension

The next section considers another type of psychological therapy called applied tension which has been developed specifically for the treatment of blood-injury-injection phobias (BII). BII is characterised by a slightly different pattern of symptoms to other specific phobias and this is why applied tension is required as an additional technique that can be combined with other CBT strategies.

Key study: Treating blood-injection-injury phobia using cognitive-behavioural therapy with applied tension – Chapman and DeLapp (2013)

Think!

What is meant by **applied tension**?

Think!

Have you ever **fainted** or seen someone faint at school or another public place? Fainting is very common and affects as many as 39 per cent of medical students at one time or another (Alboni *et al.*, 2007). Why do you think people who are prone to fainting sometimes also develop agoraphobia?

Think!

This is a really uplifting case study as it shows how a man who had been severely affected by his anxiety for over 20 years was able to overcome his phobia in just nine weeks. Can you think of any reasons why the therapist achieved such positive results with this particular client?

Introducing Dr Kevin Chapman and Dr Ryan DeLapp

Dr Kevin Chapman is a licensed clinical psychologist specialising in multiculturalism and mental health. He is the founder and director of the Kentucky Center for Anxiety and Related Disorders (KYCARDS) and a nationally recognised expert in the use of cognitive-behavioural therapy (CBT) for the treatment of anxiety and related disorders. Dr Chapman says:

> I have always been passionate about helping others who struggle with anxiety disorders, the most common type of mental health condition. Cognitive-behavioural therapy is the gold standard treatment for anxiety and related disorders and I am passionate about disseminating this treatment to the public through media engagement.

> 'As a man thinketh in his heart, so is he' (Proverbs 23:7). I like to tell my clients you are NOT your symptoms.

> (K. Chapman, personal communication, August 2021)

Blood-injection-injury (BII) phobia, including fainting at the sight or thought of blood, affects around 3.5 per cent of the population, but as Chapman and DeLapp (2013) show, it is treatable. Through combining CBT and techniques like applied tension (AT), people can stay conscious in the presence of their feared stimuli, which is essential to the success of exposure therapy; otherwise, new learning cannot take place. T's childhood included many experiences that made him vulnerable to BII phobia, suggesting that the causes may be due to nurture rather than nature, but Öst (1992) showed that this phobia has a stronger genetic component than some other specific phobias.

>> Can you think why fainting at the sight or thought of blood/injury might have helped our early humans to survive? Quite a few possibilities have been suggested but testing evolutionary hypotheses can be difficult.

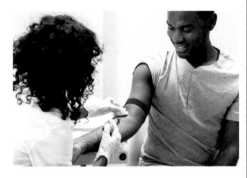

▲ Figure 6.47

Context

The diphasic response

The treatment of BII phobia differs from other phobias as it includes strategies to reduce the risk of fainting (sudden loss of consciousness). For many people with BII phobia, the presence (or even the thought) of blood or medical-related stimuli can trigger a **diphasic (or two-part) biological response**. As with all phobias, the person experiences an increase in blood pressure and heart rate on seeing or imagining blood or a medical procedure, but unlike other phobias this increase is followed by a sudden decrease in blood pressure and heart rate. The second part is called **vasovagal syncope**. This can cause fainting due to reduced blood flow to the brain. Although this condition is not serious, fainting can lead people to injure themselves, such as knocking their head when they faint.

The role of disgust

People with BII often have a stronger than average disgust response. This is associated with fainting as disgust triggers activity in the parasympathetic nervous system, such as reducing blood pressure. This said, only one specific type of disgust predicts fainting in people with BII phobia. **Animal reminder disgust** refers to repulsion experienced when reminded of our own, human, 'animalness', such as the sight of blood or veins. This type of disgust has been found to predict fainting in BII-phobic patients, but **core disgust** (anxiety relating to contamination) did not (Olatunji *et al.*, 2006).

Left untreated, BII phobia can seriously impact a person's mental and physical health due to avoidance of routine check-ups and failure to seek medical attention. This means research into the most effective forms of treatment is critical.

Currently, three techniques are combined to target the symptoms of BII phobia (see Table 6.13).

▼ Table 6.13 Techniques for treating BII phobia

Type of therapy	Purpose of therapy
Cognitive therapy	To challenge and restructure irrational beliefs/thoughts
Behavioural therapy	To encourage approach behaviour and reduce avoidant behaviour; this may include *in vivo* graduated **exposure** (as with systematic desensitisation; see page 328) and may also include **modelling** (observation and imitation of a trusted peer/therapist)
Applied tension	To reduce the risk of fainting (see below)

Anxiety around self-injections has successfully been reduced using CBT (Cox *et al.*, 2004), but evidence suggests that CBT is more effective in reducing fear than disgust, and Olatunj *et al.* (2006) suggest that additional sessions may be necessary for people with BII phobias compared with other phobias. Ayala *et al.* (2009) reviewed five randomised control trial (RCT) studies assessing the efficacy of various treatments for BII phobia. Therapy was effective for around 75 per cent of participants and the review suggested all the therapeutic approaches assessed resulted in similar levels of improvement.

▶ AIM

The aim of this study was to provide insight into 'active mechanisms of change' (Chapman and DeLapp, 2013, page 331) throughout a nine-week course of applied tension and manualised cognitive-behavioural therapy for an adult male patient with BII phobia.

▶ METHODOLOGY

The **case study** method was used to collect quantitative data from self-reported questionnaires and qualitative data from a diagnostic interview.

Case history

T was a Hispanic male, aged 42. He self-referred following more than 20 years of intense fear/panic in medical situations, such as doctors' waiting rooms, and suffered from vasovagal syncope during blood tests and other procedures. He perceived these procedures as 'dangerous' and experienced distress relating to his physical symptoms, which included racing heart, hot flashes, cold chills, dizziness and unsteadiness additional to the fainting. T's child had autism spectrum disorder and he felt a sense of guilt and shame due to being unable to attend regular medical appointments with his child.

As a child, T's mother 'joked' he might have a heart problem. His grandmother suffered anxiety relating to medical emergencies; each day, she listened to an ambulance dispatch scanner and T was also exposed to this. Also, he had witnessed the deaths of his grandfather, uncle and aunt from illnesses, including cancer.

T's exercise routine included running, cycling, weight training and swimming, giving the impression of being in control of his health. In reality, he had not visited a doctor in years, except for a psychiatrist, who prescribed anti-anxiety medication.

Assessment

A variety of self-report questionnaires were used to collect quantitative data about T's symptoms (see Table 6.14). A diagnostic interview confirmed his BII phobia diagnosis. He had also experienced a major depressive episode in college.

▼ Table 6.14 Self-report questionnaires completed as part of T's initial assessment

Measures	Description	T's scores
The Beck Anxiety Inventory (BAI)	21 items; items are rated from 0–3	**Baseline:** 41 (severe anxiety)
		12-month follow-up: 7 (low anxiety)
The Fear Survey Schedule II (FSS-II)	Assesses fear towards 51 objects/situations; items are rated on a 7-point scale	**Baseline:** 6 ('terror') for blood and 5 ('very much fear') for death, illness, death of a loved one, untimely or early death and hypodermic needles
		12-month follow-up: none of the items was scored as 'very much fear' or 'terror'
The Blood-Injection Symptom Scale (BISS)	17 items assessing sensations experienced during situations involving blood or injections	**Baseline:** T answered 'Yes' for all 17 items
		12-month follow-up: 4/17 sensations were experienced when exposed to medical-related stimuli: feeling anxious, heart pounding, feeling nauseous and sweating

TREATMENT AND ASSESSMENT OF PROGRESS

T completed nine sessions of CBT, including applied tension as detailed in the *Mastering Your Fears and Phobias (MYFP)* manual (Craske *et al.*, 2006). T and the therapist worked collaboratively to set weekly goals. T completed homework between sessions, including reading assignments, practising applied tension five times a day and completing graduated exposure tasks (such as watching online videos of blood tests, finger-prick blood test, testing his blood pressure and attending medical appointments). He also completed the Phobic Encounter Record (PER) between sessions, where he rated his anxiety from 0 to 100 and listed his thoughts, feelings and behaviours when exposed to blood and/or medical-related stimuli.

▼ Table 6.15 Description of T's sessions

Session	Description of session
1–3	Psychoeducation covering phobias, vasovagal syncope, the importance of **self-monitoring** using the PER, cognitive restructuring, thinking errors and the graduated exposure, i.e. remaining in the feared situation until new learning has taken place. T prioritised objects and situations for treatment from doctors/hospital (greatest priority) through to airplanes (lowest priority). **Progress:** Reading helped T to understand anxiety at the hairdressers earlier in the week. He had felt 'panicky' but remained in the situation and reflected on his thoughts until he felt calm.
4	Creating a ten-item fear hierarchy, each item rated from 0 to 100. The therapist explained that T would be asked to rate his level of distress on the **Subjective Units of Discomfort Scale (SUDS)** (0–100) to monitor changes in his anxiety. **Progress:** T felt optimistic and had bought a blood pressure cuff and a heart rate monitor to prepare him for phobic encounters.
5	T was asked to do item 1 from the fear hierarchy at home. The therapist explained and modelled applied tension (AT) to reduce the risk of fainting while applying the tourniquet and looking at his vein. **Progress:** T reported no phobic encounters yet but felt he was more aware of cues relating to potential fainting, anxiety and fear.
6	T watched YouTube videos of people having blood tests (item 2 on hierarchy). SUDS increased from 30 to 35 minutes into the first video. He used AT as the blood was seen going into the tube. SUDS stayed at 35 and he said it was 'not bad'. SUDS dropped to 20 at the end of the first video. He said he felt 'slight nausea but not a big deal'. Further videos were shown with closer camera angles. T reported similar SUDS. **Progress:** T experienced 'immense success' on item 1; SUDS was 40, but said, 'it was fine'.

▼ Table 6.15 Description of T's sessions

Session	Description of session
7	T pricked his finger to check for blood sugar and looked at his own blood. SUDS were 45 before the test, dropping to 20, even without AT. T pricked two more fingers (SUDS=20) and said he was 'about there'. **Progress:** T's wife checked his blood sugar three times using the finger-prick test. SUDS was 45; he used AT twice but managed the third test without. He looked at his blood for five minutes.
8	T and his therapist observed people giving blood at a 'blood bank' (a centre where people donate blood) (SUDS=65 before the procedure, dropping to 45 within five minutes and 30 within ten minutes). He did not use AT and did not feel faint. He watched a second person give blood and said his SUDS score was 0. He agreed to go for his own blood test in the coming week. **Progress:** T said he would make an appointment for his own blood test.
9	T took his own blood pressure (SUDS=55, dropping to 20). When he took it again, his SUDS remained at 20. He said he would make an appointment for a blood pressure test in the week and telephone the therapist if he needed an additional session. **Progress:** T's blood test went well; he only used AT at the start. SUDS=40, quickly dropping to 0. SUDS peaked at 25 in a second test on his other arm.

Applied tension procedure

1 Find a comfortable chair.

2 Tense the muscles of your arms, torso and legs.

3 Hold the tension for 10 to 15 seconds.

4 Release for 20 to 30 seconds.

5 Repeat five times.

Following his ninth session, T took his own blood pressure at a drug store (pharmacy). He had his blood pressure taken by a nurse and was examined by a doctor. He did not need to use AT and described his SUDS as 'rather low'. He said he had 'never felt better in my life' and did not need any more treatment sessions.

Follow-up

Four months later, T thanked the therapist and had several doctor's appointments booked. Ten months later, he was still doing well and 12 months post-treatment he completed follow-up questionnaires, to allow comparisons to be made between his baseline and follow-up scores (see Table 6.14).

▶ CONCLUSIONS

Psychoeducation, objective recording, cognitive restructuring and graduated exposure were highly effective when combined with applied tension in the treatment of a man with a severe BII phobia. This was, in part, related to increases in self-efficacy achieved through a highly individualised treatment plan of a sufficient duration to meet his needs.

 ## Methodological strengths and weaknesses

A strength of this **case study** was the collection of both quantitative and qualitative data. For example, SUDS scores were taken before, during and after T was exposed to items on his fear hierarchy, allowing changes in T's anxiety to be monitored within and between sessions. The collection of qualitative data provided a sense of T's subjective experience of recovery. This triangulation of data gathering is important as it increases the overall credibility of the findings.

Another strength is that, although only one patient's case is described, clinicians should be able to determine whether the findings would **generalise** to their own clients. The researchers provided detailed information about the man's family history and past and present symptoms, including depressive disorder (in remission), panic disorder in relation to medical stimuli only, obsessive-compulsive disorder and social anxiety. The detailed case history means readers can draw their own conclusions about whether the findings would transfer to the setting in which they might be working and their own clients.

A weakness of this study is the use of **self-reported** data in the form of the SUDS, which may not have been valid. As he was being asked to give his answers orally, he might have given the answers that he perceived the therapist expected to hear. T also suffered with social anxiety, meaning he might have been even more motivated to give positive answers. This is important as it means the data may not reflect T's genuine anxiety levels.

A final weakness of this study is the lack of a control group. Randomised control trials sometimes include a sham-treatment group to test the extent to which expectancy effects influence participants' recovery journeys. For example, participants might believe they are learning skills to reduce the risk of fainting but really this is not the case. This is important as in this study it is difficult to determine how much of T's recovery was due to the specific type of therapy employed and how much was a product of his increased motivation and desire to change his behaviour, for the sake of his family.

Ethics

Ethically, this study is excellent as T's anonymity is maintained through the use of his initial. Furthermore, the therapist worked collaboratively with him, ensuring progress through the fear hierarchy occurred at his own pace. This is important as both protecting his anonymity and not moving on until he felt ready protected T from psychological harm. Furthermore, the therapy T received massively improved his quality of life and could in fact save his life, as he is now able to attend medical appointments for routine check-ups. The way that the study was conducted and reported minimised harm to the client, while maximising benefits both to T and to therapists, who may find the detailed information provided in the study useful for their own clients.

Application to everyday life

This case study demonstrates that people with BII can be treated in outpatient community settings with great success. This may be linked to patient satisfaction, which increases compliance and improves attendance at treatment sessions. From a practical point of view, BII is harder to treat than other specific phobias as patients also need to learn to use AT. This can increase the number of sessions required, which also increases the financial cost. Another practical issue is the lack of access to specialist clinics like the one attended by T; he had to travel 2.5 hours for his appointments and this increased the financial cost and time required to access therapy.

ISSUES AND DEBATES

Idiographic versus nomothetic

This case study takes an idiographic approach, providing a detailed record of the way manualised CBT with AT was personalised to the specific needs of T, a man with severe BII. Despite the advantages of this approach, the focus on just one person means it is impossible to know whether the therapy would be as successful for other individuals. If the study included a larger number of people, it would be possible to calculate average SUDS scores before and after CBT + AT treatment and to compare the spread of the data in each set to better understand how individual differences affect treatment efficacy. Taking a more nomothetic approach could be helpful as the focus on a single patient and therapist may be misleading as this treatment programme may not be as effective for everyone, especially people being treated by less experienced or skilful therapists.

REFLECTION

- What factors do you think made CBT + AT so successful for this particular patient?
- If you were conducting research in this area, how might you improve this study and/or design your own study to investigate the use of AT as a way of improving the efficacy of cognitive-behavioural therapy in the treatment of BII phobia?

LEARNING LINKS

At AS Level, you learned about the case of a nine-year-old boy who received a combination of behavioural and cognitive therapy for his specific phobias of buttons (Saavedra and Silverman, button phobia). As with Chapman and DeLapp, the researchers linked the boy's phobia to disgust in response to the feared stimuli. In BII phobia, it is thought that disgust leads to increased activity in the parasympathetic nervous system (falling blood pressure) and subsequent fainting (Page, 2003). However, not all researchers agree. When shown 'disgusting' blood-related images, Vossbeck-Elsebusch et al. (2012) found no difference in the level of disgust reported by people with BII phobias with and without a history of fainting and they did not find that higher self-reported disgust was related to higher parasympathetic nervous system activity (such as decreased heart rate or blood pressure). Does this mean therapists should stop targeting disgust in the treatment of BII phobia?

STUDY TIP

This is a key study, so you need to learn the background and context, aim, case history and stages involved in T's treatment carefully. You should also try to remember some of the specific quantitative findings (SUDS) and qualitative findings (T's comments following different encounters with blood and medical procedures).

To remember the stages in T's therapy, why not draw a comic strip or storyboard? To help remember the numbers, you could make up a rhyme, such as 'In session *eight*, T watched blood donors *donate*, T's SUDS was *65* but donating saves *lives*, the donor was a hero and T's SUDS was soon *zero*.'

Putting in a little extra effort to process information at a deeper level like this should help you to remember it better and the rhyming words should act as memory cues.

▶ TEST YOURSELF

1   Medical student Tamwar had always wanted to be a doctor but when he was asked to perform a blood test in front of the other students, he fainted. Tamwar was upset and embarrassed and decided to research why this happened in the hope that he could somehow stop it from happening again.
    a   Explain one biological reason why Tamwar might have fainted at the sight of blood. [2]
    b   Explain one way that Tamwar could stop himself from fainting at the sight of blood in future. [4]
2   a   Outline what is meant by idiographic versus nomothetic. [2]
    b   Phoebe and Freddie are discussing whether Chapman and DeLapp (2013) took an idiographic or a nomothetic approach in their study about treating blood-injection-injury phobia. Phoebe thinks they took an idiographic approach, but Freddie thinks, because they collected SUDS scores, the study was nomothetic. Explain whether you agree with Phoebe or Freddie. [4]
3   a   Describe the study by Chapman and DeLapp (2013) on treating blood-injection-injury phobia using cognitive-behavioural therapy with applied tension. [6]
    b   Evaluate this study by Chapman and DeLapp (2013), including a discussion about generalisations from the findings. [10]
4   From the key study by Chapman and DeLapp (2013) on treating blood-injection-injury phobia using cognitive-behavioural therapy, describe two ways in which the researchers collected data using self-reports. [4]
5   Explain one strength of Chapman and DeLapp (2013) with reference to the longitudinal design. [2]
6   Outline one reason why people might think Chapman and DeLapp's findings are subjective. [2]

KEY TERMS
MOCI
obsession
obsessive-compulsive disorder
compulsion
thought-event fusion
thought-action fusion
insight
clomipramine
typology
Y-BOCS

6.5 Obsessive-compulsive disorder
6.5.1 Diagnostic criteria (ICD-11)

Think!
What was the compulsive behaviour that Charles (in Rapoport, 1989) was unable to stop? Which type of OCD does this fit in best with (see Table 6.16)?

METHODOLOGY

interviews

case studies

validity

quantitative and
qualitative data

Think!

Imagine you could ask one closed and one open question to each of the following people. What would you ask them?

Charles; Charles' mother; Charles' father; Judith Rapoport; Charles' science teacher

Think!

Hodgson and Rachman (1977) are thinking of revising the **MOCI**; they ask you to help them. Make a list of the top three ways you think they could improve the validity and reliability of the test.

Some people may have a compulsion to clean. How many different **obsessions** can you think of that might be driving her behaviour?

▲ Figure 6.48

As the name suggests, people with **obsessive-compulsive disorder** (OCD) experience obsessions, meaning repetitive and persistent thoughts and images. These thoughts and images are unwanted and intrusive, meaning the person feels unable to control them, although they may try to ignore or suppress them. **Compulsions** are repetitive acts or behaviours. They can be physical (such as touching/tapping things in a certain way) or mental (such as counting to a certain number in your head).

The ICD-11 states that compulsions are often carried out in response to an obsession, possibly to **neutralise** negative thoughts. For example, a person may imagine a loved one being involved in an accident and become anxious believing that their thoughts will make an accident more likely to happen in real life. This is called **thought-event fusion**. They may then feel compelled or driven to carry out certain behaviours in order to stop the accident from happening, so neutralising the power of the negative thought. Compulsions are often not rationally linked to the obsession in any way – for example, counting cannot alter the probability of whether an accident happens or not. However, the individual may find it impossible not to carry out the compulsive act.

OCD is only diagnosed if the obsessions and compulsions are time-consuming, meaning they take up more than one hour per day. Like the other disorders in this chapter, a diagnosis is only made if the symptoms cause significant distress and/or have a negative impact on a person's life, personally, socially or at school or work.

When people receive a diagnosis of OCD, a **specifier** may be added, which gives information about whether the person has poor–absent or fair–good **insight** into their condition. People who lack insight into their condition may be convinced that their obsessional thoughts are true and that their compulsions are necessary to control events in the world. For example, a woman who cleans obsessively may be convinced that, without doing so, she will cause a family member to become ill or even die of food poisoning. People with fair–good insight are often aware that their obsessional thoughts are untrue; however, anxiety may reduce this insight.

Types of obsessions and compulsions

Thought-event fusion is just one type of obsession, but a number of different types of obsessions and compulsions have been identified (see Table 6.16 for examples).

▼ Table 6.16 Types of obsessions and compulsions

Obsession	Compulsion
Contamination: A carer may be terrified of passing germs onto a client, for fear of them getting ill or even dying.	Cleaning: An employee may feel forced to clean floors and surfaces multiple times and wash their hands until they are sore.
Harm/safety: A parent may have obsessive thoughts about their children being involved in accidents, fires, floods, etc.	Checking: A parent may check they have locked all the doors and windows, or that they have turned off electric appliances multiple times.
Symmetry/order: A student may feel uncomfortable unless everything around them is perfectly aligned and in its 'right' place.	Counting, ordering and arranging of possessions: A student may spend hours organising items on their desk or in their room before starting schoolwork.
Forbidden thoughts/taboos: A person might have sexual thoughts.	Ritualistic physical and/or mental acts in an attempt to neutralise: The person may say prayers repeatedly or carry out ritualistic washing to 'purify' themselves.

Focus on: Rapoport (1989)

▶ CASE HISTORY

From the age of 12, Charles became obsessed that there was something sticky on his skin. This led to him spending three hours at a time in the shower. After months of behavioural therapy and various medications, he began seeing Rapoport at the age of 14. She described him as open, appreciative and friendly. Before the onset of his disorder, he had been doing well at school, especially in biology. Gradually, his symptoms worsened and he was unable to go to school. Washing took up too much of his day and he was unable to concentrate on schoolwork. Charles' mother tried to help him by rigorously cleaning everything in his room and the rest of the house. Visitors were asked to wash their hands to avoid contamination but eventually she stopped asking people to the house at all. The father found his wife and son's behaviour difficult and managed this by working longer hours.

▶ SYMPTOMS

- Charles was obsessed with stickiness and called it 'terrible', 'some kind of disease'.
- The worst thing he could think of was touching honey.
- He washed for three hours at a time – for example, passing the soap from one hand to the other after a certain amount of time had passed.
- He showed general slowness with daily routines, such as dressing, which could take two hours.
- Charles became very distressed when Rapoport explained that she wanted to do an EEG (see page 7), which would involve putting sticky paste on his scalp; he stayed up washing all night following the day of the EEG.
- Charles was sad because his sisters and other children would call him 'crazy'.

▶ TREATMENT

Charles was given **clomipramine** (a tricyclic antidepressant; see page 276). This helped in the short term. Within a month, Charles was able to pour and touch honey, but one year later he relapsed. He had become tolerant to the drug, meaning he needed increasingly large doses to produce the same effect. His symptoms returned, although in a more manageable way.

Evaluating Rapoport (1989)

One strength of Rapoport's study of Charles was that she **interviewed** him extensively about why he could not stop washing. This allowed Rapoport to collect **qualitative data** where Charles was able to explain his experiences in his own words. For example, when asked what would happen if he did not complete his washing routines, Charles said, 'maybe some sickness would come' and 'it might be bad luck'. This helped to increase the validity of the study as instead of forcing Charles merely to circle a number on a scale or tick a box, he was able to explain why he behaved as he did.

A weakness of this **case study** is that it only provides information about a single participant. Charles was aged 14 at the time of the study and Rapoport explains that OCD symptoms often can change over the years; younger children often count, check and repeat movements, while adults tend to ruminate (worry about and analyse their thoughts) (Rapoport, 1989, page 339). This is important as this case study only spans two years in the life of an adolescent patient; had Rapoport studied an older or younger patient, her findings might have been different.

Measures

The Maudsley Obsessive-Compulsive Inventory (MOCI)

Hodgson and Rachman (1977) aimed to develop a **typology** to classify the many different types of OCD symptoms. They hoped it could be useful to researchers investigating the causes and treatments for OCD. This said, they questioned whether this new nomothetic approach would be as useful as the idiographic approach that had prevailed until this point. In order to develop their questionnaire, they interviewed 30 people with OCD and developed a list of 65 true and false statements. These were given to two groups of patients from the Maudsley Hospital, in London, England. Half the people experienced obsessional thinking and the other half had anxiety but no obsessional thinking. The researchers narrowed down the list to the 30 items which were most useful in differentiating people with obsessive thinking from those with anxiety and no obsessive thinking, such as 'I avoid using public telephones because of possible contamination' and 'I frequently get nasty thoughts and have difficulty in getting rid of them' (Hodgson and Rachman, 1977). The two major types of OCD identified were cleaning and checking, but two minor types were also identified, slowness and doubting.

Evaluating the MOCI

One strength of the MOCI is that it has high test-rest reliability. For example, Hodgson and Rachman (1977) asked 50 students to complete the MOCI and then reassessed them one month later. Eighty-nine per cent of the 1500 pairs of scores generated were the same, showing the test to be highly consistent. This is important because a test that is not reliable could lead to inaccurate diagnoses, meaning a person's OCD could become worse due to lack of support or appropriate treatment.

A weakness of the MOCI is that it uses fixed-choice questions. People can only choose between the answers 'true' or 'false'. People may not know how to respond if a statement is only true some of the time or they do not understand the question. For example, when asked to respond to 'I use only an average amount of soap', people may be unsure what is average if they personally have always washed excessively. This is important as if the available options do not reflect what the respondent really thinks or feels, the data will lack validity, meaning they may not receive an accurate diagnosis.

The Yale-Brown Obsessive-Compulsive Scale (Y-BOCS)

The **Y-BOCS** is a **semi-structured interview** schedule including five items relating to obsessions and five items on compulsions (Goodman *et al.*, 1989a). Respondents are asked to rate each item on a 0–4 scale in relation to the severity of their symptoms in the last week. Scores of 8–15 are considered mild, 16–23 moderate, 24–31 severe and 32–40 extreme. Interviewers may also wish to use an accompanying checklist which lists more than 50 types of obsessions and compulsions divided into 15 categories. Typically, interviews take approximately 30 minutes.

How much of your time is occupied by obsessive thoughts?

0 (None)   1 (Less than one hour a day)   2 (1–3 hours a day)   3 (3–8 hours a day)   4 (More than 8 hours a day)

How much of an effort do you make to resist the compulsions?

0 (Always make an effort to resist, or don't even need to resist)   2 (Try to resist most of the time)

3 (Reluctantly yield to all compulsions)   4 (Completely and willingly yield to all compulsions)

▲ Figure 6.49 Sample items from the Y-BOCS

Evaluating the Y-BOCS

One weakness of the Y-BOCS is that it asks people to consider the severity of their symptoms in the last week. This could be a problem if people experience their symptoms in different ways throughout the week. For example, symptoms might be worse on days when the person is not at work as their mind is less occupied with other things. This is important because without qualitative data to put the scores into context it may be difficult for a clinician to get an accurate impression of the impact that the symptoms are having on a person's overall functioning.

A strength of this psychometric test is it has strong inter-rater reliability. This means that when two or more interviewers use the scale to assess the same person, there is a high level of agreement between them regarding the severity of the person's symptoms. Goodman *et al.* (1989a) tested this using 40 people with OCD, each of whom were assessed by four different interviewers. Agreement between them was excellent and this shows that the Y-BOCS is a reliable measure of OCD symptom severity.

One difference between the MOCI and Y-BOCS is that the MOCI is self-reported whereas the Y-BOCS is completed by a clinician as part of a semi-structured interview. Interestingly, scores on the MOCI and the Y-BOCS are only weakly correlated (Goodman *et al.*, 1989b) and this is thought to be related to the way the data is collected.

>> Which scale do you think would give a more valid measure of the person's OCD symptoms? You may have to think more deeply here about your understanding of the term validity and how it applies to psychometric testing.

▲ Figure 6.50

► LEARNING LINK

In this section, you learned about the case study of Charles, who was treated by Judith Rapoport. The case has similarities with that of Saavedra and Silverman (button phobia) (see page 114). Both studies were longitudinal in nature, tracking the progress of the child over time. In each case, the same therapist saw the child many times in order to deliver the therapy sessions and to collect data, to monitor the efficacy of the treatment programme.

Can you think why the validity of the data might change over time? Do you think it gets better or worse as the study goes on, and why? Think about the changing nature of the relationship between the therapist and the child and how this might have affected how the child interacted with the therapist. You should also think about how the therapist's behaviour may also have changed over time.

STUDY TIP

To help you to remember the details of the MOCI and the Y-BOCS and to think more deeply about their relative strengths and weaknesses, you could compare them using a Venn diagram. Draw two overlapping circles, one for each test. Any similarities between the two should be placed in the overlapping segment in the middle and ideas that differentiate one scale from the other should be placed in the corresponding circle.

> **TEST YOURSELF**

1 Barry cannot take his car out without checking each tyre 20 times. He touches the tyres in a special way and often starts his checks again if he feels he has not checked properly. Barry does not really know why he does this but says 'it is important'. Outline the difference between an obsession and a compulsion using Barry as an example.   [2]

2 Explain one similarity and one difference between the Maudsley Obsessive-Compulsive Inventory (MOCI) and the Yale-Brown Obsessive-Compulsive Scale (Y-BOCS).   [4]

3 a With reference to one study, describe the diagnostic criteria (such as ICD-11) of obsessive-compulsive disorder.   [6]

   b Evaluate the diagnosis of obsessive-compulsive disorder (such as ICD-11), including a discussion of psychometrics.   [10]

4 Explain what is meant by psychometrics using the MOCI as an example.   [2]

5 Interviews are sometimes used to investigate OCD. Explain why data from semi-structured interviews may not be reliable, using the diagnosis of OCD as an example.   [2]

6 Rapoport collected both quantitative and qualitative data in her case study of a boy who could not stop washing. Identify one way she collected each type of data. [2]

KEY TERMS

BDNF

low activity allele

SLITRK5

DRD4

D4 dopamine receptors

allele 2

knock-out mice

6.5.2 Explanations of obsessive-compulsive disorder

Biological explanations

Think!

What is **BDNF** and which family of genes is it related to?

Think!

Imagine your friend has had their genome mapped as a birthday gift. They have found out that they are carrying the **low activity allele** of the COMT gene and are worried about increased risk of OCD. What would you say to reassure your friend? Try and think of at least three things to say to them.

Think!

Shmelkov *et al.* (2010) identified **SLITRK5** as a gene that increases risk of OCD. Why should people be cautious when drawing conclusions from this study?

Genetic

Lewis (1936) found that 37 per cent of people with OCD had at least one parent who also had the disorder and 22 per cent had a sibling who had OCD. This classic family study, conducted in London, UK, showed that OCD appears to run in families. This means that if one member of the family has OCD, then other biologically close family members have a higher probability than typical of also having the disorder.

Twin study evidence also supports the idea that OCD is genetic. Carey and Gottesman (1981) found a concordance rate of 87 per cent for monozygotic (MZ) twins but only 47 per cent for dizygotic (DZ) twins. This very high rate for MZ twins suggests OCD is one of the most heritable of all mental disorders. The fact that the rate for DZ twins is so much lower shows that the high rate in MZ twins is due to nature, not nurture, as DZ twins share the same social environment, yet only one of them develops OCD. This suggests the affected twin has inherited a different combination of genes to their sibling.

Candidate genes

In 2013, 230 genes had been linked to OCD (Taylor, 2013) and, by now, this figure is likely to be much higher. This shows that OCD is another example of a polygenic disorder. Research also suggests that different genes are linked to the different types of OCD (e.g. contamination, checking).

5-HTT and serotonin

Vulnerability to OCD has been linked to various genes, including those that code for serotonin receptors and transporter molecules as well as MAO-A, an enzyme that breaks down serotonin. Specifically, a mutation of the 5-HTT gene, also linked to depression, has been identified as particularly interesting (Ozaki *et al.*, 2003). However, it appears that carriers of this mutation are also more vulnerable to a range of other psychiatric disorders, making it unclear why some people develop OCD specifically.

DRD4, COMT and dopamine

DRD4 is a gene that codes for **D4 dopamine receptors**, suggesting that an imbalance of dopamine may also be involved in vulnerability to OCD. A specific allele of this gene (called **allele 2**) appears to be less common in people with OCD (Millet *et al.*, 2003), suggesting it may somehow protect people from developing the disorder.

On page 242, you learned that the COMT gene codes for an enzyme that breaks down dopamine and has been linked to the development of schizophrenia. It has also been found that the 'low activity allele' of this gene is more common in people with OCD. Decreased levels of this enzyme could cause an excess of dopamine and this may increase vulnerability to OCD.

SLITRK5 and BDNF

A family of genes called the SLITRKs are involved in the development of new synapses and thus our ability to learn from new experiences. Specifically, a gene called SLITRK5 has been linked to OCD. It is unclear how this gene increases the risk of this disorder, but this may be linked to an important protein called BDNF. This protein maintains our neural networks and keeps them working effectively. Anything that decreases BDNF is likely to result in abnormal cognition and behaviour.

Evaluating the genetic explanation

ISSUES AND DEBATES

Determinism versus free will

A strength of the genetic explanation of OCD is that biological determinism is supported by research evidence. For example, Shmelkov *et al.* (2010) artificially silenced the SLITRK5 gene in a sample of so-called **knock-out mice**. These mice displayed compulsive grooming (licking all the fur from their faces) and burying marbles placed in their cages, a behaviour similar to hoarding seen in some humans with OCD. Due to similarities in their nervous systems, the results of this study of rodents suggests that symptoms of OCD in humans may also be determined by genetic factors. However, the study was performed on mice and although animal experiments have their advantages in terms of increased reliability and lack of demand characteristics, studies such as this may overlook the role of free will. Mice do not possess the level of consciousness that allows humans to make unpredictable decisions based on reflection and contemplation. For example, a human may be genetically programmed to show compulsive behaviour but may resist their urges in an attempt to conform in a public place. Such pressures do not operate in the same way for rodents meaning the results of Shmelkov et al. (2010) may not be generalisable to humans.

Nature versus nurture

A weakness of the genetic explanation is that it fails to explain cultural differences in OCD symptoms, therefore overlooking the role of nurture in the development of this disorder. Although the prevalence of OCD is roughly the same across the world, the nature of people's obsessions and compulsions may be culturally dependent. For example, Fontenelle et al. (2004) found that 70 per cent of people with OCD in Brazil had obsessions relating to aggression and violence compared with just 16 per cent in a sample from Singapore. The researchers cite an escalation in violent crime associated with accelerated urbanisation throughout Brazil as a potential contributing factor. This shows that caution must be exercised when making generalisations about OCD from one culture to another as environmental influences (nurture) clearly shape the nature of this disorder. This said, Fontenelle et al. (2004) also highlight the role of OCD as an evolutionary mechanism that increases survival value (nature). The involuntary creation of risk scenarios (obsessive thoughts about danger) based on specific threats from the immediate environment (such as violent crime) may protect us by encouraging avoidance of dangerous situations, but if taken too far (as in OCD), it may lead to maladaptive behaviour.

Biochemical

Serotonin, dopamine and BDNF

As explained above, in relation to the 5-HTT gene, it appears that an imbalance of serotonin may increase vulnerability to OCD. This may be linked to irregularities associated with the transport of serotonin from the synapse back into the presynaptic cell, abnormalities relating to the receptors on the postsynaptic cell and/or problems with enzymes, such as MAO-A, which break down serotonin. Abnormalities relating to D4 dopamine receptors may also increase vulnerability to OCD, while anything that affects the production of BDNF may increase the risk of developing this disorder.

The role of oxytocin

One of the key symptoms in OCD is repetitive behaviour, a symptom which is also seen in people with autism spectrum disorder (ASD). Hollander et al. (2003) had found that oxytocin (for example, administered in nasal drops) could reduce this symptom in people with ASD and this led other researchers to question whether oxytocin may have a role to play in OCD, given the cross-over in some of the symptoms.

Based on the work of Hollander et al. (2003), one might think people with OCD would have low levels of oxytocin, but interestingly, higher levels of oxytocin are associated with more severe OCD symptoms (Humble et al., 2013), particularly in people who develop the condition at a young age and are resistant to drug treatments. This could be explained by upregulation, whereby a lower number of receptors on the postsynaptic cell cause a greater amount of oxytocin to be released. Evidence to support this comes from a study in Brazil where it was revealed that people with OCD have greater methylation of the OXTR gene (Cappi et al., 2016). DNA methylation decreases gene expression, silencing or turning genes off so they cannot do their job. As the OXTR gene codes for oxytocin receptors, this suggests that irregularities in oxytocin may increase vulnerability to OCD.

Evaluating the biochemical explanation

One strength of this explanation is that understanding of the role of serotonin and other neurotransmitters has led to the development of drug treatments which have provided relief for many people whose lives have been disrupted by the disabling effects of OCD. For example, Rapoport's patient, Charles, experienced significant relief when he began taking clomipramine (a tricyclic antidepressant) that allowed him to return to school and resume his education. Although not everyone agrees with the use of psychotropic drugs, especially in the treatment of children, the biochemical explanations have helped many people who may not have been able to access psychological therapy. This said, the positive effects of clomipramine were relatively short-lived for Charles, who developed a tolerance to the drug and relapsed within a year. This suggests that the biological explanation has only been partially useful in helping to inspire effective treatments for OCD.

ISSUES AND DEBATES

Reductionism versus holism

A weakness of the biochemical explanation is that it is reductionist and fails to fully consider the role of environmental factors that may be involved in maintaining the disorder. For example, repetition of compulsive behaviours is negatively reinforced, making these behaviours even more frequent as they become associated with a reduction in anxiety. This oversight in the biochemical explanation is important as it means that it may be possible to treat OCD using behavioural therapy, whereas the biochemical explanation may give the mistaken impression that OCD cannot be treated without medication. This said, the biochemical explanation could be seen to be more holistic as processes such as methylation of the OXTR gene (leading to a reduction in oxytocin receptors) result from an interaction between nature and nurture, studied in a branch of biology called epigenetics. Cappi et al. (2016) explain that life events that occur within key critical periods can lead to epigenetic reprogramming, which can affect future neurotransmission. This is important as it helps to explain why people at different life stages are differentially affected by the same life events.

As with Rapoport's patient, Charles, compulsive handwashing is a common symptom in children and adults with OCD across the world, including in Mexico, where it affects 62 per cent of people with the diagnosis (Fontenelle et al., 2004). What does it tell you about nature versus nurture if a behaviour has similar prevalence across all cultures, despite differences in cultural beliefs and values?

▲ Figure 6.51

▶ LEARNING LINK

Think back to the study by Perry et al. (personal space) (see page 143). They studied the effects of oxytocin on personal space and how it differed depending on whether the person was high or low in empathy. The role of oxytocin in obsessive-compulsive disorder is unclear but evidence suggests people who are genetically predisposed towards lower oxytocin levels sometimes have the most severe symptoms.

Can you think how personal space and obsessive-compulsive disorder might be related? Do you think people with OCD prefer more or less personal space? How might this vary depending on the social context?

STUDY TIP

Thinking about how each of the topics you are studying is linked to the featured issues and debates is a good way of deepening and enriching your evaluation. In this section, we have mentioned nature versus nurture, reductionism versus holism and cultural differences.

You could have a table with three columns: one column for each of the different theories and studies in this section, and a column for each side of one of the featured debates.

Can you come up with points to support both sides of the debate? For example, you could say, 'On the one hand, genetic explanations are an individual explanation of OCD as each person inherits a unique combination of genes. On the other hand, situational factors can affect our genes via the process of methylation.'

Thinking about both sides of the debates like this is challenging but will help to increase cognitive flexibility.

▶ TEST YOURSELF

1   Miguel's psychiatrist has explained that there are two biological explanations of obsessive-compulsive disorder (OCD): the genetic and the biochemical explanations. Miguel thinks they sound very similar. Suggest one difference between these two explanations that Miguel's doctor could explain to him. [2]

2   State one strength and one weakness of the biochemical explanation of OCD. [2]

3   a   Describe the genetic explanation of OCD. [6]

    b   Evaluate the genetic explanation of OCD, including a discussion of nature versus nurture. [10]

4   Suggest how you would recruit suitable participants to investigate genetic explanations of OCD. [2]

5   Explain two ethical guidelines relating to the use of animals in investigations into the biological explanations of OCD. [4]

6   Explain one ethical guideline relating to the use of human participants in investigations into the genetic explanation of OCD. [2]

KEY TERMS

thinking error

personal responsibility

thought-action fusion

thought-event fusion

orderliness

parsimoniousness

obstinacy

perfectionism

Psychological explanations

Think!

Can you name three **thinking errors** that make people more vulnerable to obsessive-compulsive disorder?

Think!

Serena Williams, the former world number 1 tennis player, has many context-specific compulsions, including bouncing her ball a certain number of times before serving and always taking certain items onto the court with her. Can you think of any behaviours that you feel you just have to do in a certain way? Why do you think you behave in this way?

Think!

If Lopatka, Rachman and Freud were put in a room together and told to come up with a plan to test the behavioural explanation of OCD, what do you think they would come up with? What could they learn from each other?

Freud believed that OCD is determined by experiences of potty training in infancy, suggesting that this is the first time that the developing child becomes aware of the connection between their own behaviour and their parents' approval. What would be the best research method(s) to use to test Freud's theory?

Cognitive (thinking error)

For many of us, thoughts like 'Did I leave my hair straighteners on?' and 'I hope my teacher likes my essay' are passing thoughts, just two of the 6000 thoughts that neuroscientists now believe are part of a day in the life of the average human (Tseng and Poppenk, 2020). Cognitive psychologists believe that people with OCD find it much more difficult to ignore certain thoughts and images, mistakenly believing that all thoughts are meaningful or significant – that is, 'there must be a reason for every thought that I have'.

This mistaken assumption is common in people with OCD, who also exhibit a number of other thinking errors which can mean passing thoughts can turn into obsessions. For example, over-estimation of **personal responsibility** means believing that you alone are responsible for ensuring harm does not happen to others or indeed oneself. It is easy to see how this could turn into compulsive washing, cleaning and checking in an attempt to reduce anxiety triggered by obsessive thoughts about germs, accidents and other risks to health and safety.

Another common thinking error in people who develop OCD symptoms is **thought-action fusion** (TAF). Here people believe that imagining behaving a certain way increases the probability that you will actually behave this way – for example, imagining yourself deliberately smashing a classmate's new laptop means you believe that you may actually do this in real life. Likewise, **thought-event fusion** refers to the belief that imagining a certain event will make it more likely – for example, imagining your friend dropping their laptop will make it more likely to happen.

In summary, for cognitive psychologists, it is not the content of the initial thought that causes obsessional thinking but the way that certain thoughts are labelled and interpreted. For example, the thought may be labelled as shameful or disgusting and the person attributes this thought to dispositional factors – that is, that they are a shameful and disgusting person.

Behavioural (operant conditioning)

In order to understand how obsessive thoughts lead to compulsive actions, it is necessary to turn to **operant conditioning**, one of the three learning theories outlined on page 87, where we applied these principles to the maintenance of phobias. Avoiding the feared stimulus was negatively reinforcing, as it removed unpleasant feelings of anxiety. In OCD, compulsive behaviours develop as they help to reduce negative feelings such as anxiety, fear, guilt and shame associated with the thinking errors described above. Any actions that the person takes that reduce these negative emotions are reinforced, as they make the person feel better, meaning the behaviours become more likely. Such behaviours sometimes also occur in non-clinical samples. For example, many professional sportspeople, including Michael Jordan and Serena Williams, report rituals that they go through before major events, believing that failure to conduct these behaviours will lead to negative outcomes.

Psychodynamic

Freud's psychodynamic explanation of obsessive-compulsive disorder draws on many of the same concepts as his theory of phobias. He believed that mental health symptoms are a form of defence mechanism in that they protect the person from becoming aware of unresolved conflicts from the unconscious mind, often between the id and superego. When the id's desires are not satisfied, they may be expressed through obsessional thoughts, while compulsive acts may result from excessive guilt generated by an overly dominant superego. For Freud, such problems are determined by experiences in early childhood, including the desire to gain approval from parents. On page 323, you learned about the psychosexual stages and how unresolved conflicts at any one of these stages can lead to specific adult personality types through the process of fixation.

Freud linked obsessive-compulsive disorder to unresolved conflict in the anal stage of development (ages 1–3). At this age, the child learns that parental approval relies upon the ability to retain faeces until they are in the 'correct' place – the potty or toilet. Potty training that is too early (so that the child is physically incapable of achieving success) or too harsh (punishing the child for soiling) can result in the child becoming fixated in this stage, meaning elements of this period of development are incorporated into the developing personality. For example, the person may be obsessive about cleanliness and **orderliness** and may be highly conscientious. Other traits may also appear, including **parsimoniousness** (meanness) and **obstinacy** (stubbornness). This is sometimes referred to as an anally retentive personality and is also associated with **perfectionism**, a trait that has also been associated with OCD.

Evaluating the psychological explanations

Experimental evidence supports the idea that heightened sense of personal responsibility increases the urge to check. Thirty people with 'checking-type' OCD were asked to lock a door and turn a stove on and off. In comparison to a control group, they self-reported less urge to check and less distress when told that they would not be held responsible for any negative outcomes (Lopatka and Rachman, 1995). This supports the idea that thinking errors may have a causal role in the development of OCD. This said, behaviour may have been affected by demand characteristics as it was a repeated measures design and the participants may have felt even more anxious than usual as they were being watched as part of an experiment.

Idiographic versus nomothetic

A strength of the psychodynamic explanation is that it is supported by idiographic research, in which the focus is the subjective experiences of each individual sufferer. For example, Freud, (1909) described the case of 'the Rat Man'. Tormented by intrusive thoughts about being gnawed by rats, his patient was terrified that his father and girlfriend, Gisela, would also be tortured in this way unless he conducted ritualistic counting and praying. His symptoms improved when Freud helped him to recover memories of sexual desire and repressed hatred of his father, who had tried to stop his romance with Gisela. Freud's idiographic approach helped him to build a detailed understanding of the origins of the man's symptoms and, despite the lack of scientific support for psychodynamic theories of OCD, some therapists still believe there is a place for a psychoanalytic approach in treating late-onset OCD and people with comorbid borderline personality disorder (Chlebowski and Gregory, 2009). Research that takes a nomothetic approach, i.e. looking for trends amongst larger groups, can easily lose sight of the personal context in which symptoms are experienced and may be less helpful in explaining atypical cases.

Individual and situational explanations

A strength of the psychological theories is that they explain individual differences that lead some people to develop OCD while others do not. For example, the cognitive explanation suggests that some people are more prone to thinking errors that make them vulnerable to OCD. Psychological theories also help to explain differences between people with OCD. For example, the psychodynamic approach helps to understand obsessions around forbidden topics and taboos that may reflect the id's socially unacceptable desires, but it is also able to explain obsessions with cleanliness and neatness in terms of fixation in the anal stage. These theories provide individual explanations as they see the causes of the disorder as something that relates to relatively stable personality traits, e.g. the extent to which a person takes personal responsibility, however it is important to recognise that the severity of OCD symptoms changes over times; some days may be better than others. Based on self-report data, Brierley *et al.* (2021) concluded that situational factors, including having a meal, hot weather and watching television, were all significantly associated with worsening of OCD symptoms in their sample of 742 people with OCD.

Nature versus nurture

A weakness of the psychological approaches, in general, is their failure to acknowledge the role of nature in the development of OCD. For example, Thobois *et al.* (2004) reported a case of OCD that developed in a man who underwent surgery to remove a blood clot from his caudate nucleus. This is one of three brain structures that make up the 'worry circuit', which is thought to be abnormal in people with OCD. As the man showed no symptoms of OCD before his surgery, the study suggests that this structure is important in inhibiting compulsive urges. This is important as it can be inferred that anything that interferes with the functioning of this brain structure, including genetic factors, may increase vulnerability to OCD and psychological theories tend to ignore this possibility.

LEARNING LINK

This section has links not only with the concepts from the cognitive and learning approaches but also with the concept of brain localisation, as seen in the evaluation point above about Thobois *et al.* (2004).

The only approach that has not been considered is the social approach, but social context can also have an impact on OCD symptoms. For example, 'tight cultures' have very clear norms regarding social behaviour and failure to conform is not tolerated. In highly religious cultures, this can lead to a specific type of OCD called scrupulosity, where obsessions may relate to sinful thoughts and compulsions to purify the mind through prayer and other rituals specific to the person's religion. In such cases, it is critical for clinical psychologists to have a thorough understanding of the cultural context to understand what the person's symptoms mean to them. This can only really be gained through taking an idiographic approach.

STUDY TIP

As you read through any new explanation or theory, it is always worth thinking, 'How would I test this explanation'?

Think about how you would conduct an experiment or a correlation, an interview or an observation. What features of the theory would you investigate? Dividing each theory into a set of no more than six bullet points and thinking how each one could be tested is a great way of not only training yourself to think like a psychologist but also strengthening your memory for the theory.

> **TEST YOURSELF**

1 Caspar has obsessive-compulsive disorder (OCD). He checks his homework for at least five hours every night. If he finds a mistake, he rewrites the entire piece of work and becomes very distressed if he cannot find his 'lucky pen'. Explain Caspar's symptoms using one or more explanations of OCD. [4]

2 Outline one similarity and one difference between the psychodynamic and the behavioural explanations of obsessive-compulsive disorder. [4]

3 a Describe one or more psychological explanation of OCD. [6]
   b Evaluate one or more of the psychological explanations described in part a. [10]

4 Jessica has asked her participants to complete the Y-BOCS and a psychometric test measuring personal responsibility (from 0 to 25, where a high score indicates high responsibility). She wants to know whether there is a correlation between these two co-variables. Write a suitable non-directional hypothesis for Jessica's study. [2]

5 Mimi is conducting a postal questionnaire where she will ask people with and without a diagnosis of OCD about their childhood. Give two forced-choice questions Mimi could ask in a questionnaire. [4]

6 Explain one strength and one weakness of longitudinal studies as a way of investigating psychological explanations of OCD. [4]

KEY TERMS

selective serotonin reuptake inhibitors (SSRIs)

granisetron

placebo effect

tricyclics

maintenance dose

withdrawal symptoms

clomipramine

tolerance

risperidone

side effects

non-compliance

METHODOLOGY

case studies

reliability

6.5.3 Treatment and management of obsessive-compulsive disorder
Biological treatments

Think!

Why do you think the combination of **selective serotonin reuptake inhibitors (SSRIs)** and **granisetron** is described as paradoxical?

Think!

Imagine you are a doctor meeting a patient with OCD. You have decided to prescribe an SSRI. You know that the way patients perceive the pills they are given is important as it can increase or decrease their efficacy (**placebo effects**). How will this influence what you say and how you behave with your patient when you talk to them about their new medication? This is an important question as it shows how situational factors can affect the efficacy of biological treatments.

Think!

The study by Askari *et al.* (2012) had quite extraordinary results. It was a double-blind randomised control trial conducted with 42 patients from two outpatient clinics. What further information would you want about the study before suggesting that granisetron should be used as a standard treatment for OCD?

Many medical consultations have taken place remotely in recent years, making it more difficult for both doctors and patients to benefit from aspects of nonverbal communication like eye contact and touch.

» Do you think people with OCD who have been treated remotely will respond differently to their prescribed medications as a result?

» How could you do a study to find out? What problem might you have with the validity of your investigation?

▲ Figure 6.52

Biological treatments for obsessive-compulsive disorder include the use of SSRIs and other medications designed to increase monoamine neurotransmitters, such as **tricyclics** and monoamine oxidase inhibitors (MAOIs), all of which you learned about on page 276. All of these medications are generally administered orally as tablets. As previously noted, people do not usually notice any improvement initially and when antidepressants are used to treat OCD, the time lag can be up to 12 weeks. People also generally need to stay on medication for at least one year to prevent relapse and a **maintenance dose** may be necessary as an alternative to ceasing medication completely. This period will need to be managed carefully with advice from a medical professional as some drugs used in the treatment of OCD can lead to unpleasant **withdrawal symptoms** if they are ceased too quickly. Gradually reducing the dosage over a period of weeks or months can minimise any such problems.

Tricyclics

Tricyclics increase serotonin, dopamine and noradrenaline and can be an effective treatment for OCD as well as unipolar depression. Charles, the boy from the case study by Rapoport (1989) (see page 339), was prescribed a tricyclic drug called **clomipramine**. This drug had a major impact on his daily functioning within just four weeks and allowed him to pour honey from a spoon, something he could never have achieved before due to his obsession with stickiness, which he perceived as a 'disease'. Sadly, after 12 months, Charles built up a **tolerance** to the drug, which meant it no longer worked for him and his symptoms returned, although thankfully in a more manageable way that allowed him to function relatively well during the school day.

SSRIs

SSRIs increase serotonin in the synapse by blocking presynaptic transporter molecules. The exact mode of action for these drugs is still unclear. Although synaptic serotonin is immediately increased, improvement in symptoms is often not observed for some considerable time. This suggests that when symptoms do improve, this possibly results from down regulation – for example, the brain compensates for the increased serotonin by reducing the amount that is released from the presynaptic cell. Due to the many interactions between different brain chemicals, it is also possible that serotonin levels regulate the release of other neurochemicals which trigger the reduction in symptoms.

Augmenting SSRIs with other drugs

Antipsychotics

Fortunately, it is possible to enhance the effects of SSRIs in people who have previously been treatment-resistant by offering additional drugs, such as **risperidone** (an atypical antipsychotic; see page 251). This combination has been shown to be clinically effective (leading to a reduction in Y-BOCS scores of at least 35 per cent) in 72 per cent of patients (Selvi *et al.*, 2011).

Serotonin antagonists

Furthermore, a seemingly paradoxical combination of an SSRI and granisetron (a serotonin antagonist, i.e. a drug that blocks serotonin receptors) achieved a 100 per cent success rate in a study by Askari *et al.* (2012). All patients improved by 35 per cent on the Y-BOCS and 90 per cent were symptom-free after just two months. These results demonstrate that biological treatments can have a remarkable impact if the correct combinations can be found and measures can be put in place to support the individual with potential **side effects**.

Evaluating biological treatments

One strength of SSRIs is that their use with people diagnosed with OCD is supported by research evidence that suggests the impact is not simply a placebo effect. For example, in a relatively large meta-analysis of 17 randomised control trials, Issari *et al.* (2016) found a significantly greater improvement in patients' symptoms in the treatment groups compared with the placebo group. The amount of relief provided by the SSRIs appeared to diminish over time, but this was moderated by offering higher dosages. This is an important finding as it demonstrates that SSRIs, a relatively cheap and low-effort treatment, can provide swift relief for some people with OCD.

A practical weakness of SSRIs is that they can lead to unpleasant side effects in the initial weeks, and sometimes longer. For example, they may result in constipation, diarrhoea, nausea, vomiting headaches, dizziness, anxiety and sleep problems. All of these problems could lead to **non-compliance** – that is, people not taking their medication. This means that psychological therapies may be a better option for people who suffer more severe side effects and who may feel unable to cope with side effects that make them even more out of control.

> ## ISSUES AND DEBATES

Individual and situational explanations

A weakness of biological treatments for OCD is that up to 60 per cent of people report no improvement in their symptoms (McDougle *et al.*, 1993) following standard drug treatments. For those who do experience relief, the reduction in symptom severity may only be between 20 and 30 per cent (Pigott and Seay, 1999). However, greater understanding of the polygenic nature of OCD (i.e. that vulnerability to OCD is influenced by unique combinations of hundreds of different genes) means that over time medicine may become more personalised. For example, doctors may be able to decode exactly which genes are influencing each patient's symptoms and tailor their treatments accordingly. This would be an example of an individualised approach to treatment. However, it should not be forgotten that even with biological treatments, situational factors are also critical to their success. Research suggest that the quality of the therapeutic alliance, i.e. the rapport between doctors and their patients impacts the effectiveness of the treatment.

> ## LEARNING LINKS
>
> Biological treatments like the ones described here are prescribed by medical doctors. In the social approach, you learned about how behaviour, thoughts and feelings are dependent upon social context and our relationships with other people.
>
> You can think of the doctor–patient relationship in this way: how will the patient's behaviour be affected by the doctor? How will factors like age, gender and race affect the nature of this relationship? What impact will this relationship have on whether the person complies with their treatment, whether the patient expects the drugs to work and, in turn, the degree of improvement the person actually experiences?

> ## STUDY TIP
>
> Consolidating how drug treatments work can be fun! Why not make synapses from sweets or modelling clay, with different colours for the different parts, such as receptors, neurotransmitter molecules, transporter molecules and the different drugs?
>
> You could use sticky notes to label the different parts and processes and take photographs to embed into your revision notes. Test yourself frequently on the biological terminology as it can be easy to forget unless you rehearse it regularly.

TEST YOURSELF

1 Jane has been prescribed an SSRI for obsessive-compulsive disorder (OCD). Her obsessions keep her awake at night and her tiredness means she finds it difficult to stay awake in meetings when she is at work. Outline one advantage and one disadvantage of SSRIs as a treatment for Jane. [4]

2 SSRIs may be prescribed for children with obsessive-compulsive disorder. Outline two ways that these drugs could affect a child at school. [2]

3 a Describe biological treatments for obsessive-compulsive disorder, including SSRIs. [6]

  b Evaluate biological treatments for obsessive-compulsive disorder, including a discussion of individual and situational explanations. [10]

4 Marjorie has been prescribed an SSRI for OCD. Outline one individual factor and one situational factor that could influence whether the SSRI is effective. [2]

5 Dr Fritz is investigating the effectiveness of SSRIs with a group of people with obsessive-compulsive disorder. He has asked them to complete the Y-BOCS to see whether their symptoms have improved since they began taking medication. Explain two ways that Dr Fritz could check the reliability of his data. [4]

6 a Outline what is meant by idiographic versus nomothetic. [2]

  b Suggest why an idiographic approach might be useful in evaluating the effectiveness of biological treatments for OCD. [2]

KEY TERMS

exposure and response prevention (ERP)

homework

Subjective Units of Distress Scale (SUDS)

hierarchy

habituation

safety behaviours

Psychological therapies

Exposure and response prevention

Think!

Systematic desensitisation and **exposure and response prevention (ERP)** may seem very similar. From what you have learned on these pages, what are the main similarities and differences between the two?

Think!

Imagine you are a therapist. You are meeting the foster parents of a child who has been referred to your clinic for ERP therapy for obsessive-compulsive disorder.

What will you tell the foster parents about this therapy and what advice can you give them about how to ensure the child in their care makes the best possible progress over the next few weeks?

Think!

Cognitive-behavioural therapists always work collaboratively with their clients. The therapist's role is to support the client, who takes responsibility for their own recovery. Can you think of any reasons why this type of therapy may be more effective with people who identify more with individualistic than collectivist cultural values? If you can't remember what these terms mean, see page 225.

ERP involves experiencing high levels of anxiety through exposure but then habituating to the stimuli without being allowed to carry out compulsions like handwashing or counting. Take a look at Figure 6.53. How do we know that the woman is *not* touching the doorknob as part of an ERP therapy session? If this was how she carried out her **homework** exercise, what do you think her therapist would say?

▲ Figure 6.53

ERP is a type of cognitive-behavioural therapy used specifically with people with obsessive-compulsive disorder. The exposure element makes it similar to systematic desensitisation (see page 328) used to treat people with phobias. But there are some important differences. First, people are asked to identify obsessional thoughts that trigger compulsive behaviours and then identify environmental triggers that cue these thoughts. These cues are given **Subjective Units of Distress Scale (SUDS)** ratings, just like Chapman and DeLapp (2013) used in the treatment of T, the man with blood-injection-injury phobia (see page 309).

Triggering situations are arranged into a **hierarchy** from the lowest to highest SUDS rating and at this point the client and therapist can embark on the first exposure (to the situation or objects with the lowest rating).

ERP is only effective if exposures last long enough for the person to **habituate** to the stimulus, meaning that arousal levels reduce to the point where the person is no longer anxious. This is assessed by asking the person to report their SUDS rating, with the exposure ending when the SUDS had reduced by at least 50 per cent.

Typically, a person with OCD will reduce their own anxiety by carrying out compulsive actions like handwashing or counting, but in ERP the therapist's role is to ensure that the person is prevented from carrying out these maladaptive behaviours so that they learn that anxiety can and will reduce on its own. Therapists and clients often work on the same exposure many times until the situation is given a SUDS rating of 0. ERP therapists, like all cognitive-behavioural therapists, will encourage their clients to practise every day (homework) and keep records of their progress to share during the next session.

One important point about ERP is that it does not include any training in relaxation strategies and people are strongly advised not to use anti-anxiety medication before sessions. As the therapy progresses, people are encouraged to increase their anxiety levels to the highest possible point as it is argued that new learning can only take place when the person consciously experiences a marked reduction in anxiety in the absence of compulsive behaviour. Clients are also advised to avoid **safety behaviours**, like only touching objects with their fingertips rather than touching things like doorknobs or taps with their whole hand.

Evaluating exposure and response prevention

A strength of ERP is that it has been shown to be more effective than drug treatments such as clomipramine. In a double-blind, randomised, placebo-controlled trial, 86 per cent of people who were treated using ERP achieved a clinically relevant reduction in symptoms, whereas the rate was only 48 per cent in the clomipramine group (Foa *et al.*, 2005). This is an important finding as drug treatments leave many people with residual symptoms and have unpleasant side effects, as well as leading to problems with tolerance and withdrawal. This study shows that there is a credible alternative that is not only tolerated better by many, but also more effective.

Another strength of ERP is its practical applications with a diverse population with differing needs. For example, Lehmkuhl *et al.* (2008) demonstrated how the standard principles described above can be adapted for a child with autism spectrum disorder, who showed improvement significantly in just ten sessions. Also, Lovell *et al.* (2006; see page 356) have shown that ERP can also be adapted for telephone delivery within half the time of face-to-face therapy, cutting costs and allowing more people to access therapy. This is important as therapies need to be flexible in order that they can be adapted to the differing needs of diverse communities, particularly with global rates of OCD increasing, subsequent to the Covid-19 pandemic.

A weakness of ERP is that it can be difficult for inexperienced therapists to deliver, reducing its applications to real-world settings. Gillihan *et al.* (2012) explain seven common pitfalls that can reduce the efficacy or ERP, including failing to work with relatives and friends who may be reinforcing OCD reassurance-seeking behaviour and allowing clients to distract themselves as a way of tolerating exposure rather than being fully aware of their own bodily processes as anxiety decreases. These pitfalls mean less experienced therapists must be carefully supervised by more experienced colleagues, further increasing waiting times.

A final weakness of ERP is that old compulsions may be replaced with new ones unless the therapist is able to reveal the core underlying fear. For example, Gillihan *et al.* (2012) states that a religious person may be tormented by forbidden thoughts triggered by the number six, a number associated with the Devil. These thoughts may lead the person to engage in many hours of rituals in an attempt to neutralise their thoughts. Although ERP may help treat this problem, unless the core fear is revealed (e.g. fear of going to Hell), the person may continue to suffer with new compulsions.

Focus on: Lehmkuhl *et al.* (2008)

▶ AIMS

To investigate the efficacy of CBT for a 12-year-old child with a dual diagnosis of autism spectrum disorder (ASD) and obsessive-compulsive disorder. There was little to no research looking at cognitive-behavioural therapy for obsessive-compulsive disorder, although CBT has been used effectively to treat social anxiety in children and young people with ASD.

▶ CASE HISTORY

Jason was diagnosed with autism spectrum disorder aged two (see Table 6.17 for symptoms). He had a full-time learning support assistant at school, as well as regular speech and language therapy, and his family had attended various interventions to support his development. Aged 11, he was diagnosed with OCD when ritualistic and avoidant behaviours began to interfere with his social and academic life and began to cause significant impairment. At the beginning of therapy, Jason's score on the children's version of the Y-BOCS was 18 (moderate).

▼ Table 6.17 Symptoms relating to Jason's dual diagnosis

Symptoms relating to Jason's diagnosis of...	
Autism spectrum disorder	**Obsessive-compulsive disorder**
<ul><li>sensory issues around touch and sound</li><li>banged his head and bit himself</li><li>limited and repetitive language</li><li>repetitive play; preferred objects to toys</li><li>poor social relationships</li></ul>	<ul><li>obsessions: contamination</li><li>compulsions: handwashing and checking of food 'use by dates'</li><li>avoidance: would not touch doorknobs, library books and other children's papers and school equipment; would not sit on public benches and chairs</li></ul>

▶ TREATMENT

- Jason attended ten 50-minute cognitive-behavioural therapy sessions over 16 weeks at a local hospital.
- Cognitive restructuring and imagined exposure were not possible as Jason could not identify his obsessional thoughts so the therapist adapted the therapy to suit Jason's needs.
- The therapist helped Jason to identify distressing feelings and taught him coping strategies like saying 'nothing bad is going to happen' to reduce anxiety.
- She used phrases like 'beating OCD' and 'not letting OCD be the boss'.
- She used a chart to reward Jason's progress with the homework exercises and created other visual ways to

develop his self-awareness, such as how thoughts and feelings affect behaviour.
- She encouraged Jason to expose himself to unpleasant situations, like touching doorknobs and lift (elevator) buttons in the hospital, and observed biological signs of stress, like sweating and blushing, to ensure that Jason was exposed for long enough for new learning to take place.
- Jason's parents and teachers were involved so they could help him practise his new strategies at home and school.

JASON'S PROGRESS

Jason found the exposure element of the therapy difficult but, with encouragement, his avoidance reduced and he was proud of his achievements. The final sessions focused on one of Jason's hoarding behaviours. His Y-BOCS score had now dropped 15 points from 18 to 3 and the therapist began preparing him to finish therapy – for example, putting strategies in place to prevent relapse. Jason was followed up at three months and he was still doing well, with no signs of relapse.

CONCLUSION

If CBT is personalised to meet children's individual developmental needs, it can be effective as a treatment for children with autism and OCD.

ISSUES AND DEBATES

Use of children

A strength of this case study is that Lehmkuhl *et al.* (2008) were able to successfully adapt a therapy designed for use with adults to suit the specific needs of a child. An important consideration when working with children is to build a rapport with the whole family, as this will help to ensure that strategies worked on in therapy transfer more consistently to the home environment. Family members may also be able to provide additional information that will help the therapist to tailor the treatment programme to the child's interests if the child is unable to communicate these for themselves. This is especially important for very young children or those with additional needs, like Jason.

Evaluating Lehmkuhl *et al.* (2008)

A weakness of this study is that the **case study** method means generalisations should only be made with caution. Jason was a white American 12-year-old with average IQ and a diagnosis of autism spectrum disorder. It is difficult to know whether ERP would be as effective for children without autism or adults or teenagers with autism. The researchers commented that Jason received a great deal of professional support as a young child; this is important as it means that his results may not even generalise to other children with autism who may have had less previous experience with therapists and other practitioners.

A strength of the study was the collection of qualitative and quantitative data from observation, interview and psychometric tests (such as an IQ test and the Y-BOCS) and a detailed examination of secondary data (such as medical records). The idiographic nature of the study allowed the researchers to gain insight into the practical issues involved in adapting ERP for people with autism spectrum disorder. The collection of quantitative data from a commonly used test means the result can be compared with other studies where the Y-BOCS has been used pre-and post-treatment. This is important as, although case studies only use a single participant, comparison with other studies using the Y-BOCS can help to determine the reliability of the findings. For example, a randomised control trial with 46 adults with ASD supported the efficacy of ERP for this population (Russell *et al.*, 2013).

Like the case study of Charles (Rapoport, 1989) on page 339, Lehmkuhl *et al.* (2008) focuses on a child as the research participant, 12-year-old Jason. What similarities and differences can you identify between these two studies? Drawing a Venn diagram could help you to organise your ideas.

LEARNING LINKS

Some therapists mistakenly suggest that their clients think about something else while they are undergoing exposures, to help them to tolerate the stimulus until it is removed. This underlines the key principles of ERP and will hinder progress.

Thinking about Andrade's (doodling) study from AS Level may help you to understand why. She explained that when we are daydreaming or focusing our mind on things other than our immediate environment, we tend to lack concentration and be more forgetful. Staying fully focused on the exposure is important, otherwise new learning cannot take place.

STUDY TIP

The research method in Lehmkuhl *et al.* (2008) is a case study. If you understand the strengths and limitations of this method, then you should be able to apply them to this study to create detailed evaluation, with breadth and depth.

To learn this section, you could roll a dice and, if the number is odd, you have to come up with a weakness; if you roll an even number, you have to come up with a strength. If you want to make the game harder, roll again and the number will determine the type of point you have to make. For example, 1: generalisations, 2: reliability, 3: application to real life, 4: validity, 5: ethics, 6: objectivity/subjectivity.

▶ TEST YOURSELF

1 Beau is obsessed with order and compulsively tidies up for six hours every day. He cannot spend time with his wife or children until every last possession has been stored in its correct location, and this is causing tension. His wife has suggested he sees a therapist. Explain one psychological therapy using Beau as an example. [4]

2 Compare one biological and one psychological treatment for obsessive-compulsive disorder (OCD). [4]

3 a Describe exposure and response prevention (ERP) as a psychological therapy for OCD. [6]

   b Evaluate ERP, including a discussion of the use of children in psychological research. [10]

4 a Plan a participant observation to investigate the effectiveness of exposure and response prevention as a therapy for OCD. Your plan must include details about:

      i   whether your observation will be structured or unstructured

      ii how you will analyse your data. [10]

   b State one way that the plan makes the study valid. [2]

   c Explain one weakness of the plan with reference to validity. [2]

   d Explain one way that your plan considers ethical guidelines. [2]

KEY TERMS

cognitive-behavioural therapy (CBT)

exposure and response prevention (ERP)

mode of delivery

non-inferiority trial

comorbid

Key study: Telephone administered cognitive-behavioural therapy (CBT) – Lovell *et al.* (2006)

Think!

How did the researchers decide whether a participant's treatment was successful – in other words, that their improvement was 'clinically relevant'?

Think!

Imagine you are a therapist offering **exposure and response prevention (ERP)** therapy to people with OCD. You have just been told that the clinic where you work is changing from face-to-face to telephone-based therapy. At morning break, the therapists are all chatting about the change. Some think it is a good thing, others disagree. You listen to the views on both sides. How do you think you would feel about this? Would you be for or against telephone therapy at your clinic?

Think!

This study suggests that telephone therapy can be as effective as face-to-face therapy for people with OCD, but the therapy was tested only on adults. Do you think this **mode of delivery** would be as effective with children? Can you think of any factors other than age that might reduce the effectiveness of telephone therapy for some groups of adults?

▲ Figure 6.54 Karina Lovell

Karina Lovell is Professor of Mental Health at the University of Manchester, UK. Karina trained as a mental health nurse, completed a course in **cognitive-behavioural therapy (CBT)** and then worked in various clinical NHS positions. She completed a BA, MSc and PhD part time and in 1998 moved from London to Manchester and commenced work at the University of Manchester as a lecturer. She is past president of the BABCP, fellow of EANs and a patron of the National Phobic Society. Karina is currently Director of Research and Professor of Mental Health at the University of Manchester School of Nursing, Midwifery and Social Work.

Although telephone-based therapy may improve access to therapy for some people in wealthy nations like the UK, where this study took place, it assumes that people have access to a private telephone in a safe space, where they can speak confidentially. Many people do not have the luxury of a private telephone in a safe space, even in the wealthier nations.

>> How could this be addressed?
>> What ideas do you have about improving access to culturally relevant therapy in rural areas of lower socioeconomic status?

▲ Figure 6.55

Context

Each year, costs associated with OCD reach $8.4 million in the USA alone. This huge cost underlines the critical importance of finding ways of supporting people the world over, helping them to recover from this disabling but treatable disorder. As noted on page 255, standard cognitive-behavioural therapy involves weekly, in-person sessions, lasting up to an hour. This mode of delivery has several limitations, including the time commitment and the financial costs (for both the patient and the provider). Lengthy waiting lists mean many people are unable to access support when it is most needed and often difficulties with mobility and transport make therapy sessions impractical. These problems have prompted health services in the UK to trial new modes of delivery, including online and telephone-based therapy. Aiming to reduce contact hours and reach people who find it hard to get to physical clinics, a small pilot study and one larger study returned promising outcomes, and the study described below is the first large-scale randomised control trial of telephone-based ERP for people with obsessive-compulsive disorder.

AIMS AND HYPOTHESES

To compare two modes of delivery for one-to-one ERP as a treatment for obsessive-compulsive disorder: telephone treatment versus face-to-face treatment. The study is referred to as a **non-inferiority trial** and studies like this are often used when it would not be practical or ethical

to have a placebo group, thus the study aimed to test the hypothesis that the experimental treatment (telephone ERP) is not less effective than the control treatment (face-to-face ERP) – that is, both modes of delivery will result in similar outcomes.

METHODOLOGY

This is a randomised control trial with quantitative data collected through self-report questionnaires, including a ten-item checklist to assess compulsive behaviour from the Yale-Brown Obsessive-Compulsive Disorder Scale (Y-BOCS; see page 340), the Beck Depression Inventory (BDI; see page 261) and a questionnaire designed specifically to measure client satisfaction (out of 32; the higher the score, the higher the satisfaction). The study could also be referred to as an experiment with independent measures and a longitudinal design.

Sample

Participants were aged 16–65 and were an opportunity sample of 72 people with obsessive-compulsive disorder selected from two outpatients departments in Manchester, UK. All participants scored at least 16 on the Y-BOCS and were already diagnosed with OCD as their main problem. Some people were excluded, including people who had **comorbid** substance misuse or suicidality. Anyone who had taken medication for depression or anxiety in the last three months was also excluded.

PROCEDURE

The participants were randomly allocated to the two groups: face-to-face (n=36) or telephone treatment (n=36). Researchers who were unaware of each participant's mode of delivery (i.e. blind) assessed the participants twice, four weeks apart, to establish a baseline and again at three follow-up sessions – at one, three and six months later.

Experienced, trained therapists (one at each clinic) delivered each type of therapy (telephone and face-to-face). Therapy manuals and twice monthly supervision (including reviewing the therapists' notes) ensured the therapy was faithful to the principles of ERP.

▼ Table 6.18 Description of treatment

	The face-to-face group (n=36)	The telephone group (n=36)
Number and type of sessions	Ten one-hour sessions, one-to-one with the therapist	Two one-hour face-to-face sessions, one at the beginning and one at the end of the programme; eight weekly telephone calls, each lasting up to 30 minutes
Session content	The treatment was explained – for example, to reduce anxiety/fear through gradual, repeated exposure to anxiety-producing situations. The Y-BOCS data was used to create a fear hierarchy. The initial session (face-to-face) covered the same material as the control group. Subsequent sessions followed a similar format to the face-to-face group, but less time was allocated.	
Homework expectations	Weekly homework targets were agreed. Suggested homework time was one hour a day. Progress was recorded. Therapist monitored progress and helped with target-setting and problem solving.	Same as face-to-face, except homework record sheets were sent by post.
Support between sessions	Patients were encouraged to ask a relative or friend to help them to solve any problems during the programme.	Same as face-to-face.

RESULTS

There was no significant difference in the severity of obsessive-compulsive symptoms between the two treatment groups at the baseline assessment or at any of the four follow-up assessments. There was a slight difference in the depression scores between the two modes of delivery, despite random allocation; the telephone group had slightly higher scores to begin with and, therefore, the reduction in scores is particularly impressive.

Client satisfaction scores immediately after treatment also showed no significant difference; the telephone group scored 28.7 and the face-to-face group 29.8. Treatment was seen as successful (clinically relevant)

if an individual's symptoms decreased by two standard deviations or more from the baseline mean.

Using this definition, 77 per cent of the telephone group and 67 per cent of the face-to-face group were treated successfully using exposure and response prevention. Overall, both OCD and depression symptoms dropped twice as much as would have been necessary to accept the hypothesis that telephone therapy was no less effective than face-to-face therapy, despite the reduced contact time. Table 6.19 shows the mean averages (and standard deviations) for the Y-BOCS and BDI at the two baseline assessments, immediately following treatment and at the three follow-up assessments.

▼ Table 6.19 Average Y-BOCS and BDI scores obtained at baseline and follow-up for the two modes of delivery

| | Y-BOCS scores | | | | BDI scores | | | |
| | The face-to-face group (n=36) | | The telephone group (n=36) | | The face-to-face group (n=36) | | The telephone group (n=36) | |
	Mean	SD	Mean	SD	Mean	SD	Mean	SD
Baseline visit 1	25.5	5.5	25.9	4.9	15.7	8.5	20.2	10.4
Baseline visit 2	23.7	5.8	24.9	4.7	14.1	9.1	19.1	10.6
Immediately after treatment	13.4	7.7	14	6.9	9.3	8.5	11.2	8.0
One-month follow-up	13.7	8.5	14	7.3	10.3	8.4	12.7	10.1
Three-month follow-up	12.9	7.7	12.6	7.5	10.6	8.4	10.1	8.4
Six-month follow-up	13.3	8.6	14.2	7.8	11.1	9.1	11.5	9.5

CONCLUSIONS

Telephone-delivered exposure and response prevention therapy for OCD is as effective as face-to-face therapy despite the majority of sessions being 50 per cent shorter. This equates to a saving of 40 per cent of the therapists' time, allowing more people to gain access to therapy.

 ## Methodological strengths and weaknesses

One strength of the study was the fact that the researchers took two baseline measures using the Y-BOCS and the BDI. Each pair of scores varied by less than two points on the scales, demonstrating that, in the absence of therapy, there is minimal change in symptoms over four weeks. This was a strength because the study did not include a control group for the full course of the study and it could have been argued that the reduction in symptoms was the result of spontaneous recovery. However, this minimal difference in the baseline tests suggests this is highly unlikely. Furthermore, the two baseline tests are a good example of test-retest as a way of checking the **reliability** of the baseline scores and the consistency of these scores over time suggests that the baseline data was indeed reliable.

One weakness of the study was that the blinding procedure broke down for some of the participants, meaning that the validity of the data may have been compromised. For example, 13 per cent of participants either directly or indirectly revealed which group they were in at one of their follow-up assessments. This is important as it means that the researchers may have unintentionally behaved differently towards participants once they knew which group they were in and this could have affected the way the participants completed the questionnaires about symptoms and client satisfaction.

Another strength of the study was the random allocation of participants to the two modes of delivery as this increases validity due to control of participant variables. For example, both groups comprised similar numbers of males and females with similar mean ages. Other important demographic variables relating to marital status and employment status were also very similar across both groups. This is important as without this degree of similarity it would be hard to claim that the telephone treatment was effective face-to-face as it may only have worked because of differences in participant variables between the two groups.

This said, there was one participant variable that was not well controlled despite random allocation; the initial average depression score was higher in the telephone group, suggesting that telephone therapy may have been less effective in comparison to face-to-face therapy for people with less severe depression. In practice, telephone treatment may well be an effective solution for people with OCD mixed with significant depression due to the impact of the latter on energy and motivation. These additional symptoms may mean people find it more difficult to leave the house for therapy and, therefore, may not complete the intervention, unless it is by telephone.

A further weakness in this study was attrition, meaning participants dropping out over the course of the study. For example, five people dropped out between the two baseline assessments, three in the face-to-face group dropped out before the end of the intervention and three of this group were unavailable at the six-month follow-up. This can reduce the similarity between the two groups (in terms of participant variables) meaning it is difficult to assess whether the similar degree of success between the two modes of delivery was genuine or whether the telephone treatment only appeared non-inferior due to the specific characteristics of the sample. In this study, the people who dropped out of the face-to-face group had higher Y-BOCS scores immediately after treatment than those who did not drop out and the researchers note that had these people been available for assessment at six months, the average Y-BOCS score for this group might have been higher (suggesting less overall improvement). This would have increased the difference in outcome for the two groups, with the telephone group appearing slightly more effective.

Ethics

Lovell *et al.* (2006) explain a number of points which demonstrate how ethical guidelines were upheld. For example, of the 86 people eligible for the study, nine were excluded following screening and one was withdrawn by the clinician. The screening was not only to ensure that the people had OCD as their primary mental health problem but also to deselect any participant with suicidal intent. Risk management when working in mental health is critical and the therapists may have felt that the amount of support provided to the telephone group was insufficient to meet this level of need. The decision was made to protect participants from harm. Furthermore, one person was later withdrawn from the telephone group for the same reason. The study was approved by ethics committees in South Cheshire and Stockport.

Application to everyday life

This study demonstrates that it may be possible to save more than 40 per cent of a therapist's time by delivering therapy over the telephone, thus freeing them up to treat more patients. This said, the study was run by two experienced therapists with a high degree of supervision and training, meaning the results should be generalised with caution to clinical settings where staff have less expertise. What is unclear from this study is whether delivering therapy over the telephone is as satisfying for the therapists as face-to-face sessions. This is an important research question that could be answered through idiographic methods (see below). If this mode of delivery is less satisfying due to increases in individual cases per therapist, necessitating increased paperwork, this could lead to stress, burnout and poor retention of therapists. This could lead to the hidden cost of training more future therapists to fill the void, countering the initial saving.

Idiographic versus nomothetic

This study takes a nomothetic approach to the measurement of treatment efficacy. For example, clinically relevant improvement was defined as a decrease in Y-BOCS scores of more than two standard deviations of the baseline mean. This was a strength of the study as the use of quantitative data provided an objective way of deciding whether a person's treatment was successful or not, also increasing the reliability of the data. A more idiographic approach would have required the use of different research methods, such as semi-structured interviews or even a participant observation whereby a researcher with OCD engaged in telephone therapy or the therapists themselves were interviewed about their experiences of the two different modes of delivery. Collection of qualitative data via either method would have been interesting and may have provided additional contextual information that could help to improve the service even further.

Cultural differences

One weakness of Lovell *et al.* (2006) is the results may not be generalisable to people in countries other than the UK. Hofstede *et al.* (2022) describes the UK as highly individualist with a low power distance index (see page 226). This suggests people may respond well to one-to-one private telephone therapy with ERP practitioners, who, like other cognitive behavioural therapists, work collaboratively with their clients. In contrast, people from more collectivist, high power distance cultures may not respond as positively to this type of therapy. This said, research conducted in Iran demonstrates that ERP, albeit face-to-face, can lead to an impressive reduction in symptoms, assessed using the Y-BOCs that were still evident at a 6-month follow up (Khodarahimi 2009). It should be noted, however, that the sample in this study comprised only males meaning the results may not generalise to females. Overall, this suggest that ERP can be effective in cultures that vary widely on Hofstede's cultural dimensions.

REFLECTION

- Do you think telephone therapy is the best mode of delivery for people with obsessive-compulsive disorder? What would the limitations be?
- Can you think of any other ways that therapy can be delivered other than face-to-face or telephone? What type of clients might your suggestion suit best?

LEARNING LINK

This study used self-report data to assess changes in symptoms over time in an experimental study with a longitudinal design. In some ways, the study is similar to the study by Hölzel *et al.* (mindfulness and brain scans), which investigated the biological and psychological effects of an eight-week Mindfulness-Based Stress Reduction programme. There are some important differences, however.

Why not draw a Venn diagram to compare these two studies and see how many similarities and differences you can think of with regard to how the study was carried out but also the strengths and weaknesses? One key area to focus on is subjectivity and objectivity of the data collected. Once you have completed this activity, you may like to think about whether there are any objective ways of measuring biological changes that people may or may not experience following ERP therapy, telephone-based or face-to-face.

STUDY TIP

A great deal of data has been provided in this section and clearly you do not need to remember all of these numbers. However, drawing your own conclusions from larger datasets like this is an excellent way of processing the information at a deeper level and really starting to understand mathematical concepts like standard deviation.

Here you have the opportunity to see the variation in people's scores, which puts the mean averages in context. Imagine you are writing a newspaper headline – what data would you use from Table 6.19 to convey how effective telephone therapy can be? You could even try calculating the percentage decrease in symptom severity from before and after treatment.

> ## TEST YOURSELF
> ....
>
> 1 Ichiro is having telephone therapy for obsessive-compulsive disorder (OCD). He finds it difficult to talk about his private thoughts as he has only met his therapist for one hour, face-to-face. Explain one strength and one weakness of telephone therapy for OCD using Ichiro as an example. [4]
>
> 2 Describe two findings from the study by Lovell *et al.* (2006). [4]
>
> 3 a Describe the study by Lovell *et al.* (2006) on the treatment of OCD using telephone-administered cognitive-behavioural therapy (CBT). [6]
>
>   b Evaluate the study by Lovell *et al.* (2006), including a discussion of individual and situational explanations. [10]
>
> 4 Lovell *et al.* (2006) conducted a study to investigate the effectiveness of telephone-administered CBT. Explain what is meant by 'randomised control trial' and 'test-retest reliability' using Lovell *et al.* (2006) as an example. [4]
>
> 5 Explain why Lovell *et al.'s* (2006) study of the effectiveness of telephone-administered CBT is an example of the nomothetic approach. [2]
>
> 6 Sandra is investigating how the introduction of telephone-administered therapy has affected therapists at a local clinic. Explain how she could conduct a case study to investigate this issue. [4]

7 Consumer Psychology

Learning outcomes

In this chapter, you will learn about five key areas of Consumer Psychology. You will learn one key study (shown in brackets) within each section, as well as a number of supporting studies.

The five areas are:
- the physical environment (North *et al.*, 2003)
- the psychological environment (Robson *et al.*, 2011)
- consumer decision-making (Hall *et al.*, 2010)
- the product (Becker *et al.*, 2011)
- advertising (Snyder and DeBono, 1985).

▲ Figure 7.1 Shoppers on a busy street in Beijing, China

Where there are people, there is psychology!

Psychology is everywhere, and these people are in Beijing, the bustling capital of the People's Republic of China. This chapter includes various compulsory studies, including ones conducted in the UK (North *et al.*, 2003), USA (Robson *et al.*, 2011; Snyder and DeBono, 1985), Sweden (Hall *et al.*, 2010) and Germany (Becker *et al.*, 2011), but you will also learn about many other pieces of research to help you to evaluate the concepts, theories, treatments and therapies covered in this option. For example, on page 423, you will learn about a study that explores correlations between consumer decision-making models and wellbeing in three cultures: the USA, Western Europe and China (Roets *et al.*, 2012).

7.0 Introducing Consumer Psychology

What is Consumer Psychology?

If you purchased this book for personal use, or indeed any other product or service at any point in your life, then you are a consumer. Consumer Psychology is the science of how and why we decide between different retailers, brands and products, why we end up picking up so much more than we anticipated in the supermarket, why we spend so long browsing online stores and why we feel we just have to have one more pair of jeans! Consumer psychologists often work as independent consultants advising sales and marketing teams on how to engage with customers and promote new product lines or services and encourage us all to spend, spend, spend!

At AS Level, you learned about a study conducted by Watson and Rayner (1920), where a baby boy, Albert, was classically conditioned to show fear towards a white rat. The same year, John Watson left academia and took up a position at an advertising agency. He recognised how consumer behaviour could be manipulated by appealing to people's emotions when promoting products such as baby powder, toothpaste and face cream. Just like Albert was made to fear the rat by pairing it with a loud bang, products could be made more appealing by pairing them with stimuli that produced positive feelings. Watson, for example, revived sales on a certain brand of face cream by seeking endorsement from Queen Marie of Romania, a glamorous international royal (Buckley, 1989).

Over time, the field of Consumer Psychology has developed apace, with researchers exploring how the different aspects of the physical and psychological environment, aspects of the product itself and interactions between sales representatives and customers can influence purchase intentions and behaviour. Consumer Psychology draws upon all four approaches of the Cambridge International AS Level; although much of the research initially focused on learning theories (such as classical and operant conditioning) and cognitive processes including attention, memory and decision-making, more recently the field of neuromarketing has begun to investigate what we can learn about consumer preferences, decisions and motivation from biological responses, using technology such as brain imaging, eye-tracking and other objective measures.

Careers in Consumer Psychology

If you would like to take your studies of Psychology beyond A Level, Consumer Psychology is an exciting and growing field. There are various possible routes, starting with a bachelor's degree in psychology or economics, followed by a master's in business, marketing, behavioural economics, consumer behaviour or organisational psychology.

Unlike other applied areas of psychology, such as clinical, the job title 'consumer psychologist' is not protected by the British Psychological Society. This means that in the UK there is no official set of qualifications that you must have in order to call yourself a consumer psychologist. This said, the majority of employers will expect a postgraduate degree as a minimum and some may also expect a doctorate depending on the nature of the work.

7.1 The physical environment

7.1.1 Retail store design

Exterior store design

Think!

What is meant by **patronage intentions**?

Think!

Can you think of any memorable **storefronts** or **window displays** that you have seen? If so, what type of store was it and who would you say the **target customer** was?

Think!

How might you design a field experiment to investigate the influence of exterior retail atmospherics on consumer behaviour? What would your independent and dependent variables be? What would you control? What ethical guidelines would you need to consider?

It may not be easy for smaller shops and restaurants to encourage new customers to give them a try, especially in places where there is a great deal of competition from big brand names and chain stores, but large global stores may also need to think carefully about their exteriors. Can you think of any changes that might be necessary due to cultural differences between consumers from different countries?

▲ Figure 7.2

The retail industry is highly competitive and retailers are always looking for new ways to attract their target consumers. One strategy is to create a specific mood or image that becomes associated with the store, encouraging shoppers to enter and explore the store and stimulating sales. The term **retail atmospherics** is used to describe features of the store environment that can be modified to create this image/mood, including the **store exterior**, interior, layout and design, point-of-purchase and decoration (Berman and Evans, 1998).

Types of store exterior design

The store exterior refers to the outside of the shop or store. Despite this being the first point of contact that potential shoppers have with the store, there has been little scientific research investigating how variables such as storefront, window displays and **landscaping** affect shoppers' attitudes and behaviour. Existing research in this area is often based on the **stimulus-organism-response (SOR) model**, which examines how physical aspects of the store (the stimulus) affect consumers' emotional responses, interactions with staff and potential purchases. This is considered further on page 384 where we discuss Mehrabian and Russell's (1974) **PAD model**, which identifies three dimensions of consumers' emotions (pleasantness, arousal and dominance). Each of these dimensions affect whether shoppers approach, enter and stay in a store or whether they avoid, ignore and/or move away from the store.

Storefronts

Storefronts include entrances, exits and window displays as well as properties of the building such as height, size and colour. Aspects of the surrounding area, including other shops and facilities, such as parking, are also an important consideration in terms of a consumer's overall impression of a store. Creating an appealing storefront that invites shoppers in to find out more about what is on offer is central to creating a positive first impression. This can be particularly important for small, independent retailers where the branding or name of the store may be unfamiliar.

Window displays

Window displays are critical for attracting potential customers. Shoppers use these displays to make quick judgements to form an overall impression about whether the store is likely to meet their needs and preferences. Again, this may be particularly important for smaller retailers where customers may be less familiar with their products and services. While it

KEY TERMS

patronage intentions

storefront

window display

target customer

retail atmospherics

store exterior

landscaping

stimulus-organism-response (SOR) model

PAD model

visual merchandising

METHODOLOGY

questionnaires

qualitative versus quantitative data

objective versus subjective data

ecological validity

may be expensive or impractical to alter the building itself, an attractive window display provides a quick, cost-effective way to change the overall look of the shop. This can lead to significant increases in customers and sales.

Sen *et al.* (2002) suggest that customer satisfaction and sales can be further increased by matching displays to the self-image of the target customer (the typical person the shop hopes to sell to) and that this is more effective than presenting information about promotions or products alone. Larger, themed displays using warm colours and lighting that emphasise specific products are better at attracting attention than smaller displays. New products have been found to sell better when showcased in this way, particularly when displayed alongside accessories (Edwards and Shackley, 1992). These might include seasonal holidays and special events, but Mower *et al.* (2012) (see below) also suggest using local themes that might be reflected in the windows of other small independent retailers in the area, such as incorporating local produce, flowers and plants.

Landscaping

Landscaping refers to any plants and other vegetation outside the store, which adds to the overall impression formed. Research suggests that plants create positive emotional responses when introduced into urban settings, improving mood and perceived quality of life (Sheets and Manzer, 1991). Sales and distance travelled were greater in shopping areas that included trees and other vegetation, and customers spent longer and more money in stores that included landscaping (Wolf, 2005, 2009). Furthermore, Chebat and Morrin (2007) found that shoppers rated the quality of the environment and products as higher in stores that used flowers, plants and trees to introduce colour to their decor.

Focus on: Mower *et al.* (2012)

▶ AIMS

This study aimed to investigate the influence of window displays and landscaping on customers' mood (e.g. pleasure and arousal), liking of the external environment and intention to purchase products from a small apparel (clothing) boutique. The researchers expected that these exterior retail atmospherics would have positive effects on liking and that this would be positively correlated with mood and sales. They hoped that their findings would be helpful to small retailers.

▶ METHODOLOGY

Mower *et al.* conducted an experiment with **independent measures**. Firstly, participants read one of four short descriptions about shopping for jeans at a small boutique. The structure and colour of the shop were the same in all four descriptions but differed in terms of the presence or absence of window displays and/or landscaping (the two **independent variables**). The display was a female mannequin wearing a fashionable outfit against a modern backdrop and the landscaping was large, glazed pots containing flowers and ivy. **Quantitative data** was collected using an online **questionnaire** including six questions measuring pleasure and arousal, four questions measuring liking of the store exterior, landscaping and window displays and three questions about patronage intentions (that is, likelihood of buying products, recommending the shop and returning items).

▶ RESULTS

The presence of landscaping and window displays did not have a significant effect on pleasure or arousal, but it did increase liking of the external environment and patronage intentions. Pleasure, arousal and liking were all positively correlated with patronage intentions. Further analysis suggested that liking increased pleasure and arousal and this increase had a positive influence on patronage intentions.

▶ CONCLUSIONS

Mower *et al.* concluded that landscaping and window displays are important determinants of positive consumer responses, as higher liking of the store exterior was associated with higher patronage intentions.

Evaluating Mower *et al.* (2012)

A strength of this study was the use of **quantitative data** from the **questionnaire** items relating to liking, pleasure, arousal and patronage intentions, as these allowed comparisons to be made between the four fictional stores. Using quantitative data meant that Mower *et al.* (2012) could calculate means and standard deviations to see whether either of the exterior atmospherics led to quantifiable differences in patronage intentions. This was useful because, had the researchers collected **qualitative data** about people's attitudes towards the different storefronts, the data may have been more difficult to compare, making the findings more difficult to communicate to store managers.

A weakness is that the findings may lack **ecological validity**, as they were based on a fictional shopping trip to a store described online. The participants may have found it difficult to imagine the store based on the written description and their scores would have been based on different imagined stores depending on their past shopping experiences. In a real shopping situation, where the participants were spending real time and money searching for something they genuinely needed, variables such as landscaping and displays may have had a different effect on actual spending, which is not the same as patronage intentions.

Evaluating research into exterior store design

A strength of the research into exterior atmospherics is that it can be used by small shops to increase their consumer appeal with relatively small and inexpensive changes. This is more important than ever, given the impact of the global pandemic on independent retailers. Store managers are well advised to invest in exterior landscaping and to recruit skilled window-dressers to create stimulating and culturally appropriate window displays to attract consumers and improve profits.

> **ISSUES AND DEBATES**

Cultural differences

An issue with most of the research in this area is that it has been primarily conducted in Western, individualist cultures and, therefore, it does not take account of cultural differences in consumer behaviour. Law *et al.* (2012) note that visual merchandising – that is, displays (both in store and in windows) – can lead to different emotional responses depending on the cultural identity of the consumer and the nature of the product. This suggests that global chain stores should adapt the exterior atmospherics for stores in different parts of the world in line with local expectations and norms, rather than opting for a one-size-fits-all method, which could lead to 'approach' behaviour in some cultures and 'avoidance' in others.

The shop owner in Figure 7.3 has made sure the paint is fresh and clean and a pleasing colour but the actual window display isn't attractive. How do you think this shop owner could improve his store exterior to promote the service that he provides and his products?

▲ Figure 7.3

> **LEARNING LINKS**

Mower *et al.* (2012) collected self-report data about how people thought they might behave when shopping for jeans. Participants responded to a written description of the shops, without any visual stimuli. Think back to the social approach and Perry's study of personal space. In Experiment 2, participants were asked to choose between two images multiple times, indicating which room layout they preferred. How could this procedure be adapted to investigate the effects of differing store exteriors?

STUDY TIP

To help you to remember the details of the study by Mower *et al.*, why not create your own materials as though you were planning to replicate the study? You will need four short descriptions of a small clothing store. All descriptions should be exactly the same, except one will have landscaping and no window display, one will have a window display and no landscaping, one will have both landscaping and a window display, and one will have neither landscaping nor a window display. Remember to keep your descriptions of the landscaping and window display identical across the descriptions.

You will also need to create a list of rating scales to measure pleasure, arousal, liking and patronage intentions. Having created the materials, you could even collect some data. If you decide to do this, you will also need to design a suitable informed consent form and will need to think about how you will ensure that all data is confidential. Always check your ethical documentation with your teacher before collecting any data.

▶ TEST YOURSELF

1   Farida has purchased some large plants to decorate the outside of her hairdressing salon. Suggest one reason why this might lead to more customers coming into the salon.   [2]

2   Describe two findings from psychological research into store exterior design.   [4]

3   a   Describe what psychologists have discovered about types of store exterior design, such as storefront, window displays and landscaping.   [6]

   b   Evaluate what psychologists have discovered about types of store exterior design, including a discussion about ecological validity.   [10]

4   Research into exterior store design sometimes uses questionnaires to collect quantitative data. Explain one strength and one weakness of researching the influence of exterior store design on consumer behaviour in this way.   [4]

5   Martine is conducting semi-structured interviews with store managers from a local shopping centre. It is two weeks before a busy national holiday.

   a   State one open and one closed question that Martine could ask about store exteriors and their effect on consumer behaviour.   [2]

   b   Explain one strength of Martine using a semi-structured interview for her research on store exteriors.   [2]

6   Suggest one way in which window displays and landscaping can be studied, other than self-reports, e.g. questionnaires and interviews.   [2]

Interior store design

Think!

What is the main difference between the **freeform** and the **racetrack layout**?

Think!

Many people shop online for at least some of their purchases but also still enjoy browsing and buying from real shops and markets too. Which type of shopping do you prefer? How do your shopping habits differ when you are online compared with visiting real stores? How do these differences affect your enjoyment and spending?

Think!

The study by Vrechopoulos *et al.* (2004) focused on grocery shopping. How might the **interface design** differ for virtual shoe shopping (e.g. for trainers)?

Vrechopoulos *et al.* took a nomothetic approach in their study comparing different virtual store layouts. Participants in Vrechopoulos *et al.* (2004) provided their opinions about their online shopping experience using rating scales and average scores were calculated from the 40 participants in each group.

>> Can you think of any advantages of taking a nomothetic approach to researching store layouts?

>> Do you think it would have been more useful to take an idiographic approach?

▲ **Figure 7.4**

(a) Grid store layout

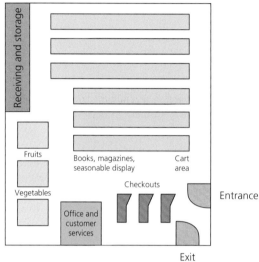

(b) Freeform store layout

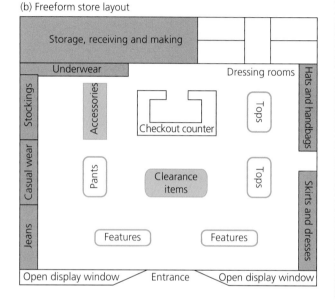

(c) Racetrack store layout

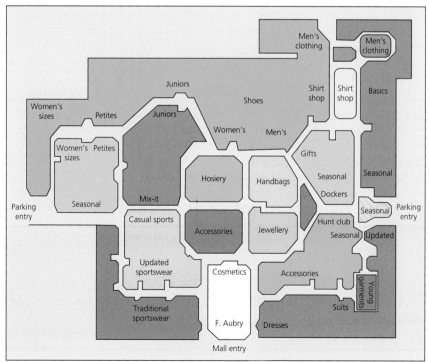

▲ **Figure 7.5 (a, b, c) Examples of the grid, freeform and racetrack layouts used in the study by Vrechopoulos *et al.* (2004)**

Types of store interior design

Interior means inside, and in this section we discuss how **store interior** can have a significant impact on consumer attitudes and behaviour. Layout refers to the way that the shop floor is organised, including the arrangement of the stock and the routes that customers take around the store. Layout can have a significant effect on many aspects of consumer behaviour, from price acceptability and purchase intentions to average time in store, amount spent on planned and unplanned purchases, customer satisfaction, ongoing preferences, repeat trade and recommendations to other potential customers. Conventional 'bricks and mortar' shops fall into three main categories of layout and, as we will see below, website designers have used these to inspire shopping sites too.

Grid layouts

In a **grid layout**, displays are organised into a rectangular arrangement, including long parallel aisles. Common in supermarkets where efficiency is often key, shoppers move around relatively swiftly, selecting predetermined items from their shopping lists. Shoppers often are familiar with the location of their regular products having visited the store multiple times.

Racetrack layouts

According to Lewison (1994), the racetrack layout provides an unusual, interesting and entertaining shopping experience where shoppers follow a designated route through a number of individual themed areas.

Freeform layouts

Favoured by large department stores, customers move in any direction among the displays, the majority of which are different styles, sizes and shapes. Shoppers enjoy browsing among the displays, which are organised in an asymmetric manner, often spending longer in stores with freeform layouts than grid or racetrack layouts.

Virtual store layouts

Online shopping, also known as ecommerce, is a huge growth area, increasing by 74 per cent since the outbreak of COVID-19, with the average consumer spending 58 minutes per week browsing e-shopping sites and 38 minutes actively making purchases (Edwards *et al.*, 2021). It is also estimated that 70 per cent of all product searches now begin online, underlining the importance of creating a user-friendly interface between the online customer and the store. Research suggests that **virtual store layout** is as important as real-life store layout in increasing the number of customers who visit the online store (Lohse and Spiller, 1998) and their willingness to make purchases (Burke, 2002).

A survey of 551 retail websites from six countries revealed that 51 per cent have a virtual freeform layout, 21 per cent use virtual grids and 1.5 per cent use virtual racetracks, with 26 per cent not falling into any of the conventional categories (Vrechopoulos *et al.*, 2002). However, at this point, there was very little research assessing how these virtual layouts affect online consumer behaviour and whether findings from conventional stores can be applied to online shopping behaviour (Eroglu *et al.*, 2001).

Focus on: Vrechopoulos *et al.* (2004)

▶ AIM

Vrechopoulos *et al.* (2004) aimed to investigate the effects of three different virtual store layouts on consumer behaviour when shopping for groceries. Specifically, they aimed to examine how the layouts affected planned purchases, ease of navigation within the store, perceived entertainment and time spent within the store. The researchers hypothesised that the grid layout would be most useful, the freeform layout would be the easiest to use but also lead to the longest time shopping, but the racetrack layout would be the most entertaining.

KEY TERMS

freeform layout
racetrack layout
interface design
store interior
grid layout
virtual store layout
virtual shopping

METHODOLOGY

questionnaires
qualitative versus quantitative data
objective versus subjective data
ecological validity

METHODOLOGY

This was a laboratory experiment with independent measures, whereby each participant interacted with only one of the virtual store layouts. Layout (grid, freeform and racetrack) was the independent variable and the dependent variables were perceived usefulness, ease of use and entertainment. Each variable was measured via self-report rating scales and time spent online, measured by the computer system.

Background colour, display techniques, products, prices and promotional banners were controlled across the three different virtual layouts and all participants were allowed the same amount of money to spend online: £20 or 12,000 GRD (Greek Drachma). Participants were given blank shopping lists and access to a list of available products in the online store so that they could plan their purchases. Products included well-known brands of cola, lager and crisps (chips), as well as own-brand products. The researchers delivered the actual groceries ordered by the participants from two well-known supermarkets in London and Athens.

The participants were 120 academics, students, employees, business executives and researchers from universities in London, in the United Kingdom, and Athens, in Greece. All were experienced internet users and shoppers. Twenty participants from each country were allocated to each of the three store layouts.

RESULTS

The freeform layout was perceived as significantly more useful and entertaining than the grid or the racetrack. This contrasted with the researchers' expectation that the grid would be most useful and racetrack most entertaining. Grid was perceived as significantly easier to use than freeform or racetrack, with freeform easier than racetrack, which again contrasted with the expectation as the prediction was that freeform would be the easiest to use. The greatest amount of time spent shopping was for those using the racetrack layout and this again was unexpected as it was predicted that the freeform layout would lead to the longest shopping times.

▼ Table 7.1 Mean average scores for the three virtual store layouts for the four dependent variables

	Grid	Freeform	Racetrack
Perceived usefulness	4.0	4.8	3.5
Ease of use	5.7	5.0	4.2
Entertainment	3.6	4.3	3.4
Time in virtual store (seconds)	747.5	817.8	971.3

CONCLUSION

The results suggest that different virtual grocery store layouts do lead to significant differences in perceived usefulness, ease of use, entertainment and duration of online shopping, but these differences do not follow the same pattern as seen in conventional stores.

Evaluating Vrechopoulos *et al.* (2004)

A strength of this study is that the findings have relatively high **ecological** validity as the researchers attempted to make the online shopping experience as similar to a real-life situation as possible. For example, participants were given a list of products before going online, they were allowed to create their own shopping list and the groceries that had been selected were delivered afterwards. This was important as it meant that, although the money invested was not their own, they were thinking carefully about what they wanted to purchase, suggesting that their behaviour was more true to life than it would have been if they did not expect to receive the shopping at the end.

A weakness of the study is that the researchers only collected **quantitative data** using rating scales and this does not provide the researchers with any insight into why certain scores were assigned for perceived usefulness, ease of use and entertainment. For example, people may have given the same high score but for different reasons: one person might have liked the racetrack as it helped them to remember items they had missed from their shopping list; others might have valued the opportunity to see new product ranges. This is important as collecting both quantitative and qualitative data might have allowed the researchers to gain greater insight into not just which layout was preferred, but why. Despite the weaknesses of quantitative data, the analysis is typically more objective, e.g. researchers simply calculated the average perceived usefulness of each online store layout. The inclusion of qualitative data could have led to a more subjective analysis where researchers' preconceptions about customer attitudes (e.g. that the racetrack would be most entertaining) could have affected the ways they interpreted the participants' answers.

Evaluating research into types of store interior

> ### ISSUES AND DEBATES

Cultural differences

One issue with research into virtual shopping environments is that researchers do not always take account of cultural differences when drawing conclusions about the most profitable layout. On page 422, we will discuss models of consumer decision-making and investigate, for example, how cultural differences can affect the likelihood of impulse (unplanned) purchasing. For example, the racetrack layout encourages unplanned purchasing as the shopper is exposed to products that may not be on their shopping lists; while people from some cultures may find this enjoyable and fun, others may find it frustrating, meaning they leave the store more quickly as the experience does not meet with their cultural expectations.

Reductionism versus holism

Another issue with research in this area is that it is reductionist in that it only considers the impact of one situational variable (store layout) when predicting complex aspects of consumer behaviour. Above, we have noted how cultural differences may affect the way people perceive different layouts, but individual differences in terms of personality, age, gender and socioeconomic status are all likely to affect the perceptions of these different online shopping experiences. Furthermore, the nature of the product, such as low-value versus high-value or necessities versus luxury items, may also influence preferred virtual layout. This is important as redesigning an online shopping site can be extremely expensive, meaning businesses need to take a holistic view of the full range of variables that affect profits in order to minimise the risk of costly mistakes.

> ### LEARNING LINKS

The study by Vrechopoulos *et al.* (2004) is a laboratory experiment with independent measures and quantitative data was collected using a self-report. Think back to the learning approach and you will remember the study by Bandura *et al.* (aggression), another laboratory experiment. Like many laboratory experiments, this study lacked ecological validity and may have been affected by demand characteristics. But not all laboratory studies are the same. Always try to think of points that are relevant to the actual study you are evaluating, not just the method of that study. Vrechopoulos *et al.* (2004) found ways to increase ecological validity, but do you think demand characteristics were still an issue or not?

STUDY TIP

The term '**temporal validity**' refers to the idea that findings may no longer be useful if society has undergone significant changes since the study was conducted. Vrechopoulos *et al.* was conducted in 2004 and technology and the popularity of ecommerce has changed dramatically since the start of the twenty first century. Try to write your own evaluative paragraph using the PET structure (point, example, this is important because…) to explain why this study lacks temporal validity. What needs to be done to check whether these findings are still relevant today?

> **TEST YOURSELF**

1 Compare the grid layout and the racetrack layout. You must refer to psychological research in your answer. [4]

2 Describe the procedure of one study investigating the effect of store interior design on consumer behaviour. [4]

3 a Describe what psychologists have discovered about different types of store layout, such as grid, freeform and racetrack. [6]

    b Evaluate what psychologists have discovered about different types of store layout, such as grid, freeform and racetrack, including a discussion of qualitative versus quantitative data. [10]

4 Questionnaires are often used to investigate how aspects of the physical environment, such as store interiors, influence consumer behaviour.

    a Suggest one rating scale and one forced/fixed-choice question that could be used to measure the effect of store interior on consumer behaviour. [2]

    b Explain one strength and one weakness of using questionnaires to investigate the influence of the physical environment on consumer behaviour. [4]

5 Dougie decides to compare consumers from Chile and the USA to see whether they differ in how useful they perceive the virtual freeform store layout.

    a Write a suitable non-directional hypothesis for Dougie's study. [2]

    b Explain how Dougie could use volunteer sampling to recruit participants for his study. [4]

6 Research into store layout is sometimes affected by demand characteristics. Explain one way that you could conduct a study into store layout that would reduce the effect of demand characteristics. [2]

7.1.2 Sound and consumer behaviour

Key Study: Music in restaurants – North *et al.* (2003)

▲ Figure 7.6 Professor Adrian North

Introducing Adrian North

Adrian North is Head of Psychology and Speech Pathology and a Professor of Psychology at Curtin University, in Western Australia. He specialises in the social and applied psychology of music. His research interests include music and wellbeing in specific populations – for example, suicidality among rock fans and the use of digital music in everyday life to improve mood. He is also interested in the impact of music on consumer behaviour, including purchasing and advertising, as well as theories of musical preference and taste.

> **Think!**
>
> How did the researchers operationalise pop music and classical music in this study?

> **Think!**
>
> Do you ever eat in restaurants with your friends and family? What sort of music would you prefer, if any? Would this differ if you went for a meal with friends compared with parents or grandparents?

KEY TERM

atmospherics

METHODOLOGY

validity

generalisations from findings

Think!

Do you think this study has good temporal validity? How could you check? If the temporal validity was poor, what could you do to improve the study?

North *et al.* (2003) were careful to control many aspects of their study into the effect of music on customer spending in restaurants controlled the tempo of the pop music compared with the classical music but the classical tracks did not include vocals whereas the pop tracks did.

How does this lack of control affect the findings? Imagine if North *et al.* (2003) had compared opera (classical but with vocals) with dance music (without vocals) – do you think the opera would have led to greater spending or not?

Context

Psychological research has suggested that the **atmospherics** of a restaurant can influence consumer behaviour, but limited research has been conducted into the effects of music specifically. Areni and Kim (1993) found that when classical music was played in a wine cellar, customers were more likely to purchase a more expensive wine than when top-40 pop music was played ($7.43 versus $2.18), even though the type of music did not affect the number of bottles purchased. North and Hargreaves (1998) played classical music, pop music, easy listening music and no music in a campus student cafeteria. The playing of classical music was linked to the perception of the location being more upmarket (high-quality). When questioned, the consumers estimated that they would spend more while the classical music was played than any other genre or no music at all. However, the first study only looked at the single product of wine and the latter used a restricted sample of undergraduates and intended spending only. Therefore, North *et al.* wanted to investigate the effects of music on consumers in real restaurants with a wider range of consumers and purchases.

AIM

North *et al.* (2003) aimed to explore whether playing classical music would lead to higher customer spending than when pop music was played.

METHODOLOGY

The research method was a field experiment in the naturalistic setting of a restaurant in a small, affluent (rich) town in Leicestershire, UK. The menu was *à la carte* (offered individual items) and quite expensive. The study took place over three weeks and the experimenter who collected the data was also a waitress.

The independent variable was the type of background music played in the restaurant. Classical and pop music were compared with a control condition of no music. The classical music included pieces by Vivaldi, Handel and Strauss, while the pop music included tracks by Britney Spears, Culture Club and Ricky Martin.

The design was independent measures, as each participant only experienced one type of music or none.

The dependent variables were the mean spend per person for each table for starters, main courses, desserts, coffee, bar drinks, wine, overall drinks bill, overall food bill and total spend. Researchers also recorded the total time spent in the restaurant from being seated to paying the bill.

Sample

The sample was the 393 customers who ate in the restaurant between February and March 2002. There were roughly the same number of male and female customers and none of them were aware they were taking part in a study.

PROCEDURE

The music in each genre (pop versus classical) was well-known and was played at a consistent volume on two 76-minute CDs using a continuous, random programme. Each type of music (including no music) was played on six nights and the order was counterbalanced so that the order of the music styles used each evening varied from week to week (see Table 7.2). Situational variables such as lighting, menu and temperature were kept constant for the duration of the experiment. Each table of diners counted as one data point and the total spend per person was the total bill for the table divided by the number of people at that table. The researchers also recorded how long each table of diners stayed in the restaurant. Data was collected from opening time at 19:00 to closing time at 23:30.

▼ Table 7.2 Order of the three music conditions, counterbalanced to avoid order effects

	Week 1	Week 2	Week 3
Monday	Classical	Pop	No music
Tuesday	Pop	No music	Classical
Wednesday	No music	Classical	Pop
Thursday	Classical	Pop	No music
Friday	Pop	No music	Classical
Saturday	No music	Classical	Pop

RESULTS

Classical music significantly increased the mean spend per person for starters, coffee, total spend on food and overall spend. There were no significant differences in spending for desserts, drinks from the bar, wine, main courses or total spend on drinks.

▼ Table 7.3 Total spend per person for variables with significant differences between conditions

	Condition		
	Classical music	Pop music	No music
Starters	£4.92	£4.04	£3.93
Coffee	£1.07	£0.80	£0.54
Total spend on food	£24.13	£21.91	£21.70
Overall spend	£32.51	£29.46	£29.73

CONCLUSIONS

The main conclusion was that using classical music can increase customer spending. This extra spending was mainly on the starters and the coffees rather than on main courses. These findings supported earlier research by Areni and Kim (1993) and North and Hargreaves (1998), who also found that classical music increased customer spending.

The first possible explanation for this increased spending is that the classical music enhanced other aspects of the restaurant, which increased spending. However, this is challenged by the student cafeteria results, where classical music contrasted with other aspects of the setting (e.g. decor). The second possible explanation is that most of the customers preferred classical music, so their pleasure transferred to ordering more from the menu. This could not be checked as the restaurant did not consent to an anonymous questionnaire on their customers' musical preferences. The third and preferred explanation is that classical music is associated with an 'upmarket' experience which primes (prepares) customers to spend more.

Methodological strengths and weaknesses

One strength is that situational variables relating to atmospherics other than the music were controlled. For example, each night the diners were exposed to the same lighting, decor, temperature and menu, and the same waitress. This is important as it means that differences in average spending from night to night were more likely to have been due to differences in music as other potential confounding variables were controlled. This suggests that the finding that classical music increased spending was **valid.**

A second strength is the naturalistic setting of this field experiment on the effects of music on spending. The findings were based on real diners spending their own money in a real *à la carte* restaurant and diners were unaware that the researchers were collecting data on their spending and time spent in the restaurant. Nothing was altered except the genre of the background music, with the restaurant serving its usual menu to normal diners. This means the diners were more likely to be behaving naturally, suggesting that the findings have greater ecological **validity** than studies like Vrechopoulos *et al.* (2004; see page 370) where shoppers knew they were part of a study and were not investing their own money.

A weakness is that the high socioeconomic status of the area in which the study was conducted limits how far these findings can be **generalised**. The restaurant is described as being in an affluent area and having above-average prices, suggesting the diners were potentially wealthier than people in other areas of Britain. This is important as it means the findings may not apply in other parts of the country and indeed to other cultures, in countries where other musical styles may be associated with upmarket dining, such as traditional music from that culture. Overall, the ability to **generalise** from this study is limited by the specific demographic of the customers of this one specific restaurant.

A second weakness is the absence of knowledge about the musical preferences of the diners. These diners were not a random sample; they were people who had chosen this particular restaurant and it is possible that they shared a particular musical taste, particularly if the restaurant normally played this type of music. Lack of knowledge about this key participant variable weakens the validity of the conclusions about classical music, as it may not be the music itself that increases spending but liking and/or familiarity with the genre that increases spending.

 ## Ethics

An ethical strength of the research was that diners' privacy was not invaded in any way and this is important given that the study took place in a naturalistic setting, where participants did not know a study was taking place. Although participants' spending was recorded without obtaining consent, according to the British Psychological Society's ethical guidelines, consent is not needed if people are in a public place, as in a restaurant. Spending and time in the restaurant were the only data recorded and the participants' dining experience was not disrupted in any way, suggesting there are no ethical issues with the study.

 ## Application to everyday life

The findings from this study have an important real-life application for upmarket restaurants, which may wish to play classical music in order to increase customer spending. While further research needs to be carried out to confirm whether these findings are seen in a range of other establishments and locations, there is unlikely to be any damage to businesses by making this change to support a more upmarket experience for customers and it may, indeed, bring the business some benefits.

Reductionism versus holism

One issue with this study is that the findings appear to be rather **reductionist** – that is, the implication is that diners will spend more while listening to classical music compared with pop music or no music. It must be remembered that classical music did not increase spending on all courses, only starters and coffee. This suggests that the music has differing effects during different episodes within the dining experiences. Perhaps, while the diners are settling in and more aware of the wider environment, the music affects spending more (i.e. when they are choosing whether to have a starter). Also, the music may have a greater impact towards the end of the meal when diners are beginning to think about leaving. If they feel more relaxed, they may be more inclined to extend the evening.

In order to fully understand the role of background music, it may be important to consider how different types of music affect spending at different points during the evening and how this interacts with aspects such as the size of the group of diners and purpose of the meal, whether it be a celebration with family, a romantic encounter or a business meeting. Taking a more **holistic** view of how the background music genre interacts with other individual and situational variables may help to increase profits even more.

Determinism versus free will

While many restaurant managers may be delighted to discover that something as simple as downloading a new classical playlist could significantly improve their profits, this deterministic view should not be overstated. Diners are not robots; their programmes cannot be hacked through strategic use of Beethoven's greatest hits! Music is just one factor in a complex set of atmospherics that vary according to the target audience, and it should be remembered that diners may choose to exercise their free will at any point, declining that extra coffee or liqueur, regardless of the soundtrack.

> REFLECTION

- To what extent do you think it is possible to generalise from this study's findings?
- If you were going to research the effect of background music on restaurant customers, what improvements or modifications would you suggest to the procedure in this study? How could the study be developed to improve reliability, validity and the ability to generalise the findings?

The data in North *et al.* (2003) was quantitative and the waitress used the till to calculate the bills for each table. What are the advantages of using the till to calculate the bills? Can you think of any problems that could have arisen with the accuracy of the bills? How could North *et al.* have improved their study to ensure the reliability of the data?

▲ Figure 7.7

> LEARNING LINKS

Do you remember the study by Andrade (doodling) from the cognitive approach? The study looked at how doodling at the same time as listening to a boring message increased concentration and memory. Andrade explained that increasing arousal (through doodling) decreased the likelihood of daydreaming through boredom and this improved performance on the task. Eating in a restaurant is not exactly a boring task, quite the opposite hopefully, but it is interesting to think about how exposing the brain to music (versus no music in the control condition) while conducting a second task (choosing from a menu) affects decision-making. Do you find background music helps you to pay attention better in some situations compared with others? Does this differ when you are alone compared with when you are around other people?

STUDY TIP
Drawing a bar chart to visually present the data in Table 7.3 would be a great way to help you to remember the information better. When plotting the graph, you will need to engage with the figures at a deeper level than you would when just looking at them. The extra time and effort invested should help you to remember the data better, in the long term. Even if you do not remember the actual figures, comparing the sizes of the bars visually should help you to see which conditions were associated with higher spending and which with lower spending, for example.

TEST YOURSELF

1 Shona and Mack own a coffee shop. Shona says she prefers playing classical music as the customers buy more expensive drinks and are more likely to add a cake. Mack prefers pop music and thinks this attracts more customers.
Explain whether you agree more with Mack or Shona. You must refer to research evidence in your answer. [4]

2 Describe the aim of the study by North *et al.* (2003) on the effects of music on spending in restaurants. [2]

3 a Describe the study by North *et al.* (2003) on musical style and restaurant customers' spending. [6]

 b Evaluate the study by North *et al.* (2003) on musical style and restaurant customers' spending, including a discussion of individual and situational explanations. [10]

4 Explain how North *et al.* (2003) calculated the mean spend per person. [2]

5 Identify the sampling technique used in North *et al.* (2003). [1]

6 Outline two controls used in the study by North *et al.* (2003). [2]

Background noise and taste

Think!

In the study by Woods *et al.* (2011), did **white noise** increase or decrease taste intensity?

Think!

Imagine you work in a noisy restaurant. If Woods *et al.* (2011) are right, do you think people will be more or less likely to add extra salt to their meals? Will they be more or less likely to complain that their food is bland?

Think!

Think about how the findings of this study compare with the findings of North *et al.* (2003). If you were a restaurant owner, how could you use the findings of these two studies to increase customer satisfaction and profits?

With reference to the findings of Zampini and Spence (2004), will the girl enjoy her crisps more with or without wearing her headphones? What might Wood *et al.* (2011) have to say about this?

▲ Figure 7.8

KEY TERMS
white noise
gustatory cues
olfaction
gustatory stimuli
sweetness
saltiness
crunchiness

METHODOLOGY
generalisations from findings
validity

Gustation

It is not just taste or smell that influences people's perception of food. Other important factors such as colour, expectations and even the sound of ourselves chewing can affect how flavours are perceived. These are called **gustatory cues** – the term 'gustation' refers to anything that is linked to our sense of taste. The term **olfaction** is used to refer to our sense of smell. **Gustatory stimuli** are chemicals that interact with our taste buds producing the experiences of different tastes, such as sweet, salty and bitter. Interactions between visual and olfactory cues and gustation have been thoroughly researched, but researchers have only relatively recently begun to explore interactions between auditory (sound) cues and taste (Spence, 2015).

Crispiness

Have you ever tried eating crisps while wearing earmuffs? Research by Zampini and Spence (2004) suggests it probably is not advisable if you want to really enjoy your snack! These researchers artificially increased the volume of the resulting crunch when their participants bit into a potato crisp (chip). Making the sound louder improved the perception of crispness/freshness, while decreasing the volume increased the perception of staleness. This suggests background noise that interferes with our ability to detect auditory cues, such as crispiness, may affect our perception of the food. But can sound interfere with our perception of other gustatory cues?

Masuda *et al.* (2008) found that pretzels were rated as less moist when listening to white noise (continuous sound with no pattern or rhythm, similar to a radio that is between stations). Again, it is thought that the noise may have blocked sounds which help us to make judgements about the gustatory aspects of food. This may be because sound also stimulates neural networks found in areas of the brain more commonly associated with taste perception. Animal research suggests that sounds and smell cross over in this way and stimulation of certain neurons using sound can actually alter the way they respond to smell (Wesson and Wilson, 2010).

Sound and sweetness

It appears that background noise can also affect gustatory stimuli that are not linked to biting and chewing. For example, participants liked a sweet solution more when exposed to 90 dB background noise, yet the same was not true for a salty solution (Ferber and Cabanac, 1987). The researchers claimed the noise was stressful, thus increasing sugar cravings and liking for sweet stimuli.

Reasons sound may affect taste perception

Some researchers believe that brain structures for processing sensory information are sometimes activated by more than one type of sensory information (Schroeder and Foxe, 2005). For example, research in rats revealed that 19 per cent of the neurons in the olfactory tubercle (an area primarily associated with processing smell) were activated by sound (Wesson and Wilson, 2010). Another possibility is that the brain uses information from more than one sensory modality when making judgements about intensity – for example, taste intensity was compared with sound intensity, meaning the loud noise made the taste seem 'quieter' (less intense). A final possibility according to Woods *et al.* (2011) is that the noise distracted attention away from the taste and made it seem less intense.

Focus on: Woods *et al.* (2011) – Experiment 1

AIM

Woods *et al.* aimed to investigate whether non-sound-related gustatory food cues (e.g. **sweetness** as opposed to crispness, **saltiness** as opposed to moistness) are reported to be less intense in noisy conditions versus quiet conditions. Secondly, they aimed to investigate whether this effect is only observed with crunchy/hard foods, where the sound that they make when eaten typically helps us to make a judgement about how much we like the food or are enjoying it.

METHODOLOGY

This repeated measures laboratory experiment had two independent variables: background noise (baseline, quiet or loud) and hardness of the food (crunchy versus soft). The dependent variables were self-reported saltiness, sweetness and liking. Forty-eight students blind-tasted four foods while wearing headphones to block the sound of their own chewing. In the background sound condition, they would hear either quiet (45–55 dB) or loud (75–85 dB) white noise. In the control condition, there was no white noise. See Table 7.4 for details of the foods. Participants rated each food for liking, sweetness and saltiness by placing a mark on a line to represent their opinion (e.g. 'somewhat intense').

▼ Table 7.4 Gustatory stimuli were presented broken into mouth-sized pieces, 1 cm cubed or 2 cm squared in size. The 'dummy' stimulus was a very plain biscuit, neither salty nor sweet

	Sweet	Savoury
Soft	Flapjack	Cheese
Crunchy	Biscuit	Crisps
'Dummy' stimulus		

Participants closed their eyes; when the researcher touched their hand, they took a piece of food from the plate and ate it. After swallowing, they opened their eyes and rated the saltiness, sweetness and their liking for the food.

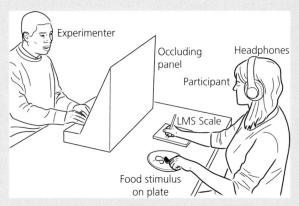

▲ Figure 7.9 A cartoon depiction of the experimental set-up

RESULTS

Background noise significantly affected measures of sweetness and saltiness, which were both rated as less intense in the loud condition compared with the quiet condition. In comparison to the baseline (the control condition), sweetness was rated much lower in the loud condition than in the quiet condition. Food seemed saltier in the quiet condition and distinctly less salty in the loud condition. Finally, foods were also liked more in the quiet condition compared with the baseline and liked less in the loud condition; however, the effect of sound did not affect liking as significantly as it did for perception of sweetness and saltiness.

The analysis found no difference in the effect of background sound on the hard versus the soft foods, suggesting that sound affected the perception of sweetness, saltiness and liking in both types of food. Likewise, liking for foods was not affected by hardness or softness.

CONCLUSIONS

Background noise reduces the intensity of sweetness and saltiness, regardless of hardness of the food. This shows that auditory cues can interfere not just with sound-mediated food cues (e.g. the **crunchiness** of a crisp as a sign of freshness), but also with purely gustatory cues; taste is actually experienced in a quiet versus a noisy environment. Although there was some indication that noise increases liking for sweet foods, this may have been due to chance.

Evaluating Woods *et al.* (2011)

A strength of this study was that the researchers controlled for individual differences in participants' taste perception. For example, a repeated measures design was used, meaning participants tasted all the foods in all three conditions (loud, quiet and no sound) and this removed participant variables as a source of bias. Also, sweetness and saltiness ratings were made in comparison with a plain biscuit (dummy stimulus) to establish a baseline for each participant. This was an important feature of the study as it ensured that conclusions about the effect of background sound on taste perception were valid.

Another strength was the standardisation of many situational variables that could have affected gustation. For example, details of the exact food brands are given in the original paper, portion size was regulated, water was always sipped between trials to wash away any remnants of the previous food, headphones eliminated any extraneous background noise and foods were tasted with eyes closed so that other cues could not interfere with gustation. These controls are important as they make the study replicable, meaning the reliability of the findings can be checked – for example, whether there really is no difference in the effect of background noise on hard versus soft foods.

Evaluating background noise and taste

ISSUES AND DEBATES

Applications to everyday life

A strength of the research in this area is that it can be usefully applied to real-world settings in catering and hospitality. For example, an awareness of the interaction between different senses such as hearing and taste can be exploited to create innovative and memorable dining experiences for consumers. One example is the popularity of ramen noodle, solo-dining restaurants in Japan, where background noise and social interaction are minimised, meaning diners can maximise the taste of their meal. Considering ways in which restaurant atmospherics interact with the product (i.e. the meal) is a powerful way of improving customer satisfaction, repeat business, recommendations and profitability.

This said, a weakness of the limited evidence in this area is that it has primarily been conducted under laboratory conditions, meaning the conclusions lack ecological validity. Tasting individual foods (pretzels or potato chips) and, in some cases, flavoured solutions (sugar or salt) is not the same as eating something you have chosen for yourself as part of a dish made up of multiple ingredients. Furthermore, wearing headphones and tasting with eyes closed creates a very unusual sensory experience that is not the same as the multisensory way that our brains usually process information. This suggests that researchers now need to move into the field - for example,

exploring interactions between different sensory cues in real-world settings, such as restaurants where diners have chosen their own menu and can be observed to see whether they are likely to add (or ask for) additional seasoning, for example, under noisy conditions.

Individual and situation explanations

The truly fascinating research in this area clearly demonstrates that, contrary to common sense, taste perception is more than a matter of individual differences, i.e. some people like their food saltier/sweeter than others. Situational factors can also affect the ways in which people experience taste, e.g. background noise, including music. Further research may help to explain how and why certain genres of music enhance enjoyment (and spending) for example, relaxing music may moderate the impact of unpredictable noises, e.g. conversations going on around us. It is also likely, however, that there are individual difference in the extent to which such external cues affect our enjoyment of food, e.g. cultural differences relating to where, when and with who we typically eat and also conditions such as autism and ADHD in which sensory experiences can be exaggerated, synesthesia (where sensory experiences in one modality can trigger experiences in another) and misophonia, which is an intolerance of certain sounds.

LEARNING LINKS

Andrade's study of doodling (2010) showed that concentration and memory while listening to a boring message could be enhanced through carrying out a low-effort task (doodling) that increased arousal enough to stop participants from daydreaming and failing to listen. Perhaps diners need to maintain an optimal level of arousal in order to fully concentrate on, and maximise, the taste experience.

Experimental chef Heston Blumenthal from the UK has found many fascinating ways to increase arousal and encourage immersive taste experiences. For example, in his audible-edible experience called the *Sound of the Sea*, diners enjoy a beautifully presented fish dish while listening to the sounds of rolling waves and seagulls on an iPod served in a shell. Before drawing conclusions about the effect of sound on taste, it may be important to consider whether the sound is congruent or incongruent with taste experience. Imagine you have the opportunity to create a multi-sensory dining experience – what dish/food would you serve and how would you use music and/or sound to enhance the taste? How could you measure the success of your dish?

STUDY TIP

Psychology is made up of theories and studies and it is important that when you learn the studies you genuinely understand why they were being conducted, so what they were testing and what the results mean in terms of the theory. This section presents a number of reasons why sound may affect taste (e.g. the masking of sounds from our own mouths, links between stress and sugar cravings and a number of suggestions about how the brain and the mind process information from different senses). Make sure you understand what the findings of Woods *et al.* (2011) tell us about these explanations before moving onto the next section. Think about it, Woods *et al.* found that white noise decreases the intensity of sweetness and saltiness, neither of which are linked to noises made when biting or chewing. What does this tell us about the conclusions drawn by Zampini and Spence (2004)?

TEST YOURSELF

1   Head chef Pierre believes sound influences taste and refuses to let diners eat in his restaurant unless they are wearing headphones. Explain one reason why Pierre may be correct in his beliefs about the influence of sound on taste.   [2]

2   Describe two ways that sound and/or music can affect consumer behaviour.   [4]

3   a   Describe what psychologists have discovered about how sound and noise affect the perception of food taste.   [6]

    b   Evaluate what psychologists have discovered about how sound and noise affect the perception of food taste, including a discussion of validity.   [10]

4   Research suggests that sound is an important determinant of food perception.

    a   Plan an investigation into food perception in a sample of people with differing levels of hearing impairments. Your plan must include:
        –   details about sampling technique
        –   a directional or non-directional hypothesis.   [10]

    b   For one piece of psychological knowledge that has informed your plan:
        i   Describe this psychological knowledge.   [4]
        ii   Explain how two features of this psychological knowledge informed your plan.   [4]

KEY TERMS

arousal
ambience
pleasure
dominance
valence

METHODOLOGY

questionnaires
quantitative and
qualitative data
objective and subjective
data

7.1.3 Retail atmospherics

Model of the effects of ambience

> **Think!**
>
> What did Mehrabian and Russell mean by **arousal** in terms of consumer behaviour?

> **Think!**
>
> Your school/college canteen has introduced some changes in an attempt to change the **ambience** of the dining hall. How could you measure the emotional and behavioural impact of these changes?

> **Think!**
>
> Do you think individual differences in age, gender, culture, personality, mental health or employment status will affect emotional reactions to different atmospherics? How might the same atmospherics lead to differing behaviours between consumers?

How would you describe the shoppers' mood in Figure 7.10 in terms of **pleasure**, arousal and **dominance**? How are their emotions likely to affect their behaviour in the store? If you were a supermarket owner, how would you try to create a positive ambience that will suit the widest range of shoppers?

▲ Figure 7.10

Figure 7.11 displays a wide range of emotional responses and how they relate to two of Mehrabian and Russell's dimensions: arousal and **valence** (pleasure-displeasure). If you were a restaurant owner, would you think it was more important to create a high-arousal or a low-arousal ambience? Do you think the time of day might affect this?

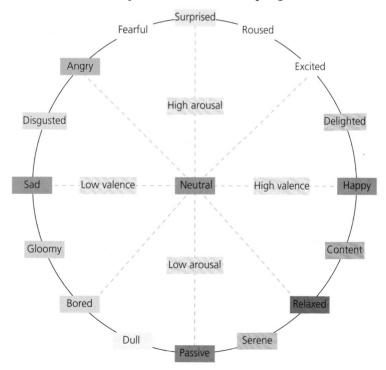

▲ Figure 7.11 Arousal and valence of emotional responses

Our emotions can be affected by aspects of the environments in which we find ourselves. For example, upbeat music can lift our mood making us feel alert, whereas candlelight and scents like lavender can make us feel relaxed. Both environments are likely to be associated with positive feelings, such as happiness or contentment. On page 365, the term 'atmospherics' was used to refer to aspects of the environment (e.g. stores, restaurants or shopping centres/malls) that can be altered to affect consumer behaviour. The atmospherics shape the ambience of the setting, which refers to the character or atmosphere of a place.

Consumers' decisions and behaviour are influenced by their emotional state, such as whether to stay in a store or leave, whether to chat to a sales assistant or ignore them, whether to leave an item in our supermarket trolley or put it back, and this means that research into how atmospherics influence our emotions, cognition and behaviour are very useful to businesses in terms of raising customer satisfaction and profitability.

Mehrabian and Russell's pleasure-arousal-dominance (PAD) model

The three-dimensional pleasure-arousal-dominance (PAD) model was developed by Mehrabian and Russell (1974) to explain how aspects of the environment can affect consumers' emotional responses and behaviour. Mehrabian and Russell believed that the complete range of human emotional responses or 'states of feeling' could be represented with reference to these three independent emotional dimensions.

Pleasure

Mehrabian and Russell used the term 'valence' to refer to whether an environment produces feelings that are positive or negative. A store with high positive valence would, therefore, refer to a generally pleasant environment, leading to happy consumers. Stores such as this are likely to be more profitable. The P in PAD, therefore, stands for pleasure-displeasure, where pleasure refers to happiness and satisfaction and displeasure refers to a state of pain, unhappiness and dissatisfaction. When consumers are happy, approach behaviours are more likely (e.g. entering and staying longer in the store). When they are unhappy, avoidance behaviours are more likely (e.g. passing by or leaving a store).

Arousal

The A stands for arousal. This refers to how stimulated, alert, energised and excited the consumer is. Consumers with a low level of arousal (i.e. feeling overly relaxed, calm or sleepy) are likely to be disengaged from the products surrounding them; therefore, environments that creates a certain level of arousal are likely to be more profitable. However, settings that create levels of arousal that are too high may be overwhelming, leading customers to leave and profits to fall.

Dominance

The final dimension in Mehrabian and Russell's model is dominance, which refers to the extent to which the consumer feels in control/autonomous. If a consumer feels restricted, this may lead them to feel uncomfortable, making them less likely to stay in the setting. Researchers agree less about how dominance is linked to consumer behaviour and decision-making (Bakker *et al.*, 2014), but it is easy to see how feeling in control can increase a customer's positive affect (emotion). For example, imagine entering a café you are familiar with. The café now operates a little differently; you now order from the counter instead of being served at a table. The initial uncertainty this situation creates could reduce the customer's feeling of being in control, potentially increasing arousal and decreasing pleasure. The impact of situations such as this is likely to be affected by individual differences between consumers (e.g. personality), making outcomes more difficult to predict.

The model suggests that the ambience of a restaurant, bar, store, shopping mall or other consumer environment depends on the pleasure, arousal and dominance experienced by the customers. In other words, ambience is a vital factor in whether people wish to visit such places.

Evaluating the PAD model

A strength is that research evidence using objective measures supports the role of arousal as a key determinant of consumer behaviour. For example, Groeppel-Klein (2005) measured electrodermal activity (EDA) as a measure of phasic arousal, meaning arousal triggered by aspects of the situation rather than individual differences between participants. Participants shopped in an experimental fruit and vegetable store, where products were displayed to increase pleasure and arousal. EDA was higher in the experimental store compared to a control store where the same products were displayed but in a less appealing manner. Consumers also purchased more products in the experimental store, showing that arousal was affected by atmospherics and increased purchasing. This is a strength as it shows that the PAD model is useful in predicting consumer behaviour.

A weakness of the PAD model is that research suggests that the role of emotions has been overstated. For example, Chebat and Michon (2003) found that ambient odours were not associated with increased pleasure or arousal but were associated with increased sales. Their findings suggest that the odours increased the perception of the quality of the product. This suggests that cognitive factors may influence consumer behaviour more than emotional factors, although this study focused on shopping as opposed to restaurants or bars where emotional factors may be more important.

ISSUES AND DEBATES

Applications to everyday life

A strength of the PAD model is that it can be easily applied to increase profitability in retail and hospitality settings. Since arousal levels need to be high but not too high, managers must think about ways in which stock is displayed so that it is exciting but not overwhelming. Likewise, customers need to feel in control but also supported in their shopping experience; limited or ambiguous signage could decrease customer satisfaction through decreasing dominance. Creative and thoughtful strategies to increase pleasure, arousal and dominance, by thoroughly understanding their customers' needs, should help managers to improve the consumer experience and profits.

Cultural differences

Another weakness of the PAD model is that it does not consider cultural differences in terms of the way atmospherics may differentially affect pleasure, arousal and dominance. For example, Lee and Lee (2021) measured self-reported arousal, pleasure and dominance using rating scales. They found that red lighting was least pleasant and most arousing for all participants, but those who identified as Asian showed the greatest self-reported displeasure for red and purple lighting compared with participants who identified as Caucasian. This is important as it suggests that store and restaurant managers should consider the ethnicity of their customer-base before making expensive decisions about interior atmospherics, including colours and lighting.

When customers feel positive and experience relatively high levels of arousal, they are likely to interact more with other customers and staff and take longer exploring what the venue or store has to offer (Aziz *et al.*, 2018). How could customers' high levels of arousal increase profit over the longer term? Can you think of any negative effects on short-term profits?

▲ Figure 7.12

▶ **LEARNING LINKS**

In the study by Dement and Kleitman (sleep and dreaming), the researchers compared objective and **subjective data** in the form of EEG measures of brain wave activity and self-reports about dream content and duration. The study by Groeppel-Klein (2005) used an objective measure of arousal to see how this affected consumer behaviour. Many of the studies prior to this had used self-reported subjective measures of arousal. What is the strength of using objective measures of variables such as arousal? Would it be possible to measure pleasure objectively?

STUDY TIP

The PAD model assumes that individuals process situations in similar ways, supporting determinism – that is, certain atmospherics will increase arousal and purchasing. When you are faced with a model like this, have a think; are there any individual differences that might exist between people that would lead them to respond differently to the same atmospheric conditions? You could collect some data of your own to see whether personality variables such as extraversion-introversion affect pleasure from different coloured lighting (e.g. red versus blue). Write a bullet-pointed procedure for a study to address this aim.

▶ **TEST YOURSELF**

1 Ashwin is shopping for a new pair of trainers but the shop is untidy, there is no assistant available to answer his questions and he cannot find the size he is looking for. He decides to buy the trainers online instead. Explain Ashwin's behaviour with reference to the pleasure-arousal-dominance (PAD) model. [4]

2 Explain one strength of the pleasure-arousal-dominance (PAD) model of ambience as a way of explaining consumer behaviour. [4]

3 a Describe what psychologists have discovered about the physical environment and consumer behaviour. [6]

   b Evaluate what psychologists have discovered about the physical environment and consumer behaviour. [10]

4 Explain one weakness of using self-reports to measure pleasure, arousal and/or dominance. [2]

5 Suggest one ethical issue that could apply in research into the effects of ambience on consumer behaviour. [2]

6 Explain one reason a psychologist may prefer to collect qualitative data rather than quantitative data when conducting research into the effects of ambience on consumer behaviour. [2]

The effects of odour

Think!

What is meant by the term **scent marketing**?

Think!

Have you ever bought something because you smelled the aroma before you saw the product? What sort of products do you think this applies to? Do any of your favourite shops have a certain smell that you now associate with their products?

Think!

Can you think of any potential improvements to the study by Chebat and Michon (2003)? Are there any questions, open or closed, that you would like to add to their questionnaires?

How does the smell of spices, pine and orange make you feel? What memories do they evoke? If you were using these scents to sell a product, which product would you choose and why? Can you think of any products that might sell less well if accompanied by this scent?

▲ Figure 7.13

KEY TERMS

scent marketing

olfactory system

limbic system

signature scents

ambient scent/odour

METHODOLOGY

questionnaires

quantitative and qualitative data

objective and subjective data

Odour and shopper pleasure-arousal-dominance

The human **olfactory system** – that, is our sense of smell – is ancient in evolutionary terms. It allows identification of good and bad food, friendly and unfriendly people and familiar and unfamiliar places. Olfactory nerves connect to the **limbic system**, which links it to brain structures responsible for memory and emotion. This helps to explain why certain scents/smells are so evocative, and it is this quality that makes them an ideal atmospheric that can be exploited by businesses aiming to manipulate consumers' cognition and behaviour.

Scent marketing

Research in this area has led to the development of scent marketing, a strategy used to increase sales and encourage brand loyalty through the use of carefully selected scents. Specific fragrances, especially those that evoke positive memories or associations, may be diffused throughout the environment or in specific areas of a store in an effort to influence the customer experience and increase profits. Many businesses have developed **signature scents** that have become an important part of their brand identity. For example, a famous toy shop in London, UK, uses a coconut-flavoured scent. The tropical smell may be associated with holidays, bringing feelings of relaxation that make parents more likely to spend money on their children. This reasoning seems plausible and researchers have focused on whether the power of scent marketing lies in the ability to influence aspects of people's mood, including Mehrabian and Russell's three variables of pleasure, arousal and/or dominance.

Pleasure and arousal

Due to the links between the olfactory and limbic systems, some researchers believe that scent marketing increases sales by creating a positive mood shift in their customers that can be measured through increased feelings of pleasure and arousal. Pleasant scents may encourage approach behaviours, whereby customers are likely to explore stores for longer and interact more with products, staff and other customers, whereas unpleasant scents may lead to avoidance behaviour. Research suggests that simple, pleasant scents like orange can be more effective than complex, layered scents like orange, basil and green tea (Herrmann *et al.*, 2013) and this may be because they require less processing. Scents can also be used to raise arousal levels, which may also encourage greater approach behaviour. For example, scents such as peppermint, thyme and rosemary are thought to be invigorating, whereas lavender and cinnamon are more relaxing (Chebat and Michon, 2003).

Dominance

An intriguing study by Madzharov *et al.* (2015) examined how scent marketing may be linked to Mehrabian and Russell's third variable of dominance. They compared the influence of warm versus cold scents (e.g. vanilla versus eucalyptus) on perception of crowding in the shopping environment, product preferences and purchasing behaviour. Warm scents led to consumers feeling more crowded and purchasing more luxury/premium items. The researchers linked this finding to dominance as the shoppers who purchased luxury items also anticipated greater respect from others as a consequence of the purchase. Their purchases were interpreted as a way of regaining control (through respect from others) in what they perceived as an overcrowded setting.

Emotion versus cognition: how does scent marketing really work?

While scent marketing may work by improving mood, it is also argued that pleasure and arousal increase not because of the smell but because of the way the smell alters our evaluation of the shopping environment and the products; if we believe the products are better quality, we may feel more excited, interested and happy, making purchases more likely. The following study attempted to reveal whether scent marketing affects consumer behaviour via an emotional or a cognitive route.

Focus on: Chebat and Michon (2003)

▶ AIMS
....

To explore whether scents affect consumer behaviour by improving our mood, supporting Mehrabian and Russell's pleasure-arousal-dominance (PAD) model or by creating a more favourable evaluation of the product or store, therefore supporting the role of cognition in consumer behaviour.

▲ Figure 7.14 The emotional route   ▲ Figure 7.15 The cognitive route

Does scent marketing increase sales via an emotional or a cognitive route? Look at the findings of this study. Which of the two models was supported?

▶ METHODOLOGY
....

This was a field experiment with data collected from questionnaires from an opportunity sample of shoppers in a Montreal shopping mall. The independent variable was the presence or absence of a light pleasant citrus fragrance in the mall's main corridor. The fragrance combined orange, lemon and grape and was pumped into the environment for three seconds, every sixth minute, from ten diffusers. The dependent variables were self-reported perceptions of product quality, the shopping mall environment, pleasure and arousal and total spending on non-grocery items.

▶ RESULTS
....

Ambient scent significantly improved perception of the mall environment and product quality. Customers found the scent arousing but the positive effect of the scent on perception was not mediated by pleasure.

▶ CONCLUSIONS
....

Scent leads to increased spending due to the effect it has on perception of the shopping environment and product quality, which in turn increases arousal and pleasure. The study, therefore, supports cognitive factors as the cause of increased spending, as opposed to emotional factors.

Evaluating Chebat and Michon (2003)

One strength was that, despite using the natural settings of the mall and real shoppers, the researchers managed to control various aspects of the shopping environment. For example, the mall owners stated that the two weeks chosen for the data collection are typically identical in terms of sales volume and number of shoppers and all special promotions were cancelled for the duration of the study. This means that any differences in shoppers' perceptions of the mall and the products and their average levels of pleasure and arousal should be due to the manipulation of the ambient scent and not uncontrolled situational variables.

A further strength was the control of other scents in the environment that could have influenced the shoppers' responses. For example, the researchers state that there were no aggressive smells coming from any of the shops in the mall during the time of their data collection. They also asked the students who were collecting the data not to wear any perfume. This is important as it means that the ambient orange scent should have been the dominant scent for all participants, thus increasing the validity of the findings.

One weakness is that the data was only collected from shoppers in February/March, a time of year that would generally be very cold in Canada, meaning that the findings may only apply to this time of year. Evidence suggests that scents can be divided into warm (e.g. vanilla and cinnamon) and cold (e.g. eucalyptus and mint) and it is possible that different scents create differing perceptions and moods depending on the season. This is important as it means that marketers may need to consider the impact of different scents at different times of year and in different climates.

A further weakness was that the **questionnaires** only collected **quantitative data** about shoppers' mood and perceptions. For example, shoppers were asked to rate products on scales ranging from 'outdated' to 'up to date' and to rate the mall on a scale from 'boring' to 'stimulating' and this did not allow them to express their attitudes and opinions in their own words. This suggests that the researchers may have missed important data about how the shoppers interpreted their shopping experiences; this is especially relevant as the study highlighted the role of cognitive factors in shaping consumer behaviour.

> ## ▶ LEARNING LINKS
>
> Piliavin *et al.* (subway Samaritans) was also a field experiment. Remind yourself of the strengths and weaknesses of field experiments in terms of validity, reliability and ethics. Now think about whether these points apply to the study by Chebat and Michon (2003). It is important that your points always relate specifically to the study that you are discussing; use specific details of the procedure to support your arguments, where possible.

> ## STUDY TIP
>
> The effects of ambient scents is a fun topic for conducting your own mini-experiments and this is a great way to consolidate your understanding of methodological concepts. You could design your own study where you ask participants to rate images of different products either on scented or unscented paper. You could try using scents that are related or unrelated to the product. Try keeping the paper in a sealed box with strong smelling soaps, such as lemon, pine or rose. You do not have to write up all elements of your study but practising writing hypotheses and thinking about how you will analyse your data will help you to start thinking like a psychologist.

> ## ▶ TEST YOURSELF
>
> 1   Misha works in a small gift shop. She suggests to her manager that they could try using ambient odours/scents to increase sales. Misha wants to use a strong orange scent, but her manager thinks the smell is too overpowering. Explain how the odour might affect consumers in the gift shop with reference to one research study.   [4]
> 2   Outline the procedure of one study investigating the effects of odour on shopper pleasure-arousal-dominance.   [4]
> 3   a   Describe what psychologists have discovered about retail atmospherics.   [6]
>   b   Evaluate what psychologists have discovered about retail atmospherics.   [10]

4 Adam sells houses. He advises homeowners to use certain fragrances in their homes to encourage potential buyers to make an offer, such as the smell of baking bread in the kitchen, flowers in the hallway and pine-scented cleaning products in the bathroom.

   a Plan an observation to investigate the influence of odours on house buyers. Your plan must include details about:

     – the type of observation (e.g. overt/covert, participant/non-participant, structured/unstructured, naturalistic/controlled)

     – how the data will be collected and analysed.   [10]

   b i State one reason for the type of observation that you chose.   [2]

      ii Explain one weakness of the type of observation that you chose.   [2]

The effects of crowding

Think!

What is the difference between social and spatial **crowding**?

Think!

Do you love being part of a crowd or hate it? Maybe you are somewhere in between? Maybe it depends on the situation? What sort of factors do you think affect how we feel when in a crowded store and how would it affect consumer behaviour?

Think!

How could Machleit *et al.* (2000) improve their study? Can you think of five improvements? Make sure you can justify how your changes will improve the findings.

Look at Figure 7.16 and think about how you would feel. How would you score your feelings of pleasure (feeling pleased/happy), arousal (feeling excited/stimulated) and dominance (feeling in control) on a scale of 0–8, where 0 is low and 8 is high?

▲ Figure 7.16

Crowding and the PAD model

The pleasure-arousal-dominance (PAD) model suggests that responses to our environment are shaped by how the environment makes us feel (Mehrabian and Russell, 1974). One factor that can affect the way the shopping environment makes us feel is crowding. This can take two forms:

» **Social crowding** describes the psychological state experienced when a shopper's demand for personal space exceeds the available space due to the volume of other shoppers (Stokols, 1972).

» **Spatial crowding** is the discomfort experienced when a shopper's freedom to move around the store is restricted, due to cramped store layout and/or poorly organised stock.

Poor use of space within a store or an ill-conceived layout, or spatial crowding, may also increase social crowding. This demonstrates the importance of careful planning in terms of how customers move around the store and how much time they may require to explore certain areas so that the volume of people in any one area does not get too high.

KEY TERMS

crowding

social crowding

spatial crowding

METHODOLOGY

questionnaires

quantitative and qualitative data

objective and subjective data

While the subjective experience of crowding may be dependent upon cultural norms and past experience, typically it is thought that crowding decreases customer satisfaction, meaning shoppers perceive the store, its products, customer service and so on, as poorer than stores that are less crowded. As with other atmospherics, such as music and ambient smells, crowding can affect approach and avoidance behaviour, ultimately affecting spending.

One explanation of the relationship between perceived crowding and satisfaction is that crowding affects our emotions and our emotions affect how satisfied we feel about the shopping experience. For example, Hui and Bateson (1991) found that perceived crowding reduces pleasure and increases stress associated with a perceived lack of control. This can be linked to Mehrabian and Russell's dominance variable, as lack of control would lead to feeling less dominant within the shopping environment. Crowding may also increase arousal and tension but may also lead to feelings of excitement and social connection to other shoppers. The effect of arousal on consumer behaviour may be moderated by personality differences. While some people enjoy the buzz of being around other shoppers, others may find high levels of emotional arousal overwhelming.

Focus on: Machleit *et al.* (2000)

AIM

This study aimed to investigate whether the relationship between perceived crowding and satisfaction is mediated by positive and negative emotions and arousal. Machleit *et al.* (2000) also aimed to explore how expectation and tolerance of crowding and type of shop (e.g. discount store) moderate the strength of the relationship between perceived crowding and satisfaction.

METHODOLOGY

A volunteer sample of American students were asked to complete a retrospective self-report questionnaire following their next shopping trip, even if no purchase was made. The questionnaire asked where they shopped and what for (e.g. groceries, books or electronic appliances) and included many rating scales measuring perceived crowding (social and spatial), crowding tolerance and expectation, emotional responses and satisfaction (see Table 7.5).

▼ Table 7.5 Example items from the shopping questionnaire used in Machleit *et al.* (2000)

Perceived crowding	Social: *The store seemed very crowded to me.*
	Spatial: *I felt cramped shopping in the store.*
Perceived satisfaction	*I was satisfied with my shopping experience at the store.*
Feelings/emotions	Positive emotions: *I felt delighted.*
	Negative emotions: *I felt nervous.*
	Pleasure: *Pleased* versus *annoyed.*
	Arousal: *Excited* versus *calm.*
Expectation of crowding	*More shoppers than were expected* versus *fewer shoppers than were expected.*
Crowding tolerance	*I avoid crowded stores whenever possible.*

RESULTS

As expected, the greater the perceived crowding, the less pleasure the shoppers reported (negative correlation) but unexpectedly, there was a negative correlation between perceived crowding and arousal – that is, the more perceived crowding, the less arousal. Perceived crowding was also positively correlated with negative emotions such as anger and negatively correlated with positive emotions such as joy.

The relationship between spatial crowding and decreased pleasure was stronger than the relationship for social crowding. Social and spatial crowding had similar effects on negative emotions – for example, the more shoppers felt crowded, the stronger their negative emotions. Perceived social and spatial crowding were both negatively correlated with satisfaction and this relationship was only partially mediated by emotion, showing that crowding can decrease satisfaction regardless of how it makes us feel.

Satisfaction was significantly lower when shops were more crowded than expected. The strength of the relationship between crowding and satisfaction was influenced by individual differences in tolerance for crowding. Finally, social crowding was unrelated to satisfaction in stores where a high number of customers may be expected, such as discount and outlet stores.

► CONCLUSIONS

The relationship between perceived retail crowding is not straightforward and is affected by situational factors, including the type of store and individual differences, such as expectations and tolerance for crowding.

Evaluating Machleit *et al.* (2000)

One strength of Machleit *et al.* (2000) is that it was a field study where participants chose which store to visit, meaning their behaviour was natural. For example, they were going about their normal lives, shopping for what they needed/wanted in a wide range of stores, from hypermarkets to shoe shops. This is important as the mundane realism of the task increases the ecological validity, meaning the findings about the relationship between crowding and satisfaction should apply to a wide range of everyday shopping situations.

A weakness of Machleit *et al.* (2000) is that the sample was limited to university students, who are not representative of the general population (participant bias). Firstly, the mean age was 23, suggesting the results may not generalise to older adults or teenagers. Furthermore, the students were studying marketing, suggesting that they may have had insight into what was being researched. This is important as it means that they may have responded in ways that they thought would confirm the researchers' expectations, meaning their results may lack validity.

► ISSUES AND DEBATES

Cultural differences

Much of the research into the effects of crowding on consumer behaviour has been conducted in individualist cultures such as the USA, where the importance placed on personal autonomy may mean shoppers are more dissatisfied in crowded shopping environments.

Crowds hinder our ability to meet personal goals, yet in collectivist cultures group goals are more important, meaning crowding may affect consumer behaviour differently in other cultures. This is supported by Anninou *et al.* (2018), who found that Chinese shoppers felt less stress related to perceived crowding in a superstore than shoppers from the UK.

► LEARNING LINKS

At AS Level, you studied the work of Simon Baron-Cohen *et al.* (eyes test) (see page 60) relating to people with autism, who often find crowds extremely distressing. This can be due to sensory overload and increased need for personal space. Consumers with autism are likely to prefer to shop when stores are less crowded due to their reduced tolerance of crowds. Many store owners are now introducing 'quiet hours' for consumers with additional needs and their families. This is a good example of the way businesses can become more inclusive and take account of individual differences between consumers. Can you think of any other alterations that could be made to stores to accommodate the needs of people with autism?

STUDY TIP

As you read about each new study, think about how you could use elements from what you have learned to design your own study. This should help consolidate the details of what you have read but will also help you to think about aspects of research methodology in general. For example, you might want to think about how you could study perceived crowding and emotion but in a laboratory experiment. How could you use virtual reality to design a follow-up study to further explore some of Machleit *et al.*'s findings?

> **TEST YOURSELF**

1 Nathan is shopping for a book for his brother. The shelves are very close to each other, and he finds it hard to decide which book to buy as other people keep pushing in front of him. Nathan feels irritated and decides to give his brother a token to choose his own book.

Using Mehrabian and Russell's pleasure-arousal-dominance model, explain two reasons why Nathan did not buy a book at the store. [4]

2 Compare the procedures of one study on the effects of odour on shopper pleasure-arousal-dominance and one study on the effects of crowding on shopper pleasure-arousal-dominance. [4]

3 a Describe what psychologists have discovered about the effects of crowding on consumer behaviour. [6]

b Evaluate what psychologists have discovered about the effects of crowding on consumer behaviour. [10]

4 Saabira and Farid are shopping in a large department store. Saabira says it is too crowded and she wants to leave but Farid says he is having a great time and wants to stay. Outline one reason for the difference in Saabira and Farid's reaction to the crowded store. [4]

5 Research on crowding and consumer behaviour sometimes involves questionnaires. These can be given to shoppers to complete while they are in the store, or they may be posted to shoppers to complete at home.

Describe one advantage of the use of postal questionnaires as a way of researching the effects of crowding on consumer behaviour. [2]

6 Suggest one way of investigating the effect of cultural differences on perceived crowding in retail environments. [4]

7.2 The psychological environment

7.2.1 Environmental influences on consumers

Wayfinding in shopping malls

Think!

What do you understand by **legibility**?

Think!

Think about a shopping centre or mall that you have visited recently and one of your favourite shops within the mall. Can you draw a map of how to find the shop from the entrance you usually use? Maybe get together with a classmate (either in real time or remotely) and swap maps. Do you notice any differences in the way you have drawn your maps, such as number of landmarks?

How could you design an experiment using virtual reality to explore spatial factors affecting **wayfinding**? What would the independent and dependent variables be? Would you go for a directional or a non-directional hypothesis?

Have you ever used a 'You Are Here' (YAH) map? Often these YAH maps are poorly aligned with the environment in which they are located – that is, the arrow on the map is not actually pointing at the landmark that is directly in front of the person reading the map. This requires some mental realignment on the part of the viewer and some people are considerably better at this than others! On a scale of 1–10, how would you score your map-reading skills? How could you achieve a more objective score?

▲ Figure 7.17

KEY TERMS

legibility
wayfinding
signage
orientation
building configuration

METHODOLOGY

questionnaires
generalisations from findings
reliability

Wayfinding (or finding your way) is part of daily life, such as moving from where you sleep to where you eat or navigating from shop to shop in a mall. The two most important physical factors for wayfinding are the general layout of the building and the quality of information about the environment, such as graphics and architecture (Passini, 1998).

Shopping malls can be complex places to navigate due to the many intersecting avenues of stores. For this reason, mall designers must think carefully about how shoppers will move around and how they will find the shops they wish to visit while also discovering new stores. The psychology of wayfinding can, therefore, increase sales and benefit businesses while improving the quality of the shopping experience for consumers. Happy and satisfied customers are more likely to return and recommend the shopping centre/mall to others, further improving business.

Shoppers typically feel more comfortable when they have an approximate understanding of their location relative to familiar stores or restaurants and when they know where to find the nearest exit, restroom/toilet, food and drink area and so on. **Signage** using pictograms (to overcome language barriers) helps shoppers to navigate their way around the shopping environment and may convey other important information.

Legibility

When people enter a new or familiar space, indoors or outdoors, they use their information-processing abilities to take in environmental information, understand and use it. Different architectural structures have different spatial configurations, and some are easier to navigate than others because they provide clearer information which is easier to process and use. Lynch (1960) refers to this as the legibility of the space, meaning a space which 'facilitates obtaining and understanding of environmental information' (Dogu and Erkip, 2000). Therefore, good legibility is an important factor in mall design and can be improved with well-designed maps and signposts. Features such as font, size, colour, contrast between lettering and background, position and illumination can all affect shoppers' comprehension of maps and signage.

Features	Description	Example	Possible problems
Visible cues	Access to visible, familiar cues or landmarks within or outside a building.	A fountain/water feature, escalators or lifts/elevators in the middle of the mall might provide a central landmark to help shoppers to orientate themselves.	Such features need careful consideration, however, as if they block shoppers' ability to 'see through' the whole mall, they can reduce the ability to form a mental map.
Architectural design	Architectural differentiation between different areas of a building that aid orientation and spatial recall. Creating a sense of identity/character for different zones will help shoppers to break the mall down into smaller chunks, making it easier to recall.	The walls of different 'zones' of a mall might have different colours or finishes or there might be different lighting.	Use of colour needs to be well-considered as while contrasting colours can be eye-catching, they can also be confusing.
Signage	Using signs and room numbers for identification or directional information.	Signage with arrows showing toilets, parking, food and drink, exits, etc.	Too much visual 'noise' can be confusing and distracting so signs need to be well-designed and use pictograms to overcome language barriers.
Building layout	The building configuration can influence how easy it is to understand the overall plan of the building. A well-organised, simple floor plan will help shoppers move easily around the shopping environment.	Malls where shoppers can look down onto lower floors from upper galleried areas may help them to encode an effective mental map of the layout of the mall.	Malls where corridors/avenues of shops look very similar can be confusing, making mental mapping difficult.

The extent to which shoppers explore their environment is generally determined by the level of information available to them; often they only visit stores with which they are familiar and that they have visited in the past. Movement outside this territory depends upon the level of information available that allows them to learn more about new areas.

Focus on: Dogu and Erkip (2000)

▶ AIM

This study aimed to investigate the effect of spatial factors on wayfinding and orientation in a shopping mall in Turkey. Dogu and Erkip (2000) hypothesised that signage would be more important than building configuration in helping people to navigate the mall. They also predicted that more frequent visitors to the mall would be better at finding their way around and that there would be gender differences in wayfinding behaviour.

▶ METHODOLOGY

Questionnaires were given to 155 adult shoppers at Karum, a mall in Ankara, Turkey. The data collection took place on weekends when the mall was busy. Karum has a fountain at the main entrance, which leads shoppers to a central atrium (a skylighted area) where the main elevator (lift) delivers shoppers to the three floors of stores. Signs use pictograms except the words 'WC' (toilet) and 'Exit' and shops are numbered, although the system is described as 'confusing'. 'You Are Here' (YAH) maps are located on all three floors. These maps have an arrow placed at the location of the map within the mall to help shoppers orient themselves. The YAH maps at Karum were not very noticeable and the accompanying directory of stores was poorly organised.

The questionnaires included closed multiple choice questions and included items about familiarity and perception of the setting (e.g. legibility, including usefulness of the 'You Are Here' maps) and wayfinding strategies, including self-confidence regarding ability to give directions to a stranger. Shoppers were asked to point in the direction of a randomly chosen store.

RESULTS

Shoppers did not find signage more helpful than building configuration for wayfinding and orientation, but those who found the signs sufficient were more likely to say they found wayfinding easy within Karum. Sixty per cent said the signs were insufficient and 68 per cent found the YAH maps insufficient. Despite many saying these maps were useful, 47 per cent claimed there were no such maps at Karum, showing the maps were not well positioned.

Frequency of visits and amount of space browsed within Karum were related but these variables were not associated with better wayfinding. Unlike previous research, there was no gender difference in the accuracy of the pointing task; both males and females showed around 63 per cent accuracy. However, more males than females made close guesses (29 per cent compared with 18 per cent). Shoppers said they avoided giving directions to stores on the secondary/back corridors, which were more complicated to identify.

CONCLUSION

The central open space (atrium) allowed high visual perception of the whole space and this improved Karum's legibility, evidenced by the majority of shoppers' positive evaluation of wayfinding in the mall. The lack of gender difference in wayfinding was seen as reflecting women's greater familiarity with Karum. Aspects of the interior space design, landmarks, floor plan and signage combined with shoppers' familiarity and preferences to help them orient themselves within the mall.

Evaluating Dogu and Erkip (2000)

A strength of this study is that the researchers not only gathered self-reported data using the questionnaire, they also asked participants to perform a standardised wayfinding task. This was the final task which involved pointing in the direction of a randomly selected store. This was a strength as it is an ecologically valid way of gathering data as shoppers could be asked for directions by a fellow shopper in the mall. Furthermore, the task is more likely to reflect shoppers' genuine wayfinding ability than the questionnaire data, as some participants may have poor self-awareness regarding their spatial awareness, meaning they may perform better or worse in the pointing task than their self-reported data suggests.

A weakness of the questionnaire is that there is no way of knowing whether the participants were correct in the answers that they were providing. For example, one item asked 'I know which direction I am facing within the building, without thinking about it. Always, sometimes, never.' This question is problematic as just because a person thinks they know which direction they are facing does not mean that they are actually correct. Participants were asked their gender at the beginning of the questionnaire, so this may have given rise to stereotype threat, which means that women, who stereotypically are thought to have poorer spatial awareness than men, may have underestimated their ability. This means that the data the women provided may have been less valid.

A weakness of the study is the small sample size and the fact that the study only examined one mall in Ankara at weekends. The researchers comment that the study was done at the weekend when the shops tended to be very busy and this can be disorienting and make wayfinding more difficult. This means that wayfinding ability may have been better if the study was done during the week when the mall may have been less busy. Furthermore, the researchers themselves comment that wayfinding may be affected by cultural differences and this means that the findings may not be **generalisable** to other malls on other days of the week or to malls in other parts of the world.

Nomothetic versus idiographic

A strength of Dogu and Erkip (2000) was the use of a nomothetic approach to the data collection. Closed questions in the self-report questionnaires allowed the researchers to gather quantitative data that is easy to analyse using descriptive statistics. For example, participants were asked 'Usually, how much of the building do you get around in each visit? A few shops, a certain floor, all or almost all' and 'What is the most "lost" you have ever become in this building? Never, just momentarily disoriented, totally lost.'

The fact that answers are given in three categories means that the analysis is likely to be more objective and reliable than if the researchers had asked open questions where the qualitative data would have required greater interpretation. Nomothetic research allows conclusions to be generalised to a wider target population and arguably more applicable than taking an idiographic approach where the researchers set out only to provide detail about one specific store or shopping centre, leaving it to readers to make decisions about whether the findings are transferable to other similar settings.

LEARNING LINKS

Dogu and Erkip (2000) predicted a sex difference in wayfinding, but would such a difference be due to biological differences or different learning opportunities relating to gender stereotyping? In the biological approach, you learned about the study by Hassett *et al.* (monkey toy preferences) (page 15), where the researchers linked the differing levels of testosterone and oestrogen to the monkeys' preferences for wheeled or plush toys. Higher testosterone in males has also been identified as a potential cause of superior spatial ability. However, a double-blind, randomised placebo-controlled trial showed that a dose of testosterone increased women's mental rotation skills and ability to represent their direction in a virtual reality environment, but it did not significantly improve their ability to navigate the virtual environment (Pintzka *et al.*, 2016). This suggests the association between testosterone and wayfinding is complex and must not be oversimplified. If differences in wayfinding are due to nurture not nature, how might cultural differences impact wayfinding skills?

STUDY TIP

Relating studies to the issues and debates is a critical evaluation skill. The learning link above highlights how this study could be linked to nature versus nurture. To help you to think more deeply about the research in this section on 'Environmental influences on consumers', you could create a table with each of the A Level issues and debates as the columns and the studies as the rows. In the boxes, you could note down your thoughts about how each study relates to each issue/debate.

TEST YOURSELF

1. Christobel and her friends are visiting a mall on a school trip to Rome. They have an hour to explore and want to visit as many of their favourite shops as possible before returning to the school minibus.
   Explain two features of the mall that might affect how many shops Christobel and her friend can visit before they have to return to the minibus. [4]

2. Wayfinding in shopping malls can be difficult even when there are signs and 'You Are Here' maps available. Explain one or more reasons why signs and 'You Are Here' maps can sometimes make it more difficult for shoppers to find their way. [4]

3. a Describe what psychologists have discovered about environmental influences on consumers. [6]
   b Evaluate what psychologists have discovered about environmental influences on consumers. [10]

4. Give one strength and one weakness of questionnaires as a way of investigating wayfinding in shopping malls. [4]

5. Explain one ethical guideline that researchers should consider when carrying out research into wayfinding in shopping malls. [4]

6. Explain two ways that a researcher might analyse quantitative data about the differences in wayfinding between males and females. [2]

Shopper behaviour and spatial movement patterns

Think!

What would you say the main differences are between raiders and explorers?

Think!

Do you (and your family) follow a set route when visiting the supermarket? Which areas of the shop do you visit the most/least? When you look at Gil *et al.*'s shopper types, do you recognise yourself or anyone else as a specialist, native, tourist, explorer or raider? Do you think these categories are affected more by individual differences between people or situational differences in the store layout or the type of shopping trip the person is on?

Think!

Gil *et al.* (2009) told their participants that their shopping movements would be tracked in-store by the CCTV cameras, but the cameras themselves are unobtrusive. What type of observation would you classify this as and how does this affect the validity of the data?

In Gil *et al.* (2009), participants consented to being tracked using CCTV and interviewed when exiting the supermarket. How could they ensure that ethical guidelines were followed regarding the way that the CCTV footage and interview transcripts were stored and used during and following the analysis?

▲ Figure 7.18

KEY TERMS

specialist, native, tourist, explorer and raider patterns

space syntax

short, round, central and wave shopping trips

Space syntax

Space syntax research models and analyses the relationship between spatial design and social, organisational and economic performance. While the study by Dogu and Erkip (2000) (page 395) examined how aspects of building configuration affect the movement of shoppers through a mall, the following study examines movement within one specific type of store: a supermarket. Here shopper movement patterns are constrained by the layout of aisles and shelf units, which tend to follow a regular and grid-like format.

The use of CCTV tracking

CCTV cameras are typically used for surveillance – to monitor customers' behaviour and to deter thieves. However, this study demonstrates how CCTV can provide useful data to increase profits and customer satisfaction. The existing CCTV cameras in one supermarket were used to track shoppers as they moved through the store. This was done to determine whether shoppers behave in a homogeneous manner (i.e. shoppers all behave in similar ways to each other), shaped by the store layout (situational factors), or whether there are individual differences between shoppers. This possibility had already been supported by research into exhibition-goers (Peponis *et al.*, 2003, 2004).

METHODOLOGY

questionnaires

generalisations from findings

reliability

Focus on: Gil *et al.* (2009)

▶ **AIM**

Gil *et al.* (2009) aimed to investigate the extent to which spatial configuration impacts movement around the store, duration of store visit and interaction with other shoppers and staff. They were also interested to reveal whether certain groups of shoppers showed distinctive movement patterns.

METHODOLOGY

Data was gathered using interviews and **naturalistic observations** of shoppers at a supermarket. The researchers also created a detailed plan of the shop floor, which identified the location of different products. An opportunity sample of more than 480 shoppers was recruited at the store. The shoppers were asked for basic details including age, gender, group size, carrier type and clothing. Coloured tabs were provided so that the shoppers could be identified when exiting the store. As the shoppers moved around the store, their movements were tracked by the CCTV camera operators. On leaving the supermarket, the shoppers were interviewed about their spending, whether they used a list and other shopping habits. Using the CCTV footage, the researchers were able to record many dependent variables, including time spent in each location, total duration of visit, average walking speed, duration of interaction with products, the percentage of the store sections visited more than once and the percentage of the store they visited.

RESULTS

Analysis of the shop floor plan revealed that the central aisle was the most accessible space in the store, followed by the two parallel aisles, while the non-food aisles (e.g. CDs, DVDs, books, etc.) were the most segregated spaces. Although spatial layout was linked to movement needs, shopper behaviour was mainly based on product location. Milk, bread, fruit and vegetable sections had the greatest level of shopper interaction, whereas baby products and non-food products were interacted with least. There was a correlation between spatial accessibility and movement patterns but not between accessibility and product interactions. The researchers identified four different types of supermarket visit (**short**, **round**, **central** and **wave**; see Table 7.7) and five distinct types of shopper (**specialist**, **native**, **tourist**, **explorer and raider**; see Table 7.8). There were wide individual differences in terms of the demographics of the shopper in each type/category, although raiders were more likely to be male and lone females were more likely to be explorers.

▼ Table 7.7 Types of shopper visit

Type of visit (n = number of participants)	Shoppers' movement
Short trip (n = 32)	A quick, in-and-out visit, few specific targets
Round trip (n = 173)	Up and along the main/furthest aisles with short episodes in the side aisles, mainly in the vegetable, fruit and bread sections
Central trip (n = 110)	Up the main aisle, then into the top aisles, back down the main aisle to the bottom side aisles and out
Wave trip (n = 166)	Up the main aisle, zigzagging left and right along the side aisles to the exit at the far end

▼ Table 7.8 The five types of shopper

Type of shopper (n = number of participants)	Description of shopper movements	Aim of shopping trip
The specialist (n = 19)	A long time spent looking at a few items	Top-up or non-food shop
The native (n = 161)	A long trip to specific aisles, likely to make purchase	Main or top-up shop
The tourist (n = 101)	Fast movers staying mainly in the main aisles near the entrance, unlikely to purchase	Food or non-food shop
The explorer (n = 67)	The longest trips, slowly doubling back down the aisles, buying a great deal	Main shop
The raider (n = 113)	Fast-moving and decisive shoppers, clear preference for main aisles unless necessary to go further; highest number of male shoppers	Top-up or for tonight

CONCLUSIONS

Gil *et al.* (2009) concluded that shoppers' movements within grid layout supermarkets are not homogenous, and different groups of people with different purposes adopt distinctive spatial strategies for their shopping.

Evaluating Gil *et al.* (2009)

A strength of this study was the use of a normal, everyday location – the supermarket – where participants were recruited on entering the store. As the shoppers were not recruited in advance and were going about their usual shop, spending their own money, they were more likely to behave naturally than in studies where participants were given a shopping list and/or money to spend by the researchers. This is a strength because the naturalistic setting increases ecological validity, meaning findings should be representative of everyday supermarket-shopping behaviour.

A further strength is that it provides detailed procedures that can be easily replicated. For example, any store that already has CCTV cameras fitted throughout could replicate the study and the use of quantitative data to categorise the shoppers means that the data analysis should also be reliable. This means that stores can be compared in terms of the different shopper types (e.g. explorer, native) and types of shopping trip (e.g. round, wave). This is important as the researchers only examined behaviour in one supermarket and, therefore, replications are necessary in order to see whether these categories apply to other types of store, such as DIY stores or discount stores.

A weakness is that, although the CCTV cameras were unobtrusive, the observational data may not be valid. This is because the shoppers were recruited prior to the observation and so were aware that their shopping behaviour was being monitored. This means that they may have consciously or unconsciously modified their behaviour, such as reduced browsing time, as they knew they would be interviewed afterwards, thus taking time out of their day. Had the researchers simply put posters up in the store telling the shoppers that there were CCTV cameras monitoring the store, the data might have been more valid and the study would still have been ethical.

A further weakness is that the researchers used opportunity sampling from one supermarket and did not provide details about the time of day or whether it was a weekend or weekday. The type of people who visit supermarkets at weekends and weekdays may vary considerably in terms of employment/socioeconomic status. Furthermore, as the researchers tried hard to ensure that they had an equal split of males and females, this means that not everyone who entered the store had an equal chance of being selected, resulting in sampling bias. This is important as it is possible that if the study used random sampling and included data from different days of the week and different times of day, a different distribution of shopper types and shopping visits may be found.

ISSUES AND DEBATES

Reductionism versus holism

Gil *et al.* (2009) took a holistic approach to their data collection using a variety of methods, e.g. naturalistic observation and interviewing. This helped them to capture a wide range of different types of information about the differing motivations of their participants. The identification of the five types of shopper is an example of an individual explanation for the customer movement patterns. However, the additional use of the CCTV footage allowed them to understand how features of the store layout affected the shoppers in general: a situational explanation. Gil *et al.* demonstrates how different ways of collecting data can be used within the same study to develop comprehensive explanations that encompass the complex range of factors that influence customer behaviour.

LEARNING LINKS

At AS Level, you studied Hassett *et al.* (monkey toy preferences) and Bandura *et al.* (aggression). Both of these studies were experiments that used observation as a way of gathering data. Fagen *et al.* (elephant learning) used controlled observation. How does Gil *et al.* (2009) differ from these studies and how is it similar? How does the methodology used by Gil *et al.* (2009) affect validity, reliability and ethics?

STUDY TIP

To help you remember the different types of shopper and shopper visit styles, why not write them all onto pieces of paper and fold them up. Working with a friend, each pick one character and one shopper visit style. Without telling your partner what you got, each draw a cartoon of your shopper, maybe with a speech bubble showing what they might be thinking or saying to other shoppers as they move around the store. Next, make a floor plan of your own local supermarket (you could do this together). Now move your character around the floorplan following the shopper visit style that you randomly selected. Your partner should guess which shopper type and shopper visit style you are portraying. Then swap over.

TEST YOURSELF

1 Francisca is having a dinner party; she spends ages in the supermarket looking for all the ingredients for the recipes she intends to make. Just an hour before her guests are due to arrive, she realises she does not have enough wine glasses and runs back to the supermarket to get some more.

Outline two of the five spatial behaviour types that Francisca might have shown on her two shopping trips. [4]

2 Describe two findings relating to spatial movement patterns in supermarkets. [4]

3 a Describe what psychologists have discovered about shopper behaviour using CCTV tracking. [6]

b Evaluate what psychologists have discovered about shopper behaviour using CCTV tracking. [10]

4 Psychologists sometimes use naturalistic observations as a way of investigating environmental influences on consumers. Explain one strength and one weakness of this methodology for investigating shopper behaviour. [4]

5 Jorge is investigating time spent interacting with non-food products and the five spatial behaviour patterns.

Write a suitable fully operationalised null hypothesis for his study. [2]

6 Explain one way that Jorge could ensure that his study is reliable. [2]

KEY TERMS

eye magnets

gaze motion patterns

silent salesperson

congruent

incongruent

nudge

edge bias

edge avoidance

middle bias

METHODOLOGY

field experiment

objective and subjective data

generalisations from findings

validity

7.2.2 Menu design psychology

Think!

What does Pavesic (2005) mean by **eye magnets** and how can they be used to alter a diner's **gaze motion** when looking at a menu?

Think!

You are a chef at Poppy's Pie Shop. Each week, Poppy receives a box of vegetables from the supermarket next door which have not been sold and need to be used up quickly. This week the box is full of parsnips. You decide to make a batch of parsnip pies but how will you adapt the menu to get the regular customers to think about parsnip pie instead of their usual favourites?

Think!

Do you think it is more important to devote space in a menu to describing the dishes or to presenting photographs and/or illustrations of the food? How could you design a study to find out which is most helpful to diners and the impact on profits?

Pavesic (2005) says a restaurant's menu is like a silent salesperson. How are a well-designed menu and a good waiter or waitress similar? What makes a good waiter or waitress? How could these features be used to inform menu design? Can you think of one important way that menus and salespeople are different and that makes menus even more important?

▲ Figure 7.19

Focus on: Pavesic (2005)

▶ THE SILENT SALESPERSON

Pavesic describes a restaurant's menu as a **silent salesperson**. The menu is one of the first things customers see outside or inside the restaurant. This is why menus are such an important marketing tool. A well-designed menu can create a positive mindset, educate and even entertain, as well as increase the average spend per diner. They may also increase customer loyalty, meaning diners are more likely to return and recommend the restaurant or café to others.

▶ MENUS: THE RESTAURANT'S BUSINESS CARD

In addition to the silent salesperson, Pavesic also calls the menu the restaurant's business card, stating that colour and style should be **congruent** with the decor and price range of the dishes. Like business cards, customers often take print menus home as souvenirs or reminders of their visit. As such, an attractive and well-organised menu may also be an important advertisement for the restaurant. The main message of this article is that the time, effort and money spent on the restaurant decor should be matched by that spent on the menu design. A simple overhaul of the layout and design can cheaply and rapidly increase profits and bring greater customer loyalty. Pavesic provides a useful checklist of common menu mistakes (see Table 7.9), all of which could have a negative impact on the restaurant's success.

▼ Table 7.9 Common mistakes in menu design

Common mistakes	Explanation
Inadequate management commitment	Not treating the design of the menu as important, not being involved with it, not realising the impact on sales.
Hard to read	Not checking font size, crowding and background colour so the print fails to stand out clearly and items may not be seen.
Overemphasised prices	Putting prices in a column so people reading will choose a dish based on price, possibly ignoring more costly items.
Monotonous design	Not varying the graphic design to make certain items stand out, not making the menu look interesting.
Poor salesmanship	Not emphasising in a visual way the items you most want to sell so they may be overlooked.
Poor use of space	Not using part of the menu, such as the back, to identify the restaurant, address and contact details, as some guests will take the menu away. Menus can be your business cards.
Incongruent	Failing to match the menu design to the restaurant, communicating a lack of care about the business.
Too big	This can make the menu difficult to hold, flap around or get in the way.

ORGANISATION AND SEQUENCING

As noted in Table 7.9, menus need to highlight the most profitable dishes, including dishes that use fresh ingredients to avoid waste and those that are easy and quick to prepare. Pavesic refers to the use of 'eye magnets', graphic techniques which attract the diners' eyes to specific areas of the menu. Careful use of boxes, borders, different colours, interesting fonts, shadows and arrows, for example, help organise the menu items, speeding up the processing time needed to make a selection. Items which are gluten-free or suitable for vegans can be signposted with a graphic/icon. Anything that decreases time spent looking at the menu helps to increase revenue as it means customers receive, consume and pay for their orders more quickly, leaving tables free for further diners.

LIGHTENING THE COGNITIVE LOAD

One reason organisation is so important is that Pavesic suggests diners spend an average of 109 seconds before choosing their meal, suggesting that if menus are too long and complicated, diners simply won't process all of the information. Pavesic notes that 60–70 per cent of menu choices come from the same 18–24 dishes; limiting the number of options to this number will cut the cost of ingredients for dishes that are rarely ordered. Therefore, shorter menus make sense economically as well as psychologically, as they are easier to process and less overwhelming.

Eye-tracking, 'heat' and gaze motion maps

Eye-tracking is commonly used by Consumer Psychology researchers as an **objective** measure of visual attention. Trackers often use pupil centre corneal reflection (PCCR), whereby the exact location of a person's gaze can be detected and monitored by projecting an invisible beam of light into the eye and tracking the direction of the reflection using a camera. Eye-trackers can be fitted into glasses so that they are wearable, meaning that eye-tracking studies can be conducted both in the laboratory and also in more naturalistic settings, such as supermarkets or restaurants. The data can be sent wirelessly to a researcher's tablet or computer for analysis where images similar to an fMRI can show where and for how long a person looked, such as which area of the supermarket shelf, product packaging or menu. These images are called 'heat' maps.

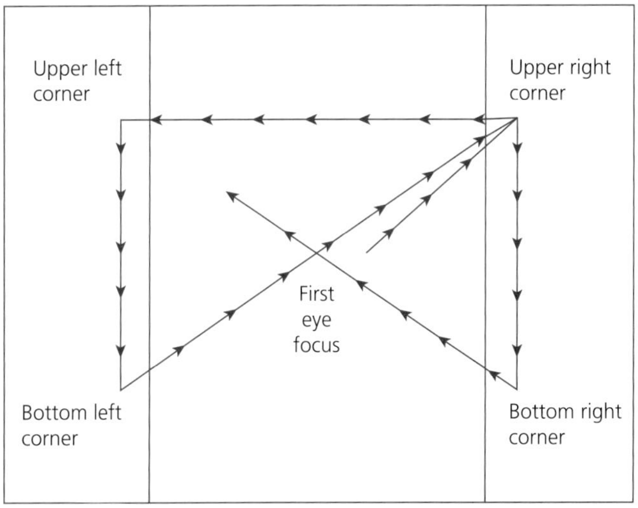

Eye-trackers can also be used to create gaze motion plots or maps to show how the eyes move around or scan a document such as a menu (see Figure 7.20). Menus often group dishes into courses, which are listed in the order in which they would be eaten, such as starter, main course, dessert, coffee. Although this may seem logical, the list-style menus mean diners are not guided to the dishes the owner/chef wishes to promote. The gaze motion map in Figure 7.20 illustrates the typical way in which diners scan a three-panel, two-fold menu. One application of this research is to adapt the layout of the menu so that the most profitable dishes are showcased in the positions that the eye-tracker suggests the diner looks at either first or last or for the longest amount of time, such as the centre and corners.

▲ Figure 7.20 Typical eye movement track when reading a two-page, three-column menu (Pavesic, 2005)

Primacy and recency effects

Cognitive psychologists have long known that people tend to remember items from the beginning and the end of a list more than they remember the items from the middle (Murdock, 1962) and researchers have questioned whether this effect might also extend to making choices from a menu. For example, are diners more likely to select dishes from the beginning and the end of a menu when dishes are arranged in lists? If this were so, restaurateurs would be well advised to place their most profitable, cost-effective, dishes into these positions in order to **nudge** diners into making choices that will benefit the restaurant the most.

This strategy was investigated in a study by Dayan and Bar-Hillel (2011); however, their motivation was to improve the health of diners rather than increase profits. They argued that healthier dishes should be placed into the first and last positions to encourage diners to make more nutritious choices and reduce obesity. The term **edge bias** refers to the tendency to choose menu items in these positions; however, previous research has also suggested that, when confronted with similar items to choose between, people have a tendency to select items from the middle, in a phenomenon called **edge avoidance** (Rubinstein *et al.*, 1996). The following study serves to clarify how these terms apply to menu psychology.

Focus on: Dayan and Bar-Hillel (2011)

▶ AIM

This study aimed to investigate the extent to which the position of food items in a menu (e.g. top or bottom versus central) affects customer choices.

▶ METHODOLOGY

Experiment 1

The first study was a laboratory experiment: 240 students were randomly allocated to one of four conditions and presented with a menu displaying four appetisers, ten entrées, six soft drinks and eight desserts (without prices). The independent variable was the way that the items were sequenced within each group (see Table 7.10). Participants were asked to choose one item from each group (appetiser, entrée, soft drink, dessert).

▼ Table 7.10 Sequencing of menu items

Condition	List order	Example
Baseline	1, 2, 3, 4	juice, Sprite, cola, Fanta
Mirror	4, 3, 2, 1	Fanta, cola, Sprite, juice
Inside-out base	2, 1, 4, 3	Sprite, juice, Fanta, cola
Inside-Out Mirror	3, 4, 1, 2	cola, Fanta, juice, Sprite

Experiment 2

The second study was a field experiment carried out in a café in Tel Aviv, Israel. Participants were genuine customers who were presented with the standard menu or an experimental menu where three of the categories of items (coffees, soft drinks and desserts) had been manipulated so that edge items were now in the middle and vice versa. Each menu was trialled for 15 days and the café staff recorded the number of times the target items were purchased (the dependent variable).

▶ RESULTS

The initial laboratory experiment revealed that all but four of the menu items were chosen significantly more often when they were presented at either end of the list (first or last) compared with the middle. The increased popularity of the items at the edge of the list extended to second and penultimate items, which were as popular as first and last items.

As with the laboratory study, the findings from the field experiment also supported an edge bias not a **middle bias**, with the majority of items being chosen more often when positioned at the extremes versus the middle of each list. For example, croissant was chosen 18 times when it was first in a list of ten items but only nine times when it was in fifth position.

▶ CONCLUSIONS

The researchers concluded that the popularity of menu items can be increased by moving them from the middle to the edge of a menu list (e.g. first or last) and this is the case regardless of the nature of the item (e.g. appetiser or dessert) and the length of the list.

Figure 7.21 shows the menu of the Good Morning café. Based on the advice from Pavesic (2005) and the findings of the study by Dayan and Bar-Hillel (2011), what advice would you give the owner of the café, who is thinking about redesigning their menu?

▲ Figure 7.21

Evaluation of menu psychology research

A strength of the research by Dayan and Bar-Hillel (2011) is that they conducted both laboratory and field experiments, meaning the **reliability** and validity of the findings are both high. For example, in the laboratory study, the researchers were able to control variables that may have affected the dishes chosen, such as removing the prices of individual items, thus increasing the ability to replicate the study and test for reliability. Although it was not possible to control factors such as the waiting staff who served each table or the time of day, the naturalistic location means the findings have greater ecological **validity**. This is important as it means that cafés that adopt a similar strategy are likely to see the same results, with customers favouring edge items.

A weakness of Dayan and Bar-Hillel's study is the fact that the data was only carried out in a single location, a seven-table coffee shop in a capital city location. The customers were mainly students and young professionals. The coffee shop was open past midnight and served drinks, cakes and ice creams. This means that the findings may not be **generalisable** to different types of restaurant where customers may be older and diners are coming to enjoy a meal of several courses.

ISSUES AND DEBATES

Applications to everyday life

A strength of the research into menu psychology is that it is highly applicable to everyday life in terms of both increasing profits and encouraging healthier choices. Pavesic's (2005) suggestions about the use of eye magnets and Dayan and Bar-Hillel's (2011) conclusions regarding re-ordering menu items to encourage diners to make certain choices could each be implemented quickly and cheaply. Small and significant changes such as these could boost profits rapidly, helping businesses, large and small, to stay afloat during financially difficult times.

Determinism versus free will

A weakness of the advice is that it is over deterministic. In reality it may not be able to predict diners' behaviour so easily as the advice may not apply equally to all types of restaurant and all types of customer. Restaurants that are frequented mainly by regular customers, such as people getting their lunch in the middle of a working day, may find that changing the menu order makes little difference as people that repeatedly order dishes they have enjoyed in the past. Diners in expensive restaurants, especially those who are highly knowledgeable about food, may enjoy studying the menu extensively and, therefore, are less likely to be affected by eye magnets. This suggests that advice may fail to take customers' free will into account.

▶ **LEARNING LINKS**

In the social approach, you learned about how behaviour may be affected by the presence of other people and by cultural norms. Pavesic (2005) suggests that people only spend 109 seconds looking at menus, but this may be due to the presence of fellow diners and waiting staff, and results may be different when diners are choosing dishes alone or at home online. Also, Pavesic is based in Atlanta, USA and it is possible that results may be different in cultures that are less time-pressured. Do you think any of Pavesic's common menu mistakes are more culturally universal than others?

STUDY TIP

To consolidate your knowledge of menu design, why not design an experiment and collect some data? Create your own menus and then lay them out in different ways or in a different order. For example, the independent variable could be the use of eye magnets or no eye magnets, and the dependent variable could be the number of times the dishes highlighted by the eye magnets are chosen from the menu. Sharing your menu on social media would allow you to attract many participants. You could ask them to complete an online form to record their choices. You could analyse your data by working out the percentage of the participants who chose one of the target dishes from each menu and draw an appropriate graph to present your findings.

▶ **TEST YOURSELF**

1   Businessman Gordon is visiting Bobo's Bistro. Profits are so low that owner Bobo is worried he might lose his business. Gordon says some simple changes to Bobo's menu could help.

   a   Explain two or more possible features of the menu that may be having a negative impact on the restaurant's profits.   [4]

   b   Outline one piece of advice Gordon might give to Bobo that could have a positive impact on the restaurant's profits.   [2]

2   Explain how the use of eye-tracking has contributed to menu design psychology.   [2]

3   a   Describe research into menu design psychology, including menu item position.   [6]

   b   Evaluate research into menu design psychology.   [10]

4   Explain one strength and one weakness of using field experiments to study menu design psychology.   [4]

5   Clarice's kiosk sells cakes to passers-by as they walk along the seafront. She records the number of customers who order each of ten different cakes listed on her menu. Write a suitable non-directional hypothesis for Clarice's research based on what you have learned about menu design psychology.   [2]

6   Mauritz is interviewing diners at Noga's Noodle Bar to gather qualitative data about their attitudes towards the menu. Noga is worried that Mauritz's data will be too subjective.

   a   Explain what is meant by subjective with reference to research into menu design psychology.   [2]

   b   Explain one way Mauritz could collect more objective data from Noga's customers regarding how they view the noodle bar's menu.   [2]

The effect of food name on menu item choice

Think!

Which style of menu was perceived as most appropriate for a business meeting by participants in Lockyer's (2006) study?

Think!

Think about your favourite meal. How would you describe this meal to create a mouth-watering mental image that would persuade others to select your favourite from a menu rather than their own?

Think!

Focus groups are often used in market research. Do you think a focus group would have data that is more or less valid than an individual structured interview? What makes you think this?

'This is not just a pudding, this is a melt in the middle Belgian chocolate pudding served with extra thick Channel Island cream' (from a Marks and Spencer advert, 2005). If this pudding was on Lockyer's (2006) menu, how would you change the wording to make the description seasonal, elaborate or organic?

▲ Figure 7.22 A chocolate pudding with cream

KEY TERMS

focus groups

menu engineering

content analysis

cluster analysis

transcript

METHODOLOGY

objective and subjective data

generalisations from findings

validity

In 2004, the British high street retailer Marks and Spencer launched an iconic 'not just food' advertising campaign. The adverts featured mouth-watering descriptions of everything from broccoli to chocolate puddings sending sales rocketing by 3500 per cent (Vizard, 2019). These advertisements, by London agency Y and R, recognised the power of descriptive language in terms of marketing food products, another important feature of a well-designed menu.

Lockyer (2006) states that, 'Words create moods in many ways and each word contains a powerful magic.' In this case, the magic should elicit a mouth-watering mental image in the mind of the diner that not only helps them to make a selection, but also generates a sense of pleasure and anticipation. Descriptions should be informative so that diners understand what each dish comprises but should also set the tone of the restaurant, communicating the chef's unique point of view, be it natural, organic ingredients or sophisticated flavour combinations.

The following study explores how **menu engineering** through the manipulation of food descriptions impacts consumers' attitudes and likelihood of choosing certain dishes. It is an excellent example of the use of both qualitative and quantitative data in action. One of the data-gathering methods used is focus groups, a special type of group interview, commonly used in market research. The qualitative data that was gathered was analysed using **content analysis**, a technique that can be conducted manually by the researcher or digitally, as was the case in this study. Computer software was used to detect patterns in the words used by participants to communicate their ideas, grouping them into categories in a technique known as **cluster analysis**.

Focus on: Lockyer (2006)

> ## AIM
>
> Lockyer (2006) aimed to investigate how the choice of wording on a restaurant menu affects the selection of menu items.

> ## METHODOLOGY
>
> Letters were sent to random addresses in Hamilton, New Zealand, offering book vouchers and refreshments for participation in a focus group. Forty-eight participants replied (72 per cent female) and were divided into four groups. The groups discussed five versions of a menu offering the same dishes but with different descriptions (see Table 7.11). Before the discussion, participants were asked to indicate how appealing they found each menu, from 1: most appealing, to 5: very unappealing. They were then asked to write why they had rated the menus in this way on a big sheet of paper which was used as a focus for the discussion. Demographic details were also gathered using a questionnaire and all data was anonymous.

▼ Table 7.11 Selection of comments made about the chicken dish described on the five test menus

Menu	Description of chicken dish	Example comments from the survey
French	Poulet sauté chasseur	'It is exciting to try something that sounds fancy.'
English with French	Chicken sautéed in butter and served with sauce Chasseur	'Sensible, not too over the top.'
Seasonal	Spring chicken cooked and served in a sauce flavoured with new season mushrooms, shallots and tomatoes	'Sounds new, nice and healthy.'
Elaborate	The most tender chicken cooked till golden and served with a delicious sauce finished with tomatoes, shallots and mushrooms	'Mouth-watering description, very suitable.'
Organic	Free-range organic chicken cooked and served with mushrooms, shallots and tomatoes in a naturally produced sauce	'I like the sound of the food being organic – makes you think it is fresh.'

> Following the focus groups, the researchers used the information gathered to create a survey to test the validity of the initial findings. The surveys included open and closed questions, including Likert-type rating scales. Approximately 1800 surveys were distributed to randomly selected homes in Hamilton and there were 200 usable responses.

> ## RESULTS
>
> As shown in Table 7.12, the majority of the participants favoured the seasonal menu (42 per cent), whereas the French menu was favoured by just one person. The French menu was in fact the least favourite (very unappealing) for the majority; likewise, only 2 per cent rated the seasonal menu as very unappealing. Table 7.13 presents a selection of key words that were identified in the cluster analysis of the **transcripts**. Overall, the participants agreed on the importance of explanations as long as they are simple, precise and appealing, and that dishes that are mouth-watering and sound fresh and natural are preferred.

▼ Table 7.12 Frequency with which each menu was rated most and least appealing

	Percentage of the sample who found each menu...		Menu selected by the survey group as 'most likely to be chosen' for...
	'Most appealing'	'Very unappealing'	
French	2	42	
English with French	20	4	
Seasonal	42	2	Business meeting
Elaborate	9	29	Any occasion
Organic	27	22	Meal with mother-in-law

▼ Table 7.13 Sample of key words arising from computer analysis of the focus group transcripts

Clusters of key words	Interpretation
Fresh, interesting, pure, natural, healthy	Words that can give clues to the feel of the restaurant.
Feel, image, mystique	Menu descriptions give clues about the dining experience; there should be some mystery and not something the diners would cook at home.
Occasion	Different wordings may be appropriate for different types of occasion, such as a romantic meal and a business meeting.
Trends, organic, season	Reflected current trends for organic, fresh food.

▶ CONCLUSIONS

Menu wording has an impact on the selection of items; clear and precise descriptions are favoured but occasion can also influence the style of description that is preferred.

Evaluating Lockyer (2006)

A strength of this study is that researchers collected both qualitative and quantitative data, meaning that the weaknesses of each type of data were balanced by the other. For example, in the focus groups, participants could express their attitudes towards the different menus in their own words, meaning the data was more valid as their responses were not constrained by the assumptions of the researchers. However, the sample sizes were small (n = 48) as focus groups are time-consuming to run, meaning the data may not be **generalisable**. This weakness was minimised by the survey data, however, which supported the original findings yet represented the views of 200 respondents. This rich collection of data means that restaurateurs can be confident when using the advice to review their own menus as it is likely to be both valid and generalisable.

This said, the findings may only be generalisable to the people of Hamilton, New Zealand, where the study was conducted, and this is a weakness. Although random sampling was used to select the households of potential participants, these people are only representative of people living in a major urban area and, therefore, may not represent the attitudes of people living in more suburban or rural areas, or in other cultures.

One possible weakness is the use of focus groups, where people sometimes censor what they say to conform with the majority. For example, people may agree that the French menu seems *romantic* and *fancy* rather than admitting that they felt intimidated by not understanding what the dishes were. This means that the findings may lack validity as they do not reflect the genuine views of everyone in the group and are skewed by the opinion of more confident/dominant individuals. This said, the survey data was completed anonymously and individually, suggesting that the findings did represent the majority of the sampled group.

▶ ISSUES AND DEBATES

Applications to everyday life

A final strength of this study is the clear application it has for everyday life. Changing aspects of a restaurant such as the decor or retraining and recruiting new staff may be expensive and time-consuming; these changes may also lead to unexpected outcomes, such as losing regular customers. However, altering the wording of the menu is an affordable and small change that could lead to major benefits without the likelihood of any great loss of income. Menus can be printed in small quantities to see whether they make a positive impact and they can be altered on a weekly basis to reflect the changing seasons and available produce.

LEARNING LINKS

At AS Level, you learned about three different sampling techniques: opportunity sampling, random sampling and volunteer (self-selecting) sampling. Can you remember which of these provides the most representative sample, meaning the findings of the study can be generalised with greatest confidence? Which sampling technique was likely to provide the least representative sample? Which sampling technique would you say is being used in Lockyer (2006) and how does this affect the generalisability of the findings? The researchers offered a book voucher to encourage people to participate in the focus groups. How might this have affected the generalisability of the findings?

STUDY TIP

To help you to think about the difference between objective and subjective ways of collecting and analysing data, why not create a washing line in your classroom or study area using a piece of string. If there is nothing to tie the ends to, you could put it up with pins on a noticeboard. One end of the washing line should be labelled objective and the other end subjective. Next, cut out some colourful pieces of paper and on each one write the name of one of the studies you have learned about in this topic. You could cut the paper into the shape of chef's aprons to tie in with the restaurant/menu theme. Now peg your 'study' aprons to the line in order, from most objective to least objective/most subjective.

Remember, objectivity is about ensuring that data collected is not affected by the participant or the researcher's opinions/emotions; this is usually achieved when data relates to some aspect of the participants that they cannot control (e.g. biological responses) and does not require any type of interpretation on the part of the researcher. Why not create 'pockets' on each apron by sticking on an extra piece of paper? Now you can write the reasons to explain their position on the washing line and place them in the pocket. Good points could go on green paper and bad points on red paper.

TEST YOURSELF

1   Imran has a small business selling street food at festivals. There is a lot of competition and he needs his stall to stand out from the crowd. He asks his friend Otis to help him improve his menu. Explain one piece of advice that Otis might give Imran about how to improve the names of his dishes. [2]

2   Compare the use of laboratory experiments and field experiments to investigate the effects of menu design. [4]

3   a   Describe what psychologists have discovered about the effect of food names on menu item choice. [6]

    b   Evaluate what psychologists have discovered about the effect of food names on menu item choice. [6]

4   Research in Consumer Psychology often uses focus groups, where participants work in groups to discuss an issue. Explain one way that consumer psychologists using focus groups can follow ethical guidelines. [4]

5   Surveys are a useful way of collecting a large amount of both quantitative and qualitative data when researching menu design. Suggest one way that a researcher might analyse and/or present quantitative data from a survey about menu design. [2]

6   A researcher prepares two versions of a menu, one with short, precise descriptions and one with longer descriptions including details about where the ingredients were produced. Explain one or more controls that the researcher would need to consider to make sure that any conclusions from this study are valid. [4]

7.2.3 Consumer behaviour and personal space

Think!

Banquette seating is popular in many urban restaurants where space may be costly and restaurants must pack their diners in to cover their costs. What were the three distances that Robson *et al.* (2011) investigated and how do they relate to Hall's zones (see page 417)?

Think!

Do you have a favourite place to go out to eat? If so, approximately how far are the tables from one another? Would it be possible to fit more tables in by decreasing the space between the tables? How would the atmosphere of the place change if tables were closer together and/or further apart? Would it still be your favourite place to eat?

Think!

This study used questionnaires with pictures of restaurant settings. How might you investigate people's attitudes to table spacing in the real world? Why might this be challenging?

Key study: Consumers' responses to table spacing – Robson *et al.* (2011)

Introducing Stephani Robson

Dr Stephani Robson is a Canadian restaurant psychologist, specialising in seating and hotel design. She is a senior lecturer at Cornell School of Hotel Administration in the USA. Her career started in food-service design where she designed kitchen facilities for hotels, restaurants, airports, hospitals and universities. Her PhD examined consumer behaviour in restaurants and her research explores how consumers' intentions, satisfaction and behaviour are affected by environmental design.

▲ Figure 7.23 Dr Stephani Robson

KEY TERMS

banquette

METHODOLOGY

observations

quantitative and qualitative data

ethics

Robson *et al.*'s (2011) study shows how decreased table spacing can reduce satisfaction, but can you think of any reasons that it might increase enjoyment of the dining experience? Think back to Mehrabian and Russell's (1974) PAD model (page 84).

Context

According to Robson *et al.* (2011), restaurants with banquette seating can increase their revenue by 37.5 per cent if the distance between the tables is reduced from 18 inches (46 cm) to 6 inches (15 cm), as the extra space means six additional diners can be accommodated. While this strategy may seem like an obvious choice, 64 per cent of British restaurant customers felt being closely packed together reduced satisfaction with their dining experience (Smithers, 2010) and this dissatisfaction may translate into avoidance behaviours, such as leaving earlier than anticipated. This can lead to decreased spending and less likelihood of returning and/or recommending the venue to others.

Dissatisfaction associated with tightly packed tables may result from invasion of diners' personal space and reduced privacy. Individual, situational and cultural differences affect the amount of personal space individuals require. This means levels of dissatisfaction may vary for different types of diner, venue or occasion. Restaurant managers should consider demographic details of their target customers (e.g. sex, age, ethnicity and group size) before making decisions about table spacing.

On page 143, we discussed the correlation between interpersonal distance and degree of familiarity between individuals. For example, the less familiar we are with a person, the more uncomfortable we may feel when the person invades our personal space. This suggests that the amount of space that we require, or the size of our invisible personal space 'bubble', decreases with familiarity. On page 417, we also note that the shape of the personal space bubble is larger in front and behind us and smaller at the sides. Decreased distance between tables to the diner's right and left may, therefore, be more acceptable than decreasing the space between tables placed to the rear of the diner. This said, diners may still feel that their privacy is being invaded if others are so close that conversations can be easily overheard.

Previous research had examined seating preferences (Sommer, 1965), including spacing between chairs at a table, but before this study there was no research looking at table spacing.

▼ Table 7.14 Factors affecting the need for personal space

Individual versus situational differences	Factor affecting personal space requirements	More personal space required, e.g. increased space between tables	Less personal space required, e.g. decreased space between tables
Situational	Familiarity with others in the group	Strangers and/or acquaintances	Friends, relatives, loved ones
	Size of party	Larger groups of diners but also dining alone	Smaller groups of diners
	Balance of social status/power	People of unequal status/power, e.g. a group of line managers and their employees	Partners of equal status
	Overall size of the environment	Smaller environments	Larger environments
Individual	Age	Older individuals	Younger individuals
	Gender	Males	Females
	Cultural differences	People from North America or Northern Europe	People from Asia, the Mediterranean and Latin America
	Experience of reduced personal space	Familiar with having more space, e.g. people living in rural areas	Familiar with having less space, e.g. people living in crowded urban environments

▶ AIMS

This study aimed to determine how much space between tables is seen as 'adequate' in different dining scenarios, such as dining with a friend versus a business colleague. Specifically, Robson et al. examined 'whether tight table spacing influences guest attitudes and preferences' (2011, page 411) and whether this is influenced by cultural differences.

METHODOLOGY

This study was an experiment as there were two independent variables that were manipulated by the experimenters: firstly, the distance between restaurant tables and, secondly, who they were dining with. Participants were randomly allocated to one of the nine groups in this independent measures design. The dependent variables were the participants' emotional, intentional and anticipated behavioural reactions to the various scenarios. The data was gathered using a two-part, web-based questionnaire.

Sample

A link to a web-based survey was shared with a diverse national sample via a professional sampling company. There were 1013 American respondents: 81 per cent identified as white, with the remainder identifying as either black (7 per cent), Hispanic: any race (4 per cent), Asian (3 per cent) or other (4 per cent); 53 per cent identified as female and 45 per cent as male. Ages ranged from less than 21 (6.1 per cent) to over 50 (39 per cent). The majority lived in suburban areas and dined out once or twice a month.

PROCEDURE

Participants provided demographic details in the first part of the internet questionnaire (see above). The next section started with an image of restaurant tables placed either 6 or 12 inches (15 or 30 cm) apart (corresponding to Hall's intimate zone) or 24 inches (60 cm) apart (Hall's personal zone) (see page 417 for more on Hall's zones). Robson et al. chose these distances having studied the floor plans of new restaurants featured in hospitality industry magazines (see Table 7.15).

Before completing the questionnaire, respondents were told whether they should answer as though

they were having dinner with a business colleague, friend or romantic partner, each of whom would be associated with different levels of stress/arousal. Next, participants completed 32 seven-point rating scales, where 1 = strongly disagree and 7 = strongly agree (see Table 7.16 for example items). Robson et al. constructed the questionnaire using 12 items to measure emotional responses from the Stress Arousal Check List (SACL) and 16 items to measure perceived control, privacy and comfort.

▼ Table 7.15 Robson et al.'s justification for the spacing of tables in the photographs

Inter-table distance	Relation to Hall's zones	Reason this distance was selected
6 inches (15 cm)	Intimate	Common in New York restaurants
12 inches (30 cm)		Mean inter-table distance based on floor plan review from hospitality magazines; suitable intermediary (medium distance)
24 inches (60 cm)	Personal	Distance diners prefer based on previous research (Robson et al., 2010)

▼ Table 7.16 Example statements from the web-based 32-item questionnaire used in Robson et al. (2011)

		1 Strongly disagree	2 Disagree	3 Somewhat disagree	4 Neither agree nor disagree	5 Somewhat agree	6 Agree	7 Strongly agree
Beliefs	Sitting at this table, I would...							
	have an exciting meal experience							
	disturb the next table if I had to get up							
Emotional responses	Sitting at this table would make me feel...							
	tense							
	influential							
Behavioural intentions	If the host showed me to this table, I would ask to be seated elsewhere							

▶ RESULTS

Table spacing

Participants consistently reported that they felt more uncomfortable and dissatisfied when tables were 6 inches apart compared with 12 inches and 24 inches; the less distance between the tables, the more they reported feeling crowded and that they had less privacy. Respondents in the 6 inches group also reported worries about being overheard and/or disrupting other diners and reported higher stress scores. The majority of respondents in this group (70 per cent) agreed that they would ask to be reseated if possible.

In the 12 inches group, most respondents still reported negative feelings. However, this was the distance where respondents reported feeling most in control compared with 6 or 24 inches. Although respondents in the 24 inches group reported the least negativity, 35 per cent reported that they would still feel crowded and uncomfortable even at this greater distance.

Individual differences

▼ Table 7.17 Influence of individual differences on thoughts/feelings about table spacing

Factor	Effect on thoughts/feelings about table spacing
Age	• No consistent outcomes regarding emotional and behavioural responses, except younger respondents felt: – more stressed at 24 inches than older respondents – more positive, comfortable and in control at 6 inches than respondents aged over 35.
Gender	• Female participants felt more stress, less control and greater discomfort than male participants, who felt more arousal at each distance. • Female participants were significantly more uncomfortable even at 24 inches in all scenarios, e.g. with a friend, colleague.
Ethnicity	• Little impact on diners' reported stress or arousal levels. • Asian participants were more comfortable and in control at both increased proximity (6 inches) and decreased proximity (24 inches) than other groups. • Hispanic participants expressed greater control and comfort at 12 inches than other groups, who still found this interpersonal distance to be too close.
Frequency of restaurant visits	• Frequent diners were more comfortable with all table spacing distances than less frequent visitors.
Area where respondent currently lives	• No difference between respondents from urban versus rural areas in terms of stress, control or comfort. • People from urban areas experienced greater arousal at all table distances than people from less densely populated areas.

Situational differences

Closely spaced tables in the date scenario (dinner with a romantic partner) led to more stress and discomfort being reported. Closer table spacing for dining with a friend led to moderate levels of discomfort and stress in comparison with a romantic partner. Close table spacing had little impact in a business scenario, although comfort was rated as lower.

▶ CONCLUSIONS

Consumers dislike closely spaced tables in restaurants and this was generally the case regardless of individual differences. Generous spacing is more desirable, especially for romantic dates.

 ## Methodological strengths and weaknesses

One strength of Robson *et al.* (2011) is that many controls were introduced to increase the validity of the findings regarding the impact of individual and situational factors on satisfaction. For example, all respondents were asked whether they had experience in the restaurant industry, how often they ate in restaurants and whether they lived in urban or rural areas. This helped to control for participant variables that might have affected people's attitudes towards table spacing as people from more densely populated places with greater experience might have more favourable opinions about the closely packed tables.

A second strength was the special care taken when designing the web-based questionnaire. For example, a pilot study was conducted using an opportunity sample of ten participants of different ages, ethnicities and locations, who then sent the web link to their email contacts, to gather responses from 282 participants. This pre-testing of the items helped to ensure that the quantitative data was both valid and reliable.

A weakness was the reliance on solely **quantitative data** gathered through the use of closed questions. For example, the vast majority of items asked respondents to rate their agreement with statements such as 'It would be fine with me if I sat at this table' on seven-point rating scales, meaning respondents were unable to express their thoughts and feelings about banquette-style seating or experiences of other types of restaurant in their own words. This is important as respondents may have shared useful information, but this was not possible as the answer options were pre-determined by the researcher.

A final weakness is that the findings can only be generalised with caution. Although the sample size is relatively large, Robson *et al.* (2011) note that there were 'notable imbalances across age groups, ethnicities and dining frequency' – for example, there were very few responses from diners under the age of 21 (6 per cent) and the majority were white Americans (81 per cent), with very few Asian-American respondents (3 per cent). This is important as it means that there may be greater cultural differences than this study suggests; as the questionnaire was in English, Americans who do not speak English as their first language may not have participated. This means that the dining preferences of bicultural Americans may not be reflected in these findings.

 ## Ethics

An ethical strength of this research is that participants' confidentiality was maintained. Although the researchers collected some personal data, such as gender and ethnicity, they did not record any details which would identify individual participants. This is important as other ways of investigating attitudes around table spacing could have invaded people's privacy had they been approached to complete a survey while dining in a restaurant, for example.

 ## Application to everyday life

Recommendations from this study can be readily actioned by restaurant owners and designers in creating and modifying dining environments that utilise the available space to the greatest financial effect while maintaining high customer satisfaction. Tables should be spaced at least 12 inches apart. Fewer tables with greater spacing may be financially advantageous as this distance is preferred by consumers of all demographics, meaning they are likely to stay longer, spend more and are more likely to return, possibly bringing new customers with them. This suggests that longer-term profits may outweigh short-term losses. Furthermore, it may be advisable to find an alternative to banquette-style seating, as space and budget allow, especially for those restaurants that attract many couples as opposed to business lunches, for example. Another option to increase customer satisfaction when space is limited is to use booths or dividers so that customers cannot see each other even if they are in close physical proximity. Physical barriers such as this increase psychological distance and provide greater privacy.

> ## ISSUES AND DEBATES

Cultural differences

Robson *et al.* (2011) aimed to investigate cultural differences in people's attitudes towards table spacing in restaurants through the use of a culturally diverse sample. However, less than 20 per cent of respondents identified as non-white (e.g. black, Hispanic and Asian) and participants were American, meaning that those people who came from non-white ethnic groups were also part of an ethnic minority. Being part of a minority may affect people's preferences when visiting public places such as restaurants and this could affect feelings of being in control, need for privacy and/or the probability of asking to be reseated, for example. For this reason, it is difficult to conclude whether cultural differences affect attitudes and behavioural intentions or not without replicating the study in a number of different countries.

- If you were conducting research on restaurant table spacing, what differences might you expect to find in other countries and cultures? Why might this be?

- This study used a questionnaire to gather data about people's attitudes and behavioural intentions, but it only asked closed questions. Can you think of any open questions that you would like to have included?

LEARNING LINKS

At AS Level, you looked at the key study by Perry *et al.* (personal space). Perry *et al.* investigated people's preferred interpersonal distance from others depending on their relationship to that person, as well as preferred interpersonal distance for an intimate meeting. Neither Perry *et al.* nor Robson *et al.*'s studies took place in a real-life setting. What were the main disadvantages of these studies' research methods? Do you think the result would differ in a real-world setting? Why might this be the case?

STUDY TIP

One way to help you to remember the details of this study would be to carry out a partial replication. Create your own mock restaurant by laying two tables out with cutlery, place mats, glassware, maybe a vase of flowers and a menu. Measure the distance between the tables carefully before taking your three photographs for 6, 12 and 24 inches. Use some of the questions from Robson *et al.*'s (2011) questionnaire, which can be found on the last page of their original paper. Whenever you are collecting data, it is essential that you follow ethical guidelines and take local cultural sensitivities into account. Ask your teacher to help you to decide whether your study is ethically acceptable. Once you have collected some data, you can think about how you will analyse it using the correct descriptive statistics and graphs.

TEST YOURSELF

1 Winston runs a sushi restaurant. The restaurant gets busy in the summer but can be very quiet in the winter. Winston needs to seat as many diners as he can during the summer months to make his business work.
Explain one advantage and one disadvantage of decreasing the space between the tables at Winston's restaurant. [4]

2 Describe two features of the sample used in the study on table spacing by Robson *et al.* (2011). [4]

3 a Describe the study by Robson *et al.* (2011) on consumers' responses to table spacing. [6]
  b Evaluate the study by Robson *et al.* (2011), including a discussion about cultural differences. [10]

4 Explain one strength and one weakness relating to the use of quantitative data in the study by Robson *et al.* (2011). [4]

5 Lola and her mum visit Café Munchkin. The tables are widely spaced throughout the enormous room. Lola does not like it at Café Munchkin and says it makes her feel tense, but her mum thinks it feels exclusive and very comfortable.
Explain two reasons why Lola and her mum might have different attitudes about Café Munchkin. You must refer to Robson *et al.* (2011) in your answer. [4]

6 a Outline what is meant by cultural differences using the example of personal space. [2]
  b Suggest a suitable procedure to investigate cultural differences and personal space in restaurants. You must *not* use questionnaire/self-report as your research method. [4]

KEY TERMS

proxemics

personal space

arousal

alpha and beta personal space

intimate, personal, social and public zones

overload

behavioural constraint

social system

point of intrusion

buffers

METHODOLOGY

observations

quantitative and qualitative data

ethics

Hall's zones

> **Think!**
>
> What did Hall mean by **proxemics**?

> **Think!**
>
> Imagine you are studying the menu in a restaurant. Your concentration is affected by other diners' conversations going on around you and the waiting staff are hovering behind you waiting impatiently to take your order. How will your decision-making be affected as you try to choose something to eat?

> **Think!**
>
> Imagine you wanted to replicate the study of queuing and defensive behaviour by Milgram *et al.* (1986). You want to create a behavioural checklist to record people's behaviour. What would you need to do to create this list and how would you ensure that the observations were reliable?

Hall published his work on the four distance zones in the 1960s. Do the zones have temporal and population validity – that is, do you think the size of these zones are relevant today and in countries other than the USA? What size should the zones be based on in your experience of your own culture?

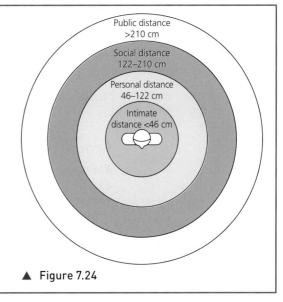

▲ Figure 7.24

What is personal space?

Hall (1966) suggested that we have a physical space around ourselves, like a bubble, in which we feel comfortable. When our **personal space** is invaded by other individuals coming too close to us, we feel uncomfortable and experience increased **arousal** and negative emotions. We may respond by attempting to move away from them to maintain our 'personal space'.

Individual differences and personal space

The size of our personal space bubble varies depending on both individual factors and situational factors. Individual factors include gender, age, culture and examples of neurodiversity, such as autism and traumatic brain injury (TBI), which may also affect personal space requirements. The size of the personal space bubble is also smaller at the sides and larger at the front and behind us, meaning we may be more comfortable with someone sitting close to us on the bus but not if they are sitting right in front of us, not least because eye contact may also be uncomfortable at this angle.

Sociocultural context and situational factors

Social context can also affect who we allow to enter our personal space. For example, when we are on a crowded commuter train, we may not feel threatened by strangers stepping into our personal space, but we would feel uncomfortable if the same person sat 'too close' to us in an empty train carriage.

In the 1960s, anthropologist Edward T. Hall used the term proxemics to refer to the study of how humans use personal and public space. He identified four distance zones (see Figure 7.24 and Table 7.18 below) (Hall, 1966) and noted how our relationship and familiarity with others affects how close they can come before we begin to feel uncomfortable. As an anthropologist, Hall travelled widely and was particularly interested in cultural differences in proxemics, noting that in many Middle Eastern cultures it is common for people to stand much closer to one another without feeling any sense of discomfort. In fact, efforts to maintain interpersonal distances may be seen as abnormal and hostile.

Hall divides cultures into 'contact' and 'non-contact' cultures, where the norm in 'contact' cultures is for closer interpersonal distances and more touching, and in 'non-contact' cultures it is for greater distances and less touching between people. He also used the terms **alpha personal space** for objective, measurable external distances between people and **beta personal space** for the individual's subjective distance assessment.

▼ Table 7.18 The four distance zones (Hall, 1966)

Zone	Who can enter?	Size of zone
Intimate	Romantic partner, children and other close family and friends	<46 cm
Personal	Friends, family, colleagues	46–122 cm
Social	Acquaintances, strangers	122–210 cm
Public	The wider, more impersonal space, reserved for public lectures/speeches, etc., more anonymous	>210 cm

Arousal, overload and behavioural constraint

When people invade our personal space, our brains become highly active as we try to process whether the person is a threat and how we should manage the situation. This may lead to increased biological arousal as our body prepares to respond. Whether the response is positive or negative will depend on how the situation is interpreted. In situations where the desire for privacy and personal control over our surroundings is high, invasion of our personal space may lead to more negative emotions. Under these circumstances, there is the potential for sensory and cognitive **overload**, meaning the individual may be unable to cope with the amount and rate of environmental inputs (Milgram, 1970). This may lead the individuals to employ various forms of **behavioural constraint** to reduce further stimulation, such as averting eye contact, reducing social interaction and making attempts to maintain interpersonal distance.

Hall (1966) suggested that we have a physical space, a 'bubble', in which we feel comfortable. How could you design a study using virtual reality to investigate arousal, overload and behavioural constraint in the context of either dining in a restaurant or shopping? How would you collect both objective and subjective data to measure these variables?

▲ Figure 7.25

Evaluating Hall's zones

One strength of Hall's zones is that, despite the work being conducted in the 1960s, more recent research supports the existence of the intimate, personal and social zones of differing radius and supports. For example, Sorokowska *et al.* (2017) surveyed 8943 participants from 42 countries, aged 17–88, and found wide cultural differences which showed a negative correlation between mean annual temperature and preferred distance – for example, the hotter the country, the less need for personal space. Despite these cultural differences, the mean preferred distances for a stranger, an acquaintance and a 'close person' (e.g. spouse/best friend) matched Hall's social, personal and intimate zones. This evidence suggests that the research has strong temporal validity in terms of the zones themselves, although the mean amount of personal space required when interacting with different people has increased over the years.

One weakness of Hall's zones is the implication that we all have a similar size and shape of bubble, yet research suggests this is not the case. Parsons *et al.* (2004) demonstrated that people with autism and low verbal skills tend to violate norms about personal space significantly more than matched controls in a virtual reality environment – for example, bumping into people in a virtual café. People with autism and stronger verbal skills require more personal space than average. This research is important as individual differences between people from neurodiverse groups are often overlooked despite conditions like autism being increasingly recognised throughout the world.

The social structure of a queue

Defending your place in a queue

The concept of queuing involves waiting for a 'turn' in a line or sequence – for example, to be served at a supermarket till or to buy a ticket at the cinema. Typically, people join the end of the line when they arrive, meaning that people are served in chronological order, 'first come, first served'. Queues are social structures comprising two or more people ranked in order of temporal priority. We benefit by being in front of those who arrive later, generally accepting that those before us will be served first. In cultures where queuing is common, people expect all of the members of the queue to respect the social norms and queue-jumpers can cause indignation and trigger defensive behaviour (Cooley, 1964).

A queue, therefore, can be defined as a small-scale **social system** which:
- ⟫ regulates the order in which people can gain access to goods or services
- ⟫ possesses a distinctive, usually linear, spatial form
- ⟫ requires those involved to have pre-existing knowledge of this form and how it functions (Schwartz, 1975).

Queues can involve standing in line, taking a number which gives the position in the queue or waiting in a designated space for an appointment. The formality of the queuing depends on the knowledge and observation of socio-psychological rules and norms associated with the conflict between delaying individual progress and protecting the queue from being disrupted by later arrivals. Signs, rails or ropes may be used to show how and where people should queue, such as where the end of the line is, and queues may even be managed by specific personnel who help to direct people as to where to stand and discourage intentional or unintentional queue-jumping – that is, people who intrude into the queue, positioning themselves somewhere other than the end of the line. Milgram *et al.* (1986) were interested in exploring reactions to such **intrusions** in naturalistic settings and conducted a field experiment to investigate how defensive behaviour of other queue members affects the likelihood of queue-jumpers being accepted or rejected.

Focus on: Milgram *et al.* (1986)

▶ AIM

To observe the reactions to an intruder who attempts to jump the queue in a public place. The researchers predicted that people would be less likely to show defensive behaviour if other members of the queues also behaved passively, apparently accepting the behaviour.

METHODOLOGY

This field experiment took place at railroad ticket counters, betting parlours and other locations in New York, in the United States of America. Data was collected by observation. Confederates attempted to intrude into 129 naturally occurring queues at the point labelled 0 (see Figure 7.26) by saying, 'Excuse me, I'd like to get in here.' The independent variable was whether or not the people at positions +1 and +2 were also confederates or whether they were genuine, unsuspecting participants. These additional confederates were referred to as

buffers, as they stood between the next genuine participant and the intruder. They faced forward and behaved passively, not objecting to the intrusion. Milgram *et al.* (1986) also manipulated the number of intruders; in some trials, two intruders attempted to join the queue in position 0. An observer stood nearby, collecting physical, verbal and non-verbal responses, and the dependent variable was the number of times other queue members demonstrated defensive behaviour – that is, objecting to the intruder(s).

-2   -1   0   +1   +2   +3   +4   +5   +6   +7

▲ Figure 7.26 '0' marks the position of the experimental intruder in the queue

RESULTS

▼ Table 7.19 Milgram *et al.* (1986) findings

Defensive behaviours	Examples	Percentage of queues where this behaviour was observed
Physical	Pushing, sleeve tugging and tapping on shoulder	10%
Non-verbal	Hostile glares and/or gestures	15%
Verbal objection and/or disapproval	Ranging from polite to hostile, such as 'Excuse me, you have to go to the back of the line' and 'Hey buddy, we've been waiting. Get off the line and go to the back.'	22%

Objections were made in 54 per cent of queues with one intruder and no buffer and this decreased to 25 per cent with one buffer and only 5 per cent with two buffers. The presence of a second intruder (with no buffer) increased objections by 37 per cent; objections were made in nearly all of the queues observed (21/23). However, when there was a buffer, this figure dropped to 25 per cent, meaning the number of objections was unaffected by the number of intruders if there was a buffer. In the queues with two intruders and two buffers, there was a slight, unexpected increase in objections (30 per cent).

CONCLUSIONS

Objections are more likely if there is more than one intruder and less likely if queue members adjacent (next) to the intruder(s) do not object to the intrusion.

Evaluating Milgram *et al.* (1986)

A strength was that the **observations** made by Milgram *et al.* (1986) were both qualitative and quantitative. For example, they recorded whether or not queue members objected and coded their responses as verbal, non-verbal and physical as well as recording the exact nature of what happened and any dialogue, such as tugging a sleeve and/or saying 'Um... are you waiting to buy a ticket?' Combining both types of data meant that not only was Milgram's data objective as he recorded observable behaviour, he was also able to attempt to interpret the intentions behind the behaviours by examining what was actually said as well as done.

A weakness of this study is that all observations took place in New York, USA, where people were queuing for relatively trivial services/items. Although missing trains or failing to place a bet may be costly, it is not life-threatening as it might be for people queuing to get over the border in a war zone or waiting for emergency aid in a natural disaster. This is important as the results may have been very different with people being less tolerant of single intruders and more likely to object and possibly physically eject the queue-jumper regardless of the passive behaviour of buffers.

ISSUES AND DEBATES

Individual and situational explanations

Milgram's research focuses situational explanations of queuing behaviour, e.g. that people are more likely to defend their position if there is more than one queue jumper and less likely to object the greater the proximity from the queue jumper, e.g. the more buffers (additional people between them and the queue jumper). However, he fails to acknowledge the role of individual explanations relating to personality, gender and cultural differences that might also be important determinants of behaviour towards queue jumpers. For example, queue members' amygdala reactivity may determine the extent to which the jumper is seen as a threat and this may be affected by biological factors relating to genes and hormones as well as factors relating to social context/environment.

▶ LEARNING LINKS

At AS Level, you learned about Milgram's (1963) study of obedience. The study prompted a scathing attack from critic Diana Baumrind (1964), who attacked Milgram's research with reference to serious ethical concerns. The American Psychological Association (APA) have published clear ethical guidelines since Milgram's original study, yet the study described on this page conducted in 1986 still raises a variety of ethical issues. How many ethical issues can you think of for this study? Remember, for something to be an issue, there needs to be arguments for and against it. To help with this, think about why Milgram used confederates in this study. How did this improve the study? How does a study like this differ from studies using virtual reality or surveys to measure the effect of the psychological environment on consumer behaviour?

STUDY TIP

Milgram *et al.* (1986) is a great study to practise your evaluation skills. Although we have provided a couple of points here, there are many more that you can make. Think about the size of the sample, sampling technique and characteristics of the participants. What does this information tell you about the extent to which the findings can be generalised? What were the independent and dependent variables? How were these operationalised? How does this link to the validity and reliability of the study? Remember, when you are making evaluation points, always include details that show your knowledge of the study combined with your understanding of research methodology.

▶ TEST YOURSELF

1   Holly and her friends are celebrating her birthday at a restaurant, but the tables are positioned very close to each other and Holly feels uncomfortable and overwhelmed as she studies the menu. Explain how overload and arousal may be affecting Holly's ability to read the menu.   [4]

2   Describe one quantitative and one qualitative finding from research into queuing.   [4]

3 a Describe what psychologists have discovered about consumer behaviour and personal space. [6]

b Evaluate what psychologists have discovered about consumer behaviour and personal space. [10]

4 Sapphire and Leroy have noticed that people often seem to really enjoy waiting in the queue when going to concerts to see their favourite band. They wonder whether having a shared interest in the band will affect how queue members behave towards people who try to intrude into the queue ahead of them.

a Plan a study to investigate responses to queue-jumping in people waiting for a concert. Your plan must include:
   – details about the type of data and how it will be collected
   – your aim and/or hypothesis. [10]

b For one piece of psychological knowledge that has informed your plan:
   i Describe this psychological knowledge. [4]
   ii Explain how two features of this psychological knowledge informed your plan. [4]

KEY TERMS

utility theory

rational action

prospect theory

rational actor

utilitarian value

self-interest

satisficing theory

bounded rationality

suffice

aspiration level

reference point

loss aversion

framing

risk aversion

7.3 Consumer decision-making

7.3.1 Consumer decision-making

Think!

Utility theory is a theory of **rational action**. What does this mean?

Think!

Imagine you are in the supermarket buying shampoo and faced with a huge number of choices. There are so many different brands that you cannot decide what is best. In the end, you take one of the first ones that you saw. It is moderately priced and looks good enough. Which theory best describes your consumer decision-making?

Think!

How might you use **prospect theory** to explain compulsive shopping during sales?

Models of consumer decision-making

Prospect theory attempts to explain seemingly irrational consumer decision-making using the concepts of a personal reference point and general loss aversion. Have you had the experience of explaining why you took a certain decision to buy a product in terms of its value to you and how you perceived the risk of a loss?

▲ Figure 7.27

Utility theory

Utility theory argues that consumers think rationally about the possible outcomes of their decision to purchase a product by consulting all the available information. They consider the utility (usefulness) to themselves, and then buy or do not buy the item. The consumer is viewed as a **rational actor**. For example, before buying a chocolate bar, you would decide its **utilitarian value** to you: are you hungry and is this the sort of chocolate that you like? If the answer to both is yes, utility theory would predict that you would buy the chocolate. You are acting in your own **self-interest**.

Interestingly, while maximising the utilitarian value of your purchase seems sensible in terms of increasing happiness, Schwartz (2000, 2004) argues that due to the problem of collecting enough information, and rising standards concerning what is an acceptable purchase, we may feel regret that we may have not made a perfect choice. This links to the later research by Roets *et al.* (2012), discussed below.

Evaluating utility theory

One strength of utility theory is that it explains how people make optimal (best) choices, given enough useful information. For example, if you know that you really need a new pair of jeans before you go out tonight, you will consider the price you can pay, the style and colour you prefer and how quickly you can get your preferred pair; you will make a rational choice, choosing the jeans with the highest utilitarian value to you. This demonstrates the validity of utility theory, as it has been used by economists to explain consumer decision-making for more than 300 years.

> ## ISSUES AND DEBATES
>
> ### Reductionism versus holism
>
> One weakness of utility theory is that it is reductionist. It ignores many other factors that are important to us when we decide to buy a product. You may make a rushed decision to buy during a sale. This can be so exciting that people become addicted to sales shopping, which is definitely *not* a rational decision made after careful consideration! This shows how emotion can affect a consumer's decision to purchase.

Satisficing theory

Satisficing theory was developed by Herbert Simon (1956) in response to the rationality of utility theory. Satisficing theory is a practical theory that acknowledges that we cannot possibly have enough information about a product to make a totally rational choice. Even if all the information were available, we have cognitive limits and so, instead of being completely rational actors, we operate with **bounded rationality** (Simon, 1991). Our rationality is bounded (limited) by our cognitive abilities, available time and the effort we are willing to make. We make 'good enough' choices by combining what will satisfy us with what will **suffice**. This requires much less time and energy than considering all possible alternatives.

When buying a car, for example, we may have specific criteria to guide our decision. We may want a five-door electric car and would like it in blue. However, when we go to the car dealer, she only has a five-door electric car in grey. She could order us a blue model, but it may be more than a month before it arrives. Satisficing theory would predict that we would take the car on offer, as being five-door and electric were a 'must', but we can be satisfied with the grey colour – it will suffice. We do not want to spend many hours just to find a blue car. The level at which we will be satisfied varies from person to person according to our personalities and experience. Herbert Simon identified this as a person's **aspiration level**.

Evaluating satisficing theory

One weakness of Simon's satisficing theory is that an individual aspiration level is rather vague and difficult to predict. How and why one person is satisfied with a product when another would want something different means that the theory cannot accurately account for all consumer decision-making. Some of us are subject to a personal confirmation bias that will steer us towards buying one particular brand of trainers, for example, while others would make a different decision. This inability to have a more precise definition of aspiration level means that this part of the theory lacks validity. Aspiration level is a subjective concept and difficult to measure empirically; it can only be inferred through our purchases. 'He bought that because of his aspiration level; his aspiration level must be this because he bought that' is an example of circular reasoning.

> ## ISSUES AND DEBATES

Applications to everyday

One strength of satisficing theory is that it has a clear application to everyday life. If everyone followed utility theory and examined all information in order to maximise the utilitarian value of their purchase, they would put in many hours and much effort. We will instead choose the first product that is 'good enough', rather than spend a lot of our resources looking for the perfect buy. It reflects the reality that consumers make decisions based on individual as well as situational factors.

Prospect theory

Prospect theory explains why people sometimes behave irrationally rather than rationally when making decisions (Kahneman and Tversky, 1979; Tversky and Kahneman, 1992). They added the idea that people interpret losses and gains from their own **reference point**. So the value of something (rather than being a rational utilitarian value or determined by an individual aspiration level) is set by our own reference point, with losses being feared more than gains are valued. This is a human characteristic known as **loss aversion**. We value a small certain gain over a large uncertain one, and we hate to lose, especially if our reference point, for example, is a position of poverty.

However, prospect theory argues that it is possible to **frame** a given problem in more than one way to influence the decision that is made. It demonstrates that we will make a riskier decision in the face of certain loss.

The example used in Tversky and Kahneman (1981) is that of an unusual disease that was expected to kill 600 people. They conducted an independent measures laboratory experiment with two groups who were given different descriptions of the potential consequences of a programme designed to combat the disease.

Programme A was framed in terms of certain gain (Group 1) or certain loss (Group 2); Programme B was framed in terms of probability of gain (Group 1) or probability of loss (Group 2):

Group 1 – framed in terms of potential gains:
» A: 200 people will be saved, or
» B: There is a one-third probability that 600 people will be saved and a two-thirds probability that no people will be saved.

(Seventy-two per cent voted for A.)

Group 2 – framed in terms of potential losses:
» A: 400 people will die, or
» B: There is a one-third probability that nobody will die and a two-thirds probability that 600 people will die.

(Seventy-eight per cent voted for B.)

In both groups, the participants showed loss aversion. In Group 1, the possibility of losing everyone was too awful, so the majority chose the certainty of saving 200 people; in Group 2, the certainty of losing 400 people was too awful and the majority would rather gamble on the possibility that nobody would die. People are more likely to pursue certain gains (be **risk averse**) and avoid certain losses (be risk seeking).

Evaluating prospect theory

Cultural differences

One weakness of prospect theory is its inability to account for cultural differences in levels of loss aversion. Wang *et al.* (2016) found that people in collectivist cultures were less loss averse than those in individualistic cultures. This may be to do with the extent to which the impact of such losses will be experienced collectively rather than affecting the individual. This limits the generalisability of the theory to collectivist cultures.

ISSUES AND DEBATES

Applications to everyday life

One strength of prospect theory is that it has a clear application in everyday life. Tversky and Kahneman's example showed that people will engage in risk-seeking behaviour in order to avoid a loss. Advertisers know this and frame their marketing campaigns to focus on how their products could protect consumers from potential losses. Chen and Liang (2006) investigated how consumers could be persuaded to shop online by focusing on the potential losses of time and money related to shopping in their local stores or supermarkets.

LEARNING LINKS

In individualist cultures, maximisers report less happiness than satisficers. You read above how utility theory and maximising the utilitarian value of your purchase does not necessarily lead to happiness. Roets *et al.* (2012) conducted a study comparing the correlation between consumer decision-making models and wellbeing in three cultures: the USA, Western Europe and China, and found that it was only in the individualist Western societies, where choice is highly valued, that maximising was associated with discontent. In China, although maximising could lead to regret, it did not lead to unhappiness, as abundance of individual choice is not seen as the route to happiness in this collectivist society.

STUDY TIP

It is always useful to think about how the content relates to the issues and debates outlined on page 224. Take the debate about idiographic versus nomothetic approaches in psychology; you could draw a line with idiographic at one end and nomothetic at the other and then decide where on the line each of the three theories fits. Is utility theory more nomothetic or more idiographic? As it treats everyone as rational and allows no room for individual differences, it probably belongs more towards the nomothetic end of the line. Where would you place satisficing and prospect theory? Try placing the theories on a line for free will versus determinism? Are the theories more similar with regard to this debate?

TEST YOURSELF

1   Samira is going to the sales. She buys a dress without trying it on because it is reduced by 70 per cent. She tells her friend Juana later that she 'could not bear to miss the chance – it was so cheap'.
    Suggest which model of consumer decision-making describes Samira's decision to purchase the dress. [2]
2   Compare utility theory and satisficing theory. [2]
3   a   Describe what psychologists have found out about models of consumer decision-making. [6]
    b   Evaluate what psychologists have found out about models of consumer decision-making, with a discussion about determinism versus free will. [10]
4   Explain one strength and one weakness of using an experiment to investigate consumer decision-making. [4]

5   Explain one way that a researcher could take an idiographic approach to investigate consumer decision-making.   [2]
6   Psychologists often use self-reports when researching how consumers make decisions. Suggest one way that a psychologist could use forced-choice questions to investigate consumer decision-making.   [2]

KEY TERMS
compensatory
non-compensatory
heuristics
cognitive bias

Strategies of consumer decision-making

Think!

What is the difference between **compensatory** and **non-compensatory** strategies of consumer decision-making?

Think!

You are a researcher investigating consumer decision-making strategies. You are being interviewed on the radio. The interviewer asks whether your research has changed the way you make your own decisions when shopping. How might you answer this question? Do you think your decision-making strategies are affected more by your research in some situations than others? If so, why is this?

Think!

The growth of online comparison websites has made it much easier and quicker to use compensatory strategies. The fact that such websites are used globally may also have reduced cultural differences in the consumer decision-making strategies used by consumers across the world. How would you design a study to investigate change in consumer decision-making strategies across time and place?

Online shopping is very popular as it takes a lot of time and effort out of making purchases. Are there ways in which online shopping makes consumer decision-making more difficult? Discuss whether there are consumers for whom online shopping is particularly useful. Are there any for whom it may be a bad choice?

▲ Figure 7.28

Compensatory strategy

This is a decision-making strategy that is used when you have to consider only a few alternative products. You weigh up the positive and negative attributes (qualities) of the different products and allow for positive attributes to compensate for the negative ones. It is a rational strategy that involves deciding on all the attributes that could have an effect on your decision. You then decide on which are the most important ones and work out an overall value for each product based on how each scores in regard to these attributes. This should allow you to choose the option with the best value.

Negative attributes can be compensated for by higher value positive attributes. For example, you may find that a plane ticket that is a higher price than a ferry ticket (negative attribute of plane) may be the better choice because it is a direct flight to your destination (positive attribute of plane), while the ferry involves a long bus journey on arrival (negative attribute of ferry).

Evaluating compensatory strategy

A strength of compensatory strategy is that it uses detailed comparison to result in maximising the utilitarian value of a choice. Todd and Benbasat (2000) describe how the recent growth of comparison websites and online decision-making tools allows us to use compensatory strategy with little effort. They argue that this development has increased the likelihood of people using compensatory decision-making strategies as it enables them to find sufficient information and to compare products quickly and easily. The popularity of these websites demonstrates the appeal of compensatory strategy for consumers but also that they may find it difficult to use such a strategy without the aid of technology.

> **ISSUES AND DEBATES**

Reductionism versus holism

One weakness of compensatory strategy is that it is reductionist. It reduces a product to the numerical value of its attributes and the consumer decision-making process to a mathematical calculation. Not only does this ignore the consumer's emotions, but it increases the time and effort needed to make a decision. Therefore, compensatory strategy is a less desirable strategy for some consumers.

Non-compensatory strategy

The non-compensatory strategy of consumer decision-making is used when there is a large choice of products and a lack of full information or a lack of time to process the available information. Instead of weighing up all the positive and negative attributes of a product, consumers select the one that seems to have the fewest or no negative attributes. Sometimes there will be a negative attribute that is immediately unacceptable and the product will be rejected straight away. So, unlike the compensatory strategy, a negative attribute cannot be compensated for by a positive attribute. For example, you want to buy a new smartphone with at least an 8 megapixel camera. Even though there are phones available with many different positive attributes, if they have not got this camera then you will dismiss them straight away. No positive attribute can compensate for the lack of an 8 megapixel camera.

This strategy shortcuts the compensatory process to make decision-making somewhat easier. In the example of whether to buy a plane ticket or a ferry ticket, a person on a tight budget would immediately dismiss the plane ticket as too expensive (an unacceptable negative attribute) without considering its positive attributes.

This strategy involves using **heuristics** (cognitive shortcuts). Three choice heuristics are associated with non-compensatory strategy:
1   Conjunctive heuristic: You set a minimum acceptable cut-off level for each positive attribute and choose the first product or several products that meet this criterion. In the example of the phone above, the 8 megapixel camera would have scored a perfect 5/5 or 10/10 on your scale. Anything below that would have been rejected. This is sometimes used to reduce the choice rather than to make an immediate final choice.
2   Lexicographic heuristic: You decide on a particular product on the basis of its perceived most important attribute. If you now have several phones to choose from that all have the camera you want, rather than shut your eyes and point, you may look at size or brand, or whatever is now most important to you. This is where personal preference is important.
3   Elimination-by-aspects heuristic: This concept was developed by Tversky (1972), who argued that we select according to a sequence, eliminating choices that do not have our most important attribute, then our second most important and then our third most important attribute and so on, until we are left with one choice. To take our phone example again, once we have eliminated all those without the camera we want, we might then eliminate those that are too large to fit in our pocket comfortably, and finally eliminate those that are not the brand we prefer.

While heuristics are usually associated with **cognitive bias** and irrationality, people develop them over time based on experience and, therefore, they should not be dismissed as wrong. Behavioural economists like Gerd Gigerenzer (2008) argue that heuristics work and provide real-life solutions to diverse problems. This is part of the argument that economics is too concerned with rationality when people are not necessarily rational.

Evaluating non-compensatory strategy

> ## ISSUES AND DEBATES
>
> ### Idiographic versus nomothetic
> One strength of non-compensatory strategy is that it allows quick decisions when faced with many choices. In the example given above, once a phone does not have at least an 8 megapixel camera we can reject it, speeding up the decision-making process. Less time spent making decisions leaves more time to enjoy taking photos with our phone! Like satisficing theory, it sets a personal aspiration level of what is 'good enough' by immediately excluding those which are not. Therefore, it is a more idiographic strategy than is compensatory strategy.
>
> ### Applications to everyday life
> One weakness of non-compensatory strategy is that it can exclude products that would have been suitable. The choice of attributes is personal and can be easily influenced by friends, family and advertising. Your final phone with the 8 megapixel camera may actually be too expensive for you to buy, but because you want it so much, price has not been placed on your list of attributes as you decide you will take out the credit option even though the interest rate is high. The larger ones you eliminated earlier that had that particular camera were more affordable and, therefore, may have been a better choice. Therefore, this is a strategy that has an application to everyday life but is not necessarily a good strategy.

Partially compensatory strategies

Partially compensatory strategies are when we make our decisions in a serial fashion, rather than in a 'one-off' way. There are two partially compensatory strategies:

1 Majority of conforming dimensions: This is when we take the first two possible products and evaluate them across all attributes, keeping the one that scores more highly across more attributes and dismissing the other. With our phone, we would look at two mobile phones that both have the camera we want, and rate them for their look, ease of use, size, price, availability, brand and any other attribute that is important to us. Once we have decided, we then move on and evaluate the winner against the next phone on our list and so on, until we are left with one. This may prevent us from dismissing the cheaper but larger phone, as happened with the non-compensatory strategy.

2 Frequency of good and bad features: This is similar to compensatory strategy in that all possible products are compared regarding the cut-off values for their relative attributes and those having most attributes that meet or exceed the cut-off values are chosen. Given that the cut-off value for the 8 megapixel camera was 5/5 (top marks), you can see that this method would weight the decision in favour of phones with the necessary camera but would also ensure that others were considered, as price, size, availability and brand, for example, would all be possible attributes.

Evaluating partially compensatory strategies

One strength of partially compensatory strategies is that they combine the rationality of compensatory strategies with the heuristics of non-compensatory strategies. There is no need for complicated calculations to maximise the utilitarian value of the product, but the chance of being swayed completely by your emotions and state of mind is also diminished. They take a more holistic approach to the choice by weighing up all the possible attributes but also including individual preference in the weighting of these. Therefore, they are less reductionist than compensatory strategies.

One weakness of partially compensatory strategies is that they can be as time-consuming as compensatory strategies as you compare your choices either one by one or across many different attributes before making a decision. This takes time and effort, especially as the attributes on which you choose to focus may not necessarily be those found as default on most comparison websites. Therefore, they may not meet the need for speedy decision-making.

Internet shopping and decision-making: website design

Website design influences consumer decision-making. All of the decision-making strategies discussed above involve comparison of products. When we want to compare products, we often look online, so it is important that online sites include features that allow us to easily compare their product with others in order to be successful.

Focus on: Jedetski *et al.* (2002)

▶ AIM

To investigate if consumer decision-making strategies are affected by whether a website allows for comparison with alternatives and the number of alternatives it permits. Jedetski *et al.* (2000) predicted that, when websites allow for comparison of alternatives, participants will use a compensatory decision-making strategy, but if there was no comparison of alternatives permitted, they would use a non-compensatory strategy. They also predicted that non-compensatory strategy would be more commonly used when the number of potential products was 100 or more compared with 30 or less.

▶ METHODOLOGY

Twenty-four participants were instructed to purchase answering machines, baby monitors, golf clubs and toasters from either the *CompareNet* or *Jango* websites. *CompareNet* had more filters and allowed side-by-side comparison of a few attributes and products at a time. *Jango* lacked this facility and the participants could only sort as a list and without comparison of attributes. The independent variables were whether the website allowed for comparisons of alternatives (*CompareNet*) or not (*Jango*) and the number of products available, categorised as 30 or less and 100 or more. Decision-making strategies were observed and noted. Participants were also asked to indicate their agreement with the following four statements on seven-point Likert rating scales:
● I am confident that I made a good decision.
● My overall satisfaction with the website was high.
● The amount of frustration I felt when using the website was low.
● The amount of time required to make a decision was appropriate.

▶ RESULTS

Non-compensatory strategy was used on *Jango* far more than it was on *CompareNet* and when there were more than 100 different alternative products to consider. Participants who used *CompareNet* reported greater satisfaction than *Jango* users (5.67 versus 4.65), but this was unrelated to decision-making strategy and may have related to other differences between the two websites. Likewise, there appeared to be no effect of decision-making strategy on self-reported confidence, frustration and/or perception of time.

▶ CONCLUSION

The findings confirm the argument that many difficult-to-compare alternatives mean that non-compensatory strategy is used, whereas if comparison of alternatives is easy, compensatory strategy is more likely to be used. This research supports Todd and Benbasat's (2000) argument (page 427) that the growth of consumer comparison tools has led to compensatory strategy being more likely to be used than previously.

Evaluating Jedetski *et al.* (2002)

Internal validity: A strength is that the use of an independent measures design meant that participants bought items from only one website, meaning their decision-making could not be affected by order effects. This increases validity of the findings regarding the use of compensatory versus non-compensatory strategies. This said, ecological validity was low as participants were asked to purchase products they didn't want or need meaning that in real life they may have used a different strategy. A further strength is that the use of seven-point Likert scales meant participants were not forced to agree or disagree and could select the middle value if they were not sure about their level of confidence or satisfaction, for example. This said, the small sample size of 22 in each group and the comparison of only two websites means that generalisation should be made with caution.

ISSUES AND DEBATES

Determinism versus free will

One strength of Jedetski's research is that it demonstrates how decisions regarding online purchases of goods like baby monitors, golf clubs and toasters are determined by the type of comparison tools available, rather than by individual free will. When there are many difficult-to-compare alternatives and a site with a comparison tool that lacks filters, then consumers choose a non-compensatory strategy, using heuristics to quickly reject as unacceptable products that have negative attributes for them personally. This is a deterministic explanation of how we come to choose by the product brand, main attribute or acceptable price. We feel as if we are exercising our free will, yet this study shows that given a better comparison tool we would probably have used a compensatory strategy, taken our time and made a rational decision, weighing up all the attributes of a certain product.

However, one weakness of Jedetski's conclusion is a lack of explanation of why the online tool that allows easy comparison and rational choice does not result in any more consumer satisfaction. Logically, as the non-compensatory strategy can result in excluding products that would have been suitable, consumers should report more confidence in their choices and greater satisfaction with a compensatory strategy. But this was not the case. There was no relationship between the strategy used and self-reported confidence or overall satisfaction with purchases from two online sites. Jedetski was unable to explain this except to say that other differences between the two websites may account for this. The study is convincing in its argument that the sophistication of the online comparison tool determines the type of choice made, but so long as the consumer has the illusion of free will and personal choice, then they are equally happy to make quick heuristic-based decisions.

Heuristics are cognitive shortcuts we may use when the number of product choices seems too large for us to attempt a rational and detailed comparison. Think of a recent purchase you made where you had many choices. How did you decide which product to buy? Which strategy is most like the one that you used? Did you use a combination of strategies? Explain your answer.

▲ Figure 7.29

LEARNING LINKS

Look back at the models of decision-making that you have just studied. Can you see a match between these models and the strategies that consumers use? How might Simon's (1956) satisficing theory explain non-compensatory strategy?

STUDY TIP

Most of the research into consumer decision-making strategies is ethnocentric as it has generally taken place in individualistic, Western societies. This means that cultural differences between consumers may not be taken into account. When this is the case, the validity of the findings is reduced and it limits the extent to which generalisations can be made. Whenever you are considering research studies, it is always helpful to think about where in the world they were conducted. However, it is important to think critically; some behaviours may be less affected by cultural differences than others.

> ## TEST YOURSELF

1 Meena is trying to buy a new coat, but there are so many choices online that she is finding it difficult to make up her mind.
   a   Suggest one strategy that Meena could use to make a quick decision. [2]
   b   Suggest a different strategy if she has more time and fewer alternatives from which to decide. [2]
2 Explain one strength and one weakness of one strategy of consumer decision-making. [4]
3   a   Describe what psychologists have discovered about strategies of consumer decision-making. [6]
   b   Evaluate what psychologists have discovered about strategies of consumer decision-making, including a discussion about reductionism. [10]
4 Explain one strength and one weakness of using the experimental method to investigate strategies of consumer decision-making. [4]
5 Suggest an alternative method for investigating strategies of consumer decision-making. [2]
6 Outline one way in which website designers could apply findings from research into consumer decision-making strategies. [2]

7.3.2 Choice heuristics

Think!

What is the recognition heuristic and under what conditions is it likely to influence consumer decision-making?

Think!

Jenna owns a small grocery shop and finds that many of her customers tend to buy the same brands again and again. She would like to encourage them to expand their choices, but first needs to identify which heuristics they are using. Which heuristics are Jenna's customers using and how might she encourage them to sometimes choose alternative products?

Think!

Heuristics are based on our experiences and our personal preferences. They are used to speed up decision-making and to allow for our individual feelings about a product to be considered. However, they can lead to less than optimal choices. Is there any way in which we could protect ourselves against making poor buying choices without having to use a time-consuming and effortful compensatory strategy?

Heuristics are used to speed up our buying decisions, such as which shampoo to choose. Talk with your friends about their favourite brands of phone, shampoo, pizza or any other product about which you all have a strong opinion. What are everyone's opinions based on and would it be easy to change anyone's opinion, including yours? Why or why not?

▲ Figure 7.30

availability heuristic

representativeness
heuristic

recognition heuristic

inference

take-the-best heuristic

anchoring heuristic

intuition

METHODOLOGY

experiments

quantitative and
qualitative data

objective and subjective
data

Choice heuristics

Heuristics are methods or techniques that we use to help us make a decision or solve a
problem more quickly. The term was developed by Herbert Simon, along with bounded
rationality and satisficing. You have already learned a little about heuristics through
prospect theory (framing; page 424) and non-compensatory strategy (conjunctive,
lexicographic and elimination-by-aspects heuristics; page 427). Now we look in more detail
at how heuristics affect consumer decision-making.

There are five main heuristics used to explain consumer decision-making:

» **Availability heuristic**: This is a mental shortcut that is based on how quickly something
comes to your mind. For example, when deciding which shampoo to buy, you may well
choose your current brand or one that you have just seen advertised because it comes to
mind the fastest. If you had more information, you might have chosen a different brand.
Less easily remembered brands are ignored, even if they may have been more suitable.
Advertisers know this and try to fix a positive association in our minds between their
brand of product and how it would meet our needs.

» **Representativeness heuristic**: This is based on comparing a product with how it
represents an image we have of ourselves or an image it represents of how we may
benefit by using it. If the supermarket-brand shampoo is in good-quality packaging that
reminds us of a top brand through its colour and style, then we may buy it. We are even
more likely to do so if it is advertised using a picture of a person who looks as we would
like to look. It is representative of luxury (at a reasonable price) and of our desired
image.

» **Recognition heuristic**: This heuristic simplifies our choices when we are faced with
products or brands that are largely unfamiliar to us. This can happen when you travel to
a different country and go to buy your shampoo in the local shop. You are faced with a
shelf of several choices, and suddenly you see a brand that you recognise and have used
before, so you buy that and do not have to take a chance on the others. This works by
inference – the one that is recognised usually has the higher value to us. Of course, if
you have used it before and did not like it, then you may have decided to try one of the
others; the value of recognition is not absolute. However, it is easiest to be 'safe' and go
with what we know. It is an example of what the behavioural economists Gigerenzer and
Goldstein (1996) call 'one-reason decision-making'.

» **Take-the-best heuristic**: This is a very simple heuristic that is also an example of
one-reason decision-making. We base our decision on a single important reason. 'This
shampoo is for blonde hair. I have blonde hair and so I will buy this shampoo.' We decide
on the attribute that is most important to us and ignore all others.

» **Anchoring heuristic**: This heuristic is used when a consumer uses prior knowledge of a
similar product to act as a standard against which to measure other options. For example,
if a store positions a shampoo (Brand A) next to a more expensive option (Brand B), it
is likely to sell better than if it was presented alongside a cheaper option (Brand C). B
makes A seem like a bargain, whereas C may make A seem overpriced. If the shampoo we
eventually buy is a lower price but in a similar bottle and marketed in a similar way to a
more expensive product that attracts us, then it looks like a good deal. Beautiful, shiny
hair at a moderate price! Product manufacturers will sometimes introduce a higher-priced
item before a very similar lower-priced one just to influence consumers' decision-making.

Applying heuristics to decision-making styles

We have spent the last few pages looking at *how* heuristics are used in consumer decision-
making. But there has been little research on *why* particular heuristics are chosen. We know
there are some situational factors that guide us towards one or other heuristic, such as the
number of alternative products from which to choose, lack of knowledge about a certain
product and the alternatives, time pressure and cognitive limitation. However, researchers
also believe that heuristics are linked to individual decision-making styles.

Focus on: Del Campo *et al.* (2016)

AIM

To investigate whether the use of the recognition or take-the-best heuristic depends on individual decision-making styles.

METHODOLOGY

Del Campo *et al.* (2016) conducted a laboratory experiment based on a choice problem, where different heuristics usually lead to different choices. They used time pressure to create a situation where participants were pushed to rely on heuristics and then recorded the heuristics used by participants with different decision-making styles.

They used five decision-making styles developed by Scott and Bruce (1995):

1   Rational – making decisions in a logical and systematic way by considering various options.
2   Intuitive – using **intuition** to make decisions that 'feel right', by relying on instincts and not conscious reasoning.
3   Dependent – preferring to consult others before making a decision.

4   Avoiding – delaying making decisions until the very last moment.
5   Spontaneous – making quick and impulsive decisions.

Del Campo *et al.* said that consumers would score differently on each of these, but nobody would have only one style. In that way, they are different dimensions of a decision-making process.

They conducted their experiment in Austria and replicated (repeated) it in Spain. Participants were randomly allocated to a time pressure (40 seconds) or no time pressure condition and asked to make one purchase from five different choices of eggs. After their decision, the participants had to explain why they had chosen these eggs and were also asked to complete a 25-item questionnaire on their decision-making style.

RESULTS

The researchers found that time pressure increased participants' use of the take-the-best heuristic in Austria, but not in Spain. No significant difference was found between dependent or avoiding decision-making styles and use of the recognition heuristic, which might have

been expected, as those who are uncertain regarding decisions are supposed to prefer this heuristic. However, a significant positive correlation was found in Austria, but not in Spain, between the spontaneous decision-making style and using the recognition heuristic.

CONCLUSION

Del Campo *et al.* (2016) concluded that the distribution of decision-making styles was similar across the two cultures and there was some correlation between decision-making styles and the recognition or the take-the-best heuristic. However, there were also

large differences between the results in the two countries, which suggests that cultural factors might also be important in which heuristics were used. Thus, choice heuristics rely on both individual and situational explanations.

Evaluating del Campo *et al.* (2016)

One weakness is that the researchers measured purchase intentions using an online questionnaire, which is not the same as asking people to spend their own money on real products. The participants were shown pictures of five different cartons of eggs with a description of the product and asked which they would choose and why. This is a weakness as in real life participants might have used different strategies due to the distraction of other shoppers, noise in the store and the fact they were shopping for a variety of other items, not just the eggs. This suggests that the findings lack validity.

Individual and situational explanations

One strength of del Campo *et al.*'s research is that, although it is an **experiment**, researchers manipulated and measured the effect of situational and individual factors affecting a routine decision we all make frequently. They investigated the effect of the situational factor of time pressure (shown previously to increase the use of heuristics) and the individual factor of decision-making styles on a shopping decision over which eggs to buy in two different cultural contexts. This means it engages in both individual and situational explanations.

Evaluating choice heuristics

Applications to everyday life

One strength of choice heuristics as an explanation of consumer decision-making is that they have application to everyday life. We all have favourite brands and we all tend to go for the familiar or the one that seems a good enough choice when faced with too many alternatives. Research has confirmed the existence of choice heuristics and, therefore, this is a reliable theory of consumer decision-making.

Cultural differences

One weakness of choice heuristics as an explanation of how we decide to buy one product and not another is that, while heuristics exist, as del Campo *et al.* (2016) found, there is cultural variation in how they are used. Therefore, the definitions of when they might be used cannot be generalised to all cultures until there has been more cross-cultural research.

We have looked at how time pressure affects decision-making, with the use of certain heuristics increasing when time is short, but del Campo *et al.* (2016) found that the use of certain choice heuristics varied between cultures, with Austrian and Spanish participants showing a different response to time pressure. Think about how the time available might affect your decision-making when shopping. Do you think time pressure may affect you more if you are from a culture where people are concerned with punctuality than if you are from a more laid-back culture and relaxed about being late back after lunch because you were shopping? If so, it might not be that decision-making styles directly affect choice heuristics, but how time pressure impacts your decision-making style, which then affects which heuristic you use.

▲ Figure 7.31

► LEARNING LINKS

At AS Level, you learned about experiments as a method of gathering quantitative data. Del Campo *et al.* (2016) gathered quantitative data in their experiment. What are the strengths and limitations of gathering quantitative data to compare two cultures? How could del Campo *et al.* have gathered qualitative data in their study?

STUDY TIP

You may find it helpful to look back over the pages on models, strategies and heuristics of consumer decision-making and construct a table or spider diagram comparing them, to find patterns and links. For example, how might bounded rationality be relevant to heuristics, or maximising utility value relate to compensatory strategy?

> ## TEST YOURSELF

1   Peter is going shopping for new shoes in his lunch hour, but he has an important meeting after lunch and must not be late back to work.

   Suggest how two choice heuristics might affect Peter's decision-making while he is shoe shopping. [4]

2   a   Describe the anchoring heuristic. [2]

   b   Explain one situational factor that might make you use this heuristic. [2]

3   a   Describe what psychologists have discovered about choice heuristics. [6]

   b   Evaluate what psychologists have discovered about choice heuristics, including a discussion about application to everyday life. [10]

4   You want to investigate whether individual or situational factors are more important when it comes to choice heuristics.

   a   Plan a study to find out whether individual or situational factors are more important for choice heuristics in consumer decision-making.

      Your plan must include:

      –   details about which individual and which situational factor you will measure.

      –   your research method. [10]

   b   For one piece of psychological knowledge that has informed your plan:

      i   Describe this psychological knowledge. [4]

      ii   Explain how two features of this psychological knowledge informed your plan. [4]

Point of purchase decisions

KEY TERMS

suggestive selling

point of purchase

> ### Think!

What is **suggestive selling** and can you give an example?

> ### Think!

Jerome manages a small grocery shop near a secondary school in a busy area. He notices that he has about 100 chocolate bars that will be past their sell-by date in a month. He wonders how he can sell them before then. What suggestions might you give Jerome to help him sell the chocolate bars?

> ### Think!

Wansink *et al.* (1998) showed that consumer decision-making is affected by individual differences, such as individual internal anchors that limit the effect of external anchors on **point of purchase** decisions, but can you think of any external (situational) reasons for not buying multi-packs or not agreeing to buy an extra item that 'goes with' your purchase?

METHODOLOGY

experiments

quantitative and qualitative data

objective and subjective data

Point of purchase decisions are made by the consumer after they enter the store, or once they are already on the website. These decisions can be influenced by careful advertising next to the product, such as 'buy one, get one free' or 'reduced just for today' signs, which are effective ways to get us to buy more than intended. If you have ever left a supermarket with things that were not on your shopping list, the chances are that you have been subject to point of purchase displays that changed your purchase decisions.

KEY TERMS
multiple unit pricing
multiple unit packaging

Multiple unit pricing

Even though a consumer may only currently need one of a certain product, they may be persuaded to buy more than one by a display that offers a lower price per item if they buy two or more together, rather than buying one singly. This is known as **multiple unit pricing**. Alternatively, **multiple unit packaging** of identical products may encourage consumers to buy more than they need in one go at a reduced price per item. This is common with cheaper items, like socks, underwear or batteries, where buying extra could be seen to be a useful way of saving money in the long term. Manning and Sprott (2007) conducted a laboratory experiment to investigate the effect of multiple unit pricing on point of purchase consumer decision-making regarding cheap items. They found that only the '8 for $8' condition generated a significant increase in buying compared to those in the single item pricing condition. Low-quantity multiple unit pricing ('2 for $2' or '4 for $4') was no more effective than the single item pricing condition.

Suggestive selling

When a salesperson asks a customer if they would like to make an additional purchase, they are using suggestive selling (also known as upselling). Often the additional sale is smaller than the original purchase and is a complementary product – something that goes naturally with what has already been bought. Perhaps the customer would like to buy some special polish to go with the new shoes, a scarf to go with the coat or extended insurance for the computer or phone? The consumer has already made a decision to purchase an item, so selling them something extra that is a much lower price is made easier.

Focus on: Wansink *et al.* (1998)

▶ AIM

To investigate how consumers decide how many of a certain product to buy. The researchers proposed an anchoring and adjustment model of how people make such decisions. Anchoring and adjustment is when a person (in this case, the consumer) adjusts their estimate of the cost to them, and therefore their decision on whether to buy, based on a specific anchor price.

▶ METHODOLOGY

Two field experiments and two laboratory experiments were conducted. The first three experiments tested the impact of external anchors on purchase quantity decisions. The fourth experiment investigated whether internal anchors moderate the effect of the anchor-based promotions.

▶ FIELD EXPERIMENT 1

Eighty-six shops took part for one week, and they were randomly allocated to either a single item promotion price or multiple item promotion price condition. A list of 13 products, including toilet rolls, paper towels, breakfast cereal, sweets, frozen dinners and soft drinks, was drawn up and the researchers compared multiple unit pricing with single unit pricing. This is manipulating the anchor: '1 for *x* amount' is a lower anchor than '3 for *x* amount', even though per item the promotional price may be the same.

Sales of these goods were counted and calculated as a percentage increase over the average weekly sales for the previous six months.

Results

Multiple item promotional pricing resulted in a 32 per cent increase in sales over the single item promotional pricing.

FIELD EXPERIMENT 2

This was an observational study conducted in three supermarkets on three consecutive evenings between 20:00 and 21:00. Campbell's soups were advertised at 79 cents per can. The regular price was 89 cents. A sign was erected in each of the supermarkets saying, 'Campbell's soup sale 79 cents a can'. In Supermarket 1, an accompanying sign said, 'No limit per person'. In Supermarket 2, this was changed to 'Limit of 4 per person' and in Supermarket 3 the sign said, 'Limit of 12 per person'. The purchase limit condition was rotated every evening, so every supermarket operated every condition. This was another manipulation of the anchor through supermarket purchasing limits.

Results

Purchasing limits increased sales even with this small discount of 10 cents per can. Shoppers who bought soup from the displays with no limit purchased 3.3 cans of soup. Buyers with limits of four cans bought an average of 3.5 cans and those with limits of 12 cans bought an average of 7.0 cans. This showed that the buyers in the 12-can limit condition purchased significantly more cans than those in either of the other two conditions.

LABORATORY EXPERIMENT 1

In this experiment, 120 student participants were each offered six products at one of three price levels: no discount, 20 per cent discount or 40 per cent discount. All of them were also given either suggestive selling claims that included either no product quantity anchor ('buy them for your freezer') or an explicit product quantity anchor ('buy 18 for your freezer'). They were not told whether the price was a discount and were asked to predict how many they would buy.

Results

Both the anchor and the discount level significantly and separately increased purchase quantity intentions. The external anchor increased intended purchase quantities even without a discount.

LABORATORY EXPERIMENT 2

In this experiment, which was similar to laboratory experiment 1, 139 students were each given a shopping scenario involving 25–30 per cent discounts on single units of well-known snack products. The external anchor was a no purchase limit, or a limit of either 14, 28 or 56. The internal anchor had three levels:

1 No internal anchor.
2 Default internal anchor: After seeing the product discounts and whichever purchase limit had been allocated, participants were asked, 'How many of this product do you usually buy at a time?' After writing down a number, each participant indicated how many they intended to buy this time.
3 Expansion internal anchor: After seeing the product discounts and limit, participants were asked, 'On each of the lines below, please write down a different situation in which you might imagine yourself consuming this product.' After listing

different situations in which they may use the product, they were asked, 'How many of this product do you think you might use in the next month?' Finally, they indicated how many they intended to buy this time.

Results

Purchase intentions in the no internal anchor condition averaged 7.1, though this increased with purchase quantity limits. Purchase intentions in the default anchor condition remained fairly steady, at an average of 5.2, regardless of the purchase quantity limits. Purchase intentions in the expansion anchor condition averaged 10.3, again with little variation according to the purchase quantity limits. This suggests that the external anchor only had an effect in the no internal anchor condition.

OVERALL CONCLUSIONS

Point of purchase external anchors, such as multiple unit pricing, purchase quantity limits and suggestive selling, can increase consumer purchasing. However, this is true only in the absence of individual internal anchors. If consumers use individual internal anchors, these can significantly increase or decrease the amount bought. This suggests that point of purchase decisions are affected by both individual and situational factors.

Evaluating Wansink *et al.* (1998)

One strength of this study is that the findings from the field **experiment** observations were supported and extended by the findings from the laboratory experiments and subsequent interviews. Moreover, under laboratory conditions, the researchers were able to investigate internal anchors separately from external anchors, something that could not have been done just using observation. Therefore, the research has high reliability.

One weakness of this research is that the main method used to investigate anchoring and adjustment in consumers is experiments. There is a lack of self-reported qualitative data regarding consumers' point of purchase decisions. This means that the reasons for consumer actions are inferred from the quantitative data rather than supplied directly by the study participants. This could mean that the findings lack validity.

Evaluating the examples of point of purchase decisions

ISSUES AND DEBATES

Applications to everyday life

One strength is that examples of point of purchase decision-making strategies have an application to everyday life. Multiple unit pricing and suggestive selling are not only used in shops but are also common with online shopping, which is a growing area. For example, if you buy a book online, you will often be shown what other books were bought by people who made this purchase and online clothing stores may suggest a coordinating accessory before payment. This shows that point of purchase examples can be generalised to online purchases as well as in-person shopping.

Reductionism versus holism

A weakness is that point of purchase explanations are reductionist by only considering a limited number of factors in consumer decision-making. They are just looking at anchoring through multiple unit pricing and suggestive selling and not necessarily considering the economic status or family circumstances of the consumer. For example, an elderly person living alone on a limited pension is much less likely to respond to multiple item pricing as they will think of the combined price and the quantity as limitations rather than advantages. In this way, these examples have limited usefulness and suggest that research with a more holistic outlook, e.g. investigating point of purchase decision-making in specific subsets of consumers may be beneficial.

Purchase decision-making is affected by individual and situational factors. Are there products that you can think of that consumers probably would not buy in multi-packs? Why is this? Is there a characteristic that they have in common? Would some of these items be better sold through suggestive selling and, if so, why

LEARNING LINKS

At AS Level, you learned about observations as a method of gathering quantitative data. The second field experiment in Wansink *et al.* (1998) used covert observation of the number of cans of soup bought by shoppers. Think of other studies that have used observation to gather quantitative data. What tool needs to be developed in order to record the observations? What are some of the problems with this method?

STUDY TIP

Point of purchase decisions are mainly suggested to have situational explanations. Make a list of the situational and individual explanations for consumer point of purchase decisions from your reading and from your experience. Look back through your notes and see how some of these relate to heuristics, not just anchoring as proposed by Wansink *et al.*, but some of the other heuristics you learned about when looking at non-compensatory strategy and choice heuristics.

TEST YOURSELF

1 Maria's boutique has seen a significant drop in sales of scarves and gloves lately, due to warm weather. She is wondering how, with autumn approaching, she can promote them so that sales increase.
   Explain one point of purchase technique Maria might use to increase her sales of scarves and gloves. [2]

2 Research has suggested that many consumer decisions are made at point of purchase. Outline what is meant by point of purchase decision-making. [2]

3 a Describe what psychologists have discovered about point of purchase decision-making. [6]
   b Evaluate what psychologists have discovered about point of purchase decision-making, including a discussion about individual and situational explanations. [10]

4 Explain one strength and one weakness of the use of quantitative data to investigate consumer decision-making at point of purchase. [4]

5 Mykola needs help planning a study to investigate consumer decision-making at point of purchase. He has decided to gather qualitative data.
   a Suggest one way that Mykola could recruit a suitable sample for his study. [2]
   b Suggest two open questions that Mykola could ask his participants in order to collect qualitative data about point of purchase decision-making. [2]

7.3.3 Mistakes in decision-making

KEY TERMS
dual systems
intuitive
probability
extrapolation

METHODOLOGY
experiments
interviews
reliability

Think!

What is the difference between System 1 and System 2 thinking?

Think!

Jenny is going food shopping. She is on a very tight budget and has little money for extras. How could she help herself resist System 1 thinking while she is in the shop? Are there any examples of when System 1 thinking might be justified and not represent a mistake in decision-making?

Think!

Kahneman's 'thinking fast and slow' theory of System 1 and System 2 thinking is based on empirical evidence from experiments that has then been applied to consumer decision-making. What issues might be raised when generalising from a series of experiments to real life?

Some activities might involve System 2 thinking in one person but System 1 thinking in someone else. Is there an activity that you do that involves System 2 thinking, but for someone you know involves System 1? An example might be playing a musical instrument: you may be learning the keyboard and engaging System 2 as you read the music and hunt for the correct keys; your friend is an expert player who unconsciously positions their hands just right and plays while hardly needing to look at the music. Try and think of some examples that apply. What does this suggest about System 1 and System 2 thinking?

Thinking fast and slow

The behavioural economist Daniel Kahneman wrote a book in 2011 called *Thinking Fast and Slow*. It describes how a **dual systems** approach (using System 1 and System 2) explains decision-making under different individual and situational conditions. The terms 'System 1' for intuitive thinking and 'System 2' for more rational thinking were first used by Stanovich and West (2000) to explain why people do not always act as we expect them to, or make decisions based on logic. They are the two different ways humans have of tackling cognitive problems and making decisions. The point Kahneman makes in his book is that highly selective perception and memory shape what comes to mind, before we make decisions and choices.

System 1 thinking

System 1 thinking is fast and often unconscious. It takes less effort than System 2 and is used far more often, especially when we are under time pressure or faced with the cognitive overload of too many choices and we need to make a decision. The heuristics that you have learned about on the previous pages are examples of System 1 thinking. This is linked to the determinism versus free will debate, as the use of System 1 **intuitive** thinking by consumers suggests that their purchasing decisions are determined by forces outside their control, such as external anchors, and a tendency to prioritise easily available information over rationality.

Consumer decision-making and System 1 thinking

If you look back at consumer decision-making models, you will see that, although Simon's theory of satisficing and his concept of bounded rationality that result in a 'good enough' purchasing decision seem to suggest System 2 thinking, they are closer to System 1.

Decision-making is speeded up by omitting some analysis of alternatives and we come away happy with our purchase. Non-compensatory strategy is explicitly System 1: it involves three different heuristics and you have also learned about five different choice heuristics that affect consumer decision-making.

These heuristics can lead to mistakes in decision-making: the availability heuristic prevents us from trying new products that do not come to mind as easily as a well-known brand; the anchoring heuristic means that we can be overly affected by multiple unit pricing; and the representativeness heuristic convinces us that if we buy this particular product then we too can look like the people in the advertisements.

At first it might seem as if consumer decision-making is wholly governed by System 1. However, this is not entirely true, as we will see in a moment, but by knowing how heuristics affect us, especially at point of purchase, we can pause, consider and sometimes resist their pressure.

System 2 thinking

System 2 thinking is slower and takes more effort, which is why it is only used when there is a need for analytical and rational choices. The two systems are parallel but not completely separate: System 2 will use information from the speedy System 1 to make choices and System 1 will use the years of experience and learning from System 2 to make professional or specialised decisions much faster than an inexperienced person could. A good example of this is an experienced chess player being able to see several moves ahead to plan a checkmate, while their less experienced opponent is feeling quite confident that they are going to win this time. This thinking combines the rationality of System 2 with the speed of System 1.

Consumer decision-making and System 2 thinking

System 2 thinking is most evident in the utility theory model or the compensatory strategy of consumer decision-making, where we engage in careful statistical comparison between alternative products, eliminating gradually until we have maximised the utility value of our choice. However, there is also an element of System 2 thinking in point of purchase decisions. When faced with a variable purchase limit for a product acting as an external anchor ('buy

14/28/56 of these snacks'), Wansink *et al.* (1998) found that consumers who used the number that they usually purchased as an internal anchor could resist the external pressure. This careful consideration of what they usually did is an example of System 2 thinking.

So, do we always have to use System 2 thinking when we make purchasing decisions? Only if we have many hours to spare when shopping! Also, although System 2 may be less likely to lead to mistakes in decision-making, we can never be sure that we have made the right purchase. You may remember that Schwartz (2000, 2004) argued that the problem of collecting enough product information, together with rising standards concerning what is an acceptable purchase, combine to make us discontented as we feel regret that we may have made an imperfect choice, even when we take our time and compare a product on all attributes.

Moreover, System 2 does not often overrule System 1 thinking. Daniel Kahneman and his colleague Amos Tversky conducted many experiments to show how susceptible we are to System 1 thinking. To demonstrate anchoring bias, they had participants spin a wheel of fortune rigged to stop at 10 (low anchor) or 65 (high anchor). They then asked them a completely unrelated question: 'What is your best guess at the percentage of African nations in the United Nations?' Participants who had spun 10 guessed an average of 25 per cent, while those who had spun 65 guessed 45 per cent. Their estimates were obviously 'anchored' by the number they had spun, even though it was irrelevant (Shleifer, 2012, p. 8). This is what happens when multiple item promotional pricing makes us buy ten pairs of socks for £25 when one pair would only have cost us £2.75 and the other nine pairs are just lying in our wardrobe. We cannot resist the external anchor.

Focus on: Shleifer (2012)

▶ DESCRIPTION

Shleifer reviewed Kahneman's book and described some of the economic research that had been developed based on his use of System 1 and System 2 thinking, heuristics and biases. For example, heuristics such as the representativeness heuristic encourage us to expect trends to continue, to ignore rational explanations and focus instead on our memories, our attention and our perception. The representativeness heuristic can be used to explain why we think what has happened in the past will continue to happen in the future; investors buy stocks and shares as the market is rising, and sell as it is falling, when logically they should do the opposite. Shleifer (2012) points out that System 1 thinking tells us that the fast-rising stocks could be the next Google, instead of warning us that 'what goes up must come down'.

Shleifer (2012) suggests that unhealthy consumer behaviour, such as smoking, over-consumption of alcohol or even not saving enough for our retirement, could all be addressed through campaigns that encourage System 2 thinking by using internal anchors. The campaigns themselves would have to appeal to System 1 thinking, or they may not capture consumer attention.

Evaluation of the thinking fast and slow explanation for mistakes in decision-making

One strength of this explanation is that it is applicable to everyday life. Shleifer (2012, pp. 4–5) summarises an excellent example of the representativeness heuristic from Tversky and Kahneman (1981):

> An individual has been described by a neighbor as follows: 'Steve is very shy and withdrawn, invariably helpful but with very little interest in people or in the world of reality. A meek and tidy soul, he has a need for order and structure, and a passion for detail.' Is Steve more likely to be a librarian or a farmer?

Most participants use System 1 thinking to reply incorrectly that Steve is more likely to be a librarian, as he seems more representative of a stereotypical librarian than a farmer. They ignore the fact that there are five times as many farmers as librarians in the USA and there are actually very few male librarians. Their decision clearly breaks the law of **probability**; it is definitely more probable that Steve is a farmer. Once this is pointed out to participants, then System 2 will engage and they may change their answer, though some will still cling to the first answer they gave because it 'feels right'. System 1 can be hard to overrule.

This can be applied to explain why we choose a certain product that is representative of a self-image that we desire and ignore that it has been designed to have a very wide appeal and it is no more representative of us than of many others. Our decision is distorted by our automatic representation of the product as for 'people like me'.

Another strength is that the theory has wide empirical support. Shleifer (2012) shows how economists have used the concepts of System 1 and System 2 thinking to model consumer decision-making regarding financial investments. Consumers decide their investments using **extrapolation** of information from past experience and pour money into high-performing stocks without considering that alternatives may offer a better deal over the long term. The role of investment advisors is to engage System 2 thinking and perform market analysis to advise their customers. The fact that there is empirical support for thinking fast and slow increases the validity of the theory when explaining mistakes in decision-making.

One weakness is that, although some economists suggest that System 1 thinking is solely responsible for mistakes in consumer decision-making, this is not true. System 2 thinking can also sometimes lead to wrong decisions. Dijksterhuis (2004) split participants into three groups and asked them to make a decision regarding renting one of four possible flats in Amsterdam. One flat had more positive attributes than the other three and was the clear best choice. Individuals in the groups were given either no time, three minutes or three minutes with a distraction task (preventing System 2 thinking) to make their decision. The participants who had three minutes but with a distraction task preventing them from exercising System 2 thinking made the best choice. The researchers carried out a number of similar studies and concluded that good decisions are made unconsciously, which is against what behavioural economists would predict with System 1 thinking. This suggests that the theory cannot completely account for all consumer decision-making, which means it lacks validity under some circumstances.

Another weakness that limits the generalisability of the theory is that Kahneman's research was carried out largely in Western individualistic cultures. We read earlier that del Campo *et al.* (2016) found that the use of certain choice heuristics varied between cultures, with Austrian and Spanish participants showing a different response to time pressure. Similarly, heuristics are used when faced with an abundance of choice, but Roets *et al.* (2012) argued that an abundance of individual choice is not seen as particularly important in China, which is a collectivist society. Therefore, it could be inferred that there is less importance placed on thinking fast when making purchasing decisions. This means that the theory lacks some cross-cultural validity.

Have you ever gone shopping in a culture that is not your own, such as when you first move to a new country, or when you are on holiday? Maybe you usually go to a big supermarket, but more recently have started visiting smaller local shops, or vice versa. What did you notice about your fellow shoppers? Were they making quick decisions, or standing lost in thought in front of an abundance of choice? Maybe they were ringing a friend or partner to ask for advice. Discuss what their behaviour, and yours, suggests about factors that affect the validity of some of the theories that you have learned so far.

▲ Figure 7.32

STUDY TIP

Many of the examples given by Kahneman in his book are not directly applied by him to consumer decision-making. Write a list of the most common heuristics that you have read about in this section on consumer decision-making and try to match them to Kahneman's examples.

► LEARNING LINK

At AS Level, you learned about oxytocin, a hormone that was investigated by Perry *et al* (personal space) to see how it affected interpersonal distance. This hormone has also been shown to affect consumer decision-making. For example, Liu *et al.* (2013) found a correlation between oxytocin levels (measured in blood samples) and impulse purchasing measured on self-report questionnaires, although this was only true of female participants. It is important to realise, however, that the act of impulse buying could increase oxytocin rather than the other way around. For example, Alexander *et al.* (2015) found increased oxytocin in a group of participants given online coupons compared with a control group. Do you think people are more likely to use System 1 or 2 thinking when experiencing high levels of oxytocin? How does this link to the debate on free will and determinism?

► TEST YOURSELF

1   Omar is the manager of a large grocery store in an area with many elderly residents. He finds they are resistant to buying some products as they feel they are just not for 'a person like me'. Outline one way that Omar could try to improve the sale of these products. [2]

2   a   Outline what is meant by determinism versus free will. [2]
    b   Give one example of how the theory of fast and slow thinking is deterministic. [2]

3   a   Describe what psychologists have found out about the link between thinking fast and slow and mistakes in decision-making. [6]
    b   Evaluate what psychologists have found out about the link between thinking fast and slow and mistakes in decision-making, including a discussion about individual and situational explanations. [10]

4   Zena runs a clothes shop and decides to conduct some interviews with her customers about how they make their decisions about what to purchase.
    a   Give one open and one closed question that Zena could ask her customers to find out about their decision-making when purchasing clothes in her shop. [2]
    b   Explain one way that Zena could recruit a representative sample. [2]

5   Explain one strength and one weakness of using an experiment to investigate mistakes in decision-making. [4]

Key study: Choice blindness when tasting food items – Hall *et al.* (2010)

KEY TERMS

concurrent detection
choice blindness
incentives
retrospective detection
sensory change detection

Think!

What did Hall *et al.* (2010) mean by **concurrent detection** in this study?

Think!

Do you think you would notice if you chose and ordered a dish in a restaurant and the waitress gave you something different? If you think you would notice, can you think of any circumstances that might make it more likely that you would not notice? How likely do you think you would be to mention it to the waitress?

Think!

Can you think of any reasons other than **choice blindness** that might have led to such low rates of detection in this study?

Introducing Lars Hall

Dr Lars Hall is a director of the Choice Blindness Lab at Lund University Cognitive Science (LUCS) in Sweden. Hall and his colleagues, including Petter Johansson, study cognitive processes relating to preferences, attitudes, emotion and speech production.

The shoppers in the study by Hall *et al.* were asked to taste different jams. What was different about the jams in Hall *et al.* (2010) compared with Figure 7.33?

▲ Figure 7.33

Context

Choice blindness

The term 'choice blindness' was first used to explain the findings of another study conducted by Lars Hall and colleagues (Johansson *et al.*, 2005). Participants were shown pictures of two faces and asked which one they found most attractive. When the researchers secretly switched the cards over and showed the participant the face they had rejected, the switch was only detected in 26 per cent of the trials. This failure to recall a choice immediately after we have made it is known as choice blindness. Hall *et al.* (2010) wanted to see whether choice blindness would occur for taste and smell in the real-life setting of a supermarket. They invited passers-by to either taste jams or smell tea blends and choose their favourite before secretly switching them to see if the consumer noticed. They also wanted to see whether choice blindness was affected by **incentives** and if people would pay more attention if they were able to take the product home.

▶ AIMS AND HYPOTHESES

Hall *et al.* (2010) aimed to investigate whether consumers would demonstrate choice blindness in the naturalistic environment of a supermarket when asked to choose between products with differing tastes and smells.

The researchers predicted that participants would be less likely to exhibit choice blindness when:

- the pairs of products were dissimilar in smell/taste to each other
- the participants indicated that they liked one product significantly more than the other
- they were offered an incentive for their participation in the study, such as a free gift to take home.

▶ METHODOLOGY

This was a field experiment as it took place in the naturalistic environment of a supermarket and it had three independent variables that were manipulated by the experimenters: whether the participants were told they would receive a free gift, whether they were presented with teas/jams that were similar to each other or different and whether the experimenter secretly switched the products over or not.

Sample

The study used an opportunity sample of 180 supermarket shoppers, from Lund, in Sweden, 118 of whom were female. The age range was 16–80 (mean age 40.2). The shoppers were recruited by asking them whether they would like to take part in a quality control test.

Materials

The pairs of jams and teas were chosen in a pre-test. Participants rated the similarity of eight pairs of jams and seven pairs of teas on a scale from 1 (very different) to 10 (very similar). The pairs were matched for colour and consistency. The researchers chose the pair that was most similar and two pairs that were most dissimilar (see Table 7.20). The jams and teas were presented in jars divided in the middle into two compartments with lids on both ends (see Figure 7.34). This meant that the jar could be secretly flipped over and the rejected product offered to participants in the experimental condition, in place of their original choice. The shoppers were told that the original packaging had been removed so that their choices were only affected by the taste (jam) or the smell (tea).

▼ Table 7.20 Pairings of jam and tea

	Similar pair	Dissimilar pairs	
Jams	*Blackcurrant* and *Blueberry*	*Ginger* and *Lime*	*Cinnamon apple* and *Grapefruit*
Teas	*Apple pie* and *Honey*	*Caramel & cream* and *Cinnamon*	*Pernod* (aniseed/ liquorice) and *Mango*

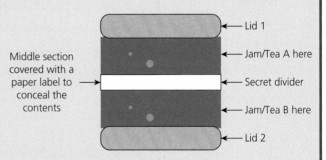

▲ Figure 7.34 The two-compartment jar

PROCEDURE

A stand was set up in an outer aisle of the supermarket beverage section disguised as an independent tea and jam quality assessment. The area had moderate noise and flow of customers and neutral ambient odour. Passing shoppers were invited to taste two jams and to smell two teas as part of a 'quality control survey'.

Half of the shoppers were told they would be given a free gift of their preferred tea or jam (the incentive). The participants either tasted the pair of jams or smelt the pair of teas and rated how much they liked each product on a ten-point rating scale (from 'not at all good' to 'very good'). Next, they stated which product they preferred (e.g. blueberry or blackcurrant).

Immediately after they stated their preference, they were asked to sample their preferred option again. While the participant was recording their ratings, the experimenter secretly flipped the jars over so that the participant was offered the product they had rejected, believing it to be their preferred option. After their second taste of the supposedly preferred product, they were asked to verbally explain why they made their choice and to rate how difficult they found it to discriminate (tell the difference) between the two products, again using a ten-point scale (from 'very difficult' to 'very easy') and how confident they were in their choice (from 'very unsure' to 'very certain').

The procedure was repeated for the second pair of products, so those that tasted the pair of jams first now smelt and rated the pair of teas, and vice versa.

The researchers conducted the same number of trials with a control group. The procedure was identical except the jars were not flipped. This meant that the participants always tasted their genuine preferred product on the third taste/smell.

After taking part, each participant was asked whether they had noticed anything unusual about the samples and was debriefed.

The dependent variable

The researchers measured whether the participants detected the mismatched jam/tea or not. If participants voiced concern about the manipulated product:

- immediately after tasting/smelling it, the response was classed as **concurrent detection**
- at the end of the experiment (before or after the debriefing), the response was classed as **retrospective detection**
- tasting or smelling different the second time round (e.g. stronger/weaker, sweeter), the response was classed as **sensory change detection**.

RESULTS

The majority of shoppers failed to detect the mismatch between the intended and the actual outcome of their choice, believing that the final taste or smell experienced corresponded with their initial choice.

▼ Table 7.21 Percentage of participants who detected the mismatched jam/tea

	Type of detection			Total detection
	Concurrent	Retrospective	Sensory change	
Jam	14.4%	6.2%	12.4%	33%
Tea	13.8%	6.9%	11.5%	32.2%

Although the majority failed to detect the mismatch even when tastes and/or smells were very different (e.g. Pernod versus mango), there were differences in the detection rate between the most and least similar jam and tea pairs. There was a significantly greater difference in liking for the two products in pairs where the switch was detected, although this was only true in the jam condition.

Unexpectedly, detection was less common in those who were offered a free gift (19.6 per cent) than those who were not (46.3 per cent), although this was only true of the tea condition.

There was no difference in the participants' confidence or their ability to tell the difference between the two products in the manipulated (jars flipped) and unmanipulated (jars not flipped) conditions.

Figure 7.35 shows that detection rates were higher for pairings that were rated as more dissimilar (e.g. cinnamon apple versus grapefruit), but even under such circumstances choice blindness still affected more than 50 per cent of shoppers.

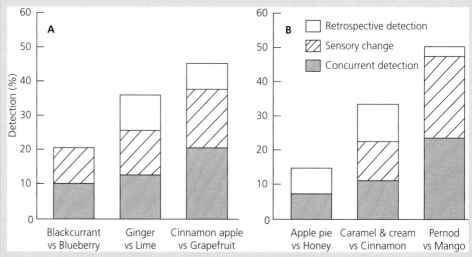

▲ Figure 7.35 Comparative bar charts showing the rate of different types of detection for the six pairings of teas and jams

CONCLUSIONS

The majority of consumers show choice blindness even when products are rated as significantly different from each other. This shows that choice blindness occurs in naturalistic as well as laboratory settings and affects senses such as taste and smell as well as vision. The findings suggest that choice blindness is not due to difficulties in differentiating between the products and occurs even when the outcome of our choices has real-world consequences – as in this study the participant's choice affected which free gift they would receive.

Methodological strengths and weaknesses

One strength was that the procedure was carefully controlled, meaning the researchers were able to establish whether the free gifts or similarity of products affected choice blindness. For example, the researchers randomised which tea/jam pairs were presented and whether the jar was flipped for the jam or the tea. This was important as it increases the validity of the findings.

A further strength was the natural setting of the supermarket, which decreased the likelihood of demand characteristics. The researchers presented themselves as independent consultants conducting quality tests with the customers. This means that customers were less likely to expect any form of deception, unlike studies conducted in laboratory settings where participants may have been more likely to question why they were asked to taste the same product twice.

A weakness of conducting the study in a naturalistic setting such as a supermarket is that it is not possible to control all variables, meaning the procedure may not be completely standardised for each shopper. For example, noise levels may vary, meaning some shoppers are more distracted than others by announcements over the store loudspeakers or other customers talking next to the stall. This is important as it means it may not be possible to replicate certain aspects of the environment and so the findings cannot be tested exactly for **reliability**.

A further weakness linked to the naturalistic setting is that it may be difficult to control the extent to which participants spoke to each other, thus contaminating the results. Although the researchers conducted the debriefing out of earshot of the stall, it is possible that participants told other shoppers about the opportunity to taste products and receive free gifts and may have told them about aspects of the procedure. This is important as it means that some participants may have seen through the deception, meaning their behaviour was not natural, and therefore decreasing the validity of their responses.

Ethics

A strength is that ethical procedures were followed in this study. The study was approved by the Regional Swedish Ethics Board in Lund and, after the experiment finished, participants were interviewed and gave their written consent for their data to be used. No participant is identifiable and so confidentiality was maintained.

Application to everyday life

Research in this field has interesting implications for the food industry as the phenomenon of choice blindness demonstrates that the link between personal preferences and decision-making is not as clear as some researchers and managers may think. In this study, it was easy to manipulate consumers into thinking they liked a certain product and it showed that their memory of previous products was poor. A deeper understanding of consumer decision-making based on mistakes such as these will doubtless be helpful to businesses in terms of encouraging shoppers to purchase products with which they have limited experience and do not actually prefer.

> ISSUES AND DEBATES

Individual and situational explanations

This study demonstrates that the majority of people are prone to choice blindness; however, this phenomenon is affected by both individual and situational factors. For example, up to 50 per cent of participants in the dissimilar products conditions reported that they had detected the switch, showing that only half the sample were affected by choice blindness under these conditions. One example of individual differences between those that did detect the switch is that, on average, 14 per cent pointed out the difference at the time they tasted the product (concurrent detection), while others reported simply that the second product seemed different (sensory change) and others noted the switch during the debrief (retrospective detection). These differences may be due to differences in reporting as opposed to actual perceptual differences – people may have felt unsure whether they should mention it or not, and this may be underpinned by personality differences. Situational factors also appear to affect choice blindness as the jams/teas that were more similar were more likely to elicit choice blindness and the offer of a free gift unexpectedly increased choice blindness.

▶ REFLECTION

- What does this study tell us about the links between consumer preferences and decisions? Do consumers really prefer the products they have chosen or are there other factors which put them in the mood for buying other than whether they actually like the product or not?
- If you were conducting research in this area, how would you adapt the procedure for consumer environments where it is less easy to exert control, such as open-air markets? Can you explain the changes you are suggesting?

▶ LEARNING LINK

At AS Level, you looked at social processes such as obedience (Milgram, obedience) in the social approach and social sensitivity (Baron-Cohen *et al.*, eyes test) in the cognitive approach. How might concepts from these studies help to explain the results of this study?

STUDY TIP

Sometimes role-playing complex procedures can help to consolidate them and help you to remember them in the long term. Why not try and make a container similar to the one used by Hall *et al.* (2010) and then role-play the study, taking turns to play the part of the two different researchers and the customers? You could write all the different roles onto pieces of paper and randomly choose which part you will play. Remember, customers fell into four groups: those who showed choice blindness and three different types of detector. If you intend to taste/smell real teas and jams, remember to check whether anyone in your class has an allergy to any of the ingredients.

▶ TEST YOURSELF

1. The key study by Hall *et al.* (2010) investigated choice blindness in consumers who tasted two different jams and said which one they preferred. Describe the container in which the jams were presented. [2]
2. Outline one finding from Hall *et al.* (2010) relating to sensory change detection. [2]
3. a Describe the study by Hall *et al.* (2010) on choice blindness when tasting food items. [6]
   b Evaluate this study by Hall *et al.* (2010), including a discussion about experiments. [10]
4. State the operationalised dependent variable in the study by Hall *et al.* (2010). [2]
5. Explain one strength and one weakness relating to the reliability of the study by Hall *et al.* (2010). [4]
6. Explain one way in which Hall *et al.* (2010) could have checked whether their findings were reliable. [2]

Consumer memory for advertising

Think!

What is the difference between **retroactive** and **proactive interference**?

Think!

Have you ever gone shopping for a particular item that you saw advertised some time ago in your local shopping centre, but when you get there, you cannot remember which brand it was because the online searches you have done for similar items have become confused with your earlier memory? What type of memory interference are you experiencing?

KEY TERMS

retroactive interference
proactive interference
explicit memory
implicit memory
interference theory

Think!

Burke and Srull (1988) measured **explicit memory** to identify mistakes in consumer memory for advertising. How might they have changed their study to measure consumer **implicit memory**?

Have you ever bought a can of drink or another product and found that it is not what you expected? Research has shown that competitive advertising can interfere with our memory of what we bought last time and cause us to confuse it with another similar-looking product of the same type. Think of examples of companies designing their product to look very similar to that of a brand leader. How might the brand leader react to this?

▲ Figure 7.36

METHODOLOGY

experiments

interviews

reliability

For advertising to be memorable, consumers need to understand and perceive it to have value and meaning for them. As you will learn when you look at advertising in more detail, memory for advertising, or for anything else, can be divided into two types: explicit memory, which refers to information we are conscious of, and implicit memory, which refers to information we are not consciously aware of. Both types of memory are important to advertisers, but particularly implicit memory, as if an advertisement's message is remembered by us implicitly, we are unlikely to resist it. For example, if we see a certain chocolate bar on the supermarket shelf, we may pick it up and put it in our basket without much thought and certainly without recalling a billboard advertisement for the chocolate that we passed hours before, suggesting we deserve a treat!

However, memory can be unreliable. Memory is an active, constructive process and language and images from advertising can become mixed with the consumer's own experiences to give a false picture. **Interference theory** explains this: forgetting occurs because the retrieval of certain memories from the long-term memory store interferes with the retrieval of other items. Generally speaking, the interference causes slower learning and poorer memory (Roediger and Karpicke, 2006). They become tangled and compete for attention. This can happen through retroactive interference or proactive interference.

Retroactive interference and consumer memory

Retroactive interference refers to forgetting a previously remembered event or skill because you have learned a new skill or about a new event. New memories interfere with old memories. The more similar the new memories are to the old memories, then the more likely they are to interfere with them. An example is remembering your new postcode when you move to a new house, but then forgetting the old postcode when you want to ask to have your letters forwarded from your old address.

When applied to consumer memory, this means that brand information learned in the past can become forgotten because of newly learned facts about another brand or a different product in the same brand.

Proactive interference and consumer memory

Proactive interference is the opposite of retroactive interference; you struggle with learning a new skill or remembering a new event because your previous strong memory from the past interferes. For example, you may learn to drive in the UK, but then need to drive a rental car in France. You have to transfer your skills learned when driving on the left-hand side of the road, in a driver's seat positioned on the right-hand side of the car, to driving on the right-hand side of the road, sitting in the driver's seat on the left-hand side of the car. Your previous driving memories compete and interfere with your new ones.

As might be expected, when applied to consumer memory, this means that new brand information learned recently from either a new brand or from another product of the same brand competes and interferes with brand information from the past.

Burke and Srull (1988) developed a series of experiments to test their hypotheses about this competitive interference and consumer memory for advertising.

Focus on: Burke and Srull (1988)

▶ AIM

To investigate the retroactive and proactive effects of competitive advertising.

▶ METHODOLOGY

Experiment 1: retroactive effects

In experiment 1, 144 psychology students were split randomly into six groups of 24. They were told that they would see a number of magazine advertisements on a computer screen. Three groups were told they were to rate how likely they would be to buy each of the products. The other three groups were told that they should rate the interest value of each of the advertisements.

Twelve one-page, text-only (no pictures) advertisements were used, with the advertisement headline and content. The researchers identified three out of the twelve as target advertisements that were to be tested for recall later. The position of these three was counterbalanced within the groups to reduce any possible order effect; however, they were all presented *early* in the sequence. A target advertisement could also appear in the following context:
- a varied product context, with other advertisements promoting different brands in different types of product
- a same product context, with a different advertisement promoting a different brand in the same product type
- a same brand context, with a second advertisement promoting the same brand in the same product class, but representing a different model.

After a short distraction task, each participant was given a surprise recall test. They each had two minutes to recall each of the three target advertisements after being prompted with the brand name, model and product type name (such as 'garden machinery' or 'cleaning products'). The order of recall was randomised for each subject, tape recorded and later analysed by a naïve researcher (who did not know to which group participants had been allocated).

Experiment 2: proactive effects

The procedure was identical to that in experiment 1, except that this time the target advertisements were presented *late* in the sequence of twelve advertisements.

▶ RESULTS

Experiment 1

Participants remembered almost twice as much information if they reviewed the target advertisements with the intention of rating the brands on purchase likelihood rather than interest. Levels of recall were best in the varied product context but much worse in the same product or same brand context, and worst of all when the targeted advertisement had appeared very early in the sequence, rather than somewhat later. However, this difference was much greater for those who rated the advertised brands on interest. Rating brands on likelihood of buying the product increased accurate retrieval of the advertisement details.

Experiment 2

Similarly to experiment 1, participants remembered more accurately when the target advertisements were in the varied product context and less well when they were in the same product or same brand context. However, this time the purpose of the review (for buying or for general interest) was not as relevant. Although participants who rated the product on their likelihood of buying it did remember better than those who rated it on interest, the difference was small.

▶ CONCLUSION

Experiment 1 demonstrated that retroactive interference affected recall of target advertisements, although this was decreased when participants were rating the advertisements on their likelihood of buying the product. Experiment 2 demonstrated that proactive interference affected recall of target advertisements, whether participants were rating the advertisements on interest or on likelihood of purchase.

Evaluating Burke and Srull (1988)

One strength is that many variables in the **experiments** were well controlled. For example, all participants had the same amount of time to recall the advertisements (two minutes); there was random allocation to groups; the recall of each participant was recorded and rated by researchers who did not know to which group the participant had been assigned; and position of target advertisements and of competitive advertisements was standardised and counterbalanced. These design features mean that the study can be easily replicated to check for the reliability of the findings.

A weakness is that in each experiment the advertisements were displayed on a computer. This research study was conducted two years before the world wide web and so the participants would have been unused to seeing advertisements on screen. Therefore, the materials lacked face validity and the results lack ecological validity, as we cannot assume they represent a real-life situation.

Another strength is that the individual motivation of the consumer is shown to have a mediating effect on their memory for a particular brand, especially in the case of retrospective interference. So this adds an individual explanation for what is usually seen as an effect of situational factors, namely the context in which the target brand is shown. This shows that, in the case of retrospective interference in particular, remembering or forgetting the target brand is an interaction of individual and situational factors.

A final weakness is that we know that advertising and marketing strategies often operate through implicit memory. Yet these experiments measured explicit memory and explicit interest in buying. It may be that when the participants are actually faced with the product in the target advertisements, their implicit memories will prompt them to buy, whereas they could not explicitly retrieve accurate information about the advertisement under experimental conditions. This suggests that the findings may lack validity, suggesting that advertising may affect consumers differently in the real world.

Memory for online advertisements may be an interaction of individual and situational factors. When you go online and look at advertisements for products, are you often just browsing or are you always intending to buy? Do you find that you have a better memory for what you see if you have a serious intent to buy rather than when you are just looking through products? How does this link to Burke and Srull's (1988) research?

▲ Figure 7.37

Determinism versus free will

The research in this section suggests that perception and memory determine our choices, even when we feel as if we are exercising our free will. For example, Shleifer (2012) shows how unhealthy consumer behaviour can be traced to the representativeness heuristic that encourages us to expect trends to continue, to ignore rational explanations and focus instead on our memories,

our attention and our perception. We feel healthy, even though we smoke, and we expect this to continue into our older age, whereas rational System 2 thinking would tell us that it cannot. Even when we appear to choose freely, it is against a backdrop of choice blindness, competitive advertising and memory interference that individually and together mean that free will has a very small part to play in consumer choice.

LEARNING LINK

At AS Level, you learned about the study by Pozzulo *et al.* (line-ups) in the cognitive approach, where child witnesses had to pick out targets from line-ups where the target was either present or absent. You learned that children's memories can be affected by both cognitive and social factors. If you redesigned the Burke and Srull study using child participants, do you think the results would be any different? Can you think of anything you would need to do differently if you used children instead of adults as the participants?

STUDY TIP

Write some Consumer Psychology study cards, with the key idea on one side and a study and/or key study on the other. For example, for this topic, you would have 'Consumer memory interference and advertising' on one side of the card and 'Burke and Srull (1988)' on the other. You can add to these as you go through the Consumer Psychology unit, and maybe colour-code them for each section. They will be a useful revision tool.

TEST YOURSELF

1   Ellie is organising an online advertising campaign to promote several different brands of make-up for different companies. The campaign will include 12 separate advertisements, each for a different product.
    a   Explain how proactive interference might affect the sales of the 12 products. [2]
    b   Suggest one way Ellie could reduce the effect of memory interference in the organisation of her campaign. [2]
2   a   Outline what is meant by individual and situational explanations. [2]
    b   Give one example of how research into consumer memory for advertising provides a situational explanation for consumer behaviour. [2]
3   a   Describe what psychologists have discovered about interference and consumer memory. [6]
    b   Evaluate what psychologists have discovered about interference and consumer memory, including a discussion about reliability. [10]
4   Research into consumer memory for advertising often uses the experimental method. Suggest another way that consumer memory for advertising could be studied apart from a laboratory experiment. [2]
5   Explain one strength and one weakness of the experimental method for investigating consumer memory for advertising. [4]
6   Give two features of advertisements that a psychologist might need to consider when selecting suitable examples to use in an experiment on interference and consumer memory. [2]

7.4 The product

7.4.1 Packaging and positioning of a product

KEY TERMS

central gaze cascade effect

horizontal centrality

eye-tracking

expectation disconfirmation

fixation

saccade

gaze cascade

planogram

METHODOLOGY

generalisations from findings

objective and subjective data

validity

Think!

During a visual search, when does the **central gaze cascade effect** take place: the beginning, the middle or the end?

Think!

Mr Bucket owns a sweet shop. A customer has asked him to make some gifts to give to the guests at her wedding. He has some ribbons and paper flowers that he could use to trim the gifts but cannot decide whether to use transparent plastic or brown paper bags. What advice would you give Mr Bucket based on the gift-wrapping research?

Think!

You want to know how position affects sales of a popular canned drink. How could you test **horizontal centrality** using a data-gathering technique other than **eye-tracking**?

Figure 7.38 shows the Japanese art of *furoshiki*, where gifts are wrapped in fabric and trimmed with natural products. The picture also shows some other items – do you think the cookies and plants are gifts? Do gifts need to be wrapped to be appreciated?

▲ Figure 7.38

Gift wrapping

Why are gifts wrapped?

Gifts have been wrapped for centuries using both fabric and paper, and in both cases, the wrappings have symbolic meanings. Paper was first used in the second century BC in Ancient China, where the cultural tradition of gift-giving (送禮Sònglǐ) is an important way of showing respect, maintaining relationships and promoting social harmony. Gifts are typically wrapped in red and gold paper as these colours symbolise good fortune and happiness. In Korean culture, gifts are wrapped in colourful fabric squares called a *bojagi*. Hiding the identity of an object by wrapping is associated with protection, not just of the object but also of the recipient. Likewise, in Japan, the ancient art of *furoshiki* involves fabric wrappings, a practice that is gaining popularity in the West due to its sustainability.

Today, many people enjoy wrapping gifts in innovative and creative ways, using online blogs and tutorials to make their gifts look stylish, pretty or exciting. Research suggests that this is a good investment as the same gift receives greater approval when wrapped than when unwrapped and high-quality wrapping is preferred to plain or no wrapping (Howard, 1992).

It seems that the simple act of wrapping can turn any object into a gift and people tend to wrap gifts because it is a social norm to do so – people expect gifts to be wrapped (Porublev *et al.*, 2009). Wrapping also creates a sense of curiosity and anticipation: bright paper, ribbons and bows can trigger the retrieval of past happy memories. This is called cue-dependent memory. Happy memories create a positive mood that transfers to the gift inside the wrapping (Howard, 1992) and this suggests that people wrap presents to increase liking for the gift.

Types of wrapping

In the Western world, gifts were typically wrapped in tissue or brown paper and secured with strings and sealing wax until the early twentieth century, when decorative paper was popularised by brothers Joyce and Rollie Hall, the founders of the multibillion-dollar business Hallmark. In 1917, their Kansas store is said to have run out of tissue paper and the brothers encouraged shoppers to use decorative envelope lining paper instead. This trend caught on and today the global gift wrap industry, including paper, bags, boxes and trimmings, is worth around US$19 billion (Statista, 2021).

Beliefs and expectations

Patrick *et al.* (2017) showed participants a blanket and asked them to rate how expensive they thought it was. Blankets that were taken out of an opaque box tied shut with a ribbon were believed to be more expensive than those in similar boxes but with a transparent window. They found that this assumption was mediated by the belief that the items in opaque boxes were more likely to be in pristine (perfect) condition. Therefore, givers may similarly believe that unveiling gifts (i.e. taking them out of wrappings, boxes and bags) makes gifts seem higher quality, and more likely to gain approval from the recipient.

While research supports the importance of wrapping, sloppily wrapped gifts may sometimes be appreciated more than neatly wrapped. Rixom *et al.* (2019) found that students reported more favourable attitudes towards a gift of a basketball team mug when it was sloppily wrapped than when it was neatly wrapped. Even mugs for basketball teams that they did not like (undesirable gifts) were rated more favourably when presented in untidy wrappings. Further analysis showed that this effect was mediated by **expectation disconfirmation**, meaning sloppily wrapped presents created lower expectations in the recipient; when unwrapped, the gifts that exceeded expectation were, therefore, liked more – that is, the recipients were pleasantly surprised.

Look at the gifts in Figure 7.39. Are they sloppily or neatly wrapped? Which gift would be appreciated more by a friend and which by an acquaintance? Can you explain why, with reference to expectation disconfirmation?

▲ Figure 7.39

Interestingly, Rixom *et al.* (2019) also found that when gifts are believed to have been given by an acquaintance (rather than a friend), the opposite effect was revealed; recipients preferred gifts in neater wrappings. When the giver is an acquaintance, recipients perceive neatness as a measure of the importance of the relationship between themselves and the gift-giver; the neater the wrapping, the more important the relationship is perceived, and this positivity is reflected in the attitudes shown towards the gift (see Figure 7.40).

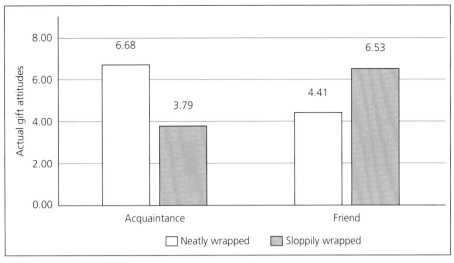

▲ Figure 7.40 Bar chart showing the effect of the neatness of wrapping on attitudes towards gifts presented by a friend versus an acquaintance

> How would you describe the difference between sloppily and neatly wrapped gifts for acquaintances?

Evaluation of gift wrapping research

Cultural differences in gift wrapping may stem from nurture (e.g. fabric versus paper, decorative versus plain paper), but the universal preference for wrapped versus unwrapped gifts suggests a biological explanation. This is supported by research from the animal kingdom, such as Trillo *et al.* (2014), who found that female spiders were more likely to mate with a male who brought her prey tightly wrapped in silk (white) than with a male who brought an unwrapped or poorly wrapped 'gift' (black/grey colour). The colour of the wrapping was associated with the condition of the male spider, with white gifts suggesting a strong, healthy potential mate and darker gifts suggesting a weaker, less healthy individual. This research suggests that gift wrapping in humans may also be linked to sexual selection, in romantic partners at least.

A weakness of much of the research into human gift-giving is that much of it has been experimental, meaning that it lacks ecological validity. For example, in Rixom *et al.* (2019), all participants were given a coffee mug that had not been chosen specifically for them and the wrappings were also generic (see Figure 7.40) and not adapted to the preferences of each individual. This suggests that results may not reflect attitudes towards sloppily wrapped gifts in the real world, where the giver is usually someone known to us personally and the gift and packaging is based on our knowledge of the recipient.

Attention and shelf position

Consumers are regularly presented with rows of products to choose from, and research consistently shows that they are more likely to choose options from the middle of the selection. For example, Christenfeld (1995) found that the product in the middle of a supermarket shelf was preferred 71 per cent of the time. This effect is known as horizontal centrality.

The use of eye-tracking

On page 403, we discussed the use of eye-tracking technology as a way of collecting objective data in Consumer Psychology. This data-gathering technique has also been used to investigate visual attention and horizontal centrality, specifically how consumers search a horizontal display and make choices. Researchers can record the location and duration (in milliseconds) of **fixations** (brief moments when the eye is stable) and **saccades** (eye movements between fixations) to create digital representations of the way an individual scans a shelf of products, for example. (See Figure 7.42 on page 457, where the longest fixations are shown in warm colours, e.g. reds and oranges, and the briefer fixations in colder colours, e.g. blues/greens.)

Studies using this technology suggest that visual attention may be directed more towards brands at the centre of a display, thus explaining horizontal centrality (Chandon *et al.*,

2007). An alternative explanation is that consumer choices are unrelated to visual attention and have more to do with belief that products displayed centre-stage (i.e. in the middle) are popular and that popularity is associated with quality (Valenzuela and Raghubir, 2009).

The central gaze cascade effect

The term 'central fixation bias' describes the tendency to fixate on the centre of a visual display in an effort to extract as much information as possible (Tatler, 2007). In Consumer Psychology, the term **gaze cascade** has been used to describe typical eye movements moments before a product is selected; the more we fixate on an item, the more we like it and the more we like an item, the more likely we are to look at it. Central fixation bias and gaze cascade combine to create the central gaze cascade effect – the tendency to fixate for longer on items in the middle of a horizontal arrangement during the final seconds before a choice is made. The additional visual attention these items receive means we are more likely to purchase these items.

Focus on: Atalay *et al.* (2012)

> ## AIM
> ....
> Atalay *et al.* (2012) aimed to investigate the effect of horizontal centrality on choice likelihood and how this effect is linked to increased visual attention and/or inferences.

> ## METHODOLOGY
> ....
> Sixty-seven students were asked to select one product from each of two **planograms** shown on a computer screen. Planograms are diagrams used in the retail industry. They provide detailed plans of how stock should be arranged and can relate to single shelves, whole aisles or the entire shop floor.
>
> The planograms in this study showed three products from three fictitious brands of vitamin supplements and meal replacement bars. Products were organised into three columns, one per brand (see Figure 7.41). The students viewed the planograms one at a time for as long as they needed before choosing one of the products.

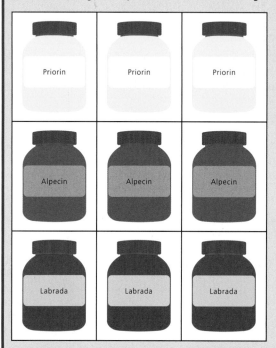

▲ Figure 7.41 Example of a 3 x 3 planogram, similar to the ones used in Atalay *et al.* (2012)

An eye-tracker monitored gaze location and duration while examining the planograms. After indicating their preferred products, all participants completed a questionnaire to measure their attitudes towards the different brands.

▶ RESULTS

Participants took an average of 35 seconds to choose their preferred vitamin supplement and meal replacement bar. During this time, the horizontally central brands received more visual attention than those on the left or right-hand side. They received more fixations and fixation lasted longer than fixations on other products. Participants fixated more on the centre of the planogram in the first 0.5 seconds of each condition and increasingly fixated on the centrally positioned products in the final five seconds before making their decision. Products in the centre of the planogram were selected 18 per cent more often than those at the sides for both meal replacement bars and vitamin supplements. There was no difference in choice frequency of products positioned to the left or the right of centre.

▶ CONCLUSION

Horizontal centrality, central fixation bias and the central gaze cascade effect were all supported, suggesting that brands positioned in the centre of the shelf receive more visual attention, making them more likely to be selected.

Evaluating Atalay *et al.* (2012)

A strength of Atalay *et al.* (2012) is the use of eye-tracking, which provides data that is more **objective** and reliable. For example, the researchers counted the number and duration of fixations on left, right and centrally positioned products in the first and last five seconds of each trial to see whether fixations at the beginning or the end of the visual search were better predictors of product choice. This is important as self-reported data on purchase intentions can be invalid, as consumers are unable to explain their cognitive processes that occur below the level of conscious awareness. Eye-tracking data, therefore, provides access to sensory data that could not be collected in any other way.

ISSUES AND DEBATES

Determinism versus free will

A weakness of experimental research into the effects of shelf position is that it is overly deterministic. Examining a planogram of fictitious products is not like browsing genuine products in a real or online shop, where decisions are affected by prior knowledge of the products from personal recommendations and advertising, not to mention distractions of other shoppers entering the visual field and the pressure of time. Lack of mundane realism means the findings may not generalise to real-world shopping behaviour where free will may override unconscious biases towards centrally positioned products.

 Eye-tracking technology can provide a 'heat map' style representation of the visual field, showing the areas that attract the most visual attention. Does Figure 7.42 support the findings of Atalay *et al.* (2012) or not?

▲ Figure 7.42

▶ **LEARNING LINK**
....

At AS Level, you learned about Dement and Kleitman's study (sleep and dreaming). Like Atalay, Dement and Kleitman also used an objective measure to capture information about processing that happens below the surface of conscious awareness. They studied dreaming using an EEG to measure and record the duration of different types of brain waves, whereas Atalay used eye-tracking to measure visual attention and the duration of fixations. Can you think of any other ways that the methodology of these two studies is similar or different? Comparing studies, theories and concepts helps to process information at a deeper level, meaning it should be easier to recall in the future.

STUDY TIP

Atalay *et al.* (2012) used planograms in their experiment. To understand more about how retailers and researchers use planograms, you could create one of your own for a product or store of your choosing, such as make-up, toys or sports equipment. The planogram should give details such as how much space (facings) will be allocated to each product, where the products will be located in relation to each other and how many different brands will be featured. There are many useful images and videos online to learn more about planograms.

▶ **TEST YOURSELF**
....

1   Sabrina works at Mr Bucket's sweet shop. He has bought many heart-shaped lollies for Valentine's Day. The big day is nearly here but there are a many lollies left. Based on your knowledge of packaging and positioning of products, suggest two ways to help Sabrina to sell all of Mr Bucket's lollies.   [4]

2   Explain two ways that gift wrapping can affect a recipient's beliefs about either the giver or the gift itself.   [2]

3   a   Describe what psychologists have discovered about attention and shelf position.   [6]

    b   Evaluate what psychologists have discovered about attention and shelf position.   [10]

4   Eye-tracking is often used by consumer psychologists. Compare the use of self-report and eye-tracking as ways of gathering data on the effect of shelf position and visual attention.   [4]

5   Shabnam and Aki are discussing how to collect some data on the beliefs about the best way to wrap a present for your employer. Shabnam thinks it is best to ask closed questions using rating scales, but Aki thinks it is better to ask open questions. Explain whether you agree more with Shabnam or Aki.   [4]

6   Vanessa's participants have ten minutes to explore a crowded shoe store. Later, she shows them photographs of six pairs of shoes and asks them to point out where they were located on a series of planograms representing the layout of the shoe shop and all the shoes.

    a   Suggest two features of a shoe shop planogram.   [2]

    b   Vanessa thinks shelf position will affect the accuracy of her participants' recall. Write a suitable directional hypothesis for Vanessa's study.   [2]

Key study: Food package design and taste perceptions – Becker *et al.* (2011)

Think!

Was **design sensitivity** an independent or a dependent variable in this study? How was it operationalised?

Think!

Penelope's usual hairspray comes in a pale blue can with a pattern of wavy lines. Yesterday she bought a new limited edition version for the brand's 50th anniversary; the can is bright pink and is covered in gold and silver stars. Penelope thinks the hairspray smells stronger and nicer than usual. Could Penelope be experiencing **cross-modal correspondence**? Why might this be?

Think!

The customers in this study had to complete multiple items where they indicated their agreement with a statement on a seven-point rating scale. How many reasons can you think of that support the argument that data collected in this way is not valid?

KEY TERMS

design sensitivity

cross-modal correspondence

colour saturation

processing fluency

congruency (congruent versus incongruent)

shape angularity

variants

manipulation check

potency

Introducing Thomas van Rompay

Second author on Becker *et al.* (2011), Thomas van Rompay supervised Liza Becker's Master's thesis and is an Associate Professor at the Department of Communication Science at the University of Twente (UT) in the Netherlands. His research explores how meaning and emotion are communicated through design, including multi-sensory experiences associated with packaging.

▲ Figure 7.43 Thomas van Rompay

METHODOLOGY

validity

generalisations

objective versus subjective data

Context

Consumers often choose food and drink products based on their appearance (Fenko *et al.*, 2010). This is especially true for products that are new to the consumer, when brand or product knowledge is limited or when they are bombarded with information and need to make a quick decision. Under these circumstances, aspects of the packaging including colour, shape and materials all provide important visual cues that shape our overall impression and lead to certain expectations of the product, such as the quality, healthiness and/or taste.

Cross-modal correspondence

Interestingly, research suggests that packaging can even modify the way a consumer experiences the taste of a product. For example, when popular soda brand *7Up* brightened the green colour of their cans by adding more yellow, consumers experienced the drink as more lemony, even though the drink itself had not been altered (Hine, 1995). This phenomenon is called cross-modal correspondence, meaning that when we experience a greater intensity in one sensory modality, this often transfers to other senses, which we also experience more intensely.

Packaging shape and colour

Research also shows that packaging shape and colour can influence product perception. For example, Berlyne (1976) suggests that angular shapes (with sharp edges/corners) are associated with energy, toughness and strength, whereas rounded shapes are associated with approachability, friendliness and harmony. As with the *7Up* study above, changing the packaging from white to orange led consumers to expect a juice drink to be sweeter and this expectation affected the way they experienced the drink (Deliza and MacFie, 2001). The following study by Becker *et al.* (2011) tests the idea that colour saturation (meaning intensity/brightness) affects taste perception – that is, the more saturated the colour, the more intense the flavour.

Processing fluency and congruence

Processing fluency refers to how easy or difficult it is to extract information from a stimulus and to understand its meaning. Congruence refers to the extent to which two stimuli 'go together' or match. The terms congruent and incongruent can, therefore, be used to describe stimuli that match or do not match, respectively. With regards to packaging, incongruent features, such as high saturation colours (associated with power and intensity) and a rounded shape (associated with harmony and approachability), may confuse the consumer (low processing fluency). The product's identity will be ambiguous and the lack of clarity will leave the consumer with negative affect (emotion). When shape and colour saturation are congruent (e.g. rounded shape and low saturation), the consumer will think and feel more positively about the product due to higher processing fluency.

Individual differences: design sensitivity

In order to experience cross-modal correspondence or for processing fluency to be affected by incongruent design elements, people must attend to the features of the packaging, including shape and colour, in the first place. Research has shown that people with a design background are more likely to experience such effects (Smets and Overbeeke, 1995).

▶ AIMS AND HYPOTHESES

Becker *et al.* aimed to investigate the extent to which the colour and shape of a product's packaging affect the taste of the product.

They hypothesised that yoghurts packaged in:
● angular pots will have a stronger flavour than yoghurts presented in rounded pots
● a high colour-saturation pot will have a stronger flavour than yoghurts presented in a low colour-saturation pot.

They also hypothesised that:
● overall attitudes towards the yoghurt will be more positive for pots with shape–colour congruence, such as angular shape and high colour saturation, than pots with shape–colour incongruence, such as angular shape and low saturated colour
● consumers with greater design sensitivity will experience more intense effects of colour and shape of packaging on taste intensity than those who are indifferent to design features.

METHODOLOGY

This was a field experiment in a large German supermarket. There were three independent variables: the colour saturation of the yoghurt pot (high versus low), the **shape angularity** of the pot (angular versus rounded) and the design sensitivity of the participants (high versus low). This was measured using a psychometric test. Participants whose scores were above the median were classed as 'high design sensitivity' and those whose scores were below the median were classed as 'low design sensitivity'. Please see page 462 for more information about this questionnaire.

Sample

The participants in the main study were an opportunity sample of 151 German supermarket customers (77 female, 74 male; mean age 31). They were approached individually in the entrance of the shop and asked if they would like to take part in 'a taste test' for a new brand of yoghurt.

PROCEDURE

The pre-test

Twenty participants rated the pairs of pots in Figure 7.44 on 12 items (called 'The Potency Scale'). This included words such as impressive, sour and pure.

The pair of pots that differed the most from each other (C) was chosen for the design of the pots in the main study. Similarly, the researchers presented two pairs of pots that varied from each other in terms of hue, saturation and brightness. Participants, again, completed The Potency Scale for these pairs and the pair that differed the most was selected. The researchers used the findings of the pre-test to design the four pots (referred to as **variants**) in Figure 7.45.

The main study: at the supermarket

Participants who agreed to take part in the taste test viewed a 20-second movie of one of the four packaging variants (see Figure 7.55) rotating through 360°. After tasting a sample of lemon yoghurt (all samples were the same), they then completed a computer questionnaire (see Table 7.22).

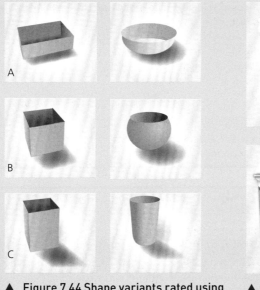

▲ Figure 7.44 Shape variants rated using the Potency Scale in the pre-test

▲ Figure 7.45 Yoghurt pot variants created from the findings of the pre-test; which pots would be considered shape/colour congruent and which would be shape/colour incongruent according to Becker *et al.* (2011)?

▼ Table 7.22 Dependent variables measured through a self-report questionnaire completed after tasting the yoghurt

	Section of questionnaire	Items	Response format	Analysis
Items relating to the product	Taste intensity evaluation	Rated the yoghurt's taste as: • sharp • bitter • mild (reverse scored).	Items were rated on seven-point scales, 1: not at all, to 7: very much so.	Taste intensity and product evaluation scores were calculated by averaging the three items; the higher the score, the more intense the flavour (taste intensity) and the more favourable the attitude (product evaluation).
	Product evaluation	Rated the product as: • superior • eye-catching • high-quality.		
	Price expectation	Suggested price for the new yoghurt when introduced into the supermarket	Eurocents	n/a
Additional item	**Manipulation check**: to check that differences in the **potency** of the packaging (colour and shape) had been perceived.	Single item: 'This product package strikes me as potent.'	Items were rated on seven-point scales, 1: not at all, to 7: very much so.	Higher average scores were expected for the high colour saturation, angular variants and lower average scores for the low colour saturation, rounded variants.

Measurement of design sensitivity

This was measured using 'The Individual Differences in the Centrality of Visual Product Aesthetics' scale (*Bloch et al., 2003*). This comprised eleven items divided into three categories:

● recognising design (acumen)
● importance of design (value)
● reaction to design (response).

Sample item: 'Sometimes the way a product looks seems to reach out and grab me.'

Items were rated on seven-point scales, 1: not at all, to 7: very much so. Sensitivity to design score was calculated by averaging the 11 items; the higher the score, the more sensitive to design.

▶ RESULTS

Manipulation check

Angular packaging was perceived as significantly more potent than rounded but there was no significant difference in perceived potency between high (100 per cent) and low (50 per cent) colour saturation packaging, except for participants with high sensitivity to design. These participants did perceive high colour saturation variants as more potent than the low colour saturation variants.

Taste evaluation

There was no difference in taste intensity between angular and rounded packaging or high and low colour saturation packaging. However, there was a significant interaction between the shape of packaging and taste intensity in the high sensitivity to design group – that is, those who were sensitive to design experienced the taste of the yoghurt as significantly more intense when the product was displayed in an angular pot compared with a rounded pot. Taste intensity was unaffected by packaging shape or colour in the low sensitivity to design group.

Product evaluation

The angular pots were rated more positively and the suggested price was higher than the rounded pots. The average suggested price was also marginally higher for the low (50 per cent) colour saturation pots than the high (100 per cent) colour saturation pots, although there was no significant difference in attitudes towards the product when displayed in high versus low colour saturation packaging.

Potency: a mediating factor affecting suggested price

Further analysis revealed that participants gave a higher average suggested price for the angular pots than the rounded pots because angularity is associated with potency – products that are perceived to be stronger and/or more impressive (higher potency) are perceived to be more expensive; therefore, the suggested price of products in angular pots is higher.

CONCLUSIONS

Angular product packaging can inspire a more intense taste experience in people who are sensitive to design features of packaging and this effect is mediated by the perception of greater product potency. This provides support for cross-modal correspondence but only for those who pay greater attention to packaging design. Contrary to previous research, colour saturation does not always lead to a more intense taste experience,

even in people who are sensitive to design. In fact, high colour saturation can have a negative impact through its association with cheapness and potentially lower quality. The study did not support the suggestion that shape–colour incongruence will lead to poorer product evaluation; however, this may have been due to the colour difference being too subtle.

 ## Methodological strengths and weaknesses

A strength of this study was the careful design of materials, which increased the overall **validity** of the findings. For example, the pre-test ensured that the packaging variants in the main study were clearly different from one another in terms of perceived potency and provided results that were in line with previous research, such as the more angular, the more potent. This was a strength as it meant that if there is any association between visual elements of packaging design and taste perception, they should be observable in the study.

This said, the difference in colour saturation between the high and low conditions (100 per cent versus 50 per cent) may have been too subtle to influence the customers' taste perception and attitudes. This is a weakness as it means that the researchers may have rejected their hypotheses about colour saturation and shape–colour congruency due to a problem with the materials and not because this variable genuinely does not affect consumers. This means that some of the findings relating to colour saturation may not be valid.

A weakness is that Becker *et al.* (2011) only examined cross-modal correspondence for one single product: lemon yoghurt, which has a sour flavour. The findings may not generalise to other products which are associated with different taste elements, such as salty, bitter or umami. Previous research suggests packaging colour can affect the perception of sweetness of fruit juice (Deliza and MacFie, 2001) and intensity of the lemon flavour of *7Up* (Hine, 1995), but the negative findings of this study regarding colour saturation and taste perception may only apply to sour tastes. Therefore, the study needs to be replicated with other tastes before concluding that colour is not such a strong cue as shape in modifying consumer experiences and attitudes.

A final weakness is that this study was conducted only on one cultural group, supermarket shoppers in Germany, and this means the findings may not be **generalisable** to people from alternative cultures with differing diets and preferences. For example, Moskowitz *et al*. (1975) found that Indian labourers (but not wealthier Indian medical students) had a preference for highly sour/bitter tastes shaped by a diet high in tamarind, a cheap and readily available sour fruit. This is just one example of the many cultural differences in taste perception, suggesting that the effects of packaging on taste perception may vary between cultural groups, especially for those groups who are less familiar with packaging and more accustomed to eating fresh produce.

 ## Ethics

Participants were deceived in this study as they were asked to take part in a taste test for a new brand of yoghurt, which they believed would be introduced to the supermarket range. They were not told that all participants were tasting the same yoghurt but being exposed to different packaging variants. They were also told that the questionnaire about design sensitivity was for customer lifestyle profiling purposes. This deception was necessary to reduce demand characteristics as participants may have consciously altered their response had they known the researchers were interested in the effect of design sensitivity on product evaluation and taste perception. As the cost to the participants is relatively low (e.g. just a few minutes of their time and the opportunity to try some yoghurt), this deception can be seen as justified, meaning that the study is ethically acceptable.

 ## Application to everyday life

This research is immediately applicable to graphic designers specialising in packaging, specifically in the food and drink industry. Evidence-based design decisions may be helpful when pitching new ideas to clients. If a client can understand the reasoning behind a certain design, they may be more likely to accept the designer's suggestions. For example, a designer may choose to use less saturated colours to make the product seem more expensive and higher quality. However, the client may be concerned that the product will not stand out against rival brands. If the designer is able to explain the findings of Becker *et al*. (2011), they may be able to persuade their client to make a decision that will result in more favourable customer feedback and improved sales.

ISSUES AND DEBATES

Reductionism versus holism

The findings of Becker *et al*. (2011) demonstrate how a reductionist approach can be helpful in gaining a deeper understanding of how our senses interact when perceiving a new product. Previous research had shown that manipulating packaging colour can affect taste perception – for example, juice in orange packaging was perceived as sweeter than the same juice in white packaging (Deliza and MacFie, 2001). Instead of manipulating the actual colour, Becker *et al*. (2011) manipulated a single element of one colour (saturation), finding that this more subtle change did not result in changes in taste perception. Reducing the complex sense of colour perception into its individual elements (e.g. saturation) and studying them individually can help researchers to gradually reveal which elements of product design result in the greatest impact on consumers in a way that a more holistic approach could not.

REFLECTION

- What improvements could you make to Becker *et al*.'s (2011) procedure and how do you think your changes might affect the findings?
- People often eat yoghurts directly from the pot, meaning the effects of packaging on taste may be different for products where the packaging is not present at the time of consumption; how could you test this idea?

LEARNING LINK

You may remember learning about how gustatory and auditory input can influence each other. For example, on page 379, it was noted that areas of the brain that usually process smell were activated by sound (Wesson and Wilson, 2010) and that background noise increased liking for sweet but not salty foods (Ferber and Cabanac, 1987). In these studies, sensory stimuli were presented at the same time but, in Becker *et al.* (2011), the visual cues (colour and shape of packaging) were presented on a laptop before being asked to rate the taste of the yoghurt. The effects are believed to be linked to expectations that are created when we access information from long-term memory to make judgements about how the product will taste. In cognitive psychology, this is known as top-down processing. How is the research by Becker *et al.* (2011) similar to the research in the previous section on gift wrapping? Think about expectations and cue-dependent memory.

STUDY TIP

A good way to remember the procedure of this study would be to create your own materials, including those used in the pre-test. This could be done by cutting pictures from magazines, drawing pictures or manipulating images in a picture editing app. The full design sensitivity questionnaire is also available online in the paper by Bloch *et al.* (2003). Why not collect some data using this questionnaire and practise carrying out a median split to sort your participants into high and low design sensitivity groups? Remember, whenever collecting data, you must check with your teacher first to ensure that you are following ethical guidelines in accordance with local cultural sensitivities.

TEST YOURSELF

1   Piers is launching a new range of non-alcoholic drinks targeted at young adults. He has an important meeting with his marketing team and needs to present some ideas for the design of the bottles. Using your knowledge of Becker *et al.* (2011), suggest two ways Piers could improve consumer attitudes towards his products.   [4]

2   Describe one finding from the study by Becker *et al.* (2011) that supports cross-modal correspondence and one finding from this study that does not support cross-modal correspondence.   [4]

3   a   Describe the study by Becker *et al.* (2011) on food package design and taste perceptions.   [6]

    b   Evaluate the study by Becker *et al.* (2011) on food package design and taste perceptions, including a discussion of validity.   [10]

4   Explain why Becker *et al.* (2011) ran a pre-test before starting their main experiment.   [2]

5   Explain one strength and one weakness relating to the use of quantitative data in the study by Becker *et al.* (2011).   [4]

6   Vasu thinks the data collected by Becker *et al.* (2011) is objective, but her friend Archie thinks it is subjective. Their teacher says they are both right but for different reasons. Explain one reason why Vasu is right and one reason why Archie is right.   [4]

7.4.2 Selling the product

KEY TERMS

customer-focused

competitor-focused

unique selling point (USP)

FAB model

product-focused

B2B

> **Think!**
>
> Which of the three sales techniques described on this page involves (a) being persuasive, (b) making comparisons, and (c) seeking clarification?

> **Think!**
>
> Can you remember the last time you bought something that involved talking to a salesperson, like a phone, laptop or some other type of specialist equipment? What selling technique do you think the person used? What makes you think this?

> **Think!**
>
> Imagine you want to conduct a correlational study on selling techniques. What would your two co-variables be? Can you think of two that might show a positive correlation (as one variable increases so does the other) and two that might show a negative correlation (as one variable increases the other decreases)?

A salesperson can adopt different selling techniques to encourage customers to buy. What advice would you give this computer salesperson to help him engage with his customers and make a sale? Should he ask more questions or give more information?

▲ Figure 7.46

Sales techniques and the buyer–seller relationship

Customer-focused techniques

Customer-focused sellers view each buyer as having a unique problem that needs to be solved – for example, the customer has started making podcasts and needs a microphone but is not sure which is the best model for them. The salesperson needs to be creative and think through everything they need to know about the buyer in order to offer them the best solution. They behave like a consultant or expert, asking questions of the buyer and clarifying their understanding of the buyer's individual needs. Sellers will use active listening techniques, like paraphrasing the buyer's answers, to ensure they have fully understood the problem and make the buyer feel that the salesperson is fully focused on offering a bespoke (customised) service.

METHODOLOGY

field experiments

Effect on buyer–seller relationship

Research suggests that customer-focused selling is positively associated with repeat trade, cooperation, trust and lack of conflict between buyers and sellers (Saxe and Weitz, 1982). Furthermore, a survey of buyers found a strong and positive relationship between this sales technique and buyer–seller relationship development (Williams, 1998).

Competitor-focused techniques

Competitor-focused sellers view the buyers 'problem' as similar to other buyers. They spend less time asking questions of the buyer in favour of offering a range of solutions that have proven successful in similar situations in the past. The technique is about drawing comparisons between the buyer and similar customers. For example, door-to-door salespeople might tell you they have sold their product already to several of your neighbours, making you think that if people 'like you' think this was a good product, it will suit you well too.

Likewise, comparisons will also be made with other similar products on the market, giving information about features that help their product to stand out, such as, 'You might be able to get this from your current internet provider, but our customer service is better than all of our closest competitors.' These features are sometimes known as the **unique selling point**, or **USP**. Sellers will concentrate on the features, advantages and benefits of their product in comparison with rival brands. This is sometimes referred to as the **FAB model** of selling and is useful for distilling product information into a manageable summary that helps customers to avoid feeling overwhelmed and to make an informed decision.

This type of selling is less about collaborating to find a solution that fits the buyer and more about informing the buyers about how they are similar to other current customers and why their product is better than other available options.

Effect on buyer–seller relationship

Williams (1998) describes competitive selling as a zero-sum (win-lose) situation and suggests that the failure to share information between buyer and seller can lead to less positive future relations between buyer and seller due to decreased customer satisfaction. The competitive nature of the selling may also be reflected in a higher level of negotiation and bargaining on the part of the buyer and this can also negatively affect the development of the buyer–seller relationship (Dabholkar *et al.*, 1994).

Product-focused techniques

Product-focused salespeople will convince their buyer that they 'need' the product and then persuade them to purchase it. Few questions are asked of the buyer – this might reveal characteristics of the buyer that do not match the product! Instead, the seller will do most of the talking, offering detailed information about the product. Unlike competitive-focused selling, comparisons with other similar products are minimised and the focus is solely on the product, how it is used and how it will fit into the buyer's life.

Effect on buyer–seller relationship

Product-based selling often includes a demonstration of the product, and research suggests that buyers in both large and small organisations, with high and low levels of authority, are equally responsive to product-based selling (DelVecchio *et al.*, 2003). This suggests that a good working knowledge of the product is seen as a basic requirement by any buyer. Salespeople who ask too many questions of the buyer (customer-oriented) or draw too many comparisons with rival products may be seen as less competent or knowledgeable regarding their own product and this could be damaging to the ongoing buyer–seller relationship. Alternatively, salespeople who are perceived as knowledgeable and have expertise in their field engender trust in the buyer, a key feature of a positive and durable relationship (Parsons, 2002).

The three selling techniques described above were identified by DelVecchio *et al.* (2003). Table 7.23 summarises the main features of these techniques.

▼ Table 7.23 Types of industrial buyer–seller relationship (DelVecchio *et al.*, 2003)

Descriptions	Customer-focused	Competitive-focused	Product-focused
Salesperson views buyers' problems as:	Unique	Similar to others	Solved by existing product
Salesperson communication behaviours	Interacting	Informing	Persuading
Salesperson communication tactics	Inquiries and clarifications	Statements and comparisons	Statements and proof

Evaluating research into selling techniques

One strength of the research by DelVecchio *et al.* (2003), which identified the three selling techniques described in this section, was their focus on buyer-responsiveness rather than self-reported data from salespeople. Previous research has shown that salespeople tend to overestimate their ability to adapt to different sales situations (Brennan and Turnbull, 1999), suggesting that their self-reported data may be biased. The data gathered by DelVecchio *et al.* (2003) is, therefore, likely to be more objective and a better source of information regarding **B2B** (business to business) selling techniques.

A weakness was the very narrow demographic represented in DelVecchio *et al.*'s sample. Eighty-five per cent of the participants were male and 88 per cent were aged 42–44, with ten years' experience in their current position and 19 years in the industry. This is a weakness as the results may not reflect those of female B2B buyers or those with less experience in the industry. This is supported by Benko and Pelster (2013), who found that female B2B buyers from large organisations tend to use sales presentations as an opportunity to explore possibilities, whereas males use the presentations to narrow down their options. These differences suggest that female buyers may be more responsive to selling techniques that provide information about competitors and allow for in-depth discussion.

ISSUES AND DEBATES

Idiographic versus nomothetic

A strength of DelVecchio *et al.*'s research was their use of the nomothetic approach, which allowed the researchers to use statistical analysis to make generalisations about the usefulness of different selling techniques. For example, they concluded that B2B buyers in larger organisations and with greater authority are more responsive to customer-focused selling than those in smaller organisations with less authority. This is a strength as it means that B2B sellers can plan their pitches based on DelVecchio *et al.*'s findings – for example, planning more time for questions when selling to larger organisations (customer-focused approach) and more time for product demonstrations to smaller organisations (product-focused approach).

Cultural differences

A weakness of DelVecchio *et al.*'s research into the three selling techniques is that it does not consider the differences that might arise when buyers and sellers differ in terms of their cultural identity. For example, Pandey and Charoensukmongkol (2019) investigated the issues faced by Thai salespeople selling to Japanese and Vietnamese buyers at international trade fairs. Japanese culture is characterised by a very high intolerance of uncertainty, meaning Japanese buyers may need to know a great deal about a product before making a decision in comparison with Vietnamese buyers. This suggests that Japanese buyers may respond better to a product-focused technique than Vietnamese buyers, regardless of the size of their organisation or level of authority.

Which selling technique is being referred to in this quote from Steve Jobs?

'People don't know what they want until you show it to them'

Steve Jobs

▶ Figure 7.47 Steve Jobs, co-founder of Apple Inc.

▶ LEARNING LINK

If we ask people how they think they would behave in a given situation, what they say often differs from how they actually behave when placed in a real-world situation. This was clearly demonstrated in the studies conducted by Asch (1951) and Milgram (obedience) that you studied at AS Level. As well as learning about the social processes of conformity and obedience, these studies have also taught psychologists to be wary of the validity of self-reported data. Much of the research into selling has asked buyers to consider how they would feel or what they would think if a seller behaved in a certain way, but it is important to remember that this does not tell us how buyers would actually respond when confronted with a salesperson in real life. Can you think of any alternative research methods that might give better insight into the behaviour of sellers and buyers?

STUDY TIP

To help you to remember the similarities and differences between the three selling techniques, why not write a script for a role play/sketch for each of the techniques (you could also act it and/or film it). Each should be centred on the same product. You could then show the films/sketches to your friends and see if they can guess which technique is being represented. You could take this further by showing one film/sketch to each person and asking them to rate the salesperson on a number of different qualities/attributes and include items to measure how likely they would be to make a purchase or return to the same company in future. Remember, before collecting any data, you must always check that you have followed ethical guidelines in your planning and considered local cultural sensitivities.

▶ TEST YOURSELF

1   Derek is preparing a presentation for an important meeting with a team of buyers at a local organic grocery store, the largest organic and whole food store in the country. He will be presenting a new range of treats that his company has created from natural ingredients. His boss has advised him to use a competitor-focused selling technique. Explain two ways Derek can make sure his presentation follows his boss's advice. [4]

2   Compare any two sales technique with reference to at least one similarity and one difference. [4]

3   a   Describe two or more sales techniques. [6]
    b   Evaluate two or more sales techniques, including a discussion of cultural differences. [10]

4   Research into sales techniques often gathers quantitative data from buyers to see which techniques they prefer. Explain one weakness of using quantitative data to investigate sales techniques. [10]

5   a   Explain what is meant by determinism versus free will. [2]
    b   Explain one reason why research into sales techniques has been criticised for being deterministic. [2]

6   Explain one or more reasons why a psychologist might decide to conduct a field experiment rather than a self-report to investigate sales techniques. [4]

METHODOLOGY

field experiments

Interpersonal influence techniques

Think!

What is meant by **reframing**?

Think!

Your friend has asked you to help at their clothing stall in a large street market. She has a large number of t-shirts to get rid of and suggests that you use the disrupt-then-reframe technique to sell as many as possible. How would you do this?

Think!

Which of Cialdini's six techniques do you think is most likely to lead to a sale, and why? How could you design a study with high ecological validity to test the effectiveness of these six techniques for closing a sale?

The disrupt-then-reframe technique has been shown to increase compliance to the requests of door-to-door salespeople, but much of the research has been conducted in European countries such as the Netherlands. Do you think the disrupt-then-reframe technique would be more or less effective in the country where you live?

▶ Figure 7.48 The disrupt-then-reframe technique has been shown to increase compliance to the requests of door-to-door salespeople, but much of the research has been conducted in European countries such as the Netherlands

Interpersonal influence and compliance techniques

The term **interpersonal influence** refers to changes in an individual's behaviour or beliefs that result from communication/interaction with one or more other individuals. At AS Level, you learned about a variety of different types of social influence, including conformity (page 130), obedience (page 133), bystander apathy and good Samaritanism (page 153). In this section, you will learn about another type of social or interpersonal influence called **compliance**. Compliance involves following an order or request, like obedience; however, unlike obedience, the person giving the orders does not have any form of **authority**.

An example of compliance from Consumer Psychology would be a salesperson with a tray of tasters saying, 'Go on in, sir, have a try of this wonderful new cheese!' or a market trader telling a passer-by to 'Come on, have a feel', while offering a selection of silk scarves. Psychologists have identified and investigated numerous compliance techniques, such as the 'foot-in-the-door' technique (where a consumer complies with a small request from a seller and is then more likely to comply with a larger request, e.g. they taste the cheese and then agree to buy some) and the 'door-in-the-face' technique (where a large request is turned down by the consumer, who is then more likely to comply with a smaller request, e.g. they refuse to purchase an expensive silk dress but agree to buy a cheaper silk scarf). In this section, you will learn more about the disrupt-then-reframe (DTR) technique.

The disrupt-then-reframe technique

The DTR technique involves the seller making a confusing or disrupting statement first, before going on to make the actual request. In a series of three experiments, Kardes *et al.* (2007) found that supermarket shoppers were 21 per cent more likely to add a discounted box of candy to their basket or cart if a confederate acting as a salesperson initially stated, 'The price is now 100 Eurocents' before stating, 'That's 1 Euro. It's a bargain!', compared with simply stating, 'The price is now 1 Euro. It's a bargain!' As the shoppers were not used to hearing prices in cents, this created a temporary sense of confusion which was resolved by the second part of the sentence. This technique has increased sales of products from cookies to lottery tickets and has helped raise revenue for various not-for-profit organisations.

The need for cognitive closure and ambiguity aversion

As well as providing supporting evidence for the DTR technique, Kardes *et al.* (2007) also proposed a possible explanation for the success of the technique: the **need for cognitive closure** (NFCC), which is mediated by perceived ambiguity.

Kruglanski and Webster (1996) define the NFCC as 'desire for a firm answer to a question and an aversion toward ambiguity' (p. 264). A stimulus is described as ambiguous if it is unclear or open to interpretation. Typically, humans dislike ambiguity; we are **ambiguity averse** and seek simple, quick solutions that are easy to process. Once an ambiguous situation has been clarified, we stop searching for further information which, if contradictory, could threaten our understanding and sense of closure! There are individual differences in the need for cognitive closure, with some people tolerating ambiguity better than others; this said, as the NFCC increases, so does ambiguity aversion.

With regard to the DTR technique, Kardes *et al.* (2007) predicted that it would be more effective with people who are high in the NFCC as the technique deliberately creates ambiguity, which is less tolerable for those high in the NFCC. Once the **disrupting message** is reframed in an easily understandable way, those high in the NFCC will feel immediately better, making them more likely to comply.

Focus on: Kardes *et al.* (2007) – Experiment 2

> ### ▶ AIM
> This field experiment aimed to investigate the extent to which the effectiveness of the DTR technique is moderated by the need for cognitive closure.

> ### ▶ METHODOLOGY
> A male confederate approached 155 students on the campus of a Dutch university, each of whom were randomly allocated to either the 'disrupt-then-reframe' experimental group or the 'reframe-only' control group. He introduced himself to the students as a member of a group working to improve student life (e.g. reducing the costs of living for students) and delivered either the DTR or the reframe message depending on the group to which the participants had been allocated.

▼ Table 7.24 Kardes *et al.* (2007) experimental and control groups

	Type of message	Purpose of message	Message
Experimental group	Disrupt message	Present ambiguous product information	'You can now become a member for half a year for 300 Eurocents.'
	Reframe message	Decrease ambiguity	'That's 3 Euros. That's a really small investment!'
Control group	Reframe message only	Present non-ambiguous product information	'You can now become a member for half a year for 3 Euros. That's a really small investment!'

All participants then completed a 20-item questionnaire measuring their level of need for cognitive closure (NFCC). Statements included 'I don't like unpredictable situations' and were rated on a six-point scale. On completion, participants were debriefed and all money received was donated to charity.

RESULTS

Thirty per cent of the DTR group paid the 3 Euro membership fee, compared with only 13 per cent of the reframe-only group. A median split was used to divide participants into a high and a low need for cognitive closure. As expected, 26 per cent more people with a high NFCC complied in the DTR group compared with the reframe-only group, whereas the difference was only 7 per cent in the low NFCC group (see Figure 7.49).

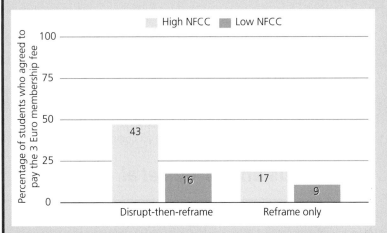

▲ Figure 7.49 Bar chart showing the percentage of students who agreed to pay the 3 Euro membership fee in the disrupt-then-reframe group compared with the reframe-only control group

CONCLUSION

The DTR technique can increase compliance with a request to join a club for a small fee in a real-world setting. This effect is moderated by the need for cognitive closure, with individuals who score higher than average being more likely to comply with the DTR request than those who score lower than average. The researchers note that the 'disrupt message' increases ambiguity. People with a high need for cognitive closure are more ambiguity averse. This means they are more motivated to decrease ambiguity than people with a low need for cognitive closure. When the reframe message disambiguates the situation, they are quick to act on the new information and comply with the request.

Evaluating Kardes *et al.* (2007)

One strength of this **field experiment** is that it was conducted in a real-world setting and the participants were unaware that they were taking part in a study about interpersonal influence. For example, they believed that the club they were asked to join was real and they were told that the 'need for cognitive closure' questionnaire was about 'students' lifestyles and opinions'. This means that their behaviour is less likely to result from demand characteristics and that the findings regarding the effectiveness of DTR have high ecological validity.

A weakness is that situational variables that could have affected the effectiveness of the DTR technique were less easy to control due to the naturalistic setting. For example, some of the students may have been in a hurry to get to lectures, whereas others may have finished studying and been on a break. Research suggests that the NFCC can be affected by time pressure (Kruglanski and Webster, 1996), making it difficult to decide whether the effectiveness of DTR was due to situational or dispositional factors.

Factors affecting the need for cognitive closure

The need for cognitive closure is affected by both situational and dispositional factors (see Table 7.25).

▼ Table 7.25 Situational and dispositional factors affecting the NFCC

Situational or dispositional	Factor	Need for cognitive closure	Effectiveness of DTR technique
Situational (external)	Situations that are time pressured and require a quick decision	Higher	Increases
	Situations that are perceived as dull, where closure provides an escape route!		
	Individuals fear being penalised or criticised for a bad decision	Lower	Decreases
Dispositional (internal)	Individual is from a high uncertainty avoidance culture, such as Japan or Guatemala	Higher	Increases
	Individual is from a low uncertainty avoidance culture, such as Hong Kong.	Lower	Decreases

ISSUES AND DEBATES

Applications to everyday life

A strength of Kardes *et al.* is that it has clear applications to everyday life in terms of training for sales staff. The disrupt-then-reframe technique is quick and easy to learn and takes just a few seconds of extra time with potential customers. Unlike techniques described below such as reciprocity, there is no additional cost to the business but everything to gain in terms of increased profits. This is important as many small businesses may not be able to afford to spend much on marketing but could increase their sales through simple changes to the scripts used by their sale teams.

Determinism versus free will

Many of us may like to think that we are responsible for every decision that we make and that when we make a purchase this is entirely our choice; while others may be easy to manipulate, we are in fact far more shrewd! We like to believe that our behaviour and attitudes are a product of free will however research such as Kardes *et al.* demonstrates just how easy it can be to fall into cognitive traps created by canny sales staff. When System 1 thinking takes charge, purchasing may be determined less by free will and more by circumstances than we care to accept.

Cialdini's six ways to close a sale

Dr Robert Cialdini has worked in the field of influence, persuasion and negotiation for almost half a decade and is referred to as the 'godfather of influence'. He is most famous for his book *Influence: The Psychology of Persuasion*. Published in 1984, the book has sold over two million copies and has been translated into 27 different languages, underlining its global influence on sales and marketing (The British Library, n.d.). In his book, he proposed six strategies for persuasion, which he called 'weapons of influence'. These strategies have been adopted by sales teams all over the world as ways to close a sale – to ensure that interactions between sellers and potential buyers result in a sale, where both parties are satisfied with the outcome.

Reciprocation

Cialdini (1984) states that humans are biologically predisposed to return favours, gifts and invitations. Likewise, we are more likely to help people who have helped us. This tendency to exchange goods and services for mutual benefit (give and take) helps to build positive and long-lasting social relationships. In turn, this means that if someone gives something to us, we immediately feel indebted to them and are more likely to do them a favour in return to feel better about ourselves. These behaviours are so ingrained that consumers may be significantly more likely to make a purchase or donate to a charity if they have already received some small token gift, such as a free pen, coffee or voucher. Sellers who under-promise and overdeliver are also using the principle of **reciprocation** because not only does this behaviour please the client, it also encourages them to come back another time as they feel obliged to them, due to their perceived generosity.

Commitment and consistency

Cialdini also believes that people typically prefer to be consistent and expect **consistency** from others. This means that once a person has made a **commitment** to an individual or company, they are likely to be loyal to them. Social norms make it difficult to withdraw from relationships where we feel committed or obliged to others and the same psychology explains why we are likely to stick to the same brand of trainers, year on year, drink at the same coffee shops and renew contracts with the same companies. This principle also explains the foot-in-the-door technique described on page 470, where making a small donation or purchase makes a person significantly more likely to make a larger donation/purchase. Once we have said 'yes' once, it is more difficult to resist further requests.

Social proof

Humans are social animals; at AS Level, you learned just how much the behaviour of other people can shape our own behaviour, even without us being consciously aware of it. When we see (or hear of) others behaving in a certain way, it makes us more likely to behave in that way too, especially if they are people with whom we identify or admire. Cialdini uses the term **social proof** to describe the way that other people's behaviour is used as evidence for how to behave, especially when we are uncertain. The more people are behaving in this way, the stronger the proof. Salespeople and advertising agencies use this principle when they lead us to believe that people like us are already happily using their products and services. This reassures us and makes us more likely to do the same.

Authority

At AS Level, you learned that people are predisposed to accept authority (see page 133), meaning an authoritative salesperson is likely to be more successful than a submissive one. Many factors are associated with authority and social power, including expertise, charisma and the ability to reward others (through discounts/special offers). Outward signs of authority such as appearance, including clothing, body language, impressive titles and prestigious offices, may also persuade buyers that the seller has authority, making them more likely to accept their recommendation and offers.

Liking

It is not easy to say no to someone friendly or **likeable** and, therefore, salespeople are well advised to spend time building a relationship with a potential customer before discussing products. This rapport-building may include paying compliments (flattery), showing an interest in their lives and asking questions in an effort to find common ground/shared interests. Such efforts help to lower the consumer's resistance, making them more likely to make a purchase.

Scarcity

When goods become **scarce**, they become more valuable, as more people want the product and know that they may not be able to achieve their goal. Every Christmas, there is a most-wanted toy/gadget that 'sells out' – parents will drive miles to acquire the perfect gift as the discomfort that comes with feeling one's freedom of choice has been limited is too much to bear! Mentioning that an item is on offer for a limited time, or that an offer is about to expire, can pique a customer's interest, making a sale more likely.

Evaluating Cialdini's six ways to close a sale

A strength of Cialdini's principles is that there is a wealth of research evidence to support their effectiveness. For example, Beltramini (1992) conducted a **field experiment** whereby 1500 customers were randomly allocated to either an experimental group or a control group. Those who received a leather business card holder as a gift from a donor company subsequently gave higher ratings of the company's products than a control group who did not receive the gift. The naturalistic business setting of this study demonstrates that the concept of reciprocity is applicable to the real world and has strong ecological validity. This said, the gift tended to improve attitudes towards the products but did not necessarily mean that customers were more likely to contact the donor company in the future, and this implies that reciprocity may need to be used in combination with a range of other culturally appropriate techniques.

> ## ISSUES AND DEBATES
>
> ### Cultural differences
>
> One weakness of Cialdini's principles is that they are eurocentric, meaning they may work best for people from individualist cultures such as the USA and northern Europe. For example, Petrova *et al.* (2007) found that the foot-in-the-door technique, which is explained via the principle of consistency and commitment, was twice as effective with American students than Asian international students studying in America. Furthermore, Cialdini *et al.* (1999) have found cultural differences in the effectiveness of different strategies. In Poland (a high uncertainty avoidance culture), a compliance technique relating to social proof was significantly more effective than one relating to commitment/ consistency. This research is important as it demonstrates that salespeople need an awareness of their clients' cultural identity before deciding on the best sales strategy.
>
> This said, it is also critical that the salesperson is able to exercise adaptability and flexibility during a pitch, as cultural stereotyping can be harmful to developing business relationships. There is often more variation between individuals within a culture than there is between cultures and not everyone will identify strongly with the culture of the country in which they live.

A salesperson should adapt their selling strategy to each individual customer. How could the sales assistant use each of Cialdini's principles to help him to sell the jacket to his customer?

▲ Figure 7.50

► **LEARNING LINK**

At AS Level and also in this chapter, we have talked about different ways of collecting objective data through measuring various biological functions, including gaze (eye-tracking), brain waves (EEG), sweat (galvanic skin response) and brain activity (fMRI). Which of these data-gathering techniques would be best for investigating how and why the disrupt-then-reframe technique works?

STUDY TIP

Whenever you have a list of items to remember, try making up an acronym or mnemonic to help you to remember them all. The initial letters for Cialdini's six principles are R, S, C, S, A, L. You could either make up a word if you can find one or a phrase like 'Really Cunning Sales-people Always Smile Lots'. If you can make the phrase describe something about the theory, all the better.

► **TEST YOURSELF**

1   At school, Marta hates it when there is no straight answer to a question, but her best friend Marisa enjoys topics that are open to discussion and exploring different interpretations. Explain which student, Marta or Marisa, will be more likely to comply with the disrupt-then-reframe technique.   [4]

2   Cialdini outlined six ways to close a sale. Explain what he meant by reciprocity, using one example from everyday life.   [2]

3   a   Describe what psychologists have discovered about selling a product.   [6]
    b   Evaluate what psychologists have discovered about selling a product, including a discussion of determinism versus free will.   [6]

4   a   Plan a field experiment to investigate how Cialdini's principle of scarcity might affect sales in a video games store. Your plan must include:
        –   details about the experimental design
        –   the independent and dependent variables
        –   a suitable directional or nondirectional hypothesis.   [10]
    b   State two reasons for your choice of experimental design.   [2]
    c   Explain one strength of the way in which you have operationalised your dependent variable.   [2]
    d   Explain one reason for your choice of directional or non-directional hypothesis. [2]

7.4.3 Buying the product

Think!

What do the terms **problem recognition** and search mean in relation to the Engel-Kollat-Blackwell (EKB) model of consumer decision-making?

Think!

What factors affect the shops that you visit? What would make you go to a store that was further from home or one that was more expensive than you would usually choose? How do you think your answers would differ from your parents or grandparents?

KEY TERMS

problem recognition
information processing
dissonance
normative compliance
informational influence

METHODOLOGY

objective and subjective data
validity

Think!

The study by Sinha *et al.* (2002) was conducted in India. Can you think of any reasons why decision-making about which products to purchase and which stores to visit might be different in this culture than studies conducted in the West? Tip: You could research the cultural values associated with India online, but remember there are always wide individual differences with regard to the extent to which people in any country identify with the values of the national culture.

The Engel-Kollat-Blackwell (EKB) model

Input and information processing

In 1968, Engel, Kollat and Blackwell published the model of consumer decision-making shown in Figure 7.51. This model takes an **information processing** approach (see page 45) and examines the stages that a consumer goes through before deciding whether or not to buy a product. The process begins with incoming information (input) about the products on offer, such as the product itself, price tags, merchandising displays, etc. The consumer must pay attention to the information in order for it to be further processed. At this point, information from long-term memory will be retrieved, such as past experiences with the product, recall of times when the product would have been useful and, most importantly, recall of other rival products/brands which serve as baselines for comparison. Consumers may need to be exposed to product information repeatedly for the sale to be successful. If it does not capture their attention and raise awareness of why the sale would be beneficial to them, the sale will be lost before the decision-making process has even begun!

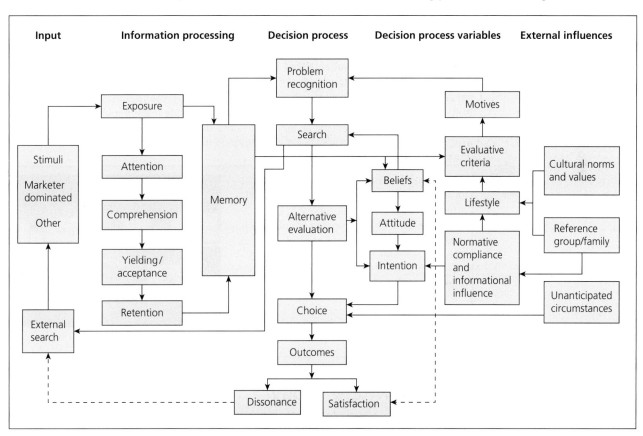

▲ Figure 7.51 The Engel-Kollat-Blackwell complete model of consumer decision-making (Engel *et al.*, 1968, p. 500)

Decision-making

The Engel-Kollat-Blackwell (EKB) model suggests that decision-making comprises five linear stages (meaning they follow a set sequence), starting with problem recognition. For the consumer to carry on considering the possible purchase, they must identify a need or problem that can be solved with this product, such as 'I need this notebook; my current one is nearly full.' Once a need/problem has been recognised, the consumer will start searching for solutions and evaluating alternatives, before potentially making a choice.

Individual differences: decision process variables

The model includes a number of factors that impact the decision-making process, each of which are personal to the prospective buyer and include beliefs, values and attitudes, all of which may be affected by past purchasing experiences, personality and lifestyle. The model also includes external/environmental factors that might affect our choices, such as family and cultural norms and socioeconomic background.

Outcomes

Once a decision has been made, whether it is to buy or not to buy, this will lead to either a sense of satisfaction and pleasure or dissatisfaction and **dissonance**, which arises when our thoughts and behaviours are in conflict – for example, we bought something that we believe we did not need, or we did not buy something when we had the chance even though we believe it was a bargain.

Evaluating the EKB model

A strength of the EKB model is that, unlike many cognitive models, it takes a holistic approach to understanding consumer decision-making. The researchers consider the complex interactions between stimulation from the external world, in terms of the marketing of the product, and our own private internal world of memories, emotions and intentions. In addition, there is an awareness of the social context of the purchase and how this will or will not help the buyers to fit in with their peers, family and wider community. This is a strength as it encourages marketing personnel to think more broadly about factors that affect our purchase decisions and to view each customer as unique.

A weakness of the EKB model is that it only explains consumer decision-making for products for which we have consciously identified a need. Although it recognises many factors impacting the decision-making process, the consumer is presented as a rational active participant and this fails to acknowledge that many people make impulse purchases for items they were not expecting to buy. This limits the usefulness of the model as it does not explain purchases where there is no pre-shopping intention.

The customer wants a new television as his old one is too small for his new apartment (he has recognised 'the problem'); the search is on! Which television should the customer buy? What information does he need to consider before making a choice? Tip: Look at the EKB model to generate as many ideas as you can.

▲ Figure 7.52

Deciding where to buy

Reasons for store choice

Shoppers are involved in decisions not just about what to shop for, but also where to shop. Stores, shopping centres and complexes need marketing strategies to attract shoppers and this can be a difficult task in the age of online shopping. The reasons shoppers choose certain stores are many and varied (see Table 7.26) and may result from a cost–benefit analysis of the advantages and disadvantages of various options – for example, a store may be known for poor staff welfare but be cheap and convenient; another may have a great product range but poor customer service.

▼ Table 7.26 Factors affecting which stores consumers will choose

Type of factor		Examples
Situational factors	Aspects of the store	Accessibility, convenience, e.g. distance from home, parking and facilities for shoppers with disabilities and/or children
		Cleanliness, organisation, price, quality and range of products/brands, customer service
	The specific nature of the shopping trip	Buying for self versus buying gifts
		Time pressure and variety of products required, e.g. a quick 'top-up' shop for essentials versus a regular weekly food shop
		Researching options/getting ideas versus definite purchase intention
Individual differences relating to the consumer	Beliefs, values and attitudes	Ethical issues linked to a shopper's personal values, e.g. staff welfare, sustainability
	Personality	For example, a person with a high need for personal gratification may visit a high-status store as it makes them feel good (Sinha *et al.*, 2002)
	Age	Research has shown that older customers are less likely to choose stores based on price or proximity and more likely to choose a store based on entertainment value as they tend to shop for recreation as well as necessity (Lumpkin *et al.*, 1985)
	Other demographic factors	Gender, socioeconomic background, past purchase experience

Shoppers may decide to visit a new store or mall as they are curious and want to experience something new. This has been the case for shoppers in developing countries, where globalisation has led to the development of large Western-style stores as an alternative to the more traditional, smaller retailers. Another reason for trying a new store might be to find a specific product that is not available elsewhere. This may be particularly true when the item is costly and, therefore, the consumer is motivated to avoid a costly mistake. In an effort to avoid a dissatisfying purchase, some shoppers may invest more time than others in the search stage of the EKB's decision-making process (see page 476). Dash *et al.* (1976) found that this type of consumer was more likely to visit a speciality store compared with those who spent less time on the search and were more likely to visit a department store.

Focus on: Sinha *et al.* (2002)

AIM

The aim of this study was to explore reasons for store preferences in an opportunity sample of shoppers in the Indian city of Ahmedabad.

METHODOLOGY

A sample of 247 shoppers were asked to complete a 43-item survey of Likert-style statements as they left a range of different types of stores primarily located in high socioeconomic areas of the city. Types of stores included those selling groceries, clothing, books, music and cigarettes. Shoppers were also asked an open question where they were asked to give up to three reasons for visiting the store.

RESULTS

The open question was answered in 96 different ways, which were classified into seven different categories. More than 70 per cent of shoppers reported *convenience* and the nature of the products (*merchandise*) as the reasons for choosing the store they had just visited. *Service* and *ambience* were also commonly reported, with other reasons including recommendations (*referrals*) from others and being a *previous patron* (customer) of the store. The final category was *other* and accounted for 4 per cent of reasons. Stores selling products that are used up quickly (consumables) were chosen for convenience, whereas stores selling non-consumables were selected due to the merchandise (product range). Shoppers were willing to travel more than 35 km to a store for a good range of merchandise and pleasant ambience.

▼ Table 7.27 Findings by age and gender

Demographic	Category	Key findings
Age	Under 20s and over 50s	Least likely to report *convenience* as their reason for choosing a certain store.
	25–40	Most likely to choose a store due to its *merchandise* and *ambience*.
	30–40	More likely than other age groups to report *service* as one of their reasons.
Gender	Males	More likely to report *convenience* as a reason for store choice than females (40 per cent compared with 30 per cent); also more likely to mention *ambience*; 'go and grab' shopping style, decisions made quickly and less time spent in-store.
	Females	More likely to report *merchandise* as a reason for store choice than males (40 per cent compared with 30 per cent); also more likely to mention *previous patronage* of the store; appeared to spend longer on the search stage of the decision-making process, considering alternatives.

CONCLUSIONS

Indian shoppers choose stores for a range of different reasons and these reasons are shaped by individual differences such as age, gender and past patronage of the store, as well as store characteristics, including proximity and merchandise.

Evaluating Sinha *et al.* (2002)

A strength of this study is that data was collected directly after shoppers left the store. This means the reasons for selecting this store should still be fresh in the minds. Had they been asked to think back to a previous shopping trip, they may have given reasons relating to their typical habits and failed to mention some of the situational factors that are often unexpected and prompt us to visit stores that we have not used before, such as 'near the restaurant I had come for'. This is a strength as it means the data should be more **valid** and give a more comprehensive overview of why people visit certain stores more than others.

ISSUES AND DEBATES

Cultural differences

A weakness was that the study only sampled people shopping at stores in one city: Ahmedabad, in the northwest of India. The researchers also comment that the stores were in higher socioeconomic areas, meaning that the shoppers are likely to have been wealthier than some of the inhabitants of the city, meaning store choice would not have been inhibited as much by price range. This limitation means that the findings of the study may not be generalisable to people from poorer neighbourhoods and to cities in other parts of India, including the south, which is characterised by differing cultural traditions, food and languages.

Idiographic versus nomothetic

A strength of this study was the nomothetic approach, which means that conclusions can be drawn about how shoppers choose stores that could then be applied to other similar cities in this area of India and potentially in other countries too. For example the questionnaires collected data using numerous Likert scales. Measures of central tendency and spread can easily be calculated and conclusions drawn that may be useful to businesses to better understand their customer base. The customers were also asked an open question but it is important to note that just because the data collected here was qualitative this does not automatically mean the researches were taking an idiographic approach. Content analysis was used to categorise the answer into different groups before working out the frequency of each category of answer. This is a good example of the way in which qualitative data can be turned into quantitative data and analsyed using statistics.

Salespeople usually have detailed specialist knowledge about the product that they sell, giving them power/authority. How is a salesperson's specialist knowledge likely to affect the buyer? Think about the EKB model and Cialdini's six principles.

▲ Figure 7.53

▶ LEARNING LINK

If you examine the EKB model closely, you will see that some of the decision-making variables mentioned are **normative compliance** and **informational influence**, which are two types of conformity, a type of social influence, which was introduced at AS Level.

- Normative compliance refers to the way in which people yield to group pressure and behave in a certain way in order to be accepted and avoid rejection. Can you think of a time when you have purchased something to fit in with friends or to go along with a family member, whether you inwardly liked the item or not?

- Informational influence occurs when we conform with people whose opinions we value due to the desire to be right. Can you think of a time when you have bought a product based on the advice of someone more knowledgeable about the product than you?

STUDY TIP

The EKB model has many components and at first glance may seem rather overwhelming! Why not make a photocopy, cut it into five vertical strips and practise putting the model back together, in the correct order (input, information processing, decision process, decision process variables and external influences). Now create another copy. This time cut it into five horizontal strips and practise assembling the decision process stages in order from top to bottom: problem recognition, search, alternative evaluation, choice and outcomes. These are the most important parts of the model. On a third copy, you could use three colours to code the decision process stages, the internal influences (e.g. memory) and the external influences (e.g. culture/family). Investing your time in this way should help you remember the components of the model more effectively than just looking without doing any additional thinking.

▶ TEST YOURSELF

1   Lots of Rosa's friends have new wireless earphones. She wants some too.
    a   With reference to the Engel-Kollat-Blackwell (EKB) model, explain the decision process that Rosa would go through before purchasing her own earphones.   [4]
    b   Describe one external influence on Rosa's decision-making according to the EKB model.   [2]
2   Outline two ways that age and/or gender influence where consumers choose to shop.   [2]
3   a   Describe what psychologists have discovered about buying products.   [6]
    b   Evaluate what psychologists have discovered about buying products, including a discussion of validity.   [10]
4   a   Explain what is meant by cultural differences.   [2]
    b   Outline one way that cultural differences could affect the consumer decision-making process described in the Engel-Kollat-Blackwell (EKB) model.   [4]
5   The second stage of the Engel-Kollat-Blackwell (EKB) consumer decision-making model is searching for information. Explain one way that a researcher could collect objective data about individual differences during the search stage.   [2]
6   Blake is investigating buying behaviour by asking shoppers questions as they leave a large discount store. Give one open and one closed question that Blake could ask to investigate consumer decision-making at the discount store.   [2]

Post-purchase cognitive dissonance

> **Think!**
>
> When is **cognitive dissonance** more likely to happen?

> **Think!**
>
> Vera and Ted go shopping for their dinner. Vera sees a nice-looking chicken pie, but Ted is looking at a delicious steak, his favourite. Vera would also much prefer steak but says they should get the pie as it is much cheaper. Why might Ted and Vera experience cognitive dissonance and how could they resolve this?

> **Think!**
>
> A consumer firmly believes in equal pay for equal work, yet buys clothes from companies that exploit workers in developing countries. How might they justify this behaviour? Can you think of any other attitudes that might conflict with a consumer's behaviour?

Nordvall (2014) investigated the cognitive dissonance shoppers experience when asked to decide between organic and non-organic products. What experimental design did Nordvall (2014) use and how might this have affected her data?

▲ Figure 7.54

What is cognitive dissonance?

Cognitive dissonance is a state of mental discomfort that arises when our beliefs/values contrast with our behaviour. This topic was first explored by Festinger *et al.* (1956) in a fascinating covert participant observation where he infiltrated a cult called the *Seekers*, whose members were convinced that the world would end before dawn on 21 December 1954. When members woke up on 21 December and nothing had happened, they experienced a state of anxiety as they realised their belief in the cult leader had been misplaced. To maintain their self-esteem, cult members justified their beliefs, believing that they had saved the world through prayer and devotion. But how does all of this relate to Consumer Psychology? One example is the mismatch between positive attitudes towards environmentally friendly organic produce and actual purchasing of these products. This is the subject of the research by Nordvall (2014), described below.

Examples from Consumer Psychology

Organic foods are generally thought to be better for the environment as well as for those who eat them and consumers often self-report their approval of such products even though they are more expensive than non-organic alternatives. However, the amount of people who say they approve of organic foods does not match the amount of organic food that is actually sold, even though consumers say organic foods are worth the extra cost. Holding green beliefs but failing to purchase organic products is one example of cognitive dissonance in the world of Consumer Psychology.

The example above relates to the absence of purchasing behaviour, but consumers often experience **post-purchase dissonance**, not least because many planned purchases require some sort of compromise (Bose and Sarker, 2012). Take the case of Sofia – she buys a new black sofa for her apartment; it is not the pink one she really wanted, which was a bit too large and rather overpriced. When her sofa arrives, she feels a slight sense of disappointment. Why did she not choose the one she really liked? Sofia is experiencing post-purchase dissonance.

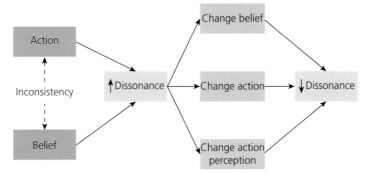

▲ Figure 7.55 Cognitive dissonance: where it comes from and how it can be reduced (Festinger, 1957)

Factors that increase dissonance

Commitment

In the study by Festinger *et al.* (1956), the researchers observed that members who demonstrated greater commitment to the cult and its beliefs experienced greater cognitive dissonance when the world failed to end. This relates to Cialdini's principles of persuasion; as humans tend to seek consistency, they are compelled to justify behaviour that appears to be inconsistent with their beliefs and values.

Involvement

In Consumer Psychology, the more motivated or committed we are to a purchase due to the time invested in searching for a suitable product, the relative cost or the emotional significance, the greater the likelihood of cognitive dissonance. High-involvement products, where buyers invest more time, effort and money, are more likely to result in cognitive dissonance than low-involvement products. This said, cognitive dissonance may also follow unplanned purchases, where no planning time has been invested. Over time, the pleasure and arousal of an impulse buy reduces and the buyer may question why they purchased an item, especially if the utilitarian value is low and the item was expensive.

Culture and religion

Cultural and religious factors may increase cognitive dissonance when participants are deciding to buy products that may be desirable in one culture but seen as undesirable or even prohibited by another (Bose and Sarker, 2012).

Ways of reducing dissonance

In the case of Sofia, she is likely to resolve her negativity by changing her attitude towards the new sofa, emphasising how comfortable it is and how perfectly it fits in with her other furniture. She may also reconstruct her memory of the size and inappropriateness of the pink sofa. This attitudinal change is called **adaptive preference formation** (Elster, 1983). Sofia has reduced the conflict between the two opposing cognitions ('I saw a sofa I really liked' and 'I didn't buy it') by restructuring her attitudes towards the sofas, so that they match her behaviour, given that this cannot be changed. Research suggests that consumers may reduce dissonance in other ways too, such as seeking reassurance through social proof – for example, reading positive online reviews from other satisfied customers (Schiffman and Wisenblit, 2015). Research also suggests that leaving positive feedback shortly after making an online purchase significantly reduces post-purchase dissonance (Richins and Bloch, 1986).

Focus on: Nordvall (2014)

▶ AIM

This study aimed to investigate whether consumers experience cognitive dissonance after making a choice between organic and non-organic groceries, a relatively low-involvement, mundane product. Previous research had demonstrated the occurrence of cognitive dissonance following the purchase of high-involvement products (e.g. computers) where the motivation to feel positive about one's purchase is high due to the level of financial investment (Elliot and Devine, 1994), but there was little research on failure to purchase low-involvement products.

▶ METHODOLOGY

A total of 100 Swedish students completed a virtual shopping trip on computers, believing the study to be about general shopping habits. There were three stages to the data collection.

Condition 1 (pre-manipulation)

There were 25 organic and 25 non-organic grocery items presented individually and randomly on the computer screen. Participants rated the frequency with which they bought these products in everyday life on a seven-point scale (1: never buy, to 7: buy very often). All grocery items were unbranded. Based on this data, the researchers paired each organic grocery item with a non-organic item with a similar rating, meaning each item in the pair was likely to be perceived as equally attractive/desirable to the participant.

The manipulation

Participants were shown the pairs of equally attractive items, one organic and one non-organic, and were asked to click on the item they wanted to add to their online 'basket'. This was done to create a sense of cognitive dissonance (i.e. 'I like this item and find it desirable but I am rejecting it in favour of the alternative').

Condition 2 (post-manipulation)

The participants were shown all 50 grocery items again, with a reminder of whether they had accepted or rejected the item in the previous stage. This time they were also asked to explain their scores with reference to the following list of ten commonly reported reasons for choosing organic products:

- health aspects
- taste
- environmental reasons
- availability
- physical appearance
- nutrient level
- price
- animal welfare
- quality
- other.

The researchers expected higher ratings to be reported for chosen items and lower ratings to be given to rejected items when compared with condition 1. Adjusting their ratings in line with their behaviour in the **manipulation** phase should allow participants to resolve the dissonance that resulted from rejecting a desirable item.

▶ RESULTS

Organic items rejected

As expected, when participants rejected an organic item, the ratings for non-organic options went up by an average of 0.28 in condition 2. Unexpectedly, ratings for the rejected organic items did not go down – they also went up by 0.15. When the results were combined, the overall difference in the ratings post-manipulation was not significant, suggesting only a marginal tendency to reduce dissonance through changing attitudes towards the accepted and rejected grocery items. Reasons given for rejecting the organic option were price and appearance.

Organic items accepted

When the researchers analysed the data for organic items that were accepted, the same findings were repeated; although there was a slight tendency to reduce the rating of the rejected non-organic product, this was not significant. However, there was very little data to analyse as the organic product was only chosen an average of 4 out of 17 times! When the organic product was chosen, the most reported reasons were animal welfare and environmental concern.

> ## ▶ CONCLUSION
>
> Even though grocery shopping is seen as a low-involvement task (compared with buying a new laptop or car, for example), cognitive dissonance still arises and is reduced by increasing positive attitudes towards the purchased item – for example, 'I know organic foods are better for me and for the environment, but non-organic products are cheaper and more attractive.'

Evaluating Nordvall (2014)

A strength of this study is that, although it is a laboratory experiment, the task has strong ecological **validity**. Many people are used to completing their grocery shopping online and, therefore, viewing products in this way would not have been unusual. This means that the participants' choices should represent how they would have behaved when doing their normal weekly shop.

A problem with the validity is that typically we are not asked to rate the items that we put into our shopping baskets. Furthermore, the fact that participants were asked to rate the same items twice may have created demand characteristics. This could reduce validity as participants may have thought they were expected to rate the chosen products more favourably. They may also have shown social desirability bias when they failed to rate rejected organic products lower the second time around as they did not want to appear to be lacking in social responsibility or environmentally unfriendly.

A strength of this study is that it has applications to everyday life in terms of increasing the likelihood of shoppers buying organic products. Understanding more about the ways consumers justify their purchasing behaviour can be helpful to retailers, who can use this information to create targeted advertising campaigns and improve the way stock is displayed and promoted in store. This is a strength as increasing sales of organic products can improve global health and help to combat climate change.

> ## ▶ ISSUES AND DEBATES
>
> ### Reductionism versus holism
>
> One issue with the methodology of this study is it could be seen as reductionist. For example, quantitative data was gathered using seven-point rating scales and conclusions were generalised based on data derived from just 100 Swedish students. Many qualitative psychologists believe that reducing people's thoughts, feelings and intentions to numbers is inappropriate and that this **nomothetic** approach fails to engage with the social context in which consumers form their opinions and make purchasing decisions.

Managers want people to leave their store feeling like the customer on the left and not the customer on the right in Figure 7.56. When people experience the negative feelings of cognitive dissonance, this bad feeling may generalise to the whole store and the customer may not visit again. How could store managers ensure that customers always leave feeling happy and confident about any purchases that they made?

▲ Figure 7.56

▶ **LEARNING LINK**

At AS Level, you learned about the study by Milgram (obedience), where participants inflicted physical harm on a stranger even though they knew this was painful and morally wrong. The moral strain they experienced is an example of cognitive dissonance. As the participants could not change what they had done, they began to think differently about why they had behaved in this way, saying, for example, that it was the learner's fault for getting the answers wrong and emphasising that he had given his consent to be shocked. Can you think of any individual/dispositional factors that might have affected the level of cognitive dissonance experienced by the participants? Do you think the same factors would affect post-purchase dissonance and adaptive preference formation?

STUDY TIP

Why not try making a slideshow to replicate the organic groceries study. Find images of organic and non-organic versions of the following ten items (all used in Nordvall, 2014): meat, sugar, rice, shrimp, milk, apples, mangos, onions, washing powder, toilet paper. Read the procedure carefully to work out what you need to do with the images. Now try role-playing the procedure with a few friends to help you to remember the details.

▶ **TEST YOURSELF**

1 Graziella has purchased a pair of leather gloves as a present for her mother's birthday despite being vegetarian and a keen supporter of animal rights.
   a Explain why Graziella might experience cognitive dissonance following her purchase. [4]
   b Suggest one way that Graziella could resolve her cognitive dissonance. [2]
2 Outline two factors that affect cognitive dissonance. You must refer to examples from Consumer Psychology in your answer. [4]
3 a Describe what psychologists have discovered about post-purchase cognitive dissonance. [6]
   b Evaluate what psychologists have discovered about post-purchase cognitive dissonance, including a discussion of objective and subjective data. [10]
4 A researcher decides to test cognitive dissonance by asking shoppers to choose between two grocery items, one organic and one non-organic. This is called a fixed-choice question. Give one strength and one weakness of fixed-choice questions as a way of gathering data in Consumer Psychology. [2]
5 a Outline what is meant by idiographic. [2]
   b Suggest one way that a researcher could investigate post-purchase cognitive dissonance using an idiographic approach. [2]
6 Carlton believes that there will be a relationship between how much an item costs and the amount of cognitive dissonance a person experiences. Write a suitable null hypothesis for his study. [2]

7.5 Advertising

7.5.1 Types of advertising and advertising techniques

METHODOLOGY

objective and subjective data

generalisations from findings

validity

Think!

What is meant by attitude change?

Think!

Imagine you have to develop an **advertising** campaign to sell school supplies like uniforms, drink bottles, pens, notebooks and calculators to parents and children. Who would your adverts feature? What **medium** would work best? What time of day would you want to target your consumers? Remember you may need to try different strategies for different **audiences** and products.

Think!

The **Yale Model of Communication** has been around for decades. How do you think advertising and consumers have changed since the model was first developed in the 1950s? What do you think the challenges are for advertising agencies that did not exist 70 years ago? How do these issues affect the temporal validity of advertising research over the years?

KEY TERMS

advertising

medium

audience

Yale Model of Communication

attitudes

communication

source

eye-tracking

EEG

marketing mix model

credibility

attention

comprehension

acceptance

motivation

central and peripheral routes

elaboration likelihood model

Using celebrities in advertisements seems to make good sense according to the Yale Model of Communication, but their use can sometimes have unexpected effects. Why might some consumers develop negative attitudes towards brands featuring certain celebrities? Think of as many reasons as you can.

▲ Figure 7.57

Advertising is all about persuasion, meaning the process by which a person, group or organisation attempts to change the beliefs, values or **attitudes** of others. Key to this, of course, is the art of **communication** – that is, the transfer and/or exchange of information between a **source** and an audience. Using different types of advertising discussed in this section, companies try to increase our awareness of their products and to encourage us to develop favourable attitudes towards their brand and product range. Ultimately, they are trying to convince us to change our consumer behaviour, to choose their products instead of a rival brand. Although attitudes do not always predict behaviour, consumer behaviour is more likely to change if advertising agencies are able to successfully create positive associations with their products.

The Yale Model of Communication

Social psychologists at Yale University, led by Carl Hovland, began developing the Yale Model of Communication during the Second World War for use by the American army. The purpose of the model was to explain why some attempts to change attitudes are more effective than others. For this reason, it has been applied to many areas of psychology, including health promotion and advertising. Hovland *et al.* (1953) focused on three main factors, which interact to determine the effectiveness of the communication (see Figure 7.58). They can be summarised as 'who said what to whom?' Later, McGuire (1968) focused on two further factors, extending the model to 'who said what to whom, how and to what effect?'

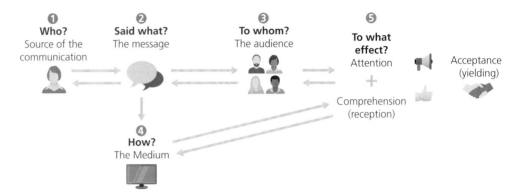

▲ Figure 7.58 Key features of the Yale Model of Communication

Who? The source

Persuasive communication is more effective in changing attitudes and behaviour when the source is either credible and/or someone with whom the audience identifies. **Credibility** refers to the extent to which the person is believable. This relates to their trustworthiness, expertise and/or authority. Audiences are more likely to identify with, and therefore be influenced by, sources who are physically attractive, popular or who promote an image that audience members admire. The arousal associated with such people also means they are likely to capture our **attention** so that we listen to what they say or watch what they are doing.

Says what? The message

Adverts that focus on important information about the product, sometimes called the hard-sell (see page 498), may be the most effective way of promoting some products to some audiences; however, many adverts rely on subtler, more subjective, image-oriented messages (see page 497), such as 'You can be as popular and successful as these people if you buy this car/breakfast cereal/insurance policy.'

Messages that present both sides of an issue/argument may be more persuasive than one-sided messages, but again this can depend on aspects of the audience, the product and the situation. Finally, the timing of the message is an important factor to be considered with regard to how effective it is likely to be. When several messages are communicated one after the other, the primacy effect and the recency effect (see page 403) suggest that the first and last messages are likely to be the most effective as they will be the most memorable. This is why adverts often end with a slogan (see page 511) as this part of the advert is likely to be best remembered.

To whom? The audience

Understanding the demographic of the product's target audience is crucial to effective advertising. Important features include age, gender and cultural background, with evidence suggesting that people who are most open to persuasion tend to be younger, less intelligent and with moderate self-esteem (Rhodes and Wood, 1992).

How? The medium/channel

How the message is transmitted is known as the medium or channel – for example, through television, radio, print (magazines, newspapers and flyers), social media, product placement in films, billboards, etc. Some audiences may be more or less likely to attend to messages conveyed via these channels than others. Different types of advertising are discussed on page 487 where we also discuss the effectiveness of different media in more detail (see Ciceri *et al.*, 2020).

To what effect? Attitudinal and/or behavioural change

An audience member's attitudes and/or behaviour cannot change if they are not paying attention to the message. Likewise, if the audience member does not understand the message, its impact will be lost (**comprehension**). Both these cognitive processes will be affected by characteristics of the source, message and the audience member themselves. McGuire (1968) referred to attention and comprehension as reception. Even messages that are understood may not affect a person's attitudes or behaviour unless the person accepts the message (**acceptance**) and this will also be affected by individual and situational factors relating to the person's **motivation** to change (Stone and Lukaszewski, 2009). McGuire (1968) refers to this stage as yielding. This is where consumers begin to integrate the content of advertising messages into their understanding of the product and how it relates to their needs.

Evaluating the Yale Model of Communication

A weakness of the model is that, although it considers interactions between several components, it is still oversimplified. For example, research suggests that advertising can change attitudes via two different routes, described by Petty and Cacioppo (1986): the **central route** and the **peripheral route**. The route that is chosen depends on the audience member's level of motivation. High motivation results in a high degree of message elaboration, meaning consumers think deeply about the advertising message. This is more likely to lead to change in attitudes and purchasing behaviour. In contrast, the peripheral route is used by under-motivated consumers who pay less attention and are less likely to understand the message. These consumers may form more general impressions about the product based on qualities of the source rather than a logical analysis of messages about the product. This alternative model of persuasion is called the **elaboration likelihood model**. Its focus on how consumers process messages in different ways demonstrates that the Yale Model of Communication does not fully explain how consumers process advertising messages.

ISSUES AND DEBATES

Reductionism versus holism

A strength of this model is that it takes a holistic approach in that it considers the interactions between a wide variety of factors. It does not underestimate the complexity of attitude and behaviour change. For example, the same source may affect audience members in different ways depending on whether they are seen as credible or attractive, while the same message may have variable impact as it will be understood to differing degrees by different people. This is important, as taking a more holistic approach to understanding consumer behaviour is likely to result in more successful advertising campaigns than might have been achieved with a more reductionist approach.

Applications to everyday life

A strength of the model is that if it is applied thoughtfully it has the potential to benefit both businesses and consumers. For example, most brands today understand that collaborating with social media influencers can increase their 'reach', i.e. their ability to get the message from a 'source' to their potential customers (the targets). However, it is important that brands choose relevant influencers whose followers fit the demographic of their target customer. Large numbers of followers suggests that the influencer has credibility and authority meaning 'targets' should pay attention to the messages they

convey. Gupta *et al.* (2015) showed that features of the source can increase the persuasiveness of advertising messages. Trustworthiness, attractiveness and expertise, in that order, were the most important qualities in influencing consumer attitudes. The emphasis on source credibility is, therefore, well supported.

This said, endorsement from attractive and popular celebrities can have the opposite effect, driving consumers away from certain brands (lack of 'acceptance'). For example, if consumers perceive a mismatch between the choice of celebrity and the product and/or brand image, this can limit the clarity of the message. In this case, the celebrity can overshadow the product and dilute the message. This is supported by qualitative research by Temperley and Tangen (2006), where consumers criticised football legend David Beckham's endorsement of a Japanese food product. The researchers concluded that celebrities who endorse too many products can damage the image of certain brands for a variety of reasons. This demonstrates that businesses that recognise the complexity of the interactions between sources (who), messages (says what) and audience members (to whom) may be better positioned to ensure that they do not waste their profits on high-profile influencers who will not leverage sales of their product.

▶ **LEARNING LINK**

At AS Level, you learned about Bandura's social learning theory and his study of aggression in preschool children. How many similarities and differences can you think of between social learning theory and the Yale Model of Communication?

STUDY TIP

When you are evaluating a theory or model, you can look at whether the claims made by the theory/model are supported by research evidence or not. You can also evaluate that evidence; if studies have weaknesses, this also weakens the evidence they provide for the theory. You can also show how the model can be applied to explain real-world events as well as comparing it to other alternative models. Remember though, if you do this, you must show how the model you are evaluating is either better or worse than the one you have compared it with.

▶ **TEST YOURSELF**

1 Howard was doing a crossword puzzle when he recognised the voice of his favourite comedian on the television. He looked up and was surprised to see the comedian on an advert for *Krinkles* crisps. Using your knowledge of the Yale Model of Communication, describe two factors that will influence whether Howard purchases *Krinkles* rather than his usual brand of crisps. [2]
2 Compare the use of EEG and eye tracking in consumer psychology. You must refer to psychological research in your answer. [4]
3 a Describe the Yale Model of Communication. [6]
   b Evaluate the Yale Model of Communication, including a discussion of application to everyday life. [10]
4 Explain two reasons why an advertising agency should be careful when deciding on who to feature in their advertisements. [2]
5 Liesel is studying consumer attitudes towards adverts featuring celebrities. She decides to collect qualitative data using interviews. Her friend says her data will be 'too subjective'.
   a Explain what is meant by subjective. [2]
   b Explain one advantage and one disadvantage of Liesel's study. [4]
6 Liesel shows her participants a video of an advert featuring a popular singer. Suggest one way that cultural differences could affect her participants' responses to the advert. You must refer to one or more features of the Yale Model of Communication in your answer. [2]

Advertising media

Think!

What was the **EEG** used to measure in Ciceri *et al.* (2020)?

Think!

Neuromarketing is becoming increasingly popular. Why do you think this is and can you think of any limitations of focusing so much on this type of data?

Think!

Waheed's children are pestering him to take them out for a burger. He says he will take them as long as he gets to decide where they go. Use Lauterborn's 4Cs **marketing mix model** to work out all the factors that will affect Waheed's choice of restaurant.

KEY TERMS

EEG
marketing mix model
neuromarketing
types of advertising
banner blindness
targeted advertising
cookies
visual attention
eye-tracking
frustration
consumer-centric

METHODOLOGY

objective and subjective data

generalisations from findings

validity

Newspapers and magazines are rapidly moving to online versions, but do these differing media change the impact of adverts on consumers? Think about the findings of Ciceri *et al.* (2020). Which of the two consumers in Figure 7.59 is more likely to change their attitudes and behaviour towards the products and services they see advertised? Are there any limitations with the study that mean we cannot be sure?

▲ Figure 7.59

Printed media

Traditionally, businesses have placed adverts in newspapers and magazines as a way of communicating with consumers. Prior to the internet, newspapers had a wide reach, meaning adverts would be seen by many people, but pages can have a cluttered appearance with many rival companies competing for the audience's attention (Schiffman and Wisenblit, 2015).

Magazines are targeted at people with specific interests (e.g. baking, golf or wildlife) and so they provide a useful channel to ensure that advertising messages are transmitted to the 'right' people. Audience members often see specialist interest magazines as a credible source and this gives the adverts that they carry more gravitas (power to influence). This is supported by research that also suggests that, in comparison with web adverts, people find print adverts as informative and useful as the articles. Print advertising is also rated as less annoying than other **types of advertising** (Elliott and Speck, 1998).

Television

In comparison with print media, television adverts are expensive to produce and broadcast. This cost was often seen as a worthy investment, however, as televised adverts reach huge audiences and allow agencies to create stimulating and emotionally arousing storylines to build a strong brand identity. This said, viewing habits have changed immeasurably in recent years. Many of us now watch our favourite shows on catch-up (i.e. without ad breaks) and through subscription streaming services such as Netflix, while adults and children are choosing to watch content on YouTube as an alternative to television.

Internet

Most print media products are now available as online versions, and many have phased out paper-based products altogether, primarily for financial reasons (Thurman and Fletcher, 2019). This means research studies such as Ciceri *et al.* (2020) (see below) are critical in investigating differences in the way that consumers process advertising messages presented online versus in print. Benway and Lane (1998) used the term **banner blindness** to describe the way that consumers avoid and/or filter out adverts placed horizontally and vertically around the sides of the screen, and Drèze and Hussherr (2003) found that participants were unable to recognise adverts they had been exposed to in their online experiment. This suggests that businesses must find other ways of capturing the attention of virtual audiences.

One way that this has been done is through **targeted advertising**. Websites include **cookies**, which allow internet browsers to record information about sites that a user visits. Information about the user's interests, activities and opinions, referred to as their psychographic profile, is combined with demographic information (e.g. age, gender, ethnicity) and used to match specific adverts to specific users, such as new parents being shown adverts for nappies and other baby products.

Smartphones and social media

Ninety-nine per cent of the world's 4.5 billion social media users access their accounts via their smartphones (Dean, 2021) and 75 per cent of Gen Z (born between 1997 and 2012) say their purchasing decisions are affected by social media ads. This figure is around 48 per cent for millennials (1981–1996) but as high as 68 per cent for Baby Boomers (1946–1964). These figures demonstrate why social media advertising is now critical to all businesses, including optimising content to be displayed on smartphones and creating appealing content for different demographics. This type of marketing may be direct, as in Facebook adverts (which are targeted using data collected via the platform; see above), or indirect.

Indirect marketing via social media includes businesses sharing informative and entertaining content to develop their brands' identity, create a dialogue with consumers and build trust and loyalty. Other indirect strategies involve user-generated content (UGC), specifically influencer content, which refers to high-quality posts shared by individuals with large numbers of followers. Influencers may or may not be paid by specific brands to mention/picture their products but due to their high levels of credibility and popularity, they can be a powerful source for turning interest into purchasing intent. However, research suggests that influencers who are transparent about their relationship with the brands they represent (advertising disclosure) have the greatest impact (Weismueller *et al.*, 2020).

Neuromarketing

Harrell (2019) defines neuromarketing as the use of physiological measures such as fMRI, EEG and **eye-tracking** to provide 'insight into customers' motivations, preferences and decision-making'. The following study by Ciceri *et al.* (2020) used two of these methods to explore differences in the way consumers interact with adverts presented in print or digital formats. As with research into menu design and shelf positioning, eye-tracking was used to measure **visual attention** by recording the length of fixations on specific areas of the page. Revisit pages 403 and 455 to remind yourself how this technology works.

EEG and advertising research

At AS Level, you studied how Dement and Kleitman (sleep and dreams) used EEG to monitor their participants' brain waves as they slept (page 6), but EEG can also be used with participants when they are awake. For example, Boksem and Smidts (2015) used EEG to accurately predict the commercial success of movies based on their trailers. This is done by monitoring brain waves associated with emotional states. The software used by Ciceri *et al.* (2020) identified five states (outlined in Table 7.28), although they only focused on **frustration**, as this emotion is commonly associated with advertising, which can make people impatient and irritable.

Data from the EEG and eye-tracking devices were synchronised so that the researchers were able to monitor changing emotional states as the participants focused on different areas of the newspaper.

▼ Table 7.28 Subjective emotional states detected by the *Emotive Affective Suite* software (Ciceri *et al.*, 2020)

Subjective emotional state	Description *Emotive Affective Suite* – software used by Ciceri *et al.* (2020)
Engagement	Alert, consciously directing attention towards a task-relevant stimuli
Excitement • Short term • Long term	Awareness/positive physiological arousal
Frustration	Irritation
Meditation	Relaxed state

Evaluating the use of neuromarketing techniques

A strength of techniques such as EEG and eye-tracking is that they provide **objective** data about the way that consumers process information. Prior to the use of these techniques, researchers relied on subjective methods, including self-reported data from questionnaires and interviews. These techniques rely on the participants' level of self-awareness and can only measure explicit processes operating at the level of conscious awareness, whereas neuromarketing techniques can measure implicit processes and are not subject to demand characteristics and/or social desirability bias. Data from studies such as Ciceri *et al.* (2020) can also be tested for reliability.

A weakness of neuromarketing is that some consumers are concerned about the ethical implications of using technology to extract information of which participants themselves are unaware. For example, EEG research has shown that altering the background colour of an advert can change a consumer's liking, suggesting that such findings could be used to stimulate so-called 'buy buttons' in the brain. This is particularly concerning when applied to groups of consumers who may be less aware of such tactics, such as children, or to sell products that could promote unhealthy behaviours, such as overeating or gambling.

Focus on: Ciceri *et al.* (2020)

▶ AIM

The study aimed to investigate differences in brain wave activity and visual attention while viewing the same newspaper presented in either a paper or a digital format, where the digital newspaper was viewed on either a desktop computer or a tablet. The study also aimed to investigate differences in recognition of adverts following the three different styles of presentation.

▶ METHODOLOGY

Seventy-two Italian regular newspaper readers were assigned to view either the paper or the digital newspaper, viewed either on a desktop or on a tablet. The groups were matched for age and gender. A mock newspaper was created containing 25 adverts. The text was converted into a pdf to be displayed on the tablet and a website to display on the desktop computers. Participants read the newspaper at their own pace but were not allowed to view pages they had already previously looked at. Brain wave activity was continually measured using an EEG throughout the time that the participants inspected the newspaper. The laptop group had their eye movements recorded via the computer screen (see page 493 for details on how this works). The paper group had the newspaper propped up on a book holder. Like the tablet group, their gaze was monitored using eye-tracking glasses. One hour later, following a distraction task, the participants were shown 50 adverts and asked to select the 25 they had seen in the newspaper.

▶ RESULTS

The desktop/website group had the lowest mean average fixation and the lowest rate of recognition, whereas the tablet group had the highest average fixation and best rate of recognition. This said, the website group showed a lower level of frustration than the other two groups.

▼ Table 7.29 Average fixation time, recognition and frustration of the three experimental groups

	Average fixation time (milliseconds)		Recognition (proportion of correct answers)		EEG frustration index (0 = pleasant, 1 = frustration)	
	Mean	Standard deviation	Mean	Standard deviation	Mean	Standard deviation
Desktop (website)	553	905	0.66	0.13	0.4	0.14
Paper	1365	1380	0.72	0.1	0.6	0.16
Tablet (pdf)	1879	1174	0.74	0.1	0.6	0.38

► CONCLUSIONS

The study supports the idea of banner blindness, that people spend less time looking at adverts on websites than they do looking at the same adverts presented on paper or in pdfs and that they are less able to remember what they have seen compared with people who view paper newspapers or pdf versions using a tablet. Frustration caused by advertising does not necessarily lead to poorer memory; in fact, negative emotion in combination with longer duration of fixation may be associated with better memory.

Evaluating Ciceri *et al.* (2020)

A strength of Ciceri *et al.* (2020) is that the procedure was very well standardised. For example, the lighting in the room was exactly the same for all participants and the tablet and computer were set to the same screen luminance. Likewise, the adverts were shown at exactly the same size. They were in the same order for all groups and participants sat the same distance from the device or book holder, which was positioned so that everyone viewed the text at the same angle. These strict controls mean that the study can be easily replicated to check the reliability of the findings regarding how advertising messages are presented, visual attention and recall.

Despite many variables being controlled in this experiment, there were some uncontrolled situational and participant variables. For example, the pdf was shown on a tablet whereas the website was shown on a desktop, meaning the size of the screen was not controlled, and different eye-tracking devices were used for the paper versus the digital groups. Furthermore, the researchers did not ask their participants how they typically read the newspaper or how much time they spend interacting with screens. These uncontrolled variables could have limited the **validity** of the finds regarding the effect of different media channels on the way adverts are processed.

► ISSUES AND DEBATES

Cultural difference

A weakness of this study is that it does not consider cultural differences as the same comprised only Italian participants and they only viewed one mock newspaper that was designed by the research team for the purpose of the study and was therefore rather artificial. Research by Jin *et al.* (2010) revealed significant cultural differences in banner advertisements from the United States, Japan, China and Korea. Significant differences were observed in size and shape of the banners and content, e.g. US banners included more text whereas Asian banners were more likely to make use of images and animation. These differences may mean that Circero *et al.*'s findings may not generalise to consumers in non-European countries. This is because banner advertisements that are designed with the differing cultural values of their target consumers in mind may be perceived as less frustrating and this may have a differential impact on fixation, frustration and recognition.

Lauterborn's 4Cs marketing mix model

In 1990, Bob Lauterborn, an American professor of advertising, reconceptualised the major marketing model of the time, the 4Ps, originally developed by McCarthy (1960). The original model conceived of marketing as a mixture of *product* (what is being offered to the consumer), *price* (how much the consumer will pay for the product/service), *place* (where the product is available) and *promotion* (how the consumer will find out about the product).

Lauterborn felt that this model was outdated and that understanding marketing from the buyer's perspective rather than the seller's would be more effective. Each P was replaced with a C as the model became more **consumer-centric**.

▼ Table 7.30 The 4Cs marketing mix model and the shift from the 4Ps

Focused shifted from...	Focused shifted to...	Explanation
Product	Customer wants and needs	You can only sell people what they want to buy; customers need to be actively 'lured' and made to believe that they want a certain product.
Price	Cost	Costs include many factors other than the price of the item and these are individual to subsets of consumers. Costs could be economic, such as petrol to get to the store versus delivery costs, or emotional, such as guilt for purchasing a product that conflicts with a consumer's values (see page 482 on cognitive dissonance and organic produce).
Place	Convenience	Modern customers are less limited by location of stores as they can buy from anywhere, online, thus increasing competition between different retailers.
Promotion	Communication	Selling should encourage a two-way dialogue with the buyer and recognise the differing impact that advertising can have on consumers; sellers should engage in active communication with buyers and buyers should be encouraged to give feedback that will be acted on. The process should be co-operative, not manipulative.

Evaluating Lauterborn's 4Cs

A strength of Lauterborn's model is that it views the buyer as an active participant in the process rather than passive and homogeneous. For example, there is an awareness that each customer will evaluate products differently according to perceived costs and benefits. This is important as Lauterborn draws attention to the idea that consumers can behave in ways that are unpredictable unless the seller makes an effort to better understand individual and cultural differences between consumers.

Although Lauterborn attempted to update the 4Ps model, huge advances in ecommerce since the 1990s mean this model is also dated. For example, the focus on communication is a good one as it recognises that advertising is not just a one-way communication between sellers and buyers, but it fails to recognise the importance of buyer-to-buyer communication, which is now a massive driver of consumer behaviour. Influencers reach huge audiences, and endorsement and product placement (see page 502) on platforms such as YouTube, TikTok and Instagram mean that businesses must consider a wider range of different channels of communication than ever before. The impact of influencers on marketing suggests that Lauterborn's model may lack temporal validity as it does not give a complete explanation of the full range of factors that affect current consumer behaviour.

If you could give a business some advice about how to increase sales through increasing communication, what suggestions would you make?

▲ Figure 7.60 Lauterborn (1990) swapped the P for promotion for C for communication

▶ LEARNING LINK

In this section, you have learned about the role of influencers in indirect advertising through social media. Think back to the Yale Model of Communication (page 487); you could use influencers as an example when talking about the source. Also think back to Cialdini's six ways to close a sale (page 474); you could use the example of influencers again when discussing social proof. Can you think of any ways that cultural differences might affect the impact of influencers on consumers in different parts of the world?

STUDY TIP

Instead of just skimming past tables and graphs, take a careful look at them (increase the duration of your fixation!) and try to ask yourself questions about what you are looking at to process the information more deeply and make it more memorable. You need to be able to interpret and understand standard deviation, a descriptive statistic that describes the amount of variation in a set of scores (see page 218). Look carefully at the data in Table 7.29. Lower standard deviation scores show that there was less variation in the scores – that is, they were more similar to the mean. Higher standard deviation scores suggest more variability – that is, scores were more diverse and further from the mean. How would you interpret the results for each of the dependent variables (fixation, recognition and frustration) for each independent variable (desktop, paper, tablet)?

▶ TEST YOURSELF

1 Saoirse is doing some research for her psychology essay on her tablet. Many of the websites that she visits include adverts either at the top or on the side of the page. Explain how Saoirse is likely to respond to these adverts. You should refer to psychological research in your answer. [4]

2 Give one similarity and one difference between television advertising and printed media advertising. [4]

3 a Describe what psychologists have discovered about different types of advertising and advertising techniques. [6]

   b Evaluate what psychologists have discovered about different types of advertising and advertising techniques, including a discussion of validity. [10]

4 Compare the use of self-reports and EEG as a way of investigating the effects of advertising on consumers. [4]

5 Explain one application to everyday life of Lauterborn's 4Cs marketing mix model. [4]

6 Suggest one way of increasing the validity of research into advertising media (e.g. print television, internet and smartphone). [2]

7.5.2 Advertising–consumer interaction

Key study: Self-monitoring – Snyder and DeBono (1985) Study 3

KEY TERMS

image-oriented

quality-oriented

self-monitoring

interaction effect

METHODOLOGY

self-reports

quantitative and qualitative data

validity

Introducing Mark Snyder

Dr Mark Snyder is Professor and McKnight Presidential Chair in Psychology at the University of Minnesota, USA. His work spans more than five decades and he has won many awards, including the Society of Experimental Social Psychology's Distinguished Scientist Award (2011) and a Lifetime Career Award from the International Society for Self and Identity (2007). His research integrates the psychology of personality, motivation and social behaviour, but he explains that the overarching theme that unifies these areas is 'how

▲ Figure 7.61 Dr Mark Snyder

individuals create their own social worlds'. Of particular fascination to Dr Snyder are differences between people who are focused on the public images that they create and convey to the world (known as high self-monitors) and people who are more attuned to showing their own true selves to those around them (known as low self-monitors). He is also committed to science in the public interest, especially in his studies of the dynamics of prosocial behaviour, including why people participate in voluntary service and social activism, such as campaigning for social justice and political change.

Think!

What were the students told about the shampoo in the **image-oriented** condition?

Think!

Imagine you own a shop selling soaps, body lotions and facial scrubs. How could you find out if your customers are high or low in **self-monitoring**? How could sales assistants use this information to encourage them to try new products?

Think!

You are shopping for new shoes. Would you be more likely to be attracted by adverts that were **quality-oriented** or image-oriented?

The chameleon is an amazing animal which changes its colour to fit in with its surroundings. Some people are referred to as social chameleons; do you think they are more likely to be high or low in self-monitoring?

▲ Figure 7.62

Context

There are two schools of advertising, each with a differing approach, the soft sell and the hard sell (Fox, 1984). Soft-sell advertisements promote the image of the product; the packaging is as important as the product itself and the advertisements have striking visual appeal. Adverts for perfumes, cars and coffees all use this approach; they create identity and depict a lifestyle that the customer may aspire to, often only featuring the product in a subtle manner. We learn little about the product but much about the type of person who uses this product – the handsome, popular man who drinks the coffee, the fun-loving, fashionable girl who drives the car.

In contrast, the hard-sell approach is focused on the product itself: how it tastes, its nutritional value, how it will help us, what it is made of and sometimes even how it is superior to rival brands. Snyder and DeBono (1985) aimed to investigate whether these two styles of advertising suit different types of consumer, targeting a specific personality trait called self-monitoring.

Self-monitoring

People who are high in self-monitoring alter their behaviour to fit in with the social situations in which they find themselves; they adapt their behaviour to be socially appropriate and can seem like a different person when in a different context. Snyder and DeBono (1985) suggest that people who fit into this category are more likely to be influenced by image-oriented (soft sell) advertising as they are motivated to attend to the type of image that they project to others in social situations. Advertisements that provide information about the image that they would project if they purchased the featured product would, therefore, be more appealing.

Snyder and DeBono (1985) state that people who are low in self-monitoring are less changeable from one situation to the next and are more concerned about demonstrating their true attitudes and values and 'being themselves' regardless of the company or circumstances. In contrast to people who are high in self-monitoring, they are more likely to respond to quality-oriented (hard sell) advertising, such as the pureness, the performance or the sustainability, as this information helps them to understand whether or not the product will reflect the qualities that matter to them.

Measuring self-monitoring

The Self-Monitoring Scale was developed by Snyder (1974). This self-report, psychometric test measures 'the extent to which an individual has the will and ability to modify how they are perceived by others'. The test comprises 25 true or false statements and, therefore, collects quantitative data using forced-choice closed questions (see Table 7.31). It measures five core elements of self-monitoring: concern with social appropriateness, use of social cues, ability to modify social behaviour, using this ability in social situations and the extent to which a person's behaviour is consistent in differing social situations. This test has been shown to be both reliable and valid (Snyder, 1974).

▼ Table 7.31 Sample items from the Self-Monitoring Scale, with likely answers of people who are either high or low in self-monitoring

Item from the Self-Monitoring Scale	High self-monitoring	Low self-monitoring
'In order to get along and be liked, I tend to be what people expect me to be rather than anything else.'	True	False
'When I am uncertain how to act in a social situation, I look to the behaviour of others for cues.'	True	False
'My behaviour is usually an expression of my true inner feelings, attitudes and beliefs.'	False	True
'I am not particularly good at making other people like me.'	False	True

AIMS AND HYPOTHESES

Snyder and DeBono aimed to investigate how a consumer's level of self-monitoring affects the impact of advertising that is either image-oriented or quality-oriented. They hypothesised that image-based advertising would be more effective in convincing high self-monitors to try a new shampoo while quality-oriented advertising would be more effective for low self-monitors.

METHODOLOGY

This study was an experiment with two independent variables: one was manipulated by the researcher (whether participants were given image-oriented or product quality-oriented information about the shampoo) and the other was a naturally occurring participant variable (whether they were a high or low self-monitorer, according to Snyder's 1974 Self-Monitoring Scale). The dependent variable was the participant's willingness to use the product, as measured by their answer to two questions (see below).

Sample

The sample comprised 40 undergraduate students from the University of Minnesota. All were studying Introductory Psychology and received course credit for participating.

PROCEDURE

All participants completed the Self-Monitoring Scale (Snyder, 1974) and a median split was used to divide them into two groups: high self-monitorers and low self-monitorers. They were telephoned by the researcher, who said they were carrying out market research for a new shampoo. Before being asked how willing they would be to try the new product, they were given some information about how the shampoo compared with other shampoos in laboratory tests. Participants were randomly allocated to either the quality-oriented or the image-oriented condition where the information emphasised either the cleanliness (quality-oriented) or the appearance (image-oriented) (see Table 7.32).

After hearing the message, they were asked to indicate how much they would like to try the new shampoo on a five-point rating scale, from 'definitely not', 'probably not', 'unsure', 'probably, yes' or 'definitely, yes'. They were also asked to indicate their willingness as a percentage, where 0 per cent was equal to 'not at all' and 100 per cent meant they would be 'definitely willing' to try the product.

▼ Table 7.32 Image-oriented vs quality-oriented messages in Snyder and DeBono (1985)

	Cleanliness	Appearance
Image-oriented advertising	About average in how it cleans your hair	Consistently above average in how good it makes your hair look
Quality-oriented advertising	Consistently above average in how clean it gets your hair	About average in how good it makes your hair look

RESULTS

The researchers found that the answers to the two questions, about willingness to try the new shampoo, were positively correlated, as you would expect, and so they combined the scores and called this measure the 'willingness to use' index, where the higher the score the greater the willingness to use the product. The researchers found an **interaction effect** between the two independent variables, meaning that the image-oriented message only made people more willing to try the product than the quality-oriented message if they had a higher than average self-monitoring score. Likewise, the quality-oriented message only made people more willing to try the product than the image-oriented message if they had a lower than average self-monitoring score.

▼ Table 7.33 Willingness to use the shampoo

Self-monitoring	Image-oriented message	Quality-oriented message
High	+0.76	−0.70
Low	−0.91	+0.92

CONCLUSION

Snyder and DeBono (1985) concluded that high self-monitoring individuals are more responsive to advertising messages that are image-oriented, whereas low self-monitoring individuals are more responsive to quality-oriented advertising messages.

 ## Methodological strengths and weaknesses

A strength of this study was that the experimenter making the phone calls was blind to whether the participant was in the high or low self-monitoring group, meaning they did not have any expectations regarding whether the participant was more or less willing to try the shampoo. This is important as knowledge of the participant's personality may have affected the researcher's tone of voice, such as sounding more positive when they expected the person to be willing to try the product. Therefore, the blinding process reduced experimenter bias, making the results more **valid**.

A further strength was the fact that the researchers collected the data about self-monitoring at a different time to the call from the pretend marketing company. This meant that the students were less likely to see the two things as being related. If they had been asked the self-monitoring questions at the same time as hearing about the new shampoo, this may have created demand characteristics, meaning they might have realised that the study was about personality and advertising. Spacing the two data collections apart increased the validity of the findings.

A weakness is that the sample was limited to university students, many of whom were young adults who may not be representative of the wider population. Given the time in which the study was conducted, the students were likely to have come from families with above-average incomes, meaning they may respond to adverts in different ways to people from lower-income backgrounds. These limitations mean that the findings may not be generalisable to people with lower levels of education, older adults or children, all of whom may respond differently to advertising messages.

Another weakness of this study was the purely nomothetic approach, which means it is not entirely clear *how* or *why* self-monitoring affects the way consumers respond to different styles of advertising. For example, conclusions were based on two questions about willingness to try the product, which provided the 'willingness to use' index. Taking a more idiographic approach, by collecting some qualitative data in addition to the quantitative part of the study, could have provided greater insight into how the consumers differed in their perception of the shampoo based on the differing messages.

 ## Ethics

One ethical issue with this study was that it involved deception. Participants were told that the telephone call came from a marketing company working on behalf of a client who was launching new shampoo, but this was not the case. While deception was necessary to increase the validity of the findings, it also means that participants did not have the opportunity to give their informed consent as they did not know what the study was really about (e.g. the effects of personality in consumer behaviour). Lack of informed consent makes people more vulnerable to psychological harm; in this study, the students may question future telemarketing calls, not knowing if they are legitimate or not.

 ## Application to everyday life

Understanding the impact of the consumer's personality on the way they respond to different styles of advertising could help marketing and advertising agencies to tailor their campaigns more effectively. For example, recognising that not everyone responds to image-oriented marketing is important; giving clear information about the strengths of the product may be a more effective strategy for many people. Furthermore, Snyder and DeBono note that low self-monitorers may find image-oriented messages aversive, making them actively less likely to try certain products, meaning that designing hybrid advertisements that simply use both types of message may not necessarily be the best solution. Instead, it may be better to create different types of advertising and think more strategically about where and when each version of the advert is shown.

Determinism versus free will

One issue with Snyder and DeBono's findings is that they could be wrongly seen as overly deterministic – that is, if you know whether someone is high or low in self-monitoring, then you can accurately predict how they will respond to certain advertising strategies. However, this is not always the case. Mark Snyder notes that someone may be high in self-monitoring in some situations and low in others, demonstrating the role of situational factors in shaping our behaviour (personal communication, 2021). This means that it may be impossible to predict how a person will respond to different styles of advertising based merely on self-monitoring and advert style.

Willingness to try the product may depend on many other factors – for example, what the product is and the situation (e.g. whether the advert is shown at the cinema with friends present or on your phone when you are browsing alone). Furthermore, free will suggests that, although advertising may affect a consumer's willingness to try a new product, in reality they may choose not to do so for reasons that could not have been foreseen.

REFLECTION

- Which features of Snyder and DeBono's study made the findings more valid and which made them less valid?
- Will high self-monitoring individuals be attracted to any products advertised through image-oriented advertising or only those products that reflect the type of image they wish to portray? How could you conduct a study to find out?

Advertisers should consider whether to use image-oriented or quality-oriented messages. If you were creating an advert for a new shampoo to be marketed mainly in Taiwan, Singapore and China, would you go for a more image-oriented or more quality-oriented campaign? Think about the values of these cultures – how do they fit in with high and low self-monitoring? Could this knowledge help to make your campaign more effective?

▲ Figure 7.63

LEARNING LINK

At AS Level, you looked at Bandura *et al.* (aggression) and the theory of social learning and Baron-Cohen *et al.* (eyes test) and the concept of social sensitivity. You also learned about the idea of social norms. How might these apply to, and aid understanding of, the conclusions of the Snyder and DeBono (1985) study?

STUDY TIP

Carrying out practical work in psychology is a great way of consolidating your understanding of the studies and becoming more confident with aspects of methodology in general. Snyder's Self-Monitoring Scale is freely available online and there is also an interactive self-scoring version that you could use to test yourself and/or collect some data from your peers. Why not find the median and split the group into high and low self-monitoring groups? You could also write your own advertising messages to promote a product, such as a new shaving gel, fountain pen or protein shake. Remember though, if you conduct any form of data collection, it is essential to ask your teacher to check that you have followed ethical guidelines, including keeping the data anonymous.

> ## TEST YOURSELF

1 Zane says he does not care what other people think of him and behaves in the same way regardless of who he is with. He is looking to buy a new watch and has seen one in an advert that he thinks would suit him.

   a State whether Zane is likely to score high or low for self-monitoring and outline one reason for your answer. [2]

   b Explain how the advert might have presented the watch in a way that was more likely to attract a customer like Zane. [2]

2 Describe the procedure of the study by Snyder and DeBono (1985) up until the point of the telephone call. [4]

3 a Describe the study by Snyder and DeBono (1985) on consumer personality and advertising. [6]

   b Evaluate the study by Snyder and DeBono (1985) on consumer personality and advertising, including a discussion of self-reports. [10]

4 Explain how Snyder and DeBono (1985) altered the telephone interview to appeal to people who had high self-monitoring personalities. [4]

5 Outline one advantage and one disadvantage of the way in which Snyder and DeBono (1985) divided the participants into the high and low self-monitoring groups. [4]

6 a Give two examples of quantitative data that were collected in the study by Snyder and DeBono (1985). [2]

   b Explain one advantage of using quantitative data in this study. [2]

KEY TERMS

mere exposure

reminder effect

product placement effect

covert

overt

implicit memory

processing fluency

explicit memory

METHODOLOGY

self-reports

quantitative and qualitative data

validity

How product placement in films affects choice

Think!

The **mere exposure** effect and the **reminder effect** are both deterministic. What does this mean?

Think!

How many films or television programmes can you think of where branded products are clearly visible on screen? Research suggests that we should like these products more and possibly buy them more because of this. Which theory from AS Level could explain this?

Think!

Most research into the **product placement effects** on consumer decision-making is experimental and produces quantitative data obtained from structured observations and questionnaires. Why do you think this is? Why might it be useful to collect both quantitative and qualitative data?

Placement of high-sugar products is banned on television in the UK (Ofcom, 2010). Do the findings of Auty and Lewis (2004) explain the outright ban of high-sugar product placement in the UK?

▲ Figure 7.64

Product placement in films is when a branded product is placed in a natural context in a film. Often the presence of the commercial brand is not even noticed by those watching the film. This technique dates back to 1895 when French pioneers of cinema, the Lumière brothers, inserted a specific brand of soap called *Sunlight* into one of their films (Ruggieri and Boca, 2013).

Just like other forms of advertising, this technique works through persuasion, but this time it is **covert** persuasion, rather than **overt**: nobody is telling you to buy the product or making promises about how it will make you feel. Nonetheless, research has shown that seeing a branded product in a film has a persuasive effect that works through **implicit memory**, which is unconscious.

Product placement is one way films get funded. The actors in a film are simply using a particular object, but advertisers will pay a great deal for their products to be used by iconic characters such as James Bond and child hero Kevin from *Home Alone*. This is not surprising, as research suggests that product placement in films may result in an increase in liking for a particular product and subsequent increases in sales (Auty and Lewis, 2004).

The effect of product placement on consumer attitudes occurs in two main ways: through mere exposure and reminders.

Mere exposure

The original mere exposure theory was developed by the American social psychologist Robert Zajonc in 1968, who conducted numerous laboratory experiments on the effect of repeated exposure of words and nonsense words on people's attitudes towards them. He found that 'mere repeated exposure of an individual to a stimulus object enhances his attitude toward it' (Zajonc, 1968, p. 23).

He followed his laboratory experiments with a field experiment conducted in the student newspapers of two large Michigan universities. For a period of some weeks, an ad-like box appeared on the front page of the paper, which contained one or more Turkish words or Turkish-sounding nonsense words. The words were manipulated to appear between one and twenty-five times over a twenty-five day period. Then in a questionnaire, the five target words were randomly arranged in a list with filler words and participants were asked to complete a seven-point Likert scale (from good to bad) for each word and also say whether they recalled seeing the word before. The words that had been displayed the most times received the most favourable ratings, confirming that there was a positive correlation between mere exposure and improved attitude (Zajonc and Rajecki, 1969).

The application of mere exposure to product placement in films is clear: we see a well-known branded product in a natural context being used by someone whom we may view as a role model, and even though we may not consciously notice the brand, this increases our liking for it, and therefore the chances that we will choose this over a competitor when we next shop. This argument makes the mere exposure effect a deterministic theory of the effects of product placement in films.

Evaluating mere exposure

One strength of mere exposure as an explanation for the success of product placement in films is that it can be measured quantitatively by observing consumer purchasing behaviour. For example, Ruggieri and Boca (2013) discovered that the mere placement of a brand in a film generated a positive attitude in high-school students regardless of whether the product was recognised, with no need for reminders. This suggests that implicit memory of the product was sufficient to trigger attitudinal change.

Cultural differences

A weakness is that mere exposure cannot explain cultural differences in the acceptance of product placement in films. For example, Gould *et al.* (2000) found that consumers from the USA were more likely to show the mere exposure effect, reporting being more likely to buy products they saw in films than consumers from France and Austria. However, the effect was measured by self-report of intended purchasing rather than observation of buying behaviour, which suggests that explicit rather than implicit memory was being measured. Nonetheless, as knowledge of the product placement technique has spread, it is likely that there will be more examples of people consciously resisting this manipulation of their purchasing decisions, and that such resistance will vary cross-culturally. Therefore, the mere exposure effect lacks some temporal validity and also lacks generalisability.

Reminders

This theory is often labelled in studies as the reminder effect. It is the argument that it is not simply mere exposure to the product in the film that results in a more positive attitude in possible consumers, but this effect is more likely if the viewers are already familiar with the film. Then the more recent viewing acts as a reminder and the product placement develops a feeling of familiarity that translates into liking. Both mere exposure and the reminder effect have been explained through **processing fluency**: individuals already familiar with a stimulus can process it more easily. Think about learning to read; once you have read a word a few times, it becomes easier to recognise and say each time you come across it – this is a good feeling! The ease of processing is experienced as pleasant and this positivity transfers to the presented stimulus. This is described by Jacoby *et al.* (1989) as a 'misinterpretation of the effects of the past producing a pleasing quality of the stimulus rather than... a feeling of familiarity' (p. 402). The reminder effect is also a deterministic theory of the effects of product placement.

The following study demonstrates the effects of product placement and reminders on children's choices.

Focus on: Auty and Lewis (2004)

> ### AIM

To investigate the effect of product placement on children, and to what extent age is a relevant factor in this effect.

> ### METHODOLOGY

A sample of 105 children aged 6–12 were randomly allocated to two groups. The experimental group watched a clip from the popular film *Home Alone* in which a family ate pizza and drank Pepsi. The control group watched a clip of the same length, from the same film, where people ate macaroni and drank milk. This film was chosen as it was very likely that the children would have seen it before. Later, the children were interviewed about their recall of the clip. Implicit memory was measured by observing whether the children chose a small can of Coca-Cola or Pepsi when given the choice. In the interview, if children in the experimental group did not mention Pepsi by name, they were prompted using questions that became increasingly specific and ended with 'What was the name of the cola?' This measured **explicit memory**, meaning their conscious memory of the product.

RESULTS

62 per cent of the children in the experimental group chose Pepsi compared with only 38 per cent in the control group. Table 7.34 shows the percentage of the experimental group who were able to name the brand of cola correctly following prompts. Explicit memory was better for older children, who also needed fewer prompts than the younger children.

▼ Table 7.34 Percentage of the experimental group who were able to name Pepsi following prompts

Age of children	Percentage of sample who were able to name Pepsi after prompting	Number of prompts required
6–7 years old	50%	4.43
11–12 years old	67%	2.06

Children in the experimental group who had previously seen the film a number of times were more likely to remember Pepsi without prompting and to choose Pepsi over Coca-Cola in the choice task. Those who had not seen the film before were no more likely than the control group to choose Pepsi, demonstrating the importance of reminders. Control group children who had seen the film before were no more likely to choose Pepsi than those who had never seen the film.

CONCLUSIONS

Product placement does appear to have an effect on children's consumer behaviour (i.e. choice of drink), demonstrating the effect on implicit memory. Explicit memory does not appear to play a part as there was no difference in choice of drink between those who accurately remembered the brand and those who did not. Age was not a significant variable; although younger children needed more prompting to remember the brand, this did not make any difference to their choice of Pepsi or Coca-Cola. Recent exposure after previous exposure (i.e. a reminder) results in attitude and behaviour change, whereas a single exposure to a branded product is not necessarily sufficient to change behaviour.

Evaluating Auty and Lewis (2004)

A strength of this study is that it filled a gap in the literature as there was very little research on product placement effects in children. This is important as children may be vulnerable to developing preferences for unhealthy products if exposed to them in films and television programmes. In 2010, Ofcom, the UK television regulator, confirmed that product placement would be allowed in programmes for adults but was not allowed in children's programmes (Ofcom, 2010). Product placement of high-sugar products (e.g. fizzy drinks like Pepsi and Coca-Cola) were banned altogether. This ruling demonstrates that studies such as Auty and Lewis (2004) are important in shaping policies which protect public health, and this is a strength of the research.

A weakness of the study is that the children were not asked previously whether they preferred Pepsi or Coca-Cola. This was done to prevent demand characteristics that may have affected the results, but prior preference for one or other of these brands is an uncontrolled variable. This may have affected the validity of the findings regarding the effects of reminders on product placement and children's consumer behaviour.

Use of children in research

The use of children in this study meant that the researchers had to be particularly careful about how they gained informed consent. The study took place within the children's own schools and their teachers were involved in allocating the children to groups. When children are at school they often have to do as they are told and have little choice over whether they wish to participate in activities or not. This means that when psychologists work in schools they need to be make sure the children understand that they can choose not to participate and also that they have the right to withdraw. Information about the study needs to be developmentally appropriate, e.g. using pictograms or comic strips. When approached by researchers, head teachers or other senior staff must decide whether each study is appropriate for children in

their school. If the activities are in keeping with the types of things the children regularly do during the school day, parental consent may not be required, so long as parents are aware that their children may occasionally be involved in such projects. This said, parents should be informed that a study is occurring and given the chance to opt-out if they do not want their children to be involved (the British Psychological Society, 2021). In this study, Auty and Lewis gained written parental consent not least because the children would be offered soft drinks after watching a film clip and this is not something that would typically occur within the school day.

Please note, ethical guidelines differ from country to country and students are advised to check codes of conduct of the professional psychological associations in whichever country they are studying.

Auty and Lewis's study used children as young as six years old. Auty and Lewis gained parental permission to offer a cola to children during a short interview and teachers randomly assigned the children to groups. What other ethical considerations did they need to be sure were met?

▲ Figure 7.65

► LEARNING LINK

Comparing studies from different parts of the chapter can help you to think more deeply about their usefulness. This will help you not only to remember them better but also to prepare yourself to write interesting and evidence-based discussions. Earlier in this chapter, you learned about the study by Ciceri *et al.* (2020), which used eye-tracking to measure visual attention and recognition to test memory for newspaper adverts. How many similarities and differences can you think of between Ciceri *et al.* (2020) and Auty and Lewis (2004)? This exercise may also help you to think about how to improve studies of the product placement effect.

STUDY TIP

It is important that you know the difference between the mere exposure effect and reminders. Although they are very similar, there are some differences. Ruggieri and Boca's (2013) research is a good study to read more about if you want to show the difference between these two theories of product placement in films. They used a self-report method of questionnaire and a Likert scale to measure brand awareness and brand preference. How might this have affected their findings? Make a list of methods used by researchers investigating product placement in films and notes on how this may affect what they find.

TEST YOURSELF

1 Samir has watched the film *Top Gun* at least ten times. He saves his pocket money for many months to buy a pair of Ray Ban's Aviator sunglasses as worn by the lead character played by Tom Cruise.

Outline how one explanation relating to product placement in films explains Samir's desire for these expensive sunglasses. [2]

2 Outline one real-life application of research into product placement in films. [2]

3 a Describe what psychologists have found out about how product placement in films affects choice. [6]

b Evaluate what psychologists have found out about how product placement in films affects choice, including a discussion about the use of children in research. [10]

4 Jenni wants to find out how product placement in films affects consumer behaviour. Help her to plan an experiment to investigate whether one exposure to a branded product in a film can affect participants' choice to buy the product.

a Your plan must include:
 – details about the sampling method
 – explanation of the data collection method. [10]

b For one piece of psychological knowledge that has informed your plan:
 i Describe this psychological knowledge. [4]
 ii Explain how two features of this psychological knowledge informed your plan. [4]

7.5.3 Brand awareness and recognition

Brand recognition in children

METHODOLOGY
experiments
interviews

KEY TERMS
logo
brand recognition
brand symbolism
theory of mind

Think!

What is a **logo**? How does a logo help with **brand recognition**?

Think!

In the 1960s and 1970s, children in many countries could buy sweet cigarettes. These were either white candy sticks with a red tip or chocolate sticks wrapped individually in white paper and sold in imitation cigarette boxes with very similar names to the real cigarette brands. Both are banned now, although white candy sticks without the red tip can still be bought in some sweet shops. Why do you think they were banned from sale? How could we test if this ban is justified?

Think!

The study by Fischer *et al.* (1991) identified cigarette brand recognition as a possible factor in leading young children to smoke later in their teen or adult life. This is quite a deterministic view of the role of brand recognition. What other factors in a young child's life may play a role in whether they smoke when older?

Very young children often have strong brand awareness, even beginning to learn to read through familiar logos on toys, food and drink packaging (Ahmad, 2021). What is it about certain logos that might appeal to a young child? Is it the association with a well-loved product or do the children come to love the product because they are familiar with the logo?

▲ Figure 7.66

Brand recognition is the extent to which consumers can correctly identify a brand based on visual indicators such as a logo and colours. We can all think of examples of brands that we recognise from a distance without being able to read the actual name above the shop doorway or on the billboard. Advertisers know that a logo (a symbol made up of text, image and colour that identifies a brand) is a powerful visual method for developing brand recognition.

Children are also consumers and, although research on children is limited, studies have shown that even three-year-olds can recognise brands through logos, even if they cannot always give the name of the product. Swiss psychologist Jean Piaget (1970) claimed that children below the age of seven do not have sufficient cognitive development to think about abstract concepts, suggesting that children of this age should not be able to understand **brand symbolism** through the use of logos.

However, McAlister and Cornwell (2010) point to the cognitive **theory of mind**, which argues that children can think symbolically at a young age if they have a developed understanding of the fact that other people sometimes think differently from them. They tested this with children aged three to five years old and found that very young children were easily able to recognise logos from brands of fast food, soft drinks and toys. When they measured the children's theory of mind through a standardised task, they found the more developed the theory of mind was, the better the child was at brand recognition. A later study by Cornwell *et al.* (2014) demonstrated that children's recognition of brands like fast foods and soft drinks was a significant predictor of child obesity.

Health concerns regarding brand recognition by children were raised in the 1990s, when it was shown that, despite recognising brands aimed at children better than those aimed at adults, three-year-olds could recognise cigarette advertisements through logos. Even though advertising cigarettes on television had been banned by the 1990s, it was still allowed on billboards, in sports sponsorship, on t-shirts and in shops.

Fischer *et al.* (1991) identified this as 'environmental tobacco advertising' and investigated young children's ability to recognise cigarette brand logos in the following study.

Focus on: Fischer *et al.* (1991)

▶ AIM

The aim of this research was to investigate the influence of advertising on very young children, by measuring product logo recognition in children aged three to six years old.

METHODOLOGY

Twenty-two brand logos were collected from a variety of printed sources, such as packaging and advertisements. Ten targeted children (including breakfast cereals and fast-food restaurants), five represented two cigarette brands and seven were aimed at adults (including brands of car and computer). None had specific image or word clues as to what they represented.

The participants were 229 male and female three- to six-year-olds from preschools (kindergartens) in Georgia, USA. They were asked to match each of the 22 logo cards, one at a time, to one of 12 named products on a game board. Each child's parent was asked whether anyone in the household smoked and how many hours a day the child watched television. They were also asked to rate how often their child asked for a particular brand, using a four-item Likert scale, labelled 'almost always' to 'never'.

RESULTS

Children had high recognition for the children's brand logos. Disney was the highest at 91 per cent and Cheerios the lowest at 25.3 per cent. However, they also had fairly high recognition for the adult brand logos, from 16.2 to 54.1 per cent, with car logos having the highest recognition rates.

While children younger than six found the Disney logo easier to recognise than the 'Old Joe Camel' cigarette cartoon logo, the six-year-olds found both logos easy to recognise. The six-year-olds achieved a 91.3 per cent recognition rate for the Camel cigarettes logo, in contrast to a 30 per cent recognition rate for the three-year-olds. This result was independent of whether or not someone in the household smoked.

CONCLUSIONS

Market researchers believe that children who are influenced at a young age by brand logos for adult products will go on to use those products in adulthood. This study shows that very young children see, understand and remember advertising aimed at adults. Given the serious health consequences of smoking, the exposure of children to environmental tobacco advertising may represent an important health risk and should be studied further.

Evaluating Fischer *et al.* (1991)

One strength of the research is that it measured brand recognition (the dependent variable) through a matching game – for example, matching the Nike logo to a picture of a sports shoe or the Apple logo to a picture of a computer. The products on the game board were named by the researcher, and each card was matched individually. This means that the task has high validity as their performance was not affected by their reading ability and they did not have to give their answers verbally, meaning brand recognition could be measured even in the youngest participants.

A weakness is that the children all came from preschools in the state of Georgia, USA and, therefore, may not have been representative of all children. Although the sample was balanced in terms of gender, with children of different ethnicities and socioeconomic backgrounds, all children were receiving formal preschool education in a Western, individualist culture. This means the findings cannot be generalised to older or younger children, those in other countries or those who are looked after/educated at home, who may differ in their brand awareness of different types of product.

Another strength of this **experiment** is that there were many controlled variables. For example, parents were also asked about children's television watching, household smoking and how often children asked for products by brand name. This allowed for an in-depth analysis of the relationship between these variables and children's brand recognition, adding to the validity and increasing the ability to replicate the study.

A weakness of the study is that there is the possibility of experimenter bias in that the researcher who worked with the children on the matching game could have provided unintentional cues that aided the children in making a correct match. The study was in part funded by an organisation called Doctors Ought to Care and the American Cancer Society, meaning the researchers may have been biased towards providing evidence which demonstrates the influence of environmental tobacco advertising on the youngest consumers in society. While it could be argued that this is critical in providing evidence to change social policy, it does mean that the findings may not be completely objective.

ISSUES AND DEBATES

Use of children in research

Fischer *et al.* (1991) carried out their research into advertisement recognition through brand logos in a kindergarten with children aged 3–6 years old. The researchers were adults who used a 'matching the card to the square on the board' game that will have been a type of game familiar to the children. Children were taken into a private room to complete this test, with the adult researcher who will have seemed to them like another teacher. While this will have probably increased their motivation to succeed in matching the cards, it will also have heightened their awareness of the researcher's

social cues. Without an impartial observer monitoring the process, it is difficult to exclude the possibility that young children, who are very prone to researcher influence and wanting to please (see Pozzulo *et al.*) will have been responding to the researcher's encouragement. Fischer *et al.* state, 'After the child placed the card on the board (whether correct or incorrect), the child was told, "That's good." No other feedback or encouragement was given.' However, body language and facial expressions are very hard to control, and children are sensitive to these. So the researcher effect is a risk when using children as participants.

Children can be very receptive to social cues from adults. How could you redesign the logos study so that the children carried out the task more independently, without the possibility of being influenced by the experimenter? Can you think of any other practical and/or ethical issues that you would need to consider in your study?

▲ Figure 7.67

▶ LEARNING LINK

You learned about theory of mind at AS Level when studying the research of Baron-Cohen *et al.* (eyes test). Review this briefly and think why it might be that McAlister and Cornwell (2010) found that young children with a well-developed theory of mind were more able to recognise brand logos. Why else might young children be able to recognise logos more easily than we might have expected?

STUDY TIP

Start a list of all the different ways that advertisers get their product recognised by people and add in a relevant study for each one. This will allow you to organise your work schematically.

> ### TEST YOURSELF

1   Colin has developed a range of colourful, safe plastic cars for small children, aged three to six years. He does not have a logo for his brand yet but thinks he will not bother with a logo as the cars are selling quite well and he thinks children of this age group probably would not notice the logo, just the car.

    Using your knowledge of brand awareness and recognition, give two reasons why Colin should develop a logo for his plastic cars.   [2]

2   Outline what is meant by brand recognition. Refer to one example in your answer.   [2]

3   a   Describe what psychologists have found out about brand recognition in children.   [6]

    b   Evaluate what psychologists have found out about brand recognition in children, including a discussion about application to everyday life.   [10]

4   Explain one way that a psychologist could recruit a random sample of children for a study of brand recognition in young children.   [2]

5   Explain one strength and one weakness of psychological research into brand recognition in children.   [4]

6   Psychologists sometimes use interviews when investigating brand recognition and awareness. Explain how interviewing could be used to study the link between brand logo recognition and unhealthy eating.   [4]

Brand awareness, brand image and effective slogans

KEY TERMS

brand awareness

slogans

jingles

brand image

priming effect

polysemous slogans

literature review

brand positioning

secondary data

Think!

What is **brand awareness**, and how are **slogans** relevant to it?

Think!

You want to develop a slogan to describe your favourite food or some other item that you like. Which of the five different types of slogan will you design?

Think!

Can you think of any reasons why it might be difficult to conduct highly controlled laboratory experiments on the effectiveness of slogans and/or jingles?

The 'Have a break, have a KitKat' slogan (Figure 7.68) has been around for years. Do you think it would make you any more likely to buy the product? Maybe not, but that's because logos and slogans, like product placement, often affect implicit as opposed to explicit memory.

▲ Figure 7.68

Brand awareness

Brand names, logos and slogans all go together to make up brand identity. Brand awareness describes the condition of consumer familiarity with a particular product's brand identity by its name. It often also includes the qualities that separate the product from other brands. A brand awareness campaign tries to familiarise consumers with a product and differentiate it from competing brands. This is one way to activate the availability heuristic or the recognition heuristic that you learned about on page 432.

KEY TERMS

experiments

interviews

Consumers confronted with choices are simply more likely to buy a familiar brand than an unfamiliar one, as that is the one they recognise or the one that comes to mind the fastest – the most available in their memory. Therefore, companies use advertising to make sure that familiar brand is theirs. It is important that advertising is directed where their target audience spends time. That is why companies are now spending a great deal of energy promoting brand awareness on social media platforms.

Brand image

Brand image is one way of increasing brand awareness. With so many different products on the market, it is impossible to be well informed about them all. As you learned earlier, it is very time-consuming to compare products and most people will take a satisficing approach and choose the 'good enough' item. More and more, their decision is based on the brand image rather than the product itself. For example, how many people have investigated carefully before deciding an Apple laptop is the product they need and how many have bought it because of the positive brand image, and the passion of Steve Jobs who dared to 'think different'? We all want to think we are creative, innovative and different.

The brand image is not just of the product itself but it is carefully designed to be an image of what the consumer may gain by buying it. Snyder and DeBono (1985) wrote that consumers who are particularly sensitive to these images are those who care overly about their own image to others. They will buy the suit that promises a 'wealthy businessman' look or the make-up that hides all blemishes and wrinkles without regard to whether these items really have the same effect on them. More recently, brand image has been shown to have an effect on teenagers' buying behaviour, which is quite logical, as they are generally a group concerned with their social image.

Effective slogans

A slogan is a short and memorable phrase used in advertising to capture a brand image. It is the link between the brand image and the consumer and can tell us more about a brand than either a brand name or a logo. Slogans have a **priming effect**, which is a cognitive bias that occurs when we are exposed to a certain stimulus that then subconsciously affects our response to something else. Therefore, slogans prime us subconsciously to think favourably about a certain product. The priming effect is often related to words and images we see during our daily lives, which clearly applies to advertisements.

Unlike the brand name, which is almost never changed (unless a company is bought by another), and the logo, which may be 'tweaked' but is not usually changed, a slogan can be changed and updated to appeal to different target consumers at different times. An example of a long-lasting slogan is Nike's 'Just do it', which has been used for more than 20 years.

Types of slogans

Different types of slogans will appeal to different target consumers, and sometimes to the same consumer at different points in their day. Think how if you have been working hard, you might be attracted by a slogan that encourages you to buy something because you need to 'Have a break' or because 'You're worth it'?

There are several main types of advertising slogans, including the following (Amarnani, 2021; Marketing Tutor, 2022):
1   Business slogans – these are informational and convey the values of the company. Communicating the company's values increases the connection with the consumer. Think of Spanish clothing retailer Zara's 'Love your curves'.
2   Descriptive slogans – these are something that consumers can visualise. Cadbury's Dairy Milk chocolate is a good example: 'A glass and a half in every bar'.
3   Persuasive slogans – these are used to try and get the consumer to give the product a try. For example, Nestlé's 'Have a break, have a KitKat'.
4   Creative slogans – these use word-play and sometimes also humour to increase the response of customers. Think of the advertisement for American laundry detergent Tide, from some years ago: 'Tide's in. Dirt's out'.
5   Emotive slogans – these spark an emotional response among consumers. They make us feel something, such as Tesco's 'Every little helps'. This stresses the supermarket's low prices as being caring support for those trying to feed their family.

Function of slogans

There are two main functions of slogans: to enhance brand awareness and to positively affect the brand image, by creating, supporting or changing that image. For example, while Nike has kept the same slogan for more than 20 years, Pepsi has changed theirs repeatedly to appeal to different consumers and to try (unsuccessfully) to get ahead of the brand leader, Coca-Cola. Changing slogans can sometimes help to increase the market value of a company, as it is perceived that these changes reflect a focused effort to improve marketing strategies, often through awareness of changes in the demographic of their consumers (Mathur and Mathur, 1995). Kohli *et al.* (2007) cite the example of the change in slogan of Campbell's soup from 'M'm! M'm! Good' to 'Never underestimate the power of soup', a change that prompted attention from the media and was seen as an effort to become more relevant to modern consumers.

Some slogans are **polysemous** – they have multiple meanings and can be interpreted differently. This means they can be used for longer and for more target consumers; they have ongoing broad appeal. Think of the multiple possible interpretations of 'Just do it'. Dimofte and Yalch (2007) investigated this and gave the example of a slogan for car insurance that says 'Safe drivers get it'. If the meaning can change depending on the interpretation of different consumers during different time periods, then the same slogan may be used over a long period of time to create and support the brand image.

Guidelines for creating effective slogans

In order to fulfil these functions, slogans have to be memorable. They must not be so long that they cannot be held in short-term memory for transfer to long-term memory, but they must convey meaning. Kohli *et al.* (2007) reviewed academic articles related to slogans and looked at industry publications for relevant case studies to identify guidelines for creating effective slogans.

> ## ISSUES AND DEBATES

Applications to everyday life

Brand image and effective slogans both go to make up the brand awareness that is part of everyday life. Short, repetitive slogans are often set to music as jingles that act as an effective 'earworm' (a catchy song that runs continually through your mind). This has a priming effect on your implicit memory and when you see a billboard, magazine, TV advertisement or website with the slogan, you will catch yourself singing the jingle. Next time you are out shopping, the item is likely to form part of your impulse buy. This is especially true for relatively small and cheap items like chocolate bars or beauty products.

Focus on: Kohli *et al.* (2007)

> ## AIM

The aim of this research was to develop a list of guidelines for creating effective advertising slogans that could be of use to business practitioners.

> ## METHODOLOGY

The researchers conducted a **literature review**, meaning they searched through many academic and business articles on slogans in order to summarise and evaluate the limited research in this area.

RESULTS

There are seven crucial points that should be remembered for slogans to be effective:

1 Keep your eye on the horizon – have a long-term view of where you want the product to be in the future. This means that you should avoid using language that becomes outdated; keep the slogan 'timeless'.

2 Every slogan is a **brand positioning** tool – a brand should have clear positioning in the mind of the target consumers and the slogan should highlight the brand's main strengths. This positioning could be linked to features of the product or the benefits of buying the product. An example given is Exedrin – 'The Headache Medicine'.

3 Link the slogan to the brand – because research has shown that the level of incorrect slogan recall is very high, the researchers recommend having the slogan on packaging as well as on advertising.

4 Please repeat that – slogans can be repeated within different advertising campaigns for better recall.

Brands that have used the same slogans consistently generate higher recall rates.

5 Jingle, jangle – **jingles**, meaning setting a slogan to a small phrase of musical notes (making it melodic and rhythmic), can enhance memory for the product. This is especially true if advertised on the radio, but music can also distract consumers from specific product information so it needs to be used carefully.

6 Use slogans at the outset – research has shown that ideas formed during the encoding of a stimulus are instrumental in influencing memory, so slogans should be used immediately to establish brand identity.

7 It is OK to be creative – while keeping it simple usually works, sometimes a more complex slogan can lead to deeper processing and better memory for the slogan, providing it is still easily understood.

CONCLUSIONS

Slogans are an important component of brand identity and this guiding framework can help provide structure to effective slogan development, which is essentially a creative process. The most effective slogans emphasise meaningful differences between the company's product and that of competitors and match with existing brand perceptions.

Evaluating Kohli *et al.* (2007)

One strength of the research is that it analyses data from company reports as well as from academic literature. The examples used in illustrating their arguments are all taken from real life: BMW, Nike and Xerox slogans are all referred to. Companies can use these ideas to improve their marketing strategies, and therefore the guidelines in the article have application to everyday life.

A further strength is that Kohli *et al.'s* recommendations are supported by research evidence. For example, Yalch (1991) conducted an experiment in which participants were asked to recall brands with which certain slogans were associated. They found that slogans that were typically presented as a jingle led to better recall than those that were not jingles. This is important as it demonstrates that turning a slogan into a jingle can enhance brand recall, meaning such products may come to mind more easily, feel more familiar and lead to increased sales.

A weakness of Kohli *et al.* (2007) is that the recommendations are based on **secondary data** (data collected by other researchers) through a literature search, meaning that, although the advice is evidence-based, the validity of the evidence may be questionable. For example, many of the studies used as supporting evidence are relatively old, some dating back to the 1960s. The review itself is also now rather dated and, given the rapid rate of change in ecommerce and social media, some of the recommendations may lack temporal validity.

A final weakness is that there are many factors that may encourage a consumer to choose one product over another and, therefore, even effective slogans may play a much smaller part than is suggested by Kohli *et al.* (2007). Therefore, the research is not a full explanation of consumer behaviour.

Determinism versus free will

Companies spend huge amounts of money advertising their products because brand awareness determines consumer choice. If people ignored advertisements, then there would be no point in having them. It is because of their effectiveness that advertising itself is a big business. Slogans and jingles are designed to be polysemous and position a brand in the consumer's mind, targeting as wide an audience as possible. However, the more aware we become of these tactics, the better positioned we are to resist them and exercise some free will over our choices. Just be sure to hum the jingle from one brand as you reach for the cheaper, and just as delicious, chocolate bar from a competing manufacturer.

Research has found that jingles lead to better recall of brands. Do you think people from different age groups and/or cultural backgrounds might respond differently to the same slogans and jingles or do reactions depend more on the nature of the product and the power of the slogan than the person? As a psychology student who knows about the priming effect, do you think you would be more able to resist the appeal of a slogan? Are there any times when you think it might not help you resist?

▲ Figure 7.69

LEARNING LINK

You learned about heuristics earlier in this Consumer Psychology chapter. Review what you learned about the framing effect and about choice heuristics. How is this relevant to slogans? Apart from priming, what other heuristics may be activated by a slogan?

STUDY TIP

Visual tools like mind maps (also called spider diagrams) help us to see the links between different parts of a topic. Construct a visual tool to link the different concepts and arguments of Consumer Psychology. You will be surprised how many overlaps and links there are in this option.

TEST YOURSELF

1 Jacintha has an advertising contract to create a slogan for an environmental charity that will demonstrate their commitment to climate action. She knows there are five main types of slogans but is unsure which would be the most effective.
  a Outline one type of slogan Jacintha could create to help the charity to achieve their goals. [2]
  b Explain why this would be the best type of slogan for this contract. [2]
2 Explain the link between slogans and brand awareness. [4]
3 a Describe what psychologists have found out about slogans. [6]
  b Evaluate what psychologists have found out about slogans, including a discussion about determinism versus free will. [10]
4 Outline two of the functions of slogans. [2]
5 Suggest two ways a company can make sure that their slogan is effective. [4]
6 Researchers have conducted experiments to investigate brand awareness. Outline one way that a researcher could measure the effectiveness of slogans as a way of increasing brand awareness. [4]

8 Health Psychology

Learning outcomes

In this chapter, you will learn about five key areas of research and application within Health Psychology. You will learn one key study (in brackets) within each section as well as a number of supporting studies. The five areas are:

- The patient practitioner relationship (Savage and Armstrong, 1990)
- Adherence to medical advice (Yokley and Glenwick, 1984)
- Pain (Brudvik *et al.*, 2016)
- Stress (Bridge *et al.*, 1988)
- Health Promotion (Shoshani and Steinmetz, 2014).

Each area will be evaluated with reference to:

- research evidence and related Research methodology
- psychological issues and debates, including applications to the real world.

▲ Figure 8.1 Beautiful Bergen in Norway, home of Brudvik *et al.*'s key study on pain (page 577)

Where there are people, there is psychology!

Psychology is everywhere and here we see people in the historical town of Bergen in Norway. This chapter contains a number of compulsory and supporting studies which will help you learn and evaluate different concepts and theories in health psychology. The studies come from countries such as Saudi Arabia (Aleem and Ajarim, 1995), the UK (Savage and Armstrong, 1990), and Israel (Shoshani and Steinmetz, 2014). One of the key studies for this option was conducted in Bergen, Norway by Brudvik *et al.* (2016). Their study investigated how children in hospital rate their pain in comparison with rating provided by their parents and doctors.

8.0 What is Health Psychology

Health psychologists focus on promoting healthier lifestyles and preventing ill health. This can involve finding ways to help people to improve their health such as stopping smoking, losing weight or looking after their teeth properly. By helping people to change their behaviour, they can help people to protect themselves from future illnesses such as heart attacks or cancer. Health psychologists also help doctors understand how to communicate effectively with their patients in order to improve diagnosis and care, as well as investigate reasons that patients do not adhere to their treatment programmes. Helping to increase adherence is another important aspect of the health psychologist's role. Furthermore, many health conditions are characterised by pain and part of the health psychologist's role is to find personalised solutions to pain management, including devising appropriate ways of measuring pain using psychometric tests such as rating scales, for example. They are also involved in measuring levels of stress and researching ways of helping people to reduce stress in order to prevent a range of future health problems.

Health psychologists use a wide variety of techniques to gather data. One of the key methods is randomised control trials, an example of which can be found on page 608 where we discuss the key study by Bridge et al. (1988) which investigates the effectiveness of a relaxation intervention on women undergoing radiotherapy for breast cancer. Another common method in Health psychology is the clinical interview. Zelikovsky and Schast (2008) used the Medical Adherence Measure (MAM), a semi-structured interview, which was designed to elicit detailed and accurate responses from patients about whether they had adhered to their treatment. Health psychologists also use the case study method to investigate unusual cases in-depth, such as Aleem and Ajarim (1995) who reported on the case of a young woman who had Munchausen Syndrome.

Careers in Health Psychology

If you would like to take your studies of Psychology beyond A Level and are interested in the field of Health Psychology, the first step to becoming a Health Psychologist is an undergraduate degree in psychology, accredited by the British Psychological Society or a Master's Level conversion course. Following this, aspiring Health Psychologists must complete an accredited Master's degree in Health Psychology followed by further doctoral-level qualifications.

Health psychologists work in a variety of settings from health research units to hospitals or community health settings. Health psychologists may also work in universities conducting research and lecturing. They may work directly with patients or people in the community or liaise with physicians and/or other healthcare workers, helping them support their patients.

For further information, visit **https://careers.bps.org.uk/area/health**.

8.1 The patient–practitioner relationship
8.1.1 Practitioner and patient interpersonal skills

Think!

What is meant by paralanguage? Can you think of two pieces of advice you could give a doctor to improve the paralinguistic aspects of their communication with patients?

Think!

People with autism sometimes have difficulties understanding non-verbal communication and sometimes do not like being touched. How could a **practitioner** improve their interpersonal skills when working with patients with Autism Spectrum Disorder?

Think!

McKinstry and Wang (1991) used **questionnaires** to research how clothing affects patients' perception of doctors. Can you think of any reasons why the data collected in this type of study might not be valid?

McKinstry and Wang (1991) varied what the male and female doctors in the photographs were wearing and measured how this affected patient's respect and confidence in them (see page 519).

» Which doctor would you prefer to see?

» Do you think other members of your family would pick the same doctor?

» Why do you think this might be?

» What advice might you give to doctors who see patients of a range of ages and from different socio-economic backgrounds?

▲ Figure 8.2 a, b, c

KEY TERMS

gesture

non-verbal communication

physician

practitioner

personal space

paralanguage

universal

METHODOLOGY

experiments

questionnaires

quantitative data

generalisations from findings

Non-verbal communication

When patients need to see a healthcare practitioner, whether that is a doctor, nurse, physiotherapist or other practitioner, it is important that the patient feels that they can trust that professional. The patient needs to have confidence in the treatment that is being suggested or that they are currently receiving. **Non-verbal communication** can provide cues to help practitioners to understand their patients' unspoken concerns.

Trust can be built through effective communication, yet when non-verbal communication conflicts with verbal communication, the non-verbal messages often override the verbal ones (Silverman and Kinnersley, 2010). For example, if a **physician** told their patient that everything was going to be all right but had a worried facial expression, the patient would focus more on the worried expression than the verbal reassurance.

Researchers have identified a variety of different types of non-verbal communication that can affect practitioner–patient interaction, including facial expressions, **gesture**, invasion of **personal space** and **paralanguage**.

Facial expressions

Research has identified seven basic facial expressions that are considered to be **universal**, (Ekman and Friesen, 1971). This means that humans across the world in different countries and cultures will recognise and interpret them in the same way. These expressions are anger, fear, joy, sadness, surprise, contempt and disgust. With regard to health psychology, patients may look carefully at their practitioner's face for clues about the seriousness of their diagnosis, for example. Practitioners may use facial expressions to interpret how a patient is feeling about a diagnosis and to help them to decide upon the best way to communicate important information (Silverman and Kinnersley, 2010).

Paralanguage

This refers to the non-verbal parts of speech including disfluencies such as 'umms and errs' and other aspects such as volume, speed and pitch. Particular tones of voice, for example, can indicate to patients that their practitioner is uninterested in them (Marcinowicz *et al.*, 2010).

Invasion of personal space

Personal space was discussed on page 143 and refers to an invisible boundary around us; if people cross that boundary, we feel uncomfortable. The boundary can be larger or smaller, depending on individual differences (for example, personality factors such as empathy and cultural differences) as well as situational factors and/or our interpretation of the social context. Practitioners often need to invade their patients' personal space to examine them and this can make patients feel uncomfortable. For example, Marin *et al.* (2018) found that patients who reported a greater invasion of their personal space by the nursing professionals on a hospital ward, were those who had more privacy at home and were lonelier.

Gestures

These include hand gestures or shrugging of shoulders. These can be used with verbal and other non-verbal communications and may be effective in helping patients understand the significance of what the practitioner is saying. However, the practitioner must be cautious and consider the cultural background of their patient because gestures can mean different things in different cultures and what might be acceptable in one culture, might be considered extremely rude in another, causing offence and damaging the ongoing nature of the relationship between practitioner and patient.

Appearance

The practitioner's physical appearance including dress, hairstyle and facial hair can affect a patient's confidence in their ability to accurately diagnose and treat them. This is exemplified below, by McKinstry and Wang (1991).

Focus on... McKinstry and Wang (1991)

▶ AIM

McKinstry and Wang (1991) studied how clothing affects the practitioner-patient relationship. Specifically, they examined whether doctors' clothing influenced the patients' respect for the doctor's opinion and how acceptable the patients found different styles of clothing.

▶ METHODOLOGY

The study involved 475 patients who had appointments with 30 doctors from five general practices in Lothian, Scotland. Participants were asked to answer a questionnaire which was administered by a research assistant who visited each surgery on five separate occasions.

Patients looked at five photographs of a male doctor and three photographs of a female doctor, differing only in the degree of formality of their clothing. The males wore either a white coat, suit, tweed jacket, cardigans or jeans and the female wore either white coat, skirt or trousers. Participants were asked, 'Which doctor would you feel happiest about seeing for the first time?' and their level of confidence in the doctor. They were also asked which photograph looked most like their own doctor. Finally, they answered closed questions about the clothes worn by each of the doctors.

▶ RESULTS

There was a highly significant relationship between the ages of the patient and their choice of doctor. Older patients gave higher scores to the male doctor in the suit and white coat and the female doctor in the white coat.

▼ Table 8.1 Percentage of top acceptability score (5) for the doctors in the different styles of clothes

	Percentage of patients							
	Male doctor					Female doctor		
Acceptability score	White coat	Suit	Tweed jacket	Cardigan	Jeans	White coat	Skirt	Trousers
5	38%	50%	30%	16%	13%	55%	47%	22%

The male doctor wearing a suit received the highest score from the greatest number of people. The female doctor was seen as most acceptable when she was wearing a white coat. Fifty per cent of participants gave the doctor wearing the jeans an acceptability rating of either 0 or 1. Only 11 per cent of participants gave the female doctor in trousers an acceptability rating of either 0 or 1, while 41 per cent of participants reported that they would have more confidence in the ability of one of the pictured doctors based on their appearance.

When asked if there was a doctor they would feel unhappy about consulting, 28 per cent (134) participants responded 'yes' (significantly more female than male participants, 104 vs 30). The male doctor in the cardigan or the male doctor in jeans and the female doctor in trousers were most likely to be mentioned.

The majority of the participants reported that the way the doctor dressed was either very important (11 per cent) or quite important (53 per cent). Thirty-six per cent thought that it was of no importance.

Some participants voted in a way that matched the clothing choice of their own doctor, suggesting their scores were affected by the outfits that seemed most familiar.

CONCLUSIONS

The findings suggest that patients prefer doctors to dress in a more traditional/conservative manner and McKinstry and Wang (1991) note that doctors may dress in a certain way in order to gain their patients' approval. Interestingly, the doctors wearing white coats received relatively high scores despite the fact that most general practitioners in the UK do not wear them.

Evaluating McKinstry and Wang (1991)

One strength is that the study used photographs of unknown doctors rather than asking participants to talk about their own doctors. This is important as personal relationships with their doctors will not have affected the scores that they gave, as if you have a poor relationship, you may give a poor score whatever they wore. This makes the findings regarding the importance of dress code more valid.

Another strength is that the structured questionnaires collected **quantitative data** which makes the results more **objective**. For example, the questionnaires asked closed questions with rating scales, from 0 to 5. This is a strength as it limits researcher bias in the interpretation of the data allowing the researchers to test hypotheses such as, 'Patients will find the male doctor in a white coat more acceptable than the male doctor in jeans'.

One weakness of the research is that the results may not be **representative** of the wider population. For example, the sample in the study came from Lothian in Scotland which means that it may not be representative of other countries or even other parts of Scotland. This is a weakness as there may be a particular characteristic of the Scottish population that may have caused the results suggesting the results are not **generalisable**.

Another weakness of the study is that the photos of the doctors were not comparable between genders. There were more photos of males than females in a greater number of outfits. For example, there was no picture of a female doctor in a suit, whereas there was a picture of a male doctor in a suit. This might explain why the white coat was voted as being most favourable for the female doctor as this was the most formal clothes that she wore, meaning results may not be valid.

> ## LEARNING LINKS
> Questionnaires have been used in a number of the studies you have learned at AS Level. For example, Pozzulo *et al.* (line-ups) used questionnaires in their research. They also used photographs as part of their materials. Can you think of any differences in the use of questionnaires between the two studies? What problems might you encounter when using questionnaires with the samples from these two studies?

STUDY TIP
When you are learning the different types of non-verbal communication, it is helpful to think of examples of each that patients/doctors might encounter. Also, it may be worth thinking about what types of non-verbal communication you may use yourself in everyday life. For example, think about how non-verbal communication is affected by the formality of the situation, such as formal versus informal.

> ## TEST YOURSELF
>
> 1 Mason is a doctor in a local practice and is interested in the effect of non-verbal communication on patients at the surgery and wants to conduct some research.
>   a Suggest one type of non-verbal communication Mason could concentrate on in his research. [2]
>   b Suggest one way Mason could research non-verbal communication other than through the use of questionnaires. [2]
> 2 Suggest one reason why research into non-verbal communication may be reliable. [2]
> 3 a Describe research into non-verbal communications with a focus on practitioner clothing. [6]
>   b Evaluate research into non-verbal communications with a focus on practitioner clothing including a discussion on generalisability. [10]
> 4 Describe one strength and one weakness of using questionnaires to study the effect of practitioner clothing on non-verbal communication. [4]
> 5 Explain one methodological issue from a study into the effect of practitioner clothing in non-verbal communication. [2]
> 6 Explain one ethical issue that researchers might have considered when investigating the effect of practitioner clothing in non-verbal communication. [2]

KEY TERMS

verbal communication

primacy effect

utilizers

underutilizers

Verbal communication

Think!

What is meant by the primacy effect? How can this affect how much information a patient remembers after they have been to see their doctor?

Think!

Have you ever attended a medical appointment where you did not understand all of the words used by the practitioner? How did this make you feel? If this happened, did you ask the practitioner to explain what they meant? If not, why was this?

Think!

What ethical considerations would there be if a researcher decided to investigate verbal communication by observing real appointments?

Dr Daria recently had a consultation with a patient about stopping smoking and gave them advice about a number of treatments that they could undertake. The consultation was conducted remotely but seemed to go well. However, the patient has asked for an appointment face-to-face as they felt like they did not fully understand what Dr Daria had been saying and they felt confused. Think about what you now know about the interpersonal skills of a doctor and a patient.

» What do you think may have gone wrong in the initial consultation?

» How could Dr Daria make sure her patient understands more about possible treatments at their face-to-face consultation?

▲ Figure 8.3

METHODOLOGY

experiments

questionnaires

quantitative data

generalisations from findings

In healthcare settings, **verbal communication** tends to focus on the way the practitioner questions the patient to gain information about their condition, and the type of language that the practitioner uses to convey information about the patient's diagnosis and treatment.

Svarstad and Mechanic (1976) found that patients often lack important knowledge about their treatment. Half of the patients that she interviewed did not know how long they should take their medication for and one fifth did not know why they were taking the medication or how frequently they should take it. This suggests that either the practitioners are not conveying the information clearly or they are not conveying it at all.

Ranjan *et al.* (2015) recommended that when practitioners have to break bad news to patients about their diagnosis or treatment, it is important for them to: use simple non-technical language, use open-ended questions to assess how prepared the patient is to receive bad news and give information in small portions to allow the patients to comprehend what is being said to them. They also recommend using empathetic statements, so patients feel supported and doctors are able to express their own sadness or emotion about the diagnosis. However, Monden *et al.* (2016) found that only 40 per cent of practitioners surveyed felt that they had the sufficient skills to deliver bad news, whilst 93 per cent thought that it was a very important skill. This highlights the importance of training for practitioners in communication. Practitioners who deliver bad news without empathy can create barriers between themselves and the patient which can in turn create hostility towards the practitioner and may even be extended to health professionals in general.

Factors that can affect verbal communication

Primacy effect

Information from the beginning of the consultation is likely to be remembered better than information from the middle. This information will be stored in the patient's long term memory (Ley, 1988).

Forgetting

Patients often remember little of their appointment with their practitioner. Richard *et al.* (2016) reported that patients remember as little as a fifth of information discussed and immediately forget between 40 and 80 per cent of what was said to them at their appointment. Ley (1988) found they recalled 55 per cent of the information which they had been told but their recall did not improve with repetition. However, categorising the information did help recall.

Traditionally, any lack of understanding or barriers to communication between patients and practitioners has been blamed on the patient but more recently attention has turned to the way practitioners communicate with their patients. One barrier to communication that psychologists have investigated is the use of medical terminology.

Focus on... McKinlay (1975)

▶ AIM

To investigate the understanding of technical language among working class families in a Scottish maternity ward.

▶ METHODOLOGY

The sample consisted of 87 unskilled, working-class families who were accessing obstetrics and gynaecology appointments. Obstetrics is a specialist area of medicine relating to pregnancy, childbirth and the time period just after the birth (postpartum) and gynaecology is an area of medicine concerned with the female reproductive organs. The sample was divided into two groups; those who attended regular appointments (**utilisers**) and those who underused the service (**underutilisers**).

They were presented with a list of 13 words that a group of practitioners working on the wards had indicated they would normally use when questioning or explaining something to a patient.

Patients heard the word spoken aloud, then heard it again in the context of a sentence. Next, they were asked to say the meaning of the word. Their responses were recorded word-for-word (verbatim).

Two of the practitioners working on the wards scored the responses in the following categories:
a   Not understood the word at all and said that they had not
b   Gave a response but the meaning was completely wrong
c   Gave an incomplete or unclear response
d   Had a good understanding.

Participants were assigned a number so the practitioners who were scoring the responses did not know whether the participants were utilizers or underutilizers. Therefore, the scoring was 'blind'.

RESULTS

There was a consistently higher word comprehension amongst those patients who used the service often (utilizers) on a number of words.

▼ Table 8.2 The percentage of the sample who showed wrong or vague knowledge compared with adequate understanding on five of the 13 words

	Utilisers		Underutilisers	
	Wrong or vague knowledge	Adequate understanding	Wrong or vague knowledge	Adequate understanding
Antibiotic	44.4	41.7	60.0	28.9
Breech	0.0	100	6.7	84.4
Mucus	22.2	47.2	33.3	33.3
Glucose	36.1	44.4	44.4	37.8
Enamel	30.6	61.1	40.0	51.1

There were a number of words where patients in both groups showed a lack of comprehension. Such as *purgative* (57.8 per cent and 72.2 per cent for the underutilisers and utilisers said they had no knowledge of the word). Patients also showed little understanding of the words *rhesus* and *umbilicus*.

McKinlay (1975) also investigated the relationship between how well they thought that patients would understand the medical terminology and how many of them actually used the words.

▼ Table 8.3 Percentage of patients that doctors expected to have 'adequate knowledge of words' compared to the percentage of patients who actually had adequate knowledge and the percentage of doctors using the words

	% of patients that the doctors 'thought' would have an adequate understanding of the words	% of underutilisers who had adequate knowledge	% of utilisers who had adequate knowledge	% of the doctors actually using the words with patients
Antibiotic	5.6	28.9	41.7	44.4
Breech	22.2	84.4	100.0	38.9
Membranes	0.0	44.4	63.9	44.4
Protein	16.7	0.0	11.1	55.6

CONCLUSIONS

- Physicians consistently underestimated the level of word comprehension of the working-class participants.
- A large percentage of doctors used certain words when communicating with patients, despite assuming that the patients would have little understanding of the majority of the words.
- The responsibility for a lack of understanding actually lies with the practitioners for using medical terminology while assuming that their patients will not actually comprehend what they are saying and for underestimating the abilities of the patients to comprehend the terminology.

Evaluating McKinlay (1975)

One strength is that the study had high **ecological validity**. For example, patients were interviewed at the clinic about words that they would be likely to hear in one of their clinic sessions. Therefore, their understanding of the words presented is likely to represent their real-life understanding of the language used in their clinics.

A weakness is that the sample were all working class mothers attending obstetric or gynaecologist appointments and are therefore unrepresentative of the target population. There may be something about this sample in terms of the type of appointments they are attending or their social class which makes the results more likely. If patients with a wider range of conditions, from more diverse social classes were included, then the results may be different; suggesting the findings might not be generalisable.

> ## ISSUES AND DEBATES

Application to everyday life

One strength of the study is that it is applicable to real-life situations. This means that the focus is moved away from the patient and towards the practitioner in terms of responsibility for communication barriers, and strategies can be put in place to improve comprehension. For example, in some hospitals new mothers look at new literature that is designed for parents who are expecting a baby to see whether the terminology used is likely to be accessible and understandable by patients from different backgrounds. This shows how the results of the study have helped to change working practices in health care.

Idiographic versus nomothetic

One possible weakness is that researchers looking at practitioner and patient interpersonal skills use a nomothetic approach and focus on groups of people. Although this can be useful in terms of generalising their findings, it can be argued that an idiographic approach would be better as qualitative methods can be used in order to discover individual needs the patients may have. It might be that those needs change depending on their circumstances. For example, a patient visiting the doctor with back problems might need a different style of communication than if they have mental health problems or receive a diagnosis of a potentially life changing illness such as cancer.

STUDY TIP

To help you learn the findings from the McKinlay study, write as many conclusions from the data in the tables as you can. Also, you can understand the use of technical language more by doing your own experiment. Think of all the technical language (terminology) you have learned in psychology since you started. Write down twenty key terms, then check the comprehension of AS Level students who have just started psychology and A Level students. Use the four categories McKinlay used and see what your results are. How do you think this would affect the learning of students if your teacher used this terminology in psychology lessons right at the start of AS Level? How would it make them feel?

▶ LEARNING LINKS

McKinlay's study can be said to have high ecological validity. This was also true of the study by Piliavin *et al.* from the social approach (see page 153). What is meant by the term 'ecological validity'? McKinlay and Piliavin differ though with regard to why they have high ecological validity. Can you see why? How could you make the ecological validity of McKinlay's study even higher?

> ## TEST YOURSELF

1 Dr Harper wants to make sure that there is a high level of understanding about treatments discussed with patients.

Suggest *one* piece of advice that could be given to Dr Harper to ensure a high level of understanding in patients. [2]

2 Explain *two* factors that can affect verbal communication. [4]

3 a Describe what psychologists have discovered about verbal communication between patients and practitioners. [6]

b Evaluate what psychologists have discovered about verbal communication between patients and practitioners, including a discussion of nomothetic versus idiographic. [10]

4 Explain *one* ethical issue that researchers might have considered when investigating the understanding of medical terminology in verbal communication. [2]

5 Explain *one* strength and *one* weakness of using interviews to investigate verbal communication. [4]

6 Suggest *one* way that verbal communication could be investigated other than using an interview. [2]

7 Compare verbal and non-verbal communication in the patient–practitioner relationship. [6]

KEY TERMS

diagnosis
false positive
false negative
terminal
cultural differences

METHODOLOGY

validity

8.1.2 Patient and practitioner diagnosis and style

Think!

What is meant by a **false positive** diagnosis?

Think!

Have you ever been to the doctor and found it difficult to explain your symptoms? Why might people find their symptoms difficult to explain? What do you think could be done to make it easier?

Think!

Differences in both the individual (practitioner and patient) and the situation can affect how a **diagnosis** is made and presented. Can you think of any individual and situational factors which could affect this process?

Making a diagnosis

Disclosure of information

For doctors to make a valid diagnosis, the patient needs to provide them with enough information. However, research has found that the amount of information given can depend on a number of factors including the gender of the practitioner. For example, Hall *et al.* (1994) found that patients gave more medical information to female practitioners, who in turn asked more questions and conducted longer visits.

There may also be certain circumstances where the patients themselves can make diagnosis difficult. For example, if they insist on more tests, even though the doctors say that they do not need them, if they ignore what the doctor is saying or if they become angry (Sarafino, 2006).

Patients understand, interpret and communicate their symptoms in a number of different ways, and this may make it difficult for the doctor to make a valid or reliable diagnosis. Some patients may lack the vocabulary to explain what is wrong with them, whereas others may unintentionally give misleading information that they have found on the internet. Some patients may be concerned that their symptoms may be something serious and avoid giving too much information about their illness or appear not worried in the hope that the doctor will say that there is nothing to worry about (Sarafino, 2006).

False positive and false negative diagnosis

Sometimes doctors get the diagnosis wrong. There are over 1300 known diseases and the doctor has between five and twenty minutes to make a diagnosis. This can be challenging for the doctor as they cannot be an expert in all areas. This is even more difficult when the patient is unable or unwilling to communicate their symptoms effectively. There are two main types of errors that doctors can make:

False positive

This is where the doctor diagnoses a patient as being ill when they are actually healthy. For example, if a doctor told you that you had an illness such as schizophrenia based on your symptoms, and you did not have it.

False negative

This is where the doctor diagnoses a patient as being healthy when they do have a diagnosable medical condition, either physical or psychological. An example of this might be if a patient had found a lump in their breast and the doctor told them it was nothing to worry about, but the patient later found out that they had breast cancer.

Presenting a diagnosis

Research has found that communication may be far less dependent on the specific words used than on the *meaning* that is conveyed by the doctor. Shapiro *et al.* (1992) conducted an experiment into how practitioners presented **mammogram** results to a group of women at risk of breast cancer. The women viewed a video clip of a practitioner giving the results who either appeared 'worried' or 'not worried'. The participants receiving the results from the 'worried physician' recalled significantly less information, reported significantly higher levels of anxiety and had significantly higher pulse rates. The findings suggest that the mood of the physician can have a significant effect on how well a patient receives difficult information about a diagnosis. This suggests that when delivering difficult news, practitioners who appear calm and unworried are likely to be more effective in reducing patients' stress.

During the Covid-19 pandemic, receiving a diagnosis of a serious illness became even more challenging due to regulations preventing patients from being accompanied by relatives or friends. Diagnoses were also frequently given over the telephone. Although this meant patients could have someone with them for support, non-verbal communication was missing, making the situation all the more difficult for both the practitioner and the patient.

Evaluating research into making and presenting diagnoses

> ISSUES AND DEBATES

Applications to everyday life

One strength of research into how doctors make and present a diagnosis is that it has applications to everyday life. For example, research has informed practitioners that keeping a calm and unworried appearance when presenting a diagnosis will mean that patients are less stressed and are likely to remember more of the information given. Understanding their diagnosis properly should help patients to make informed decisions about their treatment pathway.

Cultural differences

One issue is that **cultural differences** may influence the disclosure of information from the practitioner to the patient. For example, Elwyn *et al.* (2002) notes that in the United States of America it is common for patients to be told their diagnosis no matter how serious it is whereas in Japan, patients are often not told their diagnosis, especially if their condition is **terminal** (Noguchi, 2007). In this situation, it is more common for the family to be told the diagnosis rather than the patient. In America practitioners normally only inform family members of a diagnosis with the consent of the patient. This may also show that researchers should take a more idiographic approach when looking at diagnosis as practitioners should consider cultural factors and individual differences when making and presenting a diagnosis.

One weakness is that the research in this area often lacks ecological **validity**. For example, in Shapiro *et al.* (1992) participants were asked to watch video clips of practitioners giving a diagnosis and then comment on their body language. One problem with this is that the participants may not have felt the same emotion that they might have done if they were receiving a real diagnosis. Therefore, the findings may not be generalisable to real life settings.

Another weakness is that research in this area can present ethical issues. For example, in Shapiro *et al.*'s (1992) study the use of patients who are at risk of cancer may be unethical as even though the videos they watched were not their own diagnosis it may have caused them distress. In addition, in Noguchi (2007), Japanese patients were not informed of a terminal diagnosis. This creates a moral and ethical dilemma for the researchers as to whether patients have the right to access all the information about their health, no matter how serious the diagnosis.

Figure 8.4 shows an elderly gentleman discussing medical issues with a female doctor. What does psychological research suggest about the amount of information a female doctor receives from her patient? Are there any ways the doctor could help the patient to explain their symptoms more effectively and without high levels of stress?

▲ Figure 8.4

LEARNING LINK

One issue with research into making and presenting a diagnosis is possible ethical issues. Can you think of any studies you have learned at AS Level that have also had issues with ethics, in particular distress and possible harm?

STUDY TIP

It is sometimes easy to get confused between false positive and false negative diagnoses. Try to imagine the doctor saying 'no, you are not ill' when you are lying in bed with a fever and spots all over your body or diagnosing you as ill when you feel absolutely fine and all tests have come back okay. Which of the above is an example of a false positive diagnosis?

8

> ### TEST YOURSELF
>
> 1 Areeba is a doctor at a local practice. She is very tired and is worried about getting a diagnosis incorrect especially as she only has a small amount of time with each patient.
>   Explain two types of errors that Areeba could make when diagnosing a patient. [4]
> 2 Explain what is meant by cultural differences, with an example from presenting a diagnosis to a patient. [2]
> 3 a Describe what psychologists have discovered about making and presenting a diagnosis. [6]
>   b Evaluate what psychologists have discovered about making and presenting a diagnosis, including a discussion of validity. [10]
> 4 Patients can sometimes give misleading information to their practitioner making diagnosis difficult.
>   a Plan a study using a questionnaire to investigate to what extent patients check their symptoms on the internet before seeing their doctor and how much they use the information they have found when describing their symptoms to the doctor.
>   Your plan must include details of:
>   – the structure of your questionnaire
>   – sampling technique. [10]
>   b i State two reasons for your choice of sampling technique. [2]
>   ii Explain one strength of your choice of sampling technique. [2]

Key study: The effect of practitioner style on patient satisfaction – Savage and Armstrong (1990)

KEY TERMS

general practitioner

sharing style

directed style

paternalistic

autonomy

> ### Think!
>
> What are the differences between **sharing style** and **directed style** in doctors' consultations?

> ### Think!
>
> How would you feel if your doctor asked you what you thought was wrong with you, rather than telling you what they thought?

> ### Think!
>
> Imagine you wanted to replicate Savage and Armstrong's study but in a laboratory setting. How would your study be both similar and different?

Introducing David Armstrong

When this paper was published, Professor Armstrong was a Reader in Sociology as applied to Medicine and an Honorary Consultant in Public Health Medicine in the National Health Service, in the UK. He and his colleague Dr Dick Savage, a general practitioner from South London, also in the UK had various discussions about whether general practitioners should adopt a 'paternal' or 'patient-centred' approach. The evidence for either approach was lacking so Armstrong and Savage decided to conduct a randomised controlled trial to investigate the effects of the different approaches. Despite being a relatively small study, according to Armstrong it remains the only trial on this important question. (D. Armstrong, personal communication, 2021).

METHODOLOGY

validity

» To what extent do you think that doctors should use sharing style consultations in their practices? Do you think patients prefer this style?
» How would you investigate whether personality had an impact on the style of consultation that patients prefer?

▲ Figure 8.5

CONTEXT

A number of studies have shown that general practitioners who use a sharing style during consultations tend to achieve greater levels of patient satisfaction and their patients are more willing to follow medical advice.

A sharing style actively involves the patient in the consultation such as asking them what they think is wrong with them and how they would like the doctor to help them. The traditional style of consultation is directed style. This involves the doctor making the diagnosis after listening to the patient's symptoms and telling them what treatment they need. This is seen as **paternalistic**, where the doctor is seen as the authority figure who is in control of the patient's wellbeing for their own good, but in doing so, limits their **autonomy**.

AIMS

To investigate whether patient satisfaction is increased with a sharing style of consultation compared to a directed style.

METHODOLOGY

This study is a field experiment. It took place in an inner London general practice. Data was collected by questionnaire.

Sample

Two hundred randomly sampled patients from an inner London General Practice (aged between 16 and 75) completed two questionnaires. Originally, 359 patients were chosen but a number of them did not complete both assessments, so their data was not used.

A random number generator was used to select four patients from each surgery the doctor held over a period of four months. A patient presenting any form of symptom was eligible to be part of the study.

PROCEDURE

Patients gave consent for their appointments to be audio-recorded for a research project. Participants were randomly allocated into one of two conditions (the **independent variable**) by a set of cards that were placed on the doctor's desk, face down. The card allocating the patient to a condition was only turned over once the patient had been identified as being suitable for the study.

The two conditions were:
1 a directed style of consultation
2 a sharing style of consultation.

The doctor also had prompts which gave examples of directed and sharing styles of consultation.

▼ Table 8.4 Prompts used by the doctor in the different styles of consultation

		Style of consultation	
	Part of the consultation	**Sharing**	**Directed**
1	Judgement on the consultation	Why do you think this happened?	This is a serious problem/ this is not a serious problem
2	Diagnosis	What do you think is wrong?	You are suffering from...
3	Treatment	Would you like a prescription? What have you tried to do to help so far?	It is essential that you take this medicine
4	Prognosis	What do these symptoms mean to you?	You should be better in.... days
5	Follow up and closure	When would you like to come and see me again?	Come and see me in.... days/I don't need to see you again for this problem

Dependent variables

At the end of the consultation, the participant was given a questionnaire to complete in the waiting room and told to hand it to the receptionist before leaving. The questions asked were:
1 I was able to discuss my problem well.
2 I received an excellent explanation.
3 I perceived the practitioner to have complete understanding.
4 I felt greatly helped.
5 I felt much better.

A second questionnaire, with a stamped addressed envelope, was given to the patient. They were told to complete the questionnaire one week later and to post it back. The questions asked were the same as the first questionnaire.

After the patient left, the length of the consultation, demographics and other information from the notes were recorded on a computer.

▶ RESULTS

There were no significant differences in terms of age, sex, ethnic origin, reason for visiting the doctor or style of consultation between those participants who completed both questionnaires and those who did not.

There were no significant differences in the length of consultation between the sharing and directed styles of consultation.

On the initial questionnaire, significantly more participants who had received the directed style of consultation agreed with the statement '*I received an excellent explanation*' compared to the sharing style (45 per cent versus 24 per cent). This number reduced on the follow-up questionnaire (33 per cent versus 17 per cent), but there was still a significant difference.

Both on the initial questionnaire and on the follow up questionnaire, significantly more participants in the directed style group compared to the sharing style group (62 per cent versus 37 per cent) agreed with the statement '*I perceived the general practitioner to have a complete understanding*'.

There was no significant difference between the two groups when responding to '*I felt greatly helped*' and '*I felt much better*' in the first questionnaire. On the follow-up questionnaire, significantly more of the directed style group agreed that they felt greatly helped compared to the sharing style group.

Participants in the directed style group who rarely attended the surgery showed a significantly better perception of the doctor's explanation and understanding of their problem on the follow up questionnaire.

> ## CONCLUSIONS
> ● Directed style consultations lead to greater patient satisfaction regarding the doctor's understanding of patients' problems and the quality of the doctor's explanation. This suggests that patients prefer certainty and paternalism when they visit the doctor, and for the doctor to be an authority figure.
> ● The directed style does not provide greater satisfaction during longer consultations where advice is the main treatment and patients are thought to have either chronic or psychological illnesses.
> ● Patients with simple physical illnesses benefit more from a directed style of consultation.

 ## Methodological strengths and weaknesses

A strength of the study was that it took place in a real-life setting. For example, it used real patients coming for actual consultations with their doctor. This means that the study is high in ecological **validity** and should reflect typical patient-practitioner interactions, at least as far as the patient's behaviour is concerned.

Another strength was that it used random sampling to select participants for the study. This should mean that participants are representative of the patients in the doctors' surgery. Had the practitioner used opportunity sampling, he might have only used patients that he knew well or that he knew they generally responded well to his normal style of consultation.

A weakness of the study is that the doctor followed prompts that were on his table. The doctor may have felt less relaxed than usual during these consultations. This was probably particularly true of those consultations that were not typical of his normal interpersonal style. This could have affected how the patients responded to him and in turn how they rated him after the consultation, thus lowering the validity of the study.

Another weakness is that a significant number of the participants failed to complete both the first questionnaire (11 per cent) and the follow-up questionnaire (44 per cent). It might be that those participants who completed the questionnaires had a certain personality type, which could have impacted the **generalisability** of the data they provided.

 ## Ethics

The participants all gave consent to take part in the research, although they did not know that the research was about different consulting styles. The participants could choose not to complete either of the questionnaires and therefore had the right to withdraw. The researcher also excluded any participants with life threatening conditions or whom they perceived might be upset by taking part or incapable of completing the questionnaires.

 ## Applications to everyday life

Research into practitioner diagnosis and interpersonal style has significant applications to everyday life. By understanding which style of consultation works best for different patients, practitioners can adapt their style to suit individual patients. This may help with information disclosure meaning practitioners are able to make more accurate diagnoses.

>
> ### ISSUES AND DEBATES
>
> #### Determinism versus free will
> A great deal of research in psychology suggests that people's thoughts and behaviour are determined by genetic and environmental factors and that people have no free will over how they think and behave. However, techniques such as counselling can help patients change how they cope with a serious diagnosis. This shows that people can use their free will to change how they think, feel and approach the treatment of an illness (Boulton *et al.*, 2001). This is important because research has found that attitudes towards diagnosis of serious illnesses is correlated with survival rates from the illness and with it not recurring (Greer *et al.*, 1979).

Individual and situational explanations

Savage and Armstrong's research offers situational explanations for whether patient satisfaction is increased by either a sharing or directed style. However, it ignores individual differences that could impact on which style is more preferable to a patient. Although the directive style appeared to lead to greater patient satisfaction overall, there are likely to be individual differences whereby directive style increased satisfaction for some people more than others. For example, some patients may already have a good understanding of their medical condition and the treatment options available and therefore may prefer a more sharing style. This is important as doctors should take such factors into consideration and be flexible in terms of matching the style of communication (situational factor) to their knowledge of the patient's personality, level of understanding, cultural background (individual factors) and so on.

▶ REFLECTION

- Generalisability is one issue that is discussed when looking at research. Do you think that this study is generalisable?
- Do you feel that these results may be different in other cultures? Why do you think this may be so?

▶ LEARNING LINK

At AS Level, you looked at how Saavedra and Silverman investigated button phobia in a young boy. Do you think that he would have benefited from them using a sharing style with the boy during their research? Do you think the age of a patient affects the preferred style?

STUDY TIP

When you are learning key studies you need to make sure that you learn all of the different aspects such as the aims, research methods, procedure and so on. You could make up a set of ten questions which would test your knowledge of the different areas and then go back to them a few days after you have learned the study and see if you can answer them.

▶ TEST YOURSELF

1   Kelsey wants to conduct research into how satisfied patients are with consultations with their doctor. However, she does not want to use a questionnaire.
   a   Suggest one way Kelsey could conduct her research on patient satisfaction other than through the use of a questionnaire. [2]
   b   Outline one weakness of the research method you suggested in (a) as a way of researching patient satisfaction. [2]
2   Describe how the patients were randomly allocated into the two different conditions in Savage and Armstrong's (1990) study. [2]
3   a   Describe the study by Savage and Armstrong (1990) on the effect of a general practitioner's consulting style on patients' satisfaction. [6]
   b   Evaluate the study by Savage and Armstrong, including a discussion about applications to everyday life. [10]
4   Explain one difference between sharing and directed styles of diagnosis. [2]

From the key study by Savage and Armstrong (1990) on the effect of consulting style on patient satisfaction:
5   Describe the dependent variables used in the research. [2]
6   Outline one ethical issue that was addressed in the research. [2]
7   Explain one strength and one weakness of using a field experiment when researching the effect of consulting style on patient satisfaction. [4]

KEY TERMS

appraisal delay
total delay
utilisation delay
illness delay
perceived threat
perceived susceptibility
perceived seriousness
perceived benefits
perceived barriers
health belief model
cue to action

METHODOLOGY

interviews
case study
generalisations from findings

8.1.3 Misusing health services
Delay in seeking treatment

Think!

Why do people sometimes delay their efforts to seek treatment?

Think!

Sarafino (2006) found that using questionnaires to study treatment delay had a number of issues such as lack of understanding, therefore interviews were used instead. Can you think of any problems that may arise due to the use of interviews? Remember there are three different interview formats, two different techniques and two different question formats.

Think!

Imagine, your friend's grandmother has been having pains in her hip for the last few weeks, but she still will not go to the doctor. She says she thinks it is just old age. How would the health belief model explain her delaying treatment?

In the UK, patients can sometimes be waiting for a long time on the telephone trying to get through to their doctor, only to find out that all of the appointments have gone by the time they finally get through to the surgery. How do you think that might affect patients seeking treatment?

▲ Figure 8.6

Delay in seeking treatment is defined as the time between the patient first noticing a symptom to the time when they are first seen by a doctor. Safer *et al.* (1979) suggested that the decisions and thought processes that a person has when they first experience a symptom may be very different to those they experience when they first suspect that they may be ill. There may be many reasons why someone would delay seeking treatment. For example, they might not have a trusting relationship with their doctor. If they have had a prior experience where they might not have felt listened to, or were misdiagnosed, then it could affect how quickly they seek treatment. Another reason might be a perceived stigma around seeking treatment for mental health concerns.

Fernando *et al.* (2017) found that delays in help-seeking for mental health problems in Sri Lanka are influenced not just by the perception of stigma from the individuals but also from their family caregivers. They found that around 15 per cent of patients and carers reported delays in seeking help for their illness due to stigma-related concerns.

Bruffaerts *et al.* (2007) found that the median duration of delay in treatment was one year for mood disorders, but 16 years for anxiety in a sample of the Belgian general population. However, they suggest that the onset of these mental health concerns might be during childhood or adolescence and may be viewed by the individuals as a normal part of their everyday lives rather than being viewed in terms of mental ill health

Health belief model as an explanation for delay

According to the **health belief model** (HBM), decisions about whether to seek medical help are determined by the extent to which patients see their symptoms as a perceived threat. Sarafino (2006) suggested that the **perceived threat** felt by patients about their current symptoms may also be influenced by the information they have received from their peers or via mass media. This is particularly true for illnesses which receive a great deal of media attention such as cancer. These symptoms, and indeed the perceived threat created by them, create a **cue to action** which alerts the person that there is something wrong; these cues to action can also come from conversations with friends or information that the patient has seen on social media or the television.

The second factor discussed in the HBM is **perceived susceptibility**. This refers to the extent to which people think they are vulnerable to having the illness that they think they have. The final factor is **perceived seriousness**. This refers to how serious the person thinks that illness will be and its potential effect on their life. The Health Belief Model (HBM) suggests that people also tend to weigh up the **perceived benefits** of seeking treatment, for example better health versus the **perceived barriers** of the treatment itself such as side effects, time, cost. People who believe that treatment can be of benefit to them tend to seek treatment quicker than those who do not see the benefit.

In general, people who feel threatened by their symptoms tend to see their practitioner more quickly, whereas people who do not view their symptoms as a threat to their health may delay seeking help or avoid seeing their practitioner completely.

Safer *et al.* (1979) reported that the majority of research into delays in seeking medical care focuses simply on the time between noticing the symptom and when they are first seen at the clinic. They decided to investigate whether the time delay can be broken into different stages and factors that affect the delay. Furthermore, they asked whether different decisions and processes are involved at different stages in the delay.

> ## ISSUES AND DEBATES

Reductionism versus holism

The health belief model explanation for why people delay in seeking treatment can be thought to be holistic in its approach as it considers multiple reasons, including external influences such as friends and social media, and internal reasons such as how much of a perceived threat they believe their symptoms pose. A disadvantage of this is that it is hard to isolate which variables might have the strongest effect in delaying seeking treatment, making it difficult to create effective interventions. This suggests that research that takes a more reductionist approach may be necessary, however, it can be difficult to carry out this type of research in health psychology as it is often impossible to manipulate variables for practical and ethical reasons.

Focus on... Safer *et al.* (1979)

> ## AIM

To investigate factors that influence delays in seeking medical treatment.

> ## METHODOLOGY

An opportunity sample of 93 patients completed a 45-minute structured interview. The patients were approached in the waiting room of four clinics in an inner-city hospital. If patients reported that they were seeing the doctor or nurse about a new symptom or illness, they were asked to take part in the study.

The patient was asked questions about their symptoms and their reactions to their symptoms such as *'Do you expect the treatment will be uncomfortable?'*. The patient was also asked to state the length of delay at various stages of the illness. These stages were defined as:
- **Total delay** The time from first noticing symptoms up until the time they were interviewed at their appointment.
- **Appraisal delay** The number of days from first noticing a symptom of the illness to concluding that they were ill.

- **Illness delay** The number of days from concluding that they were ill until the time that they decided to get professional help from a physician or nurse.
- **Utilisation delay** The number of days from deciding to seek help to being interviewed at the clinic.

Patients were given a scale to measure their emotional reactions to the symptoms (for example, worried or angry). A seven-item scale was also used to measure the extent to which patients imagined negative consequences for their symptoms and treatment (for example imagining themselves on the operating table and their family crying because they are ill). Participants were also questioned about the level of pain that they were experiencing on a ten-item scale.

▶ RESULTS

- Total delay: Whether the patient also has a competing problem or issue in their life such as marriage or divorce (23.8 day delay) versus no competing problem (7.2 day delay) had the highest correlation with total delay. Level of pain was negatively correlated with total delay. Higher levels of painful symptoms led to shorter total delay (8.6 day delay) while lower levels led to longer total delays (23.8 day delay). Finally, not reading about your symptoms (11.5 days) meant shorter delays than reading a great deal about your symptoms (50.2 days).
- Appraisal delay: Pain has the highest correlation with appraisal delay with little or no pain averaging a delay of 7.5 days with those with a severe pain averaging 2.5 days. Second highest correlation was reading a great deal about symptoms (19.6 days) versus not reading about symptoms (3.5 days). The third highest correlation was the presence of bleeding (1.2 days) versus those without bleeding (4.8 days).
- Illness delay: Patients with new symptoms delayed by an average of 2.5 days, whereas those with old and frequently experienced symptoms delayed by an average of 11.3 days. Negative imagery was the next highest correlate. If the patient imagined negative consequences of being sick, the delay was 4.4 days, while those with little negative imagery delayed just 1.9 days on average.
- Utilisation delay: The highest correlation with utilisation delay was worry over cost. Patients who were very concerned delayed by 9.7 days on average, whereas those who were not concerned delayed by an average of 2.0 days. Again, pain was correlated with those patients experiencing pain delayed by an average of 1.6 days compared to 3.8 days by patients experiencing no pain. Those patients who felt their symptoms could not be cured delayed by an average of 4.3 days, whereas those who felt they could be cured delayed by an average of 1.8 days.

▶ CONCLUSIONS

- Strong sensory signals such as bleeding or severe pain reduce the delay in seeking medical help for symptoms.
- Factors such as use of negative imagery, concerns over the cost of treatment and whether or not the patient feels they could be cured all contribute to delayed help-seeking behaviour.
- Researching symptoms is associated with delaying help-seeking behaviour.

Evaluating Safer *et al.*

One weakness with Safer *et al.*'s research was that it used retrospective data. They asked patients to recall exact timings of when they first experienced symptoms, when they first realised that they were ill and when they decided to seek help. It might be that patients were inconsistent with their ability to accurately recall the time delays, especially considering they may have been under considerable stress. This affects the **reliability** of the results.

Another weakness is there are ethical issues with Safer *et al.*'s research. Firstly, they were interviewing people who were unwell. The interviews took 45 minutes which is a considerable amount of time when someone is feeling unwell and in fact, two participants had to withdraw from the research as they became too ill to continue. They were also asking patients to imagine negative consequences of their treatment, including 'my family crying because I was ill'. This could cause distress and potentially harm the participants.

One strength of the research is that Safer *et al.* conducted a pilot study in which participants were given the questionnaires to complete themselves. However, they found that many patients had trouble reading the questions. Therefore, in the main study, they used **interviews** and read the questions aloud. By conducting a pilot study, they were able to identify a flaw in the design and rectify it before testing their main sample. This demonstrates the benefit of pilot studies.

Another strength is that research into treatment delay has applications to everyday life including the development of strategies to reduce appraisal delay. For example, people could be urged to seek treatment for reasons other than sensory symptoms such as pain and to reduce utilisation delay you could ensure people are given information about help with costs. This means that the findings have benefits to wider society and to the health of individuals.

> ### STUDY TIP
>
> Creating podcasts can be a great way of learning a study, especially as you will be able to learn while doing other things like exercising or travelling to school.

> ### LEARNING LINKS
>
> Safer *et al.*'s findings suggest that pain and bleeding reduce patients' delay in seeking treatment. Think back to the learning approach at AS Level and the principles of operant conditioning that you learned about in the core studies. How could the shorter time a patient took to visit their practitioner be an example of negative reinforcement? Think about what the result of a consultation with the practitioner may be. Will this make it more or less likely they will go back to their practitioner with problems in the future?

> ### TEST YOURSELF
>
> 1 Emelia is worried about the number of patients who seem to be making appointments after experiencing symptoms for a number of months. She is putting together an action plan to reduce these delays.
>   Suggest two ways that Emelia could reduce the delays in people seeking treatment from doctors. [4]
> 2 Explain what is meant by appraisal delay. [2]
> 3 a Describe what psychologists have discovered about delays in seeking treatment. [6]
>   b Evaluate what psychologists have discovered about delays in seeking treatment, including a discussion about ethical issues. [10]
> 4 Explain one methodological weakness of using interviews to investigate why patients delay seeking treatment. [2]
> 5 Explain two ethical issues researchers would have to consider when researching why people delay in seeking treatment. [4]
> 6 Outline one disadvantage of using retrospective data to research delays in seeking treatment. [2]
> 7 Compare two explanations for why people delay in seeking treatment for an illness. [4]

KEY TERMS

Munchausen syndrome
malingering
falsification
faecal matter
deep vein thrombosis
factitious disorder
immune deficiency
neutrophil disorder
peregrination

METHODOLOGY

interviews
case study
generalisations from findings

Munchausen syndrome

> ### Think!
>
> What is the main difference between Munchausen syndrome (also known as **factitious disorder**) and **malingering**?

> **Think!**
>
> Why might case studies be the best research method for studying a condition like Munchausen's syndrome?

> **Think!**
>
> Imagine, you are a doctor, how might it feel to discover that your patient has been deliberately pretending to have symptoms of a serious illness?

Why do you think a nomothetic approach may not be appropriate for investigating Munchausen's syndrome? Imagine you have the opportunity to interview Richard Asher about the patients he worked with in London. Think of three open and three closed questions you could ask him based on the features identified in Table 8.5.

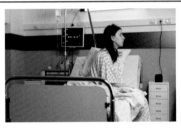

▲ Figure 8.7

The term **Munchausen's syndrome** was originally used by psychiatrist Richard Asher (1951) to refer to a group of patients in London, UK. These patients had gone to dramatic lengths to deceive doctors into believing that they were suffering from serious medical conditions, often requiring multiple surgeries. People with Munchausen syndrome tend to travel widely, sometimes even changing their names in the hope of receiving further treatments from doctors who are unaware of the deception. The name comes from a German aristocrat, Baron von Münchhausen, who was well known for exaggerating and deceiving people. Today, the disorder is more commonly referred to without the 's' and is used interchangeably with the term 'factitious disorder'. However, the term Munchausen syndrome tends to only be used in severe and chronic cases (Tatu, 2018) and cases where the symptoms are mainly physical, as opposed to physical and psychological (Aleem and Ajarim, 1995).

The word *factitious* comes from the Latin word for 'artificial' or 'contrived' and the DSM-5 (see page 117) indicates that a diagnosis of factitious disorder is made when a patient falsifies (fakes) physical or psychological signs or symptoms or induces an injury, illness or impairment of some sort (American Psychiatric Association, 2013). The diagnosis is only made when there is no obvious external reward other than the attention received and/or feelings of power associated with controlling medical professionals.

Falsification can take a variety of forms. For example, people may exaggerate genuine symptoms of a pre-existing medical condition or fabricate (make up) symptoms. Individuals may falsely report having neurological symptoms such as seizures, fainting or dizziness. Laboratory test results may be manipulated by deliberately adding blood to urine samples or by ingesting a substance, such as insulin. People may injure themselves or even induce illnesses through actions as unusual as injecting themselves with **faecal matter** (solid bodily waste), see Aleem and Ajarim (1995) below. Whatever the method chosen, this deceptive behaviour may lead healthcare professionals to perceive the person as more unwell than they actually are.

Munchausen syndrome is thought to be very rare, but the genuine prevalence is hard to establish due to the deception involved and, as noted above, the fact that patients often use different names as a way of receiving continued support for their falsified symptoms.

Diagnosing Munchausen syndrome

Jaghab *et al.* (2006) encourage practitioners to be alert to three signs of a possible case of Munchausen syndrome:
1 Lengthy medical records, including multiple admissions to different hospitals.
2 Willingness to submit to any medical procedure regardless of pain, discomfort or risk.
3 Inconsistencies between the patient's history and medical observations.

Before diagnosing this condition, practitioners must first rule out other possible causes of the patient's symptoms, including possible mental disorders, such as delusional disorder. Here the patient would genuinely believe that they were ill whereas in Munchausen syndrome patients actively deceive others. The disorder can be difficult to diagnose due to similarities with other disorders including substance abuse disorders and impulse-control disorders.

Table 8.5 lists the essential features and supporting features that Aleem and Ajarim (1995) indicate must be present in order to diagnose this condition. These are based on a list originally suggested by Folks and Freeman (1985).

▼ Table 8.5 Diagnostic features of Munchausen syndrome (Aleem and Ajarim, 1995)

Essential features	Supporting features
Pathological lying (pseudologia fantastica)	Borderline and/or antisocial personality traits
Peregrination (traveling or wandering)	Deprivation in childhood
Recurrent feigned or simulated illness	Equanimity for diagnostic procedures
	Equanimity for treatments or operations
	Evidence of self-induced physical signs
	Knowledge of or experience in a medical field
	Most likely to be male
	Multiple hospitalisations
	Multiple scars (usually abdominal)
	Police record
	Unusual or dramatic presentation

Patients are at risk of significant psychological distress and/or impairment through causing physical harm to themselves and friends, family and healthcare professionals are also likely to suffer as a consequence.

Malingering

An important aspect of the diagnosis of Munchausen syndrome is that the person does not receive any obvious external reinforcement or reward for their behaviour. When a person feigns or exaggerates symptoms but there is an obvious gain or incentive, the person may be said to be malingering. It is therefore critical that the practitioner is able to establish whether the person will benefit in any way, either by avoiding some negative, for example avoiding work, conscription into the military or punishment, including criminal prosecution or gaining something positive such as obtaining medications or drugs (to use or sell), receiving sickness or disability benefits, improved social housing or financial compensation. Malingering is thought to be more common in legal and military professions (avoiding dangerous duty) and comparatively less common in ordinary civilian life.

Focus on... Aleem and Ajarim (1995)

▶ AIM

To present a case study of Munchausen syndrome in a patient who was referred for a possible case of **immune deficiency** (when a person's immune system is not working properly).

▶ METHODOLOGY/FINDINGS

Aleem and Ajarim (1995) published a case study of a 22-year-old female university student who was referred to their hospital with a possible case of immune deficiency or **neutrophil disorder**. (A disorder when patients have lower than normal white blood cells. This can result from an infection or cancer.)

Family history

The young woman was described as intelligent. Her father was a teacher and was described as friendly and supportive. She had six sisters and was the third child. Her mother had breast cancer. None of her family worked in medical related jobs.

Symptoms

She was initially investigated at the age of 17 due to issues relating to her menstrual cycle (periods). She developed symptoms of **deep vein thrombosis** (when a blood clot forms in one or more veins). The medication to treat this was not effective. She was admitted to hospital aged 22 with a painful swelling on her breast. She told doctors that she had had similar swellings previously over her abdominal wall which had required repeated surgical drainage. This procedure had taken place at various other hospitals over 20 times. On examination, doctors found multiple scars over her abdominal wall.

She presented at the hospitals with various complaints such as painful swelling in her groin and weakness in her legs. CT scans and an ultrasound diagnosed a hematoma (where blood has pooled and collected under the skin). She underwent surgery and recovered well. Further testing showed no abnormalities to her immune system.

An abscess meant that she later required further surgical drainage. Cultures were taken from her abscess. Cultures are samples taken from an abscess or wound which are then tested for bacteria or viruses. A variety of bacteria were found in the cultures. After approximately four days in hospital, she developed a similar abscess on her other breast which had to be surgically drained as well.

Suspicions

At this stage, the woman's physicians became suspicious and started to consider whether her problem was factitious because there was no explanation for her abscesses and the bacterial growth within them.

A psychiatric consultation was organised without alerting the woman to the physician's suspicions. The psychiatrist reported that she was extremely defensive and rationalised all her responses to questions. She only showed superficial emotion about her problem but seemed to be under a great deal of stress. It was thought that she might benefit from psychotherapy but with little chance of improvement. A diagnosis of Munchausen syndrome was made.

Evidence of Munchausen syndrome

One day, when the patient was not in her bed, a nurse found a syringe full of faecal matter. When the patient returned, one of the other patients informed her of what the nurse had discovered. She became very angry and against medical advice left the hospital immediately and no further follow-up was possible. Faecal matter contains bacteria and viruses that lead to infections that can cause abscesses (infected tissue) or sepsis, a potentially fatal reaction to an infection.

Evaluating Aleem and Ajarim (1995)

A strength of this **case study** is that it offers detailed insight into a rare disorder. By reflecting on the signs and symptoms that the patient displayed, it may help other practitioners to diagnose Munchausen syndrome. It is an appropriate research method to use for this disorder as it is a rare condition and it would be both practically difficult and have ethical issues if researchers were to try and use an experimental method.

Another strength of research into Munchausen syndrome is that it provides practitioners with a greater amount of information about the symptoms and reasons for it occurring. For example, Jaghab *et al.* (2006) discussed a number of key symptoms that may be present in someone with Munchausen syndrome. This type of research has allowed for more reliable diagnosis of this rare syndrome, allowing patients to start treatment more quickly, thus reducing the likelihood of severe harm to themselves or others.

However, a weakness of using a single case study is that the patient may not have been typical of all individuals who have Munchausen syndrome making it difficult to generalise from the findings to other patients with this disorder. If practitioners use this case study as a template to which other potential cases are compared, they may miss something because the disorder presents differently for different people.

Another weakness of case studies is that the **qualitative data** provided may be subject to interpretation by the researchers. For example, the researchers may have interpreted the information provided about the woman's first hospitalisation differently due to already knowing about the syringe that was discovered. Had they not known about this information she may have been viewed differently. This means that the information given from the case study may not be reliable as interpretation depends on the researcher's past experience.

> ## ISSUES AND DEBATES

Idiographic versus nomothetic

As Munchausen's syndrome is relatively rare, an idiographic approach is appropriate as there are so few cases that generalising from small samples in a more nomothetic manner may not be considered valid. A strength of this way of working is that researchers often provide rich in-depth information about the patient, which means that readers who are also practitioners are able to decide whether the findings may be applicable/transferable to their own clients. However, when working with patients with Munchausen's it is important that practitioners keep an open mind as the condition may manifest in different ways in different individuals. This again underlines why taking an idiographic approach is so important.

> ## LEARNING LINK

Aleem and Ajarim (1995) used a case study method, as did Saavedra and Silverman (button phobia), which you learned about at AS Level. How are these two studies both similar and different in the ways that they gathered their data? Think about the topic areas studied. What does this tell you about the usefulness of case studies to test rare disorders?

STUDY TIP

To help you learn the Aleem and Ajarim (1995) study, why not create a storyboard. This is a good way of organising the material into a logical order in a visual way. You could cut the storyboard up into individual frames (parts of the story) and ask a friend to organise them into the correct order with your help. If they find this task very difficult you may need to include more detail in each frame.

> ## TEST YOURSELF

1 Jagdip is worried about her friend Mia as she always seems to be ill. She goes to the doctors constantly, but they never seem to find anything physically wrong. Jagdip started learning about Munchausen syndrome at college and is wondering whether Mia may be suffering from it.
   Suggest two symptoms that may suggest that Mia has Munchausen syndrome. [4]

2 Explain what is meant by idiographic, giving one example from research into Munchausen syndrome. [2]

3 a Describe what psychologists have discovered about:
   – Munchausen syndrome
   – malingering. [6]
  b Evaluate what psychologists have discovered about the following disorders, including a discussion of qualitative data.
   – Munchausen syndrome
   – malingering. [10]

4 Explain why the case study as a research method is appropriate for studying Munchausen syndrome. [4]

5 Explain one ethical issue researchers might encounter when using a case study to research Munchausen syndrome. [2]

6 Outline one disadvantage of using case studies to research rare disorders such as Munchausen syndrome. [2]

KEY TERMS

unintentional non-adherence

intentional non-adherence

regime

METHODOLOGY

generalisations from findings

8.2 Adherence to medical advice

8.2.1 Types of non-adherence and reasons why patients do not adhere

> **Think!**
>
> Can you give an example of non-adherence to medical advice? What are the possible consequences of this type of non-adherence?

> **Think!**
>
> Imagine you are a doctor and half of all your patients have not taken their medication properly, with many admitting they stopped as soon as they felt better. Others admitted that they just forgot to take them or that there were too many side effects. How could you improve adherence to medication in your patients?

> **Think!**
>
> It can be difficult to study whether people are adhering to medical advice or not. Can you think of any methodological problems you may encounter when trying to find out whether people are taking their medication properly?

Research has shown that one reason why patients fail to adhere to their treatment regime might be the side effects. How could doctors persuade patients to adhere? Do you think it is ethical for them to do so?

▲ Figure 8.8

Types of non-adherence

Adherence to medical advice is the ability of a patient to follow specific guidance from a health professional. Non-adherence, therefore, can be defined as the failure to follow the advice from a health professional such as not taking medication or following a treatment plan. There are a number of reasons that patients may not adhere, such as a poor relationship with their doctor, poor communication or time and cost. The consequences of not following advice can be severe and in some instances fatal. The two types of non-adherence discussed on these pages are failure to follow treatments and failure to attend appointments.

Failure to follow treatments

It is thought that a third to half of all medications given by doctors are either not taken correctly or not taken at all. The costs of not taking this medication can be both personal and economic. Although it may be easy to blame the patient, a more holistic outlook is necessary. Perhaps the patient did not understand what they needed to do, perhaps the side effects of a medication were so bad that they were unable to work or maybe the patient felt better and did not realise that they needed to carry on taking the whole course.

The reasons for failure to follow treatments tend to fall into two categories: *intentional* and *unintentional*.

- **Unintentional:** This occurs when a patient wants to follow a treatment but there are some barriers in the way that are not in their control. This may include not remembering or understanding what the doctor said, not being able to afford to pay for the treatment or taking time off work for it, or it may be that they simply forgot.
- **Intentional:** This is when a patient deliberately decides not to follow a treatment. This may be due to the beliefs or preferences that the patient has, their levels of motivation or maybe due to them not believing that they need the treatment or that it will work.

Laba *et al.* (2012) identified six intentional factors that can influence a patient's decision-making:

1   Immediate medication harms.
2   Long-term medication harms.
3   Immediate medication benefits.
4   Long-term medication benefits.
5   Financial cost of medication.
6   Regime for taking the medication (how often, for long or any other considerations, such as taking the medication an hour before food).

Laba *et al.* (2012) found that the ability of the medication to reduce the risk of death was rated as the most important factor in adherence, followed by how severe the current side effects were and the risk of side effects in the future.

It is important that health professionals understand the reasons behind people failing to follow a treatment plan. Better understanding will enable interventions to be put in place to help increase adherence levels. For example:

»   If cost is an issue, especially in countries where health services are not free at the point of care, then efforts could be made to reduce the cost of the medication to people who cannot afford health insurance.
»   Where the **regime** of taking the medication is complex, literature explaining this to patients in an easy-to-follow way might help increase the number of patients who follow their treatment.
»   Making patients aware of ways to cope with or treat potential side effects of the medication may improve adherence.

> ## ISSUES AND DEBATES
>
> ### Reductionism versus holism
>
> It is important for practitioners to take a holistic approach when understanding why patients may not follow a treatment plan. By understanding the often complex reasons why patients do not follow their treatment plan, practitioners can find ways to effectively support their patients. If they take a reductionist approach, focusing on a limited perspective, they may miss key reasons why their patient is not following their treatment plan and any intervention is likely to be less effective.

Failure to attend appointments

The failure to attend appointments by individuals is an expensive and persistent problem across the world. Rates of non-attendance world-wide are thought to be between 5 and 39 per cent. According to the National Health Service (England) data in 2019, up to 15 million appointments are being missed every single year in England, which costs the NHS around £216 million pounds! (National Health Service, 2019). If this figure is similar across other countries, then the billions of pounds wasted each year could have been spent treating other patients and reducing waiting lists for treatment. Unsurprisingly, a previous failure to attend an appointment was a strong predictor of future failure to attend (FTA) behaviour.

Other predictors of FTA were:
»   age (either young or over 80 years old) and work commitments
»   difficulties in getting to the hospital
»   a feeling that that the appointment was unnecessary (for example, feeling better)
»   being too ill to attend
»   a fear or mistrust of hospitals
»   a fear that a serious illness might be discovered (Collins *et al.*, 2003).

Parsons *et al.* (2021) reviewed twelve studies reporting that work or family commitments, forgetting the appointment and transportation difficulties were the most commonly reported factors. The demographics that are most likely to miss appointments are:
»   younger than the age of 21
»   low social status/class
»   individuals who had missed appointments previously
»   those who have already had a mental or physical diagnosis
»   minority ethnic groups.

Problems caused by non-adherence

It is clear that both failing to attend appointments and not following treatments can have both personal and economic costs. Missed appointments can lead to medical problems that are unresolved meaning that the patient may become more vulnerable and live with untreated medical conditions. Economically, missed appointments cost health services millions of pounds in many countries. This can mean a significant amount of money which could be directed at improving health is wasted and remaining resources stretched.

Similarly, if patients do not adhere to treatment it can result in the need for further, more expensive treatment. For example, if a patient failed to take a preventative heart medication, then resulting damage to the heart might lead to the need for surgery. This has a cost to the healthcare system and to the patient themselves.

Evaluation

> ## ISSUES AND DEBATES

Application to everyday life

One strength of explanations of non-adherence is that they can be applied to real life. For example, if you understand that cost and complexity are two factors in an individual's non-adherence then strategies to overcome this can be put in place such as lowering cost or making instructions clearer. For these reasons explanations can be used to inform more effective strategies in health services to ensure adherence.

Nomothetic versus idiographic

A strength is that, by taking a nomothetic approach, explanations will be of benefit to society as a whole and are therefore ethical. For example, increased adherence would not only improve the health of the most vulnerable but also decrease the financial waste encountered in health services through lost appointments. This will enable the money to be directed to those areas that are most in need.

Cultural differences

One weakness of explanations is that they may not take into account cultural differences. For example, research showed that minority ethnicities, those of low social status and the young are more likely to not adhere. However, studies tend to look at individual countries and not take into account differences in health services. For example, cost would not be such an issue in the UK where care is free at the point of service but may be more in the USA, where healthcare is paid for. Therefore, it is difficult to suggest that any set of results would be applicable to all countries lowering the generalisability of theories.

Individual and situational explanations

A strength of research in this area is that it takes into account both individual and situational explanations of why patients may fail to attend an appointment. For example, an individual explanation would be having a fear or distrust of hospitals or in an older patient, limited mobility may make it difficult to physically get to the hospital. Situational explanations for missing an appointment might include a parent missing an appointment due to problems with childcare. By considering both individual and situational explanations, practitioners can gain greater insight into the reasons for failure to attend appointments.

> ## LEARNING LINK

Non-intentional reasons for failing to follow treatment programmes include forgetting. Memory and forgetting is part of the cognitive approach that you learned about at AS Level. By understanding how forgetting happens, psychologists can devise ways to help patients remember to take their medication.

STUDY TIP

STUDY TIP

One way of understanding the problems with non-adherence is to look at different cultures. In these pages we have looked at how many NHS appointments have been missed and how much that costs the UK. Have a look to see whether this is a problem in all countries, or whether it is more of an issue in some countries than others. Why do you feel this is? For example, is there something within particular cultures which means that they are less likely to fail to follow treatment or attend appointments? This is a very important issue to think about when you evaluate this topic area.

▶ TEST YOURSELF

1 Scarlett has noticed that a number of people are missing their doctors' appointments every day. Scarlett is finding this really frustrating as she has to turn away many people who need appointments, as there are never enough.

   a State any two characteristics of people who are more likely to fail to attend an appointment with their doctor. [2]

   b Suggest one reason why people may fail to attend an appointment with their doctor. [2]

2 Explain what is meant by individual and situational explanations with an example from non-adherence to medical advice. [4]

3 a Describe what psychologists have discovered about:
      – failure to follow treatment
      – failure to attend appointments. [6]

   b Evaluate what psychologists have discovered about
      – failure to follow treatment
      – failure to attend appointments, including a discussion on application to everyday life. [10]

4 Explain one strength and one weakness of using questionnaires to measure non-adherence to treatment. [4]

5 a Plan a study using an interview to investigate why patients fail to attend appointments. Your plan must include details about:
      – your interview technique
      – example questions you could ask. [10]

   b For one piece of psychological knowledge:
      i describe this psychological knowledge [4]
      ii explain how two features of this psychological knowledge informed your plan. [4]

Explanations of why patients do not adhere

KEY TERMS

rational non-adherence

perceived seriousness

perceived susceptibility

cues to action

demographics

hypertension

METHODOLOGY

generalisations from findings

Think!

What techniques could healthcare professionals use to persuade patients to follow their treatment?

Think!

What things would you consider (if any) before deciding to take medication?

Think!

If patients are thinking rationally about the risks versus the benefits of medication, should health professionals attempt to influence their decision about taking their medication?

How important do you think it is that practitioners consider the severity of side effects of medication on individual patients rather than just focusing on the benefits of the medication?

▲ Figure 8.9

Rational non-adherence

Rational non-adherence means that a patient directly refuses to follow a treatment regime. This act therefore is deliberate and intentional and the patient believes they have a very good reason for acting in this way. The patient therefore believes that their choice is both rational and justified. For example, they may not want to have the side effects that come with a particular medication as they feel the medication is worse than the illness. They may also believe that their diagnosis is incorrect and therefore do not believe they need the treatment in the first place. According to Sarafino (2006), reasons for rational non-adherence include:

>> believing that the medication is not helping them
>> feeling that the side effects outweigh the benefits of the treatment, especially if it is having a significant negative impact on their quality of life
>> are confused about how often and how to take the medication
>> do not have enough money to buy more of the medication
>> wanting to see if they still have the illness, if they stop taking the medication.

Bulpitt and Fletcher (1988) researched adherence in patients with hypertension (high blood pressure). The medication for **hypertension** can have a number of side effects including dizziness and sexual problems. They found that eight per cent of men stopped taking the medication due to sexual problems and over a period of five years, while 15 per cent stopped taking the medication due to tiredness, sexual problems and gout (swelling and pain in joints). The research showed that when the costs of taking the medication (side effects) outweighed the benefits then individuals will make a rational choice not to take it.

Health belief model

The health belief model looks at factors which influence whether individuals will take preventative action when faced with a potential illness or injury. This action depends on the outcome of two main assessments:

>> How much of a threat the health problem poses.
>> The pros and cons of taking action.

How much of a threat the health problem poses

When deciding how much of a threat a potential health problem poses, an individual might consider:

a **Perceived seriousness** of the problem: For example, considering how serious the problem could become if left untreated. The more serious the problem is considered to be, the more likely the individual is to take preventative action.

b **Perceived susceptibility**: The individual considers how likely they are to develop the problem. The more susceptible they think they are, the more likely they are to take preventative action.

c **Cues to action**: Cues to action can take the form of a reminder of a hospital appointment or an advertisement on social media/TV. It could also include posters around towns/cities informing people of the symptoms to look out for in certain illnesses such as cancer and to serve as a reminder to get any symptoms they might be experiencing checked by a medical professional. Those people who see the cues are more likely to take preventative action than those who do not.

d Perceived benefits and barriers: This is where the person will look at the barriers of following a treatment path such as the cost, the difficulty in getting to a treatment such as therapy sessions, or the side effects of medication and then weigh them up against the benefits of following the treatment such as improved health, approval of others, saving money, for example by stopping smoking. If there are more benefits than barriers, they are more likely to adhere.

Other factors include demographic variables such as age, sex, race and ethnic background as well as personality traits and social class.

Focus on... Laba *et al.* (2012)

▶ AIM

To explore medication taking decisions that may lead to intentional non-adherence behaviour as well as the relative importance of medication specific factors and patient background on those decisions.

▶ METHODOLOGY

The study used an initial sample of 248 Australian participants who were all English speaking with a median age of 57 years; 45 per cent were male, 55 per cent females. Of the 248 participants who began the online survey 161 completed it.

A discrete choice experiment (DCE) was conducted through the use of a web-enabled online survey. The survey presented a series of hypothetical alternatives from which the participant makes a specific choice. This information is then quantitatively analysed. Laba *et al.* (2012) used the 'The Beliefs About Medication Questionnaire (BMQ)'. This looked at the importance of eight medication factors: immediate and long-term medication harms and benefits, cost, regimen, symptom severity, alcohol restrictions, regarding a participant's preference about continuing to take medication.

For example, participants are given information on two drugs, which might include information about the potential side effects, frequency of dose, cost, ability to drink alcohol while taking it, as well as statistics on how effective it is. Participants then choose which of the two drugs would be their preference (see Table 8.6). To ensure the questions more accurately reflected what went on in practice, health terms and non-disease specific medication were used. There were ten hypothetical choice tasks to be completed on the questionnaire. Background information about the participants was also taken. Participants completed the questionnaire online.

▲ Table 8.6 Example of a discrete choice question

	Medication A	Medication B
Symptom severity	1 out of 10	7 out of 10
On medication, daily symptoms are now felt	6 days per week	2 days per week
The severity of daily medication side effects	1 out of 10	4 out of 10
For every 100 people taking this medication, the number of people who will have unwanted effects in the next ten years is:	35	95
For every 100 people with this illness, 85 will die in the next 10 years. On medication this number reduces to:	65	65
The medication is taken:	Once a day	Once a day
Can you drink alcohol?	Yes	Yes
Your monthly cost for the medication	$10	$50
Which would you prefer?		

> ## RESULTS
> ....
> - Six out of eight factors had an influence on medication choice (immediate and long-term medication harms and benefits, cost and regimen of taking the medication).
> - Participants with private medical insurance were less sensitive to the cost of the medication than those without it.
> - Side effects were found to have a greater influence over adherence than benefits to health.
> - The ability of the medication to reduce death was viewed as the most important factor in adherence to medication. This was followed by current side effect severity and risk of future side effects.

> ## CONCLUSIONS
> ....
> Patients make decisions about taking their medication based on rational choices. Adherence could be improved by reducing costs of medication, altering how and when the medication needs to be taken and educating patients on the benefits of the medication.

Evaluating Laba *et al.* (2012)

A weakness of the study is that 1668 people were initially invited to participate. However, only 244 respondents commenced the questionnaire and 161 actually completed it. This is a participation rate of 10 per cent. It might be that only a certain type of person chose to participate in the study, for example people who are interested in the topic area and therefore may be more invested in taking their medication than other people, so the results may not be representative of the target population.

> ## ISSUES AND DEBATES
> ....
> ### Application to everyday life
>
> A strength of the study is that it has application to everyday life. The results show what factors influence patients' adherence to their treatment regime. This could help healthcare professionals to design interventions to improve adherence by addressing concerns that patients have regarding their medication such as cost, complexity and the likely side effects.
>
> ### Idiographic versus nomothetic
>
> The nomothetic approach used in this study is a strength as it allowed conclusions about rational non-adherence to be generalised to the wider population. For example, quantitative data was collected using discrete choice questions about the factors influencing medication choice. This type of data can be analysed using statistics leading to findings that are more objective and reliable. This said, the lack of open questions means the participants could not explain the reasons behind their answers and the researchers may therefore have missed the opportunity to learn about factors affecting adherence that they had not previously thought about. Combining a more idiographic approach may have helped gain greater insight into these issues.

LEARNING LINK

Many studies you have learned at AS Level also use quantitative methods to study behaviour. Baron-Cohen *et al.* (eyes test) also used forced choice scenarios where participants had to choose one out of four emotions which they believed represented the emotion in the sets of eyes given. There are some studies, however, that also used qualitative methods. Can you remember what they were? Do you think qualitative or quantitative methods are best in studying topics such as non-adherence? What makes you think this?

STUDY TIP

One of the best ways of understanding concepts such as the health belief model and rational non-adherence is to apply them to novel scenarios. You could try doing some research using online new sites about people who did not follow treatment or take medication, or develop some scenarios yourself or with friends, and swap them with each other so that you can practise applying the theory.

TEST YOURSELF

1   Rei is a student doctor and is studying reasons why individuals do not adhere to medical advice.
    a   Suggest one reason why individuals do not adhere to medical advice.   [2]
    b   Outline the results of one study into non-adherence to medical advice.   [2]
2   Explain two concepts from the health belief model which may explain non-adherence.   [4]
3   a   Describe what psychologists have discovered about why patients do not adhere to treatment.   [6]
    b   Evaluate what psychologists have discovered about why patients do not adhere to treatment. Include a discussion on idiographic versus nomothetic.   [10]
4   Explain how a study into rational non-adherence can be applied to everyday life.   [4]
5   Explain one weakness of using self reports when trying to measure adherence.   [2]
6   Explain one strength and one weakness of using quantitative methods to research non-adherence to medical advice.   [4]
7   Compare the rational non-adherence and the health belief model for why patients do not adhere to medical advice.   [4]

KEY TERMS

Medication Adherence Report Scale (MARS)

Medical Adherence Measure (MAM)

diabetes

hypoglycemia

reflectance meter

metabolic control

clinical interview

METHODOLOGY

quantitative and qualitative data

validity

reliability

8.2.2 Measuring non-adherence

Think!

What type of questions are used in a semi-structured clinical interview?

Think!

Imagine you have been given medication to take for an illness. You are happy to take them but as you have to take them at the same time each day you have sometimes forgotten until later in the day and so you were worried about taking them and so decided not to; there are even some days you cannot remember whether you have taken them or not. Your doctor asks you to complete a questionnaire about whether you have completed the course properly. What problems can you see with you filling in this questionnaire? How would filling it in make you feel?

Think!

This section refers to the use of semi-structured interviews which produce qualitative data. What are the advantages of using qualitative methods in the study of non-adherence? Would the **clinical interview** method be considered nomothetic or idiographic?

How could you try to ensure that participants respond honestly to questionnaires about adherence to medication? Would a different approach be required for people of different ages?

▶ Figure 8.10

Subjective measures including clinical interview and semi-structured interviews

Self-report

Subjective measures include self-reports where the patients complete questionnaires explaining to what extent they have been adhering to their treatment plan. A frequently used questionnaire is the 10-item **Medication Adherence Report Scale (MARS)**, which has a forced choice format asking for yes/no answers and was originally designed to measure patients' adherence to medication for schizophrenia (Unni *et al.*, 2019). Patients may also be given booklets to record each time they take their medication.

Evaluation of the self-report

One strength of using questionnaires is that they are cheap and quick to administer to a large number of patients; this will increase the ability to generalise any results to the target population. You can also obtain quantitative data about attitudes to adherence which can then be statistically analysed. However, they can lack reliability because you are relying on a patient's memory, and they may not recall accurately how often they had been taking their medication.

One weakness of using questionnaires is that the validity can be an issue if patients give socially desirable answers. They may say that they have been following their treatment when they have not, because they do not want their doctor to know that they have not been taking their medication either at all or regularly. One way to overcome this is to combine the use of self-reports with biological methods such as blood tests to see whether the results correlate with each other.

Clinical interview

A clinical interview is a dialogue between patient and clinician to help the professional gain information which will help with diagnosis and treatment. A clinical interview has a focused purpose, in this case to establish levels of adherence. A clinical interview can be structured and unstructured although the focus on these pages will be the semi-structured interview. Semi-structured means that there will be some predetermined questions which can be open or closed questions, but the focus will be on more open-ended questions which will lead from the responses to the predetermined questions. For example, if the patient then says they have missed their medication three times, then more in depth questioning about their reasons for not taking it can be used. The focus for the clinical interview should be solely on the patient.

The **Medical Adherence Measure (MAM)** was designed as a semi-structured clinical interview designed to elicit detailed and accurate responses from patients about whether they had adhered to their treatment and included questions about diet, medication and clinic attendance. The success of the interview is based on a supportive patient/healthcare professional relationship so that patients feel comfortable enough to be honest about their adherence to their treatment and the focus is on the improvement of patient care. The patients, therefore, know that the focus of the interview is to support them, rather than punish them for non-adherence (Zelikovsky and Schast, 2008).

Evaluation of the clinical interview

A strength of the clinical interview is that it can provide detailed, rich qualitative data about levels of adherence as well as reasons why they may not be adhering; for example, in-depth questioning will provide detailed data that can help improve patient adherence by providing researchers with a greater understanding of patients worries and concerns. This increases both the **validity** and the usefulness of the measure.

However, a weakness is that in comparison with questionnaires, which can be administered online, it is a time-consuming and expensive method of gathering data and researchers may have access to limited funding to conduct their research, which might result in smaller sample sizes. It is also more time consuming for the patient who may have difficulties attending due to having to have time off work, for example, meaning that there may be a higher dropout rate than would occur in a questionnaire-based study, thus lowering the generalisability of the findings.

> ## ISSUES AND DEBATES

Idiographic versus nomothetic

The clinical interview uses in-depth interview techniques to discover why patients may not be adhering to their treatment routine. By using an idiographic approach, practitioners can better understand the specific issues that their patients might be facing rather than just looking at generic issues that might not be appropriate for that patient. In this regard, an idiographic rather than a nomothetic approach may be more beneficial.

Focus on... Riekert and Drotar (1999)

> ### AIM

To assess the implications of non-participation or incomplete participation in research into treatment adherence for adolescents with **diabetes**.

> ### METHODOLOGY

A total of 94 families (parents plus adolescents) were asked to take part in the study; 80 originally consented but only 52 completed the study. The adolescents were between the ages of 11 and 18, had a diagnosis of diabetes for over a year and did not have any additional illness or developmental delay. They were recruited through a clinic for monitoring their diabetes.

The adolescents completed a semi-structured (clinical) interview using the Adherence and IDDM Questionnaire-R. This assessed the adolescents' adherence to their treatment and included diet, glucose testing and preparedness for **hypoglycemia**. The questionnaire provided quantitative data. The other measurements used for the adolescents included:
- the number of blood sugar tests used (monitored electronically through a **reflectance meter**)
- **metabolic control**, as measured at the clinic every time they attended.

The parents then completed a questionnaire asking for demographic data about the whole family group such as family background, age, ethnicity, how long they had diabetes for and parental educational background. After completion of the interview the family were then given a packet of questionnaires with a prepaid return envelope to take home to complete (a 30-minute questionnaire for the parents concerning their relationship with their adolescent and a questionnaire that took approximately one hour for the children to complete concerning their relationship with their parent). Families who had not returned the questionnaires within ten days were called to remind them.

Researchers also reviewed the medical charts of all 94 adolescents who were initially requested to take part in the research to obtain the number of blood sugar tests per day that they completed and their metabolic control levels. Demographic data of the families who refused to consent to take part was also obtained.

▶ RESULTS

The demographic characteristics were similar for all three groups: participants who completed the study, those who did not return the questionnaires (non-returners) and those who did not consent to take part (non-consenters).
- The adolescents of the families who failed to return their questionnaires tested their blood sugar levels significantly less frequently than those of families who returned the questionnaire or who did not consent to take part.
- Adolescents of the families who did not return their questionnaires also had significantly lower rates of adherence to their treatment than those of families who returned their questionnaires.

▶ CONCLUSION

Lower adherence to the treatment regime by adolescents is associated with lower participation in adherence studies by adolescents and their families.

Evaluating Riekert and Drotar (1999)

One strength is that the study used a number of methods in order to ensure levels of adherence were measured accurately. For example, the adolescents completed a clinical interview and the parents completed a demographics questionnaire. Metabolic rate and use of blood sugar equipment was also measured. This is a strength as the results of the study are not reliant on one method alone. Each method has its own weaknesses so using more than one minimises these weaknesses and increases the **validity** of the research.

A weakness is that the sample was only taken from one clinic and was based upon one type of illness – diabetes. Also, there were a number of potential participants who were asked to take part but who did not consent to take part in the study. It may well be that there is something particular about this type of illness or the people that wanted to take part in the study in the first place, that means that the results found would not be generalisable to the wider population, or other illnesses.

▶ ISSUES AND DEBATES

Application to everyday life

A strength of the study is that it has application to everyday life. For example, Riekert and Drotar suggested that families who failed to complete the research tasks may have lacked planning and organisational skills, which could also have affected how adherent they were to the treatment plan. This may allow targeted interventions for those who do not take part and ensure that a routine is established and understanding is high, which in turn will raise adherence.

▶ LEARNING LINK

Research by Riekart and Drotar (1999) highlighted ethical issues about consent and how use of information without consent could cause distress. There are some occasions where a lack of consent may not be such a problem. For example, in Piliavin *et al.* (subway Samaritans) participants did not know they were part of a study but were observed in a public place. Do you feel that there are any circumstances where the breaking of ethical issues is justified?

STUDY TIP

This is a good topic area to construct a quiz on. You could devise a series of questions on the characteristics of clinical interviews and questionnaires as well as the study and then you could test your friends (the ones who do psychology) with them. It is not only answering questions in a quiz that helps your understanding but also constructing them, as you have to make sure you have the right answers and also be able to explain to others why they are the correct ones.

TEST YOURSELF

1 Ruby would like to conduct some research about the levels of adherence to medication in patients who are taking anti-anxiety medication. She decides she is going to use a questionnaire.

   a Outline one disadvantage of Ruby using questionnaires to measure adherence to anti-anxiety medication in patients. [2]

   b Explain one alternative method Sara could use to measure adherence to anti-anxiety medication in patients. [2]

2 Explain what is meant by the nomothetic versus idiographic debate, with an example from measuring adherence. [2]

3 a Describe what psychologists have discovered about the use of:
   – clinical interviews
   – questionnaires as measures of adherence to medical advice. [6]

   b Evaluate what psychologists have discovered about the use of:
   – clinical interviews
   – questionnaires as measures of adherence to medical advice with a discussion on application to real life. [10]

4 Explain one ethical issue with using self-report to measure adherence to medication. [2]

5 Outline one advantage of using more than one method in research when looking to measure adherence to medical advice. [2]

6 Explain one strength and one weakness of using biological methods such as blood sugar tests to measure adherence to medical advice. [4]

KEY TERMS

pill counting

medication dispensers

metabolism

dried blood spot sampling

plasma

viral load

METHODOLOGY

quantitative and qualitative data

validity

reliability

Objective measures

Think!

Can you name two biological measures of adherence? What are the advantages of these types of measures?

Think!

Imagine your doctor's surgery has a number of patients over 75 who are on hypertension (high blood pressure) drugs. Doctors at the surgery are worried because some of them do not seem to be stable on their medication but are not sure whether it is the medication not working or the patients not taking their medication. Think of one method that the doctors could use to find out whether it is the drugs not working or that they are not taking their medication. Can you see any problems with the method you have suggested?

Think!

One debate that has been highlighted by the measuring adherence topic is the quantitative vs qualitative data debate. Which methods that you have studied on these pages use qualitative and which use qualitative data? Which type of data do you feel is the best way of measuring adherence? Qualitative, quantitative or both?

Pill counting

An objective method of measuring adherence is to calculate the number of doses that the patient should have taken, then count the number of pills left in a bottle and to compare it with the number of pills that should remain. Typically, pill counts are conducted in person and this may be a burden to the patient as they will then be required to come to a clinic and remember their medication. In-person pill counts may also be inaccurate if there are set times for a **pill count**; patients could deliberately manipulate how many are in a packet. Unannounced pill counts are a way of overcoming this especially if these are done by telephone as this will be more practical for the patients.

Kalichman *et al.* (2008) conducted research on HIV positive men and women by completing a telephone-based unannounced pill count, providing blood specimens to look at viral loads, with 68 out of the 89 participants also receiving a second pill count through an unannounced home visit. They found a high level of agreement (92 per cent) between the telephone pill count and the home pill count. In addition, patients **viral load** (the amount of virus found in the body) as determined by the blood specimens corresponded strongly with the level of adherence determined by the telephone pill count, suggesting that unannounced telephone-based pill counts are an objective and valid method for monitoring adherence.

Evaluating pill counting

This is a simple and straightforward method of measuring adherence. However, it does not measure how many pills the patient has actually ingested. If patients are aware that their pills are going to be counted, they could simply throw some away to avoid practitioners discovering that they have not adhered to their treatment, lowering the validity of the measure.

One strength is that telephone pill counting has research support. For example, Kalichman *et al.* (2008) study showed a high level of agreement between telephone pill counts, home pill counts and viral loads in HIV sufferers. This is a strength as it suggests that telephone pill counting is a valid measure of adherence.

Medication dispensers

Medication dispensers are portable devices that allow you to organise medication by day and time. These devices provide reassurance to the patient by dispensing the correct pills at a set day/time and can use visual or audio alarms to alert the patient. The automatic medication dispenser records the date and time a pill leaves the device, and how often it has been used. Some medication dispensers also use alerts in the form of SMS and email messages as a reminder to take medication. Electronic medication dispensers have the advantage of being portable and therefore can provide long-term monitoring without affecting the patient adversely.

Evaluation of medication dispensers

One advantage of this method is that it provides a **reliable** way to measure adherence which is not affected by social desirability or errors of memory. There is also an obvious advantage to the patient who is more likely to stick to their treatment with reminders, meaning that they are less likely to relapse and be admitted to hospital.

One disadvantage of medication dispensers is that they may not get accurate results. Although the dispenser may record the medication being removed, this does not mean that the person has taken the medication. This means that this method lacks **validity**.

In addition, the usefulness of the medication dispensers may vary with age; with older patients showing lower levels of adherence even with the use of dispensers. Some found the alarms irritating, whereas others forgot to charge the dispensers up! It may also depend on reasons for non-adherence. If patients simply forget to take medication, then medication dispensers may be useful, but if they are concerned about side effects then this may not improve adherence.

Focus on... Chung and Naya (2000)

▶ AIM

To electronically assess compliance with an oral asthma medication.

▶ METHODOLOGY

The sample in the study consisted of 47 asthmatic patients, both male and female, aged 18–55. All had a history of asthma. An initial screening period of two to three weeks was then followed by a 12-week treatment period during which patients took asthma medication twice a day. Tablets were dispensed in screw top bottles which had been fitted with a TrackCap medication event monitoring system (MEMS). This system recorded the date and time each time that the cap was removed and replaced.

The instructions on the bottle/outer carton read: *'Take one tablet in the morning and one tablet in the evening approximately 12 hours apart. Do not take the tablets at mealtimes.'* Patients were also told to remove a tablet and replace the cap quickly due to tablets being sensitive to moisture. Each removal of the TrackCap was presumed to indicate a single medication use event. If the cap was removed multiple times during a very short period, then the device would recognise this but would not record the multiple openings. If the bottle was left open for 15 or more minutes, then the device would record one additional event. Patients were not required to keep diaries about their treatment and were not questioned about tablet counts, nor was it discussed in their presence.

All participants gave consent to be part of the research, but they did not know that the electronic monitoring advice was attached to the medication bottle. This was to avoid bias.

Dependent variables were:
1 Tablet count (number of dispensed tablets minus the number of returned tablets).
2 Track Cap compliance (number of events divided by number of prescribed tablets).

▶ RESULTS

- 80 per cent compliance was measured for the Track Cap and 89 per cent compliance for the tablet count. This difference could be accounted for by patients taking out more than one tablet at a time. This could be because they lost medication or were trying to hide non-compliance by removing tablets or simply that it was easier to remove them in one go, yet they still complied with the treatment regimen.
- The Track Cap data suggested that one participant removed a whole week's worth in one go. This might have been to put them in a weekly medication dispenser, so that they could keep track of whether they had taken their tablet.
- 64 per cent of participants had full adherence on the Track Cap (two tablets, 12 hours apart), 20 per cent showed under-compliance (one event a day, only one tablet) and 10 per cent showed no compliance for up to eight days.

▶ CONCLUSIONS

Medication event monitoring systems such as Track Cap can be effective in measuring compliance.

Evaluating Chung and Naya (2000)

A weakness of the study is that there were ethical issues that were not resolved despite the study receiving ethical approval. For example, participants were deceived as to how they were being monitored and it is not clear whether the participants were fully debriefed at the end of the study. This type of deception may have caused the participants upset/distress.

Another weakness of this study was that participants may have been showing demand characteristics. Rates for adherence were high for this study. However, participants were made aware that their adherence would be measured. Further research would benefit from a double-blind study where participants were not aware that their adherence was being measured to gain a more accurate understanding of to what degree patients do comply under normal circumstances.

One strength, however, was that it was a useful study to measure adherence. For example, by measuring adherence remotely using the Track Cap, researchers were able to measure adherence with minimal disruption to the patients' lives. As their adherence was measured at their own homes when they would normally take their medication, the study is also high in ecological **validity**.

Another strength is that compared to self-reports and interviews, electronic monitoring is an objective and **quantitative** analysis of adherence to medical advice. For example, although there is a chance the participants could 'cheat the system' this was far less than in self reports where social desirability bias may make them overestimate their adherence. This makes the results of the study more **valid**.

Biological measures of adherence
Blood and urine samples
Non-biological methods of adherence such as clinical interview and pill counting have the disadvantage of not being able to measure if the patient has taken the medicine or not. However, biological measures can give an objective measure of the amount of medication that has been taken.

The two main ways to biologically measure adherence is through the use of blood or urine samples. These measures not only help identify adherence but also can identify what is the most clinically effective dose for the individual patients.

>> Urine analysis: This is a fairly cheap way of collecting and testing for adherence. It is easy for the patient and totally non-invasive. In addition, urine is stable (this is when their chemical properties do not change) for up to 14 days at room temperature and with standard refrigeration. Also, urine sampling gives objective visual results unlike self-reports and for some patients where adherence is key to health, they find it reassuring that this has been evidenced through an objective test.

>> **Blood sampling**: As well as traditional methods of blood testing, **dried blood spot (DBS)** testing can be carried out. DBS testing comes from collecting several drops of blood on filter paper. Drug levels in red blood cells can then be seen. Burnier (2020) showed that DBS testing can show levels of hypertension drugs reliably and that results were as high as using **plasma**. Plasma carries blood components such as nutrients, hormones and proteins through the body. When separated from the rest of blood, plasma is a light yellow liquid which can be used for testing.

Evaluation
One strength of biological methods is that they provide an objective and visual cue for the patient and doctor about levels of adherence. Unlike subjective methods there is no social desirability bias from a blood test and therefore the results are **reliable**. The feedback from the test will allow a constructive conversation to be had between doctor and patient, especially if there are signs of non-adherence, meaning effects on health can be minimised.

One weakness of biological methods is that drug/drug and drug/food interactions or differences in individual **metabolism** (rate at which drugs are broken down/used up by the body) of the drugs may interfere with how accurate the results are. Therefore, this method should not be used if patients are on more than one type of medication. Another issue with blood tests is that they are invasive and some patients find them unpleasant and stressful. Therefore, they are not a suitable measure for all patients. Therefore an idiographic approach to measuring non-adherence may be more appropriate so that people are not made to feel more stressed or uncomfortable.

> **LEARNING LINK**

This section looks at biological ways of measuring adherence. You studied the biological approach at AS Level. Dement and Kleitman, for example, used an EEH machine to objectively identify when the participant was in REM sleep. Here, blood and urine tests are used as an objective measure of adherence. Objective tests are helpful in some ways but not others. What can researchers/practitioners not know about non-adherence from a blood or urine test?

STUDY TIP

When looking at measuring adherence, it is good to think about the objective and subjective methods which you have learned about together. Make two columns, one for objective and one for subjective and place the relevant methods in them to give you an easy visual cue about where each method sits. Then list the strengths and weaknesses of objective methods with examples and do the same for subjective methods. Then come to a judgement of which, in your opinion, is better for measuring adherence and why.

> **TEST YOURSELF**

1   Tamara's doctor asks her to take part in research on adherence to asthma medication. There are a number of ways that the doctor could conduct this research. Tamara has always been scared of needles, has high levels of anxiety and finds it difficult to talk one-to-one with her doctor.

    a   Outline two methods of measuring adherence that would not be appropriate when conducting research with Tamara.   [2]

    b   Suggest one method that would be appropriate to measure adherence with Tamara.   [2]

2   Explain how some measures of adherence could lack validity.   [4]

3   a   Describe what psychologists have discovered about:
        –   objective measures of adherence
        –   biological measures of adherence.   [6]

    b   Evaluate what psychologists have discovered about:
        –   objective measures of adherence
        –   biological measures of adherence including a discussion of reliability. [10]

4   Outline the sample used in a study on researching objective measures of adherence.   [2]

5   Outline one advantage and one disadvantage of using pill counting to measure levels of adherence.   [4]

6   Suggest one reason why using blood samples to measure adherence may not be appropriate for all people.   [2]

7   Compare subjective and objective measures of measuring non-adherence.   [6]

8.2.3 Improving adherence

Think!

How was **operant conditioning** used to try to improve adherence using the Funhaler?

Think!

Chaney *et al.*'s (2004) study looked at ways to improve adherence in small children through the use of the Funhaler. Using the principles from these pages, can you think how you would try to improve adherence in teenagers or young adults? How could you research the effect the methods you have chosen could have?

Think!

How does Chaney *et al.* (2004) have a good application to real life?

KEY TERMS

asthma

spacer device

Funhaler

positive reinforcement

operant conditioning

behavioural contracts

prompts

intervention mapping

METHODOLOGY

experiments

questionnaires

generalisations from findings

validity

Using children in research is important when looking at adherence to treatment, especially as children can have different reactions to adults when using a device or taking medication, such as increased fear. It is important however that ethical issues are taken into account when using children, especially those as young as in Chaney *et al.*'s participants. Can you think of any ethical issues from this study? How did Chaney *et al.* overcome any potential ethical issues of using children in their research?

▲ Figure 8.11

Improving adherence in children

Taking medication can be a frightening experience for young children who may not be able to fully understand the necessity of adherence. Strategies to improve adherence in children could include:

» making sure the regime is simple such as taking medication once a day
» making medicines taste pleasant
» making medication easier to take, for example liquids rather than pills
» using text messaging as a reminder with older children
» regular phone contact between practitioner and parent
» involving children fully with their treatment plans, such as taking into account their concerns) may also improve adherence (Benn, 2014).

Asthma is a condition which affects the lungs and can cause occasional breathing difficulties in all ages. Symptoms can include coughing, a tight chest and a whistling sound when breathing. **Spacer devices** are used to deliver asthma medication to children. These devices are plastic containers with a mouthpiece or mask at one end with a space to insert an asthma inhaler at the other end. As they fit over the mouth, they can be scary for children. Getting children to inhale correctly can be challenging for parents, especially if the children do not like or are scared of the device.

The **Funhaler** is based upon the principles of operant conditioning, where children will be rewarded if they use the device correctly which means they are more likely to do it again. The rewards in this case were spinners and a whistle which would activate if the device was used correctly.

Focus on... Chaney *et al.* (2004)

> ### AIM

To establish the acceptance, ease of use, and compliance of the Funhaler device compared to currently used spacer devices in a group of young asthmatic children.

> ### METHODOLOGY

The sample comprised 32 children aged 1.5–6 years old diagnosed with asthma and currently using a small volume, standard spacer device. The children were randomly recruited through seven local **general practice** or paediatric clinics. Parents were initially contacted by telephone before any home visits were conducted. Informed consent was given and parents were interviewed using a questionnaire about the current asthma device. The questionnaire included questions about problems associated with the delivery of the medication and parental and child compliance with using the device. The Funhaler was not shown to anyone at this point. After interview completion, a Funhaler device was given to be used instead of the current device for two weeks (with adult supervision).

The Funhaler

At the time of the study, this was a new inhaler attachment device for use with metered dose inhalers. It has a fun toy module that can be attached with a spinning disk and a whistle. The device is designed to encourage the child to use their inhaler effectively. By using a good technique, the toy works at its best. However, the toy itself does not affect the dose that the child receives.

Parents were contacted once by phone at a random point of the study to see whether or not they had medicated their child the previous day. They were also visited at home once at the end of the two week trial and a second questionnaire regarding use of the Funhaler was completed by the same parent, who participated in the initial interview. This included yes/no questions as well as questions with predetermined responses from which the parents could choose the most appropriate answer about using the Funhaler device and the original device and the children's response to it. For example: What was your child's attitude towards using the device? Pleasure, acceptance, no interest in the device, suspicion, mild fear/dislike/strong fear/dislike, panic or phobia.

▶ RESULTS

▼ Table 8.7 Adherence to prescribed technique

Percentage medicated the previous day			
Current device	59%	Funhaler	81%
Using the recommended 4+ breath cycles per aerosol delivery			
Current device	50%	Funhaler	80%

There was a significant difference in the percentage of children who had been medicated the previous day (showing that they had been adhering to the treatment plan), with significantly more children having been medicated using the Funhaler.

There was a significant improvement in parents being able to successfully medicate their children using the Funhaler (current device = 10 per cent, Funhaler = 73 per cent). Only three out of the entire sample continued to have problems even when using the Funhaler and did not manage to overcome them. The majority of children and their parents showed positive attitudes towards the Funhaler, compared with the current device (see Table 8.8).

▼ Table 8.8 Child's attitude towards using their device and parental approach to using the device, showing the percentage of responses

	Existing spacer device	Funhaler
Child's attitude towards using the device		
Pleasure	10%	68%
Strong fear or dislike	19%	0%
Panic or phobia	31%	0%
Parental approach to medicating their child		
Completely happy	10%	61%
Dislike	16%	0%

▶ CONCLUSIONS

- Improved adherence suggested that the Funhaler could be useful in managing young children with asthma.
- Use of the Funhaler could improve clinical outcomes in children.
- Behaviourist theories such as operant conditioning can be effective in increasing adherence to medication in children.

Evaluating Chaney *et al.* (2004)

One weakness is that as a pilot study with a small sample of Australian children it did not offer a large enough sample to be representative of a wider population. It also only showed differences in compliance between children who were already used to a conventional spacer meaning that the sample was limited not only to Australia but also to children who had already had experience of using a spacer in the first place. This lowers the **generalisability** of the findings.

Another weakness is that the involvement of the parents in the research may have led to the high level of compliance shown. It may well be that it was not the use of the Funhaler that caused the results but just participating in the study alone. For example, the parents will have wanted to show that they were not neglecting their children's health so would have put in extra effort to ensure compliance therefore the results may have been the same with a normal spacer. This lowers the **validity** of the results.

The study is useful as it offers a positive application of psychology and a device that could benefit young children with asthma and potentially reduce hospital admissions. This would benefit society as it would reduce the burden on the health services with fewer hospital admissions and in addition improve the lives of the young children with asthma, allowing them to lead a more normal life.

Another strength of the study is that the children used the Funhaler in their own home at the times when they would have ordinarily needed it and there was minimal contact with the researchers through the trial. This means that the results can be applied to real life situations as it was high in ecological **validity**.

> **ISSUES AND DEBATES**

Use of children in research

It is important that children's rights and wellbeing are paramount as they may not always have the language skills to explain why they are upset or uncomfortable, depending on their age or cognitive ability. Chaney's research took place in the children's own homes. This was beneficial as the children would be more relaxed, especially as it was the parents who administered the spacer devices. This means that their findings should have high ecological validity. It is also more ethical; as the children were trying out a new form of medication for their asthma, it was important for them to be as relaxed as possible so that they could make best use of the inhaler to improve their health. Had the study been conducted under laboratory conditions, they may have felt stressed due to the unfamiliar environment, making the device less effective. The parents in Chaney's research gave their consent for their child to take part in the research, so the researchers followed ethical guidelines.

Individual behavioural techniques
Contracts

Behavioural contracts are verbal or written contracts that patients make with their healthcare professional. This is where a patient may commit to taking their medication regularly or changing their diet, for example. The contracts will have at least one target behaviour that the patient will commit to adhering to. The ultimate aim of the contracts is to improve adherence to treatment.

A strength of using behavioural contracts is that their effectiveness is supported by research evidence. Neale (1991) found that participants who signed a behavioural contract agreeing to increase exercise and adopt a special diet to reduce cholesterol had significantly greater positive health changes than those who did not have a contract. The findings of this study suggest that the simple act of making and signing an agreement can be helpful in decreasing cardiovascular risk in as little as three months.

A weakness of behavioural contracts is that although they were effective in the short term at helping patients adhere to their treatment, they were not effective when followed over longer periods of time (Bosch-Capblanch *et al.*, 2007). In addition, Bosch-Capblanch *et al.* (2007) found that research into effectiveness of contracts was small-scale and poorly executed, lowering the **validity** of results.

Prompts

Prompts can be effective at reminding patients when to take medication, or when their appointments are so that they do not miss them. Today it is more common for healthcare providers to use automated text messages to their patients' mobile phones as prompts.

A strength of text reminders is that they can be an effective way of improving treatment adherence and increasing attendance at medical appointments. Schwebel and Larimer (2018) conducted a review of 162 studies in this area, concluding that prompts have many benefits including being convenient, cost-effective and acceptable to patients. This is an important finding as missed appointments cost health services millions, however Schwebel and Larimer (2018) also note that further research exploring the frequency and timing of prompts may be helpful in increasing their usefulness.

A weakness of using text messages is that not everybody uses them. Some elderly patients, for example, may not find them beneficial if they do not use text messaging on their phone. Therefore, it may not be a suitable method for everyone and alternative methods should be made available to patients.

Customising treatment

By tailoring treatment to best fit with the ability and lifestyle of the patient, healthcare practitioners are likely to improve adherence to treatment. Heath *et al.* (2015) describe the use of intervention mapping, an approach that uses multiple theories and research evidence to help develop effective behaviour change interventions. The process involves identifying and understanding how and why the patient needs to change. Then psychologists need to discover what is causing or having an influence over the behaviour. They then need to work out which factors inhibit that behaviour. Next, they will choose appropriate behavioural techniques that can be used for the intervention and find ways to effectively deliver the intervention. Finally, the psychologists should share their findings with other healthcare professionals.

A strength of this approach is that it is supported by research evidence. For example, Lakhanpaul *et al.* (2020) used **intervention mapping** to improve understanding of asthma in South-East Asian families in Leicester, UK. They collected qualitative data using semi-structured interviews to better understand perceptions and experiences of asthma and the families' priorities in terms of improving asthma-care services. This study demonstrates the importance of taking a community-based, culturally-relevant approach in order to dismantle barriers to treatment and customise services to suit users' needs.

Unfortunately, the approach is costly due to the time invested in collaborating with community groups and may be counterproductive if it is not conducted with appropriate sensitivity to cultural differences.

> ### ▶ LEARNING LINKS
> Chaney *et al.* (2004)'s study used the principle of **positive reinforcement** in order to improve adherence. At AS Level you learned about the study by Fagen *et al.* (elephant learning) where positive reinforcement was used to shape the behaviour of elephants. Can you remember what the elephants were being trained to do? What similarities and differences are there between these two studies? Think about the aim, procedure, results and conclusion as well as the evaluation points. Are there any reasons that positive reinforcement in humans and non-human animals would be different? Or would the principles be the same?

> ### STUDY TIP
> When you are answering any questions from this section or from your teacher, ensure that you contextualise your answers when you are evaluating. If you are evaluating a weakness of a research method in a specific study, do not just give a generic weakness of that research method. You must refer to the specific study and why it is a weakness for that study.

TEST YOURSELF

1 Sid keeps forgetting to take his medication. His doctor has warned him that if he does not improve then the likelihood is that his illness will get worse and he may end up in hospital. He wants Sid to sign a behavioural contract.
   a Explain what is meant by a behavioural contract. [2]
   b Suggest one weakness of behavioural contracts as measure to improve Sid's adherence to medication. [2]
2 Health professionals are looking at ways to improve adherence to medication in children between the ages of five and ten. Explain one strategy that the health professionals could use to improve adherence in children. [4]
3 a Describe what psychologists have discovered about improving adherence in children. [6]
   b Evaluate what psychologists have discovered about improving adherence in children, with a discussion about generalisability. [10]
4 Explain what is meant by a pilot study with an example from improving adherence. [2]
5 Explain one ethical issue that researchers need to address when using children in research. [2]
6 Explain one weakness of using experiments to research adherence to medical advice in children. [2]

KEY TERMS

diphtheria
tetanus
whooping cough
polio
measles
mumps
rubella
immunisation
pre-schooler

METHODOLOGY

experiments
questionnaires
generalisations from findings
validity

Key study: Improving medical adherence using community interventions – Yokley and Glenwick (1984)

Think!

What research method was used by Yokley and Glenwick (1984)?

Think!

Doctors are worried because in parts of the UK rates of childhood **immunisations** have dropped. Using what you have learned, how could healthcare professionals in your country incentivise parents to get their children immunised?

Think!

Imagine you wanted to replicate the study by Yokley and Glenwick (1984) study. Is there anything you would change or improve?

Introducing James Yokley

▲ Figure 8.12

Dr James Yokley has dedicated his career as a clinical psychologist to addressing unhealthy, harmful behaviour by developing social responsibility. The lack of social responsibility exhibited by multiple forms of unhealthy, harmful behaviour constantly on display in the news media overloads our health and human services system, overcrowds our jails, threatens our civil rights, tears the moral fabric of our society and prevents young people from achieving their goals in life.

In a world constantly challenged by social responsibility barriers to overcome, Dr Yokley likes to tell his students that... 'You are only limited by your creativity.'

CONTEXT

Behavioural psychology has been used to modify the behaviour of people in society in a number of ways such as promoting preventive behaviours in regard to smoking, nutrition, seat belt-wearing and speeding. Yokley and Glenwick (1984) wanted to investigate ways of increasing immunisation because at the time of their research, preventable diseases such as **polio**, **whooping cough**, **tetanus** and **rubella** still caused the deaths of over five million children across the world. Yokley and Glenwick (1984) reported 10,000 cases of preventable diseases in the USA in 1982.

AIM

To evaluate the impact of four conditions for motivating parents to have their children immunised.

METHODOLOGY

This study used a field experiment with a longitudinal design. The study was conducted in a naturalistic setting with a manipulated independent variable.

Sample

The target population consisted of children under the age of five who needed one or more inoculation for **diphtheria**, tetanus, whooping cough, polio, **measles**, **mumps** or rubella.

A sample of 2101 preschool children were chosen from a register held at a public health clinic in a Midwestern city in the USA. Of these children, 1133 (53.9 per cent) were found to be immune deficient and in need of at least one inoculation. However, due to attrition, such as parents indicating that their children were fully inoculated, the final sample consisted of 715 children. 50 per cent were female and 64 per cent white.

PROCEDURE

Research record cards were created for the participants as their medical records were not allowed to be removed from the medical centre. Only information directly relevant to the research was included. The five research assistants who were undergraduate students at the university, created the records.

In order to prevent confounding variables which could have affected the internal validity of the experiment, parents with two or more immune-deficient **pre-schoolers** were assigned to conditions as families rather than the individual children to avoid them receiving conflicting conditions.

Children or families were randomly assigned to one of four conditions (independent variables).
1 Mailed out general prompt: *'Dear parent: Unless your doctor decided differently your child needs X doses of X vaccines at X ages. If your child is behind in any of them ... I urge you to make an appointment to get your child caught up.'*
2 Mailed out specific prompt: *'To the Parents of (child's name), our records show that it is time for .... to receive the following shot(s): ... (specific list provided) .... Shots may be obtained FREE of charge at the: ... (specific clinic location, dates, and times).'*
3 Mailed out specific prompt plus extended clinic hours: This included the specific prompt plus: *'ATTENTION: FOR YOUR CONVENIENCE, TWO SPECIAL 'OFF HOURS' CLINICS ARE BEING HELD AT THE (clinic name) CLINIC (clinic address). Just sign all of your children in at the clinic and you may go out for the evening or day while we take care of them FREE of charge. Hope to see you there!'* They were told this included drinks, movies and snacks.
4 Mailed out specific prompt plus a monetary incentive: *'ATTENTION: IN AN EFFORT TO GET PARENTS TO HAVE THEIR CHILDREN IMMUNISED AGAINST CHILDHOOD DISEASES, THE AKRON HEALTH DEPARTMENT WITH SUPPORT FROM B. F. GOODRICH IS GIVING AWAY $175.00 IN CASH PRIZES TO PARENTS WHO TURN IN THE TICKET ATTACHED TO THIS PAGE.'*

Parents were told that there would be three prizes of $100, $50 and $25 and in order to be eligible for the lottery, parents had to bring their children to the clinic for immunisation and whilst there, tear off their ticket stub which had been mailed to them and put it in the clinic's lottery box.

Control groups

1 Contact control group: Received a telephone call asking about whether their child was immunised and general demographic information but no specific prompt to have their child immunised.
2 No contact control group: Received no contact during the study.

The prompts were posted out with a postage-paid postcard (addressed to the health department) for each child so that the parent could update their health clinic records if their child had already received the immunisation.

The dependent variables were:
1 The number of children receiving one or more immunisations at the clinic.
2 The number of target children attending the clinic (for any reason).
3 The total number of immunisations received by the target children.

After two months, the lottery was drawn for the money-incentive group and prizes were delivered directly to the winners' homes. A further follow up took place after three months.

▶ RESULTS

Throughout the three follow up periods, the effectiveness of the four interventions remained in the same order, with the monetary incentive being the most effective at getting the parents to bring their child to the clinic for their immunisation, followed by the specific prompt plus increased access, then the specific prompt and finally the general prompt.

The monetary incentive was significantly more effective compared to the no contact control group on all measures and to the contact control group on most measures.

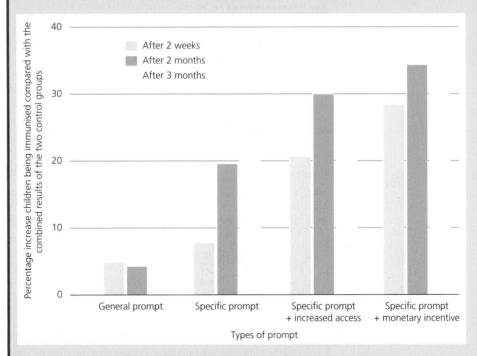

▲ **Figure 8.13 Graph to show the total number of inoculations received by the children in the different groups and the percentage increase of groups compared to the combined control groups**

> ## CONCLUSIONS
>
> ● Using behavioural incentives to motivate parents to have their children immunised is effective.
> ● A single general prompt is not enough to motivate parents to immunise their children. Although the specific prompt did show a significant percentage increase in immunisations in the first and second follow ups (at two and three months).

 ## Methodological strengths and weaknesses

A strength of this study is that participants were randomly assigned to conditions. Random assignment should mean that participant variables such as personality of the parents will not bias results. This means that the researchers can state that having the monetary incentive with the specific prompt did cause more parents to inoculate their children, increasing the validity of the results.

Another strength of this research is that it followed **standardised procedures** such as the same prompts within groups. This means it had good reliability. It also means that the research can be replicated. This is important because replication of research demonstrates that the results were not due to chance making the research more reliable.

A weakness is that the results may not generalise to other parts of the USA or to other countries because parents from different socioeconomic backgrounds or different cultures may not be motivated in the same way. For example, there may be places where there is a great deal of mistrust in immunisations and a monetary reward may not be sufficient to persuade parents to get their child vaccinated.

Another weakness is that a number of the initial sample did not take part in the study. For example, there were a number of 'return to sender' letters from both controls and the final sample was 36.9 per cent less than the original sample. This may introduce bias into the sample as there may be more of a certain sex of child or families who had two or more children without immunisations and therefore the results may not be representative of the target population.

 ## Ethics

An ethical weakness of the research is that parents did not consent to take part. They were unaware that they were participants and that their behaviour was being manipulated. In addition, there may be questions whether it is ethically correct to encourage one group with money in order to get their children immunised. A strength of the research is that following the data collection, both control groups received the specific prompt letter by post ensuring that the parents of children in these groups were also reminded that their children required further immunisations.

 ## Applications to the real world

A strength of the study is that it has practical applications. Where immunisation levels are low and certain preventable diseases are returning, incentivised programmes such as this might help increase the number of parents getting their children vaccinated.

> ## ISSUES AND DEBATES
>
> ### Use of children in research
>
> Although Yokley and Glenwick used children in their research, their focus was actually on the behaviour of their parents in getting them vaccinated and what interventions were most likely to increase the parents' likelihood of getting their children vaccinated. However, even though the focus was on the parents, it was important that they considered the children when designing the study as their interventions could have potentially negatively impacted on vaccine uptake, such as being in the control condition. However, Yokley and Glenwick ensured that the control groups received a follow-up letter reminding parents to vaccinate their children after the study was complete, ensuring that no group was disadvantaged.

REFLECTION

- Do you feel the lack of informed consent in this study was justified in order to achieve valid results?
- How could you make this study more generalisable?

Do you think that the incentives Yokley and Glenwick used would work in your country?

▶ Figure 8.14

LEARNING LINKS

At AS Level, you learned about a study by Saavedra and Silverman (button phobia). One thing that was not taken into account in this study is whether the child or parent had had some previous experience that made them reluctant to be immunised. For example, perhaps the parent had negative side effects from an immunisation. It may also be that the child or parent has a needle phobia. How would having a needle phobia impact on getting a vaccination? Can you remember from AS Level the types of treatments that could help overcome phobias?

STUDY TIP

Why not create a poster to represent the different conditions in the study by Yokley and Glenwick (1984) with drawings to make it very visual? It does not matter if you can only draw stick people! For example, think of how you can represent the different types of prompts such as the gentle reminder of the first condition and the additional parts of the later prompts such as extended hours and money. How could you visualise the different evaluation points discussed on these pages?

TEST YOURSELF

1 A group of doctors have noticed that cases of measles have increased in their area. They are having a meeting to discuss how to increase immunisation using community intervention. Explain two ways the doctors could increase the number of measles immunisations provided to children in their area. [4]

2 Explain what is meant by reliability, using an example from research into improving adherence. [2]

3 a Describe the study by Yokley and Glenwick (1984) on improving medical adherence using community interventions. [6]

   b Evaluate the study by Yokley and Glenwick (1984), including a discussion about generalisations from the findings. [10]

4 Outline one control and one experimental condition used in the study by Yokley and Glenwick (1984) on community interventions. [4]

5 Explain one ethical issue that was raised in this study. [2]

6 Explain one strength and one weakness of conducting field experiments to study participation in immunisation interventions in communities. [4]

7 Compare individual behavioural techniques and community interventions as a method of improving adherence. [6]

8.3 Pain
8.3.1 Types of pain

KEY TERMS

acute pain

chronic pain

phantom limb pain

mirror treatment

congenital insensitivity

affective

sensory

malignant

benign

METHODOLOGY

case study

Think!

What is meant by phantom limb pain?

Think!

Imagine your friend Katherine is telling her friends at school that she feels no pain. Her friend Thanaksan thinks this is a good thing because he is always banging into things. Katherine explains to her friends that it may not be as good as they think. What problems might Katherine encounter when she feels no pain at all? How will this affect her life?

Think!

One debate that could be discussed when looking at pain is whether it is affected more by individual or situational factors. What individual factors do you feel may determine how much pain people feel? Are there any situational factors that may contribute?

Another debate that is important when looking at issues such as pain is the nature versus nurture debate. This is not about the transmission of pain signals via nerves, we all know that that's a biological process but how some people can feel/take more pain than others. Some researchers suggest how much pain we feel could be influenced by nurture with culture, gender and social class all part of the reason. For example, the pain experience may change due to lower social classes enduring more stress and undertreated pain. Perhaps it is nature that some people just have a higher genetic tolerance to pain? Or perhaps it is a mixture of both. What is your experience of pain? How much does it hurt if you cut yourself or burn yourself accidentally? Is that different from your friends or family?

▲ Figure 8.15

Functions of pain

According to the ICD 11, pain is a disorder 'characterised by a sensation of marked discomfort, distress or agony ... causing physical or psychological misery, pain and distress'. People often assume that everyone feels pain in the same way, but this is not the case. A person's experience of pain is quite subjective as it has both a **sensory** (how intense it is) and an **affective** (how unpleasant the feeling is to you) component to it. For example, people who believe their pain is a threat to their health will rate the affective level as higher than someone who believes the pain is just because they exercised a bit too much at the gym (they may even see it as pleasant!) despite having similar sensory ratings. An individual's response to pain therefore may be affected by social, genetic and cognitive factors.

The main function of pain is to serve as a signal that something is wrong with the body, whether that is due to injury or illness. It also may prevent us from injuring a body part even more. If it did not hurt to walk on a broken leg you may carry on using it and cause more damage. Sarafino (2006) refers to the case of a young woman with an inability to feel pain, called **congenital insensitivity to pain**. As a child she had bitten off the end of her tongue while eating, without realising it. When tested under laboratory conditions, psychologists were unable to elicit any normal pain reactions such as raised heart rate or blood pressure in response to stimuli such as strong electric shocks.

Doctors can also use pain as a clue in diagnosing what is wrong with you. They will ask how much pain you are in, where it is and the type of pain it is. From this they can try and establish its cause.

Acute and chronic pain

Acute pain

Acute pain refers to sudden, sharp pain that lasts for less than six months, depending on the condition (ICD 11). Acute pain acts as a warning that your health may be compromised. Acute pain is complex, it can sometimes be very temporary and short-lived but at other times it can be longer lasting and cause severe pain. Symptoms can start and stop without warning, last for seconds or days but do not last all day and night. Acute pain is usually caused by something specific such as a broken bone, burning your finger on something hot or childbirth. The pain will go away once the issue is resolved. Acute pain can be extremely distressing and can cause anxiety.

Chronic pain

Chronic pain refers to pain that usually lasts longer than six months. Patients who experience chronic pain often have high levels of anxiety and exhaustion. It can affect their sleep and can have a serious impact on their ability to lead a normal life.

There are three types of chronic pain:
1. Chronic/recurrent pain: This is pain that comes in episodes with periods in between of no pain. An example of this might be migraine headaches.
2. Chronic/intractable/**benign** pain: This type of chronic pain is constant, although the severity might vary. It is not caused by a **malignant** condition such as cancer. An example of chronic/intractable/benign pain would be back pain.
3. Chronic/progressive pain: This pain: is also constant but is due to an underlying condition such as cancer and gets increasingly worse as the symptoms of the illness progress.

> ## ▶ ISSUES AND DEBATES
>
> ### Individual and situational explanations
>
> It is important to take individual experiences of pain into account when understanding a patient's perspective. Pain perception can be influenced by prior experience, the present context in which the patient is experiencing the pain, and what that pain might mean for the future for that individual. Situational factors can also impact an individual's pain perception, such as the environment that they find themselves in. If it is loud, bright and stressful, this could increase the pain perception. Therefore, both individual and situational factors can have an impact on pain perception.

Phantom limb pain

There are some types of pain which do not appear to have a cause. **Phantom limb pain** is one of these. Patients who have phantom limb pain experience pain in a limb that has been amputated and therefore no longer exists or have suffered severe nerve damage meaning the limb no longer has any functioning nerve that would normally allow the patient to feel pain. Around 80 per cent of individuals experience phantom pain after a limb loss and it is more common in women than men. It can start straight after the limb is lost or even months later.

What exactly causes phantom limb pain is unknown, but it may be explained to some degree by mixed signals from the brain. After a limb has been amputated, areas of the spinal cord and the brain lose the normal input that they get from the missing limb and adjust to this in unpredictable ways. This adjustment can trigger the message that there is something wrong and lead to pain. Research has also shown that the brain may 'rewire' that part of the sensory circuit to another part of the body. As the amputated part cannot receive sensory information from the brain it is referred elsewhere such as from a missing hand to a cheek. Therefore, when the cheek is touched it is thought the missing hand is being touched leading to the feeling of pain. Damaged nerve endings could also be a factor, as well as simply the memory an individual has of pre-amputation pain in the area.

Phantom limb pain is a chronic condition and can last for months or years. The pain can be either recurrent or intractable. The pain itself is described as 'shooting', 'burning' or 'cramping' (Sarafino, 2006).

Mirror treatment

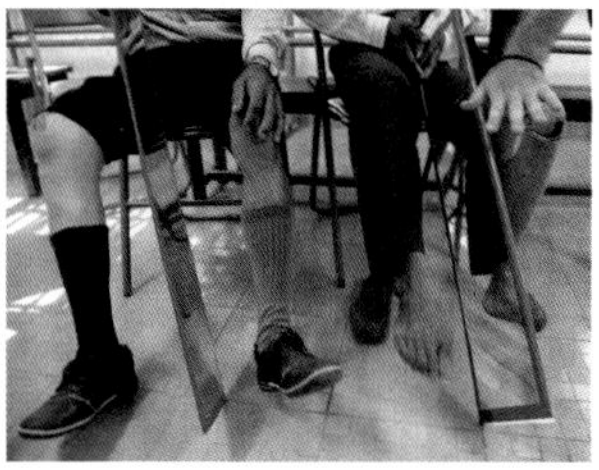

▲ Figure 8.16 Mirror treatment for phantom limb pain (PLP)

Mirror treatment has been found to be an effective treatment for phantom limb pain (Ramachandran and Rogers-Ramachandran, 1995). It uses a mirror to create the illusion of the amputated limb still being there by placing the opposing limb in front of the mirror with the amputated limb hidden behind it (see Figure 8.16). The patient then imagines moving the 'phantom' limb. Ramachandran and Rogers-Ramachandran (1995) suggest that the theory behind the success of mirror treatment lies in the reasons why phantom limb pain occurs in the first place. They suggest that it occurs due to a miscommunication problem in the brain where neurons which had originally commanded muscles in the phantom limb still exist and can send out signals such as a request to move the limb. When the brain sends these signals, they expect signals in return such as movement which says the command has been carried out. When this does not happen (as the limb does not exist) then this miscommunication causes a conflict known as **negative feedback**. To get past this negative feedback, mirror treatment 'tricks' the brain through the visual system telling neurons in the brain that the limb is moving even though it really is not. This breaks the negative feedback loop which has been telling the brain the limb is not moving and establishing new connections to 'feel' the limb again.

Focus on... MacLachlan *et al.* (2004)

> ### AIM
> ....
> To report the effects of mirror treatment on a person with lower limb amputation who was experiencing distress.

> ### METHODOLOGY/RESULTS
> ....
> MacLachlan *et al.* reported the case study of an individual named Alan who was 32 years old. He had a rare bacterial infection that resulted in him becoming extremely ill and having to have his leg amputated. He spent time in an intensive care unit and did not become consciously aware that his leg had been amputated until five weeks later. He was then sent to a specialist unit where he was referred to a clinical psychologist due to experiencing phantom limb pain.
>
> He was prescribed pain medication and advised to use a **TENS machine** (a machine that sends electrical pulses through your skin which results in the release of endorphins which stop the pain signals in the brain), but this only made the pain worse. He was then offered the opportunity to try mirror treatment (see above).
>
> By the end of the third week of exercises using the mirror treatment, Alan rated his phantom limb pain as 0. When it was at its worst before treatment, he had rated it at between 5 and 9. He felt that he had far more control over his phantom limb than he had prior to using the exercises and this control led to the substantial reduction in pain.

> ### CONCLUSION
> ....
> ● Mirror treatment is a useful and effective way to treat phantom limb pain. It avoids patients having to take pain medication which can have negative side effects and gives the patient control over their own pain.
> ● Patients with phantom limb pain have the free will to control their pain.

Evaluating MacLachlan *et al.* (2004)

The use of the **case study** methodology is a strength especially for studying a phenomenon like phantom limb pain. The case study gives detailed insight into the background of the patient and how effective the treatment was compared to other treatments, such as the pain relief medication and TENS machine. This makes it a more valid method of studying rare phenomena.

One weakness, however, is that findings cannot be generalised from one individual to the wider population. This is because their experience of using the mirror treatment may be completely different to other people who have experienced the loss of a limb, especially as we know that pain can be a subjective experience and differ due to culture and gender, for example. Therefore, the results from this case study may not be representative of other people's experiences.

Another weakness the researchers acknowledged was the possibility of a 'placebo effect'. This is where just the knowledge that you are receiving treatment can have positive effects. For example, the attention Alan had got from the clinicians as part of the treatment or even a change of dressing may have contributed to the results, lowering its validity.

ISSUES AND DEBATES

Determinism versus free will

Phantom limb pain is a distressing condition, therefore the fact that the case study shows that the use of mirror treatment could change the life of sufferers and reduce their levels of pain substantially is extremely important. In terms of determinism versus free-will the patient obviously has the free-will to attend treatment or not, however the treatment itself can be seen to be biologically deterministic. The treatments cause the brain to break the negative feedback loop and establish new connections and we, as individuals, have no control over this process as it is not within our conscious control, meaning the success of the treatment is determined by biological processes rather than individual free-will.

LEARNING LINK

MacLachlan et al. (2004) report the case study of Alan who had phantom limb pain. At AS Level, you studied Saavedra and Silverman (button phobia) who also used the case study method. Both were aiming to treat different conditions. Think about the similarities and differences between the two studies.

STUDY TIP

Phantom limb pain is an unusual problem which you may not have heard of before. There are some great videos on YouTube about phantom limb pain and also some that show how mirror treatment for phantom limb pain works. One way to really understand it is by listening to people's real-life experiences so these could really help aid your understanding.

TEST YOURSELF

1   Debs and Eddie were discussing the small accident that they had the previous night. They were both trying to move a chair to a different area of their house when they dropped it onto their fingers. Debs said that the pain was 'terrible' whereas Eddie said he hardly felt it at all. Debs experienced acute pain.
    a   Suggest one reason why Eddie and Debs had a different experience of pain.   [2]
    b   Explain what is meant by acute pain.   [2]
2   Explain what is meant by the nature versus nurture debate with an example from your knowledge of pain.   [2]
3   a   Describe what psychologists have discovered about:
        –   phantom limb pain and mirror treatment
        –   functions and types of pain.   [6]
    b   Evaluate what psychologists have discovered about:
        –   phantom limb pain and mirror treatment
        –   functions and types of pain including a discussion about case studies.   [10]

4 Outline one advantage and one disadvantage of using case studies to investigate phantom limb pain and mirror treatment. [4]

Mona is investigating chronic pain. She wants to recruit participants who she can observe at their workplace to see how their pain affects their day-to-day life.

5 Explain one way that Mona could recruit participants for her study. [2]

6 Explain two ethical guidelines that Mona will need to consider before carrying out her observational study. [2]

Theories of pain: Specificity theory and gate control theory

KEY TERMS

specificity theory

pain centre

gate control theory

nerve fibres

Transcutaneous Nerve Electrical Stimulation (TENS)

T-cells

dorsal horn

spinal cord

METHODOLOGY

case study

Think!

How does **specificity theory** explain pain?

Think!

You are having a discussion about specificity theory and **gate control theory** with your friends and they are confused about the differences between the two theories. How would you explain the differences between the two theories?

Think!

One debate which is discussed in psychology is reductionism versus holism. Which of the two theories you have learned about on these pages would you say is more reductionist? Give a reason for your answer.

Figure 8.17 shows a man rubbing his arm which is painful. Gate control theory suggests that this helps reduce pain. What different ways can you think of to distract yourself from pain?

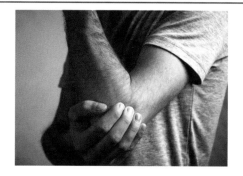

▶ Figure 8.17

Specificity theory

Specificity theory sees the mechanism of pain along the same lines as other senses such as temperature or touch. The theory suggests that we have a **sensory system** which is specifically dedicated to pain. Each sensory system, whether it is for heat, touch or pain, has dedicated receptor cells which only activate when detecting their specific stimuli. Once these receptor cells detect pain they send messages, or signals, through a dedicated pathway (along **nerve fibres**) to a specific **pain centre** in the brain. These brain centres will then process the signals received to produce the perception (experience) of pain. Specificity theory suggests that the more the pathway is used the more intense the pain felt. This early theory of pain, therefore, sees pain as a purely biological process.

Evaluation

One strength of specificity theory is that it led to the development of other more detailed theories of pain. Although it is largely discredited today it formed the basis of research for many years and it was this level of research which meant that its principles were shown to be flawed and other theories appeared. This makes the theory useful.

Gate control theory

Melzack and Wall (1965) proposed a theory of pain based on the action of **T-cells** (transmission cells). First, small, slow fibres carry the pain stimulation to the **dorsal horn** of the **spinal cord**. They pass through a 'gating mechanism' which then activates the T-cells which transmit the pain signal impulses through the spinal cord to the brain. When the output from these T-cells reaches a critical level, the person will feel pain. The more that these T-cells transmit the pain signal impulses past that critical level, the more pain the person perceives.

The gate controls how freely the T-cells are able to transmit their signal. If the gate is open, then they are able to transmit freely. However, if it is closed to some degree, the T-cells are then inhibited and unable to transmit as freely.

The extent to which the gate is open or closed depends on three factors, according to the theory:

1   How much activity there is in the slow pain fibres: The more activity there is (the greater the pain stimulus) the wider the gate opens.
2   How much activity there is in the other peripheral fibres: These large fibres carry information about harmless stimuli or mild irritations and they close the gate. For example, if someone banged their elbow and 'rubbed it better', the information about the rubbing would come through the peripheral fibres, which would close the gate, reducing the sensation of pain as less T-cells are able to transmit their pain message to the brain.
3   Messages that come from the brain to the spinal cord: Neurons in the cortex and the brainstem can send impulses relating to emotions down the spinal cord which can open or close the gate. Anxiety and boredom are thought to open the gate and positive emotions such as happiness or being distracted tend to close it.

Evaluation

A strength of gate control theory is that it is supported by research evidence. Mendell (2014) reported that patients who had their large fibres stimulated by **Transcutaneous Nerve Electrical Stimulation (TENS)** experienced pain relief for the duration of the stimulation and for 30 minutes after the treatment ended. This finding is well explained by the theory as increased activity in the large nerve fibres closed the gate leading to reduced pain.

However, one weakness of the theory is that the researchers have not yet found physical evidence of a gating mechanism in the spinal cord. Therefore, there are parts of the theory that lack evidence, suggesting that other mechanisms might be involved.

> **ISSUES AND DEBATES**

Nature versus nurture

The gate control theory of pain focuses on the nature side of the debate in its explanation of why and how we experience pain. However, it ignores environmental factors that could affect our pain perception such as treating patients in settings that do not have distracting stimuli such as plants or relaxing pictures, which could help alleviate the pain. There may also be things within the clinical environment that can make the pain worse such as hearing other patients in pain or harsh overhead lighting. It also ignores other factors that can reduce pain such as laughter and psychological treatments.

Reductionism versus holism

Another strength of the gate control theory of pain is that it takes a more holistic approach to pain as it was one of the first pain theories to refer to both the psychological factors as well as the physical/biological factors that influence how people perceive pain. This is important because it helps us understand how people can use things such as positive emotion and distraction to cope with pain. However, it still does not take into account individual differences in pain and does not suggest reasons why people with the same injuries experience pain differently.

> **LEARNING LINK**

At AS Level, you studied Andrade (doodling) whose aim was to try and discover whether doodling would increase attention/concentration. This is suggesting a distraction technique such as doodling can have a positive effect. Theories of pain also suggest that distractions could divert attention away from internal messages about pain therefore also having the positive effect of reducing pain. Do you believe distraction works for you? Have you ever doodled while listening to the teacher in class? Sometimes you may even do it without realising.

STUDY TIP

Gate theory may seem a little confusing if you just read about it, so why not try and make a three-dimensional model to understand it better? You could use cardboard tubes to represent the nerve fibres and make a 'gate' from coloured card (or whatever else you have to hand). You could use colourful balls of modelling clay or marbles to represent the pain signals moving along the fibres and reaching the gate, which is either partially open or closed. You could use another colour of clay or marble to represent the T cells. The model will help you to think about how the position of the gate affects the onward journey of the pain signals to the brain and ultimately how much pain we experience.

> **TEST YOURSELF**

1   Hajirah hits her elbow on the door on the way outside. She rubs her arm and notices that the pain goes away slightly.
    Explain, using gate control theory, why Hajirah's pain went away when she was rubbing her arm.   [4]
2   Outline what is meant by reductionism with an example from specificity theory of pain. [2]
3   a   Describe what psychologists have discovered about theories of pain.   [6]
    b   Evaluate what psychologists have discovered about theories of pain, including a discussion about application to everyday life.   [10]
4   a   Plan an experiment to test the effectiveness of distraction on the reduction of pain. Your plan must include:
        –   a directional or non-directional hypothesis
        –   details about sampling technique.   [10]
    b   State two reasons for your choice of sampling technique.   [2]
    c   Explain one weakness of your choice of sampling technique.   [2]
5   Explain one similarity and one difference between the specificity and the gate control theories of pain.   [4]

8.3.2 Measuring pain

KEY TERMS

visual analogue scale

McGill pain questionnaire

UAB Pain behaviour scale

Think!

What is meant by the term visual analogue?

Think!

Imagine you are a healthcare professional. Your patient, Erin, says she is in a great deal of pain. What questions could you ask (both open and closed) to find out more about the severity of Erin's pain?

Think!

Often in psychology we want to ensure that the data we collect is objective, but why
might it be better for data about pain to be subjective?

Subjective measures

There are a number of different ways to measure pain. **Observations** record a patient's
behaviour whereas objective measures such as EEGs record brain activity (Koyama *et al.*,
2018). However, neither of these methods measure the subjective experience of pain for
individual patients. Therefore, subjective measures such as using self-report are important
for healthcare professionals to understand the severity of the pain that the patient is
experiencing, as well as its impact on their everyday lives.

Clinical interview

Clinical interviews tend to be used to assess patients with chronic pain rather than just look
at the physiological aspects of pain. The interview will look at psychological and behavioural
factors that influence the patient's subjective reporting of pain. During the interview, the
patient's history and medical evaluation are completed.

In addition to collecting this information, the healthcare professional should also observe
how the patient behaves while discussing their thoughts and feelings. This observation will
give information about the patient's emotional state and their beliefs about the cause of the
pains. All of this information may lead to a knowledge of pain triggers or moderators which
will aid treatment planning.

As part of the clinical interview, in order to assist with treatment planning, healthcare
professionals can also use a range of psychometric tests to help them to understand the type
and intensity of the pain that the patient is experiencing, how well they are able to function in
their everyday lives and to evaluate their emotional distress and their beliefs and expectations.

Evaluation

One strength of the clinical interview is that it is an effective way to assess pain as
although there are standardised questions, the physician can ask patients to elaborate or
clarify certain things, which would not be possible with a questionnaire and allows the
treatment plan to be specifically tailored to the individual patient. This makes it more likely
the treatment will be successful, and adherence increased.

However, one weakness of the clinical **interview** is that it may not be effective for all
people. For example, if the patient is not able to communicate well about their pain or does
not have a trusting relationship with their practitioner or there are cultural factors acting as
a barrier, the clinical interview may not be an effective way to measure pain, and this may
limit its usefulness.

Psychometric measures and visual rating scales
McGill pain questionnaire (MPQ)

The **MPQ** is a self-report questionnaire used by physicians to measure subjective pain
experiences. It was designed to give **quantitative** data about the patient's pain experience
which could be statistically analysed. It was constructed by Melzack and Torgerson (1971)
who asked doctors and university graduates to put 102 adjectives into groups which
described the different aspects of pain. For this, they identified three dimensions of pain
(alongside a fourth miscellaneous category) which were subdivided into 20 questions.

1   Sensory (questions 1 to 10): What the pain feels like physically. Types of pain are put
    into different categories. Within each category, patients have a choice of between two
    and six words to describe the pain. They choose the word which best fits their pain. Each
    word is assigned a number, for example category 9 (dullness): dull 1, sore 2, hurting 3,
    aching 4, heavy 5.
2   Affective (questions 11 to 15): This is the emotional side of the pain. It looks at what
    emotions the pain makes the patient feel with words such as tiring, sickening or fearful
    amongst the choices. There is a choice between two and five words within each question,
    with each assigned a number.

3 Evaluative (question 16): What is the subjective intensity of the pain experience, measured with a five-point scale, for example, which word describes it at its worst?
  » mild, 1
  » discomforting, 2
  » distressing, 3
  » horrible, 4
  » excruciating, 5
4 'Miscellaneous' (questions 17 to 20): Looking at various aspects of pain on three-to-five-point rating scales.

When filling in the questionnaire each patient was told to pick the word which best fit their pain for each question. If none of the words in a question fit then they could leave it blank.

Patients were also asked to indicate where the pain is on a body chart with the letter E used for pain on the surface (on the skin), I used for internal pain or IE used for both. They were also asked to rate the intensity of current pain on a six-point rating scale from 0 (no pain) to 5 (excruciating). Finally, the patients filled in three questions consisting of three-point rating scales which described the pattern of pain, for example one question had brief, momentary and transient in one category.

Three major results are obtained:
1 A pain rating index (PRI): The higher the score, the higher levels of pain. A total score is given for all 20 questions, plus a sensory, affective and evaluative score.
2 The number of words chosen.
3 The present pain intensity (PPI) at the time of the questionnaire.

Evaluation

A strength of the McGill pain questionnaire is that it has been found to be reliable and valid. Ferraz et al. (1990) performed a test-retest analysis on 91 patients and found excellent reliability, (r = +0.96), meaning that the responses of the patients on the questionnaire were highly correlated when they were tested on the same questionnaire again later. In terms of validity, Byrne et al. (1982) compared results of patients with back pain to previous research and found similar results.

One weakness of using the McGill questionnaire is that **quantitative** measures of pain may limit the ability of the patient to communicate their real experience of pain. For example, some patients might find that the words used to describe the different types of pain do not fit with their subjective experience of pain or they may have to have a strong enough grasp of the English language to understand the difference between words such as transient and momentary. This means that some patients may choose certain words but misunderstand their meaning simply because they wish to give a socially desirable response.

Visual analogue scales

A **visual analogue scale** (VAS) is a **psychometric** scale that is designed to measure an attitude, feeling or characteristic that cannot be directly measured, like subjective perception of pain, along a continuum of values.

It is usually shown to the patient as a 100 mm horizontal line along which the patient marks their current intensity of pain. Each end of the line shows the extremities of what is being measured – extreme pain to no pain (left best, right worst).

They can complete a VAS on each visit to the clinic so that their healthcare professional can monitor whether their pain experience is increasing/decreasing/remaining the same.

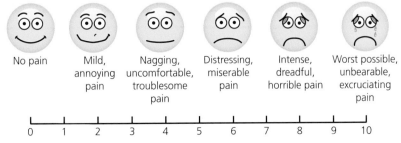

▲ Figure 8.18 An example of a visual analogue scale for measuring pain

Evaluation

One strength of VAS is that they are quick and easy to use by patients and as they are designed to show a spectrum of pain on a continuum, there are no 'gaps' in the pain intensity as there would be with a scale such as 'mild, moderate, severe'. This means that patients should feel that their pain experience is represented on the scale, making the scale more valid.

However, one weakness is that patients are not able to elaborate on their pain experience and how it impacts on their daily lives. This is a weakness as it only gives a basic measurement of pain, lowering the validity of the measure.

Behavioural/observational measures

UAB Pain behaviour scale

The UAB pain behaviour scale, views pain from a behaviourist perspective. Rather than using self-report, it measures only what pain behaviour is observable. It measures different aspects of behaviour such as verbal and non-verbal (groans, moans) complaints of pain, facial grimaces, mobility, body language and medication. They are all measured on a three-point scale and the observer has to judge how frequently each behaviour occurs across a three-week period (see Table 8.9).

▼ Table 8.9 An example of one of the measures of the UAB Pain behaviour scale

Body language (clutching, rubbing of site of pain)	M	T	W	T	F	S	S	M	T	W	T	F	S	S	M	T	W	T	F	S	S
None	1	1	1	1	1	1	1	1	1	1	1	1	1	1	1	1	1	1	1	1	1
Occasional	½	½	½	½	½	½	½	½	½	½	½	½	½	½	½	½	½	½	½	½	½
Frequent	0	0	0	0	0	0	0	0	0	0	0	0	0	0	0	0	0	0	0	0	0

Evaluation

A strength of the UAB scale is that it is quick to score and easy to use. This means that it can be used with a larger number of patients, including those who may not be able to fill in a self-report themselves. This is a strength as a wider sample will make the results more generalisable.

A weakness is that although this is a more objective scale as it is based on observable behaviours, it depends on the ability of the observer to accurately record the pain behaviour. If the observer misses or misinterprets when the patient is in pain, then the patient may feel that their subjective experience of the pain is being ignored or under-rated. In addition, correlation between scores on the UAB and on the McGill Pain Questionnaire is low, indicating that the relationship between how someone observes and records another person's pain behaviour and the self-reports of the subjective experience of pain is not a close one. Therefore, using this as a sole measure of pain may not give a full picture of what the patient is actually experiencing.

> **LEARNING LINK**
>
> At AS Level, you learned about the study by Dement and Kleitman (sleep and dreams) where the researchers measured sleep stages objectively using EEG to determine when a person was in REM or NREM according to the proportion of different types of brain wave. REM sleep was characterised by a high proportion of beta waves and NREM by a high proportion of delta waves. Recent research by Koyama *et al.* (2018) suggested that EEG can also be used as an objective measure of pain.

> **STUDY TIP**
>
> One way to learn the measurements of pain would be to create a mind map with as many links as possible between the different methods, for example looking at similarities and differences. Also, it is worth looking on the internet for an example of the different scales you have learned about, as many allow you to fill a copy in. This will allow you to understand any issues that patients may face when completing these sorts of questionnaires but also why they are an effective measure.

> ## TEST YOURSELF

1 Javid has been experiencing back pain for a number of weeks and has gone to his doctor as he feels unable to cope with it for any longer. His doctor wants to measure how much pain Javid is in currently.

   a Suggest two appropriate ways Javid's doctor could measure the severity of his pain. [4]

   b For one of the measures of pain you have suggested in part (a), explain one strength of this way to measure pain. [2]

2 Explain one weakness of the McGill pain questionnaire. [2]

3 a Describe what psychologists have discovered about subjective measures of pain. [6]

   b Evaluate what psychologists have discovered about subjective measures of pain, with a discussion about qualitative and quantitative data. [10]

4 Describe how the UAB pain behaviour scale can be used with a patient in a nursing home. [2]

5 Outline one disadvantage of using the UAB pain behaviour scale. [2]

6 Explain one strength of using psychometric testing to measure pain experiences. [2]

Key study: measuring pain: Comparing pain assessments by doctors, parents and children – Brudvik *et al.* (2016)

KEY TERMS

demographic questions

hypersensitivity

pain relief

METHODOLOGY

quantitative and qualitative data

interviews, observations

psychometrics

generalisations from findings

> ### Think!
>
> What are the similarities and differences between the pain scales used by the younger and older children, the parents and the physicians?

> ### Think!
>
> When was the last time you were in pain? Why might it have been hard to rate your pain on a scale like the ones in Figures 8.21–8.23?

> ### Think!
>
> Imagine you are a researcher, and you want to investigate children's experiences of hospital using a case study. How would you go about this? How would your study be both similar and different to Brudvik *et al.*?

Introducing Christina Brudvik

Christina Brudvik is a medical doctor and professor at the University of Bergen in Norway. Her medical interests and research are related to injury prevention, minor injury treatment and especially how to understand and improve pain relief in children with injuries. In this study, Christina and her French colleague Svein-Denis Moutte found that adults, especially the doctors, underestimate children's pain. Even if this conclusion confirms what we had expected, this type of study is important as an eye-opener for clinicians to improve their pain diagnostics and then give better pain relief. It feels rewarding to do studies that either verify or reject anticipations – and studies that hopefully can make a difference in either clinical medicine or psychology. 'In order to identify factors that affect the clinical handling of paediatric pain, we need more knowledge about how parents and physicians assess children's pain.'

▲ Figure 8.19 Christina Brudvik

Christina says, 'Good luck to you all with your further studies and research.'

Can you think of any reasons why parents and doctors might underestimate the level of pain experienced by children?

▶ Figure 8.20

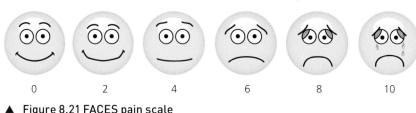

| 0 | 2 | 4 | 6 | 8 | 10 |

▲ Figure 8.21 FACES pain scale

| 0 | 2 | 4 | 6 | 8 | 10 |

| No hurt | Hurts little bit | Hurts little more | Hurts even more | Hurts whole lot | Hurts worse |

▲ Figure 8.22 Wong-Baker FACES pain rating scale

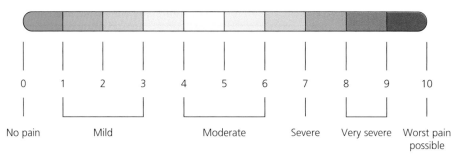

| 0 | 1 | 2 | 3 | 4 | 5 | 6 | 7 | 8 | 9 | 10 |

| No pain | Mild | | Moderate | | Severe | Very severe | Worst pain possible |

▲ Figure 8.23 A colour analogue scale

▶ CONTEXT

Research shows that hospital doctors underestimate children's pain and **pain relief** medication is administered less often, later and at lower doses than it is for adults. In some US emergency departments, pain relief medication was not given to children with fractures (broken bones) even when they were in considerable pain (Brown *et al.*, 2003). Research suggests that parents are better judges of their children's self-reported pain than nurses, yet still under-estimate their children's self-reported pain (Rajasagaram *et al.*, 2009), with fathers providing less accurate ratings than mothers (Morrow *et al.*, 2011). Other factors associated with underestimation of children's pain were the doctors' seniority and the frequency of the child's hospital visits. Agreement over pain experienced by children with cerebral palsy and chronic neurological disorders was particularly low.

▶ AIMS

Brudvik and her colleagues aimed to explore:
1 The relationship between children's self-reported pain and ratings of their pain intensity made by their parent and doctors.
2 How age, medical condition and severity of pain affect pain intensity estimates.
3 Whether pain assessment affects the administration of **pain relief**.

METHODOLOGY

This field study collected data using questionnaires at the Bergen Accident and Emergency Department in Norway. Correlation was used to analyse the data.

Sample

An **opportunity sample** of 243 paediatric patients aged 3–15 years old (mean age = 10.6), their parents and 51 doctors were recruited as they entered the hospital department. Families requiring follow-up appointments were later discounted.

PROCEDURE

Doctors and parents completed a **numeric rating scale**, where they had to rate the intensity/severity of the child's pain, from 0–10. Parents answered **demographic questions** about their child's age, gender and nationality and were asked if they had given their child any pain relief before their consultation.

Doctors were asked about their own medical experience (in years), medical specialisms and whether they were parents themselves. They were also asked whether they gave any pain relief during their consultation and whether the child's pain level seemed to match their diagnosis.

The 3–8-year-olds completed the Faces Pain Scale-Revised (FPS-R) and the Wong-Baker Faces Pain Rating scale, (see Figures 8.21 and 8.22), by pointing to the face that best matched their pain level. The researcher recorded the corresponding numerical score from 0–10. 9–15-year-olds indicated the intensity of their pain using a visual analogue scale, with a coloured 100 mm. line. Green equalled 'no pain at all' and red was 'the worst thinkable pain' (see Figure 8.23). Finally, the child's diagnosis was classified as infection, fracture, wound injury or soft tissue, ligament or muscle injury and each family's total waiting time (from arrival to consultation) was recorded.

RESULTS

Pain ratings were highest for children reporting their own pain, followed by parental ratings and finally doctors' ratings, (see Table 8.10). There was a moderate level of agreement between children and their parents but a low level of agreement between children and their doctors. Agreement between parents and physicians was also low. Pain intensity was worst for fractures and the difference in agreement between child and doctors was lowest for this group. This suggests physicians made more accurate estimates for the most painful conditions. This said, only 42 per cent of children with severe pain (judged by doctors) were given pain relief medication. Of the children who rated their pain as severe, only 14.3 per cent were given pain relief medication.

Doctors underestimated the pain of the younger children more than the older children, but this may have been due to the fact that the older children were more likely to have fractures than the younger children, who were more likely to have wounds. Occasionally, doctors overestimated pain in children with the most severe pain and the mean difference between child and doctor ratings was –0.6 for this group.

▼ Table 8.10 Average pain ratings for each participant group

	Mean	Standard deviation
Children's self-reports	5.5	2.0
Parental ratings	4.8	2.2
Physicians' ratings	3.2	2.0

> ## CONCLUSIONS
>
> Emergency Department doctors significantly underestimate pain in 3–15-year-olds, although this is less true in the case of fractures. Lack of agreement between the doctor's diagnosis and the child's self-reported pain level leads to greater disagreement in child/ doctor ratings. Anxiety and stress can exacerbate somatic (bodily) pain perception, and this may account for the particularly large discrepancies in the pain ratings of doctors and younger children, who may have been the most anxious. Brudvik *et al.* conclude that doctors should place a higher value on parental reports of their children's pain, especially when children are unable to communicate effectively for themselves.

Methodological strengths and weaknesses

A strength of this study was the relatively well standardised procedure. For example, doctors were trained to use the numerical rating scale and parents were given a detailed written description to ensure they each gave similar support to their children regarding their interpretation of the faces on the pain scales. This is important because it helps to make the study replicable, meaning the findings can be tested for reliability.

A further strength was the natural setting, where the doctors went about their usual routines, with relatively limited time to conduct their consultations. This strengthens the study's ecological validity. Had the doctors been observed away from the usual hospital setting, they may have spent more time thinking about their clinical assessment and the researchers would have gained less understanding of everyday medical practices.

A weakness is that the findings may not be **generalisable** as the study only looked at one emergency department in one Norwegian hospital. The doctors in this department did not routinely assess pain before this study, none specialised in paediatrics and, in Norway, it is not possible to specialise in emergency medicine. This is important as it means doctors in other countries may have assessed children's pain more accurately, resulting in more pain relief medication being given.

A further weakness is that although the parents rated their children's pain first, the parents and children were not completely blinded to (unaware of) each other's answers. This means the children's answers may have been influenced by their parents' reactions. For example, they might have said they felt less pain than they really did so that their answer matched their parents. This is important because it means the children's ratings may not have been completely **valid**.

Ethics

One ethical strength is that all parents gave written consent for themselves and their children to be involved in the study. This was critical as the families were especially vulnerable due to their children's injuries/illnesses, meaning they were at greater risk of psychological harm. The researchers also made sure that one of the team was always available to provide extra support or guidance about the study if the families needed it. As the children's medical condition could change very quickly, it was important that parents knew that someone was available in case they wished to exercise their right to withdraw.

Application to everyday life

A strength of this study is that it can be used to support changes in Norwegian paediatric care. For example, medical training should include the importance of listening to children (and their parents) regarding pain levels and remembering that individuals experience their pain differently even when they have the same physical condition. This is critical due to the links between pain, recovery time and long-term problems such as anxiety and **hypersensitivity**.

Also, visual analogue scales may help children to provide more useful information than asking them face-to-face, as children may under-report their pain levels due to fear of further painful procedures or just to please the doctor.

ISSUES AND DEBATES

Idiographic versus nomothetic

Brudvik *et al.*'s research illustrates the nomothetic approach in psychology. This is because they measure pain numerically using rating scales. This means researchers can use statistical analysis to determine the significance of the findings. If Brudvik's team had asked open questions in their questionnaires, they could have collected **qualitative** data. This would have allowed for a more idiographic approach and the researchers could have learned more about how and why some children experience greater pain than others, despite similar diagnoses.

REFLECTION

- To what extent do you think changes should be made to hospital practices and staff training as a result of the findings of this study?
- If you were conducting research in this area, how might you improve this study and/ or design your own study to investigate children's experiences in hospital?

LEARNING LINK

At AS Level, you looked at social processes such as obedience (Milgram) and bystander intervention (Piliavin *et al.*; subway Samaritans). How might these processes relate to the experiences of doctors, children and parents in the emergency department of a hospital? You also looked at attention (Andrade; doodling), memory (Pozzulo; lineups) and social sensitivity (Baron-Cohen *et al*; eyes test) in the cognitive approach; how might concepts from these studies help to explain differences in the pain ratings in this study?

STUDY TIP

By now you will have learned a great deal about how to evaluate studies, so why not explore some of your own evaluative points, in addition to the ones on this page; for example, how could you use social desirability bias to comment on the validity of the data gained in this study? Do you think this might affect people from some cultures more than others? If so, why?

TEST YOURSELF

1 Explain what is meant by a Visual Analogue Scale (VAS). [2]
2 Describe two findings of the study by Brudvik *et al.* (2017) on pain assessment. [4]
3 a Describe the study by Brudvik *et al.* (2017) on measuring pain. [6]
  b Evaluate this study by Brudvik *et al.* (2017), including a discussion of idiographic versus nomothetic. [10]
4 Explain how Brudvik *et al.* (2017) used the Wong-Baker scale to measure pain in children. [2]
5 Explain one strength and one weakness relating to the use of quantitative data in the Brudvik *et al.* (2017) study. [4]
6 Suggest an appropriate non-directional hypothesis for Brudvik *et al.* (2017). [2]

8.3.3 Managing and controlling pain

KEY TERMS

analgesics

paracetamol

prostaglandins

NSAIDs

opiates

novocaine

sciatica

mechanism

local anaesthetics

tolerance

METHODOLOGY

objective and subjective data

> **Think!**
>
> Why might some people prefer not to take biochemical treatments for their pain?

> **Think!**
>
> Do you ever need to take a painkiller? If so, do you always think about side effects before taking one?

> **Think!**
>
> Do you think biochemical treatments are more effective than psychological ones?

What could doctors do to help ensure patients do not become addicted to their pain medication? You have studied adherence to medical advice – what reasons can you think of which may mean that patients do not continue with their medication?

▶ Figure 8.24

Biological treatments: biochemical

Analgesics

Analgesics are a group of drugs that are used to relieve pain and are also known as painkillers or pain relievers. Although they all work to have the same effect, different drugs have different mechanisms of action (how they work) on pain. Some analgesics such as aspirin are used to relieve mild pain whilst others, such as codeine, are used for stronger pain relief.

Acetaminophen (paracetamol)

One of the most common types of painkiller is **paracetamol**. It was invented in 1893 and in the UK alone, an estimated 6300 tonnes of paracetamol are taken each year (Moore, 2016). Paracetamol is thought to reduce the intensity of pain signals to the brain and reduce fever, although scientists are still discovering exactly how it works. It can also reduce or stop the number of **prostaglandins** that your body releases as well. These substances can make you run a fever or feel more pain. Paracetamol is used for pain such as headaches, back ache and muscle pain.

NSAIDs (aspirin)

Other types of painkillers include **non-steroidal anti-inflammatory drugs** (NSAIDs) such as ibuprofen and aspirin. They work better for pain that is caused by inflammation such as injury or arthritis. NSAIDs work by blocking the body's chemicals that are associated with inflammation and pain. They block two types of enzymes, one that protects the stomach lining and the other which is produced when joints are injured or inflamed.

Opiates: Morphine and Codeine

Opiates such as morphine and codeine are strong forms of painkiller. They are mostly used to control acute, severe pain such as after surgery or trauma, for example, breaking a leg. Opioids attach to proteins known as opioid receptors in the nerve cells of the brain and spinal cord (central nervous system) as well as the gut and other parts of the body. After this has happened, the opioids block the pain messages usually sent from the body through the spinal cord to the brain leading to **analgesia**. While opioids can effectively relieve pain, they do carry some risks and can be highly addictive especially if they are used to manage chronic pain over a long period of time. Addiction happens due to **tolerance**, which means that an increasing amount of the drug is needed to achieve the same effect.

Anaesthetics

Anaesthetics cause the total loss of feeling or sensation and can be local which causes the loss of feeling in one small area of the body or general where there is total loss of sensation and usually consists of an individual being unconscious

Local anaesthetic: Novocaine

Novocaine is often used during dental procedures to numb your gum such as if you are having a filling or an extraction. Novocaine is injected near to the area affected and works by stopping the nerves in that area of the body from sending pain signals to the brain. You can tell novocaine has worked due to the numbness around the area injected within five minutes or so. Although the area is numb the individual may be able to feel pressure around the area being treated.

Indirect medication such as antidepressants

Antidepressants are used for chronic pain such as migraines, low back pain and **sciatica**. Although the painkilling **mechanism** of antidepressants is not totally understood they may increase the neurotransmitters within the spinal cord which reduce pain signals. They do not work immediately and it can take up to a week for any effect to be felt, with full effect after several weeks. Pain relief is not total and is often defined as moderate but is often more effective for nerve pain such as sciatica rather than non-nerve pain, such as back pain.

Evaluating biochemical treatments

One strength is that serious side effects are rare with paracetamol at the recommended dose (Prescott, 2000) making it a relatively safe drug. However, large clinical trials have found that paracetamol is no better than a placebo for chronic pain such as back pain or arthritis and it is only effective in small numbers of people for acute pain (Moore, 2016). Also, exceeding the dose is extremely dangerous and can lead to serious health consequences and even death.

NSAIDs have been found to be effective for reducing fever, inflammation and pain from headaches. However, because they block the enzymes that protect the stomach lining as well as the ones that are produced when the joints are injured or inflamed, they can have side effects of creating stomach irritation. Therefore, they are not suitable for people who have had a gastric ulcer, for example.

One weakness is that the research around the safety of ibuprofen is conflicting. On the one hand, an observational study has found that the use of ibuprofen for in excess of five years is associated with a 44 per cent less risk of developing Alzheimer's disease, whereas another has found that women using ibuprofen daily for more than five years puts them at a 51 per cent increased risk of breast cancer (Connelly, 2017). This is a weakness as it suggests the possibility of harm.

Another weakness is that although opioid medications have been found to be effective in treating acute pain (Rosenblum *et al.*, 2008), they can be dangerous. Higher doses can slow breathing and heart rate, so it is important that the dosage given to patients is carefully monitored. Opioids can also be addictive because they cause pleasant feelings in addition to reducing pain. This can lead to serious health problems. Therefore, it is very important that the patient follows the doctor's instructions for usage.

> ## ISSUES AND DEBATES
>
> ### Idiographic versus nomothetic
> Biological treatments for pain tend to take a nomothetic approach, assuming that pain medication will be effective for all. Paracetamol is often prescribed for pain despite the fact that research has found it to be ineffective for many people. Therefore, an idiographic approach seems to be more appropriate, especially as individuals will also experience differences in side effects to pain medication as well its effect on the pain.

Reductionism vs holism

Biological treatments for pain are reductionist as they only focus on biological mechanisms of pain. They ignore environmental factors that could affect pain perception such as the environment that the patient may be living in, e.g. being on a noisy ward with bright lights could increase the pain perception. By having a more holistic view and looking at environmental factors such as these and by changing the environment, patients may need less pain relief.

▶ LEARNING LINK

The research by Hölzel *et al.* (mindfulness and brain scans) at AS Level investigated the direct effect of mindfulness on the brain. This study has useful applications to help people increase their wellbeing. Research into the effectiveness of painkillers also has direct applications for wellbeing and helping people reduce pain. The study by Hölzel *et al.* also has interesting implications for pain management – that mindfulness could be used to reduce pain without negative side effects associated with biochemical methods.

STUDY TIP

It is important that you know the different types of pain each biochemical method is best for and how they actually work. It is very easy to get these mixed up so perhaps make some flashcards for each one or put them into some visual format.

▶ TEST YOURSELF

1 Ana has suffered from back pain for a number of months and it just will not go away. She is going back to her doctors to see whether she can get something for her pain. Suggest one biochemical treatment that may help Ana with her back pain. [2]

2 Explain one strength and one weakness of one biochemical treatment for managing and/or controlling pain. [4]

3 a Describe what psychologists have discovered about biochemical treatments for pain. [6]

   b Evaluate what psychologists have discovered about biochemical treatments for pain, including a discussion on effectiveness. [10]

4 Describe how a randomised control trial could be used to investigate biochemical treatments for pain. [4]

5 Explain one reason why a person may prefer not to use biochemical treatment to manage or control their pain. [2]

6 Explain one reason a doctor might prefer to collect subjective data about a patient's pain levels after receiving a biochemical treatment rather than objective data. [2]

Psychological treatments

Think!

How does acupuncture work to relieve pain?

Think!

Have you ever tried to think of a pleasant scene or memory to distract you from something unpleasant like having a filling at the dentist? Did it help?

Think!

One methodological issue is whether you obtain subjective or objective data in research. Which do you feel is the most useful for studying the effectiveness of pain treatments?

KEY TERMS

attention diversion

non-pain imagery or
guided imagery

acupuncture

endorphin levels

nitric oxide

cognitive redefinition

METHODOLOGY

objective and subjective
data

Figure 8.25 depicts what some people may visualise when using guided imagery as many would see this as pleasant. What senses could you use within this scene? Could there be certain smells and sounds that you could imagine from this scene? What would be your pleasant scene if you were told to use this type of treatment?

▲ Figure 8.25

Cognitive strategies

Attention diversion

Given the various side effects of biochemical treatments for pain and that some medications may not be effective for some people, it is important for people living with chronic pain that there are alternative treatments available.

One alternative is **attention diversion**. This means using distraction to help reduce the pain perception. This could be as simple as going shopping or watching a favourite television programme.

Another way is to listen to music. Music can be used to reduce the pain experience in chronic pain, but it can also be used in acute pain. For example, some women experience pain when first starting to breastfeed their new-born baby. As biochemical treatments for pain can pass into their breast milk, the mothers are limited on the pain relief that they can use. Williamson (2020) reviewed a number of trials using music to reduce pain in breastfeeding with trials conducted in India, Thailand, Malaysia and Brazil and found small positive effects in four of the trials. However, the most positive effect was found when the women were able to choose the music themselves. This is important when considering music as a treatment for pain because music is very personal and for it to be most effective, the individual needs to have an emotional engagement with the music. It is thought to work by increasing **endorphin** levels and **nitric oxide** (a substance that increases blood flow by expanding blood vessels) which helps reduce stress and tension.

Evaluation

One strength is that research in randomised control trials has found that listening to music can significantly reduce perceived pain and increase quality of life (Holden, 2013). This is beneficial because patients can reduce their pain without having the side effects which biochemical therapies can have. It can also be self-administered and can also be inexpensive.

One weakness is that the individual has to be fully committed and have a high level of belief in the ability of distraction techniques to relieve pain. For example, conventional treatments such as medication are often highly trusted in terms of pain relief and alternatives may not have the level of research or be prescribed by doctors, therefore there may be some doubt in whether it will work; especially whether the distraction techniques will result in the relief of most of the pain. If this does not happen, the patient may give up on the treatment.

Non-pain imagery

Non-pain imagery is also called **guided imagery** and is used to help reduce pain by imagining a pleasant scene that is unrelated to the pain they are experiencing. Therapists can 'guide' the patient to use their different senses to imagine the scene. For example, imagining that they are in a wood next to a campfire, and imagining the heat of the fire of their skin, the smell of the burning wood, the crackling sounds that the fire makes.

Other types of non-pain imagery involve replacing the pain sensation with something less pleasant such as imagining having an argument with someone (Sarafino, 2006) or replacing the pain feeling for one of 'tingling' or pins and needles.

The use of imagery is another way of distracting the patient from their pain. It works best if the patient is able to create a vivid image that they are engaged with, that they can imagine whenever they need it. It also works best with moderate rather than severe pain (Sarafino, 2006).

Evaluation

One weakness is that non-pain imagery is useful for short periods of pain but may be less useful for longer periods as it could be difficult to keep the visualisation up for an extended period of time. In addition, not everyone is able to visualise things in their head, therefore this method of pain reduction is not suitable for everyone.

However, one strength is that it is a useful way of helping patients manage their pain without side effects. The patients, once they have learned the technique, have control over their pain management and it can be used whenever and wherever they need it.

Cognitive redefinition

Some patients have feelings of fear or threat about potential pain experiences such as some medical procedures. **Cognitive redefinition** helps the patients think more rationally and realistically about their fear. For example, understanding what type of pain or sensations they are likely to feel during the procedure can help them reduce the pain they experience. By being given realistic information about procedures, they are able to redefine their pain experience and reduce their fear and misconceptions (Sarafino, 2006).

Another approach in cognitive redefinition is to use positive self-statements. Coping statements are based on the individual's ability to cope with the pain. For example, saying 'It hurts, but I can get through this'. Or interpretative statements such as 'Pain with a purpose', where a person in labour might reimagine the pain as being there for a good reason, to help them have their baby.

Cognitive redefinition can also be used to challenge illogical thoughts that the patient might have, which could in turn make the pain experience worse. For example, imagining stomach pain is caused by cancer, despite having tests that showed that cancer was not the cause. The therapist can then work with the patient to understand that the fears are illogical.

Evaluation

> ## ISSUES AND DEBATES
>
> ### Idiographic versus nomothetic
>
> Although cognitive redefinition may be effective for some patients, it may not work for others. Imagine a person who has learned that they are resistant to local anaesthetic. Next time they have a procedure requiring local anaesthetic, they may be fearful that the procedure is going to hurt. In this case, their fears are rational as they are based on past experience meaning cognitive redefinition may be ineffective. Therefore an idiographic approach is more appropriate to ensure whether the patients, thoughts are actually illogical or irrational.

Alternative treatments

Acupuncture

Acupuncture is a technique where fine metal needles are inserted under the skin in various parts of the body and then they are swivelled around or a mild electrical current is passed through them to create stimulation.

It is a technique that has been used for over 2000 years and originated in China. It is thought that the stimulation by the needles in different parts of the body can relieve pain.

The effectiveness of acupuncture might be explained by the gate control theory of pain. The stimulation of the needles might activate the large fibres that close the gate, stopping the pain signals getting through. However, scientists are still searching for evidence of the gate itself.

> ## ISSUES AND DEBATES

Cultural differences

Acupuncture offers an alternative treatment for pain based on ancient Chinese techniques. This shows that there are alternative pain relief techniques to traditional Western treatments such as drug therapy, which are supported by research evidence. For example, Hu *et al.* (2016) found that cancer patients who received acupuncture alongside conventional drug therapy experienced a greater reduction in pain perception than those who just had conventional drug therapy. This is a strength as it offers patients a wider range of effective treatment options rather than just Western-based medications. This is important as some people can experience serious side effects from medication. If they are able to use acupuncture as an effective pain treatment then they are able to avoid these side effects.

Evaluation

One strength of acupuncture is that it has some research support. Yuan *et al.* (2008) conducted a review of 23 trials which investigated the use of acupuncture for lower back pain and found moderate evidence that it was more effective than no treatment. This suggests that acupuncture may be a useful addition to other therapies.

Stimulation therapy/TENS

The gate control theory can also explain how Transcutaneous Electrical Nerve Stimulation (TENS) works. Electrodes are placed on the skin close to where the patient is experiencing pain and mild electrical current is passed through the skin. The current can be turned up if the pain is not reduced sufficiently. It is thought to work in a similar way to acupuncture by stimulating the large fibres that close the gate.

Evaluation

TENS has been found to be effective during labour. Kaplan *et al.* (1998) gave 104 Israeli women questionnaires after giving birth and found that the majority had found it effective in helping with their labour pains. However, its effects tend to be short-lived with chronic conditions such as phantom limb pain (Sarafino, 2006).

Evaluating psychological treatments

> ## ISSUES AND DEBATES

Determinism versus free will

One strength of psychological treatments for pain is that they are useful because they suggest that patients have free will and the ability to manage their own pain. This gives patients some control over their condition which may also be helpful in reducing their stress levels which can be raised during both acute and chronic pain. Helping patients understand that their pain is not inevitable (i.e. a product of biological determinism) may enable them to feel like they have more control over their own body and ability to control the pain themselves.

A strength is that none of the treatments have the side effects that biomedical treatments have. For example, opioids can cause addiction and severe side effects whereas psychological treatments such as TENS and acupuncture have no side effects at all. This means that adherence to psychological treatments may be higher as side effects are one of the main reasons people fail to adhere.

One weakness is that some patients, particularly those with severe pain, may be unable to manage the pain by themselves. The expectation that they should be able to cope on their own could make them feel that they have failed. It is, therefore, very important that healthcare professionals are sensitive in their use of psychological treatments, ensuring that patients do not feel like they have failed if they do not work for them.

In addition, some psychological treatments are not appropriate for all patients. For example, acupuncture may not be appropriate for people with needle phobia or visual imagery may not be appropriate for someone who cannot create mental imagery. Some people's pain may also just be too severe for psychological treatments to have an impact and therefore biochemical treatments, or a combination of the two, may be more appropriate. This suggests that practictioners should use an idiographic approach to ensure that their patients get the appropriate treatment for their individual needs.

> ## ISSUES AND DEBATES

Application to everyday life

Research into psychological treatments for pain relief is useful because it can help patients in their everyday lives. If they can learn effective techniques to manage their pain, then they can experience a better quality of life on a day-to-day basis. It is important that research is conducted into the effectiveness of these psychological treatments so that patients are not given treatments that are both ineffective and/or could potentially make them feel worse.

> ## LEARNING LINKS

At AS Level, you studied Hölzel *et al.* (mindfulness and brain scans) who looked at mindfulness for stress management. What are the similarities and differences between non-pain imagery and mindfulness?

STUDY TIP

One way to memorise sections of Health Psychology is to use the **method of loci**. This uses mental imagery to mentally place different sections such as cognitive strategies (attention diversion, non-pain imagery and cognitive redefinition) in different places in a familiar environment around your home. When you need to recall them, imagine yourself walking around your home and you should 'see' the different sections there. For example, you might imagine someone in your kitchen with headphones on listening to music for attention diversion. You can find out more about how the method of loci works by looking online.

> ## TEST YOURSELF

1 Rafeeqa is six months pregnant but has just twisted her ankle and is suffering with mild to moderate pain.
   a Suggest one psychological treatment that may be appropriate to help relieve Rafeeqa's ankle pain. [2]
   b Outline one strength of the treatment you have suggested in (a). [2]
2 Explain why using visual imagery may not be suitable for everyone who is experiencing pain. [2]
3 a Describe what psychologists have discovered about psychological treatments for pain [6]
   b Evaluate what psychologists have discovered about psychological treatments for pain, including a discussion about free will versus determinism. [10]

Acupuncture is an alternative psychological treatment that can be used to manage pain.
4 Explain acupuncture as a psychological treatment for pain. [4]
5 Outline one reason why acupuncture may not be suitable for all patients. [2]
6 Explain two strengths of using psychological treatments as a way of managing pain. [4]
7 Compare biological and psychological ways of managing and controlling pain. [6]

8.4 Stress

8.4.1 Sources of stress

KEY TERMS

GAS
fight or flight
chronic stress
epinephrine
norepinephrine
cortisol
amygdala
ACTH
pituitary gland
coronary heart disease (CHD)

METHODOLOGY

generalisations from findings

Think!

What did Selye mean by alarm in his GAS model of stress?

Think!

It is the week before you go and sit a psychology test at school. You have been worrying about it for a long while and have been up late studying for the last week. How would this high level of stress make you feel? Think about such things as your appetite, sleep and heart rate. Now your test is over, how do you feel? Do you feel excited or just exhausted? How is your appetite? What does this tell us about the stress response?

Think!

Stress can be explained in terms of both individual and situational explanations. Do you think an individual's stress response is due to individual factors such as personality/gender or situational factors such as what is happening around them? Can you think of any situational factors that may help lower someone's stress levels? Think about what you do when you are stressed.

Some degree of stress seems necessary to motivate us but when that stress becomes too much it can lead to us feeling overloaded and burned out. Why might viewing stress as a challenge rather than a threat reduce the negative health implications?

▶ Figure 8.26

Defining stress

Stress is how our body reacts when we are feeling under pressure or threatened in some way. It can be positive as it can help motivate us to do things but if we experience too much stress, we can feel overwhelmed and it can affect our physical and mental health.

According to Sarafino (2006), stress has been defined in three different ways:
1 The effect of the environment on the individual, for example major life events, environmental disasters or chronic stressors such as living in poverty or inadequate housing.
2 Stress as a bodily response focusing on how people respond to stressful events.
3 The interaction between the person and the environment, where it is not just stimulus and response but where individuals can choose how to respond to the stressor using a combination of behavioural, cognitive and emotional strategies.

The physiology of stress

The General Adaptation Syndrome (GAS)

The **General Adaptation Syndrome** was developed by Hans Selye (1936) who studied the effect of prolonged stress on the body.

He suggests that GAS consists of three stages:
1 Alarm stage: This is the first stage of GAS and it is the stage which prepares the body for a **flight or fight response** to a perceived stressor. Once the **amygdala** in the brain is alerted, a signal is sent to the hypothalamus. The hypothalamus activates the sympathetic nervous system causing the adrenal medulla to release the hormones

8

epinephrine and **norepinephrine**. The hypothalamus also signals the **pituitary gland** to release **ACTH**, which in turn stimulates the production of the hormone **cortisol** from the adrenal cortex. The body's increased arousal levels are maintained by these hormones. The alarm stage prepares the body to meet whatever challenge the 'stressor' or emergency poses. This could be running away from whatever has triggered the 'fight' or 'flight' response or 'fighting it' (hence fight or flight).

2 Resistance stage: After the initial reaction to the perceived stressor, and if the stress continues, the body tries to adapt to the ongoing demands being placed upon it. This happens around 48 hours after the onset of stress. In an attempt to remain alert, the body resists the efforts of the parasympathetic nervous system to return blood pressure, heart rate and so on to normal, by allowing higher-than-normal levels of epinephrine, norepinephrine and cortisol to continue to circulate. By now, the individual may not be showing outward signs of stress (this stage can be described as apparent coping), however they may find it difficult to respond to new stressors in the environment. Selye suggests that during this phase, individuals may begin to become susceptible to illnesses such as ulcers and high blood pressure.

3 Exhaustion stage: This final stage is experienced if the stressor continues over a long period of time. The body does not have enough resources to maintain prolonged physical arousal indefinitely and so these become severely depleted causing a weakening of the immune system. Continued stress at this stage makes the individual more likely to experience illness and physiological damage.

The fight or flight response evolved to protect us from danger within our environment such as finding a tiger standing outside our cave. However, today we rarely have to physically fight or flee from what our body tells us is an emergency situation. For example, you are more likely to experience fight or flight response if you are about to go into an exam and feel that you have not properly prepared. Some stressors cannot be easily avoided or might be long term, such as losing your job and not being able to find another one or caring for a relative who has a long-term health condition.

Evaluation

One strength of GAS is that it is a useful theory that helps us understand why people are more likely to suffer with physical illnesses when they have been under chronic stress. For example, it notes sustained levels of cortisol due to chronic stress causes suppression of the immune system. This is a strength of the theory as understanding the links between stress and illness may mean that we can attempt to identify people under stress earlier and be able to mitigate its effects in order to reduce the harmful effects of it on a person's health.

> ## ISSUES AND DEBATES
>
> ### Reductionism versus holism
> Another weakness is that the GAS model fails to take into account gender differences in stress response. For example, men are more likely to adopt the 'fight or flight' response whereas women tend to adopt a more 'tend and befriend' response (Taylor *et al.*, 2000). Tend and befriend is where women try to protect their children and themselves from harmful stress (tend) and seek out social support from others, such as friends, to help them to do this (befriend). This suggests that the GAS model is too reductionist and does not take into account the complexities of the stress response in different people.
>
> ### Idiographic versus nomothetic
> Selye's theory takes a nomothetic approach, assuming that everyone will react to stress in the same way. It does not take into account how different people react to stress. For example, some people view it as a challenge than a threat and research has shown that those people are less likely to experience the negative physical effects of stress, suggesting a more idiographic approach to stress would be more appropriate.

The effects of stress on health

Acute (short term) stress

Although it is assumed that stress is always bad for your health this is not always the case. Although long term chronic stress can have negative effects, acute stress can often do the opposite and actually be protective in terms of health. For example, if you have surgery or even a vaccination, the acute or short term stress response alongside the activation of the immune system actually enhances the immune response. If you go back to the GAS model this makes sense as the fight or flight mode is our inherent survival mechanism and therefore if that is activated, then one way to help you survive is to enhance your immune response.

Chronic stress

Prolonged stress can affect us negatively, both physically and psychologically.

Digestive system

Stress responses affect the digestive system. Chronic and prolonged stress can change your hormone levels and increase the acidity levels in your stomach (stomach acid is produced to help you digest your food). This increase in stomach acid may eventually lead to stomach ulcers. However, the more likely indirect cause of ulcers is the behavioural responses to stress that people have. People under stress often perform behaviours which may increase risk of ulcers such as smoking, drinking, use of NSAIDs such as ibuprofen (to counter stress-related headaches) and lack of sleep.

Circulatory system

The stress response increases the strain on your circulatory system due to the increase in heart rate. Stress also affects the function of the immune system by raising blood pressure. Hypertension is one the highest risk factors in **coronary heart disease (CHD)**.

Another risk for CHD is high cholesterol levels. Stress contributes to this due to the fact that the production of adrenaline and noradrenaline during the stress response affects the release of fatty acids. This leads to a clumping together of cholesterol particles which can consequently lead to blood clots and narrowing of arteries. This increases the likelihood of CHD. However, again, CHD may be more likely due to the negative coping strategies people use for dealing with stress such as overeating, drinking alcohol and smoking.

Immune system and immunosuppression

Stress affects the immune system as a whole and can lead to immunosuppression. This is due to the cortisol that is produced during chronic stress. Cortisol reduces the body's immune response which will mean people who are exposed to long term stress are more likely to become ill.

Kiecolt-Glaser *et al.* (1984) studied whether examination stress (a chronic stressor) could lead to poorer immune function. 75 American medical students had a blood sample taken a month prior to their exams (lower stress) and during the exam (high stress). From the blood sample the levels of natural killer (NK) cells were measured. NK cells are an essential part of our innate immune system and lower levels indicate poorer immune response. Participants also completed a questionnaire looking at psychological factors such as life events (major events that need adjusting to by an individual such as moving house) and loneliness. Levels of NK cells were lower in the second sample (high stress) and even more so for those who reported feeling lonely and those who scored high on life events.

Evaluation

One strength of understanding the effects of stress on health is that this knowledge can help raise awareness of the damaging effects of stress. This could lead people to take action to protect their health either through reducing their stress levels or engaging in positive coping strategies which will mean population health will go up, benefiting society.

One weakness of research into stress and health is that researchers have been unable to find one single factor which may be linked to stress and poor health. For example, is it the physiological stress response that causes cardiovascular disease or the negative coping strategies that come with high stress such as excess alcohol? This limits the usefulness of such research as we are unsure which factor could be altered to prevent such disorders or poor immune function.

LEARNING LINK

This section is linked to the biological approach. Two studies you have learned at AS Level can be linked in some way to the stress response. Dement and Kleitman looked at sleep and dreaming and how we dream during REM sleep. One of the major consequences of stress is poor sleep and insomnia. As sleep is how the mind and body repairs itself then this has consequences for health. Also, Hölzel *et al.* look at the effects of mindfulness on brain structure. It is possible that mindfulness can be used to reduce stress so this study's results could be beneficial for stressed individuals.

STUDY TIP

The GAS model can be challenging to learn. One way to do it is to create a poster with a drawing of the human body and label the different areas that are involved in GAS. You can number them too to help you remember which order GAS occurs.

TEST YOURSELF

1 Pietro is feeling really stressed. He is a manager of a local shoe company and he is struggling to recruit enough staff to cope with the amount of orders they have. His wife is also eight months pregnant and so he is worried about her and how they will cope with his long hours. He has tried to deal with his stress for months, he is constantly getting colds and struggling to sleep.
   a Outline which stage of the GAS model of stress Pietro may currently be in. [2]
   b Explain one consequence of Pietro having chronic stress. [2]
2 Outline one difference between the male and female response to stress. [2]
3 a Describe what psychologists have discovered about the physiology of stress. [6]
   b Evaluate what psychologists have discovered about the physiology of stress, including a discussion on nomothetic vs idiographic. [10]
4 Outline one study which shows that stress can weaken the immune response. [2]
5 Explain one weakness of Selye's GAS model of stress. [2]
6 Selye's GAS model of stress was based on a series of experiments where rats were exposed to stressors including pain, freezing temperatures and food deprivation.
   Explain two ethical guidelines that researchers must consider if they wish to carry out research involving animals. [4]

KEY TERMS

readjustment rating scale

Type A personality

Social Readjustment Rating Scale (SRRS)

METHODOLOGY

generalisations from findings

Causes of stress

Think!

What is meant by control and workload in relation to work-related stress.

Think!

You work long hours in the finance department of a local pie company. The company has started to lose money and you need to decide whether to make any of the workers redundant, meaning they will lose their jobs. You are getting married next year and are moving into a new house. Recently, you have been getting a lot of colds and coughs and have taken your first day off work in nearly five years. From what you have learned on these pages, what do you think are the main causes of your stress?

Think!

Stress can be caused by individual factors and situational factors. Which of the causes of stress are to do with individual factors and which are to do with situational factors? Which do you think is most important, if any?

Which of the three causes of stress do you feel is more likely to cause ill health? Are there any which you think are more relevant to you? What about gender differences? Do you think there may be differences in what causes stress in men and women?

▲ Figure 8.27

Life events: Holmes and Rahe

In 1967, psychiatrists Thomas Holmes and Richard Rahe assessed over 5000 medical records to try and discover whether there was a relationship between stress and physical illness (Holmes and Rahe, 1967). They focused on life events, which are experiences which may cause significant disruption to an individual's everyday life. These experiences could include marriage, divorce, changing jobs or even Christmas! From their research, Holmes and Rahe developed the **Social Readjustment Rating Scale** (SRRS) which measures the number of life events a person has experienced in the last 12 months from a list of 43 life events (see page 602).

They concluded that the more life events experienced in the last 12 months, the more likely a person is to become stressed and consequently suffer from ill health. They theorised that significant life events, whether positive or negative, needed adjusting to and that the more life events people have to cope with over a twelve-month period, the more likely they are to become stressed and ill.

Evaluation

> ### ISSUES AND DEBATES
>
> #### Reductionism versus holism
> One weakness of the idea of life events as a predictor of illness is that it ignores that everyday hassles such as waking up late for work or problems with friends or family can cause us stress. Kanner *et al.* (1981) developed a scale to measure how many daily hassles and uplifts people had encountered in the previous month. They tested 100 Americans on the scale as well as testing them for wellbeing and found that the hassles scale tended to be a better predictor of stress-related problems than life events. This suggests that using only life events to predict stress is reductionist.

One strength is that research has supported the idea that life events are associated with stress and ill health. Rahe (1970) studied 2500 American sailors using the SRRS alongside subsequent onset of ill health. The results showed that there was a positive correlation between life events score and illness scores. This suggests that life events contributed to stress and subsequent ill health, although as the study is correlational, it is not possible to state that stressful life events are a cause of ill health.

> ### ISSUES AND DEBATES
>
> #### Individual and situational explanations
> Life events only take into account situational explanations of stress. A weakness of this is that looking only at life events as a reason for stress ignores individual and cultural differences. The scale measures life events such as Christmas. Although some people may find Christmas stressful, many others do not see it as stressful at all with no adjustment needed. For some cultures Christmas is not even celebrated or recognised. This suggests that life events may not be a valid measure of stress.

This shows how this research suggests that our response to stress is deterministic, i.e. we react to the number of stressful life events in our life. However, if people are aware that certain life events are affecting their health then coping strategies can be put in place for them to manage it. For example, getting married is one of the highest scores on the life events scale, which suggests it has the potential to cause high levels of stress. By being aware of this the individual knows this they can put in strategies such as social support, exercise and so on which could lower levels of stress suggesting that we can exert free will over how we deal with stressors in our lives.

Work

There are a number of factors which have linked work with stress such as under stimulation, (the job is repetitive/boring), a low level of control over their work (workers have no freedom to make their own decisions about their job/working conditions) and a high workload (the amount of work a person has to do in a specific amount of time). These factors can lead to lower self-esteem, lower satisfaction and the possibility of a higher rate of ill health. Marmot *et al.* (1997) studied 10,000 civil servants from the UK and found that although there was no correlation between workload and stress a lack of control was associated with the development of coronary heart disease (CHD) in lower grade civil servants (with lower levels of control), even when accounting for lifestyle factors and personality.

Johansson *et al.* (1978) looked at Swedish sawmill workers and compared finishers (who prepared timber) to cleaners who cleaned the mill. The finishers had a lack of control over their work and high repetitiveness, but a high level of responsibility and demand. Cleaners could work at their own pace and had less responsibility. They found that finishers had higher levels of stress hormones even before starting work than cleaners and these increased during the day. Illness and absence rates were also higher amongst finishers, suggesting that low control and high demand (and repetitive work) is linked to stress-related illness.

Focus on... Chandola *et al.* (2008)

> ### AIM

To determine the biological and behavioural factors linking work stress and coronary heart disease (CHD).

> ### METHODOLOGY

In Phase 1 of the study (1985–88) 10,308 London-based male and female civil servants aged 35–66 were studied. Participants were followed for 17 years, and data gathered over seven phases, the last of which involved a clinical examination.

Self-reported work-related stress was assessed through the use of the Job Strain Questionnaire. Job strain was indicated if demands of the job are rated as high and control over their job is rated as low. Factors such as isolation at work were also considered. Total work stress was measured by adding together the number of times job strain and isolation at work was reported in Phases 1 and 2.

Participants were also assessed on incidents of coronary heart disease (CHD) (during phases 2–7) and cortisol, measured on waking and 30 minutes afterwards by providing saliva samples. Behavioural risk factors were measured in Phase 3, for example alcohol consumption, cigarette smoking, diet and physical exercise.

> ### RESULTS
> ....
>
> ● Self-reported work stress was lowest in the highest grades of the civil service.
> ● Amongst younger participants (37–49 at Phase 2) there was a significant association between work stress and incidents of CHD. However, there was little association found for the older participants (age 50–60).
> ● Greater reports of work stress were associated with poor health behaviour such as eating less fruit and vegetables and reduced physical activity.
> ● Work stress was also correlated with a morning rise in cortisol in Phase 7.

> ### CONCLUSIONS
> ....
>
> Work stress that is continuous over a period of time is a risk factor for CHD. Approximately 32 per cent of the effect of work stress on CHD can be explained by its impact on health behaviours, such as poor diet and low levels of physical activity.

Evaluating Chandola *et al.* (2008)

One strength of work-related stress explanations is that they have research support. For example, Chandola *et al*'s study is supported by Marmot *et al.* (1997) and Johansson *et al.* (1978) study results. For example, Marmot *et al.* (1997) found that CHD was more likely to occur in civil servants who had low control over their job. This is a strength as it supports the idea that low control leads to stress and consequently CHD and strengthens the reliability of these findings.

However, the samples in these studies were taken from people employed in a limited range of professions and countries. For example, Chandola *et al.* (2008) and Marmot *et al.* (1997) both used civil servants from the UK while Johansson *et al.* (1978) used sawmill workers from Sweden. However, it is possible that people from other countries and/or professions may react differently to these factors in the workplace. This is a weakness, as the samples are not reflective of the whole population and therefore may not be **generalisable**.

Another weakness is that there are conflicting research findings on the link between workload and stress. For example, Shulz *et al.* (2010) looked at data from 16,000 employees across 15 nations across Europe finding that as well as work overload being a cause of stress, work underload was also associated with high rates of ill health and absence. This is a weakness as Johansson *et al.* (1978) assumed work overload was the cause of stress and this may not be the case.

Type A personality: Friedman and Rosenman

Friedman and Rosenman were physicians working in the USA in the 1950s, with male patients with coronary heart disease. They compared the male participants' incidence of CHD to their partners/spouses, who ate a similar diet. They found that the partners/spouses were less likely to have CHD. They also noticed that certain behaviour patterns were associated with cholesterol levels and blood clotting time and these were associated with greater risk of CHD. They called these behaviour patterns **Type A personality**.

Type A personality traits include being competitive, ambitious, work-driven, time-conscious, and aggressive. In contrast, Type B personalities are more laid back, lacking the ambition and drive that typifies Type A personalities. It was seen as a particular risk factor for white, middle-class men (Friedman and Ulmer, 1985).

Having a Type A personality in the workplace can lead to CHD. Consider how Chandola *et al*'s research focused on situational variables whilst Friedman and Rosenhan's focuses on individual variables. Which explanation do you think is more persuasive?

▶ Figure 8.28

Evaluation

One strength is that the theory has research support. Friedman and Rosenman (1974) studied 3154 healthy men between 39 and 59 for eight and a half years. They were asked to complete a personality questionnaire which separated them into Type A and Type B personalities. Almost twice as many Type A people developed coronary heart disease even when adjusted for lifestyle, than Type B. This suggests that personality is associated with CHD. However, the study is correlational, meaning it cannot be concluded that Type A personality causes CHD as there may be other factors that cause both this personality type and CHD.

> ## ISSUES AND DEBATES
>
> ### Reductionism versus holism
>
> A criticism of the theory of Type A/B personality is that it is reductionist. For example, it is difficult to describe complex human behaviours in terms of specific personality traits. Many people may not fit neatly into Type A or B and may be a mixture of both dependent on context and what else is going on in their life at the time. This suggests that a holistic approach to understanding how people react to stress may be more beneficial as situational factors could also have an impact on people's reaction to stress such as social networks, work environment and home life as well as their personality.

In addition, it is difficult to determine which aspects of Type A personality actually increase the risk of CHD in an individual. Some research suggests that it is only levels of hostility that may be the leading factor in higher levels of stress and CHD rather than Type A personality as a whole. Others have suggested that the way people cope with stress is much more important than their personality. This suggests that the theory may not be valid.

> ## LEARNING LINKS
>
> Chandola *et al.* (2008) used a longitudinal study. Think back to when you studied Hölzel *et al.* (mindfulness and brain scans) at AS Level. How similar are the two studies in terms of design? Apart from topic area, what differences are there?

> ## STUDY TIP
>
> When you are planning your own studies, it is sometimes helpful to think about the studies you have learned about on your course. Imagine, for example, that you wanted to design a field experiment to investigate stress in the workplace, think about the research that you have studied such as Chandola *et al.* or Friedman and Rosenman. How could you expand on their research? Or look at a different section of the population? For example, Chandola *et al.* used civil servants. Who could you use?

> ## TEST YOURSELF
>
> 1 Dmitrij runs a factory which makes fluffy socks. He has a really good team of workers, but he is worried that absence levels are rising. He has researched a little about work-related stress and is looking to change things at work to try and lower stress and absence levels.
> Using your knowledge of work-related stress, suggest two strategies Dmitrij could use in the workplace to lower stress and absence levels. [4]
> 2 Outline the characteristics of a type A personality. [2]
> 3 a Describe what psychologists have discovered about the causes of stress. [6]
>   b Evaluate what psychologists have discovered about the causes of stress, including a discussion of reductionism versus holism. [10]
> 4 Outline the relationship between employee workload and levels of stress. [2]
> 5 Explain one strength and one weakness of life events as a cause of stress. [4]
> 6 Outline why research into work related stress may not be generalisable. [2]
> 7 Compare life events and Type A personality as causes of stress. [4]

8.4.2 Measures of stress

Think!

What happens when someone has a **perfusion fMRI** scan?

Think!

Imagine your friend is feeling stressed due to work pressures and worries over money. The doctors want to measure their stress levels, but your friend has a phobia of needles and does not like crowded and enclosed spaces. Which type of biological stress measurement would be best for your friend? Are there any issues with using the measurement you have chosen?

Think!

Generalisability is one issue that is often discussed when evaluating research in psychology. Think about the three physiological measures of stress described in this section. If you want a large sample to increase generalisability, which measure might be the best to choose and why?

Biological measures
Recording devices for heart rate

In hospitals, heart rate is often measured using **electrocardiography**. It measures the number of beats per minute. As a measure of stress, researchers have found that heart rate increases in acutely stressed individuals and decreases in chronically stressed individuals (Schubert *et al.*, 2009). It can also be measured by the doctor or nurse putting two fingers on the patient's inner wrist and counting the beats per minute using a watch (taking your pulse).

Heart rate variability (HRV) is another measurement that may indicate stress. HRV is the variation in time between heartbeats. This is measured in milliseconds. Some variation is normal and when we are relaxed variation goes up slightly, but if we are stressed then variation in heartbeats goes down. HRV can be measured in clinical settings such as hospitals by using an **electroencephalogram** (ECG). However, more recently a number of portable devices which can be used to measure HRV have been developed, including smart watch applications which detect your heartbeat optically by measuring the wave of blood flow from the wrist and then calculating the interbeat interval and produce a graph which can be viewed on a smartphone.

Recording devices for brain function: fMRI

Functional magnetic resonance imaging (fMRI) is a type of scanning machine that can detect and record brain activity using powerful electromagnets. It works by recognising changes in blood oxygenation and flow in the brain that occur when there is neural activity, such as someone thinking or doing a task. When an area of the brain is active, the blood flow to that area increases. Degrees of neural activity are represented in different colours on the scan, making it possible to see which areas of the brain are more active than others.

Focus on... Wang *et al.* (2005)

▶ **AIM**

To study the central circuitry of psychological stress using functional MRI (fMRI).

METHODOLOGY

Wang *et al.* recruited 32 participants, 25 were placed in the experimental group and 7 in the control group. The participants in the experimental group rested for 15 minutes before having their fMRI scan. Each participant had four scans of eight minutes each followed by a full anatomical scan at the end.
- Scan 1: Baseline (control) condition without a task.
- Scan 2: Low-stress condition; participants counted aloud back from 1000, to control for activation of verbal and auditory centres.
- Scan 3: High-stress condition; participants were told to perform a serial subtraction of thirteen from a four digit number and respond verbally; they were prompted to go faster during the task and if they made an error they had to restart the task.
- Scan 4: A final baseline (control) condition without a task.

The second and third scans were always done in the same order to eliminate contamination of the control condition due to higher levels of emotion due to the high stress task.

Control participants also had four scans for the same length of time but unlike in scans two and three of the experimental condition, the control group did not perform a task in any of the scans.

Participants in both groups completed a self-report stress scale (1–9) and saliva samples were collected immediately after participants entered the scanner and after each scan. Participants also reported level of effort, frustration and task difficulty after the low and high stress tasks. Heart rate was recorded every two minutes.

RESULTS

- The ventral right prefrontal cortex (RPFC) showed continued activation during and even after the stress task period suggesting that this region serves a central role in coordinating a range of biological and behavioural stress responses.
- Results supported previous research showing that RPFC activation (and therefore psychological stress) is associated with negative emotions such as sadness and fear as well as heightened vigilance.
- The sustained activation of the ventral RPFC and the detected brain regions within the RPFC such as the amygdala, even after the end of the stress tasks, is consistent with previous research findings of emotional networks; this demonstrates that perfusion fMRI is a suitable approach to measure stress.

CONCLUSIONS

- Psychological stress leads to negative emotions and vigilance.
- The ventral right prefrontal cortex plays a central role in the stress response.

Evaluating Wang *et al.* (2005)

One strength of perfusion fMRI as a technique for measuring stress is that it uses an internal contrast agent. This means that it is a non-invasive method compared to a PET scan which uses a radioactive tracer. This is a strength as it makes it safer for the participant reducing the risk of psychological harm.

Another strength is that fMRI scans are a more **objective** way of measuring stress than some other methods. For example, questionnaires or observations rely on the participants being accurate/truthful in their recall or observers interpreting behaviour the correct way, whereas fMRI requires less interpretation. This makes the use of fMRI scans a more **reliable** way of measuring stress.

One weakness, however, is that fMRI scans are often expensive and time consuming. This means that the number of participants in studies is often low, such as the 32 in the study by Wang *et al.* (2005). This reduces the **validity** of the results. It also restricts the ability to generalise the findings to a wider population.

Another weakness of the use of fMRI scans to measure stress is that it is not a direct causal measure of neural activity in the brain. For example, fMRI only measures blood flow changes within the brain rather than neural activity which makes the suggestion that any area 'causes' stress rather complex and difficult. This is a weakness as although we can say that the RPFC area is active during a stress task, we cannot say with any certainty that it is definitely associated with a particular function such as stress.

Can you think of any practical and/or ethical issues relating to the use of fMRI scanning as a measure of stress?

▶ Figure 8.29

Sample tests: salivary cortisol

Cortisol is released by the adrenal glands as part of our 'fight or flight' response to stress. It can be measured in both urine and saliva and is seen as a preferable method due to its non-invasive nature. High levels of cortisol indicate that the individual is experiencing physiological stress.

Focus on.... Evans and Wener (2007)

▶ AIM

To investigate how density and proximity of other train passengers affect stress in commuters.

▶ METHODOLOGY

During their morning commute, 208 American commuters self-reported how stressed they felt using five-point Likert scales. Near the end of their journey, they completed a proofreading task to measure motivation/persistence. A saliva sample was taken to measure cortisol levels at the end of the journey. Crowding was measured via observation; researchers noted the total number of passengers in the carriage, number of available seats per carriage and per row in which the participants were sitting. At the weekend, the researchers visited the participants' homes and another cortisol sample was taken, at the same time as the workday one. The researchers recorded the difference between the cortisol level at the weekends and on the train as a measure of stress. The participants' spouse/partner was also asked to evaluate the participants' interactions with them on a five-point rating scale using a questionnaire.

▶ RESULTS

- The density of crowding in close proximity to the participant (**proximal crowding**) was significantly correlated with cortisol levels, self-reported mood and percentage of errors on the proofreading task.
- The density of crowding within the train as a whole (**distal crowding**) was not correlated with stress.
- Longer commutes were associated with significantly higher cortisol levels indicating higher stress.
- Longer commutes resulted in poorer proofreading performance and higher levels of perceived commuting stress.
- Spousal ratings of commuter stress were not associated with longer commuting times.

▶ CONCLUSION

Proximal crowding is related to commuter stress, possibly due to invasion of personal space, whereas distal crowding is not.

Evaluating Evans and Wener (2007)

A strength of the study is that measuring cortisol in saliva samples is an **objective** way of measuring the physiological effects of stress. Evans and Wener found the difference between cortisol while commuting in the week and at the weekend in order to see whether greater increases in cortisol were associated with more densely packed carriages. This is a strength as calculating the difference in the change in cortisol levels does not require any interpretation on the part of the researcher, making the findings more **reliable**.

One weakness is that the findings were correlational. There may have been other factors that increased proximal crowding and stress. This means the researchers cannot state that proximal crowding causes increases in stress, just that these covariables are related. This is important as transport companies may use these findings to redesign their carriages in order to prevent invasion of passengers' personal space, yet this may not solve the problem if there are other unknown variables contributing to passengers' stress.

> ## LEARNING LINK
> At AS Level you learned about the study by Piliavin *et al.* (subway Samaritans) which was conducted on the New York subway. Evans and Wener's study was also conducted on public transport in a similar area, the commuter trains travelling between New Jersey and Manhattan. How do you think the demographic of passengers in these two studies would compare? How might they be both similar and different to each other? (The key here is the time of day at which the studies were conducted.) How do the limitations of the sample affect the generalisations that can be drawn from the data? Can you think of any areas of the world where you might like to replicate Evans and Wener (2007) to see how cultural differences in interpersonal distance affect commuter stress?

> ## STUDY TIP
> A good way to evaluate studies is to think about how the conclusions apply to everyday life. This study shows that long journeys and cramped carriages increase commuter stress. How could you decrease journey times and improve the layout of train carriages to improve the customer experience? Encouraging people to use trains rather than their own individual cars could also indirectly benefit the environment too, meaning the application of psychological.findings such as this are of critical global importance.

> ## TEST YOURSELF
>
> 1 Tilly commutes to work every day on the train. Her commute lasts 45 minutes and she has to change trains. Afsana also commutes to work. Her commute is 15 minutes on one train. When talking to each they wonder how commuting affects their work and their stress levels.
>   a Outline one way Tilly and Afsana could find out about their commuter stress levels. [2]
>   b Explain what Tilly and Afsana may find out about their levels of stress and performance. [2]
> 2 Explain what is meant by an objective measure of stress. [2]
> 3 a Describe what psychologists have discovered about biological measures of stress. [6]
>   b Evaluate what psychologists have discovered about biological measures of stress, including a discussion on correlations. [10]
> 4 Heart rate monitoring can be used to measure levels of stress.
>   a Explain what is meant by heart rate variability. [2]
>   b Outline how heart rate variability can be measured. [2]
> 5 Explain one strength and one weakness of using biological measurements of stress. [4]
> 6 Elliot is studying gender differences in responses to stress. He intends to use a biological measure. Write a null hypothesis for his study. [2]

KEY TERM

life events

METHODOLOGY

questionnaires

psychometrics

subjective and objective data

validity

reliability

Psychological measures

Think!

Why may a self-report questionnaire be better to test Type A personality than a semi-structured interview?

Think!

Imagine your colleague is worried about whether her levels of stress are too high. She wants to find out whether this is the case and whether she is likely to get ill. What could she do to find out her stress levels?

Think!

Self-reports may not be a valid way of measuring stress. Why do you think some people say questionnaires are low in validity?

On Holmes and Rahe's Social Readjustment Rating Scale marriage is rated as one of the most stressful life events with a mean LCU of 50 but this scale was developed in 1967. Can you think of anything that has changed since the 1960s that might mean marriage requires less social adjustment than it did when this study was conducted? Remember, such changes are not universal; marriage may still be as stressful or even more stressful in some cultures compared to others. How do changes such as these relate to temporal validity?

▲ Figure 8.30

Self-report questionnaires

Self-reports are a convenient way to measure stress as it does not involve any potentially invasive biological tests or scans and the participants can complete them either with paper and pencil or online.

Friedman and Rosenman's Personality test

The construction of Friedman and Rosenman's personality test began with their observation that diet alone could not account for the development of coronary heart disease. They studied couples who had the same diet as each other and found that the men had a higher incidence of heart disease. To try and find out the reason behind the difference they sent 150 questionnaires out to businessmen from San Francisco, USA. They were asked to indicate which of the ten habits a friend had exhibited prior to their heart attack. They also sent the same questionnaire to hospital workers who were looking after cardiac patients. A number of traits were consistently found across the responses.

Friedman and Rosenman then conducted a structured interview over a period of over eight years. They devised 25 questions to assess how people responded to everyday pressures that could lead to feelings of impatience, hostility and competitiveness. For example, they were asked how they would cope with waiting in a long queue. The interviewer used a provocative style. The interviews were audio-taped and participants' personality was rated by two researchers to ensure inter-rater reliability.

Jenkins et al. (1979) created a pen and paper version of the personality test called the Jenkins Activity Survey (JAS) in order to make the structured interview more accessible. Originally containing fifty questions, statistical analysis found a subset of 21 items that best predicted Type A behaviour. These included questions about being competitive, setting deadlines and being punctual. By scoring the questionnaire, psychologists are able to determine what personality type the individual has, such as Type A (competitive, aggressive, ambitious) or Type B (calm, relaxed, non-competitive) or a combination of both.

Evaluation

One strength of the Jenkins Activity Survey was that as a self-report questionnaire it was easier to score and could be distributed to a wider sample. For example, it could be completed online or sent out to large numbers of people. This is a strength as the reliability of the questionnaire could be tested and cross-cultural research completed. However, even online, participants may not always be honest with their answers, although, as they are anonymous, participants may be more likely to be honest.

One weakness of questionnaires to measure Type A personality is that social desirability may be a problem. Bennett and Carroll (1989) suggested that participants would not view themselves in such negative terms such as being irritable, impatient or too angry and were more likely to rate themselves as being assertive, energetic and autonomous. This is a weakness as it may mean that the results are low in validity.

Life events questionnaire

Holmes and Rahe (1967) created the Social Readjustment Rating Scale (SRRS), a **life events** questionnaire used to measure the likelihood of someone becoming ill due to the number of life events they have experienced in a year. They created a list of 43 life events based on the type of events that their patients had reported experiencing. To create the questionnaires, they had to determine how important each event was in terms of how long it would take to adjust to them and the degree of adjustment needed. They asked a sample of 394 participants to rate the life events (regardless of whether the event was positive or negative). The events were then ranked and a score assigned.

The questionnaire was scored by totalling the scores for each event experienced over a 12-month period. According to Holmes and Rahe (1967), if a person has less than 150 life change units, they have a 30 per cent chance of suffering from stress. 50–299 life change units equate to a 50 per cent chance of suffering from stress. Over 300 life units means a person has an 80 per cent chance of developing a stress-related illness.

Evaluation

A weakness of the SRRS is that Holmes and Rahe's (1967) research was correlational and only looked at the relationship between health and life events. Therefore, life events cannot be said to directly cause ill health as there could be other variables that have an effect. For example, if someone is experiencing a great deal of stress in their life, they may not be eating as healthily as they normally would. This means that poor nutrition may be having more of an impact on the person's wellbeing than the stressful life event itself.

Another weakness of the questionnaire is that it also does not take into account individual responses to life events. The scale assumes that everyone will respond to life events in the same way. For example, marriage for some people might be an extremely stressful event and take a great deal of adjustment whereas for other people, who may have already been together for years, it might be stress-free and enjoyable. This is important as it suggests that predictions about ill health based on the SRRS may not always be accurate, implying that the SRRS is low in internal reliability.

A strength of the questionnaire is that it is supported by research evidence. Scully *et al.* (2000) reviewed the use of this scale 30 years after Holmes and Rahe (1967) first used it and reported that it was still a reliable measure of stress and had been used widely to measure the effect of life events on stress and ill health. This is important as it suggests that the scale also has temporal validity.

> **LEARNING LINK**

Questionnaires are often used to gather quantitative data about individual differences between people, such as personality, intelligence, abilities and so on. For example, the life events scale measures differences in exposure to stressors and the eyes test devised by Baron-Cohen *et al.* (page 60) measured participants' ability to accurately identify emotions based on the images of people's eyes. Do you believe quantitative data is a good way of measuring people's intelligence and abilities? Think back to the issues raised by the use of the eyes test at AS Level, such as whether the scores reflect the way a person might behave in everyday life. Does this apply to measures of stress? What would the advantage be of using both methods that collect both quantitative and qualitative data, for example using semi-structured interviews in addition to questionnaires?

STUDY TIP

One great way of increasing your understanding of the strengths and weaknesses of questionnaires such as the life events questionnaire is to go and do it yourself. There are many free versions online for you to have a go. When you complete it, think about the issues you can find in it. For example, ask how many of the life events actually apply to you or your age group. What does that tell you about age ranges targeted? What about culture? Are there any life events that do not apply to your culture? All of these give you an idea of the problems the life events questionnaire faces today.

> **TEST YOURSELF**

1   Sohail has been talking to his friend who studies Psychology. His friend believes that Sohail has a Type A personality.
    a   State two characteristics that someone with Type A personality may show.   [2]
    b   Outline how having a Type A personality may affect Sohail's health.   [2]
2   Explain one weakness of structured interviews as a way of measuring stress.   [2]
3   a   Describe what psychologists have discovered about psychological measures of stress.   [6]
    b   Evaluate what psychologists have discovered about psychological measures of stress, including a discussion about validity.   [10]

The life events questionnaire can be used to measure stress.

4   Describe how this questionnaire could be used to measure a person's stress levels.   [2]
5   Suggest why life events may not be a good measure of stress.   [2]
6   Explain one strength and one weakness of using questionnaires to measure stress.   [4]

KEY TERMS

biofeedback

muscle action potential

stress inoculation training

conceptualisation

Socratic questioning

skill acquisition

self-talk

METHODOLOGY

generalisations from findings

ethics

8.4.3 Managing stress

Think!

What happens in the skill acquisition stage of Stress Inoculation Training?

Think!

Imagine you are a researcher and you are thinking of trying to replicate Budzynski and Stoyva's (1969) research. What ethical issues would you need to consider?

Think!

Practitioners and patients have to discuss a number of practical issues before a referral is made for treatment, such as time, cost and complexity of the treatment options. What are the practical issues related to biofeedback and Stress Inoculation Therapy (SIT)? Which of the two would be better for a person who works long hours? Or a person who just wants a simple treatment?

To investigate how effective a biofeedback machine would be when given correct feedback compared to no feedback or irrelevant feedback in reducing muscle action potential.

▲ Figure 8.31

Psychological therapies

Biofeedback

Biofeedback is based on the principles of operant conditioning and is a method that uses both physiological and psychological techniques. Biofeedback uses technology to enable an individual to see/hear the physiological reactions that are occurring when under stress.

In biofeedback, an individual is first taught relaxation techniques and is then connected to machines that measure muscle tension (EMG), brain activity (EEG) and sweating (SCR). When increased activity is identified by any of the machines, feedback is given to the individual. This could be a sound if muscle tension increases or a visual display of an accelerated heart rate. The individual then uses their learned relaxation techniques while seeing/listening to the feedback. These techniques will lead to a decrease in heart rate, for example, which they see on the screen. This will be rewarding to the individual as they have achieved their goal, reinforcing the individual to carry on using the techniques in the future. The individual will then learn how to transfer these skills into the real world using the same relaxation techniques when they are in a stressful situation. Portable devices can also be used.

> ### ISSUES AND DEBATES
>
> #### Determinism versus free will
>
> When an individual takes control of their stress and makes the conscious decision to attend biofeedback sessions they are exercising their freewill in an attempt to reduce their symptoms. However, the treatment itself is deterministic; heart and breathing rate for example are shaped via visual feedback (reinforcement) from the machine. The feedback therefore determines the person's physiological responses. However, the person still has a choice over whether to attend to the feedback on the screen in order to control their physiological responses meaning biofeedback presents a combination of free will and determinism.

Focus on... Budzynski and Stoyva (1969)

> ### AIM
>
> To describe a biofeedback instrument incorporating the operant conditioning principles of immediate knowledge of results and systematic shaping of responses.

METHODOLOGY

Fifteen participants completed the study. Each of the fifteen participants was randomly allocated to one of three groups, the three levels of the independent variables.

1   The experimental group – correct feedback: Participants were told that the pitch of the tone of the instrument would vary with the level of muscle tension in their forehead. They were told to relax as much as possible and to try and keep the tone low in pitch.

2   The first control group – no feedback (silence): Participants were asked to relax as much as possible, especially the forehead muscle.

3   The second control group – irrelevant feedback: Participants were told to relax deeply, especially the muscle in the forehead and were also told that the low monotonous tone would help them relax.

Electrodes used to measure the muscle (EMG) activity were placed one inch above each eyebrow and spaced four inches apart on the participant's forehead. Each participant was then told to lie quietly with their eyes closed and to concentrate on relaxing the frontalis (forehead) muscle. The forehead muscle was chosen as this muscle is difficult to relax. The idea is that if a participant could control this more difficult muscle, then the feedback procedure would be applicable to less-difficult muscles.

All participants were initially recorded on two occasions without any feedback, and the mean level of muscle action potential for the second recording was used as a baseline measure. The second one was used as participants would be better adapted to the surroundings.

All subsequent experimental recordings were taken at approximately the same time of day (late afternoon or early evening). After the first sessions, successive sessions which consisted of twenty one-minute trials, were separated by at least a day and not more than three days. Each participant was paid $1.50 for each session and were told that a bonus would be given according to their rank in the group of 15 – the lower the muscle activity the larger the bonus.

The dependent variable was the reduction in action potential in the muscles, measured by electrodes placed on the forehead muscles in microvolts (μV).

The instrument

The instrument devised (EMG) tracks muscle action potential. Muscle action potential is where the nervous system sends a signal to the brain to contract a muscle, therefore the higher the potential the more tense the muscle. The instrument emits a tone which varies depending on the level of muscle action potential. When muscle activity decreases the pitch becomes lower, as activity increases the pitch becomes higher. This means the participant can receive continuous feedback about their level of EMG activity.

RESULTS

The researchers found that there were clear differences among the groups in relation to mean levels of muscle action potential even from the very first day of feedback (Session 2). Researchers compared baseline levels (Session 1) with post-training levels (Session 5) and found:

● a 50 per cent mean decrease in action potential in the experimental group (correct feedback)

● a 20 per cent mean decrease in action potential in the second control group (silence)

● a 28 per cent mean increase in action potential in the first control group (irrelevant feedback).

Additional support for the effectiveness of the instrument was shown by one participant who had originally started in the irrelevant feedback group and had shown consistently high levels of muscle action potential. This participant was given correct feedback training for four additional sessions and their levels of muscle action potential decreased significantly following the first extra feedback session and by the third extra session it had dropped by 50 per cent from Session 5.

▶ **CONCLUSIONS**

> **CONCLUSIONS**
> ....
> The findings suggest biofeedback in the form of immediate accurate information about bodily stress (for example, muscle tension) may be a useful tool in behavioural therapy and for use with people with certain psychosomatic disorders.

Evaluating Budzynski and Stoyva (1969)

One strength of biofeedback is that it is a non-invasive way of managing stress. For example, biological treatments such as drug therapy can cause side effects such as sickness. This is a strength as it means it is a more ethical solution to managing stress levels and that individuals are less likely to stop/drop out of treatment.

> ▶ ISSUES AND DEBATES
> ....
>
> ### Applications to everyday life
> Another strength is that biofeedback can be applied to everyday life as the relaxation techniques give individuals a way of managing their own stress in different stressful situations. This would suggest it is a more long-lasting solution to stress. On the other hand, biofeedback does not address what is causing the stress as it only tries to reduce symptoms such as heart rate and muscle tension. This is an issue because even though the individual learns a way of reducing their response to the stressor, it may still be there and is therefore not effective as a long-term solution.

A weakness of the study by Buszynski and Stoyva (1969) is that the machine may be counter-productive. For example, the participants had to control the tone in order to show muscle relaxation as well as a possible bonus. It may be that trying to control the tone and perhaps not being as successful may have caused the participants even more stress. This is a weakness as some individuals may actually find the audio feedback stressful, showing that it is not effective for everyone.

Preventing stress

Three phases of stress inoculation training (SIT)

Another technique used to reduce stress is **stress inoculation training** (SIT) (Meichenbaum and Deffenbacher, 1988). SIT has three key phases although the phases can overlap with each other:

1 Conceptualisation phase

The two specific goals of this initial phase are:
- ▸ the building up of a warm, collaborative relationship between client and trainer
- ▸ increasing the client's understanding and awareness of the nature and impact of their own stress responses.

The trainer will teach the client about the concept of anxiety and the impact stress and anxiety can have on their everyday life. The client is taught how to recognise their own stress and anxiety focusing on the thoughts that they have when faced with stress. This is done through a process known as **Socratic questioning**. Socratic questioning is where focused but open-ended questions are used to discover deeply held beliefs, in this instance about their stressful experiences and their reactions to that experience.

2 Skill acquisition phase

This phase focuses on helping clients acquire new coping skills and also consolidate the skills they already possess. This will include the clients being taught self-awareness and self-monitoring skills so that they will not only have a conscious awareness of their negative thought patterns but also learn strategies to help change them. Through discussion and self-monitoring, they become aware of their own anxious **self-talk**. They can then be taught specific

self-statements that they can use to counter any negative self-statements that they may have. Other coping skills acquired include collecting information on situations that cause them anxiety. They are also taught techniques such as problem-solving and self-reward for coping.

3 Rehearsal and application

In the third phase the clients work on refining, applying and transferring their skills across increasingly demanding levels of stressors (this forms the inoculation part of the training). Role plays, simulations and imagery might be used. For example, the client might be asked to imagine a scenario where they would normally feel anxious and to imagine how they would use their skills to deal with the anxiety. The skills are actively transferred to their everyday lives through graded homework assignments and 'experiments'. The client then feeds back to the trainer about how they coped and skills can be further refined. Relapse prevention procedures are also taught which includes going through a variety of high-risk stressful situations that they may face and then rehearsing various different coping techniques to use.

Evaluation

A strength of SIT is that, unlike drug therapy for stress or anxiety, it focuses on the causes of stress rather than just the symptoms. For example, clients discuss prior stress experiences with their trainer and explore the emotions surrounding these experiences. This is a strength as dealing with the cause of stress rather than just the symptoms may lead to longer term behavioural change as the skills used in the training can be applied to a number of situations in everyday life.

> ## ISSUES AND DEBATES

Determinism versus free will

Another strength of SIT is that it does not have any side effects that medication for stress relief might have. For example, medication can cause tiredness, nausea and sleep disturbances. This is a strength as it means that likelihood of adherence to treatment is higher, as side effects are one of the main reasons that individuals drop out of treatment programmes (see page 252), and patients have control over their own stress, meaning that they have free will. This means that SIT and biofeedback can be seen as longer-term solutions to stress.

One practical weakness of SIT is that it is expensive for some clients. For example, SIT involves the trainer working intensively with the client over a number of sessions. Although in some countries cost is covered by health services, this is not the case in others meaning that it is unaffordable for some. Also, the number of sessions required may mean some clients would have to take time off work which they may not be able to afford. This is unlike medication which is a quicker and easier way of treating stress.

In addition, SIT has often been seen as a treatment which is more complex than it needs to be. For example, many believe that just teaching people relaxation techniques and to be more positive in their thinking is as successful as teaching them the whole process. This is a weakness as the more complex a treatment the more time consuming and expensive it may be, in this case, possibly unnecessarily.

> ## ISSUES AND DEBATES

Individual verus situational explanations

Stress inoculation training (SIT) is a useful therapy as it takes into account both individual and situational explanations of why an individual is experiencing stress. The use of Socratic questioning allows the therapist to understand the individual's perspective of their stress but also to learn any situational factors that might be affecting them as well and then the treatment can be tailored to the individual to address both their own perception of their stress and how they deal with situational factors such as stress in the workplace.

► **LEARNING LINK**

Biofeedback uses the principles of operant conditioning in order to reduce levels of stress. At AS Level, 1 you studied Fagen *et al.* (elephant learning) which looked at the role of positive reinforcement on elephant learning through the use of rewards for desired behaviours. What is the reward patients receive in biofeedback? Could negative reinforcement also explain why biofeedback is effective?

STUDY TIP

One great way of increasing your understanding of techniques such as biofeedback is by trying it out for yourself. There are a number of applications on various smart watches and phones which allow you to visually monitor aspects of your health such as heart rate and temperature. These work on the same principles as the management technique discussed on these pages and help you understand the theory behind the process. Do you believe there is any reason why biofeedback may make the situation worse for some people?

► **TEST YOURSELF**

1 Davinder is attending her first session of stress inoculation therapy next week but is confused about what will happen during training. She asks her doctor for more information.
   Outline how the doctor would explain stress inoculation training as a way of managing Davinder's stress levels. [4]
2 Outline one practical weakness of stress inoculation training. [2]
3 a Describe what psychologists have discovered about psychological therapies to manage stress. [6]
   b Evaluate what psychologists have discovered about psychological therapies to manage stress, including a discussion about effectiveness. [10]
4 Paula has been learning about biofeedback and wondered whether age might influence the effectiveness of the treatment.
   a Plan a correlation to investigate the effectiveness of biofeedback in people of different ages.
      Your plan must include:
      – operational definitions of the two covariables
      – how the data will be analysed. [10]
   b For one piece of psychological knowledge that has informed your plan:
      i   Describe this psychological knowledge. [4]
      ii Explain how two features of this psychological knowledge informed your plan. [4]

KEY TERMS

radiotherapy
breast cancer
chemotherapy
mastectomy
diaphragmatic breathing
lumpectomy

METHODOLOGY

generalisations from findings
ethics

Key study: Managing stress: Relaxation and imagery in reducing stress during medical treatment – Bridge *et al.* (1988)

Think!

How did Bridge *et al.* (1988) obtain their sample?

Think!

Do you think that using relaxation and imagery would help you if you were having a difficult time? What imagery do you feel would be the most relaxing for you?

Think!

Bridge *et al.* (1988) tested the use of relaxation and imagery to help women with the stress of going through treatment for breast cancer. Imagine you wanted to replicate the study by Bridge *et al.* (1988) but using a sample of A Level students about to sit their exams to see if it would help them with exam-related stress. What ethical issues would you need to consider?

Having read about the study by Bridge *et al.* (1988) and finding that the interventions did not significantly reduce stress in the younger women with breast cancer, what would you suggest researchers focus on next in order to support the younger women who may still be working through treatment or have young children to care for?

▲ Figure 8.32

Context

Research has found that receiving a diagnosis of **breast cancer** can cause significant stress in patients due to having to deal with having a serious diagnosis which may have a significant impact on their health, their ability to work and their life in general. Treatments including surgery, **chemotherapy**, **radiotherapy** and medication can be challenging physically and psychologically meaning that research into effective ways to manage stress for cancer patients is critical.

Stress reduction techniques such as relaxation and imagery have been tested in a variety of clinical settings. Patel *et al.* (1981) found that relaxation treatment helped reduce stress in patients who had hypertension. Similarly, Renzi *et al.* (2000) found that relaxation techniques reduced pain and improved the quality of sleep in patients who had had surgery. Arakawa (1995) found that progressive muscle relaxation helped reduce anxiety in Japanese patients undergoing chemotherapy.

Relaxation and imagery techniques can help patients to deal with the psychological stresses of diagnosis and treatment and could help them find the experience less stressful, increase their wellbeing and enable them to sleep better. Furthermore, previous research with cancer patients suggests that positive thought and guided imagery can prolong life (Simonton and Simonton, 1975).

AIM/HYPOTHESES

To see whether stress could be reduced in patients who had been diagnosed with early breast cancer and were being treated with radiotherapy. Specifically, the researchers aimed to investigate whether patients who received either of two relaxation treatments would show a more positive effect on their mood states than a control group of similar, untreated women. Furthermore, the researchers hypothesised that the women who received relaxation training with an imagery component would show more change than the women given relaxation training alone.

METHODOLOGY

The research method used was a randomised control trial with three conditions. Questionnaires were used as methods of assessment (dependent variables). The questionnaires used were:
1 *Leeds General Scale for the Self-Assessment of Depression and Anxiety:* A self-report measure that has previously been used to assess mood with cancer patients.
2 *The Profile of Mood States questionnaire:* A 65-item questionnaire that measures aspects such as fatigue, anger, confusion and depression.

The questionnaires were chosen as the methods of assessment as they were minimally disruptive and non-intrusive.

Sample

An opportunity sample of 139 women who had been treated either by **mastectomy** (removal of a breast due to cancer) or breast conservation **lumpectomy** for early-stage breast cancer completed the full treatment package. All women were attending a six-week outpatients' course of radiotherapy at Middlesex Hospital in the UK. All could understand English and were under the age of 70. The average age was 53.

▶ PROCEDURE

All the women had completed at least one session of radiotherapy before being invited to be part of the study. They were informed that the study was being carried out to investigate ways of reducing stress during radiotherapy and that each participant would be randomly allocated to one of three conditions (the levels of the independent variable) and were told they would be required to complete a number of questionnaires (the dependent variables). The researchers ensured that participants knew that non-participation would have no effect on their course of radiotherapy, no drugs would be administered and confidentiality would be maintained.

Participants completed The Profile of Mood States and The Leeds General Scales Questionnaire at the start of the study. All of the participants were seen individually by one of the two researchers, once a week during the six weeks of the study.

The participants were than allocated to one of the three conditions which were:
1 The control condition.
2 The relaxation treatment group.
3 The relaxation plus imagery group.

Both the 'relaxation treatment' group and the 'treatment plus imagery' group were taught relaxation techniques which involved learning how to relax individual muscles throughout the body and **diaphragmatic breathing** which slows the breathing rate and helps the individual become calmer and more relaxed. The 'relaxation plus imagery' group were also taught to imagine a 'peaceful scene' of their own choice, to help increase the relaxation. Sessions lasted for about 30 minutes. During these 30 minutes, the exercises were practised by the treatment groups, however, in the control group the women were just encouraged to talk about themselves and their interests.

The relaxation and the relaxation plus imagery groups were given audio tapes which repeated the instructions for all of the relaxation techniques that they had learnt in their groups. Both groups were asked to practise the relaxation techniques at home for a minimum of 15 minutes per day. The sessions lasted approximately 30 minutes.

Participants all completed The Profile of Mood States and The Leeds General Scales Questionnaire again at the end of the six week study.

▶ RESULTS

No significant differences were found between the three groups in terms of mood on the initial questionnaire scores. No significant differences were found between the twenty-five women who had also received chemotherapy before the study and the 114 women who had not.

Bridge *et al.* (1988) sub-divided the women into two groups: those who were younger than 54 and those who were older before they examined the data. Both the relaxation and the relaxation and imagery significantly lowered scores for the older women on measures of tension, depression and total mood disturbance compared to the control group. The relaxation and imagery showed the greatest effect.

▼ Table 8.11 Mean scores on three of the mood states scales for women who were older than 54

	Relaxation group (n = 15)	Relaxation and imagery group (n = 23)	Control (n = 24)
Tension	10.3	8.4	13.2
Depression	7.6	5.2	10.8
Total mood disturbance	60.9	47.0	72.0

There was no significant difference in the mood disturbance of the 'Relaxation' group when the data from both age groups were combined (mean: 61.7 at onset and 61.9 at the end). There was a small difference in the 'relaxation plus imagery' group (mean: 59.6 at onset and 53.9 at the end). In the control group, total mood disturbance got worse (mean: 54.4 at the onset and 64.1 at the end).

► CONCLUSIONS

- Relaxation combined with imagery is effective at reducing mood disturbances.
- Mood disturbances worsen in patients with no intervention.
- The treatments may be more effective in older women as they have more time to focus on interventions as they are less likely to be working or potentially have young children.

 ## Methodological strengths and weaknesses

A strength of the study is that it followed standardised procedures. For example, the researchers ensured that the women in the treatment groups were taught the relaxation techniques in the same way and were given practice tapes to enable them to continue with the exercises at home, following the same techniques. This is a strength as it means that you can be sure that it is the change of condition affecting the results and not the change of procedure, increasing the validity of the conclusions.

Another strength of the study is that it was a randomised controlled trial (RCT). In an RCT, participants are randomly allocated to a treatment or control condition such as in the current study where there was a control plus two treatment groups. This is a strength as it lowers the possibility of bias and participant variables such as personality being a factor in the results. This also increases the validity of the study.

A weakness is that the dependent variables were measured through self-report questionnaires. For example, the Profile of Mood States was used to measure moods such as tension, depression and mood disturbance. This is a weakness as it may have led to socially desirable responses as the women might not want to be seen as depressed or tense and therefore may not be truthful in their answers, lowering the validity of the findings.

Another weakness is that the study only used a relatively small sample of women. There were only 44–48 participants in each group, and less when these were broken down into women under and over the age of 54, with as little as 15 participants over the age of 54 in the Relaxation group. This is an issue because it means the groups were unlikely to be representative of the target population and therefore limits the ability to make generalisations.

 ## Ethics

All participants gave valid consent for taking part as they had been fully briefed about the different conditions of the study and what they would be expected to do during the study period, which included the groups/conditions as well as completing the questionnaires. Another ethical strength was that they also informed the women that the results would not appear in their medical records, they would not be penalised in any way if they refused to take part and it would not affect their radiotherapy sessions. They were also assured that no drugs would be given and confidentiality would be maintained throughout.

 ## Applications to the real world

The relaxation techniques were found to be effective in reducing tension and depression in the women who were over 54. This means that the intervention could be targeted at older women who are most likely to benefit.

> ISSUES AND DEBATES

Determinism versus free will

The study by Bridge *et al.* demonstrates that with the right support and training people can exercise free will to help manage low mood during cancer treatment. This is beneficial as anything that helps people to reduce feelings of helplessness and increase feelings of empowerment during difficult treatments such as chemotherapy and radiotherapy is important. The study demonstrates that mental wellbeing does not need to be determined by the treatments people are receiving but their attitudes towards managing the side effects.

> REFLECTION

- What are the problems with using self-reports in this study? What alternative methods could the researchers use to assess mood, depression and anxiety?
- Can you think of any other areas of health where conducting randomised controlled trials would be useful?

> LEARNING LINK

Hölzel *et al.* (mindfulness and brain scans) also looked at using relaxation techniques to reduce stress by using mindfulness. Remind yourself of the study – are there any similarities between the relaxation techniques used in this study and the mindfulness used in Hölzel *et al.*? The two studies differ in that Holzel *et al.* use more objective measures for their assessments (MRI scans). Which do you feel is the better way and why?

STUDY TIP

There may be times when you cannot use pen and paper to learn the information on these pages. Perhaps you are taking a long journey or going away on holiday. One way to maintain your learning is through the use of a podcast or recording. Record whatever you want to learn on to your phone or another device and then listen to it as you travel or even as you sleep.

> TEST YOURSELF

1 Jayne is undergoing treatment for breast cancer and she is feeling anxious and stressed.
  a Outline one method Jayne could try to reduce her stress levels. [2]
  b Suggest one weakness of the method you have suggested in part (a). [2]
2 Explain one reason why the study by Bridge *et al.* (1988) study may not be generalisable. [2]
3 a Describe the study by Bridge *et al.* (1988) on relaxation and imagery in reducing stress during medical treatment. [6]
  b Evaluate the study by Bridge *et al.* (1988) on relaxation and imagery in reducing stress during medical treatment, including a discussion on validity. [10]

From the key study by Bridge *et al.* (1988) on relaxation and imagery:
4 Outline the two treatment conditions used in the study. [4]
5 Suggest why Bridge *et al.* included a control condition in their study. [2]
6 Explain two weaknesses of using questionnaires to study relaxation and imagery in breast cancer treatment. [4]
7 Explain one similarity and one difference between biofeedback and the use of imagery to reduce stress. [4]

KEY TERMS

fear arousal

fear appeals

health promotion
campaign

perceived severity

perceived susceptibility

self-efficacy

METHODOLOGY

longitudinal studies

objective and subjective
data

ethics

8.5 Health promotion
8.5.1 Strategies for promoting health
Fear arousal

Think!

What are the effects of a strong fear appeal on individuals' health behaviour?

Think!

Imagine you are trying to organise a **health promotion campaign** with the aim to reduce smoking behaviour in students. You are trying to decide what type of images and messages would be the most likely to change behaviour. What decisions should be made to ensure that the campaign is successful?

Think!

What ethical issues do researchers need to take into account when using fear appeals in health promotion campaigns?

How would you react to a fear appeal advertisement?

▶ Figure 8.33

Fear arousal uses vivid imagery to raise public awareness of risky health behaviours and encourage health promoting behaviours as a more suitable alternative. Psychological theories suggest that fear, due an increased subjective appraisal of **perceived susceptibility** and **perceived severity**, motivates a person to change their behaviour. An example of this would be the use of **fear appeals** which use graphic images or messages within their communications. In the UK, imagery on cigarette packets shows the potential health consequences of smoking to try to stop people from smoking. Other methods include television or billboard advertisements.

The success of fear appeals is, however, affected by a number of factors. They are more likely to be successful if an individual has higher levels of **self-efficacy** and positive expectations about outcomes. For example, smokers may become afraid of cancer if they understand their susceptibility to the disease. This fear will motivate them to stop smoking but only if they are convinced that stopping smoking will lower that risk and that they have the ability to quit.

The effectiveness of fear appeals is also affected by how graphic or anxiety-provoking the campaign is. If the fear appeals become too graphic or anxiety-provoking, then the resulting behaviour will become more defensive and may lead to the individual avoiding the anti-smoking fear message rather than taking action to change their behaviour. In fact, some studies have suggested that extreme fear messages may cause individuals to deny the cancer risk to themselves and actually result in a higher level of smoking (Brown and Smith 2007).

Janis and Feschbach (1953) suggested that high fear appeals may lead to a level of emotional stress that people just cannot deal with. They suggest a number of possible reactions to extreme fear/anxiety:

» The individual may fail to pay attention to the message. They may try to change the subject but if this fails and anxiety rises to a high level then disturbances to attention may become more severe, such as distractibility and inability to concentrate.

» If anxiety becomes too high then the individual may become aggressive to the communicator as they are seen as responsible for producing the uncomfortable feelings.
» The person may simply turn off an advert if it makes them feel too uncomfortable. They may actively avoid seeing or even thinking about it again.

Low fear appeals may also be ignored as there may not be enough motivation produced to make individuals want to change their behaviour and they may not pay enough attention to it in the first place. Janis and Feshbach (1953) studied these possible effects in the following study.

Focus on... Janis and Feshbach (1953)

AIMS

To investigate potential adverse effects and resulting defensive reactions to fear appeals.

METHODOLOGY

200 Freshmen (first years) from an American high school (mean age =15) were randomly allocated to either a strong, moderate or minimal fear appeal group or a control group concerning oral hygiene. The fear appeal groups received the same essential information about the causes of tooth decay and the same recommendations. Lectures were the same length and delivered by the same speaker, using 20 illustrated slides. The independent variable was the strength of the fear appeal:

1 Strong: Included the painful and serious consequences of poor dental hygiene, for example tooth decay, gum disease, arthritic paralysis, kidney damage or blindness. The personalised threat level was raised through frequent use of the word 'you'.
2 Moderate: The dangers of poor dental hygiene were addressed in a milder, more factual manner.
3 Minimal: Fear-arousing material was replaced with neutral information such as the growth and functions of teeth.

The control group were given information about the structure and function of the eye.

Four dependent variables measured the effects of the communication:
1 A general health questionnaire to measure dental hygiene (completed a week before the lectures).
2 Self-reported feedback on the effects of the communication on a five-point scale from 'very worried' to 'not at all worried'.
3 A 23-item test on the factual content of the lectures.
4 A follow-up questionnaire to measure the effect of the lectures, completed one week later.

RESULTS

● There was no difference in the amount of knowledge remembered by the different groups.
● 42 per cent of the strong fear group thought about the condition most of the time compared to 22 per cent of the minimal fear group
● 74 per cent of the strong fear group said they felt worried a few or many times about the condition of their mouth compared to 44 per cent of the minimal fear group. This showed that the strong fear communication aroused more worry than in the minimal fear group.
● Participants who received strong fear arousal communication found the lecture more interesting than the other three groups. However, more people in the strong fear group said there was something they disliked about the illustrated talk than the other two groups.
● One week after the lectures there was only an 8 per cent increase in conformity in the strong fear group compared to 36 per cent in the minimal fear group and 22 per cent in the moderate fear group compared with the results obtained one week before the communication. The strong group did not differ significantly from the control group which unsurprisingly showed no increase in conformity.

> ### CONCLUSIONS
>
> - Strong fear appeals are effective in creating a high degree of emotional tension with the strong group expressing more concern about the state of their teeth than the other groups.
> - Overall effectiveness of persuasive communication will be reduced by the use of strong fear appeal especially if it creates a high degree of emotional tension without reassurance.
> - The level of fear appeal does not affect the amount of knowledge gained from the communication.

Evaluating Janis and Feshbach (1953)

One strength of Janis and Feshbach's study was that they used a field experiment method. The researchers went into a Connecticut high school and the lectures were included as part of the usual hygiene programme. This is a strength as this means that the study is high in ecological validity and the results should be able to be applied to other real world health promotion campaigns.

One weakness of Janis and Feshbach's study was the lack of control over the different groups speaking to each other outside of the lectures. For example, the groups could have realised that they had all been given different information which could have led to demand characteristics as they would realise they were in a study. As the students were using self-report to record their changes in beliefs and behaviour, researchers would not know if they had been honest in their responses, lowering the validity of the results.

A strength of fear arousal as a method of persuading individuals to change their behaviour is that it is still used in a variety of health promotions today. Many successful health promotion campaigns use visual imagery, for example in the UK, graphic images are used on cigarette packets including diseased lungs and arteries. This is a strength as it shows fear appeals can be applied to everyday life and are useful.

There are also ethical concerns about the use of fear appeals. While they have been found to have been effective in modifying people's health behaviour, for those people who cannot follow the guidance, it can reduce their self-esteem and increase their belief that they are unable to do anything to avoid negative consequences (Simpson, 2017).

> ### ISSUES AND DEBATES
>
> #### Individual versus situational explanations
>
> Research by Wu, Deng and Liu (2021) has looked at the effects of fear appeals during the Covid-19 pandemic using situational factors such as notification of proximity to an infected person and whether this would motivate people to make behavioural changes in order to protect themselves. They found that being notified of being in close proximity to an infected person increased anxiety and in turn improved preventative behaviours. Whilst the researchers focused on the situational factors, they also acknowledged that individual factors could have an impact on response to fear appeals, such as personality and prior experience. Therefore, it is important for researchers to consider both individual and situational factors when researching fear appeals.
>
> #### Cultural differences
>
> Research by Tannenbaum et al. (2015) reviewed the data from 127 studies on fear appeals from diverse populations. They found no evidence of cultural differences in the effects of fear appeals. This suggests that fear appeals have a universal effect regardless of culture. However, Chung and Ahn (2013) did find cultural differences when researching South Korea and the United States and suggested that different messages should be used depending on the culture to increase how acceptable the message is. Therefore, this suggests that research around cultural differences in the effect of fear appeals is conflicting, and more research is needed.

► LEARNING LINK

► **LEARNING LINK**

Saavedra and Silverman (button phobia) looked at fear in a child. Do you think it is ethical to use fear as a way of manipulating people's behaviour, even if it is to help them lead healthier lives?

STUDY TIP

One way to help you learn is to relate what you are studying to your own life. Have a look at health promotion advertisements in your country. Do they use fear appeals? How effective do you think they are at changing people's behaviour?

► **TEST YOURSELF**

1   Sydney attended her doctors' surgery for a regular appointment and saw an anti-smoking poster which had images of lungs covered in tar and rotting and missing teeth due to mouth cancer from smoking. Sydney felt shocked and just went to sit somewhere where she could not see the poster.

   a   Suggest what level of fear appeal has been used in the anti-smoking poster. [2]

   b   Explain the reasons why Sydney moved so she could no longer see the poster. [2]

2   Explain why fear appeals may cause ethical concerns. [2]

3   a   Describe what psychologists have discovered about the use of fear appeals in health promotion campaigns. [6]

   b   Evaluate what psychologists have discovered about the use of fear appeals in health promotion campaigns, including a discussion about ecological validity. [10]

4   One way to investigate the impact of fear campaigns is to conduct interviews, where participants may be interviewed in person or on the telephone. Explain *one* strength and one weakness of telephone interviews as a way of collecting data about the impact of fear campaigns. [4]

5   Suggest one open and one closed question that could be asked as part of a telephone interview to investigate the impact of fear campaigns. [2]

6   Nadiya is conducting a study comparing high and low fear campaigns relating to the health problems that can result from not eating a balanced diet. Write a suitable directional hypothesis for Nadiya's study comparing high and low fear appeals. [2]

Providing information

KEY TERM

myocardial infarction

METHODOLOGY

longitudinal studies

objective and subjective data

ethics

Think!

Lewin *et al.* (1992) is a **randomised control trial**. What does this term mean and why is this known as a **gold standard** design in health psychology research?

Think!

What type of information do you think would be most effective in helping people increase their healthy behaviours?

Think!

How would you investigate the effect of a home-based exercise plan on promoting healthy behaviour?

In order for people to live healthy lives, it is important that they have the correct information to understand what to do and how to do it. For example, to lower the risk of getting cancer, people need to know to keep fit and exercise and to minimise how much alcohol they drink and to not smoke. One approach is to use fear appeals as described in the previous chapter, but these are not always effective at changing behaviour.

Other approaches in the mass media have targeted people who already want to stop an unhealthy habit or behaviour. For example, giving people information they need in order to stop smoking such as links to equipment to help such as nicotine patches or details of stop smoking programmes to join (Sarafino, 2006).

Medical settings can also be an important place for providing healthcare information. For example, waiting rooms in hospital clinics can have booklets on preventing and coping with various diseases and illnesses that can be tailored to the specific clinic or a clinic for pregnant women might contain leaflets on healthy diet and exercise during pregnancy.

Other interventions in medical settings might include cognitive-behavioural interventions which are facilitated by healthcare professionals. Such health interventions have been found to improve activity levels, compliance with medication and quality of life (Cupples and McKnight, 1995).

Home-based exercise programmes

A **myocardial infarction** (a heart attack) is an extremely distressing event which requires both the survivor and their family not only to make some adjustments to their lifestyle but also recover psychologically. Evidence has shown that post myocardial infarction (MI) rehabilitation can both reduce distress and improve quality of life. Not providing such programmes may lead to a preoccupation with physical symptoms and a loss of confidence. Over a third of all post MI patients have a diagnosis of depression a year later. Although rehabilitation programmes within clinical settings were available within the UK, home-based interventions are not so common despite evidence they are as useful as hospital-based ones. Lewin *et al.* (1992) investigated home-based programmes as a useful tool for people who have suffered an MI.

Providing people with the right information and ways of changing their behaviour can help reduce the risk of illness returning. Have you ever been given information by your doctor to help you recover from an illness? How effective was it?

▶ Figure 8.34

Focus on... Lewin *et al.* (1992)

▶ AIM

To evaluate the effectiveness of a home-based exercise programme on people who have had an acute myocardial infarction (heart attack).

▶ METHODOLOGY

Three days after admission to a coronary care unit in the UK, 176 patients (mean age 56) were randomly assigned to one of two groups:

● *Experimental group:* Followed a self-help rehabilitation programme following discharge including exercise, relaxation and stress management programmes and self-help treatments for symptoms of anxiety and depression. Spouses were also given information, invited to also take part and to encourage compliance from the patient.
● *Control group:* Received standard care plus a placebo package of information leaflets and informal counselling.

> ### Follow up after discharge
>
> Both groups were followed up at one, three and six weeks by telephone, clinic appointment or home visit.
> - *Experimental group:* Progress with the rehabilitation programme was checked and patients were encouraged to comply with the exercises in the manual.
> - *Control group:* Patients were asked about their recovery and given general advice.
>
> Postal questionnaires were distributed at six weeks, six months and one year to measure symptoms of anxiety and depression, general health and use of health services.

▶ RESULTS

There was a significant improvement in anxiety and emotional disturbance in the rehabilitation group at six weeks and at one year compared to the control group.

Specifically, 52 per cent of the heart attack patients had significant anxiety or depression at discharge. Those who were allocated to the rehabilitation group showed significantly less depression and anxiety at six weeks, six months and twelve months compared with similarly distressed participants in the control group, in fact anxiety levels were half that of the control distressed group. In contrast, those in the distressed control group remained almost as anxious 12 months after discharge.

The control group made an average of 1.8 more visits to their general practitioner in the first six months compared to the rehabilitation group. At twelve months the control group had made a mean of 0.9 more visits. Significantly, more of the control group were admitted to hospital in the first six months (24 per cent versus 8 per cent of the rehabilitation group).

▶ CONCLUSIONS

Self-rehabilitation programmes lead to improved psychological adjustment, fewer cases of readmittance, fewer visits to the GP and a lower rate of anxiety and depression compared to standard care.

Evaluating Lewin *et al.* (1992)

A weakness of the study is that it did not include a 'no intervention' control group. Therefore, any changes seen in comparison to the control group might have been smaller than in comparison to a no intervention group. However, it would be unethical to have a no intervention control group, as patients would not know what behaviours they needed to change to prevent further heart attacks.

Another weakness is that funding ran out for the study before its completion. This meant that nearly half of both the experimental and control groups were not followed up at the six and twelve-month points. This could affect the validity of the long-term findings as such a significant number of participants were not followed up and is a weakness of longitudinal studies.

A strength of the study is that the findings have been supported by other research which have shown that interventions led by practice nurses can have a positive impact on wellbeing, such as Cupples *et al.* (1995) who found increased compliance to medication and Campbell *et al.* (1998) who found improvement in blood pressure and a 28 per cent reduction in hospital admissions. Lewin *et al.* (2002) also found that a nurse-facilitated, cognitive-behavioural, self-help intervention can help reduce depression and anxiety and the self-reported number of angina attacks. It can also help improve diet and exercise which in turn improve quality of life. This suggests that providing patients with information about how to improve their health can be effective.

Another strength of the study included controls such as ensuring that patients in the rehabilitation group did not talk to other patients who had had a heart attack about the intervention they were receiving. They also used a double-blind method so that neither the cardiologist nor the nursing care team knew which condition the patients had been assigned to. This reduced the possibility of experimental bias and increased the validity of the study.

> ### LEARNING LINK
>
> At AS Level, you learned about Albert Bandura and Social Learning Theory (page 90). He and his colleague Miguel Sabido found a way to apply this theory to everyday life in a technique called the Sabido Method (Bandura, 2003). Based on modelling, the technique has been used to create television and radio dramas that promote behavioural changes in the audience. These have been used successfully to change various health-related behaviours through embedding important information into engaging and relatable storylines (see Panford et al., 2001, who targeted sexual health in Ghana). Can you think how a scriptwriter could encourage appropriate behaviour for people who have experienced MI? How could the reactions of other family members be used to promote change?

STUDY TIP

Although many of the issues and debates and methodological issues are covered here, there are many others that could help you formulate a well-rounded and structured evaluation. For example, would this type of self-help programme help all people? Think about cultural differences or even the different types of people that it may be less effective for in your own culture. Perhaps formulate a table with all the evaluative words you have used at AS and A Level and then make copies of it. You could then use that table with every topic area to see whether there are other evaluative words that apply to a particular topic area.

> ### TEST YOURSELF
>
> 1 Soraya is 77 and has recently had a heart attack she is recovering well from. She is concerned about it happening again and is experiencing a high level of anxiety and distress now she is home.
>   Describe one form of health promotion that could be used to reduce Soraya's anxiety about having another heart attack. [4]
> 2 Outline how providing home-based exercise programmes can improve an individual's health. [2]
> 3 a Describe what psychologists have discovered about providing information as an effective health promotion technique. [6]
>   b Evaluate what psychologists have discovered about providing information as an effective health promotion technique, including a discussion on reliability. [10]
> 4 Liz is conducting a study to see whether providing information to elderly people who have heart attacks helps to reduce their risk of future heart problems.
>   Write a non-directional hypothesis for Liz's study. [2]
> 5 Explain one weakness of using self-reports to investigate the effectiveness of providing information as a means of health promotion. [2]
> 6 Suggest one reason why using a blind procedure may increase the validity of a study. [2]

KEY TERMS

taste exposure

observational learning

METHODOLOGY

use of children in research

experiments

longitudinal studies

quantitative and qualitative data

generalisations from findings

8.5.2 Health promotion

Think!

What is meant by the term **taste exposure**?

Think!

Think back to when you were around the age of the children in Tapper et al. (2003) study. Can you remember being rewarded in order to shape your behaviour in school? Also, can you think of any time your parents have tried to use any of the concepts discussed by Tapper et al., (2003) to try and get you to eat new food?

Think!

Can you think of any reasons why the results of the study by Tapper *et al.* (2003) may not be generalisable to all cultures?

Schools and healthy eating

Schools are an excellent place to promote healthy behaviours in children that will benefit them throughout their lives. Children spend a huge proportion of their lives at school and the attitudes, beliefs and behaviours learned in those years often carry through into adulthood. Therefore, promoting healthy behaviours should be an important focus for schools. However, interventions need to be well taught and high quality to have a positive impact.

Research has shown that in some countries young children do not tend to eat enough fruit and vegetables. In the UK, the Department of Health (2000) showed that less than 4 per cent of children ate the recommended five portions of fruit and vegetables a day, with one in 10 children eating no fruit.

Traditional approaches to getting children to eat their fruit and vegetables have been through education around what to eat and what not to eat but this has had limited success (Tapper *et al.*, 2003).

Tapper *et al.* (2003) focused on three different aspects of psychology when designing a health promotion which could be used successfully with children both at home and at school.

1 Taste exposure: The more you taste a novel food the more you learn to like it. For example, many people dislike foods as a child which they learn to like as an adult. Therefore, the more you get a child to taste fruit and vegetables the more they will like them and consume them.

2 Modelling: This is **observational learning** where a child may observe and imitate a role model; this is more likely if the model/s are similar perhaps in terms of age and gender, if they are admired and if there is more than one model being observed.

3 Rewards: There is a great deal of evidence to suggest rewards can shape behaviour. Operant conditioning would suggest that the use of rewards after a desired behaviour has occurred can make the behaviour more likely to occur again in the future. These rewards are more effective if they are desirable and achievable. One important aspect is that they need to be for behaviour which is both enjoyable and high status. For example, if you say to a child that they can have a pudding if they eat their vegetables that implies that the pudding is better and more enjoyable than the vegetables. The child will then think that if they have to eat vegetables to get a pudding then they must be nasty and will not enjoy them. This will mean that the child may eat them on this one occasion only, and certainly not without a pudding as a reward!

Focusing on... Tapper *et al.* (2003)

AIM

To increase the consumption of fruit and vegetables through the use of 'Food Dudes' in schools.

METHODOLOGY

Tapper *et al.* (2003) completed a variety of studies including a small-scale one in a nursery using peer modelling using a video featuring *Food Dudes* which were a group of four slightly older children who gain superpowers from eating vegetables. The *Food Dudes* do battle with the *Junk Punks* who threaten to take over the planet by destroying all the fruit and vegetables. Throughout the video, fruit and vegetables were eaten regularly. The rewards used in the studies included stickers, pens and erasers which were given when the children ate food. The results showed that modelling plus rewards was successful in increasing fruit and vegetable consumption and the changes persisted at a six-month follow up for the children in the home environment and 15 months later in the nursery.

However, Tapper *et al.* (2003) knew that to be successful, the intervention needed to be adapted to be used on a wider scale and with large groups of children.

Whole-school programme

Tapper *et al.* (2003) conducted a longitudinal whole-school intervention to be used across the whole primary age group (4–11). Children aged 4–11 in three primary schools in the UK were part of the programme.

School staff implemented the programme which consisted of:
- a *Food Dude* video with a total of six, six-minute adventure episodes
- a set of *Food Dude* rewards
- letters from the *Food Dudes* to praise and encourage the children as well as reminding them how they get the rewards
- a staff manual and briefing video
- educational support materials for teachers.

The main intervention lasted for 16 days where the children watched the videos and listened to the letters being read out. Rewards were given for children for either tasting the food or eating a whole portion.

After the intervention there was a maintenance phase where no videos were shown but rewards and letters were used intermittently.

Two more schools were tested, one of which received the *Food Dudes* programme and another which acted as control and simply received additional fruit and vegetables for the duration of the study.

Four months after the end of the intervention, the researchers assessed whether the interventions were still having a positive impact. Parents were asked to complete a questionnaire at the end of the study commenting on whether their child had enjoyed/ benefited from the intervention.

▶ RESULTS

The programme resulted in large, statistically significant increases during the week in both fruit and vegetable consumption across all three initial schools at both snack time and lunchtime. Although more fruit and vegetables were also eaten at weekends the results were not statistically significant perhaps due to the lack of rewards and cues. In the London schools, the experimental group showed significant increases in consumption compared to the control group and the increases persisted at a four-month follow up. Both parents and teachers also responded positively to the programme suggesting children enjoyed the programme but also were more enthusiastic when doing work with the *Food Dudes* theme; there was also improved attendance and increased confidence amongst children who were not normally big achievers.

▶ CONCLUSIONS

Behaviour modification programmes can be very successful at changing children's eating habits, both in the short and long term.

Evaluating Tapper *et al.* (2003)

A strength was the longitudinal design, whereby participants' eating habits were followed up four or six months after the intervention had ended. Findings showed that the intervention had a lasting effect. This is important as a normal experimental method would only see evidence of immediate impact which would not have shown any long-term benefits. In order to persuade the government to fund initiatives like this, it is essential that long-term benefits can be evidenced. However, it would be beneficial to revisit the children when they move to secondary school at 11+ to see if the intervention has lasting long-term benefits. It would also be interesting to follow the cohort into adulthood to investigate whether the healthy eating intervention was associated with future health benefits.

A weakness of the methodology was the use of questionnaires to gather data about the children's consumption of fruit and vegetables at home and school. As the parents were completing the questionnaire, they may have given socially desirable answers, stating that the children ate more fruit and vegetables than they actually did because they wanted to be seen favourably by the researchers. This will reduce the validity of the findings.

Tapper *et al.* (2003) were able to replicate their findings across three schools located across England and Wales. This suggests that the intervention might be successful within other schools across the UK. Further research is needed to see if similar interventions would work in different countries. However, the research by Wang *et al.* (2015) on middle school children in China suggests that similar interventions might be effective in other countries, increasing the generalisability of the findings of Tapper *et al.* (2003).

In response to the poor diet of many British school children, celebrity chef Jamie Oliver launched the Feed Me Better campaign to improve the quality of school dinners in England and to educate children about healthy eating. You may like to do some further research into this campaign. Can you think of any similar campaigns in your country or perhaps cultural norms are very different and children already eat a healthy diet?

▶ Figure 8.35

ISSUES AND DEBATES

Use of children in research

When researchers work with children they must design age and/or developmentally-appropriate materials. For example, Tapper *et al.* (2003) used the 'Food dude' videos and rewards that were likely to appeal to children in the age range that they were focusing on. This was especially important in this study as they were investigating an intervention that targeted children's eating habits and perception of vegetables. The materials were therefore particularly important as they could have a long term effect on the children's health, either positive or negative.

LEARNING LINK

At AS Level, you learned about Bandura (aggression), who used social learning theory to see whether children would imitate aggressive acts from adults. Similar to Tapper *et al.* (2003), Bandura investigated whether children would imitate a role model and whether imitative behaviour was increased if the model was similar to them in some way. There are a number of important differences in the way role models were used in Bandura *et al* (aggression) and the study by Tapper *et al.* Can you think of any? Who were the role models in the two studies, what were the behaviours that were being modelled?

STUDY TIP

Whenever you revise, ensure that you test yourself. That way you will know if the revision method you are using is working for you. You can do this by trying to teach the topic to someone else. For example, you could try and create a handout with a summary of the study and then go through it with a friend. You could then ask them some questions to test their understanding.

> ### TEST YOURSELF
>
> 1. Janine is a mother to two children, aged four and nine. She has never been able to get the two children to eat any fruit.
>   Explain one method that Janine could use to encourage her children to eat fruit. [4]
> 2. Identify two characteristics of a model which may make it more likely a child would imitate their eating behaviour. [2]
> 3. a. Describe what psychologists have discovered about health promotion in schools and the workplace. [6]
>   b. Evaluate what psychologists discovered about health promotion in schools and the workplace, including a discussion on longitudinal studies. [10]
> 4. Explain one ethical issue that needs to be taken into account when using children in research. [2]
> 5. Outline how operant conditioning could be used to increase health-related behaviours in children. [2]
> 6. Explain one strength and *one* weakness of using longitudinal studies to study health promotion in schools. [4]

Worksites and health and safety

KEY TERMS

token economies

lost-time injuries

medically treated compensation injuries

> ### Think!
>
> What are **token economies** and how might they be used in settings other than the workplace to promote healthy behaviour?

> ### Think!
>
> Imagine that you were organising an intervention to help people stop smoking, using token economies. What types of tokens do you think would be effective?

> ### Think!
>
> Fox *et al.* (1987) used token economies to reduce workplace accidents. What ethical issues should they have taken into consideration?

Figure 8.36 shows miners in a Navajo mine. Why do you think the token economy programme was so successful in the mines? Do you think that token economy programmes could be useful to promote other healthy behaviours?

▶ Figure 8.36

Health and safety in the workplace is an important area of focus for psychology, with 581,000 injuries occurring at work and 28.2 million workdays lost due to work-related ill health and workplace injury in the UK in 2019 and 2.8 million non-fatal workplace injuries and illnesses in 2019 in the USA.

Promoting safe work practices is essential to reducing workplace accidents. One industry that has an increased risk of accidents is the mining industry. For example, South Africa recorded 32 fatalities in the first six months of 2021, with a substantial number of other accidents recorded. Behaviour modification methods using the principles of operant conditioning, such as token economies, have been used to try and decrease accidents in workplaces, however the long-term effects of these interventions have rarely been studied.

Focus on... Fox *et al*. (1987)

> ### AIM
>
> To investigate whether token economies programmes are an effective way of reducing accidents and injuries in two mines in the USA, Shirley Basin and Navajo.

> ### METHODOLOGY
>
> Token Economy Programmes (TEPs) were introduced at two mines in response to serious health and safety concerns. Miners were divided into four hazard groups according to the amount of **lost-time injuries** (time off work for ill health due to a work injury) reported in the baseline period prior to the introduction of the TEP. Group 1 had the least hazardous jobs as they were mostly office-based. Group 4 had the most hazardous jobs, such as electricians and scraper operators, who use heavy machinery to move earth. Miners who avoided lost-time and/or **medically treated compensation injuries** (where the worker received financial compensation for an injury at work) were rewarded with monthly stamps. Stamps could be exchanged for a wide range of goods in a local store.
> - Miners in more hazardous jobs received more stamps for avoiding injuries than miners in less hazardous jobs.
> - Special payments were made to employees who made suggestions about how to prevent serious accidents or damage to equipment.
> - Miners who were injured lost monthly stamps depending on the number of days work missed, for example five or six days resulted in three months of missed stamps.

> ### RESULTS
>
> Both mines showed substantial decreases in the number of days lost during the first five years of the token economy programme. The cost of injuries at Shirley Basin decreased from $294,000 per year on average to an average of $29,000 per year, which is a 90 per cent decrease. The Navajo mine showed a similar decrease. Compared to the cost of the Token Economy Programme which averaged at around $12,000, this still represented a huge saving.
>
> No deaths or permanent disabilities occurred at the Navajo mine following the introduction of the programme. The number of days lost during 10 years of the programme was around a quarter of the national mining average at Shirley Mine and one-twelfth at Navajo mine.

> ### CONCLUSIONS
>
> Token economies are a cost-effective way of significantly reducing work-related injuries in mining leading to long-lasting changes in working practices.

Evaluating Fox *et al.* (1987)

One strength of the Fox *et al.* study is that it uses a **longitudinal research** methodology over a number of years. For example, at one mine the token economy programme ran for twelve years. This is important as it allows researchers to track changes over time, to gather a large amount of data and also to see whether the interventions implemented are effective in the long term.

One weakness of the study is that the sample may not be representative of the wider population, limiting the study's **generalisability**. For example, the two companies were in the USA and were both mining companies. The effectiveness of reward systems may only be apparent in certain countries and also there may be something about the mining community which may make them more receptive to this type of behavioural intervention (the element of risk and danger). Therefore, the results of the study may not generalise to other countries and organisations.

Finally, there may be an issue with the validity of the study. For example, the incentive of a reward may have stopped employees reporting incidents and therefore the number of accidents may not have decreased, only the reporting of them. However, a serious accident is not easily hidden so this may not be a real issue. However, a potentially bigger issue was the fact that accidents were decreasing at one mine even prior to the start of the study so there may have been sustained improvements even without the intervention, decreasing the validity of the study's findings.

> ## ISSUES AND DEBATES

Applications to everyday life

In addition, the study has important applications to real life. Time off work for accidents is a real issue for organisations in terms of employee morale and also in terms of loss of money and of work time. Therefore, if interventions such as token economy can be used effectively within a workplace to decrease accidents there is less chance of negative consequences for the employee and the cost of the programme will be less than the benefits, making the study useful.

> ## LEARNING LINK

At AS Level, you studied the learning approach which included the principles of operant conditioning. In the study by Fagen *et al.* reinforcement was used to train elephants to perform a trunk wash to test them for tuberculosis, a form of health promotion in animals. Token economies are based on the same principles. On page 102 you learned about primary and **secondary reinforcers**. Can you think what these were for the miners at Shirley Basin and Navajo? Can you think of any differences between the way that reinforcement was provided to the elephants and the miners? Tip: Think about when the reinforcers were provided in relation to the behaviours that were being targeted.

STUDY TIP

Creating online quizzes is a great way to test your learning. You could team up with some of your classmates or peers online and create quizzes for each other. Regular rehearsal of the material is important. You will need to be able to match the studies that you have learned to the correct concepts and theories that they support and retrieve the details readily when writing essays.

> ## TEST YOURSELF

1   Amalia runs a construction company and the number of accidents on her building sites has been steadily increasing over the last five years. She wants to set up a token economy programme to reduce the number of accidents.
    With reference to previous research, explain how Amalia could set up a token economy programme at her work site. [4]
2   Outline the findings of one study focusing on health and safety at worksites. [2]
3   a   Describe what psychologists have discovered about health promotion in schools and worksites. [6]
    b   Evaluate what psychologists have discovered about health promotion in schools and worksites. [6]

4 Outline one advantage and one disadvantage of the use of longitudinal studies in research into health and safety in the workplace. [4]

5 Explain one reason why it might not be useful to generalise findings from research into health and safety on worksites to other industries or types of job. Use an example to explain your answer.

6 One way to collect both qualitative and quantitative data about health and safety at worksites is to conduct interviews.

    a Suggest one open and one closed question that could be asked to workers to find out about health and safety at their workplace.

    b Explain one way that the interviewer could ensure that the data that they collect from the workers is valid.

8.5.3 Individual factors in changing health beliefs

KEY TERM

unrealistic optimism

METHODOLOGY

generalisations from findings

Think!

Do you think that optimism is always unrealistic?

Think!

Do you ever compare yourself to others and think that negative things will be more likely to happen to them?

Think!

Why might unrealistic optimism be problematic in terms of health?

Unrealistic optimism suggests that we think negative things are less likely to happen to us than other people. Do you think it is human nature to perceive ourselves as being less likely to have negative things happen to us than other people?

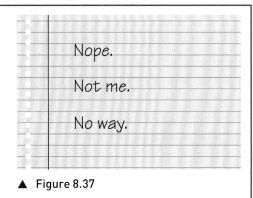

Nope.

Not me.

No way.

▲ Figure 8.37

Unrealistic optimism

Unrealistic optimism refers to the cognitive belief that negative events are less likely to happen to you than other people and positive events are more likely to happen to you. People can feel invulnerable to disease and believe that it is 'something that happens to other people' and this may lead them to disregard health advice. Unrealistic optimism may lead to more risky behaviour. For example, people with a high clinical risk of getting Covid-19 severely did not appear to be more cautious in their behaviour than those people who were at lower risk, suggesting they may have been experiencing unrealistic optimism (Gassen *et al.*, 2021). However, Gassen *et al.* (2021) also suggest that unrealistic optimism can have health benefits by reducing worry which can increase mental wellbeing.

Unrealistic optimism may be an issue in terms of individuals paying attention to and following healthcare advice if they do not perceive themselves at risk of the healthcare problem and view it instead as happening to a 'stereotypical person'.

Focus on... Weinstein (1980)

▶ AIM

To investigate whether people believe that negative events are more or less likely to happen to them than other people. Also, to investigate whether the more people feel like they have control over a negative event, the more likely they will be to think that they have a below average chance of it happening to them.

▶ METHODOLOGY

Comparative rating group

In Study 1, a diverse group of American college students estimated how much their own chances of experiencing particular life events were different to the chances of their classmates. 42 life events were used, 18 positive, (for example, owning your own home) and 24 negative (for example, being fired from a job).

The 42 life events were then randomly divided between two rating forms. The different versions of the rating form (each listing 21 events) were handed to alternate students.

Comparative rating forms

Instructions on the form said *'Compared to other students ... same sex as you .... what do you think are the chances that the following events will happen to you?'* (Ratings ranged from: much less than average to much more than average). Beneath the description of each event were the following choices: 100% less (no chance), 80% less, 70% less and so on – through to 90% more than 100% more.

Event characteristics group

The same life events were rated by 120 female students on an introductory psychology course (event rating group); they were instructed to estimate *'the percentage probability of students at the university to whom each event would occur'*.

Events were also rated for:
● controllability (1 = there is nothing one can do that will change the likelihood that the event will take place, to 5 = completely controllable)
● desirability (1 = extremely undesirable, 5 = extremely desirable)
● personal experience (1 = has not happened to anyone I know, 2 = has happened to acquaintances, 3 = has happened to friends or close acquaintances, 4 = has happened to me once, 5 = has happened to me more than once).

▶ RESULTS

Participants' scores were in the direction predicted on 37 of the 42 events (more likely to happen to them for the positive events or less likely for the negative events). However, the amount of unrealistic optimism varied greatly between the different individual events. In a number of cases, participants did not rate themselves as different from others with regard to the probability of the event. For example, participants did not rate themselves as being significantly more likely to be *'not ill all winter'*, nor did they rate themselves as being significantly less likely to be the *'victim of burglary'*.

There was a significant positive correlation between the positive events and the extent to which participants perceived them as being likely to happen to them. There was also a positive correlation between the positive events and how desirable the participants viewed the event.

Negative events were significantly correlated with how much control the participants perceived that they had over the events and their personal experience of the event. Where events were believed to be controllable, the participants had a stereotypical view of the type of person to whom this type of event would likely occur. Compared to these stereotypical people, participants deemed themselves at less than average risk.

> **CONCLUSIONS**
> ....

For both positive and negative events, unrealistic optimism appears when the event is perceived as controllable and people have some degree of emotional investment or commitment in the outcome of the event. Desirability has no significant effect on unrealistic optimism for negative events, even for life-threatening events.

Evaluating Weinstein (1980)

> **ISSUES AND DEBATES**
> ....

Idiographic versus nomothetic

One strength of the study by Weinstein (1980) is that it used the nomothetic approach. Weinstein acknowledges that an idiographic approach would not be effective in studying unrealistic optimism because it would be difficult to assess whether an individual's views were actually unrealistic. However, by investigating the extent to which groups of people underestimate their chance of negative events/over-estimate the chance of positive events he was able to demonstrate that optimism bias is a genuine systematic error and generalise his findings to the wider population.

Cultural differences

A weakness was that Weinstein only sampled students from one American university. These participants may have responded differently to people who were older and may have had a more realistic outlook. Furthermore, the findings may only be true of young adults from individualistic cultures who see themselves as in greater control of events in their lives compared with people from collectivistic cultures who tend to perceive situational factors as having a greater impact. This is important as it means that the findings regarding personal vulnerability to certain health issues may not generalise to people outside of this limited target population.

Evaluating unrealistic optimism

A strength of unrealistic optimism is that it can reduce worry and stress. This is important in situations such as the Covid-19 pandemic as it could help increase wellbeing and mental health at a very difficult time, allowing people to cope better.

A weakness of studying and measuring unrealistic optimism is that there is a conflict of opinion regarding whether the unrealistic optimism reflects rational belief or is simply an expression of people's desires and hopes for positive outcomes in their lives (Jefferson *et al.*, 2017). There is also the question of how to measure to what extent these beliefs (if they are beliefs) are false or irrational. This means that the results from research may lack validity.

> **LEARNING LINK**
> ....

Unrealistic optimism is a thinking bias that may not apply to people universally (there may be cultural differences). In the social approach, at AS Level, we introduced the idea that social behaviour may be affected by cultural norms, for example people may stand closer or further away from one another or be more likely to obey or conform to the behaviour of others. Cultural differences can also apply to the way people think. Research suggests that people from individualistic cultures such as Canada are more likely to show unrealistic optimism through underestimating negative life events, for example, than people from collectivistic cultures such as Japan (Heine and Lehman, 1995). Do you think people from collectivistic cultures are likely to be any healthier as a consequence?

STUDY TIP
One excellent way to remember the details of a study is to think how you might replicate it. Could you make a list of 18 positive and 24 negative life events that might affect people of your age group? Why not write them on slips of papers, one colour for positive and another for negative? Put them into two piles and randomly select 9 positive and 12 negative to create a list of 21 items. Put them all in a pile together and randomly select them one by one to create a randomised order. Do the same with the remaining items to create a second 21-item list. Now you have had a go at creating the materials, can you write out a set of standardised instructions and create a consent form for this study?

> **TEST YOURSELF**

1 Wilfredo and Hiram are watching a documentary about men's health featuring five men each with a different chronic health problem. Wilfredo and Hiram discuss the documentary afterwards and agree that although they feel sorry for the men, they just cannot see how these health problems would ever affect them personally.

   With reference to one research study, explain Wilfredo and Hiram beliefs about the health problems featured in the documentary. [2]

2 Explain why unrealistic optimism might lead people to disregard health advice. [2]

3 a Describe what psychologists have discovered about the role of individual factors (such as unrealistic optimism) in changing health beliefs. [6]

   b Evaluate what psychologists have discovered about the role of individual factors (such as unrealistic optimism) in changing health beliefs. [10]

4 Explain one advantage and one disadvantage of using students to study unrealistic optimism. [4]

5 Explain how Weinstein operationalised unrealistic optimism in his research into reasons for disregarding positive health advice. [2]

6 Explain one strength and one weakness of using a laboratory experiment to measure unrealistic optimism. [4]

KEY TERMS

positive psychology

pleasant life

good life

meaningful life

signature character strengths

METHODOLOGY

psychometrics

generalisations from findings

Positive psychology

Think!

What is the main basic assumption of **positive psychology**?

Think!

What daily activities help you to live a **pleasant life**? What do you believe your **signature character strengths** are that help you to live a **good life**? Do you feel that you are living a **meaningful life**?

Think!

The Values in Action (VIA) questionnaire measures signature character strengths using a series of self-reported items. Not everyone is a good judge of their own character as they may lack the necessary self-awareness. How could the validity of the Values in Action (VIA) questionnaire be improved?

By using our signature strengths we can make our lives more meaningful. Take an online version of the Values in Action (VIA) questionnaire and discuss how you could use your signature strengths to increase your happiness.

▶ Figure 8.38

Positive psychology is a relatively new approach in psychology. It was started by Martin Seligman in the 1990s and unlike other areas of psychology that focus on mental ill health, positive psychology looks at how humans in everyday life can flourish, succeed and increase their happiness and wellbeing.

Although many of the approaches in psychology are deterministic, positive psychology supports the idea of free will. According to positive psychology we can take control of our lives and do things that will improve our happiness.

Pleasant life, good life and meaningful life

One of the assumptions of the positive approach is that we can develop our strengths and virtues and use them to lead happy lives. This is broken down into three parts (see Table 8.12).

▼ Table 8.12 Seligman's three components of a happy life

Happy life components	Focuses on positive...	Description	Example
The pleasant life	Emotions	We have positive emotions and take satisfaction from daily things.	Enjoying a good book or spending time with friends.
The good life	Traits	We understand our signature strengths, the positive personality traits that are an essential part of who we are. Finding out what these are (such as humour, creativity and bravery) and using them to enhance our lives can help us lead a good life.	A person whose signature strength is creativity could examine the creative aspects their job has and focus their skills there.
The meaningful life	Institutions, e.g. democracy, family and free inquiry	This transcends making life better just for ourselves. Positive psychology suggests that we will be happiest if we use our **signature strengths** for a greater purpose, to help make other people's lives happier too. Seligman suggests that part of this includes developing positive connections with others. Positive institutions support the development of our positive traits and in turn positive emotions.	Volunteering with a charity or campaigning to help people in need.

Focus on... Seligman (2004)

▶ POSITIVE PSYCHOLOGY

The article by Martin Seligman is not a research study but an overview of a seminar course that he taught his undergraduate students at the University of Pennsylvania, in the USA. This four-week course introduced students to positive psychology and included weekly 'real-world' homework assignments. The students reviewed scientific literature examining 'the past' where they focused on contentment and satisfaction, 'the present' focusing on joy, comfort and pleasure and 'the future' on optimism, hope, trust and faith.

The students also learned about depressive realism, where unhappy people may be more accurate than happy people and the effect of major life changes on happiness, for example lottery winners who return to their pre-existing state of happiness within a year because the capacity for pleasure is 50 per cent inherited so it is quite hard to change (Brickman *et al.*, 1978).

Within the seminar, students also practised increasing their own optimism, as research shows that this increases productivity, improves physical health and lowers vulnerability to depression.

▶ HOMEWORK TASKS

Gratitude night

Research has shown that by focusing on what we are grateful for, we can increase our happiness. Seligman organised a 'Gratitude night' for his students and their families and other close people who have been important in his students' lives. The students then read testimonials to their guests, describing why and how they have been important in their lives and thanking them for everything that they have done for them.

Pleasurable day

The students learn the skills of 'savouring' which is sharing experiences with other people, taking mental photographs of the experience and collecting physical mementoes like actual photos or a ticket from a play at the theatre. They also learn how to practise mindfulness by being in the moment, slowing down and seeing things from a different perspective (see pages 29–43). Their homework is to plan and carry out a 'pleasurable day', using the skills that they have learnt.

Signature strengths

Seligman's students first identify their signature strengths by taking the Values in Action (VIA) questionnaire. This self-report scale identifies the respondent's top five strengths out of a total of 24. These strengths include optimism, kindness, love of learning, fairness and spirituality.

Students then had to choose a boring task that they needed to do and find a way of using their signature strengths to complete it. One student used his strengths of curiosity and love of learning to turn a data entry task into something much more fulfilling by looking for patterns and themes within the data.

▶ THE MEANINGFUL LIFE

The final part of the course involved moving on to the meaningful life, where again the students participated in a number of tasks:
» Creating a family tree of strengths and virtues by having their family take the VIA test and interviewing their parents about relatives who had died.
» Mentoring a younger student who was facing similar issues that they themselves had overcome.
» Writing their positive vision for the future of humankind and what their role will be in it.
» Writing their own obituary from the viewpoint of their future grandchildren.

Evaluating Seligman (2004)

A strength of positive psychology is that there is a great deal of research that supports its effectiveness in improving wellbeing. For example, Shoshani and Steinmetz (2014) found that a school-based intervention programme including exercises such as writing gratitude letters and goal setting increases self-esteem and optimism and reduces mental health symptoms in 11–15-year-olds. This is important because it demonstrates that the principles of positive psychology can be applied in real world settings and may reduce the number of children from needing to access mental health services in the future.

A further strength is that Seligman's seminar programme has many practical applications. His students were able to actively practise what they were learning in the classroom to see for themselves if it had a positive effect on their wellbeing. The programme can be generalised to other universities and schools so that students are not just learning theoretically about positive psychology but are also able to put it into practice as well.

A weakness of using a self-report scale such as the Values in Action (VIA) questionnaire as a measure of signature strengths is that people may give socially desirable answers, choosing strengths that make them look good rather than what they actually feel are their strengths. This is a weakness as it decreases the validity of the data and means people may focus their attention on tasks that are less beneficial for them.

Another weakness of positive psychology is the assumption that everyone will be happier if they think more positively. However, research has found that unpleasant thoughts can be just as important as positive ones. Rodriguez (2013) states that ignoring negative thoughts can have unwanted effects on our wellbeing and mental health as it does not allow us to accurately evaluate our experiences. Negative emotions can alert us to a problem that needs dealing with such as a bad relationship or a problem at work. Therefore, taking a nomothetic approach may not be appropriate.

> ## LEARNING LINK
>
> One of the activities that Seligman describes as a way of cultivating a meaningful life was to create a family tree of strengths and virtues by asking family members to complete the VIA questionnaire and interviewing their parents about relatives who had died. Think about your work on Bandura *et al.* (aggression) and you may wonder whether family members are likely to share similar signature strengths and virtues? Do you think you share similar strengths to those of your immediate family?

> ## TEST YOURSELF
>
> 1 Claudia has recently been diagnosed with a long term serious health problem. Her friend Lamara tells her about a book she has been reading about positive psychology and suggests it could help Claudia to feel better about her diagnosis. Explain two ways that positive psychology could help Claudia to feel better about her diagnosis. [4]
> 2 Describe what is meant by the terms 'pleasant life' and 'meaningful life'. [4]
> 3 a Describe what psychologists have discovered about individual factors in changing health beliefs. [6]
>   b Evaluate what psychologists have discovered about individual factors in changing health beliefs. [10]
> 4 a Explain what is meant by nomothetic. [2]
>   b Suggest one way in which positive psychology could be seen as taking a nomothetic approach and one way that it could be seen as taking an idiographic approach. [4]
> 5 Ariel works with young people at an after-school youth club. He wants to organise a positive psychology night. Suggest two activities that Ariel could organise for his positive psychology night to increase the young people's wellbeing. [4]
> 6 Explain one way that Ariel could collect some data to investigate whether the young people at his club had benefited from the positive psychology activities at the youth club.

Key study: Using positive psychology in schools to improve mental health – Shoshani and Steinmetz (2014)

KEY TERMS

intervention

wait list control group

METHODOLOGY

psychometrics

generalisations from findings

> **Think!**
> Why did the researchers use a **wait list control group** rather than just a control group?

> **Think!**
> The intervention in this study involved writing letters of gratitude to people who had affected the students' lives in a positive way. If you had to write one of these letters every week for one month, which four people would you choose and why?

Think!

The intervention group and the control group in Shoshani and Steinmetz (2014) were from two different schools. Why might this be a disadvantage of the study? Why do you think it could also be an advantage? There are several points that can be made on both sides; how many can you think of? If you were to repeat the study, would you use two different schools or the same school? Why?

Do you think a similar intervention would work in your school? Can you think of anything that could be done to increase the efficacy of the intervention and ensure that as many students participate as possible, including those who are likely to benefit the most?

▲ Figure 8.39

Introducing Anat Shoshani and Sarit Steinmetz

Professor Anat Shoshani is Assistant professor in the Baruch Ivcher School of Psychology and academic director of the Maytiv Center for Research and Practice in Positive Psychology at IDC. She has developed and overseen positive psychology interventions for both pre-schools and schools. One of her main research focuses is resilience of at-risk children and designing coping mechanisms for children who are exposed to war and terrorism.

▶ CONTEXT

Positive psychology is a relatively new area of psychology that was first introduced in 1998, when Martin Seligman was made President of the American Psychological Association and it became the focus of his term of presidency. Positive psychology has many applications to everyday life, such as in the workplace, in the military and also in schools. There have been many studies looking at the impact of positive psychology interventions in schools, such as using gratitude diaries (Emmons and McCullough, 2003) and focusing on signature strengths (Seligman *et al.*, 2009).

The findings have been varied with some reducing symptoms of anxiety and depression and others increasing enjoyment of school or raising attainment. However, many of the studies only look at the short-term immediate effects of the interventions.

▶ AIMS

To investigate whether participants in the positive psychology intervention group had better mental health outcomes (such as increased self-efficacy, optimism and life satisfaction and lower levels of psychological distress and mental health symptoms) throughout middle school compared with a control group. Secondly, the study aimed to reveal whether the efficacy of the **intervention** was moderated by any specific socio-demographic factors, including gender.

METHODOLOGY

The study was a longitudinal field experiment that took place over two school years. The experiment had a mixed design as it compared an intervention group and a wait list control group (independent measures) and took measures before and after the intervention period (repeated measures).

Sample

The researchers recruited 1038 adolescents in the seventh to ninth grades (aged 11.8–14.7 at the start of the study) from two large middle schools in the centre of Israel. 537 students all from one school participated in the positive psychology intervention group and 501 students from another school were in the wait list control group.

PROCEDURE

Materials

A wide range of self-report questionnaires were used to gather quantitative data using rating scales.

- *Brief symptoms inventory*; To identify clinically relevant psychological symptoms in adolescents such as depression, phobic-anxiety, anxiety, hostility using four-point Likert scales.
- *The Rosenberg self-esteem scale*: To evaluate self-worth using four-point Likert scales.
- *The General Self-Efficacy scale*: To assess how people cope with daily hassles and life events using four-point Likert scale.
- *Satisfaction with life scale*: To assess an overall satisfaction with life, for example '*In most ways my life is close to ideal*' (1 = strongly disagree, 7 = strongly agree) using a seven-point Likert scale.
- *The Life Orientation Test-Revised*: To assess how optimistic or pessimistic a person is using a five-point Likert scales.
- *Socio-demographic measures*: Questionnaire to gather background information on the students, including age, gender, country of birth and socioeconomic status.

Intervention group

The schoolteachers were trained in group dynamics and positive psychology by clinical psychologists, during 15, two-hour sessions every two weeks across the school year. A teachers' textbook including lesson plans and activities was also created to ensure that all teachers were delivering the lesson in the same way.

The teachers then conducted parallel sessions with their students. The school psychologist and counsellors randomly checked that the student sessions were being run appropriately. The classroom programme included activities, discussions, reading poems and stories and watching video clips. An important component of the programme was **gratitude** which refers to our awareness and appreciation of the positive aspects of our lives, past, present and future for which we are thankful. In this study, the intervention group discussed five or more things for which they were grateful each week and also wrote gratitude letters to people who had a positive impact on their lives.

Wait list control group

In the wait list control group, the teachers continued with their normal social science lessons, focusing on issues relating to adolescence.

▶ RESULTS

Both the intervention and the wait list control group showed slightly higher levels of psychological symptoms at the start of the study compared to Israeli normative data.

Living below the poverty level and being in a single parent household were both risk factors that were found to be positively related to participants' mental health scores prior to the intervention with participants showing higher levels of general distress, depression and anxiety.

Males also showed lower scores on the *General Efficacy Scale* and lower depressive symptoms than females at the start of the study and increased initial anxiety levels compared to females.

Participants in the intervention group showed significant decreases in psychological distress between the beginning and the end of the study (mean change = −0.22) and symptoms of depression (mean change = −0.10), whereas participants in the wait control demonstrated increased mental health symptoms.

Participants in the intervention group also showed significant increases over time for optimism, compared to the control group.

▶ CONCLUSIONS

The intervention resulted in increases in mental wellbeing and decreases in anxiety and interpersonal sensitivity, general distress, and depression. Those participants in the waiting control group showed an increase in general distress and depression symptoms. The transition in middle school has 'profound effects' on mental health but this can be counteracted by introducing positive psychology interventions. The intervention was found to be effective for both low and high-risk students.

 ## Methodological strengths and weaknesses

A strength of the study is that it used a longitudinal design. Although the positive psychology intervention only ran for one year, the students were followed up over a two-year period with measures being taken before and after the intervention in the academic year 2010–2011, but also twice during the following academic year 2011–2012. This allowed the researchers to monitor the longer-term effects of the intervention. This is a strength as evidence to support the long-lasting effects on mental health may mean other schools are motivated to integrate the intervention into their students' timetables.

A further strength was the use of a wait list control group. This allowed the researchers to determine the extent to which children's mental health changes over the time in the absence of any specific intervention. Without a control group, it would not be possible to know whether the intervention group's improved wellbeing was dependent on the intervention or natural fluctuation over time. Therefore, the inclusion of a control group was central to the validity of the study and the conclusion that improved well-being resulted from the positive psychology intervention.

A weakness is that the students completed the same self-report questionnaires at four points across two years. The students in the intervention group may have recognised that these questionnaires were a measure of the success of the programme and provided the answers that they believed their teachers hoped for. This is important as it could mean that the results were a product of demand characteristics thus weakening their validity, meaning the intervention may appear to be more effective than it actually was.

Another weakness of the study was a lack of **generalisability.** Only two Israeli middle schools were involved in the project and participants were all aged between 11 and 15 at the beginning of the study. It is possible that the intervention was more successful with this age group and for children in these two specific schools due to the high level of motivation of the teachers and support provided by Shoshani and Steinmetz, suggesting that positive psychology interventions may be less effective with older teenagers or primary school aged children.

Ethics

One issue with this study is that the wait list control group may not have been able to benefit from the positive psychology intervention, meaning that they may have been at risk of increased mental health symptoms in comparison with the intervention group. By the time the intervention was introduced for the students at the control group school some of them would have moved on to high school. This was an issue because the psychologists needed a control group to improve validity of the study, but it did mean that the programme was withheld from some students even though the psychologists knew it might be beneficial.

This said, the control group increased the credibility of the findings meaning other schools may be more likely to adopt the programme in future. The future benefits to society over the long term therefore arguably outweigh the cost of withholding the start of the intervention from the control school.

> ## ISSUES AND DEBATES
>
> ### Use of children in psychological research
>
> Shoshani and Steinmetz (2014) used children in their research. It is very important when using children as participants that they are allowed to consent and withdraw from the research, as long as they have the cognitive capability to do so. Parental consent must also be sought. In Shoshani and Steinmetz's study, they sent informed parental consent forms and student 'assent' forms. This meant that both the parents and children knew what they would be undertaking.

> ## ISSUES AND DEBATES
>
> ### Applications to everyday life
>
> This study has a direct application to everyday life as it took place in schools. It could help students who struggle with transitions between schools and other factors that go alongside the start of adolescence. It could also help reduce absenteeism from school due to anxiety. By using an intervention that is proactive rather than reactive (improving wellbeing before it becomes an issue), it could reduce the pressure on support services such as therapy for children who are struggling with their mental health. Therefore, interventions that can improve wellbeing and have a long-term benefit are very useful.

> ## ISSUES AND DEBATES
>
> ### Individual versus situational explanations
>
> Positive psychology tends to focus on situational explanations of happiness such as factors like having strong social networks or faith can increase our happiness (Myers and Diener, 1995). However, it tends to ignore individual explanations such as personality and how for some people, focusing on negative aspects and acknowledging them is important for them to be able to adjust their behaviour. For example people who have chronic illnesses may need to be able to focus on the negative aspects of their illness and how they impact on them as individuals in order to be able come to terms with how it is affecting them and adjust their coping behaviours.

> ## LEARNING LINK
>
> Hölzel et al.'s (mindfulness and brain scans) research used a longitudinal design. How does their research differ from Shoshani and Steinmetz (2014)?

STUDY TIP

One way to learn the Shoshani and Steinmetz study would be to create a mind map. If you are unsure how to create an effective mind map, there are many videos on online to show you how.

TEST YOURSELF

1 Mr Giannone is Deputy Head of Sunshine High, a large inner city school. He wants to introduce a weekly positive psychology programme that will be delivered by the teachers.

 Explain two ways that Mr Giannone could help the teachers to prepare for delivering the positive psychology programme at the school. [4]

2 Outline two findings from the study by Shoshani and Steinmetz (2014). [4]

3 a Describe the study by Shoshani and Steinmetz (2014) on using positive psychology in schools to improve mental health. [6]

 b Evaluate the study by Shoshani and Steinmetz (2014), including a discussion about psychometrics. [10]

4 Explain one issue relating to the use of children in research into wellbeing. [2]

5 Describe one of the self-report questionnaires used by Shoshani and Steinmetz (2014). [2]

6 Explain one strength of using a longitudinal design to investigate wellbeing. [2]

9 Organisational Psychology

Learning outcomes

In this chapter, we will discuss:
- the social, physical and psychological environments that may affect individual and group behaviour in the workplace.

There are five areas that will be studied, with each area explaining a key study (given in brackets) as well as a number of supporting studies.

The five areas are:
1 motivation at work (Landry *et al.*, 2019)
2 leadership and management (Cuadrado *et al.*, 2008)
3 group behaviour in organisations (Claypoole and Szalma, 2019)
4 organisational work conditions (Swat, 1997)
5 job satisfaction (Giacolone and Rosenfeld, 1987).

▲ Figure 9.1 Sunrise in Botwana, home of Dr Christianah Oyetunji, who investigates workplace psychology in schools

Where there are people, there is Psychology!

Psychology is everywhere. These women are carrying firewood in beautiful Botswana, a country in Southern Africa. One of the fastest growing economies in the world, Botswana is also the home to Christianah Oyetunji who discovered that there are cultural differences in the followership styles of lecturers in Botswana (Oyetunji 2013, page 683).

This chapter contains a number of compulsory key studies from many countries including the USA (Landry *et al.*, 2019), Spain (Cuadrado *et al.*, 2008) and Poland (Swat, 1997), but there are a number of other pieces of research included within the chapter which will support your understanding of, and allow you to evaluate, the concepts, theories and models of organisational psychology. For example, Saeednia (2011) looked at whether Maslow's hierarchy of needs (see page 640) can be measured in children through a basic needs satisfaction scale and Earley (1993) studied managers in Israel, China and the USA to see whether culture had an effect on an individual's performance in a group.

9.0 Introducing Organisational Psychology

What is Organisational Psychology?

Sometimes called 'occupational' psychology, organisational psychology is quite simply the application of psychological theories and concepts to organisations and workplaces. It is the study of how people think and behave at work, both as an individual or as part of a group. Although not as big or well known as other fields in psychology such as clinical and health, the application of psychological knowledge to the workplace is a fast-growing field, with its ultimate aim being to improve the aspects of the workplaces for both employees and the employers. Researchers aim to find ways to help people find a better work-life balance, to feel more satisfied at work and to feel safe at work. It also helps to find solutions when things do go wrong. Research has looked at issues of health and safety at work and how errors occur; whether they are accidental, or deliberate in the form of sabotage. Organisational psychologists also aim to reduce all forms of discrimination within the workforce.

Organisational psychology is not only about improving the life of the employee, but also about improving the organisation itself. It helps employers pick a person who is best for a job role and builds a better workplace culture by understanding individual and group behaviour. Organisational psychology also tries to reduce the number of people leaving and improve job retention through educating employers about what helps to motivate employees and how to increase job satisfaction.

One area that is of great importance to researchers in organisational psychology is the idea of cultural differences. Many theories within organisational psychology are based upon theories and concepts constructed in Western societies such as the USA; these have then been applied globally. Psychologists discuss the term 'cultural bias', which is where we tend to interpret theories based upon the values and beliefs of the culture we belong to. For example, can we really apply a theory about leadership which has been constructed in the USA to more collectivist cultures such as Japan or China? For this reason, many psychologists are completing research where the participants are taken from a number of different cultures, with the results from each cultural group then being compared in order to see whether cultural differences have occurred.

Careers in Organisational Psychology

If you would like to take your studies of Psychology beyond A Level, Organisational Psychology is one of the fastest-growing areas. The path begins by completing a Bachelor's degree in psychology. You will then go on to complete a Master's degree in occupational/organisational psychology and then complete two years' supervised practice. Completion of the above will allow you to use the title occupational/ organisational psychologist.

Organisational psychologists work in a wide variety of different sectors. You may work in industry with businesses of all different sizes, in the public and private sector or within the government or public services. The civil service is one the biggest employers of organisational psychologists. The prison service, the Home Office and the Ministry of Defence all employ organisational psychologists.

For further information visit: **https://careers.bps.org.uk/area/occupational**.

KEY TERMS

hierarchy of needs
self-actualisation
esteem needs
belongingness
safety needs
physiological needs
deficiency needs
growth needs
collectivist
individualistic

METHODOLOGY

validity

9.1 Motivation at work
9.1.1 Need theories
Maslow's hierarchy of needs

> **Think!**
>
> What are the four needs that must be met before an individual can reach self-actualisation? What does the term **self-actualisation** actually mean?

> **Think!**
>
> You are a manager at a big company. You are worried about your employees as they do not seem to be very motivated. You hear some employees talking about their worries about money and how they do not feel very safe at work. As an employer, how could you use what you have learned about Maslow's hierarchy of needs to ensure that motivation improves and employees feel happier in their work?

> **Think!**
>
> You learned about determinism versus free will at AS Level. Have a look at Maslow's **hierarchy of needs** and think about which needs rely on others to achieve them (are determined by others) and which can be achieved through free will. Do you notice any pattern?

Figure 9.2 shows the five levels of Maslow's hierarchy of needs. For each level of need there are a number of items that an individual has to have for that need to be met. Which needs do you feel are most important to you? Are there any that you do not feel you would need to be met before moving on to the next level of the hierarchy?

Maslow's hierarchy of needs

 Figure 9.2

Abraham Maslow (1943) proposed a motivational theory which comprises five basic needs, often shown as a hierarchy within a pyramid (see Figure 9.2). From the bottom upwards, these needs are:

1 **Physiological needs**: These are basic survival needs such as food, air, warmth and sleep. Without these needs being met a person cannot function properly.
2 **Safety needs**: This is the need for a safe and secure environment, including financial security and a safe and stable home.
3 Love and **belongingness** needs: This is the need to feel as though you belong, whether this is in society, at home or at work. This could include the need for friendships and intimate relationships, as well as the feeling of being part of a group.
4 **Esteem needs**: This is the need to feel respected; the feelings of having accomplished something. This can be divided into esteem for yourself, such as a feeling of achievement and mastery over a task and respect and recognition from others, such as increased status and prestige.
5 Self-actualisation needs: This is when your potential is fulfilled and you have accomplished everything you wanted to.

Maslow believed that we need to fully satisfy the most basic needs at the bottom of the hierarchy before moving up to the next stage. He saw the first four levels as **deficiency needs**; these are needs where we are motivated to obtain something we do not have. The longer these needs are unmet, the stronger the motivation is. The final level, self-actualisation, is a **growth need**. Here the motivation turns from trying to obtain something that is lacking, to trying to grow as a person. As you fulfil growth needs, the motivation increases to do even better.

Maslow believed that everyone has the potential to reach self-actualisation but in reality, experiences in life such as losing your job, or a divorce often meant that an individual may move back down the hierarchy at any time and may never reach the top.

Application to the workplace

An employee would first focus on the most basic needs. In the workplace, this could mean trying to satisfy:

» Physiological needs such as enough wages to buy food and be able to afford to keep warm.
» Safety needs such as having a pension and having a safe workplace environment.

If these basic needs are *not* met, then the employee may be demotivated and base their job decisions on the threats to survival that they face and are more likely to leave.

If these basic needs *are* met, then love and belongingness will become more important. This could include:

» Feeling accepted as an important part of the organisation and having some social interaction. The importance of this need may depend on personality as some people prefer not to interact with others.

Once this need is met then the higher needs of esteem and self-actualisation are next.

» Esteem needs are about feeling respected and recognised in the workplace. This could include a better job title, promotion at work, being involved in decision making or being able to do courses that mean that they learn new skills that they can use in the workplace.
» Self-actualisation needs allow the employee to grow and challenge themselves on a regular basis, but also means that a worker has greater autonomy and freedom from supervision.

If all these needs are met, then workers will be happy and secure within their workplace and have high levels of motivation.

Evaluating Maslow's needs theory

Maslow's theory may not be **valid** as he assumes that lower needs must be met before you can move on to higher level needs. However, this claim can be disputed as there are many people who live in poverty and still show love and belongingness. For example, many famous people such as Mother Teresa, lived in poverty all their life but still arguably achieved self-actualisation.

ISSUES AND DEBATES

Cultural differences

Maslow's theory does not take into account cultural differences. For example, Maslow assumes that his definition of self-actualisation is the same in all cultures. However, this may not be the case as **collectivist cultures** such as China may have a different meaning for self-actualisation than **individualistic cultures** such as the USA

Application to everyday life

One strength of Maslow's theory is that it can be applied to everyday life. Maslow's theory has made a large contribution to organisational psychology and increasing motivation in the workplace. Therefore, employers can use the theory to ensure that workers feel safe and have a stable wage, meaning that they will feel more motivated, making the theory useful.

Reductionism versus holism

Maslow's theory is more holistic than other theories of motivation, i.e. cognitive theories. For example, the theory states that it is not just physiological needs that are important in motivation but also psychological needs such as self-esteem and belongingness. Therefore, Maslow's hierarchy of needs is a more complete theory that takes a number of factors into account when looking at motivation.

Determinism versus free will

Humanistic psychologists such as Maslow are firmly on the free-will side of the debate, suggesting that free will is necessary in order to have the ability to self-actualise. For humanistic psychologists the question is 'how could a person change themselves without free will?' For example, if you cannot meet your basic physiological needs through work then you have a choice to look for another job and leave. However, there is an argument that although people do have free will, our behaviour/motivation is still, to some extent, determined by external forces outside of our control such as a lack of ability to find another job.

Focus on... Saeednia (2011): Generating a scale measuring hierarchy of basic needs

> ### AIM
....

To develop a reliable scale to measure basic needs satisfaction in children.

> ### METHODOLOGY
....

A total of 13 children plus their parents and educators were interviewed initially. This interview used open-ended questions and therefore produced qualitative data. The participants were interviewed about their basic need's satisfaction with themes such as a participant's wishes and desires, openness of the family to allow the child's independence and supportiveness of the family explored. The data gained from the interviews was coded and analysed based on Maslow's theory. The themes established in the interview were then used to construct the Basic Needs Satisfaction Scale (BNSS), which would be used to measure the extent to which basic needs are satisfied. These needs were based around Maslow's original five needs. After an initial pilot study, the BNSS was distributed to 300 participants who had been randomly chosen from an initial sample of 457 people.

> ### RESULTS
....

The study found that the reliability of the BNSS for use with children was high (0.83), suggesting that it is a consistent measure of the concepts.

> ### CONCLUSION
....

The study also showed that qualitative methods may be more appropriate for investigating Maslow's hierarchy of needs and for finding out people's desires due to the tendency of children to 'unconsciously pretend' that a need is being met, especially if the environment is not going to help the child meet that need.

The BNSS is an indicator of life satisfaction. This life satisfaction changes depending on culture. In poorer nations this often means safety, whereas in wealthier nations it is more about love and self-esteem. This is consistent with Maslow's theory.

Evaluating Saeednia (2011)

One weakness of the study is that the generalisability of the findings may be low. The sample only consisted of people who lived in wealthy areas of Tehran. Therefore, the results may not be applicable to people who live in less wealthy areas or indeed less wealthy nations.

Another weakness is the age of the participants used in the study. Although the study did try to ensure the results were correct by interviewing family and educators as well, the limited ability of children to express themselves fully may affect the **validity** of the results.

One strength of the study is that it suggests that **quantitative data** may be reliably obtained when researching Maslow's hierarchy of needs. This helps overcome the criticisms that the theory is not very scientific and its concepts not able to be tested. This will increase the reliability of the theory.

Another strength is this study provided the basis for future research. This was one of the first attempts to produce a **questionnaire** to look at basic needs in children with some success. This is important as further research can be completed and weaknesses identified to enable it to become a reliable tool to assess children's needs in the future.

> ### LEARNING LINK
> Saaednia's study used more than one method in order to make sure the results were valid. For example, this study included both qualitative interviews and quantitative (structured) questionnaires. Look back at the studies you learned about at AS Level and any you have already covered at A Level. Do any of them use different methods as part of their research?

> ### STUDY TIP
> In this chapter you will come across other need's theories and for each of these theories you should be able to discuss relevant issues and debates such as validity, application to real life and cultural differences. One of the ways you could do this is to write down each of the issues or debates and decide how these apply to the theories. For example, you could look at validity and decide whether one of the theories is more valid than the other and then try and justify your choice using the knowledge you have gained from this chapter. This will not only help your understanding of the issues raised, but also help you to select appropriate information to justify your choices.

> ### TEST YOURSELF
>
> 1 Johannes is a manager of a shoe company. He wants to change policies so that his employees feel happy and motivated at work. He has started studying Maslow's theory to see whether that may help him.
> Explain, using Maslow's hierarchy of needs, two ways Johannes could ensure that his employees' needs are met. [4]
> 2 Outline what is meant by esteem needs as discussed by Maslow. [2]
> 3 a Describe Maslow's hierarchy of needs. [6]
>   b Evaluate Maslow's hierarchy of needs, including a discussion of application to real life. [10]
> 4 Explain one strength and one weakness of one study investigating Maslow's hierarchy of needs. [4]
> 5 Outline one strength of using self-reports to study Maslow's hierarchy of needs. [2]
> 6 State one way that studies investigating Maslow's hierarchy of needs could be improved. [2]

McClelland's theory of achievement motivation (1961)

> ### Think!
> What are the characteristics of a person whose dominant need is for **affiliation**?

> ### Think!
> You are a manager at a local company and one of your employees has completed a really challenging business deal. You want everyone to know how well she has done so you call a meeting and praise her. Instead of being really happy she looks uncomfortable and embarrassed and leaves as soon as possible. What could McClelland's achievement motivation theory tell you about her reaction? What could you have done differently?

KEY TERMS
achievement
affiliation
personal power
institutional power
Thematic Apperception Test
projective testing

Think!

McClelland used the **Thematic Apperception Test** (see below) to try to measure people's different needs. Using your knowledge of the test, do you think that this is a valid measure of people's needs?

The Thematic Apperception Test was used by McClelland to measure people's needs. This is what is known as a **projective** test; people are shown ambiguous pictures and asked to make up a story about them. What story could you make up about the picture in Figure 9.3?

▶ Figure 9.3

McClelland's theory of achievement motivation (1961) built on Maslow's theory of basic needs by identifying three work-related motivational needs that he believed everyone has. These are:

>> **achievement**
>> power
>> affiliation.

McClelland suggests that these needs are universal, meaning that regardless of age, race or gender we all possess these needs and are motivated to satisfy them. He stated that we may not possess the three needs in equal amounts and one of them could be dominant over the others. This dominant motivator will then shape our behaviour at work. McClelland believed that our specific mix of motivational needs are shaped by our life experiences and our culture; they are, therefore, learned behaviours.

The three work needs

Need for achievement

This is the urge to achieve something in the work that you do, to master a task. For a surgeon, this may be performing a successful operation. For a lawyer, it may be winning a particularly difficult case. It is this need that drives people to want to work.

A person with high achievement needs will try to succeed by avoiding low reward/low risk (of failure) situations, but also by avoiding difficult to achieve high risk (of failure) situations. The low-risk situations will be avoided as success will be too easily obtained and therefore will not be seen as a 'real' achievement. If a situation has too high a risk, then people with high achievement needs will see the result as down to luck rather than their own achievement. High achievers want regular feedback so they can monitor their own progress and would rather either work alone or with other high achievers.

Those with low achievement needs will try to avoid any form of responsibility at work and have a fear of failing, so they do not try.

McClelland believed that those with high achievement needs would make the best leaders within the workplace.

Need for affiliation

People with high **affiliation** needs want social interactions with others. They want to be liked, accepted and feel part of the group. High affiliators tend to conform to group norms and will not challenge the group, as they fear rejection. They are not risk takers, prefer collaboration to competition and do not like to draw attention to themselves. For example, they may not enjoy being singled out for praise. High affiliators prefer work that leads to a large amount of time spent with others. They perform well during team activities and are well suited to customer service positions.

Those with low affiliation needs are not team players, do not desire social interaction, remain distant from others and do not seek their acceptance.

Need for power

People with a need for power are often suited to leadership positions and have a desire to be in control and have authority over others. They want to make an impact and to influence decision-making processes. People with high power needs want prestige and high status and want their viewpoint to be accepted. There are two types of power that individuals may need: **personal power** is the need to control others; **institutional (or social) power** is the need to coordinate and organise a group or team to further the goals set out by a business. The most effective managers have a need for institutional power rather than personal power.

People with *low need* for power will not seek positions of authority and influence, will remain dependent on others to make decisions and will not take the lead. They will often reduce the importance of their role when speaking to others.

Within the workplace, therefore, it is important to identify the needs of your employees, including those who will make the best leaders. Personality traits and behaviours within the workplace will help with this identification. However, McClelland used a test called the Thematic Apperception Test as a way of trying to measure individual needs.

 ## Thematic Apperception Test (TAT)

The TAT is a projective test that involves a person describing ambiguous stimuli. It tests a person's imagination and involves them being shown a series of ambiguous pictures (around 20). After each picture, the individual is then asked to immediately make up a story. The theory is that people will *project* (attribute) their own needs onto the story. For example, someone with a high need for power might create a story about someone controlling other people. Thus, the stories people create reveal their unconscious motives and needs. McClelland devised a way of scoring people's stories with regard to power, affiliation and achievement.

Evaluating McClelland's theory of achievement motivation

> **ISSUES AND DEBATES**

Cultural differences

One weakness of McClelland's theory is that it does not take into account gender and cultural differences. McClelland's theory was constructed using males working in organisations, who were from Western societies and individualistic cultures. This means that you may not be able to apply it to females or to collectivist cultures such as Japan where work needs, such as the need for power, may not exist in the same way.

Individual and situational explanations

McClelland's theory only considers individual needs and does not consider situational factors as well. For example, satisfied power needs means that the person has authority over others. However, this is only possible if other people adopt a more submissive role within the workforce; meaning that the social situation has to be right, and it is not just about their individual needs. This suggests that this is an incomplete theory and cannot explain all factors in workplace motivation.

McClelland's theory used projective tests to try and measure the needs of individuals. McClelland produced a scoring system that was relatively reliable and can be analysed statistically. However, it was still measuring unobservable personality characteristics from the preconscious mind. This is important, as any results obtained cannot be disproven.

One strength of McClelland's theory is that it can be used to find out the needs of potential and current employees. This allows organisations to place people into areas to which they are most suited and allows them to screen prospective employees so they can employ the person who is the best fit for the job advertised. This is important as it can improve factors such as productivity and staff retention.

Look at Figure 9.4.
» Which motivational needs do you think the people in the picture are showing?
» Think about what methodology you could use to try and find out whether you are correct.
» What problems do you think you may have using the methods you have suggested?

▲ Figure 9.4

▶ LEARNING LINK

You have now learned about two different theories in this section. Both theories are known as needs theories. Look at both theories and see whether you can find any similarities and differences between them. This could be what they were each trying to achieve or how you could measure these needs in a group of employees. You could look at them both in terms of strengths and weaknesses. Remember to use issues and debates which have been mentioned in this section. Also, McClelland believed that motivators are learned behaviour shaped by past experiences. Remind yourself of the studies in the learning approach (see pages 85–127). How could concepts from the learning approach explain why a person has certain achievement needs?

STUDY TIP

There are a number of things you could do to help you remember all the different characteristics for each of the work-related needs. You could try putting all the characteristics of a particular need into a visual form – this could be a picture of a person you feel represents that characteristic. You could then list all their characteristics around the picture. Drawing skill is not important; stick-people will do! For the TAT, try doing the test either on yourself or a friend or family member. You do not need to use the original images, just get some pictures together and ask people to make up a story about them. Once you have your stories (they could write them down), think about how you could use them to find out their dominant need. What do you need to do next? What problems might you have when you try to interpret your findings? This should give you an idea of the methodological issues raised when doing these types of tests.

▶ TEST YOURSELF

1 Sarah has been told by her boss that she scored highly on affiliation needs on Thematic Apperception Test.
Explain two characteristics Sarah may be showing. [4]

2 Outline one way McClelland's Theory does not take into account cultural differences. [2]

3 a Describe what psychologists have discovered about need theories. [6]
  b Evaluate what psychologists have discovered about need theories, including a discussion on application to real life. [10]

4 People have different work needs that motivate them and these may depend on life experiences and culture.
  a Plan a study using an experiment to find out whether the need for achievement changes depending on whether you have been in your job a long time or a short time. [10]
    Your study plan must include
    – a directional or non-hypothesis
    – controls.
  b For one piece of psychological knowledge that has informed your plan (for question 4):
    i Describe this psychological knowledge. [4]
    ii Explain how two features of this knowledge informed your plan. [4]

KEY TERMS

SMART goals

goal-setting theory

expectancy theory

valence

instrumentality

9.1.2 Cognitive theories of motivation

> ## Think!
>
> What are the three factors that Vroom suggested were essential for high levels of motivation in the workplace? How can each of them be applied by managers in the workplace?

> ## Think!
>
> Imagine it is six months before your examinations. Your goal is to get an A in Psychology, but you know that to do so you need to have a plan. Use Locke and Latham's five characteristics to set out some effective goals which will help you to achieve an A in your exam. Remember that although your end goal is to get an A, you can have a number of subgoals which will help you to achieve that end goal.

> ## Think!
>
> Locke and Latham looked at a large amount of previously published research from which they formulated their theory. Is the use of previously published research primary or secondary data? What problems may arise from using this specific type of data?

Over the last couple of pages, we have talked about how rewards are important for motivation in the workplace. This could be a big money bonus or praise from your manager. Think about which is more important to you. Is it the praise from people more senior than you or the money? Can you think of any occasion when having money as a bonus for completing a task would not help motivate you? Think about what it took to get that money, what it may represent.

▲ Figure 9.5

Latham and Locke's goal-setting theory

Goal setting is devising an action plan in order to motivate a person to achieve a specific goal. It is more complex than just a desire to do something but involves looking at a specific thing you want to achieve, for example achieving an A on your Psychology studies and then devising a realistic plan of how to accomplish this.

Locke *et al.* (1968) suggested that a more effective goal was one that was specific and measurable rather than one that kept outcomes general, therefore **SMART goals** are more effective than more general goals. SMART goals need to be:

>> Specific: These are goals that are well defined, clear and not too complex to understand. Ask yourself who is involved? What do I want to achieve and why? And when do I want it to be achieved by?

>> Measurable: These are goals that have specific criteria to track progress. Ask yourself, How do I know if I've reached my goal? What things do I need to look out for to ensure I am progressing?

>> Achievable: Is the goal realistic and not too hard? Do I have the resources to achieve it?

>> Realistic/Relevant: What benefit is there to you? How does the goal fit in with your wider life goals?

>> Time bound: How long do I have to achieve the goal? Does it have a start and end date clearly defined?

For Locke, a target which says, 'We want to increase sales of fluffy pink slippers by 50% in 28 days' is more effective than 'Let's get more slippers sold soon.' He believed that the best goals are those that you are not 100% sure that you will achieve, but ones where there is a realistic chance you can do so, with hard work and positive feedback.

Locke and Latham (1990) built upon Locke's earlier theories, repeating the need to set specific and challenging goals, but also outlining five characteristics of effective goal setting.
1 Clarity: The goal needs to be specific and clear, unambiguous and measurable.
2 Challenge: A goal that is too easy is demotivating, but it should not be unrealistic. Goals need to be relevant and linked to rewards.
3 Commitment: Goals must be understood and the workforce needs to be invested in them.
4 Feedback: Regular feedback through the entire process keeps people on track and focused.
5 Task complexity: Timescales need to be realistic, with sub-goals and regular reviews.

Evaluating goal-setting theory

One strength of this theory is that it is supported by evidence-based research. Locke and Latham's theory was based on over 50 years of research, and is still used widely in the workplace today, with more recent studies also supporting its concepts. This is important as it suggests that the theory is high in reliability.

Another strength is that it may improve the workplace experience for workers and managers. It allows managers to plan for a specific task and to monitor its progression; this will allow them to identify quickly when things are going wrong. It can also increase workers' motivation to succeed. This benefit to the workplace makes it an ethically sound theory.

> ### ISSUES AND DEBATES
>
> #### Reductionism versus holism
>
> One weakness of goal setting theory is that it is reductionist. The theory suggests that motivation is down to cognitive factors such as the setting of achievable and specific goals, but not other factors such as physiological needs or the importance of past experiences. Therefore, goal setting may be seen as an incomplete theory and does not explain all motivation in the workforce.
>
> #### Cultural differences
>
> Goal setting theory does not consider cultural differences as it is based upon values that are found in individualistic Western societies, such as the USA, and not more collectivist cultures where values within the workplace are different. This suggests that the theory may not be able to be generalised to all cultures, limiting its usefulness.

Vroom's expectancy (VIE) theory of motivation

Vroom's **expectancy theory** (1964) states that an individual's motivation at work can be affected by their expectation about what is going to happen in the future – the expected consequences. Vroom's theory assumes that behaviour results from the conscious and rational choices that people make, with the ultimate aim to maximise pleasure from that choice and minimise the pain associated with it. This means that any decision will look at the potential rewards (the pleasure) coming from an action, as well as the potential costs (the pain). For example, if you are asked to perform a task which you know will take up a great deal of your time and will take a great deal of effort and you know that you will not get any reward/recognition for doing it, then you will be less motivated to complete it.

Vroom suggested that performance at work is based on individual factors such as personality, skills, abilities and experience. He believed that effort, motivation, and performance are all linked and that although individuals may have different goals they will be motivated if they believe that:
» effort and performance are positively correlated
» if you perform well, you will get a reward that is desirable and satisfies a need
» the desire to satisfy a need is enough to make the effort worthwhile.

This theory is based upon the following three beliefs which affect levels of motivation:
1 **Valence:** This looks at the 'strength' of an expected reward – the perception of an outcome. This can relate to the size of the reward, for example a big or small bonus

at the end of the month, or the type of reward. For example, is the reward based on intrinsic motivation, such as a sense of achievement, or extrinsic motivation, such as a gift card or money? For rewards to be a effective a company will need to ensure they are tailored to the employee and are seen as valuable by them.

2 **Instrumentality**: This is whether you believe that if you perform well, the expected outcome/reward will happen and this will match the effort you have put in. This is affected by such factors as:
   » the trust you have in the people who are deciding who will get the outcome/reward
   » whether the process of deciding who gets the reward is simple
   » whether the relationship between performance and outcome is clear and transparent.

3 **Expectancy**: This is the perception that effort will lead to the intended performance goals/outcomes. Expectancy is affected by a number of factors such as the level of skill you possess for doing the job, whether you have the right resources and information to do the job and the amount of support you get from others. Within the workplace, providing training to enhance skills and mentoring to provide support may help raise expectancy.

Vroom used a formula to represent whether motivation would be high in a worker:

Motivation = Valence × Instrumentality × Expectancy

If any of the three are low, then motivation will be low. However, the common theme is the idea of reward; therefore, if the reward is small then motivation as a whole will tend to be low.

Evaluation of Vroom's expectancy theory

One weakness of expectancy theory is that it may not always apply to real life. This is because often within the workplace, rewards are not correlated directly with performance and other factors such as position, effort and responsibility are not taken into account. This, therefore, limits the theory's validity.

Another weakness of expectancy theory is that it assumes that people always make rational and conscious choices. For example, it assumes that people will know consciously what rewards are best for them and that their decisions are based upon what gives the biggest rewards. This may not be the case, with short term need, personality and other processes also having an effect. This suggests that the theory may not apply to all individuals.

A strength is that results from research have suggested that the theory can predict the choices people will make. Redmond (2009) suggested that valence, instrumentality and expectations all correlated highly in terms of predictability. This makes it a useful theory in terms of workplace motivation.

> ### ISSUES AND DEBATES

Individual and situational explanations
Vroom's expectancy theory suggests that individual factors such as personality, skills, abilities, and experiences are most important in performance at work. This is different to other theories such as Maslow's hierarchy of needs as this assumes that all people are the same.

Idiographic versus nomothetic
Nomothetic approaches try and make generalisations about the world through the use of methods such as experiments/questionnaires and involves establishing laws that apply to the general population. Vroom's expectancy theory establishes an equation that can be used to determine the behaviour of all workers; this means that it establishes a law that can apply to all rather than looking at the individual and what uniquely motivates them in particular.

Determinism versus free will
Vroom's expectancy theory suggests that behaviour/motivation is determined by our expectations about the rewards and costs of a particular action; with potential rewards being the largest determinant of motivation; this is environmental determinism. This ignores that idea of free will where people may be motivated no matter the reward or cost of the action.

LEARNING LINK

Vroom's expectancy theory talks about correlations between the three beliefs of valence, instrumentality and expectancy. Think back to what you learned about correlations in your AS Level research methods. What are the strengths and weaknesses of the correlational method? Did any of the studies from AS Level also use the correlational method?

STUDY TIP

There is a great deal of information to learn on these two theories. One way of trying to learn each theory is to practise with some novel scenarios. Perhaps think of an important goal you want to reach at school to be able to do a particular job in the future, or even to be able to afford the latest phone. Write down your end goal and then try and work out how any of the theories would help you reach that goal. Or think of times when you have not been motivated to complete a task; look at Vroom's theory and see whether it can help you understand why you were unmotivated. Perhaps the valence was not high or your expectations were low. Applying the theories to real life situations will help you understand them.

TEST YOURSELF

1 a Outline what is meant by valence in relation to Vroom's expectancy theory. [2]
  b Explain one similarity between Vroom's expectancy theory and one other cognitive theory of motivation. [2]
2 Davinda is trying to increase sales of her new range of fluffy pink unicorn T shirts. She has called a meeting to try and motivate her staff to get more sales over the next couple of months. She has been reading about Locke and Latham's goal setting theory to try and get some ideas.
  Explain two ways that Locke and Latham's theory can help her improve sales of her fluffy pink unicorn T shirts. [4]
3 a Describe cognitive theories of motivation to include:
    – Locke and Latham's goal setting theory
    – Vroom's expectancy theory. [6]
  b Evaluate cognitive theories of motivation, including a discussion of application to real life. [10]
4 Locke and Latham proposed a cognitive theory of motivation.
  Explain what is meant by a SMART target. [2]
5 Motivation, according to Locke and Latham, is down to cognitive factors.
  Explain why Locke and Latham's theory could be said to be reductionist. [2]
6 Explain two strengths of Locke and Latham's theory of motivation. [4]

9.1.3 Motivators at work

Think!

How can **intrinsic motivation** increase motivation at work?

Think!

Nettie is a team leader at Harriet's hat shop. She is really pleased with her team and their standard of work and wants to make sure that it continues. How could Nettie use Deci's **self-determination** theory to ensure her workforce stays motivated and production levels stay high?

KEY TERMS

intrinsic
extrinsic
self-determination
appraisal
autonomy
relatedness
competence
profit sharing
performance related pay
empowerment
active listening

METHODOLOGY
generalisations from findings

Think!

One debate you have learned about is determinism versus free will. What is meant when a theory is said to be deterministic? Do you think this applies to self-determination theory? Give a reason for your answer.

There are a number of different types of intrinsic and extrinsic motivators. These include motivators such as pay, bonuses, respect and praise. What type of motivator do you feel that Figure 9.6 is portraying? What type do you feel would motivate you more at work or at school?

▲ Figure 9.6

Extrinsic motivation at work

Extrinsic motivation is when behaviour is driven by external factors. This could be rewards such as money or avoiding negative consequences such as having money taken off your salary because you are late. Extrinsic motivation is driven by operant conditioning which uses rewards and punishment to increase or decrease the likelihood of a behaviour being repeated. The benefit of extrinsic motivation is that employees can see direct, observable results of their behaviour. This can focus energy and increase motivation. However, one problem is cost, especially for a large team. It can also be quite short term and can lead to burnout and demotivation, especially if used frequently just to get results.

Types of extrinsic motivation at work

1 Pay: This is the obvious form of extrinsic motivation. You may enjoy the job that you do, but you are motivated to go to work in order to receive a salary so you can pay your bills and enjoy life by going on holidays and spending money on other things that you enjoy.
2 Bonuses: Extra rewards may be given yearly but can be at shorter intervals. They are usually based on individual or company targets, and they motivate the employee to put in effort during a specific time span to earn a lump sum of money. They can also be non-monetary rewards.
3 **Profit sharing**: This is where an organisation awards an employee a percentage of their profits. This is based upon an organisation's profits over a set period of time, usually once a year. Profit sharing works only if it is done fairly, but if so, it can increase morale (mood) and productivity.
4 **Performance-related pay**: This is a reward given out when work reaches a required standard. Individual performance is reviewed regularly against agreed objectives. This is an **appraisal**. Then employees are put into performance groups which determines the reward. The reward is usually a cash bonus or a raise in salary. However, targets need to be realistic and achievable or motivation will decrease.

Intrinsic motivation at work

Unlike extrinsic motivation which comes from external factors, intrinsic motivation is to do with internal emotions and is when behaviour is driven by factors such as the feeling of satisfaction at reaching a target, recognition from a manager and praise. Intrinsically motivated behaviours in the workplace are those which are motivated due to a feeling of being valued, and a sense of belonging.

Types of intrinsic motivation at work

1 Recognition: Recognition involves giving verbal appreciation to recognise an employee's performance. This may take place formally, such as in an appraisal or meeting, or informally such as a manager's conversation to say how well you are doing. Recognition

could involve some form of reward such as 'employee of the month', but it needs to be linked to job performance rather than reaching targets.

2 Praise: Praise can enhance intrinsic motivation but over-praising can reduce it. Telling someone well done is motivating but it has to have some meaning and needs to be targeted. For example, if a manager says it constantly or just uses it to say an employee has met a target then it may not increase motivation. You should use praise even if things have not gone as well as hoped for as this will also help keep motivation going.

3 Respect: This can have a direct impact on motivation and productivity. This can be through **active listening**, not insulting people or criticising their ideas. If a person has a problem, listen to them and do not downplay their feelings.

4 **Empowerment**: Workers are motivated more when they can make the decisions that affect their work, such as how and when to approach a task. Giving workers **autonomy** shows high levels of trust and confidence in them and that you value their contributions. It gives them a sense of ownership about their work. Empowerment also happens when mastery of a task is achieved and workers feel like they can accomplish more.

5 Sense of belonging: People need to feel as though they are a valued member of the workforce and be proud to be part of it. This can include having trusting relationships with others. If they feel like they belong, are respected and that people value their input then they will be intrinsically motivated to work.

Deci and Ryan's (1985) self-determination theory

Self-determination refers to a person's ability to manage themselves, make confident choices and think on their feet. There are two key assumptions to this theory:

1 A need for growth drives behaviour: Many people are keen to grow and improve and gaining mastery over a challenge is an essential part of self-development. This is linked to intrinsic motivation.

2 Autonomous motivation is important: Self-determination theory focuses mostly on intrinsic motivation such as an increase in autonomy, although it does acknowledge that human beings can be motivated by outside factors such as money and fame (extrinsic). If behaviour is purely self-determined, then it will be intrinsically motivated and done for pure pleasure and internal satisfaction. Non self-determined behaviours are those where a task just has to get done and there is no pleasure and little choice in what a person does; this demonstrates a lack of control, or autonomy.

Self-determination theory suggests that there are three basic needs to be fulfilled so that an individual experiences intrinsic motivation:

1 Autonomy: This is the need for self-governance and independence; being in control of your own behaviour and destiny. Autonomy can be increased by allowing workers choice over how they work. Workers will lack autonomy if they feel controlled by others or if they have to meet constant deadlines. Feelings of autonomy can be decreased if extrinsic rewards are constantly given for a behaviour, especially if the behaviour had already been intrinsically motivated. Eventually, a worker's motivation will change to only caring about obtaining the reward and not about satisfaction with the job.

2 **Relatedness**: This is the need to build relationships with others, and a need to feel a sense of attachment and belonging to others. This is where you feel part of a social group. Without these sorts of connections, self-determination is much harder to achieve mainly due to the feelings of isolation and lack of support it brings. If a worker is respected by others and people care about their feelings, then relatedness increases; if a worker is criticised or they are excluded from a particular group then it will decrease.

3 **Competence**: This means having the right qualities to perform a task, such as a particular skill, IQ (a measure of intelligence), judgement or strength. When a worker has competence, they can interact effectively with their environment and can achieve their goals; they obtain mastery over their environment. If a task is too hard or a worker receives too much negative feedback about their work, then competence will decrease, but if a task is well matched to the person's skill or they receive feedback that is positive, then competence will increase. Constructive feedback also helps competence as it helps the worker know where they have gone wrong so they can improve their skills.

Evaluating motivators at work

One strength is that there is research support. Deci and Ryan (1999) reviewed 128 experiments which looked at the effect of extrinsic rewards on intrinsic motivation. They found that rewards that depended upon completion of a task or were performance related decreased intrinsic motivation due to people not taking responsibility for motivating themselves and only focusing on short-term gain, whilst positive feedback enhanced free will and autonomy, increasing intrinsic motivation. Also, Kohn (1994) showed that if an organisation used rewards to control behaviour, then more surveillance and competition will follow, further decreasing intrinsic motivation.

There may be different motivators in individualistic and collectivist cultures. For example, in some collectivist cultures the need for individual autonomy may be far less than in individualist cultures. Hagger *et al.* (2013) found that intrinsic motivation was higher in individualistic groups when offered personal choice on a task, than in collectivist groups where intrinsic motivation was higher when asked to do a task by a manager. Different aspects of motivation will be more important to different cultures and these theories fail to take these cultural differences into account.

> ## ISSUES AND DEBATES
>
> ### Determinism versus free will
>
> One weakness of self-determination theory is that it suggests that people's behaviours are determined by the specific types of motivation that they receive. For example, if they receive extrinsic motivators all the time then their intrinsic motivation will decrease. This may not be the case for all individuals, and individual differences in personality may need to be considered. It may be for some that they will be motivated whatever reward that they do or do not get, or it may be that some external unrelated factors will increase motivation and no reward within the workplace will make a difference.
>
> ### Application to everyday life
>
> Also, self-determination theory can be applied to a number of real-life situations. If managers know that 'controlling' rewards like target-related pay decrease motivation in the workforce, while intrinsic motivators such as a collaborative atmosphere increase motivation, then they can use this information to ensure the workforce's needs are met. This may increase worker satisfaction and productivity, making the theory useful. One weakness of theories into motivators at work is that they tend to be ethnocentric, meaning they have been constructed using a Western idea of motivation in the workforce.

> ## ► LEARNING LINK
>
> All the concepts on these pages are linked to the key study which you will learn on the following pages (see page 654). It is important that you also use the key study when learning about motivators at work as it will give you a more holistic view of the theory. The study also covers intrinsic/extrinsic motivation and self-determination and links it to the workplace, which will help you contextualise the theories.

> ### STUDY TIP
>
> There is a great deal of information on these pages. One way of condensing the information whilst learning is to read through the pages and then use your memory to try and write down what you have learned. What you will find is that the first time you will have many gaps but if you repeat the process then you will find that you will get to a point where you have written down what you need to learn, but in a shortened form. You could also use flashcards and split them into intrinsic motivation, extrinsic motivation and self-determination theory.

> ## TEST YOURSELF

1 Frederico's current job pays a basic salary monthly, but he gets extra money every six months if specific sales targets have been met. He also has an appraisal every six months to see whether he will get a wage rise.
   a Suggest which type of motivation is being used in Frederico's workplace   [2]
   b Explain one weakness of using the type of motivation you have identified in a).   [2]
2 Suggest two ways organisations could use self-determination theory to increase motivation in the workplace.   [4]
3 a Describe what psychologists have discovered about:
      – intrinsic and extrinsic motivation in the workplace
      – self-determination theory of motivation.   [6]
   b Evaluate what psychologists have discovered about:
      – intrinsic and extrinsic motivation in the workplace.
      – self-determination theory of motivation.
      Include a discussion about reliability.   [10]
4 Explain one difference between intrinsic and extrinsic motivation.   [2]
5 Suggest why theories looking at motivators at work may not take into account cultural differences.   [2]
6 Explain two ways self-determination theory can be applied to real life.   [4]

KEY TERMS

self-determination theory

extrinsic and intrinsic motivation

functional meaning

informational

psychological needs

motivation

autonomy

Key study: Applying self-determination theory to motivational rewards – Landry *et al.* (2019) Study 1

Think!

How did the use of different instruction paragraphs at the start of the study affect participants' performance on the task?

Think!

Have you ever been offered money to complete a task in a certain amount of time? How did you feel when you completed the task? Did you feel a sense of achievement for completing it on time or were you just glad that you had earned the money?

Think!

Landry *et al.* used volunteer students from a university course as participants in their research. There are both strengths and weaknesses of using this type of sample in research. Can you think of one strength and one weakness?

Landry's study suggests that offering monetary rewards does not always mean that performance will increase. Do you agree with this? Can you think of any time where money would be the key factor in whether you increase performance? Does this depend on who is giving the reward, for example, someone you know and like or someone you do not?

▲ Figure 9.7

▶ CONTEXT

Organisations often use money as a way of attracting individuals to work for them, and to try and improve the motivation of their current workforce. Previous research has shown, however, that monetary rewards may only lead to a temporary improvement of performance as employees focus on the external rewards of completing an activity (extrinsic motivation) rather than the internal enjoyment or satisfaction of completing it (intrinsic motivation).

Self-determination theory suggests that extrinsic motivators such as money should not always be seen as negative; rather it is how they are applied that will determine what **functional meaning** employees give to them. If the employee believes that the monetary reward is **informational** and supports **autonomy**, then motivation and performance will improve as **psychological needs** are met. If the employee sees the rewards as controlling and just dependent on completing a task, then lower motivation and performance will occur as needs are frustrated.

▶ AIMS AND HYPOTHESES

Using concepts from self-determination theory, this study aimed to explain whether monetary rewards can have a beneficial effect (or not) on employees' **motivation** and performance.

Hypothesis 1: Presenting rewards in an autonomy-supportive way to convey an informational meaning leads to greater performance than presenting them in a controlling (or autonomy-threatening) way so as to confer a controlling meaning.

Hypothesis 2: The effect of informational rewards on performance is mediated by greater psychological need satisfaction, leading to higher intrinsic motivation, whereas the effect of controlling rewards on performance is mediated by greater psychological needs frustration, leading to greater extrinsic motivation (Landry *et al.*, 2019, p. 3).

▶ METHODOLOGY

This was a laboratory experiment. Quantitative data was also produced through the use of self-reports (questionnaires).

Sample

One hundred and twenty three student volunteers (mean age = 23 years) were recruited through an 'Introduction to Organisational Behaviour' course at a Canadian university. All students were randomly assigned to either the autonomy-supportive (informational) condition (n=65) or the autonomy-threatening (controlling) condition (n=58). 60 per cent of the students were female.

▶ PROCEDURE

Initially, all participants were asked to read an instruction paragraph about a task they would be asked to perform and the reward they were to be given on completion. This paragraph was either:
a   Autonomy-supportive: The paragraph would be supportive and encouraging, giving an informational meaning to the reward. For example, participants were told 'the monetary reward was ... a token of appreciation for their contribution.'
b   Autonomy-threatening: This would pressurise the participant, giving a controlling meaning to the reward. For example, participants were told 'the monetary reward was ... to reinforce the performance standards of the task.'

The reward given was a $10 gift card for a local coffee shop.

After reading the instructions, participants were given two minutes to correctly solve 25 four-letter anagrams. This task has been used in many previous research studies and is considered a valid measure of performance. After completion, a performance score was obtained using a **standardised procedure**.

Self-report measures

1 All participants were also asked to rate on a seven-point Likert scale (1 = strongly disagree, 7 = strongly agree) the extent to which they felt their psychological needs had been satisfied or frustrated using the Basic Psychological Needs Satisfaction Scale and the Psychological Needs Thwarting Scale.
2 Participants reported their intrinsic and extrinsic motivation using a seven-point Situational Motivation Scale by responding to the stem, 'Why are you currently engaged in this activity?' There were then a number of responses such as, '... because I think that this activity is interesting' for intrinsic motivation.

Control measures

To control for individual differences, participants rated on a three-point scale how valuable the reward was to them. This controlled for individual differences due to the perceived value of the reward. In addition, participants completed a scale to measure positive and negative affect (emotions/feelings) to control for individual differences in affect arising from reading instruction paragraphs.

▶ RESULTS

▼ Table 9.1 Means and standard deviations (SD) for each condition

Variables	Autonomy supportive condition (n=65), Mean (SD)	Controlling condition (n=58), Mean (SD)
Needs satisfaction	5.79 (0.73)	5.39 (0.92)
Needs frustration	2.41 (1.01)	2.83 (1.01)
Extrinsic motivation	3.10 (1.44)	3.95 (1.25)
Intrinsic motivation	5.31 (1.03)	4.56 (1.01)
Performance	0.76 (0.16)	0.54 (0.21)

The results from Table 9.1 support Hypothesis 1, as participants in the autonomy-supportive condition scored significantly higher on performance (0.76) than participants in the controlling condition (0.54).

In terms of Hypothesis 2, participants in the autonomy-supportive condition reported significantly higher psychological needs satisfaction (5.79) compared to the controlling condition (5.39). Greater psychological needs satisfaction predicted greater intrinsic motivation and also better performance. In the controlling condition, there was higher reported needs frustration (2.83) compared to the autonomy supportive condition (2.41) and in turn this predicted greater extrinsic motivation. Extrinsic motivation did not predict performance.

Further support for Hypothesis 2 came from indirect effects where psychological needs satisfaction acted as a mediator between the condition and intrinsic motivation and between the condition and performance. The mediating effect of needs frustration and extrinsic motivation was also significant. However, the indirect effect of extrinsic motivation as a mediator between psychological need satisfaction and performance was not significant.

▶ CONCLUSIONS

● Presenting rewards in an autonomy-supportive way (informational) leads to an increased performance on tasks compared to rewards presented in a controlling way.
● Rewards presented in an autonomy-supportive way led to increased needs satisfaction which leads to healthier forms of motivation such as intrinsic motivation and better performance, due to individuals engaging more in the activity they are being rewarded for.

Methodological strengths and weaknesses

One strength of this study is that a number of control measures were used. For example, participants were asked to rate on a three-item scale how valuable the reward was to them. This controlled for individual differences due to the perceived value of the reward, increasing the validity of the study.

Another strength of this study was that quantitative data was produced on a variety of measures. For example, participants completed a number of self-reports which used Likert scales, as well as receiving a score based upon their performance on the task. Quantitative data is objective and allows statistical tests to be used and comparisons to be made, increasing the reliability of the results.

One weakness of this study was sampling bias. Although a fairly high number of participants was used (153), they were all from the same course within the same Canadian university. This means that they may all have similar characteristics to each other, leading to problems with generalising the findings to different cultures, or even different universities or courses.

Another weakness of this study is the use of laboratory experiments. This study took place in an artificial environment rather than in a real workplace where actual changes in employee performance on real life tasks could be monitored. This lowers the ecological validity of the findings.

 ## Ethics

At the beginning of the study, Landry *et al.* gave a detailed explanation of the procedure to all participants. This meant that valid consent was obtained from all participants and no deception was used. Confidentiality was maintained throughout the study and there was no suggestion of distress or psychological harm. Indeed, there may be a benefit ethically from the study for both the organisations and the individuals, as it showed that if rewards are offered in a supportive and encouraging way then needs satisfaction is higher for the individual and motivation and performance is increased for the organisation.

 ## Application to everyday life

A strength of this study is that the results help increase our understanding of motivational theories and how they can affect the motivation and performance of workers. The results have shown how to use monetary rewards in the workplace in order to benefit both the worker and the organisation. For example, if monetary rewards are used in a supportive and encouraging way, they can increase motivation and performance. However, this study was completed in an artificial environment and therefore there may be questions as to whether the results can be applied to real life workplaces and situations, which is a slight weakness of the study.

> ### ISSUES AND DEBATES
>
> #### Individual and situational explanations
>
> Studies such as Landry *et al.* raise issues relevant to individual and situational explanations. The question may be whether motivation is due to individual factors such as personal satisfaction and belief in your own competence or situational factors such as monetary rewards. This study can also be said to be reductionist as it suggests that performance is dependent on self-determination and does not take into account the effect on performance of other factors such as personality, pre-existing competence, experience and age.
>
> #### Reductionism versus holism
>
> This study can be said to be reductionist as it suggests that performance is dependent on self-determination and does not take into account the effect on performance of other factors such as personality, pre-existing competence, experience and age.

Individual and situational explanations

Studies such as Landry *et al.* raise issues relevant to individual and situational explanations. The question may be whether motivation is due to individual factors such as personal satisfaction and belief in your own competence or situational factors such as monetary rewards. For example, the study suggests that how a reward is presented to an individual is important in workplace performance and needs satisfaction, suggesting that situational factors are more important than individual factors such as personality and self-belief.

Idiographic versus nomothetic

The Landry *et al.* (2019) study uses experimental methodology and questionnaires to look for general laws that could explain whether monetary rewards can improve workplace performance and motivation. This is a nomothetic approach that does not take into account the uniqueness of the individual, but tries to apply results to the general population.

▶ REFLECTION

* If you wanted to conduct research into motivators in the workplace, how would you improve this study to ensure more valid results? Would your improvements remove the weaknesses we have talked about in this study? Would there be other issues that you would have to overcome?
* Can you see any ethical issues that may occur when using monetary rewards in the workplace? Try and think of what we have learned about in this study in terms of how they are presented in the workforce?

▶ LEARNING LINK

Think back to the studies you have learned about at AS Level. Were any of them similar to Landry *et al.* in using experimental methodology alongside self-reports to obtain quantitative data in their research? Can you think of the strengths of using these different methods to obtain quantitative data in your chosen studies? Are there any other studies where mixed research methods could be used to obtain more valid results?

STUDY TIP

One way to increase your understanding of a study is to try and relate it to some part of your own life. For example, for this study try and think of a time where you have been asked to complete a task either at home or in a workplace and you got a reward for doing so. Was this reward an amount of money for completing it or did you get encouragement to do it, and praise for doing it well? How did this make you feel and what affected your motivation more? How could you relate the concepts in this study to your experience? If you cannot remember any such experience, ask family members or friends.

▶ TEST YOURSELF

1 Outline the autonomy supportive condition in terms of the instruction paragraph. [2]
2 Explain one weakness of the Landry *et al.* (2019) study in terms of validity. [2]
3 Describe the sample in Landry *et al.* (2019) study on motivational rewards in the workplace. [4]
4 a Describe the study by Landry *et al.* (2019) on applying self-determination theory to understand the motivational impact of cash rewards. [6]
   b Evaluate this study by Landry *et al.* (2019), including a discussion on generalisability of findings. [10]
5 Explain how quantitative data was collected in the Landry *et al.* (2019) study. [4]
6 a Explain one control that was used in the Landry *et al.* (2019) study. [2]
   b Explain one strength of using controls in research. [2]

9.2 Leadership and management
9.2.1 Traditional and modern theories of leadership

KEY TERMS

transformational

charismatic

great person theory

universalist theories

idealised influence

METHODOLOGY

generalisations from findings

Think!

What is meant by a **universalist theory?** Can you describe the characteristics of any type of leadership that is discussed as part of universalist theory?

Think!

Think back to all the people you have either already met such as family, friends and work colleagues, or people you would like to meet such as sports stars or celebrities. Now think of all the types of leadership you have looked at on these two pages; would any of the people you have met/want to meet come under any of these headings?

Think!

You have learned about the reductionism versus holism debate. Do you believe that universalist theories are reductionist or more holistic? Discuss how you came to this conclusion.

Figure 9.8 shows the classic logo for Apple, the creators of the iPhone and the MacBook. The co-founder of Apple was Steve Jobs; research him online, watch some videos of his speeches and discuss what type of leader you believe he was and why.

▶ Figure 9.8 Apple logo

Universalist theories

Some of the earliest, and simplest, theories of leadership are known as universalist theories. These theories search for a set of characteristics (or traits) that are held by effective leaders. Universalist theorists argue that these characteristics mean that leaders would be effective whatever the situation they find themselves in.

Great person theory

The main assumptions of **great person theory** are that:

» Leaders are born and not made and possess certain sets of characteristics which are inherited.
» The greatest leaders arise when there is the greatest need.

Great Person Theory was first outlined in the nineteenth century with the writings of Thomas Carlyle who, in times of upheaval and uncertainty, looked for the strength and wisdom which he believed was no longer coming from the church. Carlyle believed that a great person may be in human form but has still been sent by God and 'gifted with divine inspiration.'

For Carlyle, 'The history of the world is but the biography of great men' (Carlyle 1841).

This heroic and almost mythical quality is of course very difficult to study scientifically, with Carlyle concentrating on some of the most influential men of his time such as Martin Luther, and in particular Shakespeare, but only in qualitative form.

For Carlyle, and indeed Great Person Theory, there is a belief that if great leaders of the past were born today, they would still rise up to lead because of their inherited traits/characteristics.

Evaluating great person theory

One strength of the great person theory is that the idea of it having a genetic basis has some real-life support. Great leaders often become leaders without any training and also despite not wanting to be leaders in the first place. This real-life support, therefore, suggests that this theory is valid.

> ## ISSUES AND DEBATES
>
> ### Nature versus nurture
>
> Great person theory only talks about the nature side of the debate, and not the nurture side. For example, it suggests that leadership characteristics are 'gifts from God' and that only those born with these can become great leaders. This is a weakness as it assumes that no one can be trained to be a good leader and also does not explain why some individuals with the suggested characteristics do not go on to become leaders.

Charismatic leadership theory

Similar to great person theory, all charismatic leaders possess similar characteristics or traits that can help identify them as potential leaders. These main characteristics are:

- ›› Charisma: Meaning they have the ability to attract or influence followers.
- ›› Popularity: Meaning that they can form relationships/connections with other people.
- ›› Sensitive to their environment: They can identify threats and risks as well as opportunities.
- ›› Good communicators: They can inspire people through sharing their vision.
- ›› Followers respect and adore the charismatic leader and so follow their guidance.
- ›› They set high performance standards not only for others but also for themselves.

Evaluating charismatic leadership theory

One strength of **charismatic leadership** theory is that it can be studied quantitatively. Cicero *et al.* (2007) used a field study methodology with a questionnaire to look at the link between charismatic leadership and work productivity, finding that there was a positive correlation between the two variables. Quantitative research is objective and allows statistical analysis to be performed, making the results more reliable and the theory more credible.

> ## ISSUES AND DEBATES
>
> ### Individual and situational explanations
>
> Charismatic leadership theory focuses purely on individual factors. For example, it suggests that good leadership is based upon internal characteristics such as charisma, ability to motivate and inspire and being able to understand others emotional needs. This is a weakness as it ignores situational factors, such as the environment or the social class structure, meaning that it is not a complete theory.
>
> ### Application to everyday life
>
> If, as believed by both charismatic and great person theory, great leaders have similar characteristics or traits, then employers could use forms of testing, i.e. psychometric testing, to identify these traits in employees. Indeed, psychometric testing is an integral part of the recruitment process for many organisations and may help employers find the right candidate, or the right person to be promoted within the company. This shows that universalist theories can be applied to everyday life.

Transformational leadership theory

A **transformational** leader is one that stimulates and inspires their followers to work harder to achieve a particular outcome. They are concerned with the needs of their followers and aim to help them look at problems in a different way. Transformational leaders inspire positive change in their followers, who will be taught to look after their own interests alongside the interests of the group.

Transformational leaders seek to increase the motivation and performance of their followers through tying their sense of identity and self to the group and the organisation. The transformational leader becomes a role model for their followers, allowing followers to take greater ownership of their work and to understand their own strengths and weaknesses.

Warrilow (2012) discussed four characteristics of transformational leaders:

1 **Idealised influence**: This is the degree to which a leader behaves in an admirable way, taking a stand on issues that followers identify with and having a clear set of values and morals. This leader is a role model for others.
2 Inspirational motivation: The degree to which a leader has a vision that appeals to followers. They are optimistic about future goals and give meaning to the current ones.
3 Intellectual stimulation: The degree to which the leader challenges and encourages creativity in their followers. This allows them to overcome any obstacles in the way of their goal.
4 Personal and individual attention: The degree to which the leader attends to individualised needs, acts as a mentor and respects everyone's contribution to the team that fulfils the need for self-fulfilment and self-worth; this helps the follower to grow as a person.

Evaluating transformational leadership theory

One strength of transformational leadership is that there is research support which suggests that this type of leadership is effective. Studies such as Rubin *et al.* (2005) found that individuals with characteristics that identify them as transformational leaders were evaluated as highly effective, performing at a high level and increasing levels of productivity. This research support, therefore, suggests that the theory has high validity.

One weakness of transformational leadership is that it assumes that this type of leadership is always beneficial to the workforce whatever the situation. Numerous studies such as Stevens *et al.* (1985) have found that situational variables can mean that transformational leadership can have a negative effect on followers, leading to emotional stress, burnout and work conflict. This is important, as if the theory encourages this type of leadership when organisations are looking for a leader, despite the psychological harm it can cause, it could be said to be unethical.

> ### ISSUES AND DEBATES
>
> #### Reductionism versus holism
>
> All universalist theories are more on the reductionist side of the reductionism versus holism debate. All three theories reduce leadership down to having specific characteristics or traits; assuming that all people with these traits will become great leaders. This ignores the role of learning in leadership, and also the role of the situation, i.e. the workplace. It may be that someone has all these traits but never becomes a leader due to factors within the workplace that stop them from doing so, suggesting that all three theories are not completed theories of leadership.

> ### LEARNING LINKS
>
> Universalist theories suggest that situational factors are not important when looking at leadership. Look back at your AS Level studies. Which ones would disagree with this idea and suggest that actually the situation you find yourself in is more important in influencing how you behave?

> ### STUDY TIP
>
> All of these theories have similarities and differences to each other. Although the strengths and weaknesses here have been separated for each theory, it may be useful to look at them all together and come up with some evaluation points that can be used for universalist theories as a whole. This may be linked to some of the debates and methodological issues of whether you can generalise these leadership characteristics to all cultures and/or ethical issues.

▶ **TEST YOURSELF**

1 Antonio has just been appointed manager for a local food production company. When discussing why they had appointed Antonio as manager, the company directors say that he is popular with everyone in the workforce and that when he communicates with the workforce, he seems to inspire them and they seem to respect him and will follow him.

   a Explain which type of leadership Antonio may be using with the workforce. [2]

   b Explain one weakness of the type of leadership discussed in a. [2]

2 Outline one difference between the great person and charismatic theories of leadership. [2]

3 a Describe what psychologists have learnt about universalist theories of leadership. [6]

   b Evaluate what psychologists have learnt about universalist theories of leadership, with a discussion of individual v situational factors. [10]

4 Explain what is meant by universalist theories of leadership. [2]

5 Managers in local workplaces want to discover whether leaders really show the characteristics suggested by universalist theories.

   a Plan a study using a questionnaire to investigate the most common characteristics of leaders in the workplace.

     Your plan must include:

     – questionnaire format

     – sampling technique. [10]

   b i State two reasons for your choice of questionnaire format. [2]

     ii Give one weakness of your choice of questionnaire format. [2]

     iii Explain one reason for your choice of sampling technique. [2]

KEY TERMS

temporal validity

initiating behaviour

consideration behaviour

employee and production orientation

Behavioural theories of leadership

Think!

What were the two types of leadership behaviour found in the Michigan University research project?

Think!

You are doing some research on leadership theories and have been asked to do a presentation to workplace directors on whether you believe leadership is due to nature or nurture and the implications your findings will have for the directors at their companies. For example, you could think about areas such as research support or the era (time) in which the theories were developed. Remember to come to a judgement about which side you think is stronger (or if neither of them is) and what that could mean for a company.

Think!

When completing the LBDQ questionnaire, responders had to indicate how many times a leader showed a particular behaviour. Can you think of any issues that may arise when asking workers to state a certain type of behaviour their group leader/manager has shown?

The workplace in the late 1940s was different from today in terms of type of work, who went to work, and how long people were in the same job. Research more about the workplaces in the late 1940s when Ohio and Michigan universities did their studies. Does this have any implications for the **temporal validity** of the explanations?

▲ Figure 9.9

Behavioural theories of leadership began as a response to the inability of universalist theories to isolate and measure the inherited characteristics needed to be a leader (see page 659). Behaviourist theories moved away from trying to measure specific characteristics or personalities, and concentrated more on observed behaviours, looking specifically at how an individual must behave to be a successful leader.

Two research projects, one by Ohio University and one by Michigan University, investigated effective leaders and their behaviours. Both research studies used mainly surveys and their samples consisted of not only the leaders themselves, but also their followers. Both came to similar conclusions and together are known as the behavioural theories of leadership.

The main difference between behavioural theories and universalist theories is that behavioural theories believe leadership can be learned and therefore concentrate more on the nurture rather than the nature side of the debate.

Ohio University behavioural explanations

Researchers at Ohio State University (1948) believed that studying leadership as a personality trait was worthless and instead decided to research how people acted when they were leading a group or organisation. To do this, the researchers asked followers (such as members of the leaders' work group) to complete a questionnaire about their leaders. When completing the questionnaire, the followers had to indicate how many times a leader had engaged in a particular behaviour.

The initial questionnaire consisted of over 1800 items which described potential leadership behaviours. From the responses given to these 1800 items, the Leader Behaviour Description Questionnaire (LBDQ) was formulated. The LBDQ comprises 150 statements about leadership behaviours. The LBDQ was then completed by a sample of workers in the military, education and industry. Each participant answered how frequently a particular behaviour was displayed, on a five-point rating scale, with answers ranging from never to always.

The quantitative results showed that there were two clusters of behaviour associated with leadership:
1 **Initiating (structural) behaviours**: These are task-related behaviours where the leader gives structure to the workforce. This can include behaviours which:
    ›› set clear expectations for followers
    ›› enable improvement through the use of feedback, including constructive criticism
    ›› set performance standards including the maintenance of policies and procedures
    ›› emphasise the importance of meeting milestones and targets
    ›› coordinate work tasks within the group.

    A high level of this type of behaviour means that there are few uncertainties for employees, although in the extreme this type of behaviour can lead to a leader making all decisions for their workers, leaving them with no autonomy, and punishing those who do not meet expectations.
2 **Consideration (nurturing) behaviours**: These are people-related behaviours which focus on the relationships and welfare of the workers. They include:
    ›› listening to the workers and other members of the organisation
    ›› seeing people as equals and treating them with respect
    ›› being friendly, supportive and available to workers
    ›› showing empathy for others and increasing trust amongst the team.

    This type of behaviour indicates that the leader will work on the trust between themselves and others and will look to create supporting and warm relationships within a team. This type of leader will use active listening, will seek to understand the strengths and weaknesses of each member and will look for areas where the team members can grow.

These behaviours are independent of each other and therefore you could be low or high on both. For example, you could be low on initiating (structural) behaviours and also low on consideration (nurturing) behaviours.

Many studies were done to look at the effectiveness of the two types of behaviour, suggesting that initiating (structural) behaviours were more effective in terms of leadership than consideration (nurturing) behaviours.

Evaluating the Ohio University explanations

One strength of the Ohio University explanation is that it provided a way of studying leadership quantitatively. For example, using surveys which included a five-point scale to indicate how often behaviours occur. This is a strength as it allows for objective analysis which is not subject to the interpretation of the researcher; this makes the study's findings more reliable and the explanation more scientific.

> ## ISSUES AND DEBATES
>
> ### Reductionism versus holism
>
> One weakness of the Ohio State University explanation is that it is reductionist, as it concentrates on learned aspects rather than inherited aspects. Rather than believing that leadership is based on traits that are inherited or 'gifted from God', it solely concentrates on behaviours which can be learned. This is a weakness as it is likely that leadership is more holistic and is a combination of both learned and inherited aspects, with individuals having an innate quality that makes them more likely to be a leader, which will then become more effective with training and experience.

Michigan University behavioural explanations

Michigan University explored leadership behaviour by looking at its impact on small groups. Starting with interviews, a questionnaire similar to the LBDQ was formulated. The results of this research identified the following two different types of leadership behaviour:

1 **Employee orientation** is when a leader takes an interest in human beings as people, valuing them as individuals and making sure they pay attention to their personal needs. This cluster of behaviours can be seen to be very similar to the consideration behaviours found in the Ohio University studies.
2 **Production orientation** is leadership behaviour that looks at the technical and production elements of the job. Workers are seen as a means to an end and just there to get the work done. This type of behaviour is similar to the initiating behaviours of the Ohio University studies.

Unlike the Ohio University explanation, initially Michigan University saw these two aspects as opposite ends of the same spectrum, and therefore if you are high in employee orientation behaviours then you will be low in production orientation behaviours.

However, as further research was completed, Michigan University rethought this approach and stated that, as with the Ohio university findings, these were two distinct behaviours and you could be high or low on both. In addition, the Michigan University studies found that employee orientation was more effective than production orientation behaviour, which is the opposite to the Ohio university findings.

Evaluating the Michigan University explanations

> ## ISSUES AND DEBATES
>
> ### Individual and situational explanations
>
> One weakness of Michigan University explanations is that they ignore situational factors in leadership behaviours. Many studies on leadership behaviours are inconclusive about which types are more effective. Therefore, it may be that rather than a type of leadership being the most important at any one time, the situational aspects, such as type of task, personality of the workforce and even how experienced workers are, may affect which type of behaviour is most effective.

Nature versus nurture

In contrast to universalist theories of leadership, which are more on the nature side of the debate, behaviourist theories are clearly more on the nurture side of the debate. Both the Michigan and Ohio university studies still concentrate on characteristics that make individuals good leaders but believe that these characteristics can be learned. The likelihood is, however, that neither side is correct and that there are aspects of your personality (nature) that make you more likely to be a good leader, but these can be enhanced through training and the right environment at work (nurture)

Application to everyday life

One strength of the Michigan University explanation is that it can be applied to real life. Unlike universalist theories, the Michigan University explanation means that leaders can be trained to use behaviours that are seen as more effective in that they are more employee orientated. Leaders can also be appointed based upon them having these specific behaviours. This is a strength as it allows the explanations to be used in the workplace to increase productivity, making the explanations useful.

LEARNING LINK

Ohio University used self-reports to look at leadership. However, there are a number of issues with self-reports when studying behaviour. Have a look back at what you have learned about self-reports in your research methods unit, as well as the use of self-reports in studies, and discuss the issues that researchers have to be aware of when using this type of methodology.

STUDY TIP

One important aspect that needs to be considered when learning about leadership theories, and any studies that support them, is who devised the theory and where. You always need to consider whether the theory considers cultural differences and if not what the implications are for the theory. Think about what you know about workplaces in your country and try to write down whether you feel the theories discussed so far apply.

TEST YOURSELF

1 Janet is meeting with the managers of her local bank. She is discussing how to increase productivity within the company using the behavioural theories for information.
   a Suggest one type of behaviour that may increase productivity in the bank. [2]
   b Suggest one way the company could find out about the types of behaviours shown by the leaders in the company. [2]
2 a Describe one behavioural theory of leadership. [2]
   b Evaluate how the leadership theory you have described in (a) is reductionist. [2]
3 Compare one behaviourist theory and one traditional theory of leadership. [2]
4 a Describe what psychologists have found about behavioural theories of leadership. [6]
   b Evaluate what psychologists have found about behavioural theories of leadership, including a discussion on individual vs situational factors. [10]
5 Describe how the Leadership Behaviour Description Questionnaire (LBDQ) was created. [2]
6 Explain one strength and *one* weakness of using self-reports to study leadership behaviour. [4]
7 Suggest an alternative way of studying leadership behaviour in the workplace. [2]

KEY TERMS
adaptive leaders
dysfunctional
whistleblowers
creative deviants

Heifetz's six principles in meeting adaptive challenges

Think!

What does it mean to 'get on the balcony' according to Heifetz's model?

Think!

Your company is not performing well; productivity is down and you are worried you may have to make some workers redundant. You know that the values and beliefs of the company have to change but you are unsure of how to get the workers to agree to changes. The changes include different shift patterns, adjusting values in the workplace to increase public trust and increasing worker performance through goal setting. Use Heifetz's theory to explain two strategies you could use to ensure that the changes can be implemented with support and adaptive challenges overcome.

Think!

One methodological issue that often comes up with models of leadership is whether you can generalise your findings/model to a wider population. Why might Heifetz's model not be generalisable to all types of workplaces/populations?

Think back to a time when you have had to adapt to new challenges or when something has gone wrong and you have had to find a way to overcome the problem. This could be on your own or part of a group. What types of behaviours do you feel helped you overcome an issue or adapt to change? Do you feel those behaviours were different depending on whether you were alone or in a group? Do they relate at all to the six principles you have learned on these pages?

▲ Figure 9.10

What are adaptive challenges?

Workplaces today face many different challenges. Changes in society, customers and rivals, as well as technological advances mean that organisations have to reflect and change their values, develop new practices, and learn innovative ways to operate. For a leader within a workplace, their biggest responsibility is mobilising the workplace to react to these challenges and be adaptive themselves in their work.

Adaptive work is required when our beliefs are challenged and the values that had made us successful are no longer effective, and when competing values and perspectives emerge. For example, when a certain shift pattern or way of working becomes less effective, then the company will restructure their business in order to adapt to these challenges and change the way they run their business.

For many leaders adapting to change is the most difficult challenge they may face for two possible reasons:
1 To make change happen, managers and leaders have a responsibility to change their belief that it is only they who can solve a problem. With adaptive challenges this is not the case, as the solution resides within the workforce as much as, if not more than, its leader.
2 Adaptive challenges can be distressing for those going through them. New roles, behaviours and relationships are often part of the changes, and often workers want the responsibility for this to be taken off them and placed on the leaders. However, this will not work, and so this expectation has to be unlearned. Leaders have a responsibility to ask tough questions, show workers the reality of the situation and challenge any issues that arise.

Heifetz and Laurie (1997) offered six principles for leading adaptive work.

1 Get on the balcony: Business leaders must view patterns within the workplace as if they were away from the situation. For leaders, this means it is good to be away from the centre of the action. Getting on the balcony means taking a more objective overview and this, in addition to working amongst the rest of the workforce, may help to identify power struggles, work avoidance and/or resistance to change. Without this capacity to move back and forth to the balcony, there are many ways in which the habits formed in an organisation can sabotage adaptive work and leaders can quickly become a prisoner of the system.

2 Identify the adaptive challenge: When a threat appears, the company and its leaders need to identify the threat rapidly and respond to it effectively to make efficient and sustainable changes. If they do not do this, then the company may become bankrupt and fail. The example used by Heifetz was the one of British Airways, where passengers themselves were nicknaming the business '—— Awful'. Company CEOs identified their adaptive challenge as 'creating trust throughout British Airways' and had the team integrating with both employees and customers in various areas of the business, asking people to identify which values and beliefs needed to change. A number of conflicts within the workforce were discovered and the workforce was seen as **dysfunctional**. Once this was established, the team worked to change the values of the workforce. As collaboration between workers increased, the reputation of the company became more positive.

3 Regulate distress: Adapting to change can lead to distress. It is important that leaders realise that people need to learn new things at a steady pace and not too fast or they will become overwhelmed. On the other hand, eliminating all forms of stress does not provide an incentive to change in the first place, so there is a delicate balance to maintain. There are three tasks needed to regulate distress:

   a Leaders must create a holding environment where people are allowed to let off steam or express their views without feeling constrained. This can include leaders allowing groups to talk about the challenges ahead and discuss and debate competing views.

   b A leader must shape norms, manage conflict and shape the direction in which the workforce goes. They must maintain the rate of change, define key issues and not change too much too soon.

   c A leader must have a presence amongst the workforce. They must understand the pain of change, whilst holding steady and maintaining just the right amount of tension.

4 Maintain disciplined attention: A diverse workforce will have different values, beliefs and habits in their work life. This diversity is a strength as it allows for contrasting views to be heard. Rather than avoiding contrasting issues, leaders need to confront them and allow them to be discussed and debated. They must not allow individuals to be scapegoated for their views but allow the conversation to lead to collaboration and compromise and show that this is the way to solve conflicts.

5 Give the work back to the employees: Everyone needs to take responsibility for their work. Often when challenges arise workers can become passive and expect leaders to take responsibility for the challenges that they face and solve any problems. Many workers are okay being told what to do, but many leaders also like telling people what to do and assuming control over workers. Letting people take the initiative and take risks when solving problems means that leaders need to support and not control. The leader's responsibility is to make sure their workers have confidence in themselves to do this, and this means it is equally important that the leaders also have self-confidence.

6 Protect voices of leadership from below: This means that **whistleblowers, creative deviants** and those exposing conflicts and contradictions within the workplace should be protected and heard. Their perspectives are often seen as creating a dysfunctional workforce and therefore are silenced, but actually their voices can mean a fresh approach can be taken and serious conflicts avoided. Silencing these voices due to bad timing, seeming unreasonableness or lack of clarity, may mean loss of important information that could have helped the company to grow.

Evaluating Heifetz's six principles

> ## ISSUES AND DEBATES

Application to everyday life

One strength of any model is in its application to real life. In this case, the six principles of **adaptive leadership** as suggested by Heifetz can be put into practice successfully within companies that are struggling with productivity and customer satisfaction. This was seen with British Airways who managed to change their business model to increase customer satisfaction and profitability. This is a strength as it shows that the model is useful and that it can be used in a positive way to improve businesses and indeed the work-life of the workforce.

Individual and situational explanations

Another strength of the model is that it takes situational aspects of the workplace into account. Most models of leadership only look at individual characteristics or behaviours that identify effective leaders; this is not the case for the Heifetz model as it shows that workplaces are dynamic and are often changing and new problems may arise. Therefore, leaders need to adapt and change their behaviour to meet the challenges and maintain productivity and collaboration showing the importance of situational factors.

Reductionism versus holism

One weakness of the model is that it is reductionist. Models such as Heifetz's adaptive leadership model break down leadership into components such as identifying the adaptive challenges and stepping on the balcony. This is a weakness as leadership should be looked at holistically to include other factors within the workforce, such as the different personalities of the workers and the type and size of the business, which are not considered under this model.

The Heifetz model may not be able to be **generalised** to all cultures. Heifetz's model focuses on the Western representation of the workforce. Therefore, it assumes that concepts such as stepping on the balcony and protecting voices of leadership from below are applicable to all cultures, which may not be the case. This is not to say that the model itself is culturally biased, but there needs to be consideration of whether all parts apply in all cultures.

> ## LEARNING LINK
>
> Heifetz identifies the potential role of whistleblowers and creative deviants in his six principles for leading adaptive work; these are people who do not always conform to expectations and may rebel against workplace practices and rules that they see as pointless or harmful in some way. Think about how people such as this might have behaved in the Milgram study (obedience). Why do you think people like this sometimes have difficulties at work but ultimately may be integral to the company's success?

STUDY TIP

It is important to use the questions on these pages, as well as any given to you by your teacher. This will help you to understand whether there are areas you either do not know so well or do not understand. Always try and ask for feedback on any questions that you attempt.

> ## TEST YOURSELF

1 One of Suvetra's team members has come to see her as she has observed that the mood within the team is low. Suvetra knows that there has been considerable change within the company recently and she admits that perhaps the change has gone too fast.
   a Explain which of Heifetz's six principles Suvetra's company has not been following, which has led to low mood in the team. [2]

    b Explain one way that Suvetra can raise the mood of the workers, using Heifetz's principles. [2]

2 Explain why models such as Heifetz may not be applied to all cultures and workplaces. [2]

3 a Describe what psychologists have learned about adaptive leadership. [6]

    b Evaluate what psychologists have learned about adaptive leadership, including a discussion about reductionism versus holism. [10]

4 Heifetz's six principles talked about adjusting to adaptive challenges.

    a Explain what is meant by adaptive challenges. [2]

    b Explain how *one* of Heifetz six principles can be applied to a real-life situation. [2]

5 Jonathan wants to find out how workers are coping with the challenges and changes that have happened in the last month.

Plan a study using an observation to find out whether workers are coping with the challenges and changes over the last month. Your plan must include details about:

– behavioural categories

– type of observation. [10]

6 State two reasons for the type of observation you have chosen. [2]

9.2.2 Leadership style

Think!

Explain the difference between **personal**, **private** and **public leadership** according to Scouller's 3P Model of Leadership.

Think!

Coralie's workplace distributes medication to people in their home. Over the last few days, a high number of workers off sick has meant that they have got behind in their work and were in danger of not getting medication to patients on time. This may lead to increased illness or even death of patients and so inexperienced agency workers have been brought in. As a leader, Coralie needs to make a decision quickly on how they can catch up with work before patients are in danger. Using Muczyk and Reimann's theory, explain what style of leader behaviour would be effective in helping the workforce to catch up.

Think!

One debate that is often discussed when talking about leadership theories is the situational versus individual debate. How do the two theories discussed on these pages fit in terms of this debate? Does one take situational factors into account more than the other? Does one take into account both?

 Muczyk and Reimann's theory discusses four different dimensions of leadership. Have you encountered any of the four types of leadership, linked to these dimensions, in your everyday life, such as a **directive autocrat**? Do the circumstances match the explanations given by Muczyk and Reimann?

Muczyk and Reimann's four styles of leader behaviour

Muczyk and Reimann (1987) believed that there are five dimensions that can be applied to leadership. They suggested that two of them: **participation** and **direction** were situation dependent. This means that leaders may choose different approaches to how they make decisions, for example how much participation the workforce has in the decision-making process and how these decisions are then carried out, such as the amount of direction (or control) over how the decision is executed, depending on the situation.

KEY TERMS

participation

direction

autocratic

public leadership

private leadership

personal leadership

self-mastery

METHODOLOGY

generalisations from findings

Muczyk and Reimann suggested that culture plays a huge part in the debate over what is an effective leader. Most studies and theories about leadership are conducted by American researchers, leading to an assumption that leaders everywhere should act in a way preferred by American culture: one consisting of democratic leadership and individual autonomy. They did not agree that this should be the case, or that there should be a universal leadership theory constructed. To avoid this, they use a 'contingency and situational' construct which accounts for different cultures. This means that autocratic and directive elements of leadership may be needed in societies outside the USA.

They suggested four styles of leadership:

1   Directive autocrat: This style means that there is no employee participation in decision-making and there is a large amount of directive, or close monitoring, on execution of decisions. Although not popular in places such as the USA where democratic leadership is preferred, Muczyk and Reimann explained that this may be efficient in a crisis where decisive and quick action needs to be taken. This type of leadership is often chosen when the workers are inexperienced or when the relationship between leaders and the workforce has broken down. For this to be effective the leader must be comfortable acting in such a way and still treat workers with respect.

2   Permissive autocrat: This style means that there is no employee participation in decision-making but there is far less directive, or close monitoring, over the execution of decisions by workers. This is again suited where quick decisions need to be made but also where the workforce has enough experience or the tasks to be done are simple enough or structured enough for the workers to complete them with more autonomy. Also, policies and procedures, incentives and professional standards are seen as a substitute for direct control and should be in place.

3   Directive democrat: This style means a large amount of employee participation in decision making but a large amount of directive, or close monitoring, of workers who are then executing that decision. Therefore, workers can take part in the decision-making process but once it is made then workers are supervised closely to make sure they are carrying the decision out properly. It is only appropriate when the tasks are complex and where speed of decision-making is not that important.

4   Permissive democrat: The style means a large amount of employee participation in decision-making and no close monitoring during the execution of the decision. This allows workers to participate in making decisions and then have autonomy in how these decisions are carried out. This works well in organisations where workers have both information and motivation for the task, where they are experienced and where proper policies and procedures are in place.

When looking at whether one style would be best for an organisation long term, it was acknowledged that changes in style may be needed as the organisation adapts to changing circumstances. Usually, a change is gradual with a movement from directive autocrat to permissive democrat often occurring as an organisation matures.

Evaluating Muczyk and Reimann

One strength of Muczyk and Reimann's theory is that it takes into account cultural differences. The theory suggests that to be an effective theory you need to consider cultural aspects of leadership and that autocracy and directive leadership may be more applicable to non-American cultures than democratic leadership. This is a strength as it means that the theory can be applied across cultures and not only to Western democracies such as the USA.

> **ISSUES AND DEBATES**

Reductionism versus holism

One weakness of Muczyk and Reimann's theory is that it still breaks leadership down into four specific styles. This can be said to be reductionist as it suggests that all leadership can be categorised into four key elements of behaviours: directive or permissive, autocratic or democratic. This is a weakness as there are many other theories that suggest a wider variety of behaviours which lead to effective leadership, and not only these four types, meaning it is not a complete theory of leadership.

Individual and situational explanations

Muczyk and Reimann believed that out of five dimensions of leadership behaviour, two are situation dependent (consideration and participation). They believed that leaders will decide how much workers are involved in the decision-making process, and how decisions are carried out dependent on the situation that they find themselves in. They also believe that different cultures may need different types of leadership and different times; suggesting that many aspects of leadership and decision-making processes may be based on the situation rather than individual characteristics of the leader themselves.

Scouller's levels of leadership

Scouller (2011) believed that leadership can be seen as a process that involves four dimensions:

1 Motivating purpose: Setting a purpose and direction that is inspiring to people means that they will work together collaboratively and willingly towards a goal.
2 Task progress results: Paying attention to the pace and quality of progress towards the goal.
3 Upholding group unity and spirit.
4 Attending to individual effectiveness.

For Scouller, leadership is not inherited but learned. He believed that leaders need to continually improve themselves technically and psychologically to become effective. Scouller's model, therefore, aimed to help leaders understand their role better and help them understand how they can better themselves.

For Scouller, a leader needs to ensure that their leadership meets the four dimensions explained above, and for this to happen they must work on three levels of leadership (3Ps) at the same time. The three Ps in Scouller's model are:

» **public leadership**
» **private leadership**
» **personal leadership.**

1 Public leadership (outer level): This focuses on the first, second and third dimensions (motivation, task progress and group unity). This includes a leader's actions in a group setting, such as in a meeting or when they are trying to influence the whole organisation. 34 behaviours need to be addressed during public leadership and these are grouped into five categories:
   » setting the vision
   » ensuring unity of purpose
   » achieving the group task
   » building trust and a sense of togetherness
   » creating peer pressure to ensure high performance standards.
   These behaviours aim to set group aims and make sure the job is completed.
2 Private leadership (outer level): This focuses on dimensions 2 and 4 (task progress and attending to individual effectiveness). This is the leader's one-on-one handling of the group. Private leadership acknowledges that team spirit is essential and that all group members have different levels of self-confidence, resilience, experience and motivation. For this reason, as well as being part of a group, they all need individual attention. There are fourteen different behaviours placed into two categories:
   » Individual task behaviours: Appraisal, disciplining, goal-setting and reviewing.
   » Individual building and maintenance: Relationship building and assessment of people's talents, competence and commitment.
3 Personal leadership (inner level): This covers all four dimensions as it works on the basics of a leader's effectiveness. This is shown by their leadership, presence, technical ability, skills and attitudes and **self-mastery**. This is the most influential of the three levels, driving a leader's emotional intelligence, impact, skill, judgement and insight. Personal leadership has three categories:
   » Technical: Updating skills such as time management, individual and group psychology. Practising skills that support public and private behaviours.
   » Attitude towards others: Believing people are as important as you are. This is important as it will determine how much they trust you as a leader.
   » Self-mastery: Working on self-awareness, enabling you to let go of beliefs that limit you, connect with your values and act authentically in the service of those you lead.

Scouller's model is classed as an integrated model, as it tries to include elements of many other theories including trait, behavioural, situational and functional theories.

Evaluating Scouller's levels of leadership

One weakness of Scouller's theory is that the basis of its leadership model is formed from a Western point of view. For example, areas such as self-mastery, appraisal and goal setting are based upon traditional values and beliefs in Western societies, and a particular structure of work. This may not be applicable to all cultures and all types of work and therefore could be said to be culturally biased.

> ### ISSUES AND DEBATES

Reductionism versus holism

One strength of Scouller's theory is that it is more holistic than other theories. Scouller's model includes elements of other theories such as leaders' different qualities (trait) and effect of the situation on behaviour. This is a strength as it is a more complete theory of leadership than other theories that concentrate on one specific area and are therefore more reductionist in nature.

> ### LEARNING LINK

Cultural differences are an important part of psychology, and psychological studies have sometimes been accused of only taking a Western point of view. Some studies however, such as Milgram (obedience), have tried to research different cultures to see whether they get the same results. Can you think of any other studies at AS Level, or even in your other option at A Level where cultural differences have/have not been taken into account?

STUDY TIP

To help summarise and learn the information on these pages try using flashcards and give yourself a maximum word count per card. Try to include the key words and phrases you need to remember, as well as the important evaluation issues. Also, remember that although we have included evaluation issues here, there are more, and so you could try and include some evaluation issues of your own.

> ### TEST YOURSELF

1 Hannah is going into a meeting with other members of the workforce. She wants to discuss the aim and values of the company for the long-term future.
   Using Scouller's model of leadership:
   a Explain which type of leadership will be most effective in the meeting.   [2]
   b Explain which other type of leadership may be needed with other less confident members of the group.   [2]
2 Explain why Scouller's theory is more holistic than other theories of leadership.   [2]
3 a Describe what psychologists have found out about leadership style.   [6]
   b Evaluate what psychologists have found out about leadership style, with a discussion of cultural differences.   [10]
4 Managers want to use Muczyk and Reimann theory to see whether directive or permissive leadership is more effective when trying to complete a task in a limited amount of time.
   a Plan a study using an experiment to find out whether directive or permissive leadership is more effective when completing a task.
      Your plan must include:
      – details about sampling technique
      – a directional or non-directional hypothesis.   [10]
   b i Describe the psychological knowledge that informed your plan.   [4]
      ii Explain how you used two features of this psychological knowledge to plan your experiment.   [4]

Key study: Women's access to managerial positions: An experimental study of leadership styles and gender – Cuadrado *et al.* (2008)

KEY TERMS

narrative

role congruity theory

pilot study

meta-analysis

stereotypes

gender incongruent

gender-stereotypical

Think!

What were the four experimental conditions in Cuadrado *et al.*'s (2008) study?

Think!

Daveed has noticed that the female managers in his company focus a considerably more on building up relationships with workers and involving them in decision-making than the male managers, who tend to make all the decisions themselves. Daveed wants to find out how the workers feel about the two different styles. He has researched Cuadrado *et al.*'s (2008) study but wants to study how the workers feel in a little more depth. How could Daveed take a more idiographic approach to evaluation of leadership styles in his company?

Think!

Explanations in psychology sometimes refer to differences between individuals and sometimes to differences between situations, but what do individual and situational explanations mean? Do you believe that the leadership styles discussed by Cuadrado *et al.* are due to personality factors (an individual explanation) or is it the situation in which leaders are placed that causes them to use a particular leadership style? Does your decision have any implications for an organisation?

Isabel Cuadrado is currently an associate professor of Social Psychology at the University of Almeria in Spain. Her interests include different types of leadership, gender stereotypes and prejudice. Cuadrado has a significant number of publications which focus on women's position within society, including different attitudes towards women in leadership positions, gender differences in leadership style and prejudice towards women in general. Her most recent work focuses more on prejudice and stereotypes and looks particularly at how adolescents perceive Chinese and Romanian immigrants.

Cuadrado *et al.*'s study assumes that the female leadership style is now the preferred style in a workplace. Can you think of anything that may suggest that this is not correct? For example, which style of leadership do you think you would respond to? Is this the same for everyone?

▲ Figure 9.11

▶ CONTEXT

Research has often looked for reasons why women are underrepresented in leadership positions. Explanations such as less effective leadership styles have been suggested, with the focus on autocratic versus democratic and task-oriented versus relationship-oriented styles. For Eagly and Johnson (1990), leadership studies provide an opportunity for researchers to see whether leadership is **gender-stereotypical** with males seen as more autocratic and task-oriented and women seen as more democratic and relationship-oriented.

Eagly *et al.* (1992) performed a **meta-analysis**, looking at how leaders are evaluated by others. They found that female leaders obtained poorer evaluations than males if they adopted stereotypically male leadership styles when the people evaluating them were men. However, it was not the case that men had poorer evaluations than women if they adopted stereotypically female leadership styles. In addition, when conducting a study on gender and effectiveness, results showed men were seen as more effective as leaders than women when completing stereotypical male activities, and women were seen as more effective than men when completing stereotypical female tasks. Also, males tended to favour men more than women when they were evaluators, but female evaluators showed no preference.

The above results link to the **role congruity theory** of prejudice towards female leaders, which is where men and women are evaluated less favourably when they are selected to perform tasks which are not **congruent** with their gender. As leadership roles tend to be male sex-typed, women are then treated less favourably.

▶ AIMS AND HYPOTHESES

To verify experimentally one of the assumptions of the role congruity theory of prejudice towards female leaders: that women who occupy leadership roles are evaluated less favourably than men when they adopt stereotypically masculine styles.

1 Female leaders will receive less favourable evaluations than male leaders when they adopt stereotypically masculine leadership styles (autocratic and task-oriented).
2 Male leaders will not receive less favourable evaluations than female leaders when they adopt stereotypically feminine leadership behaviours (democratic, relationship-oriented, individualised).
3 Female leaders will receive worse evaluations from male evaluators than from female evaluators.
4 Male leaders will receive similar evaluations from male and from female evaluators.

▶ METHODOLOGY

Cuadrado *et al.* (2008) used an experimental design with four experimental conditions. **Dependent variables** were measured through the use of structured questionnaires.

Sample

Participants were 136 second-year social psychology students from the National Open University of Spain. 53 per cent were women and 47 per cent were men (mean age of 29 years). Each participant was randomly assigned to each experimental condition (34 in each group). The participants received credit for their participation.

▶ PROCEDURE

Prior to the start of the study all participants were randomly assigned to one of four experimental conditions:
1 Female leader with a male stereotypical leadership style (autocratic/task-oriented).
2 Male leader with a male stereotypical leadership style (autocratic/task-oriented).
3 Female leader with a female stereotypical leadership style (democratic/relationship-oriented).
4 Male leader with a female stereotypical leadership style (democratic/relationship-oriented).
There were 34 participants in each condition.

The study uses a **narrative**, or written account, which describes a leader's behaviour in an organisational setting in order to investigate their hypotheses.

The narrative

The narrative used in Cuadrado *et al.*'s (2008) study was especially written for the research and manipulated the leader's sex and leadership style.

Participants were told to imagine that they were part of an emergency service in a public hospital. This was chosen as it is a gender-neutral setting but within the setting there are doctors (a stereotypically masculine role) and nurses (a stereotypically female role).

Participants were asked to evaluate a supervisor who was occupying that position for a trial period. The narrative described the supervisor's behaviour, with the only differences being related to the manipulation of the variables of sex and leadership style.

Dependent variables

After reading the narrative, participants completed an anonymous questionnaire which they were told would help with the evaluation process. The questionnaire included a number of different measures:

1 A list of fourteen adjectives (seven positive and seven negative) selected from previous research. Participants rated the degree to which they thought the words were applicable to the supervisor using a seven-point rating scale (where 1 = never and 7 = always). The positive adjectives included intelligent, honest and clever and the negative adjectives included careless, forgetful and bossy.
2 The supervisor's leadership capacity was measured using a seven-point rating scale (where 1 = totally negative/disagree and 7 = totally positive/totally agree). Four items were used, including: 'How would you evaluate X's general leadership capacity' and 'X is a competent supervisor'.
3 The leadership effectiveness of the supervisor was measured using a seven-point rating scale (where 1 = totally negative/disagree and 7 = totally positive/totally agree). Five items were used, including: 'How would you evaluate X's general achievement as a supervisor', and 'X does not perform his/her work as supervisor well enough'.

A **pilot study** using 40 participants had been carried out prior to the main study to test all aspects of the investigation. The participants evaluated the different versions of the narrative as credible, concise, true and clear.

▶ RESULTS

▼ Table 9.2 Means of leader's sex, leadership style and their interactions on adjective list, leadership capacity and leadership efficacy

Dependent variables	Leader's sex		Leadership style		Sex × Style Interaction			
	Male	Female	Stereotypically male (SM)	Stereotypically female (SF)	Male SM	Female SM	Male SF	Female SF
Adjective list	4.92	4.90	4.32	5.51	4.30	4.34	5.55	5.47
Leadership capacity	4.76	4.73	4.00	5.48	3.83	4.17	5.63	5.36
Leadership efficacy	4.87	4.74	4.21	5.41	4.18	4.21	5.52	5.33

The results show that, independent of sex, leaders who adopt a stereotypically female leadership style obtain significantly more favourable evaluations on all three dependent variables. Both males and females received considerably less favourable evaluations when male stereotypical leadership styles were adopted. Therefore, the results do not support Hypothesis 1.

Hypothesis 2 is supported as there were no differences in the evaluations received by male and female leaders when they adopted stereotypical female styles. However, care needs to be taken with these results due to the fact that neither sex was evaluated unfavourably when adopting **gender incongruent** styles.

Hypotheses 3 and 4 were not supported as the mean evaluation value of the leaders were virtually identical in males and females on all three dependent variables. The evaluations made by men and women were also similar on the three dependent variables.

There was also no significant difference in evaluation when looking at the interaction between sex and style.

CONCLUSIONS

- Female leaders do not receive less favourable evaluations than males when using stereotypically male leadership styles.
- Males do not favour leaders of their own sex.
- Stereotypically female leadership styles are more valued than stereotypically masculine leadership styles in modern organisations.

Methodological strengths and weaknesses

One strength of Cuadrado et al.'s study is that the measurements used for the dependent variables produced quantitative data. For example, rating scales were used to measure leadership effectiveness, leadership capacity and the adjective list. Quantitative data is objective and not subject to interpretation and therefore will be more reliable.

Another strength is that Cuadrado et al. used a standardised procedure. For example, each participant received the same narrative, with the only difference being the manipulated variables. They were also given the same measurements for the dependent variables and the same instructions. This is a strength as it means that the study can be replicated easily and therefore tested for reliability.

One weakness of Cuadrado et al.'s study is the artificiality of the task used in the study. For example, a narrative or written account was used. This task may not accurately reflect the true dynamics of a workplace and other variables which may come into evaluations, and there were also no consequences to the evaluations given. This suggests that the validity of the task will be low and may not be applicable to real life.

One weakness of Cuadrado et al.'s study is that the sample may not be representative of the wider population. For example, although participant numbers were relatively large, they were also psychology students from one university in Spain. This is a weakness as psychology students may have more knowledge about the theoretical basis of the study. Also, it may be that the results may not be replicated in other countries with different cultural norms. This means that **generalisability** of the results may be low.

Ethics

There were no real ethical concerns with this study. All data remained confidential, although knowing that all participants were on a second year social psychology course may have led them to be more identifiable. There was no potential for harm as this was a narrative task rather than a real-life situation, with no consequences for any manager or worker. All participants received credit for completion, so some may have felt pressured to continue even if they did not want to, raising the ethical question of the right to withdraw.

ISSUES AND DEBATES

Application to everyday life

The study has good application to everyday life as it showed that stereotypical female management styles were evaluated more highly and seen as more effective than stereotypical male leadership styles. This can be applied in the workforce and training targeted to ensure that managers, and potential managers, are aware of the different styles and how to get the best out of their workforce.

Idiographic versus nomothetic

Cuadrado *et al.*'s (2008) study takes a nomothetic approach to the study of gender and leadership, as they use experimental methodology including the use of structured questionnaires to measure the dependent variables. This type of approach ensures standardisation of method, but also provides very little detailed information about why participants evaluated the leaders as they did. An idiographic approach where qualitative methods were used, including the use of unstructured questionnaires and interviews, would give the researchers more insight into the reasons behind the evaluations given.

Reductionism versus holism

Reductionism is reducing down complex behaviour into small parts in order to make it easier to study scientifically. In this case, Cuadrado broke down leadership effectiveness and capacity into rating scales and also a series of adjectives, which they also rated as being applicable to a novel scenario. This type of method does not give any insight into individual reasons behind rating an individual in a certain way and is, therefore, reductionist.

▶ REFLECTION

- Cuadrado *et al.* (2008) used a narrative task in order to evaluate leadership styles. What other ways could you evaluate leadership styles in order to make the study more valid?
- Cuadrado *et al.* (2008) used psychology students from Spain in order to investigate different leadership styles. It has been suggested that this may not be the best sample to use. As well as psychology students knowing more about theory, what other issues may there be? Think about the typical age of students.

▶ LEARNING LINK

Cuadrado *et al.* (2008) used an experimental methodology with a narrative task which has been suggested to be lower in validity and may not be applied to real life. A number of studies at AS Level took an experimental methodology such as Andrade (2010), Baron-Cohen *et al.* (2001) and Perry *et al.* (2015). Think about the tasks used in these and other studies. Do they also have the issue that their validity may be low? Or are there any that have higher validity and can be more applicable to real life situations?

STUDY TIP

When learning key studies, it is important that you know the aims, hypotheses, procedure, results and conclusions of the study as well as being able to evaluate it. One way you could try and learn the study is to create a storyboard which goes through all the aspects. You could even draw researchers evaluating amongst themselves what has gone right and wrong in the research. You could also organise a debate where one side could argue that this was good research, whereas the other side could respond that there were too many problems and then have a vote at the end.

▶ TEST YOURSELF

1 Tamara has been researching different leadership styles and has been interested to find out that there is a stereotypically female leadership style.
   a State two features of a stereotypically female leadership style. [2]
   b Outline what research has shown about the effectiveness of stereotypically female leadership styles when compared to stereotypically male leadership styles. [2]
2 Explain measurements that can be used to evaluate different leadership styles used in the workplace. [4]

3 a Describe the study by Cuadrado *et al.* (2008) on women's access to managerial positions. [6]

b Evaluate the study by Cuadrado *et al.* (2008) on women's access to managerial positions, including a discussion on generalisability of findings. [10]

From the key study by Cuadrado *et al.* (2008) on women's access to managerial positions:

4 Describe the narrative that was used in the study by the researchers to investigate their hypotheses. [4]

5 Explain two findings from Cuadrado *et al.*'s (2008) study. [2]

6 Explain two reasons why Cuadrado *et al.*'s (2008) study may be high in reliability. [4]

9.2.3 Leaders and followers

Think!

Kouzes and Posner suggest five practices that make an exemplary leader. What are they? Which one do you think is the most important?

Think!

Walter wants to find out what leadership practices different managers use with the workforce in his company and whether different levels of management use different practices. How could Walter use Kouzes and Posner's research to help him find out which practices the different managers use?

Think!

Kouzes and Posner used both qualitative and quantitative data to formulate the LPI. What are the strengths of using both types of data in research?

Psychometric tests are a particular type of test which find out about a person's personality, skills and knowledge. They often use rating scales and 'forced choice' statements. What do you think may be a problem with this type of test? Can you see the reasons why they may be useful?

▲ Figure 9.12

KEY TERMS

leadership practice inventory

five practices

METHODOLOGY

self-reports

psychometrics

Kouzes and Posner's Leadership Practices Inventory

When Kouzes and Posner began researching leadership, their main aim was to try and get away from the idea that leadership was inherited and that only a certain few people can become leaders. They mainly researched middle and senior managers over a spell of 30 years and used both qualitative and quantitative methods in order to produce not only their **Leadership Practices Inventory**, but also their five practices of exemplary leadership.

Kouzes and Posner's **five practices** of exemplary leadership, therefore, were based upon thousands of case studies, a large number of interviews and millions of survey questionnaires. During these interviews, surveys and case studies, leaders were asked about their own best leadership experiences.

The five practices

When all of these responses were analysed Kouzes and Posner suggested that:

'When making extraordinary things happen in organisations, leaders engage in what they call The Five Practices of Exemplary Leadership.' (Kouzes and Posner, 2017)

These five practices are:

1 Model the way: Leaders should inspire and motivate others. Leaders must model the way and set an example, because if they do not then why would people trust or follow them?

Leaders need to be clear about what they believe in and show that they can take a strong stand on issues. They need to be true to themselves, always tell followers the truth; be honest with them. Leaders need to do what they say they are going to do. Leaders need to remain humble when praise is given, allowing workers to get the praise instead. They should understand completing a task or project is a group effort and they cannot do it alone. As Kouzes and Posner (1997) stated, 'Becoming a leader begins when you come to understand who you are, what you care about, and why you do what you do.'

2   Inspire a shared vision: Kouzes and Posner believed that having a vision of the exciting possibilities for the future and also getting others to share that vision is the characteristic that separates leaders from non-leaders. The results of thousands of LPI responses show that credibility is the single most important asset a leader can have, suggesting that 'if you don't believe in the messenger you won't believe the message.' The leader also needs to be forward-looking, leading in the present but also keeping an eye on what will happen tomorrow.

3   Challenge the process: This includes the search for opportunities, taking risks and experimenting. For Kouzes and Posner (1997), 'only challenge provides the opportunity for greatness.' Leaders do not wait for things to happen; they make them happen; they are the ones that seek change. They challenge the status quo, not waiting for an opportunity to arise, but making one happen. They should not fear failure, as often leaders learn to lead through the process of trial and error. They need to remember, however, that they cannot do this without workers, who often are the ones that turn ideas into action.

4   Enable others to act: This practice fosters collaboration and strengthens the team. It empowers workers to make decisions and creates trustworthy relationships where people feel like they are an important part of a team.

5   Encourage the heart: For Kouzes and Posner, leadership is not just about the head but about the heart. They recognise that accomplishing aims takes dedication and commitment, and to help that a leader should recognise accomplishments and contributions of others both publicly and privately. Leaders inspire others through their drive and their courage, and look to make heroes and heroines of other people. Leaders can encourage performance using incentives and rewards, as well as verbal praise and recognition: something that often costs the organisation nothing but means everything to the worker.

The Leadership Practice Inventory (LPI)

Kouzes and Posner formulated the LPI to measure these five practices. The LPI is a **psychometric** measure which uses a questionnaire. The initial formation of the LPI started with case studies, interviews and self-reports completed by participants which were then analysed to formulate the five practices. There are two parts to the LPI: the LPI self which is completed by the leader who rates themselves on the frequency they believe they engage in specific behaviours; and the **LPI observer** which is completed by up to 10 other people (both superiors and followers) who rate the frequency that they believe the leader engages in specific behaviours.

Both versions of the questionnaire are the same and comprise 30 questions, with six of these questions dedicated to each of the five practices. The questions are forced choice and answered using a ten-point rating scale where 1 is almost never, 5 is occasionally and 10 is almost always. The respondents can then see their results, and how they compare with the average rating of other people. Some of the statements included are:

14. Treats people with dignity and respect (Enable)

3. Seeks challenging opportunities to test skills (Challenge)

7. Describe a compelling image of the future (Inspire)

1. Sets a personal example of what is expected (Model)

10. Expresses confidence in people's abilities (Encourage)

Evaluating Kouzes and Posner

One strength of Kouzes and Posner's five practices and the LPI in particular is that it is a self-report method which uses a ten-point rating scale. Rating scales allow the researcher to collect quantitative data. This is a strength as it is more objective and not subject to experimenter bias and therefore is more reliable.

Another strength of Kouzes and Posner's research is that later research studies have found the LPI to be both reliable and valid. Kouzes and Posner (1993) involved 2876 managers and observers from a wide variety of organisations and found that the results from the self and observer were identical in terms of rank order, there were no significant differences between genders and that the type of organisation did not significantly affect the scores. Therefore, the results did not show gender bias, there were no significant signs of social desirability, and that the LPI is applicable across organisations.

One weakness of Kouzes and Posner's research is the use of psychometric tests to establish which five practices a leader uses. Psychometrics may be subject to social desirability bias and also exaggeration and lying. It may be that the leader completing the survey has an awareness of what the test is looking for or the observer may not like their leader and therefore deliberately lie on the test. This is a weakness as it may mean that the results of the study are not measuring the practices accurately, lowering the validity of the measure.

> ## ISSUES AND DEBATES

Cultural differences

One weakness of Kouzes and Posner's research and of the LPI is that the researchers may not have taken into account cultural differences. The five practices are based upon a Western ideal of leadership, and the LPI is a psychometric test with statements which may not consider differences in language and culture. Indeed, in a study into the LPI's reliability and validity, significant differences in scores were found that were deemed to be due to cultural differences. This is a weakness as the results of the LPI may only reflect cultural and language differences rather than which of the five practices the leader uses, lowering its usefulness and ability to be generalised to the wider population.

Idiographic versus nomothetic

Nomothetic approaches try and make generalisations about the world through the use of methods such as experiments/questionnaires. Kouzes and Posner's LPI is a psychometric test (questionnaire) to measure their five practices in exemplary leadership, and therefore this is a more nomothetic approach. However, it is worth noting that formulating the five practices Kouzes and Posner used not only a more scientific approached but also qualitative methods such as case studies and in depth interview. Therefore, although the LPI itself is a more nomothetic approach, the initial research to formulate it used more idiographic methods as well.

Application to everyday life

The LPI could be used within organisations to identify the types of behaviours their leaders are using, or indeed not using. If, for example, it is found that that a leader is not practising one element of Kouzes and Posner's five practices, for example not using verbal praise and encouragement enough (encouraging the heart) then they can be made aware of this from their results on the LPI and improve their performance and as a consequence, that of their followers.

> ## LEARNING LINK

There are a number of studies at AS Level which have used self-reports. Have a look at the types of self-reports they have used and see whether you can see any difference between the self-reports used in those studies and the ones used for Kouzes and Posner's model. For example, do they all use rating scales or do they use different types of questions? Which do you feel may be more useful?

STUDY TIP

Sometimes the best way to understand the strengths and weaknesses of a measurement such as the LPI is to actually do it yourself. There are examples of the LPI test online and many of them allow you to take the test and get a score. Obviously, the results will not apply to you if you are not a leader or manager in your spare time, but it will allow you to understand how the test is completed and the possible strengths and weaknesses of it. Can you think of any type of person that may find the completion difficult?

TEST YOURSELF

1 Dylan is an organisational psychologist who has been asked to work with Sunil's company to find out about the leadership practices in the workforce.
  a Explain how Dylan could find out about the leadership practices in the workforce. [2]
  b Explain one leadership practice that Dylan is looking for. [2]
2 Explain what is meant by a psychometric test. [2]
3 a Describe what psychologists have discovered about leadership styles. [6]
  b Evaluate what psychologists have discovered about leadership styles, including a discussion about validity. [10]

The Leadership Practice Inventory has been used as a way of measuring leadership practice in the workplace.
4 Explain how the LPI was formulated by Kouzes and Posner. [2]
5 Describe how the LPI can be used to measure leadership practices in the workforce. [2]
6 Explain one strength and one weakness of using the LPI as a way of measuring leadership practices in the workforce. [4]

Followership (Kelley, 1988)

Think!

Explain what is meant by **critical thinking** and active participation.

Think!

Ezekiel has been an employee at Norbert's food company for over 20 years. He is well respected by the rest of the workforce and is trusted by the managers. He does not seem to need specific orders and always seems to know what to do and when. He is competent at all different parts of his job.

Alain is constantly looking for a different job with a different company. He always gets on with what he has to do but is often found having conversations with other workers about what is wrong in the organisation. He has never been happy since he did not get the team leader's position last year.

Which followership styles are Ezekiel and Alain showing?

Think!

How could you find out the type of followership style workers are showing in a local company? Can you think of any weaknesses of using this type of methodology?

One of the debates you will have learned in psychology is the nomothetic versus idiographic debate. What do these terms mean? Which approach do you think Kelley's theory of followership takes: nomothetic or idiographic? Give a reason for your answer.

▶ Figure 9.13

What is followership?

An organisation's success or failure has often been said to be based on how well they have been led. For this reason, research and theory has concentrated on the great leaders of today and yesterday. In addition, focus has been on how organisations can

KEY TERMS

active/passive thinking
conformist
alienated
pragmatic survivors
exemplary
critical thinking

recruit the best leaders or train people to become one. However, you cannot forget the people the leaders lead: the followership. Research on followership did not really start until the 1950s but became prominent with Kelley's theory in 1988. Early research saw followers as passive participants, but now most research sees leadership as a shared process between interdependent leaders and followers.

But what do we mean by followership? Crossman and Crossman (2011) reviewed literature and defined followership as:

'The ability to effectively follow the directives and support the efforts of a leader to maximise a structured organisation.'

Others would suggest followership is more person-centred. For example:

'The process of attaining one's individual goals by being influenced by a leader into participating in individual or group efforts towards organisational goals in a given situation.' (Wortman, cited in Crossman and Crossman, 2011).

In general, followership may be defined as the willingness to cooperate in working towards defined goals showing a high degree of teamwork. It is the willingness to follow a leader but playing an active not passive role in the process.

Kelley's (1988) two dimensions

Just as bosses may not be good leaders, workers may not be good followers. Through their careers, many bosses have also played the follower role. In fact, most people in their careers are more likely to be followers than leaders, yet they have neither the glamour nor the training that leaders have.

But what separates an effective follower from an ineffective one? For Kelley (1988), workers who are enthusiastic, intelligent and self-reliant make effective followers, but all have different motivations with some preferring being a follower rather than a leader, while others see it purely as a stepping stone to leadership.

Kelley (1998) suggested that these different motivations cannot separate effective and ineffective followers though and instead came up with two underlying dimensions that help explain differences:

1 Whether they are independent **critical thinkers** or dependent non-critical thinkers. Does the follower question, reason and analyse information/ideas given to them to form a judgement about a situation? Are they aware of what is going on around them and solve problems? Or do they just accept whatever is told to them without question?
2 Whether they are passive or active in terms of participation. Does the follower sit back and wait for others to do something, or do they get up and do it themselves?

Kelleys' five followership styles

These two dimensions led to the following five followership styles:

1 **Passive** (or sheep): 'Sheep' are passive and uncritical. They lack initiative and a sense of responsibility. They will perform the tasks asked of them but then they will stop. They score low in independent thinking and they are passive in terms of participation.
2 **Alienated**: These followers are critical and independent in their thinking but passive when they are performing their job. There has often been an event within their role that has turned them against their job such as being passed over for promotion or just being in the same job too long. They have become cynical, negative and resentful, but do not very often openly go against their boss and are happy just to whisper on the sidelines.
3 **Pragmatic** survivors: Often living by the motto 'better safe than sorry', they see how things are at any one moment and can shift their type of followership depending on what is needed at the time. These followers are often seen as an 'early warning system' in an organisation and often can see things going bad before others can. For this reason, this type of follower is the best at surviving change in the organisation.
4 **Conformist** (or 'Yes' people): They depend on the leader for inspiration and are usually totally obedient and never question orders. Bosses weak in self-confidence seem to like and form alliances with them but they can cause an organisation to lose enthusiasm and initiative. They score high on active participation but low on independent critical thinking.
5 **Exemplary**: These followers are the most effective and show the highest levels of performance, mainly due to their high levels of independent critical thinking. They carry

out their duties with enthusiasm and assertiveness. They are the risk-takers and problem-solvers, and often get high approval ratings from fellow workers and leaders. They will challenge a leader if they disagree with a decision and will provide alternative solutions. Followership of this type can be a source of pride and fulfilment for many, and they are satisfied in their work life and do not need to become leaders. Exemplary followers can succeed without strong leadership and many feel they offer as much to an organisation as leaders do, especially in task-based situations. They do not see the leader as a hero, but as a person who manages change. Effective followers manage themselves well, are committed to the organisation, build up their skills and are courageous and honest.

Evaluating Kelley (1988)

One strength of Kelley's followership styles is that research evidence has supported the idea that exemplary followership leads to higher performance. Favara (2009) studied 175 workers in one organisation using three questionnaires to measure followership style, job satisfaction and job performance. Favara found a significant positive correlation between exemplary leadership style and job satisfaction and performance. Therefore, the findings of Favara's research support Kelley's theory that the independent active nature of exemplary followers means they are more likely to show higher performance levels, making the theory more reliable.

ISSUES AND DEBATES

Application to everyday life

One strength of Kelley's followership styles theory is that it is of benefit to organisations and businesses. Kelley was one of the first theorists to look at types of followership, rather than types of leadership, and this gives organisations an idea of what an effective follower should be and how effective followership can be obtained within businesses. This is a strength as organisations can shift focus from just looking for effective leaders to also seeking effective followers. This could help increase morale and productivity, meaning that the theory can be applied effectively to everyday life.

Cultural differences

One weakness of Kelley's followership styles is that it may not be generalisable to all cultures. It may be that some of the five types of followership only apply to Western cultures. Oyetunji (2013) studied lecturers in Botswana universities who self-reported their followership style as well as their perception of their own job performance and found that although exemplary followers should be the most effective, the opposite was the case. Passive followers saw themselves as the best performers, with the other styles less so. Oyetunji (2013) suggested that these results could be due to cultural differences, especially as some cultures do not favour workers challenging leaders. Therefore, Kelley's five followership styles may only apply to certain cultures, limiting its generalisability.

Reductionism versus holism

Another weakness of Kelley (1988) is that it breaks followership down into specific, identifiable components. For example, it suggests that followers are one of five types, depending on where they score on two separate dimensions: critical thinking and passivity. This is a weakness as it does not consider other factors such as the situational aspects of a task or organisation or that followers may not fit into a specific type at all and just be a mixture of all five types. This makes the theory of followership types reductionist.

LEARNING LINK

One of Kelley's five followership styles is the conformist (yes people) style. Kelley suggested that followers using this style are usually obedient to leaders. Milgram's study (1963) at AS Level also looked at obedience. Milgram believed that there may be a type of personality which may be more obedient but found that situational factors are more important than individual factors. What implication does Milgram's conclusion have for Kelley's theory? Does it suggest that individuals will stick to a followership type throughout their work career? Are there any of Kelley's types which would agree with Milgram that the situation is more important than individual characteristics?

STUDY TIP

Many of the theories in this topic area use self-reports to measure leadership and followership types/behaviours. Therefore, it is very important that you learn the different types of self-reports, such as structured or unstructured, and the strengths and weaknesses of each of them. For example, think about reliability and validity as well as cultural differences and generalisability.

▶ TEST YOURSELF

1 Jamil's friend at work has been studying about followership behaviour and has said that Jamil uses a pragmatic survivor style.
   a Suggest characteristics that Jamil may be showing that led to his friend's suggestion. [2]
   b Explain the relationship between the style you have mentioned in (a) and levels of performance in the workplace. [2]
2 a Outline what is meant by generalisability, using an example from followership styles. [2]
   b Explain one similarity between two followership styles, as discussed by Kelley (1988). [2]
3 a Describe what psychologists have discovered about followership styles. [6]
   b Evaluate what psychologist have discovered about followership styles, with a discussion about usefulness. [10]
4 Outline the dimensions which informed Kelley's five styles of leadership. [2]
5 Suggest why Kelley's theory is more on the individual side of the individual vs situational debate. [2]
6 Explain two strengths of Kelley's study on followership styles. [4]

KEY TERMS

forming

storming

norming

performing

adjourning

triangulation

dynamic

METHODOLOGY

generalisations from findings

9.3 Group behaviour in organisations
9.3.1 Group development and decision-making

Think!

What are the five stages of group development as suggested by Tuckman and Jensen (2010)?

Think!

Janet's workplace has just won a big contract to supply a major company with uniforms. This is the biggest contract that they have ever won and Janet knows that she needs to form a team to try and work out how to complete the order.

The team comprises three other people and Janet has tried to include a mix of people with different skills and ideas:
- Thomas knows everything about making uniforms and meeting deadlines. Sometimes Janet thinks he has read every book about it and he is the person everyone goes to for information.
- Gulika is quiet but has fantastic attention to detail. She can see every error and can ensure all goods are of high quality.
- Simon keeps everyone together. If anyone is unhappy, they go to Simon and he will listen and suggest a solution.

Which team roles are each of the members displaying according to Belbin? What are the weaknesses of each of the roles?

Think!

Take a look at the two theories on these pages; would you categorise them as situational or individual explanations? Or a mix of both?

Look at Figure 9.14. What stage of Tuckman and Jensen's group development do you think they are at? And why? Think of a time you were in a group at school or at work. Do you believe you went through the five stages Tuckman and Jensen discussed? Are there any problems you can see with trying to use linear models which suggest you move from one stage to another?

▲ Figure 9.14

Tuckman and Jensen's (2010) stages of group development

For teams to be effective in the workplace, they need to work together collaboratively. This does not happen automatically and for a while the group is unsure how to function as a team and how to achieve their goal. Tuckman (1965) reviewed 55 different articles that studied small group development. From these articles he tried to find specific concepts which were common during the development of groups. The concepts discovered formed the basis of his original model which included four developmental stages:

1 **Forming**: Group members get to know each other and try to see which behaviours will and will not be acceptable to the group. This is a period of uncertainty and people look for guidance. A member who asserts authority may be seen as a potential leader. Team members will question what the team offers them and what they are expected to do. They also worry about fitting in.

2 **Storming**: This is the most critical stage of group development. This stage is often characterised by high levels of conflict as individual personalities start to emerge. Performance may decrease as members focus on areas where they do not agree, rather than moving forward. This is a time when subgroups may form, usually led by the strongest personalities. To get through this stage, members need to 'storm' through conflicting ideas by using questioning and by challenging ideas; this will lead to higher levels of creativity. If they do not, resentment may follow.

3 **Norming**: Most conflict is resolved and the group is unified in its approach to the goal. During this stage, leaders are confirmed and members' roles allocated. However, some groups get to this stage without going through the storming stage which may lead to differences not being resolved. The danger of this stage is that dominant members may take over and quieter members become reluctant to challenge ideas. 'Groupthink' can happen, where the desire for unity means irrational decisions may be made.

4 **Performing**: Cooperation has been well established, the team has matured and is organised. What was once a set of individuals is now functioning as a team. Goals and roles are agreed on, conflicts are dealt with as and when they arise and the group is proud of their team's success. Creativity and innovation are major parts of this stage.

Tuckman and Jensen (2010) revisited the model a few years later and looked at 22 review articles which attempted to study Tuckman's original four stages. Tuckman acknowledged that the four-stage model was based on small-scale research and therefore wanted to see if further studies had been completed. Although many of the studies supported a vast majority of Tuckman's stages, only one (Runkel, 1971) set out specifically to empirically test his model. Runkel's research mainly supported the four stages, although the methodology used was prone to observer bias. Two studies and a review did identify termination as a final stage, with the 'death' of the group important especially with the connections made between members. For this reason, Tuckman and Jensen added a fifth stage:

5 **Adjourning**: Most of the team's goals have been accomplished and final tasks are being completed and results documented. As work lessens, members may be assigned to other groups and the group moves apart. This may cause regret, so some formal 'ceremony' may happen or new members may move in and the process restarts.

Evaluating Tuckman and Jensen (2010)

One strength of Tuckman and Jensen's (2010) model is that it is a **dynamic** model which has changed based upon increased theoretical knowledge. For example, a fifth stage was added due to the review of 22 articles which looked at Tuckman's original four-stage model. The ability to change the model due to more recent information and evidence increases the validity of the theory. However, there may still be a question about whether splitting group behaviour into distinct linear stages is realistic as often stages may overlap and be revisited; this will question the validity of the model.

One weakness of Tuckman and Jensen's (2010) five-stage model is that it lacks empirical evidence and therefore reliability of the theory is still largely untested. Tuckman himself admitted that more empirical research needed to be done. Indeed, the amended version was based on mainly theoretical articles rather than studies. However, 22 articles were reviewed by Tuckman and Jansen with the vast majority broadly supporting Tuckman's model, especially with the fifth stage amended, suggesting that reliability may be high.

Belbin's nine team roles

In the 1970s, Meredith Belbin began to observe teams in order to study group dynamics. Individuals would also complete a number of psychometric tests so that personality and behaviour could be included. As research progressed, he realised that behaviour was more important than factors such as intelligence, with nine team roles identified.

1 Plants: These are inventors and innovators. They prefer to operate by themselves or at some distance to other team members, using their imagination and different working methods. Their function is often to challenge standard working practices and to solve complex problems. Too many plants may not help, however, as they focus on their own ideas and not those of the group.

2 Resource investigators: Enthusiastic extroverts. They are natural communicators and negotiators and are good at developing new contracts. Good at picking up other people's ideas and promoting them, they have a warm outgoing nature and are generally relaxed. However, their enthusiasm can fade quickly.

3 Co-ordinators: Help others to work towards shared goals. Trusting and confident, they are quick to spot individual talents and use them to pursue shared objectives. They function well in charge of a diverse team and perform better with colleagues of near equal rank. However, they may manipulate others to achieve their own objectives.

4 Shapers: Highly goal orientated and have great drive and energy; overcoming obstacles through determination. Shapers are competitive and like to win. They often get promoted as they impress people with their decisive leadership style. Performing well when quick and decisive action is needed, they can also be argumentative and aggressive.

5 Monitor evaluators: Serious-minded and can be seen as over-enthusiastic. They are slow in making decisions, preferring to carefully think things over. With their high critical thinking ability, they are unlikely to make reckless mistakes, as they deal in facts and logic and not in emotion. They are good at weighing up pros and cons of a decision but can be seen as being overly critical, slow and boring.

6 Implementers: Practical and possess self-control and discipline. They work hard and are regarded as not being interested in their own personal agendas. Seen as reliable and successful, because they are efficient and do what needs to be done in a systematic way. However, they are rigid and may not accept new ways of doing things.

7 Teamworkers: Sociable and generally supportive and concerned about others. They are flexible and adapt to different situations. They are diplomatic and caring and good listeners and so are popular with colleagues who feel unappreciated. They are missed when they are not around. They want to avoid conflict, so can be indecisive when faced with difficult decisions.

8 Completer finishers: Great attention to detail, strive for perfection and correct errors. Quite introverted but are trusted to do work of the highest standard and complete it on time. Perfect when tasks need accuracy and will demand the same high standards from others. However, this often creates anxiety, and they may be reluctant to trust others to do work.

9 Specialists: See learning and furthering their knowledge as their reason to exist. Specialists will be seen as experts and people will turn to them for help and guidance. Although not viewed as natural team players, they can be used as a source of research, and should command respect due to their in-depth knowledge. They do not like social discussions and can be stubborn when challenged about the validity of their knowledge.

Belbin constructed the Belbin Self Perception Inventory to measure individual team roles; his questionnaire is based on individual responses to forced-choice statements about behaviours. Alongside this, observer statements are used with six other people making statements about the individual. These are not fixed choices and the six responses are correlated to measure validity of the inventory.

Evaluating Belbin's nine team roles

> ### ISSUES AND DEBATES

Idiographic versus nomothetic

The strength of Belbin's theory is that it takes a nomothetic, scientific approach using reliable and valid methods. Belbin used observation and psychometric tests to construct the model and used the Belbin Self Perception Inventory to measure team roles. These are quantitative methods which produce objective and reliable data. They also use observer statements to check the validity of the results. However, the use of self-reports can be seen as a weakness as they are subject to social desirability bias and forced-choice answers may not reflect actions in real life, and do not allow for responders to give reasons for their answers. The observer reports also may be affected by external conflicts and situational variables, reducing their validity.

Cultural differences

One weakness is that Belbin's theory may not apply to all team roles in all cultures. The different team roles are based upon a Western idea of team roles and although Belbin believed they should apply to all teams, some of them may not apply to cultures which are more collectivist and rely more on collective action and team working. This means that the findings of Belbin's theory and inventory may not be generalised to all cultures and so the theory has limited application.

> ### LEARNING LINK

Belbin used observations to construct his theory, and also used self-reports alongside the observations to measure an individual's team roles. Which studies at AS Level also use observations as their methodology? Do any of the same strengths and weaknesses apply here or not? Did any studies use observations alongside other methods to obtain results? What is the strength of using **triangulation** (using a number of methods together)?

STUDY TIP

A version of the Belbin Self Perception Inventory is available online. The results themselves are not important but completing it may improve your understanding about the strengths and weaknesses of such methods. As you are doing this, try and think of the problems people may encounter in using it. Think of cultural differences and how that makes it more difficult to use. Think about how the statements are constructed and how you score yourself on them. Also think about observers having to write down information about you as a person to see whether they agree with you. How does this make you feel? All of these issues are important in terms of evaluation, not only of this test specifically but also of self-reports in general.

> ## TEST YOURSELF

1   Zander wants to identify his team role at work. He asks Sunil whether he knows of any way he could find out.

   a   Suggest one way Zander can identify his team role at work.   [2]

   b   Explain one weakness of the measurement you have suggested in (a).   [2]

2   Suggest two characteristics of teamworkers as detailed in Belbin's nine team roles.   [4]

3   a   Describe what psychologists have found out about group formation and decision making.   [6]

   b   Evaluate what psychologists have found out about group formation and decision making, including a discussion on validity.   [10]

4   Carrie-Ann wants to find out whether teams actually go through Tuckman and Jensen's five stages of group development.

   a   Plan an observation to investigate whether groups go through Tuckman's five stages of group development.

      Your plan must include:

      –   details about the type of observation used.

      –   details about the sampling method used.   [10]

   b   For one piece of psychological knowledge that has informed your plan:

      i   Describe this psychological knowledge.   [4]

      ii   Explain how two features of this knowledge have informed your plan.   [4]

KEY TERMS

groupthink

group norms

cohesiveness

social identity

mind guards

conformity

group isolation

illusion of unanimity

Faulty decision-making, explanations and strategies to avoid it

> ### Think!

Define what is meant by the term **groupthink**. Outline one real life example of groupthink occurring.

> ### Think!

A group of team leaders are working together to try and discover why productivity in the factory has gone down. The discussion has centred around the workforce being at fault, suggesting that they are lazy and cannot be bothered to work. A couple of group members were worried about how the workers are being portrayed and suggest it is more about how the workers are treated and the poor quality of the equipment, but every time they try to speak up members of the group suggest that they were wrong. The group has now been meeting for many weeks. The two members who expressed doubts no longer want to raise their doubts and have started to believe that the group is right. They believe that the group would never say this about workers if it was untrue. Managers are worried that the group is showing symptoms of groupthink. Do you think the manager is right? Are any of the symptoms of groupthink being demonstrated here?

> ### Think!

Do you think that groupthink is determined more by individual or situational factors. What makes you think this?

Asch's (1951) classic study (see page 132) looked at conformity and specifically how social pressure from majority influence can lead conformity to a group. Research Asch's study and suggest reasons why this study may support groupthink as a theory. Are there any issues with using Asch's study to support groupthink?

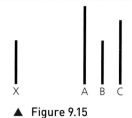

▲ Figure 9.15

Groupthink: features and examples

When critical decisions are being made, it is important to ask whether it is better to have a group making the decision or does having more than one person make it more likely that a faulty decision is made? Answering this question is difficult because you not only have to assess whether a decision is correct, but also the circumstances at the time and the information the group is working with. One possible cause of faulty decision-making is **groupthink** which happens due to social pressures.

The term groupthink (Janis, 1971) is used to try and understand why highly competent members of a group stick with a decision or a course of action that they have made, even when it is obvious to members that it is going wrong and they know that the consequences of that decision are negative.

Explanation

Janis (1971) explained that groupthink occurs when the desire for agreement becomes so powerful that it takes over from objective appraisal of the decision being made. The development of **group norms** and a strong sense of **social identity** and **cohesiveness** within the group suppresses critical thinking and means that significant group pressures are put on anyone who dares to object to the decision being made. In addition, **group isolation** may also cause groupthink. This is where the group has no outside information to help them make a more balanced decision. Janis specified social norms and stress as two indicators of whether groupthink will occur.

»» Social norms: Although it would be expected that as the group becomes more cohesive the more a member would feel able to challenge a decision, the opposite is the case. **Conformity**, therefore, actually increases as cohesiveness increases due to the individual's desire not to cause any conflict. More concerning is the idea that members actually all think a proposal is a good one but have not examined it properly or looked at pros and cons. Some may have doubts but set them aside and agree with the group.

»» Stress: Janis (1971) suggested that the strong psychological pressures a group faces when they work closely together, share the same values and most importantly face a crisis situation that puts the whole group under stress, all make groupthink more likely.

Golkar (2013) expanded this explanation of groupthink, agreeing that high stress is a factor and can interact with low self-esteem, which may have come about through past failures as well as recent difficulties in making decisions; this will lower self-efficacy and increase chances of groupthink. Groupthink is also more likely to occur if the decision to be made creates a moral dilemma.

Janis (1971) specified eight symptoms (features) of groupthink:

»» Invulnerability: Group members have an illusion of invulnerability which leads them to being over-optimistic and taking risks. They also fail to spot warnings of danger.

»» Rationale: Ignoring warnings and other negative feedback, group members rationalise their beliefs. For example, before the Pearl Harbor attack in the Second World War, warnings were ignored about the possibility of a Japanese attack as it was rationalised that the Japanese would never dare cause an all-out war with America.

»» Morality: Members believe that their group has high morals and so this allows them to ignore the moral consequences of decisions.

»» **Stereotypes**: Members have stereotypical beliefs of outgroups.

»» Pressure: Members apply pressure to any individual who expresses doubts about a decision or the validity of an argument.

»» Self-censorship: Members avoid expressing any opinion that deviates from the group opinion.

»» **Illusion of unanimity**: This is the assumption that any member who remains silent agrees with the group.

»» **Mindguards**: These are people in the group who guard members from outside dissenting voices that may break the consensus and their belief in the morality of the decision taken.

Examples

1   The Challenger Disaster. In 1986, NASA launched the Challenger spacecraft which exploded within 73 seconds of take-off. Groupthink has been suggested to be part of the reason it happened. For example:

>> NASA managers maintained that everyone was in agreement with the launch even though Thiokol engineers had expressed doubts on and off about the temperature at the timing of the launch and said take-off should be aborted. (Illusion of unanimity)

>> These engineers suffered pressure from NASA managers to reverse their doubts as there had already been three attempts at launch. In addition, there was pressure from their own company where there were worries about losing contracts with NASA. (Pressure)

>> Experts were not even consulted to give information to Jesse Moore who made the final decision to launch, so he was protected from what was seen as troublesome ideas. (Mindguards)

>> The group had worked together for many years and was a cohesive unit; engineers were isolated from the decision-making process (group isolation) and stronger leaders from NASA pushed against the engineering group.

2 The Bay of Pigs (1961) invasion took place when American soldiers attempted to overthrow the Cuban Government. President Kennedy wanted to overthrow Fidel Castro and other members of his planning group knew it, so they made decisions to please the president that were not based on objective information. They used negative stereotypes of the 'enemy' group and moved forward without any openness to new information. The result was a disaster and came close to the USA starting a war with Russia.

Strategies to avoid groupthink

1 Invite one or more outside experts or senior managers to each meeting and encourage them to challenge the ideas of the group members. However, there is a chance that if this happens everyone will then act differently and not express views fully or be honest.

2 At every meeting of the group, a member should play 'devil's advocate' and go against the majority view. This person should challenge ideas and get individuals or the group to justify their decisions. However, this is only effective if the group thinks the person playing devil's advocate really believes what he says. If not, it will not be taken seriously and could be ignored, which could perhaps even encourage groupthink.

3 Senior managers at an organisation should inform group members that they are all equally responsible for the decisions being made and that they will all face the consequences of their decisions. This may reduce the air of invulnerability some groups may feel. However, this may inhibit members from making the decision in the first place, and instead making the 'safe' decision rather than the correct one due to fear of the consequences.

4 Each group member should be assigned the role of critical evaluator with priority to air any doubts that they may have. This means the group leader must be able to take and act on constructive criticism. This may lead to the decision-making process taking a long time and lead to conflicts between the group, meaning it becomes dysfunctional and cannot make a decision at all.

Evaluating groupthink

> ### ISSUES AND DEBATES

Application to everyday life

A strength of groupthink as an explanation is that it can be applied to real life. Janis (1971) used real-life examples such as the Bay of Pigs invasion to construct her theory, and more recently it has been applied to the Iraq War and the Challenger disaster. If it can explain real-life situations, then strategies to ensure they do not happen again can be implemented. This will decrease the chances of negative consequences happening due to faulty group processes, increase health and safety and make the theory useful for both big and small organisations.

Individual and situational explanations

In addition, groupthink is a more holistic explanation of faulty decision-making as it takes into account the effects of personality, as well as the influence of the situation. Janis (1971) believed that situational aspects such as conformity, group cohesiveness, social identity and stress were important in creating groupthink, although acknowledging that a leader with a strong personality would also increase it. In addition, Golkar (2013) believed that an individual with low self-esteem and low self-efficacy would be more susceptible to groupthink, suggesting that personality factors were an issue. Therefore, the theory considers different effects of personality and different situational influences, making it a more complete theory.

One weakness of groupthink theory is the lack of supporting empirical research. Aldag and Fuller (1993) noted that support for groupthink tends to come from retrospective case studies, and these are subject to bias and faulty memory. In addition, the case studies used involved political decision-making at the highest level, which is not typical of real-life organizational situations. Indeed, Fuller and Aldag (1998) continued their criticism by suggesting that groupthink has become a populist model, which is talked about in the news and social media and that every faulty decision is suggested to be groupthink despite the lack of empirical research, meaning that other factors are ignored.

In addition, the case studies used to support and construct groupthink were all based upon decisions made in individualist cultures such as the USA. For example, the Bay of Pigs invasion and the decision to ignore warnings before the Pearl Harbor attack were both faulty decisions made by North American groups. It may be that the decision-making process is different in collectivist nations where the group is more important than the individual and therefore there may be different processes in play, limiting its application in those different cultures. However, the process of formation of groups may indeed be universal, and groupthink is still a popular and widely used theory across the world, meaning that the concerns about generalisability to all cultures may be misplaced.

▶ LEARNING LINK

Although Milgram's studies (1963) look at obedience to authority rather than conformity, there may be an argument that groupthink may be due to a strong leader of the group, a legitimate authority figure that the group may not want to disobey in terms of the decision: the same as the suggestion with Milgram's participants. In addition, the participants in Milgram's study were willing to carry on despite doubts and potentially harming another person. This can be linked to groupthink as the group would carry on with the decision-making despite the potential negative consequences that may occur. Finally, both Milgram and, later, Janis (1971) acknowledged the importance of situational factors on behaviour.

STUDY TIP

Groupthink is an interesting concept and has become a theory that is very popular in everyday life. When learning about groupthink it is important to learn all three parts: the explanations, the examples and the strategies to overcome it, as you could be asked questions on any of these parts. When learning the strategies, remember that there are reasons why they may not work. Make sure you learn these properly as well. Although two real life examples have been explained here, there are many more. Try and find some examples that are not about political leaders but look for some from different cultures or smaller businesses. If you find this hard then this may support the evaluation issues discussed on these pages.

▶ TEST YOURSELF

1 José has been reading about groupthink and is concerned that it may happen within his organisation, especially as a group has been set up to discuss changes to workplace practices.

Suggest two strategies that José may put in place within his organisation to stop groupthink from happening. [4]

2 Explain one situational factor which may be a reason for groupthink occurring in an organisation. [2]

3 a Describe what psychologists have discovered out about groupthink. [6]

b Evaluate what psychologists have found out about groupthink, including a discussion about reductionism vs holism. [10]

4 Outline the role of stress in groupthink. [2]

5 Suggest how mindguards in a group setting make it more likely that groupthink will occur. [2]

Retrospective case studies have been used to study the idea of groupthink.

6 Explain one strength and one weakness of using case studies to study groupthink. [4]

KEY TERMS

sins of commission

imprecision

sins of omission

confirmation bias

heuristics

fundamental attribution error

extra-evidentiary bias

Forsyth's cognitive limitations and errors

Think!

What is meant by sins of omission? Can you give any examples?

Think!

Parvinder's pharmaceutical company is having problems with some of their workers whom the managers believe have not been working hard enough. A group has been formed to make a decision on whether the workers need to be given a warning or not. After a week Parvinder dropped into the meeting and was concerned because the group members were arguing about a rumour about one of the workers despite being told that they had to ignore it. Also, people were constantly talking about how some of the workers just had a bad attitude, and how 'you can tell that they probably just don't care about others at all and have a bad personality', rather than looking at the situation they work in. What cognitive errors may the group be showing?

Think!

The two theories you have learned about are groupthink and cognitive limitations and error. Can you think of a similarity and a difference between these two theories?

Cognitive errors are often used to make decisions simpler and easier. For example, **heuristics** or 'rules of thumb' exist to help us make quicker decisions and **confirmation bias** means that individuals or groups only really seek out information that confirms their own beliefs. Can you think of any time you have experienced this? Is there any type of career where confirmation bias or the use of heuristics could actually have serious consequences?

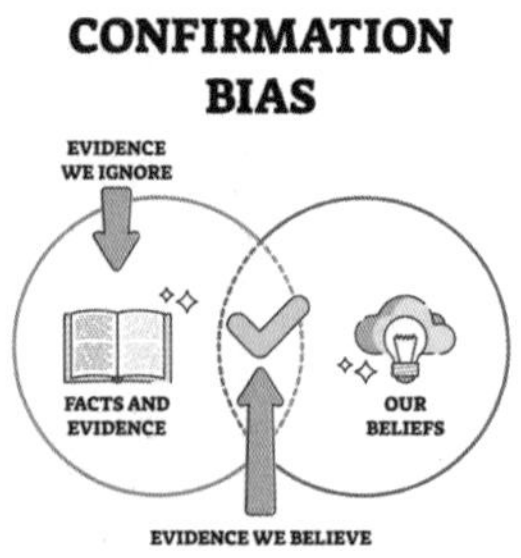

CONFIRMATION BIAS

EVIDENCE WE IGNORE

FACTS AND EVIDENCE

OUR BELIEFS

EVIDENCE WE BELIEVE

▲ Figure 9.16

When working within a group, members are often under significant cognitive demand. We often dread going into staff meetings, discussion groups or brainstorming sessions as we see them as a waste of time, where members get sidetracked talking about things that are not relevant and decision-making is a slow process. Before, during and after a meeting, group members have to consider the consequences of their actions, both as individuals and as a group. However, even though being in a group has many advantages over the individual such as more resources, more capacity to process that information and better error detection, groups still do not always make the right decisions.

According to Forsyth (2006), psychologists have identified a number of biases that may distort judgement and therefore group decisions. For example, we may jump to conclusions too quickly and stick to them despite new information, or we may overestimate the accuracy of our judgements.

Decisional sin

Forsyth (2006) in his book *Group Dynamics* discussed the three general categories of potential biases first identified by Kerr *et al.* (1996):

1 **Sins of commission**: This is where a group misses out information in some way, including when a group carries on basing their judgements or decisions on false or irrelevant information. Some examples of sins of commission are:
   a Belief perseverance: This is where information is relied on which has already been reviewed and found to be inaccurate.
   b Sunk cost bias: This is where a group is reluctant to change their course of action because they have made an investment of money or time and they do not want to lose that investment.
   c **Extra-evidentiary bias**: This is when information is used by an individual or group when they have been explicitly told to ignore it.
   d Hindsight bias: The tendency to overestimate the accuracy of your prior knowledge of an outcome.

2 **Sins of omission**: Failing to seek out information, overlooking useful information or not checking for errors within the information.
   a Base rate bias: Failure to pay attention to relevant information about general trends and tendencies.
   b **Fundamental attribution error**: Stresses dispositional (personality) causes when attributing the cause for people's behaviour and ignores situational factors. This tends to be observed in individualist cultures such as the USA and not in collectivist cultures such as Japan.

3 Sins of **imprecision**: Relying on mental rules of thumb or heuristics that oversimplify decisions or introduce errors into the decision-making process.
   a Availability heuristics: This is basing a decision just on information that is readily available.
   b Conjunction bias: Failing to recognise that the probability that two events occur together is always going to be less than only one of the events occurring.
   c Representativeness heuristics: Relying heavily on factors which seem to make sense but in the end are misleading.

Groups can also show confirmation bias which is where the group, or individuals within the group, do not seek out information which may contradict their original conclusion, whilst seeking out information that will confirm it. This can be made worse when individuals within the group continue to do this but others do not, meaning that a group solution or decision cannot be reached. Kerr *et al.* (1996) looked at the level of confirmation bias in individuals and groups and found that the tendency for confirmation bias is even stronger in groups than it is with individuals.

Strategies to avoid cognitive errors

» Educate yourself on cognitive errors in order to understand why they occur in the first place. By becoming more aware of the potential errors, you are more likely to spot them when they happen and be able to minimise their effects.

» To overcome fundamental attribution error, get group members to actively think of times when situational factors were a factor. Ask yourself whether you would have acted in a particular way; list possible explanations including situational ones. Standing up and actively having to justify your opinion always helps!

» Make sure the group is not just one unified group with similar opinions. Instead ensure it has diversity and that the leader's appointment will not overpower the group and suppress challenge.

Strategies to avoid confirmation bias

Researchers studied confirmation bias by creating groups that were:

» unanimous in their initial preference
» composed of at least one member who took a minority position on the issue
» composed of two minority members.

It was found that unanimous groups showed stronger confirmation bias than those with more diverse members. In fact, groups with two minority members actually were better than individual members in terms of overcoming confirmation bias.

Evaluating cognitive limitations and errors

One strength is that the theory of cognitive errors and limitations in group decision-making has been supported by research. For example, Osmani (2016) looked at the effect of heuristics and cognitive biases on group decision making and found that confirmation bias is more common in groups than in individuals when making decisions: when groups were presented with two projects, one with a sunk cost and one without a sunk cost, while only 26 per cent of the group recommended the project when it had no sunk cost, 86 per cent recommended it when it did have a sunk cost. The results provide support to the idea that cognitive errors play a significant role in faulty decision-making, making the theory reliable.

> ## ISSUES AND DEBATES
>
> ### Application to everyday life
>
> One strength of Forsyth's cognitive limitation theory is that it has application to everyday life. If it is understood that the formation of groups may increase the likelihood of judgemental bias, and that this is made worse by groups who are unanimous in terms of their previous beliefs, then care can be taken during the group formation stage to ensure that there is a diversity of opinion within the group, and there are members that are not afraid to challenge the group. It also suggests that training in group decision making may be beneficial. Therefore, the principles set out in Forsyth's theory may be said to be useful.
>
> ### Reductionism versus holism
>
> One weakness of Forsyth's theory of cognitive limitations is that it can be said to be reductionist. This is where complex behaviours are broken down into its simplest form. In this case suggesting that cognitive errors are the reason for faulty decision-making is reductionist. It does not take into account factors such as stress (which were discussed in alternative theories such as groupthink) and factors such as sleep deprivation which may affect decisions. This makes Forsyth's theory simplistic and suggests that it is not a complete theory of decision-making.
>
> ### Cultural differences
>
> Another weakness of Forsyth's theory is that it fails to take into account cultural differences. It may be that some of the cognitive errors suggested in the theory only apply to Western, individualistic cultures rather than collectivist cultures. Indeed, Forsyth suggested that the fundamental attribution error can only really be observed in individualistic cultures rather than collectivist cultures, suggesting that only parts of the theory can be applied to organisations in collectivist cultures. This means that the theory is not generalisable.

> ## LEARNING LINK
>
> Cultural differences are a major issue when looking at topic areas in organisational psychology and you may have already learned a significant number of topics where there could be an issue with generalisability of theories and models to both collectivist and individualistic cultures. This may also be true of topic areas in the other area you are studying and also in your AS Level studies. Milgram (obedience), for example, often got accused of not taking into account cultural differences, but his study has been replicated in a number of cultures both collectivist and individualistic and the results compared. Can you think of any other studies that have not taken into account cultural differences?

STUDY TIP

The terms 'collectivist' and 'individualistic' cultures have come up many times in organisational psychology and it is important, therefore, that you understand some of the key characteristics of these cultures, how they could affect the values and morals of an individual and therefore their behaviour. Think of your own country; do you think it is more individualistic or more collectivist?

▶ TEST YOURSELF

1 Alanna has been asked to make a presentation to her managers about the dangers of heuristics in group decision making.
  Suggest two heuristics that Alanna may focus on during her presentation. [4]

2 Explain one way that groups can lessen the effect of confirmation bias on decision making. [2]

3 Compare groupthink and Forsyth's cognitive limitations and errors theory as explanations for faulty decision making. [4]

4 a Describe cognitive limitations and errors as a reason for faulty decision making. [6]
  b Evaluate cognitive limitations and errors as a reason for faulty decision making, including a discussion of application to real life. [10]

5 Jemima wants to find out whether the information she has researched about cognitive errors are a factor in the team leaders' group decision making in her company.
  Plan an observation to find out whether cognitive errors are a factor in group decision making in Jemima's company.
  Your plan must include:
  – the type of observation used
  – types of behavioural categories used. [10]

6 a For one piece of knowledge that informed your plan for question 4, describe this psychological knowledge. [4]
  b Explain how two features of this psychological knowledge informed your plan. [4]

9.3.2 Individual and group performance

KEY TERMS

social loafing
social facilitation
co-action effect
audience effect
social inhibition
evaluation apprehension
social impact theory
diffusion of responsibility

METHODOLOGY

quantitative and qualitative data

Think!

What is meant by the terms **social facilitation** and **social loafing**?

Think!

Dante works in a large homeware store. He has been reading about social facilitation and is interested in whether the theory is correct. Dante has noticed that when the managers are more visible on the shop floor, people do not talk as much to each other and work levels seem to slow down. How could Dante investigate social facilitation and drive theory at his workplace?

Think!

What do you know about collectivist and individualist cultures? How do you think cultural differences might affect social loafing?

Look at Figure 9.17 Imagine you were the person doing the presentation. How would it make you feel? Would being in this position motivate you or make you feel anxious? Think of the reasons why you feel this. Are any of your reasons similar to the explanations on these pages?

▲ Figure 9.17

Do people perform better when alone or in a group? This is a question many people have tried to answer. Many believe that groups are more effective than individuals when performing a task. The suggestion is that as groups have many members, they will have more resources, and therefore be able to make decisions more effectively. However, this is not always the case and there are a number of variables that can affect not only group performance as a whole, but also an individual's performance within that group.

Social facilitation

Social facilitation can be defined as the tendency to perform a task better or faster in the presence of others, rather than alone. Triplett (1898) was one of the first psychologists to study this phenomenon. Whilst watching bicycle races Triplett saw that cyclists were faster when they competed against others, rather than when they rode alone against the clock. Triplett studied 40 children who played a game that involved turning a small reel as quickly as possible. The results showed that the children turned the reel slightly quicker when the game was played in pairs compared to when played alone, suggesting people may perform better in the presence of others.

The presence of others may be:
>> people working with you (**co-action effect**) or
>> the presence of an audience (**audience effect**).

Two factors affecting social facilitation are:

Drive theory

Drive refers to the increased levels of **arousal** and internal motivation used to reach a goal. Zajonc (1966) suggested that in the presence of others, people will perform simple and well-known tasks better and complex or novel tasks worse (due to **social inhibition**) than if they were alone.

Drive theory suggests that a more difficult or unfamiliar task will cause higher levels of arousal than a familiar or simple task. The presence of others will then add to this arousal. If the task is a difficult one, levels of arousal are already high so adding the presence of others will take us past our optimum level of arousal and cause stress. This results in the dominant response (the behaviour most likely to occur – the habitual behaviour) being something that we can easily do, rather than something that is new or demanding, which in the case of a difficult task is likely to be wrong. In addition, arousal levels may be affected by individual differences. If an individual is socially anxious in the first place, then their baseline arousal levels may be higher than those who are not socially anxious, meaning audience effects are going to be greater in the socially anxious person.

This is supported by the Yerkes–Dodson theory of optimal arousal which says that you reach your peak level of performance with a certain level of stress, but too much or too little arousal results in poorer performance.

Evaluation apprehension

This is the anxiety a person feels when they are worried about being judged by others. The worry is that we may be judged negatively, or within a group setting that our ideas may be rejected. This leads to a heightened sense of arousal due to evaluation apprehension, which can both inhibit and enhance our performance. We are aroused, therefore, by the presence of an audience as we have learned that they may evaluate our performance and are not just passive spectators. As with drive theory, if you are confident in yourself and the task you are performing is simple or well-rehearsed then the presence of others will enhance your performance, whereas if you are not confident or the task is complex and under-rehearsed then your performance will be inhibited. Also, if the people observing are more influential than you, or even more experienced than you, this can cause higher levels of arousal and evaluation apprehension.

Schmitt *et al.* (1986) studied 45 college undergraduates, splitting them into one of three conditions:

» work alone
» work in the presence of an individual wearing a blindfold and headphones
» work in the presence of an evaluating experimenter.

Before the participants realised that the experiment had begun, each of them was asked to perform a simple task (typing their name repeatedly) or a complex task (typing their name backwards with ascending numbers in between the letters). Compared to the 'alone' condition, participants were faster on the simple tasks and slower on the more complex task in both 'audience' conditions although results were more pronounced for the 'evaluating' condition. This provides support not only for **evaluation apprehension** but also for the argument that the presence of an audience on its own can produce **social facilitation**.

Social loafing

Social loafing is the idea that once people work within a group situation they may put in less individual effort and therefore become individually less productive. Max Ringelmann was first to study the effect when he saw that people do not reach their potential in groups: although groups often still outperform individuals, they do not do so at the rate expected if every individual was working at maximum capacity. In one study, Ringelmann (1913) asked people to pull a rope attached to a pressure gauge. He found that the more people that were pulling on the rope the further below their potential they would perform. He suggested this was due to both coordination loss and motivation loss. Although he suggested loss of coordination in the group was the main reason for social loafing, he acknowledged that loss of motivation played a part.

Social impact theory

Latané (1981) explained social loafing through **social impact theory**. Social impact is where the thoughts, feelings and behaviours of an individual are influenced by the real or imagined presence or actions of other people. Social impact theory suggests that the amount of influence other people have depends on their strength, immediacy, and number; with the number of other people seen as most important in social loafing.

The theory states that when individuals work together, social influence is diffused (spread) across all the group members, and as the size of the group increases in number, each person has less individual influence. **Diffusion of responsibility** is where each group member will be less likely to take responsibility for an action if other people are present; this becomes more prominent the more people are present. In this case, therefore, the more members of the group there are, the less the individual is likely to reach their potential as they will sit back as they think others 'will get the job done'. Social loafing becomes more likely if the person is not being individually evaluated on their own performance as they can become more anonymous.

Latané (1981) studied social loafing and group size. They asked subjects to stand in a semi-circle and to either clap or shout as loud as they could individually, and then with their other group members. The level of noise was measured and was found to increase with group size, but not in proportion to the number of group members. People made less noise individually as the numbers in the group went up, supporting the idea of group size having an effect on social loafing.

Evaluating theories of group and individual performance

A strength is that there is support from research evidence. For example, the concept of social facilitation was first studied by Triplett and then further support for evaluation apprehension and drive theory was supplied by Schmitt *et al.* (1986). Additionally, Latané conducted several studies that support social impact theory and its link to social loafing. These studies were scientific in nature and gained quantitative objective data that allowed for comparisons to be made within groups and for hypotheses to be tested; this makes the theory more reliable.

> ## ISSUES AND DEBATES

Individual and situational factors

One strength of the theories on social facilitation is that they acknowledge both individual and situational factors. For example, drive theory explains social facilitation as an internal physiological process which is also moderated by individual factors such as natural levels of social anxiety in the person. However, evaluation apprehension suggests that situational factors such as whether or not other people are overtly evaluating you; or are more influential than you (such as a manager); and whether or not you have rehearsed a task can all affect levels of social facilitation. Therefore, these theories can be seen as more complete than others that just rely on either individual or situational factors.

Cultural differences

However, there are weaknesses in terms of the research support. For example, cultural differences may not be taken into account as the majority of research used people from individualist cultures, suggesting that the results may not be applicable to collectivist cultures (see page 225). Also, the fact that individual personality differences may affect group and individual performances means that it may be worth taking a more idiographic approach to the study of group behaviour and look at the individuals themselves. It may well be that this is more important than culture, and that people within collectivist cultures who are more individualistic in their values would be as subject to social loafing as anyone from an individualistic culture.

Application to everyday life

In addition, most of the research studies were laboratory experiments with artificial tasks such as clapping and shouting. This means that the results are low in ecological validity and may not be applicable to real life situations like the workplace. Indeed, Latané himself actually used cockroaches to study social loafing, which leads to questions about whether the results could be applied to humans at all.

> ## LEARNING LINK

At AS Level, you studied Piliavin *et al.* (subway Samaritans) and looked at whether diffusion of responsibility affected helping behaviour on a subway train. Social loafing also discusses diffusion of responsibility and whether it decreases levels of motivation of individuals in group situations, as people may expect other people to contribute, just as in helping situations where in an emergency, if many people are around then they may expect the other people to help. Of course, many of Latané's social loafing studies used artificial situations in laboratory environments, whereas Piliavin *et al.* used a field experiment which has more mundane realism.

STUDY TIP

There are a number of words and phrases that you have not come across before on these pages, such as social loafing, Yerkes–Dodson Law, evaluation apprehension and others. Why not make yourself a mix and match game using all of the key terms? Write a term on a small piece of card and then on another write the definition. Do this for all the key terms you need to know on a particular spread and then mix them up. Come back to them a little while later and see if you can match the right word with the right definition. To make it harder you could also mix them up with key terms from other sections.

> ## TEST YOURSELF
>
> 1 Sarah and Tom have been working on a task at work for a week and have managed to meet their targets every day. Josie and Simone have joined them this week and at the end of the week Sarah and Tom were told that although the total amount completed this week had gone up, individually they were now 10 per cent under their targets.
>
>   Suggest two reasons why Tom and Sarah's individual performances went down after Josie and Simone joined them. [4]
>
> 2 Outline what is meant by the nomothetic approach, using an example from social facilitation/social loafing theories. [2]
>
> 3 Explain one similarity and one difference between social facilitation and social loafing. [4]
>
> 4 a Describe what psychologists have discovered about: [6]
>   - individual and group performance focusing on social facilitation
>   - individual and group performance focusing on social loafing.
>
>   b Evaluate what psychologists have discovered about:
>   - individual and group performance focusing on social facilitation
>   - individual and group performance focusing on social loafing.
>   Include a discussion on ecological validity. [10]
>
> 5 a Plan a study using a laboratory experiment to investigate the effect of the presence of others on performance at work.
>   Your plan must include:
>   - details about your sampling technique
>   - a directional or non-directional hypothesis. [10]
>
>   b State two reasons for the sampling technique you have chosen. [4]
>
>   c State one strength and one weakness of the sampling technique you have chosen. [4]

KEY TERMS

ingroup

outgroup

individualist

efficacy

collective orientation

self-interest motive

cognitive bias

Group performance across cultures

> ### Think!
>
> What is meant by an **ingroup** and an **outgroup**?

> ### Think!
>
> Dennis is interested in testing his theory that employees who work in the same department as each other will believe that the people that they work with are more likely to have similar characteristics to themselves than are people who work in different departments. How could Dennis test his theory?

> ### Think!
>
> Can you think of a strength and a weakness of using a nomothetic approach when studying group performance in the workplace?

What do we mean if we say that explanations of behaviour are deterministic? Why would psychologists suggest that explanations of cultural differences in social loafing may be deterministic?

▶ Figure 9.18

Social loafing in individualistic and collectivistic cultures

A number of research studies have looked at the effect of culture on social loafing. Social loafing (see page 697) is the reduced performance of an individual when placed in a group situation. Many studies such Latané *et al.* (1979) supported the idea of social loafing, although they did find that factors such as accountability reduced the effect.

The dimension of individualism versus collectivism seems relevant to social loafing with regard to one attribute: an individual's willingness to give up personal interests for the good of an ingroup where members share common interests and goals. A member of a collectivist society only tends to belong to a few ingroups and these emphasise cooperation, goal attainment and ingroup harmony. In contrast, a member of an **individualist** society may find their pursuit of individual goals is not consistent with being part of an ingroup, leading to the individual possibly dropping out of the group if their personal goals become unachievable. Also, if an individualist's actions within a group are not noticed by the other group members, then their focus will be on the attainment of personal goals, even if this means that they rely on the efforts of others to get there.

Earley (1989, 1993) studied the effect of culture on social loafing using a shared responsibility task. The study found that social loafing was present in managers from the USA who had individualist beliefs, but not in managers from China with collectivist beliefs. Results also showed that an individualist's performance in a group setting was worse than when working alone; it was the opposite for collectivists who worked better in a group. The major finding from this study, therefore, was that social loafing does not seem to appear in all cultures. Interestingly, accountability did not affect levels of social loafing in collectivist groups; in fact, performance levels were highest for collectivists in the highest shared responsibility groups.

Earley (1989) theorised that the results were due to the different motives of the two groups. The Chinese managers had a **collective orientation** which leads to them placing group goals higher than their own self-interest, seeing as their responsibility to act for the good of the group. They take pride in achieving group goals. However, the individualist has a **self-interest** motive and believes that group rewards should be based on individual performance. Contributing to the collective good may therefore go against their own self-interest unless rewards are based on contribution levels. For many individualists, if their contribution to the group does not get noticed then they will have little incentive to continue as they can 'loaf' without fear of sanctions.

One important aspect of Earley's (1989) study to note is that he did not suggest those in collectivist cultures would never social loaf, only that the conditions in which they would do would be substantially different from those in individualist cultures. This is something Earley explored further in his later 1993 study where he looked at whether the lack of social loafing is more about working with an ingroup who you identify with than culture. If collectivist members work with an outgroup with whom they do not identify, then social loafing may occur, since they will not feel the need to achieve outgroup goals and they, like the individualists in his earlier study, will be free to pursue their own interests.

Earley's process model of group performance

Cultural influences in different societies may mean that individualists feel more **efficacy** when performing alone, while collectivists feel more efficacy when performing with a group. Earley (1993) suggested that whilst this is true for individualists, for collectivists it will depend on the type of the group. For collectivists, efficacy is definitely higher with an ingroup but not with an outgroup or when alone. These general expectations of efficacy would be based on their past experiences of ingroup success.

Earley suggested a **cognitive bias** occurs where individuals assume that anyone who is part of an ingroup is similar to themselves, and that any outgroup member is different. For this reason, collectivists will assume that they and everyone in the ingroup will work better in a group, whereas individualists will assume that they and everyone in their group will work better alone, because that is what they themselves prefer to do.

Earley suggested, therefore, that collectivists will anticipate greater rewards as well as feeling higher levels of efficacy, both alone and as group members, and as a result will perform better while working with people in an ingroup than an outgroup or alone. Individualists will anticipate receiving more rewards and high levels of efficacy and as a result will perform better, when working alone than working in any group.

Focus on... Earley (1993)

▶ AIM

- To see whether collectivists perform worse when working with an outgroup rather than with an ingroup.
- To see whether anticipated rewards and group and individual efficacy expectations will mediate the effects of group context and collectivism-individualism on performance.

▶ METHODOLOGY

Earley used a volunteer sample of 165 entry or middle managers: 45 Israelis, 60 Chinese and 60 Americans aged between 25 and 40 who held a bachelor's degree or higher. The study consisted of an experiment where participants performed tasks under conditions of varying group membership. There were three types:
- Alone
- Member of a ten-person outgroup: Participants were told that these individuals were from different regions of their country and had been through the experiment previously. Differences in characteristics were emphasised.
- Member of a ten-person ingroup: Participants were told that other group members were people from the same region as them and had been through the experiment previously. Similarities in characteristics were emphasised.

In the outgroup or ingroup condition, participants were not in the physical presence of others but were told they were part of a group. Each participant was randomly assigned to a group and were in a room together with other participants, but they were told these were not members of their group.

The task

Each participant was seated individually at a table and read a set of instructions which told them about the task, instructed them to work earnestly and not to skip any items. The task consisted of dealing with a simulated 'in-basket' of 40 items and included writing memos, prioritising client interviews and rating job applications. These were chosen as they were familiar tasks within the participants' own workplaces. This task had been used successfully in Earley's (1989) study with Chinese and American managers and was piloted successfully with Israeli managers prior to the start of the study.

Each participant was given five sample items to be worked on for five minutes and this practice trial output was used by experimenters as feedback to provide participants with an estimate of how they would perform in the task.

Dependent measures

- Performance was measured as the number of correctly completed in-basket tasks within the space of 60 minutes.
- Individualism-collectivism was measured using a five-point scale where participants responded to items such as 'If the group is slowing me down, it is better to leave it than work alone'. The higher the score the more collectivist an individual is.
- Individual and group self-efficacy was measured using a performance scale where self-efficacy expectations for performance on tasks were rated between 0 and 100 (with 100 being certainty that performance can be achieved).

RESULTS

▼ Table 9.3 Mean scores on performance and individualism versus collectivism scales

Variables	China			United States			Israel		
	Alone	Outgroup	Ingroup	Alone	Outgroup	Ingroup	Alone	Outgroup	Ingroup
Performance (Mean)	18.49	18.37	23.83	24.55	16.21	16.57	20.79	18.63	23.18
Individualism vs. collectivism	3.73	3.76	3.61	2.99	2.76	2.55	3.71	3.58	3.95

- Individualists performed better alone than in ingroups and outgroups.
- Collectivists performed less well in outgroups and working alone than in ingroups.
- Self-efficacy levels and expected performance partially mediated the effects of group condition and individualism-collectivism on task performance.
- Measures of both group and individual self-efficacy and anticipated performance were higher for collectivists (China and Israel) in ingroups than in outgroups and alone.

CONCLUSION

- Individual and group efficacy will increase in collectivists if there is high identification with the group they are working in.
- Individual loafing may occur in collectivists when working alone.
- Although collectivism-individualism affects group performance, the type of group, whether ingroup or outgroup, may be a more important factor.

Evaluating Earley (1993)

One strength of Earley's study is that it uses quantitative methodology such as questionnaires and rating scales. For example, each participant had to complete structured questionnaires to measure their self-efficacy, anticipated performance and collectivism-individualism and also got a quantitative performance score at the end of the task. This is a strength as the results found will be objective and not subject to interpretation, increasing the reliability and replicability of the study.

Another strength of this study is that it extended Earley's (1989) research and showed that suggesting collectivists do not social loaf at all was too simplistic, and that actually it was a complex interaction between collectivism, type of group membership and anticipatory self-efficacy and performance. This is a far more holistic approach to the idea of social loafing in different cultures and therefore enhanced researchers' understanding of this complex phenomenon and provided a base for future research.

ISSUES AND DEBATES

Application to everyday life

One weakness of the study is that it was an experiment which took place in an artificial setting, rather than a workplace. Earley himself was not clear to what extent the artificial manipulation of the group and the task itself actually reflected the true dynamics of a real organisation. For example, although there was an ingroup condition the question may be whether that really reflects the close ingroup membership formed in a workplace; in the end these were still strangers. Therefore, it may be suggested that Earley's study lacks ecological validity and thus may not be applicable to real life work situations.

Idiographic versus nomothetic

In addition, the use of experiments alongside structured questionnaires meant that a nomothetic approach was taken. This is where quantitative methodology is used and group averages obtained, which are then analysed to make predictions about a group in general. For example, in this case predictions were made that collectivists as a group would perform better within an ingroup than in an outgroup or alone. This may be seen as a weakness, as although this type of approach allows for replication and generalisability, it also simplifies a complex behaviour so much that you do not get to learn about any of the reasons why an individual behaved in this way. This is something that qualitative, idiographic methods such as case studies would be able to show.

▶ LEARNING LINK

At AS Level, there were studies that looked at the effect of being part of a group on behaviour. For example, Piliavin et al. (subway Samaritans) looked at whether diffusion of responsibility would affect whether a person showed helping behaviour. One difference between Piliavin and Earley is that Piliavin et al.'s study was a field experiment and therefore had higher ecological validity. Can you think of any changes in results that may have happened if Earley's studies were performed within an actual workplace?

STUDY TIP

One important tip is to ensure that you know all of the issues and debates you have learned at AS and A Level really well. It is not enough for you to learn them just in relation to a particular topic area, but you must understand the concept as well. One way to do this is to make a quiz for your friends or class where you ask for the meaning of a particular word and you give them multiple choice answers and they have to select the correct word. You could then have bonus points for them being able to apply that word to a topic area they have learned. You could include some operant conditioning here by giving the individual with the most right answers a reward. What you will find is that not only will this help your class learn, but it will also help you as well.

▶ TEST YOURSELF

1 Jazeel, a manager of a shoe factory in Israel, is conducting a meeting with Miley who is a manager in a shoe factory in the United States. Miley is discussing how difficult it is to get her employees to work together effectively in a group rather than working alone. Jazeel suggests it may be something to do with cultural norms and values.
Outline one difference between a collectivist and individualist society. [2]

2 Explain one difference between an individualist and collectivist culture. [2]

3 a Describe what psychologists have discovered about:
   - the effect of individualism and collectivism on group performance
   - the effect of ingroup and outgroup membership on group performance. [6]
   b Evaluate what psychologists have discovered about:
   - the effect of individualism and collectivism on group performance
   - the effect of ingroup and outgroup membership on group performance, with a discussion on cultural differences. [10]

4 Outline what is meant by a collectivist orientation with an example from group performance. [2]

5 Explain how collectivism-individualism can be measured with an example from group performance. [2]

6 Explain one strength and one weakness of using experiments to measure the effect of culture on group performance. [4]

KEY TERMS

electronic performance monitoring

vigilance

METHODOLOGY

quantitative and qualitative data

Key study: Performance monitoring of employee productivity: concentration levels when being monitored – Claypoole and Szalma (2019) Experiment 1

Think!

How were the participants made aware that they were going to be evaluated in terms of performance on the sustained attention task?

Think!

So-called reality television programmes require people's behaviour to be filmed, often 24 hours a day. People on these programmes are usually aware that their behaviour is being monitored for these programmes. From what you have learned in this key study and previous knowledge about social facilitation, how do you now feel this could affect their behaviour, both individually and as part of a group?

Think!

What is meant by **ecological validity**? What are the consequences for studies such as this one if they are low in ecological validity? How could you improve this study to make it higher in ecological validity?

James L Szalma is the director of Human Factors and Psychology PhD programme at the university of Florida. He received a Bachelor of Science in Chemistry, and a MA in Applied experimental/human factors. His laboratory looked at how characteristics interact with characteristics of the person to influence performance and stress. His primary research interests are training for threat detection and how characteristics of tasks and operators interact with each other to influence performance on tasks that require sustained attention.

At the start of the study all participants were asked to surrender their phones and watches. Why do you think that they were asked to do this? How would keeping them have changed the results? Does this have any consequences for workplaces?

▲ Figure 9.19

CONTEXT

Companies monitor their workers' productivity through a variety of means. This could be as simple as asking a worker for an account of their day. One problem with this is that workers will want their employer to see them in a positive light, so accounts may not be totally accurate. In recent years, electronic systems are becoming increasingly important in monitoring, with a survey finding that over 70 per cent of organisations in the USA are using them to manage performance (American Psychiatric Association, 2007).

Research has suggested that the use of **Electronic Performance Monitoring (EPM)** may improve productivity and performance, although contradictory research suggested that EPM may also impair it (Davidson and Henderson, 2000). This depends on task difficulty, where the more difficult the task the more likely EPM may impair performance. Social facilitation suggests that evaluation apprehension (see page 696) may impair performance on a difficult task, and it has been suggested that this will be the same with an electronic 'observer'. Aiello and Svec (1993) found that performance on a complex task was impaired for those monitored by a person or an electronic monitor, compared to those who completed the task alone.

Although most research has focused on the effects of EPM on performance, the tasks researched have been limited, with everyday tasks such as driving and medical screening not included. These types of tasks need sustained attention, or **vigilance**, for extended periods of time with lapses of attention leading to possible errors or accidents. Therefore, the effects of EPM should be explored in cognitive tasks where sustained attention is needed.

▶ AIM

To determine whether typical social facilitation effects such as improved performance could be observed when using an electronic presence on a sustained attention (vigilance) task.

▶ METHODOLOGY

This was a laboratory experiment comprising two conditions – control and electronic presence.

Sample

One hundred and six participants (mean age 20.57, range 18–37) were recruited via a psychology experiment website, from a university in the south of USA. All participants were undergraduates and all were volunteers, although they did receive credit for completion of the study. There were 65 females and 41 males and all participants were randomly assigned to either the control condition or the Electronic Monitor condition.

▶ PROCEDURE

When participants first arrived at the research laboratory, they were asked to surrender electronic devices such as watches, and phones. Participants were then randomly assigned to either the control or the electronic monitor experimental condition.

The two conditions
- The control condition had no form of social presence throughout the whole experiment. Participants completed the entire experiment alone in an experimental room that had no webcam or video camera.
- The electronic presence condition consisted of two forms of electronic monitoring: a webcam and a video recorder. Instructions prior to the start of the task told participants that 'the experiment uses electronic presence to monitor performance'. The webcam was on top of the computer screen. The participants were told that the webcam 'sends live video feed to the office next door so that performance and engagement can be evaluated during the task.' The video recorder was behind the computer screen and the participants were told that the video recorder 'was used to record performance so it can be evaluated later.' (Nothing was actually recorded.)

Both devices used visual and audio cues to ensure the sense of their presence was maintained.

In both conditions, participants completed a demographics questionnaire prior to the task. Following the completion of the questionnaire, a research assistant would review the instructions with participants, answer questions and then leave. The participant then completed a 3-minute practice session and then a 24-minute sustained attention (vigilance) task.

The vigilance task

Participants were required to monitor a computer display of two-digit numbers. When a critical signal appeared on the screen, they had to respond by pressing the spacebar on a standard keyboard. A critical signal was defined as two-digit numbers that had a difference of 0 or +/– 1. i.e., 77, 65, or 01. Numbers were shown for 1000 milliseconds and participants could respond at any time during that period. During the 24-minute task, five critical signals were presented in each six minute period on watch, a total of twenty altogether. Timing of these signals was randomised during each period but kept constant across participants. Once the task finished the participants were debriefed. The task lasted no more than an hour.

▶ RESULTS

▼ Table 9.4 Correct detections, overall proportion of false alarms and over median response time in milliseconds (ms)

	Electronic presence (n=53)		Control (n=53)	
	Mean	SD	Mean	SD
Correct detections	0.6906	0.20	0.6038	0.21
False alarms	0.0059	0.01	0.0201	0.05
Response times	767.34	67.41	802.02	75.67

The proportion of correct critical signal detections went down the longer the task went on which was consistent with previous research. Participants in the electronic presence condition detected significantly more critical signals (M=0.6906) than those in the control condition (M=0.6038). False alarms decreased significantly across both conditions, although those who were monitored by the electronic presence had significantly fewer false alarms (M=0.0059) than in the control condition (M=0.0201). Median response time increased significantly across both conditions; however, participants monitored by the electronic presence were faster (M=767.34) than those that did the task alone (M=802.03).

▶ CONCLUSION

● Social facilitation, including EPM, can be used to improve performance on sustained attention tasks that are cognitively demanding but boring.
● Video based monitoring is effective as a method of electronic monitoring and is less intrusive than other forms of EPM.

 ## Methodological strengths and weaknesses

One methodological strength is that the study used a laboratory experiment methodology. This means that they used a standardised procedure and controls. This included the same task being used for both groups, with the only difference being the electronic monitor which was being manipulated. This allows researchers to replicate the study in the future in order to see whether they will achieve the same results, thus increasing reliability.

Another strength is that the study produced quantitative data. For example, the response times, numbers of correct detections and false alarms were recorded. This type of data is objective and not subject to experimenter bias. It also means that statistical comparisons can be made across the two experimental groups and judgements subsequently formed, which increases the reliability of the results.

One weakness is that the sample used may not be representative of the wider population as a whole or workers within organisations in particular. This is because the sample comprised undergraduate students from a university in the Southern US. As these students were at university, they may not be representative of the wider population, who may have more experience of sustained attention tasks. In addition, the students had responded to an experimental website, and only a certain type of person may respond, causing response bias.

Finally, the task used in the research may lack validity. Sitting at a screen looking at two-digit numbers and tapping a space bar if there is a difference of more than one between the numbers, is not something you would do in everyday life; there are also no significant negative consequences to the action. If the task involved driving, medical screening or something similar, then the results may be different. This lowers the validity of the task and the study.

Ethics

Claypoole and Szalma (2019) protected the confidentiality of the participants by making sure all responses were private and anonymous. Informed consent was also gained from each participant. The study gained consent from the American Psychological Association code of ethics committee. The only possible concern was the use of credits for study, which may mean that some participants may not feel they could stop before the end due to having received money for completing the task. Also, this study's results suggested that electronic monitors can be used to improve productivity and performance. However, constant monitoring of workers to evaluate performance may cause high levels of stress, leading to possible harm. In addition, participants were told they were being recorded when they actually were not, which is deception; however, at the end of the study, all participants were debriefed and any questions answered.

> ## ISSUES AND DEBATES
>
>
>
> ### Application to everyday life
>
> This study can be applied to real life and be a cost-effective solution for organisations. If such common devices such as webcams and video cameras can increase performance in tasks that require sustained attention, then organisations can use them to increase productivity in the workforce. However, there also needs to be a discussion about constant surveillance over workers, which may lead a significant proportion to not perform as well. This suggests that although these devices can be used, they could end up being counterproductive, and even harmful to the workers.
>
> ### Cultural differences
>
> When discussing social facilitation, it is worth remembering that cultural differences may play a part in how people react to the presence of others, whether real or electronic. Work practices are different across the world and it may be that some countries use far more sustained attention tasks than others, meaning that participants would perform better on this type of task. Also, countries also use different levels of electronic surveillance which means that some people will be used to seeing video cameras and webcams and therefore would not be anxious in their presence, whilst for some the opposite may be the case.

> ## REFLECTION
>
> - Can you think of any more ethical issues with the use of an electronic presence to monitor performance and productivity? Think of issues such as types of pay or people who may have additional needs in the workplace.
> - Do you think there are any issues with only using quantitative methods to monitor performance? For example, does it really tell you about the quality of the work done or is it just to do with the quantity of work done?

LEARNING LINK

Claypoole and Szalma (2019) used a laboratory experiment to test the use of an electronic presence in organisations. At AS Level, in the social approach (page 128) you read about a study by Bateson *et al.* (2006) who found that even an image of a pair of eyes can increase prosocial behaviour. Lone participants put an average of three times as much money into an 'honesty box' in exchange for a drink when a pair of eyes was displayed than when there were no eyes present. Bateson *et al.*'s (2006) study suggests that people may just need to be cued to think about being watched in order to improve their workplace performance.

STUDY TIP

It is really important that for each key study you learn the aims, procedure, findings and conclusions as well as the evaluation. Using a technique like Cornell note taking where you create your own questions to test yourself on what you have learned can be a really useful technique. Each time you learn a new section of material, it is worth investing just a little additional time 24 hours later to consolidate it and then revisit it periodically until the end of your course to make sure all new learning remains accessible in your memory. Regular retrieval will help with this.

TEST YOURSELF

1 Outline what is meant by electronic monitoring in organisations. [2]
2 Suggest two reasons why Claypoole and Szalma's (2019) study may not be applicable to real life. [4]
3 a Describe the study by Claypoole and Szalma (2019) on Electronic Performance Monitoring and sustained attention. [6]
   b Evaluate the study by Claypoole and Szalma (2019) on Electronic Performance Monitoring and sustained attention, including a discussion about ethical issues. [10]
4 Describe one finding from research into Electronic Performance Monitoring and sustained attention. [2]
5 Suggest one way that Electronic Performance Monitoring can be studied other than using a laboratory experiment. [2]
6 Explain two strengths of using laboratory experiments to study Electronic Performance Monitoring. [4]

KEY TERMS

inter-individual
intra-individual
inter-group
intra-group conflict
social identity theory

9.3.3 Conflict at work

Think!

What is the difference between **intra-individual** and **inter-individual conflict** in the workplace?

Think!

Johannes has noticed a significant increase in arguments amongst a number of workers in different departments over the last two months. He would like to find out the reasons behind the arguments. How could Johannes find out the reasons behind the conflict at work?

Think!

What is meant by **holism** in psychology? Are the explanations of conflict at work presented here holistic? Why do you think this?

There are many instances of individual and group conflict in real life. Figure 9.20 shows football supporters following their team. Rivalry between supporters of different teams can be extremely positive but can also lead to hostility and conflict. From your knowledge of different types of conflict, what type of conflict would this be? What would be the main reason for this conflict occurring? When there is an international match, these same supporters would then stop their rivalry and support their national team together. What could this tell you about how to overcome conflict in the workplace?

▲ Figure 9.20

Levels of group conflict

Conflict in the workplace often happens due to miscommunication between employees regarding their goals and beliefs. It can also occur when those individuals believe that the other employee/group is about to affect them negatively in some way. The conflict may be

» personal such as a breakdown in relationships
» task related
» due to procedural issues between employees.

Workplace conflict has been categorised into four different levels:

Intra-individual conflict

This is a conflict that an individual experiences within themselves. It could be where an employee's goals, values and objectives differ from those of the organisation. It can also be when an employee is uncertain about what is expected of them or when you do not think you are good enough to do a role. Goal conflict is also a reason for intra-individual conflict. This is when a particular action will result in an outcome that can be both positive and negative. There are three possible types of intra-individual conflict:

1   A situation where a person has a choice between two outcomes that are both positive, such as a choice between two jobs that are both attractive.
2   A situation where a person has a choice between two outcomes which are both negative. Maybe threatened with punishment or having to complete a task they dislike, such as travelling a long distance for a job.
3   A situation in which a person must decide between something that has both positive and negative outcomes, for example being offered a good job in a bad location.

Inter-individual conflict

This is conflict/disagreements between different individuals such as co-workers, managers and other employees. In reality, some form of interpersonal conflict is often inevitable as people have different personalities, expectations and attitudes. Inter-individual conflict does not always have to be negative, as working through this type of conflict is productive and is an important skill to learn within the workplace as it can actually improve relationships. According to Barki and Hartwick (2004), inter-individual conflict has three different components:

» Behavioural (interference): This is where someone is interfering with the objectives of another worker. An example would be if a person deliberately ensures obstacles are put in the way to stop you accomplishing a goal.
» Cognitive (disagreement): A disagreement between two people which highlights their different objectives and values. It might be that two managers of different areas have conflicting ideas about where a budget should be spent and who should have a greater allocation of money.
» Affective (negative emotions): This is the negative emotional states of two people: the anger, stress and frustration they feel when conflict occurs.

Intra-group conflict

This is where there is conflict between two or more members of a single group. This is sometimes inevitable due to the different opinions you may get about how to complete a task. There are three types: process conflict, such as different opinions on how to complete a task, relationship conflict such as personality clashes, and task conflict such as the disagreement about the actual content of the task. **Intra-group conflict** often occurs in businesses where there are many different backgrounds, cultures, ages and work experience. (Although this diversity can also have a positive effect.)

Inter-group conflict

Inter-group conflict is conflict between different groups and teams; this can have both positive and negative effects. For example, group cohesiveness and loyalty may increase due to intergroup conflict but there also may be negative effects such as an 'us' and 'them' mentality forming. This is linked to **social identity theory** where our own group is the in-group and the other group is the out-group. When these types of groups are formed, we will then exaggerate the negative aspects of the out-group whilst enhancing the positive aspects of our in-group, meaning that our own self-image will be enhanced.

One of the main reasons for intergroup conflict is competition for scarce resources. If resources are tight or the budget is small, there may be conflict about which group can use the resources provided. This is linked to competitiveness, where the need for respect from others leads to competition and therefore conflict.

Causes of organisational group conflict

Miles (1980) suggests that there are number of factors that may increase the likelihood of organisational group conflict:
1 The more an individual or group has to work and collaborate together, the more likely it is that conflict will occur. This is because avoidance of conflict is more difficult if you are dependent on each other for task completion. The most likely outcome is that differences in values and goals may become more apparent.
2 Status inconsistencies may cause conflict, especially if there are different policies surrounding such things as time off or levels of pay between groups.
3 Communication problems: Misunderstanding or misinterpreting each other can cause conflict.
4 Individual differences: Personality, skills and abilities can all cause conflict – some may be more aggressive, authoritarian, dominant or less tolerant than others.

Other factors which may cause conflict are:
1 Lack of trust especially if a group or individual is dependent on others for completion of common goals.
2 Scarce resources: This could be when different groups are competing for a budget and one group may feel they are not being dealt with fairly.
3 Organisational changes such as structure, division of work, responsibility and possible redundancy. It can cause division and frustration if a member of the group suddenly becomes team leader with authority over the group of which they were previously a member.

Causes of interpersonal group conflict

Causes of interpersonal group conflict can be both individual and situational. For example:
» Competition for scarce resources (situational): This could be two managers who are competing for the same promotion within an organisation or two people competing for an award for the highest sales figures.
» Personality differences (individual): Some people just struggle to get on with each other without any specific reason.
» Clashes of values and interests: For example, one department within an organisation (maybe the engineering department) focuses on quality and complex designs, whereas manufacturing focuses more on cost and therefore values simplicity.
» Power and status differences (situational): Organisations are political and these status differences can cause conflict.

» Poor communication: This is probably the most common cause of interpersonal conflict. This could be individual, as when the two people in conflict do not talk to each other effectively, or organisational when two employees have been given different information about a task.

Evaluating types of conflict at work

The idea of competition for scarce resources causing group conflict is based upon realistic conflict theory which has research support. Sherif (1962) investigated the idea that competition for scarce resources would increase hostility and conflict. Twelve-year-old boys at camp had to compete with each other for a prize. This led to increased hostility amongst the boys to the point where the study was terminated, showing that competition creates conflict. Therefore, explanations of group conflict have research support, increasing their reliability.

> ## ISSUES AND DEBATES

Individual and situational explanations

When looking at types of conflict and reasons for group conflict at work it is worth looking at the individual vs situational debate. Very clearly there is an element of both when looking for reasons for conflict. For example, on the individual side there are personality differences such as one person being authoritative and one person being shy, whereas on the situational side there is poor communication, organisational changes and competition for scarce resources. This shows that just changing situational factors may not be enough to resolve conflict and that you need to look at the personalities of your workers as well.

Application to everyday life

Leading on from this, another strength is that it is clear that knowing what is causing conflict will allow organisations to try and resolve the conflict and increase staff morale and productivity; showing that these explanations have application to real life. For example, if you are aware that poor communication increases the likelihood of conflict within the workforce then you can ensure that there are increased opportunities for workers to ask questions of employers and more senior staff members, and that there are different outlets such as websites and notice boards where important information is released. Therefore, these explanations for conflict are useful.

Cultural differences

One weakness is that cultural differences may not have been taken into account when looking at group conflict. Explanations take a very individualistic view on group conflict, highlighting the importance of status, respect and personality. In certain collectivist cultures it may be that individual status and power is not at all important. Therefore, some of the explanations may not be applicable, meaning that theory may not be generalisable to all cultures.

> ## LEARNING LINK

Although looking at obedience, Milgram's study can be linked to some aspects of workplace conflict. Many of the participants' reactions (see page 133) show that they were experiencing distress as their own values and morals were in conflict with what they were being asked to do in the task. This study also demonstrates the power of having two negative outcomes to a decision, in this case not completing the task or potentially hurting someone, neither of which the participant wanted to do. What sort of conflict were Milgram's participants experiencing?

STUDY TIP

One way you can try and learn the different types of group conflict is to try and come up with real life examples of times when the specific type of conflict occurred. This could be real life instances which you could research or maybe even trying to make up examples yourself for each type of conflict. Then give the examples to your friends or even your class to see whether they could guess the type of conflict that is occurring. If they can then, this shows your understanding of the term.

> **TEST YOURSELF**

1   In Patterson's healthcare company, a group of workers picks orders of medication to send to patients in their home. There have been a number of arguments between two workers within the group, who accuse each other of not being honest about how many orders they have picked so they can have the highest figures. This leaves both workers angry and frustrated.

    a   Outline which type of conflict is being shown by the workers.   [2]

    b   Suggest one cause of their conflict.   [2]

2   Explain what is meant by the individual vs. situational debate, giving an example from causes of organisational/inter-individual conflict.   [2]

3   a   Describe what psychologists have discovered about conflict at work.   [6]

    b   Evaluate what psychologists have discovered about conflict at work, including a discussion on cultural differences.   [10]

4   Outline one explanation for organisational conflict.   [2]

5   Explain how theories/explanations of conflict at work can be applied to real life.   [2]

6   Explain one way in which theories into conflict at work can be said to be holistic.   [2]

KEY TERMS

literature review
collaborating
compromising
accommodating
competing
avoiding
social stigma
psychosocial

Thomas-Kilmann's five conflict-handling modes

Think!

Can you name the four different phases of workplace bullying?

Think!

Jamie is a psychologist who has been brought into a local company to try and teach the employees about conflict resolution and how they can improve their own ability to resolve issues in the best way possible. Jamie wants to find out how the employees currently handle conflict. How could Jamie investigate the different conflict styles of the employees? How could this information be used to improve the employees' ability to resolve conflicts?

Think!

Ethical considerations are critical in all psychological research, not least when exploring sensitive topics such as bullying. Which ethical considerations would be particularly important when researching workplace bullying?

Conflict in some ways is a natural response to having interactions with others. No two people have exactly the same expectations and values, meaning differences of opinions are likely to arise at some point. The question is, therefore, how can you handle the conflict that occurs to ensure an effective resolution?

In conflict situations an individual's behaviour can be described along two dimensions:
1   Assertiveness: The extent an individual tries to satisfy their own concerns.
2   Cooperativeness: The extent an individual tries to satisfy other people's concerns.

These two dimensions of human behaviour can then be used to come up with five different ways of responding to conflict.

1 **Competing**: This is when a person is assertive and uncooperative. They pursue their own concerns often at the other person's expense. They will use whatever power is necessary to win their argument. Competing means to stand up for your rights, to defend a position you either believe is correct or just in order to win the argument.

2 **Accommodating**: This a person who is unassertive and cooperative. The individual will neglect their own concerns in order to satisfy the concerns of other people. This could be obeying an order when you do not want to or taking another person's view ahead of your own.

3 **Avoiding**: This person is unassertive and uncooperative. This person does not follow their own concerns, nor those of the other person. They just do not deal with conflict at all and avoid it for as long as possible.

4 **Collaborating**: This is a person who is assertive and cooperative. This person will work with others to find a solution that resolves their concerns. This may be through exploring a disagreement to learn from each other's thoughts and trying to find a creative solution.

5 **Compromising**: This person is moderately assertive and cooperative. Their objective is to find a mutually acceptable solution that in some ways satisfies both parties. Compromisers give up more than competitors but less than accommodators. It is the true middle-ground solution.

Each person can use any of the five modes, but many are better at some than others; this can be due to personality or situational factors and pressures. A person's style is measured through the use of the Thomas-Kilmann Instrument (TKI) which uses forced-choice answers to pairs of statements linked to each of the five conflict types.

Evaluating Thomas-Kilmann's conflict styles

One weakness is that types of conflict modes for individuals are measured using the Thomas-Kilmann Instrument (TKI). This is a questionnaire with forced-choice answers. Each question involves a pair of statements about how the individual responds to conflict situations, and the person taking the test has to choose one which is most applicable to them. One weakness of this style of questionnaire is that it is subject to social desirability bias where a person may choose an answer which makes them look better, but also it may be that the person does not agree with either statement but still must choose one; this lowers the validity of the instrument.

> **ISSUES AND DEBATES**

Application to everyday life

Once an individual understands the different styles of conflict resolution, they can use this to apply the best approach to a situation. They can also recognise their own strengths in terms of the style they are most comfortable using but it can also make them consider other styles that they use less. Perhaps this will lead them to adjust their style depending on the situation they face. However, this does assume that style can be learned and is not just a feature of our own personalities; it may be that changing styles is far more difficult than just changing your learning.

Idiographic versus nomothetic

Nomothetic approaches tend to try and look for certain laws or generalisations that apply to all people, usually using more scientific methods such as experiments, or structured questionnaires, which give quantitative data. Thomas-Kilmann's conflict styles take the nomothetic approach through the use of forced choice questionnaires, which assume that in conflict situations all behaviour can be measured along two dimensions; and that these dimensions account for all individual differences in behaviours (hence the five different responses to conflict). These five styles can then therefore be applied to all people in those situations. It may be, however, that a more idiographic approach through the use of case studies or in depth interviews may show that there are far more ways of responding to conflict, and that there are far more reasons for those responses than assertiveness and co-operation dimensions.

Focus on Einarsen (1999): The nature and causes of bullying at work: types, phases and causes

▶ AIM

To review and summarise research and literature on the nature and causes of conflict at work, using the concept of bullying.

▶ METHODOLOGY

Einarsen (1999) uses a review article methodology to look at why and how bullying occurs in the workplace. A review article uses secondary sources such as other research studies to summarise the current understanding of a topic area, in this case bullying.

▶ RESULTS

Nature (types) of bullying

Einarsen suggested that behaviours involved in bullying were mostly verbal and very seldom included physical violence. Norwegian studies suggested that physical abuse or threats of such abuse, is only present in around 2.4 per cent of cases. Amongst Norwegian victims of workplace bullying, social isolation, insults and ridicule were all more common acts (Einarsen et al., 1994).

Within the review article five types of bullying were identified:
1 Work-related bullying which could include changing your work tasks or making them more difficult.
2 Social isolation.
3 Using ridicule to attack you personally or attack your private life. This could include insulting remarks or gossip.
4 Verbal threats where you are criticised, yelled at or humiliated in front of others.
5 Physical violence or threats of violence.

Phases of bullying

Bullying is not an either-or action but evolves gradually over time. During early phases the victim is subject to aggressive behaviour, which is indirect and not too obvious, but later on more direct aggressive acts may appear. At this point victims are isolated and humiliated. In the end both psychological and physical violence may occur. Einarsen et al. (1994) suggest four phases of bullying:
1 Aggressive behaviour: Subtle aggression is directed against one or more people in a work group.
2 Bullying: This is where the aggression becomes a little more open, direct and frequent. At this point the victim starts to become less able to defend themselves either due to the bullying itself or due to some existing psychological factor.
3 Stigmatisation and victimisation: After a period of time the bullying leads to a **social stigma** being placed on the victim. This mark of disapproval sets the victim apart from others as bullying often focuses on the perceived inadequacies of the victim's personality such as lack of self-confidence or social anxiety.
4 Trauma: The whole situation then becomes hugely traumatic and begins to affect the victim's physical and mental health badly.

Causes of bullying

Research on the causes of bullying have focused on two areas: the personality of the victims as well as **psychosocial factors**. In an interview study of 30 Irish victims of bullying, all victims blamed the personality of the bully (Seigne, 1998), whilst other factors such as the bully being placed into a position of power were also discussed. When looking at causes of bullying you can look at three areas:

1 The bully: Bjorkqvist *et al.* (1994) suggested there are three possible reasons for bullying: a competition for status and job positions, feelings of envy and the bully being uncertain about themselves.

2 The victim: Victims of bullying have been described as being overachievers with unrealistic beliefs about their own abilities as well as the resources and demands of the task. They were also seen as highly rigid. Victims often see themselves as more accurate, honest and punctual than others and this could be seen as highly annoying to other workers.

3 The workplace: Four factors at work can lead to more bullying: deficiencies in work design, deficiencies in leadership behaviour, a socially exposed position of the victim and low moral standards in the department.

CONCLUSION

More empirical research needs to be done on bullying and needs to focus on the feelings of the person being victimised as well as the causes of bullying behaviour. There is a need to address different types of bullying such as predatory and dispute-related bullying and future studies must take these differences into account.

Evaluating Einarsen (1999)

One weakness of Einarsen's work is that it used a review article methodology. This type of methodology uses secondary sources such as other research studies to summarise current understanding of bullying. Although this allows the topic area to be studied without the need for primary research, you do not know how previous researchers have come to their conclusions or whether their methodology was robust; this can lower the reliability of the research findings.

Another weakness is that Einarsen's review findings suggest that the personality of the victim is partly at fault for the bullying such as victims being 'overachievers' with unrealistic beliefs about their own abilities and being annoying to others. This is suggesting that the personality of the victim rather than the actions of the bully are partly the reason for the bullying. This is a weakness as it could be said to be unethical to even partly blame victims for their experiences and could put them at risk of further psychological harm.

ISSUES AND DEBATES

Reductionism versus holism

Einarsen's findings consider both the situational and individual aspects of bullying. For example, he discussed the role of personality in both the victim and the bully whilst acknowledging the relevance of situational factors such as problems in workplace leadership, design and morality. The research also considers the subjective experience of the victim. This is a strength as it is a fairly complete explanation of bullying and acknowledges that it is not enough to just look at the personality of the victim or the bully to reduce bullying, you need to take into account workplace deficiencies as well.

Application to everyday life

Another strength is that the explanation can be applied to real life. For example, identification of the different stages of bullying is important as an increased awareness of the early signs of bullying may mean that it can be stopped far more quickly, meaning that less damage is done to the victim and to the reputation of the organisation; this makes the study findings highly useful.

► **LEARNING LINK**

Conflict resolution styles are measured using a structured questionnaire with forced-choice answers. Which studies have you learned at AS or A Level that use this style of questionnaire or self-report? What problems may be faced by researchers looking at the validity and reliability of such measures?

STUDY TIP

This study brings up a very important issue about how the reporting of research into an event or behaviour such as bullying could potentially cause harm to the readers of the report. One of the ethical guidelines that researchers must consider is that their research needs to minimise harm and maximise benefits to the people being researched and to the wider population to whom the results will be generalised. Suggesting that a victim's personality is even partly to blame for them being bullied may cause distress. Look back at the studies you have learned in this section and at AS Level. Are there any that may possibly cause harm? Or are there any that have great benefit to the person and no possible harm at all? It is an issue that is often overlooked but it is a very important one.

► **TEST YOURSELF**

1 Sadie is aware that bullying in the workplace can be a problem and wants to make sure she can spot this kind of bullying so that she can stop it at the earliest opportunity.
   a   State two types of bullying that Sadie could look out for in the workplace. [2]
   b   Explain one reason why this type of bullying could be happening. [2]
2 Explain one ethical issue that could be raised by research into the nature and causes of bullying. [2]
3 a   Describe what psychologists have discovered about the nature, causes and stages of bullying. [6]
   b   Evaluate what psychologists have discovered about the nature, causes and stages of bullying, including a discussion on situational versus individual factors. [10]
4 Describe one finding from research into the phases of bullying in the workplace. [2]
5 Outline what type of data is collected when researchers use a structured questionnaire, using an example from conflict at work. [2]
6 Suggest two ways Thomas-Kilmann's conflict-handling modes can be applied to real life. [4]

9.4 Organisational work conditions
9.4.1 Physical work conditions

KEY TERMS

Hawthorne effect

temporal validity

scientific worth

relay experiments

neurotic

illumination experiment

METHODOLOGY

experiments

questionnaires

longitudinal studies

quantitative and qualitative data

Think!

What is meant by the **Hawthorne effect**?

Think!

Gabrielle is aware of the Hawthorne effect and the Hawthorne studies, but still wants to find out whether the physical work environment, and in particular the level of noise, is affecting the levels of productivity in the workplace. How could Gabrielle minimise the possibility of the Hawthorne effect in her research to ensure she gets valid results?

Think!

Do you believe that the results of the original Hawthorne studies are reliable and/or valid? Do you still think the studies apply today or is **temporal validity** low? Why do you think this?

These pages have looked at how the presence of a researcher can affect behaviour.

» Can you think of any occasions where you have been observed?

» How did this make you feel? Did it make a difference who was observing?

» Do you believe you showed your natural behaviour in that situation?

▲ Figure 9.21

Impact of physical work conditions on productivity

Workers who are satisfied with their job are often more productive. Böckerman and Ilmakunnas (2012) found that increasing workers' job satisfaction had a positive relationship to their manufacturing output at work. Workers spend a great deal of time in the buildings they work in and therefore the environment is very important. Some of the factors that may affect performance in work are:

1 Temperature: Several studies have shown that temperature may impact physical health and performance, which may then affect productivity. If you are too hot or too cold in your workplace then you will become distracted and focus less on your work. Lorsch and Abdou (1994) found that when air conditioning was introduced into a too hot workplace, workers felt more comfortable and productivity went up between five and fifteen per cent. Other studies have suggested that workers exposed to cold temperatures at work may make up to 44 per cent more mistakes and be less productive.

2 Noise: Noise issues in the office are something that cannot really be avoided. When noise is very low productivity increases and errors reduce. Noise can be an ambient stressor and this is not only due to speech but other sounds such as photocopiers, keyboards and chairs scraping on the floor. Smith (1989), however, found that the effects of intensity of noise are still unclear and that type of noise may be more relevant.

3 Light: A number of research studies have shown that there is an association between lighting and work performance, with 80 per cent of workers saying having good lighting at work is important to them. There is evidence that lighting can have as much of an effect as any other workplace factor. Poor lighting can give a worker headaches due to the strain it puts on a worker's eyes, although too intense artificial light can have the same effect.

Other factors may include humidity and levels of carbon dioxide.

The Hawthorne effect

The **Hawthorne effect** is a term which suggests that levels of performance increase when people know they are part of a research study, such as when they are being observed or part of an experiment. This could mean that the results obtained in a study may be due to the presence of the researcher rather than the manipulation of variables.

The original Hawthorne studies (Mayo *et al.*)

The original studies were conducted in the 1920s, on employees at the Hawthorne plant of the Western Electrical Company in Chicago, USA. The original aim of the studies was to look at the effect of levels of lighting on the productivity of the workers.

The '**illumination experiment**' looked to see whether there was a relationship between the work environment and productivity, for example, the level of lighting in a factory. The researchers hypothesised that higher illumination would lead to better productivity. There were two groups in the study:

1 In the experimental group, the levels of illumination were systematically decreased.

2 In the control group, the levels of illumination were constant.

Both groups showed increased levels of performance even when the lighting got lower, and it was not until lighting was at moonlight level that participants started to complain they could hardly see what they were doing and productivity consequently did not increase. The experiment showed that lighting did not affect productivity and instead another factor was more important. It was suggested that it was due to employees knowing that they were in the study. Being observed and paid attention to made them more productive.

The **relay test room experiment** – leading on from the illumination study, Mayo *et al.* conducted a series of experiments where they changed one part of the work environment such as rest periods, working day or other physical conditions, for a group of five women. The results of the relay test studies provided support for the illumination experiment and the Hawthorne effect as whatever was changed (whether fewer or more rest periods, for example) the women worked harder and more efficiently.

Later studies such as Wikstrom and Bendix (2000) acknowledged that while the original studies seemed to show the Hawthorne effect, there may be other factors which had impacted the results such as relief from a strict supervisor, increased attention, having a different workday and believing they may have an influence in work practices.

Focus on... Kompier (2006)

▶ HAWTHORNE EFFECT IS A MYTH

Kompier (2006) in his work, *The Hawthorne effect is a myth*, agreed that there are other ways to look at the Hawthorne studies, suggesting five reasons why the Hawthorne effect itself is a myth, 'that has become a legend'.

1   The myth of **scientific worth**: The methodological quality of the original case studies is low. There is a lack of scientific rigour, many uncontrolled variables, and it is virtually impossible to identify any causal relationships. The number of participants was also small.

2   The myth of continuous improvement: In many of the original studies it was concluded that performance improved. For many, however, there were periods of time where productivity went down and this was ignored or downplayed by the researchers.

3   The myth of social factors being more important than physical factors and pay: The researchers suggested that the reason behind improvement was due to change in supervision, such as the extra attention workers received, and not economic interest. Some of the studies did not support this: when incentivised pay was introduced in one study productivity increased and when it was taken away it promptly dropped, suggesting pay is a key factor.

4   The myth of wholehearted cooperation: There was a suggestion that in the first test study everyone cooperated with the experiment and with management. Any form of conflict was denied. However, worker resistance and annoyance towards management was documented, with some even facing disciplinary action. One study even finished early due to worker conflict.

5   The myth of the **neurotic** worker: Whenever conflict within the workforce was even mentioned it was blamed upon the mental health of the worker or situations outside of the factory's control, such as family issues. This then put the blame on the individual rather than the situation they found themselves in at work. Negative attitudes regarding the work environment were then dismissed as 'obsessive thinking'.

But why does the 'myth' of the Hawthorne effect still continue? For Kompier (2006) it may be that psychologists think the story is just too good to be untrue and it has become something of a legend. Perhaps there are certain elements that are true? For example, it may well be that social factors are important in work productivity, but the point is that they are not the only motivators as suggested by the original researchers. Perhaps social scientists are just too far removed from the workplace, so they feel like the idea that the workers have feelings and attitudes is a scientific breakthrough! Perhaps it just fits in nicely with already established theories such as social influence, so seems credible. Whatever the reasons are, the 'myth' of the Hawthorne effect is still alive and being taught in a school near you today.

Evaluating the Hawthorne theories/studies

One strength of the Hawthorne studies and consequent idea of the Hawthorne effect is that it provides a baseline for all future research due to its use of a number of different techniques and methods. The studies used a mix of **quantitative and qualitative methods**, interviews and observations, blood pressure and heart rate monitoring. They also built up a strong collaboration between a factory and a university, something that has been used in many different studies since then. This means that the studies were highly useful and this methodology continues to be used effectively in organisational psychology.

The support for the Hawthorne effect came from one set of **field experiments** which was conducted at an electrical plant in Chicago, USA. Although the amount of data collected is a strength of the study, it was only obtained from one area of the USA. This may mean that the results obtained were only applicable to Western individualist cultures such as the USA, or perhaps even that particular type of workplace within the USA. There may be specific characteristics of that type of work or organisation that meant that the presence of an outside researcher was going to increase productivity levels. Therefore, there may be a problem with generalisability in terms of the results.

> ### ISSUES AND DEBATES
>
> #### Application to everyday life
>
> Another strength is that the studies used to support the Hawthorne effect are applicable to real life situations and have high ecological validity. All of the original studies took place within a 'real life' electrical plant in Chicago, using workers who were going about their normal shifts. The only variables that were manipulated were things like lighting and length of breaks which are conditions that are often changed in a real work environment. The use of the workers within a real work environment means that the results obtained can be applied to real life situations, as the study was high in ecological validity. In addition, the fact that the study was not about researcher presence at all, but lighting in the workplace means that the Hawthorne effect was an unintended consequence of the study, suggesting it is high in validity and applicable to real life.
>
> #### Determinism versus free will
>
> One weakness of the Hawthorne effect is that it is deterministic. The Hawthorne effect is the idea that our behaviour is determined by social situations and social interactions. In this study it is suggested that the attention and the real or imagined presence of others, especially if that social presence is someone seen to be higher in terms of authority, has caused a behaviour change. However, this is a weakness as it ignores the role of free will in behaviour, suggesting that the individuals had no choice but to behave in this way. In fact, Kompier (2006) showed that not all participants followed this pattern of behaviour, some dissented and complained about the new practices and for some areas productivity did fall. The idea that not everyone responded to the researchers' attention in the same way shows that free will is present in behaviour.

> ### LEARNING LINK
>
> This study shows how the real and imagined presence of others may affect behaviour and therefore links directly to the social approach (page 128). In this case it was a positive change, but you have seen how this may also lead to negative behaviours. Milgram's study (obedience) showed how situational aspects change behaviour: the presence of an authority figure leads to obedience, even when it causes the participant distress.

STUDY TIP
There may be a time where you may have to use more than one topic to answer any of the questions below. For example, in this section you may need to use Oldham and Brass (1979) (see page 721) and the Hawthorne effect. For this reason, it may be worth trying to find common evaluation themes within the two. Both Oldham and Brass and the Hawthorne studies were conducted in real life environments and therefore can be seen to have high ecological validity. There are more – try and see how many similarities and differences you can find in terms of evaluative issues.

> TEST YOURSELF

1 Selma is a team leader at an engineering company. She and her work colleagues are discussing the Hawthorne effect. Selma says she has noticed that people do change their behaviour when she is around, but her colleagues disagree and say the Hawthorne effect is just a myth.

Suggest two reasons why Selma's work colleagues may believe that the Hawthorne effect is not real and is just a myth. [2]

2 Explain what is meant by the determinism versus free will debate using an example from your knowledge of the Hawthorne effect. [2]

3 a Describe what psychologists have discovered about physical work conditions, focusing on the Hawthorne effect. [6]

 b Evaluate what psychologists have discovered about physical work conditions, focusing on the Hawthorne effect, and including a discussion about generalisability. [10]

4 Outline why the Hawthorne studies were highly useful. [2]

5 Suggest one way in which the Hawthorne effect is deterministic. [2]

6 Suggest two ways the Hawthorne studies could be made more generalisable to other organisations. [4]

KEY TERMS
social relationships
collaboration
interpersonal satisfaction
internal work motivation

Impact of the design over the work environment: Open plan offices

Think!

What is the main difference between the traditional office structure and open plan offices?

Think!

Zoe is thinking about changing the office structure in her company as she thinks that the employees do not communicate very well with each other. What will Zoe need to consider before making her decision to change from a traditional office structure to an open plan office?

Think!

The study by Oldham and Brass (1979) used two different methods to look at the effect of open plan offices on workers. What are the advantages of using both questionnaires and interviews in this study? Is there any other type of research methodology you could have used? Explain your choice.

Figure 9.22 depicts an open plan office.

» Would you like to work in this office?

» What reasons would you give for your answer?

» Are there any types of work which you do not think open plan offices would be good for?

▲ Figure 9.22

An open plan office is an office where all employees work on the same floor within the same open space. The open plan office was designed to get rid of individual rooms or areas, in favour of a space which was intended to increase **collaboration**, creativity and productivity in a world of work which is increasingly complex, and where skill and idea sharing is important. For some, the ability to network with colleagues will be an advantage, although for some the ability to work in a private and quiet space of their own would be preferable.

In recent years the open plan office has become more popular. James *et al.* (2021) identified three main factors that have influenced the move toward this style of office:

» The type of work being done: Work has become more knowledge based and complex.

» Changes in technology: Advancements in portable computers (laptops) and freely available internet means work can be done anywhere and more people are working from home, leaving desks unoccupied.

» Cost: Open plan offices are more space efficient by fitting more people in a space, they are cheaper to build as fewer walls and doors are needed and they have lower running costs (James *et al.*, 2021).

Research findings about the impact of open plan offices on health, and **social relationships** have been contradictory. Some studies such as Oommen *et al.* (2008) looked at the positive and negatives of open plan offices and have shown that open plan offices have a number of positives such as higher levels of communication, high levels of collaboration and increased flexibility to work in different areas. However, they were also found to have negatives such as high levels of noise, loss of concentration, issues with privacy and various health issues such as increased stress, people were more likely to get flu, experience fatigue and have increased blood pressure. James *et al.* (2021) conducted a review of thirty-one papers which looked at the effect on the individual working in an open plan office and found that working in an open plan office was associated with more negative outcomes on measures such as health, satisfaction, social relationships and overall stress. Environmental concerns included a lack of privacy, poor lighting, excessive noise and poor temperature control.

Focus on... Oldham and Brass (1979)

▶ AIM

To examine the changes in employees' reactions to work after moving from a conventional office to an open plan office design.

▶ METHODOLOGY

76 employees at an American newspaper moved from a conventional office to a new open plan office, with no interior walls, no filing cabinets more than three feet high and no private offices. These workers completed a questionnaire eight weeks before the move and twice after the move at nine and eighteen weeks. Their results were compared with those of two control groups (see Table 9.5).

▼ Table 9.5 The three groups compared by Oldham and Brass (1979)

Group	Moved from...	Moved to...	Questionnaires completed...
Experimental group; (n=76) non-supervisory staff members, e.g. copy editors, receptionists	Old conventional office	New open plan office	Eight weeks before the move, nine and 18 weeks after
Non-equivalent control group; five members of the press room	Old conventional office	New conventional office (private cubicles)	Eight weeks before the move, nine and 18 weeks after
Quasi-control group (n=26) randomly selected at beginning of study	Old conventional office	New open plan office	Only at nine and 18 weeks after the move

The questionnaire used seven-point rating scales to measure characteristics of the work environment including work satisfaction – the degree to which employees were satisfied and happy with their jobs, **interpersonal satisfaction** – the degree to which employees were satisfied with co-workers and supervisors and **internal work motivation** – the degree to which an individual experiences positive internal feelings when performing effectively on the job.

Management and employees were questioned informally to gather extra qualitative data on their reactions to the open plan office and interviews were used to see whether other changes in the working environment may have occurred simultaneously. The researchers also asked about concentration levels.

▶ RESULTS

Quantitative findings

Employees' internal motivation and satisfaction with work and colleagues declined sharply after moving from the traditional office to the open plan office. There was largely no difference between the scores of the experimental group tested three times and the quasi-control group, showing that the decreased motivation and satisfaction was not a result of order effects resulting from completing the questionnaire before and then after the move. The non-equivalent control group showed no difference in their scores before and after the move suggesting that changes in the experimental groups scores were not related to the move itself but to the difference in office structure.

Qualitative findings

Many interviewees described the open plan office as a 'fishbowl', 'cage' or 'warehouse'. They discussed their feelings about a lack of privacy and inability to concentrate due to noise with one referring to it as 'Grand Central Station'.

▶ CONCLUSION

- Moving from conventional offices to open plan office styles can have a negative effect on workers' levels of motivation and satisfaction.
- Environmental factors such as noise levels and lack of privacy can have negative effects on an employees' concentration levels.

Evaluating Oldham and Brass (1979)

One strength of the research by Oldham and Brass (1979) is that it used a standardised procedure throughout the weeks studied. For example, all the employees were given the same structured **questionnaire** whenever it was filled in and the data collection points were at the same time for every participant dependent on their experimental group. The use of a standardised procedure is a strength as it allows researchers to repeat the study which will ensure the study's results are reliable.

In addition, Oldham and Brass (1979) was a **longitudinal study**, which involves monitoring a population over a sustained period of time; in this case three different data points, i.e. eight weeks before the move and then nine and 18 weeks afterwards. This allowed researchers to obtain a large amount of data and see changes over time. For example, Oldham and Brass findings showed that satisfaction with work and colleagues decreased sharply after the move/over time. This type of result could not be obtained through the use of a snapshot study, which could only have discovered how the workers felt in any one moment of time.

Another strength is the use of both **qualitative and quantitative data** to support their results. For example, questionnaires were used across all three data collection points which used seven-point rating scales for the outcomes measured. Also, qualitative data was collected through the use of informal interviews with the employees where they expressed their feelings about the open plan office. The ability to use both types of data increases the validity of the results as, for example, the initial results showing that workers had negative feelings about open plan offices was supported by their comments in the interviews.

One weakness of Oldham and Brass's study is that it only used data from one company in the Midwest of the USA. It may well be that the company had particular characteristics that meant that open plan offices did not suit the workers, or it may be that there were other issues within that caused the results collected. In addition, it may be that cultural factors may have contributed to the results and perhaps these results would not be replicated in other countries. Therefore, the fact it was only done on one company limits the **generalisability** of the results of the study.

In addition, the study was done in 1979 when open plan offices were not as popular as they are today and the type of work within those offices was different; this may lower the **temporal validity** of the study. For example, it was in the 1990s when open plan offices became increasingly popular due to the technological advances of that period and the rise of portable computers. It may be that these technological advancements meant that open plan offices would be more favourably looked on by employees as they could see the flexibility it gives them. However, James *et al.* (2021) found a similar negative reaction to open plan offices in his more recent study suggesting perhaps the results would be the same now as they were in 1979.

> ### ▶ LEARNING LINK
>
> This study used both qualitative and quantitative methods to look at the work environment. Are there any studies you have learned at AS Level or A Level that have used both types of methods? What do you think are the advantages of using both? Are there any disadvantages?

> ### STUDY TIP
>
> You do not need to learn the supporting (Focus on...) studies in as much detail as the key studies but it is important to learn enough about them that you are able to discuss the research with reference to particular issues and debates and/or methodological issues. For example, you should be able to discuss the advantages and disadvantages of using experiments, questionnaires, longitudinal studies, quantitative and qualitative data to investigate physical work conditions, with reference to studies such as Kompier (2006) and Oldham and Brass (1979). Can you think of any other relevant issues or debates? Try listing all the relevant issues and debates that relate to these studies and how each relates to the research.

▶ **TEST YOURSELF**

1   Sunni is worried that the new type of open plan office his company has moved into is not successful and his employees seem demotivated.

Suggest two reasons why the open plan office may have caused Sunni's staff to become demotivated. [4]

2   Explain one strength of using questionnaires to study the impact of the design of the work environment on employees. [2]

3   a   Describe what psychologists have discovered about the impact of the design of the work environment on employees. [6]

b   Evaluate what psychologists have discovered about the impact of the design of the work environment on employees, including a discussion on temporal validity. [10]

4   Researchers sometimes use interviews and questionnaires to look at the impact of the design of the work environment on employees.

Describe one finding from research on the impact of the design of the work environment on employees. [2]

5   Suggest one way the impact of the design of the work environment could be studied other than through the use of questionnaires and interviews. [2]

6   Explain two ways research into the impact of the work environment may be limited in its generalisability. [4]

KEY TERMS

backward rotation

forward rotation

flexi-time

on call

rapid and slow rotations

circadian rhythms

phase advance

phase delay

METHODOLOGY

questionnaires

quantitative and qualitative data

validity

9.4.2 Temporal conditions of work environments

Think!

What is meant by **flexi-time working**?

Think!

Tiffany has just been interviewed for a job in a factory. The interviewers explained to her that the job required her to work three different shifts within a week – she would start with an early shift, then a late shift, then a night shift. What type of shift pattern is Tiffany describing? Can you think of any weakness associated with this type of shift pattern?

Think!

How could an organisation investigate which shift pattern is the most effective for their workforce? Think about research methodology, sampling and ethical issues.

Rotational shift work

Rotational shift work is often used in manufacturing sectors when production needs to be continuous. Employees work a shift for a set period of time, for example a week, and then move on to another shift. Rotational shifts allow organisations to run two or three shifts a day, seven days a week. Workers will take turns working eight to twelve hours a day on all the different shifts. For example, a worker may work an early shift from 6 a.m. till 2 p.m., a late shift from 2 p.m. till 10 p.m. and then perhaps an overnight shift from 10 p.m. till 6 a.m. Some workplaces work a two-shift pattern as dedicated staff work permanent night shifts.

»   **Forward rotation shifts:** This is a strategy used to decrease the disruption of **circadian rhythms** which govern the sleep-wake cycle. Known as a **phase delay**, this type of shift system moves from a morning shift, to evening shift then possibly to a night shift before the cycle begins again.

»   **Backward rotation shifts:** This is a counterclockwise or **phase advance** shift system where a worker will begin with the night shift, then move to the evening shift and then to the morning shift. This type of shift is known for *poorer health outcomes*.

There are different types of shift dependent on how fast workers move through the shift pattern. This can range from a few days to a number of weeks.

Rapid rotation shifts

These involve shifts that change frequently. It may be that a worker will work an early shift for one week and then the next week change to late shifts the following week and night shifts the week after and so on. However, there are a number of **rapid rotation** shift types which are quicker than this, where shifts are rotated every two to three days over a seven- or eight-day period.

Examples

Metropolitan shift pattern

This is a fast, forward rotation shift pattern which involves four working teams and three eight hour shifts to enable an organisation to have 24/7 working. Each team does two early shifts (6 a.m.–2 p.m.), two late shifts (2 p.m.–10 p.m. shifts) and two night shifts (10 p.m.–6 a.m.) and then has two days off; free weekends will come once every eight weeks. One issue with this quick rotation is if people are off sick it is difficult to cover a shift due to working time arrangements (such as having to have a certain period of time off before the next shift).

Continental shift pattern

Like metropolitan shift patterns, continental shifts are fast forward rotation shifts using four teams and allowing 24/7 coverage in the workplace. They consist of:
» Week 1: Two early shifts, three late shifts, and two nights shifts (full seven days working).
» Week 2: Two days off, three early shifts, two late shifts.
» Week 3: Two night shifts, three days off, two early shifts.
» Week 4: Two late shifts, three night shifts, two days off.

Continental shifts are still popular and allow for more frequent weekends off (one in four) than metropolitan shifts, however their main disadvantage is the long seven consecutive workdays, as seen in Week 1.

Slow rotational shifts

This is a shift pattern where there are longer intervals between the changes of shift. It could be that shift patterns only change once every two weeks, but it could be even longer than that. For example, workers would work day shifts for six weeks then change to night shift for six weeks.

Slow rotations provide more consistency and regular patterns for workers, allowing them to plan time outside of work. In addition, the body will adjust easier to regular schedules.

On-call work patterns

Many professions such as aviation, medicine and engineering use **on-call** work patterns. This is where workers have to provide 24-hour coverage, seven days a week and so are on 'standby' to respond to a time critical situation. This is most common in places such as hospitals where an emergency means that a person must deal with a problem immediately.

There are generally two types of on-call working:
1 You leave your workplace, for example at evenings and weekends, but can be called back to work during these periods. This means the person is free to do what they want to in the period at home and only time spent in their place of work is counted as working hours. However, there are some restrictions that they may need to follow such as:
   a They need to be able to get to the workplace within a certain time period, such as fifteen minutes from the time they are notified.
   b They must live in a location within a set distance, for example no more than five miles away.
   c Alcohol consumption is not allowed when on-call at home.
   d They must be awake at set times, such as between 12 a.m. and 2 a.m.
   e They must always be contactable by phone.

2　You are at your workplace when on call. For some professionals such as junior doctors a period of time on call means that they will remain at their place of work but will be given somewhere to sleep. If you remain on site, then the whole of the period on call will be classed as working time.

Nicol and Botterill (2004) found that on-call work can play a role in increasing stress and decreasing mental health. It can also decrease the quality and quantity of sleep and leave people more tired after their on-call periods. The disruption caused by being on call can also affect social and family life.

Flexi-time

Flexi-time is a flexible way of work where a worker completes a set number of hours per day but their starting times, lunch times and finishing times are chosen within the limits set by the employer. This allows workers to fit their work hours around their personal circumstances and commitments outside of work, such as childcare or transport to school. Flexi-time therefore does not change the total hours worked or the responsibilities the workers have.

Some organisations allow workers to start and finish whenever they like but many employers have core times within the day (usually their peak time for being busy) when employees have to be at work. For example:

>> Arrival at work: Can be between 7 a.m. and 10 a.m.
>> Lunch hours: Can be between 12 p.m. and 2 p.m.
>> Flexible leaving time: Between 4 p.m. and 6 p.m.
>> Core working hours (at desk): 10 a.m.–12 p.m. and 2 p.m.–4 p.m.

Flexi-time's freedom increases satisfaction and morale amongst the workforce, with reduced stress and fatigue. Traffic rush-hours can be avoided and people are in the office for a longer number of hours per day. It also allows people to work whilst having family commitments. However, flexi-time requires more discipline in workers and also an ability to track when everyone is working and where!

Evaluating design of work

One issue when looking at different types of working patterns and how they affect individuals is the idea of individual differences. This is whether our own differences in physiology and personality may affect the type of work patterns which may suit us best. It is easy to suggest that certain types of shift patterns benefit the individual more and that other types of shift patterns damage health, but this is too simplistic and suggests that we all react the same. This is not the case, and some people may be more suited to working nights or early mornings so we cannot look for **generalisations** and need to look more at the individual.

When researching shift work and the different patterns, researchers tend to use **questionnaires** asking questions about health, accidents, near misses and so on (see page 180). Questionnaires allow for a larger sample as they are simple to distribute and allow for quantitative data to be collected and statistically analysed. This will give researchers an idea about the effects of shift work patterns on the individual and be useful to organisations. However, questionnaires can be subject to a poor response rate and social desirability bias which can lower the **validity** of the research.

> ## ▶ LEARNING LINK
>
> As many people who work shift work will tell you, shift work can disrupt your sleep wake cycles and your circadian rhythms. Dement and Kleitman (sleep and dreams) looked at the stages of sleep and in particular the time you dream, which is during rapid-eye movement (REM) sleep. It is known that sleep is the time when repair and healing takes place in your body and brain. How do you think the different shift types described in this section could affect a person's health and wellbeing?

STUDY TIP

To help you to understand and remember the differences between the different shift patterns, you could print out a few weeks from an online calendar. Using different colour pens for different shift patterns, try marking up when different people would be working – you could give the workers names to help remember them better, for example Mickey Metropolitan and Coby Continental. Try to think about how the shift patterns might affect each of your workers. Personalising the shift patterns in this way and creating a bit of a story might help you to remember them better.

▶ TEST YOURSELF

1 Demi wants to go back to work after having her children, but she is worried about fitting work around them. She also does not drive, so does not really want to be travelling on trains during the traffic rush hour.
   a Suggest which shift pattern would be better for Demi when she returns to work. [2]
   b Explain one weakness of the type of shift pattern you suggested in part (a). [2]
2 Explain why taking into account individual differences is important when looking at different types of shift work. [2]
3 Jamie and Alex have started new jobs. Alex is working a forward rotational shift and Jamie is working a backward rotational shift.
   Compare Alex and Jamie's possible health outcomes due to working these shift patterns. [2]
4 a Describe what psychologists have discovered about different types of shift work. [6]
   b Evaluate what psychologists have discovered about different types of shift work. [10]
5 Outline what is meant by on-call working. [2]
6 Suggest whether a nomothetic or idiographic approach may be preferable when researching the different types of shift work. [2]
7 Explain one strength and one weakness of using questionnaires to study effects of different shift patterns. [4]

KEY TERMS

rotational shift work
sleep deprivation
morbidity
stage 2 sleep

METHODOLOGY

questionnaires
quantitative and qualitative data
validity

Effect of shiftwork on health and accidents

Think!

What is meant by **rotational shift work**?

Think!

Toby has been asked to move from day shifts to permanent night shifts in his job as a care worker. He thinks it is a good idea as it means he spends more time with his family but is a bit worried as some people have suggested that it may affect his health negatively. What negative effects do you think Toby might experience relating to the change from day to night shifts?

Think!

Gold *et al.* (1992) used questionnaires to find out about a number of consequences of shift working. How and why might the topic being studied affect the truthfulness of participants' responses in this study?

Imagine you are a night shiftworker:
» What do you think would be the hardest part of working a night shift?
» Is there any part of working a night shift that you would like?
» Is there anyone you know who would be better off on a night shift and why?

 ▶ Figure 9.23

Effects of shiftwork on health

Ansiau *et al.* (2017) were commissioned by the Institute of Safety and Health (IOSH) to look at the long-term effects of shift work on the following:

1 Sleep quality: There is a general agreement that shift work affects the quality and duration of sleep and this is widespread despite individual differences. The researchers found that the time shift workers spent asleep was reduced by around two hours a day, but their quality of sleep also declined due to the reduction of Rapid Eye Movement and **stage 2 sleep**. They found that those who gave up shift work at a younger age continued to report poor quality sleep showing longer term effects.
2 Quality of life: Researchers found that shift workers reported more chronic fatigue than non shift workers. There were no real differences in other indicators such as social isolation and stress.
3 Physical health: The researchers found that shift workers and former shift workers are more likely to suffer from obesity, peptic ulcers, gastro-intestinal problems, failure to control blood sugar levels and cardiovascular disease. This was especially true for those who had worked shifts for over ten years, even controlling for gender and age.
4 Cognition: There was a significant association between shift work and poorer cognitive performance including poorer attention and **episodic memory**. Those who had quit shift work more than five years previously had no differences in cognitive performance, suggesting that it was a temporary issue whilst shift work was ongoing.

Cardiovascular disease (CVD)

Torquati *et al.* (2018) reviewed 21 studies which looked at the link between CVD and shift work and found that the risk of CVD was 17 per cent higher amongst shift workers than day workers whilst the risk of Coronary Heart Disease (CHD) **morbidity** was 26 per cent higher. Abu Farha and Alefishat (2018) looked specifically at night shift workers in Jordan and found that there was a positive association between night shift work and CVD and clogged arteries, with more frequent and longer night shifts increasing into the risk.

Reproductive effects

Harrington (2001) found that shift work, and especially night work, is of higher risk to women of childbearing age. This may be due to disruptions to the menstrual cycle and increased stress because of the conflicts between night shifts and family life. Increased risk of abortion, low birth weight and premature birth have all been seen as outcomes of shift work.

Shift work and accidents

The cause of accidents is complex and it cannot be suggested that they are due to shift work alone. However, there is a link between shift work and increased fatigue leading to lower performance levels and higher rates of accidents. Ryu *et al.* (2017) studied shift workers in factories in South Korea, finding that current shift workers were 2.7 times more likely to have a work-related injury, whilst past shift workers were 1.7 times more likely, compared to workers who have never worked shifts. Shift work duration only affected this level of risk in women and not men.

The 1986 Challenger disaster happened at night in circumstances where managers had fallen behind in the planning of the shuttle launch, leading to little more than two hours of sleep on the night before the launch. Poor judgement and human error were suggested as part of the cause for this disaster, with actions partially brought about through **sleep deprivation**.

Evaluating the link between shift work and poor health/accidents

The link between shift work and health/accidents is purely correlational. There may be other factors that have caused physical health problems and accidents rather than just shift work. Individuals may have a poor diet, external problems that have caused high stress or they may be inexperienced at their job. All of these may cause health problems such as CVD or errors at work, suggesting that the link is too simplistic and there are many factors that need to be taken into account.

> ISSUES AND DEBATES

Application to everyday life

One strength of researching the effects of shift work is that it has application to real life. If research shows that shift work has negative consequences, then organisations can adapt working patterns to reduce errors and improve health. For example, instead of rotational shifts they could do phase delay shifts. However, this is all dependent on whether the workforce wants and would adapt to those changes, or whether the type of work can be completed on a different shift pattern.

Determinism versus free will

One weakness of suggesting that shift work affects health and performance negatively is that it is deterministic, suggesting that health/accidents are caused by external forces over which we have little control. This is too simplistic as the individual has control over other aspects of their life which may help lessen the impact of shift work such as good nutrition, ensuring the environment at home is good enough for sleep and reducing external stress, for example.

Focus on... Gold *et al.* (1992)

> ## AIM

To examine the impact of work schedule on the sleep schedule, sleepiness and accident rates of female nurses in a Massachusetts hospital.

> ## METHODOLOGY

Questionnaires were distributed to 878 nurses (mean age 33.9) and other auxiliary hospital staff. The nurses recorded for the current week, the following week and the previous two weeks their work shift category at the hospital, and any other job. Types of shift included:
1 Rotator (four days/evening, then four days of nights).
2 Day/evening shifts but no nights.
3 Nights – eight shifts in a month, no days or evenings.
4 Day/evening with occasional nights.
5 Nights with occasional days/evenings.

The nurses were also asked whether their job involved a variable work shift such as a day shift sometimes and a night shift at other times. Sleep-wake times were recorded throughout. Information was also collected about sleep quality, alcohol consumption, medication taken, falling asleep at work or when driving to and from work, accidents, errors and 'near-miss' accidents in the past year. Sleep and wake times were used to see whether a nurse obtained 'anchor sleep' which was at least four hours of sleep during work days and days off.

> ## RESULTS
> ....
> - Rotators reported fewer hours of sleep, more accidents and more near misses than those on regular day or evening shifts, as well as night shift workers.
> - Falling asleep at work occurred at least once a week in 35 per cent of rotators, 32.4 per cent of night nurses and 20.7 per cent of day/evening nurses who worked occasional nights.
> - Rotators had 3.9 times the odds of falling asleep whilst driving and night nurses had 3.6 times the odds compared to day/evening nurses.
> - Adjusting for the effects of alcohol and medication, the odds of reporting any accident or error were twice as high for rotators as for day/evening nurses and there were 2.5 times the odds of near-miss accidents.

> ## CONCLUSION
> ....
> Sleep deprivation and disruption of the circadian rhythms experienced in a rotating shift pattern are associated with lapses of attention and increased error rates on performance tasks.

Evaluating Gold *et al.* (1992)

The strength of Gold *et al.*'s (1992) study was that **quantitative data** was collected on the amount of sleep and the numbers of near misses or errors. Quantitative data is objective, and therefore reliable, and statistical comparisons and analysis can be performed. However, the use of questionnaires can also cause problems due to social desirability bias. Sleeping whilst driving or working could cause a negative reaction at work and therefore participants may not be honest in their answers. This may mean that the answers collected are not measuring true levels of errors, lowering **validity**.

However, Gold *et al.*'s (1992) research is that it only used nurses and other staff from one hospital in Massachusetts, USA. This leads to doubts about generalisability to other countries, cultures or even other states in America. However, over 800 nurses were recruited which is a significant number which may increase **generalisability**. In addition, these are physiological reactions to shift work which may be the same wherever the worker came from, suggesting the use of only one hospital may not be so much of a problem as first thought.

> ## ISSUES AND DEBATES
> ....
>
> ### Application to everyday life
> Another strength is that it has high application to real life and therefore can be useful to organisations. If it is found that a particular shift pattern is causing illness or potential danger to the worker, or to the clients they are working with, then the organisation can adjust the shift pattern or put in place support to ensure that this does not occur.
>
> ### Idiographic versus nomothetic
> The study itself takes a more nomothetic approach rather than idiographic. A nomothetic approach analyses trends to provide general rules of behaviour and usually uses quantitative methods. In this case a wide variety of nurses was asked to fill in questionnaires about shift work, meaning that we can suggest that shift work in general causes health issues. However, it may be worth taking a more idiographic approach and using qualitative methods such as case studies, as we would be able to gain more insight into the reasons why shift work causes the individual such problems and whether there are specific external factors, such as family issues, that are making the problem worse.

▶ LEARNING LINK

You have learned about the Challenger disaster when looking at the effect of groupthink on decision making. The mention of it on these pages makes the important point that we should never just assume that there is a single factor that causes any type of behaviour or action. Psychologists often look at single factors because it is easier to research, however we must be aware that other factors can lead to a behaviour occurring. In this case, the Challenger disaster may be partly due to groupthink, but these pages show that sleep deprivation and poor-quality sleep can lead to faulty decision-making and poor judgement, leading to a disaster that cost all astronauts their lives.

STUDY TIP

It is important that you have a sound understanding of all key terms so you can use them appropriately when writing about health and accidents. For example, rotational shift work, as you know, is when a worker changes shifts every week, and we know this is the most damaging for health according to research. However, if you do not understand this term, it may be that you would not know about the right health effects. Quiz yourself on the key terms regularly; remember the terms highlighted at the top of each section are all defined in the glossary. There may be other terms that are not highlighted that you feel you need to know so add them as well.

▶ TEST YOURSELF

1 Jarrod's biscuit factory has seen a significant increase in the number of absences amongst workers at the company. The only thing that has changed is that they brought in shift working nine months ago.
   Suggest two reasons why the introduction of shift working may be the reason why the number of absences has gone up. [4]
2 a Outline what is meant by the determinism vs free-will debate. [2]
   b Explain why it could be deterministic to suggest that shift work causes ill health and accidents. [2]
3 a Describe what psychologists have found out about the link between shift work and accidents/ill health. [6]
   b Evaluate what psychologists have found out about the link between shift work and accidents/ill health, with a discussion about nomothetic vs idiographic approaches. [10]
4 Zara wants to find out whether night shifts or day shifts have the worst effect on workers' health within her company.
   a Plan a study using a questionnaire to find out whether day shift or night shift has the worse effect on workers' health. Your plan must include details about:
      – questionnaire format
      – sampling technique. [10]
   b State two reasons for your choice of questionnaire format. [2]
   c Give one weakness of your choice of questionnaire format. [2]

KEY TERMS

errors of commission

errors of omission

sequence

system errors

token economy

METHODOLOGY

longitudinal studies

objective and subjective data

generalisations from findings

9.4.3 Health and safety

Think!

What is the main difference between an error of commission and an error of omission?

Think!

Vihaan is concerned about the number of people absent from work due to minor accidents in the workplace. This became even worse when Fredrick got his arm trapped in machinery at work which led to him being off work for two months. Vihaan wants to find a way of reducing accidents at work so that there is less absence. How could Vihaan reduce accidents at his workplace?

Think!

Fox *et al.*'s study took place in 1987 at two mining companies in the USA. Can you suggest any weaknesses of the study based upon the information given in this first sentence?

The Three Mile Island incident is one error that has been studied extensively. Research what happened at Three Mile Island, suggest some reasons why the incident happened and try to relate them to what you have learned. What could have been done to try and prevent this incident from occurring?

▶ Figure 9.24

Accidents at work

Human errors in operator machine systems

Whenever an operator processes information from the environment, makes a decision and takes action, there is always the possibility that an error can occur. An error can occur consciously such as misjudging the height of a vehicle at a low bridge, or unconsciously such as accidentally tripping a switch which turns something off. Errors can be classified in a number of ways:

» An **error of commission**: This is when an operator performs an action which is incorrect/inappropriate or an additional action which should not have been done in the first place. This could have been pressing a button twice or opening a valve on a machine that should be closed.

» An **error of omission**: This is where an operator fails to perform an action which they were meant to do such as failing to put a lock on to stop a machine being operated accidentally or failing to press a stop button on a machine. In many cases these errors occur because someone has forgotten to do something

» An **error of sequencing**: This is where an operator does a series of actions out of the order in which they were supposed to be done.

» An **error of timing**: This is where an operator does an action at the wrong time – too early or too late.

System errors in operator machine systems

The other type of error that can have negative consequences involves a problem with the system itself. This could be an error in the controls of the machine or an error with the display itself.

A display is any device which provides information to the machine operator.

» Visual displays: These include lights, dials and digital readouts. They can show measures such as temperature, speed or time. Visual displays are better for complex messaging.

» Audio displays: These can include pre-recorded messages and tones. These are important if working in a dark room; if the message is time dependent and if the worker is not static.

For example, on an aircraft a pilot will have a visual display which tells them their altitude and how fast they are descending or ascending. However, an audio display such as the TCAS (traffic collision avoidance system) will inform the pilot of a problem, warning them to pull up if they are too near another aircraft.

In order to reduce **system errors**, companies should:

» Make sure that the right kind of display is used for the information needed to be input. For example, a dial is not the best choice if you need an accurate reading – a digital display is preferable.

» Group displays logically – if more than one display is for a single system then group them together.

» Put a relevant display next to a relevant control. If a display shows you the speed of a machine, then put the control which adjusts speed near to it.

» Use colour to enhance the display and warn of danger but do not make it too bright or vivid, which may cause eye strain.

Controls are anything that a worker uses to operate a system such as a lever, switch, handle, keyboard or joystick. Companies should reduce likelihood of errors by:

» Grouping the controls logically and arranging them in the order in which they are to be used and by their frequency of use.

» Making sure controls can be easily reached and operated. Make sure you have a system to protect any controls where it is critical that they should not be accidentally operated. In this case, something like turning a key should be used to operate.

» Label each control so its function is clear, such as 'Emergency shutdown, push down to operate'. Use colour coding.

Despite all precautions, things do go wrong with automated systems, so it is vital that backup systems are in place and operators are trained in the correct procedure to follow if something goes wrong. For all electronic automated systems wherever possible there should be a manual backup.

Evaluating human and system errors

> ### ISSUES AND DEBATES

Application to everyday life

Researching the reasons behind accidents at work has obvious application to real life. To be able to reduce accidents you need to understand why they occur in the first place. Once that understanding is there, then you can develop systems to make their occurrence less frequent, as discussed with visual and audio displays. This includes having back-up systems for systems failures and regular appraisals and observations to ensure fewer human errors occur.

Individual and situational explanations

When looking at human errors you can discuss the individual versus situational debate. In this case many of the errors could be due to situational factors such as poor layout of displays and controls, poor training or distractions. However, there could be some individual factors occurring, such as lack of self-esteem or a lack of confidence in their ability to perform the job or a lack of coordination which makes them trip or fall.

Reducing accidents at work: Token economy

A **token economy** is a system based upon principles of operant conditioning where specific behaviours are rewarded with tokens (secondary **reinforcers**) which are then exchanged at a later date for a desired reward (primary reinforcer). Tokens can be in the form of trading stamps and the rewards can be anything from activities to privileges at work.

Focus on... Fox *et al.* (1987)

In 1985, there were 500 accidents, and 40,000 work related injuries in mines that meant workers had to have at least one day off work. Most previous interventions to reduce accidents had been relatively short term, meaning that the long-term effectiveness was unknown.

▶ AIM

To investigate the use of a token economy in which miners were given tokens for not having accidents or injuries for specified periods of time.

▶ METHODOLOGY

The study was carried out at two open-pit mines, one in Wyoming and one in Arizona, USA. The two settings used similar mining procedures and accidents had occurred at both mines. The participants were the employees at the two mines. Both mines had similar health and safety policies, such as on the job hazard training and yearly refresher training. Each week the health and safety staff inspected all areas of the mine for any correctable hazards and violations of health and safety policy.

Workers in each mine were divided into hazard groups based on lost time injuries during the baseline period. Group 1 jobs were the least hazardous, where workers spent 75 per cent of their time in the office; Group 4 jobs were the most hazardous, such as electricians, scrapers, and operators.

Individual employees were given trading stamps at the end of the month with their wages if they had suffered no lost time injury or compensation injury that required a doctor's care. The number of stamps awarded went up depending on the level of hazard of the job. Safety groups also awarded extra stamps for those employees who came up with safety suggestions that prevented serious injury or death or prevented accidents or damage to property. Employees who had had an accident received no stamps for that month if they had been off for 1–2 days, or for two months if they had been off for 3–4 days, and so on. Failure to report an accident also resulted in a loss of tokens. The token economies went on for over a decade at both mines. The trading stamps could be exchanged at neighbouring stores carrying hundreds of items.

▶ RESULTS

At both mines there were substantial decreases in the number of days lost during the first years of the token economies. In terms of lost time injuries, the trend went down significantly during the second year of the token economy, but not the first. Costs of injuries and accidents fell significantly, and the cost-benefit ratio showed that the money saved from the decline in accidents more than compensated for the cost of the trading stamps.

▶ CONCLUSIONS

Behavioural programmes can be effectively administered and can be maintained for long periods of time.

Evaluating Fox *et al.* (1987)

One strength of the Fox *et al.* study is that it uses a **longitudinal research** methodology over a number of years. For example, at one mine the token economy programme ran for twelve years. This is important as it allows researchers to track changes over time, to gather a large amount of data and also to see whether the interventions implemented are effective in the long term.

In addition, the study has important applications to real life. Time off work for accidents is a real issue for organisations in terms of employee morale, loss of money and work time. Therefore, if interventions such as token economy can be used effectively within a workplace to decrease accidents there is less chance of negative consequences for the employee and the cost of the programme will be less than the benefits, making the study useful.

One weakness of the study is that the sample may not be representative of the wider population, limiting the study's **generalisability**. For example, the two companies were in the USA and were both mining companies. The effectiveness of reward systems may only be apparent in certain countries and there may be something about the mining community which may make them more receptive to this type of behavioural intervention, for example the element of risk and danger. Therefore, the results of the study may not generalise to other countries and organisations.

Finally, there may be an issue with the **validity** of the study. For example, the incentive of a reward may have stopped employees reporting incidents and therefore the number of accidents may not have decreased, only the reporting of them. However, a serious accident is not easily hidden so this may not be a real issue. However, a potentially bigger issue was the fact that accidents were decreasing at one mine even prior to the start of the study so there may have been sustained improvements even without the intervention, decreasing the validity of the study's findings.

► LEARNING LINK

Fox's study is based on the principles of operant conditioning which suggests that desired behaviour will increase if it is rewarded in some way; in this case safety behaviours were rewarded with trading stamps. Fagen *et al.* (2014) used secondary reinforcement to train elephants. This is based on the same learning principles as Fox *et al.* used in the mines. However, the question for this study is whether we can generalise from animal studies to humans: are the cognitive processes the same for elephants and humans?

STUDY TIPS

One way of learning about how to reduce accidents is to research serious accidents that have happened in the world and to try and see if you can apply what you have learned on these spreads to those accidents. For example, you could look at the Herald of Free Enterprise disaster or the Challenger disaster to see whether they were due to human errors or system errors or a mixture of both.

► TEST YOURSELF

1   Omar wants to find ways to make the displays they use at work more effective and less prone to error such as pressing the wrong buttons.
    Suggest two ways that Omar can make the displays used more effective and less prone to errors.   [4]

2   Outline what is meant by validity, using an example from research about reducing accidents at work.   [2]

3   Outline one difference between a system error and a human error.   [2]

4   a   Describe what psychologists have discovered about health and safety in the workplace.   [6]

    b   Evaluate what psychologists have discovered about health and safety in the workplace, including a discussion about longitudinal studies.   [10]

5   a   Plan an experiment to test the effectiveness of token economies to reduce accidents in the workplace.
        Your plan must include:
        –   details about the sampling technique
        –   a directional or non-directional hypothesis.   [10]

    b   Describe one piece of psychological knowledge which informed your plan.   [4]

9 ORGANISATIONAL PSYCHOLOGY

accident prevention
industrial plants
accident protocols
line managers

Monitoring accidents at work

How does Swat (1997) define an accident at work?

Managers at Giselle's sweet factory are worried about the number of people who are having days off work. She notices that the way that people report accidents is not very reliable and she wonders whether more accidents are happening than those written down. Use Swat's (1997) study to suggest how Giselle could improve her accident reporting system.

Swat's study used a longitudinal research methodology. What are the strengths and weaknesses of longitudinal studies?

Key study: Monitoring of accidents and risk events – Swat (1997)

Krzysztof Swat began his academic career by studying Sociology at the University of Lodz in Poland. He then went on to complete a PhD in Economics at the same university in 1983. His main areas of interests include organisation and management, and ergonomics. It was his interest in ergonomics that led Swat to his position of research assistant professor at the Nofer Institute of Occupational Medicine Institute, a position he held for over 17 years until 2001. The study outlined in this chapter draws upon his areas of interest and stemmed from his desire to find causes of accidents at work and as a result prevent them from happening in the first place.

Think about any time you have had a minor accident such as falling over or banging into something. Think of how you felt. Is there any reason why your accident may not have been reported if it had happened in the workplace?

▶ Figure 9.25

▶ CONTEXT

There is no universal way of monitoring accidents and every country, and even every organisation, has a different way of monitoring them. Two types of monitoring have been discussed in terms of accident prevention.
1 Active monitoring: These are all the formal and informal checking activities that are carried out by line managers to ensure accidents do not occur.
2 Reactive monitoring: This looks at safety through looking at accidents and incidents that have occurred. It looks at the incident types and frequency of accidents, sickness rates, near misses and property damage.

Swat (1997) found that Poland's system of documenting accidents was ineffective. No detail on losses resulting from accidents and incidents was available. The medical costs associated with accidents were just included in the overall health care system costs, and therefore they did not affect the insurance plans of the affected organisations. Also unplanned events, such as machine issues, which may interrupt production were not monitored.

> **AIM**
> ....
> To develop an organisationally useful method of recording risk events in organisations which could help find causes of accidents and consequently prevent them.

> **METHODOLOGY**
> ....
> This was a case study with a longitudinal design which took place between 1994 and 1997 and used already available secondary data on accidents and minor injuries in four different **industrial plants** in Poland. Interviews with line managers, safety supervisors and employees were also conducted.
>
> ## Sample
> Four industrial plants from different industrial branches (foundry, machinery, meat processing and furniture) in Lodz, Poland were chosen. All of the plants chosen were rather old and had equipment which was a number of years old. A total of 2964 workers were employed in the plants in 1993.

> **PROCEDURE**
> ....
> The number of accidents recorded in 1993, within each of the four plants, was the first and most common source of information about risk at work. The 83 accidents which occurred in 1993 were analysed for frequency, accident severity and their direct and indirect causes. In the study:
> - An accident was defined as a 'case which had been formally reported as an accident by the... safety supervisor'. In other words, a sudden undesired event which was connected with the workplace resulting in health impairment in the worker. In Poland, this would only mean an accident that resulted in sick leave or death.
> - Accident frequency was defined as 'the number of injury accidents resulting in sick leave per 100 employees within a year'.
> - Accident severity rate was the number of sick days per accident.
>
> Three types of information were used about accidents: collective accident reports from safety supervisors, the researchers' own investigations of **accident protocols** and interviews with the safety supervisors and **line managers**.
>
> The second source of information on risk at work used in the study came from minor incidents from 1994 which did not result in death, serious injury or serious damage. Only the meat processing plant was analysed, with an incident being defined as 'any sudden event which resulted in personal injury.' Data on first aid cases reported to the meat plants was analysed as well as interviews with 96 employees, who were told to report even small injuries.

> **RESULTS**
> ....
> ## 1 Accidents
> ▼ Table 9.6 Accident frequency rate (per 100 employees)

Foundry	Machinery plant	Meat processing	Furniture	Average for all plants
5.9	2.1	2.8	2.3	2.8

▼ Table 9.7 Accident severity rate (number of sick days per accident)

Foundry	Machinery plant	Meat processing	Furniture	Average for all plants
38.8	61.2	41.4	41.2	44.6

Five different accident types were proposed from these results which could be used for monitoring:

1 Falls and slips
2 Accidents connected with manual work
3 Accidents connected with working parts of machinery
4 Accidents connected with sources of energy
5 Others

▼ Table 9.8 Frequency rates for types of accidents (per 100 employees) on average in all plants

Fall and slip	Manual work	Working parts	Sources of energy	Other
0.7	1.1 (highest in Meat processing 1.2)	0.7 (highest in Foundry 2.6)	0.2 (highest Foundry 0.9)	0.1

The study found four essential causes of accidents:

1 Insufficient supervision
2 Poor workplace organisation (such as inadequate personal protection)
3 Technical factors
4 Individual error of the worker

Insufficient supervision was seen in the highest number of accidents (89 per cent), with technical problems the least (11 per cent). However, there were overlaps between these causes, with a number of incidents having more than one cause.

Poor housekeeping (maintenance) was also seen frequently as a cause of accidents and Swat (1997) suggested that this classification should be used when monitoring accidents. Frequency and type of accident was very much related to the levels of housekeeping within the plant. Examples of types of housekeeping accidents are:

1 Falls on slippery floors
2 Faulty staircases leading to slips and falls
3 Use of improper tools
4 Unsuitable clothes

Housekeeping contributed, in total, to 65 per cent of the accidents in the foundry, 47.8 per cent in the meat processing area, 37.5 per cent in the furniture area and 33.3 per cent in the machinery section, showing that housekeeping needs to be considered as a risk factor in workplaces.

2 Incidents

Note: The frequency rate of incidents in the meat factory increased from 2.8 to 3.5 between 1993 and 1994 with manual accidents being the main reason.

In terms of incidents in the meat factory in 1994, there were 254 injuries requiring medical treatment (218 of these were manual injuries and most likely to lead to injuries of the left hand), 23 cases with sick leave days (remember sick leave days are the only ones usually reported in Poland so these are the only figures they would normally have) of which five were serious leading to over 30 sick days each. Interviews with employees suggested the real total of incidents could be as high as 520, meaning that 95 per cent of incidents are never reported.

CONCLUSION

● Accidents should be recorded according to the circumstances in which they occurred and their type, for example where they were related to manual work or to energy sources. The comparison of frequency indicators for accident types both nationally, and within the different sections of the plants, may supply information on the extent of safety management faults.
● Lesser incidents should be noted, especially those needing first aid. That would supply more data for these types of incidents which would help safety management more than just knowing about the few serious incidents.
● Poor housekeeping should be noted as a cause. Poor operation is a frequent source of incidents and this therefore is a central risk factor and should be incorporated into safety monitoring systems.

Methodological strengths and weaknesses

One strength is that a variety of different data collection methods were used. For example, the data from the established accident monitoring procedures was used alongside information from interviews with managers and employees. This is a strength as it means that organisational data can be compared with the results of the interviews to identify differences. In this case it showed that the company data was not comprehensive enough and many incidents were missed, allowing changes to monitoring procedures to be suggested.

In addition, a **longitudinal design** was used which allowed the researchers to look at organisations over a period of three years. Longitudinal studies are often used to look at trends over time and allow a greater amount of detail to be obtained than shorter studies. For example, in this case accident rates over a period of a year for three of the plants, and over two years for the meat processing plant, were compiled and analysed alongside the interviews. This is a strength, as it leads to a more comprehensive understanding of the subject, in this case accident monitoring at work.

One weakness is that the research methods used have issues of **subjectivity**. Although the information officially collected by the organisations could be said to consist of quantitative and objective data, it is subject to omissions, where employees may not record or even report a particular accident or the line manager may not want a number of incidents reported because it would cause them issues with their managers. In addition, the researcher used their own analysis to look at the different plants, which again may lead to researcher bias and subjective interpretation to support their aims.

There are also issues concerning the **generalisability** of case studies. Although four different trades were studied, these are a very small proportion of the types of organisations in countries such as Poland; it may be that there is something specific about those organisations that caused the accidents recorded. In addition, the fact that only organisations in Poland were studied would also affect generalisability. However, it is worth noting the case study very often has no intention of generalising outside of one particular country and this may be the case with Swat (1997) who was focusing on the particular monitoring problems within Poland.

 ## Ethics

There were no specific ethical issues mentioned within the study, although no particular businesses were identified and therefore confidentiality was upheld. It may be, however, that there was only one meat factory within that area in Poland, so they may be more easily identified. There was no harm from the study and results could have a benefit to the workers due to increased monitoring of accidents leading to greater **accident prevention**, meaning that the results are beneficial and therefore ethical.

 ## Application to everyday life

This study has obvious application to real life as it will allow organisations within Poland and in other countries to formulate a more robust accident monitoring system. This will allow them to identify how many accidents occur and also to look at the causes and be able to work on prevention of accidents rather than reaction to accidents.

 ## ISSUES AND DEBATES

Idiographic versus nomothetic

Although this study takes a nomothetic approach by looking at general trends in accidents which can be applied across a number of different trades and countries, it may be worth taking a more idiographic approach and looking at the individual, with more qualitative forms of data collected. This would allow researchers to investigate individual reasons behind accidents which could then be analysed using thematic analysis and used for accident prevention.

> REFLECTION

- Do you feel that this study takes an individual or situational explanation of accidents in the workplace? Or does it suggest both are important? What does this mean for organisations?
- How could you make this study more generalisable? Can you think of any issues with your suggestions?

LEARNING LINK

This study used a case study with a longitudinal design to look at accident reporting over a period of three years. Are there any studies at AS Level which also used a case study method? Or a longitudinal design? What are the common features of case studies? Can you think of any practical problems of doing case studies?

STUDY TIP

One of the best ways to consolidate your understanding of the concepts you are studying, such as accident monitoring, is to find out how accidents are reported in places that you know. This could be your school, a workplace or even a place where your parents work. From what you have learned from this study, how effective do you think these ways of reporting are? Could anything you have learned help to improve them?

TEST YOURSELF

1 Using information from Swat (1997), suggest two ways that accident reporting could be improved within organisations. [4]
2 Explain how accidents were defined in Swat's (1997) study. [2]
3 a Describe what psychologists have discovered about monitoring of accidents. [6]
  b Evaluate what psychologists have discovered about monitoring of accidents, including a discussion of generalisability. [10]

The key study by Swat (1997) used accident data already recorded by the organisations to study accident monitoring.

4 Outline what is meant by accident severity and frequency. [2]
5 Describe the different types of accidents that were discussed by Swat (1997). [2]
6 Explain one strength and one weakness of using interviews to study accident monitoring at work. [4]

KEY TERMS

hygiene factors

motivational factors

intrinsic

extrinsic

strikes and slowdowns

satisfiers

METHODOLOGY

generalisations from findings

9.5 Satisfaction at work
9.5.1 Theories of job satisfaction

Think!

How are **hygiene** and **motivational factors** linked to **extrinsic** and **intrinsic motivation**?

Think!

Babak is confused. Recent changes to his business have ensured that all his workers have a good salary, flexible working hours and access to a health care plan, but they still seem unmotivated and levels of productivity are not going up at all. Why might the workers not be motivated to increase productivity? What could Babak do to improve this?

Think!

Think back to the debate about reductionism versus holism. Do you believe Helzberg's theory is reductionist or does it take a more holistic approach to job satisfaction? Give reasons for your answer.

Think about things that motivate you to complete a task. Do you feel like you are motivated more by hygiene factors or motivational factors? Do you have any friends or family that are motivated by different factors? What does that tell you about the two factor theory?

▶ Figure 9.26

Herzberg's two factor theory

Background

Herzberg *et al.*'s (1959) theory was the result of a five-year research programme looking at job attitudes. At the time of the study there was a need to gain a better understanding of people's attitudes to work, as it was a time of **strikes and slowdowns**. During the first stage, Herzberg conducted a literature review of 2000 studies between 1900 and 1955. Although the results showed contradictory findings, Herzberg *et al.* (1959) developed an initial hypothesis which stated that satisfaction and dissatisfaction could not be measured on the same continuum.

Herzberg *et al.* (1959) then set out to study his hypothesis empirically by using the critical incident technique. This research was conducted at nine sites close to Pittsburgh, USA. 203 accountants were studied and researchers used semi-structured interviews where participants were asked to describe any time they had felt good or bad about their job. After describing this, they were asked for another description at the other end of the continuum. In other words, they were asked for a bad story if their first one was good. The participants were then asked to rate their experience on a scale of 1 to 21 (1 = hardly affected feelings and 21 = had a serious impact on feelings). Herzberg found that Maslow's theory of self-actualisation (see page 640) was the key to understanding good feelings about the job.

From the data, the two factor theory of motivation was constructed, with job satisfaction divided into two categories.

Hygiene factors (context of job)

These are factors which do not lead to feelings of positive satisfaction in the long term, but if they are not present then they can lead to negative feelings. The two factor theory suggests that meeting the lower level needs of individuals would not motivate them to put in extra effort but would only prevent them from becoming dissatisfied. These are factors that are extrinsic in nature and granted by other people. For the organisation trying to use this theory it means that meeting the extrinsic needs of the employee will mean that their employees will be free from unpleasant working conditions and levels of dissatisfaction will decrease, but workers will still feel neutral and will be neither satisfied nor motivated. Types of hygiene factors include:

» Pay: This should be appropriate and reasonable for the job done, as well as competitive to those in the same industry.

» Company policies: Policies should not be too rigid. They should be fair and clear and include flexible working hours, breaks, holidays and so on.

» Physical working conditions: The work environment should be safe and clean and work equipment should be well maintained.

» Interpersonal relations: Relationships with peers, superiors and other workforce members should be appropriate and acceptable; there should be no conflict.

Motivational factors (content of the job)

Motivational factors increase job satisfaction; and are known as **satisfiers**. Employees find these types of factors intrinsically rewarding. Intrinsic factors are effective in creating more long-term positive effects on employee performance, and these factors meet the basic needs for psychological growth. These factors will create additional interest in their job for employees, and when employees are interested and satisfied then their productivity and efficiency will improve. Motivational factors include:

- ▸▸ Recognition: Employees need praise and recognition for their work from managers.
- ▸▸ Sense of achievement: Employees need to feel that they have accomplished something.
- ▸▸ Growth and promotional opportunities: There must be a chance of career progression in order to motivate a person to perform well.
- ▸▸ Responsibility: Employees must hold themselves responsible for their work. Employers should minimise control but retain accountability.

Helzberg *et al.* (1959) suggested that extrinsic and intrinsic factors are related to each other. The presence of extrinsic factors may reduce worker dissatisfaction but will not provide satisfaction. On the other hand, the presence of intrinsic factors will help a person's inner growth and will lead to high performance and productivity but the absence of them will just lead to neutrality and not satisfaction or dissatisfaction. In simple terms, extrinsic factors will mean that a person will be willing to work, whilst intrinsic factors will decide the quality of their work. Therefore, organisations should ensure that both intrinsic and extrinsic factors are satisfied.

Evaluating Herzberg's two factor theory

Herzberg's theory is supported by psychological theories that have been shown to be credible. For example, the idea of productivity being improved through meeting personal growth needs, such as the need for relationships or ability to obtain promotion is linked to Maslow's needs theory (see page 640), whilst the idea of extrinsic and intrinsic motivation being linked to motivation at work has been studied extensively. Therefore, the idea that Herzberg's two factor theory has theoretical support means that it is more credible.

Herzberg's theory of job satisfaction fails to consider individual differences within the workforce. It assumes that the needs for all employees are the same and that such things as recognition or responsibility are vital in terms of increased productivity and performance. However, it may be that different people are motivated by different needs due to their personal circumstances, but also due to their personality: some people may not need intrinsic motivators to produce high quality work. Therefore, this failure to take into account individual differences lowers the validity of the results.

> ## ▸ ISSUES AND DEBATES
>
> ### Application to everyday life
>
> One strength of Herzberg's theory of job satisfaction is that it can be applied to real life to increase job satisfaction in workers and improve the quality of their work life. If, as suggested by Helzberg, workers need both hygiene factors and motivational factors in order to be motivated and increase productivity then they must concentrate not only on increasing pay or improving practical work conditions but also ensure that factors as recognition and promotional opportunities are present. However, it may be that individual and cultural differences play a part in the type of motivators that are most important to the workers. Therefore, there may need to be a more idiographic approach to investigating job satisfaction so that factors can be tailored to a particular workforce.

Cultural differences

In addition, the Herzberg theory of job satisfaction does not consider cultural differences. Herzberg's theory was constructed using semi-structured interviews with employees in Pittsburgh, USA. Therefore, it may be that different cultures have different needs, or maybe people in some cultures are motivated by extrinsic needs more than people in the USA. For example, Edward and Teoh (2009) studied workers in two universities in Kuala Lumpur and found that the presence of extrinsic factors positively contributed to job satisfaction, whilst the absence of intrinsic factors did not only neutralise feelings as suggested by Herzberg but actively demotivated the workers. Therefore, research has shown that cultural factors play a significant role in what does and does not motivate workers and that Herzberg's theory may not be applicable across all cultures.

▶ LEARNING LINK

This subtopic has many links to other topic areas within the organisation chapter. For example, Herzberg acknowledges that needs theories such as Maslow's hierarchy of needs are vital in understanding job satisfaction. Also, you have learned about the importance of intrinsic and extrinsic motivation in the workplace and how important it is that extrinsic motivators are used as a way of promoting autonomy to improve production. For this reason, the cultural differences in China and Kuala Lumpur that were discussed in the evaluation may be due to how the different motivators were presented to the workers rather than different motivators being important. For example, perhaps in the USA extrinsic motivators are used as a way of controlling the workforce whereas in other cultures they are used as a way of promoting autonomy.

STUDY LINK

The theme throughout these pages is the idea that you cannot consider this theory in isolation or as a stand-alone theory. Many of the study links supplied have been links to the topics at AS Level, but many also apply to what you are studying at A Level. A large number of topic areas within organisational psychology are linked to each other and can help you understand a study or theory. In this case it is Maslow's theory which can help you understand the concepts of intrinsic and extrinsic motivation, but there are many other examples you can find in this chapter. Look through some of the topics you have already learned and see whether you can see the similarities to other areas.

▶ TEST YOURSELF

1   Aaron is the manager at a car factory. He wants to increase motivation on the shop floor and has started reading about Herzberg's two factor theory.
    Suggest two factors that Aaron could use to improve motivation on the shop floor.   [4]
2   Outline what is meant by hygiene factors of motivation.   [2]
3   a   Describe what psychologists have discovered about job satisfaction in the workplace.   [6]
    b   Evaluate what psychologists have discovered about job satisfaction in the workplace, with a discussion about cultural differences.   [10]
4   Suggest one reason why Herzberg's theory of job satisfaction can be said to be reliable.   [2]
5   Herzberg suggests that job satisfaction is affected by hygiene and motivational factors. Plan a study using an interview to investigate the factors which affect job satisfaction in the workplace.
    Your plan must include details about:
    –   sampling technique
    –   interview technique.   [10]
6   a   State two reasons for the choice of interview technique you used in Question 4.   [4]
    b   Give one weakness of your choice of interview technique.   [2]

KEY TERMS

psychological states

core characteristics

person-fit approach

task identity

job rotation

enrichment

job design

job enrichment

job enlargement

Hackman and Oldham's job characteristics theory

> **Think!**
>
> Which three types of Hackman and Oldham's job characteristics may lead to workers believing that their job is valuable and worthwhile?

> **Think!**
>
> Think about the characteristics of your ideal job? What would they be? Do you feel this ideal job is possible? If not, why not?

> **Think!**
>
> How do you think cultural differences might affect the 'ideal job'?

Hackman and Oldham's theory, developed in the 1970s, is one of the very few which take a **person-fit approach**, taking into account a person's personality, behaviours, and accomplishments in order to describe the perfect fit for a job. In addition, the beliefs, values and ethnic background all contribute to how a person responds to a job. The theory is comprised of five **core characteristics** that are combined with three **psychological states** to determine job outcomes:

Psychological states

The three psychological states are:

1 Experienced meaningfulness of the work: The degree to which the employee feels that the job they are doing is valuable and worthwhile.
2 Experienced responsibility of work: The degree to which the employee feels personally responsible for the results of the work they do.
3 Knowledge of the actual results of the work activities: The degree to which an employee knows how effectively they are performing in the job.

Job characteristics

The five core characteristics are:

1 Skill variety: This looks at the diversity of the job; whether the worker engages in a wide range of activities that need a number of different skills and talents.
2 Task identity: This is where a job requires completion of a 'whole' piece of work. You do a job from beginning to end with a visible result.
3 Task significance: This is whether the job has a substantial impact on people's lives; this could be within an organisation or in wider society.

These three characteristics are linked to the psychological state of experienced meaningfulness of work.

4 Autonomy: Does the job provide freedom, independence and discretion in terms of work schedule and how it is to be carried out? For example, can an employee make their own decisions?

This characteristic is linked to the psychological state of experienced responsibility of work.

5 Feedback from the job itself: Does the employee have clear feedback about the effectiveness of their performance at their job?

This characteristic is linked to the psychological state of knowledge of the actual results of work activities.

All the above have an effect on job outcomes. If all psychological needs are met then employees will have high internal work motivation, high 'growth' satisfaction, high general job satisfaction and high work effectiveness.

Evaluating Hackman and Oldham's theory

One weakness of the theory is that there may be limits to its generalisability. Such theories tend to be based upon organisations in Western countries such as the USA and it may be that the five core characteristics do not apply to employees in collectivist countries where such things as task diversity and autonomy may not be as important. However, a study by Ayandele and Nnamseh (2014) studied the validity of the theory amongst workers in the African civil service and found that the results supported the model not only in terms of culture but also in terms of the different types of organisations, suggesting that this may actually be a fairly universal theory of job satisfaction.

> ## ISSUES AND DEBATES

Application to everyday life

One strength of the theory is that it can be applied to real life situations. The five characteristics described by the theory could be easily used as a checklist when a job is being created or reviewed. For example, when looking at a job you could ensure that there is enough task variety, that employees are given enough control over decisions, and that there are regular appraisals where employees are given feedback about their performance. This means that the theory can be used to improve work satisfaction and productivity and therefore this makes the theory useful.

Reductionism versus holism

Hackman and Oldham's theory takes a more holistic approach to job satisfaction. Whereas theories such Herzberg's two factor theory focus on external factors such as pay, working conditions, responsibility, etc. Hackman and Oldham acknowledged the role of personality, beliefs, values, culture and ethnicity as well as workplace elements in job satisfaction. This makes it a more holistic, and universal, theory of job satisfaction.

Focus on... Belias and Sklikas (2013)

> ## TECHNIQUES OF JOB DESIGN

Job design is a tool which is used by organisations to meet the needs of their employees whilst still safeguarding the interests of the organisation and can be defined as 'the specification of the contents, methods, and relationships of jobs in order to satisfy technological and organisational requirements as well as the social and personal requirements of the job holder' (Armstrong, 2003, p. 494).

Job design should begin with task requirements (what should be done) and then look at a number of motivating characteristics such as responsibility, autonomy and self-control. Three important factors in job design are:

1 **Job rotation**: This allows employees to rotate from one job to another. For this to be effective four factors need to be taken into account:
   a Gender
   b Physical demands of the job.
   c Knowledge, skills and capacities of the employee.
   d The demands and the time needed to perform other tasks.
   Job rotation can improve productivity, increase training opportunities and reduce boredom. Importantly, it can control musculo-skeletal disorders which are more common in workers who do one job constantly and therefore use the same parts of the body all the time. One issue with job rotation, however, is a lack of knowledge and skills, but also gender stereotypes which may stop people from moving into a job commonly associated with people of a different gender to themselves.
2 **Job enlargement**: This is where a job is expanded to include more or different tasks. This is to stimulate the interest of the employee through greater variety in their work. There are two approaches to job enlargement: the first is horizontal enlargement to reduce the boredom of the work by adding more tasks at the same skill level; the second is vertical enlargement, which is how the employee decides the job is done. The main goal of this is to enhance the status and self-fulfilment of the employee.

3 **Job enrichment**: This is the development of practices which challenge and motivate employees to raise their performance levels. This includes including a greater variety of work, requiring higher levels of knowledge, giving workers autonomy and responsibility and providing opportunities for personal growth. The two main features of job enrichment are variety and feedback. Employee motivation positively correlates with feedback, resulting in behaviour which can improve job performance and effectiveness.

Evaluating techniques of job design

One strength of job design theory is that it can be useful to businesses in order to improve performance in the workplace. Chen and Lu (2012) found that job design had a positive impact on employee motivation and performance. This shows how job design can improve motivation, job satisfaction and performance, meaning that organisations can increase productivity through non-monetary means such as autonomy and responsibility which links to the idea of intrinsic motivation which has been shown to be more effective in the long term.

> ### ISSUES AND DEBATES

Idiographic versus nomothetic

One weakness of job design theory is that it takes an idealistic view of the workplace and assumes that all types of organisations have the ability to implement the factors suggested. For example, there are some types of work where it is not possible to have job rotation or there is not the ability to expand a job role. It is also perhaps too simplistic to suggest that rotation or expansion of job roles will increase satisfaction when for some individuals this may actually increase their stress levels. Perhaps this is why taking an idiographic perspective would be better than trying to formulate general trends for all workers. Internal factors like personality or external factors related to family life or personal life may mean that what would be seen as a positive for one person, could be viewed negatively by another.

> ### LEARNING LINK

In the evaluation it was suggested that taking an idiographic approach may be better to really understand job satisfaction in employees. At AS Level, you studied Saavedra and Silverman who used a case study methodology to study a young boy with a button phobia. This is an idiographic methodology with qualitative data obtained alongside quantitative data. How could you use an idiographic approach to study the theories discussed on these pages?

STUDY TIP

There is a great deal of information on these last few pages, but also many different elements of the theories. You need to find a way that allows you to learn these theories in a straightforward way. Try different ways of revising and see which one leads to the best results in class tests and assignments. For example, you could try making colourful mind maps or storyboards and displaying them somewhere that you will look at regularly or how about recording your notes and listening to them on headphones? Some people even suggest listening to notes while they fall asleep.

> ## TEST YOURSELF
>
> 1 Louis has a vacancy at his sock factory. He has had a high turnover of staff and he is trying to work out how to retain his staff for longer.
>
> Suggest two ways Louis can try and ensure his staff are happier and want to stay at his company, using techniques of job design. [4]
>
> 2 Outline one psychological need Hackman and Oldham believed had to be fulfilled for an employee to be satisfied at work. [2]
>
> 3 a Describe what psychologists have discovered about:
> - job characteristics theory
> - techniques of job design. [6]
>
> b Evaluate what psychologists have discovered about:
> - job characteristics theory
> - techniques of job design including a discussion about usefulness. [10]
>
> 4 Hackman and Oldham's job characteristic theory takes a person-fit approach. Outline what is meant by a person-fit approach. [2]
>
> 5 a Explain what is meant by a nomothetic approach to research. [2]
>
> b State one strength and one weakness of a nomothetic approach, with reference to theories of job satisfaction. [4]
>
> 6 One way to investigate job satisfaction is to carry out self-report questionnaires. Explain two ethical guidelines that would be important when conducting research into job satisfaction self-report questionnaires. [4]

KEY TERMS

psychometric tests

job descriptive index

remuneration

adjectives

dimensions

METHODOLOGY

quantitative and qualitative data

psychometrics

validity

reliability

9.5.2 Measuring job satisfaction

> ### Think!
>
> How was the Quality of Work Life questionnaire constructed?

> ### Think!
>
> Roland is a manager in a local shrimp company. He is trying to find out about job satisfaction in his workplace. He wants to use a questionnaire. How could Roland use a questionnaire to measure job satisfaction? Are there any issues that Roland needs to be aware of when using the questionnaire?

> ### Think!
>
> **Psychometric tests** such as the **JDI** and the QWL scale have often been criticised as only considering individual factors such as motivation and personality rather than situational factors. What situational factors do you believe could affect quality of working life (QWL)?

Think about quality of work life and job satisfaction. What would be the most important factor that would make you satisfied at work? Ask friends what their most important factor would be and why that factor is so important to them. What does this tell you about trying to use a rating scale as a way of measuring job satisfaction in organisations?

▲ Figure 9.27

Job satisfaction rating scales and questionnaires

In recent times employee satisfaction has been researched extensively. Alongside all the numerous theories that have been constructed about job satisfaction, there is also the question of how it can be investigated. Whether an employee is satisfied with their job or not is often studied through the use of a questionnaire or interview. This is usually a self-report questionnaire given to the employee. This will hopefully protect their anonymity, allowing them to express themselves more freely. One of the most popular job satisfaction questionnaires is the Job Descriptive Index (JDI) constructed by Smith in 1969.

The Job Descriptive Index

The Job Descriptive Index, or JDI (Smith *et al.*, 1969), still remains one of the most widely used measures of job satisfaction today. Smith *et al.* (1969) wanted to measure job satisfaction through the use of words, mainly **adjectives**, so that the employees could describe their feelings about their jobs.

The researchers initially did their own surveys with employees to create a 72-item questionnaire which could assess a number of different factors, or dimensions, that represent job satisfaction. The questions are descriptive and are answered using a three-point Likert scale (Yes, No, or Undecided). After testing, each word is given a numerical value that reflects how well it describes a satisfying job.

The five dimensions tested are:
1 The satisfaction with the job in general: Question: How do you feel about your day to day responsibilities? Words used could include 'repetitive', 'fascinating', 'rotten'.
2 Satisfaction with the level of supervision: Are you receiving enough help and support? Words used within this section include 'supportive', 'unkind'.
3 Salary/pay: What do you think of your pay? Is it enough? The words used can include 'adequate', 'underpaid'.
4 Satisfaction with co-workers: Do you receive respect and work well as a team? Words used include 'frustrating', 'helpful', 'lazy'.
5 Opportunities for promotion: Words used could include words such as 'very limited', 'good', 'dead end job'.

Example question of the Job Descriptive Index (JDI): Pay

Think of the pay you currently get. How well does each of the following words describe your present pay?

In the line beside the word write:

Y for 'Yes, it describes my pay.'

N for 'No, it doesn't describe my pay.'

? for 'I cannot decide.'

– Adequate for normal day to day expense

– Fair

– Barely able to live on the income

– Bad

– Comfortable

– Not as much as I deserve

– Well paid

– Enough to live on

– Underpaid

The scales were scored between 1 and 3. For example, positive items such as 'well paid' that were given a 'yes' would be scored as 3, the '?' as 2 and 'no' as 1. For negative items such as 'bad' a 'yes' would be scored as 1, the '?' as a 2, and 'no' as a 3. This means that the higher the score on the dimension, the more job satisfaction there is.

Walton's Quality of Working Life (QWL)

The concern for an employee's quality of life in a job is attracting research interest both in terms of academic research and within organisations; mainly to try and improve conditions as negative consequences can affect workers and organisations. According to Walton (1973) it does not matter what occupation you are in; most employees are affected by dissatisfaction at work. Walton (1973) suggested eight categories as measure of QWL:

1 Adequate and fair compensation: Salary/remuneration (pay) should be fair.
2 Safe and healthy working conditions: Employers should try to provide better working conditions. Flexi hours and protection against noise and pollution are part of this.
3 Opportunity to use and develop human capacity: Employees should be allowed sufficient autonomy. Workers need to be able to use their skills and abilities.
4 Opportunities for growth and security: Opportunities for promotion should be provided.
5 Social integration in the work organisation: Employees need a sense of belonging to the organisation they belong to.
6 Constitution in the work organisation: Employees need personal privacy and have a right to expression and to equal treatment.
7 Work and total life span: Some employees have to work late or have to travel for work so may be away from their family for a long time, affecting QWL.
8 Social relevance of work life: Organisations who do not take social responsibilities seriously, for example no pollution control, low quality policies.

The QWL evaluation scale

Timossi et al. (2008) used Walton's eight dimensions of quality of working life to develop a scale which could be used to measure each dimension. The process in scale development was:

» To simplify the terminology used within the eight dimensions to more everyday terms, such as salary, work conditions and tiredness.
» To formulate a set of questions involving the original and adapted terms.
» The questions would have a simplified statement and then the original term in brackets so as to link back to Walton's original work.
» Standardisation of the questionnaire using Walton's eight criteria and 35 subcriteria, with each represented by a question.
» Formulation of a response scale using a five-point rating scale.

Example question

In regard to a fair and appropriate salary (compensation):
1 How satisfied are you with your salary (remuneration)?

Very dissatisfied	Dissatisfied	Neither satisfied nor dissatisfied	Satisfied	Very satisfied
1	2	3	4	5

(Timossi et al., 2008, p. 6)

Evaluating scales to measure job satisfaction

One strength is that research support has shown that both the JDI and the QWL scale have high levels of reliability and validity. For example, Kinicki et al. (2002) performed a meta-analysis (a statistical review of previous studies) and found that the JDI questionnaire had high internal consistency as well as test-retest reliability which supported the idea that job satisfaction is a dynamic state which can change depending on circumstances and experience. The QWL scale also had internal consistency, with Timossi et al. (2008) finding a correlation coefficient of 0.96, meaning that it was reliable. In addition, both scales are based on theoretical constructs which increases their validity.

Another strength is that quantitative data was obtained in the JDI. Each of the answers given within the questionnaire was assigned a score dependent on its relationship to the domain measured and whether it was a negative or positive word. These scores were then added to give a final total for that domain. The higher the score was, then the higher the levels of satisfaction were. This meant that there is no subjectivity in the results as the results were just given objective scores which did not need interpretation. This increases the reliability of the data collected.

The JDI and the QWL scale are forms of **psychometric tests**, which have a number of strengths. Psychometric tests allow managers to have a greater insight into the motivations, traits and characteristics (or in this case the levels of satisfaction) of their workers. They do this through the use of a standardised and objective measure and they are also simple to use and allow for a greater distribution with little cost. This means that psychometric testing is a practical and useful means of measuring job satisfaction within the workplace.

However, as with any use of questionnaires, there is a chance of socially desirable answers or an employee who does not answer truthfully. In addition, anxiety at taking the test may also bias responses. Moreover, the use of forced-choice answers may not reflect an individual's real feelings especially as the JDI used a three-point scale and the QWL used a five-point scale, with one of these measures in the JDI being 'undecided'. This undecided category may be the one an anxious person would choose if they were unsure of how to respond. Therefore, this may lower the **validity** of the data.

ISSUES AND DEBATES

Individual and situational explanations

Scales that measure job satisfaction tend to look at situational aspects of an individual's job rather than individual factors such as personality and self-esteem, etc. For example, the JDI and the QWL asked questions about rate of pay, levels of supervision, who you work with and opportunities for promotion, all of which are situational factors within the workplace that could affect how you feel about work. Interestingly though, you could make a case for individual factors having an effect on the answers to the scales, i.e. how you feel about your co-workers may be dependent on your own personality and how this matches with theirs. For example, if you are more introverted you may not feel as comfortable with workers who are more sociable and talkative, so although scales tend to focus on (and measure) the situation you find yourself in at work, individual factors may also have an effect on those answers.

LEARNING LINK

Both the JDI and QWL scale used psychometric tests with rating scales and questionnaires to measure domains such as job motivation and satisfaction. Earlier in your organisational studies you also learned about psychometrics. Look back at how they were used and the issues that were raised. Were the same issues raised here? What does this tell us about psychometrics? Do you feel they are more useful for some measures than for others?

STUDY TIP

One way of understanding the strengths and weaknesses of certain scales is to try and complete them yourselves. When you do this often it brings up other issues that you had not previously considered. For example, think about the terms used in the questionnaire. Are they easy to understand? Could there be a different understanding dependent on culture or gender? Are you tempted to answer in a certain way? Try and come up with some more evaluation points based upon your experiences of answering the questions on the scales.

TEST YOURSELF

1 Eugene wants to use psychometric tests in order to measure job satisfaction in the workplace. Suggest two reasons why psychometric tests are a good way to measure job satisfaction. [4]
2 Explain the difference between individual and situational explanations, using an example from measures of job satisfaction. [2]

3 Compare two different measurements of job satisfaction in terms of similarities and differences. [4]
4 a Describe what psychologists have discovered about:
- the Job Descriptive Index (JDI)
- the Quality of Working Life (QWL) scale. [6]
b Evaluate what psychologists have discovered about:
- the Job Descriptive Index (JDI)
- the Quality of Working Life (QWL) scale, including a discussion about reliability of the scales. [10]
5 Questionnaires are often used to study job satisfaction and quality of working life. Outline two categories of quality of working life as suggested by Walton (1973). [4]
6 Suggest one reason why measurements of job satisfaction may be culturally biased. [2]
7 Explain two weaknesses of using questionnaires to investigate job satisfaction. [4]

9.5.3 Attitudes to work

KEY TERMS

functional

job involvement

organisational commitment

institutional stars

apathetic employees

corporate workers

lone wolves

career enhancing

calculative

normative

medical

corporate citizen

METHODOLOGY

generalisations from findings

Think!

What are the four types of absence suggested by Blau and Boal? How are these absences linked to organisational commitment and job involvement?

Think!

Siobhan has been reading about the four types of workers defined by Blau and Boals. She would like to find out what types of workers there are in her organisation. How could Siobhan use the model to find out the type of workers employed in the organisation?

Think!

Can you think of any situational and individual factors which might influence levels of absence in the workplace?

Think about any times you have been absent from your job or even your lessons. What were your reasons for being absent? Do you feel they fit into any of the categories Blau and Boal discussed? Are there any issues with having categories of absence such as on this model?

Blau and Boal's absenteeism and organisational commitment model

The costs to organisations of high staff turnover and absenteeism are high and are one of the main reasons why a significant amount of research has been conducted to discover the reasons behind high levels of absenteeism. Work satisfaction is often the focus of such research, but over 15 per cent of absenteeism cannot be attributed to lack of satisfaction and therefore other variables need to be discussed.

Organisational commitment is one variable that has been researched as a cause of turnover and absenteeism, with around 34 per cent of staff turnover being accounted for by this alone (Hom *et al.*, 1979). **Job involvement** has also been said to be a possible reason for staff turnover in 16 per cent of cases, although its link to absenteeism is less well known. One problem with research is that issues such as the type of absenteeism is not recorded and the relationship between variables such as job involvement and absenteeism may only be true of a certain type of absenteeism, but not of others. However, it may well be that job involvement and organisational commitment may interact with each other to affect both absenteeism and turnover and most research has only looked at them separately.

The model

Different interpretations of what is meant by organisational commitment and job involvement had previously led to variations in study results. Therefore, Blau and Boal operationalised both concepts:

1 Job involvement: Could be defined as the extent to which an individual identified with their job (Blau, 1985).
2 Research has identified two categories of organisational commitment: **Behavioural**, where an individual is committed to an organisation because it has become too costly for them to leave and **attitudinal**, where commitment is more positive and is defined as a state where an employee identifies with an organisation and its goals and they wish to maintain membership of this group. This model uses the attitudinal definition of organisational commitment.

Types of absence

Blau and Boal (1987) also separated absenteeism into four types.

1 **Medical**: This is an absence that is a response to infrequent and uncontrollable events. This could be illness, injury or family demands such as a sick child. One identifying feature of this type of absence is that it is a random occurrence with no pattern emerging.
2 **Career enhancing**: This absence allows the employee to further other career goals. These absences are a little more difficult to detect, although they may peak just before quitting a job or (if furthering goals is within the organisation) just before a transfer.
3 **Normative**: Absence is a habitual response to the norms of the organisation regarding absence. This could be an 'excused absence' as some organisations allow people to take personal days off. With this absence a pattern will begin to show and therefore both frequency and timing of the absence may be predicted.
4 **Calculative**: This is when an employee uses a certain amount of unexcused and excused absence days as permitted by the company. This could be an employee who has very low commitment and knows how many days they can take off before severe penalties are imposed. Frequency and total number of days off would normally be greatest for this type of absence.

Organisations, therefore, should ensure that type and frequency of absence are recorded in detail to ensure patterns are spotted.

The framework of the model

Blau and Boal (1987) separated organisational commitment and job involvement into high and low categories, such as a high job involvement/low job involvement and high organisational commitment/low organisational commitment. These were then combined into four cells:

1 High job involvement – high organisational commitment
2 High job involvement – low organisational commitment
3 Low job involvement – high organisational commitment
4 Low job involvement – low organisational commitment

From these categories, Blau and Boal (1987) described four types of individuals and predicted their levels of absence and turnover.

1 **Institutional stars**: These are the employees who have high levels of organisational commitment and high levels of job involvement. Work is important to their self-image and therefore they will spend a large amount of time and effort working on a task. These employees identify strongly with the organisation and will therefore put a great deal of effort into maintaining the organisation, eventually becoming mentors. When these types of people leave the company, it will be voluntarily and the result of their loss will be felt highly as they are hard to replace. The type of absence you will see with this employee is medical. Absences will be random and at the lowest level of any of the four types, due to their commitment and involvement.
2 **Lone wolves**: These have high levels of job involvement but low levels of organisational commitment. Work is important to them, but they do not identify with the organisation or its goals. These employees will show high levels of individual task effort, but less

effort on maintaining group relationships. This type of employee would leave an organisation voluntarily if a better opportunity arose elsewhere. Due to their lack of integration in the company, their leaving would have less impact than if an institutional star left. Absences tend to be of the career enhancing type as they believe in maximising their career opportunities and may go against organisational absence policy if it furthered their own individual agenda. Levels of absence will be positively correlated with turnover.

3 **Corporate citizens**: These have low levels of job involvement but high levels of organisational commitment. Their work is not personally important, but they identify strongly with the organisation and its goals. This type of employee focuses less on individual tasks but more on group tasks. Their knowledge of policies allows them to become mentors to less experienced employees. Their loyalty is high but their commitment to specialist roles is low; they will conform to behavioural expectations and are important to maintain group cohesiveness. Corporate citizens usually do not leave voluntarily. This type of employee will have normative types of absence where their absences will be excused and part of the existing norms of the organisation, such as taking personal days.

4 **Apathetic employees**: These employees have low job involvement and low organisational commitment. Work is not important to their self-image and they do not put a great deal of effort into tasks. They will apply the minimum amount of effort to get by. They work for pay and promotions. Their type of absence will be calculative where they take advantage of company absence policy and have as many days off as they can without getting punished. If these types of employees leave voluntarily, they will not be missed and would hopefully be replaced by employees of other types.

Evaluating the Blau and Boal model

One weakness of Blau and Boal's model is that it may not take into account cultural differences. The model is based upon individualistic societies and their workforces and therefore it may not apply to collectivist cultures. There are different cultural norms towards such issues as absenteeism in different countries and different responses in terms of sanctions. This model also does not consider the notion that maintaining group relations is far more important in some cultures than individual pursuit of career enhancement. This suggests, therefore, that the model is limited in terms of generalisability, affecting its usefulness.

Another weakness is that the model was developed in the 1980s and therefore may have low temporal validity. Workplaces are different places today than they were in the 1980s, due to a decline in manual jobs and a rise in technological and clerical work. Also, there are far more flexible working patterns which allow people to work from home and to work round their family commitments. This change in the workplace means that the concepts of organisational commitment and job involvement as defined by Blau and Boal may not apply today and may need to be redesigned for the modern workforce.

> ### ISSUES AND DEBATES

Application to everyday life

One strength of the model is that it has high application to everyday life. Absenteeism costs organisations a great deal of money in terms of sick pay, lost time and work time disruption. If organisations can establish patterns of absenteeism within the workforce, they may be able to address reasons for it before they become an issue. For example, the management could discuss how they can raise the commitment levels and job involvement in the workforce. The model, therefore, could be beneficial to the organisation and the workforce, increasing its usefulness.

Reductionism versus holism

The model is more holistic as it considers both internal and external factors when looking at commitment and job involvement. Blau and Boal acknowledged that individual factors such as personality, levels of self-esteem and self-image all play a part in involvement and commitment to an organisation. However, they also suggested that situational factors such as organisational goals, career prospects within the workforce, and even absence policies and procedures could also have an effect. This makes Blau and Boal's model more complete and therefore gives a better overall explanation of attitudes to work. However, some research studies have suggested that the model is still too narrow and should focus on behavioural commitment as well as attitudinal commitment, as situational factors such as not being able to afford to leave and family circumstances are very important.

LEARNING LINK

The evaluation of this model has suggested that temporal validity may be low. Remind yourself what temporal validity means and then have a look at the studies you learned about at AS Level and try and suggest which of those has high temporal validity and which has low temporal validity. For example, read again about Piliavin's findings (1969) on helping behaviour or Milgram's findings (1963) on obedience. Would we find the same results today?

STUDY TIP

Why not make yourself a revision game? Perhaps make cards of the different types of individual employees such as lone wolves or corporate citizens and then write another set of cards which have low organisational commitment on them and a set with high organisational commitment. Afterwards, do the same for job involvement. You could even then do a third set showing the type of absences. Cut them out individually and mix them up. See if you can match the type of employee with their levels of commitment and involvement and type of absence.

TEST YOURSELF

1   Jamal likes his job at the jigsaw factory and often comes up with innovative solutions to the problems with the machine, but he often argues with the other staff and never comes to work parties. He has been absent several times in the last three months and the other workers think he has been going for job interviews.
   a   Explain which type of worker Jamal is according to Blau and Boal's model.   [2]
   b   According to the model, explain whether Jamal's organisational commitment and job involvement are likely to be high or low.   [2]
2   Explain one reason Blau and Boal's model may have good application to real life.   [2]
3   a   Describe what psychologists have discovered about absenteeism in the workplace.   [6]
   b   Evaluate what psychologists have discovered about absenteeism in the workplace, including a discussion on cultural differences.   [10]
4   Outline what is meant by job involvement according to Blau and Boal's model.   [2]
5   Plan a study using a questionnaire to find the main reason for absenteeism in the workplace.
   Your plan must include details about:
   –   questionnaire format
   –   sampling technique.   [10]
6   Explain one strength and one weakness of using questionnaires to study attitudes in the workplace.   [4]

KEY TERMS

workplace sabotage
instrumental sabotage
demonstrative sabotage
self-presentation theory

Key study: Reasons for employee sabotage in the workplace – Giacalone and Rosenfeld (1987)

Think!

What is meant by **accounts** as discussed by **self-presentation theory**?

Think!

Safira wants to find out about potential reasons for **workplace sabotage** in organisations in Cranton, a small city in the UK. She wants to make sure her study is reliable and ethical. How could Safira conduct her study?

Think!

Giacalone and Rosenfeld stated that their study was only the start of the process for research into sabotage and that researchers should study both individual and situational factors within the workforce to see whether this affects levels of sabotage. What individual factors do you feel may make an individual more likely to commit workplace sabotage?

Dr Robert A Giacalone is currently the Raymond and Eleanor Smiley Chair in Business Ethics at the Boler School of Business, John Carroll University. In his current position, he also serves as the Director of the Ginn Institute for Corporate Social Responsibility. Dr Giacolone has edited/authored 10 books and 160 articles on a variety of topics including ethics and values and exit interviewing. He is currently co-editor of the book series 'Ethics in Practice' and has had consulting roles with many large organisations such as the US Army, the US Navy, and the Federal Reserve Bank (Boler College of Business, 2021).

▶ CONTEXT

Organisational sabotage can be defined as a behaviour by an employee on the payroll which is intended to inflict a production or profit loss on an organisation. The cost of this type of action is hard to establish and is increasing. There has been very little research on workplace sabotage due to the nature of the issue; sabotage is an anti-social act which can contain violence and destructiveness but is also a criminal act in many cases.

The aims of sabotage seem to fall into two categories:
1 **Instrumental sabotage:** Trying to achieve limited demands and/or a change in socio-political power.
2 **Demonstrative sabotage:** This is a protest against management, injustice and a rejection of accepted values.

Allen and Greenberger (1980) suggested that sabotage may be a way for workers to have a feeling of mastery and control over their environment, to feel as though they are not at the mercy of management. Self-presentation theorists suggest that employees may use accounts, or reasons, for sabotage events in order to minimise the seriousness of an act. These will make the action feel less socially undesirable or even justified.

This study therefore looks at individuals who may or may not accept many motives for sabotage, with individual differences playing a part in the number and type of accounts, or reasons, a person will accept. It may be that the more accounts for sabotage that a person will accept, the more likely they are to engage in sabotage or at least the more likely they are to justify its occurrence.

> ## AIMS

- To explore if those who accepted more reasons for acts of sabotage would be more likely to justify sabotage and see it as more acceptable.
- To explore if there are differences in the types of sabotage that would be seen as justifiable.

> ## METHODOLOGY

This study collected data using structured questionnaires in the form of a seven-point rating scale.

Sample

Subjects were a volunteer sample of 38 labourers who worked at an electrical factory in northeast USA. All of the participants belonged to the union.

> ## PROCEDURE

The procedure can be split into two parts.

1 Constructing the questionnaires

The sabotage methods questionnaire and sabotage reasons questionnaire:

In the first part of the study, a retired employee who had worked at the factory was asked to provide a list of types of sabotage methods used by employees. He produced a list of 29 types of sabotage which were placed in four categories:

- work slowdowns
- destruction of machinery, premises or products
- dishonesty
- causing chaos.

The same retiree also produced a comprehensive list of reasons that employees thought sabotage occurred and what reasons they gave for justifying it. This resulted in a list of 11 reasons/justifications for sabotage including:

- self-defence
- revenge
- protection from the boss
- protect your own job
- the company/foreman deserved it
- the company/foreman hurt me previously
- release of frustrations
- just for fun.

2 Using the questionnaires

The participants were asked by a non-supervisory colleague (someone who was not a foreman or from management) to rate the items on each questionnaire on a seven-point scale, with one being 'not at all justifiable' and seven being 'totally justifiable'.

Participants were told that their responses were to be used in an industrial psychology seminar and management would not see their answers. They were also told not to write their names or other identifying information on the questionnaires. The questionnaires were presented as a pack so that the responses on both questionnaires for each participant were kept together.

The responses on the sabotage reasons questionnaire were summarised for each sabotage reason and a median score was reached from the results. Two groups were formed based on whether their total was above or below this median value. These groups were called low reason acceptors and high reason acceptors. In other words, those who were above the median score justified more reasons for sabotage (high acceptors) and those below the median score justified less reasons for sabotage (low acceptors).

The responses to the sabotage methods questionnaire were also summarised creating median results for the four sabotage methods.

▶ RESULTS

▼ Table 9.9 Mean scores for each of the four methods of sabotage (total taken from the 29 methods in total split into the four categories)

	Work slowdown	Destruction	Causing chaos	Dishonesty
High acceptors	25	19.8	13.5	15.5
Low acceptors	18.9	13	8.8	12.4

For three of the four types of sabotage: work slowdowns, destruction (of machinery, premises or products) and causing chaos, high reason acceptors saw these as being more justified forms of sabotage than low reason acceptors did. However, for dishonesty there were no significant differences between the two groups although high acceptors did see dishonesty as slightly more justifiable. Giacalone and Rosenfeld suggest the results for dishonesty may be because it is the only one that could lead to monetary gain for the saboteur, and that it was not an effective method to demonstrate against injustice or management. Perhaps some types of civil disobedience are seen as more socially desirable, but this is not the case for dishonesty.

In terms of reasons for sabotage the most justifiable reasons (with 1=unjustifiable and 7=very justifiable) were to protect your job (M=3.47), self-defence (M=3.37) and protect yourself from the boss (M=3.16), with the least justifiable being release of frustration (M=1.97) and just for fun (1.29).

▶ CONCLUSIONS

- Importance in future research needs to be placed on the recognition of sabotage rather than concentrating on the root cause of the problem.
- Focusing on recognition and deterrence may help reduce potential for accidents and risk exposure as well as financial losses.
- The more accounts (reasons) an individual will accept for sabotage, the higher the level of justification for all different types of sabotage except for dishonesty.

Methodological strengths and weaknesses

One strength of the study is the use of questionnaires. For example, every participant used a seven-point rating scale to show whether or not a particular method or reason for sabotage was justifiable. This enabled researchers to obtain quantitative objective data which allowed for statistical analysis and comparisons to be drawn and conclusions formed, increasing the reliability of the study.

A further strength is that the participants were asked to complete the questionnaires by a non-supervisory colleague. This was a person at the same level as them, rather than someone who has control over them. This is a strength, as being asked by a supervisor or manager to complete a socially sensitive questionnaire on sabotage could be intimidating and decrease the chances of truthful responses, which would lower the validity of the results.

One weakness of the study is that the categories used in the reasons and methods questionnaires were constructed from the viewpoint of one retired employee. It may be that the retired employee had a narrow point of view on sabotage or had not had any experience of it himself. This is a weakness, as his individual view of reasons for and methods of sabotage may not be representative of the reasons for and methods of sabotage of all workers, lowering the validity of the questionnaires.

Another weakness is that the results may not be able to be generalised to other organisations in different countries or even different occupations. For example, the study took place in the USA at one electrical factory with all participants being members of a union. It may be that other occupations or countries have a completely different outlook on sabotage and therefore results may be very different. Also, the fact that the workers had to be in a union to participate may also limit generalisability, as it may be only a certain type of worker will join a union.

Ethics

One ethical weakness is that the participants were told that the results would be presented in an industrial psychology seminar, whereas they were used in a research paper. This means the participants were deceived. However, information about the participants was kept confidential. The participants were asked not to write their names on the questionnaires. Each questionnaire was provided in a packet containing both questionnaires so that labelling was not required, further increasing the anonymity of the participants. One issue also to be aware of is the idea that the researchers were studying something that may be illegal, so if there was an employee who was clearly in favour of all types of sabotage, would it be unethical for that person not to be made known?

> ## ISSUES AND DEBATES

Application to everyday life

Giacalone and Rosenfeld saw their study as an initial investigation into sabotage and considered that further research was needed to determine the relationship between perceived justifiability and performing an act of sabotage or the willingness to report sabotage. This development of their approach through further research could help encourage the reporting of acts of sabotage or identify employees at risk of performing sabotage, making the workplace at less risk of these acts.

Individual and situational factors

One area of further research which Giacalone and Rosenfeld proposed was the investigation of the impact of individual differences on how employees perceived the justifiableness of sabotage. In addition, situational workplace factors may be worthwhile investigating to see if workplace conditions affect employees' beliefs about sabotage.

Idiographic versus nomothetic

The study used a nomothetic approach to workplace sabotage as it looked for general laws/trends, using structured questionnaires, which can then be applied to all workforces in terms of why, and what type of, workplace sabotage may be seen as justified. This may be a simplistic view to workplace sabotage as it is not possible to really look for general trends as to why some people find sabotage acceptable or not. Perhaps using idiographic methods, such as unstructured interviews and focus groups, will provide more in-depth reasons about sabotage, and why people find it acceptable.

> ## REFLECTION

- To what extent do you think that the research is generalisable to other workplaces and professions?
- If you were conducting research in this area, how might you improve this study and/ or design your own study to investigate sabotage in the workplace?

> ## LEARNING LINK

At AS Level, you looked at social processes such as obedience in the study by Milgram (1963) and bystander intervention in the 'Subway Samaritans' study by Piliavin *et al.* (1969). How might social influence be involved in sabotage? How could moral strain affect a saboteur after their act of sabotage and would this depend on their classification as a low or high acceptor?

STUDY TIP

By now you will have learned a great deal about how to design studies, so why not explore some of your own evaluative points in addition to the ones on this page? For example, how could questionnaires on the topic of employee sabotage be designed to reduce the possibility of participants not being truthful due to social desirability bias?

▶ TEST YOURSELF

1   Devante has heard about employees in his organisation who have deliberately stopped products from leaving the building. His friend is shocked at this and wonders why anyone would do such a thing.
    State two reasons why employees in an organisation may commit sabotage in the workplace.   [2]

2   Explain one possible reason why dishonesty mean scores were not significantly different between high and low acceptors.   [2]

3   a   Describe the study by Giacalone and Rosenfeld (1987) on reasons for employee sabotage in the workplace.   [6]

    b   Evaluate the study by Giacalone and Rosenfeld (1987) on reasons for employee sabotage in the workplace, including a discussion on generalisability.   [10]

4   From the key study by Giacalone and Rosenfeld (1987) on sabotage in the workplace, describe how the two questionnaires used in the study were constructed.   [4]

5   Suggest one way that the ethical guidelines were followed in the study by Giacalone and Rosenfeld (1987).   [2]

6   Suggest one reason why Giacalone and Rosenfeld (1987) told the participants that their answers would be used in a seminar, not for a research project.   [2]

Acknowledgements

The publishers would like to thank Laura Swash for writing Sections 7.3.1–7.3.3 and Sections 7.5.2–7.5.3 in Chapter 7 and Carl Piaf for Section 9.5.3: Key Study – Reasons for employee sabotage in the workplace – Giacolone and Rosenfeld (1987) in Chapter 9.

The Publisher would like to thank the following for permission to reproduce copyright material.

pp.22, 23, 25, 28 Hassett, J. M., Siebert, E. R., & Wallen, K. (2008). Sex differences in rhesus monkey toy preferences parallel those of children. Hormones and behavior, 54(3), 359-364; p.96 Bandura, A., Ross, D., & Ross, S. A. (1961). Transmission of aggression through imitation of aggressive models. The Journal of Abnormal and Social Psychology, 63(3), 575–582; doi:10.1037/h0045925; pp.107, 109, 220 Fagen, A., Acharya, N., & Kaufman, G. E. (2014). Positive reinforcement training for a trunk wash in Nepal's working elephants: Demonstrating alternatives to traditional elephant training techniques. Journal of Applied Animal Welfare Science, 17(2), 83-97; p.121, Saavedra, L. M., & Silverman, W. K. (2002). Case study: Disgust and a specific phobia of buttons. Journal of the American Academy of Child & Adolescent Psychiatry, 41(11), 1376-1379; p.138 Milgram, S. (1963). Behavioral study of obedience. The Journal of abnormal and social psychology, 67(4), 371; p.220 Chapman, E., Baron-Cohen, S., Auyeung, B., Knickmeyer, R., Taylor, K., & Hackett, G. (2006). Fetal testosterone and empathy: evidence from the empathy quotient (EQ) and the "reading the mind in the eyes" test. Social Neuroscience 1(2), 135-148; p.221 Saavedra, L. M., & Silverman, W. K. (2002). Case study: Disgust and a specific phobia of buttons. Journal of the American Academy of Child & Adolescent Psychiatry, 41(11), 1376-1379; p.238 Freeman et al. "Can Virtual Reality be Used to Investigate Persecutory Ideation?", The Journal of Nervous and Mental Disease, Volume 191, Number 8, August 2003: https://www.psych.ox.ac.uk/files/research/can-virtual-reality-be-used-to-investigate-persecutory-ideation.pdf; p.261 Beck, A. T., Steer, R.A., & Brown, G.K. (1996). "Manual for the Beck Depression Inventory-II". San Antonio, TX: Psychological Corporation; p.285 Kleptomania Symptom Assessment Scale (K-SAS); pp.304-5 Alex Blaszczynski, Lia Nower, "Imaginal Desensitisation: A Relaxation-Based Technique for Impulse Control Disorders, Journal of Clinical Activities", Assignments & Handouts in Psychotherapy Practice; p.308 Sample items from the "Generalised Anxiety Disorder Assessment (GAD-7)", Generalised Anxiety Disorder Questionnaire (GAD-7), © Egton Medical Information Systems Limited; p.341 Sample items from the Yale-Brown Obsessive-Compulsive Scale (Y-BOCS); p.369 Levy, M., & Weitz, B. A. (2001). "Retailing management" (4th ed.). McGraw-Hill, IRWIN; p.380 Woods, A. T., Poliakoff, E., Lloyd, D. M., Kuenzel, J., Hodson, R., Gonda, H., Batchelor, J., Dijksterhuis, G. B. and Thomas, A., (2010). "Effect of background noise on food perception". Food Quality and Preference, 22(1), 42–47; p.403 Pavesic, D. (2005). The Psychology of Menu Design: Reinvent Your 'Silent Salesperson' to Increase Check Averages and Guest Loyalty. Hospitality Faculty Publications. Paper 5; pp.454-5 Rixom, J. M., Mas, E. M. & Rixom, B. A. (2019). "Presentation Matters: The Effect of Wrapping Neatness on Gift Attitudes". Journal of Consumer Psychology, 30(2), 329-338; p.461 Becker, L., van Rompay, T. J. L., Schifferstein, H.N.J. & Galetzka ,M. (2011). "Tough package, strong taste: The influence of packaging design on taste impressions and product evaluations". Food Quality and Preference 22, 17– 23; p.467 DelVecchio, S. K., Zemanek, J. E., McIntyre, R. P., & Claxton, R. P. (2003). "Buyers' perceptions of salesperson tactical approaches". Journal of Personal Selling & Sales Management, 23(1), 39-49; p.477 Engel, J. F., Kollat, D. T., & Blackwell, R. D. (1968).Consumer Behavior. New York: Holt, Rinehart and Winston; p.564 Yokley, J. M. & Glenwick, D. S. (1984). "Increasing the immunization of preschool children; an evaluation of applied community interventions". Journal of Applied Behavior Analysis, 17(3): 313–25; p.668 Asch, S. E. (1951). Effects of group pressure upon the modification and distortion of judgments. In H. Guetzkow (Ed.), Groups, leadership and men; research in human relations (pp. 177–190). Carnegie Press.

Every effort has been made to trace all copyright holders, but if any have been inadvertently overlooked, the Publishers will be pleased to make the necessary arrangements at the first opportunity.

The authors would like to thank the following people for their support in writing this book: Stephanie Cheung-Tsang for help with translation, Dr Joanna Nye for her help with the section on yoga, Professor Pamela Heaton for her advice on autism spectrum disorder, all the researchers who supplied photos, quotes and help with their biographies, including Dr Lissette Saavedra, Dr Wendy Silverman, Dr Britta Hölzel, Dr Ariel Fagen, Dr Anat Perry, Dr Joanna Pozzulo, Professor Kim Wallen, Professor Tom Sensky, Dr Jitender Aneja, Professor Daniel Freeman, Professor Chris Frith, Dr Eleanor Longden, Dr Eileen Luders, Dr Kevin Chapman, Professor Karina Lovell, Dr Stephani Robson, and Dr Christina Brudvik. Also, thanks to Julia Rotter, the photographer who captured Britta Hölzel. Huge thanks to Professor Jackie Andrade for her suggestions and support. Thank you so much to Dr Mark Forshaw for his help in finding the original Friedman and Rosenhan Type A personality interview questions.

Photo credits

The Publisher would like to thank the following for permission to reproduce copyright material.

p.viii © Milanmarkovic78/stock.adobe.com; p.xii © Drazen/stock.adobe.com; p.1 © Pavel Kasak/stock.adobe.com; p.4 © Yay Images/stock.adobe.com; p.6 © The University of Chicago; p.9 © Prostorina/stock.adobe.com; p.10 © Viacheslav Lakobchuk/stock.adobe.com; p.16 Professor Kim Wallen; p.17 © Jahmaica/stock.adobe.com; p.19 © Anna Om/stock.adobe.com; p.21 © Professor Kim Wallen; p.25 © Ekkapol/stock.adobe.com; p.27 © Lost_in_the_Midwest/stock.adobe.com; p.29 © Julia Rotter; p.30 Luders E, Kurth F, Toga AW, Narr KL and Gaser C (2013) Meditation effects within the hippocampal complex revealed by voxel-based morphometry and cytoarchitectonic probabilistic mapping. Front. Psychol. 4:398. doi: 10.3389/fpsyg.2013.00398; p.33 © Mangostar/stock.adobe.com; p.34 © Gorodenkoff/stock.adobe.com; p.37 © Zdenka Darula/stock.adobe.com; p.40 © NLshop/stock.adobe.com; p.44 © Alicia/stock.adobe.com; p.45 © AA+W/stock.adobe.com; p.50 c © Professor Jackie Andrade, b © WavebreakMediaMicro/stock.adobe.com; p.52 © Howtogoto/stock.adobe.com; p.57 © Anton/stock.adobe.com; p.59 © Darla Hallmark/stock.adobe.com; p.61 © Brian Harris/Alamy Stock Photo; p.70 c © Dr Joanna Pozzulo, b © Couperfield/stock.adobe.com; p.74 © UpperCut Images/Getty Images; p.77 © Gary718/Shutterstock.com; p.79 © Andrey Popov/stock.adobe.com; p.81 © Burdun/stock.adobe.com; p.85 © SasinTipchai/stock.adobe.com; p.86 © Denisismagilov/stock.adobe.com; p.90 © Jose Gil/Shutterstock.com; p.101 Dr Ariel Fagen; p.102 © Yesac/stock.adobe.com; p.105 © Prasert/stock.adobe.com; p.111 © Michaeljung/stock.adobe.com; p.114 l © Dr Wendy Silverman, r © RTI International; p.115 © Satura_/stock.adobe.com; p.119 © Polya_olya/stock.adobe.com; p.123 © Myboys.me/stock.adobe.com; p.128 © PhotoSpirit/stock.adobe.com; p.129 © Filipe.Samora/Shutterstock.com; p.133 © Interfoto/Personalities/Alamy Stock Photo; p.135 © Imagesbykenny/stock.adobe.com; p.140 © F11photo/stock.adobe.com; p.143 Dr Anat Perry; p.159 © Fabio formaggio/123 RF.com; p.165 © SeanPavonePhoto/stock.adobe.com; p.174 © Good Studio/stock.adobe.com; p.187 © Michele/stock.adobe.com; p.189 © Professor Kim Wallen; p.191 © Rawpixel.com/stock.adobe.com; p.196 © JackF/stock.adobe.com; p.211 © Henner Damke/stock.adobe.com; p.226 © Godji10/stock.adobe.com; p.227 © Prostock-studio/stock.adobe.com; p.228 © Pixel-Shot/stock.adobe.com; p.229 © Pathdoc/stock.adobe.com; p.230 © Aliaksei/stock.adobe.com; p.232 © Vibe Images/stock.adobe.com; p.234 t Dr Jitender Aneja, b © AJay/stock.adobe.com; p.236 Daniel Freeman; p.240 © Syda Productions/stock.adobe.com; p.242 © Designua/stock.adobe.com; p.246 Professor Chris Frith; p.247 Dr Eleanor Longden; p.251 © t Gina Sanders/stock.adobe.com, b © Aleksandra Gigowska/stock.adobe.com; p.253 © Will & Deni Mcintyre/Science Photo Library; p.256 Tom Sensky; p.259 © Elnur/stock.adobe.com; p.268 © Blindturtle/stock.adobe.com; p.269 © Iushakovsky/stock.adobe.com; p.271 © Leif Skoogfors/Corbis HistoricalGetty Images; p.274 © Kalpis/stock.adobe.com; p.278 © Pressmaster/stock.adobe.com; p.280 © Stasnds/stock.adobe.com; p.282 © Rob/stock.adobe.com; p.284 © Alinsa/stock.adobe.com; p.286 © Komarov Dmitriy/stock.adobe.com; p.290 © Maksym Yemelyanov/stock.adobe.com; p.299 © Lightfield Studios/stock.adobe.com; p.302 © Ivan Kruk/stock.adobe.com; p.311 © GoodIdeas/stock.adobe.com; p.313 © Daria_serdtseva/stock.adobe.com;

PHOTO CREDITS

p.316 © BillionPhotos.com/stock.adobe.com; p.317 © Happy monkey/Shutterstock.com; p.320 © Wong sze yuen/Shutterstock.com; p.322 © Evannovostro/stock.adobe.com; p.325 © Alfa27/stock.adobe.com; p.327 © Lightfield Studios/stock.adobe.com; p.329 © Stanislaw Mikulski/stock.adobe.com; p.331 Dr Kevin Chapman; p.332 © Andrey Popov/stock.adobe.com; p.338 © Karenfoleyphoto/stock.adobe.com; p.341 © Seventyfour/stock.adobe.com; p.345 © Ruslanita/stock.adobe.com; p.350 © Sofiko14/stock.adobe.com; p.353 © Anusak/stock.adobe.com; p.357 t Karina Lovell, c © Kittiwat/stock.adobe.com; p.363 © Mehdi33300/stock.adobe.com; p.365 © Jakartatravel/stock.adobe.com; p.367 © Monkey Business/stock.adobe.com; p.369 © Dubo/stock.adobe.com; p.373 © Professor Adrian North; p.377 © Pressmaster/stock.adobe.com; p.379 © Cherryandbees/stock.adobe.com; p.380 tl © Moving Moment/stock.adobe.com, tr © ImagesMy/stock.adobe.com, cl © Radub85/stock.adobe.com, cr © Roman Fernati/stock.adobe.com, b © Rimglow/stock.adobe.com; p.383 © WavebreakMediaMicro/stock.adobe.com; p.385 © Mavoimages/stock.adobe.com; p.387 © Anna_ok/stock.adobe.com; p.390 © IR Stone/Shutterstock.com; p.394 © Frantic00/Shutterstock.com; p.398 © APchanel/stock.adobe.com; p.402 © Syda Productions/stock.adobe.com; p.405 © Kraphix/Shutterstock.com; p.407 © Dimasobko/stock.adobe.com; p.411 Dr Stephani Robson; p.418 © Vrx123/stock.adobe.com; p.422 © Oneinchpunch/stock.adobe.com; p.426 © Scanrail/stock.adobe.com; p.430 © Karuka/stock.adobe.com; p.431 © Apicha/stock.adobe.com; p.434 © Hanohiki/stock.adobe.com; p.442 © Gina Sanders/stock.adobe.com; p.444 © Zyabich/stock.adobe.com; p.449 © Art_zzz/stock.adobe.com; p.451 © Fizkes/stock.adobe.com; p.453 © Jfunk/stock.adobe.com; p.454 Rixom, J. M., Mas, E. M. & Rixom, B. A. (2019)."Presentation Matters: The Effect of Wrapping Neatness on Gift Attitudes". Journal of Consumer Psychology, 30(2), 329-338.; p.457 © Monopoly919/stock.adobe.com; p.459 © Thomas van Rompay; p.466 © Kadmy/stock.adobe.com; p.468 © Ray Tang/Shutterstock.com; p.470 © Robert Kneschke/Shutterstock.com; p.475 © Monkey Business/stock.adobe.com; p.478 © Sergey Ryzhov/stock.adobe.com; p.481 © Dan Dalton/KOTO/stock.adobe.com; p.482 © JackF/stock.adobe.com; p.485 © Nehopelon/stock.adobe.com; p.487 © Cubankite/Shutterstock.com; p.491 © Deagreez/stock.adobe.com; p.496 © Stoatphoto/stock.adobe.com; p.497 t Dr Mark Snyder, b © PBaishev/stock.adobe.com; p.501 © Vector Tradition/Shutterstock.com; p.502 © Cjmacer/Shutterstock.com; p.506 © New Africa/stock.adobe.com; p.508 © Sindler1/stock.adobe.com; p.510 © Dmitry Lobanov/stock.adobe.com; p.511 © Gudellaphoto/stock.adobe.com; p.515 © Mangostar/stock.adobe.com; p.516 © Grigory Bruev/stock.adobe.com; p.518 l stockyimages/stock.adobe.com, c Noey smiley/stock.adobe.com, r Prostock-studio/stock.adobe.com; p.522 © Rocketclips/stock.adobe.com; p.528 © Monkey Business/stock.adobe.com; p.530 © Eggeeggjiew/stock.adobe.com; p.534 © Natalia Romero/EyeEm/Getty Images; p.538 © DC Studio/stock.adobe.com; p.542 © John T Takai/Shutterstock.com; p.546 © Monkey Business/stock.adobe.com; p.550 © Daisy Daisy/stock.adobe.com; p.558 Lightfield Studios/stock.adobe.com; p.562 Dr James Yokley; p.566 © Jes2uphoto/stock.adobe.com; p.567 © Lertluck Thipchai/stock.adobe.com; p.569 © Tang Chhin Sothy/AFP/Getty Images; p.571 © Andranik123/stock.adobe.com; p.577 Christina Brudvik; p.578 © Pressmaster/stock.adobe.com; p.582 © Volanthevist/Moment/Getty Images; p.585 © Andrew Mayovskyy/stock.adobe.com; p.589 © Desdemona72/stock.adobe.com; p.593 © Krakenimages.com/stock.adobe.com; p.595 © 10'000 Hours/DigitalVision/Getty Images; p.599 © Monty Rakusen/Image Source/Getty Images; p.601 © Ivashstudio/stock.adobe.com; p.604 © ABO Photography/Shutterstock.com; p.609 © Photographee.eu/Shutterstock.com; p.613 Roquillo/stock.adobe.com; p.617 © JohnnyGreig/E+/Getty Images; p.622 © Richard Splash/Alamy Stock Photo; p.623 © Uncredited/AP/Shutterstock; p.629 © Emerald_media/Shutterstock.com; p.633 © Dmitry Pistrov/Shutterstock.com; p.638 © Lucian Coman/Shutterstock.com; p.640 © Laplateresca/stock.adobe.com; p.644 © Konradbak/stock.adobe.com; p.646 © Fizkes/stock.adobe.com; p.647 © Asada/stock.adobe.com; p.651 © Studio Romantic/stock.adobe.com; p.654 © Pathdoc/stock.adobe.com; p.659 © Dvoevnore/stock.adobe.com; p.662 © Stokkete/stock.adobe.com; p.666 © Pathdoc/stock.adobe.com; p.673 © Ndabcreativity/stock.adobe.com; p.678 © Sinseeho/stock.adobe.com; p.681 © Rawpixel.com/stock.adobe.com; p.685 © Deagreez/stock.adobe.com; p.692 © VectorMine/stock.adobe.com; p.696 © The six/stock.adobe.com; p.699 © ChenPG/stock.adobe.com; p.704 © Djile/stock.adobe.com; p.709 © Photocreo Bednarek/stock.adobe.com; p.717 © Syda Productions/stock.adobe.com; p.721 © KOTO/stock.adobe.com; p.728 © Sushiman/stock.adobe.com; p.732 © Erik Bergin Photos/stock.adobe.com; p.736 © Studio Romantic/stock.adobe.com; p.741 © BillionPhotos.com/stock.adobe.com; p.747 © Fizkes/stock.adobe.com

Index